ADVANCED ACCOUNTING

5th Edition

ADVANCED ACCOUNTING

REVISED BY

Allan R. Drebin

Professor of Accounting and Information Systems
J.L. Kellogg Graduate School of Management
Northwestern University

Published by

A58 **SOUTH-WESTERN PUBLISHING CO.**

CINCINNATI   WEST CHICAGO, ILL.   DALLAS   PELHAM MANOR, N.Y.   PALO ALTO, CALIF.

ISBN: 0-538-01580-2

Library of Congress Catalog Card Number: 81-84619

1 2 3 4 5 6 7 8 9 K 1 0 9 8 7 6 5 4 3 2
Printed in the United States of America

Preface

ADVANCED ACCOUNTING is a textbook for the student who has completed introductory and intermediate studies, and who understands the basic concepts and theoretical framework of accounting. The Fifth Edition of ADVANCED ACCOUNTING, as did previous editions, deals with the accounting and financial reporting issues related to special forms of economic units, both profit-seeking and not-for-profit. Its objective is to prepare the student to apply basic accounting principles to the special situations found in such organizations. The textbook is designed to serve the needs of the management student who requires an understanding of the reports and statements issued by complex organizations, as well as the accounting major who requires a sound understanding of theory and practice to qualify for admission to the accounting profession.

In preparing the Fifth Edition, the primary concern was to incorporate the numerous institutional and authoritative changes that have taken place since publication of the previous edition, while retaining the basic instructional and expository approaches that have proved so successful over many years of use. Substantive changes have been made in the section on consolidated statements to reflect authoritative pronouncements dealing with purchase accounting, the equity method, and the treatment of intangibles. The special problems arising in accounting for foreign branches and subsidiaries are discussed in the context of current authoritative pronouncements as well as the controversy surrounding alternative approaches to the translation issue. The impacts of major revisions in the bankruptcy law and in governmental accounting principles have been recognized.

Chapter sequence and subject matter have generally been retained from the previous edition. The text covers partnerships, installment sales, consignments, home office and branch accounting, consolidations, fiduciary accounting, and governmental accounting. Material on compound interest procedures has been deleted, since it is now generally included in intermediate-level courses.

Several decisions regarding theoretical concepts and expository style had to be made in the course of the revision. The most important of these is the use of what might be described as a "modified entity theory" approach to consolidations. This is used whenever the controlling interest is less than 100 percent. The effect of this approach is to recognize all identifiable assets and liabilities at their full market value at the date of acquisition, but recognize goodwill only to the extent that it has been paid for by the controlling interest. This is consistent with current authoritative pronouncements which require that acquired resources be recorded at their fair values at acquisition, but also require that goodwill be recognized only to the extent that total cost exceeds the fair values of net assets acquired. Alternative treatments were considered but not used. These include recording assets at their prior book values plus the controlling interest's portion of the increase in value (resulting in a meaningless composite value) or imputing goodwill to the minority interest (defying the cost principle).

In presenting the material on consolidated statements, concepts are developed first by reference only to the balance sheet, with procedures for preparing the income statement reserved for a final chapter. This approach, which has proved successful in earlier editions, permits the student to concentrate on the net impact of the various eliminations and adjustments without being overloaded with procedural complexity. When the income statement is introduced, a straightforward work sheet in which debits equal credits is used to analyze the transition from trial balance to completed statements. Adjustments required by the equity method are developed logically in the course of consolidation, which eliminates the need for the assumption that these adjustments have previously been made.

In the final analysis, the effectiveness of the approaches used will depend on their acceptance by instructors and students. With this in mind, the author would be grateful for any comments from users that might be helpful in making improvements in subsequent editions. The author's aim is to continually refine the instructional effectiveness, while maintaining theoretical rigor and authoritative validity. It is sincerely hoped that the many users of the previous edition who have encouraged this revision will find that it lives up to its heritage.

The author would like to express his thanks to Professor Arthur Neiminsky of California State University, and Mr. Louis Peterson of Coopers and Lybrand for their helpful comments. The cooperation of the American Institute of Certified Public Accountants in permitting the use of materials adapted from the Uniform C.P.A. Examinations, and the National Council of Governmental Accounting for permitting the use of material derived from their authoritative pronouncements, is gratefully acknowledged.

Allan R. Drebin

Contents

Part Four   Fiduciaries

1
Partnerships — Formation and Operation

The partnership is defined as "an association of two or more persons to carry on as co-owners a business for profit."[1] "Persons" are considered to include individuals, partnerships, corporations, and other associations. The partnership is a legal relationship originating from a voluntary contract between parties, which may be oral or written or simply implied from the acts of the parties. No formal sanction or recognition by a governmental unit is required in its formation.

NATURE OF THE PARTNERSHIP

The partnership form of organization is widely used. As in the case of the corporate form, the partnership makes possible the pooling of resources for some common business purpose. The partnership has been employed for both small and large-scale operations. Many partnerships represent an association of no more than two persons; some units, however, represent an association of dozens of persons. The partnership may be a small enterprise selling goods or services at a single location, or it may be a large enterprise with branches or offices at many different locations. Most accounting and law firms with offices throughout the nation, as well as many sales, construction, and engineering firms of national scope, are organized as partnerships.

Certain important characteristics of the partnership form of organization deserve special note.

Mutual Agency

Each partner is an agent of the partnership for the purpose of its business. Acts of a partner bind the partnership, provided they are within the

---

[1]This is the definition given in the Uniform Partnership Act, which has been adopted by a majority of the states. The discussion of partnerships in this and succeeding chapters is based upon the Uniform Partnership Act except where reference is made to other law.

1

partner's express or implied authority. Acts of a partner that do not fall into the category of carrying on business in the usual manner will not bind the partnership unless there is special authorization from copartners.

Limited Life

Since the partnership is a relationship originating from a contract between certain parties, any change in the relationship terminates the contract and dissolves the partnership. The withdrawal of a partner or the death of a partner, for example, automatically dissolves the partnership. Continuity of the partnership in these circumstances can be provided for by prior agreement, however.

Unlimited Liability

The liability of partners is not limited to the amounts of their investments. Persons entering into contracts with an "association of individuals" can look to these separate individuals for payment of their claims if partnership property is insufficient to satisfy such claims. Partners, therefore, may be held personally liable and their separate assets may be attached to meet partnership obligations.

Ownership of an Interest in a Partnership

Properties invested in a partnership are no longer separately owned but belong to the association of individuals comprising the partnership. The party who invests property in a partnership gives up the right to the separate enjoyment and use of such property. In transferring property to be identified with the partnership, an *interest* as a co-owner is acquired. Unless otherwise provided by agreement, this interest gives the partner an equal voice in the management of the partnership, the right to inspect the books of account of the firm, and the right to obtain an accounting of firm activities. Under certain circumstances, partners may pledge, transfer, or sell their interests in partnership properties.

Participation in Partnership Profits

Each partner shares in the profits of the partnership. However, an agreement that calls for a sharing of profits alone does not of itself create a partnership. A party may agree to accept a share of business profits as compensation for services or for the use of certain properties, but a partnership will not be recognized in the absence of definite intent on the part of the parties to enter into this form of relationship.

PARTNERSHIP AS AN ASSOCIATION OF INDIVIDUALS AND AS A SEPARATE ENTITY

The partnership is defined as an association of persons. It involves a pooling of assets and calls for an accounting for each partner's interest in the pooled assets. It is founded upon an agreement between persons, and it terminates with the expiration of the agreement or a change in the parties to the agreement. Furthermore, a contractual relationship between a partnership and other parties is actually a contract between partners, jointly and individually, and such other parties, since partners can be held liable in their private capacities for claims that cannot be satisfied by the firm. For certain purposes, however, the partnership takes on the attributes of a separate entity. For example, it acquires, holds, and transfers properties in its own name, and it enters into contracts with others. Partners act as agents of the firm. The partnership is thus alternately viewed as an association of individuals and as a separate business entity.

CHOOSING BETWEEN PARTNERSHIP AND CORPORATE FORM

When several persons decide to pool their resources in a single business venture, they must choose between organizing as a partnership or as a corporation. This decision calls for a careful evaluation of the relative advantages and disadvantages of the two forms of enterprise under the particular circumstances. Among the advantages to be considered in choosing the partnership form are the relative ease of its formation and dissolution, the personal character of the organization in its relationships with others, and the relative freedom and flexibility that it enjoys in its activities. Conversely, the disadvantages include the personal liability of partners for debts of the organization, the lack of business continuity, and the difficulties in transferring ownership interests. When there is a need for a large amount of capital in establishing a business, parties will normally find it necessary to adopt the corporate form of organization.

The relative income tax positions of the two forms of business also require careful consideration. Under present federal income tax laws, the partnership is a tax-reporting entity but not a tax-paying entity. Income tax laws require the partnership to file an informational return that summarizes partnership operations and shows the distribution of income among owners. Partners must report their distributive shares of the partnership income on their individual income tax returns, whether or not such income is distributed and made available to the partners. Corporations, on the other hand, are taxpaying entities. Business income of the corporation is subject to corporate tax rates. Corporation income after income taxes is also taxed as income of the stockholder when it is distributed as dividends or when it is distributed in liquidation.

Federal income tax legislation provides that under certain circumstances and subject to special limitations, corporations that can qualify as "Subchapter S" corporations may elect a special tax status in which they are treated for tax purposes essentially as a partnership. The income or loss is attributed to stockholders and the corporations pay no federal income taxes. When a corporation can qualify as a "Subchapter S" corporation and elects such special tax status, the corporate tax return becomes no more than an informational return, and stockholders report as income subject to individual tax rates their pro rata shares of the taxable income of the corporation, whether distributed by the corporation or retained by it.[2]

Income tax factors, both those that normally apply as well as those that are elective under special conditions, may play important parts in choosing between the partnership and corporate forms of organization. A review of the tax factors relating to the partnership and to the corporation should be made with each change of the tax laws and tax rates to determine whether there would be any advantage in changing the form of an existing business.

KINDS OF PARTNERSHIPS

Partnerships are classified as trading and nontrading partnerships, and distinctions are made among general partnerships, limited partnerships, and joint-stock companies.

Trading and Nontrading Partnerships

A partnership whose main activity is the manufacture or the purchase and the sale of goods is known as a *trading partnership*. A partnership that is organized for the purpose of rendering services is known as a *nontrading partnership*. A firm of accountants, attorneys, or realtors would be considered a nontrading partnership. The distinction between trading and nontrading partnerships is significant in determining the proper limits of a partner's implied powers to act on behalf of the firm.

General and Limited Partnerships

A *general partnership* is one in which all partners may publicly act on behalf of the firm and in which each partner can be held individually liable for obligations of the firm. Such partners are known as *general partners*. Statutes of most of the states permit the formation of a *limited partnership*, wherein the activities of certain partners are limited and the personal liability of these parties in turn is limited to a stated amount, which may be the amount actually invested.[3] Such partners are known as *limited* or *special partners*. Laws under which limited partnerships may be organized provide that at least one member of the firm shall be a *general partner* whose liability is unlimited. When limited partners act in a manner that would indicate to others that they are general partners, their liabilities to outsiders become the same as general partners. A limited partnership must hold itself out to the public as such and must comply with the provisions of the limited partnership act under which it is formed.

---

[2]Several requirements must be met if a corporation is to qualify as a "Subchapter S" corporation. The corporation may not have more than one class of stock or more than 25 stockholders. It must derive no more than 20% of its gross receipts from royalties, rents, dividends, interest, annuities, and gains from the sales or exchanges of stock or securities during the taxable year. Furthermore, not more than 80% of its gross receipts can originate from sources outside of the United States.

[3]The Uniform Limited Partnership Act has been formulated to bring about uniformity in the formation and operation of the limited partnership.

Joint-Stock Companies

A partnership may be formed with a capital structure in the form of transferable shares. Such an organization is known as a *joint-stock company*. Ownership of shares is usually evidenced by a stock certificate and gives a party the right to participate in the management of the firm, to share in the profits, and to transfer holdings. Transfer of shares does not affect the continuity of the organization. The liability of each member of a joint-stock company is unlimited, as in the case of a general partnership. The joint-stock company, then, has features of both the partnership and corporate forms of organization. The joint-stock company has its origin in the common law, although in several states it is now regulated by statutory law.

ARTICLES OF PARTNERSHIP

The partnership is created by an agreement that must possess all of the essential elements required of any enforceable contract. Although a partnership may be formed by an oral agreement, it is always preferable that the agreement be in writing so that misunderstandings and disputes between parties as to the nature and the terms of the contract may be avoided or reduced to a minimum. The agreement in writing is referred to as the *articles of partnership*.

The articles of partnership should contain all of the terms relating to the establishment of the partnership. The articles should set forth fully and clearly the agreement that has been reached on important matters such as:

(1) The partnership name, the parties entering into the agreement, and the location of the business.
(2) The effective date of partnership formation and the duration of the contract.
(3) The character and the scope of the business and its location.
(4) The investments by each partner and the values assigned to such investments.
(5) The rights, powers, and duties of the partners, as well as any limitations upon the authority of partners.
(6) The books and accounts of the partnership and the fiscal year that is adopted.
(7) The profit-and-loss-sharing ratio, including any special provisions for the recognition of differences in investment and service contributions.
(8) Special interest charges and credits relating to investments by partners, and special compensation allowed for services rendered by partners.
(9) Partners' investments and withdrawals subsequent to formation and their treatment in the accounts.
(10) Life insurance on partners and treatment of insurance premiums, recoveries on policies, etc.

(11) Special procedures for settlement of a partner's interest upon withdrawal or death.

(12) Methods for resolving disputes between partners.

If any change is made in the partnership agreement after formation, such a change requires the approval of all of the parties. When certain matters are not covered by agreement, reference is made to partnership law in resolving any differences between the partners.

INTEREST IN CAPITAL AND SHARE IN PROFITS

The accounting problems peculiar to a partnership relate to the measurement of the individual partners' ownership equities or *interests* in the firm. A partner's interest in a firm should be distinguished from the right to share in firm profits. A partner's interest is summarized in an individual capital account and consists of the original investment, subsequent investments and withdrawals, and the partner's share of firm profits and losses.

Partners may agree to share profits and losses in any manner, irrespective of capital interests. In the absence of an express agreement, partnership law provides that profits and losses shall be divided equally; when there is an express agreement as to profits but none as to losses, losses are divided in the same ratio as profits.

The significance of the foregoing is indicated in the following illustration. A and B enter into partnership. A and B invest assets and are to receive credit of $30,000 and $10,000 respectively for their contributions. The partners agree to share profits and losses equally. Partnership activities are summarized at this point as follows:

	Net Assets	A, Capital	B, Capital
Investments..	$40,000	$30,000	$10,000

A has a $30,000 interest in the firm, which has a total capital of $40,000; A's interest may be referred to as a ¾ or 75% interest. B's interest is $10,000, which is a ¼ or 25% interest.

Assume that subsequent partnership activities result in a net income of $25,000. Partnership accounts will report the following:

	Net Assets	A, Capital	B, Capital
Investments..	$40,000	$30,000	$10,000
Net income..	25,000	12,500	12,500
Total..	$65,000	$42,500	$22,500

The agreement between A and B provides that profits are to be divided equally. Therefore the interests of both A and B increase by $12,500. Not only have interests changed in amount, but they have also changed relative to each other and are no longer in a 3:1 relationship. The changes in interests, absolute or relative, have no effect on the profit-and-loss ratio, however; the partners will continue to share future profits and losses equally. If liquidation takes place at this point and assets realize book value, A is entitled to $42,500 and B to $22,500, as reported in their capital accounts.

Assume in the example above that instead of net income of $25,000, operations result in a net loss of $25,000. The loss is divided equally, and the accounts will report the following:

	Net Assets	A, Capital	B, Capital
Investments...............................	$40,000	$30,000	$10,000
Net loss.....................................	(25,000)	(12,500)	(12,500)
Total..	$15,000	$17,500	($ 2,500)

B's capital account now shows a debit balance of $2,500. This balance may be regarded as a receivable because it represents a claim by the partnership against B. If the firm is liquidated at this point and net assets realize book value, B will be required to contribute $2,500 in settlement of this deficiency; A will receive $17,500, consisting of the proceeds from asset realization, $15,000, and the amount recoverable from B, $2,500.

The problems arising in the determination of partners' respective ownership interests as a result of investments, withdrawals, and profits and losses are discussed in detail in the remaining pages of this chapter. The significance of the respective ownership interests when a partnership dissolves is considered in the chapters that follow.

RECORDING PARTNERS' INVESTMENTS

Investments by partners may be made in the form of cash or other assets as provided in the partnership contract. When assets other than cash are invested, it is necessary for the partners to agree upon the value of such assets. The assets are recorded in accordance with the agreement, and the partners' capital accounts are credited for the amounts of the respective investments.

The importance of proper valuation of assets invested by partners cannot be overemphasized. The values originally assigned to assets are credited to the partner investing the assets and become a measurement of the partner's interest; subsequent sales of these assets at amounts other than book value result in profit and loss items that are divided in the profit-and-loss ratio. If equity is to be achieved, then, assets invested by partners should be reported at their fair market values; only increases or decreases in the values of such assets taking place during the term of partnership will be allocated among the partners.

CHANGE FROM SOLE PROPRIETORSHIP TO PARTNERSHIP

Frequently an individual who operates a business joins with others in forming a partnership. The assets and the liabilities of the business may be transferred to the newly formed partnership. When the individual's business books are to be employed for the new partnership, entries are made on these books to give effect to the new organization. When new books are to be opened for the partnership, entries are required on the individual's books to record the transfer of the net assets to the firm, and entries are made on the new books to show the beginning asset, liability, and capital balances of the partnership.

To illustrate, assume that E and F form a partnership. E has been operating a business that is to be carried on by the new partnership; F is to invest cash of $25,000. Just before the partnership is formed, a balance sheet is drawn up for E's business as follows:

E
Balance Sheet
June 30, 19X7

Assets			Liabilities and Capital	
Cash..		$16,200	Liabilities	
Accounts receivable............	$20,000		Accounts payable................	$24,000
Less allowance for doubt-				
ful accounts.................	1,200	18,800	Capital	
Merchandise inventory		21,400	E, capital	40,400
Supplies		1,600		
Furniture and fixtures..........	$12,000			
Less accumulated depre-				
ciation.........................	5,600	6,400		
Total assets......................................		$64,400	Total liabilities and capital.................	$64,400

It is agreed that E shall withdraw the cash and that the partnership shall take over the remaining assets and assume the liabilities. However, the following adjustments are to be made in recognizing the asset transfer and in establishing E's interest:

Accounts receivable: Uncollectible accounts of $1,000 are to be written off; a 4% allowance for doubtful accounts is to be recognized on remaining accounts.

Merchandise inventory: Goods previously valued at cost calculated in terms of last-in, first-out are to be recognized at their present market value of $26,600.

Furniture and fixtures: Replacement value is $15,000, but the asset is considered to be 50% depreciated and has a fair market value of $7,500.

Goodwill: E is to be allowed credit for goodwill of $10,000 that is considered to be related to E's business.

Participant's Books are Retained for Partnership

If E's books are retained for the new partnership, the following entries may be made:

Transaction	Entry		
To record the restatement of E's investment as agreed:	Allowance for Doubtful Accounts......................................	440	
Decrease in accounts receivable ...... $ 1,000	Merchandise Inventory.............	5,200	
Decrease in allowance for doubtful accounts (to report allowance at 4% of $19,000, or $760).............. 440	Accumulated Depreciation........	5,600	
Increase in merchandise inventory ... 5,200	Goodwill	10,000	
Increase in furniture and fixtures:	Accounts Receivable.............		1,000
Decrease in cost balance.. $4,500	Furniture and Fixtures..........		4,500
Elimination of accumulated depreciation................. 5,600 1,100	E, Capital..............................		15,740
Establishment of goodwill................ 10,000			
To record the withdrawal of cash by E.	E, Capital...................................	16,200	
	Cash		16,200
To record the investment of cash by F.	Cash	25,000	
	F, Capital..................................		25,000

A balance sheet for the partnership follows:

E and F
Balance Sheet
June 30, 19X7

Assets			Liabilities and Capital		
Cash..		$25,000	Liabilities		
Accounts receivable	$19,000		Accounts payable................		$24,000
Less allowance for doubtful accounts	760	18,240			
Merchandise inventory		26,600	Capital		
Supplies		1,600	E, capital	$39,940	
Furniture and fixtures..........		7,500	F, capital	25,000	64,940
Goodwill...............................		10,000			
Total assets		$88,940	Total liabilities and capital..................		$88,940

New Books Are Opened for the Partnership

If new books are opened for the partnership, entries on the new books are made as follows:

Transaction	Entry		
To record investment by E.	Accounts Receivable...............	19,000	
	Merchandise Inventory.............	26,600	
	Supplies	1,600	
	Furniture and Fixtures.............	7,500	
	Goodwill	10,000	
	Allowance for Doubtful Accounts.............................		760
	Accounts Payable		24,000
	E, Capital..............................		39,940
To record investment by F.	Cash	25,000	
	F, Capital................................		25,000

If new books for the partnership are opened, books for the sole proprietorship must be closed. Asset, liability, and capital accounts may be closed by a single compound entry. If desired, it would be possible to record the restatement of assets and the recognition of goodwill on the individual's books. This would be followed by a compound entry to close all of the account balances as adjusted.

CONSOLIDATION OF BUSINESSES

The accounting procedures described in the preceding section are also applied when two or more businesses are consolidated in the formation of a partnership. The articles of partnership should indicate clearly how the interests of the partners are to be determined. It is also important that the parties agree upon the valuations to be assigned to assets and liabilities. Books of one of the constituent units may be used for the newly formed partnership or a new set of books may be opened.

PARTNERS' ACCOUNTS

Accounts for recording transactions with partners consist of (1) capital accounts, (2) drawing or personal accounts, and (3) receivable and payable accounts.

Capital and Drawing Accounts

Partners' original investments are recorded in capital accounts for each partner. Transactions between the partnership and the individual partners resulting in changes in the partners' ownership interests may be summarized in the capital accounts or in separate drawing accounts. Changes in partners' interests arise from transactions such as the following:

Increases

(1) Investments in the partnership of cash, merchandise, or other assets.
(2) Assumption or payment by the individual partners of partnership obligations.
(3) Collection by the partnership of personal claims of partners.
(4) Profits from partnership operations.

Decreases

(1) Withdrawals from the partnership of cash, merchandise, or other assets.
(2) Collection of partnership claims by individual partners.
(3) Assumption or payment by the partnership of personal indebtedness of partners (individual income taxes, life insurance premiums, etc.).
(4) Losses from partnership operations.

The partnership agreement should indicate clearly those special considerations that are to apply as a result of absolute and relative changes in partners' interests. Entries can then be made in the accounts in a manner that will appropriately recognize changes in interests.

Normally, increases or decreases in capital that are interpreted as permanent capital changes are recorded directly in the capital accounts. Drawings by partners in anticipation of profits, and other increases and decreases of relatively minor amounts that are not viewed as of a permanent character, are recorded in the drawing accounts. At the end of the accounting period, profit or loss is summarized in the income summary account and the balance in this account is transferred to the drawing accounts. The resulting debit and credit balances in the drawing accounts are transferred to the partners' capital accounts.

In certain instances it may be desirable to maintain a permanent distinction between the original or fixed capitals and subsequent increases or decreases in capitals resulting from partners' investments and withdrawals and from profits and losses. This is the case, for example, when it is agreed that partners are to be credited with interest on capital balances that exceed original or fixed balances and are to be charged with interest on capital deficiencies. When a permanent distinction between original balances and changes in those balances is to be maintained, profits, losses, investments, and withdrawals may be summarized in the drawing accounts and these balances may be left open and carried into succeeding fiscal periods. A credit balance in a drawing account would indicate that the partner had withdrawn less than the increases in the partner's interest; a debit balance would indicate that withdrawals had exceeded such increases. When only profits, losses, and withdrawals against profits are summarized in the drawing accounts and these accounts are left open, the distinction between the capital and the drawing accounts of the partnership parallels the distinction between the invested capital and the retained earnings accounts of the corporation. Individual partner's capital and drawing balances would be combined in reporting each partner's total interest on the balance sheet.

Receivable and Payable Accounts

A withdrawal by a partner, made with the assumption of ultimate repayment to the firm, normally calls for the recognition of a special receivable balance. The amount receivable from the partner may be recorded by a charge to the account Advances to Partner or the account Notes Receivable from Partner, whichever is appropriate.

An advance to the firm by a partner, made with the assumption of ultimate repayment by the firm, normally calls for recognition of a special payable balance. The amount owed to the partner may be recorded by a credit to the account Loans Payable to Partner or the account Notes Payable to Partner, whichever is appropriate.

In certain instances, partners may agree to invest fixed amounts, with any subsequent withdrawals or investments to be recognized as partnership receivables and payables. Receivables from partners may be reported on the balance sheet as assets; payables to partners, as liabilities. When current settlement of these balances is anticipated, they would be recognized as current assets or current liabilities.

The partnership agreement should state clearly any interest provisions with respect to fluctuating capital balances. In the absence of a special agreement, the Uniform Partnership Act provides that partners are entitled to interest on capital that exceeds the amounts they agreed to contribute; however, the Act does not require that partners be charged for interest on withdrawals that reduce their invested capital. When partner receivable and payable balances are recognized, special agreements should be made concerning the rate of interest that is applicable on these balances.

DISTRIBUTION OF PROFITS AND LOSSES

Partners may agree to the distribution of profits and losses in any manner they wish. The agreement on this matter should be specific and complete so that misunderstandings and disputes may be avoided.

Profits and losses are generally divided in one of the following ways:

(1) Equally.
(2) In an arbitrary ratio.
(3) In the ratio of partners' capitals.
(4) Interest to be allowed on partners' capitals, the balance to be divided on some arbitrary basis as agreed.
(5) Salaries or bonus to be allowed for partners' services, the balance to be divided on some arbitrary basis as agreed.
(6) Interest to be allowed on partners' capitals, salaries to be allowed for partners' services, the balance to be divided on some arbitrary basis as agreed.

As a basis for illustrating each of these methods, assume that a profit of $36,000 is determined for the firm of A and B at the end of a fiscal year. Regular withdrawals by partners in anticipation of profits have been summarized in the drawing accounts; permanent capital changes have been summarized in the capital accounts. Drawing and capital accounts at the end of the year appear as follows:

A, Drawing			B, Drawing		
Jan. 1 to Dec. 31	6,000		Jan. 1 to Dec. 31	19,000	

A, Capital			B, Capital		
		Jan. 1	50,000	Mar. 1	5,000	Jan. 1	70,000
		Apr. 1	10,000			Nov. 1	10,000

Profit and Loss Division Equally

Agreements between partners frequently call for the division of profits and losses equally. In the absence of a specific agreement to the contrary, both common and statutory law provide that profits and losses shall be divided equally, regardless of asset and service contributions. The entry for the partnership of A and B to record the division of the profit of $36,000 equally would be as follows:

Income Summary	36,000	
A, Drawing		18,000
B, Drawing		18,000

A's share of profits: ½ of $36,000 = $18,000
B's share of profits: ½ of $36,000 = 18,000
Total.................................. $36,000

The resulting balances in the drawing accounts may now be closed into the capital accounts.

Profit and Loss Division in Arbitrary Ratio

In order that differences in partners' capital or service contributions may be recognized, partners may agree to share profits in some arbitrary ratio that expresses such differences. For example, assume that, since the experience, ability, and reputation of A are factors of special significance to the success of the firm, A and B agree to divide profits in the ratio of 3:2. The entry to record the division of the profit of $36,000 is:

Income Summary	36,000	
A, Drawing		21,600
B, Drawing		14,400

A's share of profits: $3/5$ of $36,000 = $21,600
B's share of profits: $2/5$ of $36,000 = 14,400
Total.................................. $36,000

If operations had resulted in a loss of $36,000, A would have borne $3/5$ of the loss and B $2/5$ unless the agreement provided that losses were to be distributed in a manner other than the profit ratio. It would be possible, of course, for A and B to agree to share profits 3:2 but to share losses equally or in some other manner.

In certain cases, partners may agree to share part of the earnings in a particular ratio and the balance differently. For example, A and B could agree to divide profits up to $20,000 in the 3:2 ratio and any profits in excess of this amount equally.

Profit and Loss Division in the Ratio of Partners' Capitals

When properties invested by the partners represent significant contributions to the success of the firm, partners may agree to divide profits in the ratio of partners' capitals. When profits are to be divided in the capital ratio, the agreement should indicate specifically whether the ratio is to be defined in terms of:

(1) Original capitals.
(2) Capitals at the beginning of each fiscal period.

(3) Capitals at the end of each fiscal period.
(4) Average capitals for each fiscal period.

Original capitals. If the agreement between A and B provides that the periodic division of profits shall be based upon original capitals, reference would be made to the amounts originally invested by the partners.

Capitals at the beginning of each fiscal period. If the periodic division of profits is to be based upon capitals at the beginning of each period, the beginning balances as reported by the capital accounts would provide the basis for allocation. Assuming this agreement for A and B, the entry to record the division of the profit of $36,000 for the year is:

```
Income Summary ...........................................        36,000
    A, Drawing...................................................                 15,000
    B, Drawing...................................................                 21,000
```

```
A, Capital, January 1................................................   $  50,000
B, Capital, January 1 ..............................................       70,000
Total capitals, January 1 .........................................   $120,000

A's share of profits: 50,000/120,000 of $36,000 =     $  15,000
B's share of profits: 70,000/120,000 of $36,000 =        21,000
Total...................................................................... $  36,000
```

Capitals at the end of each fiscal period. If the partnership agreement provides for a division of profits based upon partners' capitals at the end of each year, calculations for the division of profits will be made as follows:

```
A, Capital, December 31 ...........................................     $  60,000
B, Capital, December 31 ...........................................         75,000
Total capitals, December 31 ......................................     $135,000


A's share of profits: 60,000/135,000 of $36,000 =      $  16,000
B's share of profits: 75,000/135,000 of $36,000 =          20,000
Total......................................................................    $  36,000
```

Average capitals for each fiscal period. If the division is to be based upon average capitals for the year, calculations will be made as follows:

	Date	Investment Balance		Number of Months Unchanged	Month-Dollars	
A:	Jan. 1	$50,000	×	3	$150,000	
	Apr. 1	60,000	×	9	540,000	$ 690,000
				12		
B:	Jan. 1	$70,000	×	2	$140,000	
	Mar. 1	65,000	×	8	520,000	
	Nov. 1	75,000	×	2	150,000	810,000
	Total			12		$1,500,000

A's share of profits: 690,000/1,500,000[4] of $36,000 = $ 16,560
B's share of profits: 810,000/1,500,000 of   36,000 =   19,440
Total .... $ 36,000

When partners wish to distribute profits in terms of relative investments, the use of average capitals, which provides for the recognition of
capital changes during the period, normally offers the most equitable
method. An agreement for the use of average capitals also acts as an incen-
tive for additional investments when these can be profitably employed.
When this method is to be used, the agreement should indicate clearly what
investments and withdrawals are to be recognized in calculating average
capitals. For example, an agreement may provide that all of the changes in
partners' interests are to be recognized; here recognition would be given to
investments and withdrawals reported in partners' drawing accounts as
well as in capital accounts. Or, the agreement may provide that regular
drawings are to be permitted in anticipation of accruing profit and that
calculations shall be made without regard to drawings. Under the latter
agreement, it would be desirable to limit entries in the drawing accounts to
regularly allowed drawings, with amounts withdrawn in excess of such allowances, as well as amounts invested, being recorded directly in the capital accounts. The capital accounts will then reflect the data that are to be
considered in calculating the average capital ratio.

In the example, partners' investments were expressed in terms of
month-dollars. In making month-dollar calculations, partners may agree to
consider investments and withdrawals made during the month as having
been made as of the beginning of the month, as of the beginning of the
following month, or as of one of these dates depending upon whether the
change took place before or after the middle of the month. Any unit of time
can be used in calculating the ratio of average capitals. Thus, when investments and withdrawals are made during the month, greater accuracy in
calculating respective investments can be obtained by using weeks or the
actual number of days, thereby determining the ratio of partners' capitals in
terms of week-dollars or day-dollars.

Profit and Loss Division with Allowance
of Interest on Partners' Capitals

In the preceding section it was suggested that when investments in
properties represent significant contributions to a firm, partners can agree
to distribute profits or losses in accordance with relative capital contributions. For example, when individuals pool their cash for investment in the
commodities or securities markets, they may feel that an equitable alloca-

---

[4]It would be possible to determine each partner's average capital for the year by dividing the sum of the
month-dollar products for each by 12. For example: A's average capital = $690,000 ÷ 12, or $57,500; B's
average capital = $810,000 ÷ 12, or $67,500. Or average capitals may be calculated by multiplying the investment balances during the year by the fractions of the year for which such balances are unchanged. For
example, A's average capital = ($50,000 × 3/12) + ($60,000 × 9/12), or $57,500; B's average capital = ($70,000 ×
2/12) + ($65,000 × 8/12) + ($75,000 × 2/12), or $67,500. The use of balances reduced to year-dollars will not
change the ratio between partners and will result in exactly the same profit or loss for each partner.

tion of profit or loss calls for division according to relative investments. However, there are instances when partners may feel that, while respective capitals need to be considered, division of profits in the capital ratio will not be equitable for the following reasons: (1) investments represent only one factor contributing to the success of the joint enterprise and the arrangement for profit distribution should recognize all of these factors; (2) in the event of loss, the partner making the larger investment absorbs the greater part of the loss, with no recognition of any special capital contribution.

Interest on capital balances. In providing for the recognition of differences in investments as well as the other factors responsible for successful operations, partners may agree to allow interest on capitals, with any profit or loss after interest divided in some arbitrary ratio. An agreement for interest should indicate the interest rate that is to be applied. It should also indicate whether calculations are to be made in terms of capital balances as of a certain time or on average capitals for the period. The law makes no provision for remuneration to partners for their investments in the absence of an agreement to that effect.

To illustrate the allowance of interest on partners' capitals, assume that A and B agree to allow interest on average investments at 6%; any profit or loss balance is to be divided equally. Assuming no entries for interest during the course of the period, entries to record the allowance of interest and the remaining distribution of profit follow:

Income Summary		7,500	
A, Drawing			3,450
B, Drawing			4,050

A: $50,000 at 6% for 3 months	$ 750	
$60,000 at 6% for 9 months	2,700	$ 3,450
B: $70,000 at 6% for 2 months	$ 700	
$65,000 at 6% for 8 months	2,600	
$75,000 at 6% for 2 months	750	4,050
Total interest allowable		$ 7,500

Income Summary		28,500	
A, Drawing			14,250
B, Drawing			14,250

Original balance in income summary account	$36,000
Less allowance for interest	7,500
Balance to be distributed equally	$28,500

The profit distribution may be summarized in a single entry as follows:

Income Summary	36,000	
A, Drawing		17,700
B, Drawing		18,300

The effect of an allowance for interest is to distribute only a limited amount of the profit in the capital ratio. In the case of A and B, 6% of combined average capitals, or $7,500, was distributed in the ratio of average capitals, the balance being distributed equally.

When the partnership agreement provides without qualification that interest is to be allowed on investments, interest must be allowed even though operations have resulted in earnings that are less than the allowable interest or in a loss. After the entry for interest in such a case, the debit balance in the income summary account is transferred to the partners' drawing accounts in the profit-and-loss ratio. For example, assume that operations for A and B prior to the recognition of interest had resulted in a loss of $10,000. Entries to close the income summary account would have been as follows:

Income Summary	7,500	
A, Drawing		3,450
B, Drawing		4,050
Interest allowable on capitals.		
A, Drawing	8,750	
B, Drawing	8,750	
Income Summary		17,500

Original balance in income summary account	(Dr.)	$10,000
Allowance for interest	(Dr.)	7,500
Balance distributable equally........................	(Dr.)	$17,500

The net effect of the foregoing on capitals is:

		A		B		Total
Allowance for interest.................	(Cr.)	$3,450	(Cr.)	$4,050	(Cr.)	$ 7,500
Less distribution of resulting loss	(Dr.)	8,750	(Dr.)	8,750	(Dr.)	17,500
Net effect	(Dr.)	$5,300	(Dr.)	$4,700	(Dr.)	$10,000

If profit and loss were distributed in the ratio of partners' capitals, B would have been charged with the greater share of the loss. If profit and loss were distributed equally, B would have absorbed a loss of $5,000. The provision for interest, however, secured a $600 advantage for B over A.

Assume that partnership operations had resulted in a loss of only $500. The allowance for interest and the distribution of the total loss would result in an increase in B's capital with a reduction in A's capital equal to the loss plus the increase accruing to B. The net effect on capitals would be:

		A		B		Total
Allowance for interest..................	(Cr.)	$3,450	(Cr.)	$4,050	(Cr.)	$7,500
Less distribution of resulting loss..	(Dr.)	4,000	(Dr.)	4,000	(Dr.)	8,000
Net effect...................................	(Dr.)	$ 550	(Cr.)	$ 50	(Dr.)	$ 500

Here, too, the agreement for interest resulted in a $600 advantage for B. Partners can provide by agreement, of course, that profit or loss shall be distributed in some arbitrary manner without recognition of interest when the results from operations fail to cover a specified interest allowance.

Interest on excess investments. It may be agreed to allow interest on the excess of the average investment of one partner over that of another. If this were the agreement between A and B, the income summary account would be debited for $600 [6% × ($67,500 − $57,500)] and the drawing account of

B would be credited for this amount. Any income summary balance would then be transferred to the partners' drawing accounts in the agreed ratio.

The agreement for interest may take still other forms. For example, an agreement may provide for fixed capital contributions from individual partners, with interest allowed on amounts in excess of such fixed amounts and interest charged on any deficiencies. In other instances, interest may be allowed on capitals in excess of a fixed proportion of total capital, or interest may be charged on capital deficiencies in terms of such a fixed proportion.

Interest on temporary advances or loans. When a partnership makes a temporary advance to a partner or receives an amount as a temporary loan from a partner and these transactions are recognized as creating debtor or creditor relationships between the partner and the firm, interest charges and credits on such transactions are recognized as interest expense and interest income. Interest accruals are recognized periodically on these items just as on other receivable and payable balances. When settlement for interest is made by cash, entries to record the collection of interest or the payment of interest are made in the usual manner. When settlement is not to be made in cash but by adjustments to partners' capitals, interest on an advance to a partner is recorded by a charge to the partner's drawing account and a credit to Interest Income; interest on a loan made by a partner to the firm is recorded by a charge to Interest Expense and a credit to the partner's drawing account.

Recognition of revenue and expense items may be called for in other relationships between a partnership and the individual partners. In certain instances, for example, a partnership and an individual partner may enter into a landlord-tenant relationship. In other instances, the parties may enter into a seller-buyer relationship. Such relationships call for accounting procedures similar to those just described.

Profit and Loss Division with Allowance of Salaries or Bonuses to Partners

Partners may wish to provide for a division of profits that recognizes differences in their abilities and experience or in the time devoted by them to the business. Partners may agree to an arbitrary ratio for this purpose. However, the use of an arbitrary ratio to recognize personal differences is subject to the same limitations as those found in the use of the capital ratio to recognize capital differences; i.e., it may fail to provide satisfactory recognition of the several factors contributing to the success of the enterprise and it may prove inequitable in the event of loss when the partner who has made the greater personal contribution to the firm is charged with the greater part of the loss.

Salaries. In recognizing differences in personal contribution as well as other factors that are responsible for the success of the enterprise, it may be agreed that partners shall be allowed salaries, with any profit or loss balance after salaries divided in some arbitrary ratio. The law makes no provision for remuneration for partners' services in the absence of an agreement thereto; however, the Uniform Partnership Act does provide that, when a partnership must be liquidated as a result of the death of a partner, surviving partners are entitled to reasonable compensation for their services in winding up the business.

To illustrate the application of a salary arrangement, assume that A and B agree to the allowance of monthly salaries of $1,500 and $1,250 respectively; any profit or loss balance is to be shared equally. Amounts actually withdrawn by partners during the year were recorded in their drawing accounts as summarized on page 12. The profit of $36,000 before recognition of salaries is distributed to the partners by the following entries:

Income Summary...	33,000	
A, Drawing		18,000
B, Drawing		15,000

A: Salary for 12 months at $1,500	$18,000
B: Salary for 12 months at $1,250	15,000
Total salaries allowable	$33,000

Income Summary...	3,000	
A, Drawing		1,500
B, Drawing		1,500

Original balance in income summary account....	$36,000
Less allowance for salaries.............................	33,000
Balance distributable equally	$ 3,000

The foregoing may be summarized in a single entry as follows:

Income Summary...	36,000	
A, Drawing		19,500
B, Drawing		16,500

When an agreement provides for salaries without qualification, salary distributions must be made even though profit is inadequate to cover salaries or there is a loss. After salaries are recorded in such a case, the income summary account shows a debit balance that is transferred to the partners' accounts as agreed.

The allowance of salaries to A and B of $18,000 and $15,000 will provide a $3,000 advantage to A in all distributions. If the partners do not wish such an advantage to remain effective when profit does not cover salaries or when a loss is incurred, their agreement should include provisions for scaling down or suspending salaries under these circumstances.

When fixed salary amounts are paid to partners at regular weekly or monthly intervals, a salary account for each partner may be charged. After nominal accounts are closed into Income Summary and the net profit is determined, the salary accounts may be transferred to the income summary account in determining the balance of the profit that remains to be distributed. When salaries are allowed but the partners do not necessarily withdraw the allowed amounts at regular intervals, the partners' drawing accounts instead of salary accounts should be debited for all cash withdrawals. Consideration of the amounts allowed as salaries should be deferred until the books are closed. At that time the income summary account is debited and each partner's drawing account is credited with the amount allowed as salary for the entire period. The balance in the income summary account is then divided as agreed.

When an agreement permits partners to make withdrawals, it is important that the nature of such withdrawals be clearly defined. For example, assume that an agreement permits partners to withdraw specified amounts periodically. Is it the intent of the parties simply to permit partners to draw cash out of the business in anticipation of profits, or is it their intent to consider allowed withdrawals as partial profit distributions? If the first interpretation is applicable, profit or loss distribution will be made without regard to drawing account balances, and withdrawals will be subtracted from distributive profit shares in arriving at each partner's capital change for the period. If the second interpretation is applicable, drawing account balances will be closed into Income Summary, from which the distribution to partners will be as agreed.

Bonuses. In some instances a managing partner is allowed a bonus that is to be based on the earnings of the business. The bonus is commonly stated as a percentage of profits, but the agreement should indicate whether the percentage is to be applied to the profit determined before deduction of the bonus or after deduction of the bonus. To illustrate, assume that A, the managing partner, is allowed as a bonus 20% of the profit before the bonus is deducted. The bonus would be $7,200, determined by applying the 20% rate to the profit from operations, $36,000. But if A is allowed a bonus of 20% of the profit after deduction of the bonus, the bonus would be calculated as follows:

The bonus plus the net profit after deduction of the bonus = $36,000.
Let X = the net profit after deduction of the bonus
And $.20X$ = the bonus allowed to A.
Then: $1.20X = \$36,000$
            $X = \$30,000$
          $.20X = \$6,000$, the bonus allowed to A.

To record the bonus allowed to A, the income summary account is charged and A's drawing account is credited. The balance in the income summary account is then distributed as agreed.

In addition to the statement as to how the bonus calculation is to be made, the bonus agreement should indicate whether the bonus rate is to be applied to the full increase in capital, including all extraordinary and nonrecurring items that receive current recognition, or only to the net income as measured by normally recurring revenue and expense items.

Profit and Loss Division with Allowances for Interest and Salaries

Partners may agree to allowances of both interest and salaries as a means for dividing profits equitably. When both salaries and interest are allowed, the income summary account may be charged and the drawing accounts credited for both classes of allowances at the end of each period. Any balance in the income summary account is then divided in the agreed ratio. The entries for salaries, interest, and the transfer of a remaining balance in the income summary account are the same as those illustrated in earlier sections.

Profit Distribution on the Income Statement

A full analysis of the distribution of earnings may be reported at the bottom of the income statement. Assume that the firm of A and B previously referred to has agreed to the following: monthly salaries of $1,500 and $1,250 respectively; interest at 6% on average capitals; and any profit or loss balance to be divided equally. This can be reported on the income statement as follows:

	A	B	Total
Net income for year..			$36,000
Net income divided as follows:	A	B	Total
Amount allowed as salaries............................	$18,000	$15,000	$33,000
Amount allowed as interest............................	3,450	4,050	7,500
	$21,450	$19,050	$40,500
Less reductions made equally for amount by which salaries and interest exceed net income...	2,250	2,250	4,500
Net income distribution......................................	$19,200	$16,800	$36,000

Interest for Partners' Investments and Salaries for Partners' Services Treated as Expenses

In the foregoing discussions, net income was viewed as the return to the partners for their full contribution to the business as owners — capital as well as personal service. Interest and salary allowances to partners were regarded as means of providing for an equitable distribution of such income. The partnership was viewed as an association of individuals; accounting for the partnership paralleled that for the sole proprietorship, where no compensation to an owner for capital or services was recognized in measuring net income.

It is possible to record allowances to partners for interest and salaries as expense items rather than as distributions of net income. If the partnership is viewed as a separate entity, special compensation allowed to partners may be regarded the same as the compensation accruing to the stockholders of a corporation who, at the same time, have entered into relationships with the corporation as creditors and employees. Frequently the partners themselves may prefer to view interest and salary allowances as expenses of operation and may call for statements that summarize net income after such charges. Federal income tax laws provide that fixed or guaranteed payments to partners for the use of capital or for services must be reported for tax purposes just as though they were paid to outsiders.

When partners' interest and salaries are treated as expenses, charges for these items are made to expense accounts rather than to the partners' drawing accounts; expense balances are then closed into the income summary account in arriving at the earnings distributable in the agreed profit-and-loss ratio. On the income statement, partners' interest and salaries would be listed with the other expenses in arriving at the net income or loss. Whether partners' interest and salaries are treated in the accounts as expense items or as distributions of net income, the ultimate distributions of partnership earnings among the partners are exactly the same.

CORRECTIONS IN PROFITS OF PRIOR PERIODS

When a misstatement of earnings for a prior period is discovered, the profit-and-loss-sharing agreement for the fiscal period in which earnings were misstated must be considered in correcting the capital accounts. The correct earnings for the prior period, as well as the proper share of the profit or loss to which each of the partners was entitled, should be calculated. The share of the profit that each partner actually received is compared with the share that should have been received in arriving at the corrections that are required in the capital accounts.

STATEMENT OF CHANGES IN PARTNERS' CAPITAL ACCOUNTS

The balance sheet and the income statement for a partnership are accompanied by a third statement that reports the changes that have taken place in the partners' interests during the period. The statement of changes in partners' capital accounts may be prepared in the following form:

A and B
Statement of Changes in Partners' Capital Accounts
For Year Ended December 31, 19X1

	A	B	Total
Capitals, January 1, 19X1	$50,000	$70,000	$120,000
Additional capital investments	10,000	10,000	20,000
	$60,000	$80,000	$140,000
Less capital withdrawals		5,000	5,000
Balance	$60,000	$75,000	$135,000
Net income for year	19,200	16,800	36,000
	$79,200	$91,800	$171,000
Less personal drawings	6,000	19,000	25,000
Capitals, December 31, 19X1	$73,200	$72,800	$146,000

QUESTIONS

1. What are the essential characteristics of a partnership?

2. Under what circumstances is the partnership viewed as a separate entity? Under what circumstances is the partnership viewed as an association of individuals?

3. In what respects is the partnership form of organization similar to the corporate form? What are the essential differences between the two forms of organization?

4. Distinguish between (a) trading and nontrading partnerships; (b) general and limited partnerships.

5. What is the nature of the joint-stock company?

6. State at least twelve matters in regard to the partnership relationship that should be fully covered in the partnership agreement.

7. What is the significance of a partner's *interest* in a firm? What is the significance of a partner's *share in the profits* of a firm?

8. Give four sources for (a) an increase in a partner's interest in a firm, (b) a decrease in a partner's interest.

9. (a) Indicate the source of partner receivable and payable balances and the treatment of such balances on the statements. (b) How would you record interest charges and credits emerging from such relationships?

10. State the common bases employed in the distribution of partnership profits. Under what circumstances would each of the bases named be the most acceptable?

11. In the absence of an agreement:
   (a) Is interest allowed on capital investments?
   (b) Is interest charged on partners' drawings?
   (c) Is interest allowed on partners' advances to the firm beyond their agreed investments?
   (d) Is compensation allowed partners for extra time devoted to the partnership?
   (e) Is compensation allowed for special services of a partner relative to firm liquidation?

12. (a) What is the purpose of allowing interest on invested capital? (b) What are the possible treatments for such interest in the accounts? (c) What is the effect of the allowance of interest when operations result in a loss?

13. In forming a partnership with Jackson, Macey suggests that interest of 6% be allowed on average capitals, the balance of any profit to be distributed in the ratio of average capitals. Jackson insists that there is no need for the interest provision if profits are to be distributed in the ratio of average capitals. Is this correct?

14. Martin and McCrea are partners sharing profits 2:1 respectively. Martin borrows cash from the firm and ultimately returns the amount borrowed together with interest. McCrea wants to be credited for the full amount of the interest collected. Do you agree?

15. A partnership agreement permits partners A and B to withdraw $100 per week. The profit and loss ratio is 2:1 respectively. What two interpretations may be made of this agreement? Which interpretation will A prefer?

16. (a) What is the purpose of allowing salaries to partners? (b) What is the ultimate effect upon capitals if partners' salaries are treated as an expense as compared with their treatment as distributive shares of profit?

17. The partnership of S and T uses buildings that are owned by T, for which T is to receive rent of $10,000 per year. At the end of the first year of operations, the accountant charges rent and credits T for $10,000. T insists that the full charge for rent should be made against S. Comment on T's statement.

18. What are the advantages of reporting partners' salaries and interest on the income statement as expenses as compared with recognition of these items as partial distributions of net income?

19. X and Y divide profits and losses according to capital balances at the beginning of each year. In 1982, securities acquired in 1972 at a cost of $10,000 are sold for $35,000. Partner X insists that the profit should be recognized as having accrued over a 10-year period at the rate of $2,500 per year; the profit and loss ratio for the past 10 years, then, should be applied to the annual increments in arriving at the distribution of the $25,000 gain. (a) Evaluate this proposal. (b) How should a controversy on this point have been avoided?

EXERCISES

1. Peters admits Quarles as a partner in business. Accounts in the ledger for Peters on November 30, 19X6, just before the admission of Quarles, show the following balances:

Cash...	2,600	
Accounts Receivable..	12,000	
Merchandise Inventory......................................	18,000	
Accounts Payable		6,200
Peters, Capital..		26,400

It is agreed that for purposes of establishing Peters' interest the following adjustments shall be made:

(1) An allowance for doubtful accounts of 2% of accounts receivable is to be established.
(2) The merchandise inventory is to be valued at $20,200.
(3) Prepaid expenses of $650 and accrued liabilities of $400 are to be recognized.

Quarles is to invest sufficient cash to obtain a ⅓ interest in the partnership.
(a) Prepare the entries to adjust the account balances in establishing Peters' interest and to record the investment by Quarles. (b) Prepare a balance sheet for Peters and Quarles.

2. P and R, partners, divide profits and losses on the basis of average capitals. Capital accounts for the year ended December 31, 19X2, are shown below. The net profit for 19X2 is $13,500. Prepare summaries to show how the profit is divided. (Changes in capitals during the first half of a month are regarded as effective as of the beginning of the month; changes during the second half of a month are regarded as effective as of the beginning of the following month.)

P, Capital				R, Capital			
Mar. 9	5,000	Jan. 1	30,000	Sept. 4	4,000	Jan. 1	33,000
Oct. 26	7,500	July 1	10,000			Apr. 14	15,000
		Sept. 22	10,000				

3. Boyle and Clark are partners sharing profits in the ratio of 3:2. The partnership agreement states that each partner is to be allowed drawings of $3,000 annually. Each partner withdrew this amount during 19X9, drawing accounts being charged. The net profit for 19X9 was $10,000. What entries are necessary to close the accounts at the end of the year if the balances in the drawing accounts are recognized as (a) partners' drawings and (b) partners' salaries?

4. A, B, and C form a partnership and agree to maintain average investments of $100,000, $50,000, and $50,000 respectively. Interest on an excess or on a deficiency in a capital contribution is to be computed at 6%. After the interest allowances, A, B, and C are to share any balance in the ratio of 5:3:2. Average amounts invested during the first six months were as follows: A, $120,000; B, $55,000; C, $40,000. A loss from operations of $2,500 was incurred for the first six months. How is this loss distributed among the partners?

5. Allen and Powers are partners. The partnership agreement provides that Allen "shall receive a bonus of 25% of the profits." What two interpretations of this phrase are possible? Assuming a profit of $20,400, what amount would be allowed as a bonus in each case?

6. R, S, and T, attorneys, decide to form a partnership and agree to distribute profits in the ratio of 5:3:2. It is agreed, however, that R and S shall guarantee fees from their own clients of $60,000 and $50,000 respectively, that any deficiency is to be charged directly against the account of the partner failing to meet the guarantee, and that any excess is to be credited directly to the account of the partner with fees exceeding the guarantee. Fees earned during 19X4 are classified as follows:

From clients of R	$100,000
From clients of S	40,000
From clients of T..................	10,000

Operating expenses for 19X4 are $20,000. Prepare the entries to close the nominal accounts into the income summary account and the latter into the capital accounts at the end of 19X4.

7. Partners A and B share profits 3:1 after annual salary allowances of $4,000 and $6,000 respectively; however, if profits are not adequate to meet the salary allowances, the entire profit is to be divided in the salary ratio. Profits of $9,000 were reported for the year 19X8. In 19X9 it is ascertained that in calculating net income for the year ended December 31, 19X8, depreciation was overstated by $3,600 and the ending inventory was understated by $800. Prepare the correcting entry that is required in 19X9.

PROBLEMS

1-1. Allen and Bailey entered into partnership on March 1, 19X0, investing $62,500 and $37,500 respectively. It was agreed that Allen, the managing partner, was to receive a salary of $15,000 per year and also 10% of the net profit after adjustment for the salary; the balance of the profit was to be divided in the ratio of original capitals. On December 31, 19X0, account balances were as follows:

Cash..........................	$ 35,000	Payables....................	$ 30,000
Receivables...............	33,500	Sales........................	116,500
Fixtures.....................	22,500	Allen, Capital.............	62,500
Purchases.................	98,000	Bailey, Capital	37,500
Returns and Allow-			
ances....................	2,500		
Operating Expenses ...	30,000		
Allen, Drawing...........	10,000		
Bailey, Drawing..........	15,000		
	$246,500		$246,500

Inventories on December 31, 19X0, were: merchandise, $36,500; supplies, $1,250. Prepaid taxes and insurance were $475 and accrued liabilities totaled $775. Depreciation on fixtures is to be computed at 20% per year.

Instructions: (1) Prepare the adjusting and closing entries on December 31, 19X0.

(2) Prepare an income statement, a balance sheet, and a statement of changes in partners' capital accounts for the period ended December 31, 19X0.

1-2. On July 1, 19X6, Baker and Carr decided to pool their assets and form a partnership. The firm is to take over business assets and assume business liabilities, and capitals are to be based on net assets transferred after the following adjustments:

(1) Carr's inventory is to be valued at $14,000.
(2) An allowance for doubtful accounts of 5% is to be established on the accounts receivable of each party.
(3) Accrued liabilities of $800 are to be recognized on Baker's books.
(4) Carr is to be allowed goodwill of $10,000 and is to invest the additional cash necessary to have a 60% interest in the new firm.

Balance sheets for Baker and Carr on July 1 before adjustments are given below:

	Baker	Carr
Cash..	$ 7,500	$ 4,500
Accounts Receivable...................................	18,000	15,000
Inventory	16,000	12,000
Equipment..	10,000	12,000
Accumulated Depreciation..........................	(4,500)	(1,500)
	$47,000	$42,000
Accounts Payable	$13,800	$10,000
Capital...	33,200	32,000
	$47,000	$42,000

Carr's books are to be continued as the partnership books after July 1.

Instructions: (1) Prepare the entries to adjust and close Baker's books.

(2) Prepare the required entries on the books of Carr upon the formation of the partnership.

(3) Prepare a balance sheet for the firm of Baker and Carr as of July 1, 19X6.

1-3. The capital accounts for Cross and Deming at the end of 19X1 are as follows:

Cross

January 1	Balance..	35,000
May 1	Investment...................................	15,000
October 1	Withdrawal.................................	10,000

Deming

January 1	Balance..	25,000
April 1	Withdrawal...................................	5,000

Net income for the year ended December 31, 19X1, is $30,000.

Instructions: Prepare journal entries to record the transfer of net income to the capital accounts under each of the following assumptions. (Show the procedure used in calculating the respective amounts in the explanation after each entry.)

(1) Net income is divided 65% to Cross, 35% to Deming.

(2) Net income is divided in the ratio of investments at the beginning of the period.

(3) Net income is divided in the ratio of average investments.

(4) Interest at 8% is allowed on average investments and the balance of net income is divided equally.

(5) Salaries of $20,000 and $16,000 are allowed to Cross and Deming respectively, and the balance of net income is divided in the ratio of investments at the end of the period.

(6) Cross is allowed a bonus of 33⅓% of net income after bonus, and the balance of the net income is divided in the ratio of investments at the beginning of the period.

1-4. The capital accounts of Clark and Dobson show the following facts for the fiscal year ended December 31, 19X4:

Clark			Dobson		
Jan. 1	Balance.........	$26,000	Jan. 1	Balance.........	$16,500
Mar. 30	Investment.....	3,000	May 18	Investment.....	5,000
May 10	Investment.....	7,000	Aug. 24	Withdrawal.....	2,000
July 25	Withdrawal.....	4,000	Dec. 31	Balance.........	19,500
Dec. 31	Balance.........	32,000			

The income summary account shows a credit balance of $23,800 on December 31.

Instructions: Prepare the journal entries to transfer the balance in the income summary account to the capital accounts if the profit is to be distributed on each of the following bases. (Show the procedure used in calculating the respective amounts in the explanation after each entry.)

(1) In the ratio of investments at the beginning of the fiscal period.

(2) In the ratio of average capitals. Investments and withdrawals are to be considered as made at the beginning of the month if made before the middle of the month and are to be considered as made at the beginning of the following month if made after the middle of the month.

(3) Interest of 6% on average capitals, salaries to Clark and Dobson of $15,000 and $10,000 respectively, and any balance equally. (Investments and withdrawals are to be considered as in part [2].)

(4) Allowance to Clark of a bonus of 25% of the net profit after bonus, interest of 6% to be allowed on the excess of the average investment of one partner over that of the other, and any balance in ratio of 3:2 to Clark and Dobson respectively. (Investments and withdrawals are to be considered as in part [2].)

(5) Salaries of $1,500 and $1,000 a month to Clark and Dobson respectively, provided annual earnings are sufficient to cover the allowance; if earnings are insufficient, the profit shall be distributed in the salary ratio; if operations result in a loss, it shall be distributed equally.

1-5. The following account balances appear in the ledger for the firm of Evans and Gale at the end of 19X7 before the profit for the year has been transferred to the partners' accounts:

Evans, Drawing	7,200	
Gale, Drawing	12,500	
Evans, Loan		17,500
Evans, Capital		50,000
Gale, Capital		50,000
Income Summary		30,250

The following information is to be considered in closing the income summary account and the drawing accounts:

(1) The cost of installing equipment at the beginning of 19X7, $2,700, was charged to expense. The installation relates to equipment with a 10-year life.

(2) The loan to the firm was made by Evans on March 1, 19X7. No entry has been made for interest on the loan, which is 6% and is to be paid to Evans at the time the loan is repaid.

(3) The partnership agreement permits Evans and Gale to withdraw weekly sums of $150 and $225 respectively, these amounts to be regarded as salaries. Actual withdrawals by partners differed from allowed amounts and are summarized in the drawing accounts.

(4) Gale, the managing partner, is entitled to a special bonus of 25% of the net profit after deduction of all special allowances to partners (including the bonus), and any remaining profit is to be distributed equally.

Instructions: (1) Prepare the entries required to close the accounts.

(2) Prepare a statement of changes in partners' capital accounts for 19X7.

1-6. Miller, Nash, and Otis formed a partnership on January 1, 19X5, investing $40,000, $24,000, and $20,000 respectively. Partners agree to the following distribution of profits:

(1) Annual salaries are to be allowed partners as follows:
Miller, $4,800
Nash, $6,000
Otis, $6,000
(2) Interest is to be allowed on partners' capitals as of the beginning of each year at the rate of 6%.
(3) Miller, the managing partner, is to be allowed a bonus of 20% of the net profit after treating as expenses partners' salaries, interest, and bonus.
(4) Profits and losses after partners' salaries, interest, and bonus are to be divided equally.

The partnership fiscal period is to be the calendar year. Activities of the partnership for 19X5, 19X6, and 19X7 are summarized below:

| | Profit or Loss Before Interest, Salaries, and Bonus | Cash Withdrawals | | |
		Miller	Nash	Otis
19X5	Loss — $ 2,760	$ 6,000	$ 7,240	$ 8,000
19X6	Profit — 12,000	6,980	8,160	8,860
19X7	Profit — 29,400	10,200	12,000	10,600

Instructions: Prepare a statement of changes in partners' capital accounts covering the three-year period, 19X5–19X7.

1-7. Bedford and Brown formed a partnership on January 1, 19X0, investing $40,000 and $60,000 respectively. Partners agree to share profits as follows:

(1) Bedford and Brown are to be allowed salaries of $800 and $1,000 per month respectively, and each salary allowance is to be increased by $100 per month beginning January 1, 19X2.
(2) Interest is to be allowed on partners' capital balances as of the beginning of each year at the rate of 5%.
(3) Profits and losses after salaries and interest are to be divided equally.

The partnership fiscal period is the calendar year. Net income for the firm and drawings of the partners for the period January 1, 19X0, to September 1, 19X2, are summarized below.

| | Net Income Before Salaries and Interest | Drawings | |
		Bedford	Brown
Jan. 1 — Dec. 31, 19X0	$35,000	$8,800	$14,200
Jan. 1 — Dec. 31, 19X1	24,000	6,500	8,000
Jan. 1 — Sept. 1, 19X2	8,500	4,000	5,500

On September 1, 19X2, the partners received a cash offer of $90,000 for total net assets of the firm and accepted the offer. Net assets were turned over to the purchaser, and the cash was distributed to the partners in final settlement.

Instructions: Prepare a statement of the partners' capital accounts that shows all of the changes in capital that took place over the period January 1, 19X0, to September 1, 19X2, when the firm was dissolved.

1-8. Balance sheet data for the firm of M, N, and O as of January 1, 19X9, follow:

Assets	$122,500	Liabilities................	$ 62,500
		M, Capital	20,000
		N, Capital	20,000
		O, Capital................	20,000
	$122,500		$122,500

Partners share profits and losses equally after the allowance of a salary to O, the managing partner, of $750 monthly.

As a result of operating losses sustained at the beginning of 19X9, M advanced $15,000 to the firm on April 1; it was agreed that 6% interest would be allowed on the loan. With continued losses, the members decided to liquidate. O agreed to take over partnership equipment in part settlement, the transfer being made at an agreed value of $4,000. On November 1, $20,000 cash was available for distribution to partners after sale of remaining assets and the payment of partnership obligations to outsiders. O had withdrawn salary for January and February but had not received salary for the period March 1 to November 1; no other cash payments had been made to partners. Available cash was distributed on November 1 and the firm was declared dissolved.

Instructions: Prepare a statement of partners' capital accounts, showing partners' capital and loan balances together with all of the changes in such balances that took place during 19X9.

1-9. Marsh, Norton, Olin, and Parks are partners. Their interests in the capital and their profit and loss ratios are as follows:

Marsh	40%
Norton	30
Olin	20
Parks...	10

To provide a means by which the remaining partners might purchase a deceased partner's interest from the partner's estate, a life insurance program was inaugurated whereby life insurance proceeds would be paid to the remaining partners in proportion to their percentage ownership in the partnership. Since each partner was in effect insuring the life of each of the other partners, it was agreed that partners would not pay any part of the premiums on policies covering their own lives.

In 19X3 the premium on all policies amounted to $9,000, which was charged as an expense on the books and thereby deducted from the year's profit. The profit was then credited to the partners in proportion to their ownership percentages. Investigation of the insurance premiums revealed:

Premium on life of Marsh...........	$3,500
Premium on life of Norton..........	1,400
Premium on life of Olin..............	2,300
Premium on life of Parks	1,800

Instructions: Prepare the correcting entry that should be made to the partners' capital accounts in order to reflect properly the agreement as to the insurance. Give your supporting computations in good form.

(AICPA adapted)

1-10. The Trading Company, a partnership, was formed on January 1, 19X8, with four partners, D, E, F, and G. Capital contributions were as follows:

D	$100,000
E	50,000
F	50,000
G	40,000

The partnership agreement provides that partners shall receive 5% interest on the amounts of their capital contributions. In addition, D is to receive a salary of $10,000 and E a salary of $6,000, which are to be charged as expenses of the business.

The agreement further provides that F shall receive a minimum of $5,000 per annum from the partnership and G a minimum of $12,000 per annum, both including amounts allowed as interest on capital and their respective shares of profits. The balance of the profit is to be shared in the following proportions:

D	30%
E	30
F	20
G	20

Instructions: Calculate the amount that must be earned by the partnership during 19X8, before any charge for interest on capital or partners' salaries, in order that D may receive an aggregate of $25,000 including interest, salary, and share of profits. Show your calculations in statement form.

(AICPA adapted)

1-11. X, Y, and Z have been partners throughout 19X5. Their average capital balances for the year and their balances at the end of the year before closing the nominal accounts are as follows:

	Average Capital Balances	Capital Balances Dec. 31, 19X5
X	(Cr.) $90,000	(Cr.) $60,000
Y	(Cr.) 3,000	(Dr.) 1,000
Z	(Cr.) 7,000	(Cr.) 10,000

The profit for 19X5 is $75,000 before partners' drawing allowances are charged and before interest on average balances at the agreed rate of 4% per annum is determined. X is entitled to a drawing account credit of $10,000, Y of $7,000, and Z of $5,000 per annum. The balance of the profit is to be distributed at the rate of 60% to X, 30% to Y, and 10% to Z.

The partners desire to distribute cash to themselves so that, after credits and distributions as indicated in the preceding paragraph, the balances in their accounts will be proportionate to their profit-sharing ratios. None of the partners is to pay in any money, but they desire to distribute the lowest possible amount of cash.

Instructions: Prepare a statement of the partners' accounts, showing balances at the end of 19X5 before closing, the allocations of the net profit for 19X5, the cash distributed, and the closing balances.

(AICPA adapted)

1-12. The law firm of B, C, and D has decided to dissolve partnership as of June 30, 19X7, and has called you in to render an accounting. The only records maintained are the checkbook and a daily record of cash received. The firm has been in existence for 4 years. Partners have equal capital investments and profits are divided equally. The partnership records show the following information concerning business assets:

	Cost	Accumulated Depreciation January 1, 19X7
Office furniture and fixtures..	$1,500	$ 450
Books................................	900	180
Automobile — B	2,000	600
Automobile — C	1,000	200
Automobile — D	3,000	600
	$8,400	$2,030

Cash receipts to June 30, 19X7, amount to $60,000. A summary of cash disbursements follows:

Rent..	$ 1,400
Wages and salaries......................................	2,102
Entertainment...	4,000
Automobile and miscellaneous	1,000
Withdrawals — B	9,000
Withdrawals — C	10,000
Withdrawals — D	12,000
	$39,502

There are no liabilities on June 30, 19X7. The capital accounts of the partners as of January 1, 19X7, were equal. Depreciation has been charged against partnership profits. Automobiles are depreciated over a 5-year period and office furniture and fixtures and books over a 10-year period. The bank balance at June 30, 19X7, is $29,998. The three partners have agreed to distribute the office furniture and fixtures in kind and they feel that the distribution will be equal. The automobiles, which were purchased from partnership funds, will be retained by the partners to whom they have been assigned. The books will be distributed to B.

Instructions: Prepare a statement of changes in partners' capital accounts from January 1, 19X7, to June 30, 19X7, and the final cash distribution to each partner.

(AICPA adapted)

1-13. A, B, and C, attorneys, agree to consolidate their individual practices as of January 1, 19X9. The partnership agreement includes the following features:

(1) C had leased office space and is bound by the lease until June 30, 19X9. The monthly rental is $600. The partners agree to occupy C's office space until the expiration of the lease and to pay the rent. The partners concur that the rent is too high for the space and that a fair rental value would be $450 per month. The excess rent is to be charged to C at year-

end. On July 1 the partners moved to new quarters with a monthly rental of $500.

(2) Each partner's capital contribution is the net amount of the assets and liabilities taken over by the partnership, which are as follows:

	A	B	C
Cash....................................	$ 5,000	$ 5,000	$ 5,000
Accounts receivable..............	14,000	6,000	16,000
Furniture and library	4,300	2,500	6,200
	$23,300	$13,500	$27,200
Accumulated depreciation......	$ 2,400	$ 1,500	$ 4,700
Accounts payable	300	1,400	700
	$ 2,700	$ 2,900	$ 5,400
Capital contributions..............	$20,600	$10,600	$21,800

Partners guarantee the collectibility of their receivables .

(3) No salaries are to be paid to the partners. The individual partners are to receive 20% of the gross fees billed to their respective clients during the first year of the partnership. After operating expenses are deducted, the balance of the fees billed is to be credited to the partners' capital accounts in the following ratios: A, 40%; B, 35%; C, 25%.

   On April 1, 19X9, D is admitted to the partnership, and is to receive 20% of the fees from new business obtained after April 1, after expenses applicable to that new business are deducted. Expenses before uncollectible accounts expense are to be apportioned to the new business in the same ratio as fees from the new business are to total gross fees.

The following information pertains to the partnership's activities in 19X9:

(1) Fees were billed as follows:

A's clients...............................	$22,000
B's clients..............................	12,000
C's clients...............................	11,000
New business:	
Prior to April 1.....................	3,000
After April 1	12,000
Total	$60,000

(2) Total expenses, excluding depreciation and uncollectible accounts expenses, were $19,350, including the total amount paid for rent. Depreciation was to be computed at the rate of 10%. Depreciable assets purchased during 19X9, on which one-half year's depreciation was to be taken, totaled $5,000.

(3) Cash charges to the partners' accounts during the year were:

A...	$ 5,200
B	4,400
C...	5,800
D	2,500
	$17,900

(4) Of A's and B's receivables, $1,200 and $450 respectively proved to be uncollectible. A new client billed in March for $1,600 had been adjudged bankrupt and a settlement of 50 cents on the dollar was made.

Instructions: Prepare a statement of changes in partners' capital accounts for the year ended December 31, 19X9. Supporting computations should be in good form.

(AICPA adapted)

2
Partnerships — Dissolution upon Ownership Changes

A partnership is said to be dissolved when the original association for purposes of carrying on activities has ended. For example, a partnership is automatically dissolved by the death of a partner. When there is dissension among partners, a court may decree the dissolution of a partnership upon the request of one or more of the partners. The withdrawal of one or more partners through the sale of their interests also dissolves the original association.

With dissolution of a partnership, the authority of the partners to carry on business as a going concern is ended. Although dissolution brings to an end the association of individuals for their original purpose, it does not mean the termination of business or even an interruption in its continuity. Upon the death or retirement of a partner, the business may continue as a new partnership composed of the remaining members.

CONDITIONS RESULTING IN DISSOLUTION

The conditions that result in the dissolution of a partnership are classified and summarized below.

Dissolution by Act of the Parties

Certain acts by members of a partnership result in dissolution. Under this heading may be included:

(1) Termination of time or accomplishment of purpose. If a definite time for termination is stated in the partnership agreement, or if a particular objective is to be accomplished, termination of the time or accomplishment of the objective fulfills the partnership contract and the firm may dissolve. When a partnership does not have a fixed life or when it continues after stipulated conditions have been fulfilled, it is known as a *partnership at will*.

(2) Mutual agreement. Partners may mutually agree at any time to a change in membership or to termination of their association.

(3) Withdrawal of partners. Partners have the power to withdraw from a partnership at any time, thus dissolving the firm. If, however, a partner exercises this power in contravention of the partnership agreement, he or she becomes liable to the other partners for damages that may be sustained through such action. In other words, partners have the *power* to withdraw from a partnership at any time, but they must also have the contractual *right* to do so if they are to avoid liability for damages. An exception to this rule is found in the *partnership at will*, from which partners may withdraw at any time without liability to the other partners. One or more partners may also withdraw from a partnership without liability upon the unanimous consent of all partners.

Dissolution by Operation of the Law

A partnership is automatically dissolved upon the occurrence of certain contingencies recognized by law, namely:

(1) Death of any member of the partnership.
(2) Bankruptcy of any partner or of the partnership.
(3) Any event that makes it unlawful for the business to be carried on or for individual members to carry on as a partnership.
(4) War against a country of which a member is a citizen.

Dissolution by Judicial Decree

A court may decree dissolution on application by or for a partner upon evidence of any of the following circumstances:

(1) Insanity of a partner or the inability of a partner for any cause to fulfill his or her part of the partnership contract.
(2) Conduct of a partner that affects unfavorably the business being carried on.
(3) Internal dissension among partners.
(4) Impossibility of profitable continuation of the business.
(5) Other reasons that render dissolution equitable, such as fraud or misrepresentation in the formation of the partnership.

ACCOUNTING FOR DISSOLUTION

The remaining pages of this chapter consider the problems that arise upon dissolution as a result of (1) the admission of a new partner, (2) the withdrawal of a partner, (3) the death of a partner, and (4) the incorporation of a partnership. The special accounting problems incident to the winding up of a business, including those relating to the realization of business assets, settlement of obligations, and settlement with respective partners, are considered in Chapters 4 and 5.

ADMISSION OF NEW PARTNERS

Admission of a new partner is possible only with the consent of all of the partners. Such an admission brings about a new association of individuals and represents the formation of a new partnership; the original partnership is considered dissolved by common consent. A partnership agreement is binding only while the relationship between the original parties to the agreement remains unchanged. Upon the admission of a new partner, an agreement should be drawn up that states the partners' interests upon formation of the partnership, the distribution of future profits and losses among partners, and all of the other considerations relative to the new association.

The newly formed partnership may continue to use the books and the records of the original firm, but certain account balances will generally require restatement. As long as the original partnership continues in operation, conventional practice does not call for the current recognition of changes in asset values; gains or losses on properties owned by the business emerge only upon ultimate disposition of the properties. But the admission of a new partner involves the formation of a new firm wherein contributions by the participating members must be completely and accurately recognized.

Present market values should be determined for the assets that are to be identified with the new organization and account balances should be restated to report such values. Inventories should be restated at present replacement values. Adequate allowances should be established for receivables. Marketable securities should be reported at their current market values. Noncurrent assets should be reported at present appraised values. All liabilities should be determined and reported on the books. The foregoing changes give rise to profit or loss allocable to the original partners in the original profit-and-loss-sharing ratio. If such changes are not reported in the accounts, an incoming partner will participate in gains and losses that took place prior to admission.

Ordinarily an incoming partner makes some asset contribution for an interest in the newly organized firm. However, a person may be admitted as a partner without an investment and without the recognition of a capital interest. Under such circumstances, a capital interest will emerge as a result of future investments, withdrawals, and profit and loss distributions.

Although a person admitted into a partnership becomes a co-owner in all of the partnership property as of the date of admission, the new partner's liability on existing debt is limited under the provisions of the Uniform Partnership Act. The Act provides, "A person admitted as a partner into an existing partnership is liable for all the obligations of the partnership arising before his admission as though he had been a partner when such obligations were incurred, except that this liability shall be satisfied only out of partnership property." In the event of business insolvency, then, personal assets of a new partner cannot be seized in satisfaction of claims related to the original organization; but the new partner's personal assets can be seized in satisfaction of liabilities that arise from activities of the new organization.

A person may acquire an interest in a partnership by (1) the purchase of such an interest from one or more of the original owners, or (2) the investment of assets that increase the capital of the partnership.

Acquisition of Interest by Purchase

Partners have the power to sell part or all of their interest in a firm. If all the partners agree to the admission of the buyer of the interest as a partner, the admission dissolves the old partnership and brings into existence a new one. If the partners do not agree to the admission of the new party as a partner, the Uniform Partnership Act provides that the party simply acquires, in accordance with the contract, the profits, and upon the dissolution, the interest, to which the original partner would have been entitled. The transfer of the interest does not, of itself, dissolve the firm, nor does it entitle the buyer to interfere in the management of the business. If, under terms of the partnership agreement, the original partner does not have the right to transfer his or her interest but nevertheless does so, claims may be raised against that partner by the remaining partners for any losses that they incur through this action.

When an individual acquires a portion or all of the interest of a partner in a business, the interest acquired is recorded as the capital of the new partner and the capital of the selling partner is correspondingly reduced. The payment for the interest is not recorded on the books of the partnership, for this is simply a transaction between two individuals acting in their private capacities. To illustrate, assume that A and B are partners, each with a capital of $30,000 and sharing profits equally. C purchases ½ of B's interest for $18,000. A approves the admission of C as a partner. The original partnership books are to be retained by the new firm of A, B, and C. The only entry required on the books is:

B, Capital...	15,000	
C, Capital...		15,000

This entry is made regardless of the amount paid by C to B. The total capital of the partnership remains $60,000. A has a 50% interest in the new firm, B a 25% interest, and C a 25% interest.

The fact that C has acquired a 25% interest in the partnership of A, B, and C does not necessarily mean that profits and losses will be shared in the same percentage. Upon C's admittance, the partners should agree upon the future distribution of profits and losses. In the absence of an agreement, A, B, and C will share profits and losses equally.

Parties may feel that accounts fail to report the value of net assets satisfactorily and may decide to adjust valuations prior to the admission of the new partner. Net assets should be restated and the revaluation gain or loss recognized in the capital accounts of the original partners in their profit and loss ratios. When the price paid by an incoming partner is regarded to offer evidence of goodwill identified with the business but not reflected on the books, this intangible may be established on the books before the transfer of the interest is recorded.

Acquisition of Interest by Investment

When an individual acquires an interest by making an investment, the assets and the capital of the partnership are thereby increased. For example, assume that D and E have capitals of $20,000 and $10,000 respectively and share profits equally. Assets are properly valued. F is admitted as a partner upon investing $12,000. Profits and losses of the new firm are to be divided equally. The original partnership books are to be maintained for the new firm of D, E, and F. The investment is recorded as follows:

```
Cash.................................................................................  12,000
   F, Capital........................................................................       12,000
```

In recording the investment, F's admittance must conform to the terms of the agreement. In the absence of a specific agreement, the investment by F would be recorded as indicated. F receives credit for the actual amount invested; the interests of D, E, and F in the newly formed partnership are $20,000, $10,000, and $12,000. F's interest is 12/42, or approximately 29%.

Assume that the agreement between D, E, and F provides that F is to invest a sum sufficient for a ¼ or 25% interest in the new firm. In this case, the combined capitals of the original members, $30,000, would represent ¾ of the new capital, and the incoming partner would be required to invest $10,000 for a ¼ interest. Capitals for partners D, E, and F, then, would be $20,000, $10,000, and $10,000 respectively; interests of D, E, and F would be $20,000/$40,000 or 50%, $10,000/$40,000 or 25%, and $10,000/$40,000 or 25% respectively.

Investment with allowance of bonus or goodwill to old partners. When a partnership has operated with considerable success, the partners may admit a new member with the provision that (1) part of the new partner's investment shall be allowed as a bonus to the old partners, or (2) partnership goodwill shall be established and credited to the old partners.

Bonus. In the preceding section, capitals for D and E totaled $30,000 and F was credited for the $10,000 investment in acquiring a ¼ interest in the new partnership. Assume, however, that the partnership of D and E has operated with such success that F is willing to invest $12,000 for a ¼ interest. Since the net firm assets prior to F's investment are $30,000, an additional investment by F of $12,000 will increase the net assets to $42,000. If a capital account for F is credited with $12,000 and no change is made in the capital accounts of D and E, F's interest in the partnership will be 12/42, which is greater than the ¼ interest agreed upon previously. Since net assets after F's admission total $42,000, a credit of $10,500 to F will equal a ¼ interest. The amount by which the investment exceeds the interest allowed F may be considered a bonus to the old partners. The bonus is divided between the old partners in the original profit and loss ratio. Since D and E shared profits equally, the bonus of $1,500 results in an increase of $750 in each partner's capital. Assuming that the original books are to be used for the new partnership, the entry to record the investment by F is as follows:

```
Cash...........................................................................  12,000
    D, Capital..............................................................            750
    E, Capital..............................................................            750
    F, Capital..............................................................         10,500
```

Goodwill. But assume that F, while accepting a ¼ interest in the partnership, insists on being credited for the entire investment of $12,000. The valuation by F of a ¼ interest at $12,000 may be used as a basis for recording goodwill identified with the net asset contribution made by D and E to the new organization. If F's capital of $12,000 is to represent ¼ of the total capital, this total will have to be $48,000 and the combined capitals of D and E will have to be $36,000. Since the capitals of D and E now total $30,000, these balances must be increased by $6,000. Goodwill is debited and the original partners' capital accounts are credited for $6,000. The profit and loss ratio is used in distributing the capital increase of $6,000. The entries to record F's investment are as follows:

```
Goodwill.......................................................................   6,000
    D, Capital..............................................................          3,000
    E, Capital..............................................................          3,000

Cash...........................................................................  12,000
    F, Capital..............................................................         12,000
```

Since nothing is said about the profit-and-loss-sharing ratio in the foregoing, it is assumed that future profits and losses will be divided equally among D, E, and F.

Comparison of bonus and goodwill methods. In the previous examples, Partner F obtains a ¼ interest in assets and a ⅓ share of profits upon admission by the use of either the bonus method or the goodwill method. Although either method can be used in achieving the required interest for the new partner, the two methods offer the same ultimate results only (1) when the incoming partner's percentage share of profit and loss and percentage interest in assets upon admission are equal, and (2) when the former partners continue to share profits and losses between themselves in the original ratio. For example, if in the preceding examples F's share of profits was limited to 25% and D and E were to share remaining profits 37½% and 37½%, both the bonus and the goodwill methods would give the same ultimate results. To illustrate, balances in the examples were found to be as follows:

	Goodwill	Other Assets	D, Capital	E, Capital	F, Capital
When bonus method is used............................		$42,000	$20,750	$10,750	$10,500
When goodwill method is used............................	$6,000	$42,000	$23,000	$13,000	$12,000

Assume that assets ultimately realize no more than $42,000, failing to confirm the existence of goodwill. If the goodwill method is used in recording F's investment, the failure to realize goodwill will result in a loss distributable to partners in the profit and loss ratio. Ignoring intervening changes in proprietorship, capital balances for D, E, and F in each case will be:

	Goodwill	Other Assets	D, Capital	E, Capital	F, Capital
When bonus method is used............................		$42,000	$20,750	$10,750	$10,500
When goodwill method is used............................	$6,000	$42,000	$23,000	$13,000	$12,000
Deduct write-off of goodwill (loss distributed in profit and loss ratio, 37½%, 37½%, 25%)....	6,000		2,250	2,250	1,500
	–0–	$42,000	$20,750	$10,750	$10,500

The goodwill method ultimately gives account balances that are identical with those obtained through use of the bonus method.

On the other hand, assume that assets ultimately realize $48,000, validating the existence of goodwill. If the bonus method is used in recording F's investment, the realization of $6,000 in excess of asset book values will result in a gain distributable to partners in the profit and loss ratio. Ignoring intervening changes in proprietorship, capital balances for D, E, and F in each case will be:

	Goodwill	Other Assets	D, Capital	E, Capital	F, Capital
When goodwill method is used............................	$6,000	$42,000	$23,000	$13,000	$12,000
When bonus method is used............................		$42,000	$20,750	$10,750	$10,500
Add recognition of goodwill (gain distributed in profit and loss ratio, 37½%, 37½%, 25%)....	$6,000		2,250	2,250	1,500
	$6,000	$42,000	$23,000	$13,000	$12,000

Whether goodwill proves to be existent or nonexistent, then, the goodwill and the bonus methods give identical results when the incoming partner's share of profits is equal to the original interest acquired and the former partners continue to share profits and losses in their original ratio. If these conditions are not fully met, however, results will be different.

When an incoming partner's percentage share in profits exceeds the percentage interest allowed in assets upon admission, choice of the bonus method as compared with the goodwill method results in ultimate advantage to the new partner and corresponding disadvantage to the original partners. Recognition of goodwill upon admission increases the new partner's capital by the percentage share in assets, while recognition of goodwill later increases the new partner's capital by the percentage share in profits, which is larger than the percentage share in assets. When the new member's share in subsequent profits is less than the share in assets upon admission, the goodwill method results in ultimate advantage to the new member and disadvantage to the others; recognition of goodwill upon admission provides the new partner with a greater capital increase than recognition of goodwill later, which would be limited to the profit and loss percentage. Further advantages and disadvantages may accrue to the original partners through a change in the profit and loss ratio between them.

To illustrate, in the original examples previously given, it was stated that, upon admission, F was granted a ¼ interest in assets but a ⅓ share in future profits; D and E were to share remaining profits equally. Under these circumstances, use of the bonus method offers ultimate advantage to F and corresponding disadvantage to D and E. Assume that assets ultimately realize only $42,000 and thus fail to confirm the existence of goodwill. The ultimate write-off of goodwill results in capital balances as follows:

	Goodwill	Other Assets	D, Capital	E, Capital	F, Capital
When bonus method is used		$42,000	$20,750	$10,750	$10,500
When goodwill method is used	$6,000	$42,000	$23,000	$13,000	$12,000
Deduct write-off of goodwill (loss distributed equally)............	6,000		2,000	2,000	2,000
	–0–	$42,000	$21,000	$11,000	$10,000
Gain or (loss) through use of bonus method.			($ 250)	($ 250)	$ 500

The same advantages and disadvantages will emerge, assuming that assets ultimately realize $48,000, thus validating the existence of goodwill. Capital balances in each case will be as follows:

	Goodwill	Other Assets	D, Capital	E, Capital	F, Capital
When goodwill method is used	$6,000	$42,000	$23,000	$13,000	$12,000
When bonus method is used		$42,000	$20,750	$10,750	$10,500
Add recognition of goodwill (gain distributed in profit and loss ratio, equally)	$6,000		2,000	2,000	2,000
	$6,000	$42,000	$22,750	$12,750	$12,500
Gain or (loss) through use of bonus method.			($ 250)	($ 250)	$ 500

Asset revaluation. It must be observed that the foregoing discussion assumes that values assigned to net assets on the original partnership books are acceptable. If F's investment of $12,000 for a ¼ interest in the firm is based upon a recognition of the fact that net assets on the books at $30,000 are actually worth $36,000, appropriate entries would be required to restate assets at their current values and to raise the capitals of the original owners accordingly. Then, neither bonus nor goodwill requires recognition in recording the investment of the new partner.

The importance of a fully detailed agreement between partners has already been emphasized. Complete statements as to the profit-and-loss-sharing agreement as well as partners' interests in firm assets upon partnership formation are particularly important. In the latter case, not only the fractional interest but also the precise dollar interest should be indicated.

Investment with allowance of bonus or goodwill to new partner. A partnership may be in urgent need of additional funds or the partners may desire the services of a certain individual. In such instances a new member may be admitted with the provision that (1) part of the capitals of the old partners shall be allowed as a bonus to the new partner, or (2) goodwill shall be established and credited to the new partner.

Bonus. Assume that the firm of D and E in the previous examples needs additional capital as well as the services of F. D and E agree to allow F a ²/₅ interest for an investment of $12,000. If a capital account for F is credited with $12,000 and no change is made in the capital accounts of D and E, F's interest will be 12/42, which is less than a ²/₅ interest. Since the net assets of the partnership after F's admission total $42,000, a credit of $16,800 to F will equal a ²/₅ interest. The amount by which the interest allowed F exceeds the $12,000 investment may be considered a bonus contributed by the old partners. The bonus is subtracted from the capitals of D and E in the original profit and loss ratio. Assuming that the original partnership books are to be used for the new firm, the entry to record the investment by F is as follows:

Cash..	12,000	
D, Capital...	2,400	
E, Capital..	2,400	
F, Capital..		16,800

Goodwill. Assume, however, that D and E are unwilling to have their capital accounts reduced, although they are willing to allow F a ²/₅ interest in the firm for an investment of $12,000. The present capital balances of the partners may be used as the basis for determining the interest to be allowed F and the goodwill to be added to the partnership's books. If the sum of the capitals of D and E, $30,000, is to represent ³/₅ of the total capital, the total capital will have to be $50,000 and F's interest will have to be $20,000. Goodwill is debited for the difference between the amount invested by F and the amount to be credited to F's capital account. The entry to record F's admission is:

Cash..	12,000	
Goodwill..	8,000	
F, Capital..		20,000

Comparison of bonus and goodwill methods. Partner F obtains a $2/5$ interest in assets and a $1/3$ share of profits by the use of either the bonus method or the goodwill method in the previous example. Although either method can be used in achieving the required interest for the new partner, the ultimate effects upon the partners' capitals will not be the same. Under the circumstances given, F will prefer to be admitted with an allowance for goodwill because the percentage interest in assets upon admission to the firm is greater than the percentage share in subsequent profits. The nature of the comparisons that might be made in evaluating the two methods from the points of view of the different parties is similar to that described in the previous section.

Asset revaluation. The foregoing discussion assumes that values of net assets on the original partnership books are acceptable. If F's investment of $12,000 for a $2/5$ interest in the firm is based upon a recognition of the fact that net assets reported on the books at $30,000 are actually worth only $18,000, appropriate entries would be required to restate these assets and to reduce the capital balances of the original owners accordingly. Neither bonus nor goodwill, then, requires recognition in recording the investment of the new partner.

Bonus and goodwill determinations when not specifically stated. An agreement may indicate that an incoming partner is to receive an interest that is greater or smaller than that which would be recognized if the partner were simply to receive credit for the amount invested. Such an agreement, however, may fail to point out whether the required interest is to be accomplished through recognition of bonus or goodwill. In the absence of an express statement, the conditions for admission must be carefully analyzed in recording the partner's interest in the firm. A series of examples follow.

Assume that X and Y share profits equally. Capital accounts are as follows just before Z's admission:

$$\text{X, Capital...............} \quad \$25,000$$
$$\text{Y, Capital...............} \quad \$35,000$$

Example	Analysis	Entry		
(1) Z invests $20,000 for a ¼ interest.	Since recognition of Z's investment at $20,000 will result in a ¼ interest (20,000/80,000), neither bonus nor goodwill is implied by the agreement.	Cash .... Z, Capital	20,000	20,000
(2) Z invests $30,000 for a ¼ interest.	Since recognition of Z's investment at $30,000 will result in more than a ¼ interest (30,000/90,000), a ¼ interest is achieved either by (1) crediting Z with $22,500 (¼ × $90,000) and recording the excess as a bonus to original partners or (2) crediting Z with $30,000 by recording goodwill and raising capitals of the original partners $30,000 (capital of original partners to be ¾ of new capital, or 3 × $30,000, or $90,000; present capital, $60,000).	Cash .... X, Capital Y, Capital Z, Capital *or* Cash .... Goodwill ... X, Capital Y, Capital Z, Capital	30,000 30,000 30,000	3,750 3,750 22,500 15,000 15,000 30,000

Example	Analysis	Entry		
(3) Z invests $30,000 for a $25,000 interest; total capital $90,000.	Since total capital is limited to $90,000, the sum of the original capital and Z's investment, then an investment of $30,000 by Z for a $25,000 interest implies a $5,000 bonus to original partners.	Cash .... X, Capital Y, Capital Z, Capital	30,000	2,500 2,500 25,000
(4) Z invests $30,000 for a ¼ interest in a total capital of $100,000.	Since Z is to receive an interest of $25,000, which is $5,000 less than the amount invested, and since total capital is to be $10,000 more than total invested capital, the implication is a bonus of $5,000 to original partners together with goodwill of $10,000 to original partners.	Cash .... Goodwill ... X, Capital Y, Capital Z, Capital	30,000 10,000	7,500 7,500 25,000
(5) Z invests $30,000 for a ½ interest.	Since recognition of Z's investment of $30,000 results in less than a ½ interest (30,000/90,000), a ½ interest is achieved either by (1) a $45,000 credit to Z (½ × $90,000), representing the $30,000 investment and a bonus of $15,000, or (2) a $60,000 credit to Z, representing the $30,000 investment and goodwill of $30,000 (capital of the new partner to be ½ of the new capital, or $60,000, since present capital is $60,000).	Cash .... X, Capital.. Y, Capital.. Z, Capital *or* Cash .... Goodwill ... Z, Capital	30,000 7,500 7,500 30,000 30,000	45,000 60,000
(6) Z invests $30,000 for a $40,000 interest in a total capital of $90,000.	Since the total capital is limited to $90,000, the sum of the original capital and Z's investment, then an investment of $30,000 for a $40,000 interest implies a bonus of $10,000 allowed to the incoming partner.	Cash .... X, Capital.. Y, Capital.. Z, Capital	30,000 5,000 5,000	40,000
(7) Z invests $30,000 for a ½ interest in a total capital of $100,000.	Since Z is to receive a $50,000 interest (½ × $100,000), which is $20,000 more than the amount invested, and since total capital is to be $10,000 more than total invested capital, the conditions for admission imply goodwill of $10,000 and also a bonus of $10,000 to the new partner.	Cash .... Goodwill ... X, Capital.. Y, Capital.. Z, Capital	30,000 10,000 5,000 5,000	50,000

SETTLEMENT WITH A WITHDRAWING PARTNER

A partner has the power to withdraw from a firm at any time. A partner who has the right to withdraw under the terms of the contract is entitled to claim the full amount of his or her interest in the firm. A partner who exercises the power to withdraw in violation of the partnership agreement and without the mutual consent of all participants becomes liable to the other partners for any damages they sustain through this action. Under the latter circumstances, a withdrawing partner's claim may suffer impairment in part or in whole by the damages attributable to the withdrawal.

The withdrawal of a partner may bring about the complete termination of the business. On the other hand, the business may be continued without interruption, with settlement being made with the withdrawing partner by (1) the purchase of his or her interest by another member of the firm or (2) the transfer of partnership cash or other assets in satisfaction of his or her interest. Under the latter circumstances, withdrawal of the partner would be considered to dissolve the old partnership and bring into existence a new one. The purchase of a withdrawing partner's interest by a remaining partner results in a transfer of the retiring member's capital to the capital account of the partner making the purchase; the actual amount paid to the retiring partner is a transaction outside of the partnership and is not recognized on the partnership books. Settlement by partnership payment to the withdrawing member results in a reduction in firm assets accompanied by cancellation of the withdrawing partner's capital. If settlement is deferred beyond the date of withdrawal, the capital account of the withdrawing partner is closed and a liability account is credited for the amount to be paid in settlement.

The partnership agreement should indicate any special procedures that are to be applied in measuring the interest of a withdrawing partner. The agreement should indicate what recognition is to be made of market values of property items and of any partnership goodwill in arriving at a settlement. It should also indicate how payments are to be made in settlement of the interest. Failure to anticipate these problems in the original agreement may give rise to controversy among partners. In the absence of appropriate provisions in the original agreement, parties will have to make special agreements for settlement at the time a withdrawal occurs.

It should be observed that the withdrawal of a member from a partnership and settlement with the firm does not relieve the withdrawing partner of personal liability on existing partnership claims in the absence of an agreement with creditors to that effect.

The withdrawal of a partner ordinarily calls for an appraisal of partnership assets and a restatement of asset and capital balances in terms of the revaluation. Gains and losses from revaluation are carried to the partners' capitals in the profit and loss ratio. The interest of a withdrawing partner, then, will include changes that have taken place in asset values during the life of the partnership, changes that in a going concern would normally await the realization of assets.

Revaluation of assets is required, not only in arriving at a fair determination of a retiring partner's interest, but also in stating properly the interests of the continuing partners. With the formation of a new firm and with new arrangements for profit and loss distribution, beginning capital balances should report fairly the investments of the partners.

Partners may agree to pay a withdrawing partner an amount equal to his or her capital balance. On the other hand, partners may agree to pay a withdrawing partner an amount that is greater or smaller than the balance reported in his or her capital account.

Payment to Withdrawing Partner of Amount that Exceeds Capital Balance

A partner who withdraws from a firm that has been unusually prosperous may demand an amount that exceeds his or her capital balance. Remaining partners may be willing to settle on this basis instead of terminating the business, a procedure that might otherwise be forced upon them by the retiring partner. Under such circumstances, partners may agree that (1) the excess amount paid shall be treated as a bonus to be absorbed by the continuing partners, or (2) the excess amount paid shall be used as a basis for recording partnership goodwill.

Bonus. Assume that the capital accounts of J, K, and L are $10,000 each, that assets are properly valued, and that the partners share profits 50%, 25%, and 25% respectively. The partners agree to pay $11,500 in settlement of L's interest. If the excess of $1,500 is to be considered a bonus chargeable to J and K, the entry is:

```
L, Capital............................................................... 10,000
J, Capital ..............................................................  1,000
K, Capital...............................................................    500
     Payable to L......................................................            11,500
          To record agreement to pay $11,500 in full settlement of
          L's interest, the bonus allowed being charged to J and K in
          the ratio existing between them, 50:25.
```

Goodwill. Assume, however, that J and K are unwilling to have their capital accounts reduced, although they are willing to pay $11,500 in settlement of L's interest. The allowance of $1,500 in excess of L's interest may be regarded as a payment for goodwill related to the partnership but not recorded on its books. Since L shares in net asset increases to the extent of 25%, $1,500 may be regarded as 25% of the presently existing goodwill; the total goodwill, then, is $6,000. The following entries recognize the partnership goodwill as thus determined and report the obligation to the withdrawing partner:

```
Goodwill.................................................................. 6,000
     J, Capital ..........................................................             3,000
     K, Capital...........................................................            1,500
     L, Capital...........................................................            1,500
          To set up partnership goodwill of $6,000 as determined by
          settlement with L who is allowed $1,500 for a 25% interest
          in goodwill.

L, Capital................................................................ 11,500
     Payable to L........................................................            11,500
          To record agreement to pay L $11,500.
```

The recognition of goodwill of $6,000 and its distribution to all of the partners is consistent with the practice of recognizing the full change in other asset values and of carrying the effects of such changes to all of the capital balances. But there are some who would support the recognition of goodwill only to the extent of the amount allowed to the withdrawing partner; the books, then, will report only the goodwill that is actually "purchased" by the continuing organization. Those who support this approach to goodwill do not suggest that revaluation of other assets be limited to only that portion of the change that is applicable to the equity of the withdrawing partner; however, to counter the charge of inconsistency, this group would raise the argument of conservatism. If, in the previous illustration, goodwill is to be recognized only to the extent of the excess payment to L, the entry would be as follows:

L, Capital..	10,000	
Goodwill..	1,500	
Payable to L..		11,500

      To record agreement to pay $11,500 for L's interest in the
      firm, the excess being regarded as payment for L's share of
      goodwill.

Comparison of bonus and goodwill methods. Although either the bonus method or the goodwill method can be used in recording the withdrawal of L, the two methods offer the same results only when the remaining partners continue to share profits between themselves in the original ratio. For example, assume in the preceding examples that J and K agree to share profits of the firm of J and K in the same manner as in the past, or 2:1 (50:25) respectively. If the bonus method is employed and any goodwill is recognized at a later date, its recognition will have exactly the same effect upon the capitals of J and K as its recognition upon the withdrawal of L. On the other hand, if the goodwill method is employed and goodwill has to be written off as a loss, reductions in the capitals of J and K will be the same as those made in using the bonus method upon L's withdrawal. But assume that J and K decide to divide profits of the new firm equally. With a change in the profit and loss arrangement providing an advantage to K, the bonus method will result in ultimate gain to K: if the bonus method is employed and any goodwill is recognized at a later date, K's share of the increase will be greater than the charge to K's capital upon L's withdrawal. On the other hand, if the goodwill method is employed and goodwill has to be written off as a loss, K's share of the decrease will be greater than the credit to K's capital upon L's withdrawal. In view of the differences that are found in each case, it is important that the parties agree to the exact procedure that is to be followed.

Payment to Withdrawing Partner of Amount that is Less than Capital Balance

A partner who is anxious to withdraw may be willing to accept less than the balance reported in his or her capital account. Willingness to accept such a reduced amount may arise from the realization that a forced sale of the firm's assets may result in a loss and a decrease in an interest as great as or greater than that which can be effected through agreement. When a withdrawing partner agrees to accept less than the amount reported in his or her capital account, such a difference may be viewed (1) as a bonus accruing to continuing partners, or (2) where goodwill has been previously recorded, as an offset against the goodwill balance.

Bonus. Assume in the previous example that L agrees to accept $8,500 in full settlement of a $10,000 interest. If the difference of $1,500 is to be regarded as a bonus to the continuing partners, the entry is:

L, Capital..	10,000	
Payable to L...		8,500
J, Capital		1,000
K, Capital..		500

To record agreement to pay $8,500 in full settlement of L's interest, a bonus of $1,500 accruing to J and K in ratio existing between them, 50:25.

Goodwill. Assume, however, that the partnership books show a goodwill balance. L's capital account balance reflects this intangible in part. Under these circumstances, partners may view the payment of an amount that is less than L's capital balance as indicating a shrinkage in goodwill rather than an increase in the continuing partners' capitals. Assuming that L is paid $8,500 for an interest reported at $10,000, with the credit excess being treated as a reduction of goodwill, the entry would be as follows:

L, Capital..	10,000	
Goodwill...		1,500
Payable to L...		8,500

To record agreement to pay $8,500 in full settlement of L's interest; the credit of $1,500 arising from settlement reduces Goodwill.

It would be possible to recognize the entire shrinkage in partnership goodwill implicit in the settlement with L. Since a reduction of $1,500 applies to a 25% interest, the full goodwill shrinkage may be considered to be $6,000, and the following entry may be made:

J, Capital	3,000	
K, Capital...	1,500	
L, Capital	10,000	
Goodwill...		6,000
Payable to L...		8,500

Comparison of bonus and goodwill methods. Although either the bonus or the goodwill method can be used to record the withdrawal of L, it should be observed that here, as in the case of earlier examples involving problems of bonus and goodwill, the alternative methods offer the same ultimate results only when the remaining partners continue to share profits between themselves in the original ratio.

SETTLEMENT WITH AN ESTATE

The death of a partner dissolves the partnership. In the absence of special provisions to the contrary, profit and loss should be summarized, the partnership assets should be appraised, and the decedent's interest in the firm should be established as of the date of death. Profit or loss from the date the books were last closed is determined and transferred to the capital accounts in the existing profit and loss ratio. The change in asset values arising from revaluation is likewise carried to the capital accounts in the profit and loss ratio. It is then the obligation of the partners to wind up the business. Assets are sold, liabilities are paid off, and settlement is made with the partner's estate and surviving partners.

Partners may provide by agreement that in the event of the death of a partner the business shall be continued by surviving partners. Partners may agree to settle for the interest of the deceased partner (1) by payment from partnership assets, (2) by payment from individual partners who acquire the interest, or (3) by payment from partnership insurance proceeds with surviving partners acquiring the deceased partner's interest. When the business is to be continued by the surviving partners, the death of a partner results in the dissolution of the original partnership and the formation of a new partnership. The interest of the deceased partner as of the date of death should be transferred to a liability account. Payments made to the estate are recorded as reductions in the payable balance.

The partnership agreement sometimes provides that the interest of a deceased partner shall not be calculated until the end of the regular fiscal period when the books are closed. In such instances it may be provided that the interest of a deceased partner shall be determined by allowing a pro rata share of the profits of the period up to the date of death with interest on the capital balance from that date until the date of settlement with the estate. In other cases it may be provided that the usual share of profit shall be allowed even though the decedent's services are lost to the firm for part of the fiscal period. The agreement may also provide for the recognition of goodwill in arriving at the interest of the decedent.

In some instances it may be provided that the estate or some heir shall continue in the place of the deceased partner. An entry to transfer the capital of the deceased partner to an account with the new partner is then necessary.

INCORPORATION OF A PARTNERSHIP

Partners may decide to incorporate in order to secure the advantages found in the corporate form of organization. When a charter is granted recognizing a corporation, the corporation will act to acquire the net assets of the partnership in exchange for its stock. The stock received by the partnership is distributed to the partners in settlement of their equities. The corporation thus takes over the assets and assumes the liabilities of the partnership; the partnership is dissolved and the partners now become stockholders in the newly formed corporation. In recording activities of the new unit, the partnership books may be retained, or a new set of books may be opened.

Partnership Books Retained

If the partnership books are retained, entries are necessary to report (1) the changes in asset and liability values and in the partners' interests prior to incorporation, and (2) the change in the form of proprietorship. A revaluation account may be debited with losses and credited with gains from revaluation, and the balance in this account may subsequently be closed into the capital accounts in the profit and loss ratio. However, with relatively few adjustments, the capital accounts may be debited or credited directly for losses and gains from revaluation. The issuance of stock in exchange for the partners' interests is recorded by debits to the partners' capitals and credits to the appropriate corporate capital accounts.

New Books Opened for the Corporation

If new books are opened for the corporation, all of the accounts of the partnership are closed. In closing the accounts of the partnership, the transfer of assets and liabilities to the corporation, the receipt of stock in payment of net assets transferred, and the distribution of stock to the partners are recorded. If it is desired to provide a full summary of the transactions that terminated the partnership, entries may also record the restatement of net assets and partners' interests.

Entries are made on the new books of the corporation to record the assets that were acquired, the liabilities that were assumed, and the stock that was issued in payment for net assets.

QUESTIONS

1. What is meant by dissolution of a partnership?

2. Give three causes for dissolution under each of the conditions listed below:

    (a) Dissolution by act of parties.
    (b) Dissolution by operation of law.
    (c) Dissolution by judicial decree.

3. (a) What is a *partnership at will?* (b) Under what circumstances does this factor assume significance?

4. A partner may acquire an interest *by purchase* or *by investment.* (a) How do these differ? (b) What entries are made on the partnership books in each instance?

5. A and B are partners sharing profits equally. C purchases one half of B's interest and the three parties agree to share future profits equally. At the time of C's admission, certain assets have a fair market value that is materially in excess of their book value. C suggests that there is no need to restate assets. Do you agree?

6. R and S are partners. T is admitted with a ¼ interest and is given a capital credit that exceeds the cash investment. (a) What are two methods of recording the investment? (b) If T's share of partnership profits is to be 33⅓%, which method will T prefer?

7. Jane Prather, Ellen Morris, and Sylvia Osher are attorneys. Osher decides to retire on January 1, 19X8, but claims that statements as of December 31, 19X7, fail to measure her interest adequately. (a) What special problems are faced in settlement with Osher? (b) How would you recommend that these problems be met?

8. William Meadows and Peter Saliers have been partners for many years when Meadows decides to withdraw. The firm has followed the practice of reporting inventories for statement purposes at cost or market, whichever is lower. Meadows feels that, for purposes of withdrawal, his interest should be measured with regard to the replacement value of the inventory, which is considerably in excess of cost; Saliers is opposed to the recognition of the inventory at its higher replacement value since such a procedure is inconsistent with past practice. What position do you support?

9. Harry Mellon retires from the firm of Kelley, Long, and Mellon. What are the possible positions that may be taken in recording the settlement, assuming that (a) Mellon is paid more than the balance in his capital account and (b) Mellon is paid less than the balance in his capital account?

10. What special accounting problems arise in the calculation of a deceased partner's interest and in settlement with the estate?

11. (a) What special accounting problems arise upon the incorporation of a partnership? (b) What opening entries are required, assuming that partnership books are retained for the corporation?

EXERCISES

1. Burke, Carter, and Drew are partners sharing profits 40%, 35%, and 25%. Partners' original capitals were in this ratio, but on June 30, 19X3, capital balances are as follows: Burke, $60,000; Carter, $50,000; and Drew, $50,000. Partners want to bring capital balances into the profit and loss ratio.

    (a) Assuming that the capital balances are to be brought into the profit and loss ratio by payments outside of the firm among partners, the total firm capital to remain the same, what cash transfers are required between partners and what entry would be made on the firm books?

    (b) Assuming that the capital balances are to be brought into the profit and loss ratio by the lowest possible cash investment in the firm by partners, what additional investments are required and what entry would be made on the firm books?

2. Shirley Bell and Paul Myers are partners who have capitals of $10,000 each and who share profits in the ratio of 60:40. Keith Rand pays Myers $4,000 for ½ of his interest in the firm. (a) What are the capital balances of each partner after Rand's admission? (b) How will profits be shared in the absence of express agreement?

3. O, P, and Q are partners sharing profits in the ratio of 3:3:2. R is admitted as a partner and is to be allowed ¼ of the profits, the remaining profits to be divided between O, P, and Q in the original ratio. What is the new profit and loss ratio for the firm of O, P, Q, and R?

4. The capital balances for Cook and Dempsey are $40,000 each; partners divide profits equally. Evans is admitted to a ⅓ interest in net assets and in net earnings upon investing cash of $25,000. Record Evans' admission, using three alternative procedures and indicating the conditions that would support each alternative.

5. Fears and Harper are partners who have capitals of $30,000 and $20,000 and who share profits 75% and 25% respectively. They agree to admit Landis as a partner upon payment of $30,000. What entries would be made on the firm books, assuming that:

- (a) One third of the capital balances of the old partners are transferred to the new partner, with Fears and Harper dividing the cash between themselves.
- (b) One third of the capital balances of the old partners are transferred to the new partner, with Fears and Harper dividing the cash between themselves. However, before recording the admission of the new partner, goodwill is recorded on the firm books so that Landis' capital may be equal to the amount paid for the interest.
- (c) The cash is invested in the business and Landis is credited with a ¼ interest in the firm, with the bonus method being used in recording the investment.
- (d) The cash is invested in the business and Landis is credited with the full amount of the investment, which is to be 25% of the new firm capital.
- (e) The cash is invested in the business and Landis is credited for $40,000, which is to be 33⅓% of the new firm capital.

6. Mason and Norris are partners who have capitals of $6,000 and $4,800 and who share profits in the ratio of 3:2. Oster is admitted as a partner upon investing cash of $5,000, with profits to be shared equally.

- (a) Assume that Oster is allowed a 25% interest in the firm. (1) What entries would be made in recording the investment if the goodwill method is used? (2) What entries would be made if the bonus method is used? (3) Which method will be preferred by Oster? How much will Oster gain by the use of this method?
- (b) Assume that Oster is allowed a 40% interest in the firm. (1) What entries would be made in recording the investment if the goodwill method is used? (2) What entries would be made if the bonus method is used? (3) Which method will be preferred by Oster? How much will Oster gain by the use of this method?

7. A, B, and C are partners sharing profits in the ratio of 3:3:2. Investments are $60,000, $40,000, and $30,000 respectively. The partners agree to admit D on the following basis: D is to pay A $40,000 for ½ of A's interest; D is also to invest $30,000 in the business. The total capital of the partnership is to be $200,000, of which D's interest is to be $50,000 upon admission. What are the entries to record D's admission?

8. A, B, and C have capital balances of $11,200, $13,000, and $5,800 respectively and share profits in a ratio of 3:2:1. D invests cash in the partnership for a ¼ interest. Give the entry to record D's admission under each of the following conditions:

- (a) D receives a ¼ interest in the assets of the partnership, which includes credit for $2,000 of goodwill that is recognized upon admission.
- (b) D receives a ¼ interest in the assets of the partnership and B is credited with $2,000 of the bonus to the old partners that is recognized on D's admission.

(continued)

(c) D receives a ¼ interest in the assets of the partnership and B is credited with $2,000 of the goodwill that is recognized prior to D's admission.

9. John Halls, Cary Jones, and Marsha Kepple are partners with capital balances on June 30, 19X9, of $30,000, $30,000 and $20,000 respectively. Profits are shared equally. Kepple withdraws from the partnership. The partners agree that Kepple is to take certain furniture and fixtures at their secondhand value of $1,200 and a note for the balance of her interest. The furniture and fixtures are carried on the books as fully depreciated. What entry would be made to record the settlement with Kepple?

10. Roades, Stone, and Tracy are partners sharing profits in the ratio of 3:2:1 respectively. Capital accounts are $50,000, $30,000, and $20,000 on December 31, 19X1, when Tracy decides to withdraw. It is agreed to pay $30,000 for Tracy's interest. Profits after the retirement of Tracy are to be shared equally. (a) Give three possible entries to record Tracy's retirement. (b) Which of these methods will be preferred by Stone? What is the amount of the gain to Stone through use of this method as compared with the other alternatives?

11. Carter, Doyle, and Eton share profits in the ratio of 5:3:2. Eton is permitted to withdraw from the firm on December 31, 19X4. The partnership balance sheet on this date is as follows:

Assets		Liabilities and Capital	
Receivable from Eton.	$ 5,000	Liabilities.................	$ 40,000
Goodwill...................	40,000	Payable to Doyle........	15,000
Other assets..............	95,000	Carter, capital...........	35,000
		Doyle, capital............	30,000
		Eton, capital.............	20,000
		Total liabilities and	
Total assets..............	$140,000	capital...................	$140,000

(a) Give three alternative solutions to record the withdrawal, assuming that Eton is paid $22,000 in full settlement of the capital interest and $5,000 claim balance. Which solution do you prefer?
(b) Give three alternative solutions to record the withdrawal, assuming that Eton is paid $12,000 in full settlement. Which solution do you prefer?

PROBLEMS

2-1. Collins and Cox are partners sharing profits 60:40. A balance sheet prepared for the partners on April 1, 19X8, is shown on page 55.

On this date the partners agree to admit Curry as a partner. Terms of the agreement are summarized below.

Assets and liabilities are to be restated as follows:

(a) An allowance of $2,300 is to be established for possible uncollectibles.
(b) Inventories are to be restated at their present replacement cost of $86,250.

(c) Equipment is to be restated at a value of $17,500.

(d) Accrued liabilities of $1,950 are to be recognized.

Collins, Cox, and Curry will divide profits in the ratio 5:3:2. Capital balances for the new partners are to be in this ratio, with Collins and Cox making cash settlement outside of the partnership for the required capital adjustment between themselves, and Curry investing cash in the partnership.

Cash..................	$ 24,000	Payables.............		$ 44,500
Receivables.........	46,000	Collins:		
Inventories..........	82,500	Capital account	$75,000	
Equipment.......... $35,000		Less drawing		
Less accumulated		account		
depreciation..... 22,500	12,500	balance	8,500	66,500
		Cox:		
		Capital account	$50,000	
		Plus drawing		
		account		
		balance	4,000	54,000
Total assets......................	$165,000	Total liabilities and capital ..		$165,000

Instructions: (1) Prepare the entries on the partnership books to give effect to the foregoing.

(2) Prepare a balance sheet for the newly formed partnership.

2-2. Cross and Dodd are partners sharing profits 60% and 40% respectively. On July 1 their interests in the firm are as follows: Cross, $23,000, Dodd, $18,600. Evans is admitted as a partner upon the investment of $16,000.

Instructions: Record the investment by Evans in journal form, assuming that:

(1) The new partner is given credit for the actual investment made.

(2) The new partner is given a ⅓ interest, with a bonus contributed by the old partners.

(3) The new partner is given a ⅓ interest, with goodwill recorded upon admission.

(4) The new partner is given a ¼ interest, with a bonus allowed to the old partners.

(5) The new partner is given a ¼ interest, with goodwill recorded upon admission.

2-3. J and K are partners with capitals of $10,000 and $40,000, respectively, and sharing profits 1:3.

Instructions: Prepare the journal entries required to record L's admission under each of the following assumptions:

(1) L invests $30,000 for a ¼ interest, with the total firm capital to be $80,000.

(2) L invests $30,000 for a ⅓ interest, with the total firm capital to be $90,000.

(3) L invests $30,000, with $10,000 considered a bonus to the old partners. Prior to L's admission, goodwill of $12,000 is to be recorded on the firm books. *(continued)*

(4) L purchases a ¼ interest in the firm, with ¼ of the capital of each old partner transferred to the account with the new partner. L pays the partners cash of $20,000, which they divide between themselves.

2-4. M and N are partners with capitals of $40,000 and $20,000 respectively. They share profits in the ratio of 3:1. The partners agree to admit O as a member of the firm.

Instructions: Prepare the required entries on the firm books to record the admission of O under each of the following assumptions:

(1) O purchases a ¼ interest in the firm. One fourth of each partner's capital is to be transferred to the new partner. O pays the partners $15,000, which is divided between them in proportion to the equities given up.

(2) O purchases a ⅓ interest in the firm. One third of each partner's capital is to be transferred to the new partner. O pays the partners $16,000, which is divided between them in proportion to the equities given up.

(3) O purchases a ⅓ interest in the firm. One third of each partner's capital is to be transferred to the new partner. O pays the partners $30,000, which is divided between them in proportion to the equities given up. Before O's admission, however, goodwill is recorded on the firm books so that O's ⅓ interest will be equal to the amount of the payment.

(4) O invests $30,000 for a ¼ interest in the firm. Goodwill is recorded on the firm books prior to O's admission.

(5) O invests $30,000 for a 50% interest in the firm. M and N transfer part of their capitals to that of O as a bonus.

(6) O invests $40,000 in the firm. $10,000 is considered a bonus to Partners M and N.

(7) O invests $40,000 in the firm and is allowed a credit of $12,000 for goodwill upon admission.

(8) O invests $25,000 for a ¼ interest in the firm. The total firm capital is to be $85,000.

(9) O invests $27,500 for a ¼ interest in the firm. The total firm capital is to be $110,000.

(10) O invests $24,000 for a ⅓ interest in the firm. The total firm capital is to be $84,000.

2-5. X and Y are partners whose capitals on December 31, 19X2, before the books are closed, are $38,500 and $21,500 respectively. The partnership agreement provides for distribution of profits as follows: monthly salaries of $750 to X and $600 to Y are to be allowed; any balance is to be distributed equally. If profits are insufficient to cover the salary allowance, the profit is to be distributed in the salary ratio; in the event of a loss, distribution is to be made equally.

The profit from operations for 19X2 was $18,000, and this was transferred to the capital accounts. Equipment with a book value of $18,900 was destroyed by fire on December 12. Pending settlement with the insurance company, the full amount of the fire loss was reported as a claim against the insurance company.

On March 1, 19X3, the firm recovered $13,500 in full settlement of the fire loss (the fire loss determined at this time is regarded as a correction in the profit for 19X2). On April 1, Z was admitted as a partner upon the investment of $48,000 in the firm. Profits after Z's admission are to be divided equally. It was agreed that the books should not be closed until the end of the year, but that the profit determined from operations at that time should be considered to have been earned pro rata during the year. The profit from operations for 19X3 was $36,000, and this was transferred to the capital accounts.

Instructions: Prepare a statement of changes in partners' capital accounts, showing all of the changes that took place in the capital accounts in 19X2 and 19X3.

2-6. Caine, Osman, and Roberts formed a partnership on January 1, 19X4, agreeing to distribute profits and losses in the ratio of original capitals. Original investments were $62,500, $25,000, and $12,500 respectively. Earnings of the firm and drawings by each partner for the period 19X4–19X6 follow:

	Net income (loss)	Drawings		
		Caine	Osman	Roberts
19X4	$44,000	$15,000	$7,800	$5,200
19X5	18,500	15,000	7,800	5,200
19X6	(10,500)	10,000	5,200	5,200

At the beginning of 19X7, Caine and Osman agreed to permit Roberts to withdraw from the firm. Since the books of the firm had never been audited, the partners agreed to an audit in arriving at the settlement amount. In withdrawing, Roberts was allowed to take certain furniture and was charged $1,500, although the book value was $4,500; the balance of Roberts' interest was paid in cash.

The following items were revealed in the course of the audit:

	End of 19X4	End of 19X5	End of 19X6
Understatement of accrued expenses	$ 400	$ 500	$ 650
Understatement of accrued revenue	250	100	150
Overstatement of inventories..................	1,500	2,000	2,000
Understatement of depreciation expense on assets still held........................	150	350	200

Instructions: (1) Prepare a statement of changes in partners' capital accounts, covering the period January 1, 19X4, to the time of Roberts' withdrawal, reporting corrected earnings balances for each year and corrected capital balances for each partner.

(2) Prepare the entries that are required at the beginning of 19X7 to correct the books and to record the transfer of assets to Roberts in final settlement.

2-7. The balance sheet for the firm of A, B, and C shows capitals on December 31, 19X9, of $22,500, $24,000, and $40,000 respectively. A, B, and C had shared profits equally since the firm was organized in 19X2, but beginning January 1, 19X9, partners had agreed to share profits in the ratio 1:1:2 respectively. On December 31, 19X9, C decided to retire and the partners agreed to make the following corrections in arriving at the amount to be paid for C's interest:

(1) Accounting for the partnership in past years had not recognized accrued revenue and accrued expense items. It was agreed that capitals should

be restated in terms of accrual accounting. Accrued items were:

	December 31, 19X8	December 31, 19X9
Accrued revenues......	$ 600	$ 800
Accrued expenses......	2,400	6,000

(2) Certain expenditures had been recognized as expenses, but it was agreed that these are to be capitalized as additions to buildings and depreciated at 5% per year. Such expenditures totaled $6,000 in 19X8 and $8,000 in 19X9. Depreciation for only one-half year was to be recognized for the year in which the expenditures were made.

(3) The merchandise inventories had been reported annually on a *lifo* basis. It was agreed that these are to be restated on a *fifo* basis. Inventory values at *lifo* and *fifo* were as follows:

December 31, 19X8		December 31, 19X9	
Lifo	Fifo	Lifo	Fifo
$38,000	$56,000	$39,500	$62,500

Instructions: (1) Prepare a statement of changes in partners' capital accounts, reporting corrections in net incomes for prior years in arriving at corrected capital balances as of December 31, 19X9.

(2) Prepare the entry or entries required on the partnership books to give effect to the foregoing corrections.

2-8. Ross and Sears are partners whose capital accounts on December 31, 19X3, before the firm's books are closed, are $50,000 and $30,000 respectively. The drawing account for Ross shows a debit balance of $8,200; for Sears, a debit balance of $6,800. The partnership agreement with regard to profits provides that (1) each partner is to be allowed an annual salary of $9,000, and (2) Ross is to receive 60% and Sears 40% of the profits after allowance of salaries.

The income summary account on December 31 has a credit balance of $14,000 before any entry for the allowance of salaries, and this balance is closed into the partners' capital accounts. The balances of the drawing accounts are also closed into the capital accounts.

On January 2, 19X4, Thomas is admitted as a partner upon the investment of $20,000 in the firm. The partners allow a bonus on the investment so that Thomas may have a ⅓ interest in the firm. The new agreement provides that profits are to be distributed as follows: Ross, 35%; Sears, 25%; and Thomas, 40%. Salaries are not allowed.

On December 31, 19X4, the partners' drawing accounts have debit balances as follows: Ross, $7,500; Sears, $5,000; and Thomas, $6,800. The income summary account has a $15,000 debit balance. Accounts are closed.

The partners decide to liquidate. All of the assets are sold in January, 19X5. After creditors are fully paid, cash of $17,500 remains available for partners. This is distributed to the proper parties.

Instructions: Prepare a statement of changes in partners' capital accounts, showing all of the changes that took place since January 1, 19X3.

2-9. Partners D, E, F, and G share profits 40%, 30%, 15%, and 15% respectively. Their partnership agreement provides that in the event of the death of a partner the firm shall continue until the end of the fiscal period. Profits shall be considered to have been earned proportionately during this period, and the deceased partner's capital shall be adjusted by the proper share of the profit or loss until the date of death. From that date until the date of settlement with the estate there shall be added interest at 6% computed on the adjusted capital. The remaining partners shall continue to share profits in the old ratio. Payment to the estate shall be made within one year from the date of the partner's death.

Partner G died on November 16. On December 31, the end of a six-month period, account balances on the partnership books before the income summary account is closed are as follows:

Cash............................	$ 7,500	Notes Payable	$ 15,000
Accounts Receivable..	70,000	Accounts Payable	70,500
Inventories.................	95,000	D, Capital...................	42,000
Machinery and Equip-		E, Capital...................	37,500
ment	45,000	F, Capital...................	24,000
Store Furniture and		G, Capital...................	22,500
Fixtures.................	16,500	Income Summary	
		(7/1-12/31)	22,500
	$234,000		$234,000

The income summary account is closed on December 31. On this date, F decides to retire. D and E agree to pay the balance in F's capital account after distribution of profits, less 20%, and issue a partnership 60-day, 6% note to F in settlement.

Instructions: (1) Prepare all of the necessary journal entries as of December 31.

(2) Prepare a balance sheet for the firm of D and E as of December 31.

2-10. The partnerships of A & B and of C & D started in business on July 1, 19X5; each partnership owns one retail appliance store. It was agreed as of June 30, 19X8, to combine the partnerships to form a new partnership to be known as Four Partners' Discount Stores.

The June 30, 19X8, post-closing trial balances of the partnerships appear on page 60.

The following additional information is available:

(1) The income-sharing ratios for the former partnerships were 40% to A and 60% to B, and 30% to C and 70% to D. The profit-and-loss-sharing ratio for the new partnership will be A, 20%; B, 30%; C, 15%; and D, 35%.

(2) The beginning capital ratios for the new partnership are to be the same as the profit-and-loss-sharing ratios for the new partnership. The capital to be assigned to A & B will total $225,000. Any cash settlements among the partners arising from capital account adjustments will be a private matter and will not be recorded on the partnership books.

(3) The partners agree that the allowance for doubtful accounts for the new partnership is to be 3% of the accounts receivable balances.

(4) The beginning inventory of the new partnership is to be valued by the *fifo* method. The inventory of A & B was valued by the *fifo* method, and the inventory of C & D was valued by the *lifo* method. The *lifo* inventory represents 85% of its *fifo* value.

(5) Depreciation is to be computed by the double-declining balance method with a 10-year life for the depreciable assets. Depreciation for 3 years is to be accumulated in the beginning balance of the accumulated depreciation account. A & B computed depreciation by the straight-line method, and C & D used the double-declining balance method. All assets were obtained on July 1, 19X5.

(6) After the books were closed, an unrecorded merchandise purchase of $4,000 by C & D was discovered. The merchandise had been sold by June 30, 19X8.

(7) The accounts of A & B included a vacation pay accrual. It was agreed that C & D should make a similar accrual for their 5 employees, who will receive a 2-week vacation at $100 per employee per week.

	A & B Trial Balance June 30, 19X8		C & D Trial Balance June 30, 19X8	
Cash	$ 20,000		$ 15,000	
Accounts receivable	100,000		150,000	
Allowance for doubtful accounts		$ 2,000		$ 6,000
Merchandise inventory	175,000		119,000	
Land	25,000		35,000	
Buildings and equipment	80,000		125,000	
Accumulated depreciation		24,000		61,000
Prepaid expenses	5,000		7,000	
Accounts payable		40,000		60,000
Notes payable		70,000		75,000
Accrued liabilities		30,000		45,000
A, capital		95,000		
B, capital		144,000		
C, capital				65,000
D, capital				139,000
	$405,000	$405,000	$451,000	$451,000

Instructions: (1) Prepare a work sheet to determine the beginning balances of the new partnership after giving effect to the above information. Formal journal entries are not required. Supporting computations, including the computation of goodwill, should be in good form.

(2) Prepare a schedule computing the cash to be exchanged between A and B, and between C and D, in settlement of the affairs of each original partnership.

(AICPA adapted)

2-11. Linden and Mills have been operating a business for several years as partners, during which time they have divided profits equally. They need additional capital to expand their business and have agreed to admit Jackson to the partnership as of January 1, 19X6, with a ⅓ interest in profits and in the capital.

Jackson is to invest cash equal to ½ of the combined capital of the present two partners, which is to be redetermined.

The average partnership profits after partners' salaries, for the past two years, are to be capitalized at the rate of 10% per annum, which will redetermine the aggregate capital of the two present partners. Before such capitalization of profits, the accounts are to be adjusted for errors and omissions.

The business has not followed a strict accrual basis of accounting. As a result, the following items have been omitted from the books:

Item	Balance 12/31/X3	Balance 12/31/X4	Balance 12/31/X5
Accrued expenses......................	$3,201	$2,472	$4,360
Prepaid expenses......................	1,010	1,226	872
Accrued income.......................	—	250	475

In addition, no provision has been made for loss on uncollectible accounts. It is agreed that a provision of $4,500 is needed as of December 31, 19X5, of which $600 is for 19X4 accounts. Charge-offs have been made to expense in 19X3 of 19X2 and prior accounts, $1,200; in 19X4 of 19X3 accounts, $3,100, and of 19X4 accounts, $400; in 19X5 of 19X4 accounts, $2,280, and of 19X5 accounts, $525.

The inventory at December 31, 19X5, contains some obsolete goods carried at a cost of $4,300. A 20% write-down is to be made to reduce these items to their present value.

In 19X4 and 19X5, salaries of $3,000 for each partner were taken out of the business and charged to expense before profits were determined. It has been agreed that the salaries should have been $4,000 each.

The following financial data are available:

Balance Sheet
December 31, 19X5

Cash..........................	$ 7,000	Accounts payable	$ 43,200
Accounts receivable...	42,500	Notes payable	25,000
Notes receivable........	6,000	Accumulated depreciation of fixtures....	5,300
Merchandise	64,000	Linden, capital	22,000
Store fixtures	12,400	Mills, capital	36,400
	$131,900		$131,900

	19X3	19X4	19X5
Profit per books............................	$ 8,364	$ 8,585	$10,497
Linden, capital	20,000	24,000	22,000
Mills, capital	25,000	33,000	36,400

Instructions: (1) Prepare working papers to summarize the adjustments for errors and omissions and the redetermination of capital accounts as well as the receipt of Jackson's capital contribution as of January 1, 19X6. Prepare a schedule showing the computation of the amount Jackson pays into the partnership in support of the entry on the working papers.

(2) Prepare a balance sheet for the new partnership as of January 1, 19X6.

(AICPA adapted)

2-12. Alston and Bailey, equal partners in the A and B Stores, sold a ⅓ interest in Store No. 3 to Carter, manager of that store, on January 1, 19X0. The new partnership will operate as the ABC Co. Alston and Bailey will continue to operate other stores. The balance sheet of Store No. 3, at January 1, 19X0, was as follows:

Assets			Liabilities and Capital		
Merchandise		$63,000	Liabilities		
Furniture and			Accounts payable		$20,000
fixtures	$22,000				
Accumulated			Capital		
depreciation	10,000	12,000	Alston	$30,000	
Prepaid expenses		3,900	Bailey	30,000	60,000
Utility deposits		1,100	Total liabilities and		
Total assets		$80,000	capital		$80,000

Furniture and fixtures, which have an estimated remaining life of 5 years, were revalued at $18,000 according to the agreement of sale. Each partner contributed $1,000 as working capital, which was credited to the appropriate drawing account.

The following transactions for 19X0 were all in cash:

Sales	$620,000
Merchandise purchases	493,000
Salaries and wages (including salary of $9,000 to Carter, as manager)	77,000
Expenses	25,400
New furniture purchased 7/1/X0 (estimated life — 10 years)	3,000

You are also given the following information:

Merchandise inventory, December 31, 19X0	$ 60,000
Prepaid expenses, December 31, 19X0	3,000

Before the books were closed as of December 31, 19X0, the check record was kept open until all 19X0 bills were paid.

The partnership agreement provides for a salary of $750 monthly to Carter. All remaining profits are divided equally.

Each partner's drawing account shows a net debit balance of $3,000.

Instructions: (1) Prepare a schedule showing the cash payment that Carter made to Alston and Bailey.

(2) Prepare an income statement of the ABC Co. for the year ended December 31, 19X0, including a schedule showing the distribution of profit and loss to the partners.

(AICPA adapted)

2-13. Western Company is a family partnership engaged in the wholesale trade. It closes its books on December 31. During the year, all transactions are recorded on a cash receipts and disbursements basis. However, at the end of the fiscal year, adjustment is made to what was termed the "inventory account" for all items necessary to reflect operations and financial position on an accrual basis.

Partner E died on October 31, 19X8. E's will left equal shares in the estate to partners A and C and an outsider, F. All remaining partners, together with F, agreed that the business of Western Company would continue as a partnership of A, B, C, D, and F, with partners' interests on November 1, 19X8, as computed on a proper accrual basis to October 31, and after distribution of E's interest on that date. (Assume that E's estate is distributed immediately.)

Depreciation of plant assets may be ignored.

Balances as shown by the books of the firm were as follows:

	January 1, 19X8	October 31, 19X8
Cash	$ 42,000	$ 55,000
Inventory account	195,000	195,000
Plant assets	60,000	59,000
Accruals	29,000	16,000
Notes payable	100,000	60,000
Partners' equities	168,000	168,000
Sales	—	2,000,000
Purchases	—	1,725,000
Operating expenses	—	210,000

In addition to the foregoing, the following information concerning the inventory account was available:

At January 1, 19X8: accounts receivable, $80,000; merchandise, $200,000; freight claims receivable (on incoming merchandise), $2,000; prepaid expenses, $10,000; accounts payable, $90,000; allowances due customers, $7,000. At October 31, 19X8: accounts receivable, $83,300; merchandise, $221,000; freight claims receivable (on incoming merchandise), $1,500; prepaid expenses, $6,000; accounts payable, $85,000; allowances due customers, $8,000.

Partners' equities and profit-and-loss-sharing ratio were as follows:

	Equities	Profit and Loss Ratio
A	$10,500	6.25%
B	52,500	31.25
C	77,000	37.50
D	7,000	12.50
E	21,000	12.50

Instructions: (1) Prepare an income statement for the period January 1 to October 31, 19X8.

(2) Prepare a balance sheet as of October 31, 19X8.

(3) Prepare a statement of partners' equities on November 1, 19X8.

(AICPA adapted)

2-14. The East Bay Motel has been owned by Catron and Johnson on a 50% partnership basis. On April 1, 19X2, Catron bought Johnson's interest and dissolved the partnership. You have been engaged to act as a consultant to the accountant of the East Bay Motel. The trial balance on page 65 was taken from the books of the motel as of March 31, 19X2. The books were last closed December 31, 19X1.

Upon a careful inspection of details of the settlement between Catron and Johnson, you learned that no adjustment for supplies, taxes, interest, and insurance had been recorded on March 31, 19X2.

The following settlement transactions occurred on April 1, 19X2:

(1) The partnership bank account was closed by drawing equal checks payable to each partner.

(2) Catron paid Johnson $235 to be applied as follows: one half of petty cash, $50; one half of supplies inventory, $185.

(3) It was necessary for Catron to borrow additional funds on the motel property. Complete refinancing was worked out with the Second National Bank as set forth in the following disbursement statement prepared by the bank:

Amount of loan from Second National Bank.................			$84,000
Amount of check from Catron			500
Total			$84,500
Less payoff of mortgage due ABC Life Insurance Co.		$56,150	
Amount due Johnson............................	$28,950		
Plus ½ unexpired fire insurance premium due Johnson, prorated April 1, 19X2, to April 1, 19X3; original premium was $3,180	500		
	$29,450		
Less:			
½ penalty due ABC Insurance Co.	$1,325		
½ interest due ABC Insurance Co. from Feb. 6 to Apr. 1, 19X2	250		
½ real estate taxes from Jan. 1 to Apr. 1, 19X2	150		
Total	1,725		
Amount due Johnson..		27,725	83,875
Total			$ 625
Less financing costs...			625
			–0–

(4) In addition, Johnson accepted a $30,000 second mortgage payable in equal monthly installments.

(5) An appraisal of the motel property indicated the following values:

Land	$ 45,500
Building..............................	78,000
Furniture and fixtures...........	18,200
Total	$141,700

Cash..	630	
Petty Cash	100	
Prepaid Insurance..	1,360	
Land	32,500	
Building...	75,000	
Accumulated Depreciation — Building		15,000
Furniture and Fixtures..	30,000	
Accumulated Depreciation — Furn. and Fix.		10,800
Mortgage Payable — ABC Life Insurance Co..........		53,000
Catron, Capital		28,265
Johnson, Capital...		28,265
Room Income		17,249
Wages	3,545	
Advertising and Supplies	2,755	
Repairs and Utilities...	2,234	
Office Expense	114	
Taxes	166	
Depreciation	3,770	
Interest	405	
	152,579	152,579

Instructions: Prepare a work sheet that includes columns to show:

(1) Adjustments necessary to bring accounts into agreement with data as presented, showing facts of the dissolution agreement.
(2) Income statement for the period January 1, 19X2, to March 31, 19X2.
(3) Balance sheet as of March 31, 19X2.
(4) Adjustments for dissolution.
(5) Beginning balances for Catron's books.

(AICPA adapted)

3
Partnerships — Liquidation

It has already been suggested that the dissolution of a partnership does not mean the formal termination of the business. Dissolution of a partnership was recognized in connection with the reorganization of the business as a new unit. In other instances dissolution was recognized as a condition that called for winding up business affairs. Under the latter circumstances, the association of partners was considered ended for purposes of carrying on activities in the usual manner; but partners could still engage in activities leading to final settlement of business affairs, and the partnership agreement continued to govern the association until such time. The term *dissolution*, then, refers to the termination of the partnership as a going concern.

LIQUIDATION DEFINED

The process of winding up a business normally consists of the conversion of a portion or all of the assets into cash, settlement with creditors, and the distribution of remaining assets to the ownership groups. The conversion of assets into cash is referred to as *realization*; the payment of claims is referred to as *liquidation*. The latter term is also used in a broader sense to refer to the complete winding-up process.

Upon liquidation of a partnership, the accountant must be able to advise as to the proper distribution of assets among individual partners. Improper distributions, resulting in overpayment to certain parties with corresponding loss to others, may result in personal liability on the part of the person authorizing such distributions.

PROCEDURE IN LIQUIDATION

When a partnership is to be liquidated, the books should be adjusted and closed and the net income or loss for the period should be carried to the partners' capital accounts. The partnership is then ready to proceed with liquidation.

As assets are converted into cash, any differences between the book values and the amounts realized represent gains or losses to be divided among partners in the profit and loss ratio. Such gains and losses are carried to the capital accounts. The capital balances then become the basis for settlement.

In the course of liquidation, when a partner's capital account reports a debit balance and that partner has a loan balance, the law permits exercise of *the right of offset*, that is, the offset of a part or all of the loan against the capital deficiency. A debit balance in the capital account in the absence of a loan balance or after offset of a loan balance indicates the need for a contribution by the deficient partner. The inability of a partnership to recover a capital deficiency will mean that remaining partners will have to absorb such an amount.

As cash becomes available for distribution, it is first applied to the payment of outside creditors. It may then be applied in settlement of partners' loan and capital balances. The Uniform Partnership Act provides that partners' loans shall rank ahead of partners' capitals in order of payment. For practical purposes, however, this provision is not effective. When a distribution of cash is made before all of the losses are known, payment should not be made on loan balances or such portions thereof as may be required to offset possible capital deficiencies. In some instances, then, it may be appropriate to apply cash to the payment of capital balances of certain partners even though loan balances of others remain unpaid.

PAYMENTS TO PARTNERS AFTER REALIZATION IS COMPLETED

The accounting procedures that are followed upon partnership liquidation are illustrated in this and the next chapter. Examples in this chapter assume that distributions are made to partners only after realization of assets has been completed and the full loss or gain from realization is known. Examples in the next chapter illustrate the procedures that are followed when distributions are made to partners during the course of liquidation and before the full loss or gain from realization has been determined.

For purposes of the discussions to follow, it is assumed that the firm of A, B, C, and D decides to liquidate. All partnership assets are to be converted into cash. A, B, C, and D share profits and losses 30%, 30%, 20%, and 20% respectively. A balance sheet prepared on May 1, 19X7, just before liquidation, reports the following balances:

Assets		Liabilities and Capital	
Cash	$ 10,000	Liabilities	$ 75,000
Other assets	180,000	B, loan	6,000
		D, loan	5,000
		A, capital	42,000
		B, capital	31,500
		C, capital	20,500
		D, capital	10,000
Total assets	$190,000	Total liabilities and capital	$190,000

A number of examples will be offered that assume the realization of varying amounts of cash for other assets of the partnership. The assumptions are listed below.

Example 1. Realization of assets, $140,000, with loss on realization fully absorbed by partners' capital balances.

Example 2. Realization of assets, $120,000, with loss on realization requiring transfer from partner's loan account to capital.

Example 3. Realization of assets, $100,000, with loss on realization resulting in a capital deficiency for one partner.

Example 4. Realization of assets, $80,000, with loss on realization resulting in capital deficiencies for more than one partner.

Example 5. Realization of assets, $60,000, with cash insufficient to pay creditors:

    (a) When all of the partners are personally solvent.

    (b) When certain partners are personally solvent and others are personally insolvent.

Loss on Realization Fully Absorbed by Partners' Capital Balances

Example 1. Assume that the noncash assets of the firm of A, B, C, and D, with a book value of $180,000, ultimately realize $140,000. The loss of $40,000 is distributed in the profit and loss ratio. The capital balances of the partners, in this case, are large enough to absorb their shares of the total loss on realization. Under these circumstances the distribution of cash presents no problem. Cash is first applied to the payment of outside creditors, and the balance is applied to the payment of partners' loan and capital balances. These events are summarized in the following statement of liquidation.

A, B, C, and D
Statement of Liquidation
May 1–31, 19X7

	Cash	Other Assets	Liab.	B Loan	D Loan	Capitals and Profit-Sharing Percentage			
						A, Cap. (30%)	B, Cap. (30%)	C, Cap. (20%)	D, Cap. (20%)
Balances before liquidation.......	10,000	180,000	75,000	6,000	5,000	42,000	31,500	20,500	10,000
(a) Sale of assets and distribution of loss	140,000	(180,000)				(12,000)	(12,000)	(8,000)	(8,000)
	150,000		75,000	6,000	5,000	30,000	19,500	12,500	2,000
(b) Payments to creditors........	(75,000)		(75,000)						
	75,000			6,000	5,000	30,000	19,500	12,500	2,000
(c) Payment to partners.........	(75,000)			(6,000)	(5,000)	(30,000)	(19,500)	(12,500)	(2,000)

The journal entries to record the sale of the assets and the distribution of cash are as follows:

Transaction	Entry		
(a) Sale of assets for $140,000; loss distributed to A, B, C, and D, 30%, 30%, 20%, and 20% respectively.	Cash	140,000	
	A, Capital	12,000	
	B, Capital	12,000	
	C, Capital	8,000	
	D, Capital	8,000	
	Other Assets		180,000
(b) Payment to creditors.	Liabilities	75,000	
	Cash		75,000
(c) Payment to partners.	B, Loan	6,000	
	D, Loan	5,000	
	A, Capital	30,000	
	B, Capital	19,500	
	C, Capital	12,500	
	D, Capital	2,000	
	Cash		75,000

The following points should be noted in this example:

(1) The loss on the realization of assets is divided among the partners in the same way as losses from operations. If there had been a gain on realization, the partners' capital accounts would have been credited. When assets are sold in a number of lots, a separate account to summarize gains and losses may be opened. After the realization of all assets, the debit or credit balance in the account is transferred to the capital accounts in the profit and loss ratio.

(2) Outside creditors are paid in full before payments are made to partners on either loan or capital balances.

(3) Partners' net interests in firm assets are determined before any payment is made to partners. When the books report amounts receivable by the firm from individual partners as a result of advances or as a result of charges for goods or services, such balances would be offset against partners' capitals. Settlement is then made in accordance with amounts reported by partners' loan and capital accounts.

Loss on Realization Requiring Transfer from Partner's Loan Account to Capital

Example 2. Assume that the noncash assets of the firm of A, B, C, and D realize $120,000. The sale of the assets for $120,000 results in a loss of $60,000 that is divided among the partners in the profit and loss ratio. Distribution of this loss requires a charge to D of $12,000 and results in a debit balance of $2,000 in D's capital account. Instead of requiring D to make an additional investment, $2,000 is transferred from D's loan account to offset the deficiency. Partners are then paid amounts equal to their loan and capital account balances. The following statement summarizes the liquidation process.

A, B, C, and D
Statement of Liquidation
May 1–31, 19X7

	Cash	Other Assets	Liab.	B Loan	D Loan	Capitals and Profit-Sharing Percentage			
						A, Cap. (30%)	B, Cap. (30%)	C, Cap. (20%)	D, Cap. (20%)
Balances before liquidation.......	10,000	180,000	75,000	6,000	5,000	42,000	31,500	20,500	10,000
Sale of assets and distribution of loss.............	120,000	(180,000)				(18,000)	(18,000)	(12,000)	(12,000)
	130,000		75,000	6,000	5,000	24,000	13,500	8,500	(2,000)
Payment to creditors..........	(75,000)		(75,000)						
	55,000			6,000	5,000	24,000	13,500	8,500	(2,000)
Offset of D's loan against debit balance in capital account					(2,000)				2,000
	55,000			6,000	3,000	24,000	13,500	8,500	
Payment to partners..........	(55,000)			(6,000)	(3,000)	(24,000)	(13,500)	(8,500)	

The entry to record the application of D's loan to the capital deficiency would be as follows:

Transaction	Entry
Transfer from D's loan account to capital account of the amount required to absorb the capital deficiency.	D, Loan..................................... 2,000 D, Capital............................. 2,000

Loss on Realization Resulting in Capital Deficiency for One Partner

Example 3. Assume that the noncash assets realize $100,000, resulting in a loss of $80,000. In distributing the loss of $80,000, D is charged for $16,000. This results in a debit balance of $6,000 in D's capital account. The offset of the entire amount of D's loan account against capital still leaves D's capital account with a debit balance of $1,000. If D pays the firm $1,000 at this point, the capital deficiency is canceled and the partners can distribute cash to A, B, and C in final liquidation. If, however, recovery from D is not made at this point and the partners decide to distribute the available cash, the distribution should recognize the possibility that D may fail to meet the obligation to the firm. The available cash, then, should be distributed in a manner that leaves the capitals of A, B, and C with balances that can absorb the possible loss of $1,000. If D subsequently contributes $1,000, this cash is paid to A, B, and C according to the balances in their accounts.

The following statement of liquidation is based on the assumption that available cash is distributed to A, B, and C, and that D subsequently contributes the deficiency.

A, B, C, and D
Statement of Liquidation
May 1–31, 19X7

	Cash	Other Assets	Liab.	B Loan	D Loan	Capitals and Profit-Sharing Percentage			
						A, Cap. (30%)	B, Cap. (30%)	C, Cap. (20%)	D, Cap. (20%)
Balances before liquidation	10,000	180,000	75,000	6,000	5,000	42,000	31,500	20,500	10,000
Sale of assets and distribution of loss	100,000	(180,000)				(24,000)	(24,000)	(16,000)	(16,000)
	110,000		75,000	6,000	5,000	18,000	7,500	4,500	(6,000)
Payment to creditors..........	(75,000)		(75,000)						
	35,000			6,000	5,000	18,000	7,500	4,500	(6,000)
Offset of D's loan against debit balance in capital account					(5,000)				5,000
	35,000			6,000		18,000	7,500	4,500	(1,000)
Payment to partners (per schedule)	(35,000)			(6,000)		(17,625)	(7,125)	(4,250)	
						375	375	250	(1,000)
Additional investment by D....................	1,000								1,000
	1,000					375	375	250	
Payment to partners	(1,000)					(375)	(375)	(250)	

In this example, cash of $35,000 is available to pay A, B, and C, whose combined loan and capital balances are $36,000. In determining the amount to be paid to these partners, the loss of $1,000 which will have to be absorbed by A, B, and C in the event of D's insolvency must be considered.

The amounts to be paid to partners may be referred to as their *free interests*. The free interest is calculated, as shown in the schedule on page 72, by combining each partner's loan and capital balance prior to the distribution of any cash and subtracting from this total any balance that must remain available to absorb possible future losses.

When the amount of cash that may be paid to a partner is determined, cash is first applied to any outstanding loan and any residual is applied to the capital balance. Partner D, however, receives no cash for the loan account, despite the fact that the other partners receive payments for capital balances. The legal priority of a partner's loan balance is nullified by the right of offset. The distribution of cash in any manner other than that shown will result in the overpayment of certain partners and the underpayment of others and will require cash transfers among partners later if D's obligation to the firm is not met.

A, B, C, and D
Schedule to Accompany Statement of Liquidation
Amounts To Be Paid to Partners
May 1–31, 19X7

	A (30%)	B (30%)	C (20%)	D (20%)
Capital balances before distribution of cash..............	18,000	7,500	4,500	(1,000)
Add loan balance...		6,000		
Partners' total interests	18,000	13,500	4,500	(1,000)
Restricted interests — possible loss of $1,000 to A, B, and C if D fails to contribute amount of deficiency (ratio: A, B, C — 30:30:20)	(375)	(375)	(250)	1,000
Free interests — amounts to be paid to each partner..	17,625	13,125	4,250	
Payment to apply on loan		6,000		
Payment to apply on capital.....................................	17,625	7,125	4,250	
Total cash distribution..	17,625	13,125	4,250	

The entries to record the additional investment by D and the distribution of this amount to A, B, and C follow:

Transaction	Entry
Additional investment by D to meet capital deficiency.	Cash... 1,000 D, Capital............................. 1,000
Payment to partners in final settlement.	A, Capital................................ 375 B, Capital................................ 375 C, Capital................................ 250 Cash..................................... 1,000

If D makes settlement directly with the other partners, the following entry is made:

Transaction	Entry
Payment by D directly to A, B, and C in settlement of indebtedness to copartners.	A, Capital................................ 375 B, Capital................................ 375 C, Capital................................ 250 D, Capital............................. 1,000

If the firm cannot collect its claim against D, the entry to record the loss would be:

Transaction	Entry
Charge-off of D's uncollectible balance against capitals of A, B, and C, in the ratio 30:30:20 respectively.	A, Capital................................ 375 B, Capital................................ 375 C, Capital................................ 250 D, Capital............................. 1,000

Loss on Realization Resulting in Capital Deficiencies for More Than One Partner

Example 4. Assume that the noncash assets realize $80,000, resulting in a loss of $100,000. In distributing the loss of $100,000, D's capital account is charged for $20,000. This results in a debit balance of $10,000 in D's capital account. The offset of D's entire loan balance of $5,000 against capital still leaves a capital deficiency of $5,000. If $5,000 is recovered from D at this point, the capital deficiency is canceled and the partners can wind up activities by distributing the cash to partners A, B, and C. If, however, recovery from D is not made at this point and the partners decide to distribute the available cash, the interests of A, B, and C should be left with balances sufficient to absorb the possible loss from D. The recognition of such a loss will result in a debit balance in C's capital. In anticipating all contingencies, it becomes necessary to consider the possibility of such an additional loss to A and B.

If D subsequently invests $5,000, this cash may be distributed to the partners according to the balances reported in their capital accounts. Under these circumstances C would not be required to make a further contribution. An investment by D is assumed in the following statement of liquidation.

A, B, C, and D
Statement of Liquidation
May 1–31, 19X7

	Cash	Other Assets	Liab.	B Loan	D Loan	Capitals and Profit-Sharing Percentage			
						A, Cap. (30%)	B, Cap. (30%)	C, Cap. (20%)	D, Cap. (20%)
Balances before liquidation	10,000	180,000	75,000	6,000	5,000	42,000	31,500	20,500	10,000
Sale of assets and distribution of loss	80,000	(180,000)				(30,000)	(30,000)	(20,000)	(20,000)
	90,000		75,000	6,000	5,000	12,000	1,500	500	(10,000)
Payment to creditors..........	(75,000)		(75,000)						
	15,000			6,000	5,000	12,000	1,500	500	(10,000)
Offset of D's loan against debit balance in capital account					(5,000)				5,000
	15,000			6,000		12,000	1,500	500	(5,000)
Payment to partners (per schedule)	(15,000)			(5,250)		(9,750)			
				750		2,250	1,500	500	(5,000)
Additional investment by D....................	5,000								5,000
	5,000			750		2,250	1,500	500	
Payment to partners	(5,000)			(750)		(2,250)	(1,500)	(500)	

Cash of $15,000 was available to pay A, B, and C, whose combined loan and capital balances totaled $20,000. In determining how the cash was to be distributed, the free interest for each partner was calculated by means of the following schedule.

A, B, C, and D
Schedule to Accompany Statement of Liquidation
Amounts To Be Paid to Partners
May 1–31, 19X7

	A (30%)	B (30%)	C (20%)	D (20%)
Capital balances before distribution of cash................	12,000	1,500	500	(5,000)
Add loan balance..		6,000		
Partners' total interests..	12,000	7,500	500	(5,000)
Restricted interests — possible loss of $5,000 to A, B, and C if D fails to contribute amount of deficiency (ratio: A, B, C — 30:30:20)	(1,875)	(1,875)	(1,250)	5,000
	10,125	5,625	(750)	
Restricted interests — additional possible loss of $750 to A and B if C fails to contribute amount of possible deficiency (ratio: A, B — 30:30)...............................	(375)	(375)	750	
Free interests — amounts to be paid to each partner....	9,750	5,250		
Payment to apply on loan		5,250		
Payment to apply on capital..	9,750			
Total cash distribution	9,750	5,250		

The possible loss of $5,000 in the event of D's insolvency was first considered. Since A, B, and C share profits 30%, 30%, and 20%, this ratio was applied in arriving at the partners' restricted interests of $1,875, $1,875, and $1,250 respectively. C's capital, however, was inadequate to absorb a share of the possible additional loss. The potential loss to C, $750, was then considered a further restricted interest applicable to A and B. Since the profit and loss ratio for A and B is 30% and 30%, or equal, further reductions of $375 each were applied to A and B in arriving at their free interests.

The distribution of $15,000 developed in the schedule resulted in payment on A's capital balance before B's loan was fully liquidated. If B insists that full settlement be made on the loan balance before cash is paid on capital balances, in view of the priority given partners' loans in the Uniform Partnership Act, the liquidator must consider all of the contingencies that are faced in terminating the partnership. A future loss through failure to recover cash from deficient partners will give rise to a debit balance in B's capital account. Cash paid to B in satisfaction of the loan balance, then, will have to be recovered to absorb such a capital deficiency, and failure to effect such a recovery could render the liquidator liable to a partner suffering a loss through a premature distribution. Under these circumstances, the liquidator must insist on one of the following procedures:

(1) Recognize the legal priority of partners' loans but make payment to a trustee under the condition that the cash can be recovered to offset

a capital deficiency if one should arise; when the possibility of a need for offset is gone, the cash can be released to the partner.

(2) Defer settlement until the full amount of the loss that each partner will be required to absorb in final settlement, including charges arising from failures of copartners to meet their proper share of firm losses, is ascertained; application of loan balances against capital deficiencies can then be effected and appropriate cash distribution made.

(3) Distribute cash in a manner that recognizes the possibility of future losses, including charges that may arise from failures of copartners to meet their proper share of firm losses; payment on loan balances, as well as capital balances, then, will be withheld when such balances may be required to absorb losses.

If all parties are informed as to the nature and significance of the problem, they should have no objection to the distribution of cash as suggested in (3). Distributions of cash when loan and capital balances are involved are the same as the distributions that would be made if total interests were in the form of capital balances.

Realization Resulting in Cash Insufficient To Pay Creditors

Example 5(a). Assume that the noncash assets of the firm of A, B, C, and D realize only $60,000. Assume further that all partners are personally solvent and capable of meeting any obligation to the firm that may emerge from liquidation. A loss of $120,000 is charged against the partners' capital balances and available cash of $70,000 is paid to creditors. Appropriate offset of loan balances against capital deficiencies is made. In this case, creditors are left with unpaid balances totaling $5,000; partners A and B have positive equities of $6,000 and $1,500 respectively in the firm, while partners C and D owe the firm $3,500 and $9,000 respectively. If C and D make payments to the firm in settlement of their obligations, the cash of $12,500 may be distributed to creditors and to A and B in full settlement. A statement of liquidation under these conditions is shown on page 76.

It has already been suggested that, insofar as business-creditor relationships are concerned, the partnership is not viewed as a separate entity but as an association of individuals, all personally responsible for partnership obligations. In the previous example, settlement with creditors was achieved through contributions to the partnership by capital-deficient partners. Assume that creditors, however, finding that partnership assets are insufficient to meet partnership liabilities in full, proceed against the individual partners. If they are successful in collecting the balance of $5,000 owed to them from A, for example, A's interest in the partnership would increase by $5,000. Upon ultimate collection of capital deficiencies of $3,500 and $9,000 from partners C and D respectively, A would be paid $11,000 and B $1,500. When liquidation is completed by full recovery from deficient partners, the same results are achieved regardless of who makes payment to creditors. Under each of the previous assumptions, A and B recover $6,000 and $1,500 respectively, and C and D contribute $3,500 and $9,000 respectively.

A, B, C, and D
Statement of Liquidation
May 1–31, 19X7

	Cash	Other Assets	Liab.	B Loan	D Loan	Capitals and Profit-Sharing Percentage			
						A, Cap. (30%)	B, Cap. (30%)	C, Cap. (20%)	D, Cap. (20%)
Balances before liquidation..........	10,000	180,000	75,000	6,000	5,000	42,000	31,500	20,500	10,000
Sale of assets and distribution of loss	60,000	(180,000)				(36,000)	(36,000)	(24,000)	(24,000)
	70,000		75,000	6,000	5,000	6,000	(4,500)	(3,500)	(14,000)
Payment to creditors............	(70,000)		(70,000)						
			5,000	6,000	5,000	6,000	(4,500)	(3,500)	(14,000)
Offset of loans against debit balances in capital accounts .				(4,500)	(5,000)		4,500		5,000
			5,000	1,500		6,000		(3,500)	(9,000)
Additional investment by C and D	12,500							3,500	9,000
	12,500		5,000	1,500		6,000			
Payment to creditors............	(5,000)		(5,000)						
	7,500			1,500		6,000			
Payment to partners.............	(7,500)			(1,500)		(6,000)			

Example 5(b). In the foregoing example it was assumed that all of the
partners were personally solvent and able to meet whatever indebtedness
was incurred in arriving at final settlement. Assume, however, that certain
partners are personally insolvent. Under these circumstances the law requires a *marshaling of assets* that calls for the following procedure: partnership assets must first be applied to the settlement of the partnership's
own liabilities, and each partner's separate assets must first be applied to
the settlement of the partner's own liabilities. Thus, creditors of an insolvent partnership may claim only that portion of a partner's separate property that is not required for the satisfaction of personal obligations; separate
property in excess of personal obligations may be claimed by firm creditors
regardless of the partner's interest in the firm, whether positive or negative.
On the other hand, creditors of an insolvent partner may make claim to
partnership property only after firm creditors have been satisfied in full; the
claim of separate creditors, however, is limited to the remaining positive
interest of the particular partner. The Uniform Partnership Act makes the
following further provision:

> When a partner has become bankrupt or his estate is insolvent, the claims
> against his separate property shall rank in the following order:
> I. Those owing to separate creditors.
> II. Those owing to partnership creditors.
> III. Those owing to partners by way of contribution.

A deficiency in a partner's capital account is therefore not to be included in the separate creditor total against which personal property is first applied under the Uniform Partnership Act, but is to be met only after other personal and partnership creditors are fully satisfied.

To illustrate application of the foregoing rules, assume again the sale of the assets of the firm of A, B, C, and D at $60,000, payment to creditors of $70,000, and offset of loan balances against capitals. Liabilities of $5,000 are unpaid. The personal status of each of the partners at this point, together with the interest of each in the firm, both positive and negative, are given below.

Partner	Personal Status Exclusive of Firm Interest		Firm Status	
	Assets	Liabilities	Interest in the Firm	Obligation to the Firm
A	$10,000	$20,000	$6,000	
B	20,000	15,000	1,500	
C	25,000	15,000		$3,500
D	10,000	10,000		9,000

The personal assets of A and D must be applied in total to payment of personal creditors. However, the personal assets of B and C exceed the respective personal debts, and partnership creditors have recourse against either partner for the balance of their claims. The fact that B has a positive interest in the partnership is no defense if partnership creditors choose to hold B. Furthermore, A's personal creditors who cannot be fully satisfied from A's personal assets will look forward to further satisfaction of their claims through final liquidation of the partnership and ultimate settlement of A's positive interest.

Assume that partnership creditors collect from B. Before final settlement is made by the partners, the claim against D, who is personally insolvent, is charged against the capitals of A, B, and C in the ratio 30:30:20. C, who is indebted to the firm and personally solvent, makes appropriate payment to partners A and B, who have positive equities in the firm; the amount recoverable on A's interest is applied to payment of A's individual creditors. Assuming settlement in this manner, the statement of liquidation would be completed as shown on page 78.

If partnership creditors collect from C instead of B, final settlement will produce the same net results. B will be required to contribute $1,875, the difference between the charge to B's capital for D's deficiency, $3,375, and B's unpaid loan balance of $1,500; C, after paying personal creditors, will be required to contribute $750 to cancel a capital deficiency of $5,750, consisting of a debit capital balance of $3,500, increased by the charge for D's deficiency, $2,250. Contributions by B and C totaling $2,625 will be paid to A.

A, B, C, and D
Statement of Liquidation
May 1-31, 19X7

	Cash	Other Assets	Liab.	B Loan	D Loan	Capitals and Profit-Sharing Percentage			
						A, Cap. (30%)	B, Cap. (30%)	C, Cap. (20%)	D, Cap. (20%)
Balances (see page 76).....................			5,000	1,500		6,000		(3,500)	(9,000)
Payment to creditors by B.....................			(5,000)				5,000		
				1,500		6,000	5,000	(3,500)	(9,000)
Amount due from D and uncollectible, charged to A, B, and C in the ratio 30:30:20 respectively						(3,375)	(3,375)	(2,250)	9,000
				1,500		2,625	1,625	(5,750)	
Payment by C to A and B...................				(1,500)		(2,625)	(1,625)	5,750	

QUESTIONS

1. Burke and Collins invest $25,000 and $5,000 respectively in forming a partnership. No agreement is made concerning profit distribution. A loss of $5,000 is incurred at the end of the first six months of operations. Liquidation of the partnership results in an additional loss of $10,000. Collins insists that operating losses may be divided equally but that losses from liquidation should be divided in the ratio of capital investments. (a) Is there any merit to Collins' contention? (b) What is the status of the partners after the foregoing takes place?

2. What is meant by the *right of offset* as applied to the liquidation of a partnership?

3. (a) What priorities are recognized under the Uniform Partnership Act in the distribution of cash upon partnership liquidation? (b) What limitations would you apply in recognizing such priorities?

4. Mead and Norris, who share profits equally, have loan and capital balances as follows:

	Mead	Norris
Loan balance.........	$25,000	$10,000
Capital balance......	50,000	60,000

All of the assets are sold for $35,000, and Mead suggests that this be applied to the payment of loan balances in final settlement. Do you approve?

5. A, B, and C are partners sharing profits 3:3:2. The partnership is dissolved. Upon distribution of the partnership loss from liquidation, C's capital account

shows a debit balance of $10,000. C is personally insolvent. How is this balance treated?

6. Just before partnership liquidation, capital accounts for A, B, and C, who share profits 2:1:1 respectively, are as follows: A, credit balance, $40,000; B, credit balance, $25,000; C, debit balance, $12,500. Under what circumstances, if any, will C share in the distribution of cash after realization of partnership assets?

7. A, B, and C are partners sharing profits equally. The partnership and also certain partners are insolvent and the partnership is liquidated. Upon distribution of the partnership loss from liquidation, a statement is drawn up summarizing the status of each partner as follows:

| Partner | Personal Status (Exclusive of Firm Interest) | | Firm Status | |
	Assets	Liabilities	Interest in Firm	Amount Owed to Firm
A	$30,000	$10,000	$5,000	
B	5,000	10,000		$ 5,000
C	15,000	10,000		15,000

Assume that provisions of the Uniform Partnership Act apply.

(a) Against whom can firm creditors proceed for the recovery of their unpaid claims?
(b) What are the rights of the individual creditors of each partner?
(c) From whom can A's interest be recovered?

EXERCISES

1. Knox and Wheeler are partners, and their capital balances are $15,000 and $10,000 respectively. The firm owes Wheeler $4,000 on a note. Profits are shared equally. Upon liquidation, cash of $6,000 becomes available for distribution to the partners. How is this cash to be distributed?

2. A, B, and C formed a partnership in 19X0, agreeing to divide profits 2:1:1 respectively. In the middle of 19X1, with operations going unfavorably, the partners decided to dissolve the relationship. From the following facts, prepare a summary of partners' capital balances that indicates what, if anything, remains to be done in final settlement.

	A	B	C
Value of net assets contributed to firm...	$50,000	$22,500	$20,000
Partnership net income, 19X0, $30,000, divided 2:1:1	15,000	7,500	7,500
Drawings — 19X0..............................	15,000	10,000	10,000
Net assets at time of dissolution valued at $65,000, distributed to partners 2:1:1	32,500	16,250	16,250

3. J and K share profits 40% and 60% respectively. After sale of all firm assets, ledger accounts show the balances reported below. Both partners are personally insolvent and unable to contribute to the partnership. Prepare all of the entries to summarize partnership activities, including the appropriate distribution of cash on hand.

Cash............................	$ 2,000	Salary Payable to J.......	$ 500
Receivable from K........	1,500	J, Capital	9,500
Loss from Liquidation...	24,500	K, Capital....................	18,000
	$28,000		$28,000

4. L, M, and N are partners sharing profits 3:3:2 respectively. The partners decide to liquidate. The partnership books report the following balances with respect to land and buildings:

Land		$15,000	Mortgage payable (secured	
Buildings	$25,000		by land and buildings)	$16,000
Less accumulated			Accrued interest on	
depreciation.......	7,500	17,500	mortgage	160

The land and buildings are worth $30,000 on the market, and L agrees to take over the property at this value and to assume all the indebtedness on the property. Record the transfer on the firm books.

5. X, Y, and Z form a partnership on January 1, 19X3, investing $15,000, $10,000, and $10,000 respectively; profits are to be shared in the ratio of 2:1:1 respectively. It is agreed that 6% (½ of 1% per month) is to be charged on withdrawals that decrease capitals below the original investments. On March 1, X withdraws $5,000. Business is unsatisfactory and it is decided to dissolve the partnership. Partnership assets realize $5,000 and the accountant distributes this cash to the proper parties on November 1, 19X3. All parties are solvent, and proper settlement is made among partners the same day. Prepare a statement of partners' capitals that summarizes the activities that took place in 19X3.

6. The capitals of Ames, Baker, and Caldwell, who are partners, are $14,000, $10,000, and $14,000, and profits are shared 30%, 20%, and 50% respectively. Upon liquidation, all of the partnership assets are sold and sufficient cash is realized to pay all of the claims except one for $2,000. Caldwell is personally insolvent, but the remaining partners are able to meet any indebtedness to the firm. State how settlement would be made.

7. A, B, C, and D are partners with capitals of $5,500, $5,150, $6,850, and $4,500 respectively. A has a loan balance of $1,000. Profits are shared in the ratio of 4:3:2:1 by A, B, C, and D respectively. Assets are sold, liabilities are paid, and cash of $6,000 remains. How should this cash be divided?

PROBLEMS

3-1. Gordon and Haller began partnership operations on January 3, 19X6, investing cash of $25,000 and $15,000 respectively. Gordon is to be allowed an annual salary of $12,000, and the balance of any profit or loss is to be distributed in the ratio of original capitals. Operations are unsuccessful and a balance sheet prepared on December 31, 19X6, shows the following:

Gordon and Haller
Balance Sheet
December 31, 19X6

Assets		Liabilities and Capital	
Cash............................	$13,350	Accounts payable	$17,500
Accounts receivable		Gordon, capital............	25,000
(net)........................	10,000	Haller, capital..............	15,000
Merchandise	17,500		$57,500
Equipment (net)	8,500	Less loss for 19X6........	3,150
Advance to Haller	5,000		
		Total liabilities and	
Total assets.................	$54,350	capital.....................	$54,350

Interest at 6% is to be charged on the withdrawal of $5,000 made by Haller on July 1. No entries have been made for the interest charge or for the salary allowance to Gordon.

Liquidation takes place at the beginning of 19X7. As a partial settlement, Gordon agrees to take over the merchandise at a value of $14,000. Accounts receivable are sold at a 20% discount and equipment is sold for $6,800. Payment is made to creditors and the remaining cash is distributed to the partners.

Instructions: Prepare the entries to close the loss for the year and to record the dissolution of the partnership.

3-2. A, B, and C, who share profits and losses in the ratio of 2:2:1 respectively, decide to liquidate on December 31, 19X9. Below is a condensed balance sheet prepared just prior to liquidation:

A, B, and C
Balance Sheet
December 31, 19X9

Assets		Liabilities and Capital	
Cash..........................	$ 20,000	Trade liabilities...........	$112,000
Other assets..............	340,000	B, loan......................	5,000
		C, loan......................	8,000
		A, capital	95,000
		B, capital	60,000
		C, capital	80,000
		Total liabilities and	
Total assets...............	$360,000	capital...................	$360,000

Instructions: For each case below prepare a statement of liquidation, with supporting schedules where necessary, assuming that cash is realized for the other assets as indicated and that all available cash is immediately distributed to the proper parties. Assume that partners who find themselves indebted to the firm invest additional cash and such cash is distributed as a second installment to the proper parties.

(a) $250,000. (c) $170,000. (e) $90,000.
(b) $185,000. (d) $125,000.

3-3. Carl, Decker, and Eaton form a partnership on July 1, 19X4, each partner investing $25,000. On August 1, 19X4, Carl was advanced $10,000 by the firm. On September 1, 19X4, Decker made a loan to the firm of $20,000. Interest is to be charged on advances to partners and credited on loans by partners at the rate of 6%. Business is unsatisfactory and the partners decide to dissolve. Eaton is allowed special compensation of $2,500 for managing the sale of assets and settlement with creditors. On December 31, all assets have been sold, outside creditors have been paid, and cash of $35,000 is distributed to partners. All partners are personally solvent and final settlement is made among partners on February 10, 19X5.

Instructions: Prepare a statement of changes in partners' capital accounts covering the period July 1, 19X4 to February 10, 19X5.

3-4. The following balance sheet was prepared just prior to liquidation and dissolution of the partnership of A, B, C, and D. Profits are shared by A, B, C, and D in the ratio of 4:2:1:1 respectively.

A, B, C, and D
Balance Sheet
April 30, 19X8

Assets		Liabilities and Capital	
Cash.........................	$ 20,000	Liabilities..................	$180,000
Other assets..............	380,000	D, loan......................	12,500
Receivable from A......	25,000	A, capital	155,000
		B, capital.................	37,500
		C, capital	20,000
		D, capital.................	20,000
		Total liabilities and	
Total assets..............	$425,000	capital...................	$425,000

"Other assets" are sold for $200,000 and available cash is distributed to the proper parties. Partner B is personally insolvent, but the other partners are able to meet any personal indebtedness to the partnership. The solvent partners make appropriate contributions to the partnership, and this cash is distributed in final settlement.

Instructions: (1) Prepare a statement of liquidation, together with a supporting schedule if necessary.

(2) Give the entries that would be made to record the dissolution of the partnership.

3-5. M, N, O, and P share profits in the ratio of 2:1:1:1 respectively. The partnership cannot meet its obligations to creditors, and dissolution is authorized on November 1, 19X1. A balance sheet for the partnership on this date shows balances as follows:

M, N, O, and P
Balance Sheet
November 1, 19X1

Assets		Liabilities and Capital	
Cash...........................	$12,500	Liabilities....................	$30,000
Other assets...............	40,000	P, loan.........................	2,500
		M, capital	5,000
		N, capital....................	5,000
		O, capital....................	5,000
		P, capital	5,000
		Total liabilities and	
Total assets................	$52,500	capital....................	$52,500

The personal status of partners on this date is as follows:

	Cash and Cash Value of Personal Assets	Personal Liabilities
M	$30,000	$20,000
N	5,000	15,000
O	20,000	17,500
P	15,000	20,000

"Other assets" of the partnership are sold and $12,000 is realized.

Instructions: (1) Assuming dissolution under provisions of the Uniform Partnership Act and contributions by appropriate parties in meeting the claims of partnership creditors, prepare the entries that would appear on the partnership books in winding up the business.

(2) State the amounts that will be paid to the personal creditors of each of the partners.

3-6. The balance sheet for the firm of W, X, Y, and Z on June 15, 19X9, just prior to liquidation, is as follows:

W, X, Y, and Z
Balance Sheet
June 15, 19X9

Assets			Liabilities and Capital	
Cash.....................................		$14,000	Accounts payable	$40,000
Merchandise inventory		27,500	W, loan	1,000
Accounts receivable.............		30,000	Z, loan.................................	2,500
Store fixtures	$15,000		W, capital	13,500
Less accumu-			X, capital	7,500
lated deprecia-			Y, capital	5,000
tion................	12,500	2,500	Z, capital	4,500
Total assets.........................		$74,000	Total liabilities and capital	$74,000

W, X, Y, and Z share profits in the ratio of 5:5:3:2 respectively. Noncash assets realize a total of $24,000. The personal status of partners exclusive of firm equities is as follows:

	Cash and Cash Value of Personal Assets	Personal Liabilities
W	$30,000	$16,500
X	15,000	18,500
Y	20,000	17,500
Z	5,000	8,500

Instructions: (1) Prepare the journal entries to record the sale of the assets, the distribution of the loss on the sale of the assets, and the payment of available cash to creditors.

(2) Assuming dissolution under provisions of the Uniform Partnership Act, prepare the journal entries to complete the liquidation if the creditors collect their unpaid balance from W and the partners then make proper settlement among themselves.

(3) Assuming dissolution under provisions of the Uniform Partnership Act, prepare the journal entries to complete the liquidation, assuming that the creditors collect their unpaid balance from Y instead of W and the partners then make proper settlement among themselves.

3-7. A and B, a trading partnership, decide to admit C as a partner on January 1, 19X5. They agree with C as follows:

C is not to contribute any tangible assets, but C's share of the profits is to be credited to a capital account until a $^1/_5$ interest has accumulated. C is to share profits and losses to the extent of $^1/_5$. In addition to the profits, C is to receive a salary of $3,000 per year, payable monthly. A and B are to receive no salary; they are to share profits and losses equally.

The balance sheet of A and B at December 31, 19X4, is as follows:

A and B
Balance Sheet
December 31, 19X4

Assets		Liabilities and Capital		
Cash.............................	$ 1,500	Accounts payable		$ 8,000
Accounts receivable.....	10,000	Capital accounts:		
Merchandise	7,500	A...............	$10,000	
Furniture and fixtures...	1,500	B	5,000	15,000
Goodwill......................	2,500			
		Total liabilities and		
Total assets.................	$23,000	capital.....................		$23,000

During the six months ended June 30, 19X5, the business has sustained unusual losses and it is decided to dissolve the partnership.

The balance sheet at June 30, 19X5, is shown on page 85.

Accounts receivable were sold for $9,000, the buyer assuming all responsibility for collection and loss, if any. Merchandise realized $6,500; furniture and fixtures, $500.

Examination of the books discloses that C has not drawn any salary for four months and that B has advanced to the partnership $2,500 by way of a temporary loan. These liabilities are included in the sum of $12,500 shown as accounts payable. C is insolvent.

A and B
Balance Sheet
June 30, 19X5

Assets		Liabilities and Capital		
Cash............................	$ 500	Accounts payable		$12,500
Accounts receivable.....	12,500	Capital accounts:		
Merchandise	5,000	A...............	$10,000	
Furniture and fixtures...	1,500	B	5,000	
Goodwill......................	2,500		$15,000	
		Less deficit (loss on trading for 6 mos.)......	5,500	9,500
		Total liabilities and		
Total assets.................	$22,000	capital.....................		$22,000

Instructions: Prepare a statement of liquidation.

(AICPA adapted)

3-8. You are engaged to assist in terminating the affairs of A and B Discount Sales, a partnership under liquidation. Allen owns Toy Wholesalers and contributed $10,000 in inventory for a 50% interest in A and B Discount Sales on January 3, 19X2. Ball owns Appliance Wholesalers and contributed $2,000 cash and $8,000 in inventory for a 50% interest on the same date. All profits and losses are to be shared equally.

In the course of your examination you determine the following facts:

(1) An incompetent part-time bookkeeper had discarded all cash register tapes and invoices for expenses and purchases. The bookkeeper was also employed by Appliance Wholesalers.

(2) The partners state that the only existing payables are to themselves, as follows:

Toy Wholesalers........................	$ 9,740
Appliance Wholesalers..............	5,260
	$15,000

(3) You are able to prepare the following summary of cash transactions from bank statements and canceled checks:

Beginning cash balance		$ 2,000
Receipts:		
Sales...	$70,000	
Inventory liquidation.....................................	7,000	77,000
		$79,000
Disbursements:		
Purchases	$36,000	
Operating expenses	26,000	
Leasehold improvements (5-year lease)...........	6,000	
Liquidating expense.......................................	4,000	72,000
Balance, December 31, 19X2...		$ 7,000

(4) On December 31, 19X2, $7,000 was paid to the partners, $3,500 to each, to apply on the $15,000 liability.

(5) The partners state that the dollar amounts of regular sales of toys and appliances were approximately equal and that the dollar amounts of liquidating sales of toys and appliances were also approximately equal. There was a uniform markup of 40% of cost on toys and 25% of cost on appliances. All sales were for cash. The ending inventory of shopworn merchandise was liquidated on December 31, 19X2, for 50% of the retail sales price.

(6) The partners believe that some appliances may have been returned to Appliance Wholesalers, but the bookkeeper failed to record the returns on the books of either organization.

Instructions: (1) Compute the unrecorded amount of appliances returned to Appliance Wholesalers, if any.

(2) Prepare an income statement for A and B Discount Sales for the period January 3 to December 31, 19X2.

(3) Prepare a statement of partners' capital accounts.

(AICPA adapted)

3-9. M owns a 75% interest in MN partnership and N owns a 25% interest. The partnership is to dissolve and the only assets to be distributed are 145 shares of Arthur Co. with a cost basis to the partnership of $14,500 and a market value of $35,000; 45 shares of Bay Corporation with a cost basis to the partnership of $4,500 and a market value of $15,000; and 210 shares of Cory Stores with a cost basis to the partnership of $21,000 and a market value of $30,000. *Under tax rules, the basis of the distributed assets in the hands of the distributee will be in proportion to the partnership's basis.*

Since M is a director in Arthur Co., M and N agree that M is to receive all 145 of those shares.

Instructions: Prepare a schedule showing the distribution of the stocks so that each partner will receive an equitable share from a market value and from an income tax point of view. Submit your supporting computations in good form.

(AICPA adapted)

3-10. X, Y, and Z are partners sharing profits in the ratio of 4:3:2 respectively. The partnership and two of the partners are currently unable to pay their creditors. The partnership balance sheet and the personal status of the partners are as follows:

X, Y, and Z Partnership
Balance Sheet
November 15, 19X8

Cash...........................	$ 500	Accounts payable	$37,000
Other assets................	60,500	X, capital	10,000
		Y, capital	6,000
		Z, capital	8,000
		Total liabilities and	
Total assets.................	$61,000	capital......................	$61,000

Personal Status of Partners
(Excluding Partnership Interests)

Partner	Cash and Cash Value of Personal Assets	Liabilities
X	$31,000	$20,000
Y	9,450	11,900
Z	4,000	5,000

Instructions: (1) Prepare a schedule showing distributions to partnership and personal creditors in the event of dissolution under provisions of the Uniform Partnership Act, assuming that "Other assets" are sold for $33,500.

(2) Prepare a computation showing the minimum amount that must be realized from the sale of partnership assets other than cash so that the personal creditors of Y will receive full settlement of their claims.

(AICPA adapted)

4
Partnerships — Installment Liquidation; Joint Ventures

When partnership liquidation takes place over an extended period of time, it is frequently desirable to make cash distributions to partners as cash becomes available. In adopting an installment payment procedure, particular care must be taken to avoid an overpayment to any partner. This calls for special procedures to determine the partners who may properly participate in successive cash distributions. Just as in earlier examples of liquidation, cash can be made available to partners only after the claims of creditors have been fully satisfied or sufficient cash has been set aside for this purpose.

PROCEDURES FOR DETERMINING INSTALLMENT DISTRIBUTIONS

In the examples of liquidation that were given in Chapter 3, the total loss or gain on asset realization was known and this balance was divided among the partners in the profit and loss ratio. In making distributions it was necessary to consider only the possibility of losses that might arise upon failure of deficient partners or potentially deficient partners to meet their indebtedness to the firm. Distributions were made to partners in a manner that left their accounts with balances sufficient to absorb these possible losses.

When distributions are made during the course of liquidation, the amount that will be realized on assets that remain to be sold is not known and consequently the amount of the loss that partners will have to absorb is not determinable. Under these circumstances, each distribution to partners should be made as though it were the last. Such an assumption calls for the recognition of (1) the possibility of a total loss on all remaining assets, and (2) the possibility that deficient partners or potentially deficient partners may be unable to meet their indebtedness to the firm. The practical effect of such a procedure is to provide distributions that bring the partners' interests into the profit and loss ratio as rapidly as possible. Once the profit and loss ratio is achieved, further distributions can be made in the profit and loss ratio. The partners' interests will thus remain in the profit and loss ratio and be able to absorb properly any future loss.

Profit and Loss Ratio Achieved with First Installment

Assume that A and B are partners sharing profits 60:40 respectively. The balance sheet as of October 1, 19X4, is as follows:

A and B
Balance Sheet
October 1, 19X4

Assets		Liabilities and Capital	
Cash	$ 15,000	Liabilities	$ 20,000
Other assets	105,000	A, capital	75,000
		B, capital	25,000
Total assets	$120,000	Total liabilities and capital	$120,000

The partners decide to liquidate. During October, assets with a book value of $70,000 realize $55,000. The liabilities of $20,000 are paid. Account balances on the partnership books at the end of October are as follows:

	Cash	Other Assets	Liabilities	A Capital	B Capital
Balances before liquidation	15,000	105,000	20,000	75,000	25,000
Sale of assets and distribution of loss	55,000	(70,000)		(9,000)	(6,000)
	70,000	35,000	20,000	66,000	19,000
Payment to creditors	(20,000)		(20,000)		
Balances	50,000	35,000		66,000	19,000

At this point $50,000 is available for distribution and owners' interests total $85,000. Since the amount to become available to partners in the future is not known, the present distribution is made as though it were the last. A schedule is prepared in arriving at the distribution, as follows:

A and B
Schedule To Accompany Statement of Liquidation
Amounts To Be Paid to Partners
October 31, 19X4

	A	B
Capital balances before distribution of cash...	66,000	19,000
Restricted interests — possible loss of $35,000 if nothing is realized on remaining assets, chargeable to partners 60:40	(21,000)	(14,000)
Free interests — amount to be paid to each partner...................................	45,000	5,000

The distribution of cash in this way leaves A with a capital of $21,000 and B with a capital of $14,000. Capitals now are in the profit and loss ratio of 60:40. No matter what future losses may be, neither partner will have been overpaid and thus be required to return cash to the firm.

With the capital balances in the profit and loss ratio, future cash distributions may be made in the profit and loss ratio. Assume that in November assets with a book value of $25,000 are sold for $10,000 and in December remaining assets of $10,000 are sold for $12,500. A statement summarizing the complete process of liquidation follows:

A and B
Statement of Liquidation
October 1–December 31, 19X4

	Cash	Other Assets	Liabilities	Capitals and Profit-Sharing Ratio	
				A, Cap. (60)	B, Cap. (40)
Balances before liquidation..........	15,000	105,000	20,000	75,000	25,000
October — sale of assets and distribution of loss........................	55,000	(70,000)		(9,000)	(6,000)
	70,000	35,000	20,000	66,000	19,000
Payment to creditors	(20,000)		(20,000)		
	50,000	35,000		66,000	19,000
October — installment to partners (per schedule)..........................	(50,000)			(45,000)	(5,000)
		35,000		21,000	14,000
November — sale of assets and distribution of loss....................	10,000	(25,000)		(9,000)	(6,000)
	10,000	10,000		12,000	8,000
November — installment to partners in profit and loss ratio ..	(10,000)			(6,000)	(4,000)
		10,000		6,000	4,000
December — sale of assets and distribution of gain...................	12,500	(10,000)		1,500	1,000
	12,500			7,500	5,000
December — installment to partners in profit and loss ratio ..	(12,500)			(7,500)	(5,000)

Entries to record the course of liquidation are as follows:

Transaction	Entry		
October — sale of assets for $55,000, book value, $70,000; loss distributed 60:40.	Cash .... A, Capital .... B, Capital .... Other Assets	55,000 9,000 6,000	70,000
Payment to creditors.	Liabilities .... Cash	20,000	20,000
October — payment to partners, leaving capitals with balances that can absorb any future loss.	A, Capital .... B, Capital .... Cash	45,000 5,000	50,000
November — sale of assets for $10,000, book value, $25,000.	Cash .... A, Capital .... B, Capital .... Other Assets	10,000 9,000 6,000	25,000
November — payment to partners in profit and loss ratio.	A, Capital .... B, Capital .... Cash	6,000 4,000	10,000
December — sale of assets for $12,500, book value, $10,000.	Cash .... Other Assets .... A, Capital .... B, Capital	12,500	10,000 1,500 1,000
December — payment to partners in profit and loss ratio.	A, Capital .... B, Capital .... Cash	7,500 5,000	12,500

In this example, if settlement with the partners had been deferred until all of the assets were sold, the cash distribution would have been exactly the same as the total cash made available through the installment procedure. When the partnership assets with a book value of $105,000 are sold for $77,500, a loss of $27,500 results. A would be charged with 60% of this amount, or $16,500, and B would be charged with 40%, or $11,000. A and B, then, would be entitled to $58,500 and $14,000 respectively, exactly the same amounts they ultimately received through installment distributions.

A cash distribution that is viewed as though it were the last should be no different when partners' interests are composed of loan and capital balances than when interests are limited to capital balances alone. The right of offset makes the distinction between loan and capital balances meaningless for this purpose. If the interests of A and B were composed of loan and capital balances, these would be combined and the amounts to be withheld would be applied to the sum of these balances in arriving at the proper cash distribution. However, loan and capital balances should not be merged in the accounts in view of the interest that may accrue on loan balances, and the legal distinction that is made between loan and capital balances. When it is determined that cash is to be made available to a certain partner, cash is first applied to the reduction of the loan balance.

Profit and Loss Ratio Achieved Subsequent to First Installment

In the example in the preceding section, partners' interests were brought into the profit and loss ratio with the first distribution. Thereafter distributions were made in the profit and loss ratio. In considering the possibility of a loss on all remaining assets, it may be found that the interests of certain partners are inadequate to meet such a contingency. The possibility that deficient partners may not meet their indebtedness to the firm must then be recognized. Under these circumstances, the first distribution will not succeed in bringing the partners' interests into the profit and loss ratio. Furthermore, the determination of subsequent distributions will require a consideration of the possible loss on remaining assets. Each distribution, however, should bring partners' interests closer to the profit and loss ratio; upon achieving the profit and loss ratio, further distributions may be made in that ratio.

To illustrate the procedure that is used, assume that X, Y, and Z are partners sharing profits in the ratio of 50:30:20. A balance sheet prepared just prior to liquidation follows:

X, Y, and Z
Balance Sheet
July 1, 19X9

Assets		Liabilities and Capital	
Cash	$ 10,000	Liabilities	$ 52,500
Other assets	230,000	X, loan	12,500
		Y, loan	10,000
		X, capital	65,000
		Y, capital	50,000
		Z, capital	50,000
Total assets	$240,000	Total liabilities and capital	$240,000

Assets are sold, and the cash from asset realization is distributed at the end of each month. Asset realization takes place as follows:

July: Assets, book value of $ 70,000, are sold for $50,000.
August: Assets, book value of $ 30,000, are sold for $20,000.
September: Assets, book value of $ 25,000, are sold for $12,500.
October: Assets, book value of $105,000, are sold for $50,000.

The course of liquidation is summarized on the statement of liquidation and supporting schedules that follow.

X, Y, and Z
Statement of Liquidation
July 1–October 31, 19X9

	Cash	Other Assets	Liab.	X Loan	Y Loan	Capitals and Profit-Sharing Ratio		
						X, Cap. (50%)	Y, Cap. (30%)	Z, Cap. (20%)
Balances before liquidation....................	10,000	230,000	52,500	12,500	10,000	65,000	50,000	50,000
July — sale of assets and distribution of loss.........	50,000	(70,000)				(10,000)	(6,000)	(4,000)
	60,000	160,000	52,500	12,500	10,000	55,000	44,000	46,000
Payment to creditors	(52,500)		(52,500)					
	7,500	160,000		12,500	10,000	55,000	44,000	46,000
July — installment to partners (Schedule A)....	(7,500)							(7,500)
		160,000		12,500	10,000	55,000	44,000	38,500
August — sale of assets and distribution of loss ..	20,000	(30,000)				(5,000)	(3,000)	(2,000)
	20,000	130,000		12,500	10,000	50,000	41,000	36,500
August — installment to partners (Schedule B)....	(20,000)				(10,000)		(500)	(9,500)
		130,000		12,500		50,000	40,500	27,000
September — sale of assets and distribution of loss.........................	12,500	(25,000)				(6,250)	(3,750)	(2,500)
	12,500	105,000		12,500		43,750	36,750	24,500
September — installment to partners (Schedule C)	(12,500)			(3,750)			(5,250)	(3,500)
		105,000		8,750		43,750	31,500	21,000
October — sale of assets and distribution of loss ..	50,000	(105,000)				(27,500)	(16,500)	(11,000)
	50,000			8,750		16,250	15,000	10,000
October — installment to partners in profit and loss ratio	(50,000)			(8,750)		(16,250)	(15,000)	(10,000)

X, Y, and Z
Schedule A — To Accompany Statement of Liquidation
Amounts To Be Paid to Partners
July 31, 19X9

	X (50)	Y (30)	Z (20)
Capital balances before distribution of cash............................	55,000	44,000	46,000
Add loan balances..	12,500	10,000	
Partners' total interests..	67,500	54,000	46,000
Restricted interests — possible loss of $160,000 if nothing is realized on remaining assets	(80,000)	(48,000)	(32,000)
	(12,500)	6,000	14,000
Restricted interests — additional possible loss of $12,500 to Y and Z if X is unable to meet the possible deficiency (ratio Y and Z — 30:20)...	12,500	(7,500)	(5,000)
		(1,500)	9,000
Restricted interests — additional possible loss of $1,500 to Z if Y is unable to meet the possible deficiency		1,500	(1,500)
Free interest — amount to be paid Z on capital			7,500

X, Y, and Z
Schedule B — To Accompany Statement of Liquidation
Amounts To Be Paid to Partners
August 31, 19X9

	X (50)	Y (30)	Z (20)
Capital balances before distribution of cash............................	50,000	41,000	36,500
Add loan balances...	12,500	10,000	
Partners' total interests..	62,500	51,000	36,500
Restricted interests — possible loss of $130,000 if nothing is realized on remaining assets	(65,000)	(39,000)	(26,000)
	(2,500)	12,000	10,500
Restricted interests — additional possible loss of $2,500 to Y and Z if X is unable to meet the possible deficiency (ratio Y and Z — 30:20)..	2,500	(1,500)	(1,000)
Free interests — amount to be paid to each partner.................		10,500	9,500
Payment to apply on loan..		10,000	
Payments to apply on capital...		500	9,500
Total cash distribution..		10,500	9,500

X, Y, and Z
Schedule C — To Accompany Statement of Liquidation
Amounts To Be Paid to Partners
September 30, 19X9

	X (50)	Y (30)	Z (20)
Capital balances before distribution of cash............................	43,750	36,750	24,500
Add loan balance	12,500		
Partners' total interests..	56,250	36,750	24,500
Restricted interests — possible loss of $105,000 if nothing is realized on remaining assets	(52,500)	(31,500)	(21,000)
Free interests — amount to be paid to each partner.................	3,750	5,250	3,500
Payment to apply on loan..	3,750		
Payments to apply on capital...		5,250	3,500

In arriving at the amounts to be paid to individual partners, effect was given to the possibilities of (1) a complete loss on remaining unsold assets and (2) failure to recover anything from partners who may become deficient under such circumstances. Such losses are considered only for purposes of determining the appropriate distribution of cash. Partners' capital accounts in the ledger would be affected only by the profits and losses that emerge on the actual disposal of partnership assets.

PROGRAM FOR DISTRIBUTION OF CASH

The procedure that has been described can be used in all cases involving liquidation by installments. Such a procedure requires calculations and the preparation of a schedule for each proposed distribution until partners' interests are brought into the profit and loss ratio. In some instances it may be desirable to prepare in advance a program for the distribution of whatever cash may become available during the course of liquidation. As cash is received from the sale of assets, it can then be distributed to partners in accordance with this program.

To indicate the nature of the alternative approach, assume that capital accounts for F and G just before partnership liquidation are as follows:

F, Capital   G, Capital

$30,000 $25,000

Assume further that F and G share profits and losses equally. Since F will not be required to absorb a greater amount of any losses on liquidation than G, the first cash to be made available to partners should be paid to F. F's capital account can be reduced $5,000 before it will equal G's balance. Once the capital accounts are in the profit and loss ratio, further cash distributions can be made in the profit and loss ratio — equally in this case.

Assume, however, that F and G share profits 75% and 25% respectively. In this case, G should receive first cash. Losses chargeable against G are only 25/75 or ⅓ of the amount chargeable against F. Under these circumstances there can be no objection to cash distributions that reduce G's capital to ⅓ of the balance in F's capital account before F is allowed to share in cash distributions. G, then, should receive the first $15,000 of available cash. With capitals in the profit and loss ratio, further cash distributions are properly made to F and G in the profit and loss ratio, 75:25.

The fact that G's prior claim to cash amounted to $15,000 was readily determined in the preceding example. Frequently, however, capital balances and profit and loss ratios do not lend themselves to such ready analysis, and special calculations are necessary to determine a priority program. These calculations applied to the example just given are shown as follows.

Procedure	Explanation
Calculate loss-absorption abilities of partners:	Partners' interests are divided by their respective profit and loss shares to find the maximum losses that they can absorb. This calculation shows that a loss of $40,000 will consume all of F's capital, but it will take a loss of $100,000 to consume G's capital.

	Capital		Profit and Loss Ratio		Loss That Will Absorb Each Partner's Interest
F	$30,000	÷	.75	=	$ 40,000
G	$25,000	÷	.25	=	$100,000

Calculate priorities in terms of excess loss-absorption capacities:

G's loss-absorbing capacity is greater than that of F by $60,000. Payments may be made to the point where G's loss-absorbing capacity is no greater than that of F. To find the loss-absorbing capacity of a partner's interest, the interest was divided by the partner's share of profit and loss; to find the amount of capital represented by an excess loss-absorbing capacity, such excess is multiplied by the partner's share of profit and loss. G's excess loss-absorbing capacity, $60,000, multiplied by the .25 profit and loss share, gives the interest represented by this excess.

Excess of G's Loss-Absorbing Capacity		G's Share in Profit and Loss		Prior Claim of G
$60,000	×	.25	=	$15,000

After priorities have been met, further distributions can be made in the profit and loss ratio.

After $15,000 is paid to G, partners' interests are in the profit and loss ratio. Further distributions can now be made in this ratio.

Development of Priority Payment Program Illustrated

Development and application of a priority payment program when more than two partners are involved is illustrated in the section that follows. The example is based upon the data that were given for the firm of X, Y, and Z on page 92.

For X, Y, and Z, dividing interests of $77,500, $60,000, and $50,000 by .50, .30, and .20 gives loss-absorption balances of $155,000, $200,000, and $250,000 respectively. This indicates that Z should receive first cash. Z's interest may be reduced by payments to the point where the loss-absorption capacity for Z is no greater than that for Y. At this point cash should be distributed to both Y and Z. The interests of Y and Z may be reduced by the joint payments to the point where the loss-absorption capacity for Y and for Z is no greater than that for X. At this point, the interests of X, Y, and Z will be brought into the profit and loss ratio, and further cash distributions are properly made in the profit and loss ratio. Development of this payment program appears as follows.

X, Y, AND Z
Program of Priorities for Cash Distribution in Partnership Liquidation
July 1, 19X9

	X	Y	Z	Payments		
				X	Y	Z
Capital balances............................	65,000	50,000	50,000			
Loan balances...............................	12,500	10,000				
	77,500	60,000	50,000			
Profit and loss ratio........................	50%	30%	20%			
Loss-absorption balances (interests divided by partners' profit and loss percentage)........................	155,000	200,000	250,000			
Allocation I: Cash to Z, reducing loss-absorption balance to amount reported for Y; reduction of $50,000 requires payment of .20 × $50,000			(50,000)			10,000
	155,000	200,000	200,000			
Allocation II: Cash to Y and Z to reduce their loss-absorption balances to amount reported for X; reductions of $45,000 require payments as follows: To Y, .30 × $45,000, or $13,500 To Z, .20 × $45,000, or $9,000....		(45,000)	(45,000)		13,500	9,000
	155,000	155,000	155,000		13,500	19,000
Allocation III: Further cash distributions may be made in the profit and loss ratio.						

In developing a priority payment program for partners at the start of liquidation, the maximum loss that can be absorbed by each partner's interest is first calculated. Loan balances are combined with capital balances in arriving at partners' interests, and these interests are divided by the partners' respective profit and loss ratio expressed in percentages. Cash is then applied in a manner that brings the partners' interests ever closer to the point where they can absorb the same partnership loss.

The information that is provided in the payment program for X, Y, and Z may be summarized as follows:

(1) The first $10,000 available to partners should be paid to Z.
(2) The next $22,500 should be paid to Y and Z in the ratio of 30:20.
(3) Amounts that exceed $32,500 should be paid to X, Y, and Z in the profit and loss ratio of 50:30:20.

Installment Distributions Based on Payment Program

To show the application of the payment program, it will be assumed that cash is available for distribution to partners X, Y, and Z at monthly intervals as indicated in the earlier example. Cash available for partners, then, is as follows:

July.......................................	$ 7,500
August....................................	20,000
September...............................	12,500
October	50,000

Installment distributions are calculated as follows:

July Installment — $7,500

		Payable to		
		X	Y	Z
Allocation I — payable to Z..	$10,000			
Amount payable to Z in July......................................	7,500			7,500
Allocation I balance	$ 2,500	—	—	7,500

August Installment — $20,000

		Payable to		
		X	Y	Z
Allocation I — balance payable to Z.............................	$ 2,500			
Amount payable to Z in August..................................	2,500			2,500
Allocation II — payable to Y and Z, 30:20.....................	$22,500			
Amount payable to Y and Z in August........................	17,500		10,500	7,000
Allocation II — balance	$ 5,000	—	10,500	9,500

September Installment — $12,500

		Payable to		
		X	Y	Z
Allocation II — balance payable to Y and Z, 30:20........	$ 5,000			
Amount payable to Y and Z in September.................	5,000		3,000	2,000
Allocation III — payable to X, Y, and Z, 50:30:20..........	$ 7,500	3,750	2,250	1,500
		3,750	5,250	3,500

October Installment — $50,000

	Payable to		
	X	Y	Z
Allocation III — payable to X, Y, and Z, 50:30:20..........	25,000	15,000	10,000

The cash distributions to X, Y, and Z developed from the payment program are exactly the same as the distributions on pages 93–94 that were calculated by considering the possible loss on unsold assets and making distributions in terms of partners' free capitals. Just as in the earlier example, cash that is paid to partners would first be applied against any loan balances that they might have. Entries to record the course of liquidation of the firm of X, Y, and Z and a statement of liquidation summarizing activities for the four-month period, then, would be the same as in the earlier example.

There may be instances when it is difficult or actually impossible to determine the loss or gain related to the sale of individual assets during the course of liquidation. In such instances, the recognition of loss or gain may be postponed until all of the assets are sold; at that time the difference between the book value of assets and the total amount realized from their sale would be recognized as the loss or gain from liquidation and would be reported in the capital accounts. Whether losses or gains are recognized currently or upon termination of liquidation will have no effect upon cash distributions, for losses and gains are transferred to capital accounts in the profit and loss ratio and the objective of the cash distribution procedure is to bring partners' interests into the profit and loss ratio at the earliest possible time.

The preparation of a priority payment program and the determination of cash distributions in accordance with such a program may prove relatively complex when there are many partners and profits and losses are not shared in a simple manner. In these circumstances, it may be more convenient to determine cash distributions by use of the first method, which involves the recognition of the possible loss on remaining assets at the time of each cash distribution.

JOINT VENTURES

A special commercial undertaking by two or more individuals or business units that is terminated upon the fulfillment of the established objective is known as a *joint venture*. Thus the term would be applied to a joint undertaking for a specific purpose such as the development or sale of a tract of land, the construction of a bridge or dam, the purchase and sale of a block of securities, or the exploration and drilling for oil or gas.

The association of parties in a joint venture constitutes a partnership, and partnership law governs throughout the course of the relationship. However, since the joint venture exists only for a specific purpose, the powers and the duties of the members are limited to that purpose. Each partner to the venture may contribute cash, merchandise, or services, and in turn shares in the profit or loss resulting from the undertaking. Since this is a partnership, absence of a specific agreement with respect to the sharing of profit and loss results in equal division. Participants may, by agreement, provide for the allowance of interest on investments, commissions or bonuses on sales, and salaries for services so that differences in contributions to the joint venture in the form of capital, ability, and time may be recognized in distributing profits. Generally, one member of the joint venture is designated as the managing partner and is allowed special compensation for acting in this capacity. The managing partner submits statements to the other partners summarizing venture transactions.

There are two methods of accounting for a joint venture: (1) separate books for the joint venture are maintained; (2) separate books are not maintained, but accounts for the joint venture transactions are carried on the individual books of one or more of the participants. When a joint venture is to be carried on over a relatively long period and a number of involved transactions are anticipated, it is best to open a separate set of books. However, when the joint venture is to be of short duration and of a relatively simple character, there may be no need for separate books.

When separate books for the joint venture are maintained, joint venture transactions are recorded on the separate books in exactly the same manner as for partnership relationships discussed earlier. When a partner maintains individual books summarizing business as well as personal activities, the interest in a joint venture, just as any interest in a partnership, is recognized and accounted for as an investment. The investment account is debited for the original investment in the undertaking and for subsequent investments and shares of profits that increase the partner's interest; the investment account is credited for withdrawals and shares of losses that decrease the partner's interest. The debit balance in the investment account on the partner's individual books, then, will agree with the credit balance measuring the partner's interest on the joint venture books.

When separate joint venture books are not kept, activities of the venture will have to be summarized on the partners' individual books. If each partner maintains a set of books and each set of books is to be complete, it will be necessary for each partner to notify copartners of all of the transactions entered into on behalf of the joint venture. In reporting joint venture activities on the individual books, a joint venture account is debited for all joint venture costs and is credited for all joint venture revenue. Each partner also maintains accounts with each of the other partners to indicate ownership interests of these parties in the venture. In following these practices, the balances in the joint venture account and in the accounts with copartners will be the same on the books of each member during the course of the venture.

Separate books:

Transactions	Partnership Books		
(1) A transferred land to the joint venture at agreed current value of $100,000; the land cost A $75,000.	Land... A, Capital	100,000	100,000
(2) B made settlement on contracts for grading, landscaping, water and sewer, and other land improvements, $60,000.	Land... B, Capital.............................	60,000	60,000
(3) C transferred cash to A for joint venture purposes, $40,000.	Cash.. C, Capital	40,000	40,000
(4) A paid advertising, commissions, and other selling expenses, $37,500.	Selling Expenses........................... Cash	37,500	37,500

(5) The lots were sold for a total of $250,000; $50,000 was received in cash and the balance in installment notes.	Cash..
	 Notes Receivable ....
	   Land...................................
	   Gain on Sale of Land..................
		50,000
		 200,000
			160,000
			 90,000

(6) The installment notes were sold without recourse at a 10% discount.	Cash... Interest Expense .... Notes Receivable	180,000 20,000	200,000

(7) Net income of the joint venture was summarized and closed into the partners' accounts:
 Net income................................ $32,500
 Special compensation to A............................ $ 5,000
 Balance, $27,500 divided 100:60:40 to A, B, and C:
    A................................... 13,750
    B................................... 8,250
    C................................... 5,500
                 $32,500
	Gain on Sale of Land....................
	   Selling Expenses......................
	   Interest Expense......................
	   A, Capital ....
	   B, Capital..............................
	   C, Capital ....
		90,000	37,500
			 20,000
			 18,750
			 8,250
			 5,500

(8) A distributed cash in final settlement of the joint venture.	A, Capital .... B, Capital................................. C, Capital................................. Cash	118,750 68,250 45,500	232,500

Accounting for the Joint Venture Illustrated

The alternative accounting procedures that may be employed for a joint venture are illustrated in the example that follows. Assume that A, B, and C enter into a joint venture for the purchase, development, and sale of a parcel of land. A is designated the managing partner; upon termination of the joint venture, special compensation of $5,000 is to be allowed to A and the balance of the profit is to be divided in the ratio of the partners' investments. Transactions and the entries that are required under the alternative procedures are given on pages 100–103.

Separate Books of A			Separate Books of B			Separate Books of C		
Investment in Firm of ABC.....	100,000							
Land............		75,000						
Gain on Transfer of Land to Joint Venture (or Capital)........		25,000						
			Investment in Firm of ABC.....	60,000				
			Cash............		60,000			
						Investment in Firm of ABC.....	40,000	
						Cash............		40,000
Investment in Firm of ABC.....	18,750		Investment in Firm of ABC.....	8,250		Investment in Firm of ABC.....	5,500	
Income from Firm of ABC..		18,750	Income from Firm of ABC..		8,250	Income from Firm of ABC..		5,500
Cash..............	118,750		Cash..............	68,250		Cash..............	45,500	
Investment in Firm of ABC............		118,750	Investment in Firm of ABC............		68,250	Investment in Firm of ABC............		45,500

When separate joint venture books are not maintained, a joint venture account on the partner's individual books is debited with all joint venture costs and expenses and is credited with all joint venture revenue. A debit balance in the joint venture account during the course of the venture would be recognized as the net amount invested in the joint venture. A credit balance in the investment account upon conclusion of the venture indicates that revenue of the venture has exceeded costs and expenses and there has been a profit; the investment account is closed by a debit and the partners'

No separate books:

Transactions	Books of A (Managing Participant)		
(1) A transferred land to the joint venture at agreed current value of $100,000; the land cost A $75,000.	Joint Venture...................... 100,000 Land...............................		75,000
	Gain on Transfer of Land to Joint Venture (or Capital).....................................		25,000
(2) B made settlement on contracts for grading, landscaping, water and sewer, and other land improvements, $60,000.	Joint Venture...................... 60,000 B...................................		60,000
(3) C transferred cash to A for joint venture purposes, $40,000.	Joint Venture Cash.............. 40,000 C...................................		40,000
(4) A paid advertising, commissions, and other selling expenses, $37,500.	Joint Venture...................... 37,500 Joint Venture Cash...........		37,500
(5) The lots were sold for a total of $250,000; $50,000 was received in cash and the balance in installment notes.	Joint Venture Cash.............. 50,000 Joint Venture Notes Receivable................................... 200,000 Joint Venture...................		250,000
(6) The installment notes were sold without recourse at a 10% discount.	Joint Venture Cash.............. 180,000 Joint Venture...................... 20,000 Joint Venture Notes Receivable..........................		200,000

(7) Net income of the joint venture was summarized and closed into the partners' accounts:
Net income.. $32,500
 	
Special compensation to A .... $ 5,000
Balance, $27,500 divided 100:60:40 to A, B, and C:
   A.............................. 13,750
   B 8,250
   C.............................. 5,500
                $32,500
	Joint Venture...................... 32,500
	   Income from Joint Venture
	   (or Capital) ....
			18,750

	B...................................		8,250
	C...................................		5,500
(8) A distributed cash in final settlement of the joint venture.	Cash................................... 118,750 B....................................... 68,250 C....................................... 45,500 Joint Venture Cash...........		232,500

accounts are credited. A debit balance in the investment account upon conclusion of the venture indicates that costs and expenses have exceeded revenue and there has been a loss; the investment account is closed by a credit and the partners' accounts are debited. Accounts with copartners report the interests of these parties in the net assets of the joint venture; a credit balance indicates an accountability by the joint venture to the copartner; a debit balance indicates an accountability by the partner to the joint venture.

Books of B			Books of C		
Joint Venture......................	100,000		Joint Venture......................	100,000	
A..................................		100,000	A..................................		100,000
Joint Venture......................	60,000		Joint Venture......................	60,000	
Cash..............................		60,000	B..................................		60,000
A..................................	40,000		A..................................	40,000	
C..................................		40,000	Cash..............................		40,000
Joint Venture......................	37,500		Joint Venture......................	37,500	
A..................................		37,500	A..................................		37,500
A..................................	250,000		A..................................	250,000	
Joint Venture..................		250,000	Joint Venture..................		250,000
Joint Venture......................	20,000		Joint Venture......................	20,000	
A..................................		20,000	A..................................		20,000
Joint Venture......................	32,500		Joint Venture......................	32,500	
Income from Joint Venture			Income from Joint Venture		
(or Capital)......................		8,250	(or Capital)......................		5,500
A..................................		18,750	A..................................		18,750
C..................................		5,500	B..................................		8,250
Cash...............................	68,250		Cash...............................	45,500	
C..................................	45,500		B..................................	68,250	
A..................................		113,750	A..................................		113,750

In reporting joint venture operations on the individual books of the partners, assets and liabilities other than the joint venture investment balance — for example, joint venture cash, joint venture receivables, and joint venture payables — are generally recognized only on the books of the managing participant. Balances on the books of the remaining participants are limited to the investment in the joint venture and balances with coparticipants. It would be possible to report all of the joint venture asset and liability balances on the books of each partner, but this would call for extended bookkeeping by all of the parties during the course of the relationship.

If a joint venture runs beyond the end of the regular fiscal period of the individual members, the question of whether any profit is to be recognized upon the uncompleted venture arises. If the venture is highly speculative and a successful outcome is in any way uncertain, conservatism would suggest that no profit be recognized until its completion. In some instances it may be possible to measure the success of the joint venture at a given stage with the certainty that its completion will not result in an impairment of accumulated profits. When this is the case, recognition of profit before completion of the venture is justified. When joint venture activities are recorded on the individual books of the partners, recognition of profit before completion of a venture is recorded by a debit to the joint venture account for the profit accrual and credits to the partners' accounts. Recognition of loss before completion of a venture would require debits to the partners' accounts and a credit to the joint venture account.

When separate books are not kept, a partner's interest in a joint venture is calculated from the account balances related to the venture that appear on the partner's individual books. Accounts with debit balances represent joint venture assets, costs yet to be recovered or realized, or claims of the joint venture against copartners; accounts with credit balances represent outsiders' claims or copartners' interests in venture assets. The difference between the debit and the credit balances on each partner's books measures the individual's own interest in the joint venture. For example, interests of partners A, B, and C in the illustration on pages 102–103 are calculated after transaction (3) as follows:

A's Interest			B's Interest			C's Interest		
Joint venture cash	$ 40,000		Joint venture		$160,000	Joint venture		$160,000
Joint venture	160,000		Less credits:			Less credits:		
	$200,000		A	$60,000		A	$60,000	
Less credits:			C	40,000	100,000	B	60,000	120,000
B	$60,000		B's interest		$ 60,000	C's interest		$ 40,000
C	40,000	100,000						
A's interest		$100,000						

Maintenance of records by a managing participant alone is sufficient to account for joint venture activities and to give the required data for settlement at the conclusion of the venture. However, when joint venture accounts are maintained by all of the parties, there is a check upon the accuracy of the records of the managing participant and the settlement with coparticipants upon termination of the venture.

Corporate Joint Ventures

Corporations frequently join forces to engage in a particular business venture. This may occur when one company owns valuable resources such as mineral rights or patents which the other company has the ability to exploit. Although these relationships may take the form of a limited-life project similar to those discussed previously, they are often of a continuing nature.

The Accounting Principles Board defined a corporate joint venture as "a corporation owned and operated by a small group of businesses (the 'joint venturers') as a separate and specific business or project for the mutual benefit of the members of the group."[1] Corporate joint ventures do not usually have stock that is publicly traded. Thus the reporting issues generally concern the treatment of these ventures in the financial statements of the individual venturers. With regard to this aspect, the APB concluded that:

> ...the equity method best enables investors in corporate joint ventures to reflect the underlying nature of their investment in those ventures. Therefore, investors should account for investments in common stock of corporate joint ventures by the equity method, both in consolidated financial statements and in parent-company financial statements prepared for issuance to stockholders as the financial statements of the primary reporting entity.[2]

The equity method, which is generally applicable to substantial corporate investments as well as joint ventures, is discussed in Chapter 10.

QUESTIONS

1. If cash is to be paid to partners as soon as it is available during the course of liquidation, what rules can be stated for making such distributions?

2. In developing schedules for the distribution of available cash, it is found that certain partners' capital balances are insufficient to meet the possibility of a full loss on all remaining assets. The liquidator suggests that such "deficient" partners make contributions to the partnership so that they will be able to meet any possible future contingency. Do you support such a position?

3. A, B, and C decide to liquidate. Partner A, who has a substantial loan balance in the partnership, insists that this loan balance be paid off with the first proceeds from liquidation. (a) Under what circumstances would you agree to such an action? (b) Under what circumstances would you oppose such an action?

4. D and E share profits equally. During the course of liquidation, the liquidator determines that available cash should be paid on D's capital account since its

---

[1]*Opinions of the Accounting Principles Board, No. 18*, "The Equity Method of Accounting for Investments in Common Stock" (New York: American Institute of Certified Public Accountants, 1971), par. 2(d).

[2]*Ibid.*, par. 16.

balance exceeds the total of Partner E's loan and capital balances combined. Partner E objects to such a distribution, insisting that available cash must first be applied to partners' loans. Under these circumstances, what action should the liquidator take?

5. Accounts for the partnership of A, B, C, and D in dissolution show D with an accrued salary balance of $1,500. D maintains that this is a preferred claim that should be paid off with the first available cash. Do you agree?

6. What is meant by a partner's "restricted interest"? How are restricted interests shown in the ledger?

7. (a) Describe the purpose and the advantages of a priority program for the distribution of available cash during the course of liquidation. (b) Identify the steps involved in the preparation of such a program.

8. Define a joint venture.

9. Describe two methods of accounting for a joint venture. What factors determine the method to be adopted?

10. Parker and Peters join in a venture. Parker invests $10,000 and Peters $2,000; profits are to be shared equally. The venture is unsuccessful and, upon its conclusion, cash of only $2,500 remains to be distributed to members. State how settlement should be completed.

EXERCISES

1. Partners A and B share profits 40% and 60% respectively. The receiver in charge of liquidation of the partnership wishes to distribute available cash to the partners. How should the cash be distributed, assuming the following balances:

Cash............................	$ 5,000	Salary payable to A	$ 500
Other assets...............	32,500	A, capital	12,800
		Loan payable to B	5,000
		B, capital.....................	19,200
Total	$37,500	Total	$37,500

2. Partners A, B, C, and D, who share profits 5:3:1:1 respectively, decide to dissolve. Capital balances at this time are $60,000, $40,000, $30,000, and $10,000, respectively. Before selling the firm's assets, the partners agree to the following:

(1) Partnership furniture and fixtures, with a book value of $12,000, is to be taken over by partner A at a price of $15,000.
(2) Partnership claims of $20,000 are to be paid off and the balance of cash on hand, $30,000, is to be divided in a manner that will avoid the need for any possible recovery of cash from a partner.

Prepare the entries to record the foregoing.

3. A balance sheet for the partnership of J, K, and L, who share profits 2:1:1 respectively, shows the following balances just before liquidation:

Cash	Other Assets	Liab.	J, Cap.	K, Cap.	L, Cap.
$12,000	$59,500	$20,000	$22,000	$15,500	$14,000

In the first month of liquidation, $32,000 was received on the sale of certain assets. Liquidation expenses of $1,000 were paid, and additional liquidation expenses of $800 are anticipated before liquidation is completed. Creditors were paid $5,600. Available cash was distributed to the partners. Prepare the entries that are called for as a result of the foregoing.

4. Partners D, E, F, and G share profits 50%, 30%, 10%, and 10% respectively. Accounts maintained with partners just prior to liquidation follow:

	Advances (Dr. Balances)	Loans (Cr. Balances)	Capitals (Cr. Balances)
D		$ 5,000	$40,000
E		10,000	30,000
F	$4,500		15,000
G	2,500		25,000

At this point, cash of $18,000 is available for distribution to the partners. Prepare the entry to record the distribution of cash, together with calculations in support of the distribution.

5. The balance sheet of the partnership of Q, R, S, and T just prior to liquidation shows:

Assets	Liab.	Q, Loan	Q, Cap.	R, Cap.	S, Cap.	T, Cap.
$90,000	$20,000	$5,000	$20,000	$20,000	$20,000	$5,000

Q, R, S, and T share profits in the ratio of 2:1:1:1 respectively. Certain assets were sold for $45,000. Creditors were paid the full amount owed, partners were paid $20,000, and cash of $5,000 was withheld pending future developments. Prepare the journal entries to record the foregoing, including the distribution of cash to the partners.

6. Capital and loan balances for partners W, X, Y, and Z, who share profits in the ratio of 4:3:2:1 respectively, are as follows just prior to liquidation:

Z, Loan	W, Cap.	X, Cap.	Y, Cap.	Z, Cap.
$5,000	$50,000	$55,000	$20,000	$10,000

Prepare a statement showing how available cash would be distributed to the partners during the course of liquidation after the creditors are paid in full. State which partner would receive the first cash available and at what point and to what degree each of the remaining partners would participate in cash distributions.

7. Capital and loan balances for partners J, K, and L, who share profits 40%, 40%, and 20% respectively, are as follows just before liquidation:

J, Loan	J, Capital	K, Loan	K, Capital	L, Loan	L, Capital
$10,000	$15,000	$10,000	$35,000	$15,000	$20,000

(a) Prepare a program to show how available cash would be distributed to the partners during the course of liquidation after creditors are paid in full. State which partner would receive the first cash available and at what point and to what degree each of the remaining partners would participate in cash distributions.

(b) Assuming that cash of $25,000 is available as a first distribution to partners, what entry would be made to record the distribution?

8. Partners A, B, and C have capital balances of $11,200, $13,000, and $5,800 respectively and share profits in the ratio 4:2:1.

(a) Prepare a schedule showing how available cash will be distributed to partners as it becomes available.
(b) How much must the partnership realize on the sale of its assets if A is to receive $10,000 as a final settlement?
(c) If A receives a total of $3,200 in cash, how much will C have received at this point?
(d) If A is personally insolvent and B receives a total of $1,800 in final liquidation of the firm, what was the partnership loss on liquidation?

9. Barnes and Carter join in a venture for the sale of football souvenirs at the Rose Bowl game. Partners agree to the following: (1) Barnes shall be allowed a commission of 10% on net purchases, (2) members shall be allowed commissions of 25% on their respective sales, (3) any remaining profit shall be shared equally. Venture transactions follow:

Dec. 30. Barnes makes cash purchases, $95.
Jan. 1. Carter pays venture expenses, $15.
Jan. 1. Sales are as follows: Barnes, $80; Carter, $60 (members keep their own cash receipts).
Jan. 6. Barnes returns unsold merchandise and receives cash of $25 on the return.
Jan. 6. The partners make cash settlement.

Separate books for the venture are not kept. What entries would be made on the books of Barnes and Carter?

10. Joint venture activities for M, N, and O having proved to be unprofitable, the parties agree to dissolve the venture. Accounts with the venture and coparticipants on the books of M, the managing partner, are as follows just before dissolution and liquidation:

Joint Venture Cash	$12,000	
Joint Venture	6,500	
N, Capital		$14,500
O, Capital		6,500

The balance of joint venture assets on hand is sold by M for $3,500. M is allowed special compensation of $300 for winding up the venture; remaining profit or loss is distributed equally.

(a) Prepare the entries that will appear on the books of M in winding up the venture and making settlement with coparticipants.
(b) Prepare the entries that would appear on the separate books of N and O upon venture liquidation and settlement.

PROBLEMS

4-1. The balance sheet for Ross, Scott, and Tucker, partners sharing profits in the ratio of 4:3:3 respectively, shows the following balances on April 30, 19X0, just before liquidation:

Assets		Liabilities and Capital	
Cash.........................	$ 31,500	Liabilities...................	$ 43,500
Other assets..............	125,000	Tucker, loan...............	3,000
		Ross, capital	60,000
		Scott, capital	35,000
		Tucker, capital	15,000
		Total liabilities and	
Total assets..............	$156,500	capital...................	$156,500

In May, part of the assets are sold for $30,000. In June, the remaining assets are sold for $21,000.

Instructions: Prepare a statement of liquidation with supporting schedules as illustrated on pages 93–94. Assume that available cash is distributed to the proper parties at the end of May and at the end of June. Assume further that partners are solvent and that any partner who is deficient makes appropriate payment to the partnership in July and this is distributed in final settlement.

4-2. Fall, Gibson, and Hoffman are partners sharing profits in the ratio of 3:1:1 respectively. On June 30 their capital accounts show balances of $82,500, $40,000, and $15,000 respectively. The partners sell the firm's assets, pay off creditors, and make cash distributions to partners at the end of each month from asset proceeds as follows:

July, $10,000; August, $16,500; September, $25,000.

Instructions: Prepare a statement of liquidation with supporting schedules as illustrated on pages 93–94. Assume that partners are personally solvent and that any partner who is deficient makes appropriate payment to the partnership in October and this is distributed in final settlement.

4-3. Partners A, B, and C share profits in the ratio of 5:3:2 respectively. On June 30, 19X6, just before liquidation, assets, liabilities, and capital balances are as follows:

			Capitals	
Assets	Liabilities	A	B	C
$150,000	$30,000	$52,000	$48,000	$20,000

Cash is realized for assets, as follows, and amounts realized are distributed at the end of each month to the appropriate parties.

	Asset Book Value	Cash Proceeds
July..................................	$30,000	$36,500
August...............................	17,500	11,500
September..........................	22,500	10,000
October	80,000	36,500

Instructions: Prepare a statement of liquidation to summarize the course of liquidation. Provide schedules or calculations in support of monthly distributions.

4-4. The balance sheet of the partnership of D, E, and F on January 1, 19X5, just prior to liquidation, shows the following balances:

Assets		Liabilities and Capital	
Cash..........................	$ 15,000	Liabilities...................	$ 80,000
Other assets..............	265,000	D, loan........................	10,000
		F, loan........................	5,000
		D, capital...................	75,000
		E, capital	60,000
		F, capital	50,000
Total assets..............	$280,000	Total liabilities and capital...................	$280,000

D, E, and F share profits in the ratio of 5:3:2 respectively. Noncash assets are sold and all available cash is distributed to the proper parties at the end of each month. Liquidation takes place as follows:

	Book Value of Assets Sold	Cash Realized on Sale of Assets
January	$ 90,000	$ 55,000
February..........................	60,000	22,500
March.............................	65,000	15,000
April..............................	50,000	20,000
	$265,000	$112,500

Instructions: (1) Prepare a statement of liquidation with supporting schedules as illustrated on pages 93–94.

(2) Prepare the necessary monthly journal entries to record the course of realization and liquidation.

4-5. K, L, M, and N are partners sharing profits 2:1:1:1 respectively. On December 31, 19X6, they agree to dissolve. A balance sheet prepared on this date is shown on page 111.

The results of liquidation are summarized below.

19X7	Book Value of Assets Sold	Cash Realized on Sale of Assets	Costs of Liquidation Paid	Payments to Creditors	Payments to Partners	Cash Balance Withheld (Undistributed)
January	$75,000	$60,000	$1,000	$55,000		$4,000
February...	30,000	18,000	1,100	15,000	$4,400	1,500
March.......	30,000	10,000	1,200		9,300	1,000
April.........	16,500	4,000	1,600		3,400	

Assets		Liabilities and Capital	
Assets	$151,500	Liabilities...................	$ 70,000
		K, loan.......................	5,000
		N, loan	2,500
		K, capital..................	22,000
		L, capital	21,500
		M, capital	17,000
		N, capital..................	13,500
		Total liabilities and	
Total assets..............	$151,500	capital...................	$151,500

Instructions: (1) Prepare a statement of liquidation with supporting schedules as illustrated on pages 93–94.

(2) Prepare the necessary monthly journal entries to record the course of realization and liquidation.

4-6. The partners of Stanford Company agreed to dissolve their partnership and to begin liquidation on February 1, 19X2. Rogers was designated as the partner in charge of liquidation. It was agreed that distributions of cash to the partners were to be made on the last day of each month during liquidation, provided sufficient cash was available.

The partnership agreement provided that profits and losses were to be shared on the following basis: Quade, 20%; Rogers, 30%; Stanford, 30%; and True, 20%. The firm's condensed balance sheet as of February 1, 19X2, was as follows:

Assets		Liabilities and Capital	
Cash...........................	$33,440	Accounts payable	$ 7,120
Goodwill......................	20,000	Loan from Quade	5,000
Other assets...............	44,510	Capital:	
		Quade	8,040
		Rogers.....................	32,160
		Stanford	36,340
		True	9,290
		Total liabilities and	
Total assets................	$97,950	capital.....................	$97,950

The liquidating transactions for February and March, other than cash distributions to partners, are summarized by months as follows:

	Cash	
	February	March
Liquidation of assets with a book value of:		
$22,020...	$16,440	
$14,950...		$16,110
Paid liquidation expenses as incurred	2,740	2,460
Paid to creditors on account	5,910	1,210

Instructions: Prepare a statement and supporting schedules showing the total amounts of cash distributed to the partners at the end of February and

March and the amounts received by each partner in each distribution. Assume that Rogers made the distributions in such a manner that eventual overpayment to any partner was precluded.

(AICPA adapted)

4-7. Partners F, G, and H divide profits 60%, 25%, and 15% respectively. A balance sheet on June 30, 19X2, just before partnership liquidation, shows the following balances:

Assets		Liabilities and Capital	
Cash............................	$ 5,000	Liabilities.....................	$35,000
Other assets................	92,500	F, capital	45,000
		G, capital.....................	10,000
		H, capital.....................	7,500
		Total liabilities and	
Total assets.................	$97,500	capital......................	$97,500

Certain assets are sold in July for $50,000 and available cash is distributed to appropriate parties. Remaining assets are sold in August for $15,000, and cash is distributed in final settlement.

Instructions: (1) Prepare a program showing how cash should be distributed to partners as it becomes available.

(2) Prepare the entries that are required to record the course of liquidation in July and August.

4-8. R, S, and T share profits in the ratio of 5:3:2 respectively. A balance sheet prepared just prior to partnership liquidation shows:

	R	S	T
Capital balances............................	$60,000	$45,000	$20,000
Loan balances...............................	22,500	15,000	6,500

Assets are sold and cash is distributed to partners in monthly installments during the course of liquidation as follows:

January	$ 7,500
February.................................	20,000
March.....................................	45,000
April (final distribution).............	15,000

Instructions: (1) Prepare a program to show how cash should be distributed during the entire course of liquidation.

(2) Using the program developed in (1), prepare schedules summarizing the payments to be made to partners at the end of each month.

(3) Prepare a statement of liquidation to summarize the course of liquidation.

4-9. Partners W, X, Y, and Z share profits in the ratio of 3:3:1:1 respectively. A balance sheet prepared just before partnership liquidation shows:

	W	X	Y	Z
Capital balances............	$70,000	$70,000	$30,000	$20,000
Loan balances...............	20,000	5,000	25,000	15,000

The partner in charge of liquidation reports the following proceeds from the sale of partnership assets during January and February and distributions of cash to partners at the end of each month:

	Cash Proceeds from Sale of Assets	Cash Distributed to Partners	Cash Retained (Undistributed)
January	$40,000	$25,000	$15,000
February	35,000	40,000	10,000

Instructions: (1) Prepare a program to show how cash should be distributed during the entire course of liquidation.

(2) Using the program in (1), prepare schedules summarizing the payments to be made to partners at the end of January and February; indicate what part of the payments are to be applied against loan balances and what part against capital balances.

4-10. The ABC Partnership is being dissolved. All liabilities have been liquidated. The balance of assets on hand is being realized gradually. The following are details of partners' accounts:

	Capital Account (Original Investment)	Current Account (Undistributed Earnings Net of Drawings)	Loans to Partnership	Profit and Loss Ratio
A	$20,000	$1,500 Cr.	$15,000	4
B	25,000	2,000 Dr.	—	4
C	10,000	1,000 Cr.	5,000	2

Instructions: Prepare a schedule showing how cash payments should be made to the partners as assets are realized.

(AICPA adapted)

4-11. Partners Adams, Burke, Cox, and Drake have decided to dissolve their partnership. They plan to sell the assets gradually in order to minimize losses. They share profits and losses as follows: Adams, 40%; Burke, 35%; Cox, 15%; and Drake, 10%. The partnership's trial balance as of October 1, 19X3, the date on which liquidation begins, is as follows:

Cash......................................	200	
Receivables...........................	25,900	
Inventory, October 1, 19X3	42,600	
Equipment (net)	19,800	
Accounts Payable		3,000
Adams, Loan...........................		6,000
Burke, Loan		10,000
Adams, Capital		20,000
Burke, Capital		21,500
Cox, Capital...........................		18,000
Drake, Capital		10,000
	88,500	88,500

Instructions: (1) Prepare a statement as of October 1, 19X3, showing how cash will be distributed among partners by installments as it becomes available.

(2) On October 31, 19X3, cash of $12,700 became available to creditors and partners. How should it be distributed?

(3) Assume that, instead of being dissolved, the partnership continued operations and earned a profit of $23,625. How should that profit be distributed if, in addition to the aforementioned profit-sharing arrangement, it was provided that Drake receive a bonus of 5% of the net income from operations after treating the bonus as an expense?

(AICPA adapted)

4-12. The partnership of Arthur, Brown, and Cook is winding up the affairs of their partnership. The trial balance of the partnership at June 30, 19X6, is as follows:

Cash.....................................	6,000	
Accounts Receivable..............	22,000	
Inventory	14,000	
Plant and Equipment (net)......	99,000	
Receivable from Arthur...........	12,000	
Receivable from Cook.............	7,500	
Accounts Payable		17,000
Arthur, Capital.......................		67,000
Brown, Capital.......................		45,000
Cook, Capital........................		31,500
	160,500	160,500

The partners share profits and losses as follows: Arthur, 50%; Brown, 30%; and Cook, 20%.

The partners are considering an offer of $100,000 for the accounts receivable, inventory, and plant and equipment as of June 30. The $100,000 would be paid to the partners in installments, the number and amounts of which are to be negotiated.

Instructions: (1) Prepare a cash distribution schedule as of June 30, 19X6, showing how the $100,000 would be distributed as it becomes available.

(2) Assume the same facts as in (1) except that, instead of accepting the offer of $100,000, the partners decide to liquidate their partnership. Cash is distributed to the partners at the end of each month. A summary of the liquidation transactions follows:

July: $16,500 — collected on accounts receivable; balance is uncollectible.
$10,000 — received for the entire inventory.
$ 1,000 — liquidation expenses paid.
$ 8,000 — cash retained in the business at end of the month.

August: $ 1,500 — liquidation expenses paid.
As part payment of capital, Cook accepted a piece of special equipment which had a book value of $4,000. The partners agreed that a value of $10,000 should be placed on the machine for liquidation purposes.
$ 2,500 — cash retained in the business at end of the month.

September: $75,000 — received on sale of remaining plant and equipment.
          $ 1,000 — liquidation expenses paid.
          No cash retained in the business.

(3) Prepare a schedule of cash payments as of September 30, 19X6, showing how the cash was actually distributed.

(AICPA adapted)

4-13. Carter and Drew join in a venture for the sale of certain novelties during a convention. Carter acts as managing partner. Partners agree to the following: Carter shall be allowed a commission of 5% on gross purchases; members shall be allowed a commission of 30% on their respective sales; any remaining profit is to be shared equally. Venture transactions follow:

June 12. Drew gives Carter $350 to be used for venture purposes. Carter purchases merchandise for $1,000, paying $400, the balance payable within 10 days.
  14. Carter pays expenses chargeable to the venture, $150.
15–18. Sales by Carter and Drew are as follows (cash proceeds are kept by parties making the sales): Carter, $970; Drew, $790.
  18. Carter pays additional venture expenses, $120.
  20. Unsold merchandise is returned by Carter, credit of $140 being allowed on the return. The balance owed is paid. Settlement between partners is completed.

Instructions: Prepare the journal entries to record the foregoing transactions on the books of each member. (Separate books for the venture are not kept.)

4-14. Lane, Morris, and Newman form a joint venture for the sale of certain merchandise. Lane and Morris are to contribute the merchandise. Newman is to act as the sales agent and is to be allowed 5% of gross sales. Lane and Morris are to be allowed 6% a year on their original investment. The balance of any profit on the venture is to be divided equally among the three parties.

On March 1, Lane and Morris contributed merchandise of $22,000 and $30,000 respectively. Between March 1 and June 1, Newman sold venture merchandise on account for $80,000, of which $76,500 was collected, allowed sales discounts of $1,350, and wrote off $2,150 as uncollectible. Newman paid joint venture expenses of $19,520 out of joint venture cash. On June 1 the venture was terminated and unsold merchandise on hand was returned to Lane and Morris at the following values: Lane, $5,000; Morris, $3,800. Cash settlement was completed by Newman on this date.

Instructions: (1) Assuming that a set of separate books for the venture is not kept, prepare the journal entries to record the foregoing on the books of each participant.

(2) Assuming that a separate set of books for the venture is kept, prepare the journal entries to record the foregoing on (a) the joint venture books and (b) the individual books of each participant.

4-15. Moore, Norris, and Olson own adjoining properties of 15, 10, and 6 acres respectively. It is agreed to pool these properties and to develop, subdivide, and sell the land as a joint venture. It is further agreed that a valuation of $3,500 shall be allowed for each acre contributed to the venture. Profits are to be divided as follows:

(1) A bonus of 10% of the selling price is to be allowed to partners making lot sales.
(2) Upon conclusion of the venture, a salary of $6,000 is to be allowed Olson, who is to act as managing partner; Olson is to take care of all of the venture receipts and expenditures.
(3) The net profit after allowance of bonus and salaries is to be divided equally.

Olson pays $50,000 for improvements that are completed in April. The property is subdivided into 155 lots that are offered for sale as follows:

	Number	Sales Price per Lot
Lots, Class I	40	$1,900
Lots, Class II	115	1,500

All of the lots are sold for cash in May and June. Sales by members of the venture are as follows:

	Number of Lots Sold	
	Class I	Class II
Sales by Moore......	10	30
Sales by Norris	15	40
Sales by Olson.......	5	10

Remaining lots are sold by sales agents. Advertising, sales agent's salaries and commissions, and miscellaneous selling expenses paid in June are $34,200. The profit from the venture is calculated and Olson distributes cash to members in final settlement.

Instructions: (1) Assuming that a separate set of books for the venture is not kept, prepare the journal entries to record the foregoing on the books of each partner.
(2) Assuming that a separate set of books for the venture is kept, prepare the journal entries to record the foregoing on (a) the venture books and (b) the books of each member.

4-16. A, B, and C agree to sell hot dogs on July 3 and 4. A agrees to construct a stand on the front lawn of C and charge the cost to operations. C will be paid $25 for the cost of sod replacement and cleaning up the lawn after July 4. A, B, and C decide that profits, if any, will be distributed first by the $25 payment to C and then by a 40% commission on individual sales. The balance will be distributed 75% to A and 25% to B. They agree that a cash box will only complicate matters and that all purchase and sales transactions will be out of pocket and the responsibility of the individual. Sales to A, B, and C are to be at cost, except that the ending inventory may be purchased at 50% of cost. All other sales are to be made at 100% markup on cost.
The activity of the venture is as follows:

July 2: A constructs the stand on the front lawn of C at a cost of $100.
July 3: A pays $1,000 for supplies. C pays $50 for a permit to operate the concession.
July 4: A purchases additional supplies for $1,500, using $500 contributed by B and $1,000 of personal money.

July 4: Sales for the day were as follows:

A.. $1,700
B 2,600
C.. 600

July 5: C pays $90 for fire extinguishers and these are distributed equally
between A, B, and C for their personal use at home.
C agrees to pay $50 for the stand.

July 5: The balance of the inventory was taken by A.

Instructions: Prepare a work sheet analysis of the transactions that will give
A, B, and C the following information:

(a) Net profit or loss from the operation.
(b) Distribution of profit or loss to A, B, and C.
(c) The final cash settlement.

(AICPA adapted)

5
Installment Sales

The sale of real estate is often made on a deferred payment plan whereby the seller receives a down payment and the balance in a series of payments over a number of years. Similar installment payment plans have been widely adopted by dealers in personal property as well as by those selling personal services. The installment payment plan is commonly offered on sales ranging from automobiles to air travel.

Selling on the installment basis raises questions regarding the appropriate pattern of revenue recognition. Although revenue is normally recognized on an accrual basis in the period in which a sale is made and an enforceable contract received, the uncertainty of collecting accounts to be received over an extended period of time may suggest the postponement of revenue recognition until the probability of collection can be reasonably estimated.

PROTECTION FOR THE SELLER

With collection periods that may range up to 3 years on the sale of personal property, a seller usually seeks protection in the event of a buyer's failure to complete payment on the contract. When personal property is sold, the risk of loss from failure to complete the contract can be minimized by the repossession of such property. To provide the credit seller of goods with this protection, various devices have been developed, including pledge, assignment, chattel mortgage, chattel trust, trust deed, factor's lien, equipment trust, conditional sale, and trust receipt. Today the traditional distinctions among these security devices, based largely on form, are no longer retained. Instead, Article 9 of the Uniform Commercial Code provides for the creation of a "security interest" and delineates the rights of creditors, debtors, and third parties with respect to that security interest (without regard to what the parties have chosen to call their agreement).

Despite the ability of a seller to repossess property in the event of contract default, losses in carrying installment contracts may be heavy. The installment contract, offering liberal credit arrangements, may attract many customers whose credit risk is high. Furthermore, with payments spread over an extended period, there is the possibility of a change in the customer's ability to pay. The depreciation or the obsolescence on goods sold may exceed the payments made, and goods subject to repossession may not be worth as much as the unpaid balance of the contract. Repossession itself may be a costly process. Furthermore, sales on the installment basis mean continuing bookkeeping and collection costs, and in certain instances important servicing and repair costs that must be borne by the seller. These factors must be considered by the seller in establishing an installment sales policy.

In attempting to reduce or avoid repossession losses, the seller should consider adopting the following safeguards in installment contracts:

(1) The required down payment should be large enough to cover the decline in the value of an article in its change from "new" to "used."
(2) The period between installment payments should not be too long, preferably not more than one month.
(3) The periodic installment payments should exceed the decline in the value of the article that takes place between payments. When the value of an article exceeds the unpaid balance of the contract, the buyer will not want to default on the contract.

METHODS OF GROSS PROFIT RECOGNITION ON INSTALLMENT SALES

Two general approaches may be taken in recognizing gross profit on installment sales: (1) the gross profit may be related to the period in which the sale is made, or (2) the gross profit may be related to the periods in which cash is collected on the installment contract.

Gross Profit Recognized in the Period of Sale

Installment sales may be regarded as calling for treatment that is no different from that employed for regular sales. Gross profit may be recognized at the time of the sale, the point at which goods are exchanged for legally enforceable claims against customers. Such a procedure will call for recognition in the period of sale of the charges involved in carrying installment sales contracts as well as the charges related to contract defaults and uncollectibles. This is done by debiting appropriate expense accounts and crediting allowances for the charges that can be anticipated. The charges that are anticipated will depend on the individual business unit and its own particular experiences with installment contracts. The recognition of gross profit on installment sales in the period in which the sales are made is relatively simple in application and sound in theory.

Gross Profit Related to the Periods in Which Cash Is Collected

Installment sales may be regarded as calling for special treatment whereby gross profit is related to the periods in which the installment receivables are collected rather than to the periods in which the receivables are created. The inflow of cash rather than the time of sale becomes the criterion for revenue recognition. In adopting such an approach, several alternative procedures can be applied. The installment sales plan that is employed must be considered carefully in making a choice as to the procedure that will measure net income most satisfactorily.

Procedures that relate gross profit to collection periods are:

(1) *Collections regarded as first the recovery of cost.* Collections on a contract are regarded as representing first the recovery of product cost. After recovery of cost, all further collections are regarded as profit. This procedure is too conservative under most circumstances; it can be supported only when there is doubt as to any recoverable value associated with either the balance of the installment contract or the goods subject to repossession.

(2) *Collections regarded as first the realization of profit.* Collections are regarded as representing first the realization of the gross profit on the contract. After recognition of the full profit on the transaction, all further collections are regarded as a recovery of cost. This procedure lacks sufficient conservatism under most circumstances in view of the probability that defaults and repossessions over the life of contracts will impair the original profit margin.

(3) *Collections regarded as both return of cost and realization of profit.* Each collection on a contract is regarded as representing both a return of cost and a realization of gross profit in the ratio in which these two factors are found in the original sales price. This method serves to spread the gross profit on an installment sale over the full life of the installment contract. Continuing expenses on an installment contract are matched against the gross profit that is recognized in successive periods; the possible failure to realize the full amount of the gross profit in the event of default by the buyer is anticipated.

Method (3), providing for the recognition of gross profit in proportion to collections, is referred to as accounting by the *installment method* or *installment basis*. When gross profit is regarded as contingent upon the collection of cash, there is normally stronger support for its recognition over the entire collection period than for the alternative procedures mentioned.

THE INSTALLMENT METHOD

In applying the installment method in the accounts, the difference between the contract sales price and the cost of goods sold is recorded as deferred gross profit. This balance is recognized as revenue periodically in the proportion that the cash collections of the period bear to the sales price. Stated differently, the original gross profit percentage on the sale is applied to periodic collections in arriving at the amounts to be recognized as revenue. At the end of each period a deferred gross profit balance remains on the books and is equal to the gross profit percentage applied to the balance of installment receivables as of this date.

The deferral of gross profit is, in effect, the deferral of sales revenue accompanied by the deferral of cost of goods sold related to such sales revenue. The deferral of gross profit may suggest the deferral of expenses that were incurred in the promotion of installment sales. Ordinarily, however, such a practice may be difficult to defend. Although merchandise cost may be viewed as creating an asset value which can be carried over to subsequent years, selling and administrative expenses do not generally create such values. Furthermore, serious difficulties would be faced in selecting the expenses to be deferred and determining the allocation procedures to be applied in such deferrals. Revenue on installment sales recognized in periods subsequent to the period of sale will not be free of charges; certain costs will be continuing — bookkeeping, collection, and product servicing, for example — while other costs will emerge at different intervals — losses related to defaults and repossessions and losses from uncollectible accounts. The installment method of accounting normally implies the deferral of gross profit but the recognition of selling and administrative expenses in the period of their incurrence.

The installment method of reporting gross profit can be used for federal income tax purposes by dealers in personal property regularly selling on the installment plan. A taxpayer who receives at least one payment after the tax year in which the sale occurs can also use the installment method to report a gain on: (1) the casual sale of personal property other than inventory, and (2) any sale or other disposition of real property. Expenses cannot be deferred for tax purposes.

The entries that are required in accounting for installment sales are illustrated in the following pages. The installment method of accounting is first illustrated by means of a simple example involving the sale of real estate. This is followed by illustrations involving the sale of merchandise.

Sale of Real Estate on Installment Basis

Assume that on October 1, 19X2, the Westwood Realty Co. sells to S. F. West for $50,000 property that it owns and carries on its books at $30,000. The company receives $10,000 on the date of the sale and a mortgage note for $40,000 payable in 20 semiannual installments of $2,000 plus interest on the unpaid principal at 12%. Commissions and other expenses on the sale amounting to $1,500 are paid. Regular installments of principal and interest on the mortgage notes are received by the seller in 19X3. The entries that follow are those that would appear on the seller's books if (1) gross profit is recognized in the period of sale, and (2) gross profit is recognized periodically in proportion to collections. It is assumed that the seller's fiscal period is the calendar year.

Transaction	Entry	
	Recognition of Profit in Period of Sale	Recognition of Profit Periodically in Proportion to Collections

October 1, 19X2
Sold real estate (Parcel A), book value, $30,000, for $50,000.
	Receivable from
	S. F. West............ 50,000
	  Real Estate
	  (Parcel A) 30,000
	  Gain on Sale
	  (Parcel A) 20,000
		Receivable from
		S. F. West........... 50,000
		  Real Estate
		  (Parcel A) 30,000
		  Deferred Gross
		  Profit (Parcel A) 20,000

Received down payment, $10,000, and mortgage note for balance, $40,000.	Cash 10,000
	Mortgage Note 40,000
	  Receivable from
	  S. F. West.......... 50,000
		Cash 10,000
		Mortgage Note 40,000
		  Receivable
		  from S. F. West 50,000

Paid expenses on sale, $1,500.	Selling Expenses . 1,500
	  Cash 1,500
		Selling Expenses . 1,500
		  Cash 1,500

December 31, 19X2
To adjust accounts for:
(1) Accrued interest on mortgage note, $40,000, at 12% for 3 months, $1,200.
(2) (Reporting by installment method) Gross profit realized: gross profit rate, 40% ($20,000 gross profit ÷ $50,000 sales price); cash collected, $10,000; gross profit realized, 40% of $10,000, or $4,000.*
	Accrued Interest
	on Mortgage Note 1,200
	  Interest Income 1,200
		Accrued Interest
		on Mortgage Note 1,200
		  Interest Income 1,200
		
		Deferred Gross
		Profit (Parcel A)... 4,000
		  Realized Gross
		  Profit (Parcel A) 4,000

To close nominal accounts.	Gain on Sale
	(Parcel A) 20,000
	Interest Income... 1,200
	  Selling Expenses 1,500
	  Income
	  Summary......... 19,700
		Realized Gross
		Profit (Parcel A)... 4,000
		Interest Income... 1,200
		  Selling Expenses 1,500
		  Income
		  Summary......... 3,700

January 1, 19X3
To reverse accrued interest established at end of previous period.
	Interest Income... 1,200
	  Accrued
	  Interest on
	  Mortgage Note . 1,200
		Interest Income... 1,200
		  Accrued
		  Interest on
		  Mortgage Note . 1,200

April 1, 19X3
Received semiannual installment on mortgage note, $2,000, and interest on $40,000 at 12% for 6 months, $2,400.
	Cash 4,400
	  Mortgage Note . 2,000
	  Interest Income 2,400
		Cash 4,400
		  Mortgage Note . 2,000
		  Interest Income 2,400

October 1, 19X3
Received semiannual installment on mortgage note, $2,000, and interest on $38,000 at 12% for 6 months, $2,280.
	Cash 4,280
	  Mortgage Note . 2,000
	  Interest Income 2,280
		Cash 4,280
		  Mortgage Note . 2,000
		  Interest Income 2,280

*For income tax purposes, a nondealer in real estate cannot recognize expenses of a casual sale of real estate as business expenses but can deduct such expenses in computing the "gross profit" on the sale. Sale of the property by a nondealer, then, would be recognized as giving rise to a gross profit of $18,500, or 37% of the sales price; although expenses of $1,500 on the sale would not be recognized in 19X2, total profit recognized over the life of the contract would be limited to $18,500.

Transaction	Entry	
	Recognition of Profit in Period of Sale	Recognition of Profit Periodically in Proportion to Collections
December 31, 19X3 To adjust accounts for: (1) Accrued interest on mortgage note, $36,000, at 12% for 3 months, $1,080. (2) (Reporting by installment method) Gross profit realized: gross profit rate, 40%; cash collected, $4,000; gross profit realized, 40% of $4,000, or $1,600.	Accrued Interest on Mortgage Note 1,080 Interest Income 1,080	Accrued Interest on Mortgage Note 1,080 Interest Income 1,080 Deferred Gross Profit (Parcel A)... 1,600 Realized Gross Profit (Parcel A) 1,600
To close nominal accounts.	Interest Income... 4,560 Income Summary......... 4,560	Realized Gross Profit (Parcel A)... 1,600 Interest Income... 4,560 Income Summary......... 6,160

If installments are collected regularly until the note is paid off, entries would continue to be made in the manner illustrated. The method of accounting for the installment sale does not affect the entries to record the amounts earned each year as interest. However, the net gain on the sale of property is recognized differently under the two methods: recognition of the profit in the period of sale results in a gain of $18,500 ($20,000 − $1,500) in 19X2; recognition of profit periodically in proportion to collections results in a gain of $2,500 ($4,000 − $1,500) in 19X2 and a gain of $1,600 (40% of $4,000) in each of the next 10 years.

If there should be a default on contract payments, the seller may proceed to repossess the property that was sold. The entry that is made upon repossession depends upon the method originally employed in recording the profit on the sale. If the profit on the sale was recognized at the time of the sale, the entry shows the reacquisition of the property at its present fair market value, the cancellation of the balance of the claim against the buyer, and the gain or the loss on the repossession. If profit was recognized by the installment method, cancellation of the balance of the claim against the buyer is accompanied by cancellation of the deferred gross profit balance related thereto; the property would still be recorded at its fair market value, but the gain or loss upon repossession would be measured by the difference between the property item that is recognized and the installment contract balances that are canceled.

Assume in the previous example that the buyer fails to meet the installment due on April 1, 19X4. The seller surrenders the mortgage note with an unpaid balance of $36,000 and repossesses the property. On this date an appraisal of the property shows it to have a fair market value of $28,500. The entries under each method would be as follows:

Transaction	Entry	
	Recognition of Profit in Period of Sale	Recognition of Profit Periodically in Proportion to Collections

Reacquired real estate (Parcel A) valued at $28,500; surrendered mortgage note with unpaid balance of $36,000.	Real Estate (Parcel A) 28,500
	Loss on Repossession (Parcel A) 7,500
	  Mortgage Note . 36,000
		Real Estate (Parcel A) 28,500
		Deferred Gross Profit (Parcel A)... 14,400
		  Mortgage Note . 36,000
		  Gain on Repossession (Parcel A) 6,900

In each case, a second entry would also be necessary to write off as a loss the accrued interest of $1,080 on the mortgage note that was recognized at the end of 19X3 but that was found to be uncollectible in 19X4.

The loss and gain figures in each case can be proved by the following calculations:

		Recognition of Profit in Period of Sale	Recognition of Profit Periodically in Proportion to Collections
Total amount collected....................		$14,000	$14,000
Loss in value of repossessed property:			
Original basis...............	$30,000		
Fair market value upon recovery......................	28,500	1,500	1,500
Net gain		$12,500	$12,500
Gain recognized prior to repossession...............................		20,000	5,600
Gain (loss) on repossession		($ 7,500)	$ 6,900

When the installment method is used in reporting profits and a number of properties are sold at different gross profit rates during the year, separate accounts may be maintained to show the deferred gross profit on each sale. At the end of the year, summaries of the amounts collected on individual contracts provide the basis for calculating the gross profits that have been realized.

Sale of Merchandise on Installment Basis

The procedures that are employed in accounting for sales of merchandise on an installment basis are similar to those just illustrated. In recording transactions it is necessary to distinguish between regular sales and installment sales and to provide the other data for arriving at the gross profit that is to be recognized as a result of collections on installment accounts.

To illustrate accounting for the sale of merchandise on an installment basis, assume that a balance sheet for the Kelton Co. on January 1, 19X7, reports the following balances:

Cash................................	$ 25,000	Accounts payable.............	$ 40,000
Merchandise inventory	100,000	Deferred gross profit on in-	
Accounts receivable (regu-		stallment sales, 19X6	22,800
lar)	15,000	Deferred gross profit on in-	
Installment contracts re-		stallment sales, 19X5	7,000
ceivable, 19X6..............	60,000	Capital stock	100,000
Installment contracts re-		Retained earnings............	50,200
ceivable, 19X5..............	20,000	Total liabilities and stock-	
Total assets......................	$220,000	holders' equity..............	$220,000

Installment sales in 19X6 and 19X5 were made at gross profit rates of 38% and 35% respectively. On January 1, 19X7, with installment contracts receivable of 19X6 totaling $60,000 still on hand, the balance sheet reports deferred gross profit of 38% of this amount, or $22,800; with installment contracts receivable of 19X5 totaling $20,000, the balance sheet reports deferred gross profit of 35% of this amount, or $7,000.

Transactions and entries for the Kelton Co. relating to regular and installment sales for 19X7 follow:

Transaction	Entry		
January 1–December 31 (1) Regular sales consisted of cash sales, $250,000, and sales on account, $200,000; installment sales were $150,000.	Cash................................ Accounts Receivable (Regular) .... Sales (Regular) .... Installment Contracts Receivable, 19X7................. Installment Sales..........	250,000 200,000 150,000	 450,000 150,000
(2) Purchases of merchandise on account were $425,000.	Purchases....................... Accounts Payable	425,000	 425,000
(3) Receipts in addition to those from cash sales were from the following sources: Accounts receivable (regular).......... $190,000 Installment contracts receivable, 19X7....................................... 80,000 Installment contracts receivable, 19X6....................................... 40,000 Installment contracts receivable, 19X5....................................... 15,000	Cash................................ Accounts Receivable (Regular)....................... Installment Contracts Receivable, 19X7......... Installment Contracts Receivable, 19X6.......... Installment Contracts Receivable, 19X5..........	325,000	 190,000 80,000 40,000 15,000
(4) Payments were applied to the following: Accounts payable........ $435,000 Less discounts taken 5,000 $430,000 Operating expenses 120,000	Accounts Payable .... Operating Expenses .... Purchases Discount ...... Cash............................	435,000 120,000	 5,000 550,000
Adjusting and closing, December 31 (5) To record cost of goods relating to installment sales, $90,000.	Cost of Installment Sales .. Shipments on Installment Sales...................	90,000	 90,000
(6) To close installment sales and cost of installment sales accounts and to record gross profit on installment sales for year, $60,000 (40% of installment sales).	Installment Sales............. Cost of Installment Sales........................... Deferred Gross Profit on Installment Sales, 19X7.	150,000	 90,000 60,000

Transaction	Entry		
(7) To record the gross profit realized as a result of collections on installment contracts of 19X7, 19X6, and 19X5, as follows: 19X7 accounts, 40% of $80,000 ..... $32,000 19X6 accounts, 38% of $40,000 ..... 15,200 19X5 accounts, 35% of $15,000 5,250	Deferred Gross Profit on Installment Sales, 19X7.... Deferred Gross Profit on Installment Sales, 19X6.... Deferred Gross Profit on Installment Sales, 19X5.... Realized Gross Profit on Installment Sales, 19X5–19X7	32,000 15,200 5,250	 52,450
(8) To close beginning inventory, purchases, purchases discount, and shipments on installment sales accounts into Income Summary, thus summarizing the goods available for regular sales ($430,000).	Income Summary............. Shipments on Installment Sales............................. Purchases Discount .... Merchandise Inventory, January 1, 19X7............ Purchases.....................	430,000 90,000 5,000	 100,000 425,000
(9) To record ending inventory, thus summarizing cost of goods relating to regular sales ($310,000).	Merchandise Inventory, December 31, 19X7.......... Income Summary..........	120,000	 120,000
(10) To close regular sales into Income Summary, thus summarizing gross profit on regular sales ($140,000).	Sales (Regular) .... Income Summary..........	450,000	 450,000
(11) To close realized gross profits on installment sales of current and prior years into Income Summary, thus summarizing total gross profit ($192,450).	Realized Gross Profit on Installment Sales, 19X5–19X7 .... Income Summary..........	52,450	 52,450
(12) To close operating expenses into Income Summary, thus summarizing the income before income tax ($72,450).	Income Summary............. Operating Expenses	120,000	 120,000
(13) To record estimated income tax payable at 40% of the $72,450 income before tax, or $28,980.	Income Tax .... Income Tax Payable	28,980	 28,980
(14) To close income tax into Income Summary, thus summarizing net income ($43,470).	Income Summary............. Income Tax	28,980	 28,980
(15) To transfer net income to Retained Earnings ($43,470).	Income Summary............. Retained Earnings.........	43,470	 43,470

Unless the gross profit on both regular and installment sales is the same, it will be necessary to maintain a record of the cost of merchandise shipped on installment sales. This cost is recorded by a debit to Cost of Installment Sales and a credit to Shipments on Installment Sales. The latter balance will be recognized as a subtraction item from the sum of the beginning inventory and purchases in determining the goods available for regular sales.[1] The ending inventory subtracted from goods available for regular sales gives the cost of regular sales.

---

[1] It would be possible to credit the purchases account instead of Shipments on Installment Sales. The use of a separate shipments account that is recognized as an offset against the sum of the beginning inventory and purchases, however, preserves the information concerning total purchases for the period.

In the illustration, the cost of installment sales is determined to be $90,000; the gross profit on such sales is then $60,000, or 40% of installment sales of $150,000. In calculating the cost of goods relating to regular sales, the amount of goods available for such sales is first determined. This is found to be $430,000 — the sum of the beginning inventory, $100,000, and purchases, $425,000, less purchases discount, $5,000, and shipments on installment sales, $90,000. Cost of goods relating to regular sales is $310,000 — goods available for sale, $430,000, less the ending inventory, $120,000.

When a perpetual inventory system is maintained, purchases are recorded directly in the inventory account. As sales occur and are recorded, the accounts Cost of Installment Sales and Cost of Regular Sales are debited and the inventory account is credited.

There are instances when the gross profit rates vary significantly within the different departments of a particular business. When the gross profit rates are different but the ratio of collections to sales for each department is approximately the same each period, an average gross profit rate can be applied to total collections for each period in arriving at the realized gross profit. When the collection ratios are not the same, however, satisfactory measurement of realized gross profit requires that sales, costs, and collections be summarized separately for each department. Sales and cost figures by departments will supply departmental gross profit rates, and these rates can be applied to collections identified with the respective departments in arriving at realized gross profit.

Alternative procedure for calculating realized gross profit. In the illustration on pages 125–126, the realized gross profit was calculated by applying the gross profit percentage for the year in which the contracts originated to the amounts collected on such contracts. The realized gross profit can also be determined by calculating the amount of deferred gross profit as of the end of the period and reducing the deferred gross profit account to this balance. This procedure applied to the facts for the Kelton Co. is as follows:

	19X7	19X6	19X5
Balance of deferred gross profit before adjustment	$60,000	$22,800	$7,000
Deferred gross profit at the end of 19X7:			
On installment contracts receivable of 19X7, 40% of uncollected balance of $70,000	28,000		
On installment contracts receivable of 19X6, 38% of uncollected balance of $20,000		7,600	
On installment contracts receivable of 19X5, 35% of uncollected balance of $5,000			1,750
Reduction in deferred gross profit balances at the end of 19X7 — gross profit realized as a result of collections during 19X7	$32,000	$15,200	$5,250

Use of special journals in recording installment sales. Sales and cash transactions are normally recorded in special sales and cash journals. The sales journal normally provides special columns for cash sales, regular sales on account, and installment sales. The cash receipts journal provides a column for collections of regular accounts receivable as well as special columns for collections on installment contracts receivable of the current and prior periods. When gross profits are to be determined on a departmental basis, special journals may be designed to offer further classification of sales, costs, and installment contract receivables and collections by departments.

Aging accounts in installment method accounting. In the illustration, accounts were set up for both installment contracts receivable and deferred gross profit by years; collections were related to receivables classified as to date of origin. It is possible to employ one control account and subsidiary ledger for all of the installment accounts and to summarize the entire deferred gross profit in a single account. When such an arrangement is followed, however, it will be necessary at the end of each period to analyze and classify installment receivables according to the year of their origin. The appropriate gross profit percentages can then be applied to the receivable totals by years in arriving at the deferred gross profit balance.

Preparation of Financial Statements When the Installment Method Is Used

The balance sheet of a business with installment sales will include the contracts receivable and the deferred gross profit balances related to sales on the installment plan. When current assets are viewed as including those resources "reasonably expected to be realized in cash or sold or consumed during the normal operating cycle of the business," installment contracts receivable qualify for inclusion under the current heading regardless of the length of time required for their collection. In reporting installment contracts receivable under the current heading, disclosure of the maturity dates of such contracts will provide readers of the balance sheet with a better appreciation of the company's financial position; accordingly, annual maturities of receivables should be indicated either by parenthetical or footnote disclosure or by listing receivables according to their annual maturities.

Conflicting positions have been taken with respect to the appropriate classification on the balance sheet of the deferred gross profit balance. It has been suggested that this balance be reported as:

(1) A liability item to be included under the deferred revenues heading.
(2) An asset valuation account to be subtracted from installment contracts receivable.
(3) A capital item to be included as a part of retained earnings.

Deferred gross profit on installment sales is generally reported in the liability section of the balance sheet as deferred revenue. Accountants following this practice take the position that the installment sale has actually increased the working capital position of the company but that the recognition of an increase in capital must await the conversion of the installment receivable into cash.

This position, however, is subject to serious challenge. If it is maintained that the installment sales procedure is followed because there is no assurance of the realization of revenue beyond the amount currently recognized, then the deferred gross profit balance is more properly viewed as an asset valuation account. The recovery of cash on installment contracts shrinks the valuation account requirements and thus makes possible the recognition of revenue in periods subsequent to the sale.

On the other hand, when the collection of installment contracts is reasonably assured, it can be maintained that the installment sale has given rise to gross profit as in the case of a regular sale, except that the profit should not be recognized as fully subject to income taxes or available for dividends until collections are made. Such an approach suggests the reclassification of the deferred gross profit into three elements:

(1) An allowance for the continuing expenses that are still anticipated in the collection of installment contracts receivable, including charges arising from defaults and repossessions. Such an allowance would be subtracted from the installment receivable balance.
(2) An obligation for the income taxes on the portion of the gross profit that has not yet been recognized on the tax return. Such income tax liability would not be combined with balances reporting income taxes that have already accrued since this amount will become payable only as installment contract receivables are realized in cash in subsequent periods.
(3) The balance representing net earnings identified with installment contracts. This amount can be reported as a special retained earnings balance that is not to be used as a basis for dividends until installment receivables are collected.

With such a reclassification of the deferred gross profit balance, profits on installment sales would be recognized as having accrued for financial statement purposes although maintaining a deferred status for tax purposes. In the illustrations in this chapter, deferred gross profit is reported as a liability in accordance with generally prevailing practice.

An income statement for a business with both regular and installment sales may show the gross profit for each class of sales and the total gross profit. Data concerning collections on installment contracts, the gross profit rates applying to such collections, and calculations of realized gross profit are reported in a supporting schedule.

A balance sheet, an income statement, and a schedule providing an analysis of the gross profit on installment sales for the Kelton Co., prepared at the end of 19X7, are given on pages 130–131.

Kelton Co.
Balance Sheet
December 31, 19X7

Assets	Liabilities and Stockholders' Equity
Current assets:	**Liabilities**
Cash... $ 50,000	**Current liabilities:**
Accounts receivable (regular)........ 25,000	Accounts payable......... $ 30,000
Installment contracts receivable:	Income tax payable....... 28,980 $ 58,980
19X7........................... $70,000	**Deferred revenues:**
19X6........................ 20,000	Deferred gross profit on
19X5...................... 5,000 95,000	installment sales:
Merchandise inventory................. 120,000	19X7...................... $ 28,000
	19X6...................... 7,600
	19X5...................... 1,750 37,350
	Total liabilities .... $ 96,330
	Stockholders' Equity
	Capital stock.................. $100,000
	Retained earnings:
	Balance,
	January 1 .... $50,200
	Add net
	income for
	19X7............. 43,470 93,670
	Total stockholders' equity 193,670
	Total liabilities and stockholders'
Total assets $290,000	equity $290,000

Kelton Co.
Income Statement
For Year Ended December 31, 19X7

	Installment Sales	Regular Sales	Total
Sales..	$150,000	$450,000	$600,000
Cost of goods sold:			
Merchandise inventory, Jan. 1, 19X7 .... $100,000			
Purchases $425,000			
Less purchases discount 5,000 420,000			
Merchandise available for sale $520,000			
Less merchandise inventory, Dec. 31, 19X7..... 120,000	90,000	310,000	400,000
Gross profit..	$ 60,000	$140,000	$200,000
Less deferred gross profit on 19X7 installment sales (see gross profit schedule)..	28,000		28,000
Realized gross profit on current year's sales	$ 32,000	$140,000	$172,000
Add realized gross profit on prior years' sales on installment basis (see gross profit schedule)...			20,450
Total realized gross profit...			$192,450
Operating expenses..			120,000
Income before income tax...			$ 72,450
Income tax..			28,980
Net income			$ 43,470

Kelton Co.
Analysis of Gross Profit on Installment Sales
Schedule to Accompany Income Statement
For Year Ended December 31, 19X7

Gross profit rate on installment sales, 19X7:
 Gross profit, $60,000 ÷ installment sales, $150,000.. **40%**

Deferred gross profit on installment sales, 19X7:
 (Installment contract receivables, $150,000, less collections, $80,000) × 40%............ **$28,000**

Realized gross profit:

	19X7	19X6	19X5
Collections on installment contracts receivable...........................	$80,000	$40,000	$15,000
Installment sales gross profit percentage	40%	38%	35%
Realized gross profit...	$32,000	$15,200	$ 5,250

Trade-Ins

In certain sales on the installment plan, companies will accept a trade-in as part payment on a new contract. When the amount allowed on the goods traded in is a value that will permit the company to realize a normal gross profit on its resale, no special problem is involved. The trade-in is recorded at the value allowed, Cash is debited for any payment accompanying the trade-in, Installment Contracts Receivable is debited for the balance of the sales price, and Installment Sales is credited for the amount of the sale. Frequently, as a special sales inducement, an overallowance is given on the trade-in. Such an overallowance is, in effect, a reduction in the sales price, and the accounts should properly report this fact. Under such circumstances, the trade-in should be recorded at no more than the company would pay on its purchase; the difference between the amount allowed and the value of the article to the company should be reported either as a charge to an overallowance account or as a reduction in Installment Sales. In either case, the gross profit on installment sales should be regarded as the difference between the cost of the goods sold and net sales — the installment sales total less any trade-in overallowances.

To illustrate application of the foregoing, assume that a certain article that cost $675 is sold for $1,000. A used article is accepted as down payment, and $300 is allowed on the trade-in. The company estimates reconditioning costs of $20 on this article and a sales price of $275 after such reconditioning. The company normally expects a 20% gross profit on sales of used goods.

The value of the trade-in and the amount of the overallowance are calculated as follows:

Amount allowed on trade-in...			$300
Value of article traded in:			
Sales value of article..		$275	
Less: Reconditioning costs...	$20		
Gross profit to be realized on resale, 20% of $275..	55	75	200
Overallowance...			$100

The sale can now be recorded as follows:

Merchandise — Trade-Ins	200	
Overallowances on Installment Sales Trade-Ins	100	
Installment Contracts Receivable, 19X0	700	
Installment Sales		1,000
Cost of Installment Sales	675	
Merchandise — New		675

The cost percentage on the installment sale is calculated as follows: cost, $675; net sales, $1,000, less overallowance, $100, or $900; cost percentage, 675/900, or 75%. The gross profit on installment sales, then, is 25%, and 25% of $200, the down payment on the sale, may be considered realized to date. The article traded in is recorded at $200. This cost when increased by reconditioning costs measures the utility of the article to the business and permits a normal gross profit on its resale.

It was assumed in the example just given that the company employs a perpetual inventory system for merchandise. When a periodic inventory system is employed, trade-ins are recorded in a separate nominal account and this balance is added to purchases in summarizing cost of goods sold at the end of the period.

Defaults and Repossessions

Default on an installment contract and repossession of the article sold calls for an entry on the books of the seller that reports the merchandise reacquired, cancels the installment receivable together with the related deferred gross profit balance, and records the gain or loss on the repossession. As in the case of goods acquired by trade-in, a repossessed article should be recorded at an amount that will permit a normal gross profit on its resale.

To illustrate the procedure for defaults and repossessions, assume the following data:

Total installment sales in 19X5	$100,000
Gross profit rate on installment sales in 19X5	36%

In 19X6 a customer defaults on a contract for $600 that had originated in 19X5. A total of $250 had been collected on the contract in 19X5 prior to the default. The article sold is repossessed; its value to the company is $180, allowing for reconditioning costs and a normal gross profit on resale. The entry to record the default and the repossession follows:

Merchandise — Repossessions	180	
Deferred Gross Profit, 19X5	126	
Loss on Repossessions	44	
Installment Contracts Receivable, 19X5		350

Cancellation of the installment contracts receivable balance of $350 is accompanied by cancellation of deferred gross profit of $126 (36% of $350). The repossessed merchandise is reported at a value of $180. A loss of $44 is recognized on the repossession, representing the difference between the installment contract balances canceled, $224 ($350 − $126), and the value assigned to repossessed goods, $180.

When perpetual inventories are maintained, repossessed goods are debited to the inventory balance; when periodic inventories are employed, repossessions are recorded in a separate nominal account and this balance is added to purchases in calculating cost of goods sold. When goods are repossessed in the year in which the sale is made and before the gross profit percentage has been calculated, it may be necessary to assume a gross profit percentage in recording the gain or loss from the repossession. A correcting entry is made at the end of the period when the actual gross profit percentage is determined.

If the repossessed merchandise in the preceding example is recorded at a value in excess of $224, the difference between the balance in the installment contracts receivable account and the deferred gross profit account, a gain will be reported on the repossession. Ordinarily, however, conservatism would suggest that no more than the unrecovered cost, the difference between the receivable balance and the deferred gross profit balance, be assigned to the repossessed goods. No gain, then, would be reported at the time of the repossession; recognition of any gain would await the sale of the repossessed goods.

Any gain or loss on defaults and repossessions is normally recognized on the income statement as an addition to or a subtraction from the realized gross profit on installment sales.

Use of the Installment Method

The installment method of revenue recognition has been a controversial issue. In accounting for installment sales, the accountant is faced with the question: Should gross profit be related to the period in which the sale is made or should it be related to the periods in which the sales price is realized in cash? In answering this question the accountant must consider all of the circumstances in the particular situation, and select the alternative that leads to the fairest expression of financial operations and position.

The American Accounting Association Committee on Concepts and Standards Underlying Corporate Reports cautioned against adoption of the installment method unless such a practice can be fully justified. The Committee commented:

> There is no sound accounting reason for the use of the instalment method for financial statement purposes in the case of closed transactions in which collection is dependent upon lapse of time and the probabilities of realization are properly evaluated. In the opinion of the Committee, such income has accrued and should be recognized in financial statements, even though deferred for tax purposes.[2]

The American Institute of Certified Public Accountants concurred with this view. It issued the following statement which was subsequently adopted by its membership:

---

[2]*Accounting and Reporting Standards for Corporate Financial Statements and Preceding Statements and Supplements,* "Accounting Principles and Taxable Income" (Madison, Wisconsin: American Accounting Association, 1957), p. 33.

> Profit is deemed to be realized when a sale in the ordinary course of business is effected, unless the circumstances are such that the collection of the sale price is not reasonably assured.[3]

In *Opinion No. 10*, the Accounting Principles Board repeated the above statement and continued:

> The Board reaffirms this statement; it believes that revenues should ordinarily be accounted for at the time a transaction is completed, with appropriate provision for uncollectible accounts. Accordingly, it concludes that, in the absence of the circumstances referred to above, the installment method of recognizing revenue is not acceptable.[4]

In clarification of the circumstances in which the installment method could be supported, the following observation was made:

> The Board recognizes that there are exceptional cases where receivables are collectible over an extended period of time and, because of the terms of the transactions or other conditions, there is no reasonable basis for estimating the degree of collectibility. When such circumstances exist, and as long as they exist, either the installment method or the cost recovery method of accounting may be used. (Under the cost recovery method, equal amounts of revenue and expense are recognized as collections are made until all costs have been recovered, postponing any recognition of profit until that time.)[5]

The strong support of the APB for the accrual method led to some abuses, however, in situations in which the accrual method was inappropriate. In particular, retail land sales companies which were selling on the installment basis with very small down payments and considerable risk of customer default cited the APB opinion as support for recognizing all the revenue on a sales contract at the time an initial agreement was reached with a purchaser. Subsequent cancellations and defaults by customers caused an erratic pattern of reported earnings for such companies. As a result, the AICPA formed a committee on land development accounting to look into the appropriate methods for revenue recognition in such transactions.

The Committee was apparently influenced by the Securities and Exchange Commission, which proposed that the installment method of accounting be adopted by land developers. The Committee essentially approved the use of either the accrual or installment methods for retail land sales, but limited the use of the accrual method to situations in which *all* of four very stringent criteria are met. These are as follows:

(1) The properties clearly will be useful for residential or recreational purposes at the end of the normal payment period.

---

[3]*Accounting Research and Terminology Bulletins — Final Edition, No. 43*, "Restatement and Revision of Accounting Research Bulletins" (New York: American Institute of Certified Public Accountants, 1961), p. 11.

[4]*Opinions of the Accounting Principles Board, No. 10*, "Omnibus Opinion-1966" (New York: American Institute of Certified Public Accountants, 1967), par. 12.

[5]*Ibid.*

(2) The project's improvements have progressed beyond preliminary stages, and there is evidence that the work will be completed according to plan.

(3) The receivable is not subject to subordination to new loans on the property (except for home construction purposes).

(4) Collection experience for the project indicates that collectibility of receivable balances is reasonably predictable and that 90% of the contracts in force six months *after sales are recorded* will be collected in full.[6]

If these four criteria cannot be met, then the installment method would be considered appropriate. These criteria provide objective guidance in determining whether the collection of the sales price is reasonably assured. In this sense, it may be regarded as a clarification of, rather than a departure from, the prior APB sanctions regarding use of the installment method.

There may be adequate support for the use of the installment method when real estate is sold with a small down payment and installments covering a number of years and there is a possibility of default through a change in market conditions or the inability or unwillingness of the buyer to complete the contract. However, it would appear that in conventional sales of personal property on the installment plan, the instances where use of the installment method can be justified are rare.

A dealer who sells personal property on the installment plan and recognizes the entire gross profit in the period of sale for financial statement purposes can still choose to employ the installment method for income tax purposes. The installment method is normally chosen for tax purposes as a means of postponing the recognition of income until installment collections are made and cash is actually available to meet the tax liability.

In using the installment method only for income tax purposes, there may be significant differences between net incomes reported on the successive tax returns and net incomes as stated on the books. Periodic tax payments, then, may be significantly different from the amounts that would be applicable to the net incomes reported on the books. For example, in the year in which the installment method is used for the first time, the income tax that is paid will be less than the amount applicable to book income in view of the income on current sales that is deferred for tax purposes. In subsequent periods, taxes paid may be greater or smaller than amounts applicable to book income depending upon the differences between the amount of income on prior period sales that is recognized and the amount of income on current sales that is deferred for income tax purposes. Differences between financial and tax reporting for installment sales require the application of interperiod income tax allocation procedures whereby the charge for income taxes is adjusted periodically to the balance that is applicable to net income as reported on the books.

---

[6]Committee on Land Development Companies, *Accounting for Retail Land Sales* (New York: American Institute of Certified Public Accountants, 1973), pp. 7–8.

To illustrate application of the foregoing, assume that the Kelton Co. in the illustration on pages 124–127 reports gross profit on installment sales in the period of the sales for financial statement purposes but reports gross profit by the installment method for income tax purposes. Income for 19X7 before tax would be reported on the income statement as $80,000 — regular and installment sales, $600,000, less cost of goods sold, $400,000, and operating expenses, $120,000. Receivable balances would require analysis in arriving at deferred gross profit balances requiring recognition for tax purposes. Income per books would be restated to income for tax purposes by the following adjustments:

Income before income tax, per books	$ 80,000
Add deferred gross profit at end of 19X6	29,800
	$109,800
Deduct deferred gross profit at end of 19X7	37,350
Income by installment method	$ 72,450

Assuming income taxes at 40%, the Kelton Co. would recognize a deferred tax liability of 40% of $29,800, or $11,920 for 19X6. In adjusting the accounts at the end of 19X7, an entry to recognize income tax would be made on the books as follows:

Income Tax (40% of $80,000, income per books)	32,000	
Income Tax Payable (40% of $72,450, income per tax return)		28,980
Deferred Income Tax Payable (40% of $7,550, increase in deferred gross income balance)		3,020

In employing the installment basis for income tax purposes while recognizing the entire gross profit on installment sales as well as the tax charges assignable to such profit on the books, the Kelton Co. will report operations for 19X7 as follows:

Sales	$600,000
Cost of goods sold	400,000
Gross profit	$200,000
Operating expenses	120,000
Income before income tax	$ 80,000
Income tax	32,000
Net income	$ 48,000

INTEREST ON INSTALLMENT CONTRACTS

Installment contracts frequently provide for a charge for interest on the balance due. The interest charge is ordinarily payable with the installment payment that reduces the principal. Although interest is included in the payment, use of the installment method requires that only that portion of a payment which reduces the principal balance of the installment contract receivable should be considered in computing the gross profit realized.

The arrangement for the periodic payment of interest generally takes one of the following forms:

(1) Interest is computed on the balance of the principal owed between installment periods. This is sometimes referred to as *long-end* interest.
(2) Interest is computed on the amount of the installment due, from the date the contract was entered into until the date of the installment payment. This is sometimes referred to as *short-end* interest.
(3) Periodic payments are equal in amount and represent interest on the balance of the principal owed between installment periods, the remainder a reduction in the principal balance.
(4) Interest throughout the payment period is computed on the original principal.

To illustrate the foregoing payment plans, assume that on June 30 equipment is sold for $400 on an installment basis. Terms of the sale call for a down payment of $100, the balance to be paid in 6 monthly installments with interest at 12% . The payments that would be made according to each of the plans listed are described in the following paragraphs.

Periodic Interest on Balance of Principal Owed Between Installments

If 6 principal payments of $50 are to be made together with the interest due on the balance of the principal owed between installment dates, payments would be made as shown in the following table.

Date	Interest on Balance Owed (1% per Month)	Contract Payment Due	Total Payment	Balance of Principal
June 30				$400.00
June 30		$100.00	$100.00	300.00
July 31	$ 3.00	50.00	53.00	250.00
Aug. 31	2.50	50.00	52.50	200.00
Sept. 30	2.00	50.00	52.00	150.00
Oct. 31	1.50	50.00	51.50	100.00
Nov. 30	1.00	50.00	51.00	50.00
Dec. 31	.50	50.00	50.50	None
	$10.50	$400.00	$410.50	

The sale and the first two installment payments would be recorded as follows:

Transaction	On the Books of the Buyer	On the Books of the Seller

June 30
To record the installment sale, $400, and the down payment, $100.
	Equipment....... 400.00
	  Installment
	  Contracts
	  Payable 400.00
	Installment
	Contracts
	Payable 100.00
	  Cash............. 100.00
		Installment
		Contracts
		Receivable 400.00
		  Installment
		  Sales............ 400.00
		Cash................ 100.00
		  Installment
		  Contracts
		  Receivable 100.00

July 31
To record the first payment of $50 and interest at 12% for 1 month on the balance owed of $300.
	Installment
	Contracts
	Payable 50.00
	Interest
	Expense........... 3.00
	  Cash............. 53.00
		Cash................ 53.00
		  Installment
		  Contracts
		  Receivable 50.00
		  Interest
		  Income 3.00

August 31
To record the second payment of $50 and interest at 12% for 1 month on the balance owed of $250.
	Installment
	Contracts
	Payable 50.00
	Interest
	Expense........... 2.50
	  Cash............. 52.50
		Cash................ 52.50
		  Installment
		  Contracts
		  Receivable 50.00
		  Interest
		  Income 2.50

Periodic Interest on Installment Due

Assume the same facts except that interest is to be paid periodically upon the amount of the installment due, from contract date to the date of the installment payment. Payments would be made as shown in the following table.

Date	Interest from Date of Sale to Date of Payment (1% per Month)	Contract Payment Due	Total Payment	Balance of Principal
June 30				$400.00
June 30		$100.00	$100.00	300.00
July 31	$ .50	50.00	50.50	250.00
Aug. 31	1.00	50.00	51.00	200.00
Sept. 30	1.50	50.00	51.50	150.00
Oct. 31	2.00	50.00	52.00	100.00
Nov. 30	2.50	50.00	52.50	50.00
Dec. 31	3.00	50.00	53.00	None
	$10.50	$400.00	$410.50	

In this plan, interest payments do not agree with the interest actually accruing on the unpaid principal. Assuming the preparation of monthly financial statements, accrued interest based on the principal balance would have to be recognized at the end of each month. The amount of interest paid may then be offset against this balance.

The interest accrual as well as the installment payments at the end of July and August would be recorded as follows:

Transaction	On the Books of the Buyer	On the Books of the Seller
July 31 To record accrued interest at 12% for 1 month on balance owed of $300.	Interest Expense... 3.00 Accrued Interest on Contracts Payable............. 3.00	Accrued Interest on Contracts Receivable .... 3.00 Interest Income . 3.00
To record the first payment of $50 and interest at 12% for 1 month on payment of $50.	Installment Contracts Payable . 50.00 Accrued Interest on Contracts Payable................ .50 Cash................. 50.50	Cash..................... 50.50 Installment Contracts Receivable .... 50.00 Accrued Interest on Contracts Receivable .... .50
August 31 To record accrued interest at 12% for 1 month on balance owed of $250.	Interest Expense... 2.50 Accrued Interest on Contracts Payable............. 2.50	Accrued Interest on Contracts Receivable .... 2.50 Interest Income . 2.50
To record the second payment of $50 and interest at 12% for 2 months on payment of $50.	Installment Contracts Payable . 50.00 Accrued Interest on Contracts Payable................ 1.00 Cash................. 51.00	Cash..................... 51.00 Installment Contracts Receivable .... 50.00 Accrued Interest on Contracts Receivable 1.00

Although the charges for interest are greater than the payments for interest in these entries, the charges go down periodically while the payments go up. After the final payment, total payments for interest will be equal to the sum of the charges that were recognized. Changes in the accrued interest balance are summarized below.

Date	Increase for Accrual (Cr.)	Decrease for Payment (Dr.)	Balance of Accrued Interest on Contracts Payable (Cr.)
July 31	$3.00	$ .50	$2.50
Aug. 31................	2.50	1.00	4.00
Sept. 30	2.00	1.50	4.50
Oct. 31	1.50	2.00	4.00
Nov. 30................	1.00	2.50	2.50
Dec. 31................	.50	3.00	None

Equal Periodic Payments that Represent Interest and Principal

When periodic payments are to be equal in amount and are to represent interest on the unpaid principal and an amount to be applied against the principal, the equal payments are found by actuarial calculations. By the use of actuarial tables it can be determined that an obligation of $300 accruing interest at 12% is discharged by 6 equal monthly payments of $51.76.[7] The following table shows payments and the allocation of such payments between interest and principal.

Date	Contract Payment Due	Portion of Payment Applying to Interest Accruing on Principal (1% per Month)	Balance of Payment Representing Reduction in Principal	Balance of Principal
June 30				$400.00
June 30	$100.00		$100.00	300.00
July 31	51.76	$ 3.00	48.76	251.24
Aug. 31	51.76	2.51	49.25	201.99
Sept. 30	51.76	2.02	49.74	152.25
Oct. 31	51.76	1.52	50.24	102.01
Nov. 30	51.76	1.02	50.74	51.27
Dec. 31	51.78*	.51	51.27	None
	$410.58	$10.58	$400.00	

*A final payment of $51.78 is required to cancel the interest for the last month together with the unpaid principal on this date.

Payments apply first to the accrued interest on the principal to the date of payment and then to a reduction in the principal. Entries to record the equal periodic payments at the end of July and August are as follows:

Transaction	On the Books of the Buyer	On the Books of the Seller

July 31
To record the first regular payment of $51.76, representing payment of accrued interest to date, $3.00 (1% of $300), and principal, $48.76.
	Interest Expense... 3.00
	Installment
	Contracts Payable . 48.76
	  Cash................. 51.76
		Cash.................... 51.76
		  Interest Income . 3.00
		  Installment
		  Contracts
		  Receivable 48.76

August 31
To record the second regular payment of $51.76, representing payment of accrued interest to date, $2.51 (1% of $250.62), and principal, $49.25.
	Interest Expense... 2.51
	Installment
	Contracts Payable . 49.25
	  Cash................. 51.76
		Cash.................... 51.76
		  Interest Income . 2.51
		  Installment
		  Contracts
		  Receivable 49.25

Periodic Interest Computed on Original Principal

Assume the same facts except that periodic interest payments are to continue at 12% of the original principal for the duration of the contract. Payments are made as follows:

---

[7]$300 is the present value of an ordinary annuity of 6 rents at interest of 1%.

Date	Interest Based on Original Principal (1% per Month)	Contract Payment Due	Total Payment	Balance of Principal
June 30...............				$400.00
June 30...............		$100.00	$100.00	300.00
July 31	$ 4.00	50.00	54.00	250.00
Aug. 31...............	4.00	50.00	54.00	200.00
Sept. 30	4.00	50.00	54.00	150.00
Oct. 31	4.00	50.00	54.00	100.00
Nov. 30...............	4.00	50.00	54.00	50.00
Dec. 31...............	4.00	50.00	54.00	None
	$24.00	$400.00	$424.00	

Although each of the first three methods resulted in interest at 12% per year, the method just illustrated results in an effective interest charge that is actually more than double the 12% rate. While the average amount owed during the course of the contract was $175 [($300 plus $50) ÷ 2], the interest charge for the 6-month period totaled $24, resulting in an interest rate of more than 27% ($48 interest per year ÷ $175, the average amount owed).

QUESTIONS

1. What are the two basic approaches to the recognition of gross profit on sales made on the installment plan? Give the theory underlying each approach.

2. What three procedures may be followed when the recognition of gross profit is to be related to the cash that is realized on installment contracts? Evaluate each procedure and indicate the circumstances under which each procedure may be considered particularly suitable.

3. What practices should be followed if losses on the repossessions of merchandise are to be minimized?

4. (a) Describe the *installment method* of accounting. (b) Give two methods for the periodic calculation of realized gross profit.

5. Would you recommend that expenses related to installment sales be deferred when gross profit on such sales is deferred? Give reasons.

6. Describe the form for a cash receipts journal that might be used to record collections on both regular accounts receivable and installment contracts originating over a three-year period.

7. L. P. Monarch wishes to adopt the installment method for profit recognition on installment sales but wishes to keep bookkeeping detail at a minimum by maintaining one customers ledger. What special procedures are required in following such an arrangement?

8. Compare the financial statements for a business that does not sell on the installment basis with those for a business that does sell on the installment basis.

9. State how each of the following balances would be classified on the financial statements: (a) installment contracts receivable, (b) repossessed merchandise, (c) overallowances on trade-ins, (d) loss on repossessions.

10. Describe the positions that may be taken in reporting deferred gross profit on installment sales on the balance sheet. Which position do you favor? Why?

11. Burke and Baggett use the installment method in the accounts and report the entire deferred gross profit balance as a part of the company's capital. Would you have any objections to such a procedure?

12. (a) At what value would you recommend that articles traded in be entered on the books? (b) How would you treat trade-in overallowances in the accounts? (c) How should such overallowances be recognized in arriving at the gross profit on installment sales?

13. The Markham Company reports the difference between the installment contract receivable balances and the deferred gross profit balances that are canceled upon a repossession as the cost of the repossessed goods. Under what circumstances, if any, would you object to such a procedure?

14. Describe four different interest plans that may be found in an installment sales contract.

EXERCISES

1. At the end of 19X7, R. A. Brady sells for $10,000 property acquired in 19X0 at a cost of $4,250. Terms of the sale are $4,000 down with the balance to be paid in annual installments of $1,000. Indicate the profit to be recognized by Brady in 19X7 and in each of the next 6 years, assuming that:

- (a) Collections on the contract are first considered a return of the property cost; after recovery of the cost, collections are regarded as profit.
- (b) Collections are first considered realization of the profit on the contract; after recovery of the profit, collections are regarded as a return of cost.
- (c) Each collection is considered both a return of cost and of profit in the ratio in which these are found in the sales price.

2. In July, 19X1, C. P. Walters sold for $24,000 real estate that had cost $9,000, receiving $3,500 cash and a mortgage note for the balance payable in monthly installments. Installments received in 19X1 reduced the principal of the note to a balance of $20,000. The buyer defaulted on the note at the beginning of 19X2, and the property was repossessed. The property had an appraised value of $16,500 at the time of repossession. Prepare the entries that would be made on the books of the seller in 19X1 and 19X2, assuming (a) that the full profit is recognized when the sale is made and (b) that the gross profit on the sale is recognized in proportion to the periodic collections.

3. The Fuller Company reports profits on the installment basis. Perpetual inventory records are kept for stock on hand. Sales during 19X8 are summarized on page 143. Prepare the entries to record the transactions and to close the accounts for 19X8.

(a) Sales on installment basis, $250,000.

(b) Collections on installment accounts, $120,000.

(c) Shipments of merchandise on installment sales; cost, $200,000.

(d) Repossessions of merchandise sold on installment basis; installment accounts canceled, $20,000; repossessed merchandise valued at $14,500.

(e) Expenses paid, $16,000.

4. J. C. Clendenin accounts for installment sales by reporting income in the proportion of the collections to the selling price. On December 31, 19X3, the books show account balances as follows:

Installment Contracts Receivable		Deferred Gross Profit	
19X1	$10,000	19X1	$ 8,000
19X2	40,000	19X2	26,000
19X3	90,000	19X3	105,000

The gross profit rates were: 19X1, 35%; 19X2, 30%; 19X3, 40%.

(a) What adjusting entries are required on December 31, 19X3?

(b) How much was collected in 19X3 on accounts receivable of each year?

5. The Charles B. Croft Store accounts for installment sales on the installment basis. At the beginning of 19X4, ledger accounts include the following balances:

Installment Accounts Receivable, 19X2...........................	$15,000
Installment Accounts Receivable, 19X3...........................	48,000
Deferred Gross Profit, 19X2	6,300
Deferred Gross Profit, 19X3	18,000

At the end of 19X4, account balances before adjustment for realized gross profit on installment sales are:

Installment Accounts Receivable, 19X2...........................	None
Installment Accounts Receivable, 19X3...........................	$12,000
Installment Accounts Receivable, 19X4...........................	65,000
Deferred Gross Profit, 19X2	6,300
Deferred Gross Profit, 19X3	18,000
Deferred Gross Profit, 19X4	30,000

Installment sales in 19X4 were made at 66⅔% above cost of merchandise sold. What are the entries to record the gross profit realized in 19X4?

6. The books of Donald Murphy show the following balances on December 31, 19X6:

Accounts Receivable..	$627,500
Deferred Gross Profit (before adjustment)	76,000

Analysis and aging of the accounts receivable reveal the following:

Regular accounts..	$415,000
19X5 installment accounts...	32,500
19X6 installment accounts...	180,000

Sales on an installment basis in 19X5 were made at 30% above cost; in 19X6, at 33⅓% above cost. Prepare the entry to adjust the deferred gross profit account at the end of 19X6.

7. The Walsh Co. sells new automobiles. A new automobile costing $2,500 was sold at the end of 19X9 for $3,600; an old automobile was accepted as down payment and an allowance of $1,500 was allowed on the trade-in. The company anticipates reconditioning costs of $150 on this automobile and a resale price of $1,400. Its used car sales are expected to produce a 25% gross profit. Prepare entries to record the sale of the automobile, to adjust and close the accounts, and to recognize the gross profit on the sale by the installment method.

8. Weiss and Company sells refrigerators at 20% above cost and accounts for sales by the installment method. In 19X2 repossessions of $15,000 were made on unpaid installment contract balances. Repossessed units had a total resale value of $13,500. The company records such repossessions at a value that will permit the normal margin on sales. Prepare the entry to summarize the repossessions for 19X2.

9. In October, 19X5, the Phillips Co. repossessed a piano that had been sold in 19X4 at a gross profit of 45%. The uncollected installment contract balance on the date of the repossession was $800. Nothing was collected in 19X4; $300 was collected in 19X5, including interest of $40, and collections were properly recorded. The repossession was recorded by a debit to Sales Returns and a credit to Installment Contracts Receivable for $800, closing the latter account. The value of the piano on the date of repossession was $380. The company recognizes income by the installment method. What entry or entries are required on December 31, 19X5, to correct and bring the accounts up to date?

10. The Cook Trading Company recognizes profits on installment sales on its books at the time of sale, just as it recognizes profits on regular sales. For income tax purposes the company reports profits on the installment basis. The 19X7 income statement prepared by the company from its accounts showed $112,000 income before income tax. The following data were recognized at the end of 19X6 in preparing the tax return:

> Accounts receivable on December 31, 19X6, included:
>> 19X5 installment accounts of $40,000; deferred gross profit of $12,000 was considered related to this balance.
>> 19X6 installment accounts of $80,000; deferred gross profit of $26,000 was considered related to this balance.

> The following data are available at the end of 19X7:

> Accounts receivable on December 31, 19X7, include:
>> 19X5 installment accounts of $12,500.
>> 19X6 installment accounts of $25,000.
>> 19X7 installment accounts of $60,000; installment sales in 19X7 were made at approximately 66⅔% above cost.

From the foregoing data calculate the income to be reported on the tax return, showing how this amount is developed.

11. On October 31, 19X3, Paul Barnes sold for $75,000 property that had cost $60,000. He received $20,000 down; the balance is payable in monthly installments, with the first payment due at the end of November. Barnes decides to report the profit on the sale on the installment basis. What entries would be made for the sale, for the receipt of installments at the end of November and December, and for the recognition of profit for 19X3, assuming that:

(a) Monthly payments are sums consisting of $600 to apply against the principal plus interest on the unpaid balance at 12%.

(b) Monthly payments are equal amounts of $600 that include interest at 12% on the unpaid amount of the obligation, with any excess reducing the principal.

PROBLEMS

5-1. Wilson Corporation, which operates on the calendar-year basis, purchased business property on June 30, 19X1, for $100,000 cash. The appraised value of the land was $10,000 and the remaining life of the building was estimated to be 50 years. Depreciation has been accumulated by use of the straight-line method.

On June 30, 19X5, the property was sold for $150,000, for which payment was received as follows:

(1) $25,000 cash on date of sale.

(2) Four non-interest-bearing notes due as follows:

$30,000 — 6/30/X6
$30,000 — 6/30/X7
$50,000 — 6/30/X8
$15,000 — 6/30/X9

Wilson Corporation elected to record the gain on the sale of the property by the installment method, since the collection of the receivable is not reasonably assured.

Instructions: (1) Prepare the necessary journal entries and computations to record the sale on June 30, 19X5.

(2) Prepare the necessary journal entries and computations to record the collection of the notes at their maturities.

(3) State the sections of the balance sheet in which the account balances at December 31, 19X5, should be shown.

(AICPA adapted)

5-2. The Four Star Investment Company was organized in January, 19X4. It is engaged in acquiring unimproved land and dividing it into lots for sale as home-sites. Realizing that the project was speculative, the company decided to recognize gross profits on sales of lots (after deducting any commissions payable to salespeople) in the proportion that cash collected each year bears to the sales price. The transactions for 19X4 were as follows:

(a) Purchased 120 acres of land for subdivision at a cost of $48,000, payable in cash, and divided the land into lots 100 feet wide and 120 feet deep, obtaining a total of 310 lots. The remaining area was devoted to streets and other general purposes. The lots were priced according to location as follows: The A lots were listed to sell for $1,500 each, B lots for $1,000 each, and C lots for $800 each. There were 80 A lots, 100 B lots, and the remainder were C lots.

(b) Costs and expenses incurred in 19X4 were as follows:

Legal fees for purchasing land, surveying fees, etc................ $ 6,000
Grading contract... 22,500
Water and sewerage system contract................................... 18,490
Paving contract.. 26,630
Building model home, which is to be offered for sale and is
   expected to yield a profit... 13,500
Advertising and publicity.. 7,300
General office expense, of which one fourth is considered ap-
   plicable to the period after development of the lots has
   been completed 23,600
Sales manager's salary.. 9,000
Sales commissions 2,210

(c) Sales during 19X4 were as follows, all at the standard prices:

A lots — 26; B lots — 32; C lots — 12

All lots were sold with a ¼ down payment, except 6 of the A lots that were collected for in full. The notes taken were payable in 3 installments starting 1 year from date of sale. Ignore interest on the notes.

Instructions: Prepare a statement, supported by all necessary computations presented in good form, showing the net profit of the company for 19X4.

(AICPA adapted)

5-3. The Warren Furniture Company reports income on the installment basis and uses perpetual inventory accounts. The following data are available:

Sales Year	Percent of Gross Profit	Installment Receivables on January 1, 19X7	Collected During 19X7	Installment Receivables on December 31, 19X7
19X5	46%	$30,000	$30,000	—
19X6	42	50,000	34,000	$ 16,000
19X7	40	—	60,000	140,000

Instructions: For these data, prepare all the 19X7 journal entries, including those required for the recognition of gross profit at the end of the year.

5-4. The trial balance at the top of page 147 was prepared for Western Equipment, Inc., on December 31, 19X4.

The inventory of merchandise on December 31, 19X4, was $60,000.

The following account balances were reported in the post-closing trial balance prepared on January 1, 19X4:

Installment Accounts Receivable, 19X3............................. $150,000
Installment Accounts Receivable, 19X2............................. 30,000
Deferred Gross Profit, 19X3 45,000
Deferred Gross Profit, 19X2 9,600

Instructions: (1) Calculate the gross profit percentages on installment sales for 19X2, 19X3, and 19X4.

(2) Prepare a balance sheet and an income statement with a supporting schedule providing an analysis of gross profit on installment sales.

(3) Prepare the adjusting and closing entries.

Cash...	27,500	
Installment Accounts Receivable, 19X4................	55,000	
Installment Accounts Receivable, 19X3................	12,000	
Installment Accounts Receivable, 19X2................	3,000	
Accounts Receivable..	17,000	
Inventory, December 31, 19X3	52,000	
Other Assets	40,000	
Accounts Payable		40,000
Deferred Gross Profit, 19X3		45,000
Deferred Gross Profit, 19X2		9,600
Capital Stock..		100,000
Retained Earnings		68,400
Sales..		125,000
Installment Sales...		320,000
Purchases..	350,000	
Cost of Installment Sales.................................	232,000	
Shipments on Installment Sales		232,000
Operating Expenses	151,500	
	940,000	940,000

5-5. The following trial balance was prepared for the Grossett Sales Corporation on December 31, 19X8.

Cash...	25,000	
Installment Accounts Receivable, 19X8........	80,000	
Installment Accounts Receivable, 19X7........	20,000	
Installment Accounts Receivable, 19X6........	5,000	
Accounts Receivable..................................	40,000	
Inventory, December 31, 19X7	30,000	
Other Assets	52,000	
Accounts Payable		75,000
Deferred Gross Profit, 19X7		96,000
Deferred Gross Profit, 19X6		22,500
Capital Stock...		100,000
Retained Earnings		44,500
Sales..		192,000
Installment Sales......................................		500,000
Purchases...	455,000	
Repossessed Merchandise...........................	10,000	
Cost of Installment Sales............................	310,000	
Shipments on Installment Sales		310,000
Loss on Repossessions	13,000	
Operating Expenses	300,000	
	1,340,000	1,340,000

The following account balances were found in the post-closing trial balance prepared at the beginning of 19X8:

Installment Accounts Receivable, 19X7............................	$240,000
Installment Accounts Receivable, 19X6............................	50,000
Deferred Gross Profit, 19X7	96,000
Deferred Gross Profit, 19X6	22,500

The inventory of new and repossessed merchandise on December 31, 19X8, was $35,000.

At the end of December, before preparing the trial balance, the bookkeeper made the following incomplete entry:

Repossessed Merchandise	10,000	
Loss on Repossessions	13,000	
Installment Accounts Receivable, 19X8		5,000
Installment Accounts Receivable, 19X7		10,000
Installment Accounts Receivable, 19X6		8,000

Instructions: (1) Calculate the gross profit percentages on installment sales for 19X6, 19X7, and 19X8.

(2) Prepare the required correcting entry for the repossessions.

(3) Prepare a balance sheet and an income statement with a supporting schedule providing an analysis of gross profit on installment sales.

(4) Prepare the adjusting and closing entries.

5-6. The Lawrence Appliance Co. recorded installment sales of $600,000 in 19X1. A record was kept of the different articles sold on the installment basis. At the end of the year the total cost of goods sold on the installment basis was calculated at $405,000. The total collections on installment sales for the year were $360,000. The estimated value of the merchandise repossessed was $24,000, and balances owed on the repossessions were $40,000. Perpetual inventory accounts were not maintained.

Instructions: Prepare the journal entries required for the data above, including the entries (1) to set up the total realizable gross profit at the end of the year, (2) to record the repossessions, and (3) to record the realized gross profit.

5-7. The Wabash Appliance Co. reports gross profit on the installment basis. The following data are available:

	19X0	19X1	19X2
Installment sales	$240,000	$250,000	$300,000
Cost of goods — installment sales	180,000	181,250	216,000
Gross profit	$ 60,000	$ 68,750	$ 84,000
Collections:			
19X0 installment contracts	$ 45,000	$ 75,000	$ 72,500
19X1 installment contracts		47,500	80,000
19X2 installment contracts			62,500
Defaults:			
Unpaid balance of 19X0 installment contracts		$ 12,500	$ 15,000
Value assigned to repossessed goods		6,500	6,000
Unpaid balance of 19X1 installment contracts			16,000
Value assigned to repossessed goods			9,000

Instructions: Prepare all of the 19X2 entries for installment sales, collections, defaults and repossessions, and the recognition of gross profit. Assume the use of perpetual inventory accounts.

5-8. The Bledsoe Co. accounts for sales of merchandise on the installment basis. At the end of each year it recognizes gross profit on these sales, considering collections during the year to be composed of cost and gross profit elements.

The balances of the control accounts for installment contracts receivable at the beginning and the end of 19X8 were:

	January 1, 19X8	December 31, 19X8
Installment contracts receivable:		
19X6	$ 24,020	—
19X7	344,460	$ 67,440
19X8	—	410,090

As collections are made, the company debits Cash and credits Installment Contracts Receivable. During 19X8, upon default in payment by customers, the company repossessed merchandise having an estimated resale value of $1,700. The sales had been made in 19X7 for $5,400, and $3,200 had been collected prior to default. The company recorded the default and repossession by a debit to Inventory of Repossessed Merchandise and a credit to Installment Contracts Receivable — 19X7 for the uncollected balance.

The company's sales and cost of sales for the 3 years involved are summarized below:

	19X6	19X7	19X8
Net sales	$380,000	$432,000	$602,000
Cost of sales............................	247,000	285,120	379,260

Instructions: (1) Prepare journal entries to record the recognition of profits at December 31, 19X8.

(2) Using two acceptable methods, prepare the entry to record the repossession and discuss the relative merits of each method.

(AICPA adapted)

5-9. The Wallace Co. started business on January 1, 19X1. Separate accounts were set up for installment and cash sales, but no perpetual inventory record was maintained. On the installment sales, a ⅓ down payment was required, with the balance payable in 18 equal monthly installments. At the end of each year the company adjusted its books to the installment basis by using a deferred gross profit account. When contracts were defaulted, the unpaid balances were charged to uncollectible accounts expense, and sales of repossessed merchandise were credited to this account. The expense account was adjusted at year-end to reflect the actual loss.

Information about the transactions of the Wallace Co. are shown at the top of page 150.

Instructions: (1) Compute the gross profit percentages for 19X1 and 19X2.

(2) In T-account form, reproduce the ledger accounts for installment contracts receivable.

(3) Calculate the net loss on defaulted accounts for 19X1.

(4) Prepare a schedule showing the realized gross profit for 19X2 that would be reported on the income statement.

(AICPA adapted)

	19X1	19X2
Sales:		
New merchandise for cash......................	$ 21,348	$ 29,180
New merchandise on installment (includ-		
ing the one-third cash down payment)....	188,652	265,320
Repossessed merchandise.......................	600	700
Purchases...	154,000	173,585
Physical inventories at December 31:		
New merchandise at cost.......................	36,400	48,010
Repossessions at realizable value	150	160
Unpaid balances of installment contracts de-		
faulted:		
19X1 sales...	2,865	3,725
19X2 sales...		3,010
Cash collections on installment contracts,		
exclusive of down payments:		
19X1 sales...	42,943	61,385
19X2 sales...		55,960

5-10. The Parker Furniture Company commenced business operations on January 1, 19X2. All sales are made on installment contracts, and inventory records are on a periodic basis. Contract receivables are kept separate by years. At the end of each year, adjustments for realized gross profits are made through a deferred gross profit on installment sales account. Defaulted contracts are recorded by debiting the loss on defaults account and crediting the appropriate contracts receivable account for the amount unpaid at the time of default. All repossessed merchandise and trade-ins should be recorded at realizable values. The following information is taken from the accounts of the Parker Furniture Company.

	19X2	19X3
Contracts receivable (unpaid balances):		
19X2 accounts	$ 62,425	$ 3,175
19X3 accounts		101,375
Installment sales	138,675	220,925
Purchases...	160,000	154,600
New merchandise inventory, December 31,		
at cost..	60,154	73,042
Loss on defaults		5,000

Additional information:

In the process of your audit you find that the following items were not included in the inventory taken on December 31, 19X3:

(1) Merchandise received as a trade-in on December 15, 19X3, for which an allowance was given. The realizable value of the merchandise is $500, which was the allowance for the trade-in. This merchandise was not recorded on the books at the time it was received.

(2) Repossessed merchandise, originally sold in 19X2, representing the only default and repossession by the company to date, had a realizable value of $2,000 at the time of repossession and at December 31, 19X3. This repossessed merchandise has not been recorded.

Instructions: (1) Prepare the adjusting entry to record the trade-in merchandise.

(2) Compute the gross profit percentages for 19X2 and 19X3.

(3) Prepare the entry necessary to adjust the loss on defaults account.

(4) Reconstruct the deferred gross profit on installment sales account by years through December 31, 19X3, showing in good form all computations for the amounts included in the account.

(AICPA adapted)

5-11. F. A. Sloan purchased two adjoining 75-foot business lots in 19X0. Lot 1 was purchased for $36,000 early in that year and Lot 2 was purchased for $24,000 later in the year. Sloan made three 50-foot lots out of the original two by taking 25 feet from each to make Lot 3. The cost of this third lot was determined by allocating a portion of the cost of the original two lots to it. Sloan then built a store on Lot 3 at a cost of $36,000. It was completed and paid for on June 30, 19X5, and had an estimated life of 20 years.

The three pieces of property were sold during 19X5 on the following terms:

Lot	Sales Price	Date of Sale	Down Payment	Equal Installment Payments
1	$36,000	Oct. 31	$ 7,200	$1,200 every 2 months
2	40,000	Mar. 31	3,600	$1,600 every 3 months
3	84,000	June 30	12,000	$5,000 every 6 months

Each installment payment is to be applied first to accrued interest on the principal amount owed at the rate of 12%, the balance to a reduction of principal.

The purchaser of Lot 3 did not complete the contract, failing to meet the installment due on June 30, 19X6, and the property was repossessed.

Instructions: (1) Prepare journal entries to record the transactions for 19X5 on Sloan's books.

(2) Prepare the entry to record the realized gross profit when the books are closed on December 31, 19X5.

(3) Record the repossession of Lot 3 in 19X6. (Assume that upon repossession the lot is recorded at original cost; the building, at original cost less depreciation to date based upon original estimates.)

5-12. The Ladero Company was formed on July 31, 19X0, and sells household appliances at retail on installment payment contracts. The following information was taken from the accounts of the Ladero Company:

	Year Ended July 31	
	19X2	19X1
Installment contracts receivable:		
19X1 contracts.....................................	$ 4,000	$ 63,000
19X2 contracts.....................................	80,000	
Sales...	250,000	150,000
Merchandise inventory, new, at cost	42,250	32,250
Purchases...	155,000	
Selling and administrative expenses.............	70,000	
Loss on defaulted contracts........................	8,550	500
Allowance for defaulted contracts................	4,500	4,500

The CPA's audit at July 31, 19X2, disclosed the following:

(1) When a contract is in default, the merchandise is repossessed and the contract is written off to Loss on Defaulted Contracts. Information regarding repossessed merchandise is kept on a memo basis and is not recorded on the books. Any income derived from the sale of this merchandise is credited to Loss on Defaulted Contracts. No repossessed merchandise was sold in 19X1 or 19X2 for more than the unpaid balance of the original contract. An analysis of the loss on defaulted contracts account follows:

Contracts written off:		
19X1 contracts.......	$ 7,500	
19X2 contracts.......	3,000	
	10,500	
Less sale of repossessed merchandise:		
19X1 contracts.......	$1,600	
19X2 contracts.......	350	1,950
Balance		$ 8,550

The market value of the repossessed merchandise inventory on hand at July 31, 19X2, was $400, all of which was repossessed from 19X1 contracts. There was no merchandise repossessed during the year ended July 31, 19X1.

The $4,000 balance of 19X1 installment contracts receivable is considered collectible.

(2) The gross profit ratio for 19X1 was 40%.

(3) The company's financial statements are prepared on the accrual basis, and the installment method of reporting income is used for income tax purposes. The company uses the direct write-off method for income tax purposes for losses on defaulted contracts.

Instructions: (1) Prepare a schedule to compute the adjustment to the balance of the account Allowance for Defaulted Contracts that the CPA would suggest at July 31, 19X2. The rate of uncollectible accounts expense for 19X2 is expected to be the same as the experience rate for 19X1 based on sales.

(2) Prepare a schedule computing taxable income on the installment sales method for the year ended July 31, 19X2. The following supporting schedules should be in good form:

Computation of realized gross profit on 19X1 sales.

Computation of losses on defaults on 19X1 contracts and 19X2 contracts.

(AICPA adapted)

5-13. On September 30, 19X6, A. C. Barr bought an automobile for $3,600. A down payment of $1,600 was made, with the balance due in 10 monthly installments, the first to be made at the end of October.

Instructions: (1) Assume that Barr is to make monthly payments of $200 plus interest on the unpaid balance at 12%. Set up a table showing the principal and interest payments and the principal amount owed after each payment.

(2) Assume that Barr is to make monthly payments of $200 plus 12% interest on each installment for the full time the payment was owed. Complete a table

with columns showing (a) the interest paid, (b) the principal paid, (c) the total payment, (d) the interest accruing on the balance of the principal between interest dates, (e) the principal balance, and (f) the accrued interest balance.

(3) Assume that Barr is to make equal monthly payments, each payment to apply first as interest at 12% on the unpaid principal and the balance as a reduction in principal. Such equal payments are calculated to be $211.16. Complete a table showing the payments, the interest and principal portions of each payment, and the principal amount owed after each payment.

(4) What is the approximate effective annual interest rate if monthly payments are $200 plus interest at 12% charged on the original principal amount of $3,600?

5-14. The Weber Corporation purchased a machine for $60,000 on July 31, 19X2. The company paid $12,000 down and gave a note for the balance payable in 48 monthly installments, the first one due on August 31.

Instructions: (1) Assuming that interest at 12% on the balance of the principal is added to regular monthly payments of $1,000, prepare the journal entries for the acquisition of the machine and for the payments at the end of August, September, and October, 19X2.

(2) Assuming that interest at 12% on the individual payments only from the date of purchase to the date of payment is added to regular monthly payments of $1,000, prepare the journal entries for the interest adjustments and for the monthly payments at the end of August, September and October, 19X2.

(3) Assuming that monthly payments are to be equal amounts of $1,264.02 as calculated actuarially, representing interest at 12% on the unpaid principal and the balance a reduction of principal, prepare the journal entries for the monthly payments at the end of August, September, and October, 19X2.

5-15. On September 30, 19X7, Harmony Instruments, Inc., sold for $1,600 a piano costing $1,000. The down payment was $160, and the same amount was to be paid at the end of each succeeding month. Interest at 1% a month was charged on the unpaid balance of the contract, with payments applying first to accrued interest and the balance to principal.

After paying a total of $640, the customer defaulted. The piano was repossessed in February, 19X8. It was estimated that the piano had a value of $560 on a depreciated cost basis. The company uses perpetual inventory accounts and enters the total deferred gross profit at the time of sale.

Instructions: Prepare the journal entries to record:

(1) The installment sale.
(2) The monthly collections.
(3) The recognition of realized gross profit at the end of 19X7.
(4) The repossession in 19X8.

5-16. The Jackson Appliance Company started business on January 1, 19X7. Separate accounts were established for installment and cash sales, but no perpetual inventory record was maintained.

On installment sales, the price was 106% of the cash sale price. A standard installment contract was used whereby a down payment of ¼ of the installment price was required, with the balance payable in 15 equal monthly installments.

(The interest charge per month is 1% of the unpaid cash sale price equivalent at each installment.)

Installment receivables and installment sales were recorded at the contract price. When contracts were defaulted, the unpaid balances were debited to Uncollectible Accounts Expense. Sales of defaulted merchandise were credited to Uncollectible Accounts Expense.

Sales:	
Cash sales..	$126,000
Installment sales	265,000
Repossessed sales..	230
Inventory, January 1, 19X7:	
Merchandise inventory	58,060
Purchases, 19X7:	
New merchandise	209,300
Inventories, physical, December 31, 19X7:	
New merchandise	33,300
Repossessed inventory...	180
Cash collections on installment contracts, 19X7:	
Down payments..	66,250
Subsequent installments...	79,341
(Average 6 monthly installments on all contracts except on defaulted contracts)	

Five contracts totaling $1,060 were defaulted, in each case after 3 monthly installments were paid.

Interest should be recognized in the period earned.

Instructions: (1) Calculate the gross profit percentage for 19X7.

(2) Prepare a schedule, showing by payment for the first 7 months: the cash sale price equivalent, the contract balance, the amount of interest earned, and the cash collected on a $1,060 installment sale contract.

(3) Calculate the net gain or loss on defaulted contracts during 19X7.

(4) Calculate the realized gross profit for 19X7.

(AICPA adapted)

6
Consignments

Goods may be transferred by their owner to another party who is to act as sales agent, with legal title to the goods retained by the owner until their sale. Such a transfer is known as a *consignment*. The party who owns the goods in such a relationship is known as the *consignor*; the party who undertakes to sell the goods is known as the *consignee, factor*, or *commission merchant*.

NATURE OF THE CONSIGNMENT

From a legal point of view the transfer of goods represents a bailment, with the consignee possessing the goods for the purpose of sale as specified in the agreement between the consignor and the consignee. The consignor holds the consignee accountable for goods transferred to the latter's care until the goods are sold to a third party. Upon such sale, the consignor recognizes a transfer of title to the goods and also revenue from the sale. The consignee, on the other hand, cannot regard consigned goods as his or her property; nor is there any liability to the consignor other than an accountability for consigned goods. The relationship between the consignor and the consignee is one of principal and agent, and the law of agency governs the determination of the rights and the obligations of the two parties.

Consignments may have advantages for many products, including household appliances, books, magazines, newspapers, and novelty items. The consignor may prefer the consignment of goods to dealers for the following reasons:

(1) The consignment may be the only way in which a wider marketing area can be secured by a producer, manufacturer, or distributor, particularly when (a) the goods are just being introduced and the demand for the product is unknown or uncertain; (b) sales in the past have proven unprofitable to the dealer; (c) the goods are costly,

requiring a large investment on the part of the dealer if purchased; and (d) price fluctuation or product perishability is such that the dealer will agree to sell goods only if the risk of loss is borne by another. The dealer, incurring neither the liability nor the risk involved with purchase of the goods, is generally willing to accept goods on a consignment basis.

(2) Selling specialists may be obtained by the consignor, particularly for the sale of grain, livestock, and produce. The compensation for such services is frequently a commission, which may be a percentage of sales price or a fixed amount for each unit of goods sold.

(3) The retail selling price of consigned goods can be controlled by the consignor who still owns the goods. This may be difficult or impossible when the goods are actually sold to the dealer.

The consignee may favor the acquisition of goods by consignment for the following reasons:

(1) The consignee is protected from the risk of failing to move the product or selling it at a loss. This factor may be particularly important in the case of new products or products that are being sold in a certain area for the first time.

(2) The risks of physical deterioration and price fluctuation are avoided. These are important considerations where risks are particularly prevalent, as in the trade of livestock, fresh produce, and other perishable products.

(3) Working capital requirements are reduced because the cost of the consignment inventory is carried by the consignor.

OPERATION OF THE CONSIGNMENT

In the transfer of goods on consignment, a written contract should be prepared expressing the nature of the relationship and covering such matters as: credit terms to be granted by the consignee to customers; expenses of the consignee to be reimbursed by the consignor; commissions or profits to be allowed the consignee; care and handling of consignment inventories and proceeds from consignment sales; remittances and settlements by the consignee; and reports to be submitted by the consignee.

The rights and the duties of the consignee are established and defined by the laws of bailments and of agency, as modified by the Uniform Commercial Code.[1] Most important among these are the following:

Consignee's rights:

(1) The consignee is entitled to reimbursement for necessary expenditures on consigned goods and also to compensation for sales. Necessary expenditures depend upon the nature of the goods consigned and ordinarily include freight, insurance, taxes, storage, handling

---

[1]To maintain priority over general creditors of the consignee, the consignor must comply with the filing provisions of Article 9 of the Uniform Commercial Code, relating to security interests.

charges, repairs under warranties, and such other charges as are by custom borne by the consignor. Expenditures that are authorized by special agreement or that are chargeable by law to the account of the consignor, as well as amounts allowed as compensation on sales, represent liens by the consignee on consigned goods or on the sales proceeds. If the proceeds from consignment sales are insufficient to cover such charges, the consignee may claim such deficiency from the consignor.

(2) The consignee has the right to offer the customary warranties on goods that are sold, and the consignor is bound by the terms of such warranties.

Consignee's duties:

(1) The consignee must protect the goods of the principal in a reasonable and prudent manner consistent with the nature of the goods and the circumstances of the consignment. If the consignee has been given special instructions, those instructions must be followed diligently in order to avoid liability.

(2) The consignee must sell the consigned goods at the price that is authorized or, in the absence of a set price, at a price that will best satisfy the interests of the principal. Ordinarily, as a result of trade custom or contract, the consignee is accountable to the consignor for consignment sales in full, regardless of whether sales are made for cash or on account. On the other hand, there are instances when the consignee may be authorized by agreement or permitted by the custom of the trade to sell goods on account, with losses to be borne by the consignor and remittances to be made only after collections on account have been made. But the right of the consignee to sell goods on such a basis does not diminish the responsibility of exercising reasonable care in the sale of goods and in the collection of accounts. If these principles are observed, the consignee cannot be held liable for losses on collections. A consignee may agree to guarantee the accounts resulting from consignment sales. A *del credere agent* is a consignee who agrees to absorb such losses when they would otherwise be charged against the principal. Normally extra compensation is allowed for assuming the additional risk.

(3) The consignee must keep goods of the consignor apart from other merchandise. If physical separation is not practicable, the goods should be marked or records maintained that will make it possible to identify consigned goods. Consignment accounts receivable should not be combined with the consignee's own receivables. From a legal standpoint, cash proceeds from consignment sales should be kept separately until remittance is made. In practice, however, cash from consignment sales is frequently combined with the consignee's own cash in the absence of an agreement specifically calling for separation.

(4) The consignee must report regularly on the progress of consignment sales. The report that is rendered by the consignee is known as an *account sales*. This report lists the goods received on consignment, the goods sold, sales prices, expenses, the amount owed, and the

amount remitted. Records must be kept by the consignee to support the information reported on the account sales.

ACCOUNTING FOR THE CONSIGNMENT

The factors that distinguish the consignment from a sale must be recognized when the transfer of goods and subsequent transactions are recorded. The accounting procedures followed by the consignee and the consignor depend upon whether (1) consignment transactions are to be summarized separately and profits on individual consignments are to be calculated separately from profits on regular sales, or (2) consignment transactions are to be merged with other transactions of the consignee, with no attempt to distinguish between profits on consignment sales and profits on regular sales.

When profits on consignment sales are to be separately determined, the consignee maintains a consignment-in account for each consignment. This account is charged for all expenses that are to be absorbed by the consignor; it is credited for the full proceeds from consignment sales. The commission or profit on consignment sales is ultimately transferred from the consignment-in account to a separate revenue account, and the resulting balance in the consignment-in account reports the amount that is owed to the consignor in settlement.

When consignment transactions are to be combined with regular transactions, the consignee's entries for consignment sales are accompanied by entries debiting Purchases or Cost of Goods Sold and crediting the consignor for the amount to be paid for the goods sold. The consignee debits the consignor's accounts for expenses that are to be absorbed by the consignor. The resulting balance in the account with the consignor reports the amount owed in final settlement.

When profits on consignment sales are to be separately determined, the consignor maintains a consignment-out account for each consignment. This account is debited for the cost of merchandise shipped to the consignee and for all other expenses related to the consignment; it is credited for sales made by the consignee. Profit or loss from consignment sales is ultimately transferred from the consignment-out account to the income summary account in which the net result from all activities is summarized.

When consignment transactions are to be combined with other transactions and a single operating income or loss is to be calculated, the consignor records consignment revenues and expenses in the accounts that summarize regular operations.

Accounting for the Completed Consignment

To illustrate the entries that are required when final settlement of a consignment occurs before financial statements are prepared, assume that on June 6, the Western Co. ships 10 radio sets to R. Green on consignment. The sets are to be sold at an advertised price of $85. The consignee is to be allowed a commission of 20% and is to be reimbursed for any transportation costs. On July 24, Green sends cash to the consignor in settlement of the account together with the following account sales:

	R. GReen SEATTLE, WASHINGTON ACCOUNT SALES		NO. 2671

Sales for account of <u>Western Co.</u>
<u>Riverside, California</u>

DATE <u>June 30,</u> 19 <u>X3</u>

Account sales of <u>6 radio sets, Model AX 154</u>

DATE	EXPLANATION	AMOUNT	
6/6—6/30	Sales: 6 sets @ $85		$510
	On Hand: 4 sets		
	Charges: Freight in	$ 25	
	Commission (20% of Sales)	102	127
	Balance		$383
	Remittance enclosed		383
	Balance due		—

The transactions and the entries to record the transactions on the books of the consignee and of the consignor are listed on pages 160 and 161. The transaction explanations in the following paragraphs are identified by number. It is assumed that the consignee and the consignor do not maintain perpetual inventory records but use the periodic inventory system in arriving at cost of goods sold.

Consignee's records — if consignment profits are separately determined. *(1) Transfer of goods to the consignee.* The consignee records the receipt of goods on consignment by a memorandum in the journal or in a separate book maintained for such purposes. A supplementary record showing all of the detail with respect to goods received on consignment should be kept. Sometimes the receipt of goods is recorded in a memorandum entry. If the goods are billed at cost, at sales price, or at some arbitrary figure, the billed price may be used in making the entry. A memorandum entry in the example, using the sales price, would be:

Merchandise on Consignment.. 850
    Consignments Received — Western Co. 850

The detail to support the balance in the consignments received account may be maintained in a subsidiary ledger. When the goods are sold and an account sales is rendered, the memorandum entry is reversed.

Transactions	Consignee's Books	
	If consignment profits are separately determined	If consignment profits are not separately determined
June 6 (1) Shipment of 10 radio sets on consignment, cost to consignor, $50 each.	(Memorandum) Received 10 radio sets from Western Co. on consignment, to be sold at $85 each. Commission allowed is 20%. Reimbursement to be allowed for costs of freight.	(Memorandum)
June 6 (2) Expenses of consignor identified with consignment. Freight to consignee........... $60		

June 6–July 20
(3) Expenses of consignee chargeable to account of consignor:
    Freight in $25
	Consignment In —
	Western Co.................. 25
	    Cash......................... 25
		Western Co.................. 25
		    Cash......................... 25

June 6–July 20
(4) Sales of sets for cash, 10 at $85, or $850. (Charge by consignor is sales price, $850, less 20% commission, $170, or $680.)
	Cash............................ 850
	    Consignment In —
	    Western Co............... 850
		Cash............................ 850
		    Sales 850
		Purchases.................... 680
		    Western Co............... 680

July 20
(5) Charge by consignee for commissions on sales, 20% of $850, or $170.
	Consignment In —
	Western Co.................. 170
	    Commissions on
	    Consignment Sales.... 170	

July 20
(6) Remittance in settlement of account together with account sales rendered by consignee.
	Consignment In —
	Western Co.................. 655
	    Cash......................... 655
		Western Co.................. 655
		    Cash......................... 655

(2) Expenses of the consignor identified with the consignment. The consignee is not affected by transactions of the consignor.

(3) Expenses of the consignee identified with the consignment. The consignee records expenses that are to be absorbed by the consignor by debiting Consignment In and crediting appropriate asset or liability accounts. When an expense account on the consignee's books was originally debited with an expense that is to be absorbed entirely or in part by the consignor, Consignment In is debited and the expense account is credited for the amount chargeable to the consignor.

(4) Sales by the consignee. The consignee records consignment sales by debiting the appropriate asset account and crediting Consignment In.

(5) Commission or profit accruing to the consignee. The consignee records the commission or profit on consignment sales by debiting Consignment In and crediting an appropriate revenue account. After the commission or profit is recorded, the credit balance in Consignment In shows the amount that is owed to the consignor in final settlement.

Since no part of the consignee's expenses has been assigned to consignment commissions or profits, the consignment revenue account must be regarded as a gross profit balance. Such revenue, then, should be added to

Consignor's Books	
If consignment profits are separately determined	If consignment profits are not separately determined
Consignment Out — R. Green .... 500 Merchandise Shipments on Consignment. 500	(Memorandum) Shipped 10 radio sets to R. Green on consignment, sets to be sold at $85 each. Consignee is to be allowed commission of 20% and is to be reimbursed for costs of freight.
Consignment Out — R. Green.................... 60 Freight Out* 60	

Cash.. 655
Consignment Out — R. Green 195
  Consignment Out — R. Green   850
Consignment Out — R. Green 95
  Consignment Income   95
	Cash 655
	Freight.. 25
	Commissions 170
	  Sales 850

*It is assumed that the freight-out account was originally charged for freight on consignment sales as well as on other sales.

the gross profit from the consignee's own sales in preparing an income statement. In certain instances, the consignee may wish to develop net earnings balances for consignment operations and for regular operations. Such an income statement presentation will call for an allocation of operating expenses between the two classes of operations.

(6) *Remittance and account sales rendered by the consignee.* The consignee records remittances of cash to the consignor by debiting Consignment In and crediting Cash. If payment is made for the full amount owed, the entry to record the payment closes the consignment-in account.

In some instances a consignee is required to advance cash to the consignor upon receiving goods on consignment. Such advances are recognized as reductions in the amount owed to the consignor when settlement is made. Advances may be recorded by a debit to an asset account, Advances to Consignor, and a credit to Cash. When remittance is made by the consignee for the difference between the amount owed on consignment sales and the amount originally advanced, the account reporting the liability to the consignor is debited, the advances account is credited, and Cash is credited.

If goods are received on a consignment basis from a number of different parties, Consignments In may be set up as a controlling account, with debits and credits recorded in individual consignment accounts in a subsidiary ledger. When there are relatively few consignments, a separate account for each one may be carried in the general ledger.

Consignee's records — if consignment profits are not separately determined. *(1) Transfer of goods to the consignee.* The consignee records the receipt of goods on consignment by a memorandum entry.

(2) Expenses of the consignor identified with the consignment. The consignee is not affected by the transactions of the consignor.

(3) Expenses of the consignee identified with the consignment. The consignee debits the consignor's account for expenses chargeable to the consignor and credits appropriate asset or liability accounts or expense accounts if expenses were originally recorded in expense accounts.

(4) Sales by the consignee. The consignee records consignment sales like regular sales. Each sales entry is accompanied by an entry to record the charge made by the consignor for goods sold: Purchases or Cost of Goods Sold is debited and the consignor's account is credited.

(5) Commission or profit accruing to the consignee. The consignee makes no entry for commission or profit on consignment sales. The earnings on consignment sales will be reflected in the consignee's gross profit as a result of the preceding entries.

(6) Remittance and account sales rendered by the consignee. The consignee records payments to the consignor by debiting the consignor's account and crediting Cash.

Consignor's records — if consignment profits are separately determined. *(1) Transfer of goods to the consignee.* The consignor records the transfer of goods to the consignee by debiting Consignment Out and crediting Merchandise Shipments on Consignment or an inventory account when perpetual inventory balances are maintained. Merchandise Shipments on Consignment is treated as a subtraction item from the sum of the beginning inventory and purchases in determining the cost of goods available for regular sales. Transfers are recorded at cost even though selling or other arbitrary prices are assigned to the goods in statements sent to the consignee.

(2) Expenses of the consignor identified with the consignment. The consignor records expenses that are related to the consignment by debiting Consignment Out and crediting Cash or liability accounts. When an expense account was originally debited for an expense that is related to the consignment, Consignment Out is debited and the expense account is credited for the amount identified with the consignment.

(3), (4), (5) Expenses of the consignee identified with the consignment — sales by the consignee — commission charge by the consignee. The consignor makes no entries for transactions of the consignee until a statement is received from the consignee.

(6) Remittance and account sales rendered by the consignee. When the consignor receives an account sales, Cash is debited for the cash remittance,

Consignment Out is debited for the total expenses charged to the consignor's account by the consignee, and Consignment Out is credited for the gross sales reported by the consignee. It would be possible to debit Cash and credit Consignment Out for the net proceeds from consignment sales. If this procedure were followed, the entry for transaction (6) in the example would be:

```
Cash.....................................................................................    655
    Consignment Out — R. Green...................................................           655
```

The balance in the consignment-out account would be the same in either case.

When the consignor requires cash advances on consignment shipments, the receipt of cash representing an advance may be recorded by debiting Cash and crediting a liability account, Advances from Consignee. The receipt of cash in settlement of the consignment, then, will call for debits to Cash and to the advances account accompanied by entries to the consignment-out account recognizing revenues and expenses reported by the consignee.

When all of the consigned goods have been sold, the consignment account shows the net result from consignment transactions: a credit balance indicates that consignment revenue has exceeded consignment expenses, resulting in a profit; a debit balance indicates that expenses have exceeded revenue, resulting in a loss. The balance in the consignment account may now be transferred to a consignment income account. The balance of the latter account is subsequently closed into the general income summary account in which other operations of the business are summarized. The balance in the income summary account reporting the profit or loss from regular as well as consignment operations is ultimately transferred to capital.

If consignments are numerous, Consignments Out may be set up as a controlling account and data relating to each consignment may be recorded in an individual account in a subsidiary ledger. If consignments are relatively few, a separate account for each consignment may be carried in the general ledger.

Consignor's records — if consignment profits are not separately determined. *(1) Transfer of goods to the consignee.* When the consignor does not maintain perpetual inventory records, the transfer of goods to the consignee is recorded by a memorandum entry in the journal or in a separate book maintained for this purpose. A supplementary record showing all of the detail with respect to goods on consignment should be kept. Sometimes shipments are recorded in a memorandum entry. Such an entry for transaction (1) in the example would be:

```
Merchandise on Consignment — R. Green ...................................    500
    Consignment Transfers ...........................................................          500
```

The detail to support the balance in the account Merchandise on Consignment may be provided in a subsidiary record. When the consigned goods are sold, the memorandum entry is reversed.

If perpetual inventory records are maintained, the transfer of goods would require an entry as follows:

Merchandise on Consignment — R. Green 500
   Merchandise Inventory (or Finished Goods) ....:...   500

(2) Expenses of the consignor identified with the consignment. The usual accounts are charged for consignment expenses, with no attempt to distinguish between consignment expenses and expenses related to regular sales.

(3), (4), (5) Expenses of the consignee identified with the consignment — sales by the consignee — commission charge by the consignee. The consignor makes no entries for transactions completed by the consignee until a statement is received from the consignee.

(6) Remittance and account sales rendered by the consignee. When the consignor receives an account sales, Cash is debited for the cash accompanying the statement, expense accounts are debited for expenses charged to the consignor's account by the consignee, and Sales is credited for the gross sales reported by the consignee. In the absence of perpetual inventories, an entry for the ending inventories establishes cost of goods sold for the period. If perpetual inventories are employed, the cost of goods sold balance on the books relating to the regular sales must be increased by the cost of goods sold relating to consignment sales by the following entry:

Cost of Goods Sold 500
   Merchandise on Consignment — R. Green   500

With sales, cost of goods sold, and expenses reflecting combined consignment and regular operations, further adjustments are made in the usual manner. Nominal accounts may then be closed into the income summary account, and the income or loss from combined operations is ultimately transferred to capital.

Accounting for an Uncompleted Consignment

In the illustration on pages 160 and 161, the profit from consignment sales was not recognized by consignee or consignor until all the consigned goods were sold and full remittance was made. If all the consigned goods are not sold at the time the parties to a consignment prepare financial statements, it becomes necessary to compute the profit realized on the part that was sold. The nature of the problems that arise and the entries that are made on the books of the consignee and the consignor for an uncompleted consignment are illustrated in the following example.

Assume the consignment of goods as in the previous example but assume that both consignee and consignor prepare financial statements on June 30. On this date 6 sets have been sold, and the consignee submits the following account sales:

R. Green

SEATTLE, WASHINGTON

ACCOUNT SALES

NO. 2843

DATE July 24, 19X3

Sales for account of Western Co.
Riverside, California

Account sales of 10 radio sets, Model AX 154

DATE	EXPLANATION	AMOUNT	
6/6—7/20	Sales: 10 radio sets @ $85		$850
	Charges: Freight in	$ 25	
	Commission (20% of Sales)	170	195
	Balance		$655
	Remittance enclosed		655
	Balance due		–

The entries to record the transactions on the books of the consignee and the consignor are given on pages 166 and 167. The entries to be made for an uncompleted consignment on the books of the consignee and the consignor are explained in the following paragraphs.

Consignee's records — if consignment profits are separately determined. The consignee should recognize the earnings on consignment sales before preparing financial statements at the end of each period by debiting Consignment In and crediting revenue for the commissions or profit on consignment sales to date. A credit balance in the consignment-in account after this entry indicates that proceeds from consignment sales exceeded the charges to the consignor, resulting in an obligation to the consignor; a credit balance is reported on the balance sheet as a current liability. A debit balance in the consignment-in account would indicate that proceeds from consignment sales were less than the charges to the consignor. The consignee may hold the consignor for reimbursement of this amount if it is not covered by subsequent sales. A debit balance in the consignment-in account would be reported on the balance sheet as a current asset (receivable).

Consignee's records — if consignment profits are not separately determined. No entry is necessary at the end of the period if entries at the time consigned goods are sold recognize purchases or cost of goods sold and the obligation to the consignor. A credit balance in the consignor's account at the end of the period is reported on the balance sheet as a current liability; a debit balance would be reported as a current asset (receivable).

Transactions	Consignee's Books	
	If consignment profits are separately determined	If consignment profits are not separately determined
June 6 Shipment of 10 radio sets on consignment, cost to consignor, $50 each.	(Memorandum)	(Memorandum)
June 6 Expenses of consignor identified with consignment: Freight to consignee........... $60		

June 6–June 30
Expenses of consignee chargeable to account of consignor:
Freight in $25
	Consignment In —
	Western Co.................. 25
	  Cash........................ 25
		Western Co.................. 25
		  Cash........................ 25

June 6–June 30
Sales of sets for cash, 6 at $85, or $510. (Charge by consignor is sales price, $510, less 20% commission, $102, or $408.)
	Cash........................... 510
	  Consignment In —
	  Western Co.............. 510
		Cash........................... 510
		  Sales 510
		Purchases................... 408
		  Western Co.............. 408

June 30
Charge by consignee for commissions on sales, 20% of $510, or $102.
	Consignment In —
	Western Co.................. 102
	  Commissions on
	  Consignment Sales.... 102	

June 30
Remittance for balance owed, together with account sales rendered by consignee.
	Consignment In —
	Western Co.................. 383
	  Cash........................ 383
		Western Co.................. 383
		  Cash........................ 383

Consignor's records — if consignment profits are separately determined. At the end of a fiscal period, the consignor must receive an account sales in order to record the profit or loss on sales of consigned goods to date. The data disclosed by the account sales are recorded in the usual manner. The consignment-out account then shows expenses identified with the consignment and revenue from consignment sales. The profit on consignment sales to date must now be removed from the consignment-out account; this will leave the account with a debit balance representing the charges identified with the goods not yet sold. The balance in the consignment-out account is reported on the balance sheet as a part of the company's inventories.

In the example, the consignment-out account shows debits of $687, consisting of the cost of the consigned goods, $500, freight to the consignee, $60, freight in, $25, and commissions, $102. Those charges relating to consigned goods sold should be applied against current revenue; those charges relating to consigned goods still on hand are properly deferred so that they can be assigned to revenue of subsequent periods. Freight charges are ap-

Consignor's Books	
If consignment profits are separately determined	If consignment profits are not separately determined

		(Memorandum)	
Consignment Out — R. Green	500		
Merchandise Shipments on Consignment.	500		
Consignment Out — R. Green	60		
Freight Out..	60		

Cash..	383	Cash...	383	
Consignment Out — R. Green	127	Freight..	15	
Consignment Out — R. Green	510	Commissions	102	
		Merchandise on Consignment....................	10	
Consignment Out — R. Green	57	Sales		510
Consignment Income	57			
		Merchandise on Consignment....................	224	
		Income Summary		200
		Freight Out...		24

plicable to all of the goods shipped and hence are assigned to current and future revenues in the same manner as the original cost of consigned goods. The commission charge is limited to consignment sales of the current period and hence is assigned in total to current revenues. The charges to current revenue and to revenue of subsequent periods are summarized below.

	Total Charges	Charges Identified With Consignment Sales (6 sets)	Charges Identified With Consignment Inventory (4 sets)
Charges by consignor:			
Cost of consigned merchandise.................	$500	$300	$200
Freight to consignee....	60	36	24
Charges by consignee:			
Freight in....................	25	15	10
Commissions..............	102	102	
Totals...........................	$687	$453	$234

The tabulation at the bottom of page 167 shows charges of $453 relating to consignment sales. The sales figure of $510 recorded by the consignor as a credit to Consignment Out represents a recovery of consignment costs of $453 and a profit of $57. The entry to transfer the profit of $57 from the consignment-out account to a consignment income account increases the debit balance in Consignment Out from $177 to $234. Consignment Out then reports the charges relating to unsold goods on consignment, and this balance is carried into the next period.

The consignment-out account with R. Green, after adjustment at the end of the fiscal period, appears as follows.

Consignment Out — R. Green

June 6 Shipped 10 radio sets, cost		June 30 Sales, 6 sets............................		510
$50 each	500	30 Balance — cost assigned to in-		
6 Freight	60	ventory of 4 sets:		
June 30 Charges by consignee:		Cost, 4 sets at $50.......	200	
Freight in...................... 25		Additional charges:		
Commissions................ 102	127	Incurred by consignor:		
		freight (4/10 of $60) .	24	
30 Profit on sale of 6 sets to Con-		Incurred by consignee:		
signment Income	57	freight in (4/10 of		
		$25)........................	10	234
	744			744
July 1 Balance — cost assigned to 4				
sets.....................................	234			

If the consignor does not record the charges made by the consignee, but credits the consignment account for the net proceeds from consignment sales, the entry on June 30 would be:

Cash	383	
Consignment Out — R. Green		383

The balance in the consignment-out account would be the same as when charges by the consignee and gross sales are reported in the account. The adjustment for the profit of $57 would be the same as in the previous instances.

The balance in the consignment-out account is reported on the balance sheet as a separate inventory item that is added to the merchandise on hand, as follows:

Inventories:		
Merchandise on hand	$10,000	
Merchandise on consignment	234	$10,234

If preferred, the original cost of the consigned goods, $200, and the additional consignment charges that are deferred, $34, could be reported separately.

During the next period, consignment shipments, expenses, and sales are recorded in the consignment-out account in the usual manner. At the end of the period this account is adjusted once more in recognizing the profit on consignment sales of the period and the charges that are to be related to the goods still on consignment.

There may be instances in which the consignee, in rendering a statement to the consignor, fails to remit the full amount owed. In this situation, the consignor debits Accounts Receivable instead of Cash. For example, if Green reports the sale of 6 sets but remits only $150, an entry would be made as follows:

Cash..	150	
Accounts Receivable — R. Green..	233	
Consignment Out — R. Green..	127	
Consignment Out — R. Green..		510

The receipt of cash at a later date would be recorded by a debit to Cash and a credit to Accounts Receivable — R. Green.

Consignor's records — if consignment profits are not separately determined. When consignment profits are not separately determined, the consignor records the charges made by the consignee against the proceeds from consignment sales by debiting appropriate expense accounts. When the consigned goods have not all been sold at the end of a fiscal period, however, those expenses that are identified with the unsold goods on consignment should be deferred. Data on the account sales are analyzed and a compound entry is made as follows: Cash is debited for the cash remitted by the consignee or Accounts Receivable is debited for the amount due from the consignee; expense accounts are debited for charges made by the consignee on goods that have been sold; Merchandise on Consignment is debited for the consignee's charges on goods not yet sold; and Sales is credited for the total consignment sales.

Those charges incurred by the consignor that relate to unsold goods on consignment must also be set up as consignment inventory at the end of the period. In the absence of perpetual inventories, Merchandise on Consignment is debited for the sum of the original cost of merchandise and the other charges relating to the unsold goods; the income summary account is credited for the original cost of these goods, and the consignor's expense accounts are credited for the portion of the expenses relating to this inventory. If perpetual inventory records are maintained, the transfer of goods to the consignee would have been recorded originally by a debit to Merchandise on Consignment and a credit to the inventory account. Instead of recording the amount of the goods in the hands of the consignee at the end of the period, then, it would be necessary to reduce the consignment inventory balance and debit Cost of Goods Sold for the goods sold by the consignee. This entry would be accompanied by an entry to defer expenses reported on the consignor's books relating to the portion of goods still unsold.

Merchandise on Consignment, after adjustments on the books of the consignor, includes the original cost of the goods increased by the deferred expenses of both consignee and consignor relating to the unsold goods. In the example, the $234 balance for merchandise on consignment consists of: original cost of goods, $200; deferred expenses of the consignee, $10; and deferred expenses of the consignor, $24.

Consignment Reshipments

In the previous examples, freight charges, whether incurred by consignor or consignee, were costs of bringing goods to the point of the sale and hence were properly viewed as acquisition costs and assignable to the inventory. When consigned goods are returned to a consignor, expenditures identified with the original shipment of goods as well as with their return should be recognized as an expense. The reshipment of goods to a consignee, then, calls for charges that are no more than those which would normally apply to such transfer. Expenditures for the repair of defective units returned should similarly be regarded as an expense, with subsequent transfer of such units to a consignee calling for charges that are no more than normal costs. Shipping charges to customers that are necessary in completing sales, when paid by the consignor or when chargeable to the consignor require recognition as expenses of the period.

Alternative Accounting Procedures

While this chapter has dealt with the standard procedures that are employed in the consignment relationship, other methods of accounting may be employed as long as the accounts properly report the personal and legal relationships of the parties. Variations from standard procedures are often introduced to meet special requirements or to provide particular information concerning consignment activities for reporting purposes. For example, assume that the consignee desires to maintain consignment income detail but does not want to combine this information with data summarizing regular operating activities for reporting purposes. The procedure previously outlined for the consignee can be followed, but consignment sales, consignment purchases, and consignment expenses would be summarized in separate accounts. This detail can then be reported in a separate section of the income statement or it can be summarized in a supporting schedule with only the net income from consignment sales reported on the income statement.

Similarly, the consignor, while wishing to maintain consignment income detail, may wish to distinguish between these data and other operating data on the income statement. When this is the case, the previously illustrated procedure for the consignor can be followed, but separate accounts would be maintained for consignment sales, consignment cost of sales, and consignment expenses. Such procedure permits full information concerning both consignment and regular operations. Consignment income data may be reported separately on the income statement, or these data may be summarized on a supporting schedule with only the net results from consignment operations reported on the income statement.

QUESTIONS

1. Distinguish between a sale and a consignment.

2. "A consignment is regarded as a bailment." "The relationship of consignor and consignee is one of principal and agent." Explain.

3. What are the advantages of a consignment over a sale from the point of view of (a) the consignor and (b) the consignee?

4. What are the duties of the consignee?

5. Explain two methods for recording consignment activities on the books of the consignee. What will determine the procedure that is to be used?

6. Explain two methods for recording consignment activities on the books of the consignor. What will determine the procedure to be used?

7. What entries are made on the books of the consignee and the consignor for each transaction listed below, assuming that each party summarizes consignment transactions separately and calculates consignment profit apart from profit on other sales?

   (a) Goods are transferred by the consignor to the consignee.
   (b) The consignor pays expenses relating to the consignment.
   (c) The consignee pays expenses relating to the consignment but is to be reimbursed for such disbursements by the consignor.
   (d) The consignee pays expenses relating to the consignment that are not reimbursable.
   (e) The consignee sells consigned merchandise on account.
   (f) The consignee collects consignment accounts receivable.
   (g) The consignee makes settlement with the consignor.

8. What entry would be made on the books of the consignee and the consignor for each transaction listed in Question 7, assuming that each party combines consignment transactions with other transactions and calculates a single profit for both consignment and regular sales?

9. State for each account below: (a) whether it would appear on the books of the consignee or the books of the consignor, and (b) how it would be reported on the financial statements that are prepared at the end of the fiscal period.

   (a) Consignment In (credit balance).
   (b) Consignment In (debit balance).
   (c) Consignment Out (debit balance).
   (d) Commissions on Consignments (credit balance).
   (e) Income on Consignment Sales.
   (f) Merchandise on Consignment.
   (g) Consignment Expenses Deferred.
   (h) Merchandise Shipments to Consignees.

10. The Burkhart Co. is advised by a consignee that sales of consigned merchandise have been made on account and that reimbursement will follow in a later period. What treatment will this require on the books of the consignor?

11. Justify the practice of showing merchandise on consignment on the consignor's balance sheet at a figure above the original invoice cost of such goods.

12. The Burnside Co. transfers merchandise to a number of dealers on a consignment basis. At the end of each period, goods on consignment are reported on the balance sheet at cost, and all consignment expenses of the period are regarded as chargeable to current revenue. Would you approve such statements?

13. The Paulson Co. transfers merchandise on a consignment basis and records such transfers in the same manner as sales on account. (a) Do you object to this procedure? (b) What adjustments are required at the end of the period for consigned goods still in the hands of the consignee under these circumstances?

14. The Garrett Company makes the following entry upon shipping merchandise on a consignment basis:

```
Accounts Receivable — Consignees................................  xxx
    Merchandise .............................................        xxx
    Deferred Gross Profit on Consignment Sales .................     xxx
```

Do you object to this procedure? What entries would you assume are made during the period and at the end of the period?

15. A consignee returns a shipment of unsold goods. How would you recommend that the consignor treat the original charges in transferring goods to the consignee and the subsequent charges when goods are returned?

EXERCISES

1. A. M. Anderson submits the following information on an account sales.

<table>
<tr><td colspan="3" align="center">A. M. Anderson
Atlanta, Georgia
ACCOUNT SALES</td><td align="right">NO. 4819</td></tr>
</table>

DATE Dec. 31,   19 X8

Sales for account of <u>Warner and Sloan</u>
<u>Jacksonville, Florida</u>

Account sales of <u>4 electric stoves, Model 53498—4329XF</u>

DATE	EXPLANATION	AMOUNT	
12/5-12/31	Sales: 4 electric stoves @ $110		$440
	On Hand: 6 electric stoves		
	Charges: Freight in	$ 61	
	Commission (25% of Sales)	110	171
	Balance		$269
	Remittance enclosed		269
	Balance due		–

The cost of each unit to the consignor is $60. Consignee and consignor take physical inventories at year-end in calculating cost of goods sold. (a) Prepare the entries that will appear on the books of the consignee and the consignor, assuming that each party calculates consignment profits separately. (b) Prepare the entries on each party's books, assuming that consignment profits are not calculated separately.

2. A consignment-out account on the books of Parks, Inc., appears as follows. What entry would be made on November 30 to adjust the account?

Consignment Out — T. A. Fuller

Nov. 15 10 radio sets 400	Nov. 30 Sales, 4 sets.......... 340
15 Freight out............ 20	(Remittance by consignee,
30 Charges by con-	$340, less charges, $123)
signee:	
Freight in 55	
Commissions 68 123	

3. In Exercise 2, assume that Parks, Inc. does not maintain consignment-out accounts but merges consignment transactions with other transactions on its books. Assume, further, that the consignor maintains perpetual inventory records. What entries would be made on the consignor's books to record the consignment transactions?

4. On May 1 the Select Products Co. ships 5 appliances to the Jones Hardware Co. on consignment. Each unit is to be sold at $250, payable $50 in the month of purchase and $10 per month thereafter. The consignee is to be entitled to 20% of all amounts collected on consignment sales. Jones Hardware sells 3 appliances in May and 1 in June. Regular monthly collections are made by the consignee, and appropriate cash remittances are made to the consignor at the end of each month. The cost of the appliances shipped by the consignor was $155 per unit. The consignor paid shipping costs to the consignee totaling $50. The consignor recognizes profits in the period in which the consignment sales are made. Assuming that both consignee and consignor report consignment profits separately, prepare the entries that would be made on each party's books to record the transactions for May and June, including any adjustments that would be made at the end of June in preparing semiannual financial statements.

5. In December, the Whitworth Publishing Company ships 20 sets of books to a book dealer on consignment. The consignor maintains a cost accounting system and perpetual inventories; the cost of manufacturing each set is $30. At the end of December the dealer reports the sale of 6 sets at $49.75 each and remits sales proceeds less 20% representing commissions and $15 for freight paid by the consignee on the receipt of the sets. What are the entries on the books of the consignor, assuming that profits from consignments are not recorded separately on the consignor's books?

PROBLEMS

6-1. On June 1, Lee Co. shipped 25 radio sets to A. M. Fields on consignment. The sets are to be sold at an advertised price of $200. The cost of each set to the consignor was $100. The cost of shipment paid by the consignor was $75. The consignor agreed to absorb the consignee's expenditures for freight and also to allow the consignee $10 for delivery and installation of each set. Commission is to be 25% of the sales price. On June 30, Fields submitted the following summary of consignment sales:

Sets received		25
Sets sold...	8	
Sets returned to consignor (defective)......................	2	10
Sets on hand..		15
June 3–30 Sales, 8 sets at $200...............................		$1,600
Charges:		
Freight in..	$ 50	
Deliveries and installation expenses......	80	
Commissions, 25% of sales..................	400	530
		$1,070
Remittance enclosed		250
Balance owed (collections from customers not yet made)...............................		$ 820

Instructions: Prepare all of the entries to record the foregoing as well as any adjustments that are required at the end of the period on (1) the consignee's books and (2) the consignor's books. Assume that consignment profits are separately determined by both parties; neither party maintains perpetual inventories.

6-2. The Wilson Publishing Company ships 4-volume sets of *Management Encyclopaedia* to book dealers on consignment. The sets are to be sold at an advertised price of $49.50. The estimated cost per set is $25. Consignees are allowed a commission of 30% of the sales price and are to be reimbursed for freight relating to consigned goods.

On December 8, 100 sets were sent to the Culver Book Store on consignment. The consignor estimated that packing charges of $85 were related to the books shipped. The shipment cost paid by the consignor was $200. The consignee paid $30 for freight on sets received. Sixty sets were sold in December for cash. Remittance of the amount owed to the consignor was made on December 31. Both consignee and consignor take physical inventories and adjust and close their books at year-end.

Instructions: (1) Prepare an account sales to be submitted by the consignee at the end of December.

(2) Prepare the journal entries for December on the books of the consignee, assuming that (a) consignment profits are calculated separately and (b) consignment profits are not calculated separately.

(3) Prepare the journal entries for December on the books of the consignor, assuming that (a) profits from consignments are calculated separately and (b) profits are not calculated separately.

6-3. Television, Inc., agrees to transfer television sets to Brooks Co. on a consignment basis. The consignee is to sell sets at $398 and is to receive a 25% commission on the sales price. The consignor agrees to reimburse the consignee for all expenses related to the consignment. The agreement also calls for an advance payment of $100 per set by the consignee; the $100 advance is to be deducted as settlement is made for each set sold. The consignee is to provide an account sales quarterly and is to make cash remittance for the amount owed at that time.

Transactions for the period October 1–December 31 are listed below.

(a) The consignor shipped 10 sets to the consignee. The consignor maintains a cost accounting system and perpetual inventories; records show a cost for each set of $210.
(b) The consignor paid freight charges on the shipment, $165.
(c) The consignee made advance payments on the sets received.
(d) The consignee sold 6 sets for cash; expenses of delivery and installation chargeable to the consignor were $75.
(e) The consignee returned 2 sets representing a model that could not be sold and paid freight charges of $40 on the return.
(f) The consignee prepared an account sales and made cash settlement on December 31.

Instructions: (1) Prepare the account sales to be submitted by the consignee.

(2) Prepare the entries that would be made by the consignee, assuming that (a) consignment profits are calculated separately and (b) consignment profits are not calculated separately.

(3) Prepare the entries that would be made by the consignor, assuming that (a) consignment profits are calculated separately and (b) consignment profits are not calculated separately.

6-4. The Duncan Corporation manufactures refrigerators and maintains a cost accounting system and perpetual inventory records. On July 3, 19X5, 10 refrigerators were sent to the Victory Electric Store on consignment. Account sales, together with remittances, at the end of July and August were as follows:

Victory Electric Store
Denver, Colorado
ACCOUNT SALES

NO. 96185

DATE July 31, 19 X5

Sales for account of Duncan Corporation
Colorado Springs, Colorado

Account sales of 4 refrigerators, Model CV34684

DATE	EXPLANATION		AMOUNT
7/7-7/31	Sales: 4 refrigerators @ $280		$1,120
	On Hand: 6 refrigerators		
	Charges: Freight in	$150	
	Delivery	60	210
	Balance		$ 910
	Remittance enclosed		60
	Balance due		$ 850

	Victory Electric Store Denver, Colorado ACCOUNT SALES		NO. 97346	

DATE Aug. 31, 19 X5

Sales for account of Duncan Corporation
                                     Colorado Springs, Colorado

Account sales of 3 refrigerators, Model CV34684

DATE	EXPLANATION	AMOUNT
7/31	Balance due	$ 850
8/1-8/31	Sales: 3 refrigerators @ $280	840
	On Hand: 3 refrigerators	
	Charges: Freight in Delivery	
	Balance	$1,690
	Remittance enclosed	330
	Balance due	$1,360

The consignee was allowed to set the sales price but was charged $280 for each refrigerator sold. The consignee was to be reimbursed for freight and transportation charges. The consignor's cost to manufacture each unit was $196.

Sales on account by the Victory Electric Store were as follows:

July 7–July 31 4 refrigerators at $400 .... $1,600
Aug. 1–Aug. 31 3 refrigerators at $370 1,110

Collections on account were as follows:

July.. $750
August.. 600

Both consignor and consignee prepare financial statements at the end of each month.

Instructions: (1) Prepare the journal entries required on the books of the consignee for July and August, assuming that consignment sales are merged with regular sales.

(2) Prepare the journal entries required on the books of the consignor for July and August, assuming that records show separately the profit on consignments.

6-5. The Aristocrat Co. ships electric shavers to Ray Jensen on consignment. The cost of shavers to the consignor is $10.80. Sales are to be made at an advertised price of $24. The consignee is allowed a commission of 25% of sales plus an allowance for advertising not to exceed $100. The following transactions take place in December:

100 shavers were shipped to Jensen.
The Aristocrat Co. paid shipment charges on goods sent to consignee, $50.
Jensen paid for advertising consigned goods, $150.

Jensen accepted a sight draft drawn by Aristocrat Co., $400.

Jensen sold 80 shavers during the month at the advertised price.

Jensen made remittance at the end of the month for the balance owed to date.

Both consignor and consignee prepare financial statements at the end of December.

Instructions: (1) Prepare an account sales to be submitted by the consignee at the end of December.

(2) Prepare the journal entries on the books of the consignee, assuming that (a) consignment profits are calculated separately and (b) consignment profits are not calculated separately.

(3) Prepare the journal entries on the books of the consignor, assuming that (a) consignment profits are calculated separately and (b) consignment profits are not calculated separately. Assume that the consignor does not maintain perpetual inventory records but takes year-end physical inventories.

6-6. In examining the accounts of the Mack Co., the auditor determined that consignments of Product A had been recorded as sales during the fiscal period. As consignment shipments were made, receivable accounts with consignees were debited and Sales was credited. At that time, Cost of Goods Sold was debited and Inventories was credited for the cost of the merchandise shipped. Receivable accounts were credited when cash was received from consignees; costs incurred by the consignees but chargeable to the consignor were recognized when remittances were recorded. The trial balance of the Mack Co. on December 31, 19X4, follows:

Cash	18,000	
Receivables — Customers	24,000	
Receivables — Consignees	18,200	
Inventories	46,500	
Plant and Equipment (net)	50,000	
Accounts Payable		25,000
Capital Stock, $1 par		50,000
Retained Earnings, January 1, 19X4		47,500
Sales		236,000
Cost of Goods Sold	165,000	
Operating Expenses	36,800	
	358,500	358,500

An analysis of account sales as of this date revealed that 2,000 units of Product A were still unsold and in the hands of consignees. This product was charged to consignees at $5 per unit but had a cost of $3.25. Expenses of $400 chargeable to the consignor had been incurred by consignees but had not been recognized. Of this total, $125 represents expenses on consigned goods not yet sold. In addition, expenses of $260 on the consignor's books were related to consignment inventories. Because of a loss carryover from 19X3, the company will not pay any income tax for 19X4.

Instructions: (1) Prepare the journal entries that are required on the books of the Mack Co. to bring the accounts up to date and to close the accounts on December 31.

(2) Prepare a balance sheet and an income statement for the year ended December 31, 19X4.

6-7. The Morrison Co. records shipments to consignees A, B, and C as sales on account. When the sale is recorded, Cost of Goods Sold is debited and Inventories is credited for the cost of goods shipped to consignees. Expenses incurred by consignees and to be absorbed by the consignor are recognized when remittances are made by the consignees. The trial balance of the Morrison Co. on December 31, 19X0, follows:

Cash	57,750	
Accounts Receivable	50,000	
Inventories	56,000	
Plant and Equipment	85,000	
Accounts Payable		12,500
Capital Stock, $100 par		100,000
Retained Earnings, January 1, 19X0		28,500
Sales		365,000
Cost of Goods Sold	213,250	
Operating Expenses	44,000	
	506,000	506,000

The product sold by the corporation is charged to consignees at $30 but costs only $16 per unit. The consignee sets the retail price. The following account sales and accompanying remittances are from A, B, and C on December 31. Remittances and supplementary data have not yet been recorded.

	A	B	C
Units received	15	40	5
Units sold	10	25	1
Units returned (now in transit)	5	0	4
Units on hand	0	15	0
Sales	$300	$750	$ 30
Delivery	20	80	18
Cost of returning sets to consignor	25		30
Remittance enclosed	$255	$670	
Balance due from consignor			$ 18

Expenses of $85 on the consignor's books are estimated to be related to the 15 units in the hands of B. Income taxes are estimated at $45,000.

Instructions: (1) Prepare the journal entries that are required on the books of the Morrison Co. to bring the accounts up to date and to close the accounts on December 31.

(2) Prepare a balance sheet and an income statement for the year ended December 31, 19X0.

6-8. You are examining the December 31, 19X9, financial statements of the Kelly Company, a new client. The company was established on January 1, 19X8, and is a distributor of air conditioning units. The company's income statements for 19X8 and 19X9 were presented to you as follows:

Kelly Company
Statements of Income and Expense
For the Years Ended December 31, 19X9 and 19X8

	19X9	19X8
Sales	$1,287,500	$1,075,000
Cost of goods sold	669,500	559,000
Gross profit	$ 618,000	$ 516,000
Selling and administrative expense	403,500	330,000
Income before income tax	$ 214,500	$ 186,000
Provision for income tax @ 50%	107,250	93,000
Net income	$ 107,250	$ 93,000

Your examination disclosed the following:

(1) Some sales were made on open account; other sales were made through dealers to whom units were shipped on a consignment basis. Both sales methods were in effect in 19X8 and 19X9. In both years, however, the company treated all shipments as outright sales.

(2) The sales price and cost of the units were the same in 19X8 and 19X9. Each unit had a cost of $130 and was uniformly invoiced at $250 to open account customers and to consignees.

(3) During 19X9 the amount of cash received from consignees in payment for units sold by them was $706,500. Consignees remit for the units as soon as they are sold. Confirmations received from consignees showed that they had a total of 23 unsold units on hand at December 31, 19X9. Consignees were unable to confirm the unsold units on hand at December 31, 19X8.

(4) The cost of goods sold for 19X9 was determined by the client as follows:

	Units	
Inventory on hand in warehouse, December 31, 19X8	1,510	
Purchases	4,454	
Available for sale	5,964	
Inventory on hand in warehouse, December 31, 19X9	814	
Shipments to: open account customers	3,008	
consignee customers	2,142	5,150 @ $130 = $669,500

Instructions: (1) Compute the total amount of the Kelly Company's inventory at:

    (a) December 31, 19X9.

    (b) December 31, 19X8.

(2) Prepare the auditor's work sheet journal entries to correct the financial statements for the year ended December 31, 19X8.

(3) Prepare the formal adjusting journal entries to correct the accounts at December 31, 19X9. (The books have not been closed. Do not prepare the closing journal entries.) (AICPA adapted)

6-9. The Stacy Company is closing its books as of December 31, 19X7. In making an investigation of the accounts of the company, you discover the following facts:

(1) During November and December, the company shipped out stoves to two dealers, A and B, on a consignment basis. The consignment agreements provided that the stoves were to be sold by the consignee at a list price of $180 each. The consignee was to be allowed a 25% commission on each sale and was to be reimbursed for all expenses paid in connection with the shipment of the stoves. Sales on account are at the risk of the consignee.

(2) At the time of each shipment, the company debited a trade account receivable and for each stove credited Sales $120, the usual sale price received by the company, on the basis of which a gross profit of 20% on cost is realized.

(3) All cash received from these two consignees was credited to the trade accounts receivable accounts. No other entries have been made in these accounts receivable.

(4) Information as to all of the transactions with the consignees is as follows:
   (a) Stoves shipped out: to A — 100, to B — 40.
   (b) Stoves unsold by consignees as of 12/31/X7: A — 35, B — 25.
   (c) Crating and shipping cost to company — $84.
   (d) Freight paid by consignees: A — $130, B — $100.
   (e) Cash advanced by A at date of receipt of the first 80 stoves — $4,000. Cash subsequently remitted by A — $5,395.
   (f) Cash remitted by B — $575.

Instructions: Prepare any adjusting entries that should be made by the Stacy Company and list each account affected by these transactions and adjustments, showing the corrected balances after adjustment. (Assume that (1) inventories are maintained on a perpetual basis and (2) consignment profits are not separately determined.)

(AICPA adapted)

6-10. On June 1, 19X5, the Adams Corporation consigned 100 refrigerators to the Burke Company, to be sold as follows:

Cash price: $180 less 5% discount.
Time-payment plan: $180 net, ⅓ in cash on delivery, the balance in 24 monthly payments of $5. All credit sales are subject to the approval of the Adams Corporation as to credit risk. Refrigerators will be repossessed when time-payment contracts are 2 months in default and will be returned to the manufacturer for reconditioning.

The manufacturing cost of each refrigerator was $60, and $400 freight was prepaid on the shipment.

The Burke Company paid $200 truckage and deposited $7,500 cash with the consignor, thus advancing in all $7,700 to secure the consignment. This sum is to remain credited to the Burke Company until all refrigerators are sold and fully paid or repossessed. However, on December 31 of the current year, and thereafter on the last day of each month, the consignor must refund to the Burke Company the amount, if any, by which the original deposit exceeds the aggregate of (1) the full sales price of the unsold refrigerators and (2) the uncollected installments on time payment contracts.

The Burke Company will receive a commission of $30 on each refrigerator sold for cash or on approved time-payment contract. The Burke Company will promptly remit all collections, less commissions in full, on all such sales. Commissions on defaulted contracts that had been approved by the Adams Corporation will not be recoverable from the Burke Company.

On June 30 the Burke Company reported that it had sold 60 refrigerators, 20 for cash and 40 on the time-payment plan. The latter sales had been duly approved by the Adams Corporation. The amounts collected had been remitted according to agreement.

Installments on the 40 time-payment contracts were collected for July, August, and September and were remitted.

In October and November, collections were made and remitted on only 30 of these contracts, and the refrigerators sold on the 10 defaulting contracts were repossessed and returned to the Adams Corporation on November 30. The latter expects to sell these refrigerators at $100 each after spending $10 each for inward freight and cost of reconditioning.

December collections on time-payment contracts were made in full, and the Burke Company reported cash sales of 20 refrigerators, with 20 remaining in stock. The Adams Corporation received these collections and the net proceeds from the cash sales on December 31.

In accounting for installment sales, the Adams Corporation follows the plan of recognizing income only in terms of amounts collected.

Instructions: (1) Prepare the entries that will record the transactions on the books of the Adams Corporation.

(2) Prepare comprehensive summaries of these entries, showing and explaining the following resulting balances at December 31, 19X5:

(a) Consignments-out.
(b) Repossessed refrigerators.
(c) Cash.
(d) Accounts receivable — Burke Co.

(e) Profit realized.
(f) Profit not realized.
(g) Gain on defaults.

(AICPA adapted)

6-11. The West Company, which manufactures and sells gas burners to be installed in coal-burning furnaces, arranged in September, 19X3, to sell some of its products through three dealers to whom it consigned burners packed with their related parts and fixtures, with each such package identified as a burner. The contract provides that the consignee shall:

(a) Fix the sales price for all burners to be sold in the consignee's territory, subject to approval by the West Company.
(b) Pay all expenses incident to handling, selling, and collecting for the burners after delivery by West Company, except for repairs and expenses pertinent thereto required because of defective production.
(c) Retain as commission 25% of the retail price of the burners, exclusive of installation charges.
(d) Be responsible for the proper installation of burners sold and may make therefor suitable charges in which West Company shall not participate.
(e) Render within 10 days after the end of each month an account sales, accompanied by a check for the amount due the West Company as the result of transactions during the month to which the report relates.

A condensed trial balance of the West Company's accounts at September 30, 19X3, follows:

Cash	58,910	
Accounts Receivable	241,964	
Inventories:		
Finished burners and related parts and fixtures	21,200	
Work in process, materials, and supplies	42,271	
Prepaid Expenses	3,007	
Plant	128,762	
Accounts Payable		31,742
Accrued Liabilities		138,798
Capital Stock		100,000
Retained Earnings		18,978
Sales		643,947
Sales Returns and Allowances	2,648	
Manufacturing Summary	129,384	
Selling Expense	139,637	
Administrative Expense	89,423	
Allowance for Uncollectible Accounts		9,398
Accumulated Depreciation		27,632
Nonoperating Income		318
Nonoperating Expense	3,607	
Provision for Income Tax	110,000	
	970,813	970,813

All shipments debited to Accounts Receivable were credited to Sales.

Accounts Receivable included accounts with the three consignees. Upon examination, these accounts revealed the following:

Hale Plumbing Co.

Debits:

9/ 4/X3	18 burners shipped on consignment	$3,600.00
9/20/X3	Transportation charges paid on two burners returned as defective	22.00
9/27/X3	Cost of repairing two burners returned as defective	18.00
		$3,640.00

Credits:

9/30/X3	Cash received for 13 burners	1,767.75
Balance, 9/30/X3		$1,872.25

Lord Heating Equipment Co.

Debits:

9/ 6/X3	6 burners shipped on consignment	$1,200.00
9/15/X3	Transportation charges on one burner returned as defective	28.00
		$1,228.00

Credits:

9/15/X3	1 burner returned as defective	$200.00	
9/30/X3	Cash received for 3 burners	544.50	744.50
Balance, 9/30/X3			$ 483.50

Quade Furnace Company

Debits:
9/ 5/X3	12 burners shipped on consignment..............	$2,400.00
9/ 5/X3	Freight prepaid on consigned burners...........	36.00
9/30/X3	Commission on 9 burners............................	450.00
		$2,886.00

Credits:
9/30/X3	Cash received for 9 burners........................	1,344.00
Balance, 9/30/X3...		$1,542.00

Consignees reported burners on hand at September 30, 19X3, as follows:

Hale Plumbing Co.	3
Lord Heating Equipment Co.	2
Quade Furnace Co.	3

Shipping records show that on September 27, 19X3, the West Company shipped burners, freight prepaid, to replace those returned by consignees, as follows:

To: Hale Plumbing Co........................	2
Lord Heating Equipment Co.........	1

Burners on hand at the West Company's plant at September 30, 19X3, numbered 212 and were inventoried at manufacturing cost. Inventories at the beginning of the period have been closed into Manufacturing Summary, while those at the end of the period have been closed out of Manufacturing Summary. All normal adjusting entries have been made for the fiscal year ended September 30, 19X3. Unpaid commissions on sales were credited to Accrued Liabilities.

Account sales for September, 19X3, with related checks, were received by the West Company as follows:

From: Hale Plumbing Co..	October 7, 19X3
Lord Heating Equipment Co.	October 12, 19X3
Quade Furnace Co....................................	October 9, 19X3

Those from Hale Plumbing Co. and Lord Heating Equipment Co. reflect payments of $36 and $18, respectively, for transportation charges that they paid upon receiving their consignments; that from Quade Furnace Company includes a charge of $6 for the cost of repairs to a defective burner.

All entries in the West Company's accounts with the consignees, which are dated September 30, 19X3, were based on checks received and data recorded in their account sales received on the dates indicated.

Instructions: (1) Prepare an account sales for September, 19X3, as rendered by each of the three consignees.

(2) Prepare a columnar work sheet showing corrections to the accounts of the West Company, as of September 30, 19X3. No adjustment of the provision for income tax is required.

(3) Prepare a balance sheet for the West Company as of September 30, 19X3.

(4) Prepare a condensed income statement for the West Company for the year ended September 30, 19X3.   (AICPA adapted)

7
Home Office and Branch Relationships — General Procedures

In their search for increased sales, business organizations are constantly reaching out into more distant areas. Frequently the development of these areas cannot be adequately accomplished by salespeople traveling from a central office. The use of catalogs with mail orders or shipments on consignment may increase sales but may still fail to accomplish the desired results.

The establishment of sales headquarters in several districts may be the means of achieving marketing objectives. Selling activities are conducted from sales offices at different locations under the direction of the home office. Customers deal, not with the headquarters of the business, but with an outlying sales unit. Contact with the organization is more easily and quickly made. The desired goods or services are more readily available.

AGENCY AND BRANCH DISTINGUISHED

The establishment of an outlying selling unit may take the form of an *agency* or a *branch*. The distinction between an agency and a branch is based upon the functions assigned to the organization as well as the degree of independence that it assumes in the exercise of such functions. An organization that merely takes orders for goods and that operates under the direct supervision of officers of the home office is called an agency. An organization that sells goods out of a stock that it maintains and that possesses the authority to engage in transactions as an independent business unit is known as a branch.

OPERATIONS OF AN AGENCY

An agency that operates solely as a local sales organization under the direction of a home office generally carries no stock other than samples of the lines that are offered for sale. Samples of the merchandise offerings as well as advertising materials are provided by the home office. The agency is normally provided with a working fund that is to be used for the payment of expenses that can be more conveniently settled through the agency. The imprest system is often adopted for the control of agency cash.

Merchandise orders obtained by the agency are sent to the home office for approval. If the sales price and credit terms are acceptable, the home office fills the orders and ships the goods to customers. The home office may bear the responsibility for maintaining the accounts that arise out of sales, billing the customers, and making collections. Expenses of operating the agency other than those paid by the agency from its working fund are met by the home office.

ACCOUNTING FOR AN AGENCY

The typical agency does not require a complete set of books. Ordinarily, summaries of working fund receipts and disbursements and records of sales to customers are sufficient. Summaries of working fund disbursements accompanied by supporting evidence in the form of paid vouchers are sent to the home office. When the local manager or salespeople are to be paid according to the volume of sales completed, sales records supply this information.

In adopting the imprest system for the agency working fund, the home office writes a check to the agency for the amount of the fund. Establishment of the fund is recorded on the home office books by a debit to the agency working fund account and a credit to Cash. The agency will request fund replenishment whenever the fund runs low and at the end of each fiscal period. Such a request is normally accompanied by an itemized and authenticated statement of disbursements and the paid vouchers. Upon sending the agency a check in replenishment of the fund, the home office debits expense or other accounts for which disbursements from the fund were reported and credits Cash.

When the home office transfers assets other than cash to the agency, it debits asset accounts identified with the agency, such as "Agency Furniture," "Agency Samples," and "Agency Supplies," and credits the appropriate asset accounts for the cost of the items transferred.

The home office may record transactions of the agency in the revenue and expense accounts used for its own transactions if there is no desire to summarize agency operations separately. After these accounts are closed, the income summary account reports the results of combined operations.

If the home office wishes to determine the net earnings of each of its agencies as well as of the home office, it will maintain separate revenue and expense accounts for the individual sales units. A supplementary record of the cost of goods sold by each sales unit must also be kept. This record provides the data for the entries charging individual agencies and the home office with the cost of goods identified with the respective sales.

To illustrate the entries required as a result of the establishment of an agency and the entries to record subsequent activities of such a unit, assume that General Traders, Inc., established a sales agency in Toledo on

March 1. Agency revenues and expenses are recorded in separate agency accounts, and the operating results for each agency as well as for the home office are determined at the end of each month. Agency transactions for March and the entries to record the transactions on the books of the home office are as follows:

Agency Transaction	Home Office Books		
March 1 Receipt of working fund from home office.	Working Fund — Toledo Agency.. Cash......................................	1,000	1,000
March 1–31 Orders submitted by agency, approved and filled by home office.	Accounts Receivable .... Sales — Toledo Agency...........	5,000	5,000
Collections by home office on agency sales.	Cash....................................... Accounts Receivable	3,000	3,000
Disbursements by home office on behalf of agency.	Salaries and Commissions Expense — Toledo Agency............. Rent Expense — Toledo Agency.. Advertising Supplies — Toledo Agency .... Cash.......................................	250 200 450	 900
March 31 Replenishment of working fund by home office, based on paid expense vouchers submitted by the agency.	Salaries and Commissions Expense — Toledo Agency............. Misc. Expense — Toledo Agency . Cash.......................................	350 200	 550
Entries summarizing agency transactions — Data for agency adjustments: Cost of goods identified with agency sales, $3,500. Advertising supplies on hand, approximately $2/3$ of amount received.	Cost of Goods Sold — Toledo Agency .... Merchandise Shipments — Toledo Agency	3,500	 3,500
	Advertising Supplies Expense — Toledo Agency .... Advertising Supplies — Toledo Agency	150	 150
	Sales — Toledo Agency.............. Income — Toledo Agency	5,000	5,000
	Income — Toledo Agency .... Cost of Goods Sold — Toledo Agency .... Salaries and Commissions Expense — Toledo Agency.......... Rent Expense — Toledo Agency .... Advertising Supplies Expense — Toledo Agency...................... Misc. Expense — Toledo Agency	4,650	 3,500 600 200 150 200
	Income — Toledo Agency .... Income Summary..................	350	350

In the example, the cost of the goods sold by the agency is recorded by a debit to Cost of Goods Sold — Agency and a credit to Merchandise Shipments — Agency. The merchandise shipments account balance is subtracted from the sum of the home office beginning inventory and purchases in determining the merchandise available for home office sales. The ending inventory, when subtracted from merchandise available for home office sales, gives the cost of goods identified with home office sales.

Following the adjusting entries, agency revenue and expense accounts are closed into an income summary account for each agency. Agency income summary accounts are subsequently transferred to the general income summary account in which the income or loss from home office activities will also be summarized.

OPERATIONS OF A BRANCH

Although a branch operates as a separate business unit, it is subject to control by the home office. The degree of self-management to be exercised by a branch is determined by the home office. General policies and standards adopted by the business are usually applied to all of the branches. Outside of this realm, however, the branch manager may be given complete authority, with effectiveness of management and control judged on the basis of the branch financial reports.

A branch's cash and merchandise and such other assets as may be needed are supplied by the home office. The branch may purchase merchandise from outsiders to satisfy certain local needs for goods not available from the affiliated unit. The branch ships merchandise, bills its customers, makes collections on account, and deposits the sums in its own bank account. The bank balance is drawn upon in making payment for purchases of goods and services.

Although the foregoing are typical branch functions, there are instances where certain limitations are imposed upon such activities. For example, in some cases the home office may assume the responsibility of collecting branch receivables, or a branch may be required to deposit branch receipts to the credit of the home office and to make branch disbursements from a working fund operated on the imprest system. Such restrictions upon the authority of a branch serve to give it some of the characteristics of an agency. On the other hand, some agencies are assigned special functions that extend beyond the scope of the typical agency, such as maintaining accounts with customers and making collections on accounts. The accounting procedures that are illustrated in this chapter are those that would be employed for a typical agency or branch. These procedures may be modified to meet special conditions.

ACCOUNTING FOR BRANCHES

Branch accounting systems may provide for maintenance of branch records at the home office, maintenance of branch records at both branch and home office, and maintenance of branch records at the branch. When the home office keeps the complete records summarizing branch activities, branch transactions may be recorded in the home office journals and ledgers or in a separate set of records. Data to be recorded are supplied by the branch in the form of either original documents evidencing branch transactions or memorandum records summarizing branch transactions supported by the original vouchers. Duplicate copies of vouchers and summaries sent to the home office are usually retained by the branch. Accounting centralization at the home office is particularly appropriate when the branch bears some resemblance to the agency form of organization.

A system whereby both the branch and the home office maintain detailed records of branch transactions is sometimes adopted. The branch may maintain the books of original entry for all transactions in duplicate. Copies of the books of original entry are sent to the home office, where data are posted to branch accounts maintained separately or included in the home office general ledger. At the end of the period the home office adjusts and closes the branch accounts and determines the branch earnings.

Records Maintained at the Branch

Generally, the branch accounting system is maintained at the branch. The branch keeps the books of original entry and posts to ledger records. Financial statements are prepared by the branch periodically and are submitted to the home office. Statements that are submitted by the branch are usually verified by the company's internal auditors.

When complete self-balancing books are kept by the branch, an account called Home Office takes the place of the customary capital accounts. This account is credited for cash, goods, or services received from the home office and for profits resulting from branch operations. The account is debited for remittances made by the branch to the home office and for losses from operations. The home office account, then, indicates the extent of the accountability of the branch to the home office.

The home office, in turn, keeps a reciprocal account, called Branch, or Investment in Branch. This account is debited for cash, goods, or services transferred to the branch and for branch income; it is credited for remittances from the branch and for branch losses. The branch account, then, indicates the amount invested in the branch. When a number of branches are maintained, a separate account is established for each branch.

Depreciable branch assets are sometimes carried on the home office books. This procedure may be followed when depreciation rates are to be uniformly applied to certain groups of assets, whether used by the branch or the home office, and when insurance policies are to be acquired by the home office for all assets.

Certain expenses relating to branch operations are sometimes paid by the home office. Branches are notified by the home office of expenses incurred in their behalf, and such charges are recorded on the branch books so that branch income statements may provide complete summaries of the operations of the separate sales organizations. Certain items can be directly identified with individual branches and are immediately charged to the branches. Such items include taxes and insurance paid by the home office on branch assets. Other charges resulting in benefits that are not directly identified with certain branches, such as advertising for the different lines being sold, may be summarized on the home office books and charged periodically to the branches according to the volume of branch sales, the volume of shipments of merchandise by the home office to branches, or on some other equitable basis. When a home office does not sell to customers but acts solely in a supervisory capacity, it may be desirable to charge all of its expenses to the branches. Expenses that are not directly identified with branches may be combined and distributed in total as an indirect charge. When charges reported on home office books are taken up on the branch books, home office accounts should be reduced by the amounts transferred.

The home office may charge the individual branches for interest and rent on the working capital and the properties and equipment transferred to the branches. Such charges are made so that earnings of the different sales units may be reported on a comparable basis in view of the differences that are found in the investments by the home office in these units. When such charges are made, the branch recognizes these charges as expense items, while the home office reports corresponding revenue.

To illustrate accounting for the operations of a branch, assume that on October 1 the Southern Supply Company of Los Angeles establishes its first branch in San Diego. Additional branches are planned for the future. Separate books are to be kept by the branch, and financial statements are to be submitted to the home office at the end of each month. Merchandise is to be billed at cost. Branch furniture and fixtures are to be carried on the books of the home office. The branch is to be charged interest at the rate of 6% on the home office investment in the branch as of the beginning of each month. Transactions of Branch #1 and the entries to record the transactions on the books of the branch and the home office are listed below and on the following page.

Branch Transactions	Home Office Books		Branch Books	

October 1
(1) Receipt of cash from home office.
	Branch #1 6,000
	   Cash ....
		
		6,000
			Cash 6,000
			   Home Office.....
				
				6,000

(2) Receipt of merchandise from home office, billing at cost.	Branch #1 12,000
	   Shipments to
	   Branch #1 ....
		
		12,000
			Shipments from
			Home Office........ 12,000
			   Home Office.....
				
				12,000

(3) Purchase of furniture and fixtures by branch for cash, the asset to be carried on the home office books.	Furniture and
	Fixtures, Branch
	#1 3,000
	   Branch #1 ....
		
		3,000
			Home Office........ 3,000
			   Cash ....
				
				3,000

October 2–31 (4) (a) Sales on account.			Accounts Receivable.......... 6,500 Sales..............	 6,500

(b) Collections on account.			Cash 3,500
			   Accounts
			   Receivable.......
				
				3,500

Branch Transactions	Home Office Books	Branch Books
(5) Payment of expenses.		Salaries and Commissions Expense .... 400 Rent Expense...... 200 Miscellaneous Expense .... 150 Cash 750

(6) Remittance to home office.	Cash 2,000
	    Branch #1....... 2,000
		Home Office........ 2,000
		    Cash 2,000

(7) Branch charges submitted by home office:
(a) Insurance on branch assets .... $ 35
(b) Depreciation of furniture and fixtures........   50
(c) Taxes on branch assets   25
(d) Advertising   300
(e) Interest at 6% for one month on investment in branch on Oct. 1, $18,000   90
	Branch #1.......... 500
	    Prepaid Insurance 35
	    Accumulated Depreciation — Furniture and Fixtures, Branch #1....... 50
	    Taxes Payable .. 25
	    Advertising Expense 300
	    Interest Income, Branch #1 90
		Insurance Expense 35
		Depreciation Expense — Furniture and Fixtures.............. 50
		Taxes Expense 25
		Advertising Expense 300
		Interest Expense, Home Office........ 90
		    Home Office..... 500

(8) Adjusting and closing entries — data for branch adjustments:
    Merchandise inventory, Oct. 31.......................... $8,400
		Merchandise Inventory 8,400
		    Income Summary........ 8,400
		
		Sales.................. 6,500
		    Income Summary........ 6,500
		
		Income Summary 13,250
		    Shipments from Home Office.............. 12,000
		    Salaries and Commissions Expense 400
		    Rent Expense... 200
		    Miscellaneous Expense 150
		    Insurance Expense 35
		    Depr. Expense — Furniture and Fixtures..... 50
		    Taxes Expense . 25
		    Advertising Expense 300
		    Interest Expense, Home Office.............. 90

	Branch #1.......... 1,650
	    Branch #1 Income............ 1,650
	
	Branch #1 Income............... 1,650
	    Income Summary........ 1,650
		Income Summary 1,650
		    Home Office..... 1,650

Explanations for the transactions, identified by number, are given in the following paragraphs.

(1) Transfer of assets other than merchandise by home office to branch. *Home office books.* When an asset other than merchandise is transferred and the asset is to be carried on the branch books, the home office debits the branch account and credits the appropriate asset account. When the asset transferred is to be carried on the home office books, an asset account identified with the branch, such as Furniture and Fixtures — Branch, is debited and the original asset account is credited.

Branch books. Upon receiving an asset other than merchandise that is to be carried on the branch books, the branch debits the asset account and credits the home office account. No entry is required when the asset transferred is to be carried on the home office books. However, the branch would maintain a memorandum record for this asset.

(2) Transfer of merchandise by home office to branch. *Home office books.* When merchandise is transferred to the branch, the home office debits the branch account and credits Shipments to Branch. At the end of the period, the balance of the account Shipments to Branch will be subtracted from the sum of the beginning inventory, purchases, and freight in to determine the merchandise available for home office sales. When the home office maintains a perpetual inventory system, appropriate inventory accounts are credited for the goods transferred to the branch. Illustrations in this chapter assume that a branch is charged for no more than merchandise cost on interoffice transfers. Such cost should include any freight and transportation charges paid by the home office in acquiring the goods as well as in transferring the goods to the branch. The home office may, however, bill a branch for an amount that exceeds cost. Such a practice calls for special accounting procedures that are described in Chapter 8.

Branch books. When merchandise is received from the home office, the branch debits Shipments from Home Office at billed price and credits the home office account. At the end of the period, merchandise received from the home office together with merchandise purchases from outsiders is added to the beginning inventory to determine the goods available for branch sale. If the branch maintains a perpetual inventory system, inventory accounts are debited for the goods acquired from the home office.

(3) Purchase of assets by branch to be carried on home office books. *Home office books.* When the home office is notified of a branch's purchase of an asset that is to be carried on the books of the home office, the home office debits an appropriate asset account identified with the branch and credits the branch account.

Branch books. Upon purchase of an asset that is to be carried on the home office books, the branch debits the home office account and credits Cash or an appropriate liability account.

(4), (5) Current transactions involving only branch and outsiders. *Home office books.* Transactions that involve only the branch and outsiders during the period require no entries on the books of the home office.

Branch books. Transactions of the branch and outsiders during the period are recorded on the branch books in the usual manner.

(6) Remittances by branch to home office. *Home office books.* Upon receiving cash from the branch, the home office debits Cash and credits the branch account. Receipt of an asset other than cash is recorded by a debit to an appropriate asset account and a credit to the branch account.

Branch books. Upon remitting cash to the home office, the branch debits the home office account and credits Cash. Transfer of some other branch asset to the home office is recorded by a debit to Home Office and a credit to the appropriate asset account.

(7) Branch charges submitted by home office. *Home office books.* When the home office charges the branch for items that are to be recognized by the branch as expenses, the home office debits the branch account and credits appropriate asset, asset valuation, liability, expense, or revenue accounts, whichever may be appropriate; thus (a) a debit to the branch for insurance that has been paid in advance by the home office is accompanied by a credit to Prepaid Insurance; (b) a debit for depreciation on branch furniture and fixtures carried on the home office books is accompanied by a credit to Accumulated Depreciation — Furniture and Fixtures, Branch; (c) a debit for taxes on branch assets that are to be paid by the home office at some future date is accompanied by a credit to Taxes Payable; (d) a debit for branch advertising that has been paid for by the home office and is included in the advertising expense account is accompanied by a credit to Advertising Expense; (e) a debit to the branch for interest on the amount invested in the branch is accompanied by a credit to Interest Income, Branch.

Branch books. Upon notification of expenses that are to be recognized on the branch books, the branch debits the appropriate expense accounts and credits the home office account.

(8) Determination of branch net income or loss. *Home office books.* When the branch reports net income for the period, the home office debits the branch account and credits Branch Income. A net loss is recorded by a debit to Branch Income and a credit to the branch account. The income account for each branch is subsequently closed into the income summary account of the home office.

Branch books. At the end of the period the necessary adjustments are made, and the revenue and expense accounts are closed into the income summary account in the usual manner. The balance in the income summary account is then transferred to the home office account.

Preparation of Branch and Home Office Statements

The branch normally prepares a balance sheet and an income statement at the end of the fiscal period. The home office also prepares statements to show its financial position and operating results. The branch investment accounts appear as assets on the home office balance sheet. Branch balance sheets may be attached as schedules in support of the branch balances. The individual branch earnings may be shown on the home office income statement immediately after operating results of the home office, as follows:

Net income from own operations..	$6,140
Add income of branches:	
Net income — Branch #1	1,650
Total income..	$7,790

The branch income statements may be attached to the home office income statement as schedules offering the detail to support the net amounts reported on the statement.

Preparation of Combined Statements for Home Office and Branches

Although separate statements offer significant information to both home office and branch officials, such statements must be combined in fully stating a company's financial position and the results of its operations. The financial position of the business unit as a whole is fully presented only when the individual asset and liability items of the various branches are substituted for the branch investment balances and combined with the home office items. Operating results for the business as a whole are fully presented only when the individual revenue and expense items of the various branches are substituted for the branch net income or loss and combined with the home office data. Stockholders, creditors, and taxing authorities require combined statements. These parties normally have little or no interest in the separate status and operating results of individual departments or branches of a business.

In combining branch data with home office data, the elimination of certain reciprocal interoffice items is necessary. In preparing a combined balance sheet, the home office account and the branch account are eliminated, since these accounts are without significance when the related units are recognized as a single entity. Any other interbranch receivable and payable balances that may have been established are also irrelevant and without significance in stating the financial position of the business.

In preparing a combined income statement, the accounts Shipments from Home Office and Shipments to Branch are eliminated, since these balances summarize interoffice transfers that are of no significance when the related units are reported as a single entity. Other interoffice revenue and expense items are also eliminated so that the combined statement may report only the results of transactions with outsiders.

Work sheets facilitate the elimination of interoffice items and the combining of like items. Work sheets for the Southern Supply Company and its branch are illustrated below and on page 195. The combined statements are given below the work sheets. Branch data are obtained from the information on pages 189 and 190.

Southern Supply Company
Work Sheet for Combined Balance Sheet
October 31, 19X6

	Home Office	Branch #1	Eliminations Dr.	Eliminations Cr.	Combined Balance Sheet
Debits					
Cash...	6,250	3,750			10,000
Accounts Receivable.................................	18,000	3,000			21,000
Merchandise Inventory.............................	30,000	8,400			38,400
Prepaid Insurance...................................	150				150
Branch #1...	15,150			15,150	
Furniture and Fixtures, Home Office..........	14,000				14,000
Furniture and Fixtures, Branch #1..............	3,000				3,000
	86,550	15,150			86,550
Credits					
Accumulated Depreciation — Furniture and Fixtures, Home Office.............................	9,100				9,100
Accumulated Depreciation — Furniture and Fixtures, Branch #1.............................	50				50
Accounts Payable	23,300				23,300
Taxes Payable	200				200
Home Office..		15,150	15,150		
Capital Stock...	25,000				25,000
Retained Earnings	28,900				28,900
	86,550	15,150	15,150	15,150	86,550

Southern Supply Company
Combined Balance Sheet for Home Office and Branch
October 31, 19X6

Assets			Liabilities and Stockholders' Equity		
Cash..............................		$10,000	**Liabilities**		
Accounts receivable.........		21,000	Accounts payable		$23,300
Merchandise inventory		38,400	Taxes payable..................................		200
Prepaid insurance............		150	Total liabilities.................................		$23,500
Furniture and fixtures.......	$17,000				
Less accumulated depreciation	9,150	7,850	**Stockholders' Equity**		
			Capital stock	$25,000	
			Retained earnings............	28,900	53,900
			Total liabilities and stockholders' equity		
Total assets.................................		$77,400	uity		$77,400

Southern Supply Company
Work Sheet for Combined Income Statement
For Month Ended October 31, 19X6

	Home Office	Branch #1	Eliminations		Combined Income Statement
			Dr.	Cr.	
Sales...	24,000	6,500			30,500
Cost of goods sold:					
Merchandise inventory, October 1..............	38,000				38,000
Purchases..	16,000				16,000
Shipments from home office		12,000		12,000	
	54,000				54,000
Less shipments to Branch #1.....................	12,000		12,000		
Merchandise available for sale..................	42,000	12,000			54,000
Less merchandise inventory, October 31	30,000	8,400			38,400
Cost of goods sold..................................	12,000	3,600			15,600
Gross profit..	12,000	2,900			14,900
Expenses:					
Salaries and commissions expense............	1,900	400			2,300
Rent expense	1,000	200			1,200
Advertising expense	800	300			1,100
Depreciation expense — furniture and fixtures	400	50			450
Insurance expense.................................	250	35			285
Taxes expense......................................	150	25			175
Miscellaneous expense	1,450	150			1,600
Total expenses..................................	5,950	1,160			7,110
Operating income...................................	6,050	1,740			7,790
Add interest income, Branch #1..................	90		90		
Deduct interest expense, home office............		90		90	
Net income	6,140	1,650	12,090	12,090	7,790

Southern Supply Company
Combined Income Statement for Home Office and Branch
For Month Ended October 31, 19X6

Sales		$30,500
Cost of goods sold:		
Merchandise inventory, October 1.................................	$38,000	
Purchases	16,000	
Merchandise available for sale.......................................	$54,000	
Less merchandise inventory, October 31.........................	38,400	15,600
Gross profit..		$14,900
Expenses:		
Salaries and commissions expense.................................	$ 2,300	
Rent expense...	1,200	
Advertising expense..	1,100	
Depreciation expense — furniture and fixtures	450	
Insurance expense	285	
Taxes expense	175	
Miscellaneous expense	1,600	7,110
Net income...		$ 7,790

Adjustment of Reciprocal Accounts

The balances in the branch account on the home office books and in the home office account on the branch books may not show identical reciprocal balances at any one time because of certain interoffice data that have been recorded by one office but not by the other. The home office, for example, debits the branch immediately upon the shipment of merchandise to the branch. The branch, however, does not credit the home office account until it receives the merchandise, which may be several days after shipment by the home office. The fact that the reciprocal account balances are not identical is of no concern during the fiscal period. At the end of the fiscal period, however, the causes for any differences in the balances must be investigated and appropriate entries made to bring interoffice accounts into agreement before accounts for each office can be closed and individual and combined statements prepared.

The data to be considered in reconciling the two accounts may be classified as follows:

(1) Debits in the branch account without corresponding credits in the home office account.

(2) Credits in the branch account without corresponding debits in the home office account.

(3) Debits in the home office account without corresponding credits in the branch account.

(4) Credits in the home office account without corresponding debits in the branch account.

To illustrate the procedure to be followed in reconciling the branch and the home office accounts, assume that on December 31, the end of a fiscal year, but before accounts are closed, branch and home office accounts are as follows:

On Home Office Books
Branch

Nov. 30 Balance	10,500	Dec. 17 Cash received from branch..	1,500
(1) Dec. 28 Merchandise shipped to branch..............................	3,000	(2) Dec. 22 Collection of branch receivables	750

On Branch Books
Home Office

Dec. 15 Cash sent to home office.......	1,500	Nov. 30 Balance	10,500
(3) Dec. 30 Cash sent to home office.......	500	(4) Dec. 26 Correction — understatement of net income for prior year ...	200

Analysis of the accounts discloses the following:

(1) Debit in the branch account without corresponding credit in the home office account. The home office has charged Branch and credited Shipments to Branch with $3,000 for merchandise shipped to the branch at the end of the year. The shipment has not reached the branch by December 31 and

consequently no entry for the shipment appears on its books. The following entry is required on the branch books on December 31:

Shipments from Home Office — In Transit 3,000
   Home Office 3,000

The account Shipments from Home Office — In Transit is closed into the income summary account. When the income statement for the branch is prepared, the balance of the account Shipments from Home Office — In Transit is added to the balance of the account Shipments from Home Office. The total of the two accounts is then equal to the balance of the account Shipments to Branch shown on the books of the home office, and these reciprocal balances can be eliminated in preparing a combined income statement.

In addition to the previous entry, the branch in recording its ending inventory must increase its merchandise on hand by the amount of goods in transit. The merchandise in transit thus appears on the branch balance sheet and will be included as a part of the total inventory in the preparation of combined statements. If the branch maintains a perpetual inventory system, a special inventory in transit account would be debited and the home office account credited. Upon receipt of the goods, the inventory account would be debited and the inventory in transit balance closed.

(2) Credit in the branch account without corresponding debit in the home office account. The home office has debited Cash and credited Branch for $750 upon collecting an account that is carried on the branch books. This transaction has not been entered on the books of the branch. The following entry is required on the branch books on December 31:

Home Office 750
   Accounts Receivable 750

(3) Debit in the home office account without corresponding credit in the branch account. The branch has debited Home Office and credited Cash for $500 upon remitting cash to the home office. This cash has not reached the home office by December 31. The following entry is required on the home office books on December 31:

Cash in Transit 500
   Branch 500

(4) Credit in the home office account without corresponding debit in the branch account. The branch has credited Home Office upon correcting the accounts for an understatement of the net income for the preceding period. This information has not been reported on the books of the home office. The following entry is required on the home office books on December 31:

Branch 200
   Retained Earnings 200

After the foregoing entries have been made, the reciprocal accounts are in agreement as indicated in the following table.

	Home Office Books	Branch Books
	Branch account	Home office account
Balances before adjustments...............................	$11,250	$ 8,700
Adjustments:		
Additions:		
Merchandise shipped to branch........................		3,000
Understatement of branch net income — prior period..	200	
	$11,450	$11,700
Deductions:		
Transfer of cash to home office	500	
Collection of branch receivable by home office ..		750
Corrected balances	$10,950	$10,950

In addition to data relative to differences, there may be other data that require recognition on both home office and branch ledgers in bringing the interoffice accounts up to date. After entries have been made to bring the accounts up to date, individual and combined statements may be prepared and the revenue and expense accounts for each office closed.

QUESTIONS

1. What are the factors that would be considered by a company in deciding whether it should adopt a policy of sales by consignment, the establishment of an agency, or the establishment of a branch form of organization?

2. Distinguish between typical agency and typical branch operations.

3. Indicate the kind of an accounting system that might reasonably be adopted by a home office and its sales office, assuming that:

    (a) An agency is organized, the home office to take care of merchandise shipments, billing of customers, and collections on account.

    (b) An agency is organized, the home office to take care of merchandise shipments but the agency to bill customers and make collections.

    (c) A branch is established, the branch to maintain a stock of merchandise, to make collections on accounts, and to make payments for expenses from its own bank account.

    (d) A branch is established, the branch to maintain a stock of merchandise, to make collections that are deposited to the credit of the home office, and to make payments from an imprest working fund.

4. The Baker Co. adopts the imprest system for cash that is sent to its newly organized sales agencies. Describe the operation of such a system.

5. What special problems result when a home office wishes to determine the degree of success of operations for each of its agencies?

6. (a) Describe the nature of the branch and the home office accounts. (b) How are these balances reported on the separate statements of the home office and the branch? (c) How are these balances reported on the combined statements?

7. (a) Describe the nature of the accounts Shipments to Branch on the home office books and Shipments from Home Office on the branch books. (b) How are these balances reported on the separate statements of the home office and the branch? (c) How are these balances reported on the combined statements?

8. What entries will appear on the books of the home office and the branch for each of the following transactions?

(a) The home office sends cash and merchandise to a newly organized branch.
(b) The branch purchases merchandise from outsiders.
(c) The branch pays expenses.
(d) The branch sells merchandise on account.
(e) The branch makes remittance to the home office.
(f) The home office charges the branch with certain expenses previously paid by the home office.
(g) The branch reports a loss from operations.

9. (a) Identify four different transactions originating with the home office that affect the branch-home office reciprocal accounts. (b) Identify four different transactions originating with the branch that affect the reciprocal accounts.

10. The Webster Co. carries on the home office books all of the furniture and fixtures that are in use by its branches. What are the entries required by both the home office and a branch when:

(a) The home office purchases branch fixtures for cash.
(b) The branch pays for the installation of the fixtures.
(c) The branch pays for insurance on the fixtures.
(d) The home office pays personal property taxes on the fixtures.
(e) The home office records depreciation on the fixtures.

11. What are the relative merits of separate statements for the home office and for the related branches as compared with combined statements for the home office and the branches?

12. (a) What eliminations are required in preparing combined statements for a home office and its related branches? (b) Why are such eliminations necessary?

13. The Walters Co. home office charges its individual branches for interest on the net amount invested. (a) What is the purpose of such a charge? (b) What entries are made by the home office and the respective branch in recognizing such a charge? (c) How is the transaction reported on the separate statements of the home office and the branch? (d) How is the transaction reported on the combined statements?

14. The home office and the branch reciprocal accounts for the Peters Corporation are not in agreement at the end of the fiscal period. What are the four possible categories within which the reason for any differences might be found? Give an example of a situation under each that might arise in reconciling the accounts.

EXERCISES

1. Prepare the entries that are required on the home office books of the Millings Company to record:

(a) The transfer of $500 to an agency to establish a working fund.
(b) Receipt of sales orders from the agency, $5,000.
(c) Collections of agency accounts by the home office, $3,500.
(d) Home office disbursements representing agency expenses, $450.
(e) Replenishment of the agency working fund upon receipt of expense vouchers for $225.
(f) Cost of goods identified with agency sales, $3,600.

2. Prepare the entries that are required on the books of the Parker Company and the separate books of its branch to record:

(a) Transfer of cash, $1,500, and merchandise, $6,000, by home office to the branch.
(b) Branch purchases of merchandise on account, $1,500.
(c) Branch payments on account, $750.
(d) Branch sales for cash, $6,500.
(e) Branch payment of expenses, $2,200.
(f) Home office disbursements representing branch expenses, $350.
(g) Determination of a loss from branch operations, $225.

3. The home office of the Meadows Company carries all branch equipment in its own ledger. Prepare the entries that would appear on the books of the home office and the branch as a result of the following transactions:

(a) At the beginning of 19X1 the branch office acquires branch furniture on account, $2,500, terms 2/10, n/30.
(b) The home office makes payment on the invoice within the discount period.
(c) Depreciation on the equipment is recorded at the end of the year at 10%.
(d) At the beginning of 19X2 the branch furniture is traded in for new branch furniture costing $4,000; an allowance of $1,500 is received on the old furniture and the home office pays the balance.

4. The following account is found on the home office books of the Ford Corporation at the end of January. Prepare the entries affecting the home office account that will appear on the branch books for January.

Alexandria Branch

19X9			19X9		
1/ 1	Balance	67,500	1/16	Remittance from branch	2,000
1/10	Payment of branch note	2,500	1/20	Return of goods by branch	1,200
1/10	Payment for branch furniture and fixtures	10,000	1/25	Collection of branch account	150
1/16	Shipments of goods to branch	6,500	1/31	Branch loss for month	750
1/30	Expenses charged to branch	800			

5. Prepare the entries that are required on the books of the Price Co. home office and Westwood branch as a result of the following transactions:

(a) The branch writes off uncollectible accounts of $600. The allowance for doubtful accounts is maintained on the books of the home office.

(b) The home office analyzes the balance of its general and administrative expenses account and finds that $1,250 of this balance is chargeable to the Westwood branch.

(c) The shipments from home office account on the branch books is found to include a charge of $1,200 for merchandise intended for shipment by the home office to the Westwood branch but shipped to the Beverly Hills branch by mistake and retained by the latter branch.

(d) The branch authorizes the home office to increase the allowance for doubtful accounts of the branch by $850 as a result of sales for the month.

6. On December 31 the branch account on the home office books of the Ward Co. shows a balance of $8,400 and the home office account on the branch books shows a balance of $9,735. The following data are determined in accounting for the difference:

(a) Merchandise billed at $615 was shipped by the home office to the branch on December 28. The merchandise is in transit and has not been recognized on the books of the branch.

(b) The branch collected a home office account receivable of $2,500, but failed to notify the home office of this collection.

(c) The home office recorded incorrectly the branch net income for November at $1,125. The branch reported net income of $1,215.

(d) The home office was charged $640 when the branch returned merchandise to the home office on December 31. The merchandise is in transit.

(1) Prepare a statement reconciling the branch and the home office accounts. (2) What entries would be made on the branch and the home office books before financial statements are prepared?

PROBLEMS

7-1. On July 1, 19X5, the Crawford Company of New York establishes an organization in Boston to act as a sales agency. The following assets are sent to the agency on July 1:

A working fund to be operated under the imprest system......	$1,000
Samples from the merchandise stock..............................	5,000
Advertising materials and literature	1,250
	$7,250

During July the agency submits sales on account of $17,600 that are approved by the home office; cost of merchandise shipped in filling orders is $10,500. Home office disbursements chargeable to the agency are as follows:

Furniture and fixtures for agency.. $2,400
Salaries and commissions... 1,750
Rent... 800
                                                                         $4,950

On July 31 the agency working fund is replenished. Paid expense vouchers submitted by the agency are as follows:

Advertising expense.. $ 325
Miscellaneous expense.. 600
                                                                         $ 925

The following information is used in adjusting the agency accounts on July 31:

Agency samples will be useful until December 31; at that time it is believed
    they will have a salvage value of 40% of cost.
Approximately $2/5$ of the advertising materials and literature remain on hand.
Furniture and fixtures are to be depreciated on a 5-year basis.
The agency manager is to receive a bonus of 5% of all sales above $10,000 a
    month, the bonus to be paid by the home office at quarterly intervals.

Instructions: (1) Prepare the journal entries on the home office books to record the transactions and to adjust and close the accounts kept with the agency.
(2) Prepare a statement summarizing agency activities for July, 19X5.

7-2. The Wesley Co. of San Francisco operates a branch in Sacramento. A branch balance sheet on December 31, 19X8, showed the following balances:

Cash.....................		$ 3,500	Accounts payable		$ 2,000
Accounts receivable...................	$12,200		Accrued expenses...............		600
Less allowance for doubtful accounts..............	850	11,350	Home office		30,250
Merchandise inventory...................		16,500			
Prepaid expenses...		350			
Furniture and fixtures.................	$ 3,850				
Less accumulated depreciation.......	2,700	1,150			
Total assets........................		$32,850	Total liabilities...................		$32,850

Branch transactions during 19X9 are summarized as follows:

(a) Sales on account, $40,000.
(b) Purchases on account, $10,500.
(c) Goods received from home office, billed at cost, $20,000.
(d) Collections on account, $38,000.
(e) Payments on account, $10,100.
(f) Uncollectible accounts written off, $600.
(g) Cash remittances to home office, $15,000.

(h) Expenses paid, $12,400.

(i) Expenses paid by home office and charged to branch, $800.

(j) Year-end adjusting data:

Merchandise on hand, $19,400.

Prepaid expenses, December 31, $450.

Accrued expenses, December 31, $400.

Receivables estimated to be uncollectible, December 31, $800.

Depreciation for 19X9, $600.

Instructions: (1) Prepare the entries to be made by the branch to record the transactions for the year and to adjust and close the accounts at the end of the year.

(2) Prepare a branch balance sheet, income statement, and statement of changes in the home office account for the year ended December 31, 19X9.

(3) Prepare all of the home office entries in 19X9 affecting the branch account.

7-3. A balance sheet for the Eagle Co. as of January 1, 19X4, is as follows:

Balance Sheet

Assets			Liabilities and Stockholders' Equity	
Cash.....................		$ 15,000	Accrued expenses.............. $	250
Accounts receiv-			Accounts payable	33,750
able.................	$42,000		Capital stock	50,000
Less allowance			Retained earnings..............	28,200
for doubtful				
accounts.......	1,200	40,800		
Merchandise in-				
ventory............		46,000		
Store furniture				
and fixtures......	$15,000			
Less accumu-				
lated depre-				
ciation..........	4,600	10,400	Total liabilities and stock-	
Total assets......................		$112,200	holders' equity................	$112,200

On this date a branch sales office is established in Miami. The branch is sent the following assets by the home office:

(a) Cash, $1,500.

(b) Merchandise, cost, $10,200.

(c) Store furniture and fixtures previously used by the home office — cost, $3,000; age, 2½ years; depreciation rate used in the past, 10% a year. The cost of shipment and installation, $900, is paid by the branch. This cost is to be written off over the remaining life of the asset. The equipment accounts are to be carried on the books of the home office.

(d) Accounts receivable, $2,600. Accounts arose from home office sales to customers in Miami. The branch is authorized to take over the accounts and make collections.

Home office and branch transactions with outsiders during January were:

	Home Office	Branch
Sales on account	$34,600	$6,200
Collections on own accounts	40,000	2,600
Purchases on account	31,600	3,000
Payments on account	36,200	1,450
Payments of expenses (including accruals as of January 1)	9,200	1,250

The following took place with respect to accounts received by the branch from the home office: collections of $1,600 were made; accounts of $150 were uncollectible and were written off; it is believed that remaining accounts of $850 are collectible.

Interoffice transactions during January were:

Merchandise shipments to branch, cost	$1,250
Cash remittance to home office	1,000

The following information is to be recorded on January 31:

(a) Merchandise costing $600 was shipped by the home office to the branch on January 31; this merchandise is in transit and will not reach the branch until February 2. (This shipment is not included in transfers previously mentioned.)

(b) Expenses that are paid by the home office during the month and that are chargeable to the branch total $475. (These are included in the $9,200 amount.)

(c) Depreciation on furniture and fixtures is recorded at the rate of 10% a year.

(d) Merchandise inventories, excluding merchandise in transit, are: home office, $44,500; branch, $9,800.

(e) Accrued expenses are: home office, $750; branch, $350.

Instructions: (1) Prepare journal entries to record the foregoing transactions for (a) the branch and (b) the home office.

(2) Prepare individual statements for the branch and for the home office.

(3) Prepare combined statements for the branch and the home office.

(4) Prepare the journal entries to adjust and close the books at the end of the month for (a) the branch and (b) the home office.

7-4. On January 1, 19X6, the Barton Co. opened a new branch in a neighboring city. A summary of transactions for the home office and the branch for 19X6 and the balance sheet for the home office on January 1 are as follows:

Home Office Transactions

(a) Transfers of cash to branch, $42,500.

(b) Transfers of merchandise to branch (billed at cost), $50,200.

(c) Sales on account, $105,000.

(d) Purchases on account, $122,500.

(e) Collections on account, $113,600.

(f) Payments on account, $124,000.

(g) Expenses paid, $26,600.

(h) Cash received from branch, $53,400.

(i) Dividends paid, $10,000.

Adjusting data on December 31:
Depreciation for year, $1,180.
Merchandise inventory, $48,500.
Prepaid expenses, $2,050.
Accrued expenses, $1,350.

Branch Transactions

(a) Cash received from home office, $42,500.

(b) Merchandise received from home office, $50,200.

(c) Sales on account, $66,000.

(d) Purchases on account, $22,500.

(e) Collections on account deposited to the credit of the home office, $53,400.

(f) Payments on account, $12,250.

(g) Purchase of furniture and fixtures for cash, $8,000.

(h) Expenses paid, $18,000.

Adjusting data on December 31:
Depreciation, $650.
Merchandise inventory, $23,500.
Prepaid expenses, $750.
Accrued expenses, $300.

Balance Sheet

Assets		Liabilities and Stockholders' Equity	
Cash..................................	$ 59,300	Accrued expenses..............	$ 1,250
Accounts receivable...........	27,650	Accounts payable	22,800
Merchandise inventory	40,120	Capital stock, $20 par	50,000
Prepaid expenses..............	1,800	Retained earnings..............	70,420
Furniture and fix-			
tures $20,000			
Less accumulated			
depreciation..... 4,400	15,600	Total liabilities and stock-	
Total assets......................	$144,470	holders' equity................	$144,470

Instructions: (1) Prepare journal entries to record the foregoing transactions for (a) the branch and (b) the home office.

(2) Prepare individual statements for the branch and for the home office.

(3) Prepare combined statements for the branch and the home office.

(4) Prepare the journal entries to adjust and close the books for (a) the branch and (b) the home office.

7-5. The branch account on the home office books of the Sunset Co. and the home office account on the branch books on January 31, 19X1, are as follows:

Wilshire Branch

19X1			19X1		
Jan. 1	Balance	62,815	Jan. 15	Remittance	10,600
5	Merchandise ship- ments: 100 units of Product A @ $37.85	3,785	22	Merchandise returns .	410
12	Merchandise ship- ments: 200 units of Product A @ $37.85 200 units of Product B @ $44.95	16,560			
15	Advertising charge- able to branch	600			
29	Merchandise ship- ments	4,400			

Home Office

19X1			19X1		
Jan. 13	Remittance	10,600	Jan. 1	Balance	62,815
18	Merchandise returns .	410	8	Mdse. shipments.......	3,785
22	Understatement of depreciation in 19X0 .	540	16	Mdse. shipments.......	16,650
31	Remittance	16,000	20	Collection of home of- fice account	750

Instructions: (1) Prepare a statement reconciling the reciprocal accounts as of January 31, 19X1.

(2) Prepare any necessary entries for the books of the home office as well as for the branch before combined statements can be prepared.

7-6. The branch account on the home office books of Block and Bell, Inc., and the home office accounts on the branch books on January 31, 19X7, are as follows:

Beverly Hills Branch

19X7			19X7		
Jan. 1	Balance	50,615	Jan. 20	Cash received from branch....................	14,000
16	Merchandise ship- ments.....................	22,600		Remittance received from branch cus- tomer in settlement of branch account.....	65
31	Expenses chargeable to branch	215			

Home Office

19X7			19X7		
Jan. 10	Uncollectible ac- counts written off......	1,200	Jan. 1	Balance	28,415
20	Cash remittance to home office	14,000	21	Correction for income understatement for December	310
			31	Cost of merchandise sold	21,400
			31	Income for January....	1,440

Shipments from Home Office

19X7			19X7		
Jan. 31	Cost of merchandise sold	21,400	Jan. 1	Balance	22,200
31	Shipments returned to home office	840	16	Shipments from home office	21,200

The following additional data are available in reconciling the accounts:

(a) A $1,400 shipment of goods charged by the home office to the Beverly Hills branch was actually sent to the Brentwood branch.

(b) The goods returned by the branch are in transit and do not appear on the home office records.

(c) The branch failed to recognize expenses incurred by the home office and chargeable against income, $215, in calculating its income for January.

(d) The allowance for doubtful accounts on branch receivables is maintained by the home office.

Instructions: (1) Prepare a statement reconciling the reciprocal accounts as of January 31, 19X7.

(2) Prepare any necessary entries to correct and bring the accounts up to date on (a) the books of the branch and (b) the books of the home office.

7-7. Comparison between the interoffice account of the Walsh Wholesale Company with its suburban branch and the corresponding account carried on the latter's books shows the following discrepancies at the close of business on September 30, 19X2:

(a) A debit of $870 (Office Furniture) on the home office books is recorded by the branch as $780.

(b) A credit for $300 (Merchandise Allowances) by the home office is recorded by the branch as $350.

(c) The home office charges the branch $325 for interest on open account, which the branch fails to take up in full; instead, the branch sends to the home office an incorrect adjusting memo, reducing the charge by $75, and sets up a liability for the net amount.

(d) A labor charge by the home office, $433, is recorded twice by the branch.

(e) A charge of $785 for freight on merchandise is made by the home office, but the amount is recorded by the branch as $78.50.

(f) The branch incorrectly sends the home office a debit note for $293, representing its proportion of a bill for truck repairs; the home office does not record it.

(g) The home office receives $475 from the sale of a truck, which it erroneously credits to the branch; the branch does not charge the home office therewith.

(h) The branch accidentally receives a copy of the home office entry dated October 10, 19X2, correcting item (g), and records a credit in favor of the home office as of September 30, 19X2.

The balance of the branch account on the home office books shows $131,690 receivable from the branch at September 30, 19X2. The interoffice accounts were in balance at the beginning of the year.

Instructions: (1) Determine the balance of the home office account on the branch books before adjustment.

(2) Determine the correct amount of the interoffice balance.

(3) Reconcile the amount of $131,690 on the home office books with the adjusted balance of the reciprocal accounts.

(4) Prepare the journal entry or entries necessary to adjust the branch books.

(AICPA adapted)

8
Home Office and Branch Relationships — Special Problems

In addition to the general branch-home office relationships described in the preceding chapter, there are other relationships that create special accounting problems. These relationships are: (1) interbranch transfers of cash, (2) interbranch transfers of merchandise, and (3) merchandise shipments to branches involving billings at arbitrary rates above cost or at retail sales prices.

INTERBRANCH TRANSFERS OF CASH

Ordinarily, branch activities are limited to transactions with the home office and with outsiders. On certain occasions, however, the home office may authorize the transfer of certain assets from one branch to another. Instead of opening special accounts with member branches, branches will normally clear such transfers through the home office account. To illustrate, assume that upon authorization by the home office, Branch #1 sends cash of $1,000 to Branch #2. The entries to record this transfer on the home office and branch books are:

Home Office		Branch #1		Branch #2	
Branch #2....... 1,000		Home Office 1,000		Cash.............. 1,000	
Branch #1....	1,000	Cash............	1,000	Home Office .	1,000

When this procedure is followed, settlement between individual branches is not required; the net extent of branch accountability so far as affiliated units are concerned is summarized in one account, the home office account.

INTERBRANCH TRANSFERS OF MERCHANDISE

When merchandise is supplied by the home office to its branches, it may become necessary in certain instances for the home office to authorize the transfer of goods from one branch to another. Interbranch transfers of merchandise, like interbranch transfers of cash, are normally cleared through the home office account rather than through special accounts with member branches.

In the case of interbranch merchandise transfers, a special problem arises with respect to the handling of freight charges. A branch is properly charged with the cost of freight on goods it receives. In arriving at the cost of the merchandise inventory at the end of the period, freight charges are properly recognized as a part of that cost. But a branch should not be charged with excessive freight when, because of indirect routing, excessive costs are incurred. Under such circumstances, the branch acquiring the goods should be charged for no more than the normal freight from the usual shipping point. The office directing the interbranch transfer and responsible for the excessive cost should absorb the excess as an expense.

To illustrate the procedure to be followed, assume that the Superior Co. ships goods to Branch #5, billing the branch for the goods at $4,500 plus freight charges incurred, $600. At a subsequent date, the home office authorizes the transfer of these goods to Branch #8. Branch #5 pays the freight charge on the transfer, $450. If the shipment had been made by the home office directly to Branch #8, the freight charge would have been $650. Entries to record this interbranch transfer of merchandise on the books of the home office, Branch #5, and Branch #8 would be as follows:

Books of Home Office

Transactions	Entry

Original shipment of goods and charge to Branch #5 for cost of goods and freight.	Branch #5 5,100
	    Shipments to Branch #5......... 4,500
	    Cash...................................... 600

Authorization of transfer of goods from Branch #5 to Branch #8: Branch #8 charged for cost of goods and normal freight; Branch #5 credited for original charges plus freight paid on transfer to Branch #8.	Shipments to Branch #5............ 4,500
	    Shipments to Branch #8......... 4,500
	
	Branch #8 5,150
	Excess Freight on Interbranch
	Transfers of Merchandise 400
	    Branch #5 5,550

Books of Branch #5

Transactions	Entry
Original receipt of goods and charges for cost of goods and freight.	Shipments from Home Office ..... 4,500 Freight In.................................. 600 Home Office 5,100

Transfer of goods at order of home office; charge to home office for original charges plus freight paid on reshipment to Branch #8.	Home Office 5,550
	    Shipments from Home Office .. 4,500
	    Freight In............................... 600
	    Cash...................................... 450

Books of Branch #8

Transactions	Entry
Receipt of goods from Branch #5; charges recognized for cost of goods and normal freight.	Shipments from Home Office ..... 4,500 Freight In.................................. 650 Home Office 5,150

In preparing the income statement for the home office, the excess freight charge may be reported as a subtraction from the summary of branch earnings in the lower section of the statement. On the combined income statement, the charge may be reported in the cost of goods sold, selling expense, or general and administrative expense section, depending on the division of the company that is responsible for such transfers.

In the example, it was assumed that neither branch was responsible for the excess freight and the charge was therefore reported on the home office books. If excess freight results from a mistake in an order for goods by a branch or from some other branch failure, the charge should be borne by the branch and reported on its books.

Branch Billing at Amounts Other Than Cost

When a home office bills the branch for merchandise at a figure other than cost, billing is usually made at an arbitrary rate above cost or at the retail sales figure.

Billing at an arbitrary rate above cost. Billing by the home office may be made at some arbitrary rate above cost in order to withhold from branch officials complete information concerning the actual earnings from branch operations. In other instances, this policy is followed as a means of assigning a charge for goods procurement and handling as well as for the special costs that are related to the home office-branch relationship.

Upon acquiring merchandise from the home office, the branch records the charges that are listed on the invoices accompanying the goods. When billings to the branch exceed cost, the earnings determined by the branch will be less than actual earnings; the inventories reported by the branch at the billed figures will exceed cost. These factors must be recognized by the home office and given effect upon its accounting records in summarizing branch operations.

Assume that goods costing $10,000 are shipped by a home office to a branch, and the branch is billed for the goods at 20% above cost, or $12,000. The shipment may be recorded as follows:

Transaction	Home Office Books		Branch Books	

Transfer of merchandise to branch:
Home office cost, $10,000.
Billing to branch, $12,000.
	Branch #1.......... 12,000
	  Shipments to
	    Branch #1.......
	  Unrealized
	  Intercompany
	  Inventory Profit
		10,000
		
		2,000
			Shipments from
			Home Office........ 12,000
			  Home Office.....
				
				12,000

The branch records the goods at their billed price. The home office makes the following entry: Branch #1 is debited for the billed amount; Shipments to Branch #1 is credited for the actual cost of the merchandise; Unrealized Intercompany Inventory Profit is credited for the difference between the billed price and the cost of the goods shipped. Branch and home office accounts, then, are reciprocal. Merchandise shipments reported at cost can be subtracted from the sum of the beginning inventory and the purchases in arriving at the cost of merchandise available for home office sales. The balance in the unrealized intercompany inventory profit account is properly recognized as an offset against the branch account in arriving at the actual investment in the branch.

As the branch sells the goods acquired from the home office and recognizes profit for the difference between the fictitious billed price and the sales price, the difference between the cost and the billed price, reported by the home office in the unrealized profit account, is properly recognized as earned. Ordinarily, the home office defers recognition of such earnings until the end of the fiscal period. At that time the unrealized profit account is reduced to a balance equal to the unrealized profit actually present in the branch inventory, and the amount of the reduction is added to the income reported by the branch.

To illustrate, referring again to the example, unrealized profit of $2,000 is recorded on the books of the home office upon the shipment of merchandise, cost $10,000, at a billed price of $12,000. At the end of the period the branch reports an inventory of $8,400. The actual cost of the branch inventory is $7,000 ($8,400 ÷ 1.20). The unrealized profit balance of $2,000 is excessive and should be reduced to $1,400. In arriving at net income, the branch recognizes cost of goods sold at $3,600 (12,000 − $8,400). The actual cost of goods sold by the branch is $3,000 ($3,600 ÷ 1.20). The earnings reported by the branch are understated and should be increased by $600. Assuming that the branch books report net income of $5,000, entries to summarize branch activities are made on the branch and home office books as follows:

Transaction	Home Office Books	Branch Books

(a) To close branch earnings to home office account on branch books.
(b) To recognize branch earnings on home office books.
	(b) Branch #1......... 5,000
	    Branch #1
	    Income 5,000
		(a) Income
		    Summary 5,000
		    Home Office ... 5,000

To bring unrealized profit account to required balance and to correct branch earnings.	Unrealized
	Intercompany
	Inventory Profit....... 600
	    Branch #1
	    Income 600	

To close branch earnings into income summary account.	Branch #1 Income.. 5,600 Income Summary. 5,600	

The balance of Unrealized Intercompany Inventory Profit is now $1,400 and reports the overstatement in the branch investment balance at the end of the period. The credit of $600 to the branch income account on the home office books corrects the branch earnings for the overstatement of the branch cost of goods sold.

When the branch inventory consists of goods acquired from the home office at a fictitious price and also goods purchased from outsiders at cost, it is necessary to distinguish between the two classes of goods so that the home office can determine the overvaluation in that portion of the branch inventory acquired from the home office.

Billing at retail sales price. The home office may bill a branch for merchandise at its retail sales price not only to conceal information concerning branch earnings from branch officials, but also to provide a more effective control over merchandise handled by the branch. The home office, when informed of branch sales currently, is provided with a continuous record of the goods in the hands of the branch. The inventory position is calculated by subtracting sales to date from the retail sales price of goods made available to the branch. At the end of the period, a physical inventory for the branch at retail sales price should be equal to the difference between the billed price of goods available for sale and net sales for the period. If the inventory reported by the branch is not equal to this difference, the discrepancy must be investigated and explained to the satisfaction of the home office.

If the branch is billed for goods at the sales price, the branch cost of goods sold will be equal to sales, and branch activities will show a loss from operations equal to the expenses of operation. Branch accounts may be adjusted and closed in the usual manner at the end of the fiscal period, and the home office account debited for the reported loss. Branch statements may be prepared and submitted to the home office. Since the branch income statement gives no indication of the actual profitability of branch activities, its value to the branch is limited to its use for statistical and comparative purposes.

In accounting for shipments that are billed at sales price, the home office may follow a procedure that is similar to that employed for shipments at an arbitrary rate above cost. A memorandum record is maintained by the home office, showing both the cost and the billed prices for all goods sent to the branch. Upon shipping goods to a branch, the unrealized intercompany inventory account is credited for the difference between the cost and the billed price. The home office will require the branch to submit a detailed summary of the goods on hand at the end of each period. By reference to the memorandum record of shipments, merchandise items comprising the inventory may be converted from sales prices to costs and the balance that should remain in the unrealized profit account determined. The laborious process of converting sales price to cost for each item or class of merchandise may be avoided if the selling prices of all merchandise are fixed by applying a uniform percentage markup on cost. The cost of the inventory may then be calculated as illustrated in the previous section.

The amount transferred from the unrealized profit account to the branch income account reports the gross profit that has been realized as a result of branch sales. This transfer converts the loss recorded as a result of the branch report into a net income if branch operations have actually proved profitable. The balance remaining in the unrealized profit account reports the overstatement in the branch investment balance.

Combined Statements when Goods Are Billed at Amounts Other Than Cost

When affiliated units record interoffice transfers of goods at cost, the preparation of combined financial statements is a relatively simple matter. Reciprocal home office and branch account balances are eliminated and balance sheet data are then combined. Reciprocal interoffice revenue and expense balances are eliminated and income statement data are combined. When goods are billed to a branch at amounts other than cost, special problems are encountered in the preparation of combined statements. The ending inventory on the branch balance sheet reported at an amount other than cost must be restated in terms of cost in preparing the combined balance sheet. The beginning and the ending inventory balances on the branch income statement reported at amounts other than cost must be restated in terms of cost in preparing the combined income statement.

When the preparation of combined statements calls for the restatement of real and nominal accounts as well as the elimination of reciprocal accounts, it is generally desirable to develop such summaries through the preparation of work sheets that include both balance sheet and income statement data. As a basis for illustrating such work sheets, the separate balance sheets and a combined balance sheet for the Rodger Corporation and its branch on December 31, 19X2, are as follows:

Rodger Corporation
Balance Sheet — Home Office
December 31, 19X2

Assets			Liabilities and Stockholders' Equity		
Cash.................................		$ 25,000	Liabilities		
Accounts receivable..........		60,000	Accounts payable............................		$ 40,000
Merchandise inventory		100,000			
Furniture and fixtures........	$30,000		Stockholders' Equity		
Less accumulated depre-			Capital stock..................	$200,000	
ciation......................	12,000	18,000	Retained earnings	36,500	236,500
Branch	$78,500				
Less unrealized inter-					
company inventory					
profit.........................	5,000	73,500			
			Total liabilities and stockholders' eq-		
Total assets.....................................		$276,500	uity		$276,500

Rodger Corporation
Balance Sheet — Branch
December 31, 19X2

Assets		Liabilities	
Cash..........	$ 10,000	Accounts payable...........................	$ 10,000
Accounts receivable........................	20,000	Home office.....................................	78,500
Merchandise inventory	45,000		
Furniture and fixtures........ $22,500			
Less accumulated depre-			
ciation...................... 9,000	13,500		
Total assets..................................	$ 88,500	Total liabilities................................	$ 88,500

Rodger Corporation
Combined Balance Sheet for Home Office and Branch
December 31, 19X2

Assets		Liabilities and Stockholders' Equity	
Cash...	$ 35,000	Liabilities	
Accounts receivable........................	80,000	Accounts payable...........................	$ 50,000
Merchandise inventory	140,000		
Furniture and fixtures........ $52,500		Stockholders' Equity	
Less accumulated depre-		Capital stock................. $200,000	
ciation...................... 21,000	31,500	Retained earnings 36,500	236,500
		Total liabilities and stockholders' eq-	
Total assets..................................	$286,500	uity	$286,500

The branch inventory on December 31, 19X2, was composed of goods acquired from both the home office and outsiders. Goods costing $20,000 were acquired from outsiders; the balance, $25,000, was acquired from the home office and is stated at billed price, which is 25% above cost.

Transactions of the home office and the branch during 19X3 are listed and recorded as follows:

Transactions	Home Office Books		Branch Books	
Purchases on account.	Purchases....... 220,000		Purchases....... 25,000	
	Accounts		Accounts	
	Payable........	220,000	Payable........	25,000
Goods shipped to branch by home office: cost, $48,000; billed price, 25% above cost, or $60,000.	Branch 60,000		Shipments from Home	
	Shipments to		Office 60,000	
	Branch	48,000	Home Office .	60,000
	Unrealized			
	Intercompany			
	Inventory			
	Profit...........	12,000		

Transactions	Home Office Books		Branch Books	
Sales on account.	Accounts Receivable 300,000		Accounts Receivable 125,000	
	Sales	300,000	Sales	125,000
Collections on account.	Cash............... 305,000		Cash............... 115,000	
	Accounts Receivable ...	305,000	Accounts Receivable ...	115,000
Payments on account.	Accounts Payable........... 200,000		Accounts Payable........... 30,000	
	Cash............	200,000	Cash............	30,000
Payment of expenses.	Expenses 47,000		Expenses 17,750	
	Cash............	47,000	Cash............	17,750
Declaration and payment of dividends by home office.	Dividends........ 25,000			
	Cash............	25,000		
Remittances by branch to home office.	Cash............... 30,000		Home Office 30,000	
	Branch	30,000	Cash............	30,000
Adjusting data: Depreciation for year.	Expenses 3,000		Expenses 2,250	
	Accumulated Depreciation.	3,000	Accumulated Depreciation.	2,250
To close beginning merchandise inventories.	Income Summary 100,000		Income Summary 45,000	
	Merchandise Inventory, Jan. 1	100,000	Merchandise Inventory, Jan. 1	45,000
To record ending merchandise inventories: Home office .... $80,000 Branch: Acquired from outsiders .... $10,000 Acquired from home office at billed price .. 20,000 Total $30,000	Merchandise Inventory, Dec. 31 80,000		Merchandise Inventory, Dec. 31 30,000	
	Income Summary	80,000	Income Summary	30,000

    A work sheet for the preparation of combined statements is illustrated on page 217. The balances listed in the first two columns of the work sheet report the account balances of the home office and the branch as of December 31, 19X3. The trial balances are adjusted and up to date except for the ending merchandise inventories. Beginning inventories are reported in the adjusted trial balances as debits. These inventories are to be recognized in arriving at cost of goods sold. Ending inventories are listed following both trial balance debit and credit sections. Ending inventories are reported as debits so that they may be recognized as assets in the development of the balance sheet. Ending inventories are also reported as credits so that they may be recognized as subtractions from the cost of goods available for sale (beginning inventories and purchases) in arriving at cost of goods sold.

Work Sheet for Combined Statements for Home Office and Branch
December 31, 19X3

	Home Office	Branch	Adjustments and Eliminations Dr.	Adjustments and Eliminations Cr.	Income Statement Dr.	Income Statement Cr.	Retained Earnings Dr.	Retained Earnings Cr.	Balance Sheet Dr.	Balance Sheet Cr.
Debits										
Cash	88,000	47,250							135,250	
Accounts Receivable	55,000	30,000							85,000	
Merchandise Inventory, Jan. 1, 19X3	100,000	45,000		(c) 5,000	140,000					
Furniture and Fixtures	30,000	22,500							52,500	
Branch	108,500			(a) 108,500						
Purchases	220,000	25,000			245,000					
Shipment from Home Office		60,000		(b) 60,000						
Expenses	50,000	20,000			70,000					
Dividends	25,000						25,000			
	676,500	249,750								
Merchandise Inventory, December 31, 19X3 (Balance Sheet)	80,000	30,000		(d) 4,000					106,000	
Credits										
Unrealized Intercompany Inventory Profit	17,000		(b) 12,000 (c) 5,000							
Accumulated Depr. — Furniture and Fixtures	15,000	11,250								26,250
Accounts Payable	60,000	5,000								65,000
Home Office		108,500	(a) 108,500							
Capital Stock	200,000									200,000
Retained Earnings, January 1, 19X3	36,500							36,500		
Sales	300,000	125,000				425,000				
Shipments to Branch	48,000		(b) 48,000							
	676,500	249,750								
Merchandise Inventory, December 31, 19X3 (Income Statement)	80,000	30,000	(d) 4,000			106,000				
			177,500	177,500	455,000	531,000	25,000	36,500	378,750	291,250
Net Income					76,000			76,000		87,500
					531,000	531,000	87,500	112,500	378,750	378,750
Balance of Retained Earnings to Balance Sheet							112,500	112,500		

The transactions that were given on pages 215 and 216 resulted in unrealized profit on the home office books as follows:

Unrealized Intercompany Inventory Profit

	19X3
	Jan. 1 Balance relating to goods acquired from home office at 25% above cost; billed price $25,000, cost $20,000 ($25,000 − [$25,000 ÷ 1.25]). 5,000
	Jan. 1–
	Dec. 31 Merchandise, cost $48,000, billed at 25% above cost 12,000
	(Balance in account, $17,000)

The branch account on the home office books appeared as follows:

Branch

19X3		19X3	
Jan. 1 Balance 78,500		Jan. 1–	
Jan. 1–		Dec. 31 Remittances from branch 30,000	
Dec. 31 Shipments to branch 60,000			
(Balance in account, $108,500)			

The home office account on the branch books appeared as follows:

Home Office

19X3		19X3	
Jan. 1–		Jan. 1 Balance 78,500	
Dec. 31 Remittances to home office 30,000		Jan. 1–	
		Dec. 31 Shipments from home office.... 60,000	
		(Balance in account, $108,500)	

In developing combined statements, the affiliated units are recognized as one unit. Accounts for the home office and the branch must be restated so that, when combined, they will offer those balances that would have resulted if the transactions of the related units had been recorded in one set of books. In this process any balance sheet accounts that report interoffice debits and credits and that have no meaning when the related units are recognized as one unit are eliminated. Any income statement accounts that report transfers of merchandise or charges for services between affiliated units similarly require elimination. Furthermore, when merchandise accounts report values other than cost and an unrealized intercompany inventory profit account has been established, merchandise accounts will require restatement to cost and the unrealized profit account will require cancellation.

The adjustments and the eliminations that were made on the work sheet for the Rodger Corporation and its branch in arriving at a summary of the activities of related units are described as follows:

(a) The reciprocal accounts Home Office and Branch are canceled by the following elimination:

Home Office	108,500	
Branch..		108,500

(b) Account balances resulting from the transfer of merchandise between offices are canceled by the following elimination:

Shipments to Branch..	48,000	
Unrealized Intercompany Inventory Profit	12,000	
Shipments from Home Office..		60,000

(c) The original balance of $5,000 in the unrealized profit account is applied to the beginning inventory balance to reduce it to cost as follows:

Unrealized Intercompany Inventory Profit	5,000	
Merchandise Inventory, Jan. 1, 19X3..............................		5,000

(d) The ending inventory, both as a balance sheet value and an income statement value, is reduced by $4,000 to its actual cost as follows:

Merchandise Inventory, Dec. 31, 19X3 (Income Statement) .	4,000	
Merchandise Inventory, Dec. 31, 19X3 (Balance Sheet)....		4,000

Combining branch and home office accounts results in those balances that would have been obtained if one set of accounts had been maintained in recording activities of both the branch and the home office. Combined account balances are carried to appropriate Income Statement, Retained Earnings, and Balance Sheet columns on the work sheet. Following such transfers, the Income Statement columns are summarized and the net income is carried to the Retained Earnings columns. The retained earnings balance may now be determined and carried to the Balance Sheet columns. The statement columns are used in preparing the combined statements illustrated on pages 220 and 221.

The adjustments and eliminations just described are made only on the work sheet. The accounts and the ledgers of the home office and the branch are not affected. Home office and branch accounts are closed in the usual manner. Transactions of subsequent periods will continue to be recorded on the books of the home office and the branch with appropriate recognition of the special requirements that are found in employing separate self-balancing records for each of the related units.

The accounts for the home office and the branch are closed by the following entries:

Transaction	Home Office Books		Branch Books	
Closing entries: To close nominal accounts.	Sales.............. 300,000 Shipments to Branch .... 48,000 Purchases.... Expenses ..... Income Summary	220,000 50,000 78,000	Sales................ 125,000 Purchases...... Shipments from Home Office............ Expenses....... Income Summary	25,000 60,000 20,000 20,000

Transaction	Home Office Books		Branch Books	
To close branch earnings to home office account.			Income Summary.......... 5,000 Home Office...	5,000

To recognize branch earnings on home office books:
(a) Branch income per branch books, $5,000.
(b) To bring unrealized profit account to required balance and to correct branch earnings:
Balance in unrealized profit account before adjustment, 12/31/X3..... $17,000
Required balance, 12/31/X3 (billed price $20,000 − cost [$20,000 ÷ 1.25])   4,000
Transfer to branch income. $13,000
	(a) Branch.......
	  Branch
	  Income....
	(b) Unrealized
	Intercompany
	Inventory Profit
	  Branch
	  Income....
		5,000
		
		5,000
		
		13,000
		
		13,000		

To close branch earnings into income summary account.	Branch Income
	  Income
	  Summary .....
		18,000
		
		18,000		

To close combined earnings for the period to Retained Earnings.	Income
	Summary ....
	  Retained
	  Earnings ......
		76,000
		
		76,000		

To close dividends balance.	Retained Earnings .... Dividends.....	25,000 25,000		

Rodger Corporation
Combined Income Statement for Home Office and Branch
For Year Ended December 31, 19X3

Sales..		$425,000
Cost of goods sold:		
Merchandise inventory, Jan. 1, 19X3..	$140,000	
Purchases...	245,000	
Merchandise available for sale..	$385,000	
Less merchandise inventory, Dec. 31, 19X3...	106,000	279,000
Gross profit...		$146,000
Expenses..		70,000
Net income		$ 76,000

Rodger Corporation
Combined Retained Earnings Statement for Home Office and Branch
For Year Ended December 31, 19X3

Retained earnings, January 1, 19X3..	$ 36,500
Add net income for year...	76,000
	$112,500
Deduct dividends declared...	25,000
Retained earnings, December 31, 19X3..	$ 87,500

Rodger Corporation
Combined Balance Sheet for Home Office and Branch
December 31, 19X3

Assets			Liabilities and Stockholders' Equity		
Cash...		$135,250	Liabilities		
Accounts receivable........................		85,000	Accounts payable............................		$ 65,000
Merchandise inventory		106,000	Stockholders' Equity		
Furniture and fixtures........	$52,500		Capital stock..................	$200,000	
Less accumulated depre-			Retained earnings	87,500	287,500
ciation......................	26,250	26,250			
			Total liabilities and stockholders' eq-		
Total assets....................................		$352,500	uity		$352,500

QUESTIONS

1. A home office frequently authorizes the transfer of cash from one branch to another. How should such transfers be reported on the books of the home office and the respective branches?

2. Describe the nature of the special problem that arises when a home office authorizes interbranch transfers of merchandise.

3. How would you recommend that the balance of the account Excess Freight on Interbranch Transfers of Merchandise be reported on (a) the income statement for the home office and (b) the combined income statement?

4. The Martin Department Store maintains three branch stores in outlying suburban districts. While merchandise is sold at an average markup on cost of 25%, certain classes of merchandise are sold at some special sales at a smaller margin, at cost, or in some instances below cost. Retail prices are also changed as a result of wholesale price fluctuations. What are the advantages and the disadvantages to be found in billing the branches for merchandise (a) at cost, (b) at a uniform percentage above cost, and (c) at selling price?

5. The home office ships merchandise to its branch, billing the branch for such goods at a standard percentage above cost. (a) What entries are made on the books of the home office and the branch in recording the transfer? (b) What entries will be required by the home office in recognizing the sale, to outsiders, of a portion of such a shipment?

6. The home office of Frank Co. bills branches for merchandise at amounts in excess of cost and establishes an unrealized profit account on such transfers. At the end of each period, the balance of this account is reduced to the excess still reported in the branch inventory. (a) How would you treat this balance in preparing a balance sheet for the home office? (b) How would you treat this balance in preparing a combined balance sheet for home office and branch?

7. Welson, Inc., bills its branch for merchandise at an amount in excess of cost and establishes an unrealized profit account on its books. The branch subsequently finds that it does not require all of the goods and returns part of the shipment. (a) What entries would be required for such a return on both the branch and the home office books? (b) How would you recognize freight charges incurred by the home office and subsequently by the branch on the transfer and the return of the goods?

8. A branch acquires goods for sale from both its home office and outside suppliers. The home office bills the branch for merchandise at the sales price, which involves varying markups on the different classes of goods shipped. How can the home office arrive at the branch inventory cost at the end of the period?

9. What special adjustments are required in the preparation of work sheets for combined statements when an unrealized profit account is found on the home office trial balance?

10. What is the effect of the preparation of combined statements on the closing entries for home office and branch books?

11. In listing adjusted trial balance data for home office and branch in the development of work sheets for combined statements, home office and branch reciprocal balances are not equal if the home office has recognized branch earnings but the branch has not yet closed its nominal accounts. What effect does this have on the elimination of the reciprocal accounts?

12. The branches of the Bolton Co. find it necessary to borrow from banks in their respective cities at frequent intervals. The home office, however, wishes to maintain a complete record of all bank obligations on its own books. What accounting procedure would you recommend on the books of the branches and the home office when (a) a branch borrows an amount from a bank and (b) the branch repays the loan together with interest?

13. The New York branch of the Suprex Products Co. receives remittances from customers whose accounts originated in sales made by other branches. This branch keeps the cash from such collections and notifies the home office and the other branches. What entries would you recommend be made by the home office and the related branches in accounting for the collections?

EXERCISES

1. Branch A is authorized by its home office to send to Branch B $1,500 cash. How is this transfer best recorded on the books of (a) Branch A, (b) Branch B, and (c) the home office?

2. The McCall Company maintains branches that market the products that it produces. Merchandise is billed to the branches at manufacturing costs, with the branches paying freight charges from the home office to the branch. On November 15, Branch No. 1 ships part of its stock to Branch No. 5 upon authorization by the home office. Originally Branch No. 1 had been billed for this merchandise at $1,600 and had paid freight charges of $350 on the shipment from the home office. Branch No. 5, upon receiving the merchandise, pays freight charges of $250 on the shipment from Branch No. 1. If the shipment had been made from the home office directly to Branch No. 5, the freight cost to Branch No. 5 would have been $400. How should the merchandise transfers be recorded on the books of (a) Branch No. 1, (b) Branch No. 5, and (c) the home office?

3. Trial balances for the home office and the branch of the Ace Company show the following items, before adjustment, on December 31. Differences in the shipments account balances result from the home office policy of billing the branch for merchandise at 20% above cost.

	Home Office Books	Branch Books
Unrealized intercompany inventory profit	$3,600	
Shipments to branch...	8,000	
Purchases (outsiders).......................................		$ 2,500
Shipments from home office		9,600
Merchandise inventory, December 1		15,000

(a) What part of the branch inventory as of December 1 represented purchases from outsiders and what part represented goods acquired from the home office?
(b) Assuming that the branch ending inventory is $10,000, composed of merchandise from home office at billed price, $8,400, and merchandise from outsiders at cost, $1,600, what entry is necessary on the home office books to adjust the unrealized profit account at the end of the fiscal period?

4. The Marsh Co. bills its branch for merchandise at 135% of cost. On December 31 the balance in the unrealized profit account is to be calculated from the following information reported by the branch:

	Merchandise from Home Office (at billed price)	Merchandise Purchased from Outsiders (at cost)	Merchandise Total
Merchandise inventory, Dec. 1	$16,200	$ 4,000	$20,200
Merchandise into stock, Dec. 1–31	20,250	12,000	32,250
Merchandise inventory, Dec. 31	18,900	5,000	23,900

(a) What is the balance of the unrealized profit account on the home office books before any adjustment is made for branch sales for December?
(b) What entry is required on the home office books to adjust the unrealized profit account at the end of December?
(c) Assuming that the branch had returned to the home office merchandise originally acquired at a billed price of $540, what entries would be made on the branch and home office books to record this return?

5. The Berkeley branch of the Bruin Co. is billed for merchandise by the home office at 20% above cost. The branch in turn prices merchandise for sales purposes at 25% above billed price. On January 17 all of the branch merchandise is destroyed by fire. No insurance was maintained. Branch accounts show the following information:

Merchandise inventory, Jan. 1 (at billed price)	$26,400
Shipments from home office (Jan. 1–17)	20,000
Sales..	15,000
Sales returns..	2,000
Sales allowances...	1,000

(a) What was the cost of the merchandise destroyed?

(b) Prepare the entries on both the branch books and the home office books to record the loss. (Assume perpetual inventory records.)

6. On December 1, Walsh Co. opened a Newark branch, to which merchandise billed at $30,000 was shipped. During the month additional shipments were made at billed prices of $12,000. During December the branch returned merchandise that was defective and received credits of $750 on the returns. At the end of the month the branch records its inventory at $18,500, which is from the following sources:

Merchandise acquired from home office at billed price.........	$16,500
Merchandise acquired from outsiders	2,000
Total inventory	$18,500

A branch loss for December is calculated at $2,600.

The home office has followed the practice of billing the branch at 20% above merchandise cost. Further, the home office has recorded branch merchandise shipments and returns in its regular sales and sales returns accounts at this billed price.

Prepare the journal entries on the books of the home office at the end of December to recognize the results of branch operations and to correct and bring its books up to date.

PROBLEMS

8-1. On December 31, the end of a monthly period, the trial balance for the Burnside Co. Branch No. 1 reported balances as follows:

Cash............................	2,510	Notes Payable	1,000
Merchandise Inventory .	16,000	Home Office.................	23,180
Store Supplies.............	400	Sales...........................	20,500
Store Furniture............	8,000	Purchases....................	5,000
Accumulated Deprecia-		Shipments from Home	
tion — Store Furni-		Office	10,500
ture........................	320	Selling Expenses..........	4,250
Accounts Payable	3,500	General Expenses	1,840

The home office bills the branch for merchandise at 33⅓% above cost. The following data were available on December 31:

Store supplies inventory, $140.
Depreciation of furniture, 1% a month.
Accrued selling expenses, $120.
Prepaid selling expenses, $150.

Merchandise inventories:	On Dec. 1	On Dec. 31
Amount received from home office (at billed price).....................................	$12,500	$14,200
Amount purchased from outsiders (at cost)..	3,500	2,750
Total on hand	$16,000	$16,950

The home office notified the branch on December 31 that it had paid off the branch note for $1,000.

Instructions: (1) Prepare the adjusting and closing entries for the branch.

(2) On the home office books, prepare the journal entries summarizing branch operations for the month.

8-2. Branch No. 12 was established by Royal, Inc., on March 1. Merchandise was billed to the branches by the home office at 30% above cost. Branch transactions during March were as follows:

Mar. 1.	Received from home office $8,500 cash and merchandise billed at $28,600.
1.	Paid $800 representing first and last month's rent on lease.
1.	Purchased furniture and fixtures for $6,500, paying $2,000 cash, the balance to be paid in 90 days. The home office is informed of this purchase, since all branch plant assets are carried on the home office books.
Mar. 1–31.	Purchased merchandise from outsiders on account, $9,500.
	Paid on account, $3,500.
	Sold merchandise on account, $16,025.
	Received in payment of accounts: cash, $8,000; notes, $1,500.

Paid expenses:

Advertising	$ 320
Sales salaries and commissions	750
Miscellaneous selling expenses	350
Miscellaneous general expenses	300
Total	$ 1,720

Remitted to home office $2,500 cash and returned merchandise that was unsuited for branch and that was billed at $1,040.

Received summary of home office charges to branch for March:

Depreciation of furniture and fixtures	$ 65
Insurance on branch assets (the home office originally debited Prepaid Insurance for payment of insurance premiums)	50
Taxes on branch assets (accrued by home office)	40
Advertising	450
Total	$ 605

On March 31 the branch had stock on hand as follows:

Merchandise received from home office (at billed amounts)	$18,850
Merchandise purchased from outsiders (at cost)	4,800
Total inventory	$23,650

Sales salaries of $40 had accrued on this date.

Instructions: (1) Prepare the branch journal entries to record the transactions listed and to adjust and close the books at the end of the month.

(2) Prepare the journal entries that are required on the books of the home office as a result of the foregoing.

8-3. Operating data for Paxton Co. of Cincinnati and its Dayton branch for 19X8 follow:

	Cincinnati Office	Dayton Office
Sales...	$1,060,000	$315,000
Inventory, January 1 (at cost)..................	115,000	
(at billed price)........		44,500
Purchases..	820,000	
Shipments to Dayton office (at cost)	210,000	
Shipments from Cincinnati office (at billed price)..		252,000
Inventory, December 31 (at cost)	142,500	
(at billed price)...		58,500
Operating expenses................................	382,000	101,500

Records show that the Dayton branch was billed for merchandise shipments as follows:

In 19X7, cost + 25%
In 19X8, cost + 20%

Instructions: (1) Prepare income statements for the branch and for the home office for the year ended December 31, 19X8.

(2) Prepare a combined income statement.

(3) Prepare the closing entries for the branch.

(4) Prepare the entries on the home office books to summarize branch and home office operations and to close the books.

8-4. The Ruggles Co. operates a branch in Cleveland. Operating data for the home office and the branch for 19X0 follow:

	Home Office	Branch
Sales...	$256,000	$78,500
Purchases from outsiders	210,000	20,000
Shipments to branch:		
Cost to home office....................................	30,000	
Billing price to branch		40,000
Expenses..	60,000	12,500
Inventories, January 1, 19X0:		
Home office, acquired from outsiders, at cost..	80,000	
Branch:		
Acquired from outsiders, at cost..............		7,500
Acquired from home office, at billed price, which averaged 22½% above cost..		24,500

Inventories, December 31, 19X0:
Home office, acquired from outsiders, at cost.. 55,000
Branch:
Acquired from outsiders, at cost.............. 5,500
Acquired from home office, at 19X0 billed price 26,000

Instructions: (1) Prepare an income statement for the branch and an income statement for the home office for the year ended December 31, 19X0.

(2) Prepare a combined income statement for branch and home office.

(3) Prepare the closing entries on the books of the branch.

(4) Prepare the entries recognizing the branch income, followed by the closing entries on the books of the home office.

8-5. On December 31, 19X5, the end of a monthly period, the following trial balances were prepared for the Spencer Co. and its branch. Merchandise was billed to the branch by the home office at 120% of cost.

	Home Office		Branch	
Cash..	10,350		2,650	
Accounts Receivable..............	26,200		12,850	
Merchandise Inventory (December 1).............................	31,500		14,400	
Furniture and Fixtures............	8,500		3,600	
Accumulated Depreciation — Furniture and Fixtures.........		2,500		540
Unrealized Intercompany Inventory Profit		3,700		
Store Supplies.......................	940		580	
Branch	33,760			
Accounts Payable		35,400		4,200
Home Office..........................				32,040
Capital Stock..........................		65,000		
Retained Earnings	6,850			
Sales.....................................		44,850		20,000
Shipments to Branch		8,500		
Purchases................................	27,600		4,100	
Shipments from Home Office ..			10,200	
Advertising Expense...............	2,850		2,800	
Salaries and Commissions Expense...............................	4,250		2,350	
Miscellaneous Selling Expense	1,850		1,050	
Rent Expense........................	2,700		1,500	
Miscellaneous General Expense (includes taxes and insurance)..........................	2,600		700	
	159,950	159,950	56,780	56,780

The following data were available on December 31:

Merchandise inventories: home office, cost $24,200; branch, $14,600, composed of merchandise received from the home office (at billed price), $11,700, and merchandise purchased from outsiders (at cost), $2,900.

Store supplies on hand: home office, $380; branch, $300.

Prepaid expenses (credit Miscellaneous General Expense): home office, $350; branch, $120.

Accrued expenses (debit Miscellaneous General Expense): home office, $260; branch, $105.

Depreciation of furniture and fixtures is recorded at 1% a month.

A cash remittance of $1,500 had been recorded on the branch books, but the cash has not yet been received by the home office and no entry has been made.

The home office had charged the branch with the following expenses that have not yet been recorded by the branch: taxes and insurance, $220.

Instructions: (1) Prepare individual statements for the branch and the home office for December, 19X5.

(2) Prepare a work sheet for combined statements.

(3) Prepare combined statements for the branch and the home office.

(4) Prepare the entries to adjust and close the books of (a) the branch and (b) the home office.

8-6. The Joy Music Company, a Washington corporation, operates two retail music stores, one located in Seattle and the other in Tacoma. Each store maintains a separate set of accounting records; intercompany transfers or transactions are recorded in an intercompany account carried on each set of records.

Purchases of a major item of inventory, such as organs and pianos, are made under a financial arrangement whereby a local bank advances 90% of the invoice price and the company pays 10%. If the bank note remains unpaid at the end of 90 days, the company is required to pay an additional 10% of the invoice price as a payment on the note.

In August, 19X9, the Seattle store purchased an organ for which the seller's draft in the amount of $6,300 was sent to The First National Bank of Seattle, which refused to finance the purchase of the instrument. Through the Tacoma store, arrangements to provide the financing were made with The Citizens Bank of Tacoma. The bank lent the Tacoma store 90% of the invoice price, or $5,670, which the Tacoma store deposited and credited to Notes Payable. The Seattle store drew a check payable to the Tacoma store for $630, or 10% of the invoice price, debiting the Tacoma intercompany account on its books. The Tacoma store credited the intercompany account with the Seattle store for the deposit.

The Tacoma store, using the 10% received from the Seattle store and the 90% advanced by the bank, drew a check payable to The First National Bank of Seattle in full payment of the draft, debiting Notes Payable.

In November, the Seattle store made the second payment of $630 directly to the Tacoma bank, debiting the Tacoma intercompany account, and also notified the Tacoma bookkeeper that the payment had been made. The Tacoma store debited Organ Purchases and credited the Seattle intercompany account. In December, the Seattle store paid off the balance on the note, debiting Organ Purchases.

Instructions: Prepare the entries that are required on each set of books to correct the account balances.

(AICPA adapted)

8-7. The trial balances of the home office and the branch office of The Allen Company appear as follows:

The Allen Company
Trial Balance
December 31, 19X7

Debits	Home	Branch
Cash..	17,000	200
Inventory — Home Office...............................	23,000	
Inventory — Branch		11,550
Sundry Assets	200,000	48,450
Branch	60,000	
Purchases..	190,000	
Shipments from Home Office		105,000
Freight in from Home Office...........................		5,500
Sundry Expenses	42,000	24,300
	532,000	195,000

Credits		
Sundry Liabilities..	35,000	3,500
Home Office...		51,500
Sales...	155,000	140,000
Shipments to Branch	110,000	
Unrealized Intercompany Inventory Profit........	1,000	
Capital Stock...	200,000	
Retained Earnings	31,000	
	532,000	195,000

The audit at December 31, 19X7, disclosed the following:

(1) The branch office deposits all cash receipts in a local bank for the account of the home office. The audit working papers for the cash cutoff revealed:

Amount	Deposited by Branch	Recorded by Home Office
$1,050	December 27, 19X7	December 30, 19X7
1,100	December 29, 19X7	January 2, 19X8
600	December 30, 19X7	January 3, 19X8
300	January 2, 19X8	January 6, 19X8

(2) The branch office pays locally incurred expenses from an imprest bank account that is maintained with a balance of $2,000. Checks are drawn once a week on this imprest account and the home office is notified of the amount needed to replenish the account. At December 30 an $1,800 reimbursement check was mailed to the branch office.

(3) The branch office receives all of its goods from the home office. The home office bills the goods at cost plus a markup of 10% of cost. On December 31 a shipment with a billing value of $5,000 was in transit to the branch. Freight costs are typically 5% of billed values. Freight costs are considered to be inventoriable costs.

(4) The trial balance beginning inventories are shown at their respective costs to the home office and to the branch office. The inventories on December 31, excluding the shipment in transit, are

Home office, at cost $30,000
Branch office, at billing value $10,400

Instructions: Prepare a work sheet for The Allen Company and its branch office, with columns for "Trial Balance," "Adjustments and Eliminations," "Home Office Income Statement," "Branch Income Statement," and "Combined Balance Sheet." The branch income statement should be prepared on the basis of home office cost. (Formal journal entries are not required. Supporting computations must be in good form.) Number your work sheet adjusting and eliminating entries. Disregard income taxes.

(AICPA adapted)

8-8. You are engaged to audit the records of the Western Import Company, which has not previously been audited. The trial balance at December 31, 19X3, follows:

Debits	Home Office	Branch
Cash...	15,000	2,000
Accounts Receivable..	20,000	17,000
Inventory — December 31, 19X3	30,000	8,000
Plant Assets (net)	150,000	
Branch	44,000	
Cost of Goods Sold..	220,000	93,000
Expenses	70,000	41,000
Total	549,000	161,000

Credits		
Accounts Payable	23,000	
Mortgage Payable	50,000	
Capital Stock..	100,000	
Retained Earnings — January 1, 19X3..............	26,000	
Sales..	350,000	150,000
Accrued Expenses		2,000
Home Office..		9,000
Total	549,000	161,000

The following additional information is to be considered:

(a) The branch receives all of its merchandise from the home office. The home office bills goods to the branch at 125% of cost. During 19X3 the branch was billed for $105,000 on shipments from the home office.
(b) The home office credits Sales for the invoice price of goods shipped to the branch.
(c) On January 1, 19X3, the inventory of the home office was $25,000. The branch books showed a $6,000 inventory.
(d) On December 30, 19X3, the home office billed the branch for $12,000, representing the branch's share of expenses paid at the home office. The branch has not recorded this billing.

(e) All cash collections made by the branch are deposited in a local bank to the account of the home office. Deposits of this nature included the following:

Amount	Date Deposited by Branch	Date Recorded by Home Office
$5,000	December 28, 19X3	December 30, 19X3
3,000	December 29, 19X3	January 2, 19X4
7,000	December 30, 19X3	January 3, 19X4
2,000	January 2, 19X4	January 5, 19X4

(f) Expenses incurred locally by the branch are paid from an imprest bank account that is reimbursed periodically by the home office. Just prior to the end of the year, the home office forwarded a reimbursement check in the amount of $3,000, which was not received by the branch office until January, 19X4.

(g) It is not necessary to make provisions for federal income tax.

Instructions: (1) Prepare a work sheet for the company and its branch, with columns for "Trial Balance," "Adjustments and Eliminations," "Branch Income Statement," "Home Office Income Statement," and "Balance Sheet." Complete the work sheet, keying and explaining all adjustments and eliminations. (The income statement should be on a *cost* basis.)

(2) Prepare a reconciliation of the branch account and the home office account, showing the *corrected* book balances.

(AICPA adapted)

8-9. The Boston Branch, an outlet of Jones Co., receives its merchandise from its out-of-state home office at an interoffice billing price determined at 133⅓% of cost at the home office shipping point. Branch inventories are carried on the branch books at the interoffice billing price.

The Boston Branch is required to file a separate state franchise report, and for this purpose inventories are to be based on cost at the home office shipping point without regard to transportation costs.

The trial balance for the Boston Branch of Jones Co. at August 31, 19X7, appears as follows:

Cash	13,930	
Petty Cash	200	
Notes Receivable	8,000	
Interest Receivable (October 1, 19X6)	190	
Accounts Receivable	18,000	
Inventory (October 1, 19X6, at interoffice billing price)	12,000	
Sales		56,200
Sales Returns	2,500	
Sales Allowances	3,815	
Shipments from Home Office and Other Branches (at interoffice billing price)	61,840	
Freight In	3,064	
Home Office		73,149
Selling Expenses	2,910	
Administrative and General Expenses	4,150	
Interest Income		1,250
	130,599	130,599

Related accounts in the books of the home office of Jones Co. show balances at September 30, 19X7, before year-end closing, as follows:

Allowance for Doubtful Accounts — Boston Branch Accounts Receivable (to be adjusted at year-end closing to 2% of accounts receivable)..		850
Unrealized Intercompany Inventory Profit — Boston Branch 10/1/X6		3,000
Branch Furniture and Fixtures (at cost, acquired 10/1/X2)..	4,500	
Accumulated Depreciation — Boston Branch Furniture and Fixtures (depreciation accumulated through 9/30/X6)...		1,800
Boston Branch	76,223	
Shipments to Branch (at billing price)		64,800

Transactions of the branch for September, 19X7, as yet unrecorded because of illness of the branch bookkeeper, are summarized as follows:

(a) Gross sales on credit, $12,000.
(b) Sales returns, $600; sales allowances, $885.
(c) Shipments from home office at billing price, $2,960; freight paid by branch, $195.
(d) Selling expenses, $390, and administrative and general expenses, $750, paid in cash.
(e) Cash collected from customers, $6,570; note received on account, $2,100.
(f) Cash remitted to home office on September 30, 19X7, $2,500.

Other Branch Data at September 30, 19X7

(g) Interest accrued on notes receivable, $204.
(h) Accounts determined to be worthless and to be written off, $595.
(i) Actual petty cash on hand, $86. The petty cash paid out was for miscellaneous administrative expenses. A check to replenish the imprest cash fund was in transit from the home office at September 30, 19X7.
(j) Inventory of Boston Branch, September 30, 19X7, at interoffice billing price, $16,000.

Additional Facts

(k) During the year, the home office incurred clerical and other expenses of $1,270 applicable to the Boston Branch, and insurance of $185 on direct shipments to the branch. These items, recorded in the home office account Administrative and General Expenses Control, are charged currently to branch operations subsidiary accounts on the books of the home office.
(l) The freight in account on the branch books includes $300 of freight on merchandise intended for shipment to Boston Branch but erroneously shipped to Wilmington Branch and retained by the latter.

Instructions: (1) Prepare a work sheet for both branch and home office, reflecting thereon the account balances, transactions, and adjustments as these would be recorded on the books of the separate offices.

(2) Prepare a balance sheet and an income statement for the branch for the year ended September 30, 19X7, required for the state franchise report.

(AICPA adapted)

8-10. The preclosing general ledger trial balances at December 31, 19X7, for the Gorman Wholesale Company and its Atlanta Branch Office are as follows:

	Home Office Dr. (Cr.)	Branch Office Dr. (Cr.)
Cash..	36,000	8,000
Accounts Receivable...........................	35,000	12,000
Inventory — Home Office.....................	70,000	
Inventory — Branch Office...................		15,000
Plant Assets, net	90,000	
Branch	20,000	
Accounts Payable	(36,000)	(13,500)
Accrued Expenses	(14,000)	(2,500)
Home Office.......................................		(9,000)
Capital Stock......................................	(50,000)	
Retained Earnings	(45,000)	
Home Office:		
Sales...	(440,000)	
Purchases......................................	290,000	
Expenses.......................................	44,000	
Branch Office:		
Sales...		(95,000)
Purchases......................................		24,000
Shipments from Home Office		45,000
Expenses.......................................		16,000
	–0–	–0–

An audit disclosed the following data:

(a) On December 23 the branch office manager purchased $4,000 of furniture and fixtures but failed to notify the home office. The bookkeeper, knowing that all plant assets are carried on the home office books, recorded the proper entry on the branch records. It is the company's policy not to take any depreciation on assets acquired in the last half of a year.

(b) On December 27 a branch customer erroneously sent a $2,000 account payment to the home office. The bookkeeper made the correct entry on the home office books but did not notify the branch.

(c) On December 30 the branch remitted cash of $5,000, which was received by the home office in January, 19X8.

(d) On December 31 the branch erroneously recorded the December allocated expenses from the home office as $500 instead of $1,500.

(e) On December 31 the home office shipped merchandise billed at $3,000 to the branch, which was received in January, 19X8.

(f) The entire beginning inventory of the branch had been purchased from the home office. Home office 19X7 shipments to the branch were purchased by the home office in 19X7. The physical inventories at December 31, 19X7, excluding the shipment in transit, are:

Home office — $55,000 (at cost)

Branch   — $20,000 (consisting of $18,000 from home office and $2,000 from outside vendors.)

(g) The home office consistently bills shipments to the branch at 20% above cost. The sales account is credited for the invoice price.

Instructions: Prepare a work sheet with a pair of columns for each of the following: (1) Trial Balance, (2) Adjustments and Eliminations, (3) Home Office Income Statement, (4) Branch Office Income Statement, (5) Combined Balance Sheet. The work sheet should show branch income data on the basis of home office cost. Disregard income taxes. Number your work sheet adjusting and eliminating entries. (Formal journal entries are not required. Supporting computations, including the computations of ending inventories, must be in good form.)

(AICPA adapted)

9
Business Combinations

A business combination takes place when two or more business organizations come together to form a single economic unit. Business combinations take many different forms. The combination of business units is often achieved through fusion of different companies into a large single unit. Such fusion is accomplished through mergers or consolidations. Business combination is also achieved by the acquisition of control by one company over the operations of another. Control of corporate units is achieved through stock ownership or through interlocking directorates. Such control results in unified and integrated operation of business enterprises while permitting component units to retain their separate corporate identities.

A variety of objectives may be achieved by a business combination. These objectives include acquisition of a wider marketing area and higher sales volume, acquisition or development of a stronger organization and better production and management talent, reduction of costs through economies and efficiencies in operating on a larger scale, increased control over the market and improved competitive position, diversification of product lines, improved position with respect to sources of raw materials supply, and better access to capital for growth as well as lower costs on borrowings. Business units may also combine in order to obtain certain income tax advantages.

Business combinations through merger or consolidation are described in this chapter. Business combinations through control over other units by stock ownership are described in the chapters that follow.

MERGERS

A *merger* is effected upon the direct acquisition of the properties of one or more companies by another. The company taking over the properties of others retains its identity and continues operations as a larger unit; the other companies are dissolved and lose their separate identities.

Ordinarily, the acquiring unit takes over all assets and assumes all liabilities of the companies to be absorbed. Upon transfer of assets and liabilities, the acquiring company makes payment for the acquisition with cash, securities of the acquiring company, or both. Such payments are distributed to the stockholders of the companies that are to be dissolved.

Before there can be a merger, the terms of the proposed arrangement must be approved by the board of directors of each company that is a party to the action. Normally, the merger agreement must be ratified by the stockholders of the company to be dissolved, and under certain circumstances by the stockholders of the company making the acquisition. Merger agreements must also meet state statutory provisions, and in certain instances will require approval by the Securities and Exchange Commission and perhaps by other regulatory agencies.

In recording the merger on the books of a company being absorbed, nominal accounts are adjusted and closed so that the earnings to the date of the merger may be determined and transferred to retained earnings. Property accounts may be revised to conform to appraised values according to the merger agreement. Asset and liability accounts are closed, and an account with the transferee is debited for the claim resulting from the transfer of net assets. The receipt of cash or securities in payment of the claim and the distribution of such assets to stockholders in final settlement are recorded. On the books of the company making the acquisition, asset accounts are debited for the values of assets taken over, liability accounts are credited for the liabilities assumed, and an account with the transferor is credited for the net amount owed. Payment for the net assets acquired may then be recorded and the account with the transferor closed.

When payment exceeds the appraised value of assets acquired, the excess is regarded by the acquiring company as payment for goodwill. Presumably, the reason for paying an amount in excess of the net asset values that have been identified rests in the superior earnings ability of the business to be absorbed.

CONSOLIDATIONS

A *consolidation* is effected when a corporation is specifically organized to acquire the assets and to assume the liabilities of two or more previously existing companies. A new corporation is formed, and the original companies are dissolved.

Ordinarily, the newly formed company issues securities that are given in exchange for properties acquired. Stockholders of the original companies thereby become stockholders of the new unit. In some cases the new corporation may sell its stock and with such proceeds acquire the net assets of the companies to be combined.

As in the case of a merger, terms of a proposed consolidation must be approved by the board of directors of each company that is a party to the action. The proposal will also require approval by stockholders in accordance with legal provisions. Before an agreement for consolidation is completed, investigations, audits, and appraisals may be called for by the negotiating parties. Information from these sources may provide bases for determination of the relative contributions that are made by each of the companies joining in the consolidation.

A set of books is established for the new enterprise. With the transfer of assets and liabilities to the new unit, entries are made on the books of the constituent companies just as for absorbed companies that are parties to a merger. The new company debits asset accounts for the value of the assets that it takes over, credits liability accounts for the liabilities that it assumes, and credits appropriate capital accounts for the capital identified with the new enterprise.

Results of the merger and the consolidation are similar, with one unit emerging from a fusion of two or more previously existing units. Frequently, a distinction between the two forms of combination is not made in practice, a combination of either form being referred to as a merger.

PROBLEMS ARISING IN THE COMBINATION OF BUSINESS UNITS

Problems that arise in the course of business combination may be simple or complex. For example, a proposal for the outright purchase of one company by another may involve little more than an agreement as to the price to be paid for the company and the terms for such payment. On the other hand, a proposal for a consolidation that involves a number of companies and payment to dissolving units in the form of different securities may raise complex problems as to the relative contributions of the constituent units and the means for recognizing such contributions. The assistance of company managements, lawyers, accountants, appraisers, and financial analysts may be required in the course of reaching an agreement. The problems that arise in the course of a combination of several companies and the approaches that may be adopted in resolving such problems are described in the following section. Although the discussion is related to a consolidation, it is equally applicable to a merger in which similar problems may be encountered.

Contributions by Constituent Members to a Combination

When equities in an enlarged unit are to be allowed to former ownership groups, a basis for the equitable assignment of such equities will normally be sought in (1) relative net asset contributions and (2) relative earnings contributions. Although both of these factors may receive close consideration in the course of negotiations, final settlement may be largely influenced by the relative bargaining strength of the different parties.

Statements of financial position prepared by the constituent companies offer a starting point in arriving at relative net asset contributions. Individual items on these statements require special analysis and investigation by independent accountants so that they may be restated, when necessary, in a manner that will make them both complete and comparable. The discovery of clerical errors or omissions as well as errors in the application of accounting principles calls for corrections to achieve a full and satisfactory accounting. When differences in practices and procedures are encountered, items will have to be restated to offer a comparable accounting. The following matters, in particular, warrant attention and modification when necessary in achieving statement comparability: valuation methods for investments; allowances for receivables; cost determination and valuation procedures for inventories; capitalization policies for plant and equipment charges; depreciation methods for plant and equipment items; amortization policies for intangibles; provisions for contingencies; and policies for recognizing deferrals and accruals. Although alternative procedures in each of the foregoing areas may be acceptable for general accounting purposes, the special purpose for which the statements are to be employed calls for the selection of particular procedures that will provide a comparable accounting.

When accounting comparability has been achieved, further inquiry into the adequacy of the data as a basis for measuring relative net asset contributions may be in order. Asset book values summarize past costs; however, assets must be recognized not in terms of their past costs but in terms of current fair values. A new accounting entity is to be created and net asset contributions to the new unit in terms of current values are to be determined. With unrecorded changes in plant and equipment values, such as those emerging from changes in monetary values and technological advances, and with different uses to be made of such property items, special assistance by independent appraisers will be required in arriving at fair valuations for respective contributions. Inventories, particularly those reported at lifo, will require restatement at a fair market value. Investments reported at the lower of cost or market will require recognition at current market value. Intangibles at amortized cost balances will require recognition at their value to the new unit.

Income statements for the constituent units must be analyzed in order to determine the relative earnings contributions to the new organization. As with the balance sheets, the income statements should be recast in order to achieve a complete and comparable accounting. The discovery of past errors and omissions calls for appropriate corrections. When differences in income measurement procedures are found, restatement of revenues and expenses in terms of comparable procedures may be required. The following matters, in particular, warrant attention and modification when necessary: measurements of cost of goods manufactured and sold, including inventory pricing and valuation methods; charges for depreciation on plant and equipment items; amortization of intangibles; recognition of uncollectible accounts; charges for management salaries; and charges relating to retirement plans.

With earnings reported on a comparable basis, further analyses are necessary in forecasting earnings of individual companies. Earnings of the past are significant only insofar as they can be employed in evaluating the relative earnings contributions that will be made by the individual units to the new organization. Modification of past earnings, then, may be in order. Items deemed extraordinary and nonrecurring may require adjustment or elimination. If depreciable assets have been restated in arriving at the individual net asset contributions, appropriate restatement of depreciation charges relating to such assets is required for purposes of income measurement. Management salaries and also interest charges arising from financing activities must be reviewed in terms of the new organization. Fixed and variable costs must be analyzed in terms of the new organization. With comparable earnings available for a number of years, the earnings trend for each unit can be determined and applied to earnings data.

With statements that provide financial data on a comparative basis, the parties must now determine how the new company shall recognize the contributions by the individual participants. In certain instances, the parties may decide that asset and earnings contributions can be satisfactorily recognized by issuing a single class of stock. In other instances, the parties may decide that a satisfactory recognition of individual contributions is possible only through the issuance of two or more classes of securities. The problems that arise in an equitable distribution of securities under each of these arrangements are discussed in the sections that follow.

Issuance of a Single Class of Stock in a Business Combination

When the earnings rates on assets of the constituent parties are approximately the same and a single class of stock is to be issued, the parties may agree that such shares shall be issued in relation to the net asset contributions. However, when earnings rates vary and a single class of stock is to be issued, the parties may provide that earnings regarded as above normal shall be used as a basis for calculating goodwill and that such goodwill shall be added to the other net assets in measuring a company's full contribution.

The term *goodwill* as used in this sense refers to the economic value of the superior earning power of a business. Although it may be an asset of considerable value, accountants do not generally recognize goodwill as an asset except as part of a transaction involving the purchase of a going business. In accounting for business combinations, the term *goodwill* has a special significance which differs somewhat from the economic sense. The accounting treatment of goodwill is discussed later in this chapter and in Chapter 10.

To illustrate the foregoing, assume that stockholders of Companies A, B, and C agree to consolidate and form Company D. Net assets at appraised values and average adjusted earnings of the past five years, which the parties believe offer the most reliable estimate of future earnings, follow:

	Co. A	Co. B	Co. C	Total
Net asset contribution	$200,000	$300,000	$500,000	$1,000,000
Percentage of asset contribution to total assets	20%	30%	50%	
Earnings contribution	$ 30,000	$ 30,000	$ 40,000	$ 100,000
Percentage of earnings contribution to total earnings..	30%	30%	40%	

If Company D issues a single class of stock in the net asset ratio, stockholders of Companies A, B, and C will receive stock in the ratio of 20:30:50 respectively. Although an equitable division of the interest in the assets of $1,000,000 is achieved, earnings of $100,000 in the future will accrue to stockholders in the asset ratio, resulting in a loss to original stockholders of Company A and a gain to original stockholders of Company C.

On the other hand, if a single class of stock is issued in the earnings ratio, stockholders of Companies A, B, and C will receive stock in the ratio of 30:30:40 respectively. Although an equitable division of future earnings is achieved, stockholders will fail to maintain their original interests in assets. Stockholders of Company A will acquire an interest that exceeds their investment, while stockholders of Company C will acquire an interest that is less than their investment.

To avoid the inequities resulting from the distribution of a single class of stock either in the net asset ratio or in the earnings ratio, the parties decide that respective contributions shall be measured by the values assigned to net assets as increased by goodwill. It is agreed that contributions are to be determined as follows: (1) a 6% return is to be regarded as a fair return on identifiable net assets; (2) excess earnings are to be capitalized at 20% in arriving at a value for goodwill. When net asset and earnings factors are considered, contributions are calculated as follows:

	Co. A		Co. B		Co. C		Total
Net assets other than goodwill		$200,000		$300,000		$500,000	$1,000,000
Goodwill:							
Average annual earnings	$30,000		$30,000		$40,000		
Normal annual return on assets, 6%.........................	12,000		18,000		30,000		
Excess annual earnings.......	$18,000		$12,000		$10,000		
Excess annual earnings capitalized at 20%...................		90,000		60,000		50,000	200,000
Total contributions		$290,000		$360,000		$550,000	$1,200,000

Based on the above calculations, the distribution of shares to stockholders of the constituent companies would be made in proportion to their relative contributions. Assume, for example, that a total of 25,000 shares of Company D were to be issued. These shares would be distributed as follows:

Co. A: $290,000/$1,200,000 × 25,000....................................	6,042 shares
Co. B: $360,000/$1,200,000 × 25,000....................................	7,500
Co. C: $550,000/$1,200,000 × 25,000....................................	11,458
Total...	25,000 shares

A comparison of the relative net asset and earnings contributions by Companies A, B, and C and the relative claims upon net assets and earnings of the new company in each case is as follows:

	Co. A	Co. B	Co. C
Net asset contribution	20%	30%	50%
Earnings contribution	30	30	40
Claim upon net assets and earnings of new company..	24	30	46

When relative earnings contributions differ from relative net asset contributions, original relationships in both earnings and net asset contributions of the individual companies cannot be preserved by the issuance of a single class of stock. In the example, Company A with above-normal earnings gains an increased share in net assets; however, it fails to retain its original share in earnings. Company C fails to maintain its interest in net assets but gains an increased share in earnings. Company B, whose asset and earnings shares were the same, retains its original relative status in both assets and earnings.

Issuance of Several Classes of Stock in a Business Combination

If original relationships in both net assets and earnings are to be preserved, it will be necessary to issue more than a single class of stock. The following procedures must be applied in the allocation of several classes of stock of the new company to the constituent groups:

(1) Earnings contributions of the constituent companies should be capitalized at a certain rate, but this rate must not exceed the earnings rate of any of the constituent companies. This procedure determines the total stock to be issued to each company.[1]

(2) Preferred stock should be distributed to constituent companies in proportion to the net assets that they contribute. Such stock should be preferred as to assets upon dissolution, with the preferences equal to the values of properties contributed. The dividend rate should not exceed the rate used in capitalizing profits. Shares should be fully participating with common.

(3) Common stock should be issued to each company for the difference between the company's total stock as calculated in (1), and the amount it receives in preferred stock as calculated in (2).

The issuance of stock that is preferred as to assets results in the preservation of claims in the new organization that are equal to the net asset contributions. Participating preferred stock supplemented by common stock so that the total stock issued is in the earnings ratio makes possible a distribution of earnings in the earnings ratio.

To illustrate this procedure, assume contributions to Company D by Companies A, B, and C as previously indicated:

---

[1]It should be observed again that "earnings" as used in the discussions represent the estimated earnings contribution to the new unit. A company may have experienced losses in the past. However, for purposes of the business combination, it is attractive only if its properties will make some contribution to earnings of the combined unit.

	Co. A	Co. B	Co. C	Total
Net asset contribution	$200,000	$300,000	$500,000	$1,000,000
Earnings contribution	$ 30,000	$ 30,000	$ 40,000	$ 100,000
Earnings rate on net assets....	15%	10%	8%	10%

It is agreed that earnings are to be capitalized at 8% in determining the total stock to be issued. Fully participating 6% preferred stock, $100 par, and preferred as to assets of this par value, is to be issued in exchange for net assets transferred. Common stock, $100 par, is to be issued to each company for the difference between the total stock to which it is entitled and the preferred stock that it is to receive. The common stock is regarded as payment for goodwill. The stock allotment is made as follows:

	Co. A	Co. B	Co. C	Total
Total stock to be issued (earnings ÷ .08)	$375,000	$375,000	$500,000	$1,250,000
Amount of preferred stock to be issued (equal to asset contribution).....................	200,000	300,000	500,000	1,000,000
Amount of common stock to be issued (balance, representing payment for goodwill).................................	$175,000	$ 75,000	—	$ 250,000

The preferred stock issued to stockholders of Companies A, B, and C preserves their claims to assets in the new organization in amounts equal to assets contributed. The preferred and common issues provide for a distribution of earnings in the earnings contribution ratio. Annual earnings of $100,000 by the new organization will permit an 8% dividend on both participating preferred stock and common stock. Such earnings would be distributed as follows:

	Co. A	Co. B	Co. C	Total
On 6% preferred participating stock (8%)	$16,000	$24,000	$40,000	$ 80,000
On common stock (8%)	14,000	6,000	—	20,000
Total distribution	$30,000	$30,000	$40,000	$100,000
Original earnings contribution	30%	30%	40%	100%

The following observations may be made:

(1) Earnings distributions must not be less than the preferred rate on the *total* capital stock if distributions are to be made in the original earnings ratio. For example, if only $60,000 were earned and distributed, the distribution would be limited to preferred stock, with earnings accruing in the ratio of preferred holdings, or 20%, 30%, and 50%. A distribution of $70,000 comes closer to the original earnings ratio, but still fails to meet it:

	Co. A	Co. B	Co. C	Total
On 6% preferred participating stock (6%)	$12,000	$18,000	$30,000	$ 60,000
On common stock (4%)	7,000	3,000		10,000
Total distribution	$19,000	$21,000	$30,000	$ 70,000
Percentage earnings distribution	27%	30%	43%	100%

A distribution of $75,000 would permit the payment of $15,000, or 6%, to common stockholders. The earnings would then be distributed in the original ratio.

If the original earnings ratio is to be maintained at any earnings distribution level, the two classes of stock issued must offer the same dividend rights, but only one class must offer a prior claim on assets upon liquidation. Such issues can be designated Class A shares and Class B shares.

(2) Preferred stock must be participating if distributions that exceed the preferred rate on total capital stock are to be made in the original earnings ratio. If, in the example, the 6% preferred stock was non-participating and earnings of $100,000 were to be distributed, the distribution would fail to meet the earnings contribution rate of 30%, 30%, and 40%. Under these circumstances the distribution would be made as follows:

	Co. A	Co. B	Co. C	Total
On preferred stock (6%)	$12,000	$18,000	$30,000	$ 60,000
On common stock (16%)	28,000	12,000		40,000
Total distribution	$40,000	$30,000	$30,000	$100,000
Percentage earnings distribution	40%	30%	30%	100%

(3) It would be possible to enable Company C stockholders to participate in the common stock distribution by capitalizing earnings at a rate that is less than 8%. For example, if earnings are capitalized at 5%, 5% fully participating preferred stock is issued in exchange for net assets transferred, and common stock is issued for the balance of the total stock to be issued. Both classes of stock are $100 par. The stock allotment is made as follows:

	Co. A	Co. B	Co. C	Total
Total stock to be issued (average earnings ÷ .05)	$600,000	$600,000	$800,000	$2,000,000
Amount of preferred stock	200,000	300,000	500,000	1,000,000
Amount of common stock	$400,000	$300,000	$300,000	$1,000,000

Earnings of $100,000 would satisfy preferred stock requirements and would make possible a 5% distribution on common stock, with earnings distributed in the original ratio as follows:

	Co. A	Co. B	Co. C	Total
On preferred stock (5%)	$10,000	$15,000	$25,000	$ 50,000
On common stock (5%)	20,000	15,000	15,000	50,000
	$30,000	$30,000	$40,000	$100,000

Capitalization of earnings at 5% in arriving at the total par value of the stock to be issued requires the accounting recognition of goodwill of $1,000,000. Assume, however, that such a valuation for the intangible is unwarranted. Instead of issuing a certain number of common shares with a "$100 par" designation, an equal number of shares can be issued but designated "no-par." The stated value assigned to the no-par common stock would be determined by the valuation placed upon goodwill. Dividend rights of the common stock would remain the same as when a par value is assigned. If no goodwill is to be recognized, both no-par preferred stock and no-par common stock could be issued. The asset preference rights and the dividend rights of each class should be the same as in the previous cases where par values were assigned and the stock should be issued in the same ratio as in the previous cases. The asset contribution could then be recorded at $1,000,000, and this value could be assigned in some reasonable manner to the preferred and common stock.

No attempt has been made in the foregoing paragraphs to cover all of the problems arising in the allotment of securities to the parties to a business combination. However, some of the major considerations have been mentioned. The individual problems in each case must be studied carefully in ascertaining bases for security allotment. In arriving at a satisfactory allotment, there will be concern not only with achieving an equitable arrangement with the individual parties but also with establishing a sound financial structure for the new organization. The latter objective must be fulfilled if the company is to prosper and stock issues are to be received favorably on the securities market. The agreement that is finally reached will be a product of theoretical considerations, practical considerations, and compromises by the parties to the negotiation.

BUSINESS COMBINATIONS REGARDED AS "POOLING OF INTERESTS" OR "PURCHASE"

A combination brings the assets of two or more companies under single ownership and control. In certain instances the combination involves a change in original ownership, as, for example, when assets of one company are sold for cash to another. However, in other instances the combination provides for a continuation of the original ownership, as, for example, when assets of a company are transferred to another company in exchange for stock that offers the original ownership a continued interest in and control of assets. A combination that involves the elimination of an important part of the original ownership is designated as a combination by *purchase*. A combination that involves a continuation of substantially all of the original ownership is designated as a combination by *pooling of interests*.

The accounting for a combination depends upon whether the combination meets certain rigid criteria for qualifying as a pooling of interests. If the combination cannot meet all of these tests, it must be treated as a purchase.

The conditions that must be met to qualify as a pooling of interests were designed to assure that a combination does in substance reflect the combining of interests and continuity of ownership that the concept implies. These conditions, promulgated by the Accounting Principles Board, may be categorized as follows:

1. Attributes of the combining companies.
   a. Each of the combining companies is autonomous and has not been a subsidiary or division of another corporation within two years before the plan of combination is initiated.
   b. Each of the combining companies is independent of the other combining companies.[2]
2. Manner of combining interests.
   a. The combination is effected in a single transaction or is completed in accordance with a specific plan within one year after the plan is initiated.
   b. A corporation offers and issues only common stock with rights identical to those of the majority of its outstanding voting common stock in exchange for substantially all of the voting common stock interest of another company at the date the plan of combination is consummated.
   c. None of the combining companies changes the equity interest of the voting common stock in contemplation of effecting the combination either within two years before the plan of combination is initiated or between the dates the combination is initiated and consummated; changes in contemplation of effecting the combination may include distributions to stockholders and additional issuances, exchanges, and retirements of securities.
   d. Each of the combining companies reacquires shares of voting common stock only for purposes other than business combinations, and no company reacquires more than a normal number of shares between the dates the plan of combination is initiated and consummated.
   e. The ratio of the interest of an individual common stockholder to those of other common stockholders in a combining company remains the same as a result of the exchange of stock to effect the combination.
   f. The voting rights to which the common stock ownership interests in the resulting combined corporation are entitled are exercisable by the stockholders; the stockholders are neither deprived of nor restricted in exercising those rights for a period.
   g. The combination is resolved at the date the plan is consummated and no provisions of the plan relating to the issue of securities or other consideration are pending.[3]
3. Absence of planned transactions.
   a. The combined corporation does not agree directly or indirectly to retire or reacquire all or part of the common stock issued to effect the combination.
   b. The combined corporation does not enter into other financial arrangements for the benefit of the former stockholders of a combining company, such as a guaranty of loans secured by

---

[2]*Opinions of the Accounting Principles Board, No. 16*, "Business Combinations" (New York: American Institute of Certified Public Accountants, 1970), par. 46.

[3]*Ibid.*, par. 47.

stock issued in the combination, which in effect negates the exchange of equity securities.

c. The combined corporation does not intend or plan to dispose of a significant part of the assets of the combining companies within two years after the combination other than disposals in the ordinary course of business of the formerly separate companies and to eliminate duplicate facilities or excess capacity.[4]

Accounting for a Pooling of Interests

When a combination is considered to represent a pooling of interests, assets are carried forward at the values at which they were carried on the books of the constituent units. Because the combination is characterized by a continuity of the original ownerships, it is also appropriate to carry forward the capital balances of the predecessor units, including retained earnings or deficit. Normally, the capital stock balances of the constituent units are combined to determine the capital stock balance of the combined unit, and the retained earnings or deficit balances of the predecessor companies are combined and recognized as retained earnings of the combined company. Thus it is possible for a new corporation, resulting from a consolidation conforming to pooling of interests requirements, to have a positive balance in retained earnings.

When a combination is recognized as a pooling of interests, the income statement of the continuing business for the period in which the combination occurs should report the combined results of operations of the constituent units for the entire period in which the combination was effected as if the combination had taken place at the beginning of the period. When comparative financial statements are presented for periods prior to that in which the combination was effected, they should be restated on a combined basis. Financial statements should clearly disclose that a business combination has been treated as a pooling of interests.[5]

Because the stockholders' equity balances of the predecessor companies are carried forward, any costs incurred in issuing stock to effectuate the combination are considered as a current expense on a pooling of interests basis. This treatment differs from that used when stock is issued as part of a purchase combination.

Accounting for a Purchase

When a combination is considered to represent a purchase, there is a new basis of accountability for the assets acquired. With the acquisition of assets through purchase, assets should be recorded at their cost to the buyer, a cost that need not coincide with the values reported on the books of the seller.

At the time of a purchase transaction, it is necessary to determine the current fair values of the assets acquired and liabilities assumed. Although

---

[4]*Ibid.*, par. 48.

[5]*Ibid.*, pars. 63–65.

the use of appraisal values might seem to introduce market values into the accounting system, this is not the case. The purpose of estimating these values is to provide a basis for allocating the total cost involved to the individual balance sheet items. The aggregate value assigned to the net assets acquired (including goodwill) will be equal to the cost involved in the purchase transaction.

In a purchase combination, the consideration given to acquire the other company may be cash, or it may include other assets or the purchaser's own securities. When items other than cash are involved, it is important to recognize the current value of the items exchanged in determining the total purchase price. If there is a determinable market value for the company's securities, that should be used. When there is no determinable market, values may be inferred from other parts of the exchange transaction.

If the aggregate purchase price exceeds the sum of the identifiable assets less liabilities obtained, the difference is attributed to goodwill. Goodwill is recorded only when purchased, and represents an intangible asset on the books of the purchaser. Care should be taken to make sure that the excess is not due to the presence of undervalued or unidentified assets. Such assets, whether tangible or intangible, should be recognized at their current values so that goodwill may be properly determined. Any goodwill that is recognized in a purchase transaction must be amortized through periodic charges to income over a period of forty years or less.

Occasionally, a company may be purchased for less than the sum of its identifiable net assets. For example, a company that is anxious to sell may be willing to accept a price below what might be obtained through more deliberate liquidation procedures.

If the purchase price is less than the sum of the identifiable net assets, there are several alternative accounting treatments that might be considered. One might argue that the savings resulting from the bargain purchase should be recognized as current income. However, purchased assets are normally recorded at cost, and gains are normally not recognized when items are purchased but when they are sold.

Another alternative would be to treat the difference as "negative goodwill" and include the balance on the equity side of the balance sheet. Some companies have recognized an item called "consolidation surplus" as an element of stockholders' equity. This procedure is also inconsistent with the cost concept, however, because it results in asset values stated at amounts greater than their cost. It also increases stockholders' equity, which implies that the stockholders have gained from the transaction.

The current generally accepted treatment is to reduce the balances of noncurrent assets, other than investments, on a pro rata basis. In the remote case that these balances are reduced to zero and an excess of net assets over cost remains, APB Opinion No. 16 provides that:

> If the allocation reduces the noncurrent assets to zero value, the remainder of the excess over cost should be classified as a deferred

credit and should be amortized systematically to income over the period estimated to be benefited but not in excess of forty years.[6]

Any out-of-pocket costs incurred in issuing securities as part of a purchase transaction are treated as a reduction of the net proceeds from the stock issue. Such costs reduce the amount by which the stockholders' equity accounts are increased in the transaction. They are not treated as a current expense because they are considered to be part of a capital transaction.

Accounting for Purchase and Pooling of Interests Illustrated

As a basis for comparing the accounting for a purchase and a pooling of interests, assume that a combination of Companies D, E, and F is contemplated. Assets, liabilities, and capitals of the companies are reported in conformity with generally accepted accounting principles and are stated on a uniform basis. On July 1, 19X4, balance sheets for the three companies are as follows:

	Co. D		Co. E		Co. F
Assets............................	$2,000,000		$1,250,000		$1,000,000
Liabilities.........................	$ 750,000		$ 400,000		$ 350,000
Capital stock..................... (no-par)	1,000,000	($100 par)	500,000	($50 par)	500,000
Additional paid-in capital.....	350,000		150,000		100,000
Retained earnings (deficit)...	(100,000)		200,000		50,000
Total liabilities and stock-holders' equity	$2,000,000		$1,250,000		$1,000,000

On this date Company D agrees to acquire all of the assets and to assume all of the liabilities of Companies E and F in exchange for shares of stock that it will issue. Stock of Company D is currently selling on the market at $50 per share. Assets of Companies E and F are to be appraised and the companies are to receive Company D shares with a market value equal to that of the net assets transferred. The exchange of shares for net assets is calculated as follows:

	Co. E	Co. F	Total
Assets per books.................................	$1,250,000	$1,000,000	$2,250,000
Asset increase per appraisal....................	150,000	100,000	250,000
	$1,400,000	$1,100,000	$2,500,000
Liabilities per books.............................	400,000	350,000	750,000
Net assets for purposes of exchange	$1,000,000	$ 750,000	$1,750,000
Number of shares to be issued (net assets ÷ $50)......	20,000	15,000	35,000

Entries that would be made on the books of Company D on the alternative purchase and pooling assumptions and a balance sheet for Company D reflecting the combination under each assumption follow:

---

[6]*Ibid.*, par. 91.

Entries on Company D Books

If combination is deemed a purchase		If combination is deemed a pooling of interests	
Assets (at appraised values)...................... 2,500,000		Assets (at original book values)....................... 2,250,000	
Liabilities...............	750,000	Liabilities................	750,000
Capital Stock, no-par (35,000 shares)	1,750,000	Capital Stock, no-par (35,000 shares)........	1,000,000
		Additional Paid-In Capital....................	250,000
		Retained Earnings....	250,000

Company D Balance Sheet, July 1, 19X4		*Company D Balance Sheet, July 1, 19X4*	
Assets..	$4,500,000	Assets..	$4,250,000
Liabilities	$1,500,000	Liabilities	$1,500,000
Capital stock.............................	2,750,000	Capital stock..............................	2,000,000
Additional paid-in capital	350,000	Additional paid-in capital	600,000
Deficit..	(100,000)	Retained earnings	150,000
Total liabilities and stockholders' equity	$4,500,000	Total liabilities and stockholders' equity	$4,250,000

In recognizing the combination as a purchase, no special problem is encountered by Company D. As in the case of any other exchange of stock for assets, the assets are recorded at their fair values and invested capital accounts are credited. In recognizing the combination as a pooling of interests, asset, liability, and capital balances reported by Companies E and F are carried without change to the books of Company D.

If the appraised values of the identifiable assets were less than the amount of consideration given by Company D, the entries on a pooling of interests basis would not be affected. In a purchase, however, the recognition of goodwill would be required. For example, assume that the assets of Company F were fairly stated on the books, but that Company D still gives 15,000 shares of its stock in exchange for the net assets. The appraised values would be $100,000 less than previously assumed. If the combination were deemed to be a purchase, Company D would make the following entry:

Assets (at appraised values)	2,400,000	
Goodwill	100,000	
Liabilities		750,000
Capital Stock, no par (35,000 shares)....................		1,750,000

Upon completion of the combination, the receipt of Company D shares in exchange for net assets and the distribution of such shares to stockholders must be recorded on the books of Companies E and F. When the consideration for net assets is an amount other than their book value, a gain or a loss is reported on the transfer. In the transaction that was designated as a purchase, for example, payment by Company D would call for entries on the books of Companies E and F as follows:

Company E Books			Company F Books		
Stock of Co. D	1,000,000		Stock of Co. D	750,000	
Liabilities.....................	400,000		Liabilities.........................	350,000	
Assets		1,250,000	Assets		1,000,000
Retained Earnings......		150,000	Retained Earnings.........		100,000
Received 20,000 shares of Co. D stock valued at $50 per share in exchange for net assets.			Received 15,000 shares of Co. D stock valued at $50 per share in exchange for net assets.		
Capital Stock................	500,000		Capital Stock...................	500,000	
Additional Paid-In Capital.........................	150,000		Additional Paid-In Capital .	100,000	
Retained Earnings.........	350,000		Retained Earnings............	150,000	
Stock of Co. D		1,000,000	Stock of Co. D		750,000
Distributed 20,000 shares of Co. D stock in exchange for 5,000 shares of Co. E stock outstanding (4 shares for 1).			Distributed 15,000 shares of Co. D stock in exchange for 10,000 shares of Co. F stock outstanding (1.5 shares for 1).		

In the example that was given for a pooling of interests, capital stock of the acquiring company was no-par and the stated capital for the combination was recognized at an amount equal to the sum of the capital stock balances of the constituent units. This permitted the full recognition of additional paid-in capital and retained earnings balances of the constituent units. When the stated capital of a combination is to be greater or less than the stated capital of the constituent units, adjustments to additional paid-in capital and retained earnings balances are the same as those that would apply to an increase or a decrease in stated capital where no business combination is involved. Hence, when the stated capital of a combination is to be greater than the total of the stated capitals of the constituent units, the excess should be deducted from the total additional paid-in capital and, when this balance is exhausted, from the total retained earnings. When the stated capital is to be less than the total of the stated capitals of the constituent units, the difference should be recognized as an increase in total additional paid-in capital. In a combination that is deemed to be a pooling of interests, then, establishing a stated capital for the combination may involve a decrease in the retained earnings total but never an increase in this total.

To illustrate the foregoing as well as to provide a comparison of purchase and pooling accounting for a consolidation, assume that Companies D, E, and F agree to form Company G and that they transfer their assets and liabilities to this company. Assets of Company D are considered to be fairly valued for purposes of the consolidation, but assets of Companies E and F are to be revalued as stated earlier. Shares of Company G are to be issued on the basis of 1 share for every $50 of net assets transferred, as follows:

To Company D: 25,000 shares ($1,250,000 ÷ $50)
To Company E: 20,000 shares ($1,000,000 ÷ $50)
To Company F: 15,000 shares ($ 750,000 ÷ $50)

The following purchase and pooling entries are given on three different assumptions of Company G stock par value: (1) $45; (2) $35; (3) $25.

Entries on Company G Books

If combination is deemed a purchase			If combination is deemed a pooling of interests		
(1) Assets (at appraised values)..................	4,500,000		Assets (at original book values...........................	4,250,000	
Liabilities		1,500,000	Liabilities................		1,500,000
Capital Stock, $45 par (60,000 shares)...............		2,700,000	Capital Stock, $45 par (60,000 shares)		2,700,000
Additional Paid-In Capital		300,000	Retained Earnings......		50,000
(2) Assets (at appraised values)..................	4,500,000		Assets (at original book values)........................	4,250,000	
Liabilities		1,500,000	Liabilities.................		1,500,000
Capital Stock, $35 par (60,000 shares)...............		2,100,000	Capital Stock, $35 par (60,000 shares)		2,100,000
Additional Paid-In Capital		900,000	Additional Paid-In Capital......................		500,000
			Retained Earnings......		150,000
(3) Assets (at appraised values)..................	4,500,000		Assets (at original book values)........................	4,250,000	
Liabilities		1,500,000	Liabilities.................		1,500,000
Capital Stock, $25 par (60,000 shares)...............		1,500,000	Capital Stock, $25 par (60,000 shares)		1,500,000
Additional Paid-In Capital		1,500,000	Additional Paid-In Capital......................		1,100,000
			Retained Earnings......		150,000

When the combination is deemed to be a purchase, capitals are limited to invested capital balances regardless of the par value assigned to the capital stock. When the combination is deemed to be a pooling of interests, capitals of the constituent units are continued but with the following modifications:

Case (1): The increase in the value assigned to capital stock from the $2,000,000 total reported by the constituent companies to the $2,700,000 balance required elimination of the full amount of additional paid-in capital of $600,000 and a further reduction in total retained earnings of $100,000.

Case (2): The increase in the value assigned to capital stock from $2,000,000 to $2,100,000 required a reduction of $100,000 in total additional paid-in capital; the full amount of retained earnings was carried forward.

Case (3): A reduction in the value assigned to capital stock from $2,000,000 to $1,500,000 was accompanied by an increase of $500,000 in total additional paid-in capital; the full amount of retained earnings was carried forward.

Effects of Alternative Combination Procedures

The effects of the alternative combination procedures should be carefully observed. Differences initially appear on the balance sheets. However, differences in balance sheet items are subsequently reflected in revenue and expense accounts and in net income determinations.

With purchase accounting, an exchange of stock for the assets of a going concern in a period of rising prices frequently results in the recognition of assets at amounts significantly above the values reported on the books of the transferor. Furthermore, when shares are selling at high net earnings multiples, the value of the shares may exceed the appraised values of identifiable assets, thus calling for the recognition of goodwill. The recognition of assets at their values at the date of the transfer is accompanied by an increase of the same amount in invested capital balances. On the other hand, pooling accounting results in the recognition of assets at their original book values. Replacement values or current market values are ignored. Intangibles that are not already reflected in the accounts are not recognized. Transfer of the assets at their original book values is accompanied by transfer of the capital balances relating to such assets. Retained earnings are carried forward. In a merger, this may mean the elimination of a previously existing deficit and the recognition of a retained earnings balance. In a consolidation, this may mean the recognition of a retained earnings balance from the very beginning of the new organization.

With purchase accounting, restated asset balances form the basis for depreciation and other charges to revenue. When intangibles are recognized on the acquisition, they require amortization against revenue and thus affect periodic earnings. With pooling accounting, charges to revenue arising from the use of acquired assets remain unchanged. In failing to recognize any intangibles related to the acquisition, revenue is freed from charges for amortization that would otherwise apply.

The effects of the alternative treatments on the income statement may be regarded as of even greater significance than those on the balance sheet. Final net income determinations are extremely important to management, employees, stockholders, and creditors. Net earnings may affect security prices on the stock market. Net earnings also affect management bonuses, employee profit-sharing arrangements, and declarations of dividends to stockholders.

Evaluation of Pooling-of-Interests Practice

Although a purchase and a pooling of interests provide significantly different results in stating a company's financial position and reporting its earnings, the criteria for distinguishing between the two approaches have not always been clear and unequivocal. The choice between the purchase and the pooling approaches has often been determined by the accounting consequences relating to each approach.

A distinction between purchase and pooling of interests for reporting purposes was made in accounting literature as early as the 1920's. The earliest reference by the American Institute of Certified Public Accountants to the pooling-of-interests concept was in 1945. In 1950, the Committee on Accounting Procedure issued its first official pronouncement dealing with this matter. In 1957, the Committee in attempting to clarify the conditions to be considered in distinguishing between a purchase and a pooling of interests issued Bulletin No. 48, which described certain "attendant circumstances" relating to the extent to which continuity of ownership existed in a particular case. However, the distinction between a pooling and purchase situation was still regarded as being sufficiently ambiguous as to permit great latitude in choosing the accounting treatment of similar situations.

In 1970, the Accounting Principles Board issued Opinion No. 16, in which the twelve conditions that must be met to qualify as a pooling of interests were delineated. The Board felt that the necessity for a transaction to meet *all* twelve conditions to qualify as a pooling of interests would provide a definitive arrangement for classifying a combination. Although this may be true of completed transactions, it is still possible to structure transactions in such a manner as to meet (or not meet) the defined criteria. Since the pooling-of-interests treatment may be regarded as advantageous in many situations, due to the prospect of reporting higher income in subsequent years, parties negotiating business combination agreements may attempt to qualify for pooling under the existing rules. For example, one of the basic rules requires that only common stock be issued in an exchange transaction to qualify as a pooling. Thus, companies wishing to use the pooling-of-interests approach could not pay cash or issue other types of securities in the combination transaction. Another rule prohibits the acquisition of treasury stock by either of the combining companies except as part of a systematic plan established for purposes other than use in acquisitions at least two years prior to the initiation of the acquisition plan. Companies may find it economically attractive to reacquire their own shares in the market, and yet be reluctant to do so for fear it might preclude them from combining with any company on a pooling-of-interests basis for the next two years, even if no such combinations are currently contemplated.

Accounting should be neutral with respect to economic activity, but the rules involved in distinguishing a purchase from a pooling of interests may have a real impact on the conduct of business affairs. The root cause of the problem in permitting two quite different approaches to recording business combinations is the basic adherence to the cost concept for recording asset values. Thus both approaches are consistent with the premise that assets should be recorded at their cost to the current owner. The difference stems from the interpretation of whether a combination results in a new owner (and thus a new determination of cost) or the continuity of the existing owners (and thus no new basis of accountability). An accounting system based on current values, while possibly introducing different issues, would eliminate the ambiguity caused by the two different approaches to accounting for business combinations. It is interesting to note that accountants are willing to accept appraisal values for recording purposes at the time a purchase transaction is completed, but not at subsequent times.

DIVISIVE REORGANIZATIONS

The preceding sections considered the combination of business units with the ownerships in the original units being continued in the combined unit. Such a combination suggested an accounting that would reflect the change as no more than one of form. Asset values as well as ownership interests of the original units were identified with the larger unit. Frequently one encounters a reverse situation — one in which an existing corporation is divided, with the ownership of the original unit being continued in the divisions. Under these circumstances, it might well be maintained that asset values of the original unit should also be carried into the smaller units.

Divisive reorganizations are commonly classified as *split-ups, split-offs,* and *spin-offs*. A split-up is the transfer by a corporation of all of its assets to two or more new companies in exchange for all of the stock of the new companies. The original unit then distributes the stock to its stockholders as a liquidating settlement and dissolves. Owners of the original company are now owners of the separate units into which it has been divided.[7]

A split-off is the transfer of a part of a corporation's assets to a new company in exchange for the stock of the new company. The original unit subsequently distributes the stock in the new company to its stockholders in exchange for a proportionate part of their stockholdings in the original company. The latter shares are canceled and the amount of the original corporation's stock outstanding is reduced.

A spin-off is the same as a split-off except that the distribution of stock is made by the original unit to its stockholders without any surrender of stock by them.

Corporate subdivision suggests accounting problems that are similar to those encountered in corporate combination. Under what circumstances should a fresh-start approach be adopted for the new unit in stating assets, liabilities, and capital balances? Under what circumstances should a reverse-pooling approach be employed and original book values for net asset transfers be recognized on the records of the new units? In employing the latter approach, many problems will arise in allocating the capital balances between the units. Since few criteria for such allocation have been suggested, the accountant will have to consider all of the circumstances of the divisive reorganization in arriving at an approach that can find theoretical as well as practical support.

BUSINESS REORGANIZATION AND TAXES

Proposals for business combination or division cannot be considered without reference to the tax factors that will accompany such action. A

---

[7]The use of the term "split-up" in this sense is to be distinguished from the issuance of an additional number of shares by a corporation without a change in the amount of paid-in capital identified with outstanding shares.

choice between several possible courses of action may be influenced in no small part by the tax implications related to the different alternatives. In some instances, tax considerations may actually be the motivating factors in considering a certain course of action. For example, stockholders of a corporation may decide upon a merger or consolidation to lessen the burden of death taxes, to provide a means of converting business profits that would otherwise be taxable as dividends into capital gains, or to utilize operating loss carryovers that might otherwise be lost. Once a course of action providing the desired tax advantages is chosen, the transaction must be carefully planned so that it fully conforms to the particular tax requirements.

In planning either a corporate combination or a division, special attention must be focused on whether such a corporate change will be accompanied by an income tax liability. Certain reorganizations qualify as "tax-free" while others are "taxable." In a tax-free transaction, the transferor recognizes neither gain nor loss on the transfer of assets. For tax purposes, the basis of assets acquired by the transferee remains the same as it was for the original owner. In a taxable transaction, the transferor recognizes a gain or a loss on the transfer of assets. For the transferee, assets take on a new tax basis at the purchase price identified with the transfer.

The Internal Revenue Code provides that a tax-free status for all of the parties to a corporate combination or division is available only under the following circumstances:

(1) A statutory merger or consolidation — an arrangement effected in accordance with the laws of the various states.
(2) An acquisition by one corporation of the stock of another, provided that *voting stock* is exchanged for a controlling interest composed of at least 80% of the stock and the voting power of the acquired company.
(3) An acquisition by one corporation of the properties of another, provided that *voting stock* is exchanged for *substantially all* of the properties of the acquired company.
(4) A transfer of assets to another corporation in exchange for a controlling interest of at least 80% of the stock and the voting power of the acquired company. (This section applies to corporate distributions whether defined as spin-offs, split-offs, or split-ups.)

When there is a tax-free combination or division, pooling or reverse-pooling treatment in the accounts will provide a consistency between book and tax bases for property items and also between book and tax charges representing the amortization of such balances. This argument is frequently advanced as a reason for the application of the pooling approach in the accounts. In choosing between alternative methods, however, the primary question is not whether a method conforms to income tax practices, but whether it leads to the fairest expression of a business unit's financial position and operating results.

1. (a) Distinguish between combination by company fusion and combination by company control. (b) Distinguish between a combination achieved through merger and a combination achieved through consolidation.

2. Assuming a merger whereby Company A exchanges shares of its stock for the net assets of Company B, describe the entries to be made on the books of Companies A and B.

3. Assuming a consolidation whereby Company C is organized and exchanges shares of its stock for the net assets of Companies D and E, describe the entries to be made on the books of Companies C, D, and E.

4. (a) Describe the nature of the contributions that are made by the parties to a consolidation. (b) What procedures are normally employed in arriving at a satisfactory measurement of relative contributions?

5. (a) What are the limitations in the issue of a single class of stock to constituent parties to a consolidation? (b) Describe the procedure that must be followed in the allotment of securities among parties to a consolidation if both the relative net asset and the relative earnings contributions are to be preserved through such allotment.

6. Stockholders of Companies A, B, and C decide to consolidate. Asset and estimated annual earnings contributions are as follows:

	Co. A	Co. B	Co. C	Total
Asset contribution	$300,000	$700,000	$1,000,000	$2,000,000
Estimated annual earnings contribution	50,000	100,000	100,000	250,000

Representatives of Companies A and B propose that a single class of stock of the new company should be distributed in the estimated earnings ratio. Representatives of Company C propose that such stock should be distributed in the asset ratio. Criticize these proposals and suggest a more satisfactory plan for consolidation, assuming that (a) a single class of stock is to be issued and (b) two classes of stock are to be issued.

7. (a) Distinguish between a combination achieved through *purchase* and a combination achieved through *pooling of interests*. (b) What factors should be considered in making the distinction? (c) What accounting significance is attached to the distinction?

8. (a) What arguments are made in support of the recognition of original asset values on the books of a new organization viewed as having emerged from a pooling of interests? (b) Give arguments, pro and con, for the recognition of the retained earnings of constituent companies on the books of the new organization.

9. State what treatment would be applied to paid-in capital and retained earnings balances of constituent companies in a consolidation viewed as a pooling of

interests (a) when the stated capital for the new unit is to be more than the total of the stated capitals of the constituent companies, and (b) when the stated capital is to be less than the total of the stated capitals of the constituent companies.

10. Describe each of the following: (a) split-up, (b) split-off, and (c) spin-off.

11. What special accounting problems arise in a divisive reorganization?

EXERCISES

1. Balance sheets for Company Y and Company Z on June 30, 19X5, are as follows:

	Co. Y	Co. Z
Assets		
Cash	$ 100,000	$ 50,000
Receivables	350,000	250,000
Inventories	940,000	560,000
Property, plant, and equipment (net)	1,100,000	650,000
Total assets	$2,490,000	$1,510,000
Liabilities and Stockholders' Equity		
Accounts payable	$ 750,000	$ 160,000
Taxes and accruals	100,000	40,000
Long-term debt	600,000	200,000
Total liabilities	$1,450,000	$ 400,000
Capital stock, $5 stated value	$1,000,000	
Capital stock, $1 par		$ 100,000
Additional paid-in capital		250,000
Retained earnings	40,000	760,000
Total stockholders' equity	$1,040,000	$1,110,000
Total liabilities and stockholders' equity	$2,490,000	$1,510,000

The companies are contemplating a merger in which the net assets of Company Z are to be acquired by Company Y in exchange for 120,000 shares of stock of the latter company; stock of Company Y is subsequently to be distributed to stockholders of Company Z in liquidation of Company Z.

Prepare a balance sheet to give effect to the merger, assuming that it is to be regarded as a pooling of interests.

2. The Brooks Corporation acquires net assets of the Wharton Corporation for $360,000, paying cash of $160,000 and issuing 4,000 shares of its stock that has a market value of $50 per share on the date of acquisition. The Wharton Corporation balance sheet, which reflects fair values as of the date of the merger, is shown on page 258.

The Brooks Corporation common stock has a par value of $20.

(a) Prepare the entries that should be made on the books of the Wharton Corporation and on the books of the Brooks Corporation in recording the merger. (b) How should the cash and the shares of the Brooks Corporation be distributed among the Wharton Corporation stockholders?

Current assets...........	$100,000	Current liabilities.......	$ 20,000
Plant and equipment..	125,000	Long-term debt..........	30,000
		Capital stock, par $10	50,000
		Additional paid-in capital............................	35,000
		Retained earnings......	90,000
		Total liabilities and	
Total assets..............	$225,000	stockholders' equity	$225,000

3. Asset and estimated annual earnings contributions of Companies M, N, and O, parties to a consolidation, are as follows:

	Co. M	Co. N	Co. O	Total
Asset contribution...............	$1,000,000	$2,000,000	$2,000,000	$5,000,000
Estimated annual earnings contribution...	90,000	200,000	240,000	530,000

Parties agree to the following: a single class of stock, $10 par, is to be issued by the new corporation; stock is to be exchanged for net assets as indicated plus allowances for goodwill represented by annual earnings in excess of 8% on asset contributions as above, capitalized at 20%.

(a) Assuming that stock is issued equal in amount to the sum of assets and goodwill, how is the stock distributed among constituent companies? (b) What entry is made assuming that stock of $5,000,000 is issued, goodwill calculations being made simply to assure the equitable allotment of this stock? How is the stock distributed among the constituent companies?

4. Assume in Exercise 3 that two classes of stock (5% fully participating preferred stock and common stock, both issues with a par value of $10) are to be issued by the new corporation. Preferred stock is to be issued to each company in an amount equal to the asset contributions as shown. Earnings are to be capitalized at 8% in determining the total of preferred stock and common stock to be issued to each company. Common stock is to be issued for the difference between the totals determined and the preferred stock to which each company is entitled. State the number of shares of preferred stock and common stock of the new corporation to be issued to stockholders of Companies M, N, and O.

5. Balance sheet data for Companies R and S, prior to their consolidation, follow:

	Co. R	Co. S
Assets	$850,000	$600,000
Liabilities..	$250,000	$200,000
Capital stock, $100 par	400,000	250,000
Additional paid-in capital......................	50,000	100,000
Retained earnings................................	150,000	50,000
Total liabilities and stockholders' equity...	$850,000	$600,000

Stockholders of the two companies agree to a consolidation whereby Company T is to be organized to acquire the net assets of Companies R and S. Company T stock is to be no-par with a stated value, and shares are to be issued in exchange for the stock of Companies R and S on a 5-for-1 basis. The consolidation is deemed a pooling of interests, and asset, liability, and stockholders' equity balances of the predecessor companies are to be continued on the new company books.

(a) Prepare the entries that are made on the books of Company T under each of the following assumptions:

  (1) The no-par shares are given a stated value of $20 per share.
  (2) The no-par shares are given a stated value of $15 per share.
  (3) The no-par shares are given a stated value of $25 per share.

(b) Prepare the entries that are made on the books of Companies R and S in recording the transfers of net assets and the distribution of Company T stock in final liquidation.

6. Stockholders of Allen Company, Bay Company, and Cook Company agree to a merger. Bay Company and Cook Company are to accept shares of Allen Company in exchange for all of their assets and liabilities on the basis of 1 share for every $125 of net assets transferred. On December 31, 19X6, the date of the transfer, balances on the books of the separate companies are as follows:

	Allen Co.	Bay Co.	Cook Co.
Assets			
Current assets.........................	$230,000	$200,000	$230,000
Plant and equipment (net)........	450,000	250,000	370,000
Goodwill.................................	20,000		50,000
Total assets............................	$700,000	$450,000	$650,000
Liabilities and Stockholders' Equity			
Current liabilities......................	$175,000	$120,000	$190,000
Bonds payable..........................		100,000	200,000
Common stock, $100 par...........	500,000	150,000	200,000
Additional paid-in capital..........	45,000	90,000	
Retained earnings (deficit)........	(20,000)	(10,000)	60,000
Total liabilities and stockholders' equity............................	$700,000	$450,000	$650,000

The following adjustments are to be made in arriving at the net asset contributions of Bay Company and Cook Company for purposes of the merger:

(1) The inventory of the Bay Company is presently stated on a lifo basis at $100,000; the inventory is to be recognized at $160,000, representing cost calculated on a fifo basis consistent with the costing procedures of the other companies.
(2) No value is to be assigned to goodwill reported on the books of the Cook Company.

Assuming that the merger is construed as a pooling of interests and that predecessor companies' asset, liability, and stockholders' equity items are to be continued, prepare the entries that are required on the books of the Allen Company and prepare a balance sheet upon consummation of the merger.

7. Company Y offers to sell to Company X its assets at their book value plus $150,000, the latter amount representing payment for goodwill. Operating data for the past year for the two companies are as follows:

		Co. X		Co. Y
Sales..		$960,000		$800,000
Cost of goods sold....................		672,000		600,000
Gross profit............................		$288,000		$200,000
Selling expenses....	$168,000		$117,600	
General and admin-				
istrative				
expenses	72,000	240,000	50,400	168,000
Net income		$ 48,000		$ 32,000

Company X estimates the following operating changes if Company Y is merged through purchase:

(1) After the merger, the sales volume of Company X will be 20% in excess of the present combined sales volume, and the sales price per unit will be decreased by 10%.
(2) Fixed manufacturing cost has been 30% of cost of goods sold for each company. After the merger, the fixed manufacturing cost of Company X will be increased by 90% of the current fixed manufacturing cost of Company Y. The current variable manufacturing cost of Company X, which is 70% of cost of goods sold, is expected to increase in proportion to the increased sales volume.
(3) Selling expenses of Company X are expected to be 90% of the present combined selling expenses.
(4) General and administrative expenses of Company X will increase by 80% as a result of the merger.

Excess of the estimated net income over the combined present net income of the two companies is to be capitalized at 20%. If this amount exceeds the price set by Company Y for goodwill, Company X will accept the offer. Prepare a projected income statement for Company X, assuming a merger and ignoring the amortization of goodwill. State whether Company X should accept the offer.

PROBLEMS

9-1. A merger was effected on June 1 whereby the Columbia Corporation took over the assets and assumed the liabilities of the Decker Company in exchange for 8,000 shares of its own stock. A balance sheet for the Columbia Corporation just prior to the merger shows the following:

Cash, receivables,		Current liabilities	$105,000
inventories...........	$365,000	Long-term debt........	180,000
Investments............	120,000	Preferred stock,	
Plant and equipment		$100 par..............	100,000
(net)....................	400,000	Common stock, $5	
Goodwill and other		stated value	250,000
intangibles...........	100,000	Additional paid-in	
		capital.................	90,000
		Retained earnings....	260,000
		Total liabilities and	
		stockholders' eq-	
Total assets.............	$985,000	uity	$985,000

The Decker Company balance sheet consists of the following:

Cash, receivables, inventories............	$ 80,800	Current liabilities......	$ 40,000
		Long-term debt.........	60,000
Plant and equipment (net)....................	140,000	Common stock, $10 par......................	100,000
Goodwill..................	40,000	Additional paid-in capital..................	80,000
		Deficit	(19,200)
		Total liabilities and stockholders' equity	
Total assets.............	$260,800	uity	$260,800

The Columbia Corporation records the assets of the Decker Company at appraised values as follows: cash, receivables, inventories, $56,000; plant and equipment, $120,000. Liabilities are understated by certain accrued items totaling $1,200. The stock of the Columbia Corporation is selling at $12 per share, and this figure is used in recording the purchase of the Decker Company net assets.

Instructions: (1) Prepare the entries that would appear on the books of the Columbia Corporation as a result of the merger.

(2) Prepare a balance sheet for the Columbia Corporation after the merger.

(3) Prepare the entries to close the books of the Decker Company.

(4) State how stock of the Columbia Corporation should be distributed to owners of Decker Company stock upon the dissolution of the latter company.

9-2. Stockholders for Companies D, E, and F agree to the following plan in effecting a consolidation:

The new company, DEF, Inc., shall acquire all of the assets of Companies D, E, and F and shall assume all of the liabilities, issuing 6% preferred stock, $100 par value, in an amount equal to the net assets transferred excluding intangible assets. Assets are to be valued at current market or reproduction costs. Average profits for 19X2, 19X3, and 19X4 in excess of 6% of net tangible assets after revaluation are to be capitalized at 25% in determining the valuation to be placed on goodwill; 150,000 shares of no-par common are to be issued in payment of goodwill.

Balance sheets on March 31, 19X5, when the consolidation is to be made effective, follow:

	Co. D	Co. E	Co. F
Cash.................................	$ 120,000	$ 100,000	$ 30,000
Receivables......................	280,000	160,000	220,000
Inventories.......................	700,000	400,000	650,000
Plant and equipment (net) .	2,200,000	1,000,000	1,500,000
Goodwill...........................	200,000	100,000	
Total assets......................	$3,500,000	$1,760,000	$2,400,000
Accounts payable	$ 350,000	$ 310,000	$ 300,000
Bonds payable..................	1,500,000		500,000
Common stock, $100 par...	1,000,000	500,000	2,000,000
Retained earnings (deficit).	650,000	950,000	(400,000)
Total liabilities and stockholders' equity..............	$3,500,000	$1,760,000	$2,400,000

Assets are revalued as follows for purposes of the consolidation:

	Co. D	Co. E	Co. F
Inventories	$ 950,000	$ 500,000	$ 800,000
Plant and equipment	3,000,000	1,300,000	1,750,000

Average earnings for the three-year period ended December 31, 19X4, were as follows: Company D, $160,000; Company E, $120,000; Company F, $125,000.

Instructions: (1) Prepare the journal entries for Companies D, E, and F to record the revaluation of assets and the adjustments for goodwill.

(2) Prepare the journal entries for each company to record the receipt of new stock from DEF, Inc., and its distribution to stockholders in exchange for their stock. Calculate the number of shares of preferred and common stock of DEF, Inc., to be distributed to stockholders in exchange for each share of common stock in Companies D, E, and F. Show how respective goodwill balances are determined.

(3) Prepare the journal entries for DEF, Inc., to record the net assets acquired and the distribution of stock for assets acquired.

(4) Prepare a balance sheet for DEF, Inc.

9-3. Asset and estimated earnings contributions by Companies A, B, and C, parties to a consolidation in 19X0, are as follows:

	Co. A	Co. B	Co. C
Assets as appraised (before goodwill)	$3,000,000	$1,500,000	$1,500,000
Estimated annual earnings contribution	300,000	165,000	135,000

The new corporation is to be known as the ABC Corporation. Two plans are suggested for the distribution of stock in the new company to stockholders of Companies A, B, and C.

Plan A: The ABC Corporation shall issue a single class of stock in exchange for assets. Earnings of each company in excess of 6% of assets as appraised are to be capitalized at 20% in calculating the goodwill contribution by constituent parties. Stock is to have a par value of $10 and is to be issued in an amount equal to total assets transferred including goodwill.

Plan B: Two classes of stock, 6% fully participating preferred and common, are to be issued. Earnings are to be capitalized at 7½% in determining the total stock to be issued in exchange for the assets of each company. Preferred stock, par $10, is to be issued in an amount equal to assets at their appraised values. Common stock, par $10, is to be issued for the difference between the total stock to be issued to each company and the amount it is to receive in preferred. The issue of common stock is to be regarded as payment of goodwill.

Instructions: (1) Prepare the required entries on the books of the ABC Corporation and state how the stock should be distributed among Companies A, B, and C under each of the plans considered.

(2) If earnings and dividends of the new corporation are estimated for 19X0 at $750,000, state how this total would be distributed among former stockholders of Companies A, B, and C under each of the plans considered.

9-4. Stockholders of Company R and Company S agree to merge. Under the agreement, a new company, Company T, is to be formed with a single class of $100 par stock. Shares of Company T will be issued to Company R and Company S in par value amounts equal to the net asset contributions made by these companies. To secure additional capital for expansion, 20,000 additional shares will be placed on sale to the public at par.

Balance sheets of Companies R and S as of December 31, 19X4, are given below.

	Co. R	Co. S
Assets		
Cash	$ 28,500	$ 22,500
Notes receivable	52,500	30,500
Notes receivable discounted	(50,000)	
Accounts receivable	158,000	90,000
Inventories	50,500	77,500
Plant expansion fund	50,000	
Land	15,000	20,000
Buildings (net)	124,000	140,000
Machinery (net)	205,000	119,000
Other assets		7,500
Total assets	$633,500	$507,000
Liabilities and Stockholders' Equity		
Notes payable	$ 42,500	$ 22,000
Accounts payable	155,500	72,000
Bonds payable		100,000
Capital stock, $10 par	300,000	
Capital stock, $20 par		300,000
Treasury stock, Co. S, 1,000 shares at cost		(20,000)
Premium on capital stock	75,000	
Retained earnings	60,500	33,000
Total liabilities and stockholders' equity	$633,500	$507,000

It is agreed that the following adjustments are to be made in arriving at the net asset contributions by the two companies:

(a) Company R employs the lifo method of inventory valuation. The inventory of December 31, 19X4, is to be increased to $65,000 to be uniform with the fifo valuation method used by Company S.

(b) The buildings of Company S were acquired in January, 19X1, and have been depreciated at the rate of $10,000 per year. Depreciation is to be recognized on the buildings on the basis of an estimated life of 20 years, the same as that recognized for buildings by Company R.

(c) Company S has been depreciating its machinery on a decreasing-charge basis. The machinery cost $200,000 when purchased 4 years ago and was estimated to have a scrap value of $20,000 at the end of 15 years. Depreciation is to be recognized by the straight-line method consistent with the depreciation method used by Company R.

Shares are sold to the public as planned and the merger is consummated on December 31, 19X4.

Instructions: (1) Prepare all of the entries required on the books of Company R and Company S, including those to record the distribution of Company T shares to stockholders. (State the number of Company T shares that are issued to Company R and to Company S, and the basis of exchange with each stockholder.)

(2) Prepare all of the entries necessary on the books of Company T.

(3) Prepare a balance sheet for Company T as of December 31, 19X4.

9-5. Stockholders of Companies L, M, and N are considering alternative arrangements for a combination. Balance sheets reflecting uniform accounting procedures, as well as fair values, that are to be used as a basis for the combination are prepared on September 1, 19X8, as follows:

	Co. L	Co. M	Co. N
Assets	$4,000,000	$5,500,000	$500,000
Liabilities	$2,850,000	$1,500,000	$175,000
Capital stock (all $10 par)	1,500,000	1,000,000	250,000
Additional paid-in capital		400,000	125,000
Retained earnings (deficit)	(350,000)	2,600,000	(50,000)
Total liabilities and stockholders' equity	$4,000,000	$5,500,000	$500,000

Company L shares have a market price of $15. A market price is not available for shares of Company M and Company N since stock of these companies is closely held.

Instructions: Prepare a balance sheet for the combination, giving effect to each of the assumptions that follow:

(1) Company L acquires all of the assets and assumes all of the liabilities of Company M and Company N by issuing in exchange 300,000 shares of its stock to Company M and 25,000 shares of its stock to Company N. The transaction is treated in the accounts as a purchase.

(2) Company L shares are issued as in (1), but the transaction is treated in the accounts as a pooling of interests.

(3) A new corporation, L and M Company, is formed to take over the assets and to assume the liabilities of Companies L, M, and N. The new company issues no-par stock with a stated value of $5 in payment of acquisitions, as follows: to Company L, 150,000 shares; to Company M, 300,000 shares; to Company N, 25,000 shares. The transaction is treated as a pooling of interests.

9-6. The stockholders of Companies X, Y, and Z are considering a combination of their companies. Accordingly, they authorize the preparation of financial statements, giving effect to uniform procedures. Balance sheets on November 1, 19X1, that are to be used in arriving at terms for a combination are shown on page 265.

Stock of each company is no-par. Shares issued and outstanding are as follows: Company X, 1,000,000; Company Y, 20,000; Company Z, 50,000. Company X shares are quoted on the market at $10; Company Y and Company Z shares are closely held and there are no quotations for them.

	Co. X	Co. Y	Co. Z
Assets	$10,000,000	$2,000,000	$1,500,000
Liabilities.......................	$ 3,500,000	$1,250,000	$ 500,000
Capital stock..................	1,000,000	1,000,000	500,000
Additional paid-in capital.	500,000	250,000	150,000
Retained earnings (deficit).............................	5,000,000	(500,000)	350,000
Total liabilities and stockholders' equity.............	$10,000,000	$2,000,000	$1,500,000

Instructions: Prepare a balance sheet, giving effect to the combination under each of the following assumptions:

(1) Company X acquires all of the assets and assumes all of the obligations of Company Y and Company Z, and in payment issues 100,000 shares of its stock to Company Y and 150,000 shares to Company Z. The transaction is treated as a purchase.

(2) Company AAA is formed to acquire all of the assets and to assume all of the liabilities of the three companies. Payment is made by Company AAA by the issue of shares with a par value of $2.50 as follows: to Company X, 1,000,000 shares; to Company Y, 100,000 shares; to Company Z, 150,000 shares. The transaction is treated as a pooling of interests.

9-7. Balance sheets for Richards, Inc., and the Scott Corporation on June 30, 19X6, appear as follows:

	Richards, Inc.	Scott Corporation
Assets		
Cash...	$ 140,000	$ 950,000
Receivables..	450,000	730,000
Inventories...	580,000	980,000
Prepaid expenses................................	25,000	66,500
Total current assets	$1,195,000	$2,726,500
Property, plant, and equipment (net) ...	900,000	720,000
Other assets......................................	100,000	20,000
Total assets.......................................	$2,195,000	$3,466,500
Liabilities and Stockholders' Equity		
Current portion of long-term debt	$ 25,000	$ 40,000
Accounts payable	500,000	146,500
Estimated federal income tax payable ..	50,000	400,000
Total current liabilities	$ 575,000	$ 586,500
Long-term debt..................................	50,000	180,000
Total liabilities..................................	$ 625,000	$ 766,500
Capital stock, $1 par, 1,600,000 shares issued and outstanding	$1,600,000	
Capital stock, no par, 5,000 shares issued and outstanding.....................		$ 50,000
Retained earnings (deficit)..................	(30,000)	2,650,000
Total stockholders' equity...................	$1,570,000	$2,700,000
Total liab. and stockholders' equity......	$2,195,000	$3,466,500

On this date the Scott Corporation is offered 400,000 shares of Richards, Inc., in exchange for its net assets. Richards, Inc., stock has a market value of $10.50 per share. The offer is accepted and the shares transferred to the Scott Corporation are distributed to its stockholders in final liquidation.

Instructions: (1) (a) Prepare entries on the books of Richards, Inc., to record the acquisition of the Scott Corporation, assuming that the merger is recognized as a purchase and the stock issued in exchange for net assets is recorded at its market value. Net assets of the Scott Corporation are recorded at their book values which reflect current appraisals; the difference between the market value of the stock and the net assets acquired for such stock is to be recognized as goodwill. (b) Prepare a balance sheet for Richards, Inc., after the purchase.

(2) (a) Prepare the entries on the books of Richards, Inc., to record the acquisition of the Scott Corporation, assuming that the merger is recognized as a pooling of interests. (b) Prepare a balance sheet for Richards, Inc., after the pooling of interests.

9-8. Effective December 31, 19X5, X Corporation proposes to acquire, in exchange for common stock, all of the assets and liabilities of Y Corporation and Z Corporation, after which the latter two corporations will distribute the X Corporation stock to their shareholders in complete liquidation and dissolution. X Corporation proposes to increase its outstanding stock for purposes of these acquisitions. Balance sheets of each corporation immediately prior to merger on December 31, 19X5, are given below. The assets of each corporation are deemed to be worth their book values.

	X Corporation	Y Corporation	Z Corporation
Current assets....................	$ 2,000,000	$ 500,000	$ 25,000
Plant assets (net)...............	10,000,000	4,000,000	200,000
Total assets.......................	$12,000,000	$4,500,000	$225,000
Current liabilities................	$ 1,000,000	$ 300,000	$ 20,000
Long-term debt..................	3,000,000	1,000,000	105,000
Capital stock ($10 par).......	3,000,000	1,000,000	50,000
Retained earnings..............	5,000,000	2,200,000	50,000
Total liab. and stockholders' equity......................	$12,000,000	$4,500,000	$225,000

	X Corporation	Y Corporation	Z Corporation
Other data relative to acquisition:			
Shares outstanding.........	300,000	100,000	5,000
Fair market value per share.........................	$40	$40	$30
Number of shares of X Corporation to be exchanged —			
for Y Corporation assets		100,000	
for Z Corporation assets			5,000
All criteria for pooling met		Yes	No

Instructions: Prepare journal entries for the X Corporation to record the combination of the X Corporation, the Y Corporation, and the Z Corporation.

(AICPA adapted)

9-9. The balance sheets of G Corporation and D Corporation at June 30, 19X7, appear as follows:

	G Corporation	D Corporation
Assets		
Cash...	$ 25,500	$ 1,500
Receivables (net).................................	24,500	7,500
Inventories...	42,000	8,800
Due from D Corporation.........................	7,600	—
Plant assets (net)................................	59,500	35,800
Other assets.......................................	4,500	200
Total assets..	$163,600	$53,800
Liabilities and Stockholders' Equity		
Accounts and notes payable...................	$ 22,600	$35,400
Due to G Corporation............................	—	7,600
Accrued expenses................................	1,500	2,200
Federal income tax payable....................	9,500	—
Total liabilities...................................	$ 33,600	$45,200
Capital stock, $10 par	$ 50,000	—
Capital stock, $100 par	—	$25,000
Capital contributed in excess of par	30,000	32,000
Retained earnings, December 31, 19X6....	43,000	(42,300)
Net income (loss) from January 1, 19X7....	9,500	(6,100)
Dividends paid.....................................	(2,500)	—
Total stockholders' equity......................	$130,000	$ 8,600
Total liabilities and stockholders' equity ...	$163,600	$53,800

The income statements for G Corporation and D Corporation for the six months ended June 30, 19X7, appear as follows:

	G Corporation	D Corporation
Sales...	$150,000	$60,000
Cost of goods sold................................	105,000	54,000
Gross profit	$ 45,000	$ 6,000
Operating expenses..............................	31,000	8,200
Operating profit (loss)...........................	$ 14,000	($ 2,200)
Other income (deductions).....................	5,000	(3,900)
Income (loss) before income tax	$ 19,000	($ 6,100)
Provision for income tax	9,500	—
Net income (loss).................................	$ 9,500	($ 6,100)

The incomes (losses) before income tax for the two corporations for the last 6 years are as follows (income per books and taxable income are the same):

	G Corporation	D Corporation
19X1	$18,000	($10,000)
19X2	(7,500)	4,000
19X3	12,600	(15,000)
19X4	14,900	(6,000)
19X5	31,200	(7,000)
19X6	28,900	(11,100)

On July 1, 19X7, D Corporation transferred to G Corporation all of its assets, subject to all liabilities, in exchange for unissued G Corporation capital stock. Both corporations have been owned by the same group of stockholders since their inception in 19X1, although in different proportions as to individuals. The terms of the merger provided that the fair value of the stock in each case is to be its book value, except that an allowance is to be made for the value of any net operating carryover losses. Obtaining the benefit of the loss carryover deduction was not the principal purpose for the merger. (Assume a 50% income tax rate and a 5-year loss carryover period.)

Instructions: (1) Compute (a) the number of shares of G Corporation to be distributed to shareholders of D Corporation, and (b) the number of shares of G Corporation stock to be exchanged for each share of D Corporation stock.

(2) Prepare the journal entry for the books of G Corporation, recording the merger with D Corporation as a pooling of interests.

(3) Prepare the journal entries for the books of D Corporation, recording the merger with G Corporation and the distribution of G Corporation stock to the stockholders of D Corporation.

(AICPA adapted)

9-10. Y Corporation acquired all of the outstanding stock of Z Corporation as of June 30, 19X3. As consideration for the acquisition, Y Corporation gave the stockholders of Z Corporation $550,000 and 500,000 shares of previously unissued common stock in exchange for all the outstanding stock of the Z Corporation. The Y Corporation stock had a par value of $1 and a quoted market value of $2.50 both before and after this transaction.

The balance sheet of Z Corporation as of June 30, 19X3, was as follows:

Assets

Current assets:
Cash..	$120,000	
Accounts receivable.............................	240,000	
Inventories...	210,000	$ 570,000

Plant assets:

	Cost	Accumulated Depreciation	Net	
Property A	$ 310,000	$160,000	$150,000	
Property B	370,000	170,000	200,000	
Property C	480,000	180,000	300,000	
Property D	250,000	150,000	100,000	
	$1,410,000	$660,000	$750,000	750,000

Total assets..	$1,320,000

Liabilities and Stockholders' Equity
Accounts payable .... $ 470,000
Stockholders' equity:
Common stock — authorized and out-
standing, 500,000 shares of $1 par...... $500,000
Paid-in capital in excess of par.............. 100,000
Retained earnings................................. 250,000 850,000
Total liabilities and stockholders' equity $1,320,000

All receivables are considered collectible. Inventories are stated at cost, which is also equivalent to replacement cost and is not in excess of market. Properties B, C and D have been appraised at $600,000, $800,000 and $200,000 respectively. Goodwill is not considered to be a significant factor in this business.

An engineer of the Y Corporation estimates that the properties of the Z Corporation will have a 10-year useful life from July 1, 19X3, with no salvage value at the end of that period. Y Corporation uses the straight-line method of depreciating its assets.

On July 1, 19X3, Z Corporation sold Property A for $500,000 and, for the 6 months ended December 31, 19X3, reported a net income of $450,000, which included the gain from the sale of Property A and depreciation of $55,000.

The balance sheet of Z Corporation at December 31, 19X3, was as follows:

Assets

Current assets:
Cash.. $390,000
Accounts receivable.............................. 355,000
Inventories... 260,000 $1,005,000

Plant assets:

	Cost	Accumulated Depreciation	Net	
Property B	$ 370,000	$188,500	$181,500	
Property C	480,000	204,000	276,000	
Property D	250,000	162,500	87,500	
	$1,100,000	$555,000	$545,000	545,000

Total assets... $1,550,000

Liabilities and Stockholders' Equity
Accounts payable .... $ 250,000
Stockholders' equity:
Common stock....................................... $500,000
Paid-in capital in excess of par.............. 100,000
Retained earnings................................. 700,000 1,300,000
Total liabilities and stockholders' equity $1,550,000

On January 1, 19X4, Z Corporation was dissolved and all of its assets were transferred to and its liabilities assumed by Y Corporation. The transaction is to be accounted for as a purchase and not as a pooling of interests.

Instructions: (1) Prepare the journal entry of Y Corporation to record its investment in Z Corporation as of June 30, 19X3, and explain the basis for the value assigned to the investment.

(2) Prepare the journal entries to record the accounts of Z Corporation on the books of Y Corporation upon dissolution of Z Corporation and explain how the amounts were determined. (Disregard income tax implications.)

(AICPA adapted)

9-11. Presented below are balance sheets for the Ace Company at December 31, 19X4, and May 31, 19X5:

	December 31, 19X4	May 31, 19X5
Assets		
Cash...	$ 1,038,000	$ 472,000
Receivables...............................	2,550,000	3,105,000
Inventories................................	5,592,000	6,028,000
Prepaid expenses......................	308,000	297,000
Total current assets	$ 9,488,000	$ 9,902,000
Property (net)............................	6,927,000	6,804,000
Other assets..............................	635,000	604,000
Total assets...............................	$17,050,000	$17,310,000
Liabilities and Stockholders' Equity		
Accounts payable	$ 2,427,000	$ 3,052,500
Current maturities — long-term debt...................................	600,000	600,000
Accrued liabilities......................	1,096,000	922,000
Dividends payable — preferred stock.......................................	63,000	0
Estimated federal income tax......	417,000	333,500
Total current liabilities	$ 4,603,000	$ 4,908,000
Long-term debt..........................	4,200,000	4,050,000
Stockholders' equity:		
Preferred cumulative stock — 21,000 shares of $100 par, 3%, outstanding; redeemable at $102.......................	2,100,000	2,100,000
Common stock — 100,000 shares of $10 par outstanding......................................	1,000,000	1,000,000
Capital contributed in excess of par of common stock............	587,000	587,000
Retained earnings....................	4,560,000	4,665,000
Total liabilities and stockholders' equity......................................	$17,050,000	$17,310,000

The increase in Retained Earnings is net of a dividend of $.20 per share paid March 15, 19X5, on common stock.

The Ace Company proposes to sell all of its assets except cash and receivables to the Jones Company on July 31, 19X5. The sales price shall be $10,000,000 adjusted by the change in book value for inventories and property from December 31, 19X4, to May 31, 19X5. The May 31 book values of prepaid expenses and other assets are to be added to the sales price.

The settlement shall be:

(1) Jones Company 4% note for $3,000,000 payable in semiannual install-
ments of $150,000 commencing January 31, 19X6.
(2) Assumption of all liabilities except the estimated federal income tax payable and long-term debt.
(3) Balance payable in cash immediately.

The company intends to retire the preferred stock immediately after the sale.
The income for June and July is estimated at $150,000 before income taxes (as-
sume that a 50% tax rate is in effect.)

The last preferred stock dividend was declared on December 31, 19X4. The
regular common stock dividend was paid on June 15, 19X5.

Taxable income for the past 4 years follows:

19X1	$1,481,000
19X2	412,400
19X3	639,600
19X4	842,500

Instructions: (1) Compute the total sales price and settlement to be made.

(2) Compute Ace Company's gain or loss on the sale, giving effect to income
tax. (Assume that a loss can be carried back three years prior to the loss year; the
taxpayer may claim a refund for taxes paid in the years in which the carryback
may be applied.)

(3) Prepare a work sheet with columnar headings "Per Books," "Adjustments," and "Estimated Balance Sheet, July 31, 19X5", giving effect to the proposed sale and other information given. Support your adjustments with schedules or computations. Formal journal entries are not required.

(AICPA adapted)

10
Consolidated Statements — Acquisition of Subsidiary Company

In Chapter 9, discussion was limited to the joint control and operation of corporate units through merger or consolidation. The practical effects of a merger or a consolidation are frequently achieved through the ownership by one company of a majority or all of the voting stock of other corporate units. A company owning more than 50% of the voting stock of another is in a position to elect the board of directors of the latter unit and thus to control the resources and the operations of the company. While the fusion of separate companies frequently offers serious practical difficulties, acquisition of control by means of stock ownership may be relatively simple to arrange and may require a smaller investment. Furthermore, control through stock ownership may be preferred over the other possibilities because of certain financial, administrative, tax, or legal advantages found in this relationship.

CORPORATE CONTROL THROUGH STOCK OWNERSHIP

The power of a corporation to acquire stock of other corporations is generally granted by the laws of the state.[1] State law may specifically permit the organization of companies that are formed for the sole purpose of acquiring and holding stock of other corporations.

Even though a corporation may acquire a majority or all of the stock issued by other corporations, the latter units continue to retain their separate identities. From a practical point of view, the acquisition by one company of a controlling interest in the stock of another company may be equivalent to a merger or a consolidation, since properties come under unified management and control. From a legal point of view, however, regardless of the degree of corporate control that may be exercised, each company continues to be regarded as a separate entity.

---

[1]Section 5 (g) of the Illinois Business Corporation Act (Ill. Rev. Stat. 1979, Ch. 32, par. 157.5), for example, permits a corporation "to purchase, take, receive, subscribe for, or otherwise acquire, own, hold, vote, use, employ, sell, mortgage, loan, pledge, or otherwise dispose of, and otherwise use and deal in and with, shares or other interests in, or obligations of, other domestic or foreign corporations, associations, partnerships, or individuals."

Parent and Holding Company

A corporation that holds the stock of others and controls their activities is called a *parent company*. When a corporation is organized for the sole purpose of holding the stock of others and supervising their activities, it is known as a *holding company*. The chief source of revenue of the holding company is the dividends on the securities it holds; expenses are entirely of an administrative nature. A company that exercises control over others while engaged in its own trading or manufacturing activities is sometimes called an *operating holding company* to distinguish it from a pure holding company. The companies that are controlled by a parent or holding company are known as *subsidiaries*. Parent and subsidiary companies are referred to as *affiliated companies*. A company that holds a major part or all of the voting stock of another is referred to as the *controlling interest*. Those holding any remaining interest in the controlled company are referred to as the *minority interest*. A controlled company whose stock is wholly owned by affiliated units is called a *wholly owned subsidiary*.

Ownership of a majority of the voting stock of a company assures control over that unit. In practice, however, ownership of a lesser amount generally offers control for all practical purposes, particularly when remaining stockholders are widely scattered, unorganized, and willing to delegate their voting power to the dominant group. When ownership is not complete, control must be exercised in a manner that is not prejudicial to the minority interest.

Recording an Investment in a Subsidiary Company

A corporation acquires the stock of other companies by purchase for cash, by exchange for other assets, or by exchange for its own securities. An investment account is debited for the cost of the stock acquired. When cash is paid, the investment account is debited for the amount paid. When other assets are given in exchange, the investment should be recorded at the fair value of the assets given up. When a company's own securities are issued in exchange for stock acquired, the investment should be recorded at the fair value of the securities given in exchange or at the fair value of the stock acquired, whichever is more clearly evident. Any difference between the value assigned to the investment and the par or stated value of the securities should be recognized as a premium or a discount on the securities issued. Investments in the stock of subsidiary companies are reported under the "Investments" heading on the parent company balance sheet.

NATURE OF CONSOLIDATED STATEMENTS

A parent company's balance sheet that reports subsidiary holdings as investments and the subsidiary company's balance sheet that reports interests held by a parent as capital stock are complete statements of the related units as separate legal entities but not as a single business or a single economic entity. If a comprehensive view of the affiliated companies is to be provided, the legal view of separateness of the different units must be cast aside and the practical implications of the ownership of a controlling interest must be incorporated in the presentation. The statement that erases the legal boundaries between a parent and its subsidiaries and presents the financial position of the affiliates as a single unit is known as the *consolidated balance sheet*.

To avoid confusion between the terms "consolidation" and "consolidated financial statements," the term "merger" will henceforth be used to represent the creation of a new legal entity from the fusion of previously separate corporations. "Consolidated financial statements" are the accounting reports designed to show the economic effects of combining two or more separate corporations under common ownership and control, although no legal fusion exists.

In preparing a combined balance sheet for a home office and its branches, individual asset and liability balances of the branch were combined with similar home office balances. Reciprocal balances arising from interoffice transactions and having no asset, liability, or proprietorship significance in viewing the related units as a single entity were eliminated. The effect of such a procedure was to substitute for the branch investment balance on the home office books those assets and liabilities represented by this balance. In developing a consolidated balance sheet for a parent and its subsidiary companies, the subsidiary units are viewed just as though they were branches: individual assets and liabilities of the subsidiary units are combined with similar items of the parent; reciprocal items that have no significance when the related units are viewed as a single entity are eliminated. The parallel approach to consolidation for home office-branch and parent-subsidiary relationships is illustrated in the example that follows.

Assume that the Ward Appliance Company of New York wishes to establish a sales outlet in Boston, and on January 2, 19X3, establishes an unincorporated branch in that city. Home office transfers cash of $125,000 and merchandise of $100,000 to the branch. A work sheet for a combined balance sheet for the home office and the branch and the combined balance sheet appear on page 275.

Assume that the Ward Appliance Company establishes the Boston office as a separately incorporated unit. The new company is to be known as the Boston Sales Company. The Ward Appliance Company acquires all the capital stock of the Boston Sales Company for cash of $125,000. The stock is recorded on the Boston Sales Company books at a stated value of $100,000, with the excess reported as additional paid-in capital. Merchandise of $100,000 is transferred to the Boston Sales Company, and open accounts for this balance are established on the books of the two companies.

Statements expressing the financial position of the parent and the subsidiary as one unit are just as necessary as when the related unit is a branch. Because the two companies are separate legal entities, however, the

Ward Appliance Company
Work Sheet for Combined Balance Sheet for Home Office and Branch
January 2, 19X3

	Home Office	Boston Branch	Eliminations		Combined Balance Sheet	
			Dr.	Cr.	Dr.	Cr.
Debits						
Cash...............................	75,000	125,000			200,000	
Receivables......................	150,000				150,000	
Merchandise.....................	200,000	100,000			300,000	
Boston Branch..................	225,000			225,000		
Plant and Equipment..........	350,000				350,000	
	1,000,000	225,000				
Credits						
Payables	250,000					250,000
Home Office		225,000	225,000			
Capital Stock....................	500,000					500,000
Additional Paid-In Capital....	100,000					100,000
Retained Earnings..............	150,000					150,000
	1,000,000	225,000	225,000	225,000	1,000,000	1,000,000

Ward Appliance Company
Combined Balance Sheet for Home Office and Branch
January 2, 19X3

Assets

Cash...		$ 200,000
Receivables..		150,000
Merchandise...		300,000
Plant and equipment		350,000
Total assets...		$1,000,000

Liabilities and Stockholders' Equity

Payables		$ 250,000
Capital stock	$500,000	
Additional paid-in capital..	100,000	
Retained earnings..	150,000	750,000
Total liabilities and stockholders' equity..		$1,000,000

individual identities of the separate units must not be disturbed. Thus, the preparation of consolidated financial statements is viewed as a "pretend" merger; i.e., as if the two separate companies had legally merged on the date that the parent acquired its controlling interest in the subsidiary. The pro forma merger is recorded only on the work sheet, so that the accounts of the separate companies remain unchanged.

A work sheet for a consolidated balance sheet for Ward Appliance Company and its wholly owned subsidiary, Boston Sales Company, may be prepared as follows.

Ward Appliance Company and Subsidiary Boston Sales Company
Work Sheet for Consolidated Balance Sheet
January 2, 19X3

	Ward Appliance Co.	Boston Sales Co.	Eliminations		Consolidated Balance Sheet	
			Dr.	Cr.	Dr.	Cr.
Debits						
Cash.................................	75,000	125,000			200,000	
Receivables......................	150,000				150,000	
Receivable from Boston Sales Co.......................	100,000			(b) 100,000		
Merchandise	200,000	100,000			300,000	
Investment in Stock of Boston Sales Co.............	125,000			(a) 125,000		
Plant and Equipment........	350,000				350,000	
	1,000,000	225,000				
Credits						
Payables..........................	250,000					250,000
Payable to Ward Appliance Co.		100,000	(b) 100,000			
Capital Stock, Ward Appliance Co.	500,000					500,000
Additional Paid-In Capital, Ward Appliance Co........	100,000					100,000
Retained Earnings, Ward Appliance Co.	150,000					150,000
Capital Stock, Boston Sales Co........................		100,000	(a) 100,000			
Additional Paid-In Capital, Boston Sales Co.		25,000	(a) 25,000			
	1,000,000	225,000	225,000	225,000	1,000,000	1,000,000

In viewing the parent and subsidiary as a single entity, reciprocal inter-company balances must be eliminated to avoid a duplication of assets, lia-bilities, and ownership equities. The investment balance of the parent is without significance when the related units are viewed as one and is elimi-nated. If the companies were legally merged, there would be no outstand-ing stock of the subsidiary. Therefore, the subsidiary capital balances are also eliminated. The intercompany receivable and payable balances are also without significance when the related units are viewed as one. Ultimate settlement of these balances will simply result in the transfer of cash from one company to another without any effect upon total net resources or stockholders' equities. Remaining account balances are combined. A con-solidated balance sheet for the Ward Appliance Company and its wholly owned subsidiary will show exactly the same balances as those in the exam-ple on page 275, where the Boston office was organized as a branch.

It was suggested in an earlier chapter that separate balance sheets for home office and branch units were incomplete as expressions of financial position because these units represent a single legal entity, which is re-flected only through the combination of data as illustrated. In the case of parent and subsidiary companies, however, the consolidation of financial data must be viewed as presenting no more than the economic unity of the related companies. This summary of economic resources subject to central direction and control is of vital significance to both management and stockholders of the parent company; nevertheless, it must be considered as complementing the separate statements of the related units, not as substituting for them. The separate balance sheets retain their validities as presentations of the assets, liabilities, and stockholders' equities of the different legal entities. A creditor must make reference to the separate balance sheet of the particular debtor in determining the degree of protection related to a claim. A stockholder must make reference to the separate balance sheet of the particular company in determining the amount that may be available for dividends. Taxing and regulatory authorities must make reference to the separate statements of the particular companies in applying specific regulations. Only when the consolidated balance sheet is accompanied by separate statements of each of the affiliated companies is full information made available concerning the legal positions of the individual units as well as the composite economic position of such units.

Although a consolidated balance sheet for the parent-subsidiary relationship cannot be offered as a statement of legal position, such a legal position can frequently be attained if this should prove desirable. For example, in the previous illustration the Boston Sales Company will continue to operate as a separate legal entity only as long as the parent company desires. If advantages emerge for a home office-branch relationship, the parent through exercise of its voting power can authorize the dissolution of the subsidiary and its conversion into a branch. The balance sheet that was previously limited to an expression of economic position is now valid as an expression of both legal and economic position.

Preceding paragraphs have referred to the need for expressing the financial position of a parent and its subsidiaries as a single unit by means of a consolidated balance sheet. There is also a need for expressing the operations of the related units as one by the preparation of a *consolidated income statement*. In preparing a consolidated income statement, revenue and expense balances reporting transactions between affiliated units are eliminated and remaining balances summarizing operations with outsiders are combined. The consolidated income statement may be supplemented by a *consolidated statement of retained earnings* to explain the change in retained earnings on consolidated balance sheets prepared at the end of successive periods. Although a complete reporting would call for consolidated financial statements accompanied by separate statements for a parent and its subsidiaries, statements to stockholders of the parent company are normally limited to consolidated statements.

Conditions for Preparation of Consolidated Statements

Judgment must be exercised in the determination of when the preparation of consolidated statements is appropriate. Consolidated financial statements can normally be justified only when (1) a controlling financial interest is present, continuing, and assured, (2) the operations of the related companies are those of an integrated unit, and (3) consolidation offers a valid reflection of the financial status of the related companies.

Controlling interest. It is the ownership of voting stock that affords control. This factor alone, however, is not an index of the control that is actually exercised. A company may have a majority ownership of the voting stock of another company and yet fail to exert a dominant role in electing the board of directors, in developing policy, or in directing operations of the latter company. For example, a company may obtain a majority interest in an established and well-managed company and may permit this company to continue its activities as an independent unit completely free from influence or control by the parent under present favorable circumstances. Or a company may have dominant interests in foreign companies, but the foreign government may place various restrictions upon the operations of such units, including restrictions upon the transfer of properties outside of such countries. In other instances, control may be temporary in view of an impending sale of shares by the parent, issue of additional shares by a subsidiary, or legal reorganization faced by a subsidiary. In each of the foregoing circumstances, consolidated statements indicating an economic unity with full and centralized control may not be appropriate.

On the other hand, a company may have less than a majority ownership in the stock of another, yet be in a position to exert effective domination over the latter. Remaining stockholders may be completely satisfied with the policies set by the controlling company, patent rights and leasehold arrangements may afford special influence to the controlling company, and conditions of interlocking directorates may contribute to unified direction. In spite of the absence of a majority interest in the voting stock of the related company, unity under effective control is present. Although the preparation of consolidated statements may not be appropriate, the equity method of accounting, which provides some of the attributes of consolidated statements, may be used. This method is discussed in Chapter 11.

In general, as the degree of ownership of stock in a subsidiary rises, the arguments supporting the preparation of consolidated statements become more persuasive. A number of companies exercising control authorize consolidated statements only when stock in a subsidiary is wholly owned. When ownership is less than 100%, holdings in the subsidiary are recognized as no more than an investment. Many other companies feel that consolidation requires ownership of a substantial majority interest, such as holdings of 75%, 80%, 85%, or more of the stock of a subsidiary. In practice one rarely encounters consolidated statements for related companies when majority stock ownership by a parent is not present even though there may be unified control. Some authorities maintain that majority stock ownership is a prerequisite for consolidation. Control must be legally assured if the assumption of a single economic entity is to be valid. The AICPA Committee on Accounting Procedure in discussing consolidation policy stated: "The usual condition for a controlling financial interest is ownership of a majority voting interest, and, therefore, as a general rule ownership by one company, directly or indirectly, of over fifty percent of the outstanding voting shares of another company is a condition pointing toward consolidation."[2]

The Securities and Exchange Commission in Regulation S-X has adopted the rule that registrants may consolidate only *majority-owned* subsidiaries. A majority-owned subsidiary is defined as "a subsidiary more than 50 percent of whose outstanding voting shares is owned by its parent and/or the parent's other majority-owned subsidiaries."

The Internal Revenue Code recognizes consolidated statements as a means for expressing the financial position and operations for "an affiliated group," and permits the filing by a parent and its subsidiaries of a consolidated income tax return reporting the combined taxable income. For tax purposes "an affiliated group" that is granted permission to file a consolidated return is defined as one or more chains of "includible corporations" having a common parent company which is an "includible corporation" and which owns at least 80% of the voting power and at least 80% of each class of nonvoting stock (except nonvoting stock which is limited and preferred as to dividends) of at least one of the other "includible corporations," provided at least 80% of the voting power and 80% of each class of nonvoting stock of any other "includible corporation" is owned by the parent corporation and/or other "includible corporation."

Operations of the related companies. When a parent holds a controlling interest in the stock of another company but the operations of the companies are not related or complementary and the organizations do not make up a homogeneous unit, a single combined presentation of financial data might be unrealistic and without value. For example, assume that a manufacturing company owns all the stock of an insurance company, a savings and loan company, or a bank. To combine the balance sheets and the income statements of a financial institution with those of a manufacturing organization would hardly provide meaningful financial data. Although each organization has profitable operations as its objective, the means and the operations for attaining this objective are not related. The Committee on Accounting Procedure comments:

> In deciding upon consolidation policy, the aim should be to make the financial presentation which is most meaningful in the circumstances. The reader should be given information which is suitable to his needs, but he should not be burdened with unnecessary detail. Thus, even though a group of companies is heterogeneous in character, it may be better to make a full consolidation than to present a large number of separate statements. On the other hand, separate statements or combined statements would be preferable for a subsidiary or group of subsidiaries if the presentation of financial information concerning the particular activities of such subsidiaries would be more informative to

---

[2]*Accounting Research and Terminology Bulletin, No. 51*, "Consolidated Financial Statements" (New York: American Institute of Certified Public Accountants, 1959), par. 2.

shareholders and creditors of the parent company than would the inclusion of such subsidiaries in the consolidation.[3]

Financial status of the related units. Legal lines can be erased only so long as they are not relevant in an economic overall view. When the lines have certain implications that affect the overall view, the implications must be recognized either by forgoing the consolidation procedure or by their disclosure on the consolidated statements. For example, assume that a parent controls a subsidiary that is insolvent and on the verge of bankruptcy. The unsatisfactory financial position of the subsidiary may be obliterated in the process of consolidation, and the consolidated statement may thus suggest a financial position for the related organizations that is not supported by the separate legal parts. Although it may be possible for healthy associates to restore solvency to an insolvent member, there is no assurance that such a course will prove to be in the best interests of the individual units and that it will be followed. Consolidation under these conditions would not provide a full appreciation of the status of the parent and its related subsidiaries as a unit but would actually serve to obscure certain facts and to misrepresent financial position.

In preparing consolidated statements, the consolidation policies that are applied should be disclosed in some satisfactory manner. Consolidation limited to wholly owned subsidiaries, for example, may be disclosed in the heading of the statement; the exclusion of an important unit may be disclosed by special note.

Problems in Preparation of Consolidated Statements

There are many problems that arise in the preparation of consolidated statements. These problems vary with the time at which the statements are prepared, the ownership interests in affiliated units and the direct or indirect controls that are afforded through such interests, and the nature of intercompany transactions. The discussion in the remaining pages of this chapter is limited to the problems that arise in the preparation of a consolidated balance sheet at the date that control of a subsidiary is acquired. The problems that arise in the preparation of the consolidated balance sheet at dates subsequent to the acquisition of control and the special problems that are encountered in the preparation of consolidated income and retained earnings statements are considered in the chapters that follow.

ACQUISITION OF THE STOCK OF A GOING CONCERN

In the example for the preparation of a consolidated balance sheet on page 274, a parent-subsidiary relationship arose as a result of the parent's acquisition of the subsidiary's stock at the time the subsidiary was formed. The interest acquired was complete or 100%. The amount paid by the parent was equal to the book value of the subsidiary interest.

A parent-subsidiary relationship often arises through the purchase of stock from stockholders of a going concern. The interest acquired by the

---

[3]*Accounting Research and Terminology Bulletin, No. 51, op. cit.*, par. 3.

parent may be 100% or it may be a lesser percentage. With less than 100% ownership, eliminations against subsidiary capital balances will be less than 100% and the portion of subsidiary capital that is not eliminated will be recognized on the consolidated balance sheet as *minority interest* — the equity in consolidated assets related to stockholders who have retained their shares in the subsidiary. Furthermore, in a purchase of stock from a previous ownership group, the amount paid for the stock may be equal to the book value of the interest acquired, it may be more than the book value of the interest, or it may be less than the book value of the interest. The reasons for any difference between investment cost and the book value of the net assets acquired must be carefully analyzed, so that the difference may be properly expressed on the consolidated balance sheet.

Before a consolidated balance sheet is prepared, the investment cost on the parent's books and the assets, liabilities, and stockholders' equity on the subsidiary's books should be examined to determine whether they are satisfactorily stated. When errors or accounting failures are discovered, they should be corrected.

Acquisition of 100% of Subsidiary Stock at Book Value

To illustrate the procedure that is followed when all the stock of a company is acquired at book value, assume that the capital of Company S consists of 1,000 shares of capital stock, $100 par, or capital stock of $100,000, and retained earnings of $50,000. On December 1, 19X4, the book values of Company S assets represent fair values, and Company P acquires all the stock of Company S at a cost of $150,000. A work sheet for a consolidated balance sheet and the consolidated balance sheet appear as follows:

Company P and Subsidiary Company S
Work Sheet for Consolidated Balance Sheet
December 1, 19X4

	Co. P	Co. S	Eliminations Dr.	Eliminations Cr.	Consolidated Balance Sheet Dr.	Consolidated Balance Sheet Cr.
Debits						
Investment in Co. S Stock.	150,000					
Eliminate Investment				150,000		
Other Assets....................	300,000	250,000			550,000	
	450,000	250,000				
Credits						
Liabilities........................	150,000	100,000				250,000
Capital Stock, Co. P	200,000					200,000
Retained Earnings, Co. P..	100,000					100,000
Capital Stock, Co. S		100,000				
Eliminate 100%............			100,000			
Retained Earnings, Co. S..		50,000				
Eliminate 100%............			50,000			
	450,000	250,000	150,000	150,000	550,000	550,000

Company P and Subsidiary Company S
Consolidated Balance Sheet
December 1, 19X4

Assets...		$550,000
Liabilities		$250,000
Stockholders' equity:		
Capital stock...	$200,000	
Retained earnings	100,000	300,000
Total liabilities and stockholders' equity..		$550,000

On the work sheet, the investment account and the subsidiary capital stock and retained earnings balances are canceled. Remaining balances for the two companies are then combined. The assets and the liabilities of the subsidiary are thus substituted for the investment account.

If the capital of Company S consists of capital stock of $200,000 and a deficit of $50,000 and Company P acquires all the stock at book value of $150,000, the consolidated balance sheet would be exactly the same as in the preceding example, but eliminations on the work sheet would be as follows:

Company P and Subsidiary Company S
Work Sheet for Consolidated Balance Sheet
December 1, 19X4

	Co. P	Co. S	Eliminations		Consolidated Balance Sheet	
			Dr.	Cr.	Dr.	Cr.
Debits						
Investment in Co. S Stock.	150,000					
Eliminate Investment				150,000		
Other Assets...................	300,000	250,000			550,000	
	450,000	250,000				
Credits						
Liabilities........................	150,000	100,000				250,000
Capital Stock, Co. P	200,000					200,000
Retained Earnings, Co. P..	100,000					100,000
Capital Stock, Co. S		200,000				
Eliminate 100%............			200,000			
Deficit, Co. S...................		(50,000)				
Eliminate 100%............				50,000		
	450,000	250,000	200,000	200,000	550,000	550,000

Acquisition of Less Than 100% of Stock at Book Value

When the stock of a subsidiary is only partly owned and a consolidated balance sheet is to be prepared, the assumption of a single entity would still require that all assets and liabilities of the related companies be combined. However, if all assets and liabilities of the subsidiary company are to be reflected on the consolidated statement, a minority interest in the net assets so combined must be recognized.

To illustrate the procedure that is followed, assume in the previous example that Company P had acquired only 90% of the stock of Company S, paying an amount equal to the book value of the interest, or $135,000. In recognizing subsidiary net assets of $150,000 on the consolidated balance sheet, it is also necessary to recognize an accompanying minority interest of $15,000 in such assets. A work sheet for a consolidated balance sheet and the consolidated balance sheet would be prepared as follows:

Company P and Subsidiary Company S
Work Sheet for Consolidated Balance Sheet
December 1, 19X4

	Co. P	Co. S	Eliminations		Consolidated Balance Sheet	
			Dr.	Cr.	Dr.	Cr.
Debits						
Investment in Co. S Stock.	135,000					
Eliminate Investment				135,000		
Other Assets..................	315,000	250,000			565,000	
	450,000	250,000				
Credits						
Liabilities........................	150,000	100,000				250,000
Capital Stock, Co. P	200,000					200,000
Retained Earnings, Co. P ..	100,000					100,000
Capital Stock, Co. S ....,.		100,000				
Eliminate 90%..............			90,000			
Minority Interest, 10%...						10,000
Retained Earnings, Co. S ..		50,000				
Eliminate 90%..............			45,000			
Minority Interest, 10%...						5,000
	450,000	250,000	135,000	135,000	565,000	565,000

Company P and Subsidiary Company S
Consolidated Balance Sheet
December 1, 19X4

Assets...				$565,000
Liabilities				$250,000
Stockholders' equity:				
Minority interest:				
Capital stock	$ 10,000			
Retained earnings..	5,000	$ 15,000		
Controlling interest:				
Capital stock	$200,000			
Retained earnings..	100,000	300,000		315,000
Total liabilities and stockholders' equity...				$565,000

As an alternative procedure to the work sheet elimination of the interest acquired in the subsidiary, it would be possible to cancel the entire investment balance and the entire subsidiary company capital balances and list separately the minority interest in the credits section of the work sheet.

Referring to the illustration on page 283, for example, a single elimination can be applied on the work sheet as follows:

Capital Stock, Co. S	100,000	
Retained Earnings, Co. S	50,000	
Investment in Co. S Stock..		135,000
Minority Interest...		15,000

If the capital of Company S is $150,000, composed of capital stock of $200,000 and a deficit of $50,000, and Company P acquires a 90% interest for $135,000, a work sheet for a consolidated balance sheet would be prepared as follows:

Company P and Subsidiary Company S
Work Sheet for Consolidated Balance Sheet
December 1, 19X4

	Co. P	Co. S	Eliminations		Consolidated Balance Sheet	
			Dr.	Cr.	Dr.	Cr.
Debits						
Investment in Co. S Stock..	135,000					
Eliminate Investment				135,000		
Other Assets....................	315,000	250,000			565,000	
	450,000	250,000				
Credits						
Liabilities.........................	150,000	100,000				250,000
Capital Stock, Co. P	200,000					200,000
Retained Earnings, Co. P..	100,000					100,000
Capital Stock, Co. S		200,000				
Eliminate 90%..............			180,000			
Minority Interest, 10%...						20,000
Deficit, Co. S		(50,000)				
Eliminate 90%..............				45,000		
Minority Interest, 10%...					5,000	
	450,000	250,000	180,000	180,000	570,000	570,000

A pro rata share of each of the capital balances is recognized in stating the minority interest. When a subsidiary has a deficit, a pro rata share of such deficit, then, is recognized as a subtraction item in arriving at the minority interest. The consolidated balance sheet for Company P and Company S in this example would be the same as that appearing on page 283 except for the detail composing minority interest. Minority interest would consist of a capital stock interest of $20,000 less a share in the deficit of $5,000.

The minority interest does not appear on the books or on the separate financial statements of any of the affiliated companies. In practice, the minority interest is reported on the consolidated balance sheet in a number of different ways. It is sometimes reported as a liability. Occasionally it is included as a part of the stockholders' equity. However, in most instances minority interest is reported under a separate heading between liabilities and the parent company stockholders' equity. The authors are of the opinion that there is no theoretical support for viewing the interest of minority stockholders as a liability. Minority interest is not a claim to be liquidated. Quite the contrary, it points to a special stockholder's interest in the assets reported on the consolidated balance sheet. In presenting the combined resources for a number of related companies, it would appear that the stockholders' equity is best reported in two parts — one part summarizing the interest of the minority group and a second part summarizing the interest of the controlling group.[4]

Minority balances in invested capital and in retained earnings may be combined for reporting purposes, or these balances may be separately listed, paralleling the presentation of the interest of the controlling group. A minority interest in senior equity securities such as preferred stock should be displayed separately. When a consolidated balance sheet includes minority interests in a number of subsidiaries, such interests are normally reported in total and the detail is provided on a supporting schedule.

Acquisition of Subsidiary Interest at More Than Book Value

The cost of a parent's interest in a subsidiary may exceed the book value of such an interest. The reason for the difference between the amount paid and the book value of the interest acquired should be determined before the consolidated balance sheet is prepared. This explanation will determine how the excess is to be reported. The explanation may be any of the following:

(1) *Failure of subsidiary accounts to report asset value increases at time of stock acquisition.* Subsidiary asset balances may properly report past costs and satisfactory depreciation and amortization practices, but such balances may fail to reflect increases in the values of individual assets. If a company's assets were acquired through a merger regarded as a purchase, asset balances would be restated in terms of the price that was paid for the assets. Since a consolidated balance sheet reports the financial position of the firms *as if* a merger had taken place, a formal appraisal of subsidiary assets and a recognition of increases would be in order. Unlike the condition of merger, however, the subsidiary company books continue to report the account balances of a separate legal entity. An appraisal involving an increase in net assets would be reflected only on the work sheet. Such adjustments would also be required on consolidated work sheets prepared in subsequent periods.

(2) *Failure of subsidiary accounts to reflect certain intangible assets.* Subsidiary net assets may report tangible assets satisfactorily, but they may fail to reflect the existence of intangible assets that were considered by the parent in its acquisition of subsidiary holdings. Again,

---

[4]The view that the minority interest expresses a part of an enlarged stockholders' equity rather than an accountability to an outside group is frequently associated with the "entity theory of consolidations." For a full statement of the entity theory of consolidations and the support advanced for this approach, see *The Entity Theory of Consolidated Statements* by Maurice Moonitz (Foundation Press, 1951).

if the company's assets were to be acquired through merger, intangibles recognized in the purchase price would be given accounting recognition. With the acquisition of stock of a subsidiary at a price that recognizes unrecorded intangibles, such intangibles may be included by means of adjustments on the consolidated work sheet. When intangible assets are subject to amortization, adjustments to reflect such amortization will be required on work sheets prepared in subsequent periods.

(3) *Payment for achieving centralized control.* The parent's payment of an amount that exceeds the book value of the interest acquired may be viewed as the price paid to achieve the desired centralized control and the economic advantages accompanying integrated operations. Accordingly, the amount by which the investment cost exceeds the book value of the subsidiary interest may be regarded as the amount paid for goodwill. This amount will be reflected on the consolidated work sheet when the parent company's investment account and the related capital account balances of the subsidiary are eliminated, since the credit to the investment account exceeds the debits to the subsidiary capital accounts.

(4) *Excess representing a combination of factors.* In certain instances an investment excess over subsidiary book value may represent a combination of factors. For example, an excess may represent a price paid to secure control, but it may also include in part a recognition of subsidiary assets that are undervalued. Under these conditions, the identifiable assets should be adjusted to reflect current values, with any excess treated as goodwill.

When subsidiary accounts do not reflect current values of assets, a full restatement of net assets is required regardless of the degree of parent ownership in the subsidiary. When assets are undervalued, they should be brought up to their full fair values at the time of acquisition. When certain intangibles are not reported, they should be established at their full amounts. Assume in the last instance, for example, that a company acquires 80% of the stock of a subsidiary at a price that is $100,000 in excess of the book value of this interest. Such excess payment, it is assumed, fairly recognizes the value of patents owned by the subsidiary which have not been recorded in the accounts. Under these circumstances, the subsidiary patents should be recognized at $125,000 ($100,000 ÷ .80). Thus the full amount of the intangible as indicated by the price paid for the subsidiary interest will be reported on the consolidated balance sheet, together with a minority interest calculated in terms of subsidiary assets as restated.

In keeping with the premise of consolidation as a pro forma merger, any goodwill balances included in the subsidiary accounts should be eliminated. Assuming treatment as a purchase, all asset items would be revalued as of the date of acquisition, and goodwill on a consolidated balance sheet would reflect only the excess paid by the parent in acquiring its proportionate share of the current values of specifically identifiable assets of the subsidiary. None of this excess is attributable to the minority interest. Although it may be argued that a proportionate interest in goodwill may be inferred from the parent's cost and assigned to the minority stockholders, this concept is not used in practice.

Goodwill results from the application of the cost basis of recording assets. It is reasonable to assume that assets which can be evaluated at the date of acquisition would have been purchased at their current values if purchased separately. Because the purchase of an entire company represents the acquisition of a bundle of assets, the cost of identifiable items is explained, and any "unexplained" cost is recorded as goodwill. Thus, the sum of all items acquired, including goodwill, is the total cost of the acquisition.

When the difference between cost and book value is expressed as goodwill, the difference represents the cost of benefits of limited duration and should be amortized over the benefit period, not to exceed 40 years. The amortization of goodwill reduces the investment account and retained earnings, and may be accomplished by periodic entries on the books of the parent company or by adjustments limited to the successive consolidated work sheets. If the parent company uses the equity method in accounting for the subsidiary, the amortization of goodwill should be recognized on its books.

It will be assumed in each of the following illustrations and problems that, in the absence of qualifications to the contrary, an investment cost that exceeds the book value of a subsidiary interest may be designated on the consolidated balance sheet as "Goodwill." Unless indicated otherwise, it will also be assumed that this balance will be amortized over a period of 40 years.

Work sheet when subsidiary interest is acquired at more than book value. To illustrate the eliminations that are required when stock is acquired at more than its book value, assume that Company S has outstanding 1,000 shares of capital stock, $100 par, or capital stock of $100,000, and retained earnings of $50,000. Company P acquires 90% of the stock for $175,000. A work sheet for a consolidated balance sheet and the consolidated balance sheet are shown on page 288.

Elimination of reciprocal elements on the work sheet leaves an investment balance of $40,000 that is carried to the consolidated balance sheet columns as goodwill. This balance does not appear on the books or on the separate financial statements of any of the affiliated companies but only on the consolidated work sheet and the consolidated balance sheet. The investment account with a balance of $175,000 has been replaced for purposes of the consolidated balance sheet by the following items:

Debits		Credits		Net Debit Excess
Assets................	$250,000	Liabilities............	$100,000	
Goodwill	40,000	Minority Interest..	15,000	
	$290,000		$115,000	$175,000

Company P and Subsidiary Company S
Work Sheet for Consolidated Balance Sheet
December 1, 19X4

	Co. P	Co. S	Eliminations		Consolidated Balance Sheet	
			Dr.	Cr.	Dr.	Cr.
Debits						
Investment in Co. S Stock.	175,000					
Eliminate Investment				175,000		
Goodwill.........................			40,000		40,000	
Other Assets...................	275,000	250,000			525,000	
	450,000	250,000				
Credits						
Liabilities.........................	150,000	100,000				250,000
Capital Stock, Co. P	200,000					200,000
Retained Earnings, Co. P..	100,000					100,000
Capital Stock, Co. S		100,000				
Eliminate 90%..............			90,000			
Minority Interest, 10%...						10,000
Retained Earnings, Co. S ..		50,000				
Eliminate 90%..............			45,000			
Minority Interest, 10%...						5,000
	450,000	250,000	175,000	175,000	565,000	565,000

Company P and Subsidiary Company S
Consolidated Balance Sheet
December 1, 19X4

Assets...			$525,000
Goodwill			40,000
Total assets			$565,000
Liabilities			$250,000
Stockholders' equity:			
Minority interest:			
Capital stock	$ 10,000		
Retained earnings...	5,000	$ 15,000	
Controlling interest:			
Capital stock	$200,000		
Retained earnings...	100,000	300,000	315,000
Total liabilities and stockholders' equity.................................			$565,000

If the subsidiary capital of $150,000 had consisted of capital stock of $200,000 and a deficit of $50,000 and the parent had acquired 90% of the stock for $175,000, the consolidated balance sheet would be exactly the same except for the detail composing minority interest.

If the assets of Company S had been appraised at $270,000 on the date Company P acquired its shares, the specific asset values would be increased by $20,000, the appraisal increment, and the minority interest would be increased by 10% of this amount, or $2,000. Because of the appraisal increment, the total capital of Company S at the date of acquisition is now

$170,000. The amount of goodwill is the excess of the investment by Company P ($175,000) over 90% of the total capital ($153,000), or $22,000. This situation is illustrated in the following work sheet.

Company P and Subsidiary Company S
Work Sheet for Consolidated Balance Sheet
December 1, 19X4

	Co. P	Co. S	Eliminations		Consolidated Balance Sheet	
			Dr.	Cr.	Dr.	Cr.
Debits						
Investment in Co. S Stock.	175,000			(b) 175,000		
Eliminate Investment						
Goodwill......................			(b) 22,000		22,000	
Other Assets..................	275,000	250,000				
Appraisal Increase			(a) 20,000		545,000	
	450,000	250,000				
Credits						
Liabilities......................	150,000	100,000				250,000
Capital Stock, Co. P	200,000					200,000
Retained Earnings, Co. P..	100,000					100,000
Capital Stock, Co. S		100,000				
Eliminate 90%..............			(b) 90,000			
Minority Interest, 10%...						10,000
Retained Earnings, Co. S ..		50,000				
Eliminate 90%..............			(b) 45,000			
Minority Interest, 10%...						5,000
Adjustment of Asset Value, Co. S..................				(a) 20,000		
Eliminate 90%..............			(b) 18,000			
Minority Interest, 10%...						2,000
	450,000	250,000	195,000	195,000	567,000	567,000

Alternative treatments of excess investment. In the previous example, the asset accounts of the subsidiary were increased to their full value on the date of acquisition, and the excess of the parent's cost over its share of the adjusted equity was treated as goodwill. Two alternative methods of treating the excess have been suggested.

A procedure often used in practice is to recognize only the proportion of the asset valuation increase attributable to the parent's share. With this procedure, no adjustment is made to the minority interest, and the excess of the amount paid over the book value acquired minus the recognized asset increment is regarded as goodwill. In the previous example, the assets would have been increased by only 90% of $20,000, or $18,000. The total assets would have been stated on the consolidated balance sheet at $543,000. Goodwill would still have been recognized at $22,000, but the minority interest would have been $15,000.

The rationale for this treatment is that only the parent's share of the value increase represents a cost incurred in the purchase transaction. The minority interest presumably paid a lower amount to acquire their proportionate share of the subsidiary, and this amount should not be written up to the current market value. Although this approach is widely used in practice, it seems to miss the essential attribute of a consolidation as a pro forma merger.

The rules for reporting a business combination as a purchase do require the statement of assets at the cost to the acquiring company, but it is the aggregate cost of the entire acquisition that is involved. This cost must be allocated to specific assets in accordance with Accounting Principles Board Opinion No. 16 on the following basis:

> First, all identifiable assets acquired, either individually or by type, and liabilities assumed in a business combination, whether or not shown in the financial statements of the acquired company, should be assigned a portion of the cost of the acquired company, *normally equal to their fair values at date of acquisition*.
>
> Second, the excess of the cost of the acquired company over the sum of the amounts assigned to identifiable assets acquired less liabilities assumed should be recorded as goodwill.[5]

This Opinion suggests that the assets acquired should be stated at their full current value at the time of acquisition. The minority interest, which represents a claim against the assets of the combined enterprise, may be regarded as a senior equity security of the consolidated entity and should be stated at its current value. This value can best be estimated by the proportionate interest of the subsidiary company as revalued.

Another approach, which would not be considered a generally accepted practice at this time, is based on the so called "entity concept." The entity theory suggests that the amount paid by the parent company for its proportionate interest is evidence of the value of the entire subsidiary, including the minority interest. Applying this theory to the previous example, the payment of $175,000 for a 90% interest in Company S implies that the value of the entire stockholders' equity of the company is $175,000 ÷ .90, or $194,444. The minority interest would be 10% of this amount, or $19,444. Even with the restatement of assets at their current values, the minority interest was only $17,000. Thus, the additional $2,444 is regarded as an element of goodwill.

Although the entity concept has some theoretical merit, it is a departure from the cost basis and would not be allowed in current practice. Goodwill is currently limited to the excess of the amount actually paid over the values of identifiable assets. On the other hand, since there seems to be more willingness on the part of accountants to report current values of specific assets, the concept of reporting goodwill at its current value may ultimately gain acceptance.

Acquisition of Subsidiary Interest at Less Than Book Value

When stock of a subsidiary is acquired at less than its book value, the treatment of the difference on the consolidated balance sheet will be deter-

---

[5]*Opinions of the Accounting Principles Board, No. 16,* "Business Combinations" (New York: American Institute of Certified Public Accountants, 1970), par. 87. (emphasis added)

mined by the following reasons for the difference between cost and book value.

(1) *Failure of subsidiary accounts to reflect asset value declines at time of stock acquisition.* Subsidiary asset balances may properly report past costs and satisfactory depreciation and amortization practices, but such balances may fail to reflect declines in the values of individual assets. If a merger of the companies had occurred, asset balances would have been restated in terms of costs as established by the purchase price. Thus, formal appraisal of subsidiary assets and a recognition of the declines on the subsidiary company's books would be in order. Asset and capital balances of the subsidiary would be reduced and the parent's interest brought into agreement with the investment account balance. When there are practical difficulties in restating account balances on the books of the subsidiary, the parent may prefer to recognize such adjustments only on the consolidated work sheet. Such adjustments would also be required on consolidated work sheets prepared in subsequent periods. When the interest acquired by a parent is less than 100%, the difference between the investment cost and the related subsidiary book value measures only the asset overstatement related to the parent's interest. In this case, it would be appropriate to reduce the minority interest on a proportionate basis.

(2) *Reduction of goodwill.* When the stock of a subsidiary is acquired at less than its book value and the subsidiary shows goodwill on its books, this goodwill may be overvalued. In any event, the goodwill previously recorded by the acquired company should not be carried forward to the consolidated statement. According to the concept of purchase accounting, only the costs incurred by the parent over and above its proportionate share of the identifiable assets (less liabilities) should be recognized as goodwill.

When the goodwill balance of the subsidiary is eliminated, the minority interest would be reduced on a proportionate basis. If the cost of the investment is greater than the parent's equity in the net assets after the subsidiary goodwill is eliminated, this excess may appear as goodwill on the consolidated balance sheet. This item stems from the *parent's* investment, however, and is not related to the goodwill previously recorded by the subsidiary.

Some accountants have argued for treating the excess of the book value of the subsidiary over the parent's investment cost as a "negative goodwill" factor to reduce any goodwill previously recorded by the parent. This procedure is not sound, however. Each acquisition should be treated separately — the amount paid to acquire one subsidiary has no connection with the amount paid to acquire another.

(3) *Capital from consolidation.* Stock may be purchased at less than book value when subsidiary assets are satisfactorily valued and earnings are considered satisfactory, but there is evidence to indicate that a "bargain purchase" was made. Under these circumstances, a difference between the book value and cost of subsidiary holdings may be regarded as capital from consolidation and viewed as an element of stockholders' equity. Although this treatment was widely used many years ago, it is a departure from the cost basis of recording assets and is not currently an acceptable practice. The procedure is expressly forbidden by APB Opinion No. 16, which states: "No part of the excess of acquired net assets over cost should be added directly to stockholders' equity at the date of acquisition." [6]

(4) *Difference representing a combination of factors.* In many instances, a difference between the amount paid for stock and its book value is explained by a combination of factors. For example, a purchase price may be viewed as involving a recognition of assets that are overvalued, counterbalanced in part by the cost of securing control of such properties. In each instance, however, the principles are the same. The purchase of a subsidiary gives rise to a new basis of accountability from the viewpoint of consolidated statements. Assets other than goodwill should be stated at their fair values at the time of acquisition, and goodwill previously recorded by the subsidiary should not be recognized.

If eliminating goodwill and reducing identifiable assets to their current values does not explain the entire difference between book value and investment cost, then the remaining difference should be treated in accordance with APB Opinion No. 16, as follows:

> An excess over cost should be allocated to reduce proportionately the values assigned to noncurrent assets (except long-term investments in marketable securities) in determining their fair values. If the allocation reduces the noncurrent assets to zero value, the remainder of the excess over cost should be classified as a deferred credit and should be amortized systematically to income over the period estimated to be benefited but not in excess of forty years.[7]

The treatment as a deferred credit does not seem to have theoretical support, but it does result in an objective disposition of the remaining balance. The need for this procedure is not likely to arise, since it would only be applicable after all the noncurrent assets (other than securities) have been completely written off.

It will be assumed in each of the following illustrations and problems that, in the absence of qualifications to the contrary, an investment cost that is less than the parent's proportionate share of the subsidiary's book value may be identified with specific assets of the subsidiary. Although the asset reduction would normally be recognized only on the consolidation work sheet, it would reduce the minority interest on a proportionate basis as though the lowered values had been recorded on the subsidiary's books.

To illustrate the eliminations that are required when stock is acquired at an amount that is less than book value, assume that Company S has outstanding 1,000 shares of stock, $100 par, or capital stock of $100,000, and

_____

[6]*Ibid.*, par. 2.
[7]*Ibid.*, par. 91.

retained earnings of $50,000. Company P acquires 90% of the stock for $126,000. A work sheet and the consolidated balance sheet are prepared as follows:

Company P and Subsidiary Company S
Work Sheet for Consolidated Balance Sheet
December 1, 19X4

	Co. P	Co. S	Eliminations		Consolidated Balance Sheet	
			Dr.	Cr.	Dr.	Cr.
Debits						
Investment in Co. S Stock.	126,000					
Eliminate Investment				(b) 126,000		
Other Assets.....................	324,000	250,000				
Reduce to Current Value				(a) 10,000	564,000	
	450,000	250,000				
Credits						
Liabilities.........................	150,000	100,000				250,000
Capital Stock, Co. P	200,000					200,000
Retained Earnings, Co. P..	100,000					100,000
Capital Stock, Co. S		100,000				
Eliminate 90%..............			(b) 90,000			
Minority Interest, 10%...						10,000
Retained Earnings, Co. S..		50,000				
Adjust for Asset Valuation.........................			(a) 10,000			
Eliminate 90% of Net Balance			(b) 36,000			
Minority Interest, 10% of Net Balance...........						4,000
	450,000	250,000	136,000	136,000	564,000	564,000

Company P and Subsidiary Company S
Consolidated Balance Sheet
December 1, 19X4

Assets..			$564,000
Liabilities			$250,000
Stockholders' equity:			
Minority interest:			
Capital stock	$ 10,000		
Retained earnings...	4,000	$ 14,000	
Controlling interest:			
Capital stock	$200,000		
Retained earnings...	100,000	300,000	314,000
Total liabilities and stockholders' equity..................................			$564,000

A cost of $126,000 for 90% of the stock of Company S implies a total value of $140,000 for the net assets. Since the book value of the net assets of Company S is $150,000, the assets appear to be overstated by $10,000. A reduction is recognized on the work sheet by an entry that reduces the other assets account and the retained earnings balance of Company S by

$10,000. The adjusted retained earnings balance is eliminated against the investment account. Crediting the other assets for $10,000 results in a net balance of $564,000 that is carried to the consolidated balance sheet columns. This balance does not appear on the books or on the separate financial statements of any of the affiliated companies but only on the consolidated work sheet and on the consolidated balance sheet. The investment account, with a balance of $126,000, has been replaced for purposes of the consolidated balance sheet by the following items:

Debits		Credits		Net Debit Excess
Assets...............	$240,000	Liabilities............	$100,000	
		Minority Interest..	14,000	
	$240,000		$114,000	$126,000

If capital of the subsidiary had consisted of capital stock of $200,000 and a deficit of $50,000 and the parent had acquired this stock for $126,000, the consolidated balance sheet would be exactly the same except for the detail composing minority interest.

Purchase of Stock Directly from Subsidiary

Instead of acquiring stock by purchase on the open market, a parent may acquire part or all of its holdings directly from the company to be controlled. The interest that is acquired may consist of treasury stock or newly issued stock. In either case, the capital of the subsidiary is increased by the amount paid for the stock, and subsequent eliminations in the preparation of the consolidated balance sheet are based on the capital of the subsidiary after the sale of the stock.

To illustrate, assume that the capital of Company S is as follows:

Capital stock (10,000 shares, no par)...	$150,000
Retained earnings	40,000
	$190,000
Less treasury stock, 2,500 shares at cost......................................	30,000
Total	$160,000

Company P acquires the 2,500 shares of treasury stock from Company S at $20 per share and also 5,000 shares on the open market at the same price. The entries on the books of Companies P and S are:

On Company P's books:
Investment in Co. S Stock...	150,000	
Cash..		150,000

On Company S's books:
Cash..	50,000	
Treasury Stock		30,000
Paid-In Capital from Sale of Treasury Stock in Excess of Cost		20,000

Work sheet eliminations on the date of the stock acquisition will be made as follows:

	Co. P	Co. S	Eliminations		Consolidated Balance Sheet	
			Dr.	Cr.	Dr.	Cr.
Debits						
Investment in Co. S Stock.	150,000					
Eliminate Investment				150,000		
Credits						
Capital Stock, Co. S		150,000				
Eliminate 75%..............			112,500			
Minority Interest, 25%...						37,500
Additional Paid-In Capital,						
Co. S		20,000				
Eliminate 75%..............			15,000			
Minority Interest, 25%...						5,000
Retained Earnings, Co. S ..		40,000				
Eliminate 75%..............			30,000			
Minority Interest, 25%...						10,000

SUBSIDIARY ACQUISITION VIEWED AS POOLING OF INTERESTS

It was assumed in the previous pages that the acquisition of stock in a subsidiary involved the elimination of an important part of the original ownership. Under these circumstances, the "purchase" concept as previously described in Chapter 9 was applied in the development of consolidated balance sheets. Modification of subsidiary company book values in terms of the parent company acquisition costs was considered appropriate, and no recognition was made of past accumulated earnings of the company acquired.

In certain instances a parent-subsidiary relationship may occur with no substantial change in the original ownership, and all of the criteria may be met to qualify as a "pooling of interests." Under these conditions, it has been held that, as in the case of a merger or consolidation deemed a pooling of interests, the need for a new accountability does not arise: assets and liabilities of the constituent units when stated in conformity with generally accepted accounting principles and properly adjusted so that they are on a uniform basis may be combined without adjustment for purposes of the consolidated statement. Retained earnings and deficit balances may be similarly combined for consolidated reporting.

The Accounting Principles Board, in Opinion No. 16, makes it clear that the pooling-of-interests method applies to consolidated statements as well as to actual mergers:

> Dissolution of a combining company is not a condition for applying the pooling of interests method of accounting for a business combination. One or more combining companies may be subsidiaries of the issuing

corporation after the combination is consummated if the other conditions are met.[8]

To illustrate the application of the pooling-of-interests concept in the preparation of consolidated statements, assume the following balance sheet data for Company A and Company B on June 30, 19X1:

	Co. A	Co. B
Assets	$1,000,000	$400,000
Liabilities	$ 300,000	$100,000
Capital stock	500,000	250,000
Retained earnings	200,000	50,000
Total liabilities and stockholders' equity	$1,000,000	$400,000

On this date Company A acquires 90% of the stock of Company B, issuing in exchange to the stockholders of Company B its own capital stock with a par value of $240,000 and a market value of $300,000. All of the criteria for a pooling of interests are met.

The investment in Company B would be recorded on the books of Company A at the book value of the net assets acquired, as reflected on the books of Company B. The market value of Company A shares, which would be used to record the investment if a purchase were involved, is ignored in the pooling-of-interests situation. Consistent with the pooling-of-interests assumption, the parent company credits its own retained earnings account with the related share of the subsidiary's retained earnings at the time of acquisition, to the extent that total capital balances exceed the par value of shares issued. Thus, the acquisition of 90% of the stock of Company B in exchange for its own stock would be recorded by Company A as follows:

Investment in Co. B	270,000	
Capital Stock		240,000
Retained Earnings		30,000

Some accountants might argue that, on the separate parent company records, the transaction is an investment rather than a combination. Investments are normally recorded at their cost (as determined by the market value of shares exchanged), and it is usually considered inappropriate to recognize retained earnings stemming from operations of a subsidiary prior to the date of acquisition. This argument overlooks the basic premise of pooling-of-interests accounting, however. If all of the criteria for a pooling of interests are met, then the maintenance of an investment account and the existence of the separate parent and subsidiary legal entities is viewed as a matter of form rather than substance. If the companies have in reality combined, and pooling-of-interests treatment is warranted, then the formal legal structure of parent and subsidiary corporations should be ignored.

In these circumstances, consolidated statements would be most appropriate for reporting purposes. Internal records can be maintained by the

---

[8]*Ibid.*, par. 49.

parent to distinguish its own transactions from those of the subsidiary if needed for tax or other purposes. In any case, because consolidated statements are prepared on a basis that reflects what would happen if the related companies were legally merged, it is appropriate to treat the hypothetical combination as a pooling of interests if it meets all of the criteria. A work sheet for a consolidated balance sheet may be prepared as follows:

Company A and Subsidiary Company B
Work Sheet for Consolidated Balance Sheet
June 30, 19X1

	Co. A	Co. B	Eliminations		Consolidated Balance Sheet	
			Dr.	Cr.	Dr.	Cr.
Debits						
Investment in Co. B Stock.	270,000			270,000		
Eliminate Investment						
Other Assets....................	1,000,000	400,000			1,400,000	
	1,270,000	400,000				
Credits						
Liabilities........................	300,000	100,000				400,000
Capital Stock, Co. A	740,000					740,000
Retained Earnings, Co. A ..	230,000					230,000
Capital Stock, Co. B		250,000				
Eliminate 90%..............			225,000			
Minority Interest, 10%...						25,000
Retained Earnings, Co. B..		50,000				
Eliminate 90%..............			45,000			
Minority Interest, 10%...						5,000
	1,270,000	400,000	270,000	270,000	1,400,000	1,400,000

Asset and liability balances are combined on the work sheet. The determination of capital balances calls for special analysis. Because the parent company has already recognized on its own books the increase in the common stock and retained earnings balances attributable to Company B, no adjustment is required for these items. Thus the parent company's share of the subsidiary capital balances are eliminated along with the investment account.

Although there has been, in effect, a capitalization of a portion of Company B's retained earnings to provide the proper balance of par value of Company A stock, the minority interest is not affected by this procedure. Their interest is found directly by taking 10% of Company B's capital accounts.

Minority interest would normally not be a substantial factor in a pooling-of-interests situation. To qualify as a pooling, there must be in essence a complete combination of the two entities. The criteria do permit minority shareholders to own as much as 10% of the subsidiary company, but this is viewed as a practical expediency to permit pooling treatment when there are a small number of "holdout" shareholders who refuse to go along with an exchange offer. Pooling would not be permitted, for example, if the parent company offered to acquire only 90% of the stock of the subsidiary.

If the shares exchanged have a par value less than the paid-in capital balances of the subsidiary, then the entire proportionate share of the retained earnings of the subsidiary would be recognized. Assume, for example, that the par value of stock given by Company A in the previous example was less than $225,000. Under these circumstances, invested capital balances would be raised to $225,000 by recognition of additional paid-in capital, and the full amount of subsidiary retained earnings identified with the controlling interest would be recognized by the parent.

The issue of parent company stock with a par value of $100,000 in exchange for the subsidiary interest would call for the following entry by Company A at the time of the exchange:

Investment in Co. B..	270,000	
Capital Stock...		100,000
Additional Paid-In Capital		125,000
Retained Earnings		45,000

The elimination entry on the consolidation work sheet would not be affected. The investment account would still be offset against the proportionate book value balances of the subsidiary. The retained earnings balance on the consolidated balance sheet would reflect the amount recorded on the parent's books.

It will be assumed in the discussions as well as in exercises and problems in this text that a consolidation is to be regarded as arising from a purchase unless it is specifically designated as a pooling of interests.

QUESTIONS

1. What advantages are found in the unified operation of related units through stock control instead of through merger?

2. On November 15 the Murdock Company acquired 8,000 shares of the stock of the Norris Corporation at a price of $20 per share. On November 1, the Norris Corporation had declared a dividend of 50 cents per share payable on December 1 to stockholders of record November 20. How should the Murdock Company record the investment and the subsequent receipt of the dividend? Give reasons for your answer.

3. (a) What is the nature and the purpose of the consolidated balance sheet? (b) What part of the stock of a corporation should be held to justify the preparation of such a statement?

4. The Carlson Co., a company with a controlling interest in a number of subsidiaries, makes available to its stockholders only consolidated statements, since it feels that these are superior to its own separate statements. Do you have any criticism of this policy?

5. What factors must be present to justify the preparation of a consolidated balance sheet?

6. State whether a consolidated balance sheet should be prepared under each of the following circumstances:

   (a) Company A, operating a chain of retail stores, owns 100% of the stock of a subsidiary that has been established to assist stores in financing sales to customers.
   (b) Company B, operating a chain of theaters, owns 100% of the stock of a savings and loan association.
   (c) Company C owns 90% of the stock of a subsidiary company that owns 90% of the stock of a third company; all companies are engaged in the manufacture and sale of electronic components.
   (d) Company D, a manufacturing company, owns 90% of the stock of a subsidiary that engages in research and development related to operations of its parent; the subsidiary has reported losses ever since its organization.
   (e) Company E, a construction company, owns 50% of the stock of a company that engages in exploration for oil and gas; operations of the latter company have been profitable ever since its organization.

7. The Morton Co. recognizes minority interest as a liability on the consolidated balance sheet. Would you consider this practice acceptable? Give reasons.

8. (a) In preparing a consolidated balance sheet, what possibilities can you suggest for reporting the portion of the cost of an investment that exceeds the book value acquired? Indicate the circumstances under which each of the methods suggested would be appropriate.

   (b) What possibilities can you suggest for reporting an excess of book value over cost of an investment? Indicate the circumstances under which each of the methods suggested would be appropriate.

9. Distinguish the accounting concept of goodwill from the economic concept of goodwill.

10. Under what circumstances would you suggest the amortization of goodwill? What procedure would you follow in amortizing such a balance?

11. What objection can be raised to the recognition of an excess of book value over investment cost as "capital from consolidation"?

12. Under what circumstances would an excess of subsidiary book value over investment cost result in a deferred credit on a consolidated balance sheet?

13. In preparing a work sheet for a consolidated balance sheet for Company P, what eliminations are made and what balances are extended to the consolidated balance sheet column under each of the following assumptions:

   (a) Company P acquires all of the stock of Company S, paying more than book value; Company S has a deficit.
   (b) Company P acquires all of the stock of Company S, paying less than book value; Company S books report additional paid-in capital and retained earnings balances.   *(continued)*

(c) Company P acquires 80% of the stock of Company S, paying book value; Company S has a retained earnings balance.

(d) Company P acquires 80% of the stock of Company S, paying less than book value; Company S books report additional paid-in capital and deficit balances.

14. (a) A company establishes a subsidiary and acquires all of the stock of the latter company at a price in excess of the par value of the stock. How will the premium on the subsidiary's books be reported on the consolidated balance sheet? (b) Assume that a company acquires an 80% interest in a subsidiary by the purchase of two blocks of stock at amounts in excess of par value, one block of 60% from original stockholders of the company and one block of 20% directly from the corporation. How will the premium on the subsidiary's books be reported on the consolidated balance sheet?

15. (a) What circumstances would suggest that consolidation be viewed as a pooling of interests? (b) What differences are found in the preparation of a consolidated balance sheet under circumstances indicating a pooling of interests as compared with a purchase?

EXERCISES

1. For each set of the following conditions, prepare the elimination that would be made on the work sheet for a consolidated balance sheet for the Marsh Company and its subsidiary, the Nater Company. Show the elimination in a form that cancels fully the investment and the subsidiary company capital balances.

Investment by Parent		Subsidiary Capital Balances		
Amount Paid	Interest Acquired	Capital Stock	Additional Paid-In Capital	Retained Earnings (Deficit)
(a) $160,000	100%	$100,000	$20,000	$25,000
(b) 140,000	100%	100,000	80,000	(30,000)
(c) 120,000	75%	100,000	40,000	(5,000)
(d) 100,000	80%	100,000	25,000	15,000

2. Balance sheet items of Palmer Corporation and the Quinn Company are summarized as follows:

Palmer Corporation

Assets............................ $1,000,000	Liabilities........................		$ 300,000
	Stockholders' equity:		
	Capital stock	$400,000	
	Retained earnings...	300,000	700,000
	Total liabilities and		
Total assets.................... $1,000,000	stockholders' equity		$1,000,000

Quinn Company

Assets	$380,000	Liabilities..........................		$ 60,000
		Stockholders' equity:		
		Capital stock		
		(12,000		
		shares, no		
		par)............	$100,000	
		Retained		
		earnings	220,000	320,000
		Total liabilities and		
Total assets.......................	$380,000	stockholders' equity........		$380,000

Prepare a consolidated balance sheet for Palmer Corporation and its subsidiary, assuming that:

(a) All the stock of the Quinn Company is purchased for $360,000.
(b) All the stock of the Quinn Company is purchased for $310,000.
(c) 9,000 shares of Quinn Company stock are purchased at 30.
(d) 9,000 shares of Quinn Company stock are purchased at 35.

3. The Culligan Company acquires 80% of the stock of Demby, Inc. The investment in the subsidiary is recorded at a cost of $1,000,000. A balance sheet for the subsidiary on the date of acquisition shows the following:

Goodwill..................	$ 150,000	Liabilities...............	$ 350,000
Other assets	850,000	Capital stock	500,000
		Additional paid-in	
		capital	50,000
		Retained earnings ...	100,000
		Total liabilities and	
		stockholders'	
Total assets............	$1,000,000	equity	$1,000,000

Prepare any entries that would be made on the books of the parent and the subsidiary or on the work sheet prior to the preparation of a consolidated balance sheet under each of the conditions stated below:

(a) Culligan Company issues 100,000 shares of its own stock, par $10, for its interest. Culligan Company shares are selling on the market at 8½ on the date of acquisition. Any difference between investment cost and the book value of the subsidiary interest acquired is to be considered as the cost of the special advantages to emerge from integrated operations of the two companies.
(b) Culligan Company pays cash for its interest. Any difference between the investment cost and the book value of the subsidiary interest acquired is to be considered as evidence of the understatement of subsidiary company tangible assets.

4. The Barnett Company on March 1 acquires 8,000 shares of the Clair Company for $165,000 cash. Each company has 10,000 shares outstanding. Account balances of the two companies on this date are as follows:

	Barnett Co.	Clair Co.
Assets	$820,000	$210,000
Liabilities...	$200,000	$ 60,000
Capital stock	400,000	100,000
Additional paid-in capital.....................	100,000	20,000
Retained earnings..............................	120,000	30,000
Total liabilities and stockholders' equity .	$820,000	$210,000

The assets of Clair Company are understated by $45,000.
Prepare a consolidated balance sheet.

5. On June 15, Norton, Inc. purchases 8,000 shares of Burke Company common stock at 12½.

(a) Assuming that the outstanding stock of Burke Company consists of 10,000 shares, $10 par, and its books show a retained earnings balance of $45,000, (1) what eliminations would be made and (2) what balances will appear as minority interest on the consolidated balance sheet?

(b) Assuming that the books of the Burke Company show a deficit of $45,000, (1) what elimination would be made and (2) what balances will appear as minority interest on the consolidated balance sheet?

6. Balance sheets for the Porter Company and the Ross Company on July 1, 19X5, are as follows:

	Porter Co.	Ross Co.
Cash...	$100,000	$ 50,000
Goodwill.......................................	50,000	40,000
Other assets.................................	350,000	60,000
Total assets.................................	$500,000	$150,000
Liabilities....................................	$150,000	$ 35,000
Capital stock, $10 par	300,000	50,000
Retained earnings..........................	50,000	65,000
Total liabilities and stockholders' equity ...	$500,000	$150,000

On this date Porter Company acquires 80% of the stock of Ross Company for $70,000. Prepare a consolidated balance sheet on the assumption that, at the time of the purchase of Ross Company stock, the other assets of Ross Co. were appraised at $62,500.

7. Fields, Inc., acquired control of the Good Company through purchases of stock of the latter company as follows:

5,000 shares on the market, cost.....................................	$635,000
2,500 shares directly from the corporation at 130	325,000
Total investment..	$960,000

Just before purchase of the stock by Fields, Inc., the capital of the Good Company was:

Capital stock, $100 par (10,000 shares authorized, 6,500 shares issued).................	$650,000	
Additional paid-in capital............................	300,000	$950,000
Less deficit		45,000
Total capital..		$905,000

Determine as of the date of purchase (a) the cost or book value excess on the investment, and (b) the minority interest.

8. The Wexler Company seeks a sales outlet in Cincinnati. Articles of incorporation are obtained in Ohio for a company to be known as the Major Sales Company, and authorization is received for the issuance of 10,000 shares of no-par stock. On April 1, 19X8, the Wexler Company acquires all the stock of the Major Sales Company at a price of $250,000. A stated value of $10 per share is assigned to the issue. A balance sheet for the Wexler Company just prior to the formation of the separately incorporated sales office follows:

Cash..............................	$ 420,000	Liabilities........................		$ 250,000
Other assets..................	780,000	Stockholders' equity:		
		Capital stock	$500,000	
		Additional paid-in capital	150,000	
		Retained earnings...	300,000	950,000
		Total liabilities and		
Total assets..................	$1,200,000	stockholders' equity		$1,200,000

(a) Prepare the entries that will appear on the books of the two companies as a result of the formation of the Major Sales Company.
(b) Prepare a separate balance sheet for the parent company and for its subsidiary.
(c) Prepare a consolidated balance sheet.

9. The Carter Company on July 1 acquires 90% of the stock of Dome, Inc., issuing its own stock in exchange for such interest. Balance sheets for the two companies just before the acquisition are as follows:

	Carter Co.	Dome, Inc.
Assets	$1,200,000	$750,000
Liabilities...	$ 500,000	$300,000
Capital stock...	450,000	100,000
Additional paid-in capital......................	100,000	250,000
Retained earnings.................................	150,000	100,000
Total liabilities and stockholders' equity .	$1,200,000	$750,000

Assuming that the combination is viewed as a pooling of interests, prepare the journal entry to record the investment on Carter's books and prepare a consolidated balance sheet under each of the following assumptions:

(a) Carter Company stock with a par value of $300,000 is issued in exchange for shares of Dome, Inc.

(b) Carter Company stock with a par value of $400,000 is issued in exchange for shares of Dome, Inc.

(c) Carter Company stock with a par value of $500,000 is issued in exchange for shares of Dome, Inc.

PROBLEMS

10-1. The balance sheets for Rush Company and Sloan, Inc., on December 1, 19X4, the date that the former acquired stock in Sloan, Inc., from the stockholders of the latter company, are as follows:

	Rush Co.	Sloan, Inc.
Cash	$ 105,000	$ 50,000
Accounts receivable	180,000	110,000
Inventories	250,000	225,000
Investment in Sloan, Inc., stock	320,000	
Land, machinery, and equipment (net)	600,000	260,000
Total assets	$1,455,000	$645,000
Accounts payable	$ 155,000	$ 65,000
Bonds payable		200,000
Capital stock	1,000,000	480,000
Additional paid-in capital	200,000	80,000
Retained earnings (deficit)	100,000	(180,000)
Total liabilities and stockholders' equity	$1,455,000	$645,000

The stock of Sloan, Inc., has a stated value of $30 per share. The Rush Company acquired 12,800 shares at 25.

Instructions: Prepare a consolidated work sheet and a consolidated balance sheet.

10-2. The balance sheets for Company R and Company S as of December 31, 19X6, are as follows:

Company R

Cash	$ 50,000	Current liabilities	$1,750,000
Receivables (net)	300,000	Long-term debt	450,000
Inventories	1,600,000	Common stock,	
Prepayments	47,000	10,000 shares	1,000,000
Plant assets (net)	2,003,000	Retained earnings	800,000
		Total liabilities and stockholders' equity	
Total assets	$4,000,000	equity	$4,000,000

Company S

Cash and invest- ments (including stock of R)..........	$ 7,000,000	Current liabilities .. Long-term debt......	$ 7,872,000 1,615,000
Receivables (net) ..	2,400,000	Common stock, 100,000 shares..	10,000,000
Inventories...........	11,200,000	Retained earnings .	20,513,000
Prepayments	422,000	Total liabilities and	
Plant assets (net)..	18,978,000	stockholders'	
Total assets..........	$40,000,000	equity...............	$40,000,000

An appraisal on December 31, 19X6, which was carefully considered and approved by the boards of directors of Company R and Company S, placed a total replacement value, less accumulated depreciation, of $3,203,000 on the plant assets of Company R.

Company S offered to purchase all the assets of Company R, subject to its liabilities, as of December 31, 19X6, for $3,000,000. However, 40% of the stockholders of Company R objected to the price on the ground that it did not include any consideration for goodwill, which they believe to be worth at least $500,000. A counterproposal was made and final agreement was reached on the basis that Company S acquired 60% of the common stock of Company R at a price of $300 a share.

Instructions: Prepare a consolidated balance sheet for the two companies as of December 31, 19X6.

(AICPA adapted)

10-3. Balance sheets for Companies A, B, and C on December 31, 19X7, are as follows:

	Co. A	Co. B	Co. C
Cash...	$300,000	$ 50,000	$ 25,000
Goodwill....................................	100,000	25,000	25,000
Other assets..............................	350,000	275,000	250,000
Total assets..............................	$750,000	$350,000	$300,000
Liabilities..................................	$150,000	$100,000	$125,000
Capital stock, par $10	300,000	150,000	200,000
Additional paid-in capital............	100,000	50,000	25,000
Retained earnings (deficit)..........	200,000	50,000	(50,000)
Total liabilities and stockholders' equity....................................	$750,000	$350,000	$300,000

On this date, Company A acquired all of the stock of Company B for cash of $275,000 and acquired 80% of the stock of Company C in exchange for 6% notes of $125,000 that are payable by Company A in 5 years.

Instructions: Prepare a consolidated balance sheet as of December 31, 19X7, assuming that differences between investment balances and the book values of subsidiary holdings are regarded as evidence of goodwill if positive, or a reduction of other assets if negative.

10-4. Balance sheets for Companies D and E on December 31, 19X9, are as follows:

	Co. D	Co. E
Cash	$ 850,000	$ 75,000
Other assets.............................	2,200,000	425,000
Total assets	$3,050,000	$500,000
Liabilities.................................	$1,200,000	$100,000
Capital stock...................(par $50)	2,000,000	(par $10) 250,000
Additional paid-in capital..........	500,000	
Retained earnings (deficit)........	(650,000)	150,000
Total liabilities and stockholders' equity...............................	$3,050,000	$500,000

On this date, Company D acquired 80% of the stock of Company E.

Instructions: Prepare a consolidated balance sheet as of December 31, 19X9, under each of the following conditions:

(1) Subsidiary stock is acquired for cash of $350,000. The difference between the investment balance and the book value of the interest acquired is regarded as evidence of the goodwill identified with the subsidiary acquisition.

(2) Subsidiary stock is acquired in exchange for 5,000 shares of the parent company stock, and the investment account is recorded at $300,000, the current market value of the shares that are issued. The difference between the investment balance and the book value of the interest acquired is regarded as evidence of the overstatement of certain assets of Company E, and asset accounts are adjusted to bring the book value of subsidiary shares into agreement with the amount paid for them by the parent.

(3) Subsidiary stock is acquired in exchange for cash of $200,000 and 6% notes of $250,000 payable by Company D in 10 years. Inventories of Company E, reported at lifo, are restated at fifo and increased by $75,000. The difference between the investment balance and the book value of the interest acquired is regarded as the cost of achieving integrated operations.

10-5. The balance sheet data for Companies P and S as of June 1, 19X5, are summarized as follows:

Company P

Assets..	$1,250,000
Liabilities..	$ 650,000
Capital stock	500,000
Retained earnings	100,000
Total liabilities and stockholders' equity	$1,250,000

Company S

Assets	$350,000
Liabilities...	$100,000
Capital stock (20,000 shares, no par)	200,000
Retained earnings..	50,000
Total liabilities and stockholders' equity	$350,000

Instructions: Prepare a consolidated balance sheet for Company P and Company S for each of the following cases (assume that Company P has sufficient cash to make the purchase indicated):

(1) Company P purchases all of the stock of Company S at $14 a share.
(2) Company P purchases all of the stock of Company S at $11 a share.
(3) Company P purchases 19,000 shares of Company S stock at $14 a share.
(4) Company P purchases 19,000 shares of Company S stock at $11 a share.

10-6. The balance sheets of Companies A and B on March 1, 19X6, follow:

	Co. A	Co. B
Cash...	$200,000	$ 20,000
Other assets...	450,000	80,000
Total assets...	$650,000	$100,000
Liabilities...	$150,000	$ 20,000
Capital stock ($10 par)	200,000	50,000
Additional paid-in capital.......................	40,000	10,000
Retained earnings..................................	260,000	20,000
Total liabilities and stockholders' equity ...	$650,000	$100,000

Instructions: Prepare a consolidated balance sheet based on each of the following assumptions:

(1) Company A purchases all of the stock of Company B for cash, $95,000.
(2) Company A purchases 80% of the stock of Company B for cash, $60,000.
(3) Company A acquires all of the stock of Company B by issuing additional shares of its own stock and exchanging these for the outstanding stock of Company B, share for share. The market value of Company A stock at this time is $18.50 per share and this value is used in recording the investment.

10-7. Balance sheets on September 30, 19X0, immediately after Company P acquires stock in Companies X, Y, and Z, are shown on page 308.
Stock was acquired by Company P as follows:

> 22,500 shares of Company X stock at 14.
> 10,000 shares of Company Y common stock at 12½.
>   500 shares of Company Y preferred stock at 105.
> 12,000 shares of Company Z stock at 5½.

	Co. P	Co. X	Co. Y	Co. Z
Investment in Co. X stock............	$ 315,000			
Investment in Co. Y stock............	177,500			
Investment in Co. Z stock............	66,000			
Other assets........	1,000,000	$500,000	$260,000	$200,000
Total assets.........	$1,558,500	$500,000	$260,000	$200,000
Liabilities.............	$ 233,500	$180,000	$ 50,000	$ 75,000
Preferred stock ($100 par)........			50,000	
Common stock ($10 par)..........	1,000,000	250,000	100,000	150,000
Retained earnings (deficit)............	325,000	70,000	60,000	(25,000)
Total liabilities and stockholders' equity..............	$1,558,500	$500,000	$260,000	$200,000

Instructions: Prepare a consolidated work sheet and a consolidated balance sheet.

10-8. The balance sheets for Companies R, S, and T on November 1, 19X2, immediately after Company R acquired control of Companies S and T, appear as follows:

	Co. R	Co. S	Co. T
Cash......................................	$ 90,000	$ 35,000	$ 20,000
Accounts receivable...............	167,500	45,000	50,000
Inventories............................	350,000	100,000	85,000
Investment in Co. S stock	192,000		
Investment in Co. T stock	165,000		
Plant and equipment (net)	400,000	160,000	135,000
Total assets..........................	$1,364,500	$340,000	$290,000
Accounts payable	$ 160,000	$ 30,000	$ 40,000
Bonds payable.......................	150,000	100,000	60,000
Capital stock.........................	600,000	100,000	200,000
Additional paid-in capital........	200,000	30,000	20,000
Retained earnings (deficit)......	254,500	80,000	(30,000)
Total liabilities and stockholders' equity..........................	$1,364,500	$340,000	$290,000

Stock of each of the companies is no-par, total shares having been issued as follows: by Company R, 60,000; by Company S, 8,000; by Company T, 12,500. Company R acquired Company S stock at $30 per share and Company T stock at $15 per share on the open market.

Instructions: Prepare a consolidated work sheet and a consolidated balance sheet.

10-9. The balance sheets for Companies L and M on November 15, 19X8, immediately after Company L acquired control of Company M, are shown as follows:

Company L

Cash......................	$ 120,000	Payables	$ 410,000
Receivables............	340,000	Capital stock	1,000,000
Inventories.............	550,000	Additional paid-in	
Investment in		capital	250,000
Company M stock,		Retained earnings...	340,000
7,500 shares	390,000		
Plant and			
equipment (net)...	600,000		
		Total liabilities and	
		stockholders'	
Total assets............	$2,000,000	equity	$2,000,000

Company M

Cash.........................	$ 40,000	Payables...................	$145,000
Receivables...............	105,000	Capital stock, 10,000	
Inventories................	115,000	shares	200,000
Plant and equipment		Additional paid-in	
(net)......................	225,000	capital...................	100,000
		Retained earnings......	40,000
		Total liabilities and	
Total assets...............	$485,000	stockholders' equity	$485,000

Upon securing control, Company L authorized that Company M's books be audited and its plant and equipment appraised. The audit disclosed that a general contingency reserve for $25,000 was carried on the books as a payable. Appraisers reported a sound value of $350,000 for plant and equipment.

Instructions: Prepare a consolidated work sheet and a consolidated balance sheet.

10-10. Companies D and E are engaged in the exploitation, development, and production of minerals. They decide to consolidate and form Company Z with a no-par capital stock of 100,000 shares.

Under certain rights acquired for nominal considerations, the holdings of Companies D and E have proved to be very valuable, principally because of discoveries of extensive underground deposits, the cost of which was considerably less than the present intrinsic values.

A disinterested appraisal has been made, and, based upon this appraisal and other assets apart from those appraised, the capital stock of Z is to be issued to the stockholders of the subsidiary companies in the following proportions: for each share of D, 2 shares of Z; for each share of E, 4 shares of Z.

The appraisal shows the value of the properties of D to be $2,600,000 and those of E, $4,400,000.

All the stock is exchanged, with the exception of 100 shares of D. Both Company D and Company E are retained as legal entities. Later, 20,000 shares of Z stock are sold for cash at $100 a share.

The accounts of D and E, as of the date of consolidation, were:

	D	E
Cash	$ 200,000	$ 100,000
Property	1,600,000	1,800,000
Other assets	500,000	100,000
Total debits	$2,300,000	$2,000,000
Accumulated depletion and depreciation	$ 800,000	$ 600,000
Liabilities	300,000	600,000
Capital stock ($100 par)	1,500,000	1,000,000
Retained earnings (deficit)	(300,000)	(200,000)
Total credits	$2,300,000	$2,000,000

Instructions: (1) Prepare journal entries to record transactions on the books of Z.

(2) Prepare a consolidated balance sheet, assuming that the consolidation is treated as a purchase.

(AICPA adapted)

10-11. The balance sheets for Companies P and Q on November 30, 19X3, immediately after the acquisition by Company P of its holdings in Company Q, follow:

Company P

Current assets	$1,160,000	Current liabilities	$ 350,000
Investment in		Long-term debt	500,000
Company Q stock		Capital stock,	
(90,000 shares)	540,000	68,000 shares,	
Plant and		$20 par	1,360,000
equipment (net)	1,800,000	Additional paid-in	
		capital	2,040,000
		Deficit	(750,000)
		Total liabilities and	
		stockholders'	
Total assets	$3,500,000	equity	$3,500,000

Company Q

Current assets	$ 750,000	Current liabilities	$ 300,000
Plant and		Long-term debt	350,000
equipment (net)	1,750,000	Capital stock,	
		100,000 shares,	
		$2.50 stated	
		value	250,000
		Additional paid-in	
		capital	400,000
		Retained earnings	1,200,000
		Total liabilities and	
		stockholders'	
Total assets	$2,500,000	equity	$2,500,000

Company Q shares were acquired by exchanging Company P shares for Company Q shares on a 1-for-5 basis. Company P shares were selling on the market at $30 and the investment in stock of Company Q was recorded on this basis.

Instructions: (1) Prepare a consolidated work sheet and a consolidated balance sheet, assuming that the combination is recognized as a pooling of interests.

(2) Prepare a consolidated work sheet and a consolidated balance sheet, assuming that the combination is recognized as a purchase.

11
Consolidated Statements — Investments Carried by Equity Method

When stock of a subsidiary company is acquired, the cost of the stock acquisition is recorded in an investment account. Thereafter the parent company must recognize the changes that take place in its ownership equity in the subsidiary by periodic adjustments to the investment account. This practice is referred to as the *equity method*. Although the parent must use the equity method in its own external financial reports, it may choose to maintain its accounts according to the *cost method*, in which the investment account is carried without adjustment.

In developing a work sheet for a consolidated balance sheet, the method that is employed in carrying the investment must be known in order to determine the nature of the eliminations to be made. Regardless of the method employed in carrying the investment, development of the consolidated balance sheet is based on the assumption that parent and subsidiary constitute a single economic entity. Whether the investment is carried by the equity method or the cost method, then, the consolidated balance sheet must be the same.

The equity method and the development of the consolidated balance sheet when this method is used are described in this chapter. The cost method and the development of the consolidated statement when the cost method is used are described in Chapter 12.

GUIDELINES FOR USING THE EQUITY METHOD

The equity method must be used to account for all unconsolidated subsidiaries in consolidated financial statements. It must also be used by the parent company to account for investments in common stock of subsidiaries "in parent-company financial statements prepared for issuance to stockholders as the financial statements of the primary reporting entity."[1] In ad-

---

[1]*Opinions of the Accounting Principles Board, No. 18,* "The Equity Method of Accounting for Investments in Common Stock" (New York: American Institute of Certified Public Accountants, 1971), par. 14.

dition, the equity method "should also be followed by an investor whose investment in voting stock gives it the ability to exercise significant influence over operating and financial policies of an investee even though the investor holds 50% or less of the voting stock."[2] Significant influence is a matter of judgment, but the Accounting Principles Board concluded that ownership of 20% or more of the voting stock of an investee leads to a presumption of significant influence in the absence of contradictory evidence.

The rationale for requiring the use of the equity method in cases where significant influence exists is that if dividends received from the investee were treated as income (as is done under the cost method) a company would be able to manipulate its own reported income by directing the investee to declare dividends. Under the equity method, the receipt of a dividend does not affect income. Income is affected by the reported earnings (with some adjustments) of the investee. If the investee follows generally accepted accounting principles, it is less likely that directions from the investor would have an impact on these reported amounts.

ACCOUNTING PROCEDURES FOR THE EQUITY METHOD

The equity method essentially parallels the accounting approach used in the preparation of consolidated financial statements. The parent and controlled investee corporations are treated as part of an integrated whole. Although there is a legal distinction between parent and subsidiary, the accounting is based on the economic relationship involved.

Although the equity method is not considered a valid substitute for complete consolidated statements, all of the rules applicable to the preparation of consolidated reports apply to the equity method. As the Accounting Principles Board noted:

> The difference between consolidation and the equity method lies in the details reported in the financial statements. Thus, an investor's net income for the period and its stockholders' equity at the end of the period are the same whether an investment in a subsidiary is accounted for under the equity method or the subsidiary is consolidated.[3]

Adoption of the equity method calls for the following accounting procedures:

- *Subsidiary net income or net loss.* Net income increases a subsidiary's net assets and increases its retained earnings. A net loss decreases net assets and decreases retained earnings. Using the conventional equity method, the parent recognizes its share of the net income of a subsidiary by a debit to the investment account and a credit to a

[2]*Ibid.*, par. 17.
[3]*Ibid.*, par. 19.

nominal account, Equity in Income of Company X. It recognizes its share of the net loss of a subsidiary by a debit to Equity in Income of Company X and a credit to the investment account. Subsidiary net incomes and net losses are thus accrued periodically on the books of the parent. Income or loss from subsidiary operations is ultimately transferred to Retained Earnings.

● *Subsidiary dividends*. The declaration of dividends by a subsidiary decreases its retained earnings and increases its liabilities. Payment of dividends reduces cash and cancels the dividend liability. The parent company recognizes its share of the dividends declared by a subsidiary by a debit to Dividends Receivable and a credit to the investment account. The receipt of cash is recorded by a debit to Cash and a credit to Dividends Receivable. A dividend is recognized by a parent, then, as a recovery of a portion of its investment in the subsidiary and not as an element of income.

● *Difference between investment cost and book value*. The difference, if any, between the cost of the investment and the parent company's equity in the net assets of the subsidiary should be accounted for in the same manner as in a consolidated statement. Thus, if there are differences between the book values of depreciable assets and their fair values at the date of acquisition, depreciation should be based on the fair values in calculating the earnings of the subsidiary. If an excess of investment cost over book value would be reported as goodwill on a consolidated balance sheet, it should be amortized over a period of 40 years or less in determining the income attributable to the subsidiary.

● *Intercompany profits and losses*. In consolidated statements, any profits or losses stemming from transactions between companies included in the consolidated enterprise are eliminated. These eliminations are discussed in Chapter 13. In using the equity method, such profits or losses should be eliminated in a similar manner.

To illustrate the use of the equity method in carrying investments in subsidiaries and the preparation of a consolidated balance sheet subsequent to the acquisition of control, assume that on January 1, 19X1, Company P acquires 80% of the stock of Company S for $100,000. On this date Company S has capital stock outstanding of $100,000 and a retained earnings balance of $20,000. Asset and liability balances of Company S represent fair values at that time. Any goodwill recognized is to be amortized over a 40-year period.

A work sheet for a consolidated balance sheet is prepared by Company P on the date of acquisition of stock of Company S as shown on page 315.

Subsidiary Income and Dividends

To illustrate the conventional procedure for recording subsidiary income and dividends subsequent to acquisition, assume that Company S reports net income of $20,000 for the 6-month period ended June 30, 19X1. A dividend of $10,000 is declared by Company S on December 5 and is paid

Company P and Subsidiary Company S
Work Sheet for Consolidated Balance Sheet
January 1, 19X1

	Co. P	Co. S	Eliminations		Consolidated Balance Sheet	
			Dr.	Cr.	Dr.	Cr.
Debits						
Investment in Co. S Stock	100,000					
Eliminate Investment...............				100,000		
Goodwill			4,000		4,000	
Other Assets.............................	250,000	200,000			450,000	
	350,000	200,000				
Credits						
Liabilities	200,000	80,000				280,000
Capital Stock, Co. P.....................	100,000					100,000
Retained Earnings, Co. P.............	50,000					50,000
Capital Stock, Co. S......................		100,000				
Eliminate 80%			80,000			
Minority Interest, 20%.............						20,000
Retained Earnings, Co. S..............		20,000				
Eliminate 80%			16,000			
Minority Interest, 20%..............						4,000
	350,000	200,000	100,000	100,000	454,000	454,000

on December 20. Company S reports a net loss of $5,000 for the 6-month period ended December 31, 19X1. The net income of Company P for 19X1, excluding subsidiary income, is $25,000. Company P declares no dividends during the year. The following entries are required on the books of the parent in 19X1 as a result of its 80% interest in Company S.

Transaction	Equity Method in Carrying Investment Account	
June 30: Announcement of net income of $20,000 for 6-month period by Co. S.	Investment in Co. S Stock ..... 16,000 Equity in Income of Co. S ...	 16,000
December 5: Declaration of dividend of $10,000 by Co. S.	Dividends Receivable............ 8,000 Investment in Co. S Stock ..	 8,000
December 20: Payment of dividend by Co. S.	Cash .... 8,000 Dividends Receivable.........	 8,000
December 31: Announcement of net loss of $5,000 for 6-month period by Co. S. Amortization of goodwill over 40-year period.	Equity in Income of Co. S ...... 4,000 Investment in Co. S Stock .. Equity in Income of Co. S ...... 100 Investment in Co. S Stock ..	 4,000 100

Work Sheet for a Consolidated Balance Sheet

When a work sheet for a consolidated balance sheet is prepared at the time of acquisition of holdings in the subsidiary, the equity originally acquired in the subsidiary is eliminated by debiting the subsidiary company capital balances and crediting the investment account. When the parent employs the equity method for an investment in a subsidiary, the investment account balance reflects the original equity in the subsidiary, adjusted for changes that have taken place in this equity. In a work sheet for a consolidated balance sheet subsequent to stock acquisition, eliminations must be made in terms of the equity as of the date of the consolidated balance sheet. Each of the subsidiary company capital balances is debited for the percentage ownership identified with the parent, and the remaining capital balances are extended to the consolidated balance sheet columns as minority interest. The investment account is credited, and any difference between the investment account balance and the amount eliminated against it is extended to the consolidated balance sheet columns as Goodwill.

A cost or book value excess on an investment in a subsidiary is determined at the time the controlling interest is acquired. If the excess is attributed to goodwill, it must be amortized with debits to the Retained Earnings balance on the consolidated balance sheets prepared in subsequent periods. If the excess is identified with specific subsidiary assets, it would affect the minority interest as well.

On December 31, 19X1, a work sheet for a consolidated balance sheet for Company P and Company S would be prepared as follows:[4]

	Co. P	Co. S	Eliminations Dr.	Eliminations Cr.	Consolidated Balance Sheet Dr.	Consolidated Balance Sheet Cr.
Debits						
Investment in Co. S Stock	103,900			103,900		
Eliminate Investment................						
Goodwill..................................			3,900		3,900	
Other Assets.............................	283,000	205,000			488,000	
	386,900	205,000				
Credits						
Liabilities..................................	200,000	80,000				280,000
Capital Stock, Co. P.....................	100,000					100,000
Retained Earnings, Co. P..............	86,900					86,900
Capital Stock, Co. S.....................		100,000				
Eliminate 80%..........................			80,000			
Minority Interest, 20%..............						20,000
Retained Earnings, Co. S..............		25,000				
Eliminate 80%..........................			20,000			
Minority Interest, 20%..............						5,000
	386,900	205,000	103,900	103,900	491,900	491,900

[4]Balance sheet figures are based on the assumption that liabilities of each company remain unchanged for the year.

Company P recorded 80% of Company S's net income of $15,000, or $12,000. It also charged against this income the $100 amortization of goodwill for the year. Company P's retained earnings at the end of the year, then, were composed of its balance as of January 1, $50,000, subsidiary income, $12,000, and its own net income for the year, $25,000, less the amortization of goodwill, $100, for a net of $86,900. The investment account was increased by the parent's share of the subsidiary net income, $12,000, and decreased by the parent's share of dividends declared by the subsidiary, $8,000, and the amortization of goodwill, $100. The offset of 80% of the subsidiary capital account balances as of the end of the year against the investment account balance left a debit excess of $3,900 to be carried to the consolidated balance sheet columns as Goodwill. Cancellation of 80% of the subsidiary capital account balances left credit excesses totaling $25,000 to be carried to the consolidated balance sheet columns as Minority Interest.

A consolidated balance sheet prepared from the work sheet is as follows:

Company P and Subsidiary Company S
Consolidated Balance Sheet
December 31, 19X1

Assets...			$488,000
Goodwill			3,900
Total assets			$491,900
Liabilities			$280,000
Stockholders' equity:			
Minority interest:			
Capital stock	$ 20,000		
Retained earnings..	5,000	$ 25,000	
Controlling interest:			
Capital stock	$100,000		
Retained earnings..	86,900	186,900	211,900
Total liabilities and stockholders' equity.................................			$491,900

Eliminations for intercompany indebtedness. The preparation of the consolidated balance sheet generally requires the elimination of other items in addition to investment and reciprocal capital balances. Transactions among affiliated companies frequently give rise to receivables on the statements of certain members of the group and corresponding payables on the statements of others. From the standpoint of the separate legal entities, a valid debt exists. Reciprocal asset and liability balances arise from such transactions as sales, advances, and loans among affiliated companies and the declaration of dividends by subsidiaries. Although such reciprocal balances call for the transfer of cash from one party to another, the transfer will have no effect upon net assets or the capital balances of the respective units.

When the legal positions are disregarded and the parent company and its subsidiaries are viewed as a single unit, the intercompany balances lose their significance and require elimination in the same manner as interbranch items. The entire amounts of reciprocal balances are eliminated only on the consolidated work sheet, even when a minority interest is present.

In making the eliminations, liability accounts are debited and the reciprocal asset balances are credited. This procedure for advances between affiliated companies is illustrated on the following work sheet:

	Co. P	Co. S	Eliminations		Consolidated Balance Sheet	
			Dr.	Cr.	Dr.	Cr.
Debits Advances to Co. S..........	15,000			15,000		
Credits Advances from Co. P.....		15,000	15,000			

When only a portion of an asset or a liability balance is identified with an affiliate, the elimination is limited to that portion, leaving the balance related to outsiders to be shown on the consolidated balance sheet. For example, a subsidiary that is 80% owned has declared dividends of $5,000. An elimination is made as follows:

	Co. P	Co. S	Eliminations		Consolidated Balance Sheet	
			Dr.	Cr.	Dr.	Cr.
Debits Dividends Receivable	4,000			4,000		
Credits Dividends Payable..........		5,000	4,000			1,000

Eliminations for discounted notes. A note issued by one affiliate and held by another would be eliminated. However, a special problem is encountered when a note transferred to an affiliate is subsequently acquired by an outsider. Here it is necessary to recognize a liability to the outsider on the consolidated balance sheet. The elimination may be made as shown at the top of page 319.

The intercompany notes receivable and notes payable balances are canceled. Notes Receivable Discounted is shown on the consolidated balance sheet as Notes Payable, since discounting the note results in an obligation to an outsider. An alternative procedure on the work sheet would be to offset the balance of Notes Receivable Discounted against Notes Receivable, leaving the notes payable balance to be carried to the consolidated balance sheet columns.

Assume that a customer's note held by one company is discounted by an affiliated company. Notes Receivable Discounted on the original company's books and Notes Receivable on the books of the company discount-

	Co. P	Co. S	Eliminations		Consolidated Balance Sheet	
			Dr.	Cr.	Dr.	Cr.
Debits Notes Receivable (acquired from Co. S)..	5,000			(a) 5,000		
Credits Notes Payable (issued to Co. P)................ Notes Receivable Discounted (Co. S note).................... Notes Payable...........	5,000	5,000	(a) 5,000 (b) 5,000 (b) 5,000			5,000

ing the note are offset against each other. If the note is subsequently taken to a bank or to some other party outside the affiliated group and discounted, no further eliminations are required. Notes Receivable Discounted is carried to the consolidated balance sheet columns. To illustrate, assume that Company P discounts customers' notes of $10,000 held by Company S. Company P, in turn, has $5,000 of these notes discounted by a bank. Eliminations would be made as follows:

	Co. P	Co. S	Eliminations		Consolidated Balance Sheet	
			Dr.	Cr.	Dr.	Cr.
Debits Notes Receivable...........	10,000	10,000		10,000	10,000	
Credits Notes Receivable Dis- counted.....................	5,000	10,000	10,000			5,000

Corrections and adjustments prior to eliminations. Before eliminations can be made, it is necessary that balances resulting from transactions between affiliated companies be reciprocal as of the date chosen for reporting the consolidated position. It may be determined upon an examination of the books of the parent and the subsidiary that certain balances are not reciprocal because (1) one of the companies has failed to record certain information or (2) items are in transit, and only one of the companies has recognized and recorded the transfer.

When a company has failed to record certain information, it is necessary that this information be recorded in its accounts and reported on its statements. For example, assume that a subsidiary has declared a dividend at the end of the year and shows Dividends Payable on its balance sheet. The balance sheet for the parent is incomplete if it fails to show the dividends receivable from the subsidiary.

When items such as cash or merchandise are in transit, the company initiating the transfer may have recorded the transaction but the other company may have no information concerning the transfer until receipt of the item, at which time the proper entry will be made. Failure by one company to recognize such a transfer at the end of a period will result in intercompany balances that are not reciprocal; examination and analysis of the related balances will disclose the failure and the need for adjustment.

Items in transit may be recognized only on the consolidated work sheet since they will be recorded in due course by the transferee. A pair of adjustment columns may be provided for this purpose. To illustrate, assume that on December 31 a parent advances $10,000 to a subsidiary. The parent records the transfer on December 31. The subsidiary company makes no entry until the cash is received in January. The adjustment and the elimination may be shown on the work sheet as of December 31 as follows:

	Co. P	Co. S	Adjustments		Eliminations		Consolidated Balance Sheet	
			Dr.	Cr.	Dr.	Cr.	Dr.	Cr.
Debits								
Advances to Co. S..........	10,000					10,000		
Cash.............................			10,000				10,000	
Credits								
Advances from Co. P......				10,000	10,000			

COMPREHENSIVE ILLUSTRATION
OF THE EQUITY METHOD

The concepts that have been developed in this chapter are reviewed in the illustration that follows. Assume that Company P acquires a controlling interest in the stock of two companies as listed below.

April 1, 19X6, purchased 900 shares (90%) of Company S1 at $130. $117,000
July 1, 19X6, purchased 800 shares (80%) of Company S2 at $90.... $ 72,000

Capital stock, retained earnings, or deficit balances on December 31, 19X5, and earnings and dividends for 19X6 and 19X7 are as follows:

	Co. P	Co. S1	Co. S2
Capital stock (all $100 par)	$300,000	$100,000	$100,000
Retained earnings (deficit) balances, December 31, 19X5..	60,000	25,000	(10,000)
Dividends declared December 30, 19X6, payable January 15, 19X7...	10,000		5,000
Net income (loss) from own operations, 19X6...................	(30,000)	(20,000)	15,000
Dividends declared December 30, 19X7, payable January 15, 19X8...	10,000		5,000
Net income (loss) from own operations, 19X7...................	15,000	(10,000)	20,000

An appraisal of Company S1, conducted on April 1, 19X6, revealed that machinery with a remaining useful life of 5 years was undervalued by $5,000 in the accounts. All other items were stated at their fair values. The difference between the cost of the investment and the equity in book value of Company S2 is entirely attributable to a building with a remaining useful life of 15 years.

With this information, the differences between cost and book value of the investments at the time of acquisition may be determined as follows. This step is necessary first, since the disposition of these balances will have an important impact on the amounts recorded under the equity method.

Company S1

Capital stock..	$100,000
Retained earnings balance, December 31, 19X5	25,000
Loss, January 1 — March 31, 19X6	(5,000)
Net book value at acquisition..	$120,000
Adjustment for machine value	5,000
Net assets at fair value..	$125,000
Co. P share	× .90
Co. P equity in net assets	$112,500
Cost of investment...	117,000
Goodwill (to be amortized over 25 years)...................................	$ 4,500

Company S2

Capital stock...		$100,000
Retained earnings balance, December 31, 19X5		(10,000)
Income, January 1 — June 30, 19X6...		7,500
Net book value at acquisition...		$ 97,500
Cost to Company P..	$72,000	
Co. P share...	÷ .80	
Implied value of net assets..	$90,000	90,000
Reduction in building value		$ 7,500

Assuming that the equity method is used in carrying subsidiary investments, a work sheet and the consolidated balance sheet of Company P on December 31, 19X7, are prepared as shown on pages 322–324. The balances in the investment and retained earnings accounts of the parent company are determined as shown in the table on page 325.

When a parent acquires a controlling interest in a subsidiary during a year, the parent recognizes profit or loss only for the period from the date of purchase of stock to the date of the balance sheet. When the subsidiary

Company P and Subsidiary
Work Sheet for
December

	Co. P
Debits	
Cash	10,000
Notes Receivable	20,000
Accrued Interest on Notes Receivable	300
Notes Receivable from Co. S1	
Accrued Interest on Notes Receivable from Co. S1	
Accounts Receivable	45,000
Allowance for Doubtful Accounts	(900)
Advances to Co. S1	5,000
Dividends Receivable from Co. S2	4,000
Merchandise Inventory	44,000
Land	24,500
Buildings	
Machinery and Equipment	90,000
Accumulated Depreciation	(24,000)
Investment in Co. S1 Stock	92,610
Eliminate Investment	
Goodwill	
Investment in Co. S2 Stock	86,600
Eliminate Investment	
	397,110
Credits	
Notes Payable	25,000
Accrued Interest on Notes Payable	600
Notes Payable to Co. S2	
Accrued Interest on Notes Payable to Co. S2	
Accounts Payable	38,300
Advances from Co. P	
Dividends Payable	10,000
Bonds Payable	
Discount on Bonds Payable	
Capital Stock, Co. P	300,000
Retained Earnings, Co. P	23,210
Capital Stock, Co. S1	
Eliminate 90%	
Minority Interest, 10%	
Deficit, Co. S1	
Eliminate 90%	
Minority Interest, 10%	
Adjustment of Asset Value, S1	
Eliminate 90%	
Minority Interest, 10%	
Capital Stock, Co. S2	
Eliminate 80%	
Minority Interest, 20%	
Retained Earnings, Co. S2	
Eliminate 80%	
Minority Interest, 20%	
Adjustment of Asset Value, S2	
Eliminate 80%	
Minority Interest, 20%	
	397,110

Companies S1 and S2
Consolidated Balance Sheet
31, 19X7

Co. S1	Co. S2	Eliminations Dr.	Eliminations Cr.	Consolidated Balance Sheet Dr.	Consolidated Balance Sheet Cr.
3,000	12,000			25,000	
5,000	15,000			40,000	
150	350			800	
	10,000		(a) 10,000		
	200		(b) 200		
30,000	47,000			122,000	
(600)	(1,000)				2,500
			(c) 5,000		
			(d) 4,000		
35,000	56,000			135,000	
20,000	16,500			61,000	
	40,000		(e) 7,500	32,500	
60,000		(g) 5,000		155,000	
(20,000)	(6,000)	(h) 750	(f) 1,750		51,000
			(i) 92,610		
		(i) 4,185		4,185	
			(j) 86,600		
132,550	**190,050**				
5,000					30,000
150					750
10,000		(a) 10,000			
200		(b) 200			
17,200	21,550				77,050
5,000		(c) 5,000			
	5,000	(d) 4,000			11,000
	50,000				50,000
	(1,500)			1,500	
					300,000
					23,210
100,000		(i) 90,000			
					10,000
(5,000)					
			(i) 4,500		
				500	
		(f) 1,750	(g) 5,000		
		(i) 2,925			
					325
	100,000				
		(j) 80,000			
					20,000
	15,000				
		(j) 12,000			
					3,000
		(e) 7,500	(h) 750		
			(j) 5,400		
				1,350	
132,550	**190,050**	**223,310**	**223,310**	**578,835**	**578,835**

Explanation of Elimination Entries

- Entries (a) through (d) eliminate reciprocal balances between parent and subsidiaries.
- Entries (e) and (g) adjust the buildings and equipment accounts for changes in value at the date of acquisition.
- Entries (f) and (h) adjust the depreciation taken on buildings and equipment to be in line with the revaluation entries. (Buildings: $500 × 1½ years = $750; equipment: $1,000 × 1¾ years = $1,750.)
- Entry (i) eliminates the investment in Company S1 stock against the corresponding (90%) stockholders' equity accounts of Company S1, including the asset valuation adjustment. The remaining balance represents the goodwill, as adjusted for amortization.
- Entry (j) eliminates the investment in Company S2 stock against the corresponding (80%) stockholders' equity accounts of Company S2. Note that minority interests are affected proportionately by the asset adjustments.

Company P and Subsidiary Companies S1 and S2
Consolidated Balance Sheet
December 31, 19X7

Assets

Current assets:			
Cash		$ 25,000	
Notes receivable		40,000	
Accrued interest on notes receivable		800	
Accounts receivable	$122,000		
Less allowance for doubtful accounts	2,500	119,500	
Merchandise inventory		135,000	$320,300
Plant and equipment:			
Land		$ 61,000	
Buildings	$ 32,500		
Machinery and equipment	155,000		
Less accumulated depreciation	51,000	136,500	197,500
Goodwill			4,185
Total assets			$521,985

Liabilities

Current liabilities:			
Notes payable		$ 30,000	
Accrued interest on notes payable		750	
Accounts payable		77,050	
Dividends payable		11,000	$118,800
Long-term liabilities:			
Bonds payable		$ 50,000	
Less discount on bonds payable		1,500	48,500
Total liabilities			$167,300

Stockholders' Equity

Minority interest:			
Capital stock	$ 30,000		
Retained earnings	2,500		
Adjustment of asset value	(1,025)	$ 31,475	
Controlling interest:			
Capital stock	$300,000		
Retained earnings	23,210	323,210	
Total stockholders' equity			354,685
Total liabilities and stockholders' equity			$521,985

	Equity Method in Carrying Investment Accounts		
	Investment in Co. S1 (90% Owned)	Investment in Co. S2 (80% Owned)	Retained Earnings Co. P
December 31, 19X5:			
Balance of retained earnings...			60,000
April 1, 19X6:			
Purchase of 900 shares of Co. S1 stock at $130..........	117,000		
July 1, 19X6:			
Purchase of 800 shares of Co. S2 stock at $90............		72,000	
December 30, 19X6:			
Dividends declared:			
Co. S2, $5,000		(4,000)	
Co. P, $10,000			(10,000)
	117,000	68,000	50,000
December 31, 19X6:			
Net income (loss), 19X6:			
Co. S1, ($20,000)	(13,500)		(13,500)
Co. S2, $15,000		6,000	6,000
Co. P, ($30,000)			(30,000)
	103,500	74,000	12,500
Depreciation and amortization:			
Co. S1 machine, $5,000	(675)		(675)
Co. S1 goodwill, $4,500..	(135)		(135)
Co. S2 building, ($7,500)...		200	200
	102,690	74,200	11,890
December 30, 19X7:			
Dividends declared:			
Co. S2, $5,000		(4,000)	
Co. P, $10,000			(10,000)
	102,690	70,200	1,890
December 31, 19X7:			
Net income (loss), 19X7:			
Co. S1, ($10,000)	(9,000)		(9,000)
Co. S2, $20,000		16,000	16,000
Co. P, $15,000			15,000
	93,690	86,200	23,890
Depreciation and amortization:			
Co. S1 machine, $5,000	(900)		(900)
Co. S1 goodwill, $4,500..	(180)		(180)
Co. S2 building, ($7,500)...		400	400
Balances, December 31, 19X7.................................	92,610	86,600	23,210

company prepares interim statements, specific data with respect to the accrual of earnings during the year are available. In the absence of such statements and in the absence of any other specific information to the contrary, it would be assumed that profit or loss accrues evenly throughout the year. A pro rata share of the profit or loss for the period is considered to have accrued prior to date of purchase, with the balance accruing subsequent to purchase. In the example, subsidiary profit and loss balances and retained earnings balances for 19X6 are calculated as follows:

<u>Company S1</u>

Retained earnings, December 31, 19X5	$25,000
Net loss for 19X6, $20,000.	
Pro rata share of net loss to April 1, 19X6, date of acquisition of interest by Co. P, 3/12 × $20,000	(5,000)
Retained earnings, April 1, 19X6 (date of acquisition).....................	$20,000
Pro rata share of net loss, April 1 to December 31, 19X6, 9/12 × $20,000.	(15,000)
Retained earnings, December 31, 19X6	$ 5,000
Loss to be taken up by parent company: 90% of net loss of $15,000, April 1–December 31, 19X6	($13,500)

<u>Company S2</u>

Deficit, December 31, 19X5...	($10,000)
Net income for 19X6, $15,000.	
Pro rata share of net income to July 1, 19X6, date of acquisition of interest by Co. P, 6/12 × $15,000	7,500
Deficit, July 1, 19X6 (date of acquisition)	($ 2,500)
Pro rata share of net income, July 1 to December 31, 19X6, 6/12 × $15,000	7,500
	$ 5,000
Dividends declared December 30, 19X6	(5,000)
Retained earnings, December 31, 19X6	None
Income to be taken up by parent company: 80% of net income of $7,500, July 1 to December 31, 19X6	$ 6,000

Although profit or loss may accrue evenly over the year, dividends do not accrue. Dividends reduce retained earnings as of the date of their declaration.

The adjustments for depreciation and amortization are based on the assumed values at the dates of acquisition. If depreciable assets are restated at fair values at acquisition for consolidated statements, the increase or decrease in depreciation would affect the parent company's equity in the subsidiary earnings. This complete change presumably affects minority interests on a proportionate basis, so only the parent company's share is deducted from the investment account and retained earnings. On the other hand, goodwill is deemed applicable only to the parent's interest, so all of the amortization of this amount is charged to the parent's retained earnings.

Calculation of these adjustments is made as follows:

Company S1

Increase in machine value at acquisition......................................	$5,000
Remaining useful life...	÷ 5 years
Annual depreciation increase...	$1,000
Company P share	× 90%
Annual reduction in Company P income	$ 900
Reduction in Company P income for the period April 1–December 31, 19X6 (9/12 × $900)...	$ 675
Goodwill recognized at acquisition...	$4,500
Assumed life...	÷ 25 years
Annual amortization	$ 180
Amount of amortization for 19X6 (9/12 × $180)............................	$ 135

Company S2

Reduction in building value at acquisition..................................	$7,500
Remaining useful life...	÷ 15 years
Annual reduction in depreciation	$ 500
Company P share	× 80%
Reduction in depreciation applicable to Company P	$ 400
Amount of reduction in depreciation for 19X6 (6/12 × $400).........	$ 200

The reduction *in depreciation* increases *the income of Company P attributable to its investment.*

MODIFICATIONS IN THE EQUITY METHOD

The equity method in its conventional application, as illustrated, provides for accruing subsidiary profit and loss in the investment account and recognizing subsidiary capital distributions as investment realization. The investment balance, then, reflects the original cost of the investment adjusted for the parent's share of the change in subsidiary net assets since the date the interest was acquired.

Justification for the equity method is in terms of the economic unity that is represented by the two units as well as the full control that the parent exercises over subsidiary company activities. Subsidiary net income improves the position of the parent and can actually be made available to the parent in view of its control over the financial activities of the subsidiary. Losses of a subsidiary affect the parent adversely. With recognition of subsidiary earnings in the parent company accounts, the receipt of dividends from a subsidiary must be regarded as the recovery of accrued earnings or the partial realization of the investment balance.

From a legal point of view, however, periodic net incomes and losses of a subsidiary have no effect upon a parent's capital or upon its ability to declare dividends. Furthermore, all dividends received by the parent from a subsidiary, whether distributions of earnings accumulated prior to affiliation or after affiliation, represent income to the parent. The same positions are taken by federal income tax laws: a parent cannot recognize subsidiary profits and losses in calculating its taxable income, and a parent must include in its taxable income any dividends representing a distribution of the subsidiary's earnings.[5]

The equity method can be modified to offer a more satisfactory accounting for parent company capital by providing a distinction between capital that is related to changes in interests in the subsidiaries and capital that is legally realized and available for dividends. Such modification calls for the use of separate accounts to distinguish realized and unrealized earnings from the investment in the subsidiary.

To illustrate the alternative procedure that can be applied, assume that on January 1, 19X5, Company H acquires 90% of the stock of Company S. Company S's net income for 19X5 is $50,000, but dividends to stockholders for the year are only $10,000. Company H may regard itself as better off by 90% of the net income of the subsidiary, or $45,000; however, from a legal point of view its earnings and its ability to declare dividends to its own stockholders at this time is limited to $9,000.

Accounting procedures to distinguish unrealized earnings call for the following:

(1) Net income of a subsidiary is regarded as support for the recognition of an increment in the subsidiary investment. The parent debits the investment account and credits a separate unrealized income account for its share of subsidiary net income.

(2) The subsequent distribution of earnings as dividends by a subsidiary is regarded as realization of the income from the investment. The parent debits Dividends Receivable or Cash and credits the investment account for its share of subsidiary dividends. This entry is accompanied by a second entry debiting the unrealized income balance and crediting income. Any balance of unrealized income is closed to a separate restricted retained earnings account.

Use of the alternative procedure results in summarizing subsidiary operations in unrealized income and in retained earnings accounts. Earnings of the subsidiary that are not distributed in the form of dividends are recognized as unrealized income or restricted retained earnings. Earnings that are distributed and made available to the parent are recognized as retained earnings. Although the total assets and the total capital of the parent company are the same in each case, the alternative method affords a clarification of the parent company's capital.

The alternative procedure is compared with the conventional procedure in the following entries for Company H:

---

[5]A corporation is entitled to a specific deduction from gross income for dividends received from other domestic corporations subject to income taxes. This deduction is 85% of dividends received, or 100% of "qualifying dividends" received from corporations of an "affiliated group" that do not file consolidated tax returns.

Transaction	Equity Method in Carrying Investment Account	
	Conventional Procedure — Subsidiary Profit and Loss Recognized as Retained Earnings	Alternative Procedure — Subsidiary Profit and Loss Recognized as Unrealized Earnings

Announcement of net income of $50,000 by Co. S.	Investment in Co. S Stock.......... 45,000
	   Equity in Income of Co. S 45,000
		Investment in Co. S Stock.......... 45,000
		   Unrealized Earnings of Co. S.............. 45,000

Declaration of dividends of $10,000 by Co. S.	Dividends Receivable.......... 9,000
	   Investment in Co. S Stock...... 9,000
		Dividends Receivable.......... 9,000
		   Investment in Co. S Stock...... 9,000
		
		Unrealized Earnings of Co. S. 9,000
		   Dividend Income............ 9,000

Closing accounts to Retained Earnings.	Equity in Income of Co. S.............. 45,000
	   Retained Earnings.......... 45,000
		Unrealized Earnings of Co. S. 36,000
		Dividend Income . 9,000
		   Retained Earnings — Unrealized....... 36,000
		   Retained Earnings.......... 9,000

The preceding description was limited to a consideration of subsidiary net incomes and their recognition by a parent. But assume that subsidiary net losses exceed net incomes. In applying the equity method in its conventional manner, such losses are recognized as decreases in retained earnings even though the legal ability of the parent to declare dividends remains unimpaired. In fact, the amount available to the parent company for payment of dividends may exceed the balance of retained earnings even before its reduction for subsidiary losses. This situation exists when the subsidiary has declared dividends out of retained earnings accumulated prior to date of control, since the receipt of dividends legally enables the parent to redistribute such amounts to its own stockholders. Here, too, accounting procedures can be developed to provide for a presentation of capital in terms of amounts that are unrealized and amounts that are realized and legally available for dividends.

To illustrate, assume that on January 1, 19X8, Company H acquires 80% of the stock of Company T. Company T reports a net loss of $30,000 for 19X8 but pays dividends of $10,000 during the year. Company H may regard itself as worse off by 80% of the loss, or $24,000; however, the dividend distribution by the subsidiary has made $8,000 available to the parent for distribution to its own stockholders. Accounting procedures would call for (1) a negative capital balance to show the excess of subsidiary losses and dividends over income accruing to the parent since acquisition, and (2) a retained earnings balance that reflects the income that may be used as a basis for dividends. The alternative procedure for recognizing the loss and the dividend is compared with the conventional procedure as follows:

Transaction	Equity Method in Carrying Investment Account	
	Conventional Procedure — Subsidiary Profit and Loss Recognized as Retained Earnings	Alternative Procedure — Subsidiary Profit and Loss Recognized as Capital Decrease

Announcement of net loss of $30,000 by Co. T.	Equity in Income of Co. T 24,000
	  Investment in
	  Co. T Stock 24,000
		Capital Decrease
		— Losses and
		Dividends of
		Co. T in Excess of
		Earnings............. 24,000
		  Investment in
		  Co. T Stock 24,000

Payment of dividends of $10,000 by Co. T.	Cash 8,000
	  Investment in
	  Co. T Stock 8,000
		Cash 8,000
		  Investment in
		  Co. T Stock 8,000

Closing accounts to Retained Earnings.	Retained Earnings............. 24,000
	  Equity in
	  Income of Co. T 24,000
		Capital Decrease
		— Losses and
		Dividends of
		Co. T in Excess of
		Earnings............. 8,000
		  Retained
		  Earnings.......... 8,000

Although net assets and total capital for the parent company are the same in each case, again a clarification of capital is achieved through use of the alternative method. Use of the conventional method results in a reduction of $24,000 in retained earnings. Use of the alternative method results in an $8,000 increase in parent retained earnings as a result of the receipt of a dividend from the subsidiary. A negative capital balance reports a $32,000 impairment in the parent company's capital as a result of the $40,000 decrease in the subsidiary capital for the year. The negative capital balance reflecting the net write-down in the subsidiary investment would be subtracted from the retained earnings in reporting total capital on the parent company's balance sheet, but its separate identification informs readers of the legal status of the retained earnings balance.

Subsidiary earnings of $40,000 will serve to restore the investment balance to its original amount and to cancel the negative capital balance. Subsidiary earnings in excess of this amount will result in an increase in the investment balance above its original amount and an accompanying recognition of an unrealized retained earnings balance. When impairment in the investment in the subsidiary is material and appears to be permanent, it would be appropriate to apply the negative capital balance against parent company retained earnings.

When the conventional equity procedures are followed and both parent and subsidiary earnings are summarized in the retained earnings account, changes in the investment account must be analyzed in determining the portion of parent company retained earnings that can be used as a basis for dividends. When the alternative procedures are used, income that is not available for dividends is reported as unrealized retained earnings. However, for purposes of the consolidated balance sheet, this balance is properly regarded as earned, since here the legal distinction between the parent and the subsidiary disappears. When the alternative procedure is used, then, capital balances arising from the restatement of investments in subsidiaries should be combined with retained earnings of the parent company in preparing the consolidated balance sheet.

REPORTING INVESTMENTS ON PARENT COMPANY STATEMENTS

Although the consolidated balance sheet will be the same regardless of whether the cost or the equity method is used, the investment in a subsidiary should be reported in separate parent company statements by using the equity method. However, the financial statements should provide data in parenthetical or note form with respect to investment cost and dividend income, so that the legal limitations relating to the parent-subsidiary relationship may be fully understood. On the balance sheet, data should be presented relative to the cost of the subsidiary investment and to the portion of retained earnings that may be regarded as realized in view of the governing legal factors. On the income statement, further data are required with respect to that portion of current income that can be regarded as realized from a legal point of view.

Some accountants have raised objections to the use of the equity method on several grounds. First, the equity method involves basic departures from generally accepted practice in the recognition of revenue, since earnings of the subsidiary are viewed as earnings of the parent. It can be maintained that this economic view finds proper expression on the consolidated statement but not on the statement representing the separate legal entity. Second, investment balances fail to show either costs or current values of subsidiary holdings, since they are composed of a mixture of different elements — costs (or investment values) as of stock acquisition dates, modified by adjustments based upon the changes in capital reported on the books of the subsidiaries following acquisitions. Finally, the equity method calls for analysis of the accounts and special adjustments in arriving at the amount of retained earnings legally available for dividends and the amount of income that is subject to income tax.

UNCONSOLIDATED SUBSIDIARIES ON THE CONSOLIDATED BALANCE SHEET

A special problem is faced when certain subsidiaries are not consolidated in the preparation of consolidated statements. The consolidated statements purport to show financial position and operations of a number of related companies from an economic point of view. Ideally, this calls for recognizing subsidiary earnings from the time the relationship was entered into as well as combining account balances of the affiliated units. However, when combining account balances of subsidiaries with those of the parent is considered inappropriate, use of the equity method still affords the parent a means of reflecting the favorable or unfavorable implications of subsidiary ownership on the consolidated statements. The objection to the use of the equity method for separate financial statements because it does not reflect the legal entity status becomes invalid when applied to consolidated statements.

The Accounting Principles Board, in considering the problem of reporting unconsolidated subsidiaries in consolidated statements, called for the use of the equity method in all cases. "The Board reaffirms the conclusion that investors should account for investments in common stock of unconsolidated domestic subsidiaries by the equity method in consolidated financial statements, and the Board now extends this conclusion to investments in common stock of all unconsolidated subsidiaries (foreign as well as domestic) in consolidated financial statements."[6]

The Accounting Principles Board left unchanged the following statement in *Accounting Research Bulletin No. 51* relating to the disclosure of assets and liabilities of unconsolidated subsidiaries:

> Where the unconsolidated subsidiaries are, in the aggregate, material in relation to the consolidated financial position or operating results, summarized information as to their assets, liabilities and operating results should be given in the footnotes or separate statements should be presented for such subsidiaries, either individually or in groups, as appropriate.[7]

QUESTIONS

1. Explain how the parent company accounts for subsidiary profits, losses, and dividends when investments are carried by the equity method. What theoretical support can you offer for such procedures?

2. Give four different transactions that result in reciprocal intercompany balances requiring elimination in preparing a consolidated balance sheet.

3. A minority stockholder of the Phillips Co., a subsidiary of Tevis, Inc., believes that the elimination of subsidiary company receivables in the preparation of a consolidated balance sheet affects adversely the measurement of the minority interest. Evaluate this opinion.

---

[6]*Opinions of the Accounting Principles Board, No. 18, op. cit.,* par. 14.
[7]*Accounting Research and Terminology Bulletin, No. 51,* "Consolidated Financial Statements" (New York: American Institute of Certified Public Accountants, 1959), par. 21.

4. Customer notes acquired by subsidiary companies of the Landsdale Corporation are discounted by the parent company as a regular practice. The parent collects the notes at their maturity. (a) What entries are made on the books of a subsidiary company and the parent upon discounting a note? (b) How are the notes receivable and the notes receivable discounted balances reported on each company's separate balance sheet and on the consolidated balance sheet?

5. Company M, a wholly owned subsidiary of Company L, is unable to borrow cash from the bank. Accordingly, it requests an accommodation note from the parent. The parent complies with the request, and the subsidiary then discounts the note at the bank. (a) What entries will appear on the books of Company L and Company M as a result of the foregoing? (b) How will these transactions be reported (1) on Company L's separate balance sheet, (2) on Company M's separate balance sheet, and (3) on the consolidated balance sheet?

6. Describe the entries that would be made on the books of Company A and Company B, parent and subsidiary respectively, for each of the following transactions, and indicate in each case the eliminations that would be required in the preparation of a consolidated work sheet, assuming that settlement of open balances is not completed currently.

(a) Company B sells merchandise on account to Company A.
(b) Company B borrows cash from Company A, issuing a note for the amount borrowed.
(c) Company B declares a cash dividend.
(d) Company B issues first-mortgage bonds, Company A acquiring a block of the bonds directly from Company B at face value.
(e) Company A discounts notes that had been acquired by Company B, and in turn has these rediscounted at the bank.

7. The Morrison Company shipped merchandise of $5,000 to its parent, the Doheny Company, on December 29. The Doheny Company did not receive the shipment until January 6. How would you suggest this transfer be reported on the balance sheets of the two companies before balance sheet data are consolidated?

8. (a) What objections can be raised to the equity method in its conventional application? (b) What modifications can be made in this method to overcome these objections?

9. What special disclosures are recommended for subsidiary investment balances and subsidiary earnings on the separate financial statements of the parent company when investments in subsidiary companies are carried by the equity method?

10. The Walsh Corporation reports investments in majority owned and wholly owned subsidiaries on its separate balance sheet. Only wholly owned subsidiaries are consolidated for purposes of the consolidated balance sheet; but whenever the latter statement is prepared, investment balances for those subsidiaries not consolidated are stated by applying the equity method. Would you support such a procedure? Give your reasons.

EXERCISES

1. The Brown Corporation and the Curtis Corporation each have 1,000 shares of stock outstanding, $100 par. Changes in capital from January 1, 19X4, to December 31, 19X5, were as follows:

	Brown Corp.	Curtis Corp.
Retained earnings (deficit), January 1, 19X4	$50,000	($15,000)
Dividends declared and paid in December, 19X4.................................	(10,000)	
	$40,000	($15,000)
Net income (loss) for 19X4...................	30,000	(5,000)
Retained earnings (deficit), Dec. 31, 19X4	$70,000	($20,000)
Dividends declared and paid in June, 19X5	(10,000)	
	$60,000	($20,000)
Net income (loss) for 19X5...................	(5,000)	15,000
Retained earnings (deficit), Dec. 31, 19X5	$55,000	($ 5,000)

The Lucas Corporation acquired 800 shares of the Brown Corporation stock at $200 and 900 shares of the Curtis Corporation stock at $100 on July 1, 19X4. Assume that all identifiable assets are stated at their fair values. What is the goodwill on each investment for purposes of the consolidated balance sheet?

2. Assuming that investments in Exercise 1 are carried by the equity method, what entries are required on the books of the parent company for earnings, losses, and dividends of each of the subsidiaries?

3. Company A acquired 80% of the stock of Companies B and C on July 1, 19X3, for $75,000 and $120,000 respectively. Capital stock outstanding of each subsidiary is $100,000. Retained earnings changes for the companies were as follows:

	Company B	Company C
Retained earnings (deficit), January 1, 19X3	($20,000)	$30,000
Dividends paid April 1, 19X3		(5,000)
	($20,000)	$25,000
Net income (loss), 19X3......................	(10,000)	30,000
	($30,000)	$55,000
Dividends paid April 1, 19X4		(5,000)
	($30,000)	$50,000
Net income (loss), 19X4......................	15,000	(10,000)
Retained earnings (deficit), January 1, 19X5	($15,000)	$40,000

The parent company carries investment accounts on the equity basis.

    (a) What eliminations would be made in preparing a consolidated work sheet on July 1, 19X3?

    (b) What entries would be made on the books of the parent for 19X3 and 19X4?

    (c) What eliminations would be made in preparing a consolidated work sheet on December 31, 19X4?

    (d) What is the cost or book value excess on each investment that will be considered in preparing the consolidated balance sheet?

4. Company P owns 80% of the stock of Company S. In journal form, prepare the elimination that is required in each of the following cases.

    (a) Company P's books: Advances to Company S, $15,000.
        Company S's books: Advances from Company P, $15,000.

    (b) Company P's books: Notes Receivable Discounted (discounted by Company S), $10,000.
                                    Notes Receivable, $20,000.
        Company S's books: Notes Receivable (received from Company P), $10,000.
                                    Notes Receivable Discounted (discounted by bank), $8,000.

    (c) Company P's books: Notes Payable (issued to Company S), $5,000.
        Company S's books: Notes Receivable (received from Company P), $5,000.
                                    Notes Receivable Discounted (Company P's note discounted by bank), $5,000.

    (d) Company P's books: Dividends Receivable from Company S, $1,600.
        Company S's books: Dividends Payable, $2,000.

5. (a) Explain the meaning and the use of the capital accounts (1) Unrealized Earnings of Subsidiary Company and (2) Subsidiary Company Losses and Dividends in Excess of Earnings. (b) If these accounts are used with the equity method, what entries would be made on the books of Company P in recording the following:

    (1) Company P purchased 80% of the stock of Company S for $220,000 on January 2, 19X7. Company S reported capital stock of $150,000 and retained earnings of $125,000 on this date.

    (2) Company S announced a loss from operations of $15,000 for 19X7.

    (3) Company S declared and paid a dividend of $10,000 in 19X7.

    (4) Company S announced income from operations of $20,000 for 19X8.

    (5) Company S declared and paid a dividend of $10,000 in 19X8.

    (6) Company S announced income from operations of $30,000 for 19X9.

    (7) Company S declared and paid a dividend of $10,000 in 19X9.

PROBLEMS

11-1. Stockholders' equities on January 1, 19X0, on the books of Companies A, B, and C were as follows:

	Company A		Company B		Company C	
Capital stock........	($100 par)	$ 800,000	($10 par)	$100,000	($20 par)	$50,000
Retained earnings (deficit).............		350,000		110,000		(10,000)
Stockholders' equity...............		$1,150,000		$210,000		$40,000

On April 1, 19X0, Company A purchased for cash 7,500 shares of Company B stock at 16½, and on May 1, 19X0, it purchased 2,000 shares of Company C stock at 22. Any excess of book value over cost at acquisition is attributable to the value of land. Any excess of cost over book value is identified as goodwill.

Earnings announced at the end of each year and dividends declared at the end of each year, payable in January of the following year, were:

	Company A		Company B		Company C	
	Net Income (Loss) from Own Operations	Dividends per Share	Net Income (Loss)	Dividends per Share	Net Income	Dividends per Share
19X0........	($50,000)	$6	($10,000)	Passed	$ 6,000	Passed
19X1........	10,000	6	12,000	15¢	14,000	$1.00
19X2........	32,000	6	20,000	50¢	20,000	2.50

Instructions: (1) Assuming that investment accounts are carried by the equity method, prepare all the entries that would be made on the books of Company A at the end of 19X0, 19X1, and 19X2.

(2) Calculate: (a) the cost or book value excess on each investment; (b) the minority interest of each company at the end of 19X0, 19X1, and 19X2; and (c) the balance of retained earnings for the controlling interest that will appear on the consolidated balance sheet at the end of 19X0, 19X1, and 19X2.

11-2. Company W accounts for investments in its subsidiaries by the equity method. On December 31, 19X6, balance sheet data for the parent and its subsidiaries were as follows:

	Co. W	Co. X	Co. Y	Co. Z
Investment in subsidiaries..	$ 905,000			
Other assets......................	875,000	$285,000	$525,000	$635,000
Total assets......................	$1,780,000	$285,000	$525,000	$635,000
Liabilities..........................	$ 895,000	$110,000	$160,000	$185,000
Capital stock	1,000,000	250,000	300,000	300,000
Retained earnings (deficit)..	(115,000)	(75,000)	65,000	150,000
Total liabilities and stockholders' equity...............	$1,780,000	$285,000	$525,000	$635,000

Appraisals at the dates of acquisition revealed that all differences between investment cost and subsidiary book values were due to land values.

Data relative to subsidiary investments are at the top of page 337.

Instructions: (1) Prepare a consolidated balance sheet. (A work sheet is not required.)

(2) Calculate the amount that was paid by the parent for the investment in each of the three subsidiaries.

	Co. X	Co. Y	Co. Z
Investment balance, December 31, 19X6........	$160,000	$305,000	$440,000
Interest of parent represented by investment..	100%	90%	85%
Total net income (net loss) of subsidiary since date of investment by parent......................	($225,000)	$140,000	$100,000
Total dividends paid by subsidiary since date of investment by parent............................	—	60,000	120,000

11-3. Comparative balance sheets for Company H and its 90% owned subsidiary Company A appear as follows:

	Company H		Company A	
	Dec. 31 19X3	Dec. 31 19X4	Dec. 31 19X3	Dec. 31 19X4
Investment in Company A...............................	$ 950,000	$1,061,362		
Other assets..................	3,650,000	3,850,000	$1,655,000	$1,880,000
Total assets..................	$4,600,000	$4,911,362	$1,655,000	$1,880,000
Liabilities......................	$1,200,000	$1,475,000	$ 650,000	$ 750,000
Capital stock	3,000,000	3,000,000	1,000,000	1,000,000
Additional paid-in capital	250,000	250,000	50,000	50,000
Retained earnings (deficit)............................	150,000	186,362	(45,000)	80,000
Total liabilities and stockholders' equity....	$4,600,000	$4,911,362	$1,655,000	$1,880,000

The controlling interest in Company A was acquired by Company H at the end of 19X3. Company A paid dividends of $25,000 during 19X4. Company H has employed the equity method in carrying the investment in the subsidiary. Goodwill recognized at the time of acquisition is being amortized over a period of 40 years.

Instructions: (1) Prepare the entries that were made by Company H to recognize dividends and earnings of subsidiary Company A in 19X4.

(2) Prepare a balance sheet in comparative form, reporting the consolidated financial position of Company H and Company A at the end of 19X3 and 19X4. (A work sheet is not required.)

11-4. Balance sheet data on December 31, 19X2, for Companies A and B appear as follows:

	Company A		Company B
Investment in Company B (32,000 shares)	$ 416,000		
Other assets................	1,350,000		$685,000
Total assets.................	$1,766,000		$685,000
Liabilities......................	$ 480,000		$235,000
Capital stock ....(no-par)	1,000,000	($2.50 par)	100,000
Additional paid-in capital............................	500,000		160,000
Retained earnings (deficit).........................	(214,000)		190,000
Total liabilities and stockholders' equity..	$1,766,000		$685,000

The investment by Company A in Company B was made on January 2, 19X2. Company B's retained earnings on this date were $145,000. Company A received dividends of $30,000 from Company B during the year and recorded these by crediting the investment account. No other entries were made in the investment account in 19X2. All Company B assets were stated at fair values on January 2, 19X2.

Instructions: (1) Prepare a work sheet for a consolidated balance sheet as of December 31, 19X2. Use the Adjustments and Eliminations columns of the work sheet to adjust the balance sheet data to reflect the use of the equity method.

(2) Prepare a consolidated balance sheet as of December 31, 19X2.

11-5. Balance sheet data for Abbott Corporation and its subsidiaries, the Burr Co. and Carl, Inc., as of December 31, 19X8, appear as follows:

Abbott Corporation

Current assets........	$1,250,000	Current liabilities....	$ 233,500
Investments:		Bonds payable........	600,000
In Burr Co. (4,500		Capital stock	
shares)	75,000	(no-par)	1,000,000
In Carl, Inc.		Additional paid-in	
(7,000 shares)..	175,000	capital................	200,000
Plant and machinery	1,000,000	Retained earnings...	500,000
Other assets...........	33,500	Total liabilities and	
		stockholders'	
Total assets...........	$2,533,500	equity.................	$2,533,500

Burr Co.

Current assets...........	$ 85,000	Current liabilities.....	$ 70,000
Plant and machinery ...	105,000	Bonds payable.........	50,000
Other assets..............	15,000	Capital stock	
		(no-par, 5,000	
		shares)	100,000
		Deficit	(15,000)
		Total liabilities and	
		stockholders'	
Total assets..............	$205,000	equity..................	$205,000

Carl, Inc.

Current assets...........	$190,000	Current liabilities........	$ 84,000
Plant and machinery ...	85,000	Capital stock (no-par,	
Other assets..............	10,000	10,000 shares)	100,000
		Additional paid-in	
		capital....................	65,000
		Retained earnings.......	36,000
		Total liabilities and	
Total assets...............	$285,000	stockholders' equity .	$285,000

Stock of the Burr Co. was acquired at the end of 19X4 for $115,500. At that time the Burr Co. showed a Retained Earnings balance of $40,000. The excess of book value over cost was attributed to a decline in the market value of land held by Burr Co. The Burr Co. reported a loss of $10,000 for 19X8, but the loss has not yet been recognized on the books of the parent.

Stock of Carl, Inc., was acquired at the end of 19X6 for $161,000. At that time Carl, Inc., showed a Retained Earnings balance of $5,000. Carl, Inc., reported net income of $15,000 for 19X8 and declared a dividend of $4,000, which is included in the current liability total. The parent has made no entries for the subsidiary net income or for the dividend in 19X8, and has made no provision for amortization of goodwill.

The Abbott Corporation current receivables include $6,000 from the Burr Co. and $500 from Carl, Inc. The subsidiaries show corresponding payable balances.

Instructions: (1) Prepare a work sheet for a consolidated balance sheet.
(2) Prepare a consolidated balance sheet.

11-6. Balance sheets for the Ellis Co. and its subsidiary, the Fair Co., as of December 31, 19X2, are as follows:

	Ellis Co.	Fair Co.
Current assets....................................	$1,800,000	$1,150,000
Investment in Fair Co. stock................	1,220,000	
Investment in Fair Co. bonds...............	200,000	
Plant and equipment (net)	1,000,000	850,000
Other assets......................................	105,000	50,000
Total assets......................................	$4,325,000	$2,050,000
Current liabilities...............................	$1,285,000	$ 450,000
Mortgage bonds payable.....................	500,000	250,000
Capital stock:		
100,000 shares, $10 par...................	1,000,000	
100,000 shares, no-par		650,000
Additional paid-in capital....................	1,800,000	
Retained earnings (deficit).................	(260,000)	700,000
Total liabilities and stockholders' equity...	$4,325,000	$2,050,000

The Ellis Co. has owned 90% of the stock of the Fair Co. for 20 years. The parent company follows changes in its equity in the subsidiary by adjustments to its investment account.

Analysis of the Ellis Co. data discloses that this company has not recognized the net income of the Fair Co. for 19X2 and the dividend declared in December. Net income for the Fair Co. for 19X2 was $65,000. A dividend of 40¢ a share was announced by the Fair Co. on December 30, payable February 1, 19X3. Dividends declared are included in the current liabilities total.

The parent company acquired Fair Co. bonds of $200,000 at face value upon their issuance by the subsidiary.

There are intercompany trade balances totaling $65,000 at the end of the year.

Instructions: (1) Prepare the journal entries to bring the books of the parent company up to date.

(2) Prepare a work sheet for a consolidated balance sheet.

(3) Prepare a consolidated balance sheet.

11-7. Balance sheet data for the Gale Corporation and its subsidiaries, Harris, Inc., and the Ingram Corporation, as of December 31, 19X7, are as follows:

Gale Corporation

Cash..........................	$ 65,000	Accrued interest on	
Accounts receivable....	50,000	notes payable.......... $	800
Advances to Ingram		Notes payable	50,000
Corporation.............	5,000	Accounts payable	45,000
Merchandise inventory	65,000	Capital stock ($10 par)	300,000
Plant and equipment		Additional paid-in	
(net).......................	120,000	capital....................	60,000
Investment in Harris,		Retained earnings.......	136,200
Inc. (35,000 shares).	105,000		
Investment in Ingram			
Corporation stock			
(14,400 shares)	172,000		
Investment in Ingram			
Corporation bonds			
(face value,			
$10,000).................	10,000		
		Total liabilities and	
Total assets...............	$592,000	stockholders' equity .	$592,000

Harris, Inc.

Cash..........................	$ 30,000	Accounts payable .... $	76,000
Notes receivable.........	15,000	Capital stock (no-par,	
Accounts receivable....	41,000	40,000 shares)........	100,000
Merchandise inventory	50,000	Additional paid-in	
Plant and equipment		capital....................	35,000
(net).......................	90,000	Retained earnings.......	15,000
		Total liabilities and	
Total assets...............	$226,000	stockholders' equity .	$226,000

Ingram Corporation

Cash..........................	$ 9,800	Dividends payable....... $	1,500
Accounts receivable....	60,200	Accrued interest on	
Merchandise inventory	85,000	notes payable..........	600
Plant and equipment		Notes payable	25,300
(net).......................	120,000	Accounts payable	37,600
		Bonds payable............	50,000
		Capital stock (no-par,	
		18,000 shares)........	100,000
		Retained earnings.......	60,000
		Total liabilities and	
Total assets...............	$275,000	stockholders' equity .	$275,000

The Ingram Corporation has just remitted payment in full of the advance by the Gale Corporation. The latter company has not yet received the check.

The Ingram Corporation owes Harris, Inc., $10,000 on a note. This amount is included in the balances on the statements of the respective companies. Interest of $120 has accrued on this note and is included as accrued interest on the Ingram Corporation books, but the accrued interest has not been recognized by Harris, Inc.

The investment accounts are carried by the Gale Corporation on the equity basis. However, neither the net incomes of the subsidiaries for the year nor the dividend declared by the Ingram Corporation have been recorded. As of January 1, 19X7 the goodwill had a remaining useful life of 10 years. Any excess of subsidiary book value over cost was attributable to nondepreciable assets. Additional paid-in capital and retained earnings accounts at the beginning of the year were as follows:

	Gale Corp.	Harris, Inc.	Ingram Corp.
Additional paid-in capital..	$ 60,000	$35,000	
Retained earnings (deficit)	112,000	(5,000)	$50,000

Instructions: (1) Prepare a consolidated work sheet from corrected balance sheets.

(2) Prepare a consolidated balance sheet.

11-8. The balance sheets on December 31, 19X9, for Company P and its subsidiaries, Company X and Company Y, are as follows:

	Co. P	Co. X	Co. Y
Assets			
Investment in Co. X, 80% interest......	$ 225,000		
Investment in Co. Y, 95% interest......	142,500		
Advance to Co. Y.............................	50,000		
Notes receivable (acquired from Co. P)..			$ 50,000
Notes receivable discounted (notes originally acquired from Co. P)........			(50,000)
Other assets.....................................	1,230,000	$375,000	330,000
Total assets.....................................	$1,647,500	$375,000	$330,000
Liabilities			
Notes payable (issued to Co. Y)..........	$ 50,000		
Advance from Co. P..........................			$ 50,000
Other liabilities................................	277,500	$100,000	75,000
Total liabilities.................................	$ 327,500	$100,000	$125,000
Stockholders' Equity			
Capital stock....................................	$1,000,000	$250,000	$200,000
Retained earnings (deficit), January 1, 19X9.......................................	300,000	30,000	(10,000)
Net income for 19X9	60,000	25,000	15,000
	$1,360,000	$305,000	$205,000
Dividends, 19X9	40,000	30,000	
Stockholders' equity, December 31, 19X9	$1,320,000	$275,000	$205,000
Total liab. and stockholders' equity....	$1,647,500	$375,000	$330,000

Company P acquired its controlling interest in subsidiary Companies X and Y in 19X6 and has maintained the investment accounts on the equity basis. However, Company P has not recognized on its books the net income of its subsidiaries for 19X9. Dividends of $30,000 paid by Company X during the year were properly recorded by the subsidiary and the parent; but a year-end dividend of $15,000 declared by Company X has not been recorded on the books of either the subsidiary or the parent.

The balance of goodwill as of January 1, 19X9, has a remaining useful life of 25 years. Any amounts of subsidiary book values in excess of investment cost were deemed applicable to nondepreciable assets at the time of acquisition.

The charge to the account, Advance to Co. Y, on Company P's books arose as the result of an accommodation note for $50,000 issued to Company Y so that Company Y might obtain working capital by discounting this paper.

Company X owes Company P $15,500. This balance is included in the other asset and other liability totals for Company P and Company X.

Instructions: (1) Prepare a consolidated work sheet from corrected balance sheets.

(2) Prepare a consolidated balance sheet.

12
Consolidated Statements – Investments Carried by Cost Method

The consolidated balance sheet has already been described as a statement that shows the financial position of two or more affiliated companies as a single unit. This concept for consolidation is the same regardless of how subsidiary company investments are carried on the books of the parent. Whether the parent adopts the equity method or the cost method for carrying investments in subsidiaries, the final product of the consolidation process must be the same. Adoption of the cost method for investment accounting will give account balances that differ from those which result from use of the equity method. Eliminations appropriate to cost method accounting will then have to be applied in the development of a consolidated balance sheet.

The cost method is not a generally accepted procedure for reporting the impact of an investment in a subsidiary. Nevertheless, some companies may prefer to use the cost method in recording their investments in subsidiaries. If separate parent company statements are prepared, adjustments to reflect the application of the equity method would be necessary. These adjustments may be achieved through work sheet entries, without actually adjusting the parent company's accounting records.

ACCOUNTING PROCEDURES FOR THE COST METHOD

The cost method is based on the theory that the accounting for an investment in a subsidiary should be the same as the accounting for any other long-term investment in securities. The parent and subsidiary are two different companies; therefore, dividends received on stock equities require recognition as revenue, and gain or loss on the investment should await the

343

sale of the securities owned. Although there may be economic unity between parent and subsidiary, the accounting system should record the legal status of transactions stemming from the relationship.

When the cost method is adopted, the parent company accounts for an investment in a subsidiary just as it would for any other long-term investment in securities. Only the original cost of the stock of a subsidiary is reported in the investment account. Changes in the parent company's equity in a subsidiary as a result of subsidiary profits and losses are disregarded. The declaration of a dividend by a subsidiary is recorded on the books of the parent by a debit to Dividends Receivable and a credit to Dividend Income. The subsequent receipt of the dividend is recorded by a debit to Cash and a credit to Dividends Receivable.

To illustrate the use of the cost method in carrying investments in subsidiaries and the preparation of the consolidated balance sheet subsequent to the acquisition of control, assume the same facts as those previously given on page 314 in illustrating the equity method: on January 1, 19X1, Company P acquires 80% of the stock of Company S for $100,000. On this date, capital stock of Company S is $100,000 and retained earnings are $20,000. The preparation of a consolidated work sheet for Companies P and S on the date of acquisition was previously illustrated on page 315.

In employing the cost method for carrying the investment, entries are required on the books of the parent during 19X1 as follows:

Transaction	Cost Method in Carrying Investment Account
June 30: Announcement of net income of $20,000 for 6-month period by Co. S.	No entry
December 5: Declaration of dividend of $10,000 by Co. S.	Dividends Receivable .... 8,000 Dividend Income.................... 8,000
December 20: Payment of dividend by Co. S.	Cash.. 8,000 Dividends Receivable 8,000
December 31: Announcement of net loss of $5,000 for 6-month period by Co. S.	No entry

With the investment carried at cost, a work sheet for a consolidated balance sheet may be prepared as shown on page 345.

When the cost method is used, the parent company does not recognize the net change that has taken place in its equity in the subsidiary until a consolidated balance sheet is prepared. Subsidiary earnings are recognized only to the extent that they have been made available to the parent as dividends. When the consolidated balance sheet is prepared, the change in the capital of the subsidiary since the date of acquisition still remains to be recognized.

Company P and Subsidiary Company S
Work Sheet for Consolidated Balance Sheet
December 31, 19X1

	Co. P	Co. S	Eliminations		Consolidated Balance Sheet	
			Dr.	Cr.	Dr.	Cr.
Debits						
Investment in Co. S Stock ...	100,000					
Eliminate Investment.......				(a) 100,000		
Goodwill.........................			(a) 4,000	(c) 100	3,900	
Other Assets......................	283,000	205,000			488,000	
	383,000	205,000				
Credits						
Liabilities	200,000	30,000				280,000
Capital Stock, Co. P............	100,000					100,000
Retained Earnings, Co. P.....	83,000		(c) 100	(b) 4,000		86,900
Capital Stock, Co. S............		100,000				
Eliminate 80%................			(a) 80,000			
Minority Interest, 20%.....						20,000
Retained Earnings, Co. S.....		25,000				
Eliminate 80% of $20,000, Retained Earnings at acquisition .			(a) 16,000			
Minority Interest, 20% of $25,000.....................						5,000
Retained Earnings to Parent......................				(b) 4,000		
	383,000	205,000	104,100	104,100	491,900	491,900

In the development of a consolidated work sheet, the investment account reports the investment at its cost and thus reflects only the original equity acquired by the parent. The eliminations that cancel reciprocal balances are identical to those made on the date of stock acquisition. Elimination of the original equity acquired against the investment account leaves a balance that reflects the excess of the original cost of the investment over book value. This amount is designated as goodwill. Elimination of the percentage of stock acquired against the subsidiary capital stock account leaves a credit excess representing the equity of the minority interest in this balance. However, elimination of the share of subsidiary retained earnings originally acquired by the parent against the present retained earnings account leaves a balance that reflects two elements: (1) the minority's equity in retained earnings and (2) a residual amount representing the change in the parent company's equity in the retained earnings since the date of stock acquisition.

In the example, the retained earnings of Company S on December 31, 19X1, are $25,000. Elimination of the parent's share of subsidiary retained earnings accumulated prior to date of purchase, $16,000, leaves a balance of $9,000. The minority's interest in retained earnings is 20% of $25,000, or $5,000, and this amount is extended to the consolidated balance sheet columns. The remainder, or $4,000, is the retained earnings increase identified with the parent company holdings, or 80% of the increase in the subsidiary's retained earnings since the date the stock was acquired. This balance is transferred to the parent company's retained earnings account in the second elimination entry.

The parent increased its retained earnings by $8,000 upon the receipt of dividends from the subsidiary. In preparing the consolidated balance sheet, the parent now recognizes an additional $4,000 in retained earnings. Retained earnings of the parent company on the consolidated balance sheet, then, reflect an increase of $12,000, which is 80% of the subsidiary earnings of $15,000 since the stock was acquired. The amortization of goodwill, however, must also be reflected. Assuming a useful life of 40 years, the amount of $100 for the year is deducted from both the goodwill and the parent's retained earnings.

The consolidated balance sheet for Company P and Company S, which is identical to the one on page 317, is as follows:

Company P and Subsidiary Company S
Consolidated Balance Sheet
December 31, 19X1

Assets			$488,000
Goodwill			3,900
Total assets			$491,900
Liabilities			$280,000
Stockholders' equity:			
Minority interest:			
Capital stock	$ 20,000		
Retained earnings	5,000	$ 25,000	
Controlling interest:			
Capital stock	$100,000		
Retained earnings	86,900	186,900	211,900
Total liabilities and stockholders' equity			$491,900

If there had been revaluations indicated for specific asset or liability accounts, additional adjustments would be necessary. These value changes would affect the minority interest as well as the resultant goodwill figure. Since adjusted depreciation applicable to these items would not have been recognized by the parent using the cost method, work sheet recognition would be necessary.

Alternative Consolidation Technique for the Cost Method

Instead of eliminations as shown in the preceding example, it is possible to adjust the investment account on the work sheet for the change in the parent's equity in the subsidiary since the date of stock acquisition. With the investment account reporting a balance that would have been obtained if the equity method were used, eliminations are made for the parent's equity as of the date of the balance sheet. To illustrate, in the preceding example the increase in the subsidiary company's retained earnings during the period of the parent company's ownership and the portion of this increase accruing to the parent are computed as follows:

Company S retained earnings:	December 31, 19X1	$25,000
	January 1, 19X1	20,000
Retained earnings increase during period of ownership by Company P		$ 5,000
Ownership interest..		80%
Retained earnings increase accruing to Company P		$ 4,000
Less goodwill amortization		100
Increase in investment		$3,900

The investment account and the parent company retained earnings are increased by $3,900 on the work sheet. The investment account is now on an equity basis: equity method accounting would have resulted in a debit to the investment account of 80% of $15,000, or $12,000, for subsidiary earnings; a credit of 80% of $10,000, or $8,000, for subsidiary dividends; and a credit of $100 to reflect goodwill amortization. The parent company retained earnings are now on an equity basis: equity method accounting would have resulted in a credit of 80% of $15,000, or $12,000, to the parent company's retained earnings, instead of an increase limited to that portion of the subsidiary earnings received as a dividend, $8,000, and a debit of $100 to reflect the goodwill amortization.

A work sheet prepared by this alternative procedure is as follows:

Company P and Subsidiary Company S
Work Sheet for Consolidated Balance Sheet
December 31, 19X1

	Co. P	Co. S	Adjustments		Eliminations		Consolidated Balance Sheet	
			Dr.	Cr.	Dr.	Cr.	Dr.	Cr.
Debits								
Investment in Co. S								
Stock	100,000		4,000	100				
Eliminate Investment ..						103,900		
Goodwill.....................					3,900		3,900	
Other Assets	283,000	205,000					488,000	
	383,000	205,000						
Credits								
Liabilities......................	200,000	80,000						280,000
Capital Stock, Co. P	100,000							100,000
Retained Earnings, Co. P	83,000		100	4,000				86,900
Capital Stock, Co. S		100,000						
Eliminate 80%............					80,000			
Minority Interest, 20%								20,000
Retained Earnings, Co. S		25,000						
Eliminate 80%............					20,000			
Minority Interest, 20%								5,000
	383,000	205,000	4,100	4,100	103,900	103,900	491,900	491,900

Dividends From Pre-Acquisition Retained Earnings

The procedure that has been described for the cost method is normally subject to one departure from accounting that considers only the legal factors. Authorities agree that a subsidiary dividend that represents a distribution of earnings accumulated prior to the date of the subsidiary stock acquisition should be recorded by the parent not as dividend income but as a reduction in the investment balance. Such a dividend is recognized as representing, in effect, a partial return of investment or the equivalent of a liquidating dividend, since the asset transfer is accompanied by a shrinkage of subsidiary company asset and capital balances below the acquired amounts. The source of dividends, whether out of earnings accumulated prior to stock acquisition or after stock acquisition, might be ignored and dividends treated as revenue when stock holdings are relatively small and no control is exercised over dividend declarations; but with significant stock holdings and a parent-subsidiary relationship, dividends that represent no more than a transfer of assets from an affiliate to a controlling company must be recognized as such. The American Institute of Certified Public Accountants has taken this position in adopting the following rule:

> Earned surplus of a subsidiary company created prior to acquisition does not form a part of the consolidated earned surplus of the parent company and subsidiaries; nor can any dividend declared out of such surplus properly be credited to the income account of the parent company.[1]

Earnings of a subsidiary accumulated prior to the date of parent control, whether retained or distributed, should not receive recognition as retained earnings either on the separate balance sheet of the parent or on the consolidated balance sheet. Only amounts that are earned after the date of company affiliation can be viewed as giving rise to retained earnings.

To illustrate the special procedures that are used when dividends received by a parent require recognition as a return of investment, assume the following: Company P purchases 80% of the stock of Company S for $200,000. Company S has stock of $100,000 outstanding and retained earnings of $100,000. Company P acquires an equity in the subsidiary of 80% of $200,000, or $160,000, thus paying $40,000 in excess of book value of the subsidiary interest acquired. In the following year, Company S reports net income of $10,000 and distributes dividends of $30,000. Income is recognized by the parent only to the extent that dividends represent earnings of the subsidiary since the date the parent acquired the stock. The receipt of the dividend is recorded as follows:

---

[1]*Accounting Research Bulletin No. 43*, "Restatement and Revision of Accounting Research Bulletins" (New York: American Institute of Certified Public Accountants, 1953), p. 11. This rule was adopted by the membership of the Institute in 1934, and still remains in effect.

Cash	24,000	
Dividend Income		8,000
Investment in Company S Stock		16,000

Since dividends that reduce the amount of the acquired retained earnings are considered to be a recovery of the investment, the original equity acquired by the parent and reflected in the investment account has now been reduced. Subsequent eliminations on the consolidated work sheet must recognize this shrinkage. Although the original investment balance of $200,000 reflected an 80% interest in capital stock of $100,000 and retained earnings of $100,000, the present balance of $184,000 reflects an 80% interest in capital stock of $100,000 and retained earnings of $80,000.

Work sheets for a consolidated balance sheet just before and just after the dividend are shown below and at the top of the next page.

Before dividend:

Company P and Subsidiary Company S
Work Sheet for Consolidated Balance Sheet

	Co. P	Co. S	Eliminations Dr.	Eliminations Cr.	Consolidated Balance Sheet Dr.	Consolidated Balance Sheet Cr.
Debits						
Investment in Co. S Stock ...	200,000			(a) 200,000		
Eliminate Investment.......						
Goodwill.........................			(a) 40,000	(c) 1,000	39,000	
Other Assets.....................	600,000	310,000			910,000	
	800,000	310,000				
Credits						
Liabilities........................	250,000	100,000				350,000
Capital Stock, Co. P...........	500,000					500,000
Retained Earnings, Co. P.....	50,000		(c) 1,000	(b) 8,000		57,000
Capital Stock, Co. S...........		100,000				
Eliminate 80%..............			(a) 80,000			
Minority Interest, 20%.....						20,000
Retained Earnings, Co. S.....		110,000				
Eliminate 80% of $100,000 Retained Earnings at Acquisition .			(a) 80,000			
Minority Interest, 20% of $110,000						22,000
Retained Earnings to Parent.........................			(b) 8,000			
	800,000	310,000	209,000	209,000	949,000	949,000

The consolidated balance sheet that is prepared after the dividend distribution continues to show goodwill of $39,000 and parent company retained earnings of $57,000. The dividend of $30,000 resulted in a distribution of $6,000 (20%) to the minority interest and $24,000 (80%) to the parent. The consolidated balance sheet reflects a shrinkage of $6,000 in total assets, accompanied by a reduction of $6 000 in the minority interest.

After dividend:

Company P and Subsidiary Company S
Work Sheet for Consolidated Balance Sheet

	Co. P	Co. S	Eliminations		Consolidated Balance Sheet	
			Dr.	Cr.	Dr.	Cr.
Debits						
Investment in Co. S Stock ...	184,000					
Eliminate Investment.......				(a) 184,000		
Goodwill.........................			(a) 40,000	(b) 1,000	39,000	
Other Assets.....................	624,000	280,000			904,000	
	808,000	280,000				
Credits						
Liabilities	250,000	100,000				350,000
Capital Stock, Co. P............	500,000					500,000
Retained Earnings, Co. P.....	58,000		(b) 1,000			57,000
Capital Stock, Co. S............		100,000				
Eliminate 80%			(a) 80,000			
Minority Interest, 20%.....						20,000
Retained Earnings, Co. S.....		80,000				
Eliminate 80% of $80,000, Retained Earnings at Acquisition as Adjusted ($100,000 less $20,000 recognized as return of investment).................			(a) 64,000			
Minority Interest, 20% of $80,000.....................						16,000
Retained Earnings to Parent......................						—
	808,000	280,000	185,000	185,000	943,000	943,000

COMPREHENSIVE ILLUSTRATION OF THE COST METHOD

The following example is based on the same facts given in the extended illustration on pages 320–327 in Chapter 11. Shares of subsidiary companies S1 and S2 were purchased by Company P as follows:

April 1, 19X6, 900 shares of Company S1 at 130 .... $117,000
July 1, 19X6, 800 shares of Company S2 at 90 72,000

Assuming that the cost method is used in carrying subsidiary invest-ments, a work sheet for a consolidated balance sheet on December 31, 19X7, would be prepared as shown on pages 352–353. A consolidated balance sheet prepared from this work sheet would be the same as the equity-basis balance sheet that was given on page 324.

The effects of earnings and dividends upon the investment and retained earnings accounts of the parent, assuming use of the cost method, are shown in the following tabulation. The account changes using the equity method are shown for comparison.

	Equity Method in Carrying Investment Accounts			Cost Method in Carrying Investment Accounts		
	Invest-ment in Co. S1	Invest-ment in Co. S2	Retained Earnings Co. P	Invest-ment in Co. S1	Invest-ment in Co. S2	Retained Earnings Co. P
December 31, 19X5: Balance of retained earnings			60,000			60,000
April 1, 19X6: Purchase of 900 shares of Co. S1 stock at $130	117,000			117,000		
July 1, 19X6: Purchase of 800 shares of Co. S2 stock at $90		72,000			72,000	
December 30, 19X6: Dividends declared: Co. S2, $5,000 .... Co. P, $10,000		(4,000)	(10,000)			4,000 (10,000)
	117,000	68,000	50,000	117,000	72,000	54,000
December 31, 19X6: Net income (loss), 19X6: Co. S1, ($20,000) .... Co. S2, $15,000 ...... Co. P, ($30,000)	(13,500)	6,000	(13,500) 6,000 (30,000)			(30,000)
	103,500	74,000	12,500	117,000	72,000	24,000
Depreciation and amortization: Co. S1 machine, $5,000 .... Co. S1, goodwill, $4,500 .... Co. S2, building, ($7,500)	(675) (135)	200	(675) (135) 200			
	102,690	74,200	11,890	117,000	72,000	24,000
December 30, 19X7: Dividends declared: Co. S2, $5,000 .... Co. P, $10,000		(4,000)	(10,000)			4,000 (10,000)
	102,690	70,200	1,890	117,000	72,000	18,000
December 31, 19X7: Net income (loss), 19X6: Co. S1, ($10,000) .... Co. S2, $20,000 ...... Co. P, $15,000	(9,000)	16,000	(9,000) 16,000 15,000			15,000
	93,690	86,200	23,890	117,000	72,000	33,000
Depreciation and amortization: Co. S1, machine, $5,000 .... Co. S1, goodwill, $4,500 .... Co. S2, building, ($7,500)	(900) (180)	400	(900) (180) 400			
Balances, Dec. 31, 19X7	92,610	86,600	23,210	117,000	72,000	33,000

	Co. P
Debits	
Cash	10,000
Notes Receivable	20,000
Accrued Interest on Notes Receivable	300
Notes Receivable from Co. S1	
Accrued Interest on Notes Receivable from Co. S1	
Accounts Receivable	45,000
Allowance for Doubtful Accounts	(900)
Advances to Co. S1	5,000
Dividends Receivable from Co. S2	4,000
Merchandise Inventory	44,000
Land	24,500
Buildings	
Machinery and Equipment	90,000
Accumulated Depreciation	(24,000)
Investment in Co. S1 Stock	117,000
Eliminate Investment	
Goodwill	
Investment in Co. S2 Stock	72,000
Eliminate Investment	
	406,900
Credits	
Notes Payable	25,000
Accrued Interest on Notes Payable	600
Notes Payable to Co. S2	
Accrued Interest on Notes Payable to Co. S2	
Accounts Payable	38,300
Advances from Co. P	
Dividends Payable	10,000
Bonds Payable	
Discount on Bonds Payable	
Capital Stock	300,000
Retained Earnings	33,000
Capital Stock, Co. S1	
Eliminate 90%	
Minority Interest, 10%	
Deficit, Co. S1	
Eliminate 90% of $20,000, Retained Earnings on April 1, 19X6	
Minority Interest, 10% of $6,750 deficit	
Retained Earnings to Parent	
Adjustment of Asset Value, S1	
Eliminate 90%	
Minority Interest, 10%	
Capital Stock, Co. S2	
Eliminate 80%	
Minority Interest, 20%	
Retained Earnings, Co. S2	
Eliminate 80% of $2,500, Deficit on July 1, 19X6	
Minority Interest, 20% of $15,750	
Retained Earnings to Parent	
Adjustment of Asset Value, S2	
Eliminate 80%	
Minority Interest, 20%	
	406,900

Co. S1	Co. S2	Eliminations Dr.	Eliminations Cr.	Consolidated Balance Sheet Dr.	Consolidated Balance Sheet Cr.
3,000	12,000			25,000	
5,000	15,000			40,000	
150	350			800	
	10,000		(a) 10,000		
	200		(b) 200		
30,000	47,000			122,000	
(600)	(1,000)				2,500
			(c) 5,000		
			(d) 4,000		
35,000	56,000			135,000	
20,000	16,500			61,000	
	40,000		(e) 7,500	32,500	
60,000		(g) 5,000		155,000	
(20,000)	(6,000)	(h) 750	(f) 1,750		51,000
			(i) 117,000		
		(i) 4,500	(j) 315	4,185	
			(k) 72,000		
132,550	**190,050**				
5,000					30,000
150					750
10,000		(a) 10,000			
200		(b) 200			
17,200	21,550				77,050
5,000		(c) 5,000			
	5,000	(d) 4,000			11,000
	50,000				50,000
	(1,500)			1,500	
					300,000
		(j) 315	(l) 14,600		
		(m) 24,075			23,210
100,000		(i) 90,000			
					10,000
(5,000)		(f) 1,750			
		(i) 18,000		675	
			(m) 24,075		
			(g) 5,000		
		(i) 4,500			
					500
	100,000				
		(k) 80,000			20,000
	15,000		(h) 750		
			(k) 2,000		
					3,150
		(l) 14,600			
		(e) 7,500			
			(k) 6,000		
				1,500	
132,550	**190,050**	**270,190**	**270,190**	**579,160**	**579,160**

PROVING SUBSIDIARY EARNINGS ACCRUING TO PARENT

When the cost method is used, the increment to the parent's retained earnings to determine consolidated retained earnings consists of two factors: the parent company's share of the retained earnings of the subsidiary since acquisition, adjusted for the effects of revaluations of specific assets at acquisition, less the accumulated amortization of goodwill, if any. These changes would be recognized in the parent company's accounts if the equity method were used. The retained earnings accruing to the parent, reported on the consolidated work sheet on pages 352–353, may be proved as follows:

Proof of Subsidiary Retained Earnings Accruing to Parent

	Co. S1	Co. S2
Retained earnings (deficit) balances, December 31, 19X7......................	($ 5,000)	$15,000
Retained earnings (deficit) balances on date of acquisition:		
Co. S1, April 1, 19X6	20,000	
Co. S2, July 1, 19X6		(2,500)
Retained earnings increase (decrease) from date of acquisition to December 31, 19X7...	($25,000)	$17,500
Less accumulated depreciation on asset revaluations...........................	1,750	(750)
	($26,750)	$18,250
Ownership interest	× 90%	× 80%
Adjusted retained earnings increase (decrease) accruing to parent since date of acquisition...	($24,075)	$14,600
Less goodwill amortized since acquisition	(315)	
Increase (decrease) in consolidated retained earnings...........................	($24,390)	$14,600

CONSOLIDATION FOR POOLING OF INTERESTS SUBSEQUENT TO ACQUISITION

If a consolidated statement is prepared for a company and subsidiary on a pooling-of-interests basis, the work sheet requirements are greatly simplified. No goodwill would be recognized, and no adjustments would be made for asset values at acquisition, so there is no need to adjust for goodwill amortization or changes in depreciation. Furthermore, the earnings of the subsidiary for the entire year of acquisition are included in consolidated retained earnings, so it is not necessary to allocate this item for a portion of a year. Although inclusion of a full year's earnings of a subsidiary acquired during a year may seem to violate the rule against including pre-acquisition earnings in consolidated retained earnings, combinations that qualify for pooling of interests treatment are not subject to this rule. APB Opinion 16, which applies to consolidated statements as well as actual mergers, states: ". . . retained earnings or deficits of the separate companies are combined and recognized as retained earnings of the combined corporation."[2]

---

[2]*Opinions of the Accounting Principles Board, No. 16*, "Business Combinations" (New York: American Institute of Certified Public Accountants, 1970), par. 53.

Work sheet entries would be necessary to adjust for any intercompany account balances and to eliminate the investment account on the parent's books against the corresponding amounts of the subsidiary's stockholders' equity. After these adjustments have been made, the consolidated balance sheet is obtained by combining the book value balances of the parent and subsidiary.

To illustrate the development of a consolidated balance sheet on a pooling-of-interests basis, assume that Company P exchanges 1,000 shares of its own stock for all of the outstanding shares of Company S on July 1, 19X3. Company P shares have a market value of $150 each at that time.

Capital stock, retained earnings, or deficit balances on December 31, 19X2, and earnings and dividends for 19X3 and 19X4 are as follows:

	Co. P	Co. S
Capital stock (all $100 par)	$300,000	$100,000
Retained earnings balances, December 31, 19X2	60,000	25,000
Dividends declared December 30, 19X3, payable January 15, 19X4	10,000	5,000
Net income (loss) from own operations, 19X3	(30,000)	20,000
Dividends declared December 30, 19X4, payable January 15, 19X5	10,000	5,000
Net income (loss) from own operations, 19X4	15,000	(10,000)

As a result of the foregoing, the investment and retained earnings accounts of the parent company are affected in the manner shown in the following table, assuming that Company P uses the equity method:

	Investment in Co. S.	Retained Earnings Co. P.
December 31, 19X2:		
Balance of retained earnings		$60,000
July 1, 19X3:		
Acquisition of 1,000 shares of Co. S stock in exchange for Co. P common	125,000	25,000
December 30, 19X3:		
Dividends declared:		
Co. S. 5,000...	(5,000)	
Co. P. 10,000...		(10,000)
December 31, 19X3:		
Net income (loss) 19X3		
Co. S 20,000...	20,000	20,000
Co. P (30,000)...		(30,000)
	$140,000	$65,000
December 30, 19X4:		
Dividends declared:		
Co. S 5,000...	(5,000)	
Co. P 10,000...		(10,000)
December 31, 19X4:		
Net income (loss) 19X4		
Co. S (10,000)...	(10,000)	(10,000)
Co. P 15,000...		15,000
Balances December 31, 19X4	$125,000	$60,000

A work sheet for the consolidated balance sheet and the consolidated balance sheet as of December 31, 19X4, would be prepared as follows:

Company P and Subsidiary Company S
Work Sheet for Consolidated Balance Sheet
December 31, 19X4

	Co. P	Co. S	Eliminations		Consolidated Balance Sheet	
			Dr.	Cr.	Dr.	Cr.
Debits						
Cash..................................	15,000	30,000			45,000	
Notes Receivable	20,000	16,000			36,000	
Advances to Co. S	12,000			(b) 12,000		
Dividends Receivable from Co. S................................	5,000			(c) 5,000		
Investment in Co. S	125,000					
Eliminate Investment.......				(a) 125,000		
Other Assets.....................	343,000	156,000			499,000	
	520,000	202,000				
Credits						
Notes Payable...................	20,000	10,000				30,000
Advances from Co. P..........		12,000	(b) 12,000			
Dividends Payable	10,000	5,000	(c) 5,000			10,000
Other Liabilities	30,000	50,000				80,000
Capital Stock, Co. P...........	400,000					400,000
Retained Earnings, Co. P.....	60,000					60,000
Capital Stock, Co. S...........		100,000				
Eliminate 100%			(a) 100,000			
Retained Earnings, Co. S.....		25,000				
Eliminate 100%			(a) 25,000			
	520,000	202,000	142,000	142,000	580,000	580,000

Company P and Subsidiary Company S
Consolidated Balance Sheet
December 31, 19X4

Assets

Cash..		$ 45,000
Notes receivable..		36,000
Other assets..		499,000
Total assets...		$580,000

Liabilities and Stockholders' Equity
Liabilities

Notes payable		$ 30,000
Dividends payable...		10,000
Other liabilities..		80,000
Total liabilities..		$120,000

Stockholders' Equity

Capital stock	$400,000	
Retained earnings.................................	60,000	460,000
Total liabilities and stockholders' equity		$580,000

QUESTIONS

1. Compare the entries for subsidiary profits, losses, and dividends when an investment is carried by the equity method and when it is carried by the cost method.

2. The Webster Co., which is 100% owned by Mason, Inc., has suffered heavy losses since the date that control was acquired by Mason, Inc., 10 years ago. (a) How are those losses recognized by the parent if the investment is carried by the equity method? (b) How can such losses be recognized by the parent if the investment is carried by the cost method?

3. (a) What eliminations are made against the investment account on the consolidated work sheet when an investment in a subsidiary is carried at cost? (b) What alternative method for eliminations on the work sheet may be employed when the cost method is used?

4. Which method in your opinion provides a more satisfactory portrayal of an ownership interest in a subsidiary — the cost method or the equity method?

5. The chief accountant for the Wharton Co. recommends use of the cost method in accounting for investments in subsidiaries, since the equity method brings appraisal values into the books and this is contrary to company policy. (a) Evaluate this position. (b) Give other considerations that would suggest use of the cost method.

6. The Wilson Co. reports a retained earnings balance of $100,000 on the date that Dewey, Inc., acquires a controlling interest. This retained earnings balance is subsequently used as a basis for cash dividends. (a) How would you recommend that the parent record such dividends? Give reasons for your answer. (b) What eliminations are made on the work sheet subsequent to the receipt of such dividends?

7. When the cost method for a subsidiary investment is used and eliminations are made in terms of original equity acquired, a retained earnings balance accruing to the parent company is recognized on the work sheet. How can this balance be proved?

8. Use of the pooling-of-interests assumption results in the parent company's recognition of retained earnings of the subsidiary prior to the date of acquisition. How can this be justified?

EXERCISES

1. The Harper Co. and the Jerome Co. each have 1,000 shares of stock outstanding, $100 par. Changes in capital, January 1, 19X0, to December 31, 19X1, were as shown at the top of page 358.

The King Corporation acquired 800 shares of Harper Co. stock at 100 and 900 shares of Jerome Co. stock at 90 on July 1, 19X0.

	Harper Co.	Jerome Co.
Retained earnings (deficit) balances, January 1, 19X0.............	$50,000	($20,000)
Dividends paid in December, 19X0...........	(15,000)	
	$35,000	($20,000)
Net income, 19X0...............................	40,000	15,000
	$75,000	($ 5,000)
Dividends paid in December, 19X1...........	(10,000)	
	$65,000	($ 5,000)
Net income (loss), 19X1..........................	(10,000)	20,000
Retained earnings balances, December 31, 19X1..........................	$55,000	$15,000

(a) What is the cost or book value excess on each investment?
(b) What entries would be made by the parent for profits, losses, and dividends of each of the subsidiaries if investments are carried at cost?
(c) What entries would be made if investments are carried by the equity method? Assume that any excess of book value over cost of investments is attributable to nondepreciable assets, and any goodwill is amortized over a period of 10 years.

2. The McFarland Corporation, a holding company, carries investments at cost. On July 3, 19X9, it acquired 32,000 shares of Jessup Co. stock at 15. Comparative balance sheet data for the Jessup Co. revealed that retained earnings had gone up from $50,000 on January 1, 19X9, to $75,000 on December 31, 19X9, as a result of profits of $40,000 less two dividends of $7,500 each paid on June 1 and December 1. Capital stock and additional paid-in capital balances remained unchanged at $420,000 and $100,000 respectively; 40,000 shares of stock were outstanding.

(a) What entries are required during the year on the books of the holding company?
(b) What eliminations are required at the end of the year in preparing a consolidated balance sheet?
(c) What is the cost or book value excess on the investment and the retained earnings accruing to the holding company as a result of subsidiary operations?

3. Company P paid $85,000 for a 90% interest in the stock of Company A on January 1, 19X5. The investment is carried at cost. During 19X5 Company A reported a net income of $30,000 and paid dividends of $10,000. At the end of the year Company A reported a retained earnings balance of $5,000. The capital stock balance remained unchanged at $80,000.

(a) What is the elimination on the consolidated work sheet?
(b) What is the cost or book value excess on the investment and the retained earnings accruing to the parent as a result of subsidiary operations?

4. The Stockton Co. owns an 80% interest in the stock of the Turner Co., acquired on January 1, 19X0, at a cost of $400,000. Capital stock of the Turner Co. is $500,000. The subsidiary showed a deficit of $50,000 when the Stockton Co. acquired control, but profitable operations converted the deficit to a retained earnings balance of $350,000 as of December 31, 19X8. The Stockton Co. maintains its investment records on a cost basis.

(a) Give two sets of adjustments and eliminations, either of which could be used in developing a consolidated work sheet.

(b) What is the goodwill balance that will appear on the consolidated balance sheet on December 31, 19X8?

5. Merrihew, Inc., paid $175,000 for a 90% interest in the Doerr Company on January 1, 19X2. The capital of the Doerr Company was composed of capital stock, $100,000, and retained earnings, $60,000. Investments are carried by Merrihew, Inc., at cost. The Doerr Company announced a net loss of $20,000 for 19X2 and paid a dividend of $10,000.

(a) How would you advise that the foregoing be recorded on the books of Merrihew, Inc.?

(b) What is the goodwill balance on January 1 and on December 31?

PROBLEMS

12-1. The Miller Company and the North Company each have 10,000 shares of no-par stock outstanding. Capital stock balances are $80,000 and $100,000 respectively. Changes in capital, January 1, 19X6, to December 31, 19X7, were as follows:

	Miller Co.	North Co.
Retained earnings (deficit) balances, January 1, 19X6	$50,000	($25,000)
Dividends declared and paid in December 19X6	(15,000)	
	$35,000	($25,000)
Net income (net loss), 19X6	40,000	(5,000)
Retained earnings (deficit) balances, December 31, 19X6	$75,000	($30,000)
Dividends declared and paid in December, 19X7	(15,000)	
	$60,000	($30,000)
Net income (net loss), 19X7	(10,000)	24,000
Retained earnings (deficit) balances, December 31, 19X7	$50,000	($ 6,000)

The Lawrence Corporation acquired 9,000 shares of Miller Co. stock at 14 and 8,000 shares of North Co. stock at 8½.

Instructions: (1) Calculate the cost or book value excess on each purchase, assuming that the investments were made on (a) July 1, 19X6; (b) October 1, 19X7. Indicate the reduction in asset values or balance of goodwill that would be shown on a consolidated statement at each acquisition date.

(2) Assume that the investments are carried by the equity method. Any excess of cost over book value is attributable to goodwill with a useful life of 40 years, and any excess of book value over cost is indicative of a decline in the

value of machinery with a remaining life of 10 years. What entries would be made on the books of the parent to record profits, losses, and dividends of each subsidiary, assuming that the investments were made on (a) July 1, 19X6; (b) October 1, 19X7?

(3) Assume that the investments are carried by the cost method. What entries would be made on the books of the parent to record profits, losses, and dividends of each subsidiary, assuming that the investments were made on (a) July 1, 19X6; (b) October 1, 19X7?

12-2. Balance sheets for parent Company P and its 80%-owned subsidiary Company Q are as follows:

	Company P		Company Q	
	Dec. 31 19X1	Dec. 31 19X2	Dec. 31 19X1	Dec. 31 19X2
Investment in Company Q	$250,000	$250,000		
Other assets..........	735,000	700,000	$475,000	$460,000
Total assets...........	$985,000	$950,000	$475,000	$460,000
Liabilities.............	$265,000	$305,000	$115,000	$175,000
Capital stock.........	500,000	500,000	200,000	200,000
Additional paid-in capital...............	100,000	100,000	100,000	100,000
Retained earnings (deficit)..............	120,000	45,000	60,000	(15,000)
Total liabilities and stockholders' equity...............	$985,000	$950,000	$475,000	$460,000

Company P acquired its controlling interest in Company Q at the end of 19X1. An excess of book value over cost at that time was attributed to a machine with a remaining life of 10 years. The interest in Company Q was carried at cost despite the unfavorable operations of the subsidiary in 19X2.

Instructions: Prepare a balance sheet in comparative form reporting the consolidated financial position of parent and subsidiary at the end of 19X1 and at the end of 19X2. (A work sheet is not required.)

12-3. The Allen Co. acquired 12,500 shares of stock of the Burton Co., $10 par, at 14, and 8,500 shares of stock of the Crow Co., $10 par, at 7½. Purchases were made on January 2, 19X4. Retained earnings changes for the three companies for 19X4 and 19X5 and balance sheets for 19X5 are shown on page 361.

Goodwill is to be amortized over a period of 20 years. Any excess of book value over cost is attributable to depreciable assets with a remaining useful life of 10 years from the date of acquisition.

Instructions: (1) Prepare a work sheet for a consolidated balance sheet.

(2) Revise the investment account balances on the assumption that the equity method is used, and prepare a work sheet for a consolidated balance sheet.

(3) Prove retained earnings balances accruing to the parent under the cost method.

	Allen Co.	Burton Co.	Crow Co.
Retained earnings (deficit) balances, January 2, 19X4	$130,000	$ 37,500	($20,000)
Net income (net loss) from own operations, 19X4	47,500	15,000	(5,000)
Dividend income from Burton Co.	5,000		
	$182,500	$ 52,500	($25,000)
Dividends declared and paid, 19X4	(15,000)	(6,000)	
Retained earnings (deficit) balances, December 31, 19X4	$167,500	$ 46,500	($25,000)
Net income from own operations, 19X5	57,500	15,000	10,000
Dividend income from Burton Co.	7,500		
	$232,500	$ 61,500	($15,000)
Dividends declared and paid, 19X5	(20,000)	(9,000)	
Retained earnings (deficit) balances, December 31, 19X5	$212,500	$ 52,500	($15,000)

Condensed balance sheets as of December 31, 19X5:

	Allen Co.	Burton Co.	Crow Co.
Investment in Burton Co.	$175,000		
Investment in Crow Co.	63,750		
Other assets............................	361,250	$282,500	$160,000
Total assets............................	$600,000	$282,500	$160,000
Liabilities................................	$187,500	$ 80,000	$ 75,000
Capital stock	200,000	150,000	100,000
Retained earnings (deficit)........	212,500	52,500	(15,000)
Total liabilities and stockholders' equity............................	$600,000	$282,500	$160,000

12-4. The Penn Construction Co. owns controlling interests in the stock of the Roper Co. and the Scott Co. The interests were acquired on May 1, 19X0. Balance sheets for the three companies on December 31, 19X0, are shown on page 362.

The parent company has made no entries to record the profits, losses, or dividend declarations of its subsidiaries. For consolidation purposes, goodwill is to be amortized over 40 years, and any excess of book value over investment cost is attributed to specific nondepreciable assets.

Instructions: (1) Prepare the necessary journal entries to adjust the parent company accounts, assuming that the investments are carried by the cost method, and prepare a work sheet for a consolidated balance sheet.

(2) Prepare the necessary journal entries to adjust the parent company accounts, assuming that the investments are carried by the equity method, and prepare a work sheet for a consolidated balance sheet.

	Penn Const. Co.		Roper Co.		Scott Co.
Investment in Roper Co. (3,600 shares)............		$270,000			
Investment in Scott Co. (820 shares)...............		125,000			
Other assets..................		570,000		$600,000	$350,000
Total assets...................		$965,000		$600,000	$350,000
Liabilities......................		$339,000		$284,000	$220,000*
Capital stock.................	(5,000 sh.)	500,000	(4,000 sh.) 380,600	(1,000 sh.)	100,000
Retained earnings (deficit):					
Balance, January 1, 19X0......................	$116,000		($40,000)	$20,000	
Net income (loss), 19X0	30,000		(24,600)	15,000	
	$146,000		($64,600)	$35,000	
Dividends paid in Nov., 19X0	(20,000)				
Dividends declared in December, 19X0, payable in January, 19X1				(5,000)	
Balance, December 31, 19X0.................		126,000	(64,600)		30,000
Total liabilities and stockholders' equity......		$965,000		$600,000	$350,000

*Includes dividends declared of $5,000.

12-5 The Burns Co. owns 25,000 shares of stock of Coogan Co. and 8,000 shares of stock of Dailey, Inc., both acquired on March 1, 19X8. Investments are carried at cost. Balance sheets for the three companies on December 31, 19X8, are as follows:

	Burns Co.	Coogan Co.	Dailey, Inc.
Investment in Coogan, Co.........	$ 40,000		
Investment in Dailey, Inc..........	82,500		
Goodwill................	60,000	$ 25,000	
Other assets..........	612,500	100,000	$130,000
Total assets...........	$795,000	$125,000	$130,000
Liabilities..............	$212,500	$ 39,500	$ 60,000
Capital stock ....(15,000 sh.)	450,000	(30,000 sh.) 60,000	(10,000 sh.) 50,000
Retained earnings..	132,500	25,500	20,000
Total liabilities and stockholders' equity................	$795,000	$125,000	$130,000

Earnings and dividends for the companies for 19X8 are listed as follows:

	Burns Co.	Coogan Co.	Dailey, Inc.
Net income (net loss).............	$47,500	$36,000	($15,000)
Dividends paid...	50 cents per share on March 15 and the same amount at quarterly intervals thereafter.	7½ cents per share on February 5 and at quarterly intervals thereafter.	None

The foregoing information was properly recorded during the year, with investments carried by the cost method.

Instructions: Prepare a work sheet and a consolidated balance sheet. Assume that any excess of investment book value over cost is attributable to the value of nondepreciable assets. Any excess of cost over book value is regarded as goodwill to be amortized over a 10-year period.

12-6. Balance sheet data as of December 31, 19X7, for the Fuller Co. and its affiliates, Gulf Co. and Horn Co., are as follows:

Fuller Co.

Cash, receivables, and inventories....	$2,050,000	Trade creditors......	$ 640,000
Investments:		Long-term debt......	1,000,000
Gulf Co. (200,000 shares at cost)..	500,000	Preferred stock, $100 par............	350,000
Horn Co. (22,000 shares at cost)..	150,000	Common stock, $10 par..............	1,500,000
Plant and equipment...........	1,480,000	Additional paid-in capital..............	750,000
Other assets...........	15,000	Deficit	(45,000)
		Total liabilities and stockholders'	
Total assets............	$4,195,000	equity................	$4,195,000

Gulf Co.

Cash, receivables, and inventories....	$ 680,000	Dividends payable...	$ 37,500
Plant and equipment...........	350,000	Trade creditors.......	192,500
Other assets...........	20,000	Long-term debt.......	150,000
		Capital stock (no-par, 250,000 shares)...............	250,000
		Additional paid-in capital	100,000
		Retained earnings...	320,000
		Total liabilities and stockholders'	
Total assets............	$1,050,000	equity	$1,050,000

Horn Co.

Cash, receivables, and inventories....	$ 120,000	Trade creditors........	$ 70,000
Plant and equipment...........	80,000	Capital stock (no-par, 25,000 shares)...............	120,000
		Retained earnings...	10,000
		Total liabilities and stockholders'	
Total assets............	$ 200,000	equity.................	$ 200,000

Stock of Gulf Co. was acquired at the end of 19X1, when the retained earnings balance of this company was $65,000. Stock of Horn Company was acquired on June 1, 19X7. The book values of all identifiable assets of Gulf Co. and Horn Co. at the dates of acquisition reflected fair values. Horn Co. had reported a deficit on January 1, 19X7, of $17,000. The dividend declared by Gulf Co. has not yet been taken up on the books of the parent. Fuller Co. receivables include $15,000 from Gulf Co. and $450 from Horn Co. Corresponding payables are included by subsidiaries in the trade creditor totals.

Instructions: (1) Prepare a consolidated work sheet.
(2) Prove the subsidiary retained earnings balances accruing to the parent company.

12-7. On September 30, 19X4, the Valley Company acquired a controlling interest in Clark Company at a purchase price of $1,550,000. Balance sheets of the two companies on December 31, 19X5, follow:

	Valley Company	Clark Company
Cash, receivables, and inventories	$2,850,000	$1,420,000
Plant and equipment	2,650,000	1,050,000
Investment in Clark Company (165,000 shares)....................	1,418,000	
Other assets	297,000	145,000
Total assets	$7,215,000	$2,615,000
Accounts payable and accrued items...........	$1,365,000	$ 450,000
Bonds payable	1,000,000	500,000
Capital stock................ ($20 par)	2,500,000 ($5 par)	1,000,000
Additional paid-in capital	1,500,000	200,000
Retained earnings	850,000	465,000
Total liabilities and stockholders' equity ..	$7,215,000	$2,615,000

A consolidated balance sheet is to be prepared for the first time on December 31, 19X5, and for this purpose the following data are developed by analysis of the accounts of the two companies:

Clark Company had retained earnings of $175,000 on the date when Valley Company acquired control. Any excess of investment cost over book value was attributed to the value of the plant and equipment, which has a useful life of 10 years on that date.

Since the date of control by the Valley Company, Clark Company has paid dividends of $160,000; dividends received from the subsidiary have been recorded by the parent by credits to the investment account.

A remittance of $15,000 in payment of accounts payable to the Valley Company was made by Clark Company on December 31, 19X5, and is recorded on the latter company's books; the remittance was in transit on December 31 and hence is not included on the balance sheet of the Valley Company as of this date.

Instructions: (1) Prepare a consolidated work sheet.
(2) Prove the subsidiary retained earnings balance accruing to the parent.

12-8. The following are the balance sheets of P, Inc., and S, Inc., as of December 31, 19X7:

	P, Inc.	S, Inc.
Cash.	$ 432,576	$ 32,569
Accounts receivable	825,620	225,627
Inventories	1,628,429	625,375
Prepaid expenses	36,475	5,648
Total assets	$2,923,100	$889,219
Accounts payable	$ 325,647	$437,989
Income tax payable	250,000	15,000
Capital stock	300,000	50,000
Retained earnings	2,047,453	386,230
Total liabilities and stockholders' equity	$2,923,100	$889,219

As of December 31, 19X7, P, Inc., acquired from the stockholders all of the shares of stock of S, Inc., in exchange for $550,000 of P's 9%, 10-year debentures. The excess cost of acquisition (excess of the purchase price over the net assets of S) is to be amortized on P's books by charges to income over a ten-year period.

For the years 19X8 and 19X9, operations of S, Inc., resulted in *losses* of $52,376 and $15,226, respectively, and operations of P, Inc., resulted in *profits* of $387,465 and $420,009, respectively. P provided a reserve on its books by charges to income for the losses of its subsidiary. The profits shown for P are *before* provision for amortization of the excess cost of acquisition and for the losses of its subsidiary. Dividends of $150,000 were paid by P in each of the years 19X8 and 19X9.

The remaining assets and liabilities of P and S at December 31, 19X8 and 19X9, were as shown on page 366.

Instructions: From the information given, prepare a work sheet for use in preparing a consolidated balance sheet as of December 31, 19X9. Key and explain all entries made as adjustments or eliminations and prepare supporting schedules for major computations. (*Disregard any income tax effects of your entries.*)   (AICPA adapted)

	P, Inc.		S, Inc.	
	19X8	19X9	19X8	19X9
Assets				
Cash.............................	$ 426,879	$ 490,327	$ 30,194	$ 31,187
Accounts receivable.......	897,426	940,227	200,525	203,287
Inventories....................	1,826,162	1,952,173	600,476	535,711
Advances to S, Inc.	165,000	180,000		
Prepaid expenses...........	32,879	34,327	5,347	4,621
Liabilities				
Accounts payable	$ 357,428	$ 298,627	$287,688	$226,178
Income tax payable	406,000	443,500		
Advances from P, Inc.			165,000	180,000

12-9. Marsh Sales, Inc., and Kelly Realty Corp. are wholly owned subsidiaries of Dodge Co. The parent corporation manufactures electric refrigerators, electric ranges, and various other electric appliances. Refrigerators and ranges are sold only to Marsh Sales, Inc., which acts as a distributor. Other appliances are sold directly to outside distributors.

The parent and subsidiary sales corporation are tenants of property owned by Kelly Realty Corp.

The intercompany accounts on the books of each company as at December 31, 19X2, are as follows:

Dodge Co.

Investment in Marsh Sales, Inc. (at cost)..	$100,000.00	
Investment in Kelly Realty Corp. (at cost)..	175,000.00	
Due from Marsh Sales, Inc.	86,175.97	
Due to Kelly Realty Corp.		$ 1,475.00
Capital stock issued and outstanding, 100,000 shares, no-par		1,000,000.00
Retained earnings............................		410,169.50

Marsh Sales, Inc.

Due to Kelly Realty Corp.		$ 800.00
Due to Dodge Co..............................		33,910.00
Capital stock issued and outstanding, 1,000 shares, $100 par		100,000.00
Retained earnings............................		62,501.10

Kelly Realty Corp.

Due from Dodge Co.	$ 6,575.00	
Due to Marsh Sales, Inc.....................		$ 2,800.00
Capital stock issued and outstanding, 1,000 shares, no par		175,000.00
Retained earnings............................		34,109.50

An audit of the books of the three companies for the year ended December 31, 19X2, revealed the following:

(1) The books of the three companies indicate the following with respect to dividends:
  (a) The board of directors of Dodge Co., at a meeting on January 4, 19X3, declared a regular quarterly dividend of 50 cents per share, payable January 31, 19X3, to stockholders of record on January 23, 19X3.
  (b) The board of directors of Marsh Sales, Inc., at a meeting on December 28, 19X2, declared a 1% dividend, payable in cash on January 15, 19X3, to stockholders of record on December 31, 19X2.
  (c) The board of directors of Kelly Realty Corp., at a meeting on December 1, 19X2, declared a dividend of $1 per share, payable January 2, 19X3, to stockholders of record on December 15, 19X2.

No effect has been given to these dividend declarations on the books of the parent company as of December 31, 19X2. The subsidiary companies recorded the dividend declarations pertaining to their respective companies at the date of declaration.

(2) Marsh Sales, Inc., received from one of its customers a check for $4,200, covering its own invoices aggregating $2,400 and invoices of Dodge Co. aggregating $1,800. The sales corporation recorded this transaction as follows:

Cash...	4,200	
Accounts Receivable....................................		4,200

(3) Marsh Sales, Inc., advanced $5,000 in cash to Kelly Realty Corp. and made the following entry:

Dodge Co.	5,000	
Cash...		5,000

(4) On September 15, 19X2, Dodge Co. shipped 100 appliances of a new design on consignment at $20 each to Marsh Sales, Inc. Marsh Sales, Inc., made no entry upon receipt of the goods. During October, 19X2, Marsh Sales, Inc., sold all of the appliances at $25 each, crediting sales for the total thereof. Dodge Co. made no entries on its books, but included the 100 appliances in its inventory at December 31, 19X2, at its cost of $14 each.

(5) The parent corporation filed a consolidated federal income tax return for the year ended December 31, 19X1. The results of operations for the respective companies that year, before consolidation, were as follows:

Dodge Co.	($13,280)
Marsh Sales, Inc.	42,260
Kelly Realty Corp.	21,130

The federal income tax, amounting to $21,000, was paid by the parent corporation, which recorded the transaction as follows:

Income Tax Payable	21,000	
Cash...		21,000

An agreement in the files indicates that federal income taxes should be apportioned among the companies based upon the unconsolidated net profit. A company having a loss year is to pay no tax nor charge the other companies for the benefit derived from the use of its loss in the return.

The proper liability of each company was recorded as at December 31, 19X1.

(6) Kelly Realty Corp. sold certain of its furniture to Marsh Sales, Inc., at current market value, which was 75% of net book value. The realty corporation had purchased the furniture for $3,500 exactly 2 years prior to the date of sale and had taken depreciation at the rate of 10% per annum. It billed Marsh Sales, Inc., for $2,800 and recorded the transaction as follows:

Marsh Sales, Inc.	2,800	
Furniture and Fixtures		2,800

Marsh Sales, Inc., recorded the purchase as follows:

Furniture and Fixtures	2,800	
Kelly Realty Corp.		2,800

(7) As of December 31, 19X2, the books of the parent corporation and the sales subsidiary do not reflect rent for December, 19X2, due to Kelly Realty Corp. in the amounts of $6,100 and $1,400, respectively.

(8) Marsh Sales, Inc., had not recorded December, 19X2, purchase invoices submitted by the parent corporation in the amount of $48,265.97.

Instructions: (1) Prepare an itemized reconciliation of the intercompany accounts.

(2) Prepare the adjusting journal entries necessary to correct each set of books at the end of 19X2.

(AICPA adapted)

13
Consolidated Statements — Intercompany Profits; Senior Securities

The acquisition of merchandise or other assets from affiliated companies gives rise to special problems. Transactions that are properly recorded by separate companies may not be proper when the companies are viewed as a single economic unit. The existence of senior securities — bonds and preferred stocks — also causes special problems, particularly when one company in the consolidated unit acquires such securities issued by another. The factors that must be considered in each of these instances are explained and illustrated in this chapter.

INTERCOMPANY PROFITS

The sale of merchandise as well as of other properties often takes place between affiliated companies. An intercompany sale normally involves a profit to the company making the sale. This profit is properly recognized on the separate financial statements of the selling company. However, such a profit can be recognized for consolidated statement purposes only if the goods or other properties have been resold outside of the affiliated group. If the asset is still held by an affiliate, the sale must be viewed as no more than a transfer between affiliates; any intercompany profit, together with the related increase in asset cost emerging from such a transfer, must be canceled.

Intercompany Profits on Inventories

When merchandise is acquired from a related company and such goods are sold to outsiders, profit is fully realized by the company originally selling the goods as well as by the company making the sale to outsiders. These transactions need not be considered in preparing a consolidated balance sheet. For example, assume that Company P sells goods costing $6,000 to Company S, an 80% owned subsidiary, for $7,500; Company P recognizes a profit on its books of $1,500. Company S, in turn, sells the goods to outsiders for $10,000 and recognizes a profit on its books of $2,500. The effect of these transactions on a consolidated balance sheet is that assets have increased by $4,000 and this increase is balanced by the assignment of retained earnings of $4,000 between the minority interest and the controlling interest: 20% of the retained earnings of $2,500 shown by Company S, or $500, is reported as retained earnings of the minority interest; 80% of the retained earnings of $2,500 of Company S, or $2,000, together with the retained earnings of $1,500 shown by Company P, or a total of $3,500, is reported as retained earnings of the controlling interest. The income of $4,000 is fully realized and its ultimate distribution in the form of dividends to stockholders representing the minority interest and the controlling interest will be made as reported on the consolidated balance sheet.

However, assume that goods that were sold to an affiliated company have not been resold and are included in the inventory of the affiliate on the date that the consolidated balance sheet is being prepared. When a subsidiary is wholly owned and when the sale is made by a parent to a subsidiary or by a subsidiary to a parent, the elimination of the full amount of the profit that was recognized on the sale is necessary. Such a transaction must be regarded for consolidated statement purposes as no different than a transfer of goods between a home office and a branch, with neither profit nor an increase in the original cost of the goods arising from the transfer.

When the sale is made by a parent to a subsidiary that is not wholly owned, elimination of the full amount of the profit would still be in order. The controlling interest can hardly maintain that it has realized a profit on a transaction that constitutes no more than an intercompany transfer of goods. However, conflicting views are held with respect to the amount of the profit that is to be eliminated when the sale is made by a subsidiary to a parent. Some accountants maintain that since a minority interest is entitled to a portion of the profit reported by the subsidiary, regardless of whether the buyer is an affiliated company or an outsider, recognition on the consolidated balance sheet of the minority interest's share in such profit and a corresponding increase in the original cost of goods is warranted. Eliminations, then, should be limited to that portion of the profit that accrues to the parent. Others insist that no profit should be assigned either to a minority interest or to a controlling interest as long as goods are held by companies within the affiliated group.

To resolve this controversy, it would be useful to consider the rationale for reporting cost in financial statements, and for recognizing profits at the point of sale to an outside interest. It may be argued that historical cost does not provide the most relevant information concerning the current values of assets held by a company. The reason for favoring cost, however, is that it can be determined objectively and is subject to verification.

When two independent parties agree to a price in an arm's-length transaction, the values involved can be said to have been validated by the negotiation process. However, when one of the companies is controlled by the other, the independence necessary to validate the transaction is lacking. Thus in a consolidation situation in which it is assumed that the parent company controls the subsidiary, it would be improper to recognize *any* value change on the basis of transactions between companies. Note that the argument is based on validation rather than attribution. Thus it is not appropriate to consider who benefits from a transaction — the parent company or minority interests — as long as independent validation to be an accounting transaction is required.

In *Accounting Research Bulletin No. 51*, the Committee on Accounting Procedure of the American Institute of Certified Public Accountants made the following observations:

> As consolidated statements are based on the assumption that they represent the financial position and operating results of a single business enterprise, such statements should not include gain or loss on transactions among the companies in the group. Accordingly, any intercompany profit or loss on assets remaining within the group should be eliminated; the concept usually applied for this purpose is gross profit or loss.[1]

> The amount of intercompany profit or loss to be eliminated . . . is not affected by the existence of a minority interest. The complete elimination of the intercompany profit or loss is consistent with the underlying assumption that consolidated statements represent the financial position and operating results of a single business enterprise. The elimination of the intercompany profit or loss may be allocated proportionately between the majority and minority interests.[2]

Sale by parent to wholly owned subsidiary. To illustrate the elimination of intercompany profit in inventories, assume that Company P sells merchandise to its 100% owned subsidiary, Company S. At the date of the consolidated balance sheet, the subsidiary has merchandise that it acquired from the parent at a price of $10,000. The cost of the goods to the parent was $6,000.

In the preparation of separate financial statements, the parent company properly recognizes a profit of $4,000 on the merchandise transfer, and the subsidiary company properly shows the goods as part of its inventory at a cost of $10,000. In preparing a consolidated balance sheet, the intercompany profit is canceled and the merchandise inventory of the subsidiary is reduced to its original cost. The following elimination is made on the work sheet, assuming that the parent company has not recognized the intercompany profit on its own books:

---

[1]*Accounting Research Bulletin, No. 51*, "Consolidated Financial Statements" (New York: American Institute of Certified Public Accountants, 1959), par. 6.

[2]*Ibid.*, par. 14.

	Co. P	Co. S	Eliminations		Consolidated Balance Sheet	
			Dr.	Cr.	Dr.	Cr.
Debits						
Merchandise Inventory.............................		10,000		4,000	6,000	
Credits						
Retained Earnings, Co. P..........................			4,000			

It would be possible to reduce the inventory balance by means of a valuation account. Instead of crediting Merchandise Inventory on the work sheet, a credit would be made to an allowance for intercompany profits on inventories account. Reporting the inventory balance less the valuation account on the consolidated balance sheet discloses the reduction for intercompany profits that has been applied to the inventory.

The equity method of accounting requires the parent company to adjust its income to eliminate the effects of intercompany profits. Note that the equity method is meant to provide the same operating results and retained earnings balance as if a consolidated statement had been prepared. APB Opinion No. 18 states: "Intercompany profits and losses should be eliminated until realized by the investor or investee as if a subsidiary, corporate joint venture, or investee company were consolidated."[3]

To achieve this result, the parent company could make the following entry:

Equity in Income of Co. S... 4,000
    Investment in Co. S.. 4,000

When this entry has been properly recorded by Company P, it is not appropriate to reduce the retained earnings balance on the consolidated work sheet. However, it is still necessary to reduce the inventory balance to reflect the cost to the consolidated entity. This reduction is accomplished by crediting Merchandise Inventory for $4,000 as part of the work sheet entry in which the adjusted balance of Investment in Co. S is eliminated. As an alternative work sheet technique, the investment account may be debited to restore it to the balance it would have had prior to the adjustment for intercompany profits, and then the investment elimination entries may be made in the usual fashion.

The intercompany profit is fully realized in the following period when the subsidiary sells the merchandise to outsiders. At the end of the period, inventories are analyzed again and any intercompany profits included in the inventories at that time are eliminated on the work sheet.

---

[3]*Opinions of the Accounting Principles Board, No. 18*, "The Equity Method of Accounting for Investments in Common Stock" (New York: American Institute of Certified Public Accountants, 1971), par. 19a.

Sale by parent to partially owned subsidiary. Assume the same facts as in the preceding example but that Company P owns only 80% of Company S stock. The parent company reports a profit of $4,000 on the merchandise transfer and the goods are shown on the subsidiary's books at $10,000. However, with neither a profit nor an increase in the original cost of the inventory to be recognized on the consolidated balance sheet, the intercompany profit is canceled as in the preceding example. The parent's profit on the original transfer is fully realized in the following period when the subsidiary sells the goods to outsiders. The parent will also participate with the minority interest in any profit or loss on the ultimate sale.

Sale by wholly owned subsidiary to parent. Assume that Company S, a wholly owned subsidiary, sells merchandise to its parent, Company P. At the date of the consolidated balance sheet, the parent has merchandise of $10,000 that it acquired from the subsidiary; the cost of the goods to the subsidiary was $6,000. Since the parent owns 100% of the subsidiary, the entire profit of $4,000 reported on the books of the subsidiary accrues to the parent. In preparing the consolidated balance sheet, the full amount of the profit must be canceled and the inventory reduced to its original cost. If the equity method is employed in carrying the subsidiary investment, subsidiary earnings have been recognized by the parent and summarized in its retained earnings account and the charge to cancel the profit on the intercompany sale would be reflected in the investment account as well as in a reduction in the parent company retained earnings. If the cost method is employed, the subsidiary earnings have not yet been recognized by the parent and the charge may be made to subsidiary company retained earnings. In each case, the retained earnings of the controlling interest is $11,000 — the $15,000 earnings of the wholly owned subsidiary, less the $4,000 adjustment for intercompany profits. A work sheet may be developed as follows:

Assuming investments are carried by the equity method:

	Co. P	Co. S	Eliminations Dr.	Eliminations Cr.	Consolidated Balance Sheet Dr.	Consolidated Balance Sheet Cr.
Debits						
Merchandise Inventory........	10,000			(a) 4,000	6,000	
Investment in Co. S............	136,000		(a) 4,000	(b) 140,000		
Eliminate Investment.......						
Goodwill.........................			(b) 15,000		15,000	
Credits						
Capital Stock, Co. P............	200,000					200,000
Retained Earnings, Co. P.....	11,000					11,000
Capital Stock, Co. S............		100,000				
Eliminate 100%			(b) 100,000			
Retained Earnings, Co. S.....		25,000				
Eliminate 100%			(b) 25,000			

Assuming investments are carried by the cost method:

	Co. P	Co. S	Eliminations		Consolidated Balance Sheet	
			Dr.	Cr.	Dr.	Cr.
Debits						
Merchandise Inventory........	10,000			(a) 4,000	6,000	
Investment in Co. S............	125,000			(b) 125,000		
Eliminate Investment.......						
Goodwill			(b) 15,000		15,000	
Credits						
Capital Stock, Co. P............	200,000					200,000
Retained Earnings, Co. P.....				(c) 11,000		11,000
Capital Stock, Co. S............		100,000				
Eliminate 100%			(b) 100,000			
Retained Earnings, Co. S.....		25,000	(a) 4,000			
Eliminate 100% of $10,000 Retained Earnings at Acquisition........			(b) 10,000			
Retained Earnings to Parent.........................			(c) 11,000			

When the parent has purchased goods from the subsidiary, it may be argued that the inventory balance on the parent company's separate financial statements should be adjusted directly in applying the equity method. Unlike the previous case, in which goods were held by the subsidiary and the parent's equity in this inventory was included in the balance of the investment account, the parent company would show an inventory balance that included profits not validated by market transactions. Thus it would be consistent with the intent of the equity method to reduce the parent's inventory account rather than the investment account. This reduction would be recorded on Company P's books with the following entry:

Equity in Income of Co. S.. 4,000
    Merchandise Inventory 4,000

The subsequent elimination entries on the consolidated work sheet would not reflect a reduction in either the inventory or the retained earnings balance, since these adjustments would already have been made by the parent. Although the consolidated statement would not be affected by the parent company's choice of accounting treatment, the elimination entries would differ according to the procedures used on the books of the constituent companies. When the equity method is used, it will be assumed that the investment account is adjusted to eliminate intercompany profits.

Sale by partially owned subsidiary to parent. Assume that Company S is only 80% owned and that, on the date of the consolidated balance sheet, Company P has merchandise of $10,000 that it acquired from the subsidiary company. Cost of the goods to the subsidiary was $6,000. If the full amount of the intercompany profit is to be canceled and the inventory reported at its original cost, the charge might logically be made to the retained earnings of the company that reported the profit. With the parent's ownership of 80% of the subsidiary stock, only 80% of the earnings will be reported as retained earnings of the parent, while 20% will be reported as retained earnings of the minority interest. In canceling the intercompany profit, then, retained earnings of the parent should be reduced by $3,200 and retained earnings of the minority interest should be reduced by $800.

If the equity method is employed, the parent company would already have recognized its share of the elimination of intercompany profit. The charge to the minority interest can be made by debiting directly the retained earnings of the subsidiary company to reduce the balance to be extended to the consolidated balance sheet columns as minority interest. The charge can also be reported on a separate line on the work sheet. Such a charge would be carried to the consolidated balance sheet columns and ultimately subtracted from the unadjusted retained earnings of the minority interest that is extended to the consolidated balance sheet columns. If the cost method is employed, subsidiary earnings accruing to the parent are still to be recognized and the full charge for intercompany profits is made to the subsidiary retained earnings account. Amounts that are extended to the consolidated balance sheet columns as retained earnings of the minority interest and retained earnings of the parent will then be based upon the subsidiary retained earnings balance after adjustment for intercompany profits. A work sheet in each case may be developed as follows:

Assuming investments are carried by the equity method:

	Co. P	Co. S	Eliminations		Consolidated Balance Sheet	
			Dr.	Cr.	Dr.	Cr.
Debits						
Merchandise Inventory........	10,000			(a) 4,000	6,000	
Investment in Co. S	108,800		(a) 3,200	(b) 112,000		
Eliminate Investment.......						
Goodwill			(b) 12,000		12,000	
Credits						
Capital Stock, Co. P............	200,000					200,000
Retained Earnings, Co. P.....	8,800					8,800
Capital Stock, Co. S............		100,000				
Eliminate 80%			(b) 80,000			
Minority Interest, 20%.....						20,000
Retained Earnings, Co. S.....		25,000	(a) 800			
Eliminate 80% of $25,000			(b) 20,000			
Minority Interest, 20% of $25,000, less $800.......						4,200

Assuming investments are carried by the cost method:

	Co. P	Co. S	Eliminations		Consolidated Balance Sheet	
			Dr.	Cr.	Dr.	Cr.
Debits						
Merchandise Inventory........	10,000			(a) 4,000	6,000	
Investment in Co. S	100,000					
Eliminate Investment.......				(b) 100,000		
Goodwill			(b) 12,000		12,000	
Credits						
Capital Stock, Co. P............	200,000					200,000
Retained Earnings, Co. P.....				(c) 8,800		8,800
Capital Stock, Co. S............		100,000				
Eliminate 80% of Capital Stock..........................			(b) 80,000			
Minority Interest, 20%.....						20,000
Retained Earnings, Co. S.....		25,000	(a) 4,000			
Eliminate 80% of $10,000, Retained Earnings at Acquisition.			(b) 8,000			
Minority Interest, 20% of $21,000......................						4,200
Retained Earnings to Parent........................			(c) 8,800			

Net earnings of the subsidiary company for the year for consolidation purposes are $11,000, consisting of $15,000, the change in subsidiary retained earnings, less $4,000, the adjustment for intercompany profits. Parent company retained earnings in each case reflect 80% of the subsidiary company net earnings of $11,000, or $8,800.

Sale by one subsidiary to another subsidiary. Assume that Company S2, 80% owned by Company P, holds merchandise acquired for $10,000 from Company S1, 90% owned by Company P. The cost of the goods to Company S1 was $6,000. Since Company P owns 90% of the stock of Company S1, 90% of the profit of $4,000, or $3,600, would be identified with the parent; 10% of the profit, or $400, would be identified with the minority interest of Company S1. In the preparation of the consolidated balance sheet, the intercompany profit of $4,000 is eliminated.

If the equity method is used for the subsidiary investment, the elimination on the work sheet is as follows:

Investment in Co. S1... 3,600
Retained Earnings, Co. S1 (reducing minority interest)............. 400
    Merchandise Inventory 4,000

If the cost method is used for the subsidiary investment, the elimination would be:

```
Retained Earnings, Co. S1 (reducing controlling and minority
    interests).........................................................................    4,000
    Merchandise Inventory .....................................................                 4,000
```

More than one transfer within affiliated group. Calculation of the amount to be eliminated is somewhat more complicated when there has been more than one transfer within the affiliated group. For example, assume that Company P holds merchandise that was acquired at a price of $10,000 from Company S1, 90% owned by Company P. Company S1 acquired the goods at a price of $8,000 from Company S2, 80% owned by Company P. The cost of the goods to Company S2 was $6,000. In this case, the profit recognized by the parent on intercompany transfers is calculated as follows:

```
Profit recognized by parent on transfer of goods by Company S1 to
    Company P, 90% of $2,000............................................    $1,800
Profit recognized by parent on transfer of goods by Company S2 to
    Company S1, 80% of $2,000...........................................      1,600
Total profit recognized by Company P...............................      $3,400
```

If investments are carried by the equity method, the elimination on the consolidated work sheet for Company P and subsidiary companies S1 and S2 would be as follows:

```
Investment in Co. S1.............................................................    1,800
Investment in Co. S2.............................................................    1,600
Retained Earnings, Co. S1 (reducing minority interest).............     200
Retained Earnings, Co. S2 (reducing minority interest).............     400
    Merchandise Inventory .....................................................                 4,000
```

If investments are carried by the cost method, the elimination would be as follows:

```
Retained Earnings, Co. S1 (reducing controlling and minority
    interests).........................................................................    2,000
Retained Earnings, Co. S2 (reducing controlling and minority
    interests).........................................................................    2,000
    Merchandise Inventory .....................................................                 4,000
```

The merchandise is reported on the consolidated balance sheet at its original cost to the consolidated group, $6,000.

Alternative procedure for sales by partially owned subsidiaries. In the previous examples inventories acquired from related companies were decreased by the full amount of the intercompany profit, and the profit elimination was allocated between the controlling and minority interests. It was suggested earlier that although elimination of the entire amount of intercompany profit is justified on the grounds that there has been no validation of these profit amounts through arm's-length transactions, there are some accountants who object to reducing the minority interest for any of the profit elimination. If the minority interest on the balance sheet is viewed as a senior equity element, entitled to its claims before the controlling interest can participate in the residual equity, then it can be argued that the legal entitlement of these interests includes the profits properly recognized by the subsidiary company. *Accounting Research Bulletin No. 51*, while mandating the elimination of the entire amount of intercompany profit, states: "The elimination of the intercompany profit or loss *may* be allocated proportionately between the majority and minority interests."[4]

It would be consistent with this position to eliminate 100% of the intercompany profit, but debit the entire amount to the retained earnings of the controlling interest. For example, assume that inventory in the hands of the parent includes merchandise of $10,000 on which an 80%-owned subsidiary made a profit of $4,000. If the inventory were reduced to $6,000, it would reflect the cost to the consolidated entity. The parent company's retained earnings would be reduced by the entire $4,000, however, rather than $3,200 as in previous illustrations. Although this approach is technically in compliance with the current accounting rules, it results in a distortion of the economic results of the combined enterprise — results which consolidated statements are designed to show. In the example, the net effect of the purchase by the parent would be to increase its income and retained earnings by $3,200 (its proportionate share of the subsidiary profits) and then decrease its income and retained earnings by $4,000 as a result of the elimination. Thus the controlling interest is reduced by $800 as a result of the purchase transaction. The elimination of intercompany profit should give the same result as if the transaction had not taken place, but in this case it gives a worse result.

Some may object to the fact that the minority interest cannot determine their equity in the consolidated entity if the retained earnings attributed to them are reduced by intercompany profits to which they are legally entitled. Although the minority interest suffers no reduction for intercompany profits if the latter procedure is followed, the method that is chosen is of no importance to this group. The minority interest is concerned, not with the financial position and minority interest measurements reported on the consolidated statement, but with the financial data reported on the separate statements of the company in which they have an ownership interest.

For purposes of illustrations and problems in this and in succeeding chapters, it will be assumed that eliminations for intercompany profits are to be complete and are to be assigned to both the minority interest and the controlling interest.

Intercompany Profits on Depreciable Assets

The practices that are followed in eliminating intercompany profits on inventories are also applicable in eliminating intercompany profits on other assets. When a profit is recognized by an affiliated company on the sale of an asset that remains within the affiliated group, it is necessary in reporting the consolidated position to reduce the asset to cost and to reduce retained

---

[4]*Accounting Research Bulletin, No. 51, op. cit.*, par. 14 (emphasis added)

earnings by the amount of the intercompany profit. The elimination of intercompany profits when depreciable assets are involved presents special problems.

Depreciable asset constructed by parent for wholly owned subsidiary. Assume that Company P constructs certain equipment for Company S, 100% owned. Company S is charged $10,000; the cost to Company P is $6,000. If a consolidated balance sheet is prepared at the date of the asset acquisition, it is necessary to reduce the equipment to the actual cost of construction and to eliminate the intercompany profit on the transfer. If Company P maintained its investment accounts on a cost basis, the following elimination would be necessary on the work sheet:

	Co. P	Co. S	Eliminations		Consolidated Balance Sheet	
			Dr.	Cr.	Dr.	Cr.
Debits						
Equipment...		10,000		4,000[5]	6,000	
Credits						
Retained Earnings, Co. P............................				4,000		

If the equity method is used, Company P would recognize the elimination of intercompany profit on its own books by reducing its investment account, as follows:

Equity in Income of Co. S...	4,000	
Investment in Co. S...		4,000

The work sheet elimination would then be:

Investment in Co. S...	4,000	
Equipment...		4,000

On consolidated work sheets prepared in subsequent periods, the intercompany profit identified with the asset decreases in proportion to the decrease taking place in the asset as a result of the recorded depreciation. For example, if the equipment has a 5-year life, the asset would be reported at only $4/5$ of its original cost at the end of the first year, and the intercompany profit included in such cost is correspondingly only $4/5$ of the profit originally recognized. Instead of applying the reduction to the equipment account at this point, the reduction must be applied both to the asset balance and to the accumulated depreciation balance, since each of these accounts is overstated. The elimination would be made as follows:

[5] If it is considered desirable to report the reduction for intercompany profits on property items on the consolidated balance sheet, the credit would be made to a separate allowance for intercompany profits account as in the case of intercompany profits on inventories.

	Co. P	Co. S	Eliminations		Consolidated Balance Sheet	
			Dr.	Cr.	Dr.	Cr.
Debits						
Equipment		10,000		4,000	6,000	
Accumulated Depreciation of Equipment		(2,000)	800			1,200
Credits						
Retained Earnings, Co. P.............			3,200			

The asset is reduced by the intercompany profit, $4,000; the allowance is reduced by the depreciation on such intercompany profit, 20% of $4,000, or $800. Asset and accumulated depreciation balances are now reduced to a cost basis and equipment is reported on the consolidated balance sheet as follows:

Equipment	$6,000
Less accumulated depreciation of equipment.....................	1,200
Book value..	$4,800

The annual depreciation recognized by the subsidiary is 20% of $10,000, or $2,000. Depreciation in terms of actual cost, however, is 20% of $6,000, or $1,200. Since the parent company recognizes 100% of the subsidiary earnings, the parent company's retained earnings are adversely affected each year by the excessive charge of $800. Although the intercompany profit at the time of the asset sale was $4,000, the intercompany profit at the end of the first year has been reduced to $3,200. Reduction of the asset book value to cost cancels this balance. The net effect of the intercompany profit is thus entirely eliminated.

The eliminations for intercompany profit that are required on the work sheets over the life of the asset are as follows:

	Retained Earnings, Company P Dr.	Accumulated Depreciation of Equipment Dr.	Equipment Cr.
Date of transfer..............................	$4,000	—	$4,000
End of first year..............................	3,200	$ 800	4,000
End of second year	2,400	1,600	4,000
End of third year.............................	1,600	2,400	4,000
End of fourth year...........................	800	3,200	4,000
End of fifth year..............................	—	4,000	4,000

At the end of the fifth year, the cost of the equipment is completely written off. The profit of $4,000 recognized by the parent at the time of construction has been canceled entirely by excessive depreciation of $4,000 recorded by the subsidiary and recognized by the parent. No further eliminations are required.

Depreciable asset constructed by parent for partially owned subsidiary. If, in the previous example, the parent had owned only 80% of the stock of the subsidiary, eliminations each year would be the same as those given. For consolidated statement purposes, then, the asset is reported at its actual cost to the consolidated enterprise and the accumulated depreciation reflects the amortization of such cost. Here, too, the subsidiary records annual depreciation that is excessive in terms of cost by $800; however, since the parent recognizes only 80% of the earnings of the subsidiary, the parent company's retained earnings are adversely affected by only $640 each year. Since the elimination for intercompany profit decreases annually by $800, the parent company's retained earnings are left each year with a $160 credit excess. This amount is the periodic profit that accrues to the parent through charging the minority interest with depreciation on the asset at its sales price. At the end of 5 years, the cost of the asset will have been written off entirely. The parent company retained earnings will reflect an $800 net increase resulting from the original profit of $4,000 on the sale less the charges on this addition to cost carried back to the parent, 80% of $4,000, or $3,200. The increase in the parent interest was accompanied by a shrinkage in the minority interest as a result of the charges that were absorbed by the latter on the amount added to the asset cost, 20% of $4,000.

Depreciable asset constructed by wholly owned subsidiary for parent. Assume that Company P acquires certain equipment from Company S, 100% owned. Company P is charged $10,000; the cost to Company S is $6,000. The equipment has a 5-year life. Here, the subsidiary recognizes a profit of $4,000 on the transfer. Since the parent owns all of the stock of the subsidiary, the entire profit accrues to the parent and subsequent eliminations of intercompany profit must be assigned in full to the parent. In preparing a consolidated balance sheet at the date of asset acquisition, intercompany profit of $4,000 is eliminated. In subsequent periods, the amounts to be eliminated will be the same as those in the first example. The intercompany profit of $4,000 recognized by the parent on the original transfer is canceled annually through (1) the excess depreciation recorded by the subsidiary and subsequently recognized by the parent and (2) the charge that is made to the parent in reducing the asset to cost.

Depreciable asset constructed by partially owned subsidiary for parent. Assume the same facts as in the preceding example except that the subsidiary is only 80% owned. In this case, 80% of the profit of $4,000 will be recognized as retained earnings of the parent and 20% as retained earnings of the minority interest. In preparing a work sheet for a consolidated balance sheet on the date of asset acquisition, the equipment is reduced to cost and the intercompany profit is canceled by a reduction of $3,200 in the retained earnings of the parent and a reduction of $800 in the retained earnings of the minority interest.

Eliminations on work sheets in subsequent periods will also be applied against the asset balance and the related parent and minority interests.

However, as the asset balance goes down, the intercompany profit in the asset and in the parent and minority interests goes down correspondingly. Eliminations that are required on the work sheets over the life of the asset are as follows:

	Retained Earnings, Company P Dr.	Retained Earnings, Company S Minority Interest Dr.	Accumulated Depreciation of Equipment Dr.	Equipment Cr.
Date of transfer.........	$3,200	$800	—	$4,000
End of first year	2,560	640	$ 800	4,000
End of second year....	1,920	480	1,600	4,000
End of third year.......	1,280	320	2,400	4,000
End of fourth year.....	640	160	3,200	4,000
End of fifth year........	—	—	4,000	4,000

Although the minority interest is debited for $800 for consolidated statement purposes at the time of the asset transfer, the debits for each subsequent year are $160 ($1/5$ of $800) less and the minority interest shows a corresponding increase of $160. This amount is the periodic profit that accrues to the minority interest through charging the parent with depreciation on the asset at its sales price. At the end of the 5 years the full cost of the asset will be written off. The minority interest will reflect an $800 net increase, which represents the original profit of $4,000 on the sale, less the portion of the profit that was carried back to the parent, 80% of $4,000, or $3,200. On the other hand, the parent company's retained earnings is debited for $3,200 at the time of the asset transfer, but debits are $640 ($1/5$ of $3,200) less per year and the retained earnings of the parent are thus increased by $640 annually. The parent recognizes annual depreciation on the asset at 20% of $10,000, or $2,000. Depreciation in terms of actual asset cost, however, is 20% of $6,000, or $1,200. A debit of $800 for depreciation, counterbalanced only in part by an increase of $640 in retained earnings, results in an annual shrinkage of $160 in parent company retained earnings. This amount is the periodic cost to the controlling interest when the profit from a purchase made from a subsidiary is shared with a minority interest.

If the parent employs the cost method, the subsidiary retained earnings may be debited for the full amount of intercompany profits, and retained earnings identified with the minority interest and the parent interest may then be calculated in terms of this adjusted balance. As in the case of eliminations for intercompany profits on inventories, if the parent employs the equity method in carrying subsidiary investments, intercompany profits are eliminated by the parent in calculating its own income. Therefore, no reduction in the parent's retained earnings is necessary in preparing the consolidated statement. In the work sheet, the investment account should be debited for the parent's share of the profit elimination and the minority interest should be debited directly for its proportionate share.

Other transfers. When a depreciable asset is acquired by a subsidiary company from another subsidiary or when such an asset is acquired after a series of transfers within the affiliated group, careful analysis is required in arriving at the intercompany profit to be eliminated. The analyses involved are similar to those described for inventory eliminations.

Income Taxes on Intercompany Profits

The Internal Revenue Code defines "affiliated corporations" and prescribes the special conditions under which such a group can elect to file a consolidated income tax return. In filing a consolidated return, intercompany profits arising from the sale of merchandise, plant and equipment items, or other assets are eliminated. When affiliated companies do not choose to file a consolidated return or when they are not eligible for such filing, each company is required to file a separate return. In separate filings, individual companies are required to include profits arising from sales to affiliated units.

When income taxes are paid on profits on intercompany sales of assets, and assets are still in the hands of an affiliate at the time of consolidation, the taxes should be deferred or they should be recognized as increasing the cost of the assets for consolidation purposes. Eliminations against parent and minority interests, then, should be limited to the intercompany profits after income taxes.[6] For purposes of illustrations and problems, eliminations are made without regard to the income tax adjustments that would be appropriate under the circumstances described.

Acquisition of Property Prior to Date of Effective Control

When inventories or other properties are acquired from an affiliated company prior to the date of affiliation, such assets are properly shown on the consolidated balance sheet at the prices at which they were transferred. No eliminations for intercompany profits are required in such instances, since the companies were not affiliated at the time the sales were completed.

INTERCOMPANY BOND HOLDINGS

A company's acquisition of bonds of an affiliated unit gives rise to an intercompany debtor-creditor relationship similar to those already described. However, certain features of this relationship and the problems that result from such features require consideration.

Intercompany bond holdings should be eliminated. The investment in bonds may be offset against bonds payable, and only the bonds held by outsiders would be reported on the consolidated balance sheet. However, since bonds held within the affiliated group can be pledged or issued to

---

[6]*Accounting Research Bulletin, No. 51, op. cit.*, par. 17.

outsiders and thus represent a ready source of cash, it may be preferable to report holdings separately as a deduction from the full amount of bonds issued in the same manner as treasury bonds. When the latter procedure is followed, both bond investment and liability balances are extended to the consolidated balance sheet columns of the work sheet. Bonds held can then be reported on the consolidated balance sheet as follows:

Bonds payable..	$200,000	
Less bonds held by affiliated company.......................	50,000	
Bonds outstanding..		$150,000

Bonds may be issued at a premium or a discount. Bonds of an affiliated company may be acquired in the market at a price that differs from the amount at which they are carried by the issuing company. In viewing the parent and subsidiary as one company, both the intercompany bonds and any premium or discount balance related to such holdings lose their significance and must be eliminated. The amount paid for bonds is viewed as the cost of bond retirement, and any difference between the investment cost and the carrying value of the obligation is recognized as a loss or a gain from bond retirement. Furthermore, such a loss or a gain is attributed to the issuing company and thus must be identified as a parent company item or as a subsidiary company item so that it may be properly assigned to controlling and minority interests.

The examples that follow illustrate the nature of the analysis that is required. To simplify the illustrations, a discount or a premium is amortized on a straight-line basis, although a compound interest procedure is preferable.

Subsidiary Acquisition of Parent Company Bonds

Assume that Company P issued 10-year bonds of $100,000 at 90. Two years after the issue, bonds of $10,000 are acquired on the market by Company S for $9,400. In preparing a work sheet for a consolidated balance sheet, the elimination for intercompany bonds can be made as follows:

	Co. P	Co. S	Eliminations		Consolidated Balance Sheet	
			Dr.	Cr.	Dr.	Cr.
Debits						
Investment in Co. P Bonds (face value, $10,000).........................		9,400		9,400		
Credits						
Bonds Payable.............................	100,000		10,000			90,000
Discount on Bonds Payable	(8,000)			800	7,200	
Retained Earnings, Co. P.............			200		200	

The liability balance appears on the books of Company P. Regardless of who acquires the bonds, the reacquisition must be viewed as the retirement of Company P bonds, with any gain or loss accruing to the latter company. The elimination on the work sheet gives effect to such an analysis. The entire loss is identified with the parent company; no gain or loss can be related to the subsidiary company that has simply made an investment. If the parent company were to authorize the acquisition of the bonds from the subsidiary at $9,400 and the bonds were retired, the $200 loss would actually be recorded on the books of the parent company and no further reference to such intercompany holdings would be required.

In applying the equity method, the parent company would recognize the loss on its own books, and the work sheet eliminations would not include a debit to Company P's retained earnings for the amount of the loss. Instead, the investment account would be debited for $200, because that account would have been credited at the time Company P recognized its intercompany loss.

If intercompany bond holdings are reported as treasury bonds, only reciprocal discount balances are eliminated. The entire discount is canceled in the bond investment balance and the investment is raised to par by a debit to the bond account; $1/10$ of the discount on bonds payable is canceled, since $1/10$ of the issue is held within the affiliated group. The bond investment balance at par can then be subtracted from bonds payable at par when the consolidated balance sheet is prepared. The balance of the discount on bonds payable represents the discount on bonds held by outsiders. The work sheet will appear as follows:

	Co. P	Co. S	Eliminations		Consolidated Balance Sheet	
			Dr.	Cr.	Dr.	Cr.
Debits						
Investment in Co. P Bonds (face value, $10,000)......................		9,400	600		10,000	
Credits						
Bonds Payable............................	100,000					100,000
Discount on Bonds Payable..........	(8,000)			800	7,200	
Retained Earnings, Co. P.............			200		200	

The original discount of $10,000 is amortized over a 10-year period, and the discount of $600 on the acquisition is accumulated over an 8-year holding period. Therefore, one year after the acquisition of the bonds by the subsidiary, amortization of the discount on the books of Company P has reduced the discount balance by $1,000, and accumulation of the discount on the books of Company S has raised the investment balance by $75.

Assuming that intercompany bond holdings are to be eliminated, a work sheet for a consolidated balance sheet would be prepared as follows:

	Co. P	Co. S	Eliminations		Consolidated Balance Sheet	
			Dr.	Cr.	Dr.	Cr.
Debits						
Investment in Co. P Bonds (face value, $10,000).........................		9,475		9,475		
Credits						
Bonds Payable............................	100,000		10,000			90,000
Discount on Bonds Payable	(7,000)			700	6,300	
Retained Earnings, Co. P.............			175		175	

Interest transactions were recorded on the books of the two companies during the year in terms of a debtor-creditor relationship. In developing the consolidated statements, however, amounts applying to intercompany bond holdings are canceled to give effect to the single company view.

Parent Acquisition of Subsidiary Company Bonds

Assume that Company S issues 10-year bonds of $100,000 at 90. Two years after the issue, the parent acquires bonds of $10,000 at $9,400. Again, for consolidation purposes the acquisition of the bonds is considered analagous to a company's retirement of its own bonds. Here, too, the price of such a retirement differs from the carrying value of the bonds and a loss must be recognized. In this case, however, it is bonds of the subsidiary that are retired at a loss; the loss, then, is related to the subsidiary company and not to the parent. If the subsidiary is wholly owned, the full amount of the loss must be assigned to the parent company. If the subsidiary is only partly owned, the loss must be assigned in part to the minority interest and in part to the parent. Assuming that the parent owns 80% of the stock of the subsidiary, acquired ten years ago, and that intercompany bond holdings are to be treated as a retirement of bonds, a work sheet for a consolidated balance sheet may be prepared as shown on page 387.

The loss of $200 by Company S is identified with the equities that must absorb this loss: 80% of $200, or $160, is assigned to the parent company, and 20% of $200, or $40, is assigned to the minority interest. If the parent were to authorize the transfer of the bonds to the subsidiary for $9,400 and their retirement, the $200 loss would actually be recorded in the subsidiary's books and no further reference to such intercompany holdings would be required.

The same result is obtained whether Company P uses the cost method or the equity method in recording its investment. When the equity method

Assuming investments are carried by the cost method:

	Co. P	Co. S	Eliminations Dr.	Eliminations Cr.	Consolidated Balance Sheet Dr.	Consolidated Balance Sheet Cr.
Debits						
Investment in Co. S Bonds (face value, $10,000).......	9,400			(b) 9,400		
Investment in Co. S	100,000					
Eliminate Investment.......				(a) 100,000		
Goodwill			(a) 12,000	(d) 3,000	9,000	
Credits						
Bonds Payable....................		100,000	(b) 10,000			90,000
Discount on Bonds Payable .		(8,000)		(b) 800	7,200	
Capital Stock, Co. P............	200,000					200,000
Retained Earnings, Co. P.....			(d) 3,000	(c) 11,840		8,840
Capital Stock, Co. S............		100,000				
Eliminate 80%			(a) 80,000			
Minority Interest, 20%.....						20,000
Retained Earnings, Co. S.....		25,000	(b) 200			
Eliminate 80% of $10,000 Retained Earnings at Acquisition...................			(a) 8,000			
Minority Interest, 20% of $24,800......................						4,960
Retained Earnings to Parent.........................			(c) 11,840			
			125,040	125,040		

Assuming investments are carried by the equity method:

	Co. P	Co. S	Eliminations Dr.	Eliminations Cr.	Consolidated Balance Sheet Dr.	Consolidated Balance Sheet Cr.
Debits						
Investment in Co. S Bonds (face value, $10,000).......	9,400			(a) 9,400		
Investment in Co. S	109,140		(a) 160	(b) 109,300		
Eliminate Investment.......				(c) 300		
Goodwill			(b) 9,300		9,000	
Credits						
Bonds Payable....................		100,000	(a) 10,000			90,000
Discount on Bonds Payable .		(8,000)		(a) 800	7,200	
Capital Stock, Co. P............	200,000					200,000
Retained Earnings, Co. P.....	9,140		(c) 300			8,840
Capital Stock, Co. S............		100,000				
Eliminate 80%			(b) 80,000			
Minority Interest, 20%.....						20,000
Retained Earnings, Co. S.....		25,000	(a) 40			
Eliminate 80% of $25,000			(b) 20,000			
Minority Interest, 20% of $25,000, less $40						4,960
			119,800	119,800		

is used, the parent's share of the subsidiary's retained earnings since acquisition is already included in the parent's retained earnings, so no adjustment is made to that account. The investment account on the work sheet is debited for the parent's share of the intercompany loss, and the minority interest is debited for its share, so that the elimination entries are balanced.

If the bonds are held until maturity, through amortization procedures the bonds will be shown at face value on the parent's books, and the discount will be eliminated on the subsidiary's books. The reciprocal balances will be equal at that time, and no adjustment on the work sheet will be necessary to reflect the loss on bond retirement. However, the combined incomes of the two companies over the period in which the bonds were held will reflect the $200 loss. Company P will have recognized $600 of interest revenue in addition to the cash received, and Company S will have recognized $800 of interest expense in addition to the cash payments.

When a subsidiary is wholly owned, the effect on retained earnings is the same throughout the life of the bonds. When the parent acquires bonds of a partially owned subsidiary, however, there will be some shifting of the incidence of the gain or loss between controlling and minority interests. In the case illustrated, for example, the $200 loss was initially attributed to the issuing company, Company S, and thus divided between controlling and minority interests on a proportionate basis. The parent's retained earnings was reduced by 80% of $200, or $160, at the time the bonds were acquired. Over the remaining life of the bonds, Company P will recognize $600 of interest income as a result of bond discount amortization. It will also recognize its 80% share of the $800 interest expense that results from the discount amortization recorded by Company S. Consequently, Company P's retained earnings will be reduced by $40 ($640 − $600). On the other hand, the minority interest will be reduced by 20% of the $800 amortization, or $160.

SUBSIDIARIES WITH PREFERRED AND COMMON STOCK

When control is acquired in a subsidiary that has issued both preferred and common stock, it is necessary to apportion the capital of the subsidiary between the two classes of stock. The apportionment is required on the date control is acquired and regularly thereafter when consolidated statements are prepared. Changes in the equities identified with the particular holdings of the parent can then be recognized in the development of the consolidated statements.

The procedures that are followed in assigning capital to preferred and common stock are the same as those followed in calculating book values for preferred and common stock. The rights and the priorities of each issue must be carefully analyzed. The portion of the capital that is related to the preferred stock is first calculated. This amount is subtracted from the total capital in arriving at the capital related to the common stock.

Preferred stock usually has a liquidating value equal to par, par plus a premium, or a stated dollar amount. Capital equal to this value is identified with the preferred equity. When the preferred shareholders have additional priorities upon the distribution of corporate capital, appropriate additional amounts should be recognized as a part of the preferred stockholders' equity. With regard to these priorities, preferred stock may be classified as follows:

(1) *Noncumulative, nonparticipating preferred stock.* When preferred stock is noncumulative and nonparticipating, the preferred equity is limited to the preferred stock balance; remaining capital balances are identified with the common stock. A deficit would be entirely identified with the common stock.

(2) *Cumulative, nonparticipating preferred stock.* When preferred stock is cumulative and nonparticipating and when dividends on the preferred have been paid to date, the preferred equity is limited to the preferred stock balance. When there are dividends in arrears on preferred stock, an amount equal to the preferred stock balance and the dividends in arrears is assigned to the preferred; the balance of capital is assigned to common. In the event of a deficit and dividends in arrears, the amount of dividends in arrears would still be included in the preferred equity; the residual common equity would thus be impaired by the deficit as well as the dividends in arrears.

(3) *Noncumulative, participating preferred stock.* When preferred stock is noncumulative but participates with common stock in dividends in excess of a stipulated rate, a retained earnings balance should be assigned to the preferred and common stocks in accordance with the specific participation features of the preferred. A deficit would be identified with the common stock.

(4) *Cumulative, participating preferred stock.* When preferred stock is both cumulative and participating, a retained earnings balance is again assigned to the preferred stock and the common stock in accordance with the participation features of the preferred. If there are dividends in arrears on preferred stock, however, an amount equal to the dividends in arrears is first assigned to the preferred stock. In the event of a deficit and dividends in arrears on preferred stock, the amount of dividends in arrears would still be included in the preferred equity; the common equity would thus be reduced by both the deficit and the dividends in arrears.

To illustrate the capital apportionment procedures when a subsidiary has issued both preferred and common stock, assume that on December 31, 19X4, the capital of the subsidiary is as follows:

6% preferred stock, 2,000 shares, $50 par	$100,000
Common stock, 20,000 shares, $10 par	200,000
Retained earnings	30,000

Assume that the preferred stock, upon liquidation, has a value equal to its par value and, when cumulative, is entitled to the payment of dividends in arrears. For each of the possible classifications of preferred stock, the capital of the subsidiary would be apportioned as follows:

	Total Capital	Preferred Stock Equity	Common Stock Equity
(1) Preferred — noncumulative, nonparticipating	$330,000	$100,000	$230,000
(2) Preferred — cumulative, nonparticipating, dividends in arrears $12,000 (including 19X4)........................	330,000	112,000	218,000
(3) Preferred — noncumulative, fully participating...........	330,000	110,000	220,000
(4) Preferred — cumulative, fully participating, dividends in arrears $12,000 (including 19X4)........................	330,000	114,000	216,000

In (4), the retained earnings balance was allocated to preferred and common equities as though it were to be distributed currently, as follows:

	To Preferred	To Common
Prior year's dividend requirement, 6%..................	$ 6,000	
Current year's dividend requirement, 6%..............	6,000	
Preferred rate to common for current year, 6%		$12,000
Balance ratably to preferred and common	2,000	4,000
	$14,000	$16,000

If the capital of the subsidiary in this example were composed of preferred and common stock as indicated and a *deficit* of $30,000, the capital would be apportioned as follows:

	Total Capital	Preferred Stock Equity	Common Stock Equity
(1) Preferred — noncumulative, nonparticipating	$270,000	$100,000	$170,000
(2) Preferred — cumulative, nonparticipating, dividends in arrears $12,000 (including 19X4)........................	270,000	112,000	158,000
(3) Preferred — noncumulative, fully participating...........	270,000	100,000	170,000
(4) Preferred — cumulative, fully participating, dividends in arrears $12,000 (including 19X4)........................	270,000	112,000	158,000

To illustrate the procedure that may be employed in the preparation of a work sheet for a consolidated balance sheet when a subsidiary company has two or more classes of stock, assume that on January 1, 19X9, the capital of Company S consists of the following:

6% preferred stock, cumulative and nonparticipating, $100 par (dividends in arrears for 19X7 and 19X8)....................................	$100,000
Common stock, $100 par...	200,000
Retained earnings	30,000

Company S was legally able to pay dividends on preferred stock in 19X7 and 19X8. However, in view of the working capital requirements of the company, dividends on preferred stock were passed.

On January 1, 19X9, Company P acquires 400 shares of preferred stock at 115 and 1,800 shares of common stock at 125. Preferred and common equities are calculated on the date of acquisition in preparing a consolidated balance sheet. The retained earnings balance is apportioned as follows:

Retained earnings, January 1, 19X9..	$30,000
Retained earnings identified with preferred — amount required to meet dividends in arrears for 19X7 and 19X8	12,000
Retained earnings identified with common — balance	$18,000

The work sheet on January 1, 19X9, is prepared as follows:

	Co. P	Co. S	Eliminations Dr.	Eliminations Cr.	Consolidated Balance Sheet Dr.	Consolidated Balance Sheet Cr.
Debits						
Investment in Co. S Preferred Stock	46,000					
Eliminate Investment in Preferred Stock............				(a) 46,000		
Excess of Cost over Book Value			(a) 1,200		1,200	
Investment in Co. S Common Stock.......................	225,000					
Eliminate Investment in Common Stock.............				(b) 225,000		
Goodwill			(b) 28,800		28,800	
Credits						
Preferred Stock, Co. S		100,000				
Eliminate 40%................			(a) 40,000			
Minority Interest, 60%.....						60,000
Common Stock, Co. S		200,000				
Eliminate 90%................			(b) 180,000			
Minority Interest, 10%.....						20,000
Retained Earnings Identified with Co. S Preferred ..		12,000				
Eliminate 40%................			(a) 4,800			
Minority Interest, 60%.....						7,200
Retained Earnings Identified with Co. S Common ...		18,000				
Eliminate 90%................			(b) 16,200			
Minority Interest, 10%.....						1,800

The treatment of the "Excess of Cost over Book Value" attributable to the preferred stock investment requires some analysis. Unlike the acquisition of common stock, which may confer voting control and a residual equity in identifiable assets, preferred stock normally carries only the right to receive fixed payments if dividends are declared by the board of directors. As a result, it is difficult to ascribe a difference in the price paid for preferred stock either to the presence of undervalued or unrecorded assets or to the anticipated benefits of achieving centralized control. Consequently, any difference between cost and book value may be explained as it relates to changes in market levels of fixed income returns; i.e., as the level of fixed income rates expected in the market drops, the value of fixed income securities increases.

If the preferred stock carries voting rights or is entitled to participate in future earnings growth, it may be possible to identify the excess as a payment for some asset value, including goodwill. In most cases, however, it would be appropriate to treat the acquisition of preferred stock by one company in the consolidated group as the acquisition of treasury stock by the company that issued the securities.

The acquisition of a company's own stock, whether common or preferred, does not result in the recognition of gain or loss nor in the creation of any asset values. The debit that arises from acquiring the stock at more than its book value is normally charged against additional paid-in capital or retained earnings. A credit excess from acquiring stock at less than its book value would be added to additional paid-in capital. The excess of cost over book value account may be used for work sheet purposes, but the proper disposition of this item should be determined before a consolidated balance sheet is prepared.

To continue the illustration, assume that the subsidiary company reports a loss of $20,000 for 19X9 and once more passes the dividends on preferred stock. The change in the common and preferred stockholders' equities for 19X9 must be calculated before a consolidated balance sheet can be prepared at the end of the year. The retained earnings allocation to preferred and common stock on December 31, 19X9, is made as follows:

Retained earnings, December 31, 19X9...	$10,000
Retained earnings identified with preferred — amount required to meet dividends in arrears, 19X7–19X8 inclusive.............................	18,000
Deficit identified with common — balance...	($ 8,000)

The preferred stockholders' equity in the subsidiary capital is considered to have increased by $6,000 in view of the increase in dividends in arrears on preferred stock from $12,000 to $18,000. The common stockholders' equity has decreased by the loss, $20,000, and also by the amount of the dividend requirement on preferred stock for the current year, $6,000, or a total of $26,000. A corporate reorganization at some future date might conceivably result in a settlement with preferred stockholders whereby this group agrees to accept less than its full equity as calculated. However, assuming profitable operations in the future and the ability of the company to pay off preferred dividend arrearages, earnings of $26,000 will be required to restore the common stockholder group to the status that it occupied at the beginning of the year.

Since Company P controls Company S through ownership of the latter company's common stock, it may carry the investment in preferred in the same manner that it carries the investment in common. If the equity method is used in carrying investments in subsidiaries, entries are made by the parent as follows:

Investment in Co. S Preferred Stock...................................	2,400	
Equity in Income of Co. S...		2,400

To record increase in preferred stock equity in subsidiary, 40% of $6,000, additional dividend arrearage on preferred stock.

Equity in Income of Co. S..	24,120	
Investment in Co. S Common Stock...................................		24,120

To record decrease in common stock equity in subsidiary, 90% of $26,000, consisting of loss for year, $20,000, dividend requirements on preferred stock for year, $6,000, and $720 ($28,800 ÷ 40) amortization of goodwill.

A consolidated work sheet at the end of the year may be prepared as follows:

Assuming investments are carried by the equity method:

	Co. P	Co. S	Eliminations		Consolidated Balance Sheet	
			Dr.	Cr.	Dr.	Cr.
Debits						
Investment in Co. S Preferred Stock	48,400					
Eliminate Investment in Preferred Stock............				(a) 48,400		
Excess of Cost over Book Value			(a) 1,200		1,200	
Investment in Co. S Common Stock......................	200,880					
Eliminate Investment in Common Stock.............				(b) 200,880		
Goodwill			(b) 28,080		28,080	
Credits						
Preferred Stock, Co. S		100,000				
Eliminate 40%			(a) 40,000			
Minority Interest, 60%						60,000
Common Stock, Co. S		200,000				
Eliminate 90%			(b) 180,000			
Minority Interest, 10%						20,000
Retained Earnings Identified with Co. S Preferred ..		18,000				
Eliminate 40%			(a) 7,200			
Minority Interest, 60%.....						10,800
Deficit Identified with Co. S Common..........................		(8,000)				
Eliminate 90%				(b) 7,200		
Minority Interest, 10%					800	

If the cost method were used in this example, no entries would appear on the books of the parent during the year, since no dividends were declared by the subsidiary. However, retained earnings would be allocated between preferred and common stock issues just as was done on page 392.

Preferred and common equities originally acquired are eliminated, minority interests in the two classes of equities are calculated and extended to the consolidated balance sheet columns, and the earnings accruing to the parent on each class of stock are then calculated and listed, as shown in the following consolidated work sheet:

Assuming investments are carried by the cost method:

	Co. P	Co. S	Eliminations		Consolidated Balance Sheet	
			Dr.	Cr.	Dr.	Cr.
Debits						
Investment in Co. S Preferred Stock	46,000					
Eliminate Investment in Preferred Stock............				(a) 46,000		
Excess of Cost over Book Value			(a) 1,200		1,200	
Investment in Co. S Common Stock......................	225,000					
Eliminate Investment in Common Stock.............				(b) 225,000		
Goodwill.........................			(b) 28,800	(d) 720	28,080	
Credits						
Retained Earnings, Co. P.....			(c) 21,000			
			(d) 720			
Preferred Stock, Co. S		100,000				
Eliminate 40%			(a) 40,000			
Minority Interest, 60%.....						60,000
Common Stock, Co. S		200,000				
Eliminate 90%			(b) 180,000			
Minority Interest, 10%.....						20,000
Retained Earnings Identified with Co. S Preferred ..		18,000				
Eliminate 40% of Retained Earnings Identified with Preferred Stock on Jan. 1, 19X9, $12,000.....................			(a) 4,800			
Minority Interest, 60% of $18,000.....................						10,800
Retained Earnings to Parent........................			(c) 2,400			
Deficit Identified with Co. S Common.....................		(8,000)				
Eliminate 90% of Retained Earnings Identified with Common Stock on Jan. 1, 19X9, $18,000.....................			(b) 16,200			
Minority Interest, 10% of $8,000 Deficit..............						800
Retained Earnings to Parent				(c) 23,400		

Preferred and common stock issues may provide for rights and privileges that vary with certain conditions and with specified dates. Under such circumstances an apportionment of capital between preferred and common equities may be possible only if certain assumptions are made with respect to such special factors. When it is necessary to make certain assumptions in arriving at the preferred and common equities, such assumptions should be disclosed by special note on the consolidated balance sheet.

STOCK DIVIDENDS BY SUBSIDIARY

A dividend in the form of like stock has no effect upon the total capital of a corporation. Such a stock dividend likewise does not change the respective equities of the individual stockholders. The parent company, then, should recognize no change in the investment account balance or revenue upon receipt of such a dividend. However, the parent should make a memorandum entry to record the additional shares received in the form of a dividend.

To illustrate the special problems that arise in preparing a consolidated balance sheet after distribution of a subsidiary stock dividend, assume that on January 1, 19X3, Company P purchased 800 shares of Company S stock at 180. On this date, the capital of Company S is:

Capital stock (1,000 shares) $100,000
Retained earnings 60,000

A work sheet for a consolidated balance sheet on the date of stock acquisition is prepared as follows:

	Co. P	Co. S	Eliminations		Consolidated Balance Sheet	
			Dr.	Cr.	Dr.	Cr.
Debits						
Investment in Co. S Stock	144,000			144,000		
Eliminate Investment................						
Goodwill............................			16,000		16,000	
Credits						
Capital Stock, Co. S.....................		100,000				
Eliminate 80%.........................			80,000			
Minority Interest, 20%..............						20,000
Retained Earnings, Co. S..............		60,000				
Eliminate 80%.........................			48,000			
Minority Interest, 20%..............						12,000

If the investment account is carried by the equity method and the subsidiary reports net income of $30,000 for 19X3 and distributes a 50% stock dividend, the parent recognizes the subsidiary earnings by increasing the investment account and its retained earnings by 80% of $30,000, or $24,000. These accounts are also decreased by $400 for the amortization of goodwill. The receipt of the stock dividend of 400 shares is recorded by a memorandum entry. Subsequent eliminations on the work sheet for a consolidated balance sheet are made in the usual manner, since the total capital of the subsidiary did not change with the transfer from retained earnings to capital stock. At the end of 19X3, assuming that $400 amortization of goodwill has been recognized on Company P's books, eliminations are made as follows:

	Co. P	Co. S	Eliminations		Consolidated Balance Sheet	
			Dr.	Cr.	Dr.	Cr.
Debits						
Investments in Co. S Stock............	167,600					
Eliminate Investment................				167,600		
Goodwill			15,600		15,600	
Credits						
Capital Stock, Co. S......................		150,000				
Eliminate 80%			120,000			
Minority Interest, 20%..............						30,000
Retained Earnings, Co. S..............		40,000				
Eliminate 80%			32,000			
Minority Interest, 20%..............						8,000

When a subsidiary transfers to the capital stock account earnings that have accumulated after the date the parent acquired control, it would be appropriate to disclose on the consolidated balance sheet that a portion of the retained earnings of the controlling interest represents earnings that have been formally capitalized by the subsidiary. Such disclosure can be made by parenthetical remark or special note or by reporting retained earnings in two parts. However, a transfer of retained earnings to paid-in capital of the controlling interest would not be appropriate, because the consolidated retained earnings should reflect the accumulated earnings of the affiliated companies.

QUESTIONS

1. What special problem arises in the preparation of a consolidated balance sheet when inventories include goods acquired from affiliated units?

2. Describe the intercompany profit eliminations required in the preparation of a consolidated balance sheet, assuming each of the following conditions. Also describe possible alternative procedures.

(a) A parent's inventory includes goods acquired from a wholly owned subsidiary.

   (b) A parent's inventory includes goods acquired from a partly owned subsidiary.

   (c) The inventory of a wholly owned subsidiary includes goods acquired from a parent.

   (d) The inventory of a partly owned subsidiary includes goods acquired from a parent.

   (e) The inventory of a partly owned subsidiary includes goods acquired from a wholly owned subsidiary.

   (f) The inventory of a wholly owned subsidiary includes goods acquired from a partly owned subsidiary.

  3. If minority interests are regarded as outside parties, why should their share of intercompany profits be eliminated in the preparation of consolidated statements?

  4. What special problems are found in the elimination of intercompany profits on depreciable assets?

  5. Company P controls Company S through ownership of the stock of the latter company. The parent has acquired from the subsidiary certain depreciable assets which are 25% depreciated on the date a consolidated balance sheet is prepared. Describe the eliminations that are required in canceling the intercompany profit on the depreciable assets, indicating alternative procedures where possible and assuming that (a) the subsidiary is wholly owned and (b) the subsidiary is partly owned.

  6. The London Company acquires 90% of the outstanding common stock of the James Company on April 10, 19X2. The James Company had completed a building for the London Company at the end of 19X1 at a cost of $60,000, receiving $85,000 on the contract. Would you recommend any elimination for intercompany profits in preparing a consolidated balance sheet at the date of stock acquisition? Explain.

  7. What elimination is made on the consolidated work sheet when the amount at which bonds acquired by the parent of an 80%-owned subsidiary exceeds the amount at which they are carried on the books of the subsidiary?

  8. What procedure should be employed for reporting a credit excess that emerges from the elimination of bonds of an affiliate acquired at an amount that is less than the amount at which they are carried on the books of the issuing company?

  9. Describe the special problem that arises in the preparation of a consolidated balance sheet when a parent's holdings in a subsidiary company consist of both preferred and common shares.

  10. In the preparation of a consolidated balance sheet, explain how the retained earnings balance of a subsidiary company would be apportioned between preferred stock and common stock, assuming that:

   (a) Preferred is noncumulative and nonparticipating.

   (b) Preferred is cumulative and nonparticipating; dividends are 3 years in arrears.   *(continued)*

(c) Preferred is noncumulative and participates ratably with common.
(d) Preferred is cumulative and participates ratably with common; only dividends for the current year are unpaid.

11. Assume a deficit instead of a retained earnings balance in Question 10. How would such a deficit be apportioned between preferred and common shares under each of the assumptions listed?

12. (a) How does a parent recognize the receipt of a stock dividend of common shares on a subsidiary's common stock? (b) In preparing a work sheet for a consolidated balance sheet subsequent to the stock dividend, how are eliminations made, assuming that investments are carried by (1) the equity method and (2) the cost method?

EXERCISES

1. Company P owns 90% of the stock of Company S1 and 80% of the stock of Company S2. Investments are carried by the equity method. Intercompany sales of merchandise are made at a gross profit of 20% of sales. In each of the following cases, give the elimination to cancel the intercompany profit.

(1) Merchandise held by Company P, acquired from Company S1 for $10,000.
(2) Merchandise held by Company S1, acquired from Company P for $10,000.
(3) Merchandise held by Company S2, acquired from Company S1 for $10,000.
(4) Merchandise held by Company S2, acquired from Company S1 for $10,000; merchandise was originally purchased by Company S1 from Company P for $8,000.
(5) Merchandise held by Company P, acquired from Company S1 for $10,000; merchandise was originally purchased by Company S1 from Company S2 for $8,000.

2. On December 31, 19X7, the Anderson Corporation completed the construction of a building for the Jenkins Company. The charge for construction was $100,000. The cost of construction was $80,000. The life of the building is estimated at 20 years.

What elimination will be made on the work sheet for a consolidated balance sheet on December 31, 19X7, on December 31, 19X8, and on December 31, 19X9, assuming that:

(a) Anderson Corporation is the parent company and owns 100% of the stock of the Jenkins Company. (Assume that the investment is carried at cost.)
(b) Anderson Corporation is the parent company and owns 80% of the stock of the Jenkins Company. (Assume that the investment is carried at cost.)

(c) Jenkins Company is the parent company and owns 100% of the stock of the Anderson Corporation. (Assume that the investment is carried at equity.)

(d) Jenkins Company is the parent company and owns 80% of the stock of the Anderson Corporation. (Assume that the investment is carried at equity.)

3. The Thurston Corporation issued 10-year 5% bonds of $500,000 at 90 on April 1, 19X1. Interest is payable semiannually on April 1 and October 1. Scott Corporation owns 80% of the stock of the Thurston Corporation. The parent company acquired Thurston Corporation bonds of $100,000 at 94 on April 1, 19X3.

(a) What are the adjusting entries to record the accrued interest on bonds on the books of the two companies on December 31, 19X3?

(b) What eliminations will be made on the work sheet for a consolidated balance sheet on this date if the investment in the subsidiary is carried by the equity method?

4. Company P owns 80% of the stock of Company Y and 90% of the stock of Company Z. Both holdings are carried at cost. Give any adjustments and eliminations that are required on the consolidated work sheet on December 31, 19X8, as a result of the following information available on this date:

(a) Company P has in its inventory goods of $48,300 acquired from Company Z. Merchandise is sold by Company Z at 15% above cost.

(b) Company Y has in its inventory goods of $6,000 acquired from Company P. The cost of the goods was $5,000.

(c) Company P owns Company Y bonds. The investment is shown at $9,700; the face value of the bonds owned is $10,000. On this date the books of Company Y show bonds payable of $100,000 and an unamortized premium on bonds payable of $2,500.

(d) Company P shows equipment of $40,000 acquired from Company Y at the end of April, 19X2. The equipment was constructed by Company Y and was sold at a gross profit of 25% of the sales price. The equipment is being depreciated on a 20-year basis.

(e) Company Z announced a dividend of $5,000, but Company P has not yet recognized the dividend.

(f) Company Z remitted $6,000 to Company Y in payment of an advance. Company Y has not yet received the remittance.

(g) Company P as an accommodation to Company Z gave the latter company a note for $50,000. Company Z then discounted the note at the bank to obtain cash. As a result of the two transactions, Company Z shows on its books Notes Receivable, $50,000, Notes Receivable Discounted, $50,000, and Advances from Company P, $50,000.

5. The Ardmore Company has stock outstanding as follows:

Common, 5,000 shares, $100 par..	$500,000
6% Preferred, 1,000 shares, $100 par (liquidating value of shares is equal to par value)...	100,000

Assuming that the retained earnings balance at the end of 19X4 is $60,000, state what part of such retained earnings should be recognized as preferred stockholders' equity and what part as common stockholders' equity if the preferred stock is:

(a) Noncumulative and nonparticipating.
(b) Cumulative, dividends paid to date, and nonparticipating.
(c) Cumulative, dividends two years in arrears (19X3 and 19X4), and nonparticipating.
(d) Noncumulative and fully participating.
(e) Noncumulative, dividends not paid for two years (19X3 and 19X4), and fully participating.
(f) Cumulative, dividends paid to date, and fully participating.
(g) Cumulative, dividends two years in arrears (19X3 and 19X4), and fully participating.

6. In Exercise 5, assume that there is a deficit of $60,000 at the end of 19X4 instead of the retained earnings balance. How should the deficit be apportioned between preferred and common equities in each instance listed?

7. On January 1, 19X0, the Webley Corporation purchased 500 shares of Vinson Corporation preferred stock at 90 and 1,600 shares of Vinson Corporation common stock at 50. Investments are carried by the equity method. The capital of the Vinson Corporation on December 31, 19X0, was as follows:

6% Preferred stock, 1,000 shares, $100 par............................	$100,000
(Dividends of $12,000 are in arrears on December 31, 19X0; liquidating value of shares is equal to par)	
Common stock, 2,000 shares, $100 par....................................	200,000
Additional paid-in capital..	30,000
Retained earnings..	15,000

Retained earnings of the Vinson Corporation on January 1, 19X0, were $40,000. At the beginning of 19X0 there were dividends in arrears of $36,000 on the preferred stock. Dividend distributions to preferred stockholders in 19X0 totaled $30,000.

From the foregoing information, give:

(a) The eliminations that would be made on the consolidated work sheet (1) on the date of acquisition of the stock and (2) on December 31, 19X0.
(b) The cost or book value excess and the goodwill on the investment to be reported on the consolidated balance sheet as a result of the purchases.
(c) The change in the parent company retained earnings as a result of subsidiary operations during 19X0.

8. The R.E. Whitaker Corporation, a holding company, carries investments at cost. On June 30, 19X6, it purchased 16,000 shares of Lowell Company stock at 12. Capital changes of the Lowell Company are shown on page 401.

(a) What elimination is required on the work sheet for a consolidated balance sheet on December 31, 19X7?
(b) In preparing the consolidated balance sheet on December 31, 19X7, what is (1) the goodwill on the investment, (2) the minority interest, and (3) the retained earnings accruing to the parent since date of acquisition?

	Capital Stock ($5 par)	Retained Earnings
Balance, January 1, 19X6.............................	$100,000	$120,000
Profit for 19X6		30,000
	$100,000	$150,000
Cash dividends, December 19X6....................		(10,000)
Balance, December 31, 19X6.........................	$100,000	$140,000
Profit for 19X7		20,000
	$100,000	$160,000
Stock dividend issued in June, 19X7...............	50,000	(50,000)
	$150,000	$110,000
Cash dividends, December, 19X7...................		(10,000)
Balance, December 31, 19X7.........................	$150,000	$100,000

PROBLEMS

13-1. The Patterson Company owns controlling interests in the Carey Company, the Drake Company, and Eaton, Inc. These interests were acquired prior to 1970. At that time, the differences between the amounts paid for the investments and the recorded book values were attributed to goodwill in the case of Carey and to nondepreciable assets in the cases of Drake and Eaton. The Patterson Company has elected not to amortize goodwill. Balance sheets prepared for these companies on December 31, 19X2, were as follows:

	Patterson Co.	Carey Co.	Drake Co.	Eaton, Inc.
Investment in Carey Co. (18,000 shares)...................................	$ 295,000			
Investment in Drake Co. (20,500 shares)...................................	240,000			
Investment in Eaton, Inc. (17,500 shares)...................................	140,000			
Other assets	1,265,000	$475,000	$410,000	$285,000
Total assets................................	$1,940,000	$475,000	$410,000	$285,000
Payables	$ 750,000	$180,000	$125,000	$100,000
Capital stock...............................	1,280,000	200,000	250,000	200,000
Additional paid-in capital	75,000	50,000	15,000	25,000
Retained earnings (deficit)	(165,000)	45,000	20,000	(40,000)
Total liabilities and stockholders' equity	$1,940,000	$475,000	$410,000	$285,000

Stock of the Patterson Company is no par, and 50,000 shares are outstanding. Capital stock of each of the subsidiaries has a stated value of $10 per share.

The parent company recognizes profits and losses of subsidiary companies in its investment accounts and treats dividends as a reduction in investment balances. Changes in subsidiary equities, including the dividends declared by the Carey Company in December, had not been recorded in 19X2. Changes in capital in 19X2 were as follows:

	Patterson Co.	Carey Co.	Drake Co.	Eaton, Inc.
Retained earnings (deficit), January 1, 19X2	($245,000)	$50,000	$35,000	($50,000)
Net income (loss), 19X2	80,000	25,000	(15,000)	10,000
	($165,000)	$75,000	$20,000	($40,000)
Dividends declared in December, 19X2, payable in January, 19X3 ...		(30,000)		
Retained earnings (deficit), Dec. 31, 19X2	($165,000)	$45,000	$20,000	($40,000)

The parent company's inventories on December 31, 19X2, included merchandise of $75,000 acquired from the Carey Company and merchandise of $30,000 acquired from the Drake Company. Merchandise was sold to the parent by subsidiaries at a 20% gross profit on the sales price. Intercompany advances and current trade balances on December 31, 19X2, totaled $100,000.

Instructions: (1) Prepare the entries to bring the parent company's books up to date on December 31, 19X2.

(2) Prepare a work sheet and a consolidated balance sheet as of December 31, 19X2.

13-2. Prior to January 1, 19X7, the stockholders of Large Company and Small Company approved the merger of the two companies. On January 1, 19X7, 5,000 shares of Large Company common stock were issued to the Small Company stockholders in exchange for the 3,000 shares of Small Company common stock outstanding.

Balance sheets of the two companies on December 31, 19X7, were as follows:

	Large Company	Small Company
Cash...	$ 36,400	$ 28,200
Notes receivable.................................	22,000	9,000
Accounts receivable............................	20,900	21,700
Interest receivable..............................	13,000	3,300
Inventories...	81,200	49,600
Plant and equipment..........................	83,200	43,500
Accumulated depreciation	(12,800)	(9,300)
Investment in Small Company	107,800	
Total assets......................................	$351,700	$146,000
Notes payable	$ 4,000	$ 12,000
Accounts payable	42,000	19,600
Dividends payable..............................		4,500
Interest payable.................................	2,600	2,100
Notes receivable discounted	8,100	
Capital stock, $10 par	120,000	
Capital stock, $20 par		60,000
Capital in excess of par......................	58,500	20,000
Retained earnings..............................	116,500	27,800
Total liabilities and stockholders' equity...............	$351,700	$146,000

The following additional information is available:

(1) Net income for 19X7 (disregard income taxes):
    Large Company.. $21,700
    Small Company.. 10,200
(2) On December 31, 19X7, Small Company owed Large Company $16,000 on open account and $8,000 in interest-bearing notes. Large Company discounted $3,000 of the notes received from Small Company with the First State Bank.
(3) On December 31, 19X7, Small Company accrued interest of $120 on the notes payable to Large Company ($40 on the notes of $3,000 discounted with the bank and $80 on the remaining notes of $5,000). Large Company did not accrue interest receivable from Small Company.
(4) During 19X7, Large Company sold merchandise that cost $30,000 to Small Company for $40,000. Small Company's December 31 inventory included $10,000 of this merchandise priced at Small Company's cost.
(5) On July 1, Small Company sold equipment that had a book value of $15,000 to Large Company for $17,000. Large Company recorded depreciation on it in the amount of $850 for 19X7. The remaining life of the equipment at the date of sale was 10 years.
(6) Small Company shipped merchandise to Large Company on December 31, 19X7, and recorded an account receivable of $6,000 for the sale. Small Company's cost for the merchandise was $4,800. Because the merchandise was in transit, Large Company did not record the transaction. The terms of the sale were FOB shipping point.
(7) Small Company declared a dividend of $1.50 per share on December 30, 19X7, payable on January 10, 19X8. Large Company made no entry for the declaration.

Instructions: Prepare a work sheet for a consolidated balance sheet, assuming that the consolidation is to be accounted for as a pooling of interests. Formal journal entries are not required.

(AICPA adapted)

13-3. Account balances as of December 31, 19X8, for Eagon Company and Ears Company are as follows:

	Eagon Co.	Ears Co.
Current assets	$ 652,500	$560,000
Investment in Ears Co. common stock	200,000	
Investment in Ears Co. bonds	87,500	
Plant and equipment	1,400,000	685,000
Accumulated depreciation...............................	(260,000)	(420,000)
Total assets...	$2,080,000	$825,000
Current liabilities..	$ 310,000	$125,000
6% bonds payable...	500,000	250,000
Discount on bonds payable.............................	(20,000)	(15,000)
6% cumulative, nonparticipating preferred stock, $50 par...		100,000
Common stock, $10 par	650,000	300,000
Additional paid-in capital	200,000	
Retained earnings	440,000	65,000
Total liabilities and stockholders' equity...........	$2,080,000	$825,000

Eagon Company acquired 90% of the common stock of Ears Company at the end of 19X1 for $200,000. At that time Ears Company reported a deficit of $35,000 and dividends on preferred stock were $21,000 in arrears. However, dividends in arrears were cleared up at the end of 19X6 and the company has paid dividends on common as well as on preferred in 19X7 and 19X8. At the time of acquisition, Ears Company land was considered overvalued as reflected in the investment cost, although no adjustment was made on Ears books. Eagon accounts for its investments on a cost basis.

At the beginning of 19X8, Eagon Company acquired land and buildings from Ears Company at a price of $100,000; land was recorded at $60,000 and buildings were recorded at $40,000. The buildings were expected to have a remaining life of 8 years and Eagon Company recorded depreciation for 19X8 at the rate of 12½%. Ears Company had carried the land at a cost of $50,000 and the buildings at a cost of $200,000 less accumulated depreciation of $180,000, and it reported a gain of $30,000 on the sale. The land was purchased by Ears Company in 19X2.

At the end of 19X8, Eagon Company purchased $100,000 of Ears Company bonds on the market, paying $90,000, which included $2,500 accrued interest for 5 months. The accrued interest on the investment is included in Eagon Company current assets; current liabilities of Ears Company include accrued interest of $6,250 on bonded debt.

During 19X8, sales of merchandise by Ears Company to Eagon Company totaled $75,000; cost of the goods to Ears Company was $60,000. On December 31, 19X8, Eagon Company inventory included goods of $12,500 acquired from Ears Company. However, the accounts for Eagon Company do not show goods of $2,500 that are in transit. These goods had been recorded as a sale by Ears Company and had been shipped on December 30. On December 31, Ears Company showed a total of $8,500 due from Eagon Company on open account.

Current liabilities of Ears Company include a payable for dividends of $1.25 per share on common stock, declared on December 20, 19X8, and payable on February 5, 19X9. No entry for the dividends has been made by Eagon Company.

Instructions: Prepare a work sheet for a consolidated balance sheet as of December 31, 19X8.

13-4. Company P owns 85% of the stock of Company A and 90% of the stock of Company B. Account balances on December 31, 19X4, were as follows:

	Co. P	Co. A	Co. B
Cash	$ 195,000	$ 40,000	$ 20,000
Accounts receivable	116,000	150,000	160,000
Inventories	310,000	207,500	270,000
Land	40,000	40,000	30,000
Buildings, machinery, and equipment (net)	500,000	415,000	300,000
Investment in Co. A stock	425,000		
Investment in Co. B stock	459,000		
Investment in Co. A bonds	105,000		
Total assets	$2,150,000	$852,500	$780,000

	Co. P	Co. A	Co. B
Notes payable..............................	$ 100,000	$ 47,500	$ 20,000
Accounts payable........................	150,000	90,000	170,000
Bonds payable	250,000	250,000	
Discount on bonds payable...........		(15,000)	
Capital stock..............................	1,000,000	500,000	250,000
Retained earnings (deficit)	650,000	(20,000)	340,000
Total liab. and stockholders' equity..	$2,150,000	$852,500	$780,000

Stock in Companies A and B was acquired at the end of June, 19X3. An excess of book value over the investment cost of Company B was attributed to a decline in value of equipment which had a remaining useful life of 30 years at that time. All other book values of Companies A and B approximated fair values. Any goodwill recognized is to be amortized over a period of 15 years.

Changes in retained earnings have been as follows:

	Co. P	Co. A	Co. B
Retained earnings (deficit) balance, June 30, 19X3.....................................	$564,000	($30,000)	$290,000
Profit (loss) from own operations, June 30–December 31, 19X3.....................................	30,000	(15,000)	40,000
	$594,000	($45,000)	$330,000
Dividends paid by Co. P, December, 19X3..........	(30,000)		
	$564,000	($45,000)	$330,000
Dividends paid by Co. B, December, 19X3..........	13,500		(15,000)
Retained earnings (deficit) balance, December 31, 19X3	$577,500	($45,000)	$315,000
Profit (loss) from own operations, 19X4..............	90,000	25,000	50,000
	$667,500	($20,000)	$365,000
Dividends paid by Co. P, 19X4...........................	(40,000)		
	$627,500	($20,000)	$365,000
Dividends paid by Co. B, 19X4	22,500		(25,000)
Retained earnings (deficit) balance, December 31, 19X4	$650,000	($20,000)	$340,000

Intercompany sales of merchandise were made at 25% above cost. On December 31, 19X4, the following information was available:

Co. B inventory includes: merchandise acquired from Co. A for.....	$30,000
merchandise acquired from Co. P for.....	25,000
Co. A inventory includes: merchandise acquired from Co. P for.....	10,000
Co. P inventory includes: merchandise acquired from Co. A for.....	35,000

Accounts receivable and accounts payable balances included $12,500 owed by Company B to Company A, $20,000 owed by Company B to Company P, and $5,000 owed by Company P to Company A.

The parent company acquired Company A bonds of $100,000 in July, 19X3, at a premium and has been amortizing the premium over the remaining life of the bonds. Company A originally issued the bonds at the beginning of 19X0 at 90; the discount is being amortized over 20 years.

Instructions: Prepare a work sheet for a consolidated balance sheet as of December 31, 19X4.

13-5. Four years ago, Astor Company acquired 50% of the preferred stock of Barnes Corporation for $55,000 and 90% of that corporation's common stock for $195,000. At acquisition date, Barnes Corporation had retained earnings of $60,000, and dividends on the 5% cumulative preferred stock were not in arrears. The investments were recorded by Astor Company at the book value shown by Barnes Corporation at date of acquisition. The difference between cost and book values at that time was recognized as income by Astor Company.

Consolidated statements are now being prepared as of December 31, 19X5, for Astor Company and its subsidiary. The financial position of the individual companies was as follows on that date:

Astor Company

Miscellaneous assets......	$116,000	Liabilities......................	$ 50,000
Investments:		Preferred stock (4%)......	100,000
Barnes preferred	50,000	Common stock...............	100,000
Barnes common..........	234,000	Retained earnings..........	150,000
		Total liabilities and	
Total assets..................	$400,000	stockholders' equity....	$400,000

Barnes Corporation

Miscellaneous assets......	$400,000	Liabilities......................	$ 60,000
		Preferred stock (5%)*	100,000
		Common stock...............	200,000
		Retained earnings..........	40,000
		Total liabilities and stock-	
Total assets..................	$400,000	holders' equity.............	$400,000

*Preferred stock dividends are 3 years in arrears. No dividends have been paid on common since acquisition by Astor Company. Profit in 19X2 was $8,000, but losses during the past 3 years have totaled $23,000.

Instructions: Prepare a consolidated balance sheet for these companies as of December 31, 19X5, in which all significant details given in the information are fully disclosed.

(AICPA adapted)

13-6. Balance sheet data for Madison Company and Norwalk Company on December 31, 19X7 are on page 407.

Madison Company acquired 80% of the common stock and 40% of the preferred stock of Norwalk Company at the end of 19X3 for a total of $215,000. At the date of acquisition, Norwalk Company showed retained earnings of $15,000, and there were dividends in arrears on preferred for the years 19X1, 19X2, and 19X3. An appraisal at the date of acquisition indicated that nondepreciable plant assets were overvalued by $37,250 on the books of Norwalk. No adjustment has been made by Norwalk. Since the date of acquisition of its stock by Madison Company, Norwalk Company has paid dividends on preferred totaling $30,000.

On December 31, 19X7, Madison Company held merchandise of $80,000 acquired from Norwalk Company. There was also merchandise in transit of $14,000 that Madison Company had not recognized on its books. In its accounts receivable, Norwalk Company showed claims of $35,000 against Madison Company, which included the charge for merchandise in transit. The gross profit reported by Norwalk Company for 19X7 was 32%.

	Madison Co.	Norwalk Co.
Current assets	$1,175,000	$500,000
Investment in Norwalk Co. stock	215,000	
Plant and equipment	525,000	200,000
Accumulated depreciation	(335,000)	(50,000)
Goodwill	100,000	
Total assets	$1,680,000	$650,000
Current liabilities	$ 550,000	$260,000
6% preferred stock, cumulative and nonparticipating	250,000	100,000
Common stock:		
500,000 shares, no par	500,000	
50,000 shares, no par		250,000
Additional paid-in capital	120,000	
Retained earnings	260,000	40,000
Total liabilities and stockholders' equity	$1,680,000	$650,000

Instructions: Prepare a work sheet and a consolidated balance sheet on December 31, 19X7.

13-7. On January 1, 19X1, Ryan Corporation acquired stock of Snell, Inc., as follows:

7,000 shares of common, $50 par, at 60
200 shares of 6% noncumulative and nonparticipating preferred, $100 par, at 150

On this date, Ryan Corporation also acquired 4,000 shares of Todd, Inc., no-par stock at 75. This represents an 80% interest. The excess of book values over amounts paid to acquire common stock was indicative of land values at the date of acquisition.

Balance sheets of the three companies on December 31, 19X1, were as follows:

	Ryan Corporation		Snell, Inc.		Todd, Inc.	
Cash		$ 178,000		$ 20,000		$ 25,000
Accounts receivable		520,000		115,000		90,000
Merchandise inventory		1,150,000		280,000		185,000
Land		60,000		40,000		65,000
Buildings	$ 600,000		$260,000		$215,000	
Less accumulated depreciation	150,000	450,000	135,000	125,000	145,000	70,000
Machinery and equipment	$1,350,000		$400,000		$350,000	
Less accumulated depreciation	400,000	950,000	180,000	220,000	180,000	170,000
Investment in Snell, Inc., stock		450,000				
Investment in Todd, Inc., stock		300,000				
Investment in Todd, Inc., bonds (face value, $20,000)		22,000				
Total assets		$4,080,000		$800,000		$605,000

(continued)

	Ryan Corporation	Snell Inc.	Todd Inc.
Accounts payable	$1,000,000	$150,000	$ 79,800
Bonds payable	300,000		100,000
Premium on bonds payable.....			5,200
Preferred stock	500,000	100,000	
Common stock	1,500,000	400,000	220,000
Retained earnings	780,000	150,000	200,000
Total liabilities and stockholders' equity	$4,080,000	$800,000	$605,000

Changes in retained earnings for 19X1 were as follows:

	Ryan Corporation	Snell, Inc.	Todd, Inc.
Balance, Jan. 1, 19X1.................	$645,000	$116,000	$195,000
Dividends, 19X1..........................	(80,000)	(16,000)	(20,000)
	$565,000	$100,000	$175,000
Profit, 19X1...............................	215,000*	50,000	25,000
Balance, Dec. 31, 19X1...............	$780,000	$150,000	$200,000

*Includes dividends received from subsidiaries.

On February 1, 19X1, Ryan Corporation began the construction of machinery for Todd, Inc. Construction and installation of the machinery was completed on June 1 at a cost to Ryan Corporation of $75,000; the subsidiary was charged $90,000. The subsidiary recorded depreciation from June 1 at the rate of 10% a year.

Instructions: Prepare a work sheet for a consolidated balance sheet as of December 31, 19X1.

13-8. At the beginning of 19X5, the Johnson Company acquired all of the treasury stock of the Sperry Company at a purchase price of $195,000 and also 70,000 shares on the open market at a price of 12½. The price paid by Johnson Company at that time reflected the fair values of nondepreciable assets of Sperry Company. A balance sheet for the Sperry Company on December 31, 19X4, showed the following:

Assets			$1,650,000
Liabilities..			$ 375,000
Stockholders' equity:			
Capital stock, $5 par, 100,000 shares issued	$500,000		
Less treasury stock, 15,000 shares at par	75,000		
Outstanding, 85,000 shares		$425,000	
Additional paid-in capital		250,000	
Retained earnings		600,000	1,275,000
Total liabilities and stockholders' equity................................			$1,650,000

At the end of 19X5, balance sheets for the Johnson Company and the Sperry Company were as follows:

	Johnson Co.	Sperry Co.
Investment in Sperry Co. stock	$1,070,000	
Other assets	5,000,000	$1,940,000
Total assets	$6,070,000	$1,940,000
Liabilities	$1,200,000	$ 385,000
Capital stock ($10 par)	2,500,000	
Capital stock ($5 par)		750,000
Additional paid-in capital	720,000	370,000
Retained earnings	1,650,000	435,000
Total liabilities and stockholders' equity	$6,070,000	$1,940,000

An analysis of changes in retained earnings in 19X5 for each company follows:

	Johnson Co.	Sperry Co.
Balance, January 1	$1,590,000	$600,000
Stock dividend declared June 1, payable June 15		(250,000)
Cash dividends declared December 1, payable December 15	(375,000)	(150,000)
Net income for year (including dividends received from affiliates)	435,000	235,000
Balance, December 31	$1,650,000	$435,000

Instructions: Prepare a work sheet and a consolidated balance sheet as of December 31, 19X5.

13-9. The balance sheets of Company A and its subsidiaries, Companies B and C, as of December 31, 19X2, are as follows:

	Co. A	Co. B	Co. C
Assets			
Investments:			
Preferred stock of Co. B — 60%	$ 300,000		
Common stock of Co. B — 90%	800,000		
Common stock of Co. C — 90%	1,300,000		
Bonds of Co. B at cost	270,000		
Notes receivable — Co. B	20,000		
Other assets	2,000,000	$2,180,000	$2,000,000
Total assets	$4,690,000	$2,180,000	$2,000,000
Liabilities and Stockholders' Equity			
Capital stock:			
Preferred — 6%	$ 500,000	$ 500,000	$ 500,000
Common	1,100,000	150,000	500,000
Total capital stock	$1,600,000	$ 650,000	$1,000,000
Retained earnings:			
Balance — January 1, 19X2	$1,100,000	$ 150,000	$ 300,000
Net profits for the year 19X2	400,000	200,000	300,000
	$1,500,000	$ 350,000	$ 600,000
Dividends deducted	12,000	30,000	30,000
Retained earnings, December 31, 19X2	$1,488,000	$ 320,000	$ 570,000
First mortgage 6% bonds outstanding	$1,000,000	$ 600,000	
Notes receivable discounted — Co. B	10,000		
Notes payable — Co. A		20,000	
Other liabilities	592,000	590,000	$ 430,000
Total liabilities	$1,602,000	$1,210,000	$ 430,000
Total liabilities and stockholders' equity	$4,690,000	$2,180,000	$2,000,000

The dividends on the preferred stocks of the respective companies have all been paid during the year 19X2.

The bonds of Company B, which mature December 31, 19X9, were acquired by Company A on July 1, 19X2, at 90.

Company A acquired its holding of the stock in Companies B and C in 19X0 and has taken up its share of the earnings of these companies.

Instructions: Prepare a consolidated balance sheet as of December 31, 19X2.

13-10. The following information pertains to Company A and its subsidiaries, Companies S-1 and S-2:

(1) Post-closing trial balances for Company A and its subsidiaries as of December 31, 19X3, are as follows:

	Co. A	Co. S-1	Co. S-2
Investment in Co. S-1 (acquired January 1, 19X2):			
Common Stock (90%)	200,000		
Preferred Stock (40%)	40,000		
Investment in Co. S-2 (70% acquired January 1, 19X3)	56,000		
Current Assets	50,000	50,000	50,000
Machinery and Equipment	40,000	20,000	30,000
Accumulated Depreciation	(20,000)	(15,000)	(10,000)
Bonds of Co. S-2 (par $10,000)	10,100		
Other Assets	600	313,000	70,180
Current Liabilities	(20,000)	(20,000)	(20,000)
Bonds Payable — 10 yrs, 4%, due December 31, 19X8			(30,000)
Premium on Bonds Payable			(180)
Common Stock — $100 par	(300,000)	(250,000)	(60,000)
Preferred Stock — 5%, $100 par, cumulative and nonparticipating		(100,000)	
Premium on Preferred Stock		(10,000)	
Retained Earnings	(56,700)	12,000	(20,000)

(2) The investment accounts are carried at cost.

(3) At acquisition, dividends on preferred stock for two years were in arrears. Preferred stock has a liquidation value of par plus all dividends in arrears and is nonvoting.

(4) On January 1, 19X3, Company S-1 declared a common stock dividend of $50,000 from Premium on Preferred Stock.

(5) The retained earnings accounts showed the following:

	Co. S-1	Co. S-2
Balance, January 1, 19X2	($10,000)	$14,000
Profit, 19X2	7,000	7,000
Cash dividends, 19X3 — on January 1, 19X3	(5,000)	
Cash dividends, 19X3 — on December 31, 19X3		(6,000)
Income (loss), 19X3	(4,000)	5,000
Balance, December 31, 19X3	($12,000)	$20,000

(6) The inventory of Company A includes $5,000 of merchandise purchased from Company S-2; cost to Company S-2 is marked up 25%.

(7) The inventory of Company S-2 includes $2,000 of merchandise purchased from Company S-1; markup by Company S-1 is 10% of selling price.

(8) Current liabilities include the following: Company S-1 owes Company A $1,000; Company S-2 owes Company A $2,000; Company S-1 owes Company S-2 $3,000; and Company A owes Company S-1 $2,000.

(9) Machinery having a life of 10 years was purchased by Company A from Company S-1 on January 1, 19X2, for $10,000. Cost to Company S-1 was $7,000.

(10) Company S-2 neglected to amortize the premium on bonds payable for 19X3.

Instructions: Prepare a work sheet for a consolidated balance sheet as of December 31, 19X3. Assume that any excess of book value over cost of common stock investments is attributable to nondepreciable assets.

(AICPA adapted)

14
Consolidated Statements — Changes in Interest in Subsidiary

Illustrations in previous chapters have assumed that control of a subsidiary is achieved through a single purchase of stock and that the parent's interest remains unchanged throughout the period of control. A parent may acquire control of a subsidiary through several purchases of stock at different times and at varying prices. A parent may sell part of its holdings in the subsidiary, thus reducing its interest. A parent's interest may change as a result of the issuance of additional shares or the retirement of outstanding shares by the subsidiary company. The problems that arise in the preparation of the consolidated balance sheet when changes have taken place in the interests held in subsidiary companies are considered in this chapter.

SEVERAL PURCHASES: CONTROL ACHIEVED UPON FIRST PURCHASE

In some instances a parent may have a controlling interest in a subsidiary company and may subsequently increase this interest by the purchase of additional stock. To illustrate, assume that Company P acquires stock of Company S as follows:

January 1, 19X8, 800 shares (80%) at 120	$ 96,000
July 1, 19X9, 100 shares (10%) at 130	13,000
Total investment	$109,000

The capital stock of each company is $100,000, and the shares have a par value of $100. Retained earnings balances on December 31, 19X7, and earnings and dividends for 19X8 and 19X9 are as follows:

	Co. P	Co. S
Retained earnings, December 31, 19X7	$60,000	$15,000
Net income from own operations, 19X8	15,000	20,000
Dividends declared, December, 19X9	10,000	5,000
Net income from own operations, 19X9	25,000	20,000

As a first step in developing consolidated statements, the following calculations show the relationship between investment cost and book value on each acquisition:

Amount paid for 800 shares on January 1, 19X8	$96,000	
Less book value of stock acquired, 80% of $115,000 ($100,000 + $15,000)	92,000	
Excess of cost over book value of subsidiary interest		$4,000
Amount paid for 100 shares on July 1, 19X9	$13,000	
Less book value of stock acquired, 10% of $145,000 [$100,000 + $15,000 + $20,000 + (6/12 × $20,000)]	14,500	
Excess of book value of subsidiary interest over cost		(1,500)

The first acquisition, in which control was achieved, resulted in an excess of cost over book value of $4,000. The second acquisition resulted in an excess of book value over cost of $1,500. The application of purchase accounting requires the valuation of specific assets at the date of acquisition and the identification of any excess cost as goodwill, or the allocation of any cost deficiency to noncurrent assets. The acquisition of a controlling interest in a subsidiary clearly calls for the revaluation of identifiable assets, based on the presumed cost to the parent at that time. Although it might be argued that a relatively small increment in these holdings should also call for a revaluation, specific assets should be restated at their current values only at the time control is achieved. This viewpoint is consistent with purchase accounting, which involves the application of historical cost to asset valuation and does not attempt to record changes in market values. The point at which control is achieved is an occasion for recognizing a new basis of accountability — cost to the new owner. Since subsequent purchases do not involve a change in accountability, specific assets should not be revalued.

If assets are not revalued, the parent company must nevertheless account for the difference between the investment cost and these asset values. According to the Accounting Principles Board, this difference is an addition to (or deduction from) goodwill: "if the investor is unable to relate the difference [between cost and book value] to specific accounts of the investee, the difference should be considered to be goodwill and amortized over a period not to exceed forty years."[1]

If specific assets are revalued at the date control is achieved, these values must be considered in calculating goodwill involved in subsequent purchases. These changed values would not be recorded on the books of the subsidiary, but would be utilized by the parent company in preparing consolidated statements and in applying the equity method.

Assume in the previous example that the fair values of depreciable assets of Company S, with a remaining useful life of 5 years on January 1, 19X8, exceed recorded book values by $2,500. The goodwill attributable to this purchase would be calculated as follows:

---

[1]*Opinions of the Accounting Principles Board, No. 18,* "The Equity Method of Accounting for Investments in Common Stock" (New York: American Institute of Certified Public Accountants, 1971), par. 19n.

Amount paid for 800 shares on January 1, 19X8...............................	$96,000
Less fair value of net assets acquired:	
80% of $117,500 ($100,000 + $15,000 + $2,500)	94,000
Goodwill..	$2,000

In applying the equity method or in preparing consolidated statements, goodwill would be amortized over a period of 40 years (or less), and the additional depreciation of $500 per year ($2,500 ÷ 5 years) would be taken into account. All of the goodwill amortization affects the parent company's earnings, whereas only the parent's proportionate share (80%) of the depreciation increase affects its interest. The revaluation of assets and the corresponding recognition of depreciation affects the minority interest in consolidated statements and also the determination of goodwill in any subsequent purchases.

Assuming that the equity method is used, the parent's investment account and retained earnings and the subsidiary net assets from the date of control until June 30, 19X9, may be summarized as follows:

	Investment in Co. S	Company P Retained Earnings	Company S Net Assets (Fair Values)
December 31, 19X7:			
Balance..		$ 60,000	$115,000
January 1, 19X8:			
Purchase of 800 shares of Co. S stock at 120.........	$ 96,000		2,500
	$ 96,000	$ 60,000	$117,500
December 31, 19X8:			
Net income from own operations:			
Co. S, $20,000...................................	16,000	16,000	20,000
Co. P, $15,000...................................		15,000	
Amortization of goodwill ($2,000 ÷ 40)...................	(50)	(50)	
Depreciation on asset revaluation........................	(400)	(400)	(500)
	$111,550	$ 90,550	$137,000
June 30, 19X9:			
Net income from own operations:			
Co. S, $10,000.................................	8,000	8,000	10,000
Co. P, $12,500.................................		12,500	
Amortization of goodwill (6/12 × $50)....................	(25)	(25)	
Depreciation on asset revaluation (6 months)	(200)	(200)	(250)
Balance..	$119,325	$110,825	$146,750

On July 1, 19X9, the purchase of an additional 10% of Company S requires the calculation of goodwill, but not the restatement of individual assets. The net assets of Company S, as adjusted for the original revaluation and the related depreciation, are $146,750. Therefore the calculation of goodwill would be made as follows:

Amount paid for 100 shares on July 1, 19X9	$13,000
Less fair value of net assets acquired (10% of $146,750).................	14,675
Excess of fair value over cost	$ 1,675

Because assets are not revalued at this time, there is no effect on the remaining minority interest. Therefore the credit excess may be subtracted from the existing goodwill. As of July 1, 19X9, the goodwill account would have the following balance:

Goodwill as of January 1, 19X8...	$2,000
Less: Amortization through June 30, 19X9.......................................	(75)
Excess of fair value over cost, July 1, 19X9 acquisition	(1,675)
Balance, July 1, 19X9...	$ 250

The goodwill would be amortized over the remainder of the useful life of the initial goodwill amount by a charge to the parent company's earnings. The parent company will recognize 90 percent of the earnings of Company S, as adjusted, from July 1, 19X9. The portion of the depreciation on asset revaluation attributable to the controlling interest is also increased to 90 percent. The parent will not recognize any of the earnings attributable to the incremental shares purchased prior to the date they were acquired. The parent's investment account and retained earnings and the subsidiary net assets as of December 31, 19X9, may be summarized as follows:

	Investment in Co. S	Company P Retained Earnings	Company S Net Assets
June 30, 19X9:			
Balance...	$119,325	$110,825	$146,750
July 1, 19X9:			
Purchase of 100 shares of Co. S stock at 130	13,000		
	$132,325	$110,825	$146,750
December, 19X9:			
Dividends declared:			
Co. S, $5,000...	(4,500)		(5,000)
Co. P, $10,000...		(10,000)	
	$127,825	$100,825	$141,750
December 31, 19X9:			
Net income from own operations:			
Co. S, $10,000..	9,000	9,000	10,000
Co. P, $12,500..		12,500	
Amortization of goodwill [($250 ÷ 38.5) × 6/12]	(3)	(3)	
Depreciation on asset revaluation (6 months)	(225)	(225)	(250)
Balance...	$136,597	$122,097	$151,500

Assuming that the equity method is used, a work sheet for a consolidated balance sheet on December 31, 19X9, would be prepared as shown on the top of page 416.

If the cost method had been used, the investment account would have been stated at its original amount, $109,000 ($96,000 + $13,000). The $27,597 difference between this amount and the balance shown for the equity method may be explained as shown on the bottom of page 416.

Company P and Subsidiary Company S
Work Sheet for Consolidated Balance Sheet
December 31, 19X9

	Co. P	Co. S	Eliminations		Consolidated Balance Sheet	
			Dr.	Cr.	Dr.	Cr.
Debits						
Investment in Co. S Stock ...	136,597					
Eliminate Investment........				(b) 136,597		
Goodwill			(b) 247		247	
Other Assets.....................	205,500	220,000	(a) 1,500		427,000	
	342,097	220,000				
Credits						
Liabilities	120,000	70,000				190,000
Capital Stock, Co. P............	100,000					100,000
Retained Earnings, Co. P.....	122,097					122,097
Capital Stock, Co. S............		100,000				
Eliminate 90%			(b) 90,000			
Minority Interest, 10%.....						10,000
Retained Earnings, Co. S.....		50,000				
Eliminate 90%			(b) 45,000			
Minority Interest, 10%.....						5,000
Appraisal Adjustment, Co. S				(a) 1,500		
Eliminate 90%			(b) 1,350			
Minority Interest, 10%.....						150
	342,097	220,000	138,097	138,097	427,247	427,247

Retained earnings, July 1, 19X9, date of change in percentage owned [$15,000 + $20,000 + (6/12 × $20,000)]..	$45,000	
Retained earnings, January 1, 19X8, date stock was originally acquired.....	15,000	
Net increase in retained earnings, January 1, 19X8 to July 1, 19X9	$30,000	
Ownership interest during this period	80%	
Retained earnings accruing to parent, January 1, 19X8 to July 1, 19X9......		$24,000
Retained earnings, December 31, 19X9	$50,000	
Retained earnings, July 1, 19X9, date additional 10% lot was acquired	45,000	
Net increase in retained earnings, July 1, 19X9 to December 31, 19X9......	$ 5,000	
Ownership interest during this period	90%	
Retained earnings increase accruing to parent, July 1, 19X9 to December 31, 19X9		4,500
Depreciation on asset revaluation:		
January 1, 19X8 to June 30, 19X9...	$ 750	
Ownership interest during this period	80%	
	$ 600	
July 1, 19X9 to December 31, 19X9...	$ 250	
Ownership interest during this period	90%	
	$ 225	
Total depreciation adjustment		(825)
Goodwill amortization:		
January 1, 19X8 to June 30, 19X9...	$ 75	
July 1, 19X9 to December 31, 19X9..	3	
Total goodwill amortization adjustment...		(78)
Total retained earnings accruing to parent, January 1, 19X8 to December 31, 19X9		$27,597

If the cost method had been used, work sheet adjustments would be necessary to increase the controlling interest's retained earnings by $27,597. These adjustments would reflect the changes that would have been recorded if the equity method had been used, as indicated above. The equity method recognizes all of the changes in retained earnings that would be shown on the consolidated statement as part of the parent company's retained earnings. The consolidated balance sheet should be the same, regardless of the method used to account for the investment.

SEVERAL PURCHASES: CONTROL NOT ACHIEVED UPON FIRST PURCHASE

A company may obtain control of a subsidiary upon a second or subsequent purchase of the stock of that company. If the first purchase fails to give control, the preparation of a consolidated balance sheet is not warranted. Upon a subsequent purchase that makes control effective, however, consolidation is proper.

In applying the equity method, recognition of the investor's equity in earnings of the investee company would be appropriate as soon as the investor is able to exercise significant influence over the investee, whether or not control is achieved. Since significant influence is generally considered to result when the investor owns 20% or more of the voting stock of the investee, a series of purchases that results in ownership interests in excess of that amount would cause a change from the cost to the equity method. The Accounting Principles Board stated that: "The investment, results of operations . . . , and retained earnings of the investor should be adjusted retroactively in a manner consistent with the accounting for a step-by-step acquisition of a subsidiary."[2]

Upon the acquisition of significant influence or control, the parent company properly recognizes the earnings that have accrued on the interests previously held from the dates of such acquisitions. In the absence of control in the past, equity changes relating to a noncontrolling interest in the subsidiary could be viewed as only of a contingent nature and could not be given accounting recognition. When control is achieved, recognition of past changes in the parent's equity is justified. For purposes of the consolidated balance sheet, then, the parent company recognizes the subsidiary earnings relating to each lot of stock from the date it was acquired to the balance sheet date, just as when control is acquired on the first of several purchases.[3]

---

[2]*Ibid.*, par. 19m.

[3]The Committee on Accounting Procedure of the American Institute of Certified Public Accountants observed that there may be circumstances calling for exceptional treatment. The Committee stated, "If two or more purchases are made over a period of time, the earned surplus of the subsidiary at acquisition should generally be determined on a step-by-step basis; however, if small purchases are made over a period of time and then a purchase is made which results in control, the date of the latest purchase, as a matter of convenience, may be considered as the date of acquisition." (*Accounting Research Bulletin No. 51*, "Consolidated Financial Statements," New York: American Institute of Certified Public Accountants, 1959, par. 10.)

To illustrate, assume that Company P acquires stock of Company S as follows:

January 1, 19X3, 150 shares (15%) at 130	$ 19,500
July 1, 19X4, 700 shares (70%) at 140	98,000
Total	$117,500

The capital stock of each company is $100,000, and each share has a par value of $100. Retained earnings balances on December 31, 19X2, and earnings and dividends for 19X3 and 19X4 are:

	Co. P	Co. S
Retained earnings, December 31, 19X2	$65,000	$25,000
Dividends declared, December, 19X3	10,000	5,000
Net income from own operations, 19X3	20,000	10,000
Dividends declared, December, 19X4	10,000	5,000
Net income from own operations, 19X4	25,000	15,000

The parent would recognize earnings of the subsidiary at the end of 19X4 as follows:

Earnings, 19X3 (recognized by adjustment to investment account and to retained earnings):
15% of $5,000 (Co. S net income, 19X3, $10,000, less dividends paid in this period, $5,000, of which 15% was recognized as revenue by parent) ... $ 750

Earnings, 19X4:
15% of $7,500 (6/12 × $15,000) Co. S net income, January 1–June 30 ... $1,125
85% of $7,500 (6/12 × $15,000) Co. S net income, July 1–December 31 ... 6,375 $7,500

The excess of investment cost over subsidiary net assets would be determined for each acquisition separately, as follows:

January 1, 19X3, cost of 150 shares	$19,500	
Co. S book value (15% × $125,000)	18,750	
Excess of cost over book value of net assets		$ 750
July 1, 19X4, cost of 700 shares	$98,000	
Co. S book value (70% × $137,500)	96,250	
Excess of cost over book value of net assets		1,750
Total excess of cost over book value of net assets		$2,500

Fair values of identifiable assets would be determined at the date on which control is achieved. If the excess of cost over the book value of net assets at that time is attributed to specific asset values, it would be reasonable to ascribe a proportionate amount of the value change to the net assets on hand at the dates of previous purchases, thereby reducing the amount designated as goodwill.

If goodwill is indicated, a question arises as to the appropriate periods of amortization. The amount attributable to the acquisition in which control was achieved clearly should be amortized over subsequent periods. The proper disposition of amounts attributable to prior acquisitions, however, may not be so clear. On the one hand, it could be argued that retroactive application of the equity method, by which earnings attributable to periods prior to the achievement of control are recognized by the parent, suggests that the amortization of goodwill should be commenced retroactively to cover the corresponding period. This view was implied by the following statement:

> When a company in a series of purchases on a step-by-step basis acquires either a subsidiary which is consolidated or an investment which is accounted for under the equity method, the company should identify the cost of each investment, the fair value of the underlying assets acquired and the goodwill for each step purchase. . . . Goodwill associated with each step purchase acquired after October 31, 1970 should be amortized in accordance with [Accounting Principles Board Opinion 17].[4]

On the other hand, it may be argued that goodwill should be applied to only those periods for which control is obtained. It is impossible to acquire goodwill, as applied in accounting, except by acquiring the controlling interest in another corporation. Unlike identifiable assets, no part of the goodwill value is ever ascribed to minority interests.[5]

In establishing the rules for amortizing goodwill, the Accounting Principles Board conceded that its selection of a forty-year maximum useful life was an arbitrary but practical solution.[6] Nevertheless, it is clear that the intention of the Accounting Principles Board was to limit the amortization to periods in which benefits are expected.[7]

As the benefits expected from goodwill normally relate to the acquisition of a controlling interest in a company, it may be concluded that none of the cost of goodwill is attributable to periods prior to the attainment of control. Thus, the period of amortization should begin when control is achieved, and not applied retroactively to previous purchases.

The same conclusion would not be justified in the case of specifically identifiable assets that have limited lives and that are used by a subsidiary prior to the acquisition of control. The cost of using these assets should be matched with the revenues derived from their use. If the parent company is to recognize its proportionate interest in the earnings of the subsidiary for the periods prior to obtaining its controlling interest, then it should also recognize the portion of its cost attributable to these earnings.

In the previous illustration, assume that the fair values of the identifiable assets of Company S are equal to those recorded on the books. There-

---

[4]"Accounting for Intangible Assets: Accounting Interpretations of APB Opinion No. 17" (New York: American Institute of Certified Public Accountants, March, 1973), par. 2. These interpretations, which were written by the AICPA staff and reviewed by informed members of the profession, were not official pronouncements of the APB and did not establish standards enforceable under the AICPA's *Code of Professional Ethics*.

[5]The "entity theory" of consolidations, which is not currently a generally accepted principle, is an exception.

[6]*Opinions of the Accounting Principles Board, No. 17*, "Intangible Assets" (New York: American Institute of Certified Public Accountants, 1970), par. 23.

[7]*Ibid.*, par. 27.

fore, the entire excess of cost over book value, $2,500, would be attributed to goodwill. Assume further that the goodwill is deemed to have a useful life of 25 years from July 1, 19X4. Amortization of the goodwill would be $100 per year, or $50 for the last 6 months of 19X4. The investment account and retained earnings of the parent are affected as follows, assuming that the equity method is used:

	Investment in Co. S	Retained Earnings, Co. P.
December 31, 19X2:		
Balance..		$ 65,000
January 1, 19X3:		
Purchase of 150 shares of Co. S stock at 130.........	$ 19,500	
	$ 19,500	$ 65,000
December, 19X3:		
Dividends declared:		
Co. S, $5,000....................................		750
Co. P, $10,000...................................		(10,000)
	$ 19,500	$ 55,750
December 31, 19X3:		
Net income from own operations:		
Co. S, $10,000..................................		
Co. P, $20,000..................................		20,000
	$ 19,500	$ 75,750
July 1, 19X4:		
Purchase of 700 shares of Co. S stock at 140.........	98,000	
	$117,500	$ 75,750
December, 19X4:		
Dividends declared:		
Co. S, $5,000....................................	(4,250)	
Co. P, $10,000...................................		(10,000)
	$113,250	$ 65,750
December 31, 19X4:		
Adjustment for earnings on 15% interest in Co. S during 19X3, less dividends received..................	750	750
Net income from own operations, 19X4:		
Co. S, $15,000...................................	7,500	7,500
Co. P, $25,000...................................		25,000
Amortization of goodwill, July 1, 19X4 to December 31, 19X4...	(50)	(50)
Balance...	$121,450	$ 98,950

A work sheet for a consolidated balance sheet on December 31, 19X4, would be prepared as shown on page 421.

If the cost method had been used, the investment account would be stated at $117,500, the sum of the original purchase amounts ($19,500 + $98,000). In this case, additional work sheet adjustments would be required in order to recognize the $4,000 excess of subsidiary income over dividends received ($7,500 + $1,500 − $5,000) and the amortization of goodwill for 19X4. These adjustments would add $3,950 to consolidated retained earnings, making it correspond to the equity-method balance.

Company P and Subsidiary Company S
Work Sheet for Consolidated Balance Sheet
December 31, 19X4

	Co. P	Co. S	Eliminations		Consolidated Balance Sheet	
			Dr.	Cr.	Dr.	Cr.
Debits						
Investment in Co. S. Stock	121,450					
Eliminate Investment.........				121,450		
Goodwill			2,450		2,450	
Other Assets.......................	157,500	200,000			357,500	
	278,950	200,000				
Credits						
Liabilities	80,000	60,000				140,000
Capital Stock, Co. P.............	100,000					100,000
Retained Earnings, Co. P.......	98,950					98,950
Capital Stock, Co. S..............		100,000				
Eliminate 85%			85,000			
Minority Interest, 15%.......						15,000
Retained Earnings, Co. S.......		40,000				
Eliminate 85%			34,000			
Minority Interest, 15%.......						6,000
	278,950	200,000	121,450	121,450	359,950	359,950

SALE OF HOLDINGS IN SUBSIDIARY

A parent may acquire stock in a subsidiary and subsequently sell a part or all of its holdings. For example, assume that Company P completed the following transactions in stock of Company S:

January 1, 19X1, purchased 900 shares at 150.............................. $135,000
July 1, 19X2, sold 100 shares at 170.. 17,000

Each company has capital stock of $100,000 and the shares of each company have a par value of $100. Retained earnings balances on December 31, 19X0, and earnings and dividends for 19X1 and 19X2 are as follows:

	Co. P	Co. S
Retained earnings, December 31, 19X0........................	$145,000	$50,000
Dividends declared in December, 19X1........................		10,000
Net income from own operations, 19X1	30,000	20,000
Dividends declared in December, 19X2........................		10,000
Net income from own operations, 19X2	35,000*	20,000

*Before gain on sale of Company S stock.

The investment and retained earnings accounts of the parent company are affected as shown on page 422.

When a sale is made, the investment account is reduced by the carrying value of the stock sold. When the equity method is used, the carrying value consists of the original cost adjusted by earnings and dividends that have been recorded in the investment account. If there have been several pur-

	If Equity Method Is Used		If Cost Method Is Used	
	Investment in Co. S	Retained Earnings, Co. P	Investment in Co. S	Retained Earnings, Co. P
December 31, 19X0: Balance...		$145,000		$145,000
January 1, 19X1: Purchase of 900 shares of Co. S stock at 150	$135,000		$135,000	
December, 19X1: Dividends declared: Co. S, $10,000.................................	(9,000)			9,000
	$126,000	$145,000	$135,000	$154,000
December 31, 19X1: Net income from own operations: Co. S, $20,000................................. Co. P, $30,000.................................	18,000	18,000 30,000		30,000
	$144,000	$193,000	$135,000	$184,000
July 1, 19X2: Sale of 100 shares at 170. Equity method: carrying value (Jan. 1, 19X2), $16,000; gain, $1,000... Cost method: carrying value, $15,000; gain, $2,000..	(16,000)	1,000	(15,000)	2,000
	$128,000	$194,000	$120,000	$186,000
December, 19X2: Dividends declared: Co. S, $10,000.................................	(8,000)			8,000
	$120,000	$194,000	$120,000	$194,000
December 31, 19X2: Net income from own operations: Co. S, $20,000................................. Co. P, $35,000.................................	16,000	16,000 35,000		35,000
Balance...	$136,000	$245,000	$120,000	$229,000

chases of stock and part of the investment is sold, the carrying value of the specific lot sold may be found or the carrying value may be determined by the first-in, first-out method or by some other method. It is assumed in the illustrations in this chapter that the carrying value of stock sold is determined by the first-in, first-out method.

The sale of stock is recorded by a debit to Cash for the cash proceeds, a credit to the investment account for the carrying value of the stock sold, and a debit or a credit to a loss or a gain account for the difference. Thereafter, the parent in using the equity method takes up earnings and dividends according to the percentage of stock retained. In the example, the carrying value of the stock of Company S is $160 a share. This value was established at the end of 19X1, after the subsidiary earnings for 19X1 had been recorded. The sale of 100 shares is recorded as follows:

```
Cash............................................................................   17,000
    Investment in Co. S Stock .............................................        16,000
    Gain on Sale of Co. S Stock ...........................................         1,000
```

When a sale is made during a fiscal period, it would be possible to take up the estimated subsidiary earnings to the date of sale before recording the sale. Assuming that the earnings to July 1, 19X2, are estimated at $11,000 and that the equity method is used, the effect on the investment and retained earnings accounts would be as follows:

	Investment in Co. S	Retained Earnings, Co. P
December 31, 19X1:		
Balance..	$144,000	$193,000
July 1, 19X2:		
Estimated net income, Co. S, January 1–June 30, $11,000..	9,900	9,900
	$153,900	$202,900
July 1, 19X2:		
Sale of 100 shares at 170. Carrying value, $171 ($153,900 ÷ 900); loss, $100............................	17,100	(100)
	$136,800	$202,800
December, 19X2:		
Dividends paid by Co. S.......................................	(8,000)	
	$128,800	$202,800
December 31, 19X2:		
Net income, Co. S., July 1–December 31, $9,000 (net income for year, $20,000 less income already recognized, January 1–June 30, $11,000)..	7,200	7,200
Net income, Co. P, $35,000.................................		35,000
Balance..	$136,000	$245,000

The parent takes up 90% of the estimated earnings to July 1, 19X2. The investment account is then reduced by the carrying value of the lot sold as of that date. Thereafter 80% of the earnings and dividends are recorded. Although this procedure would seem more logical, the procedure illustrated on page 422 may be preferred, since it does not require an estimate of the earnings to the date of sale and results in the same balances at the end of the year.

A work sheet for Company P and Company S, assuming the use of the equity method, is shown on the top of page 424.

When the cost method is used, the investment account remains at its original cost until the shares are sold. At that point, a gain or loss equal to the difference between the carrying amount of the shares sold and the sales proceeds would be recognized by the parent. This gain or loss may be regarded as the ultimate adjustment of earnings accruing to the controlling interest from its investment in the shares sold, so no further adjustment would be made for these shares on the consolidated work sheet. The work sheet adjustments would recognize the proportionate share of subsidiary earnings retained since the date of acquisition, based on the remaining interest of the parent. A work sheet for Company P and Company S, assuming the use of the cost method, is shown on the bottom of page 424.

Company P and Subsidiary Company S
Work Sheet for Consolidated Balance Sheet
Equity Method: December 31, 19X2

	Co. P	Co. S	Eliminations		Consolidated Balance Sheet	
			Dr.	Cr.	Dr.	Cr.
Debits						
Investment in Co. S Stock	136,000					
Eliminate Investment.........				136,000		
Other Assets........................	459,000	270,000			729,000	
	595,000	270,000				
Credits						
Liabilities	250,000	100,000				350,000
Capital Stock, Co. P..............	100,000					100,000
Retained Earnings, Co. P.......	245,000					245,000
Capital Stock, Co. S..............		100,000				
Eliminate 80%			80,000			
Minority Interest, 20%.......						20,000
Retained Earnings, Co. S.......		70,000				
Eliminate 80%			56,000			
Minority Interest, 20%.......						14,000
	595,000	270,000	136,000	136,000	729,000	729,000

Company P and Subsidiary Company S
Work Sheet for Consolidated Balance Sheet
Cost Method: December 31, 19X2

	Co. P	Co. S	Eliminations		Consolidated Balance Sheet	
			Dr.	Cr.	Dr.	Cr.
Debits						
Investment in Co. S Stock ...	120,000					
Eliminate Investment.......				a) 120,000		
Other Assets......................	459,000	270,000			729,000	
	579,000	270,000				
Credits						
Liabilities	250,000	100,000				350,000
Capital Stock, Co. P............	100,000					100,000
Retained Earnings, Co. P.....	229,000			b) 16,000		245,000
Capital Stock, Co. S............		100,000				
Eliminate 80%			a) 80,000			
Minority Interest, 20%.....						20,000
Retained Earnings, Co. S.....		70,000				
Eliminate 80% of $50,000 Co. S Retained Earnings, 12-31-X0			a) 40,000			
Retained Earnings to Co. P, 80% of $20,000 Co. S Earnings Retained Since Acquisition			b) 16,000			
Minority Interest, 20%.....						14,000
	579,000	270,000	136,000	136,000	729,000	729,000

If the sale of subsidiary stock reduces the ownership percentage of the parent below the level at which the ability to exercise significant influence over the investee can be presumed, then the use of the equity method would no longer be warranted. Although the use of the equity method would be discontinued, there would be no retroactive restatement of the investment account to a cost basis. The carrying amount of the investment would be "frozen" at its value at that time, and only dividends received would be included in income. It would no longer be appropriate to treat the investee company as a subsidiary in consolidated statements, but the carrying amount of the investment would be shown as an asset in the consolidated balance sheet of the parent and its subsidiaries.

SUBSIDIARY ISSUE OR REACQUISITION OF STOCK AFFECTING PARENT'S INTEREST

A parent's interest in a subsidiary may change as a result of the issuance of additional stock or the reacquisition of stock outstanding by the subsidiary company. For example, a parent may own 15,000 shares in a subsidiary company whose shares outstanding total 18,000. The subsidiary's sale of 2,000 additional shares to outsiders changes the interest of the parent from 15,000/18,000, or 83⅓%, to 15,000/20,000, or 75%. On the other hand, the subsidiary's reacquisition of 2,000 shares from outsiders, whether such shares are held as treasury stock or are formally retired, changes the interest of the parent from 15,000/18,000, or 83⅓%, to 15,000/16,000, or 93¾%. Changes in the interest of a parent as a result of changes in the capital structure of the subsidiary require special analysis in the preparation of the consolidated balance sheet.

To illustrate the nature of the problems that arise under these circumstances, assume that on January 1, 19X6, Company P acquires 900 shares of Company S stock for $108,000. The capital stock of Company P and Company S is $100 par. Capital balances for each company on December 31, 19X5, and changes in these balances for 19X6 and 19X7 are as follows:

	Co. P		Co. S		
	Capital Stock	Retained Earnings	Capital Stock	Additional Paid-In Capital	Retained Earnings
Balances, December 31, 19X5..	$100,000	$150,000	$100,000		$10,000
Net income from own operations, 19X6		40,000			15,000
Sale of additional stock, 200 shares at 150 on January 1, 19X7			20,000	$10,000	
Dividends declared, December, 19X7		(20,000)			(15,000)
Net income from own operations, 19X7		45,000			20,000

When the equity method is used, it is necessary to determine the change in the parent company's equity resulting from the change in its ownership interest in the subsidiary. In the example, just before the issue of additional stock by the subsidiary, the parent had a 90% interest in subsidiary capital of $125,000. After the issue, the parent had a 75% interest in capital of $155,000. The parent company has obtained an increase in its equity as follows:

Equity in subsidiary capital after sale of stock, 75% of $155,000.....	$116,250
Equity in subsidiary capital just prior to sale of stock, 90% of $125,000	112,500
Increase in parent's equity as a result of change in interest.............	$ 3,750

The treatment of the increased equity in consolidated statements and in the records of the parent company using the equity method is the subject of some controversy. Some authors have suggested that the parent company recognize the increase in its equity as a gain, thus increasing the investment account and the parent's retained earnings. This approach is objectionable, however, because it results in the recognition of a gain from what is in essence a capital transaction. The parent company would not recognize any gain or loss if it issued its own shares — either common or preferred — at a price that differed from the recorded value of existing shares. Nor would it recognize any gain or loss from selling its own treasury shares at a price that differed from their acquisition cost. From the viewpoint of the consolidated entity, the outstanding stock of the subsidiary is analogous to an element of equity capital.

Furthermore, even when it uses the equity method, the parent does not record its equity in the subsidiary's capital. Therefore, it is unreasonable to treat changes in this equity, which are not attributable to the earnings of the subsidiary, as income of the parent. To emphasize this point, assume that the additional shares were sold by Company S on January 1, 19X6, and that the excess of investment cost over book value was entirely attributable to goodwill. A consolidated statement prepared *prior* to the issuance of the additional shares would reflect the following amount of goodwill:

Amount paid by Company P for 900 shares.....................................	$108,000
Fair value of net assets acquired (90% × $110,000).......................	99,000
Goodwill	$ 9,000

If Company P acquired its interest immediately *after* the issuance of the shares, however, it would calculate goodwill as follows:

Amount paid by Company P for 900 shares.....................................	$108,000
Fair value of net assets acquired (75% × $140,000).......................	105,000
Goodwill	$ 3,000

If Company P had purchased its share immediately before the additional issuance by Company S, recognizing goodwill of $9,000, it would not be reasonable for Company P to then recognize a gain of $6,000 when its equity in Company S increased due to the issuance of the additional shares. If Company P purchased its shares immediately after the additional issuance there would be no gain and goodwill would be decreased by $6,000, yet the economic effect of the two situations is identical.

The issuance of shares by a subsidiary should be treated in the consolidated statements as either a reduction in the goodwill balance or as an additional element of stockholders' equity. If it is treated as a stockholders' equity element, it should be shown on the balance sheet as "Additional Capital from Change in Equity of Subsidiary."

In the previous example, assume that goodwill is to be amortized over a period of 30 years, and that the change in equity due to the subsidiary issuance of additional stock is treated as a capital element in the consolidated balance sheet. The effect on the investment and retained earnings accounts of the parent is shown as follows, assuming that the equity method is used:

	Investment in Co. S	Retained Earnings, Co. P
December 31, 19X5:		
Balance..		$150,000
January 1, 19X6:		
Purchase of 900 shares of Co. S stock at 120.........	$108,000	
	$108,000	$150,000
December, 19X6:		
Net income from own operations:		
Co. S, $15,000..	13,500	13,500
Co. P, $40,000..		40,000
Amortization of goodwill......................................	(300)	(300)
	$121,200	$203,200
December, 19X7:		
Dividends declared:		
Co. S, $15,000..	(11,250)	
Co. P, $20,000..		(20,000)
	$109,950	$183,200
December 31, 19X7:		
Net income from own operations:		
Co. S, $20,000..	15,000	15,000
Co. P, $45,000..		45,000
Amortization of goodwill......................................	(300)	(300)
Balance..	$124,650	$242,900

A work sheet for a consolidated balance sheet at the end of 19X7 would be prepared as shown on page 428.

SUBSIDIARY TREASURY STOCK TRANSACTIONS

When a parent acquires stock in a subsidiary that holds treasury stock, the parent's interest in the subsidiary is calculated in terms of the subsidi-

Company P and Subsidiary Company S
Work Sheet for Consolidated Balance Sheet
December 31, 19X7

	Co. P	Co. S	Eliminations		Consolidated Balance Sheet	
			Dr.	Cr.	Dr.	Cr.
Debits						
Investment in Co. S Stock	124,650					
Eliminate Investment.........				124,650		
Goodwill			8,400		8,400	
Other Assets.......................	338,250	260,000			598,250	
	462,900	260,000				
Credits						
Liabilities	120,000	100,000				220,000
Capital Stock, Co. P..............	100,000					100,000
Retained Earnings, Co. P.......	242,900					242,900
Additional Capital from Change in Equity of Subsidiary...................				3,750		3,750
Capital Stock, Co. S..............		120,000				
Eliminate 75%			90,000			
Minority Interest, 25%.......						30,000
Additional Paid-In Capital, Co. S...............................		10,000				
Eliminate 75%			7,500			
Minority Interest, 25%.......						2,500
Retained Earnings, Co. S.......		30,000				
Eliminate 75%			22,500			
Minority Interest, 25%.......						7,500
	462,900	260,000	128,400	128,400	606,650	606,650

ary shares outstanding. In developing a consolidated balance sheet, the cost of the treasury stock must be assigned to subsidiary capital stock, additional paid-in capital, and retained earnings balances as though the stock were actually retired, and eliminations must be developed in terms of resulting balances. Upon the subsequent sale of treasury stock, there is a change in the parent company's equity in the subsidiary, and special analysis of the effects of such a change on the parent's equity is required in developing the consolidated statement.

To illustrate the nature of the problems that arise under these circumstances, assume that on January 1, 19X5, Company P acquires 750 shares of Company S stock for $105,000. The capital stock of each company is $100 par. Capital stock, treasury stock, additional paid-in capital, and retained earnings balances for each company on December 31, 19X4, and changes in these balances during 19X5 and 19X6 are shown on page 429.

The purchase of 750 shares of Company S stock on January 1, 19X5, when 900 shares were outstanding, gave the parent a 750/900 or 83⅓% interest. In preparing a consolidated balance sheet on the date of stock acquisition, subsidiary capital balances are restated in terms of capital stock out-

	Co. P		Co. S			
	Capital Stock	Retained Earnings	Capital Stock	Treasury Stock	Additional Paid-In Capital	Retained Earnings
Balances, December 31, 19X4...............................	$100,000	$80,000	$100,000	$15,000	$10,000*	$25,000
Dividends declared, December, 19X5		(20,000)				(9,000)
Net income from own operations, 19X5.......................		25,000				15,000
Sale of all treasury stock, 100 shares, at 165 on January 1, 19X6............................				(15,000)	1,500	
Dividends declared, December, 19X6		(20,000)				(10,000)
Net income from own operations, 19X6........................		30,000				25,000

*Capital stock was originally issued at 110, resulting in a $10,000 premium on the sale of the stock.

standing and the additional paid-in capital and retained earnings balances relating to such outstanding stock. Treasury stock is viewed as retired stock, and the payment of $15,000 for reacquired stock results in the proportionate reductions of $10,000 and $1,000 respectively, and a reduction in retained earnings for the balance. Subsidiary capital balances as of December 31, 19X4 are restated as follows:

	Capital Stock	Treasury Stock	Additional Paid-In Capital	Retained Earnings
Balance per subsidiary books....................	$100,000	$15,000	$10,000	$25,000
Cancellation of treasury stock balance......	(10,000)	(15,000)	(1,000)	(4,000)
Balances for consolidation purposes.........	$ 90,000	—	$ 9,000	$21,000

The investment and retained earnings accounts of the parent company are affected by transactions in 19X5 and 19X6 as shown on the top of page 430, assuming that the equity method is used.

A work sheet for a consolidated balance sheet on the date of acquisition of control would be prepared as shown at the bottom of page 430.

When the consolidated balance sheet is prepared, it is necessary to determine the change in the parent's equity resulting from the sale of treasury stock. The increase or the decrease in the parent company's equity is calculated in a manner similar to that illustrated for the sale of unissued shares in a previous example. In this case, the increase in the parent company's equity is determined as follows:

Equity in subsidiary capital after resale of treasury stock, 75% of $142,500	$106,875
Equity in subsidiary capital just prior to resale of treasury stock, 83⅓% of $126,000	105,000
Increase in parent's equity as a result of change in interest.............	$ 1,875

	Investment in Co. S	Ret. Earn., Co. P
December 31, 19X4:		
Balance..		$ 80,000
January 1, 19X5:		
Purchase of 750 shares of Co. S stock at 140.........	$105,000	
	$105,000	$ 80,000
December, 19X5:		
Dividends declared:		
Co. S, $9,000..	(7,500)	
Co. P, $20,000..		(20,000)
	$ 97,500	$ 60,000
December 31, 19X5:		
Net income from own operations:		
Co. S, $15,000...	12,500	12,500
Co. P, $25,000...		25,000
Amortization of goodwill (40 years)........................	(125)	(125)
	$109,875	$ 97,375
December, 19X6:		
Dividends declared:		
Co. S, $10,000...	(7,500)	
Co. P, $20,000...		(20,000)
	$102,375	$ 77,375
December 31, 19X6:		
Net income from own operations:		
Co. S, $25,000...	18,750	18,750
Co. P, $30,000...		30,000
Amortization of goodwill..	(125)	(125)
Balance..	$121,000	$126,000

Company P and Subsidiary Company S
Work Sheet for Consolidated Balance Sheet
January 1, 19X5

	Co. P	Co. S	Eliminations		Consolidated Balance Sheet	
			Dr.	Cr.	Dr.	Cr.
Debits						
Investment in Co. S Stock	105,000					
Eliminate Investment.........				105,000		
Goodwill			5,000		5,000	
Other Assets........................	140,000	160,000			300,000	
	245,000	160,000				
Credits						
Liabilities	65,000	40,000				105,000
Capital Stock, Co. P..............	100,000					100,000
Retained Earnings, Co. P.......	80,000					80,000
Capital Stock, Co. S..............		90,000				
Eliminate 83⅓%			75,000			
Minority Interest, 16⅔%						15,000
Additional Paid-In Cap., Co. S		9,000				
Eliminate 83⅓%			7,500			
Minority Interest, 16⅔%						1,500
Retained Earnings, Co. S.......		21,000				
Eliminate 83⅓%			17,500			
Minority Interest, 16⅔%						3,500
	245,000	160,000	105,000	105,000	305,000	305,000

A work sheet for a consolidated balance sheet at the end of 19X6 would be prepared as follows:

Company P and Subsidiary Company S
Work Sheet for Consolidated Balance Sheet
December 31, 19X6

	Co. P	Co. S	Eliminations		Consolidated Balance Sheet	
			Dr.	Cr.	Dr.	Cr.
Debits						
Investment in Co. S Stock	121,000			121,000		
Eliminate Investment.........						
Goodwill			4,750		4,750	
Other Assets........................	185,000	207,500			392,500	
	306,000	207,500				
Credits						
Liabilities	80,000	50,000				130,000
Capital Stock, Co. P..............	100,000					100,000
Retained Earnings, Co. P.......	126,000					126,000
Additional Capital from Change in Equity of Subsidiary....................................				1,875		1,875
Capital Stock, Co. S..............		100,000				
Eliminate 75%			75,000			
Minority Interest, 25%.......						25,000
Additional Paid-In Capital, Co. S..................................		11,500				
Eliminate 75%			8,625			
Minority Interest, 25%.......						2,875
Retained Earnings, Co. S.......		46,000				
Eliminate 75%			34,500			
Minority Interest, 25%.......						11,500
	306,000	207,500	122,875	122,875	397,250	397,250

QUESTIONS

1. What eliminations are made on a work sheet for a consolidated balance sheet when an investment account shows the acquisition of an 80% interest in a subsidiary, followed by the acquisition of a 10% interest at a later date, assuming that the investment is carried by the equity method?

2. Some accountants maintain that when control of a subsidiary is not achieved until a second or later purchase of stock, earnings should be recognized for consolidation purposes only from the date control is acquired. Others maintain that, with acquisition of control, it is proper to recognize earnings that have accrued on noncontrolling interests from the date of the original acquisitions. Which position do you support? Give reasons.

3. For the past five years, Herbert Co. has maintained an investment (properly accounted for and reported upon) in Broome Co., amounting to a 10% interest in the voting common stock of Broome. The purchase price was $700,000 and the underlying net equity in Broome at the date of purchase was $620,000. On January 2 of the current year, Herbert Co. purchased an additional 15% of the voting common stock of Broome for $1,200,000; the underlying net equity of the additional investment at January 2 was $1,000,000. Broome has been profitable and has paid dividends annually since Herbert's initial acquisition.

Discuss how this increase in ownership affects the accounting for and reporting upon the investment in Broome Co. Include in your discussion adjustments, if any, to the amount shown prior to the increase in investment to bring the amount into conformity with generally accepted accounting principles. Also include how current and subsequent periods would be reported upon.   (AICPA adapted)

4. What entry is made when a parent sells a portion of an investment in a subsidiary and the investment is carried by the equity method?

5. An investment account contains a record of the purchase of two lots of subsidiary stock, 8,000 shares or an 80% lot, followed by 1,500 shares or a 15% lot. The parent subsequently sells 1,000 shares of the second lot purchased. Describe the eliminations that are to be made on a work sheet for a consolidated balance sheet, assuming that investments are carried by the equity method.

6. The Westwood Corporation acquires 80,000 shares of stock of the Bel Air Company, which has 100,000 shares outstanding. At a later date, the Bel Air Company sells 20,000 additional shares on the market.

  (a) What entry is made on the parent company books upon the additional stock issue, assuming that (1) the parent company recognizes a gain or loss and (2) no gain or loss is recognized?
  (b) What eliminations are required on the work sheet for consolidated statements, assuming that the investment is carried by the equity method and no gain or loss is recognized by the parent?

7. The Palmer Company has owned 400,000 shares or an 80% interest in the stock of Travel, Inc., for a number of years. Travel, Inc., acquires 50,000 shares of its stock on the market and formally cancels and retires these shares. How is this transaction recognized on the books of the parent and in the preparation of consolidated statements?

8. The Mason Company, with 10,000 shares outstanding, reacquires 1,000 shares of its own stock on the market at a price below its book value. The Burton Corporation subsequently acquires 7,500 shares of Mason Company stock. In preparing a consolidated balance sheet for the Burton Corporation, what disposition will be made of the treasury stock balance?

9. In Question 8, assuming that the treasury stock is resold by the Mason Company at a price in excess of its cost, (a) what entry will be made on the subsidiary company's books, and (b) what entry will be made on the parent's books, assuming that the investment account is adjusted to reflect the change in equity in Mason?

EXERCISES

1. Company H carries its investment accounts at cost. On December 31, 19X2, it purchased 800 shares of the stock of Company R at 220. On this date it also purchased 600 shares of the stock of Company S at 70, and on July 1, 19X3, it purchased an additional 200 shares at 90. Par values of stock of Companies H, R, and S are $100 each. An analysis of the retained earnings accounts of Companies R and S follows.

	Co. R	Co. S
Retained earnings (deficit), December 31, 19X2......................	$100,000	($25,000)
50% stock dividend declared June 15, distributable June 30, 19X3	(50,000)	
	$ 50,000	($25,000)
Net income (loss), year ended December 31, 19X3 (earned proportionately during the year)	(20,000)	12,000
Retained earnings (deficit), December 31, 19X3......................	$ 30,000	($13,000)

Company H recorded the receipt of the stock dividend by a debit to the investment account and a credit to Retained Earnings. Account balances on the books of Companies H, R, and S as of December 31, 19X3, follow.

December 31, 19X3

	Co. H	Co. R	Co. S
Investment in Co. R	216,000		
Investment in Co. S	60,000		
Capital Stock...	250,000	150,000	100,000
Retained Earnings (Deficit).....................	200,000	30,000	(13,000)

Give the eliminations that would appear on the work sheet and give the balances that would appear on the consolidated balance sheet after eliminations.

2. The Parker Company made purchases of the stock of the Marlow Corporation as follows:

January 1, 19X6, 1,000 shares at 12	$12,000
January 1, 19X7, 6,000 shares at 15	90,000

The Marlow Corporation has 10,000 shares of stock outstanding. Its net earnings for 19X6 and 19X7 were $15,000 and $20,000 respectively, and dividends of $10,000 were paid in 19X6 and also in 19X7.

(a) Assuming that the Parker Company carries investments by the equity method, what entries relating to the investments would be made in 19X6 and 19X7?

(b) Assuming that investments are carried by the cost method, what entries would be made in 19X6 and 19X7?

3. An investment account on the books of Paul and Pearson, Inc., on December 1, 19X9, appeared as follows:

Investment in Ronald Company

1/1/X9 9,500 shares (95% interest) at 16...................... 152,000	7/15/X9 Cash dividend....... 1,900

On this date the company sold 2,000 shares of its Ronald Company stock at
18.

(a) What entry would be made to record the sale?
(b) Assuming that the subsidiary announces net income of $30,000 for
19X9, what entry would be made to record the earnings accruing to the
parent?

4. The Star Company purchased stock of Waldon, Inc., as follows:

> March 1, 19X8,   700 shares at 60
> September 1, 19X8, 150 shares at 70
> July 1, 19X9,   50 shares at 90

Waldon, Inc., has 1,000 shares outstanding. The company reported a
$15,000 net loss from operations for 19X8 and $40,000 net income from operations for 19X9. The Star Company carries the investment account by the equity
method. What entries would be made by the Star Company at the end of each
year?

5. In Exercise 4, assume that the first two purchases occurred as indicated but
that 50 shares were sold at 90 on July 1, 19X9.

(a) How would the sale be recorded?
(b) What entries would be made at the end of each year to record the earnings for the year?

6. On April 1, 19X0, the Bears Corporation purchased 8,000 shares of Thurston
Company stock at 12. Thurston Company capital on January 1, 19X0, and
changes in capital were as follows:

Capital stock (no par), 10,000 shares............................		$80,000
Retained earnings, January 1, 19X0	$13,000	
Net income, 19X0...	8,000	
	$21,000	
Dividends, September, 19X0	4,000	17,000
Capital, December 31, 19X0.......................................		$97,000

The investment account was carried on the Bears Corporation's books at
cost. Give as of December 31, 19X0: (a) the eliminations required on the consolidation work sheet, (b) the goodwill to be shown on a consolidated balance
sheet, (c) the minority interest, and (d) the total amount of earnings attributed to
the controlling interest because of its investment in the subsidiary.

7. In Exercise 6, assume that 1,600 shares of Thurston Company stock were
sold on October 1, 19X0, at 15.

(a) What entry would be made to record the sale.
(b) Give as of December 31, 19X0: (1) the eliminations required on the consolidation work sheet, (2) the goodwill to be shown on a consolidated balance sheet, (3) the minority interest, and (4) the total earnings accruing
to the controlling interest due to its investment in the subsidiary.

8. The Glen Development Company acquired 7,500 shares of the Ever Ready
Company on the market for $160,000 at the beginning of 19X4. At this time the

books of the Ever Ready Company showed the following: 10,000 shares of stock outstanding, $10 par; additional paid-in capital, $30,000; and retained earnings, $10,000. Any difference between investment cost and subsidiary book value at the time was attributed to land values. Net income for 19X4 was $20,000. At the beginning of 19X5, the subsidiary issued 2,500 additional shares which were sold to outsiders at 20. Net income for 19X5 was $30,000.

(a) What entries should be made on the books of the parent for 19X4 and 19X5, assuming that the parent uses the equity method and recognizes gain or loss from the change in its equity in Ever Ready?

(b) What elimination entry should be made on the consolidation work sheet as of December 31, 19X5, to reflect the issuance of additional shares by Ever Ready, assuming that the parent uses the equity method and does not recognize any gain or loss from this event?

9. In Exercise 8, assume that the additional issue of 2,500 shares was sold to the parent instead of to outsiders.

(a) What entries would be made by the parent for 19X5, assuming that the parent uses the equity method and recognizes gain or loss from the change in its equity in Ever Ready?

(b) What elimination entry should be made on the consolidation work sheet as of December 31, 19X5, to reflect the issuance of additional shares by Ever Ready, assuming that the parent does not recognize any gain or loss from this event?

10. The Holmes Company owns 9,000 shares of Pacific Wholesalers acquired at a cost of $144,000 in 19X0. At the time of the purchase, Pacific Wholesalers had stock outstanding of $100,000, $10 par, and retained earnings of $60,000. On January 1, 19X7, Pacific Wholesalers issued 2,000 additional shares at par to raise funds. At this time the company's retained earnings were $20,000. During 19X7 the subsidiary paid dividends of $12,000 and reported a net income of $15,000.

(a) What entries should be made on the books of the Holmes Company in 19X7, assuming that the investment is carried on the equity basis and Holmes recognizes gain or loss due to the change in its equity in Pacific?

(b) What entries should be made in 19X7, assuming the use of the cost method?

(c) What are the retained earnings of the parent company after consolidation on December 31, 19X7, assuming that the cost basis is used and that its own retained earnings before considering subsidiary activities are $100,000?

11. The Berry Company purchased 9,000 shares of Stern, Inc., at 22 on July 1, 19X9. On this date the capital of Stern, Inc., is as follows:

Capital stock issued, 12,000 shares, $10 par.............................	$120,000
Premium on stock...	24,000
Retained earnings..	75,000
Treasury stock, 2,000 shares at cost.....................................	(18,000)
Capital, July 1, 19X9	$201,000

(a) Assuming that a consolidated balance sheet is prepared on the date of stock acquisition, (1) give the elimination that is required on the work sheet, and (2) calculate the cost or book value excess on the investment, and the minority interest that will be reported on the consolidated balance sheet.

(b) Assuming that the subsidiary sells its treasury stock on the market at 14 and the parent recognizes gain or loss due to the change in its equity, how should the sale be recognized by the parent company?

PROBLEMS

14-1. On January 2, 19X4, the Kirby Company purchased 15,000 shares of Koger Company stock at 16 and on July 1, 19X4, purchased an additional 1,500 shares at 17. The following information is available on December 31, 19X4:

	Kirby Co.		Koger Co.
Investment in Koger Co.	$265,500		
Other assets	645,000		$475,000
Total assets	$910,500		$475,000
Liabilities	$230,500		$160,000
Capital stock (50,000 shares)	500,000	(20,000 shares)	300,000
Retained earnings (deficit):			
Balance, January 1, 19X4 .... $135,000		($ 7,500)	
Net income for 19X4 65,000		35,000	
$200,000		$27,500	
Dividends declared and paid in November, 19X4 .... (20,000)		(12,500)	
Balance, December 31, 19X4	180,000		15,000
Total liabilities and stockholders' equity	$910,500		$475,000

Instructions: Prepare a work sheet and a consolidated balance sheet as of December 31, 19X4. The Kirby Company maintains its investment accounts at cost. Specific asset accounts of Koger Co. reflected fair values on each acquisition date.

14-2. On December 31, 19X2, Company A purchased 1,200 shares of the stock of Company B at $120 a share. On April 1, 19X3, Company A purchased 600 shares of the stock of Company B at $80 a share and 1,500 shares of the stock of Company C at $70 a share. Balance sheets of the three companies on December 31, 19X3, are as follows:

	Co. A	Co. B	Co. C
Cash	$ 64,000	$ 40,000	$ 15,000
Notes receivable	30,000	30,000	20,000
Accounts receivable	60,000	50,000	40,000
Inventories	110,000	91,000	65,000
Investment in Co. B	192,000		
Investment in Co. C	105,000		
Bonds of Co. B (face value, $20,000)	19,000		
Plant and equipment	200,000	150,000	100,000
Total assets	$780,000	$361,000	$240,000

	Co. A	Co. B	Co. C
Notes payable...............................	$ 74,000	$ 35,000	$ 20,000
Dividends payable	28,000	9,000	
Accounts payable..........................	60,000	55,000	70,000
Bonds payable		50,000	
Discount on bonds payable.............		(4,000)	
Preferred stock, Co. A ($100 par)....	100,000		
Common stock, Co. A ($100 par).....	300,000		
Retained earnings, Co. A................	218,000		
Capital stock, Co. B ($50 par)		150,000	
Retained earnings, Co. B................		66,000	
Capital stock, Co. C (2,000 shares, no par).....................................			180,000
Deficit, Co. C................................			(30,000)
Total liabilities and stockholders' equity	$780,000	$361,000	$240,000

Company A records its investments at cost, but has not recognized the dividend declared by Company B on December 31, 19X3. The notes payable by Company C represent loans from Companies A and B.

An analysis of the retained earnings accounts reveals the following:

	Co. A	Co. B	Co. C
Retained earnings (deficit) December 31, 19X2.....	$210,000	$95,000	($40,000)
Stock dividend declared June 15, 19X3, distributable June 30		(50,000)	
	$210,000	$45,000	($40,000)
Net income from own operations for 19X3	36,000	30,000	10,000
	$246,000	$75,000	($30,000)
Cash dividends declared December 31, 19X3, payable January 15, 19X4.....................................	(28,000)	(9,000)	
Retained earnings (deficit), December 31, 19X3....	$218,000	$66,000	($30,000)

Instructions: Prepare a work sheet and a consolidated balance sheet as of December 31, 19X3. Assume that the fair values of identifiable assets of Company B were equal to their book values on December 31, 19X2, and that a difference between book value and investment cost of Company C is attributable to the value of nondepreciable plant assets.

14-3. The December 31, 19X9, balance sheets of Encanto Corporation and its subsidiary, Norris Corporation, are as follows:

Assets	Encanto Corporation	Norris Corporation
Cash..	$ 167,250	$101,000
Accounts receivable	178,450	72,000
Notes receivable	87,500	28,000
Dividends receivable.......................................	36,000	
Inventories	122,000	68,000
Property, plant, and equipment	487,000	252,000
Accumulated depreciation...............................	(117,000)	(64,000)
Investment in Norris Corporation.....................	240,800	
	$1,202,000	$457,000

Liabilities and Stockholders' Equity	Encanto Corporation	Norris Corporation
Accounts payable	$ 222,000	$ 76,000
Notes payable	79,000	89,000
Dividends payable		40,000
Common stock, $10 par	400,000	100,000
Retained earnings	501,000	152,000
	$1,202,000	$457,000

Encanto initially acquired 60 percent of the outstanding common stock of Norris in 19X7. This purchase resulted in no difference between cost and net assets acquired. As of December 31, 19X9, the percentage owned is 90 percent. An analysis of the investment account is as follows:

Date	Description	Amount
Dec. 31, 19X7	Acquired 6,000 shares	$ 70,800
Dec. 31, 19X8	60% of 19X8 net income of $78,000	46,800
Sept. 1, 19X9	Acquired 3,000 shares	92,000
Dec. 31, 19X9	Subsidiary income for 19X9	67,200*
Dec. 31, 19X9	90% of dividends declared	(36,000)
		$240,800

*Subsidiary income for 19X9:	
60% of $96,000	$ 57,600
30% of $96,000 × 33⅓%	9,600
	$ 67,200

Assume that Norris's net income is earned ratably during the year. Amortization of the excess of cost over the net assets acquired is to be recorded over sixty months.

On December 15, 19X9, Norris declared a cash dividend of $4 per share of common stock, payable to shareholders on January 7 of the following year.

During 19X9 Encanto sold merchandise to Norris. Encanto's cost for this merchandise was $68,000, and the sale was made at 125% of cost. Norris's inventory at December 31, 19X9, included merchandise purchased from Encanto at a cost to Norris of $35,000.

In December, 19X8, Norris sold merchandise to Encanto for $67,000, which was at a markup of 35% over Norris's cost. On January 1, 19X9, $54,000 of this merchandise remained in Encanto's inventory. This merchandise was subsequently sold by Encanto at a profit of $11,000 during 19X9.

On October 1, 19X9, Encanto sold for $42,000 excess equipment to Norris. Data relating to this equipment is as follows:

Book value on Encanto's records	$36,000
Method of depreciation	Straight-line
Estimated remaining life on October 1, 19X9	10 years

Near the end of 19X9, Norris reduced the balance of its intercompany account payable to Encanto to zero by transferring $8,000 to Encanto. This payment was still in transit on December 31, 19X9.

Instructions: Prepare a work sheet for a consolidated balance sheet for Encanto Corporation and its subsidiary, Norris Corporation, as of December 31, 19X9. Formal statements and journal entries are not required.   (AICPA adapted)

14-4. Williard, Inc., acquired 10% of the 100,000 shares of $2.50 par common stock outstanding of Thorne Corporation on January 1, 19X0, for $38,000. An additional 70,000 shares were acquired for $331,600 on June 30, 19X1 (at which time there was no material difference between the fair and book values of Thorne's assets and liabilities). Williard uses the equity method of accounting for its investment in Thorne.

The balance sheets for both companies for the year ended December 31, 19X1, are as follows:

Debits	Williard, Inc.	Thorne Corporation
Cash	$ 130,000	$ 60,000
Accounts receivable	160,000	75,000
Notes receivable	15,000	12,200
Interest receivable	2,100	1,600
Dividends receivable	8,800	
Marketable securities	31,220	9,700
Inventories	180,000	96,000
Plant and equipment	781,500	510,000
Investment in Thorne Corporation stock	405,600	
Investment in Thorne Corporation bonds	30,580	
Advance to Thorne Corporation	32,000	
Unamortized bond discount		7,500
	$1,776,800	$772,000

Credits	Williard, Inc.	Thorne Corporation
Accumulated depreciation	$ 87,000	$ 85,000
Accounts payable	34,500	16,000
Notes payable	5,500	3,800
Dividends payable	20,000	11,000
Interest payable	18,000	13,000
Other accrued liabilities	15,000	1,200
Advance from Williard, Inc.		32,000
Bonds payable	400,000	150,000
Capital stock	500,000	250,000
Capital in excess of par	14,000	29,000
Retained earnings	682,800	181,000
	$1,776,800	$772,000

The following information is also available:

(1) Data on 19X1 intercompany sales and ending inventories are as follows:

	Williard, Inc.	Thorne Corporation
Intercompany sales:		
January 1–June 30	$39,000	$24,000
June 30–December 31	$41,600	$41,000
Gross profit	30%	25%
Intercompany payable at year-end	$12,000	$ 7,000
Year-end inventory of intercompany purchases at fifo cost	$26,000	$22,000

(2) Williard, Inc., acquired $30,000 of the Thorne Corporation 6% bonds on August 31, 19X1, for $30,580 plus accrued interest. Thorne Corporation issued the 20-year bonds ten years ago at 90 and has been paying the interest on each January 1 and July 1 due date.

(3) An analysis of Investment in Thorne Corporation Stock:

Date	Description	Amount
January 1, 19X0	Investment	$ 38,000
June 30, 19X1	Investment	331,600
December 31, 19X1	80% of net increase in retained earnings of Thorne Corporation during 19X1	36,000
		$405,600

(4) An analysis of the companies' retained earnings accounts:

	Williard, Inc.	Thorne Corporation
Balance, January 1, 19X0................................	$540,000	$101,000
Net income for 19X0.......................................	55,000	40,000
Cash dividends in 19X0..................................		(5,000)
Balance, December 31, 19X0...........................	$595,000	$136,000
Net income:		
January 1–June 30, 19X1.............................	31,000	23,000
June 30–December 31, 19X1..........................	40,800	33,000
Dividends declared, December 15, 19X1............	(20,000)	(11,000)
80% of net increase in retained earnings of Thorne Corporation during 19X1....................	36,000	
Balance, December 31, 19X1............................	$682,800	$181,000

(5) Thorne's other equity accounts have not changed in the past five years.
(6) On September 1, 19X1, Williard, Inc., sold equipment with a cost of $40,000 and accumulated depreciation of $9,300 to Thorne Corporation for $20,200. Thorne Corporation recorded the equipment as having a cost of $29,500 with accumulated depreciation of $9,300. At that date the equipment had an estimated salvage value of $500 and an estimated life of ten years.
(7) Included in Williard, Inc.'s Notes Receivable are $2,000 in non-interest-bearing notes of Thorne Corporation.

Instructions: Develop a work sheet for the preparation of a consolidated balance sheet for Williard, Inc., and its subsidiary, Thorne Corporation, as of December 31, 19X1. Formal statements and journal entries are not required. Assume that both companies made all of the adjusting entries required for separate financial statements unless an obvious discrepancy exists. Income taxes should not be considered in the solution. Any amortization of goodwill is to be computed over a 40-year period.

(AICPA adapted)

14-5. The following information is available for Companies P, A, and B on December 31, 19X8:

	Co. P	Co. A	Co. B
Investment in Co. A	$105,000		
Investment in Co. B	144,000		
Other assets	689,500	$150,000	$265,000
Total assets	$938,500	$150,000	$265,000

	Co. P	Co. A	Co. B
Liabilities	$120,000	$ 52,500	$ 95,000
Capital stock (all $10 par).................................	500,000	100,000	100,000
Additional paid-in capital.................................	150,000		20,000
Retained earnings (deficit).................................	168,500	(2,500)	50,000
Total liabilities and stockholders' equity............	$938,500	$150,000	$265,000

Investment accounts are carried at cost. Book values of Company A assets reflected fair values at the times of each stock purchase. A difference between investment cost and book value of Company B was attributed to nondepreciable plant assets.

Stock of Co. A was purchased as follows:

September 1, 19X7, 7,000 shares at 10
January 1, 19X8,   2,500 shares at 14

Stock of Co. B was purchased as follows:

April 1, 19X8,   9,000 shares at 18

One thousand shares of Company B stock were sold on July 1, 19X8, at 12. Changes in retained earnings for the three companies were as follows:

	Co. P	Co. A	Co. B
Balance of retained earnings (deficit), January 1, 19X6	$222,500	($20,000)	$35,000
Dividends, November, 19X7	(20,000)		(10,000)
	$202,500	($20,000)	$25,000
Increase (decrease) from own operations for 19X7 ...	(45,000)	7,500	15,000
	$157,500	($12,500)	$40,000
Dividends, November, 19X8	(14,000)		(10,000)
	$143,500	($12,500)	$30,000
Increase from own operations, 19X8.......................	25,000	10,000	20,000
Balance of retained earnings (deficit), December 31, 19X8...	$168,500	($ 2,500)	$50,000

Instructions: Prepare a work sheet for a consolidated balance sheet as of December 31, 19X8.

14-6. Accounts of the Dodge, Elgin, and Fuller companies show the following balances on December 31, 19X6:

	Dodge Co.	Elgin Co.	Fuller Co.
Investment in Elgin Co.	$172,000		
Investment in Fuller Co.	98,500		
Other assets	389,000	$275,000	$145,000
Liabilities	164,000	80,000	50,000
Capital stock (all $100 par).............	400,000	150,000	100,000
Retained earnings (deficit)..............	95,500	45,000	(5,000)

The investment accounts appear as follows:

Investment in Elgin Co.

April 1, 19X5	1,200 shares at 125	150,000
July 1, 19X5	50 shares at 130	6,500
Nov. 1, 19X6	100 shares at 155	15,500

442

PART THREE — CONSOLIDATIONS

Investment in Fuller Co.

| Jan. 2, 19X5 | 900 shares at 110 | 99,000 | Oct. 1, 19X5 | 150 shares at 110 | 16,500 |
| July 1, 19X6 | 100 shares at 160 | 16,000 | | | |

Changes in retained earnings for the three companies follow:

	Dodge Co.	Elgin Co.	Fuller Co.
Retained earnings, December 31, 19X4................	$82,500	$10,000	$ 5,000
Dividends, 19X6	(16,000)		
	$66,500	$10,000	$ 5,000
Increase (decrease) from own operations, 19X5.....	25,000	10,000	(15,000)
Retained earnings (deficit), December 31, 19X5....	$91,500	$20,000	($10,000)
Dividends paid in December, 19X6......................	(16,000)	(5,000)	
	$75,500	$15,000	($10,000)
Increase from own operations, 19X6	20,000	30,000	5,000
Retained earnings (deficit), December 31, 19X6....	$95,500	$45,000	($ 5,000)

Book values of identifiable assets of Elgin Co. were approximately equal to fair values on April 1, 19X5. The difference between the cost of the investment in Fuller on January 2, 19X5, and book values of net assets was attributed to the value of land.

The sale of Fuller Co. stock was made at $150 a share. The investment account was credited at cost, and income for 19X5 was credited for the gain on the sale.

Instructions: Prepare a work sheet for a consolidated balance sheet as of December 31, 19X6.

14-7. Balance sheets for Companies W, X, Y, and Z on December 31, 19X7, are as follows. Investments in subsidiaries were carried at cost.

	Co. W	Co. X	Co. Y	Co. Z
Investment in Co. X (800 shares)...	$ 71,600			
Investment in Co. Y (950 shares)...	68,000			
Investment in Co. Z (900 shares)...	143,500			
Inventories	120,000	$ 55,000	$ 50,000	$ 75,000
Plant and equipment (net)............	100,000	80,000		100,000
Co. X bonds (face value, $20,000).	20,400			
Other assets	200,000	115,000	105,000	130,000
Total assets	$723,500	$250,000	$155,000	$305,000
Bonds payable		$100,000		
Discount on bonds payable...........		(4,000)		
Other liabilities	$238,500	34,000	$100,000	$150,000
Capital stock (all $100 par)...........	250,000	100,000	100,000	100,000
Additional paid-in capital		10,000		
Retained earnings (deficit)	235,000	10,000	(45,000)	55,000
Total liabilities and stockholders' equity	$723,500	$250,000	$155,000	$305,000

Retained earnings changes have been as follows:

	Co. W	Co. X	Co. Y	Co. Z
Retained earnings (deficit), December 31, 19X5......................	$185,000	($30,000)	($35,000)	$ 60,000
Net income (loss), 19X6	40,000	20,000	(25,000)	60,000
	$225,000	($10,000)	($60,000)	$120,000
Dividends paid in December, 19X6	(20,000)			(20,000)
Retained earnings (deficit), December 31, 19X6......................	$205,000	($10,000)	($60,000)	$100,000
Net income (loss), 19X7	50,000	30,000	15,000	(45,000)
	$255,000	$20,000	($45,000)	$ 55,000
Dividends paid in December, 19X7	(20,000)	(10,000)		
Retained earnings (deficit), December 31, 19X7......................	$235,000	$10,000	($45,000)	$ 55,000

Company X stock was purchased on January 2, 19X6.
Company Y stock was purchased as follows:

January 1, 19X6, 850 shares at 70..	$59,500
May 1, 19X7, 100 shares at 85	8,500
Balance in account	$68,000

The Company Z investment account shows:

April 1, 19X6, purchased 850 shares at 160.............................	$136,000
July 1, 19X7, sold 100 shares at 210..	(21,000)
	$115,000
September 1, 19X7, purchased 150 shares at 190......................	28,500
Balance in account	$143,500

Book values of identifiable assets of Companies X and Y reflected fair values on the dates of acquisition. A difference between the amount paid for Company Z stock in 19X6 and the book values of identifiable assets was attributed to nondepreciable assets at that time.

An analysis of inventories on December 31, 19X7, disclosed the following:

	Inventory Total	Acquired from			
		Outsiders	Co. W	Co. X	Co. Y	Co. Z
Co. W.....	$120,000	$ 90,000		$20,000	$10,000	
X......	55,000	40,000	$15,000			
Y......	50,000	35,000	10,000	5,000		
Z......	75,000	50,000	15,000	10,000		
	$300,000	$215,000	$40,000	$35,000	$10,000	

All intercompany sales were made at a 20% gross profit on sales price.
Intercompany receivables on December 31 totaled $65,000.

Plant and equipment of Company W included assets of $30,000 constructed by Company X in 19X6. The cost of construction to Company X was $24,000. These assets had been depreciated by Company W since July 1, 19X6, at 10% per year.

Instructions: From the foregoing balance sheets and supplementary information, construct a work sheet and a consolidated balance sheet at December 31, 19X7.

14-8. The following balances appear on the books of the Bishop Company and its subsidiary, the Carey Company, on the dates stated:

	Jan. 1 19X0	Dec. 31 19X0	Dec. 31 19X1	Dec. 31 19X2
Bishop Company:				
Investment in Carey Co. ...	$128,000	$128,000	$119,000	$140,000
Retained earnings	135,000	160,000	148,000	155,000
Carey Company:				
Capital stock..................	100,000	100,000	100,000	100,000
Retained earnings	50,000	62,000	70,000	80,000

The Carey Company's capital stock consists of 1,000 shares of $100 par each. The Bishop Company purchased 800 shares on January 1, 19X0, sold 50 shares on January 1, 19X1, and purchased 100 shares on January 1, 19X2.

The investment account was charged with the cost of stock purchased and was credited with the proceeds from the stock sold. The Bishop Company has made no other entries in the investment account and has credited income for all dividends received from the Carey Company. The difference between investment cost and the subsidiary equity acquired is recognized on the consolidated balance sheet as goodwill.

Instructions: Prepare statements showing the composition of the amounts of goodwill, retained earnings, and minority interest appearing on the consolidated balance sheets prepared on: (1) December 31, 19X0; (2) December 31, 19X1; (3) December 31, 19X2.

(AICPA adapted)

14-9. Company L acquired 90% of the outstanding stock of Company N on March 31, 19X8, for $162,000. Previously Company L acquired 30% of the outstanding stock of Company M on January 1, 19X7, for $25,000. This percentage was not considered sufficient to give Company L substantial influence over operations of Company M at that time, however. On July 1, 19X8, Company L purchased an additional 40% of the outstanding stock of Company M for $42,000, thereby gaining effective control of Company M as of that date. To increase its stockholdings in Company M without impairing working capital, Company L sold 100 shares of Company N stock on October 1, 19X8, for $20,500 and immediately used $13,800 of the proceeds to secure an additional 15% of Company M outstanding stock.

The balance sheets of the respective companies as of December 31, 19X8, are as follows:

	Co. L	Co. M	Co. N
Cash	$ 86,000	$ 12,500	$ 35,000
Notes receivable	18,000	6,000	8,000
Accounts receivable (net)	52,000	13,000	34,000
Inventories	89,500	16,000	51,000
Investment in Co. M (at cost)	80,800		
Investment in Co. N (at book value)	149,320		
Plant and equipment (net)	225,000	56,500	101,000
Total assets	$700,620	$104,000	$229,000
Notes payable	$ 9,000	$ 8,000	$ 12,000
Accounts payable	73,600	22,400	46,200
Accrued liabilities	5,320	2,600	4,800
Capital stock, $100 par	400,000	60,000	100,000
Retained earnings	212,700	11,000	66,000
Total liabilities and stockholders' equity	$700,620	$104,000	$229,000

A summary of retained earnings (deficit) from January 1, 19X7, to December 31, 19X8, follows:

	Co. L	Co. M	Co. N
Balance, January 1, 19X7	$150,000	($10,000)	$40,000
Income (loss) — 19X7:			
1st quarter	7,000	(2,000)	3,000
2d quarter	9,000	1,000	4,000
3d quarter	15,000	3,000	6,000
4th quarter	12,000	6,000	5,000
Total	$193,000	($ 2,000)	$58,000
Dividends declared and paid on July 1, 19X7	(12,000)		(3,000)
Balance, January 1, 19X8	$181,000	($ 2,000)	$55,000
Income (loss) — 19X8:			
1st quarter	6,000	2,500	4,500
2d quarter	11,500	3,000	7,000
3d quarter	13,000	3,600	6,200
4th quarter	16,200	5,900	5,300
Total	$227,700	$13,000	$78,000
Dividends declared June 1, 19X8, and paid on June 15, 19X8	(15,000)		(12,000)
Dividends declared December 1, 19X8 and paid on December 15, 19X8		(2,000)	
Balance, December 31, 19X8	$212,700	$11,000	$66,000

Income of Company L for the fourth quarter of 19X8 includes $2,500 representing the gain on the sale of 100 shares of Company N stock. (Proceeds $20,500, less March 31, 19X8, cost, $18,000.)

Inventories at December 31, 19X8, include intercompany items as follows, all goods having been acquired from affiliated companies in the last quarter of 19X8:

Company		Amount	
Purchaser	Seller	Inventory	Seller's Cost
L	M	$13,600	$12,000
L	N	5,000	4,500*
M	N	13,000	11,000
N	M	16,000	14,000

*Acquired by Company N from Company M, to whom the cost was $4,200.

Instructions: Prepare a work sheet for a consolidated balance sheet for Companies L, M, and N, as of December 31, 19X8.

(AICPA adapted)

14-10. Balance sheets for Companies P, R, and S on December 31, 19X5, were as follows:

	Co. P	Co. R	Co. S
Investment in Co. R (1,600 shares)	$ 208,000		
Investment in Co. S (1,250 shares).......	140,000		
Other assets.....................................	1,247,000	$565,000	$425,000
Total assets.....................................	$1,595,000	$565,000	$425,000
Liabilities..	$ 645,000	$175,000	$204,000
Capital stock (all $100 par)	600,000	250,000	200,000
Additional paid-in capital	50,000	10,000	
Retained earnings.............................	300,000	130,000	21,000
Total liabilities and stockholders' equity	$1,595,000	$565,000	$425,000

Company P acquired 1,600 shares of Company R stock in 19X1 and has carried the investment account on the equity basis. At the beginning of 19X5, Company R sold to outsiders 500 shares of its stock at 120. In 19X2, Company P acquired 1,250 shares of stock of Company S; this investment was also carried on the equity basis. On July 1, 19X5, Company S sold to outsiders 500 shares of its stock at par. Differences between Company P's investments and the book values of underlying assets were attributed to land values at the dates of acquisition. On December 31, 19X5, Company P owes Company R $100,000.

No entries had been made in the investment accounts for 19X5. Changes in retained earnings for the three companies for 19X5 were as follows:

	Co. P	Co. R	Co. S
Retained earnings (deficit), January 1	$265,000	$100,000	($ 9,000)
Net income for 19X5.....................	65,000	30,000	30,000
	$330,000	$130,000	$21,000
Dividends paid in 19X5..................	(30,000)		
Retained earnings, December 31.....	$300,000	$130,000	$21,000

Instructions: (1) Prepare the entries on December 31, 19X5, to bring the investment accounts on the books of Company P up to date. Assume that Co. P does not recognize any gain or loss when subsidiaries issue new shares.

(2) Prepare a work sheet for a consolidated balance sheet as of December 31, 19X5.

14-11. In April, 19X2, Craig, Inc., organized two subsidiaries, South Company and West Company. Each subsidiary issued 30,000 shares of stock, $10 par, and all of the shares were acquired by the parent company. At the end of 19X9, South Company acquired properties that were recorded at a value of $150,000 in exchange for 6,000 shares of its stock, and West Company sold 7,500 shares of its stock at 12½. Parties to the exchange and to the sale were outsiders. Craig, Inc., maintains its investment accounts on a cost basis, and does not recognize any gain or loss from changes in its equity due to subsidiary capital transactions.

Balance sheet data for the parent and its subsidiaries on December 31, 19X9, were as follows:

	Craig, Inc.	South Co.	West Co.
Investment in South Co.	$ 300,000		
Investment in West Co.	300,000		
Other assets	5,575,000	$2,650,000	$993,750
Total assets	$6,175,000	$2,650,000	$993,750
Liabilities	$1,825,000	$ 850,000	$650,000
Capital stock (all $10 par)	2,500,000	360,000	375,000
Additional paid-in capital	1,000,000	90,000	18,750
Retained earnings (deficit)	850,000	1,350,000	(50,000)
Total liabilities and stockholders' equity	$6,175,000	$2,650,000	$993,750

Instructions: Prepare a work sheet for a consolidated balance sheet as of December 31, 19X9.

14-12. Balance sheets on December 31, 19X7, for the Wells Company and its subsidiary, the Wiley Company, appear as follows:

	Wells Co.	Wiley Co.
Investment in Wiley Co. (4,500 shares)	$ 230,000	
Other assets	2,235,000	$360,000
Total assets	$2,465,000	$360,000
Liabilities	$ 600,000	$115,000
Capital stock (all $20 par)	1,000,000	120,000
Additional paid-in capital	350,000	42,000
Retained earnings	515,000	83,000
Total liabilities and stockholders' equity	$2,465,000	$360,000

The Wells Company carries its investment in the Wiley Company at cost. Its interest in the subsidiary was acquired on July 1, 19X2. At that time the book values of identifiable assets of Wiley reflected current market values, and the stockholders' equity of the Wiley Company was as follows:

Capital stock issued, 6,000 shares...	$120,000
Additional paid-in capital (premium on stock issued).................	30,000
Retained earnings...	75,000
Treasury stock, 1,000 shares at cost...	(16,500)
Stockholders' equity, July 1, 19X2	$208,500

The treasury stock was sold to outsiders by the Wiley Company in 19X6 at $12,000 in excess of its cost.

Instructions: Prepare a work sheet for a consolidated balance sheet as of December 31, 19X7.

15
Consolidated Statements — Indirect and Mutual Holdings

A parent company may control another company that itself is a parent company. Such a condition is described as one of *indirect ownership*. Sometimes a company's holdings are supplemented by those of an affiliated company. Control that is achieved through a connecting affiliate may also be regarded as a condition of indirect ownership. Occasionally one may find that a subsidiary holds a block of the stock of the parent company. Such a situation is described as one of *mutual* or *reciprocal ownership*. This chapter considers the special problems that arise in the preparation of consolidated statements when indirect and mutual holdings are encountered.

INDIRECT HOLDINGS

When a parent company owns controlling interests in companies that themselves are parents, the preparation of consolidated statements for the parent at the apex of the system requires careful analysis of capitals, earnings, and dividends, beginning with the companies on the lowest tier. The following paragraphs describe and illustrate the accounting for relationships involving a parent, a subparent, and a subsidiary. First it is assumed that a controlling interest is acquired in a company that subsequently acquires control over an affiliate. Then it is assumed that a controlling interest is acquired in a company that already exercises control over an affiliate. Finally, consolidations involving a connecting affiliate are described.

Subholdings Acquired After Parent Company Control

To illustrate the consolidation procedures when subparent holdings are acquired after the parent holdings have been acquired, assume that on January 1, 19X4, Company P purchases 800 shares of Company SP stock at 150, paying $120,000. The $8,000 difference between investment cost and book value at that time is attributed to land values. On January 1, 19X5, Company SP purchases 900 shares of Company S stock at 140, paying $126,000.

The goodwill of $18,000 arising from this purchase is to be amortized over a period of 30 years. The capital stock of each company is $100,000, consisting of 1,000 shares with a par value of $100. Retained earnings balances on December 31, 19X3, and earnings and dividends for 19X4 and 19X5 are as follows:

	Co. P	Co. SP	Co. S
Retained earnings, December 31, 19X3.......	$240,000	$60,000	$10,000
Net income (loss) from own operations, 19X4	30,000	(15,000)	10,000
Dividends declared in December, 19X5	10,000	10,000	5,000
Net income (loss) from own operations, 19X5	(20,000)	30,000	15,000

Changes in the investment accounts and the retained earnings accounts of the parent and the subparent companies are shown below and on page 451.

	If Equity Method Is Used			
	Co. P Books		Co. SP Books	
	Investment in Co. SP	Retained Earnings, Co. P	Investment in Co. S	Retained Earnings, Co. SP
December 31, 19X3, balances.....................		$240,000		$60,000
January 1, 19X4				
Purchase by Co. P of 800 shares of Co. SP stock at 150......................................	$120,000			
	$120,000	$240,000		$60,000
December 31, 19X4:				
Net income (loss), 19X4:				
Co. SP, ($15,000)	(12,000)	(12,000)		(15,000)
Co. P, $30,000		30,000		
	$108,000	$258,000		$45,000
January 1, 19X5:				
Purchase by Co. SP of 900 shares of Co. S stock at 140......................................			$126,000	
	$108,000	$258,000	$126,000	$45,000
December, 19X5:				
Dividends paid:				
Co. S, $5,000...................................			(4,500)	
Co. SP, $10,000	(8,000)			(10,000)
Co. P, $10,000		(10,000)		
	$100,000	$248,000	$121,500	$35,000
December 31, 19X5:				
Net income (loss), 19X5:				
Co. S, $15,000			13,500	13,500
Less goodwill amortization			(600)	(600)
Co. SP:				
Own operations................... $30,000				30,000
Through ownership of Co. S.. 12,900				
To Co. P, 80% $42,900	34,320	34,320		
Co. P, ($20,000)		(20,000)		
December 31, 19X5, balances....................	$134,320	$262,320	$134,400	$77,900

Equity method. When the equity method of carrying investments is used, no special problem arises until a subsidiary acquires control over another company and thus becomes a subparent. Upon assuming control, the subparent now recognizes the changes in the capital of the company it controls. The parent, in turn, recognizes the subparent's capital changes, which arise from (1) the subparent's own operations and (2) the subparent's recognition of the earnings of the company it controls.

In the example, beginning in 19X5 Company P records its share of the earnings of Company SP only after the latter has recognized the earnings accruing from operations of Company S. Earnings of Company S for 19X5 are $15,000. Company SP records in its investment and retained earnings accounts 90% of this amount ($13,500), less the goodwill amortization of $600, or a net amount of $12,900. Company P may now record 80% of Com-

If Cost Method Is Used			
Co. P Books		Co. SP Books	
Investment in Co. SP	Retained Earnings, Co. P	Investment in Co. S	Retained Earnings, Co. SP
	$240,000		$60,000
$120,000			
$120,000	$240,000		$60,000
			(15,000)
	30,000		
$120,000	$270,000		$45,000
		$126,000	
$120,000	$270,000	$126,000	$45,000
			4,500
	8,000		(10,000)
	(10,000)		
$120,000	$268,000	$126,000	$39,500
			30,000
	(20,000)		
$120,000	$248,000	$126,000	$69,500

pany SP's retained earnings increase of $42,900, consisting of earnings from the latter's own operations, $30,000, and earnings that are recognized as a result of the operations of Company S, $12,900.

The parent company is affected by the earnings of the subsidiaries of the subparent company. It is not affected by the dividends of such subsidiaries, however, since dividends have no effect upon the capital of the recipient when the equity method is employed. Declaration of a dividend by Company S results in an entry on the books of Company SP to record the dividend. Declaration of a dividend by Company SP results in an entry on the books of Company P.

A work sheet for a consolidated balance sheet at the end of 19X5 for Company P, Company SP, and Company S is prepared as follows:

Equity Method:

Company P and Subsidiary Companies
Work Sheet for Consolidated Balance Sheet
December 31, 19X5

	Co. P	Co. SP	Co. S	Eliminations		Consolidated Balance Sheet	
				Dr.	Cr.	Dr.	Cr.
Debits							
Investment in Co. SP Stock.......	134,320						
Eliminate Investment					(c) 134,320		
Investment in Co. S Stock.........		134,400					
Eliminate Investment					(a) 134,400		
Goodwill.............................				(a) 17,400		17,400	
Other Assets...........................	428,000	143,500	190,000		(b) 10,000	751,500	
	562,320	277,900	190,000				
Credits							
Liabilities................................	200,000	100,000	60,000				360,000
Capital Stock, Co. P	100,000						100,000
Retained Earnings, Co. P	262,320						262,320
Capital Stock, Co. SP		100,000					
Eliminate 80%.......................				(c) 80,000			
Minority Interest, 20%...........							20,000
Retained Earnings, Co. SP		77,900					
Eliminate 80%.......................				(c) 62,320			
Minority Interest, 20%...........							15,580
Adjustment of Asset Value, Co. SP				(b) 10,000			
Eliminate 80%....................					(c) 8,000		
Minority Interest, 20%........						2,000	
Capital Stock, Co. S			100,000				
Eliminate 90%.......................				(a) 90,000			
Minority Interest, 10%...........							10,000
Retained Earnings, Co. S			30,000				
Eliminate 90%.......................				(a) 27,000			
Minority Interest, 10%...........							3,000
	562,320	277,900	190,000	286,720	286,720	770,900	770,900

If a consolidated balance sheet for Company SP and its subsidiary Company S were desired, balance sheets for those two companies could be consolidated. The consolidated balance sheet for the subparent could then be consolidated with the balance sheet for the parent in obtaining a statement for the three companies. This statement would be the same as that which was developed by means of the single work sheet.

Cost method. If the cost method is used, a work sheet for a consolidated balance sheet would be prepared as follows:

Cost method:

Company P and Subsidiary Companies
Work Sheet for Consolidated Balance Sheet
December 31, 19X5

	Co. P	Co. SP	Co. S	Eliminations Dr.	Eliminations Cr.	Consolidated Balance Sheet Dr.	Consolidated Balance Sheet Cr.
Debits							
Investment in Co. SP Stock.......	120,000						
Eliminate Investment					(e) 120,000		
Investment in Co. S Stock........		126,000					
Eliminate Investment					(a) 126,000		
Goodwill..........................				(a) 18,000	(c) 600	17,400	
Other Assets.....................	428,000	143,500	190,000		(d) 10,000	751,500	
	548,000	269,500	190,000				
Credits							
Liabilities......................	200,000	100,000	60,000				360,000
Capital Stock, Co. P	100,000						100,000
Retained Earnings, Co. P	248,000				(f) 14,320		262,320
Capital Stock, Co. SP		100,000					
Eliminate 80%....................				(e) 80,000			
Minority Interest, 20%..........							20,000
Retained Earnings, Co. SP		69,500		(c) 600	(b) 9,000		
Eliminate 80% of $60,000 Retained Earnings on 1/1/X4...				(e) 48,000			
Minority Interest, 20% of $77,900..........................							15,580
Retained Earnings to Co. P.....				(f) 14,320			
Adjustment of Asset Value, Co. SP				(d) 10,000			
Eliminate 80%...................					(e) 8,000		
Minority Interest, 20%........						2,000	
Capital Stock, Co. S			100,000				
Eliminate 90%...................				(a) 90,000			
Minority Interest, 10%..........							10,000
Retained Earnings, Co. S			30,000				
Eliminate 90% of $20,000 Retained Earnings on 1/1/X5...				(a) 18,000			
Minority Interest, 10% of $30,000..........................							3,000
Retained Earnings to Co. SP...					(b) 9,000		
	548,000	269,500	190,000	287,920	287,920	770,900	770,900

The investment account eliminations are based on capital balances as of the date of acquisition of a controlling interest. Beginning with the most remote subsidiary, however, the retained earnings accruing to its respective parent are not extended to the consolidated balance sheet columns, but are carried to the retained earnings account of the subparent. This amount is included in the determination of the subparent's retained earnings. The calculation of the subparent minority interest is based on the subparent's retained earnings as adjusted. The balance of retained earnings, if accruing to the main parent, may be extended to the consolidated balance sheet columns. If the balance accrues to a company that is in turn controlled by another, it is carried to the retained earnings of that subparent as was done in the first instance.

In the example, after the $18,000 share of Co. S retained earnings originally acquired is eliminated, and after the minority interest in the retained earnings of Co. S, 10% of $30,000, or $3,000, is extended to the consolidated balance sheet columns, the $9,000 balance is carried to Company SP retained earnings (entry [b]). The amortization of goodwill is debited to Company SP retained earnings. The minority interest in Company SP is based on the retained earnings of Company SP as adjusted by the increase accruing from its subsidiary.

Of the retained earnings of Company SP, $14,320 represents the increase that accrues to Company P as a result of the change in the capital of Company SP, which includes the earnings accruing to the latter company from the operations of Company S. This amount is obtained by adding to Company SP retained earnings, $69,500, the $8,400 accruing to it by virtue of its ownership of 90% of Company S, and subtracting from this total, $77,900, the retained earnings acquired by Company P at the time of acquisition, $48,000, and a minority interest of 20% of $77,900, or $15,580.

As in the preceding case, it would be possible first to construct a consolidated balance sheet for Company SP and its subsidiary, Company S. This balance sheet, when consolidated with that of Company P, would be the same as the consolidated balance sheet developed from the work sheet on page 453.

Subholdings Acquired Prior to Parent Company Control

To illustrate the problems that arise when control is achieved over a company that already exercises control over an affiliate, assume that on January 1, 19X1, Company SP purchased 800 shares of Company S stock at 120, paying $96,000. The difference between the purchase price and the book value of the underlying assets at that time was attributed to the value of land owned by Company S. On January 1, 19X2, Company P purchased 850 shares of Company SP stock at 160, paying $136,000. At that time all asset accounts of Companies SP and S reflect fair values, except for the Company S land, which has not changed in value in the past year. The capital stock of each company is $100,000, consisting of 1,000 shares with a par value of $100. Retained earnings balances on December 31, 19X0, and earnings and dividends for 19X1 and 19X2 are as follows:

	Co. P	Co. SP	Co. S
Retained earnings (deficit), December 31, 19X0	$250,000	$20,000	($15,000)
Net income (loss) from own operations, 19X1	20,000	10,000	(5,000)
Dividends declared in December, 19X2	10,000	5,000	
Net income from own operations, 19X2	15,000	10,000	10,000

Changes in the investment accounts and the retained earnings accounts of the parent and the subparent companies are as shown on pages 456 and 457.

Equity Method. The implied value of the net assets of Company S on January 1, 19X1, is $120,000 ($96,000 ÷ .80). The book value of Company S at that time was only $85,000, and although the land was undervalued by $35,000, it is not amortized, and the investment account and retained earnings of Company SP would not be affected.

On January 1, 19X2, the fair value of the net assets of Company SP was $126,000. This amount consists of its own net assets of $34,000 ($130,000 − $96,000 investment) plus 80% of the net assets of Company S at current values ($120,000 − 19X1 loss of $5,000), or $92,000. Company P would recognize goodwill of $28,900 [$136,000 − (.85 × $126,000)] at the time of purchase. The goodwill would be amortized over 40 years at $723 per year by reducing Company P's investment and retained earnings accounts.

Company SP recognizes earnings of the subsidiary from the date stock in Company S is acquired. Company P became a parent at the beginning of 19X2, and at the end of 19X2, it recognizes Company SP's earnings for the year as increased by the latter company's share in the earnings of Company S. Company P is thus affected by changes in the capital of Company S only from the date it acquires control of Company SP. A work sheet for a consolidated balance sheet for Company P, Company SP, and Company S is prepared as follows:

Equity method:

Company P and Subsidiary Companies
Work Sheet for Consolidated Balance Sheet
December 31, 19X2

	Co. P	Co. SP	Co. S	Eliminations		Consolidated Balance Sheet	
				Dr.	Cr.	Dr.	Cr.
Debits							
Investment in Co. SP Stock.......	146,327				(c) 146,327		
Eliminate Investment							
Goodwill................................		100,000		(c) 28,177		28,177	
Investment in Co. S Stock.........					(b) 100,000		
Eliminate Investment	423,250	139,000	90,000	(a) 35,000		687,250	
Other Assets............................	569,577	239,000	90,000				
Credits							
Liabilities..................................	180,000	100,000					280,000
Capital Stock, Co. P	100,000						100,000
Retained Earnings, Co. P	289,577						289,577
Capital Stock, Co. SP		100,000					
Eliminate 85%......................				(c) 85,000			
Minority Interest, 15%...........							15,000
Retained Earnings, Co. SP........		39,000					
Eliminate 85%......................				(c) 33,150			
Minority Interest, 15%...........							5,850
Capital Stock, Co. S			100,000				
Eliminate 80%......................				(b) 80,000			
Minority Interest, 20%...........							20,000
Deficit, Co. S			(10,000)				
Eliminate 80%......................					(b) 8,000		
Minority Interest, 20%...........						2,000	
Adjustment of Asset Value, Co. S					(a) 35,000		
Eliminate 80%......................				(b) 28,000			
Minority Interest, 20%...........							7,000
	569,577	239,000	90,000	289,327	289,327	717,427	717,427

| | If Equity Method Is Used | | | |
| | Co. P Books | | Co. SP Books | |
	Investment in Co. SP	Retained Earnings, Co. P	Investment in Co. S	Retained Earnings, Co. SP
December 31, 19X0, balances....................		$250,000		$20,000
January 1, 19X1:				
Purchase by Co. SP of 800 shares of Co. S stock at 120......................................			$ 96,000	
		$250,000	$ 96,000	$20,000
December 31, 19X1:				
Net income (loss), 19X1:				
Co. S, ($5,000).....................................			(4,000)	(4,000)
Co. SP, $10,000				10,000
Co. P, $20,000....................................		20,000		
		$270,000	$ 92,000	$26,000
January 1, 19X2:				
Purchase by Co. P of 850 shares of Co. SP stock at 160............................	$136,000			
	$136,000	$270,000	$ 92,000	$26,000
December, 19X2:				
Dividends paid:				
Co. SP, $5,000...................................	(4,250)			(5,000)
Co. P, $10,000		(10,000)		
	$131,750	$260,000	$ 92,000	$21,000
December 31, 19X2:				
Net income, 19X2:				
Co. S, $10,000			8,000	8,000
Co. SP:				
Own operations...................... $10,000				10,000
Through ownership of Co. S..... 8,000				
To Co. P, 85% $18,000	15,300	15,300		
Less goodwill amortization...................	(723)	(723)		
Co. P, $15,000		15,000		
December 31, 19X2, balances....................	$146,327	$289,577	$100,000	$39,000

Cost method. If the cost method is used, eliminations for the investment of the subparent in the subsidiary are made in terms of the capital of
the subsidiary at the date the subparent acquired control. The earnings accruing from the subsidiary since the date of acquisition of control are transferred directly to the subparent retained earnings. Eliminations for the investment of the parent in the subparent are made in terms of the capital of
the subparent at the date the parent acquired control. For this purpose,
retained earnings of the subparent include the change in the capital of the
subsidiary accruing to the subparent up to the date the parent acquired
control. These eliminations are shown in the work sheet on page 458.

After the subparent's share of the deficit on acquisition (80% of $15,000,
or $12,000) has been eliminated, and after the deficit relating to the minority
interest (20% of $10,000, or $2,000) has been extended to the consolidated
balance sheet columns, a $4,000 retained earnings increase is carried to

| | If Cost Method Is Used | | |
| Co. P Books | | Co. SP Books | |
Investment in Co. SP	Retained Earnings, Co. P	Investment in Co. S	Retained Earnings, Co. SP
	$250,000		$20,000
		$96,000	
	$250,000	$96,000	$20,000
			10,000
	20,000		
	$270,000	$96,000	$30,000
$136,000			
$136,000	$270,000	$96,000	$30,000
	4,250		(5,000)
	(10,000)		
$136,000	$264,250	$96,000	$25,000
			10,000
	15,000		
$136,000	$279,250	$96,000	$35,000

Company SP retained earnings (see entry [b]). This amount is the sub-parent's share of the $5,000 increase in Company S retained earnings since the subparent acquired control of the subsidiary. The elimination of Company SP retained earnings is based on a balance of $26,000, or Company SP's balance of $30,000 as shown by the books, less $4,000, which is 80% of the $5,000 decrease in Company S retained earnings from the date the sub-parent's holdings were acquired to the date the parent acquired control of the subparent. The minority interest in the retained earnings of Company SP is $5,850, which is 15% of the $39,000 Company SP retained earnings and share of subsidiary earnings. The balance of earnings accruing to Company P is $11,050, which is the subparent retained earnings as adjusted, $39,000, less the elimination, $22,100, and less the subparent minority interest in retained earnings, $5,850. Amortization of goodwill, $723, is deducted from Company P retained earnings.

Cost method:

Company P and Subsidiary Companies
Work Sheet for Consolidated Balance Sheet
December 31, 19X2

	Co. P	Co. SP	Co. S	Eliminations		Consolidated Balance Sheet	
				Dr.	Cr.	Dr.	Cr.
Debits							
Investment in Co. SP Stock.......	136,000						
Eliminate Investment					(c) 136,000		
Goodwill...............................				(c) 28,900	(d) 723	28,177	
Investment in Co. S Stock.........		96,000					
Eliminate Investment					(b) 96,000		
Other Assets............................	423,250	139,000	90,000	(a) 35,000		687,250	
	559,250	235,000	90,000				
Credits							
Liabilities................................	180,000	100,000					280,000
Capital Stock, Co. P	100,000						100,000
Retained Earnings, Co. P	279,250			(d) 723	(d) 11,050		289,577
Capital Stock, Co. SP		100,000					
Eliminate 85%.......................				(c) 85,000			
Minority Interest, 15%..........							15,000
Retained Earnings, Co. SP		35,000			(b) 4,000		
Eliminate 85% of $26,000 Retained Earnings on 1/1/X2 ($30,000 − $4,000)				(c) 22,100			
Minority Interest, 15% of $39,000............................							5,850
Retained Earnings to Co. P.....				(d) 11,050			
Capital Stock, Co. S			100,000				
Eliminate 80%.......................				(b) 80,000			
Minority Interest, 20%...........							20,000
Deficit, Co. S............................			(10,000)				
Eliminate 80% of $15,000 Deficit on 1/1/X1................					(a) 12,000		
Minority Interest, 20% of $10,000 Deficit...................						2,000	
Retained Earnings to Co. SP...					(b) 4,000		
Adjustment of Asset Value, Co. S					(a) 35,000		
Eliminate 80%......................				(b) 28,000			
Minority Interest, 20%...........							7,000
	559,250	235,000	90,000	294,773	294,773	717,427	717,427

Control Achieved by Means of Connecting Affiliates

Previous illustrations in this chapter provided for three-tier arrangements in which direct control was exercised by the parent over the subparent, and direct control was exercised, in turn, by the subparent over the subsidiary. There are instances when control is not achieved through direct ownership of the stock of another company, but through the holdings of a connecting affiliate. When structures are complicated, they should be analyzed diagrammatically before the process of consolidation is begun. The following diagram on the left shows the relationships in the previous example, while the diagram on the right shows the relationships discussed in the next example.

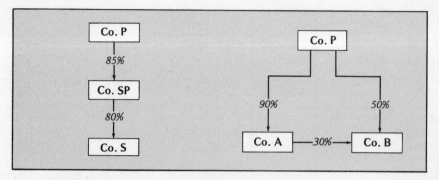

Assume that on January 1, 19X6, Company A purchases 300 shares (30%) of Company B stock at 120, paying $36,000. On January 1, 19X7, Company P purchases 900 shares (90%) of Company A stock at 150, paying $135,000, and also 500 shares (50%) of Company B stock at 160, paying $80,000. The capital stock of each company is $100,000, consisting of 1,000 shares with a par value of $100. Retained earnings balances on December 31, 19X5, and earnings and dividends for 19X6 and 19X7 follow:

	Co. P	Co. A	Co. B
Retained earnings, December 31, 19X5	$180,000	$10,000	$20,000
Net income from own operations, 19X6............	40,000	30,000	20,000
Dividends declared in December, 19X7............	20,000	10,000	10,000
Net income from own operations, 19X7............	35,000	25,000	15,000

The differences between the acquisition costs and book values at the time of purchase were identified as goodwill, which will be amortized over a period of 40 years. Since Company A paid book value for its acquisition of Company B, no goodwill would be attributed to that purchase. The amounts of goodwill to be recognized on January 1, 19X7, for Company P acquisitions are determined as follows:

Company A:

Amount paid for investment...	$135,000
Book value (90% of $146,000)	131,400
Goodwill at acquisition..	$ 3,600

Company B:

Amount paid for investment...	$80,000
Book value (50% of $140,000)	70,000
Goodwill at acquisition..	$10,000

Company P exercises direct control over Company A beginning in 19X7. Despite the absence of a majority interest by Company P in Company B, Company P is assured of control over Company B through its ownership of a controlling interest in the connecting affiliate, Company A. Investment and retained earnings accounts of the parent and subsidiary companies are affected by earnings and dividends in 19X6 and 19X7 as shown on pages 460 and 461.

	If Equity Method Is Used				
	Co. P Books			Co. A Books	
	Investment in Co. A	Investment in Co. B	Retained Earnings, Co. P	Investment in Co. B	Retained Earnings, Co. A
December 31, 19X5, balances			$180,000		$10,000
January 1, 19X6: Purchase by Co. A of 300 shares of Co. B stock at 120.............................				$36,000	
			$180,000	$36,000	$10,000
December 31, 19X6: Net income, 19X6:					
Co. B, $20,000...............					
Co. A, $30,000...............					30,000
Co. P, $40,000...............			40,000		
Recognition by Co. A of 30% of Co. B retained earnings increase for 19X6.............................				6,000	6,000
			$220,000	$42,000	$46,000
January 1, 19X7: Purchase by Co. P of 900 shares of Co. A stock at 150.............................	$135,000				
Purchase by Co. P of 500 shares of Co. B stock at 160.............................		$80,000			
	$135,000	$80,000	$220,000	$42,000	$46,000
December, 19X7: Dividends paid:					
Co. B, $10,000...............		(5,000)		(3,000)	
Co. A, $10,000...............	(9,000)				(10,000)
Co. P, $20,000...............			(20,000)		
	$126,000	$75,000	$200,000	$39,000	$36,000
December 31, 19X7: Net income, 19X7:					
Co. B, $15,000...............		7,500	7,500	4,500	4,500
Co. A: Own operations........ $25,000					25,000
Through ownership of Co. B....... 4,500					
To Co. P, 90% $29,500	26,550		26,550		
Less amortization of goodwill......................	(90)	(250)	(340)		
Co. P, $35,000............			35,000		
December 31, 19X7, balances	$152,460	$82,250	$268,710	$43,500	$65,500

Equity method. If investments are carried by the equity method, investment balances should be adjusted to an equity basis as long as substantial influence over the investee is maintained, and the subsequent accounting

If Cost Method Is Used				
Co. P Books			Co. A Books	
Investment in Co. A	Investment in Co. B	Retained Earnings, Co. P	Investment in Co. B	Retained Earnings, Co. A
		$180,000		$10,000
			$36,000	
		$180,000	$36,000	$10,000
		40,000		30,000
		$220,000	$36,000	$40,000
$135,000				
	$80,000			
$135,000	$80,000	$220,000	$36,000	$40,000
		5,000		3,000
		9,000		(10,000)
		(20,000)		
$135,000	$80,000	$214,000	$36,000	$33,000
				25,000
		35,000		
$135,000	$80,000	$249,000	$36,000	$58,000

should follow normal equity procedures. The use of the equity method is based on the presumption that the common parent, Company P, has the ability to direct transactions such as dividend declarations of Company B and thus has the potential for manipulating earnings. Indeed, if Company A owned only a 10% interest in Company B and had not previously used the equity method, Company P's acquisition of a controlling interest in both companies would indicate the need for retroactive application of the equity method by Company A.

Prior to January 1, 19X7, Company A would have regarded its 30% ownership interest as giving it substantial influence over the affairs of Company B, so the use of the equity method was justified. When another single owner holds 50% of the company, however, the validity of the assumption of substantial influence by the holder of a 30% interest might be subject to challenge. In this case, where the other substantial owner is a member of the same "family" of corporations, Companies P and A continue to recognize earnings and dividends of affiliated units, and eliminations on the consolidated work sheet are made in terms of capital balances as of the date of the consolidation. The work sheet on December 31, 19X7, is illustrated below.

Equity method:

Company P and Subsidiary Companies
Work Sheet for Consolidated Balance Sheet
December 31, 19X7

	Co. P	Co. A	Co. B	Eliminations Dr.	Eliminations Cr.	Consolidated Balance Sheet Dr.	Consolidated Balance Sheet Cr.
Debits							
Investment in Co. A Stock.........	152,460				(c) 152,460		
Eliminate Investment							
Goodwill..............................				(c) 3,510		3,510	
Investment in Co. B Stock.........	82,250				(b) 82,250		
Eliminate Investment							
Goodwill..............................				(b) 9,750		9,750	
Investment in Co. B Stock.........		43,500					
Eliminate Investment					(a) 43,500		
Other Assets...........................	284,000	222,000	225,000			731,000	
	518,710	265,500	225,000				
Credits							
Liabilities.................................	150,000	100,000	80,000				330,000
Capital Stock, Co. P.................	100,000						100,000
Retained Earnings, Co. P	268,710						268,710
Capital Stock, Co. A		100,000					
Eliminate 90%......................				(c) 90,000			
Minority Interest, 10%...........							10,000
Retained Earnings, Co. A		65,500					
Eliminate 90%......................				(c) 58,950			
Minority Interest, 10%...........							6,550
Capital Stock, Co. B			100,000				
Eliminate 50%......................				(b) 50,000			
Eliminate 30%......................				(a) 30,000			
Minority Interest, 20%...........							20,000
Retained Earnings, Co. B			45,000				
Eliminate 50%......................				(b) 22,500			
Eliminate 30%......................				(a) 13,500			
Minority Interest, 20%...........							9,000
	518,710	265,500	225,000	278,210	278,210	744,260	744,260

Cost method. If the cost method is used, the elimination of the investment of Company A in Company B is made in terms of the capital balances reported by the latter at the date Company A acquired control. For purposes of the elimination of the investment of Company P in Company A, however, the retained earnings balance of Company A must include its share of the increase in the capital of Company B up to the date of Company P control.

In the work sheet on page 464, eliminations for the capital stock of Company B held by Companies P and A are followed by eliminations for retained earnings of Company B as of the dates of the respective stock acquisitions. After the minority interest in Company B retained earnings of $9,000 has been extended to the consolidated balance sheet columns, the balance of $10,000 represents the retained earnings increase accruing to Companies P and A. The retained earnings increase accruing to Company A is 30% of $25,000, the difference between the present retained earnings balance of $45,000 and the balance of $20,000 on the date of the original stock acquisition by Company A. This increase of $7,500 is carried to Company A retained earnings (entry [b]). The retained earnings increase accruing to Company P is 50% of $5,000, the difference between the present retained earnings balance of $45,000 and the balance of $40,000 on the date of the original stock acquisition by Company P. This increase of $2,500 is transferred to Company P retained earnings. In eliminating the investment in Company A, retained earnings of the subsidiary are recognized as $46,000, which is Company A's balance of $40,000 as reported on its books, increased by $6,000 or 30% of the increase in Company B's retained earnings from the date Company A acquired stock in Company B until the date Company P acquired control of Company A.

MUTUAL HOLDINGS

A company may hold a controlling interest in a subsidiary, and the latter, in turn, may hold a part of the stock of the parent company. When there are mutual holdings, the retained earnings change of the parent for any period depends upon the retained earnings change of the subsidiary, while the retained earnings change of the subsidiary may be viewed as similarly affected by the retained earnings change of the parent. With each change dependent upon the other, algebraic calculations are required in determining the respective changes.

Mutual Holdings Arising at the Beginning of a Fiscal Period

To illustrate the procedures involved when purchases of stock at the beginning of a fiscal period result in mutual holdings, assume the following facts:

On January 1, 19X8, date of organization of Co. S, Co. P acquired 800
  shares of Co. S stock at par.. $80,000
On January 1, 19X9, Co. S purchased 100 shares of Co. P stock at 163. $16,300

Cost method:

Company P and Subsidiary Companies
Work Sheet for Consolidated Balance Sheet
December 31, 19X7

	Co. P	Co. A	Co. B	Eliminations Dr.	Eliminations Cr.	Consolidated Balance Sheet Dr.	Consolidated Balance Sheet Cr.
Debits							
Investment in Co. A Stock.........	135,000						
Eliminate Investment					(d) 135,000		
Goodwill...............................				(d) 3,600	(e) 90	3,510	
Investment in Co. B Stock.........	80,000						
Eliminate Investment					(c) 80,000		
Goodwill...............................				(c) 10,000	(e) 250	9,750	
Investment in Co. B Stock.........		36,000					
Eliminate Investment					(a) 36,000		
Other Assets............................	284,000	222,000	225,000			731,000	
	499,000	258,000	225,000				
Credits							
Liabilities................................	150,000	100,000	80,000				330,000
Capital Stock, Co. P	100,000						100,000
Retained Earnings, Co. P	249,000			(e) 340	(f) 20,050		268,710
Capital Stock, Co. A		100,000					
Eliminate 90%......................				(d) 90,000			
Minority Interest, 10%...........							10,000
Retained Earnings, Co. A		58,000					
Add Retained Earnings from Co. B..............................					(b) 7,500		
Eliminate 90% of $46 000 Retained Earnings on 1/1/X7 ($40,000 + $6,000).				(d) 41,400			
Minority Interest, 10% of $65,500...........................							6,550
Retained Earnings to Co. P.....				(f) 17,550			
Capital Stock, Co. B			100,000				
Eliminate 50% owned by Co. P				(c) 50,000			
Eliminate 30% owned by Co. A				(a) 30,000			
Minority Interest, 20%...........							20,000
Retained Earnings, Co. B			45,000				
Eliminate 50% of $40,000 Retained Earnings on 1/1/X7...				(c) 20,000			
Eliminate 30% of $20,000 Retained Earnings on 1/1/X6...				(a) 6,000			
Minority Interest, 20% of $45,000...........................							9,000
Retained Earnings to Co. A, 30% of $25,000 ($45,000 Retained Earnings, 12/31/X7 − $20,000 Retained Earnings 1/1/X6)......				(b) 7,500			
Retained Earnings to Co. P, 50% of $5,000 ($45,000, Retained Earnings 12/31/X7 − $40,000 Retained Earnings 1/1/X7)......				(f) 2,500			
	499,000	258,000	225,000	278,890	278,890	744,260	744,260

The capital stock of each company is $100,000, consisting of 1,000 shares with a par value of $100. Retained earnings balances of December 31, 19X7, and earnings and dividends for 19X8 and 19X9 are:

	Co. P	Co. S
Retained earnings, December 31, 19X7	$40,000	—
Net income from own operations, 19X8	15,000	$10,000
Dividends declared in December, 19X9	5,000	5,000
Net income from own operations, 19X9	20,000	10,000

Changes in the investment and retained earnings accounts of the parent and the subsidiary company are shown on pages 466 and 467.

Equity method. No special problem arises until 19X9 when Companies P and S record the earnings accruing to each as a result of the transactions of the other. The earnings to be recorded by each company may be computed algebraically in the following manner:

Let P = P's *increase in retained earnings*, consisting of P's net income plus the share of S's earnings accruing to P.
Let S = S's *increase in retained earnings*, consisting of S's net income plus the share of P's earnings accruing to S.

$$\text{Then:} \quad P = \$20{,}000 + .8S$$
$$S = \$10{,}000 + .1P$$

To solve for P:

$$P = \$20{,}000 + .8\,(\$10{,}000 + .1P)$$
$$P = \$20{,}000 + \$8{,}000 + .08P$$
$$P - .08P = \$28{,}000$$
$$.92P = \$28{,}000$$
$$P = \$30{,}434.78$$

To solve for S:

$$S = \$10{,}000 + .1P$$
$$S = \$10{,}000 + .1\,(\$30{,}434.78)$$
$$S = \$10{,}000 + \$3{,}043.48$$
$$S = \$13{,}043.48$$

S takes up 10% of this increase in P's retained earnings:
$$10\% \text{ of } \$30{,}434.78, \text{ or } \underline{\$3{,}043.48}$$

P takes up 80% of this increase in S's retained earnings:
$$80\% \text{ of } \$13{,}043.48, \text{ or } \underline{\$10{,}434.78}$$

It would be possible to solve for P in an alternative manner as follows:
$$P = \$20{,}000 + .8S$$
$$S = \$10{,}000 + .1P$$

Multiplying the first equation by 5 and the second equation by 4:
$$5P - 4S = \$100{,}000$$
$$-.4P + 4S = \$\ 40{,}000$$

Adding the two equations:
$$4.6P = \$140{,}000.00$$
$$P = \$\ \underline{30{,}434.78}$$

Since Company P's retained earnings increase is $30,434.78, Company S will take up 10% of this amount, or $3,043.48. Company S's retained earnings increase is now $10,000.00 + $3,043.48, or $13,043.48, and Company P takes up 80% of this amount, or $10,434.78. These entries result in total retained earnings increases on the books of Company P and Company S of $30,434.78 and $13,043.48 respectively, the amounts that were calculated algebraically.

| | If Equity Method Is Used | | | |
| | Co. P Books | | Co. S Books | |
	Investment in Co. S.	Retained Earnings, Co. P	Investment in Co. P.	Retained Earnings, Co. S
December 31, 19X7, balances...........		$40,000.00		
January 1, 19X8:				
Purchase by Co. P of 800 shares of				
Co. S stock at 100......................	$80,000.00			
	$80,000.00	$40,000.00		
December 31, 19X8:				
Net income for 19X8:				
Co. S, $10,000..........................	8,000.00	8,000.00		$10,000.00
Co. P, $15,000..........................		15,000.00		
	$88,000.00	$63,000.00		$10,000.00
January 1, 19X9:				
Purchase by Co. S of 100 shares of				
Co. P stock at 163......................			$16,300.00	
	$88,000.00	$63,000.00	$16,300.00	$10,000.00
December, 19X9:				
Dividends paid:				
Co. S, $5,000...........................	(4,000.00)			(5,000.00)
Co. P, $5,000...........................		(5,000.00)	(500.00)	
	$84,000.00	$58,000.00	$15,800.00	$ 5,000.00
December 31, 19X9:				
Net income for 19X9:				
Co. S, $10,000..........................	10,434.78	10,434.78		10,000.00
Co. P, $20,000..........................		20,000.00	3,043.48	3,043.48
December 31, 19X9, balances...........	$94,434.78	$88,434.78	$18,843.48	$18,043.48

A work sheet for a consolidated balance sheet is illustrated on page 468. The combined earnings for the year for Company P and Company S were $30,000 ($20,000 + $10,000). After eliminations are made on the work sheet, the earnings related to the controlling and minority interests are equal to the sum of: earnings reflected in an increase in retained earnings for the controlling interest, $27,391.30 (90% of $30,434.78); earnings reflected in an increase in retained earnings for the minority interest, $2,608.70 (20% of $13,043.48).

Cost method. When the cost method is used, there is no need to calculate the earnings to be recorded as a result of the operations of the affiliate. However, after eliminations have been made for the parent's equity in the subsidiary at date of acquisition, it is necessary to calculate the minority interest in the subsidiary. This figure will not be the minority percentage of the subsidiary retained earnings balance as shown, since this balance does not include the earnings accruing to the subsidiary as a result of its interest in the parent.

If Cost Method Is Used			
Co. P Books		Co. S Books	
Investment in Co. S	Retained Earnings, Co. P	Investment in Co. P	Retained Earnings, Co. S
	$40,000.00		
$80,000.00			
$80,000.00	$40,000.00		
			$10,000.00
	15,000.00		
$80,000.00	$55,000.00		$10,000.00
		$16,300.00	
$80,000.00	$55,000.00	$16,300.00	$10,000.00
	4,000.00		(5,000.00)
	(5,000.00)		500.00
$80,000.00	$54,000.00	$16,300.00	$ 5,500.00
			10,000.00
	20,000.00		
$80,000.00	$74,000.00	$16,300.00	$15,500.00

To calculate the minority interest, the subsidiary retained earnings balance may first be computed as follows:

Let P = P's *total retained earnings* balance on December 31, 19X9.
Let S = S's *total retained earnings* balance on December 31, 19X9.

Company P's total retained earnings consist of its present retained earnings balance, $74,000, plus 80% of Company S's total retained earnings, since it has owned the subsidiary since its formation. Company S's total retained earnings consist of its present balance, $15,500, plus 10% of Company P's retained earnings increase for the current year. Company P's retained earnings increase for the current year is represented by its present balance as adjusted by its share of the change in subsidiary capital, less its balance at the end of the preceding year as adjusted by its share of the change in the subsidiary capital at that time. Company P's retained earnings balance at the end of the preceding year was $63,000: the reported balance, $55,000, plus its share of the increase in the retained earnings of Company S since date of stock acquisition, 80% of $10,000, or $8,000.

Equity method:

Company P and Subsidiary Company S
Work Sheet for Consolidated Balance Sheet
December 31, 19X9

	Co. P	Co. S	Eliminations Dr.	Eliminations Cr.	Consolidated Balance Sheet Dr.	Consolidated Balance Sheet Cr.
Debits						
Investment in Co. S Stock	94,434.78					
Eliminate Investment....				(a) 94,434.78		
Investment in Co. P Stock		18,843.48				
Eliminate Investment....				(b) 18,843.48		
Other Assets	244,000.00	199,200.00			443,200.00	
	338,434.78	218,043.48				
Credits						
Liabilities	150,000.00	100,000.00				250,000.00
Capital Stock, Co. P.........	100,000.00					
Eliminate 10%			(b) 10,000.00			90,000.00
Retained Earnings, Co. P..	88,434.78					
Eliminate 10%			(b) 8,843.48			79,591.30
Capital Stock, Co. S.........		100,000.00				
Eliminate 80%			(a) 80,000.00			
Minority Interest, 20% ..						20,000.00
Retained Earnings, Co. S..		18,043.48				
Eliminate 80%			(a) 14,434.78			
Minority Interest, 20% ..						3,608.70
	338,434.78	218,043.48	113,278.26	113,278.26	443,200.00	443,200.00

Total retained earnings balances of the two companies on December 31, 19X9, may be stated as follows:

$$P = \$74,000 + .8S$$
$$S = \$15,500 + .1 (P - \$63,000)$$

The retained earnings of Company S can now be calculated as follows:

$$S = \$15,500 + .1 (P - \$63,000)$$
$$S = \$15,500 + .1 (\$74,000 + .8S - \$63,000)$$
$$S = \$15,500 + \$7,400 + .08S - \$6,300$$
$$S - .08S = \$16,600$$
$$.92S = \$16,600$$
$$S = \$18,043.48$$

The retained earnings of Company P are computed as follows:

$$P = \$74,000 + .8 (\$18,043.48)$$
$$P = \$74,000 + \$14,434.78$$
$$P = \$88,434.78$$

The minority interest of 20% of the subsidiary retained earnings balance, or $3,608.70, is now extended to the consolidated balance sheet columns. The difference between $15,500, the retained earnings for Company S, and $3,608.70, the minority interest, or $11,891.30, represents the increase in retained earnings of the subsidiary accruing to the parent company since acquisition. The work sheet is illustrated as follows:

Cost method:

Company P and Subsidiary Company S
Work Sheet for Consolidated Balance Sheet
December 31, 19X9

	Co. P	Co. S	Eliminations		Consolidated Balance Sheet	
			Dr.	Cr.	Dr.	Cr.
Debits						
Investment in Co. S Stock	80,000.00			(a) 80,000.00		
Eliminate Investment....						
Investment in Co. P Stock		16,300.00		(b) 16,300.00		
Eliminate Investment....						
Other Assets..................	244,000.00	199,200.00			443,200.00	
	324,000.00	215,500.00				
Credits						
Liabilities	150,000.00	100,000.00				250,000.00
Capital Stock, Co. P.........	100,000.00					90,000.00
Eliminate 10%			(b) 10,000.00			
Retained Earnings, Co. P..	74,000.00			(c) 11,891.30		
Eliminate 10% of						
$63,000 Retained						
Earnings on 1/1/X9			(b) 6,300.00			79,591.30
Capital Stock, Co. S.........		100,000.00				
Eliminate 80%			(a) 80,000.00			
Minority Interest, 20% ..						20,000.00
Retained Earnings, Co. S..		15,500.00				
Minority Interest, 20%						
of $18,043.48						
Retained Earnings as						
Computed.................						3,608.70
Retained Earnings to						
Co. P.......................			(c) 11,891.30			
	324,000.00	215,500.00	108,191.30	108,191.30	443,200.00	443,200.00

Mutual Holdings Arising Within Fiscal Period

Purchase of stock resulting in mutual holdings may take place within the fiscal period. In this case, the increases in retained earnings are computed on a mutual basis for only the portion of the period during which the reciprocal ownership existed.

Assume that on January 1, 19X2, Company P acquired 900 shares (90%) of Company S stock for 108,000. On April 1, 19X3, Company S acquired 100 shares (10%) of Company P stock for $20,350. Capital stock of each company is $100,000, consisting of 1,000 shares with a par value of $100. Retained earnings balances on December 31, 19X1, and earnings for 19X2 and 19X3 follow:

	Co. P	Co. S
Retained earnings, December 31, 19X1.........................	$50,000	$20,000
Net income from own operations, 19X2.........................	30,000	10,000
Net income from own operations, 19X3.........................	40,000	20,000

Equity method. Assuming that the equity method is used, changes in the investment accounts and retained earnings accounts are as follows:

	If Equity Method Is Used			
	Co. P Books		Co. S Books	
	Investment in Co. S	Retained Earnings, Co. P	Investment in Co. P	Retained Earnings, Co. S
December 31, 19X1, balances...........		$ 50,000.00		$20,000.00
January 1, 19X2: Purchase by Co. P of 900 shares of Co. S stock................................	$108,000.00			
	$108,000.00	$ 50,000.00		$20,000.00
December 31, 19X2: Net income for 19X2:				
Co. S, $10,000	9,000.00	9,000.00		10,000.00
Co. P, $30,000		30,000.00		
	$117,000.00	$ 89,000.00		$30,000.00
April 1, 19X3: Purchase by Co. S of 100 shares of Co. P stock................................			$20,350.00	
	$117,000.00	$ 89,000.00	$20,350.00	$30,000.00
December 31, 19X3: Net income, January 1–April 1:				
Co. S, ¼ of $20,000..................	4,500.00	4,500.00		5,000.00
Co. P, ¼ of $40,000..................		10,000.00		
Net income, April 1–December 31:				
Co. S, ¾ of $20,000..................				15,000.00
10% of Co. P earnings.......			4,780.22	4,780.22
Co. P, ¾ of $40,000..................		30,000.00		
90% of Co. S earnings.......	17,802.20	17,802.20		
December 31, 19X3, balances...........	$139,302.20	$151,302.20	$25,130.22	$54,780.22

Company P recorded 90% of Company S earnings for the first three months of 19X3. Since there were mutual holdings of stock thereafter, company earnings are determined algebraically for the balance of the year, as follows:

Let P and S represent earnings of respective companies for the nine-month period, April 1–December 31:

$$P = \$30,000 + .9S$$
$$S = \$15,000 + .1P$$

To solve for P:
$$P = \$30,000 + .9 (\$15,000 + .1P)$$
$$P = \$30,000 + \$13,500 + .09P$$
$$P - .09P = \$43,500$$
$$.91P = \$43,500$$
$$P = \$47,802.20$$

S records 10% of these earnings:
10% of $47,802.20 = $4,780.22

To solve for S:
$$S = \$15,000 + .1 (\$47,802.20)$$
$$S = \$15,000 + \$4,780.22$$
$$S = \$19,780.22$$

P records 90% of these earnings:
90% of $19,780.22 = $17,802.20

A work sheet for a consolidated balance sheet would be prepared as follows:

Company P and Subsidiary Company S
Work Sheet for Consolidated Balance Sheet
December 31, 19X3

Equity method:

	Co. P	Co. S	Eliminations Dr.	Eliminations Cr.	Consolidated Balance Sheet Dr.	Consolidated Balance Sheet Cr.
Debits						
Investment in Co. S Stock	139,302.20					
Eliminate Investment....				(a) 139,302.20		
Investment in Co. P Stock		25,130.22				
Eliminate Investment....				(b) 25,130.22		
Other Assets..................	242,000.00	154,650.00			396,650.00	
	381,302.20	179,780.22				
Credits						
Liabilities	130,000.00	25,000.00				155,000.00
Capital Stock, Co. P.........	100,000.00					90,000.00
Eliminate 10%			(b) 10,000.00			
Retained Earnings, Co. P..	151,302.20					136,171.98
Eliminate 10%			(b) 15,130.22			
Capital Stock, Co. S.........		100,000.00				
Eliminate 90%			(a) 90,000.00			
Minority Interest, 10%..						10,000.00
Retained Earnings, Co. S..		54,780.22				
Eliminate 90%			(a) 49,302.20			
Minority Interest, 10% ..						5,478.02
	381,302.20	179,780.22	164,432.42	164,432.42	396,650.00	396,650.00

Cost method. Assuming that the cost method is used, changes in the investment and retained earnings accounts would be as follows:

	If Cost Method Is Followed			
	Co. P Books		Co. S Books	
	Investment in Co. S	Retained Earnings, Co. P	Investment in Co. P	Retained Earnings, Co. S
December 31, 19X1, balances...........		$ 50,000.00		$20,000.00
January 1, 19X2:				
Purchase by Co. P of 900 shares of Co. S stock.................................	$108,000.00			
	$108,000.00	$ 50,000.00		$20,000.00
December 31, 19X2:				
Net income for 19X2:				
Co. S, $10,000				10,000.00
Co. P, $30,000		30,000.00		
	$108,000.00	$ 80,000.00		$30,000.00
April 1, 19X3:				
Purchase by Co. S of 100 shares of Co. P stock.................................			$20,350.00	
	$108,000.00	$ 80,000.00	$20,350.00	$30,000.00
December 31, 19X3:				
Net income for 19X3:				
Co. S, $20,000				20,000.00
Co. P, $40,000		40,000.00		
December 31, 19X3, balances...........	$108,000.00	$120,000.00	$20,350.00	$50,000.00

The Company S retained earnings balance for the purpose of computing the minority interest in this company is calculated at the end of 19X3 as follows:

Let P and S represent total retained earnings balances of Companies P and S respectively. Company P acquired Company S stock when the Company S retained earnings balance was $20,000. Company P's retained earnings total consists of its balance on the books plus 90% of the increase in Company S's retained earnings since January 1, 19X2. P, then may be stated:

$$P = \$120{,}000 + .9\,(S - \$20{,}000)$$

Company S acquired Company P stock on April 1, 19X3, when Company P's retained earnings were $90,000 ($80,000 as of December 31, 19X2, plus ¼ of $40,000, the net income for 19X3). However, the earnings of Company S from January 1, 19X2 to April 1, 19X3, although not appearing on Company P's books when the cost method is used in carrying investments, require recognition in stating Company P's retained earnings on the date Company S acquired an interest in Company P. Company P's retained earnings on April 1, then, are $103,500, or $90,000 plus 90% of $15,000 ($10,000 + $5,000, subsidiary earnings for 19X2 and for January 1–April 1, 19X3). Company S's retained earnings consist of the balance on the books plus 10% of the increase in Company P's retained earnings since April 1, 19X3. S, then, may be stated:

$$S = \$50{,}000 + .1\,(P - \$103{,}500)$$

To solve for S:

$$S = \$50{,}000 + .1\,(\$120{,}000 + .9S - \$18{,}000 - \$103{,}500)$$
$$S = \$50{,}000 + \$12{,}000 + .09S - \$1{,}800 - \$10{,}350$$
$$S - .09S = \$50{,}000 + \$12{,}000 - \$1{,}800 - \$10{,}350$$
$$.91S = \$49{,}850$$
$$S = \$54{,}780.22$$

A work sheet would be prepared as shown on page 473.

Shares of Parent Held by Affiliate Regarded as Treasury Stock

The preceding pages have described the approach that has generally been taken when there are mutual holdings within an affiliated group of companies. Equities of the parent company stockholders and the minority interests in consolidated assets are developed as of the date of the consolidated statements. Equities are determined on the assumption that net earnings are fully distributed on the date of the consolidated balance sheet, with successive distributions by the companies to their stockholders ultimately resulting in participation in earnings by the controlling interest and by the minority interest as indicated by the application of the simultaneous equations.

It is possible, however, to take a quite different approach in preparing the consolidated statement. The statement can be developed on the assumption that the shares of a parent held by a subsidiary will ultimately be resold by the subsidiary either to outsiders or directly to the parent. Such an assumption calls for the recognition of parent company shares held by an affiliate as treasury stock. There is no participation by the minority interest in parent company earnings; instead, the minority interest remains unchanged until the subsidiary sells its interest in the parent at an amount other than its cost.

Cost method:

Company P and Subsidiary Company S
Work Sheet for Consolidated Balance Sheet
December 31, 19X3

	Co. P	Co. S	Eliminations Dr.	Eliminations Cr.	Consolidated Balance Sheet Dr.	Consolidated Balance Sheet Cr.
Debits						
Investment in Co. S Stock	108,000.00					
Eliminate Investment....				(a) 108,000.00		
Investment in Co. P Stock		20,350.00				
Eliminate Investment....				(b) 20,350.00		
Other Assets	242,000.00	154,650.00			396,650.00	
	350,000.00	175,000.00				
Credits						
Liabilities	130,000.00	25,000.00				155,000.00
Capital Stock, Co. P	100,000.00					90,000.00
Eliminate 10%			(b) 10,000.00	(c) 26,521.98		
Retained Earnings, Co. P	120,000.00					
Eliminate 10% of $103,500 Retained Earnings on April 1, 19X3			(b) 10,350.00			136,171.98
Capital Stock, Co. S		100,000.00				
Eliminate 90%			(a) 90,000.00			
Minority Interest, 10%						10,000.00
Retained Earnings, Co. S		50,000.00				
Eliminate 90% of $20,000 Retained Earnings on Jan. 1, 19X2			(a) 18,000.00			
Minority Interest, 10% of $54,780.22 Retained Earnings as Computed						5,478.02
Retained Earnings to Co. P			(c) 26,521.98			
	350,000.00	175,000.00	154,871.98	154,871.98	396,650.00	396,650.00

In adopting the treasury stock approach, the parent company carries the investment in the subsidiary on its books just like any other controlling interest. The subsidiary carries the investment in stock of the parent as a long-term investment. In preparing a consolidated balance sheet, the investment in subsidiary stock is eliminated. The investment in parent stock is reported as treasury stock.

To illustrate the application of the treasury stock approach, assume the same facts as in the preceding example. Changes in the investment accounts and the retained earnings accounts of the parent and the subsidiary company would be as shown on page 474.

If Company P carried the investment in Company S at equity, the work sheet for a consolidated balance sheet would be prepared as shown on page 474; if the investment is carried at cost, the work sheet would be prepared as shown at the top of page 475.

In preparing the work sheet, investments in parent company stock are carried to the consolidated balance sheet columns at their cost. In preparing

| | If Equity Method Is Used | | | | If Cost Method Is Used | | | |
| | Co. P Books | | Co. S Books | | Co. P Books | | Co. S Books | |
	Investment in Co. S	Retained Earnings, Co. P	Investment in Co. P	Retained Earnings, Co. S	Investment in Co. S	Retained Earnings, Co. P	Investment in Co. P	Retained Earnings, Co. S
December 31, 19X1, balances...................		$ 50,000		$20,000		$ 50,000		$20,000
January 1, 19X2: Purchase by Co. P of 900 shares of Co. S stock.....................	$108,000				$108,000			
	$108,000	$ 50,000		$20,000	$108,000	$ 50,000		$20,000
December 31, 19X2: Net income for 19X2: Co. S, $10,000 ...... Co. P, $30,000	9,000	9,000 30,000		10,000		30,000		10,000
	$117,000	$ 89,000		$30,000	$108,000	$ 80,000		$30,000
April 1, 19X3: Purchase by Co. S of 100 shares of Co. P stock....................... December 31, 19X3:			$20,350				$20,350	
Net income for 19X3: Co. S, $20,000 ...... Co. P, $40,000	18,000	18,000 40,000		20,000		40,000		20,000
December 31, 19X3, balances.................	$135,000	$147,000	$20,350	$50,000	$108,000	$120,000	$20,350	$50,000

Equity method:

Company P and Subsidiary Company S
Work Sheet for Consolidated Balance Sheet
December 31, 19X3

| | Co. P | Co. S | Eliminations | | Consolidated Balance Sheet | |
			Dr.	Cr.	Dr.	Cr.
Debits						
Investment in Co. S Stock	135,000					
Eliminate Investment...............				135,000		
Investment in Co. P Stock		20,350			20,350	
Other Assets...............................	242,000	154,650			396,650	
	377,000	175,000				
Credits						
Liabilities....................................	130,000	25,000				155,000
Capital Stock, Co. P....................	100,000					100,000
Retained Earnings, Co. P..............	147,000					147,000
Capital Stock, Co. S.....................		100,000				
Eliminate 90%			90,000			
Minority Interest, 10%						10,000
Retained Earnings, Co. S..............		50,000				
Eliminate 90%			45,000			
Minority Interest, 10%						5,000
	377,000	175,000	135,000	135,000	417,000	417,000

Cost method:

Company P and Subsidiary Company S
Work Sheet for Consolidated Balance Sheet
December 31, 19X3

	Co. P	Co. S	Eliminations		Consolidated Balance Sheet	
			Dr.	Cr.	Dr.	Cr.
Debits						
Investment in Co. S Stock ...	108,000			(a) 108,000		
Eliminate Investment.......						
Investment in Co. P Stock ...		20,350			20,350	
Other Assets.....................	242,000	154,650			396,650	
	350,000	175,000				
Credits						
Liabilities	130,000	25,000				155,000
Capital Stock, Co. P............	100,000					100,000
Retained Earnings, Co. P.....	120,000			(b) 27,000		147,000
Capital Stock, Co. S............		100,000				
Eliminate 90%			(a) 90,000			
Minority Interest, 10%.....						10,000
Retained Earnings, Co. S.....		50,000				
Eliminate 90% of $20,000 Retained Earnings on Jan. 1, 19X1			(a) 18,000			
Minority Interest, 10% of $50,000......................						5,000
Retained Earn. to Parent..			(b) 27,000			
	350,000	175,000	135,000	135,000	417,000	417,000

the consolidated balance sheet, the cost of such investments may be recognized as reductions in parent paid-in capital and retained earnings balances. Capital balances of the controlling interest are thus reported in terms of the shares that are actually outstanding. In the example, ownership of 10% of the outstanding stock of Company P, at a cost of $20,350, calls for reductions of $10,000 in capital stock and $10,350 in retained earnings. The controlling interest will appear on the consolidated balance sheet as follows:

Controlling interest:
    Capital stock, 900 shares... $ 90,000
    Retained earnings... 136,650 $226,650

It would be possible to report the cost of the holdings in Company P as a subtraction from the sum of the capital balances of the parent company in stating the controlling interest on the consolidated balance sheet. If holdings in Company P are to be reported in this manner, the controlling interest would be presented as follows:

Controlling interest:
    Capital stock, 1,000 shares...................................... $100,000
    Retained earnings... 147,000
                                    $247,000
Less capital stock held by affiliated unit, 100 shares, at cost 20,350 $226,650

The American Institute Committee on Accounting Procedure in referring to mutual holdings merely observed, "Shares of the parent held by a
subsidiary should not be treated as outstanding stock in the consolidated
balance sheet."[1] The American Accounting Association Committee on Concepts and Standards went further and recommended that holdings of parent
company shares be treated as treasury stock. The Committee comments:

> Shares of the controlling company's capital stock owned by a sub-
> sidiary before the date of acquisition of control should be treated in
> consolidation as treasury stock. Any subsequent acquisition or sale by
> a subsidiary should likewise be treated in the consolidated statements
> as though it had been the act of the controlling company.[2]

The recognition of investments in parent company shares as treasury
stock on the consolidated balance sheet is both sound in theory and simple
in application. There is strong theoretical support for viewing parent holdings by a subsidiary as, in effect, reacquired shares. The need for assigning
earnings to controlling and minority interests on the assumption of a simultaneous distribution of earnings is avoided.

QUESTIONS

1. Distinguish between a condition of direct ownership and one of indirect ownership.

2. The Farris Company acquired control of the Gross Company in 19X4. The
Gross Company is a parent company, controlling activities of the Hardin Company
and the Ibsen Company. Investments in subsidiary companies are carried at cost.

(a) What eliminations are made for the investment in the Gross Company in
preparing a work sheet for a consolidated balance sheet for the Farris
Company on December 31, 19X9, assuming that subsidiary company investments were made by the Gross Company after the Farris Company
acquired control?

(b) How would your answer differ if subsidiary company investments were
made by the Gross Company prior to the date the Farris Company acquired control?

3. Company A has owned 90% of the stock of Company B since 19X2. Company
B acquired 80% of the stock of Company C upon its formation on January 1,
19X4.

---

[1] *Accounting Research Bulletin No. 51*, "Consolidated Financial Statements" (New York: American Institute of Certified Public Accountants, 1959), par. 13.

[2] *Accounting and Reporting Standards for Corporate Financial Statements and Preceding Statements and Supplements*, "Consolidated Financial Statements" (Madison, Wisconsin: American Accounting Association, 1957),
p. 44.

(a) What percentage of Company C's retained earnings will be reported as retained earnings of the controlling interest on a consolidated balance sheet for Companies A, B, and C prepared on January 1, 19X8?

(b) Assuming control by Company B over Company C as indicated but acquisition of Company A's interest in Company B on January 1, 19X8, what percentage of Company C's retained earnings will be reflected as retained earnings of the controlling interest on the consolidated balance sheet prepared on this date?

4. Company Q owns 90% of the stock of Company R and 80% of the stock of Company S. Each of the latter companies owns 40% of the stock of Company T. Can the net assets of Company T be properly included in a consolidated balance sheet prepared for Company Q? Give reasons for your answer.

5. What is meant by a condition of "mutual holdings"?

6. (a) What two views may be adopted in developing a consolidated balance sheet for two affiliates with mutual holdings? (b) Give the arguments that may be raised in support of each. (c) Which view do you support? Why?

7. Assuming that two affiliated companies have mutual holdings and recognize the earnings of each other in consolidation, what special calculations are required in the preparation of a consolidated balance sheet when (a) investments are carried by the equity method and (b) investments are carried by the cost method?

8. The Price Company, a subsidiary of Phillips, Inc., holds 500 shares representing a 2½% interest in the stock of the latter company. The shares were acquired at a price in excess of their book value and are carried at cost. Assuming that holdings of the subsidiary are not eliminated in the preparation of a consolidated balance sheet, explain two methods for reporting such acquisition on the consolidated balance sheet.

EXERCISES

1. On January 2, 19X5, the Cokely Corporation acquired 900 shares of the Gable Corporation stock at 150. On January 2, 19X6, the Gable Corporation acquired 800 shares of Hall Company stock at 105. The capital stock of each company is $100,000 and shares have a par value of $100. Retained earnings balances on December 31, 19X4, and earnings and dividends for 19X5 and 19X6 were as follows:

	Cokely	Gable	Hall
Retained earnings (deficit), December 31, 19X4...	$140,000	$50,000	($10,000)
Dividends declared in November, 19X5.....	20,000	10,000	
Net income from own operations, 19X5.....	30,000	20,000	15,000
Dividends declared in November, 19X6.....	20,000	10,000	10,000
Net income from own operations, 19X6.....	40,000	25,000	20,000

Prepare the entries affecting the investment accounts and retained earnings accounts on the books of the Hall Company, the Gable Corporation, and the

Cokely Corporation if investments are carried by (a) the equity method and (b) the cost method.

2. Retained earnings balances and income and dividend data for Companies A, B, and C are summarized below:

	Co. A	Co. B	Co. C
Retained earnings, January 1, 19X1..............	$85,000	$60,000	$10,000
Net income from own operations, 19X1	14,500	25,000	15,000
Dividends declared and paid in December, 19X1	20,000	15,000	10,000

Prepare the entries that would be made on the books of the parent company and the subparent company during 19X1, assuming use of the equity method and facts as indicated in each of the following cases:

(a) Company A acquired 90% of the stock of Company B on January 2, 19X0; Company B acquired 80% of the stock of Company C on July 1, 19X1.

(b) Company A acquired 90% of the stock of Company B on July 1, 19X1; Company B had acquired 80% of the stock of Company C on January 2, 19X0.

3. Prepare the entries that would appear in each case in Exercise 2, assuming that investments are carried by the cost method.

4. Company F owns 90% of the stock of Company G. The stock was acquired on January 2, 19X0, when Company G showed on its books a deficit of $200,000. Company P acquired 90% of the stock of Company F on January 2, 19X5, when Company F showed on its books retained earnings of $300,000. Company G's deficit had been reduced to $60,000 on this date. Investment accounts are carried at cost. The differences between investment costs and book values of net assets at acquisition dates were ascribed to specific nondepreciable assets. On December 31, 19X7, retained earnings balances for Companies P, F, and G are as follows: Company P, $3,000,000; Company F, $280,000; Company G, $40,000.

(a) What is the amount of retained earnings of the controlling interest to be reported on the consolidated balance sheet prepared for Company P and its affiliates on December 31, 19X7?

(b) What is the amount of retained earnings of the minority interest on this date?

5. Company A owns 90% of the stock of Company B, and Company B owns 80% of the stock of Company C. What elimination for intercompany profits is required on the work sheet for a consolidated balance sheet for each of the following cases, assuming that merchandise is sold at a gross profit rate of 15%? (Assume that investment accounts are carried by the equity method.)

(a) Merchandise held by Co. C, acquired from Co. A, $25,000.
(b) Merchandise held by Co. B, acquired from Co. A, $25,000.
(c) Merchandise held by Co. C, acquired from Co. B, $25,000.
(d) Merchandise held by Co. A, acquired from Co. C, $25,000.

6. On January 2, 19X4, the Marsh Company acquired 800 shares of stock in Lowell, Inc., at 110. On the same date the latter corporation acquired 100 shares of parent company stock at 140. Capital stock and retained earnings accounts on December 31, 19X4, are:

	Marsh Co.		Lowell, Inc.	
Capital stock (1,000 shares).....		$100,000		$100,000
Retained earnings, January 2, 19X4	$40,000		$10,000	
Net income for 19X4	20,000	60,000	5,000	15,000
Total capital, December 31, 19X4		$160,000		$115,000

Each company recognizes the earnings of the other on consolidated statements.

   (a) Assuming that investments are carried by the equity method, prepare the entry for each company to recognize the earnings of the affiliate for the year.
   (b) Assuming that the investment in the subsidiary is carried at cost, calculate the total minority interest that will be reported on the consolidated balance sheet at the end of 19X4.

7. Company Y owns 800,000 shares of the stock of Company Z. Company Z in turn owns 250,000 shares of the stock of Company Y. Each company has 1,000,000 shares of stock outstanding. Earnings for Companies Y and Z for 19X9 were $100,000 and $40,000 respectively before the earnings in each other were considered.

   (a) What are the earnings of Company Y and of Company Z for the year, after each company recognizes the earnings of the other?
   (b) Assuming that the earnings of $140,000 are ultimately distributed as dividends, how much will be received by the outside stockholders owning Company Y shares and by the outside stockholders owning Company Z shares?

8. Capital stock and retained earnings balances of Companies A and B on December 31, 19X7, follow:

	Co. A	Co. B
Capital stock, $100 par	$200,000	$100,000
Retained earnings (deficit).................................	50,000	(10,000)
	$250,000	$ 90,000

Company A acquired a 90% interest in Company B on June 1, 19X3, when Company B's retained earnings were $15,000. Company B acquired a 5% interest in Company A on January 2, 19X5. On this date Company B showed retained earnings of $5,000 and Company A showed retained earnings of $30,000. Investments are carried at cost. There were no differences between amounts paid to acquire investments and the corresponding book values, which reflected fair values at the dates of acquisition. In preparing consolidated statements, each company recognizes its share of the earnings of the other.

   (a) What is the total to be reported for the controlling interest on a consolidated balance sheet prepared on December 31, 19X7?

(b) What is the total to be reported for the minority interest on December 31, 19X7?

PROBLEMS

15-1. Balance sheets for Companies P, A, and B on December 31, 19X8, are as follows, and investments in subsidiaries are carried at cost.

	Co. P	Co. A	Co. B
Investment in Co. A (90%).....................	$125,000		
Investment in Co. B (15%).....................	7,500		
Investment in Co. B (80%).....................		$ 40,000	
Other assets	367,500	210,000	$75,000
Total assets...................................	$500,000	$250,000	$75,000
Liabilities	$145,000	$ 95,000	$45,000
Capital stock (all $100 par)...................	300,000	100,000	50,000
Premium on capital stock.....................	60,000	25,000	
Retained earnings (deficit)	(5,000)	30,000	(20,000)
Total liabilities and stockholders' equity..	$500,000	$250,000	$75,000

Company A's stock was purchased by Company P as follows:

January 1, 19X1, 60%, when Company A had a deficit of $15,000.
January 1, 19X4, 30%, when Company A had retained earnings of $10,000.

Any excess of investment cost over underlying book value on the first purchase was attributable to goodwill. There was no excess on the second purchase.

Company B's stock was purchased by Companies P and A on the date of Company B's organization, September 1, 19X6.

Instructions: Prepare a work sheet and a consolidated balance sheet as of December 31, 19X8.

15-2. Balance sheets for the Lane, Meyer, and Norton Companies on December 31, 19X5, follow:

	Lane Co.	Meyer Co.	Norton Co.
Investment in Meyer Co. (42,000 shares).....................................	$ 315,000		
Investment in Norton Co. (16,000 shares).....................................		$160,000	
Other assets	1,400,000	400,000	$320,000
Total assets	$1,715,000	$560,000	$320,000
Liabilities	$ 480,000	$214,500	$140,000
Capital stock.................................	1,000,000	250,000	120,000
Additional paid-in capital................			35,000
Retained earnings	235,000	95,500	25,000
Total liabilities and stockholders' equity.....................................	$1,715,000	$560,000	$320,000

Capital stock outstanding of the three companies is as follows: Lane Company, 50,000 shares; Meyer Company, 50,000 shares; and Norton Company, 20,000 shares.

Holdings of the Lane Company in stock of the Meyer Company were obtained on January 2, 19X4. The Norton Company stock had been acquired by the Meyer Company on July 1, 19X3. Any excess of cost over book values of the investments at that time was attributed to land values. Investments are carried at cost.

An analysis of changes in retained earnings and additional paid-in capital balances is as follows:

	Lane Co.	Meyer Co.	Norton Co.	
	Retained Earnings	Retained Earnings	Additional Paid-In Capital	Retained Earnings
Balances, Dec. 31, 19X2........................	$215,000	$ 60,000		($30,000)
Net income (loss), 19X3	40,000	18,000		(15,000)
Capital from reduction in stated value of capital stock, Dec. 31, $80,000:				
Recognized as additional paid-in capital................ $35,000			$35,000	
Applied to cancellation of deficit........................... 45,000				45,000
	$255,000	$ 78,000	$35,000	
Cash dividends paid in December...........	(30,000)	(5,000)		
Balances, December 31, 19X3...............	$225,000	$ 73,000	$35,000	
Net income, 19X4.................................	35,000	15,000		$10,000
	$260,000	$ 88,000	$35,000	$10,000
Cash dividends paid in December...........	(30,000)	(7,500)		
Balances, Dec. 31, 19X4.......................	$230,000	$ 80,500	$35,000	$10,000
Net income, 19X5.................................	35,000	25,000		15,000
	$265,000	$105,500	$35,000	$25,000
Cash dividends paid in December...........	(30,000)	(10,000)		
Balances, Dec. 31, 19X5.......................	$235,000	$ 95,500	$35,000	$25,000

Instructions: Prepare a work sheet and a consolidated balance sheet for the Lane Company and its affiliates on December 31, 19X5.

15-3. Companies A, B, C, and D show account balances at the end of 19X8 as shown on page 482.

Company A owns an 80% interest in Company B and an 80% interest in Company C. These interests were acquired at the beginning of 19X8. At that time, subsidiary book values of identifiable assets reflected fair values. Company C owns a 90% interest in Company D. At the time this interest was acquired, land owned by Company D was regarded as over-valued. All stock is $100 par. Investments are carried by the equity method, but no entries have been made in the investment accounts during 19X8.

The following information is to be recorded before the books are closed:

(a) Depreciation (same rates are used by each company):

Buildings...	2½%
Furniture and fixtures	20%

	Co. A	Co. B	Co. C	Co. D
Cash	$ 65,000	$ 50,000	$ 45,000	$ 20,000
Notes Receivable	45,000	25,000	5,300	10,000
Accounts Receivable	78,000	72,000	40,000	35,000
Merchandise Inventory, January 1	85,000	70,000	35,000	30,000
Land	35,000	25,000	10,000	20,000
Buildings	110,000	80,000	40,000	
Accumulated Depreciation of Buildings ..	12,000	22,000	15,000	
Furniture and Fixtures	30,000	20,000	15,000	15,000
Accumulated Depreciation of Furniture and Fixtures	15,000	12,000	5,000	4,000
Investment in Co. B	200,000			
Investment in Co. C	80,000			
Investment in Co. D			27,700	
Notes Payable	20,000	15,000	25,000	10,000
Accounts Payable	65,000	79,000	55,000	60,000
Bonds Payable	60,000		40,000	
Capital Stock	300,000	100,000	100,000	50,000
Retained Earnings (Deficit)	235,000	105,000	(10,000)	(5,000)
Sales	540,000	360,000	230,000	145,000
Purchases	290,000	180,000	140,000	80,000
Operating Expenses	220,000	165,000	95,000	50,000
Other Revenues	15,000	15,000	10,000	6,000
Other Expenses	24,000	21,000	15,000	10,000

(b) Merchandise inventories, December 31:

Company A	$100,000
Company B	85,000
Company C	35,000
Company D	30,000

(c) Dividends were declared payable January 15, 19X9, to stockholders of record December 28, 19X8, as follows:

Company A	$1.50 per share
Company B	2.00
Company D	1.00

Instructions: Prepare a work sheet for a consolidated balance sheet as of December 31, 19X8.

15-4. The following condensed balance sheets of Companies A, B, and C were prepared as of December 31, 19X5:

	Co. A	Co. B	Co. C
Current assets	$1,234,567	$ 731,282	$340,274
Investments:			
80% of Co. B stock, at cost	1,400,000	—	—
75% of Co. C stock, at cost	—	580,200	—
Plant assets (net)	3,030,933	1,282,607	514,987
Total assets	$5,665,500	$2,594,089	$855,261
Current liabilities	$ 400,500	$ 275,389	$ 93,261
Bonds payable	—	750,000	—
Retained earnings appropriated for redemption of bonds	—	250,000	—
Capital stock, $100 par	3,000,000	1,000,000	600,000
Additional paid-in capital	710,300	—	45,600
Retained earnings	1,554,700	318,700	116,400
Total liabilities and stockholders' equity	$5,665,500	$2,594,089	$855,261

Company A acquired the stock of Company B on December 31, 19X5. The stock of Company C was acquired by Company B on January 31, 19X4. Since that date Company C had total earnings of $28,400 and paid cash dividends of $40,000. Company B credited all dividends received to its income account.

Instructions: Prepare the journal entries necessary for the preparation of a consolidated balance sheet for Company A and subsidiaries as of the close of business December 31, 19X5. Show all supporting computations in good form.

(AICPA adapted)

15-5. On December 31, 19X3, the Lance Paper Company bought 90% of the $500,000 capital stock of the Miller Supply Company for $370,080, and 80% of the $200,000, 7% preferred stock of the North Printing Company for $160,000. At the time of acquisition, the book values of identifiable assets of Miller reflected fair values, except for land, which was overstated on Miller's books.

On December 31, 19X2, the Miller Supply Company had acquired 90% of the $200,000 common stock of the North Printing Company for $180,000.

Balance sheets are as follows:

Lance Paper Company
Balance Sheet
December 31, 19X4

Investments:		Accounts payable:	
Miller Supply Co.	$ 397,080	North Printing Co.	$ 10,000
North Printing Co.	171,200	Capital stock:	
Notes receivable:		Preferred	400,000
North Printing Co.	20,000	Common	800,000
Other assets (net)	724,520	Retained earnings	102,800
		Total liabilities and stockholders' equity	
Total assets	$1,312,800		$1,312,800

Miller Supply Company
Balance Sheet
December 31, 19X4

Investments:		Notes receivable discounted	$ 10,000
North Printing Co.	$ 180,000	Capital stock	500,000
Notes receivable:		Retained earnings	26,000
North Printing Co.	10,000		
Other assets (net)	346,000	Total liabilities and stockholders' equity	
Total assets	$ 536,000		$ 536,000

North Printing Company
Balance Sheet
December 31, 19X4

Accounts receivable:		Notes payable:	
Lance Paper Co.	$ 15,000	Lance Paper Co.	$ 20,000
Other assets (net)	445,000	Miller Supply Co.	10,000
		Dividends payable:	
		Preferred	14,000
		Common	16,000
		Capital stock:	
		7% Preferred	200,000
		Common	200,000
		Total liabilities and stockholders' equity	
Total assets	$ 460,000		$ 460,000

Lance consistently records on its books its share of Miller's profits.

The difference of $5,000 between the current accounts of Lance and North represents North merchandise in transit to Lance.

Miller does not record on its books its share of North profits but credits to income the North dividends when received.

Miller made a profit of $50,000 in 19X4, before considering income from its investment in North. On December 20, 19X4, Miller paid a dividend of 4% ($20,000) on its $500,000 capital stock.

North made a profit of $20,000 in 19X3, which was paid out in dividends that were duly received by the shareholders before December 31, 19X3.

North made a profit of $30,000 in 19X4, and on December 20, 19X4, declared dividends of 7% on the preferred stock and 8% on the common stock, both payable January 10, 19X5.

Provision had been made by the three companies for all known liabilities and accruals, including 19X4 federal income taxes.

Instructions: (1) Prepare a work sheet for a consolidated balance sheet.

(2) Prepare a consolidated balance sheet as of December 31, 19X4.

(3) Prepare a statement of minority interest.

(4) Prepare a statement showing the change in value of Miller Co. land, based on the acquisition cost of Lance's investment.   (AICPA adapted)

15-6. Company X acquired 80% of the capital stock of Company Y on January 2, 19X6, at a cost of $600,000. On this date Company Y held 75% of the stock of Company Z. This interest had been acquired for $187,500 on January 2, 19X0, the date Company Z had been organized. On January 2, 19X7, Company X purchased 15% of Company Z stock from a stockholder for $85,000. Book values of investments reflected fair values of identifiable assets at respective purchase dates. All investment accounts have been maintained at cost. Balance sheet data for the three companies and a summary of changes in retained earnings for the period 19X5–19X7 follow.

	Co. X	Co. Y	Co. Z
Investment in Co. Y	$ 600,000		
Investment in Co. Z	85,000	$187,500	
Other assets	640,000	637,500	$560,000
Total assets	$1,325,000	$825,000	$560,000
Liabilities	$ 350,000	$265,000	$160,000
Capital stock	1,000,000	500,000	200,000
Premium on capital stock			50,000
Retained earnings (deficit)	(25,000)	60,000	150,000
Total liabilities and stockholders' equity	$1,325,000	$825,000	$560,000
Retained earnings (deficit), Jan. 1, 19X6	($ 115,000)	($ 20,000)	$140,000
Net income (loss), 19X6	40,000	60,000	60,000
Dividends, 19X6		(15,000)	(20,000)
Retained earnings (deficit), Jan. 1, 19X7	($ 75,000)	$ 25,000	$180,000
Net income (loss), 19X7	50,000	65,000	(30,000)
Dividends, 19X7		(30,000)	
Retained earnings (deficit), Dec. 31, 19X7	($ 25,000)	$ 60,000	$150,000

Instructions: Prepare a work sheet for a consolidated balance sheet as of December 31, 19X7.

15-7. A consolidated balance sheet is being prepared for Companies P and Q. Company P has 500,000 shares of capital stock issued and outstanding, owns 350,000 shares of capital stock of Company Q, and has retained earnings of $1,050. Company Q has 400,000 shares of capital stock issued and outstanding, owns 45,000 shares of capital stock of Company P, and has a deficit of $2,100.

Instructions: Determine the amount of the deficit of Company Q applicable to the minority interest in that company.

(AICPA adapted)

15-8. Balance sheets on December 31, 19X7, for Star Properties, Inc., and Turf Corporation are as follows:

	Star Properties, Inc.		Turf Corp.
Investment in Turf Corp., 15,000 shares at cost..	$ 225,000		
Investment in Star Properties, Inc., 10,000 shares at cost			$100,125
Other assets	1,250,000		419,875
Total assets	$1,475,000		$520,000
Liabilities	$ 425,000		$180,000
Capital stock.................................(100,000 sh.)	1,000,000	(20,000 sh.)	300,000
Retained earnings	50,000		40,000
Total liabilities and stockholders' equity.............	$1,475,000		$520,000

Star Properties, Inc., acquired Turf Corporation stock when the latter company was formed in May, 19X1. Turf Corporation purchased its shares in Star Properties, Inc., on July 1, 19X4. Star Properties, Inc., showed a deficit of $10,000 on this date, while Turf Corporation had retained earnings of $15,000.

Instructions: (1) Prepare a work sheet for a consolidated balance sheet as of December 31, 19X7, assuming that each company recognizes its share of earnings on investments.
(2) Prepare a work sheet for a consolidated balance sheet as of December 31, 19X7, assuming that the subsidiary's investment in parent company stock is treated as treasury stock.

15-9. Balance sheets on December 31, 19X6, for Companies E and F are as follows:

	Co. E		Co. F
Investment in Co. F (18,000 shares at cost)........	$ 252,000		
Investment in Co. E (2,500 shares at cost)..........			$ 61,100
Other assets	1,498,000		238,900
Total assets	$1,750,000		$300,000
Liabilities	$ 450,000		$100,000
Capital stock, no par.................(50,000 shares)	1,000,000	(20,000 sh.)	200,000
Additional paid-in capital.................................	100,000		50,000
Retained earnings (deficit)...............................	200,000		(50,000)
Total liabilities and stockholders' equity.............	$1,750,000		$300,000

Company F stock was acquired by Company E on January 2, 19X1, when Company F showed retained earnings of $30,000. Company E stock was acquired by Company F on January 2, 19X4. On this date Company E and Company F retained earnings balances were $140,000 and $10,000 respectively.

Instructions: Prepare a work sheet for a consolidated balance sheet as of December 31, 19X6, assuming that each company recognizes earnings on its investment in the affiliate.

15-10. Company X and Company Y prepare balance sheets on December 31, 19X3, as follows:

	Co. X	Co. Y
Investment in Co. Y (900 shares)	$108,000	
Investment in Co. X (200 shares)		$ 26,175
Other assets	397,000	223,825
Total assets	$505,000	$250,000
Liabilities	$240,000	$115,000
Capital stock (all $100 par)	200,000	100,000
Retained earnings	65,000	35,000
Total liabilities and stockholders' equity	$505,000	$250,000

Investments in subsidiaries are carried at cost. Company X acquired Company Y stock on January 2, 19X3, when Company Y's retained earnings showed a balance of $20,000. Company Y acquired Company X stock on July 1, 19X3. Company X's retained earnings on January 1, 19X3, were $45,000. (It may be assumed that earnings accrue proportionately throughout the year and that each company recognizes earnings on its investment in the affiliate.)

Instructions: (1) Prepare a work sheet for a consolidated balance sheet as of December 31, 19X3.

(2) Revise the balances on the assumption that the equity method is used and prepare a work sheet for a consolidated balance sheet.

15-11. Parent and subparent companies record earnings and dividends of subsidiaries in investment accounts. There is no goodwill or depreciable assets related to any of the investment transactions. Prepare any journal entries affecting the investment accounts in 19X9 as a result of the following:

(1) Company P owns 1,600 shares of Company D stock. Company D has 2,000 shares of stock outstanding. Company D owns 8,000 shares of Company E common. Company E has 10,000 shares of common outstanding. Company E announces net income from operations of $20,000 for 19X9 and on December 31, 19X9, declares a cash dividend of 50 cents per share. Company D's net income for the year, before considering its earnings as a result of its ownership of Company E stock, is $30,000. (Prepare entries for Company P and Company D.)

(2) Company P owns 9,000 shares of Company F stock acquired as follows: January 1, 19X8, 8,000 shares; July 1, 19X9, 1,000 shares. Company F owns 1,000 shares of Company P stock acquired on October 1, 19X9. Company P and Company F each have 10,000 shares outstanding. Company P's net income for 19X9, before considering its earnings as a result of ownership of Company F stock, is $30,000. Company F's net income

for 19X9 is $18,000. (Assume net incomes are earned proportionately throughout the year and that both parent and subsidiary companies recognize earnings of each other. Prepare entries for Company P and Company F.)

15-12. Balance sheets for the Dodge Company, the Ely Company, and the Fields Company on December 31, 19X2, are as follows:

	Dodge Co.	Ely Co.	Fields Co.
Cash...	$ 30,000	$ 10,000	$ 15,000
Customers' notes and accounts receivable.......	90,000	50,000	60,000
Inventories...	70,000	60,000	50,000
Investments at cost:			
Stock of Ely Co. (75%).............................	100,000		
Stock of Fields Co. (80%)..........................	200,000		
Stock of Ely Co. (15%).............................			30,000
Property, plant, and equipment (net)..............	500,000	200,000	120,000
Deferred charges.......................................	10,000	5,000	5,000
Total assets..	$1,000,000	$325,000	$280,000
Notes payable...	$ 60,000	$ 50,000	$ 30,000
Accounts payable.......................................	40,000	45,000	20,000
Mortgage payable.......................................			90,000
Capital stock, $100 par...............................	500,000	200,000	100,000
Retained earnings......................................	400,000	30,000	40,000
Total liabilities and stockholders' equity...........	$1,000,000	$325,000	$280,000

The Dodge Company acquired its holdings in Ely Company and Fields Company on December 31, 19X1. The Fields Company's holdings of Ely Company stock were purchased at an earlier date at par, which was also the book value.

An analysis of retained earnings balances for the year ended December 31, 19X2, is as follows:

	Dodge Co.	Ely Co.	Fields Co.
Retained earnings at December 31, 19X1..	$280,000	$10,000	$50,000
Income for 19X2......................................	70,000	20,000	30,000
	$350,000	$30,000	$80,000
Dividends paid	(50,000)		(40,000)
Retained earnings at December 31, 19X2..	$300,000	$30,000	$40,000

Instructions: Prepare a consolidated balance sheet for the Dodge Company and its subsidiaries as of December 31, 19X2.

(AICPA adapted)

15-13. The following financial facts pertain to Corporations R and S, which had mutual holdings during and at the end of the fiscal year 19X0:

	R	S
Of the issued capital stock,		
R owns	10%	50%
S owns...	20%	10%
Net assets (exclusive of investment accounts), December 31, 19X0	$540,000	$590,000
Dividends declared during 19X0	?	18,000
19X0 net income (after taxes), exclusive of dividends...	53,000	60,000

There has been no change in the mutual holdings during the year. Each corporation carries its investment account at cost.

Instructions: (1) Compute the dollar equity of outside shareholders in the total net assets of R and S respectively.

(2) Compute the dollar amount of dividends declared in 19X0 to which the outside shareholders of R are entitled, assuming that R declared as dividends its *total* 19X0 net income.   (AICPA adapted)

15-14. Company H has agreed to purchase the minority interest in Company S. Their balance sheets show:

	Co. H		Co. S
Tangible assets	$3,764,513		$2,264,718
Goodwill	500,000		
91,000 shares of Co. S..................	1,270,000	(5,373 shares of Co. H)	622,443
Total assets	$5,534,513		$2,887,161
Creditors	$ 367,423		$ 133,675
Capital stock ....(40,000 sh.)	4,000,000	(100,000 shares)	2,500,000
Retained earnings	1,167,090		253,486
Total liabilities and stockholders' equity	$5,534,513		$2,887,161

The stock is to be acquired at asset value, but in the computation the goodwill of either company is not to be considered.

Instructions: Compute the amount that should be paid to the minority stockholders per share of Company S. Do not carry your computation further than whole cents per share.   (AICPA adapted)

15-15. The following is a summary of the balance sheets of three corporations at a given date:

	R	S	T
Total assets	$1,500,000	$2,000,000	$3,500,000
Total liabilities	$ 250,000	$ 750,000	$1,100,000
Capital stock, $100 par..................	1,000,000	750,000	2,000,000
Retained earnings	250,000	500,000	400,000
Total liabilities and stockholders' equity	$1,500,000	$2,000,000	$3,500,000

Each corporation owned a part of the capital stock of the others, carried on their respective books as follows:

	Capital Stock In		
	R	S	T
R owned		15%	15%
Carried at		$100,000	$300,000
S owned......	15%		10%
Carried at	$150,000		$175,000
T owned......	5%	5%	
Carried at	$ 50,000	$ 60,000	

The three companies agreed to consolidate and each to accept its pro rata share in the capital stock of a new corporation (P) having 1,000,000 shares of no-par value.

Instructions: Compute the percentage of the shares of Corporation P that the stockholders of R, S, and T, respectively, will receive, and the total equity or paid-in value of the consolidated capital.

(AICPA adapted)

16
Consolidated Statements — Income and Retained Earnings Statements

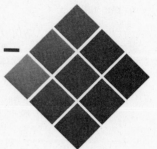

The consolidated balance sheet is a composite summary of the financial position of a parent company and its affiliates as of a given date. The considerations that lead to the preparation of the consolidated balance sheet also suggest the need for consolidated income and retained earnings statements that summarize the financial progress of the affiliated units.

The concepts underlying the preparation of consolidated income and retained earnings statements are the same as those already discussed in the previous chapters. In preparing the consolidated income statement, intercompany revenue and expense items are eliminated. Remaining balances are then combined. As in the case of the consolidated balance sheet, the consolidated income and retained earnings statements are based on the premise that the parent company and its subsidiaries represent a single economic unit.

Consolidated statements may be prepared by combining balance sheet, income statement, and retained earnings statement data on separate work sheets. Ordinarily, however, it is more convenient to prepare those statements by means of a single work sheet. Eliminations for purposes of consolidation are applied to adjust trial balances for the affiliated companies in a manner similar to that employed previously in the preparation of combined statements for a home office and its branches.

The preparation of consolidated statements will be illustrated by means of two examples. A relatively simple set of facts covering a two-year period for a trading company and its subsidiary is presented in the first example, and work sheets are illustrated for an investment carried by the equity method and for an investment carried by the cost method. A more complex set of facts for a two-year period for a manufacturing company and its subsidiary is given in the second example in which a work sheet is illustrated for an investment carried by the equity method.

WORK SHEET FOR CONSOLIDATED STATEMENTS FOR A TRADING COMPANY

For purposes of the first example, assume the following facts. The letter designation preceding each item is used later in describing the elimination required for that item and also in identifying the elimination on the work sheet.

(a) Company A acquired 80% of the stock of Company B on January 1, 19X1, at a cost of $125,000. Capital stock of Company B on this date was $100,000; retained earnings were $25,000. Goodwill arising from this purchase is to be amortized over a period of 25 years.

(b) Company A purchased merchandise from Company B as follows: during 19X1, $15,000; during 19X2, $25,000.

(c) Amounts owed by Company A to Company B on open account were as follows: December 31, 19X1, $3,500; December 31, 19X2, $6,500.

(d) Intercompany profits in inventories related to goods acquired by Company A from Company B were as follows: December 31, 19X1, $1,000; December 31, 19X2, $2,500.

(e) Company B declared dividends of $25,000 in 19X2.

A work sheet for a consolidated balance sheet for Companies A and B on the date of acquisition is prepared as follows:

Company A and Subsidiary Company B
Work Sheet for Consolidated Balance Sheet
January 1, 19X1

	Co. A	Co. B	Eliminations Dr.	Eliminations Cr.	Consolidated Balance Sheet Dr.	Consolidated Balance Sheet Cr.
Debits						
Cash	25,000	15,000			40,000	
Accounts Receivable (net).....	60,000	40,000			100,000	
Merchandise Inventory..........	85,000	40,000			125,000	
Plant and Equipment (net).....	200,000	85,000			285,000	
Investment in Co. B Stock	125,000			125,000		
Eliminate Investment.........			25,000		25,000	
Goodwill						
	495,000	180,000				
Credits						
Accounts Payable..................	75,000	55,000				130,000
Bonds Payable	100,000					100,000
Capital Stock, Co. A..............	250,000					250,000
Retained Earnings, Co. A.......	70,000					70,000
Capital Stock, Co. B..............		100,000				
Eliminate 80%			80,000			
Minority Interest, 20%.......						20,000
Retained Earnings, Co. B.......		25,000				
Eliminate 80%			20,000			
Minority Interest, 20%.......						5,000
	495,000	180,000	125,000	125,000	575,000	575,000

Equity method. Assume that the parent company carries its investment in the subsidiary by the equity method. During the year, its investment account would reflect the beginning balance, reduced by any dividends received from the subsidiary. At the end of the year, the parent would record its equity in the earnings of the subsidiary and would record adjustments for the same items that are considered in the preparation of consolidated statements, i.e., elimination of intercompany profits, amortization of goodwill, etc. Therefore it is most practical to develop the year-end equity-method adjustment concurrently with the preparation of the consolidated statements.

The parent company prepares a trial balance from its own records, taken prior to the equity-method adjustment and closing entries. It can also obtain a pre-closing trial balance from the subsidiary. If completed statements of the subsidiary are used, the accounts can be restated in pre-closing form. Thus, retained earnings balances are shown as of the beginning of the period, nominal accounts are listed in the appropriate debit and credit sections, and dividends declared are listed as a separate debit item.

The financial statements of Company B for 19X1 and 19X2 are as follows:

Company B
Income Statement
For Years Ended December 31, 19X1 and 19X2

	19X1		19X2	
Sales		$210,000		$220,000
Cost of goods sold:				
Merchandise inventory, January 1	$ 40,000		$ 75,000	
Purchases	160,000		125,000	
Merchandise available for sale	$200,000		$200,000	
Less merchandise inventory,				
December 31	75,000	125,000	70,000	130,000
Gross profit		$ 85,000		$ 90,000
Expenses		40,000		35,000
Income before income taxes		$ 45,000		$ 55,000
Income taxes		15,000		20,000
Net income		$ 30,000		$ 35,000

Retained Earnings Statement
For Years Ended December 31, 19X1 and 19X2

	19X1	19X2
Retained earnings, January 1	$25,000	$55,000
Add net income for year	30,000	35,000
	$55,000	$90,000
Deduct dividends declared		25,000
Retained earnings, December 31	$55,000	$65,000

Balance Sheet
December 31, 19X1 and 19X2

	19X1	19X2
Assets		
Cash...	$ 25,000	$ 30,000
Accounts receivable (net)	35,000	35,000
Merchandise inventory	75,000	70,000
Plant and equipment (net)	100,000	90,000
Total assets..	$235,000	$225,000
Liabilities		
Accounts payable	$ 80,000	$ 60,000
Total liabilities...	$ 80,000	$ 60,000
Stockholders' Equity		
Capital stock...	$100,000	$100,000
Retained earnings.......................................	55,000	65,000
Total stockholders' equity...........................	$155,000	$165,000
Total liabilities and stockholders' equity......	$235,000	$225,000

The pre-closing trial balances for Company A (prior to equity-method adjustments) and Company B, as of December 31, 19X1, are shown in the first two columns of the work sheet on page 494. After the pre-closing trial balances are listed, each company's ending inventory is entered twice: first as a debit immediately below the total of other debit items for the company, a position in which it represents the asset to be reported on the balance sheet; then as a credit immediately below the other credit items for the company, a position in which it represents a subtraction item from the beginning inventory and purchases in reporting cost of goods sold on the consolidated income statement. Eliminations for intercompany balance sheet and income statement items are then recorded in the eliminations columns. When adjustments or corrections of account balances are required, a pair of columns for this purpose may be included to the left of the eliminations columns.

Explanations of the eliminations on the work sheet for Companies A and B are below and on page 495. The letter preceding each explanation corresponds with that used in reporting the elimination on the work sheet.

(a1) The investment account carried by the equity method will ultimately reflect subsidiary earnings and dividends. However, earnings for the current period have not yet been recorded by the parent and no current dividend has been declared by the subsidiary. Therefore, the balance in the investment account is the beginning-of-the-year balance. This balance should correspond with the reciprocal elements of the stockholders' equity of the subsidiary, since the subsidiary's accounts represent pre-closing balances. Therefore, this elimination entry offsets the investment account balance against the proportionate share of Company B's stockholders' equity accounts. The balancing item is goodwill.

Equity method:

Company A and Subsidiary Company B
Work Sheet for Consolidated Statements
December 31, 19X1

	Trial Balances Co. A	Trial Balances Co. B	Eliminations Dr.	Eliminations Cr.	Cons. Income Statement Dr.	Cons. Income Statement Cr.	Cons. Retained Earnings Statement Dr.	Cons. Retained Earnings Statement Cr.	Cons. Balance Sheet Dr.	Cons. Balance Sheet Cr.
Debits										
Cash	35,000	25,000							60,000	
Accounts Receivable (net)	65,000	35,000		(c) 3,500					96,500	
Merchandise Inventory, 1/1/X1	85,000	40,000			125,000					
Plant and Equipment (net)	215,000	100,000							315,000	
Investment in Co. B, 1/1/X6	125,000									
Eliminate Investment				(a1) 125,000						
Goodwill			(a1) 25,000	(a2) 1,000					24,000	
Purchases	380,000	160,000		(b) 15,000	525,000					
Expenses	145,000	40,000			185,000					
Income Taxes	30,000	15,000			45,000					
Amortization Expense — Goodwill			(a2) 1,000		1,000					
	1,080,000	415,000								
Merchandise Inventory, 12/31/X1	90,000	75,000	(d) 1,000			164,000				
Credits										
Accounts Payable	60,000	80,000	(c) 3,500							136,500
Bonds Payable	100,000									100,000
Capital Stock, Co. A	250,000									250,000
Retained Earnings, Co. A, 1/1/X1	70,000							70,000		
Capital Stock, Co. B		100,000								
Eliminate 80%			(a1) 80,000							
Minority Interest, 20%										20,000
Retained Earnings, Co. B, 1/1/X1		25,000								
Eliminate 80%			(a1) 20,000							
Minority Interest, 20%								5,000		
Sales	600,000	210,000	(b) 15,000			795,000				
	1,080,000	415,000								
Merchandise Inventory, 12/31/X1	90,000	75,000		(d) 1,000					164,000	
			145,500	145,500	881,000	959,000				
Minority Int. Share of Inc. to Ret. Earn.					5,800			5,800		
Controlling Int. Share of Inc. to Ret. Earn.					72,200			72,200		
					959,000	959,000				
Consolidated Retained Earnings to Balance Sheet							142,200			142,200
Minority Interest Retained Earnings to Balance Sheet							10,800			10,800
							153,000	153,000	659,500	659,500

(a2) The goodwill figure derived in entry (a1) represents the balance of goodwill as of the beginning of the year. Further adjustment is necessary to record the amortization of goodwill for the year. The amount of annual amortization, based on a 25-year life, is $1,000 ($25,000 ÷ 25).

(b) Intercompany sales are canceled by an elimination reducing sales of Co. B and the purchases account of Co. A.

(c) Intercompany trade accounts in the amount of $3,500 are canceled.

(d) The ending inventory is reduced to cost for both the balance sheet and the income statement by the following entry:

Merchandise Inventory, 12/31/X1 (income statement).......	1,000	
Merchandise Inventory, 12/31/X1 (balance sheet)		1,000

Account balances on the work sheet may now be combined and extended to the income statement, retained earnings statement, and balance sheet columns. Revenue and expense balances and the beginning and ending inventories are carried to the income statement columns. The portion of the retained earnings of the subsidiary company identified with the minority interest as of the beginning of the period and any dividends of the subsidiary identified with the minority interest for the current period are carried to the retained earnings columns. The retained earnings of the controlling interest as of the beginning of the period and any dividends identified with the controlling interest for the current period are also carried to the retained earnings columns. Remaining balances, including the ending inventory, are carried to the balance sheet columns.

Income statement columns may now be summarized. A debit excess in the income statement columns indicates a net loss from combined activities; a credit excess indicates a net income from combined activities. The portion of the combined earnings accruing to the minority interest is calculated and carried to the retained earnings columns. This calculation may be made as follows:

Company B income, as reported	$30,000
Less intercompany profit eliminated	1,000
Adjusted income...	$29,000
Minority share	20%
Minority interest in consolidated income	$ 5,800

The elimination of the intercompany profit would not be made on Company B's own statements, but would be deducted from Company B's income (and thus proportionately from the minority interest) in the consolidated statements because Company B had sold the merchandise and it is still in the hands of the parent.

The combined earnings less the portion assigned to the minority interest are carried to a separate line in the retained earnings columns. These amounts in the retained earnings columns represent the increments to the minority and controlling interest retained earnings as a result of the year's operations. The retained earnings of the minority interest may now be determined and transferred to the balance sheet columns. The retained earnings of the controlling interest are similarly determined and transferred to the balance sheet columns. These transfers bring ending assets and ending liabilities and capital in the balance sheet columns into agreement. Consolidated statements may now be prepared as follows:

Company A and Subsidiary Company B
Consolidated Income Statement
For Year Ended December 31, 19X1

Sales		$795,000
Cost of goods sold:		
Merchandise inventory, January 1	$125,000	
Purchases	525,000	
Merchandise available for sale	$650,000	
Less merchandise inventory, December 31.............	164,000	486,000
Gross profit...		$309,000
Expenses..		186,000
Income before income taxes		$123,000
Income taxes		45,000
Net income before minority interest		$ 78,000
Minority interest in net income of subsidiary		5,800
Net income...		$ 72,200

Company A and Subsidiary Company B
Consolidated Balance Sheet
December 31, 19X1

Assets

Cash		$ 60,000
Accounts receivable (net)		96,500
Merchandise inventory		164,000
Plant and equipment (net)		315,000
Goodwill		24,000
Total assets		$659,500

Liabilities

Accounts payable		$136,500
Bonds payable		100,000
Total liabilities		$236,500

Stockholders' Equity

Minority interest:			
Capital stock	$ 20,000		
Retained earnings	10,800	$ 30,800	
Controlling interest:			
Capital stock	$250,000		
Retained earnings	142,200	392,200	
Total stockholders' equity..			423,000
Total liabilities and stockholders' equity.........................			$659,500

Company A and Subsidiary Company B
Consolidated Retained Earnings Statement
For Year Ended December 31, 19X1

	Retained Earnings — Minority Interest	Retained Earnings — Controlling Interest
Retained earnings, January 1, 19X1	$ 5,000	$ 70,000
Add net income for year...........	5,800	72,200
Retained earnings, December 31, 19X1.............................	$10,800	$142,200

The equity-method adjustment may now be recorded on Company A's books. This amount is equal to the controlling interest share of the subsidiary income, reduced by the amortization expense, which is entirely attributed to the controlling interest. It may be calculated as follows:

Income attributed to Company B	$29,000
Company A share	80%
	$23,200
Less amortization expense	1,000
Company A equity in Company B income	$22,200

The equity-method adjustment would be recorded by Company A with the following entry:

Investment in Co. B...	22,200	
Equity in Income of Subsidiary.......................................		22,200

After the accounts are closed, the retained earnings of Company A will be the same as the controlling interest retained earnings shown on the consolidated statement. The equity method is designed to provide the same final result on the separate statements of the parent company as is obtained from preparing consolidated statements.

The pre-closing trial balances and inventories as of December 31, 19X2, for Company A (prior to 19X2 equity-method adjustments) and Company B, are shown in the first two columns of the work sheet on page 498. Explanations of the work sheet eliminations are below and on page 499.

(x) Because the trial balance figures on the work sheet are taken directly from the accounting records of Company A and Company B, they reflect only transactions that have been recorded by the two companies. Work sheet adjustments that were made in prior years but not recorded in the individual company accounts would not be reflected. As a result, the trial balance figures may have to be adjusted to bring them in line with the corresponding figures shown in the previous year's consolidated balance sheet. In particular, the ending inventory of the preceding year was adjusted for consolidation purposes to eliminate the amount of intercompany profits included in the cost of this item. The adjustment would not have been recorded by the individual companies, however, since the

Equity method:

Company A and Subsidiary Company B
Work Sheet for Consolidated Statements
December 31, 19X2

	Trial Balances		Eliminations		Consolidated Income Statement		Consolidated Retained Earnings Statement		Consolidated Balance Sheet	
Debits	Co. A	Co. B	Dr.	Cr.	Dr.	Cr.	Dr.	Cr.	Dr.	Cr.
Cash	55,000	30,000							85,000	
Accounts Receivable (net)	60,000	35,000		(c) 6,500					88,500	
Merchandise Inventory, 1/1/X2	90,000	75,000		(x) 1,000	164,000					
Plant and Equipment (net)	240,000	90,000							330,000	
Investment in Co. B, 1/1/X2	127,200			(a1) 127,200						
Eliminate Investment			(a1) 24,000							
Goodwill				(a2) 1,000					23,000	
Purchases	380,000	125,000		(b) 25,000	480,000					
Expenses	135,000	35,000			170,000					
Income Taxes	40,000	20,000			60,000					
Dividends Declared, Co. A	40,000						40,000			
Dividends Declared, Co. B		25,000								
Eliminate 80%				(a1) 20,000			5,000			
Amortization — Goodwill			(a2) 1,000		1,000					
	1,167,200	435,000								
Merchandise Inventory, 12/31/X2	80,000	70,000	(d) 2,500			147,500				
Credits										
Accounts Payable	50,000	60,000	(c) 6,500							103,500
Bonds Payable	100,000									100,000
Capital Stock, Co. A	250,000									250,000
Retained Earnings, Co. A, 1/1/X2	142,200							142,200		
Capital Stock, Co. B		100,000	(a1) 80,000							
Eliminate 80%										
Minority Interest, 20%										20,000
Retained Earnings, Co. B, 1/1/X2		55,000	(x) 1,000							
Eliminate 80% of $54,000			(a1) 43,200							
Minority Interest, 20% of $54,000								10,800		
Sales	625,000	220,000	(b) 25,000			820,000				
	1,167,200	435,000								
Merchandise Inventory, 12/31/X2	80,000	70,000	(d) 2,500						147,500	
			183,200	183,200	875,000	967,500				
Minority Int. Share of Inc. to Ret. Earn.					6,700			6,700		
Controlling Int. Share of Inc. to Ret. Earn.					85,800			85,800		
					967,500	967,500				
Consol. Ret. Earn. to Balance Sheet							188,000			188,000
Minority Ret. Earn. to Balance Sheet							12,500			12,500
							245,500	245,500	674,000	674,000

profit is deemed to have been earned from the separate company point of view. The ending inventory of the preceding year becomes the beginning inventory of the current year, so that a work sheet adjustment is necessary to obtain the proper beginning inventory balance.

The inventory of Company A as of December 31, 19X1, was reduced by $1,000 to eliminate the amount of Company B's profit included in the cost to Company A. A corresponding reduction was made in the income (ultimately reducing retained earnings) of Company B. Therefore, the proper beginning balances may be obtained by making the following adjusting entry:

Retained Earnings, Co. B (1/1/X2)....................................	1,000	
Merchandise Inventory (1/1/X2).....................................		1,000

(a1) Investment account eliminations are made in terms of the reciprocal balances that are found in the real and the nominal accounts as of December 31, 19X2. In applying the equity method during the year, Company A would have reduced its investment account by the amount of dividends received from Company B. Therefore, the investment account shown on the trial balance may be explained as follows:

Balance as of January 1, 19X1..	$125,000
Plus equity-method adjustment, 19X1.....................................	22,000
	$147,200
Less Company B dividend received, 19X2................................	20,000
Pre-closing balance, 19X2..	$127,200

Because the work sheet reflects pre-closing trial balance figures, the amount of dividends declared by Company B would not have been deducted from that company's retained earnings. Thus it is necessary to eliminate Company A's proportionate share of the declared dividends, $20,000, as part of the offset to the investment account.

(a2) The goodwill figure derived in entry (a1) represents the beginning-of-the-year balance. Therefore, amortization for the current year in the amount of $1,000 is recognized.

(b) Sales made by Company B to Company A during 19X2 are eliminated along with the corresponding purchases.

(c) Intercompany trade accounts in the amount of $6,500 are canceled.

(d) Intercompany profit in the ending inventory is canceled as follows:

Merchandise Inventory, 12/31/X2 (income statement)	2,500	
Merchandise Inventory, 12/31/X2 (balance sheet)		2,500

Account balances are extended to the income statement, retained earnings statement and balance sheet columns as was done on the work sheet for 19X1. Consolidated income is calculated and identified with minority and controlling interests. The amount of subsidiary earnings included in the consolidated total must be calculated in arriving at the portion that is to be identified with the minority interest. The reduction in inventories at the end of 19X1 reduced consolidated earnings for 19X1 but will raise consolidated earnings for 19X2, the year in which the goods are sold to outsiders. Consolidated earnings for 19X2 were raised by $1,000, the intercompany profit related to 19X1 inventories, and reduced by $2,500, the intercompany profit related to 19X2 inventories. Both of these adjustments arise from intercompany profits that were included in subsidiary earnings, and are applied to the net income balance reported by the subsidiary in arriving at the earnings of the minority interest for the year. Therefore, the minority interest in Company B earnings for the year would be 20% of $33,500 (reported income of $35,000 plus $1,000 intercompany profit in beginning inventories less $2,500 intercompany profit in ending inventories).

Consolidated statements prepared from the work sheet at the end of 19X2 are as follows:

Company A and Subsidiary Company B
Consolidated Income Statement
For Year Ended December 31, 19X2

Sales		$820,000
Cost of goods sold:		
Merchandise inventory, January 1	$164,000	
Purchases	480,000	
Merchandise available for sale	$644,000	
Less merchandise inventory, December 31	147,500	496,500
Gross profit		$323,500
Expenses		171,000
Income before income taxes		$152,500
Income taxes		60,000
Net income before minority interest		$ 92,500
Minority interest in net income of subsidiary		6,700
Net income		$ 85,800

Company A and Subsidiary Company B
Consolidated Retained Earnings Statement
For Year Ended December 31, 19X2

	Retained Earnings — Minority Interest	Retained Earnings — Controlling Interest
Retained earnings, January 1, 19X2	$10,800	$142,200
Net income for year	6,700	85,800
	$17,500	$228,000
Less dividends declared during year	5,000	40,000
Retained earnings, December 31, 19X2	$12,500	$188,000

Company A and Subsidiary Company B
Consolidated Balance Sheet
December 31, 19X2

Assets

Cash	$ 85,000
Accounts receivable (net)	88,500
Merchandise inventory	147,500
Plant and equipment (net)	330,000
Goodwill	23,000
Total assets	$674,000

Liabilities

Accounts payable	$103,500
Bonds payable	100,000
Total liabilities	$203,500

Stockholders' Equity

Minority interest:		
Capital stock	$ 20,000	
Retained earnings	12,500	$ 32,500
Controlling interest:		
Capital stock	$250,000	
Retained earnings	188,000	438,000
Total stockholders' equity..		470,500
Total liabilities and stockholders' equity...................................		$674,000

The equity-method adjustment for 19X2 recorded on Company A's books is calculated as follows:

Income attributed to Company B	$33,500
Company A share..	80%
	$26,800
Less amortization expense...	1,000
Company A equity in Company B income	$25,800

This would be recorded by Company A with the following entry:

Investment in Co. B Stock...	25,800	
Equity in Income of Subsidiary.......................................		25,800

Cost method. Assume that Company A has maintained its investment account in Company B at cost. For the year ended December 31, 19X1, Company A's use of the cost method would result in the same trial balance as produced by the equity method, since it was the first year of the investment relationship and the trial balance does not reflect the year-end equity-method adjustment. For the year ended December 31, 19X2, there would be a nominal account to record the $20,000 in dividends received from Company B; the balance sheet would continue to report the investment in Company B at a cost of $125,000; and retained earnings would be reported at $120,000, the balance as of January 1, 19X2, based solely on Company A's own activities.

The work sheet for 19X1 would be identical to the one illustrated for the equity method. A work sheet for 19X2 is shown on page 502.

Cost method:

Company A and Subsidiary Company B
Work Sheet for Consolidated Statements
December 31, 19X2

	Trial Balances Co. A	Trial Balances Co. B	Eliminations Dr.	Eliminations Cr.	Consol. Income Stmt. Dr.	Consol. Income Stmt. Cr.	Consol. Ret. Earn. Stmt. Dr.	Consol. Ret. Earn. Stmt. Cr.	Consol. Balance Sheet Dr.	Consol. Balance Sheet Cr.
Debits										
Cash	55,000	30,000							85,000	
Accounts Receivable (net)	60,000	35,000		(c) 6,500					88,500	
Merchandise Inventory, 1/1/X2	90,000	75,000		(d1) 1,000	164,000					
Plant and Equipment (net)	240,000	90,000							330,000	
Investment in Co. B	125,000									
Eliminate Investment			(a1) 25,000	(a1) 125,000 (a2) 2,000						
Goodwill									23,000	
Purchases	380,000	125,000		(b) 25,000	480,000					
Expenses	135,000	35,000			170,000					
Income Taxes	40,000	20,000			60,000					
Dividends Declared, Co. A	40,000						40,000			
Dividends Declared, Co. B		25,000		(e) 20,000			5,000			
Amortization Expense — Goodwill			(a2) 1,000		1,000					
	1,165,000	435,000								
Merchandise Inventory, 12/31/X2	80,000	70,000		(d2) 2,500					147,500	
Credits										
Accounts Payable	50,000	60,000	(c) 6,500							103,500
Bonds Payable	100,000									100,000
Capital Stock, Co. A	250,000									250,000
Retained Earnings, Co. A, 1/1/X2	120,000		(a2) 1,000					119,000		
Capital Stock, Co. B		100,000								
Eliminate 80%			(a1) 80,000							
Minority Interest, 20%										20,000
Retained Earnings, Co. B, 1/1/X2		55,000								
Elim. 80% of $25,000 R. E. on 1/1/X1			(d1) 1,000 (a1) 20,000							
Minority Interest, 20% of $54,000								10,800		
Retained Earnings to Parent								23,200		
Sales	625,000	220,000	(b) 25,000			820,000				
Dividend Income	20,000		(e) 20,000							
	1,165,000	435,000	182,000	182,000						
Merchandise Inventory, 12/31/X2	80,000	70,000	(d2) 2,500			147,500				
					875,000	967,500				
Minority Int. Share of Inc. to Retained Earn., 20% of $33,500, Co. B Net Inc. after Adj.					6,700			6,700		
Controlling Interest Share of Income to Retained Earnings					85,800			85,800		
					967,500	967,500	45,000	245,500		
Minority Interest Retained Earnings to Balance Sheet							12,500			12,500
Controlling Interest Retained Earnings to Balance Sheet							188,000			188,000
							245,500	245,500	674,000	674,000

Since subsidiary activities are viewed differently when the cost method is used, certain eliminations differ from those that are required when the equity method is used. The eliminations that differ are as follows:

(a1) The balance of the investment account reports the payment for the subsidiary equity originally acquired. The parent company's percentage of capital stock and retained earnings as of the date of original acquisition of subsidiary holdings is applied against this balance, just as when the work sheet was limited to the development of the consolidated balance sheet.

The amount of the minority interest in the subsidiary retained earnings at the beginning of the current period is carried to the retained earnings columns. After the first year, a difference between the retained earnings at the beginning of the period and the sum of the elimination against retained earnings and the interest of the minority in retained earnings represents the subsidiary net earnings accruing to the parent from the date of acquisition to the beginning of the current period. This difference is extended to the retained earnings columns.

(a2) Because the amortization of goodwill would not have been recognized on the separate records of Company A, the initial elimination entry yields the original balance of goodwill at the date of acquisition of the subsidiary. Therefore, the adjustment to goodwill must provide for the amounts amortized in previous years as well as the current amount. The cumulative amount relating to previous years reduces the balance of the controlling interest retained earnings, while the current portion reduces the income attributed to the controlling interest.

(d1) In the work sheet for 19X2, the inventory at the beginning of the period is reduced by intercompany profits of $1,000. The asset reduction is accompanied by a reduction in the retained earnings of Company B. The latter charge is recognized in calculating the retained earnings of the minority interest at the beginning of the period and the retained earnings of the subsidiary accruing to the parent as of the beginning of the period.

(e) Dividend income as reported by the parent is offset against dividends declared as reported by the subsidiary. The dividends declared balance on the books of the subsidiary is canceled to the extent of the reciprocal element included therein. The balance of the account reflects the decrease for current dividends identified with the minority interest, and this balance is carried to the retained earnings columns to be recognized as such. The dividend income balance is canceled because it loses its significance when parent and subsidiary revenue and expense balances are combined to arrive at the parent's share of earnings for the period.

Remaining eliminations on the work sheet are the same as those that were required when the equity method was used. The Company B net income is calculated as follows:

Net income per books...	$35,000
Deduct adjustment for intercompany profits on merchandise:	
12/31/X2, $2,500, less 1/1/X2, $1,000	1,500
Net income for consolidation purposes...	$33,500

Work sheet columns are used in preparing the consolidated statements. These statements will be the same regardless of whether the investment account is carried at equity or at cost.

WORK SHEET FOR CONSOLIDATED STATEMENTS FOR A MANUFACTURING COMPANY

In the first example, relatively simple conditions were assumed. In the example to follow, more complex conditions are given and the special procedures under such conditions are illustrated. Consolidated statements are required for manufacturing companies at the end of the first year and at the end of the second year of a parent-subsidiary relationship. Eliminations are required for investment and related subsidiary capital balances, for intercompany profits on inventories and plant items, for intercompany indebtedness in the form of bonds, and for other reciprocal asset-liability and revenue-expense balances. The data that follow are to be considered in preparing consolidated statements for Company P and Company S at the end of 19X6 and at the end of 19X7. The letter designations preceding the items are used on subsequent pages in describing eliminations and in identifying eliminations on the work sheet.

(a) Company P acquired 80% of the stock of Company S on January 1, 19X6, at a cost of $200,000. Capital stock of Company S on that date was $200,000; retained earnings were $10,000. Goodwill arising from this purchase is to be amortized over a period of 40 years.

(b) Company P acquires part of its materials from Company S. Intercompany sales were as follows: 19X6, $25,000; 19X7, $35,000.

(c) Company S sells materials to the parent at a gross profit of 20% of sales prices. It is estimated that Company P inventories included materials acquired from Company S as follows:

	December 31, 19X6	December 31, 19X7
Finished goods......................	$2,000	$3,000
Work in process....................	3,000	5,000
Materials.............................	5,000	7,000

(d) Amounts are owed Company S by Company P on open account as follows: 19X6, $10,000; 19X7, $15,000.

(e) Dividends were declared by Company S as follows: In December of 19X6, a dividend of $5,000 was declared, and the dividend was paid in January, 19X7. In 19X7, two dividends of $5,000 each were declared; the first dividend was paid in July and the second is to be paid in January, 19X8.

(f) Company S issued bonds of $100,000 at 95 at the end of 19X6. Company P purchased one fifth of the issue from the subsidiary at this price.

(g) At the end of 19X6, Company S sold equipment to Company P for $20,000 and recognized a gain of $5,000 on the sale. The parent recognizes depreciation on the asset at the rate of 10% per year.

The following work sheet for a consolidated balance sheet was prepared on the date of stock acquisition:

Company P and Subsidiary Company S
Work Sheet for Consolidated Balance Sheet
January 1, 19X6

	Co. P	Co. S	Eliminations		Consolidated Balance Sheet	
			Dr.	Cr.	Dr.	Cr.
Debits						
Cash..................................	20,000	10,000			30,000	
Accounts Receivable (net).....	45,000	40,000			85,000	
Finished Goods	50,000	30,000			80,000	
Work in Process....................	40,000	20,000			60,000	
Materials..............................	35,000	15,000			50,000	
Land....................................	75,000	40,000			115,000	
Buildings.............................	160,000	100,000			260,000	
Machinery and Equipment.....	400,000	120,000			520,000	
Investment in Co. S	200,000					
Eliminate Investment.........				200,000		
Goodwill			32,000		32,000	
	1,025,000	375,000				
Credits						
Accumulated Depreciation —						
Buildings...........................	60,000	35,000				95,000
Accumulated Depreciation —						
Machinery and Equipment..	120,000	60,000				180,000
Accounts Payable.................	75,000	65,000				140,000
Dividends Payable	20,000	5,000				25,000
Capital Stock, Co. P..............	500,000					500,000
Retained Earnings, Co. P........	250,000					250,000
Capital Stock, Co. S..............		200,000				
Eliminate 80%			160,000			
Minority Interest, 20%........						40,000
Retained Earnings, Co. S.......		10,000				
Eliminate 80%			8,000			
Minority Interest, 20%........						2,000
	1,025,000	375,000	200,000	200,000	1,232,000	1,232,000

Assume that the parent maintains its investment in the subsidiary by the equity method. The financial statements and the schedules of the cost of goods manufactured for Company S, the subsidiary, for the years ended December 31, 19X6 and 19X7, are as follows:

Company S
Income Statement
For Years Ended December 31, 19X6 and 19X7

	19X6		19X7	
Sales...		$270,000		$365,000
Less sales returns and allowances		5,000		9,500
Net sales		$265,000		$355,500
Cost of goods sold:				
Finished goods inventory, January 1.........	$ 30,000		$ 45,000	
Cost of goods manufactured (see schedule)	180,000		245,000	
Merchandise available for sale................	$210,000		$290,000	
Less finished goods inventory, December 31....................................	45,000	165,000	65,000	225,000
Gross profit		$100,000		$130,500
Selling and general expenses		65,000		70,000
Income from operations.............................		$ 35,000		$ 60,500
Gain on sale of equipment		5,000		
Interest expense......................................				5,500
Income before income taxes.......................		$ 40,000		$ 55,000
Income taxes..		15,000		20,000
Net income		$ 25,000		$ 35,000

Balance Sheet
December 31, 19X6 and 19X7

	19X6		19X7	
Assets				
Cash..		$ 20,000		$ 25,000
Accounts receivable (net)		40,000		50,000
Finished goods		45,000		65,000
Work in process		25,000		40,000
Materials		20,000		30,000
Land		40,000		40,000
Buildings	$140,000		$140,000	
Less accumulated depreciation	45,000	95,000	50,000	90,000
Machinery and equipment	$180,000		$190,000	
Less accumulated depreciation	75,000	105,000	90,000	100,000
Total assets...		$390,000		$440,000
Liabilities				
Accounts payable		$ 60,000		$ 84,500
Dividends payable.....................................		5,000		5,000
5% bonds payable	$100,000		$100,000	
Less discount on bonds payable	5,000	95,000	4,500	95,500
Total liabilities..		$160,000		$185,000
Stockholders' Equity				
Capital stock...	$200,000		$200,000	
Retained earnings.....................................	30,000		55,000	
Total stockholders' equity...........................		230,000		255,000
Total liabilities and stockholders' equity		$390,000		$440,000

Retained Earnings Statement
For Years Ended December 31, 19X6 and 19X7

	19X6	19X7
Retained Earnings, January 1	$10,000	$30,000
Add net income for year	25,000	35,000
	$35,000	$65,000
Deduct dividends declared	5,000	10,000
Retained Earnings, December 31	$30,000	$55,000

Cost of Goods Manufactured Schedule
For Years Ended December 31, 19X6 and 19X7

	19X6		19X7	
Work in process inventory, January 1		$ 20,000		$ 25,000
Materials:				
Materials inventory, January 1	$ 15,000		$ 20,000	
Add purchases	55,000		80,000	
Materials available for use	$ 70,000		$100,000	
Less materials inventory, December 31	20,000	50,000	30,000	70,000
Direct labor		60,000		85,000
Factory overhead		75,000		105,000
Total work in process during year		$205,000		$285,000
Less work in process inventory, December 31		25,000		40,000
Cost of goods manufactured		$180,000		$245,000

The pre-closing trial balances for Company P (prior to equity-method adjustments) and Company S, as of December 31, 19X6, are listed in the first two columns of the work sheet on pages 508 and 509. The ending inventories are listed in both the debit and credit sections following the adjusted trial balance data. The eliminations for intercompany real and nominal account balances are explained in the following paragraphs. The letter preceding each explanation corresponds with that used in reporting the elimination on the work sheet.

(a1) Investment account eliminations are made in terms of reciprocal balances of both real and nominal accounts. Although the investment account has not been adjusted to reflect the income of Company S, the account has been reduced by the amount of dividends received, $4,000. Thus the balance of the investment account in the trial balance is $196,000.

(a2) The goodwill figure derived in entry (a1) represents the balance at the beginning of the year. Amortization for the current year is $800 ($32,000 ÷ 40).

(b) Sales that were made by Company S to Company P, $25,000, are eliminated.

(c) The profit recognized by Company S on transfers of materials to Company P was 20% of the sales price. Intercompany profits in Company P ending inventories are as follows: finished goods, 20% of $2,000, or $400; work in process, 20% of $3,000, or $600; materi-

Company P and
Work Sheet for
December

	Trial Balances		Eliminations				
	Co. P	Co. S	Dr.		Cr.		
Debits							
Cash	10,000	20,000					(1)
Accounts Receivable (net)	30,000	40,000			(d)	10,000	(2)
Dividends Receivable	4,000				(e)	4,000	(3)
Finished Goods, 1/1/X6	50,000	30,000					(4)
Work in Process, 1/1/X6	40,000	20,000					(5)
Materials, 1/1/X6	35,000	15,000					(6)
Land	75,000	40,000					(7)
Buildings	180,000	140,000					(8)
Machinery and Equipment	435,000	180,000			(g)	5,000	(9)
Investment in Co. S Bonds	19,000				(f)	19,000	(10)
Investment in Co. S	196,000						(11)
Eliminate Investment					(a1)	196,000	(12)
Goodwill			(a1)	32,000	(a2)	800	(13)
Discount on Bonds Payable		5,000			(f)	1,000	(14)
Sales Returns and Allowances	10,000	5,000					(15)
Materials Purchases	130,000	55,000			(b)	25,000	(16)
Direct Labor	135,000	60,000					(17)
Factory Overhead	145,000	75,000					(18)
Selling and General Expenses	80,000	65,000					(19)
Income Taxes	45,000	15,000					(20)
Dividends Declared, Co. P	40,000						(21)
Dividends Declared, Co. S		5,000			(a1)	4,000	(22)
Amortization Expense — Goodwill			(a2)	800			(23)
	1,659,000	770,000					(24)
Finished Goods, 12/31/X6	60,000	45,000			(c)	400	(25)
Work in Process, 12/31/X6	55,000	25,000			(c)	600	(26)
Materials, 12/31/X6	45,000	20,000			(c)	1,000	(27)
Credits							
Accumulated Depr. — Buildings	65,000	45,000					(28)
Accumulated Depr. — Mach. and Equip.	180,000	75,000					(29)
Accounts Payable	69,000	60,000	(d)	10,000			(30)
Dividends Payable	20,000	5,000	(e)	4,000			(31)
5% Bonds Payable		100,000	(f)	20,000			(32)
Capital Stock, Co. P	500,000						(33)
Retained Earnings, Co. P, 1/1/X6	250,000						(34)
Capital Stock, Co. S		200,000					(35)
Eliminate 80%			(a1)	160,000			(36)
Minority Interest, 20%							(37)
Retained Earnings, Co. S, 1/1/X6		10,000					(38)
Eliminate 80%			(a1)	8,000			(39)
Minority Interest, 20%							(40)
Sales	575,000	270,000	(b)	25,000			(41)
Gain on Sale of Equipment		5,000	(g)	5,000			(42)
	1,659,000	770,000					(43)
Finished Goods, 12/31/X6	60,000	45,000	(c)	400			(44)
Work in Process, 12/31/X6	55,000	25,000	(c)	600			(45)
Materials, 12/31/X6	45,000	20,000	(c)	1,000			(46)
				266,800		266,800	(47)

Cost of Goods Manufactured to Income Statement .... (48)

(49)

Minority Int. Share of Inc. to Ret. Earn., 20% of $18,000, Co. S Net Inc. After Adj. .... (50)
Controlling Interest Share of Income to Retained Earnings .... (51)

(52)

Minority Interest Retained Earnings to Balance Sheet .... (53)
Controlling Interest Retained Earnings to Balance Sheet .... (54)

(55)

Subsidiary Company S
Consolidated Statements
31, 19X6

	Consolidated Mfg. Statement		Consolidated Income Statement		Consolidated Ret. Earn. Statement		Consolidated Balance Sheet	
	Dr.	Cr.	Dr.	Cr.	Dr.	Cr.	Dr.	Cr.
(1)							30,000	
(2)							60,000	
(3)								
(4)			80,000					
(5)	60,000							
(6)	50,000							
(7)							115,000	
(8)							320,000	
(9)							610,000	
(10)								
(11)								
(12)								
(13)							31,200	
(14)							4,000	
(15)			15,000					
(16)	160,000							
(17)	195,000							
(18)	220,000							
(19)			145,000					
(20)			60,000					
(21)					40,000			
(22)					1,000			
(23)			800					
(24)								
(25)							104,600	
(26)							79,400	
(27)							64,000	
(28)								110,000
(29)								255,000
(30)								119,000
(31)								21,000
(32)								80,000
(33)								500,000
(34)						250,000		
(35)								
(36)								
(37)								40,000
(38)								
(39)								
(40)						2,000		
(41)				820,000				
(42)								
(43)								
(44)				104,600				
(45)		79,400						
(46)		64,000						
(47)	685,000	143,400						
(48)		541,600	541,600					
(49)	685,000	685,000	842,400	924,600				
(50)	....		3,600			3,600		
(51)	....		78,600			78,600		
(52)			924,600	924,600	41,000	334,200	1,418,200	1,125,000
(53)	....				4,600			4,600
(54)	....				288,600			288,600
(55)					334,200	334,200	1,418,200	1,418,200

als, 20% of $5,000, or $1,000. The intercompany profits on inventories as of December 31, 19X6, are canceled as follows:

Finished Goods, 12/31/X6 (income statement)	400	
Work in Process, 12/31/X6 (manufacturing schedule)	600	
Materials, 12/31/X6 (manufacturing schedule)	1,000	
Finished Goods, 12/31/X6 (balance sheet)		400
Work in Process, 12/31/X6 (balance sheet)		600
Materials, 12/31/X6 (balance sheet)............................		1,000

(d) Accounts receivable from Company P reported by Company S are offset against accounts payable reported by Company P.

(e) Dividends receivable of Company S reported by Company P are offset against dividends payable reported by Company S.

(f) The investment in bonds of Company S reported by Company P must be offset against the bonds payable account reported at par. One fifth of the discount on bonds payable must be canceled so that the discount reports only the amount related to bonds held by outsiders. The amount of discount on bonds payable to be eliminated is $1,000 (20,000/100,000 × $5,000).

(g) Equipment acquired by Company P from Company S at the end of 19X6 must be reduced to cost and the profit on the transfer reported by Company S, $5,000, canceled.

Account balances on the work sheet may now be combined and extended to the statement columns. Manufacturing and income statement columns are summarized and the consolidated income is determined. Net income is assigned to the minority and controlling interests, after the Company S net income has been determined as follows:

Net income per books...		$25,000
Deduct: Intercompany profit on sale of equipment to Co. P	$5,000	
Intercompany profit on merchandise transferred to Co. P	2,000	7,000
Net income for consolidation purposes		$18,000

The work sheet is then completed as in the earlier examples. Consolidated statements can now be prepared as follows:

Company P and Subsidiary Company S
Cost of Goods Manufactured Schedule
To Accompany Consolidated Income Statement
For Year Ended December 31, 19X6

Work in process inventory, January 1		$ 60,000
Materials:		
Materials inventory, January 1	$ 50,000	
Purchases	160,000	
Materials available for use.....................................	$210,000	
Less materials inventory, December 31..................	64,000	146,000
Direct labor		195,000
Factory overhead..		220,000
Total work in process during year		$621,000
Less work in process inventory, December 31...........		79,400
Cost of goods manufactured......................................		$541,600

Company P and Subsidiary Company S
Consolidated Income Statement
For Year Ended December 31, 19X6

Sales		$820,000
Less sales returns and allowances............................		15,000
Net sales...		$805,000
Cost of goods sold:		
Finished goods inventory, January 1......................	$ 80,000	
Cost of goods manufactured (see schedule)............	541,600	
Merchandise available for sale.............................	$621,600	
Less finished goods inventory, December 31	104,600	517,000
Gross profit..		$288,000
Selling and general expenses and amortization..........		145,800
Income before income taxes.....................................		$142,200
Income taxes		60,000
Income before minority interest		$ 82,200
Minority interest in net income of subsidiary		3,600
Net income...		$ 78,600

Company P and Subsidiary Company S
Consolidated Balance Sheet
December 31, 19X6

Assets

Cash..		$ 30,000
Accounts receivable (net)...		60,000
Finished goods		104,600
Work in process		79,400
Materials..		64,000
Land..		115,000
Buildings	$320,000	
Less accumulated depreciation	110,000	210,000
Machinery and equipment..	$610,000	
Less accumulated depreciation	255,000	355,000
Goodwill...		31,200
Total assets...		$1,049,200

Liabilities

Accounts payable..		$ 119,000
Dividends payable...		21,000
5% bonds payable...	$100,000	
Less bonds held by affiliated company	20,000	
	$ 80,000	
Less discount on bonds payable	4,000	76,000
Total liabilities...		$ 216,000

Stockholders' Equity

Minority interest:		
Capital stock....................................	$ 40,000	
Retained earnings...........................	4,600	$ 44,600
Controlling interest:		
Capital stock....................................	$500,000	
Retained earnings...........................	288,600	788,600
Total stockholders' equity.................		833,200
Total liab. and stockholders' equity....		$1,049,200

Company P and Subsidiary Company S
Consolidated Retained Earnings Statement
For Year Ended December 31, 19X6

	Retained Earnings — Minority Interest	Retained Earnings — Controlling Interest
Retained earnings, January 1...	$2,000	$250,000
Add net income for year...........	3,600	78,600
	$5,600	$328,600
Deduct dividends declared.......	1,000	40,000
Retained earnings, December 31......................	$4,600	$288,600

The year-end equity-method adjustment is based on Company P's share (80%) of Company S income for consolidation purposes ($18,000), less the amortization of goodwill, $800. It is recorded on the books of Company P as follows:

| Investment in Co. S .... | 13,600 | |
| Equity in Income of Subsidiary....................................... | | 13,600 |

The pre-closing trial balances and inventories as of December 31, 19X7, for Company P (prior to 19X7 equity-method adjustments) and Company S, are shown in the first two columns of the work sheet on pages 514 and 515. Explanations of the eliminations on the work sheet follow.

(x)   Because the trial balance is taken from the records of the two companies, adjustments that were made on the previous year's work sheet but not recorded by the companies must be entered as adjustments before proceeding with the other elimination and adjustment entries. In particular, the intercompany profits on sales of equipment and merchandise by Company S to Company P that were eliminated in the 19X6 work sheet must be entered because Company S would not have recorded these eliminations.

(a1) The Investment in Co. S on the books of Company P is shown with a balance of $201,600. This amount is the balance of $209,600 as of the end of 19X6 (after the equity-method adjustment), less $8,000 of dividends declared by Company S, assuming that Company P has made the adjustment for subsidiary dividend declarations, but not for the equity in Company S income. Investment account eliminations are made in terms of reciprocal balances found in real and nominal accounts as of December 31, 19X7. The debit to Retained Earnings, Co. S, is equal to 80% of the balance of Company S retained earnings after the initial adjustment ($30,000 − $7,000 = $23,000).

(a2) Amortization of goodwill for the year is recognized.

(b)   Sales made by Company S to Company P during 19X7 are canceled.

(c)   The profit recognized by Company S on transfers of materials to Company P was 20% of the sales price. Intercompany profits in the beginning inventories were canceled by entry (x). Intercompany profits in Company P ending inventories are as follows: finished goods, 20% of $3,000, or $600; work in process, 20% of $5,000, or $1,000; materials, 20% of $7,000, or $1,400.

(d) Intercompany trade balances are canceled.

(e) Dividends receivable on the stock of Company S reported by Company P are offset against dividends payable reported by Company S.

(f1) Intercompany bonded debt must be eliminated; in addition, interest income and interest expense balances relating to the intercompany debt item must be canceled. At the end of 19X6, intercompany bond holdings were eliminated by canceling reciprocal bond discount balances and applying bonds held by Company P against bonds payable of Company S. At the end of 19X7, discounts are reflected in both real and nominal balances, since discount balances have been reduced for current amortization. At the end of 19X7, elimination will involve reciprocal discount balances reflected in the discount account on the books of Company S and the investment account of Company P and also reciprocal interest balances resulting from discount amortization and accumulation on the books of Companies S and P. An elimination is made as follows:

Bonds Payable (Co. S)	20,000	
Interest Income (Co. P)	100	
Discount on Bonds Payable (Co. S)		900
Interest Expense (Co. S)		100
Investment in Co. S Bonds (Co. P)		19,100

(f2) Company S paid Company P cash interest of $1,000 in 19X7 on Company S bonds of $20,000 held by Company P. The intercompany interest is canceled as follows:

Interest Income (Co. P)	1,000	
Interest Expense (Co. S)		1,000

(g) Asset values as well as depreciation charges relating to equipment items acquired by Company P from its subsidiary must be restated in terms of cost. In considering eliminations relating to the asset and to the charges to operations arising therefrom, analysis of the asset as of the beginning and end of the period is required as follows:

	At Sales Price to Co. P	At Cost to Co. S	Intercompany Profit
December 31, 19X6:			
Equipment	$20,000	$15,000	$5,000
December 31, 19X7:			
Equipment	$20,000	$15,000	$5,000
Accumulated depreciation (10%)	(2,000)	(1,500)	(500)
	$18,000	$13,500	$4,500

	Trial Balances		Eliminations				
	Co. P	Co. S	Dr.		Cr.		
Debits							
Cash..	20,000	25,000					(1)
Accounts Receivable (net)..................	45,000	50,000			(d)	15,000	(2)
Dividends Receivable.........................	4,000				(e)	4,000	(3)
Finished Goods, 1/1/X7....................	60,000	45,000			(x)	400	(4)
Work in Process, 1/1/X7	55,000	25,000			(x)	600	(5)
Materials, 1/1/X7	45,000	20,000			(x)	1,000	(6)
Land..	75,000	40,000					(7)
Buildings....................................	185,000	140,000					(8)
Machinery and Equipment..................	450,000	190,000			(x)	5,000	(9)
Investment in Co. S Bonds	19,100				(f1)	19,100	(10)
Investment in Co. S	201,600						(11)
Eliminate Investment......................					(a1)	201,600	(12)
Goodwill.................................			(a1)	31,200	(a2)	800	(13)
Discount on Bonds Payable		4,500			(f1)	900	(14)
Sales Returns and Allowances	11,100	9,500					(15)
Materials Purchases	140,000	80,000			(b)	35,000	(16)
Direct Labor	145,000	85,000					(17)
Factory Overhead	150,000	105,000			(g)	500	(18)
Selling and General Expenses	90,000	70,000					(19)
Interest Expense		5,500			(f1)	100	(20)
					(f2)	1,000	(21)
Income Taxes.................................	50,000	20,000					(22)
Dividends Declared, Co. P	40,000						(23)
Dividends Declared, Co. S		10,000			(a1)	8,000	(24)
Amortization Expense — Goodwill			(a2)	800			(25)
	1,785,800	924,500					(26)
Finished Goods, 12/31/X7	75,000	65,000			(c)	600	(27)
Work in Process, 12/31/X7	70,000	40,000			(c)	1,000	(28)
Materials, 12/31/X7.........................	50,000	30,000			(c)	1,400	(29)
Credits							
Accumulated Depr. Buildings	75,000	50,000					(30)
Accumulated Depr. — Mach. and Equip.	205,000	90,000	(g)	500			(31)
Accounts Payable..............................	76,100	84,500	(d)	15,000			(32)
Dividends Payable	20,000	5,000	(e)	4,000			(33)
5% Bonds Payable		100,000	(f1)	20,000			(34)
Capital Stock, Co. P..........................	500,000						(35)
Retained Earnings, Co. P, 1/1/X7	288,600						(36)
Capital Stock, Co. S..........................		200,000					(37)
Eliminate 80%...............................			(a1)	160,000			(38)
Minority Interest, 20%.....................							(39)
Retained Earnings, Co. S, 1/1/X7		30,000	(x)	7,000			(40)
Eliminate 80% of $23,000..................			(a1)	18,400			(41)
Minority Interest, 20% of $23,000							(42)
Sales	620,000	365,000	(b)	35,000			(43)
Interest Income.................................	1,100		(f1)	100			(44)
			(f2)	1,000			(45)
	1,785,800	924,500					(46)
Finished Goods, 12/31/X7	75,000	65,000	(c)	600			(47)
Work in Process, 12/31/X7	70,000	40,000	(c)	1,000			(48)
Materials, 12/31/X7.........................	50,000	30,000	(c)	1,400			(49)
				296,000		296,000	(50)

Cost of Goods Manufactured to Income Statement .... (51)

(52)

Minority Interest Share of Income to Retained Earnings, 20% of $34,000, Co. S Net Income after Adj., plus (53)
  $100, Recognized Gain on Sale of Eqpt. to Parent .... (54)
Controlling Interest Share of Income to Retained Earnings .... (55)

(56)

Minority Interest Retained Earnings to Balance Sheet.. (57)
Controlling Interest Retained Earnings to Balance Sheet .... (58)

(59)

	Consolidated Mfg. Statement		Consolidated Income Statement		Consolidated Ret. Earn. Statement		Consolidated Balance Sheet	
	Dr.	Cr.	Dr.	Cr.	Dr.	Cr.	Dr.	Cr.
(1)							45,000	
(2)							80,000	
(3)								
(4)			104,600					
(5)	79,400							
(6)	64,000							
(7)							115,000	
(8)							325,000	
(9)							635,000	
(10)								
(11)								
(12)								
(13)							30,400	
(14)							3,600	
(15)			20,600					
(16)	185,000							
(17)	230,000							
(18)	254,500							
(19)			160,000					
(20)			4,400					
(21)								
(22)			70,000					
(23)					40,000			
(24)					2,000			
(25)			800					
(26)								
(27)							139,400	
(28)							109,000	
(29)							78,600	
(30)								125,000
(31)								294,500
(32)								145,600
(33)								21,000
(34)								80,000
(35)								500,000
(36)						288,600		
(37)								
(38)								
(39)								40,000
(40)								
(41)								
(42)						4,600		
(43)				950,000				
(44)								
(45)								
(46)								
(47)				139,400				
(48)		109,000						
(49)		78,600						
(50)	812,900	187,600						
(51)		625,300	625,300					
(52)	812,900	812,900	985,700	1,089,400				
(53)								
(54)	....		6,900			6,900		
(55)	....		96,800			96,800		
(56)			1,089,400	1,089,400	42,000	396,900	1,561,000	1,206,100
(57)	....				9,500			9,500
(58)	....				345,400			345,400
(59)					396,900	396,900	1,561,000	1,561,000

This analysis suggests that the asset must be reduced by $5,000 and the accumulated depreciation must be reduced by $500 so that the asset may be reported at its cost, $15,000, less accumulated depreciation based upon such cost, $1,500. The balance of equipment has already been adjusted in entry (x), but the accumulated depreciation must now be adjusted.

In assigning consolidated earnings to the minority and controlling interests, the Company S net income is calculated as follows:

Net income per books..	$35,000
Deduct adjustment for intercompany profits on merchandise 12/31/X7, $3,000, less 1/1/X7, $2,000	1,000
Net income for consolidation purposes...	$34,000

As indicated in Chapter 13, when a partly owned subsidiary sells a property item to a parent, a profit accrues to the minority interest as depreciation is recognized on the asset sales price by the parent. In this example, although a reduction of $5,000 in the asset value at the date of purchase calls for a charge of $1,000 to the minority interest, smaller reductions in subsequent periods call for correspondingly smaller charges to the minority interest. When the asset is fully depreciated, no further charge to the minority interest will be required and this group's interest will have increased by $1,000. In assigning consolidated earnings to the minority and controlling interests in the period of the asset sale, it is necessary to cancel all reference to any profit on the asset sale and hence to an increase in the minority interest arising from the sale. However, subsequent to the time of sale, as the controlling interest absorbs depreciation in terms of the asset sales price, the earnings related to the minority interest should be increased for the portion of the profit on the sale that will not be carried back to the parent. In the example, the minority interest ultimately gains $1,000, which is recognized at the rate of $100 per year. In calculating the portion of consolidated earnings relating to the minority interest for 19X7, the earnings of the minority interest are increased by $100.

QUESTIONS

1. Individual statements are available for parent Company X and subsidiary Company Y. What changes will be made in account balances in transferring statement data to the work sheet for the preparation of consolidated statements?

2. Parent Company A maintains its investments in subsidiary companies by the equity method. A work sheet for consolidated statements is prepared at the end of 19X6. Give the eliminations that would be required under each of the following sets of circumstances:

(a) Company B was organized by Company A at the beginning of 19X1, and Company A acquired all of the stock of Company B at par. Company B retained earnings increased during the period 19X1–19X5. Company B reported a profit for 19X6 and paid dividends in 19X6.

(b) 80% of the stock of Company C was acquired by Company A at the beginning of 19X3 at a price that exceeded its book value. The book values of Company C assets reflected market values at the date of acquisition. Company C capital balances consisted of capital stock, additional paid-in capital, and retained earnings. Company C retained earnings increased during the period 19X3–19X5. Company C reported a loss for 19X6, but paid dividends from past earnings.

(c) 90% of the stock of Company D was acquired by Company A at the beginning of 19X6 at a price that was less than its book value. The price paid reflected the decline in the value of land owned by Company D. Company D capital balances consisted of capital stock and a deficit. Company D operated at a loss and paid no dividends in 19X6.

3. Assuming in Question 2 that investment accounts are maintained by the parent at cost, what eliminations would be required for each of the circumstances listed?

4. Beginning and ending inventories of the Meadows Co. include goods acquired from an 80%-owned subsidiary which made a profit on the goods. What procedures would be followed in preparing a work sheet for consolidated statements if the goods acquired from the affiliate are to be reduced to their original cost to the affiliate?

5. At the end of 19X9, a parent company constructed buildings for a partly owned subsidiary at a profit. (a) What elimination for intercompany profit is required in preparing the work sheet for consolidated statements for 19X9? (b) Assuming that it was the partly owned subsidiary that constructed buildings for the parent at a profit, what elimination would be required?

6. In 19X3 a parent company sold equipment to a partly owned subsidiary at a profit. The asset has a 10-year life. (a) What elimination for the intercompany profit is required in preparing the work sheet for consolidated statements for 19X8? (b) Assuming that the foregoing facts relate to the sale of equipment by the partly owned subsidiary to the parent, what elimination would be required?

7. Company P owns all of the stock of Company S. At the beginning of 19X0, Company S issued 10-year bonds at a discount. Company P acquired half of the bond issue directly from the subsidiary. What eliminations are required on the work sheet for consolidated statements prepared at the end of 19X0?

EXERCISES

1. Company P owns 80% of the stock of Company S. Prepare the eliminations that are required for the following information, which is used in preparing a work sheet for consolidated statements on December 31, 19X5.

(a) The investment account balance is $232,000. Earnings and dividends have been recorded in the investment account since acquisition, June 30, 19X1, including dividends for 19X5. Company S capital stock outstanding is $250,000; retained earnings on June 30, 19X1, were $20,000; retained earnings on January 1, 19X5, were $50,000; net income for the year is $15,000; dividends declared by Company S during the year were $10,000, $2,500 of which is payable on January 20, 19X6.

(b) Sales made by Company S to Company P totaled $80,000 for 19X5. Sales made by Company P to Company S were $16,000. Sales are made at 25% above cost. Inventories on January 1 and December 31 included:

	Jan. 1	Dec. 31
Co. P, merchandise acquired from Co. S	$15,000	$18,000
Co. S, merchandise acquired from Co. P	1,500	4,500

(c) 5% bonds of $20,000 were acquired by Company P from Company S at par on July 1, 19X5. Interest is payable semiannually on March 1 and September 1.

(d) Company P owes Company S $30,000 on open account.

2. Assume in Exercise 1 that the investment balance is carried at cost. Prepare the eliminations that are required on the work sheet for consolidated statements.

3. Company Y owns 90% of the stock of Company Z. The investment account is carried at cost and shows a balance of $301,000 on December 31, 19X8. Company Z capital stock is $300,000; retained earnings on January 1, 19X8, were $100,000; the net income for 19X8 is $30,000; dividends declared during the year totaled $16,000, including a dividend of $4,000 in the fourth quarter payable on January 10, 19X9. The stock was acquired on June 30, 19X3, when Company Z showed a deficit of $10,000. What eliminations are required on the work sheet for consolidated statements prepared on December 31, 19X8?

4. Company P owns 80% of the stock of Company A and Company A owns 90% of the stock of Company B, both holdings acquired prior to 19X0 and carried at cost. Prepare any adjustments and eliminations that are required in preparing the work sheet for consolidated statements for the year ended December 31, 19X7, as a result of the following information:

(a) Company P has in its inventory merchandise of $48,300 acquired from Company B. Merchandise is sold by Company B at 15% above cost.

(b) Company B has in its inventory merchandise of $8,000 acquired from Company P. The merchandise was sold at a 25% gross profit rate.

(c) Company A shows equipment of $20,000 acquired from Company P at the end of October, 19X0. The equipment was constructed by Company P and was sold at a gross profit of $5,000. The equipment is being depreciated on a 10-year basis.

(d) Company B has announced a dividend of $5,000, which has not been recognized by affiliates.

(e) Company B has remitted $10,000 to Company A in payment of an advance. Company A has not yet received the remittance.

(f) During the year, sales of merchandise by Company B to Company P totaled $250,000; sales by Company P to Company B were $42,500.

5. The Werner Corporation owns 80% of the stock of the Western Company. The Western Company owns 90% of the stock of the Wilson Company. Investments are carried at equity. An analysis of the inventories of the three companies on December 31, 19X4, shows the following:

	Total	Merchandise Acquired from			
		Werner Corp.	Western Co.	Wilson Co.	Non-Affiliated Companies
Werner Corp. inventory...........	$100,000		$10,500	$1,500	$88,000
Western Company inventory....	80,000	$ 9,000		3,000	68,000
Wilson Company inventory	75,000	12,000	15,000		48,000

Merchandise is sold to affiliated units at 20% above cost.

(a) What eliminations would be made on the consolidated work sheet for consolidated statements prepared at the end of 19X4 to give effect to the foregoing information?

(b) What eliminations would be made on the consolidated work sheet for consolidated statements prepared at the end of 19X5 in recognition of the foregoing?

6. Company Y has been a subsidiary of Company X for twenty years. On January 1, 19X3, Company X completed the construction of buildings for Company Y. The contract price of the buildings was $500,000; the cost of construction was $400,000. Company Y records depreciation on the buildings at 2½% annually.

(a) What elimination would appear on the work sheet for consolidated statements for the year ended December 31, 19X7, assuming that the parent owns 100% of the stock of Company Y?

(b) What elimination would be made assuming that the parent owns only 80% of the stock of Company Y?

7. (a) Assuming the same facts as in Exercise 6 but that the construction was completed by Company Y for the parent, Company X, what elimination would be required on December 31, 19X7, if the parent owns 100% of the stock of the subsidiary?

(b) What elimination would be made if the parent owns only 80% of the stock of the subsidiary?

8. Company L has owned 100% of the stock of Company M for many years. On January 1, 19X9, Company M buys on the market $200,000 of Company L's 6% first mortgage bonds at 105. Bonds were originally issued by Company L at par on January 1, 19X6, and are payable at the end of 10 years.

(a) What eliminations would be made on the work sheet for consolidated statements prepared for the year ended December 31, 19X9? (Assume that any premium or discount on bonds is amortized on a straight-line basis.)

(b) Would the eliminations be any different assuming that the parent company owns only 80% of the stock of the subsidiary? If so, prepare the eliminations.

16-1. Financial statements for Company P and its 80%-owned subsidiary Company S for the year ended December 31, 19X8, are summarized as follows:

	Co. P	Co. S
Balance Sheet		
Investment in Co. S	$ 360,000	
Other assets	2,150,000	$550,000
Total assets	$2,510,000	$550,000
Liabilities	$ 600,000	$130,000
Capital stock	1,500,000	400,000
Retained earnings	410,000	20,000
Total liabilities and stockholders' equity	$2,510,000	$550,000
Income Statement		
Sales	$2,000,000	$650,000
Cost of goods sold	1,350,000	400,000
Gross profit	$ 650,000	$250,000
Operating expenses	500,000	185,000
Income before income taxes	$ 150,000	$ 65,000
Income taxes	60,000	15,000
Net income	$ 90,000	$ 50,000
Dividends declared	75,000	20,000
Increase in retained earnings	$ 15,000	$ 30,000

The parent has carried the investment in Company S by the equity method since acquisition of the subsidiary in 19X0. Company P has recorded the dividend received from Company S during 19X8, but failed to record its share of Company S earnings for the current year. The inventory of the parent on January 1, 19X8, included goods of $40,000 that cost the subsidiary $27,500. The inventory of the parent on December 31, 19X8, included goods of $50,000 that cost the subsidiary $31,250. During 19X8, purchases by the parent from the subsidiary totaled $135,000. Amounts owed by the parent to the subsidiary at the end of 19X8 totaled $22,500.

Instructions: Prepare a work sheet for consolidated statements for the year ended December 31, 19X8.

16-2. Adjusted trial balances for Companies A and B on December 31, 19X2, are as follows:

	Co. A	Co. B
Debits		
Merchandise Inventory, January 1	15,000	20,000
Investment in Co. B (80% interest)	112,000	
Other Assets	225,000	155,000
Purchases	105,000	60,000
Expenses	60,000	35,000
Dividends Declared	10,000	15,000
	527,000	285,000
Merchandise Inventory, December 31	25,000	15,000

	Co. A	Co. B
Credits		
Liabilities..	85,000	40,000
Capital Stock..	200,000	100,000
Retained Earnings, January 1	62,000	35,000
Sales	180,000	110,000
	527,000	285,000
Merchandise Inventory, December 31......................	25,000	15,000

The investment in Company B, acquired 8 years ago, is carried by the equity method. The company has not yet recorded the year-end equity-method adjustment. The January 1 inventory of Company A included merchandise of $5,000 that cost Company B $4,000. During the year, Company A made purchases of $20,000 from its subsidiary. The ending inventory of Company A includes merchandise of $6,000 that cost Company B $4,500.

Instructions: (1) Prepare a work sheet for consolidated statements for the year ended December 31, 19X2.

(2) Prepare a consolidated balance sheet, income statement, and retained earnings statement.

16-3. Adjusted trial balances for Companies C and D on December 31, 19X9, are as follows:

	Co. C	Co. D
Debits		
Merchandise Inventory, December 31........................	15,000	20,000
Investment in Co. D (80% Interest)...........................	60,000	
Other Assets..	355,000	240,000
Cost of Goods Sold	210,000	125,000
Expenses..	160,000	100,000
Dividends Declared...	10,000	
Total..	810,000	485,000
Credits		
Liabilities..	165,000	125,000
Capital Stock..	300,000	100,000
Retained Earnings (Deficit), January 1......................	20,000	(15,000)
Sales	325,000	275,000
Total..	810,000	485,000

The investment account is carried by the equity method, but Company C has not yet made the year-end equity-method adjustment. The difference between the amount paid by Company C for its investment and the underlying book value was attributed to land owned by Company D that had declined in value. The January 1 inventory of Company C included merchandise of $5,000 that cost Company D $4,200. During the year, Company C made purchases of $35,000 from its subsidiary. Its ending inventory includes merchandise of $3,200 that cost Company D $2,500.

Instructions: Prepare a work sheet for consolidated statements for the year ended December 31, 19X9.

16-4. Condensed financial statements for the Alpha Corporation and the Beta Corporation for the year ended December 31, 19X7, are as follows:

	Alpha Corp.	Beta Corp.
Balance Sheet		
Investment in Beta Corp. (90% interest)	$ 385,000	
Other assets	1,465,000	$800,000
Total assets	$1,850,000	$800,000
Liabilities	$ 650,000	$260,000
Capital stock...	1,000,000	500,000
Retained earnings	200,000	40,000
Total liabilities and stockholders' equity.............	$1,850,000	$800,000

	Alpha Corp.	Beta Corp.
Income Statement		
Sales...	$1,000,000	$600,000
Cost of goods sold	520,000	330,000
Gross profit...	$ 480,000	$270,000
Operating expenses	250,000	140,000
Income before income taxes	$ 230,000	$130,000
Income taxes	110,000	50,000
Net income...	$ 120,000	$ 80,000
Dividends declared	40,000	25,000
Increase in retained earnings...........................	$ 80,000	$ 55,000

The investment in Beta Corporation is carried at cost. Alpha Corporation acquired its holdings at the beginning of 19X2, when the Beta Corporation showed a deficit of $100,000. The January 1 inventory of Alpha Corporation included goods of $12,500 that cost Beta Corporation $10,000. During the year, sales by the subsidiary to the parent totaled $60,000. The December 31 inventory of Alpha Corporation included goods of $27,500 that cost Beta Corporation $20,000. Alpha Corporation owed Beta Corporation $12,500 at the end of 19X7. Dividends of $22,500 received by the Alpha Corporation in 19X7 were reported directly in retained earnings.

Instructions: Prepare a work sheet for consolidated financial statements for the year ended December 31, 19X7. Assume that any goodwill recognized is to be amortized over a period of 25 years.

16-5. Adjusted trial balances for Companies G and H as of December 31, 19X5, are shown on page 523.

The investment in Company H is carried at cost. Stock of Company H was acquired at the beginning of 19X2, when Company H showed a deficit of $15,000. The January 1 inventory of Company G included merchandise of $6,000 that cost Company H $5,000. During the year, Company G made purchases of $30,000 from its subsidiary. Its ending inventory includes merchandise of $8,000 that cost Company H $6,500. Inventories on December 31 are: Company G, $35,000; Company H, $25,000.

	Co. G	Co. H
Debits		
Merchandise Inventory, January 1............................	30,000	15,000
Investment in Co. H (90% Interest)	105,500	
Other Assets...	294,500	160,000
Purchases	90,000	60,000
Expenses...	60,000	30,000
Dividends Declared..	20,000	10,000
Total..	600,000	275,000
Credits		
Liabilities	115,000	55,000
Capital Stock..	200,000	100,000
Additional Paid-In Capital...................................	60,000	10,000
Retained Earnings, January 1	76,000	5,000
Sales	140,000	105,000
Dividend Income, Co. H Stock..............................	9,000	
Total..	600,000	275,000

Instructions: (1) Prepare a work sheet for consolidated statements for the year ended December 31, 19X5.

(2) Prepare a consolidated balance sheet, income statement, and retained earnings statement.

16-6. Adjusted trial balances for Companies L and M on December 31, 19X8, are as follows:

	Co. L	Co. M
Debits		
Merchandise Inventory, December 31................	80,000	60,000
Investment in Co. M (85% interest)	136,000	—
Other Assets...	639,000	335,000
Cost of Goods Sold	420,000	180,000
Expenses...	125,000	75,000
Dividends Declared...	25,000	10,000
Total..	1,425,000	660,000
Credits		
Liabilities	315,000	185,000
Capital Stock..	250,000	200,000
Retained Earnings (Deficit), January 1	251,500	(15,000)
Sales...	600,000	290,000
Dividend Income, Co. M Stock	8,500	—
Total	1,425,000	660,000

Stock of Company M is carried at cost and was acquired in 19X1, when Company M showed retained earnings of $30,000. The difference between the investment cost and book value at that time was attributed to a decline in the values of nondepreciable assets. During the year, Company L made purchases from Company M totaling $22,500. The January 1 inventory of Company L included merchandise acquired from Company M at $6,000. The December 31 inventory includes merchandise acquired from Company M at $4,800. Company M sells merchandise to Company L at 33⅓% above cost.

Instructions: Prepare a work sheet for consolidated statements for the year ended December 31, 19X8.

16-7. Adjusted trial balances for Reed, Inc., and its subsidiaries, the Sterling Corporation and the Taylor Corporation, on December 31, 19X4, the end of a fiscal year, are as follows:

	Reed, Inc.		Sterling Corporation		Taylor Corporation	
	Dr.	Cr.	Dr.	Cr.	Dr.	Cr.
Cash..	63,875		34,500		20,000	
Dividends Receivable	2,125					
Accounts Receivable (net)	117,000		82,500		94,500	
Merchandise Inventory, Jan. 1........	140,000		80,000		105,000	
Land and Buildings (net)................	100,000		85,000			
Furniture and Equipment (net).......	48,000		40,000		28,000	
Investment in Sterling Corporation (850 shares)...............................	244,000					
Investment in Taylor Corporation (1,600 shares)............................	188,000					
Dividends Payable..........................		6,250		2,500		
Accounts Payable		70,250		54,500		37,500
Capital Stock ($100 par)................		500,000		100,000		200,000
Retained Earnings (Deficit)		324,000		150,000		(20,000)
Sales...		730,000		470,000		420,000
Sales Returns and Allowances........	20,000		10,000		10,000	
Sales Discount	12,000		5,000		4,000	
Purchases.....................................	540,000		340,000		300,000	
Purchases Returns and Allowances.		15,000		4,000		5,000
Purchases Discount		8,000		2,000		2,500
Selling Expenses............................	80,000		50,000		45,000	
General and Administrative Expenses.......................................	55,000		25,000		30,000	
Interest Expense............................	10,000		3,000		5,000	
Interest Income..............................		3,000		2,000		1,500
Dividend Income, Sterling Corporation Stock		8,500				
Income Taxes................................	20,000		20,000		5,000	
Dividends Declared	25,000		10,000			
	1,665,000	1,665,000	785,000	785,000	646,500	646,500
Merchandise Inventory, Dec. 31	150,000	150,000	90,000	90,000	87,500	87,500

Reed, Inc., carries investment balances at cost. The Sterling Corporation stock was acquired at the beginning of 19X2, when the retained earnings of this company were $140,000. The Taylor Corporation stock was acquired on January 1, 19X3, when this company had a deficit of $15,000. Book values of identifiable assets of both subsidiaries reflected fair values at the dates of acquisition.

The Taylor Corporation sells merchandise to the parent at approximately 10% above cost. Intercompany sales during 19X4 totaled $40,000. Inventories of the parent included merchandise from the Taylor Corporation at billed price as follows:

On January 1..................... $6,600   On December 31................. $8,250

Reed, Inc., owes the Taylor Corporation $5,000 on account.

Instructions: Prepare a work sheet for consolidated statements for the year ended December 31, 19X4.

16-8. The individual and consolidated statements of Companies A and B for the year ended December 31, 19X0, are as follows:

	Co. A	Co. B	Consolidated
Cash and receivables.................	$ 35,000	$108,000	$ 97,400
Inventories..............................	40,000	90,000	122,000
Plant (net)...............................	460,000	140,000	600,000
Appraisal increase in plant (net) .			50,000
Investment in Company B	245,000		
Investment in Company A bonds.		103,000	
	$780,000	$441,000	$869,400
Accounts payable.....................	$ 70,000	$ 23,000	$ 53,000
Dividends payable....................	10,000	8,000	12,400
Bonds payable.........................	200,000	50,000	150,000
Capital stock	300,000	200,000	300,000
Retained earnings....................	200,000	160,000	231,000
Minority interest			123,000
	$780,000	$441,000	$869,400
Sales.....................................	$600,000	$400,000	$760,000
Cost of goods sold....................	(360,000)	(280,000)	(403,000)
Gross profit	$240,000	$120,000	$357,000
Operating expenses..................	(130,000)	(54,000)	(184,000)
Income from operations............	$110,000	$ 66,000	$173,000
Interest income	1,800	5,000	1,800
Dividend income	11,200		
Total.....................................	$123,000	$ 71,000	$174,800
Interest expense......................	(10,000)	(3,000)	(8,000)
Provision for income taxes	(56,000)	(34,000)	(90,000)
Loss on retirement of debt.........			(3,000)
Minority interest in net income ...			(5,400)
Net income	$ 57,000	$ 34,000	$ 68,400
Dividends...............................	(20,000)	(16,000)	(24,800)
Transfer to retained earnings	$ 37,000	$ 18,000	$ 43,600

Company A purchased its 70% interest in Company B several years ago. Company A sells its product in part to Company B for further processing, and in part to other firms. The inventories of Company B included an intercompany markup at both the beginning and the end of the year. Cash transfers are made between the companies according to working capital needs.

Early in 19X0, Company B purchased $100,000 face value of the bonds of Company A as a temporary investment, which is carried on Company B's books at cost.

Instructions: On the basis of information from an analysis of the individual and consolidated statements, answer the following six questions. Show clearly *all* computations necessary to support your answers.

(1) Does Company A carry its investment in Company B on the cost basis or the equity basis? State the reason for your conclusion.

(2) The appraisal increase represents a revaluation of the total of Company B's assets on the basis of the price paid by Company A for its interest in Company B. What was the balance of Company B's retained earnings at date of acquisition?

(3) Prepare a reconciliation schedule which will explain clearly the difference between Company A's retained earnings at December 31, 19X0, $200,000, and the consolidated retained earnings at December 31, 19X0, $231,000.

(4) What is the nature of the loss on retirement of debt on the consolidated income statement? Show the elimination entry from which it originated.

(5) Show the amounts of intercompany debts, excluding the bonds, and show which company is the debtor and which is the creditor in each instance.

(6) Prepare a schedule reconciling the sum of the cost of goods sold of Companies A and B individually with the consolidated cost of goods sold. Show clearly the intercompany markup in the beginning and ending inventories of Company B and how you determined the amounts.

(AICPA adapted)

16-9. Balance sheets and income statements of Company R and its wholly owned subsidiary Company S for the year ended December 31, 19X3, are as follows:

	Co. R	Co. S
Cash...	$ 200,000	$ 130,000
Marketable securities...................................	400,000	150,000
Accounts receivable.....................................	1,250,000	540,000
Allowance for doubtful accounts..................	(25,000)	(10,000)
Receivable from Co. S	100,000	
Inventories..	1,100,000	600,000
Treasury stock...	50,000	
Investment in Co. S (at cost)	200,000	
Advances to subsidiary................................	420,000	
Property, plant, and equipment (net)............	1,525,000	710,000
	$ 5,220,000	$2,120,000
Accounts payable...	$ 575,000	$ 185,000
Accrued expenses..	350,000	100,000
Payable to Company R.................................		90,000
Estimated federal income taxes....................	525,000	275,000
Advances from parent		420,000
Capital stock	1,000,000	150,000
Retained earnings, 1/1/X3	2,420,000	825,000
Net income	650,000	250,000
Dividends declared.......................................	(300,000)	(175,000)
	$ 5,220,000	$2,120,000
Net sales...	$10,000,000	$4,600,000
Cost of goods sold.......................................	(6,700,000)	(3,210,000)
Selling, general, and adm. expenses..............	(2,400,000)	(900,000)
Other income (net).......................................	250,000	20,000
Estimated federal income taxes....................	(500,000)	(260,000)
Net income	$ 650,000	$ 250,000

The following additional information is available:

(1) Marketable securities of the subsidiary includes shares of the parent company's stock which cost $20,000 and which were acquired for payment of bonuses.

(2) Merchandise billed at $10,000 is in transit from the parent to the subsidiary and has not been recorded by the subsidiary.

(3) There is intercompany profit of $20,000 in the portion of the subsidiary's inventory purchased from the parent. The equivalent figure at December 31, 19X2, was $10,000.

(4) The parent's equity in the subsidiary was $200,000 at the date of acquisition.

(5) Sales by the parent to the subsidiary in 19X3 totaled $1,700,000.

(6) The parent has made a service charge of $50,000 to the subsidiary, which is included in Other Income of the parent and in Administrative Expenses of the subsidiary.

Instructions: (1) Prepare a work sheet for consolidated statements for the year ended December 31, 19X3. *Key the debit and credit of each entry.*

(2) Prepare a schedule showing the changes for 19X3 in retained earnings of the companies and the entries necessary for consolidation.

(AICPA adapted)

16-10. The trial balances of Company P and its subsidiary Company S as of December 31, 19X1, are as follows:

	Co. P Debit	Co. P Credit	Co. S Debit	Co. S Credit
Cash	23,000		30,000	
Accounts Receivable	94,000		60,000	
Inventory, 1/1/X1 (at cost)	105,000		51,000	
Investment in Co. S	175,000			
Investment in Co. S Bonds	51,800			
Other Assets	445,000		210,000	
Current Liabilities		163,000		17,100
Bonds Payable, 5%				200,000
Premium on Bonds				5,400
Sales		630,000		340,000
Purchases	485,000		300,000	
Operating Expenses	92,000		70,000	
Other Expenses	22,000		15,500	
Interest and Dividend Income		12,800		
Dividends Declared	20,000		10,000	
Retained Earnings, 1/1/X1		107,000		84,000
Common Stock		600,000		100,000
	1,512,800	1,512,800	746,500	746,500

The investment in Company S represents a 90% interest that was acquired January 1, 19X1, for $175,000. At the same time, $50,000 face amount of bonds of Company S were acquired for $52,000. These bonds were twenty-year bonds that had been issued ten years ago at 106. Company S has recorded the amortization of the bond premium applicable to 19X1 as an adjustment of interest expense. The stock and the bonds were not purchased from Company S but from the public.

Included in the purchases account of Company S is a total of $180,000 of goods bought from Company P at 120% of cost to Company P. The ending inventory of Company S is estimated to include the same proportion of these purchases as other purchases.

Inventories at December 31, 19X1, at cost to each company, were: Company P, $80,000; and Company S, $45,000.

Instructions: Prepare a work sheet showing the income and the expense of each company for the year 19X1 and the consolidated income of Company P and its subsidiary.   (AICPA adapted)

16-11. The following trial balances were prepared after completion of the examination of the December 31, 19X7, financial statements of Allen Corporation and its subsidiaries, Barth Corporation and Cole Corporation. The subsidiary investments are accounted for by the equity method, but year-end adjustments to record the equity in subsidiary earnings have not yet been made.

Debits	Allen Corporation	Barth Corporation	Cole Corporation
Cash..	83,000	11,000	27,000
Accounts Receivable...............	104,000	41,000	143,000
Inventories.............................	241,000	70,000	78,000
Investment in Barth Corp.........	150,000		
Investment in Cole Corporation	162,800		
Other Investments	185,000		
Plant Assets............................	375,000	58,000	99,000
Accumulated Depreciation.......	(96,000)	(7,000)	(21,000)
Cost of Goods Sold..................	820,000	300,000	350,000
Operating Expenses	60,000	35,000	40,000
Total	2,084,800	508,000	716,000
Credits			
Accounts payable	46,000	33,000	24,000
Sales......................................	960,000	275,000	570,000
Gain on Sales of Assets	9,000		
Dividend Income.....................	6,800		
Capital Stock, $20 Par.............	500,000	200,000	100,000
Retained Earnings	563,000		12,000
Appropriation for Contingency..			10,000
Total	2,084,800	508,000	716,000

The audit working papers provide the following additional information:

(1) The Barth Corporation was formed by the Allen Corporation on January 1, 19X7. To secure additional capital, 25% of the capital stock was sold at par in the securities market. Allen Corporation purchased the remaining capital stock at par for cash.

(2) On July 1, 19X7, Allen Corporation acquired from stockholders 4,000 shares of Cole Corporation capital stock for $175,000. A condensed trial balance for Cole Corporation at July 1, 19X7, follows:

	Debit	Credit
Current Assets..	165,000	
Plant Assets (net)..	60,000	
Current Liabilities...		45,000
Capital Stock, $20 Par...		100,000
Retained Earnings...		36,000
Sales		200,000
Cost of Goods Sold	140,000	
Operating Expenses...	16,000	
Total...	381,000	381,000

(3) The following intercompany sales were made in 19X7:

	Sales	Gross Profit	Included in Purchaser's Inventory at Dec. 31, 19X7 at Lower of Cost or Market
Allen Corp. to Cole Corp..	$ 40,000	20%	$15,000
Barth Corp. to Cole Corp.	30,000	10	10,000
Cole Corp. to Allen Corp..	60,000	30	20,000
Total	$130,000		$45,000

In valuing the Allen Corporation inventory at the lower of cost or market, the portion of the inventory purchased from the Cole Corporation was written down by $1,900.

(4) On January 2, 19X7, Allen Corporation sold a punch press to Barth Corporation. The machine was purchased on January 1, 19X5, and was being depreciated by the straight-line method over a 10-year life. Barth Corporation computed depreciation by the same method based on the remaining useful life. Details of the sale are as follows:

Cost of punch press.....................	$25,000
Accumulated depreciation............	5,000
Net book value............................	$20,000
Sales price	24,000
Gain on sale..............................	$ 4,000

(5) Cash dividends were paid on the following dates in 19X7:

	Allen	Cole
June 30.....................	$22,000	$ 6,000
December 31............	26,000	14,000
Total.....................	$48,000	$20,000

(6) Allen Corporation billed $6,000 to each subsidiary at year-end for executive services in 19X7. The billing was treated as an operating expense by the subsidiaries and a reduction of operating expenses by Allen Corporation. The invoices were paid in January, 19X8.

(7) At year-end, Cole Corporation appropriated $10,000 of retained earnings for a contingent loss in connection with a lawsuit that had been pending since 19X5.

Instructions: Prepare a work sheet for consolidated statements for Allen Corporation and its subsidiaries for the year ended December 31, 19X7. The sales, costs, and expenses of the subsidiaries are to be included in the consolidation as though the subsidiaries had been acquired at the beginning of the year. You plan to deduct the current year's preacquisition earnings of Cole Corporation at the bottom of the consolidated income statement. (Formal journal entries and statements are not required. Supporting computations should be in good form.)

(AICPA adapted)

16-12. Parent, Inc., purchased for $151,000 cash 100% of the common stock and 20% of the 5% noncumulative, nonparticipating preferred stock of Subsidiary Corporation on June 30, 19X1. At that date, Subsidiary's stockholders' equity was as follows: 5,000 shares of $10 par preferred stock — $50,000; 100,000 shares of $1 par common stock — $100,000; and retained earnings — $41,000. The fair values of the assets, liabilities, and preferred stock did not differ materially from their book values. Subsidiary has made no adjustments to its books to reflect the purchase by Parent. At December 31, 19X1, Parent and Subsidiary prepared consolidated financial statements.

Transactions between Parent and Subsidiary during the year ended December 31, 19X2, follow:

(1) On January 3, 19X2, Parent sold land with an $11,000 book value to Subsidiary for $15,000. Subsidiary made a $3,000 down payment and signed an 8% mortgage note payable in twelve equal quarterly payments of $1,135, including interest, beginning March 31, 19X2.

(2) Subsidiary produced equipment for Parent under two separate contracts. The first contract, which was for office equipment, was begun and completed during the year at a cost of $17,500 to Subsidiary. Parent paid $22,000 cash for the equipment on April 17, 19X2. The second contract was begun on February 15, 19X2, but will not be completed until May, 19X3. Subsidiary has incurred costs of $45,000 as of December 31, 19X2, and anticipates additional costs of $30,000 to complete the $95,000 contract. Subsidiary accounts for all contracts under the percentage-of-completion method of accounting. Parent has made no account on its books for this uncompleted contract as of December 31, 19X2.

(3) On December 1, 19X2, Subsidiary declared a 5% cash dividend on its preferred stock, payable on January 15, 19X3, to stockholders of record as of December 14, 19X2.

(4) Parent sells merchandise to Subsidiary at an average markup of 12% of cost. During the year, Parent charged Subsidiary $238,000 for merchandise purchased, of which Subsidiary paid $211,000. Subsidiary has $11,200 of this merchandise on hand at December 31, 19X2.

Parent depreciates all its equipment over a 10-year estimated economic life with no salvage value. Parent takes a half-year's depreciation in the year of purchase.

The trial balances for Parent, Inc., and Subsidiary Corporation as of December 31, 19X2, were prepared as shown on page 531. Both companies have made all of the adjusting entries required for separate financial statements unless an obvious discrepancy exists.

Instructions: Prepare a work sheet for the preparation of a consolidated balance sheet and income statement for Parent, Inc., and its subsidiary for the year ended December 31, 19X2. Formal statements and journal entries are not required. Round all computations to the nearest dollar. Ignore income tax considerations.

(AICPA adapted)

Parent, Inc., and Subsidiary Corporation
Adjusted Trial Balances
December 31, 19X2

	Parent, Inc. Dr. (Cr.)	Subsidiary Corporation Dr. (Cr.)
Cash	43,000	31,211
Accounts Receivable	119,000	53,000
Costs and Estimated Earnings in Excess of Billings on Uncompleted Contracts	—	87,100
Dividends Receivable	500	—
Mortgage Receivable	8,311	—
Unsecured Notes Receivable	18,000	—
Inventories	217,000	117,500
Land	34,000	42,000
Plant and Equipment (net)	717,000	408,000
Investment in Subsidiary Corporation	151,000	—
Accounts Payable	(203,000)	(97,000)
Dividends Payable	—	(2,500)
Mortgage Payable	(592,000)	(397,311)
Preferred Stock	—	(50,000)
Common Stock	(250,000)	(100,000)
Retained Earnings	(139,311)	(47,000)
Sales	(1,800,000)	—
Earned Revenues on Contracts	—	(1,289,000)
Cost of Goods Sold	1,155,000	—
Cost of Earned Revenues on Contracts	—	852,000
Selling, General, and Administrative Expenses	497,000	360,000
Interest Revenue	(20,000)	—
Interest Expense	49,000	32,000
Dividend Revenue	(500)	—
Gain on Sale of Land	(4,000)	—
	–0–	–0–

16-13. On June 30, 19X6, Linskey, Inc., purchased 100% of the outstanding common stock of Cresswell Corporation for $3,605,000 cash and Linskey's common stock valued at $4,100,000. At the date of purchase the book and fair values of Cresswell's assets, liabilities, and equities were as follows:

	Book Value	Fair Value
Cash	$ 160,000	$ 160,000
Accounts receivable (net)	910,000	910,000
Inventory	860,000	1,025,186
Building	9,000,000	7,250,000
Furniture, fixtures, and machinery	3,000,000	2,550,000
Accumulated depreciation	(5,450,000)	—
Intangible assets (net)	150,000	220,000
	$8,630,000	
Accounts payable	$ 580,000	580,000
Note payable	500,000	500,000
5% mortgage note payable	4,000,000	3,710,186
Common stock	2,900,000	—
Retained earnings	650,000	—
	$8,630,000	

As of June 30, 19X6, Cresswell's furniture, fixtures, and machinery had an estimated remaining life of eight years. The building had ten years of remaining life. All intangible assets had an estimated remaining life of twenty years. All depreciation and amortization is to be computed using the straight-line method.

As of June 30, 19X6, the 5% mortgage note payable had eight equal annual payments remaining with the next payment due June 30, 19X7. The fair value of the note was based on a 7% rate.

The following trial balances for Linskey, Inc., and Cresswell Corp. were prepared. Linskey's profit and loss figures are for the twelve-month period while Cresswell's are for the last six months. Assume that both companies made all the adjusting entries required for separate financial statements unless an obvious discrepancy exists.

Linskey, Inc., and Cresswell Corp.
Trial Balances
December 31, 19X6

	Linskey, Inc. Dr. (Cr.)	Cresswell Corporation Dr. (Cr.)
Cash	507,000	200,750
Accounts Receivable (net)	1,890,000	817,125
Inventory	2,031,000	1,009,500
Buildings	17,000,000	9,000,000
Furniture, Fixtures, and Machinery	4,200,000	3,000,000
Accumulated Depreciation	(8,000,000)	(6,050,000)
Intangible Assets (net)	—	146,250
Investment in Subsidiary	7,705,000	—
Investment in Linskey 7½% Bonds Payable (net)	—	290,000
Interest Receivable	—	22,500
Discount on 7½% Bonds	24,000	—
Accounts Payable	(1,843,000)	(575,875)
Interest Payable	(200,500)	(100,000)
Mortgage Notes Payable	(6,786,500)	(4,000,000)
7½% Bonds Payable	(1,000,000)	—
8¼% Bonds Payable	(3,900,000)	—
Common Stock	(8,772,500)	(2,900,000)
Retained Earnings	(2,167,500)	(650,000)
Sales	(26,000,000)	(6,000,000)
Cost of Goods Sold	18,000,000	3,950,000
Selling, General, and Administrative Expenses	3,130,000	956,000
Management Service Income	(180,000)	—
Management Service Expense	—	180,000
Interest Expense	662,000	100,000
Depreciation Expense	3,701,000	600,000
Amortization Expense	—	3,750
	–0–	–0–

By the year-end, December 31, 19X6, the net balance of Cresswell's accounts receivable at June 30, 19X6, had been collected; the inventory on hand at June 30, 19X6, had been charged to cost of goods sold; the accounts payable at June 30, 19X6, had been paid; and the $500,000 note had been paid.

Prior to June 30, 19X6, there were no intercompany transactions between Linskey and Cresswell; however, during the last six months of 19X6 the following intercompany transactions occurred as listed on the top of page 533.

(1) Linskey sold $400,000 of merchandise to Cresswell. The cost of the merchandise to Linskey was $360,000. Of this merchandise, $75,000 remained on hand at December 31, 19X6.

(2) On December 29, 19X6, Cresswell purchased, in the market, $300,000 of Linskey's 7½% bonds payable for $312,500, including $22,500 interest receivable. Linskey had issued $1,000,000 of these 20-year 7½% bonds payable for $960,000 eight years previously.

(3) Many of the management functions of the two companies have been consolidated since the merger. Linskey charges Cresswell a $30,000 per month management fee.

(4) At December 31, 19X6, Cresswell owes Linskey two months' management fees and $18,000 for merchandise purchases.

Instructions: Prepare a work sheet for the preparation of a consolidated balance sheet and income statement for Linskey, Inc., and its subsidiary, Cresswell Corporation, for the year ended December 31, 19X6. Provide computations in good form where appropriate to support entries.   (AICPA adapted)

16-14. Adjusted trial balances for Company P and its subsidiaries Company Y and Company Z on December 31, 19X4, the end of a fiscal year, are as follows:

	Co. P		Co. Y		Co. Z	
	Dr.	Cr.	Dr.	Cr.	Dr.	Cr.
Cash..	94,500		52,500		25,000	
Dividends Receivable	2,250					
Accounts Receivable (net)	70,000		25,000		15,000	
Finished Goods, Jan. 1	60,000		30,000		22,500	
Work in Process, Jan. 1	25,000		15,000		10,000	
Materials, Jan. 1.........................	40,000		25,000		12,500	
Land and Buildings (net)...............	248,000		65,000		30,000	
Machinery and Equipment (net)......	300,000		105,000		45,000	
Investment in Co. Y........................	127,500					
Investment in Co. Z........................	64,000					
Dividends Payable..........................		4,000		2,500		
Accounts Payable		136,000		60,000		70,500
Bonds Payable.............................				100,000		
Capital Stock ($100 par).................		450,000		100,000		100,000
Retained Earnings (Deficit)		380,750		30,000		(5,000)
Sales..		892,500		245,750		105,000
Sales Returns and Allowances........	15,000		5,000		3,000	
Sales Discount	8,000		3,500		1,500	
Materials Purchases......................	260,000		61,000		30,600	
Purchases Returns and Allowances.		10,000		500		1,500
Purchases Discount		2,500		500		400
Direct Labor................................	150,000		30,000		15,000	
Factory Overhead..........................	230,000		45,000		25,000	
Selling Expenses..........................	60,000		20,500		15,000	
General Expenses	85,000		25,000		17,500	
Interest Expense...........................	2,000		7,000		5,000	
Interest Income............................		500		250		200
Gain on Sale of Equipment.............		10,000				
Income Taxes...............................	22,500		15,000			
Dividends Declared.......................	22,500		10,000			
	1,886,250	1,886,250	539,500	539,500	272,600	272,600
Finished Goods, Dec. 31................	35,000	35,000	30,000	30,000	20,000	20,000
Work in Process, Dec. 31...............	25,000	25,000	20,000	20,000	10,000	10,000
Materials, Dec. 31.........................	44,500	44,500	27,500	27,500	10,500	10,500

Company P carries investment balances by the equity method, but has made no adjustments for intercompany profits. In addition, no adjustment has been made to recognize Co. P's equity in subsidiary earnings for 19X4. Stock was acquired as follows:

900 shares of Company Y stock at 145 on January 1, 19X3, when Company Y's capital was $125,000.
800 shares of Company Z stock at 90 on January 1, 19X1, when Company Z's capital was $105,000.

The difference between the amount paid and the proportionate interest in net assets at the time of each acquisition was attributed to land values.

Companies P and Z acquired part of their materials from Company Y. During the year, sales were made by Company Y as follows (sales are made at a gross profit of 25%):

Sales to Company P..................... $45,000
Sales to Company Z..................... 15,000

It is estimated that materials acquired from Company Y are included in Company P and Company Z inventories at costs to these companies as follows:

	Co. P		Co. Z	
	Jan. 1, 19X4	Dec. 31, 19X4	Jan. 1, 19X4	Dec. 31, 19X4
Finished goods	$3,000	$4,000	$1,000	$1,500
Work in process	2,000	2,000	1,000	1,000
Materials	5,000	6,000	1,000	3,500

On January 2, 19X4, Company Y acquired machinery from Company P for which a charge of $50,000 was made. The cost of the machinery to Company P was $40,000. Company Y is depreciating the machinery on a 10-year life.

On December 31 Company P owed Company Y $12,500 on account, and Company Z owed Company Y $5,000.

Instructions: (1) Prepare a work sheet for consolidated statements for the year ended December 31, 19X4.
(2) Prepare a consolidated balance sheet, a consolidated income statement supported by a manufacturing schedule, and a consolidated retained earnings statement.

16-15. The trial balances of Company A and its subsidiaries Company B and Company C on December 31, 19X6, are shown on page 535.
The inventories at December 31, 19X6, were:

	Co. A	Co. B	Co. C
Finished goods...............................	$135,000	$145,000	$105,000
Work in process.............................	95,000	80,000	85,000
Materials.......................................	230,000	175,000	210,000

Company A purchased the entire stock issue of Companies B and C on January 1, 19X6, at the prices shown in the trial balance. During the year, each of the three companies declared and paid a 5% dividend. Company A recorded its dividends from Companies B and C by crediting Retained Earnings. The various

	Co. A	Co. B	Co. C
Debits			
Cash	75,500	50,000	60,000
Accounts Receivable (net)	350,000	190,000	420,000
Notes Receivable...........................	200,000	60,000	40,000
Materials, Jan. 1, 19X6	150,000	105,000	160,000
Materials Purchases	650,000	400,000	510,000
Direct Labor..................................	450,000	320,000	370,000
Factory Overhead	190,000	190,000	205,000
Selling Expenses	85,000	40,000	75,000
Administrative and General Expenses	45,000	25,000	35,000
Work in Process, Jan. 1, 19X6........	80,000	70,000	75,000
Finished Goods, Jan. 1, 19X6..........	90,000	65,000	80,000
Plant and Equipment......................	900,000	400,000	750,000
Investment in Co. B	875,000		
Investment in Co. C	1,199,500		
	5,340,000	1,915,000	2,780,000
Credits			
Capital Stock	3,000,000	500,000	800,000
Notes Payable...............................	110,000	80,000	60,000
Accounts Payable...........................	100,000	65,000	250,000
Bonds Payable	500,000		
Premium on Bonds	5,000		
Accumulated Depreciation	100,000	60,000	112,500
Sales..	1,400,000	1,050,000	1,250,000
Retained Earnings..........................	125,000	160,000	307,500
	5,340,000	1,915,000	2,780,000

entries for the dividends were the only entries affecting the retained earnings accounts during the year.

On December 31, 19X5, Company A's inventory of materials included goods from Company B at a price of $60,000; the cost to Company B was $40,000. On the same date Company B's inventory of materials included goods purchased from Company C for $75,000, on which Company C made a profit of $25,000.

During 19X6, Company C sold goods to Company B at a price of $200,000. These goods cost Company C $160,000. Company B still owes $30,000 on these purchases. The indebtedness is included in the accounts payable.

During 19X6, Company B sold goods costing $300,000 to Company A at a sales price of $375,000. Company A made cash advances totaling $400,000 to Company B during the year. The sales just mentioned were charged against the advances account, the $25,000 balance of which is included in Company B's accounts payable.

The inventories on December 31, 19X6, include intercompany profits as follows:

	Materials	Work in Process	Finished Goods
Company A..............................	$20,000	$5,000	$4,000
Company B..............................	30,000	6,000	5,000

Company A's bonds were issued July 1, 19X6. They bear 5% interest, payable semiannually, and mature in five years. No interest has been paid.

Allow depreciation at 5% per annum on the cost of the plant assets.

Instructions: Prepare the following consolidated statements: (1) cost of goods manufactured and sold; (2) income statement; (3) retained earnings statement (showing as the final balance the retained earnings balance appearing in the consolidated balance sheet); (4) balance sheet.

(AICPA adapted)

17
Foreign Branches and Subsidiaries

Problems of foreign exchange accounting are encountered when a business engages in operations outside the territorial limits of its home country. With multinational corporations extending their activities to every part of the world, and with sales and investment transactions commonly spanning national borders, problems of foreign exchange assume greater importance to the accountant today than ever before.

The accountant becomes concerned with problems of foreign exchange when it is necessary to express foreign transactions in terms that are meaningful to a domestic reader of financial statements. Goods may be sold and exported to buyers in foreign lands. Goods may be purchased and imported from abroad. Investments may be made in stocks or bonds issued by corporations in foreign countries or in bonds issued by foreign governments. In each of these relationships, the accountant is faced with the problem of restating, in terms of domestic currency equivalents, transactions that are recorded in a foreign currency. In addition, domestic enterprises may expand through the establishment of foreign branches and subsidiaries. If accounting records of the foreign branch or subsidiary are maintained in the local currency, complete translation of the accounts is necessary to permit combining or consolidating with parent company statements.

This chapter describes the conventional procedures that are employed in the translation of financial data reported in terms of foreign currencies. When special conditions are encountered, modification of conventional procedures to meet such special conditions may be required.

RATES OF EXCHANGE

The translation of transactions in terms of domestic currency calls for the use of *rates of exchange* that express the value relationships between a foreign country's basic monetary unit and the domestic unit. At one time, rates of exchange were based directly upon the relative pure gold content of the respective monetary units and were referred to as the *mint par rates of exchange*. With the abandonment of the gold standard, however, rates of exchange have become the products of various economic factors. *Free market rates of exchange* arise from supply and demand factors. In many countries, the government defines an *official rate of exchange*. The official rate may differ from the rate in the local market, where free market conditions determine the exchange of currencies. In some cases, different rates are quoted, depending upon the purpose for which the currency exchange is made. Even with government-defined rates of exchange, nations may limit or block the exchange or transfer of their money.

Exchange rates are subject to change. A government may act to change the official rate of exchange from time to time in response to changes that have taken place in economic or political conditions. Free market rates fluctuate daily as changes take place in supply and demand factors.

Different exchange rates, changes in these rates, and the various restrictions that may be imposed by governments upon the exchange of currencies complicate the ordinary conduct of trade between businesses or individuals in different countries. These factors also complicate the restatement of foreign transactions in meaningful fashion. Special care is necessary in interpreting transactions stated in foreign currency. When more than one exchange rate is encountered, a choice between these rates must be made in translating foreign accounts. The exchange rate chosen should be the rate that best expresses the relationship between the two currencies and that provides for the most realistic translation under prevailing circumstances. The free market rate of exchange is frequently found to be the most suitable exchange rate in meeting this objective.

QUOTATIONS OF RATES OF EXCHANGE

Rates of exchange between foreign and domestic currencies may be quoted *directly* or *indirectly*. A direct quotation states the value of a single unit of foreign currency in terms of equivalent domestic currency. For example, the British pound at a given time may be stated at an equivalent United States dollar value of $2.3625; the Danish krone may be stated at $.1695. An indirect quotation, on the other hand, states the domestic currency unit in terms of the equivalent foreign currency. Thus the United States dollar would be quoted as equivalent to .42328 of a pound; the dollar would also be equivalent to 5.8997 kroner.

Rates of exchange may be relatively stable over long periods of time; on the other hand, they may fluctuate widely even over relatively short periods. The table on page 540 lists the major currency units used in international trade and their average quoted rates of exchange for recent years. These are direct quotations expressed in United States dollars. Current rates may be found in the financial pages of daily newspapers.

FOREIGN SALES AND PURCHASES

In selling or buying goods abroad, a sale price or a purchase price is stated in terms of either the domestic currency or the foreign currency. With fluctuation in the exchange rate, one of the parties to the transaction will realize a gain or a loss resulting from the change in the exchange rate between the date the transaction is entered into and the date the account is paid. For example, an American exporter in selling merchandise abroad may bill the buyer in either United States dollars or the foreign currency. If the buyer is billed in United States dollars, there can be no gain or loss accruing to the seller from exchange rate fluctuations. Remittance of the billed dollar amount will be required of the buyer, no matter what change takes place in the exchange rate between the date of sale and the date of payment. If the buyer is billed in foreign currency, however, the American exporter will be subject to a gain or a loss arising from a change in the rate of exchange. The net gain or loss from such transactions should be recognized on the income statement.

To illustrate, assume that an American exporter sells goods to a merchant in the Netherlands, billing the buyer for $4,800. Assuming a rate of exchange for the guilder of $.48 at the date of the sale, the foreign buyer will treat this transaction as a purchase for 10,000 guilders. If the rate of exchange has changed to $.475 on the date of settlement, it will cost the buyer more than 10,000 guilders to purchase a draft for $4,800 in payment of the invoice. The buyer thus incurs a loss as a result of the fluctuation in the rate of exchange.

But assume in this example that the buyer was billed at 10,000 guilders instead of $4,800. The seller, although setting a price in foreign currency, must still record the transaction in terms of dollars. Assuming a guilder rate at the time of sale of $.48, the seller will treat the transaction as a sale for $4,800. However, a notation is made in the customer's account, stating the number of guilders required in settlement. The seller makes the following entry:

FOREIGN EXCHANGE RATES

Summary Statistics
Major Trading Currencies
(Values expressed in U.S. dollars per foreign currency unit)

Country	Currency	Average Annual Rate 1979	Average Annual Rate 1980	Spot Rate July 1, 1981
Australia	dollar	1.1177	1.1400	1.1461
Austria	schilling	.074799	.077349	.05885
Belgium	conv. franc	.034098	.034247	.02526
Canada	dollar	.85386	.85530	.8315
Denmark	krone	.1901	.17766	.13225
Finland	markka	.25732	.26892	.22242
France	franc	.23504	.23694	.1742
Germany	mark	.54561	.55089	.4142
Hong Kong	dollar	.20029	.1996	.17047
India	rupee	.12265	.12686	.11364
Ireland	pound	2.0465	2.0577	1.5100
Italy	lira	.0012035	.0011694	.000831
Japan	yen	.004572	.0044311	.00438
Malaysia	dollar	.4572	.45967	.42882
Mexico	peso	.043826	.043535	.04092
Netherlands	guilder	.49843	.50369	.3724
New Zealand	dollar	1.0223	.97337	.8440
Norway	krone	.19747	.20261	.16537
Portugal	escudo	.020437	.019980	.01567
Singapore	dollar	.46001	.46712	.46436
South Africa	rand	1.1872	1.2854	1.114
Spain	peseta	.014896	.013958	.010347
Sweden	krona	.23323	.23647	.19531
Switzerland	franc	.60121	.59697	.4822
United Kingdom	pound	2.1224	2.3258	1.8935

Source: Harris Bank

```
Accounts Receivable — Dutch Customer (10,000 guilders).......   4,800
   Sales..........................................................................................        4,800
```

Assume now that a draft for 10,000 guilders is received from the buyer at a time when the rate of exchange for the guilder has declined to $.475. Conversion of the draft into dollars results in recovery of $4,750. The seller must recognize a loss of $50 as a result of the change in the exchange rate. The seller makes the following entry:

```
Cash.........................................................................................   4,750
Loss on Currency Exchange ..................................................      50
   Accounts Receivable — Dutch Customer (10,000 guilders)....         4,800
```

The foreign buyer in these examples has a counterpart in the American importer. An American who imports goods from abroad may be billed in either domestic or foreign currency. If the billing is in domestic currency, settlement would be made in United States dollars in accordance with the sum recognized on the date of purchase; the buyer is not affected by exchange fluctuations. However, if the billing is in foreign currency, the buyer is subject to a gain or a loss from a change in the rate of exchange.

To illustrate, assume that an American importer acquires goods from a Japanese manufacturer at a billed price of 1,000,000 yen. If the rate of exchange for the yen is $.00468 on the date of the receipt of the invoice, the entry on the books of the buyer upon receipt of the goods and the invoice is:

```
Purchases................................................................................   4,680
   Accounts Payable — Japanese Creditor (1,000,000 yen).......         4,680
```

If the rate of exchange for the yen has declined to $.00467 on the date of settlement, the buyer pays only $4,670 for the required yen and makes the following entry:

```
Accounts Payable — Japanese Creditor (1,000,000 yen)..........   4,680
   Cash......................................................................................        4,670
   Gain on Currency Exchange ...............................................          10
```

If the exporter or the importer is faced with the possibility of exchange fluctuations and wishes to be protected against substantial losses from this source, it may be desirable to engage in hedging operations involving futures transactions. In the first example, the exporter who bills the buyer in guilders may, at the time of the sale of the goods, sell 10,000 guilders for future delivery on the date that the remittance from the Dutch customer is expected to be received. In the second example, the importer who is billed in yen may, at the time of the purchase of the goods, buy 1,000,000 yen for future delivery on the date that payment is due to the Japanese creditor.

TRANSLATION OF THE ACCOUNTS
OF A FOREIGN AFFILIATE

When a domestic company maintains a branch or a subsidiary company abroad, combined or consolidated financial statements for the related units require a full translation of the accounts on the statements of the foreign unit in terms of the domestic currency. Translation is necessary not only to provide meaningful data to domestic readers, but to permit aggregation of statement balances.

If exchange rates remained constant, the problem of currency translation would be relatively straightforward. Each monetary balance would be multiplied by the known exchange rate to provide the equivalent in domestic currency. With fluctuating exchange rates, however, the problems become more complex. Which rate should be used to translate each financial statement item into its domestic equivalent? The following alternative procedures have been proposed:

(1) *Current Rate*. Some accountants have suggested translating *all* financial statement items at the rate in effect at the balance sheet date. If this method were used, all items would be translated at a uniform rate.

(2) *Current — Noncurrent Method*. With this method, a distinction is made between current assets and liabilities and noncurrent assets and liabilities. Current items are translated at the current rate (as of the balance sheet date), while noncurrent assets and liabilities are translated at historical rates (the rate in effect at the time each item was acquired).

(3) *Monetary — Nonmonetary Method*. With this method, a distinction is made between monetary items and nonmonetary items, without regard to whether they are current or noncurrent. Monetary items are defined as those items that represent either money or claims to money. These items are translated at the current exchange rate. Nonmonetary items are translated at historical rates — those in effect at the time they were acquired.

Although there is much similarity between the monetary-nonmonetary and the current-noncurrent classifications, there are a few important differences. Inventories are a current asset but a nonmonetary item. Thus they would be translated at current exchange rates if the current-noncurrent method were used, but at historical rates if the monetary-nonmonetary method were used. Conversely, long-term debt is a monetary item but noncurrent. It would be translated at current rates if the monetary-nonmonetary method were used, but at historical rates with the current-noncurrent method.

(4) *Temporal Method*. The temporal method involves selecting the appropriate exchange rate on the basis of whether the item is normally shown at its historical cost or current market value in domestic financial statements. Most monetary items are assumed to be re-

ported at current values and would be translated at current exchange rates. Most nonmonetary items are reported at historical cost, so the historical rate would usually be used for these items.

The temporal method appears to be similar to the monetary-nonmonetary method, but there are some important exceptions. Inventories, for example, are normally recorded at their historical cost and thus the historical exchange rate usually would be appropriate. If inventories are reported at market values, however, as in the lower of cost or market method, then the current rate would be used. Similarly, long-term investments may be reported on a lower of cost or market basis. Investment in long-term bonds, although a monetary item, would be translated at the historical rate if reported at cost.

The temporal method was adopted by the Financial Accounting Standards Board and has thus become a generally accepted method. Although there has been considerable controversy aroused by the imposition of this method, and the authoritative pronouncements requiring its use are likely to change in the future, the use of this method will be assumed in the illustrations in this chapter. Many of the principles involved in foreign currency translation are not affected by the method used for selecting the appropriate exchange rate.

The general rules for the translation of foreign accounts by the temporal method, as recommended in Statement of Financial Accounting Standards No. 8, are summarized as follows:

Balance sheet items

Current assets. Cash, accounts receivable, and other current monetary assets should be translated at the rate of exchange prevailing on the date of the balance sheet. Inventory should follow the same rule as used in the untranslated statement. If a cost method such as *fifo* or *lifo* is used, the rate should be that which prevailed at the time the items were acquired. On the other hand, if market values are used, such as those used in the lower of cost or market method, these market values should be translated at current exchange rates.

Noncurrent assets. Plant assets, permanent investments, and long-term bonds shown at amortized cost should be translated at the rates prevailing when such assets were acquired or constructed. Any contra account balances, such as accumulated depreciation or unamortized bond discount, should be translated at the same rates as the assets to which they pertain.

Liabilities. Liabilities payable in foreign currency should be translated at the rate of exchange prevailing on the date of the balance sheet.

Capital stock. Capital stock stated in foreign currency should be translated at the rates prevailing when it was originally issued.

Income statement items

Revenues and expenses. Operations stated in foreign currency should be translated at the average rate of exchange. With wide fluctuations in exchange, the translation should be made at average rates of exchange applicable to each month, or if this is impractical, on the basis of a carefully weighted average for the reporting period.

Depreciation. Depreciation should be computed at the rates of exchange prevailing when the related assets were acquired or constructed.

The application of these rules to the translation of branch accounts is illustrated in the following section. The application of these rules to the translation of the accounts of a subsidiary company is illustrated in a later section.

ACCOUNTING FOR THE FOREIGN BRANCH

When a domestic business establishes a branch unit in a foreign country, it encounters problems similar to those already described in the chapters dealing with branch accounting. It is also faced with special problems created by branch activities that are expressed in terms of a foreign currency. These special problems arise whenever reports of the combined activities of the home office and the branch are to be prepared. Home office operations and home office relationships with the branch are summarized in terms of the domestic currency. Branch operations and branch relationships with the home office are summarized in terms of the foreign currency. Before the home office can record the earnings of the branch and prepare combined reports, account balances of the branch must be translated into a currency common with that of the home office.

In the example that follows, the procedures that are generally employed in accounting for a foreign branch will be illustrated. Assume that the ABC Company, of New York, establishes a London branch to sell the regular lines of the home office as well as goods acquired from English suppliers. A balance sheet prepared for the home office on December 31, 19X6, just before the establishment of the branch, follows:

ABC Company
Balance Sheet
December 31, 19X6

Assets			Liabilities and Stockholders' Equity		
Cash..		$ 65,000	Accounts payable		$160,000
Accounts receivable...........................		160,000	Capital stock	$200,000	
Merchandise inventory		185,000	Retained earnings............	105,000	305,000
Furniture and fixtures.......	$85,000				
Less accumulated depreciation	30,000	55,000			
			Total liabilities and stockholders' equity		
Total assets.....................................		$465,000	uity		$465,000

Transactions and entries for the home office and the branch for the year 19X7 are listed below and on the next page:

Transaction	Home Office Books (Amounts in dollars)	Branch Books (Amounts in pounds)
(1) Transfer of a draft for £10,000 by the home office to the newly organized London branch. The exchange rate on the date of the purchase of the draft was 2.41, the home office paying $24,100.	Remittances to Branch .... 24,100 Cash............. 24,100	Cash................ 10,000 Remittances from Home Office 10,000
(2) Transfer of a draft for $12,000 by the home office to the branch. The exchange rate upon receipt by the branch was 2.40, the branch deposit in the bank being £5,000.	Remittances to Branch .... 12,000 Cash............. 12,000	Cash................ 5,000 Remittances from Home Office 5,000
(3) Shipment by the home office to the branch, merchandise costing $60,000. The exchange rate when the merchandise was received by the branch was 2.40, the branch recording the shipment at £25,000.	Branch .... 60,000 Shipments to Branch 60,000	Shipments from Home Office ..... 25,000 Home Office .. 25,000
(4) Purchase by the branch, furniture and fixtures for cash of £3,600. (The exchange rate on the date of purchase was 2.40.)		Furniture and Fixtures .... 3,600 Cash............. 3,600

(5) Purchases of merchandise on account:
    Home office $200,000
    Branch..................... £ 12,000
	Purchases........ 200,000
	Accounts Payable 200,000
		Purchases........ 12,000
		Accounts Payable 12,000

(6) Sales on account:
    Home office $360,000
    Branch..................... £ 30,000
	Accounts Receivable 360,000
	Sales 360,000
		Accounts Receivable 30,000
		Sales 30,000

(7) Collections on account:
    Home office $345,000
    Branch..................... £ 25,000
	Cash................ 345,000
	Accounts Receivable 345,000
		Cash................ 25,000
		Accounts Receivable 25,000

(8) Payments on account:
    Home office $245,000
    Branch..................... £ 9,500
	Accounts Payable 245,000
	Cash............. 245,000
		Accounts Payable 9,500
		Cash............. 9,500

(9) Expenses paid in cash:
    Home office .... $ 75,000
    Branch..................... £ 9,000
	Expenses 75,000
	Cash............. 75,000
		Expenses 9,000
		Cash............. 9,000

(10) Transfer of draft for $24,000 by the branch to the home office. The exchange rate on the date of purchase of the draft was 2.40, the branch paying £10,000.	Cash................ 24,000 Remittances from Branch.. 24,000	Remittances to Home Office ..... 10,000 Cash............. 10,000

Transaction	Home Office Books (Amounts in dollars)	Branch Books (Amounts in pounds)
(11) Transfer of draft for £1,000 by the branch to the home office. The exchange rate on the date of receipt of the draft was 2.38, the home office deposit in the bank being $2,380.	Cash.............. 2,380 Remittances from Branch.. 2,380	Remittances to Home Office..... 1,000 Cash............. 1,000

(12) Depreciation for year on furniture and fixtures:
  Home office............. $ 8,500
  Branch................... £   360
	Depreciation
	Expense........... 8,500
	Accumulated
	Depreciation . 8,500
		Depreciation
		Expense........... 360
		Accumulated
		Depreciation . 360

In accounting for domestic branches, the net investment in a branch was reflected on the home office books in a single branch account, and the net accountability of the branch to the home office was reflected on the branch books in a single home office account. In accounting for a foreign branch, however, additional accounts may be introduced to facilitate the subsequent translation of branch account balances into domestic monetary amounts. Remittances between a home office and its branch may be summarized in separate reciprocal accounts on both home office and branch books, so that the dollar amount represented by the remittance-from-home-office and remittance-to-home-office balances on the branch books may be readily determined. Remittance account balances are ultimately closed into the related home office and branch accounts.

After the transactions for the ABC Company and its London branch are posted, trial balances for the two offices will appear as shown at the top of page 547.

Translation of Branch Account Balances

At the end of each fiscal period, the home office will require the foreign branch to submit financial statements in terms of the foreign currency. At the same time, the home office will require the branch to submit the trial balance and the adjusting data in support of the branch statements. These data will be used by the home office in translating branch operations in terms of the domestic monetary unit.

Financial statements for the London branch of the ABC Company appear on pages 547 and 548. Pre-closing account balances and ending inventory data, as originally submitted by the branch in terms of pounds and as restated by the home office in terms of dollars, are listed on page 548.

ABC Company and London Branch
Trial Balances
December 31, 19X7

	Home Office		Branch	
	Dr.	Cr.	Dr.	Cr.
Cash..	$ 80,280		£ 6,900	
Accounts Receivable...	175,000		5,000	
Merchandise Inventory, January 1	185,000			
Furniture and Fixtures..	85,000		3,600	
Accumulated Depreciation..................................		$ 38,500		£ 360
Accounts Payable		115,000		2,500
Branch	60,000			
Remittances to Branch..	36,100			
Remittances from Branch....................................		26,380		25,000
Home Office				15,000
Remittances from Home Office...........................				
Remittances to Home Office			11,000	
Capital Stock...		200,000		
Retained Earnings		105,000		
Sales...		360,000		30,000
Purchases..	200,000		12,000	
Shipments to Branch		60,000		
Shipments from Home Office			25,000	
Depreciation Expense...	8,500		360	
Other Expenses	75,000		9,000	
	$904,880	$904,880	£72,860	£72,860
Merchandise Inventory, December 31[1]				
Acquired from Suppliers..................................	$100,000	$100,000	£ 6,500	£ 6,500
Acquired from Home Office..............................			12,000	12,000
	$100,000	$100,000	£18,500	£18,500

ABC Company — London Branch
Balance Sheet
December 31, 19X7

Assets			Liabilities	
Cash..		£ 6,900	Accounts payable..............................	£ 2,500
Accounts receivable		5,000	Home office.......................................	31,140
Merchandise inventory		18,500		
Furniture and fixtures.............	£3,600			
Less accumulated deprecia-				
tion	360	3,240		
Total assets..		£33,640	Total liabilities...................................	£33,640

---

[1]The ending inventory is listed as both a debit and a credit in view of the need for recognizing this balance both as an asset item on the balance sheet and as a subtraction item from the sum of beginning inventory and purchases on the income statement.

ABC Company — London Branch
Income Statement
For Year Ended December 31, 19X7

Sales..		£30,000
Cost of goods sold:		
Purchases..	£12,000	
Shipments from home office	25,000	
Goods available for sale..	£37,000	
Less merchandise inventory, December 31.................	18,500	18,500
Gross profit..		£11,500
Depreciation Expense...	£ 360	
Other Expenses	9,000	9,360
Net income		£ 2,140

ABC Company — London Branch
Trial Balance Translated into U.S. Dollars
December 31, 19X7

	Adjusted Trial Balance		Translation Rate*		Translated Trial Balance	
	Dr.	Cr.			Dr.	Cr.
Cash...	£ 6,900		(C)	2.35	$ 16,215	
Accounts Receivable......................	5,000		(C)	2.35	11,750	
Furniture and Fixtures	3,600		(H)	2.40	8,640	
Accumulated Depreciation		£ 360	(H)	2.40		$ 864
Accounts Payable...........................		2,500	(C)	2.35		5,875
Home Office..................................		25,000	(R)	$60,000		60,000
Remittances from Home Office		15,000	(R)	$36,100		36,100
Remittances to Home Office	11,000		(R)	$26,380	26,380	
Sales...		30,000	(A)	2.38		71,400
Purchases	12,000		(H)	2.37	28,440	
Shipments from Home Office..........	25,000		(R)	$60,000	60,000	
Depreciation Expense	360		(H)	2.40	864	
Other Expenses.............................	9,000		(A)	2.38	21,420	
	£72,860	£72,860			$173,709	$174,239
Exchange Adjustment (to balance) ..					530	
					$174,239	$174,239
Merchandise Inventory, Dec. 31:						
Acquired from Suppliers...............	£ 6,500	£ 6,500	(H)	2.37	$ 15,405	$ 15,405
Acquired from Home Office	12,000	12,000	(H)	2.40	28,800	28,800
	£18,500	£18,500			$ 44,205	$ 44,205

*Translation rate:
  (C): Current rate — exchange rate at end of period (2.35).
  (H): Historical rate — exchange rate on date transaction was completed (rate on date of purchase
       of furniture, 2.40; rate on date of acquisition of goods from home office, 2.40; rate on date
       of acquisition of goods from suppliers, 2.37).
  (R): Reciprocal amount — dollar value on home office books for corresponding transaction.
  (A): Average rate (2.38).

The practices described in the following paragraphs are generally applied in the translation of the foreign branch balances and have been applied in the example.

Current monetary items. Current monetary items are restated at the rate of exchange in effect at the end of the accounting period. This is the rate that is expected to prevail as noncash current monetary assets are converted into cash and as cash is applied to the payment of current obligations. The application of the current rate to current monetary assets and to current liabilities affords the closest approximation to the balance that will become available for remittance to the home office.

Nonmonetary items. When a significant part of an inventory consists of goods acquired from a home office, the original dollar cost may be assigned to that part of the inventory. The rate as of the date of purchase may be applied to the balance of the inventory. This practice is followed in the example. The date of purchase would be established by reference to the particular inventory valuation method adopted — *lifo* or *fifo*. If the application of cost-or-market valuation procedure to inventories results in their restatement at market value, then the current exchange rate would be used.

Noncurrent assets are converted at the rate of exchange prevailing on the dates of their acquisition. These items are thus carried on successive statements at original dollar values without regard to fluctuations in the rate of exchange. Historical costs in dollars are expressed, regardless of the change in the value of the monetary unit, in accordance with generally accepted accounting principles.

A special problem is encountered for plant and equipment items. With many different acquisitions at different dates, special procedures must be applied in the accounts to facilitate the restatement of this class of assets. Such procedures normally involve the maintenance of two sets of values for plant and equipment accounts. Accounts may be established with two pairs of money columns — one pair of columns reporting the asset balances in terms of the monetary unit actually employed and the second pair of columns of a memorandum nature reporting the asset balances in terms of equivalent dollar amounts. Accounts will then provide balances that show costs for assets in the foreign currency and costs in equivalent dollar amounts. The dollar amounts are substituted for the foreign currency values when branch accounts are converted.

The accumulated depreciation reported by the branch in terms of the foreign currency represents the application of various depreciation rates to the different asset costs. When assets are restated, the accumulated depreciation must be restated, so that these depreciation rates are applied to the equivalent dollar acquisition costs.

To simplify the process of periodic account balance restatements, branch plant and equipment accounts and related accumulated depreciation accounts may be carried on the books of the home office. In following this policy, the branch records the purchase of a plant and equipment item by a debit to the home office account and a credit to Cash in the foreign currency. The home office is notified and it debits a branch plant and equipment account and credits the branch at the exchange rate prevailing at the date of purchase. Periodically, the home office charges the branch for depreciation on the property item by debiting the branch account and crediting an accumulated depreciation account, based on the original dollar cost identified with the asset. The branch recognizes the expense by debiting Depreciation Expense and crediting the home office. The charge is calculated in terms of the foreign currency cost of the asset.

Reciprocal accounts. Reciprocal home office-branch accounts reporting investments and cash transfers will ultimately be offset against each other and hence must be stated at the same dollar amounts. The values in foreign currency in the accounts of the branch are restated at the dollar balances reported on the home office books, as follows: (1) the home office balance is restated at the dollar balance reported in the reciprocal branch account on the home office books; (2) the remittances-from-home-office balance is restated at the dollar balance reported in the reciprocal remittances-to-branch balance on the home office books; (3) the remittances-to-home-office balance is restated at the dollar balance reported in the reciprocal remittances-from-branch balance on the home office books.

Revenue and expense accounts. Revenue and expense accounts, with certain exceptions that are mentioned later, are restated at an average rate for the current period. Average rates normally provide the best approximation to the dollar equivalents represented by the nominal account balances. The restatement of revenues and expenses in terms of the original dollar values would be a formidable task and the results would normally differ little from those obtained when averaging procedures are used.

An average rate is not applicable to the beginning and the ending inventories that enter into the cost of goods sold computation. The beginning inventory is restated at the same dollar value that was used for the inventory at the end of the previous period. The ending inventory is stated at the value that was used in its recognition as an asset item. Thus, the ending inventory is stated at the same dollar value on the balance sheet and on the income statement.

An average rate is not applied to nominal account balances that report transactions between the branch and the home office. Shipments from Home Office, for example, is restated at the dollar value that is reported for Shipments to Branch on the home office books.

Another exception to the averaging procedure is made in the case of amortization and depreciation of asset values. The debit to the expense account should be the same in dollars as the credit made to the asset account or to the contra asset account. The credit to the asset or to the contra asset is made in terms of an asset dollar value as of the date of the asset acquisition, as described earlier.

The average rate used in restating revenue and expense balances may be an average daily rate, an average weekly rate, or an average monthly rate for the year. In some cases the averaging procedure may be modified by weights to offer adequate recognition of those rates in effect during the busy seasons. An average rate is sometimes computed to reflect the rates that are applied to the transfer of earnings to the home office. The dollar balance in the remittances-from-branch account on the home office books divided by the foreign currency balance in the remittances-to-home-office account on the branch books offers such an average.

The exchange adjustment. If all of the accounts of the branch were restated at a single exchange rate, accounts after translation into dollars would be in balance; however, restatement of items at different rates leaves the accounts out of balance. When rates of exchange have fluctuated narrowly during the period, the difference between debits and credits will be small. When rates have fluctuated widely, the difference may be large. In either case, the accounts are brought into balance by recognizing a debit or a credit to an exchange adjustment balance. A debit to the exchange adjustment balance may be viewed as a loss, and a credit to this balance may be viewed as a gain. Under this procedure, asset and liability balances as translated are accepted as complete and accurate. Any trial balance difference calls for adjustment in the nominal account section. The gain or the loss is reported on the income statement as gain or loss from currency translation.

Conversion of the account balances for the London branch of the ABC Company, in accordance with the foregoing rules, resulted in a trial balance in dollars with a credit excess of $530, and hence the recognition of an exchange adjustment loss of this amount. It should be recognized that this exchange adjustment emerges only in the translation of branch account balances and receives no recognition on the books of the branch. The preparation of combined statements for a home office and its foreign branch in terms of domestic currency requires the assumption of a uniform monetary unit and the recognition of an exchange adjustment. From the standpoint of the account balances of the London branch, as measured in pounds, there has been no gain or loss.

Combined Statements for Home Office and Foreign Branch

With the branch trial balance and ending inventory amounts translated into dollars, financial statements for the branch in terms of the domestic currency may now be prepared. With branch earnings expressed in terms of dollars, the home office may recognize branch earnings on its books and summarize operations for the period. The closing entries for the home office and the branch, and the branch and home office statements as prepared by the ABC Company home office, are as follows:

Transactions	Home Office Books (Amounts in dollars)	Branch Books (Amounts in pounds)
(13) To close beginning merchandise inventory.	Income Summary .... 185,000 Merchandise Inventory, Jan. 1 185,000	

(14) To record ending merchandise inventories:
  Home Office $100,000
  Branch Office .... £ 18,500
	Merchandise Inventory, Dec. 31 100,000
	  Income Summary 100,000
		Merchandise Inventory, Dec. 31 18,500
		  Income Summary 18,500

(15) To close nominal accounts summarizing income activities.	Income Summary 140,000
	Shipments to Branch 60,000
	  Purchases..... 200,000
	
	Sales 360,000
	  Income Summary 276,500
	  Depreciation Expense......... 8,500
	  Other Expenses 75,000
		Income Summary 37,000
		  Purchases..... 12,000
		  Shipments from Home Office 25,000
		
		Sales 30,000
		  Income Summary 20,640
		  Depreciation Expense........ 360
		  Other Expenses ...,.... 9,000

(16) To close balance in income summary account on branch books into home office account.		Income Summary .... 2,140 Home Office .. 2,140
(17) To recognize branch net income on home office books: Net income per branch books, £2,140; in domestic currency, $4,881, less translation loss, $530, or $4,351.	Branch .... 4,351 Income Summary (Branch Profit)........... 4,351	
(18) To close combined income summary on home office books.	Income Summary .... 55,851 Retained Earnings 55,851	

(19) To close remittances balances into respective branch and home office accounts.	Branch 9,720
	Remittances from Branch..... 26,380
	  Remittances to Branch...... 36,100
		Remittances from Home Office 15,000
		  Remittances to Home Office 11,000
		  Home Office .. 4,000

ABC Company — London Branch
Balance Sheet
December 31, 19X7

Assets		Liabilities	
Cash................................	$16,215	Accounts payable	$ 5,875
Accounts receivable........................	11,750	Home office	74,071
Merchandise inventory	44,205		
Furniture and fixtures $8,640			
Less accumulated depr.... 864	7,776		
Total assets.....................................	$79,946	Total liabilities................................	$79,946

ABC Company — London Branch
Income Statement
For Year Ended December 31, 19X7

Sales		$71,400
Cost of goods sold:		
Purchases	$28,440	
Shipments from home office	60,000	
Merchandise available for sale	$88,440	
Less merchandise inventory, December 31	44,205	44,235
Gross profit		$27,165
Depreciation Expense	$ 864	
Other Expenses	21,420	22,284
Income before exchange loss		$ 4,881
Loss on currency translation		530
Net income		$ 4,351

ABC Company — Home Office
Balance Sheet
December 31, 19X7

Assets			Liabilities and Stockholders' Equity		
Cash		$ 80,280	Accounts payable		$115,000
Accounts receivable		175,000	Capital stock	$200,000	
Merchandise inventory		100,000	Retained earnings	160,851	360,851
Furniture and fixtures	$85,000				
Less accumulated depreciation	38,500	46,500			
Branch		74,071			
			Total liabilities and stockholders' equity		
Total assets		$475,851			$475,851

ABC Company — Home Office
Income Statement
For Year Ended December 31, 19X7

Sales		$360,000
Cost of goods sold:		
Merchandise inventory, January 1	$185,000	
Purchases	200,000	
	$385,000	
Less shipments to branch	60,000	
Merchandise available for sale	$325,000	
Less merchandise inventory, December 31	100,000	225,000
Gross profit		$135,000
Depreciation Expense	$ 8,500	
Other Expenses	75,000	83,500
Income from own operations		$ 51,500
Add net income — London branch		4,351
Net income		$ 55,851

With branch data translated into dollars, combined financial statements for the home office and branch may be prepared. A work sheet for the preparation of combined statements for the ABC Company is illustrated on page 554.

ABC Company
Work Sheet for Combined Statements for Home Office and Branch
December 31, 19X7

	Home Office	Branch	Eliminations Dr.	Eliminations Cr.	Income Statement Dr.	Income Statement Cr.	Retained Earnings Dr.	Retained Earnings Cr.	Balance Sheet Dr.	Balance Sheet Cr.
Debits										
Cash	80,280	16,215							96,495	
Accounts Receivable	175,000	11,750							186,750	
Merchandise Inventory, January 1	185,000				185,000					
Furniture and Fixtures	85,000	8,640							93,640	
Branch	60,000			(a) 60,000						
Remittances to Branch	36,100			(b) 36,100						
Remittances to Home Office		26,380		(c) 26,380						
Purchases	200,000	28,440			228,440					
Shipments from Home Office		60,000		(d) 60,000						
Depreciation Expense	8,500	864			9,364					
Other Expenses	75,000	21,420			96,420					
Exchange Adjustment		530			530					
	904,880	174,239								
Merchandise Inventory, December 31 (Balance Sheet value)	100,000	44,205							144,205	
Credits										
Accumulated Depreciation	38,500	864								39,364
Accounts Payable	115,000	5,875								120,875
Home Office		60,000	(a) 60,000							
Remittances from Home Office		36,100	(b) 36,100							
Remittances from Branch	26,380		(c) 26,380							
Capital Stock	200,000									200,000
Retained Earnings	105,000							105,000		
Sales	360,000	71,400				431,400				
Shipments to Branch	60,000		(d) 60,000							
	904,880	174,239								
Merchandise Inventory, December 31 (Income Statement value)	100,000	44,205				144,205				
			182,480	182,480	519,754	575,605			521,090	360,239
Income to Retained Earnings					55,851			55,851		
Retained Earnings to Balance Sheet							160,851			160,851
					575,605	575,605	160,851	160,851	521,090	521,090

ACCOUNTING FOR THE FOREIGN SUBSIDIARY

Domestic companies may establish subsidiary companies in foreign countries under the incorporation laws of such countries, or they may acquire controlling interests in foreign companies already organized. The accounting for the foreign subsidiary is similar to that which has already been described for the foreign branch. However, there are certain reciprocal balances that will be found in the parent-subsidiary relationship that were not found in the home office-branch relationship. These special reciprocal balances are illustrated in the following example, together with the procedures for translating these special reciprocal balances and preparing consolidated statements for the parent and the foreign subsidiary.

For purposes of illustration, assume that the ABC Company in the previous example, instead of establishing an affiliated unit in London in the form of a branch, establishes the unit in the form of a wholly owned subsidiary company known as the ABC Company of London. All of the facts given in the previous example are the same, with the exception of the form that the transactions between the affiliates take in view of the different relationship that exists.

Assume that the transactions between the home office and the branch are defined for the parent-subsidiary relationship as follows:

(1) Acquisition by the parent of all of the stock of the subsidiary company for £10,000.
(2) Long-term advance of $12,000 by parent to subsidiary company.
(3) Sale of merchandise on account by parent to subsidiary for $60,000.
(10) Remittance by subsidiary company to parent on account, $24,000.
(11) Declaration and payment of dividend by subsidiary company to parent, £1,000.

The foregoing transactions would be recorded on the books of the parent and its London subsidiary as follows. It is assumed that the parent maintains its investment balance at cost. All of the other transactions of the parent and the subsidiary would be recorded as previously illustrated on pages 545 and 546.

Transaction	Parent Company Books (Amounts in dollars)		Subsidiary Company Books (Amounts in pounds)	

(1) Acquisition by the ABC Co. of 100% of the stock of a newly organized subsidiary, ABC Co. of London, with payment made by a draft for £10,000. The exchange rate on the date of the purchase of the draft was 2.41, the parent paying $24,100.	Investment in ABC Co. of London............ 24,100
	  Cash............
		24,100	Cash.............. 10,000
			  Capital Stock.
				10,000

(2) Advance by the parent to the subsidiary, with transfer of draft for $12,000. The exchange rate upon receipt of the advance by the subsidiary was 2.40, the subsidiary deposit in the bank being £5,000.	Advances to ABC Co. of London............ 12,000 Cash............	12,000	Cash.............. 5,000 Advances from ABC Co. (New York) ($12,000)......	5,000

Transaction	Parent Company Books (Amounts in dollars)		Subsidiary Company Books (Amounts in pounds)	
(3) Sale of merchandise by the parent to the subsidiary for $60,000. The exchange rate when the merchandise was received by the subsidiary was 2.40, the subsidiary recording the shipment at £25,000. (It is assumed that merchandise was sold by the parent at its original cost.)	Accounts Receivable from ABC Co. of London............ Sales............	60,000	Purchases........ 25,000 Accounts Payable to ABC Co. (New York) ($60,000)......	25,000
(10) Payment by the subsidiary to the parent on account, with transfer of draft for $24,000. The exchange rate on the date of the purchase of the draft was 2.40, the subsidiary paying £10,000.	Cash................ 24,000 Accounts Receivable from ABC Co. of London	24,000	Accounts Payable to ABC Co. (New York) ($24,000)......... 10,000 Cash............	10,000
(11) Declaration and payment of a dividend of £1,000 by the subsidiary. Transfer of a draft for this amount was made by the subsidiary. The exchange rate on the date of receipt of the dividend was 2.38, the parent deposit in the bank being $2,380.	Cash................ 2,380 Dividend Income.........	2,380	Dividends Paid . 1,000 Cash............	1,000

After the transactions for the ABC Company and its subsidiary are posted, trial balances for the two companies will appear as follows:

ABC Company (New York) and London Subsidiary
Trial Balances
December 31, 19X7

	Parent		Subsidiary	
	Dr.	Cr.	Dr.	Cr.
Cash..	$ 80,280		£ 6,900	
Accounts Receivable...	175,000		5,000	
Accounts Receivable from ABC Co. of London.......	36,000			
Merchandise Inventory, January 1	185,000			
Furniture and Fixtures......................................	85,000		3,600	
Accumulated Depreciation.................................		$ 38,500		£ 360
Advances to ABC Co. of London..........................	12,000			
Investment in ABC Co. of London	24,100			
Accounts Payable		115,000		2,500
Accounts Payable to ABC Co. (New York)..............				15,000
Advances from ABC Co. (New York).....................				5,000
Capital Stock..		200,000		10,000
Retained Earnings		105,000		
Dividends Paid			1,000	
Sales...		420,000		30,000
Purchases..	200,000		37,000	
Depreciation Expense..	8,500		360	
Other Expenses	75,000		9,000	
Dividend Income...		2,380		
	$880,880	$880,880	£62,860	£62,860
Merchandise Inventory, December 31:				
Acquired from Suppliers.................................	$100,000	$100,000	£ 6,500	£ 6,500
Acquired from Parent......................................			12,000	12,000
	$100,000	$100,000	£18,500	£18,500

Translation of Subsidiary Company Account Balances

At the end of the fiscal period, the subsidiary company prepares financial statements in terms of its own currency. At the same time it will submit to the parent company the trial balance and the adjusting data in support of the subsidiary statements, so that the parent can translate the data in preparing consolidated statements. Preclosing account balances and ending inventory data, as originally submitted by the subsidiary in terms of pounds and restated by the parent company in terms of dollars, are listed as follows:

ABC Company — London Subsidiary
Trial Balance Translated into U.S. Dollars
December 31, 19X7

	Adjusted Trial Balance		Translation Rate*		Translated Trial Balance	
	Dr.	Cr.			Dr.	Cr.
Cash	£ 6,900		(C)	2.35	$ 16,215	
Accounts Receivable	5,000		(C)	2.35	11,750	
Furniture and Fixtures	3,600		(H)	2.40	8,640	
Accumulated Depreciation		£ 360	(H)	2.40		$ 864
Accounts Payable		2,500	(C)	2.35		5,875
Accounts Payable to ABC Company, New York		15,000	(R)	$36,000		36,000
Advances from ABC Company, New York		5,000	(R)	$12,000		12,000
Capital Stock		10,000	(R)	$24,100		24,100
Dividends Paid	1,000		(R)	$ 2,380	2,380	
Sales		30,000	(A)	2.38		71,400
Purchases from Suppliers	12,000		(H)	2.37	28,440	
Purchases from Parent	25,000		(R)	$60,000	60,000	
Depreciation Expense	360		(H)	2.40	864	
Other Expenses	9,000		(A)	2.38	21,420	
	£62,860	£62,860			$149,709	$150,239
Exchange Adjustment (to balance)					530	
					$150,239	$150,239
Merchandise Inventory, December 31:						
Acquired from Suppliers	£ 6,500	£ 6,500	(H)	2.37	$ 15,405	$ 15,405
Acquired from Parent	12,000	12,000	(H)	2.40	28,800	28,800
	£18,500	£18,500			$ 44,205	$ 44,205

*Translation rate:
  (C): Current rate — exchange rate at end of period (2.35).
  (H): Historical rate — exchange rate on date transaction was completed (rate on date of purchase of furniture, 2.40; rate on date of acquisition of goods from parent, 2.40; rate on date of acquisition of goods from other suppliers, 2.37).
  (R): Reciprocal amount — dollar value on parent company books for corresponding transaction.
  (A): Average rate (2.38).

The practices described in the following paragraphs are generally applied in the restatement of subsidiary-parent company reciprocal accounts and have been applied in the example.

Paid-in capital and retained earnings. If the subsidiary company is formed by the parent, the paid-in capital accounts are restated at the exchange rate effective as of the date of organization. At dates subsequent to formation, paid-in capital balances will continue to be converted at original rates. Retained earnings as of the beginning of the period will be reported at the amount that was recognized at the end of the preceding period — a dollar balance that brought the balance sheet of the preceding period into balance. If the subsidiary was organized prior to the date control was achieved by the parent, all balance sheet items, including paid-in capital and retained earnings balances, would be translated at the rate prevailing at the date control is achieved. At dates subsequent to the acquisition of control, paid-in capital balances would continue to be converted at the rate originally applied. Retained earnings as of the beginning of the period would be the amount reported as retained earnings on the balance sheet prepared at the end of the preceding period.

Intercompany trade account balances. Entries on the books of the parent and the subsidiary for intercompany purchases and sales are made as though the units were not affiliated. Similar practices are followed for settlements between companies. Billing in dollars by a parent to a subsidiary is recognized by an entry on the books of the subsidiary in the equivalent foreign currency at the time the goods are received, with a memorandum notation of the dollar settlement required. Subsequent payment in dollars when the foreign cost of dollar exchange is more or less than the amount originally recorded results in the recognition of a loss or a gain on exchange on the books of the subsidiary. Billing in the foreign currency by a parent to a subsidiary results in a dollar entry on the parent's books at the rate of exchange on the date of the transfer, with a memorandum notation of the foreign currency settlement amount. Subsequent payment in the foreign currency that provides a greater or a lesser number of dollars than the amount originally recognized results in a gain or a loss on exchange on the books of the parent. When the sale is made by the subsidiary to the parent, similar considerations will apply. When there are open trade account balances between the companies at the end of the period, subsidiary company balances in foreign currency are restated at the dollar balances reported on the books of the parent. Reciprocal dollar balances are then eliminated in the preparation of consolidated statements.

Intercompany advances. Advances between related companies result in intercompany debtor and creditor balances on the books of the parent and the subsidiary. As in the case of trade account balances, when settlement is to be made in currency that is foreign to the particular company, memorandum accounts are maintained to report the foreign monetary settlement requirements. With fluctuations in the exchange rate, a gain or a loss on exchange is recognized upon settlement. At the end of the period, as in the case of trade accounts, advances shown in the foreign currency are restated at the dollar balances reported on the parent's books. Reciprocal dollar balances are then eliminated in the preparation of consolidated statements.

Consolidated Statements for Parent and Subsidiary Company

The parent company investment in the subsidiary may be carried by the cost method or by the equity method. When the cost method is employed, the parent recognizes dividends received from the subsidiary as revenue. The dollars reported as dividend income on the parent company's books provide the basis for restating the dividends paid balance on the subsidiary books. In developing a work sheet for consolidated statements, eliminations for an investment account maintained at cost are made in the usual manner. Dividends received reported by the parent are applied against dividends paid reported by the subsidiary. A work sheet and consolidated statements are completed in the usual manner.

When the investment is carried by the equity method, subsidiary earnings need to be restated in terms of the domestic currency and the parent then recognizes its share of such earnings. The investment account is debited and a revenue account is credited. Thereafter, in preparing a work sheet for consolidated statements, eliminations for an investment account maintained by the equity method are made in the usual manner.

The closing entries for the ABC Company and its London subsidiary and a work sheet for the preparation of consolidated statements may be prepared as follows:

Transactions	Parent Company Books (Amounts in Dollars)		Subsidiary Company Books (Amounts in Pounds)	
(13) To close beginning merchandise inventory and Purchases.	Income Summary......... 385,000 Merchandise Inventory, January 1...... Purchases.....	185,000 200,000	Income Summary......... 37,000 Purchases.....	37,000
(14) To record ending merchandise inventories: Parent..................... $100,000 Subsidiary .... £ 18,500	Merchandise Inventory, December 31.... 100,000 Income Summary......	100,000	Merchandise Inventory, December 31.... 18,500 Income Summary......	18,500
(15) To close nominal accounts summarizing income for the year.	Sales............... 420,000 Dividend Income............ 2,380 Income Summary...... Depreciation Expense........ Other Expenses......	338,880 8,500 75,000	Sales............... 30,000 Income Summary...... Depreciation Expense........ Other Expenses......	20,640 360 9,000
(16) To close Income Summary and Dividends Paid balances to Retained Earnings.	Income Summary......... 53,880 Retained Earnings.......	53,880	Income Summary......... 2,140 Dividends Paid .... Retained Earnings.......	1,000 1,140

ABC Company (New York) and London Subsidiary
Work Sheet for Consolidated Statements
December 31, 19X7

	Parent Company	Subsidiary Co.	Eliminations Dr.	Eliminations Cr.	Income Statement Dr.	Income Statement Cr.	Retained Earnings Dr.	Retained Earnings Cr.	Balance Sheet Dr.	Balance Sheet Cr.
Debits										
Cash	80,280	16,215							96,495	
Accounts Receivable	175,000	11,750							186,750	
Accounts Receivable from ABC Co. of London	36,000			(c) 36,000						
Merchandise Inventory, January 1	185,000				185,000					
Furniture and Fixtures	85,000	8,640							93,640	
Advances to ABC Co. of London	12,000			(d) 12,000						
Investment in ABC Co. of London	24,100									
Eliminate Investment				(a) 24,100						
Dividends Paid		2,380		(b) 2,380						
Purchases	200,000	88,440		(e) 60,000	228,440					
Depreciation Expense	8,500	864			9,364					
Other Expenses	75,000	21,420			96,420					
Exchange Adjustment		530			530					
	880,880	150,239								
Merchandise Inventory, December 31 (Balance Sheet value)	100,000	44,205							144,205	
Credits										
Accumulated Depreciation	38,500	864								39,364
Accounts Payable	115,000	5,875								120,875
Accounts Payable to ABC Co., New York		36,000	(c) 36,000							
Advances from ABC Co., New York		12,000	(d) 12,000							
Capital Stock	200,000									200,000
Retained Earnings	105,000							105,000		
Capital Stock, ABC Co. of London Eliminate 100%		24,100	(a) 24,100							
Sales	420,000	71,400	(e) 60,000			431,400				
Dividend Income	2,380		(b) 2,380							
	880,880	150,239	134,480	134,480						360,239
Merchandise Inventory, December 31 (Income Statement value)	100,000	44,205				144,205				
					519,754	575,605				
Income to Retained Earnings					55,851			55,851		
Retained Earnings to Balance Sheet					575,605	575,605	160,851	160,851		160,851
							160,851	160,851	521,090	521,090

CRITICISM OF TRANSLATION PROCEDURES

The procedures required by Statement of Financial Accounting Standards No. 8, for translating balances of foreign affiliates, have aroused controversy. The dissatisfaction with the procedures centers on two main issues: the failure to reflect the true economic risks caused by exposure to foreign currency fluctuations, and the inclusion of translation gains and losses as a component of periodic income.

Regarding the economic risks of foreign currency exposure, it is contended that the temporal method procedures adjust for changes in some liability accounts without considering the linkage with related assets that may mitigate the effects of currency changes. For example, assume that a subsidiary in a foreign country acquires merchandise on account for sale in that country to be paid for in local currency. If the value of the local currency increases relative to the dollar, the accounts payable would be translated at the higher rate, resulting in a monetary loss. On the other hand, the merchandise cost would be translated at the original exchange rate in effect at the time of purchase. Thus, there would be no monetary gain recognized on the merchandise, despite the fact that customers will pay for it in the local currency which is now more valuable. The same problem would arise in the case of the foreign subsidiary's acquisition of long-lived assets that are financed with long-term debt in the local currency.

The impact of the temporal method is to provide an accurate representation of the balances that would be shown if all records were maintained in dollars in accordance with generally accepted accounting principles. It is, in effect, a manifestation of the historical cost concept applied to a foreign situation. The failure to reflect economic reality is more a function of conventional accounting assumptions than the specific problem of foreign currency translation. Yet those who object to this procedure on the grounds that it does not indicate the true economic circumstances have not called for the abandonment of the cost principle in other areas of accounting.

The gain or loss from currency translation has become a major component of income for many multinational corporations. Some accountants have objected to the inclusion of this item in the determination of income, because it tends to be subject to erratic fluctuations that obscure the measurement of operating performance. This is considered to be particularly objectionable by those who hold the view that the translation gain or loss does not reflect the true impact of the economic exposure to exchange fluctuations.

There is also evidence to suggest that many companies have engaged in hedging transactions, such as dealing in foreign currency futures markets or borrowing in dollars to finance foreign operations, which may introduce actual economic risks despite the impact of minimizing exposure to accounting gains and losses. Accounting measurement should be neutral with respect to economic activity and should portray results without affecting actual transactions.

The FASB has reconsidered its position on foreign currency translation and has issued an exposure draft of a proposed statement that would supersede Statement No. 8. In essence, the proposed statement would require *all* asset and liability accounts to be translated at the current rate in effect at the balance sheet date. The impact of this proposal would be to limit the accounting gain or loss exposure to the net equity investment of the parent in the foreign subsidiary.

Although this change might be regarded as a step toward economic realism in financial reporting, it is clearly contrary to the basic premise of consolidated reporting. It could be argued, for example, that including all of a corporate subsidiary's liabilities in a consolidated balance sheet does not reflect the true economic risk to parent company stockholders, because the parent company would not be liable for more than its own equity investment in the event of insolvency of the subsidiary. Nevertheless, consolidated statements are prepared on this basis, because it is useful to view the separate legal units as a single economic entity. When the subsidiary company accounts are developed on a basis that differs from that of the parent, the combined accounting figures lose their significance. In focusing on the risk exposure of the parent, the view of the consolidated enterprise as a single unit is distorted.

The proposed statement introduces the concept of a "functional currency," which is the currency of the primary economic environment in which the entity operates and generates net cash flows. This environment need not be the country in which the entity is located, and considerable judgment would be permitted in its determination. Account balances are first restated into the functional currency, if necessary, using the temporal method. The resulting balances are translated into dollars at current exchange rates. If the U.S. dollar is designated as the functional currency, the results would be the same as if the temporal method were used.

The proposed statement also suggests that translation gains and losses be shown as an element of stockholders' equity, without affecting periodic income determination. Although this might overcome the objections to such gains and losses obscuring income from operations, it is a departure from the "clean surplus" concept, which requires changes in stockholders' equity other than from investment transactions to be explained in the income statement.

At the date of publication of this textbook, it cannot be determined which direction the FASB will follow. Illustrations in this chapter, however, are developed within the framework of conventional practice, and the problems at the end of the chapter assume application of the procedures that have been illustrated.

SPECIAL PROBLEMS

Examples in this chapter have assumed that consolidation provided a valid reflection of the activities and the status of the affiliated units. Frequently, special factors may suggest that foreign affiliates be excluded from consolidation. Investments in the foreign units, then, would be reported on the separate statements of the domestic unit with special presentations, notations, or footnotes offering pertinent data relative to such investments. Consolidation may be given up in favor of some alternative investment presentation as a result of such factors as restrictions on the movement of foreign exchange, restrictions on the transfer of properties, special legislation regulating activities between affiliates, unfavorable legislation affecting foreign units, widely fluctuating rates of exchange, changing governments, or significant time periods between fiscal year closing dates for affiliated companies.

QUESTIONS

1. (a) What is meant by the rate of exchange? (b) Distinguish between a market rate of exchange and an official rate of exchange. (c) When more than one rate is in effect, what rate should be employed in translating foreign accounts into dollars?

2. Distinguish between a direct exchange quotation and an indirect quotation.

3. The Boston Company sells goods abroad and bills its customers in terms of their own currencies. (a) How should the company record such sales? (b) How will the company record remittances from such foreign accounts? (c) Would your answers be any different if the customers abroad were subsidiary companies?

4. Ward House, an importing concern, purchases goods from Japan and is billed for 1,000,000 yen. At the date of purchase, the exchange rate for the foreign currency is $.004501. However, at the time of settlement of the account, the yen is quoted at $.00445?

(a) Does Ward House gain or lose by the exchange fluctuation? Explain.
(b) Would your answer be different if the purchase price had been billed at $4,501?

5. Describe four different methods that have been proposed for translating the accounts of a foreign affiliate into domestic currency.

6. What practices are required by the temporal method in translating the following classes of accounts stated in foreign currencies?

(a) Accounts Receivable
(b) Merchandise Inventory stated at cost on a *lifo* basis
(c) Merchandise Inventory stated at market value which is below cost
(d) Machinery and Equipment
(e) Accumulated Depreciation of Equipment
(f) Noncurrent liabilities

7. The following accounts are found on the books of a foreign branch. Assuming the use of the temporal method, state how each account balance would be translated into domestic currency for purposes of home office and branch combined statements.

(a) Cash
(b) Beginning Merchandise Inventory
(c) Ending Merchandise Inventory
(d) Equipment
(e) Accumulated Depreciation
(f) Accounts Receivable
(g) Allowance for Doubtful Accounts
(h) Prepaid Insurance
(i) Accrued Expenses
(j) Home Office — Current
(k) Remittances to Home Office
(l) Remittances from Home Office
(m) Shipments from Home Office
(n) Sales
(o) Expenses
(p) Depreciation Expense

8. Describe several methods for arriving at an average rate of exchange.

9. (a) Distinguish between exchange gains and losses arising from transactions and those arising from translation. (b) What treatment would you recommend for gains and losses of each category?

10. Weedon, Inc., purchases goods regularly from a French supplier. Settlement is made in francs and credit terms are 60 days. On December 31, the end of the fiscal period, Weedon, Inc., books show a liability to the French supplier of $202,000, representing a purchase for 1,000,000 francs that was made when the franc was quoted at $.2020.

(a) What adjustment, if any, would you make on December 31 if the franc is quoted on this date at $.2030?
(b) What adjustment would you make on this date if the franc is quoted at $.2010? Give reasons.

11. (a) How do you explain the emergence of an "exchange adjustment" balance in converting a trial balance from a foreign currency standard to the domestic standard? (b) Describe the way in which this balance should be reported on the combined or consolidated financial statements. (c) What disposition is made of the exchange adjustment in the succeeding period?

12. The following accounts appear on the books of a foreign subsidiary company. The subsidiary was organized by the parent and is wholly owned. Assuming the use of the temporal method, state how each account balance would be translated in preparing consolidated statements for the parent and its subsidiary.

(a) Capital Stock
(b) Additional Paid-In Capital
(c) Retained Earnings (balance at the beginning of the period)
(d) Advances from Parent   *(continued)*

(e) Merchandise Inventory
(f) Plant and Equipment
(g) Accumulated Depreciation
(h) Bonds Payable
(i) Dividends Payable

13. Assume in Question 12 that only 80% of the stock of the subsidiary had been acquired several years after its formation. How would each item listed be converted?

14. Use of the temporal method for translating the financial statements of foreign affiliates and the recognition of translation gains and losses in current income have been criticized. Discuss the alternative positions that have been taken on these issues.

15. Some have suggested that the translation of long-term debt should not be made at the current exchange rate, in view of the fact that the liabilities will ultimately be paid in terms of the rate of exchange prevailing at the time they come due. It is argued that recognition of any apparent translation gain or loss prior to the due date of the obligation is premature, since such gain or loss has not yet been realized. Evaluate this position.

16. Beals Co. has a foreign branch in a country that is at war. Transfer of the foreign currency is blocked and the branch investment is considered to be in serious jeopardy. How would you recommend that this situation be recognized on the statements of the home office?

EXERCISES

1. Simpson Company, of Detroit, sells merchandise to Burdick Company, of Windsor, Canada, on November 4. The sales price is $26,000, and the exchange rate of the Canadian dollar on this date is $.9225. Settlement of the invoice is made by Burdick Company on December 20, when the exchange rate for the Canadian dollar is $.93. Prepare the entries that would be made on the books of the two companies for the transfer of goods and the settlement, assuming that (1) $26,000 represents the sales price in American dollars; (2) $26,000 represents the sales price in Canadian dollars.

2. The following transactions took place between the home office of Sawyer Company, of Cincinnati, and a branch located in Paris, France. Prepare the entries required on the books of the home office and on the books of the branch for each of the following transactions:

(a) A draft for 300,000 francs was sent to the branch. The exchange rate for the franc expressed in terms of dollars on the date of the purchase of the draft was $.2041.

(b) Merchandise costing $81,800 was sent to the branch. The exchange rate on the date of shipment was $.2045.

(c) The branch purchased furniture and fixtures for 50,000 francs. This property item is to be carried on the books of the home office, and the home office is informed of the purchase. The exchange rate on the date of the purchase was $.205.

(d) The branch sent a draft for $16,400 to the home office. The exchange rate on the date of purchase of the draft was $.205.

(e) The branch sent a draft for 60,000 francs to the home office. The exchange rate on the date of deposit of the draft in the bank was $.204.

(f) The branch returned merchandise that was unsuited for its use, on which the original billing was $4,090.

(g) The home office informed the branch of a charge for depreciation at 10% of the cost of furniture and fixtures [see acquisition in (c)].

3. On December 31, the Norway branch of James Company of Los Angeles prepared the following trial balance in krone:

Cash	3,500	
Accounts Receivable	24,000	
Remittances to Home Office	35,000	
Merchandise Inventory, January 1	28,500	
Shipments from Home Office	74,000	
Accounts Payable		7,500
Remittances from Home Office		21,500
Home Office — Current		54,000
Sales		102,000
Operating Expenses	20,000	
	185,000	185,000

Exchange rates for the krone at the beginning of the year and at the end of the year were $.21 and $.20 respectively. The average rate for the year was $.208.

On the home office books, Shipments to Branch is shown at $15,530, Remittances to Branch is shown at $4,500, Remittances from Branch is shown at $7,680, and Branch — Current is shown at $12,000.

Prepare a trial balance in United States dollars for the Norway branch as of December 31.

4. Transactions of the First State Bank of Wilmington, California, with a foreign correspondent for one month, were as follows:

Debits

July 2. Remittance, demand draft, 3,500 francs (franc rate: $.3505).
      8. Remittance, sight draft, 2,700 francs (franc rate: $.3525).
     20. Remittance, cable, 4,260 francs (franc rate: $.3558).

Credits

July 5. Sight draft, 1,900 francs (franc rate: $.3512).
     15. Cable, 4,000 francs (franc rate: $.3547).
     26. Demand draft, 3,820 francs (franc rate: $.3572).

Assuming an exchange rate of $.3575 for the franc at the end of July, determine the exchange profit or loss for July and give the balances in the account at the end of July in both foreign and domestic currency.

5. In January, 19X2, Chang Company, of San Francisco, established a wholly owned subsidiary in Hong Kong. Prepare the entries that would be required on the books of the two companies for each of the following transactions. Chang Company maintains its investment account in the subsidiary company by the equity method.

(a) In establishing the subsidiary company, the parent sends a draft for 1,000,000 Hong Kong dollars in payment for 10,000 shares. The rate for the Hong Kong dollar in terms of the American dollar is $.176 when the parent purchases the draft.

(b) In February the parent transfers to the subsidiary company merchandise billed at a price of $77,000 in American dollars. The rate of exchange at the time is $.175.

(c) In May the subsidiary sends to the parent a draft for $35,000 in American dollars in partial settlement of the amount owed. The draft is acquired by the subsidiary when the rate of exchange is $.175.

(d) In June the subsidiary company ships to the parent company merchandise billed at 175,000 Hong Kong dollars. The parent company credits the receivable account that it has with the subsidiary, using an exchange rate of $.175.

(e) In December the subsidiary company sends the parent a draft for 50,000 Hong Kong dollars, representing a dividend on the shares held by the parent. The draft is converted into cash by the parent at an exchange rate of $.174.

PROBLEMS

17-1. Adjusted trial balances for Spencer Company and its Canadian branch office on December 31, 19X9, appear on page 568.

The exchange rates for the Canadian dollar were as follows:

Beginning of year... .96
Average for year.. .94
End of year .... .92
On date of acquisition of furniture and equipment................................ 1.04

All of the branch merchandise on January 1 had been acquired from Canadian suppliers when the Canadian dollar was worth $.96 in U.S. dollars. Branch

	Home Office (U.S. Dollars)		Branch (Canadian Dollars)	
	Dr.	Cr.	Dr.	Cr.
Cash	55,200		22,000	
Accounts Receivable	61,600		32,500	
Allowance for Doubtful Accounts		1,600		1,000
Merchandise Inventory, Jan. 1	85,000		36,000	
Furniture and Equipment	125,000		60,000	
Accumulated Depreciation		40,000		42,000
Accounts Payable		36,600		20,500
Branch	78,800			
Remittances from Branch		9,350		
Remittances to Home Office			10,000	
Capital Stock		200,000		
Retained Earnings		108,050		
Home Office				80,000
Sales		300,000		172,000
Shipments to Branch		30,000		
Purchases	215,000		95,000	
Shipments from Home Office			32,000	
Expenses	105,000		28,000	
	725,600	725,600	315,500	315,500
Merchandise Inventory, Dec. 31:				
Acquired from Suppliers	120,000	120,000	22,000	22,000
Acquired from Home Office			10,500	10,500
Total	120,000	120,000	32,500	32,500

merchandise from the home office on December 31 had an original cost of $9,800 to the home office. Because of rapid turnover, remaining inventory at December 31 may be assumed to have been purchased at the end of the year.

Instructions: (1) Prepare a statement showing the translation of the branch balances into United States dollars.

(2) Prepare the entries on the home office books to recognize the branch earnings for the year and to close the home office accounts at the end of the year.

17-2. Carr and Hobbs, Inc., opened a branch in the Netherlands at the beginning of 19X2. Transactions of the branch in 19X2 are summarized as follows:

(a)	Cash received from home office, January 1	$ 39,050
(b)	Merchandise received from home office: January 1	$195,250
	June 30	$306,400
(c)	Cash remitted to home office, June 30	800,000 guilders
(d)	Purchase of furniture and fixtures for cash at the beginning of the year	150,000 guilders
(e)	Sales on account	2,000,000 guilders
(f)	Collections on accounts receivable	1,650,000 guilders
(g)	Purchases on account	100,000 guilders
(h)	Payments on accounts payable	80,000 guilders
(i)	Expenses paid	400,000 guilders

Adjusting data at the end of 19X2 were as follows:

Merchandise inventory: acquired in the Netherlands at the end of
December.. 20,000 guilders
acquired from home office...................... 205,000 guilders
Accrued expenses... 10,000 guilders
Furniture and fixtures are depreciated at the rate of 20% per year.

Exchange rates for the guilder in 19X2 were:

January 1... .3905
June 30 .... .3830
December 31...................................... .3765
Average rate...................................... .3835

Instructions: (1) Prepare the entries for the branch to record transactions for 19X2 and to adjust and close the books.

(2) Prepare a statement showing the translation of the branch balances into United States dollars.

(3) Prepare all of the entries that would be made by the home office, including the entry to recognize branch earnings for 19X2.

17-3. The trial balances on December 31, 19X4, of South Bay Importers, Inc., and its Saudi Arabian branch are as follows:

	South Bay Importers, Inc.		Saudi Arabian Branch (In Riyals)	
	Dr.	Cr.	Dr.	Cr.
Cash.....................	$ 62,500		25,000	
Accounts Receivable	85,000		145,000	
Remittances to Saudi Arabian Branch	30,000			
Saudi Arabian Branch...........................	83,000			
Inventories, January 1.........................	48,000			
Prepaid Expenses.................................	23,500		6,000	
Land..	24,000			
Building	150,000		200,000	
Accumulated Depreciation of Building....		$ 30,000		
Furniture and Fixtures	14,500		10,000	
Accumulated Depreciation of Furniture and Fixtures		7,000		
Accrued Expenses.................................		2,500		1,500
Accounts Payable.................................		46,000		86,000
Capital Stock, $100 par		300,000		
Retained Earnings.................................		97,000		
Remittances from Home Office..............				98,500
Home Office				285,500
Sales		209,500		238,500
Shipments to Branch (at cost)		83,500		
Purchases	225,000			
Shipments from Home Office.................			278,300	
Selling Expenses...................................	18,000		28,000	
General and Administrative Expenses.....	12,000		17,700	
	$775,500	$775,500	710,000	710,000

The branch purchased its building and its furniture and fixtures in the middle of the year, when the exchange rate for riyals was $.30. Both the home office and the branch recognize depreciation on buildings at the rate of 10% per year and depreciation on furniture and fixtures at the rate of 20% per year. Depreciation charges are divided equally between selling expenses and general and administrative expenses.

Inventories on December 31 are as follows: home office, $58,400; branch, 133,000 riyals (cost to home office, $43,900).

Exchange rates for the riyal during the year were:

January 1	$.32
December 31	.30
Average rate for the year	.31

Instructions: (1) Prepare a work sheet for combined statements for the home office and the branch.

(2) Prepare a combined income statement and a combined balance sheet.

17-4. Trial balances prepared for Southern Supply Company and its Canadian branch store on December 31, 19X3 are as follows:

	Home Office (U.S. dollars)		Canadian Branch (Canadian dollars)	
	Dr.	Cr.	Dr.	Cr.
Cash	$ 76,000		$ 10,000	
Accounts Receivable	66,000		20,000	
Merchandise Inventory, January 1	37,200		14,800	
Furniture and Fixtures (net)	14,400		5,000	
Remittances to Branch	24,000			
Branch — Current	23,600			
Accounts Payable		$ 18,800		$ 2,400
Remittances from Home Office				23,850
Home Office — Current				23,550
Unrealized Intercompany Inventory Profit		12,560		
Capital Stock		100,000		
Retained Earnings, January 1		77,440		
Sales		249,600		84,000
Shipments to Branch		41,600		
Purchases	224,000		12,000	
Shipments from Home Office			52,000	
Selling Expenses	22,800		12,000	
General and Administrative Expenses	12,000		8,000	
	$500,000	$500,000	$133,800	$133,800

Merchandise sent by the home office to the branch was billed at 25% above cost. Additional merchandise required by the branch was acquired from United States sources and has been recorded on the books of the branch in terms of U.S. dollars.

The merchandise inventory of the branch at the beginning and the end of the year is composed of the following:

	Jan. 1	Dec. 31
Goods acquired from outsiders, at cost.....................	$ 4,000	$ 3,600
Goods acquired from home office, at billed price........	10,800	19,400
Total...	$14,800	$23,000

The merchandise inventory of the home office at the end of the year cost $27,000.

The branch acquired its furniture and fixtures when the exchange rate for the Canadian dollar was $1.02.

Exchange rates for the Canadian dollar were as follows:

January 1..	$1.02
December 31...................................	1.03
Average during year.........................	1.024

Instructions: Prepare a work sheet for combined statements for the home office and the branch.

17-5. A branch office was established in Liverpool on January 1, 19X4, by Atlantic Sales Company of Boston. The transactions of the branch for the year are summarized as follows:

Cash received from home office	$10,000 (rate: 2.10)
	$ 5,000 (rate: 2.08)
Merchandise received from home office........................	$26,000 (rate: 2.10)
	$20,000 (rate: 2.06)
Cash remitted to home office.....................................	£ 4,000 (rate: 2.08)
	£ 4,000 (rate: 2.07)
Purchase of furniture and fixtures for cash...................	£ 500 (rate: 2.10)
Sales on account...	£35,000
Accounts receivable collected.....................................	£27,000
Purchases on account..	£10,000
Accounts payable paid...	£ 8,500
Operating expenses paid	£ 6,000

The following adjustments are required at the end of the year:

(a) Merchandise inventory, all from outside suppliers..................... £8,450
(b) Accrued operating expenses.. £ 150
(c) Depreciation on furniture and fixtures, 10%.
(d) The branch manager, in addition to salary, is to be allowed a bonus of 10% of the net income accruing to the home office after deducting the bonus (this amount is to be set up as a liability on the books of the branch).

The average rate of exchange is $2.08. The exchange rate on December 31, is $2.11.

Instructions: (1) Prepare the entries for the branch to record its activities for the year.

(2) Prepare a work sheet for the branch in both currencies.

(3) Prepare statements for the branch in both currencies.

(4) Prepare the entries to adjust and close the books of the branch.

(5) Prepare all of the entries for the home office resulting from the above information.

17-6. At the beginning of 19X1, Wilson Company establishes a wholly owned subsidiary in West Germany under the name of Rhine Corporation, with a capital of 1,000,000 deutsche marks. During 19X1, the following transactions take place:

(a) The parent sells merchandise to the subsidiary at cost, $154,000, billing the subsidiary in deutsche marks. The exchange rate for the deutsche mark on the date of sale is $.440.

(b) The subsidiary purchases furniture and fixtures at the beginning of 19X1 for 20,000 deutsche marks. The rate of exchange on the date of the purchase is $.4375.

(c) The subsidiary sells merchandise on account for 690,000 deutsche marks.

(d) Subsidiary collections on account total 600,000 deutsche marks.

(e) The subsidiary sends drafts to the parent in partial settlement of account as follows:

> 100,000 deutsche marks ....exchange rate, $.437
> 150,000 deutsche marks ....exchange rate, $.435
> 50,000 deutsche marks ....exchange rate, $.433

(f) In December, 19X1, the subsidiary acquires buildings for 400,000 deutsche marks and machinery for 450,000 deutsche marks. The rate of exchange on the date of the purchases is $.432.

(g) Operating expenses paid by the subsidiary total 46,000 deutsche marks.

On December 31, 19X1, the parent company prepares a trial balance of its accounts after adjustment, except for the ending inventory, as follows:

Cash	$ 137,500	
Notes Receivable	105,000	
Accounts Receivable	242,500	
Inventories, January 1, 19X1	250,000	
Prepaid Expenses	18,000	
Investment in Stock of Rhine Corp., 100% ownership (10,000 shares of 100 deutsche marks par), at cost	432,000	
Land	50,000	
Buildings	400,000	
Accumulated Depreciation of Buildings		$ 205,000
Furniture and Fixtures	58,000	
Accumulated Depreciation of Furniture and Fixtures		17,500
Accounts Payable		149,500
Accrued Expenses		5,500
Deposits Received on Machines Leased		86,000
Deferred Income on Leasing		39,500
Capital Stock		700,000
Additional Paid-In Capital		100,000
Retained Earnings		132,500
Sales		1,489,500
Purchases	1,038,000	
Operating Expenses	194,000	
	$2,925,000	$2,925,000

The subsidiary recognizes no depreciation on buildings and machinery for 19X1. Depreciation on subsidiary furniture and fixtures to be recognized at 20% per year. Inventories on hand on December 31, 19X1, are as follows: parent, $150,000; subsidiary, 165,000 deutsche marks. The average rate of exchange for the deutsche mark for 19X1 is $.434, and the rate of exchange on December 31, 19X1, is $.430.

Instructions: (1) Prepare the entries that are required on the books of the subsidiary to record the transactions for 19X1 and to adjust and close the accounts at the end of 19X1.

(2) Prepare trial balances for the subsidiary in deutsche marks and in United States dollars. (Indicate rates used in conversions.)

(3) Prepare a work sheet for consolidated statements.

(4) Prepare a consolidated income statement and a consolidated balance sheet.

17-7. Following are the balance sheets for Frost Corporation, of Santa Monica, California, and its Swedish subsidiary, Belt Company, on December 31, 19X9:

	Frost Corporation	Belt Co. (In kronor)
Assets		
Cash	$ 47,500	125,000
Notes receivable	25,000	80,000
Accounts receivable	69,500	225,000
Inventories	174,000	525,000
Prepaid expenses	3,500	15,000
Investment in Belt Company — 80% of shares outstanding (at cost)	90,000	
Land	96,500	
Buildings (net)	88,000	
Furniture and fixtures (net)	6,000	30,000
Total assets	$600,000	1,000,000
Liabilities and Stockholders' Equity		
Accounts payable	$ 89,600	275,000
Accrued expenses	5,400	25,000
Bonds payable	100,000	
Capital stock	250,000	500,000
Additional paid-in capital	60,000	
Retained earnings	95,000	200,000
Total liabilities and stockholders' equity	$600,000	1,000,000

Frost Corporation acquired its holdings in Belt Company on January 2, 19X9. On this date, Belt Company had a capital of 550,000 kronor, including a retained earnings balance of 50,000 kronor. The exchange rate on January 2, 19X9, was $.200. The book values of Belt Company assets reflected fair values in local currency at that time.

Belt Company acquired the furniture and fixtures in May, 19X8. Belt Company owes the parent $25,000 on account as of December 31, 19X9. This amount is included in its accounts payable as 125,000 kronor.

The December 31, 19X9 inventory of Frost Corporation includes merchandise of $36,500 acquired from its subsidiary when the exchange rate was $.192. The merchandise cost Belt Company 155,000 kronor. The December 31, 19X9 inventory of Belt Company is stated at market value, which is less than cost.

The exchange rate on December 31, 19X9, was $.194.

Instructions: Prepare a work sheet for a consolidated balance sheet for the parent and its subsidiary.

17-8. Ward Corporation acquired Pierce Corporation on January 1, 19X4, by the purchase at book value of all outstanding capital stock. Pierce Corporation is located in a Central American country whose monetary unit is the peso. Pierce Corporation's accounting records were continued without change. A trial balance, in pesos, of the balance sheet accounts at the purchase date follows:

Pierce Corporation
Trial Balance (in pesos)
January 1, 19X4

Cash	P 3,000	
Accounts Receivable	5,000	
Inventories	32,000	
Machinery and Equipment	204,000	
Accumulated Depreciation		P 42,000
Accounts Payable		81,400
Capital Stock		50,000
Retained Earnings		70,600
	P244,000	P244,000

Pierce Corporation's trial balance, in pesos, at December 31, 19X5 is shown at the top of page 575.

The following additional information is available:

(1) All of Pierce Corporation's export sales are made to its parent company and are accumulated in the account Sales — Foreign. The balance in the account Due from Ward Corporation is the total of unpaid invoices. All foreign sales are billed in United States dollars. The reciprocal accounts on the parent company's books show total 19X5 purchases as $471,000 and the total of unpaid invoices as $70,500.

(2) Depreciation is computed by the straight-line method, using a 10-year life for all depreciable assets. Machinery costing P20,000 was purchased on December 31, 19X4, and no depreciation was recorded for this machinery in 19X4. There have been no other depreciable assets acquired since January 1, 19X4, and no assets are fully depreciated.

(3) Certain plant assets that were acquired by Pierce Corporation prior to January 1, 19X4, were sold on December 31, 19X5. For 19X5, a full year's

Pierce Corporation
Trial Balance (in pesos)
December 31, 19X5

Cash	P 25,000	
Accounts Receivable	20,000	
Allowance for Doubtful Accounts		P 500
Due from Ward Corporation	30,000	
Inventories, December 31, 19X5	110,000	
Prepaid Expenses	3,000	
Machinery and Equipment	210,000	
Accumulated Depreciation		79,900
Accounts Payable		22,000
Income Tax Payable		40,000
Notes Payable		60,000
Capital Stock		50,000
Retained Earnings		100,600
Sales — Domestic		170,000
Sales — Foreign		200,000
Cost of Goods Sold	207,600	
Depreciation	22,400	
Selling and Administrative Expenses	60,000	
Gain on Sale of Assets		5,000
Provision for Income Tax	40,000	
	P728,000	P728,000

depreciation was recorded before the assets were removed from the books. Information regarding the sale follows:

Cost of assets	P14,000
Accumulated depreciation	4,900
Net book value	P 9,100
Proceeds of sale	14,100
Gain on sale	P 5,000

(4) Notes payable are long-term obligations that were incurred on December 31, 19X4.

(5) No entries have been made in the retained earnings account of the subsidiary since its acquisition, other than the net income for 19X4. The retained earnings account at December 31, 19X4, was converted to $212,000.

(6) Inventories on hand at the end of 19X5 are assumed to have been acquired evenly throughout the year 19X5. They are stated at cost, which is below current market value.

(7) The prevailing rates of exchange follow:

	Dollars per Peso
January 1, 19X4	2.00
19X4 average	2.10
December 31, 19X4	2.20
19X5 average	2.30
December 31, 19X5	2.40

Instructions: Prepare a work sheet to convert the December 31, 19X5 trial balance of Pierce Corporation from pesos to dollars. The work sheet should show the unconverted trial balance, the conversion rates, and the converted trial balance.

(AICPA adapted)

18
Insolvency — Statement of Affairs

The term *insolvency* as popularly employed and as normally defined by state statute expresses the inability of an individual or a business to meet outstanding debts as they mature. The assets of the business may exceed its liabilities, but if its liquid assets are insufficient to meet maturing obligations, the business is considered insolvent. Insolvency commonly arises because of losses from operations, the overextension of credit to customers, or excessive investments in inventories or in plant and equipment.

When an individual or a business is determined to be insolvent, creditors may assume control of the insolvent's assets in an attempt to protect their interests. In such cases, the accountant is asked to prepare a *statement of affairs*, which shows the insolvent's financial position and the status of the creditors with respect to the insolvent's assets. The statement of affairs is discussed later in the chapter.

AVAILABLE PROCEDURES IN INSOLVENCY

Creditors and the insolvent may seek to settle difficulties without recourse to the courts. They may agree to an extension of time for payment of debt, a composition of creditors, control of the debtor's assets by a creditors' committee, or other forms of "friendly adjustment." If a settlement without resorting to the courts is not mutually satisfactory, however, the creditors or the insolvent may apply to state or federal courts for legal remedies, such as reorganization or liquidation.

Extensions

If a person cannot meet obligations as they mature, creditors may agree to allow the insolvent an extension of time in which to pay the debts. Creditors generally favor the allowance of an extension of time when it is probable that, by doing so, the debtor will be enabled to pay the debts and continue in business. For creditors, the extension may mean the full recovery of their claims as well as a continuing demand for their product by this sales outlet. When it appears that an extension of time for payment will not succeed in solving the financial difficulties that have arisen, either the creditors or the insolvent will resort to other forms of action.

Composition of Creditors

Creditors may agree to accept a certain percentage of their respective claims in full settlement of amounts owed. Settlement may consist of cash payment of the agreed amount or part payment in cash and the balance in the form of notes. An agreement of this kind is known as a *composition of creditors*. Such a composition settlement may be favored by creditors in an effort to avoid the costs and delays that are involved in alternative actions. Further, such a settlement may permit the debtor to continue in business.

Control by Creditors' Committee

Debtor and creditors may agree to the formation of a creditors' committee for the control of the debtor's business. The committee generally appoints a representative who, under its direction, conducts, reorganizes, or liquidates the business. The agreement may provide for the return of properties to the debtor when claims have been met or when creditors are satisfied with the financial improvement that has been achieved. Trade associations, local credit bureaus, and adjustment bureaus frequently offer specialized services in controlling and operating a debtor's properties or in arranging settlements between the debtor and creditors without recourse to courts.

Voluntary Assignment for Benefit of Creditors

State insolvency laws provide that an insolvent may execute a voluntary assignment of all property to a trust for the benefit of the creditors. An *assignee* or *trustee* is appointed to take over the debtor's properties on behalf of the creditor group. The assignee converts the properties into cash and makes appropriate distributions of this cash among creditors. If any assets remain after claims have been fully satisfied, these assets are returned to the debtor.

Reorganization

An insolvent debtor or the creditors may apply to the bankruptcy court for the appointment of a trustee to take charge of the debtor's business. The trustee, operating as an officer of the court and under its supervision, pays off maturing obligations according to their legal priorities and attempts to restore solvency. If solvency is restored, the trustee can return the business to its owners. If the business cannot be rehabilitated and solvency restored, the court may permit the trustee to (1) reorganize the business by reducing or eliminating the equity of the debtor, or (2) wind up the business, paying creditors as much as possible from the proceeds of liquidation.

Liquidation

Bankruptcy legislation makes it possible for either a debtor or creditors to file a petition with the court asking that the debtor be declared insolvent and that the assets, with the exception of those that are exempt under the law, be sold and the proceeds distributed to the creditors. Liquidation, rather than other means of settlement, may be preferred by debtors as well as creditors. A debtor who complies with the bankruptcy provisions is legally freed from the payment of past debts even though the assets that are surrendered are not sufficient to cover these debts. The debtor is thus given a fresh start. Creditors who are parties to bankruptcy proceedings are assured of an orderly and equitable distribution of the debtor's assets.

BANKRUPTCY REFORM ACT

The Constitution gives Congress the power to establish uniform laws on the subject of bankruptcies. Prior to the enactment of federal laws on this subject, the states had power to enact legislation. The adoption of a bankruptcy law by Congress in 1898, however, supplanted state acts. The law in effect at present is the Bankruptcy Reform Act of 1978. Its provisions are contained primarily in Title 11 of the United States Code. Conditions, procedures, and relief under bankruptcy laws, then, are the same throughout the United States. With bankruptcy action, affairs of the insolvent come under the jurisdiction of a bankruptcy court, which is an adjunct to a federal district court.

Corporate Reorganization Provisions Under the Bankruptcy Act

A corporation facing insolvency may seek a change in its capital structure by applying to a bankruptcy court for reorganization under Chapter 11 of the Bankruptcy Act. Such action may also be sought on an involuntary basis through a petition by creditors.

The objective of reorganization is to develop a plan which will ultimately provide a greater return to creditors than could be provided by complete liquidation. Continuing as a going concern often results in the realization of larger values than the sale of assets under distressed conditions. If creditors determine that continued operation is not in their best interests, they may petition the court to have the case transferred to a Chapter 7 (liquidation) case.

During the period of reorganization, the affairs of the corporation may continue to be managed by the existing management (whose status is referred to as *debtor in possession*) or by a court-approved independent trustee. If management continues under the control of the debtor, the debtor must in effect act as trustee of the assets that belong to the creditors.

A reorganization plan may either impair or leave unimpaired various classes of claims and interests. The plan, however, must provide the same treatment for each claim or interest of a particular class, unless the holder agrees to a less favorable treatment. Thus it would be possible for the plan to leave intact the rights of senior security holders while offering holders of unsecured junior debt less than the full amount of their claims.

The reorganization plan must be accepted by sufficient numbers of each class of interested parties to become effective. If the interests of a given class are not impaired by the plan, it is assumed that the plan is accepted by that class. Each class of creditors that may be imparied by the plan is considered to have accepted the plan if at least two-thirds in dollar amount of claims and more than one-half in number of the allowed claimants vote in favor of the plan. A class of equity security holders accepts the plan if at least two-thirds of the outstanding securities voted are in favor of the plan.

The court will confirm a plan of reorganization only if the plan is accepted by each class, as previously outlined, and each holder of the claim or interest of such class has accepted the plan or, under the plan, will receive property of a value that is not less than the amount that the claimant would receive if the debtor were liquidated.[1] The court will confirm the plan if it meets these conditions and is satisfied that the plan is feasible and in the best interests of the creditors. The reorganization is then binding upon the corporation, its stockholders, and its creditors. In the event of failure to effect a corporate reorganization, proceedings for liquidation under Chapter 7 of the Bankruptcy Act may be initiated.

Bankruptcy Provisions Under the Bankruptcy Act

Bankruptcy proceedings begin with the filing of a petition with a federal bankruptcy court, asking for relief under the Bankruptcy Act. The Act provides for voluntary and involuntary actions in instituting bankruptcy proceedings.

The law allows a business debtor to file a petition asking to be adjudged a *voluntary bankrupt* and to be allowed the benefits of the Act. The amount owed by the debtor is immaterial.

Creditors may file a petition asking that a debtor be adjudicated an *involuntary bankrupt*. A petition for an involuntary case may be filed by three or more creditors having a total of at least $5,000 in unsecured claims. If there are fewer than twelve creditors, then any one creditor having at least $5,000 in claims may file the petition. The action may be taken either if the debtor is generally not paying debts as they mature, or if a custodian was appointed or took possession during the 120-day period prior to the filing of the petition. If the petition is not contested, relief may be granted under the appropriate chapter of the Bankruptcy Act, giving due consideration to the requests of the petitioning creditors. If the petition is contested, relief may be granted only after a trial.

The voluntary or involuntary petition filed with the bankruptcy court indicates the grounds upon which bankruptcy proceedings are sought. In

---

[1] *U.S. Code*, Title 11, Section 1129.

certain cases a *trustee in bankruptcy* may be appointed to take charge of the debtor's assets. The trustee preserves the property and safeguards it against loss. The trustee acquires all of the debtor's rights, titles, and interests in property, real or personal, tangible or intangible. If the debtor is to be liquidated, the trustee then disposes of the property and uses the proceeds for the satisfaction of the creditors' claims. A *creditors' committee* may be appointed by the creditors to make recommendations to the trustee and to the court relative to administration of the bankruptcy action. A bankruptcy judge supervises and reviews the activities of the trustee and authorizes the distribution of the proceeds from the sale of the debtor's property.

Creditors of the bankrupt must prepare statements setting forth their claims and supplying information about the consideration related to such claims, property pledged on the claims, and any other pertinent matters. Such claims and proofs must normally be filed with the court within six months of the first meeting of creditors. Except for certain debts, such as those incurred shortly before the filing of the petition, mutual debts between the debtor and a creditor are offset and only the difference is recognized.

Creditors to whom certain assets have been pledged as security are known as *secured creditors*. Creditors who have no security but who are entitled under the law to priority in payment over general creditors are known as *creditors with priority*. Creditors without security or priority are known as *unsecured* or *general creditors*.

Unpledged properties are sold by the trustee, and the cash is accumulated for ultimate distribution to creditors with priority and then to general or unsecured creditors. Properties that have been pledged to creditors as security are converted into cash, and the proceeds are applied first to the respective secured claims. If certain pledged property fails to realize an amount equal to the claim against it, the unpaid balance of the claim becomes an unsecured or general claim against the debtor. If the pledged property realizes more than the amount of the claim, the excess becomes available to the trustee for distribution to creditors with priority and to unsecured creditors.

The Bankruptcy Act provides fourteen levels of priority for payments to creditors. All claims due to one preference group must be met in their entirety before any claims of the next group may be considered. If there are only enough assets to make a partial payment to a given group, then the distribution to this group must be made on a pro rata basis. The order of priority in liquidation proceedings is as follows:

Preferential priority

1. Assets held in trust and unavoidable liens. The holders of such liens may require that specific assets be turned over or that sufficient cash be received from the liquidation of these assets to satisfy these liens.
2. Administrative expenses. These comprise the costs of preserving and liquidating the estate, including all appropriate expenses of the trustee, his attorney, accountant and other authorized con-

sultants and court costs. Within this group, a higher priority is given to repayment of borrowings by the trustee and to payments for restoration of destroyed assets that are subject to liens.

3. Claims arising during the period between the date the estate came under jurisdiction of the bankruptcy court and the appointment of a trustee. These become another group of administrative expenses.

4. Certain claims for wages, salaries, or commissions, including vacations, severance and sick leave pay. This fourth priority is limited to $2,000 for each claimant, and is further restricted to compensation, vacation, sick leave or other pay earned during the ninety days preceding the filing of the petition or the cessation of the debtor's business, whichever occurs first.

5. Claims covering commitments to make contributions to employee benefit plans. This fifth priority is limited to a total of $2,000 to all plans for each covered employee, after taking into account amounts allowed for other forms of salary claims, and is further restricted to amounts arising from services rendered within 180 days before the filing of the petition or the cessation of the debtor's business, whichever occurs first.

6. Unsecured claims of individuals who, in consumer credit transactions, made deposits to purchase property or services or to lease property. This sixth priority is limited to $900 for each claimant, and covers undelivered or unprovided property or services.

7. Tax claims secured by unavoidable liens against the debtor's property.

8. Tax and custom claims that are unsecured.

General unsecured

9. All other unsecured claims that have been timely filed, or tardily filed if the late filing was due to lack of notice or actual knowledge of the case, and which are not subordinated.

Subordinated

10. Tardily filed claims that, because the late filing was without excuse by reason of lack of notice or knowledge of the case, have lost a higher priority standing.

11. Claims for fines; penalties; forfeitures; or for multiple, exemplary, or punitive damages. These do not include claims for actual pecuniary loss. The subordination of penalties or damages is limited to claims which arose before entry of the order for relief or the appointment of the trustee. Claims arising after that date are classified as administrative expenses.

12. Claims for interest on administrative expenses or on unsecured claims.

13. Claims that are required to be or may be subordinated under Title 11 USC Section 510. These include claims for recision of, or damages arising from, the sale or purchase of a security. The court has the authority to subordinate a claim on equitable principles.

14. Any remaining assets go to the debtor.[2]

---

[2]Homer A. Bonhiver, *The Expanded Role of the Accountant Under the 1978 Bankruptcy Code* (Deloitte, Haskins, & Sells, 1980), pp. 55–56.

When claims with priority have been provided for in full, the bankruptcy judge will authorize the distribution of available funds to remaining general creditors. Distributions involve the declaration and the payment of a *dividend* to creditors. Such a dividend is a stated percentage payment on all allowed unsecured claims. Upon receipt of the final dividend, unsecured creditors must regard unpaid balances as losses.

The adjudication of a person as a bankrupt operates as an application for a discharge in bankruptcy. The court, after examining the debtor, will fix a time for filing objections to a discharge in bankruptcy. In the absence of any valid objections, the court will grant a discharge that releases the bankrupt from all obligations that arose prior to the date of the order for relief.

Under certain circumstances, a debtor will be denied a discharge if the trustee or a creditor objects. For example, a discharge will be denied if it is proved that the debtor:

(1) Destroyed, mutilated, falsified, concealed, or in certain cases failed to keep or preserve books of accounts or records.

(2) Transferred, removed, destroyed, or concealed any property with intent to hinder, delay, or defraud creditors within twelve months prior to the filing of the bankruptcy petition.

(3) Refused to obey any lawful order of, or answer any material question approved by, the court.

(4) Failed to explain satisfactorily any losses of assets or deficiencies of assets to meet liabilities.

(5) Was granted a discharge under the Act in a bankruptcy proceeding commenced within six years prior to the date of the filing of the bankruptcy petition.

A discharge in bankruptcy will also be denied if the debtor during the course of proceedings has committed certain offenses as defined by the law. Offenses named include such acts as: knowingly and fraudulently making false oaths in relation to any bankruptcy proceeding; knowingly and fraudulently concealing property belonging to the debtor's estate; knowingly and fraudulently concealing, destroying, mutilating, falsifying, or withholding any document affecting the properties or affairs of the debtor; and knowingly and fraudulently giving or offering any money, property, remuneration, reward, advantage, or promise thereof, for acting or forbearing to act in a bankruptcy proceeding. In addition to a denial of discharge, offenses are punishable by fines and imprisonment. Fines and imprisonment may be applied not only to the debtor but also to any other party committing, advising, or otherwise assisting in such offenses.

STATEMENT OF AFFAIRS

The statement of affairs is, in effect, a statement of position from a "quitting concern" point of view. Assets are reported at their estimated realizable values instead of being reported at their book values. Furthermore, instead of being classified as current and noncurrent, assets are reported as *pledged* with certain creditor groups or *free* and thus available to general creditors. Liabilities are reported at their balance sheet amounts. The liabilities, however, are not classified as current and noncurrent, but are listed in terms of their legal status or rank, i.e., as obligations *with priority, secured* obligations, and *unsecured* or *general* obligations.

The statement of affairs may be required by creditors as a means of determining what action to take with respect to an insolvent. The statement may also be requested by an assignee or a trustee as a means of informing creditors concerning the possible outcome of a particular course of action.

The statement of affairs is particularly important in Chapter 11 reorganization proceedings which require approval of the various classes of claimants. The Bankruptcy Act requires that adequate information be disclosed before there can be any solicitation of acceptance or rejection of a reorganization plan. "Adequate information" is defined in the Act as:

> . . . information of a kind, and in sufficient detail, . . . that would enable a hypothetical reasonable investor typical of holders of claims or interests of the relevant class to make an informed judgment about the plan.[3]

Before the statement of affairs can be constructed, a balance sheet is prepared and certain supplementary information is assembled. Such supplementary data consist of the following:

(1) Estimates and appraisals from reliable sources of the amounts that will be realized for each asset.
(2) Pledges of assets that have been made on specific obligations.
(3) Obligations that are expected to emerge in the course of liquidation but that are not reflected on the balance sheet.

Assets on the Statement of Affairs

The classification of assets and their presentation on the statement of affairs differ from the classification and the presentation of assets on the balance sheet. The availability of assets to unsecured creditors generally forms the basis for classification on the statement of affairs. Asset classifications are related to the liability classifications on the opposite side of the statement. Assets are ordinarily classified in groups and in the following order:

(1) *Assets pledged with fully secured creditors.* Assets that have been pledged and that are expected to realize an amount equal to or in excess of the claims on which they have been pledged are reported under this heading.
(2) *Assets pledged with partly secured creditors.* Assets that have been pledged but that are expected to realize less than the amounts of the

---

[3] *U.S. Code*, Title 11, Section 1125.

claims on which they have been pledged are reported under this heading.

(3) *Free assets*. Assets that have not been pledged and hence are not related to individual liability items are reported under this heading.

The asset side of the statement of affairs usually has columns to show (1) the book value of the asset, (2) the name of the asset, (3) the appraised value of the asset, (4) the estimated amount that will become available for unsecured creditors as a result of the realization of the asset, and (5) the estimated loss or gain on the realization of the asset.

Liabilities and Capital on the Statement of Affairs

The classification of liabilities and their presentation on the statement of affairs differ from the classification and the presentation of liabilities on the balance sheet. On the statement of affairs, liabilities are classified according to their legal priority and secured status. Liabilities are followed by capital items. Liability and capital items are normally classified in groups and in the following order:

(1) *Creditors with priority*. Creditors who must, by law, be provided for in full before anything may be paid to remaining unsecured creditors are reported under this heading. Federal and state statutes must be consulted in determining what debts are given priority in settlement with creditors. Creditors who have priority under the Bankruptcy Act were indicated on pages 581 and 582.

(2) *Fully secured creditors*. Creditors who have been pledged certain assets that are expected to realize as much as or more than their respective claims are reported under this heading.

(3) *Partly secured creditors*. Creditors who have been pledged certain assets that are expected to realize less than their respective claims are reported under this heading.

(4) *Unsecured creditors*. Creditors who are without legal priority and who have been pledged no assets are reported under this heading.

(5) *Capital*. Balances summarizing the interests of the owners in the business are reported under the heading "Capital" or "Stockholders' Equity."

The liabilities and capital side of the statement of affairs has columns to show (1) the book value of the liability or capital item, (2) the name of the liability or capital item, and (3) the amount of the liability that is unsecured.

Preparation of the Statement of Affairs

In constructing the statement of affairs, it will prove most convenient to proceed in the following manner:

(1) The section headings for the statement should first be set up, with adequate space left between these for the data to be shown.

(2) Each liability should be considered and reported in the appropriate liability section. If a liability is secured, the related asset should be considered at this time and reported in the appropriate asset section.

(3) After all liabilities have been considered, together with assets pledged on such claims, all remaining assets represent unpledged items and may be listed as such.

(4) Asset and liability data are then summarized and the statement is completed.

The preparation of a statement of affairs is illustrated in the example that follows. A balance sheet prepared for Superior Products, Inc., on May 15, 19X2, appears on page 587.

Appraisals of the company's assets indicate that forced realization of assets will result in recovery of the following amounts:

Cash	$ 1,750
Notes receivable, $14,000, and accrued interest, $300	14,300
Accounts receivable	19,500
Finished goods	14,000
Work in process after completion (estimated costs to complete: materials, $2,000; additional labor, etc., $2,500)	25,000
Materials remaining after completion of goods in process	8,500
Miscellaneous supplies	500
Prepaid insurance	—
Stock of Hanson Co. ($60 per share)	30,000
Land	
Buildings	55,000
Machinery and equipment	18,000
Goodwill	—
Patents completely written off the books in past years but with a realizable value	10,000

It is estimated that, in addition to the liabilities shown on the balance sheet, the following amounts will have to be paid:

Liquidation expenses	$12,500
Notes receivable discounted that will probably be dishonored without possibility of recovery by the company	5,000
Probable judgments on damage suits pending	20,000

Obligations of the company are secured as follows:

Obligation	Security
Notes payable of $20,000, on which interest of $400 is accrued	300 shares of Hanson Co. stock
Accounts payable of $30,000	Notes receivable
First mortgage bonds	Land and buildings

The statement of affairs for Superior Products, Inc., prepared from the balance sheet and the supplementary data, appears on pages 588 and 589. Items that should be given special attention are discussed in the following paragraphs.

Presentation of assets and liabilities. The net book value of each asset, liability, or capital item is indicated in the Book Value column. Valuation account balances are deducted from the asset accounts to which they apply

Superior Products, Inc.
Balance Sheet
May 15, 19X2

Assets

Current assets:

Cash..........		$ 1,750	
Notes receivable.........		15,000	
Accounts receivable.........	$35,000		
Less allowance for doubtful accounts.........	3,500	31,500	
Accrued interest on notes receivable.........		300	
Inventories:			
Finished goods.........	$15,000		
Work in process.........	22,000		
Materials.........	10,000		
Miscellaneous supplies.........	1,500	48,500	
Prepaid insurance.........		1,200	$ 98,250
Investments:			
Stock of Hanson Co. (500 shares).........			40,000
Plant and equipment:			
Land.........		$ 35,000	
Buildings.........	$50,000		
Less accumulated depreciation.........	5,000	45,000	
Machinery and equipment.........	$55,000		
Less accumulated depreciation.........	15,000	40,000	120,000
Intangibles:			
Goodwill.........			20,000
Total assets.........			$278,250

Liabilities and Stockholders' Equity

Liabilities

Current liabilities:

Taxes payable.........	$ 600	
Wages payable.........	1,200	
Notes payable.........	55,000	
Accounts payable.........	102,000	
Accrued interest on notes payable.........	1,200	
Accrued interest on bonds.........	750	$160,750
Long-term debt:		
First mortgage bonds.........		50,000
Total liabilities.........		$210,750

Stockholders' Equity

Capital stock.........	$100,000	
Additional paid-in capital.........	12,000	
	$112,000	
Less deficit.........	44,500	
Total stockholders' equity.........		67,500
Total liabilities and stockholders' equity.........		$278,250

and only the net values are indicated. The gross amount of each item as
well as the amount in the valuation account could be shown if desired. If
this were done, the amounts in the valuation accounts would be shown

Superior
Statement
May 15,

Book Value	Assets	Appraised Value	Estimated Amount Available	Loss (Gain) on Realization
	Assets pledged with fully secured creditors:			
$ 35,000	Land			
45,000	Buildings .... }	$55,000		$25,000
	Less claim, first mortgage bonds, and accrued interest (see contra)...................................	50,750	$ 4,250	
	Assets pledged with partly secured creditors:			
24,000	Hanson Co. stock, 300 shares (deducted contra)...	$18,000		6,000
15,000	Notes receivable...	$14,000		1,000
300	Add accrued interest	300		
	Total (deducted contra).............................	$14,300		
	Free assets:			
1,750	Cash	$ 1,750	1,750	
31,500	Accounts receivable.....................................	19,500	19,500	12,000
15,000	Finished goods	14,000	14,000	1,000
22,000	Work in process:			
	Est. value after completion........... $25,000			
	Less costs to complete:			
	Materials $2,000			
	Labor, etc.................... 2,500 4,500	20,500	20,500	1,500
10,000	Materials:			
	Required to complete goods in process .... $ 2,000			
	Balance, estimated to realize........ 8,500	10,500	10,500	(500)
1,500	Miscellaneous supplies	500	500	1,000
1,200	Prepaid insurance	0		1,200
16,000	Hanson Co. stock (200 shares)......................	12,000	12,000	4,000
40,000	Machinery and equipment	18,000	18,000	22,000
20,000	Goodwill	0		20,000
	Patents	10,000	10,000	(10,000)
				$84,200
	Estimated amount available.............................		$111,000	
	Creditors with priority (see contra)....................		14,300	
	Est. amount available to unsecured creditors without priority (approx. 64¢ on the dollar)*.....		$ 96,700	
	Estimated deficiency to unsecured creditors		54,200	
$278,250			$150,900	

*Estimated amount available, $96,700, divided by total unsecured liabilities, $150,900, equals estimated amount payable on claims, 64%, or 64 cents on the dollar.

Products, Inc., Debtor
of Affairs
19X2

Book Value	Liabilities and Stockholders' Equity		Amount Unsecured
	Creditors with priority:		
	Estimated liquidation expenses	$12,500	
$ 600	Taxes payable	600	
1,200	Wages payable	1,200	
	Total (deducted contra)	$14,300	
	Fully secured creditors:		
50,000	First mortgage bonds..	$50,000	
750	Add accrued interest	750	
	Total (deducted contra)	$50,750	
	Partly secured creditors:		
20,000	Notes payable...	$20,000	
400	Add accrued interest	400	
	Total..	$20,400	
	Less security: Hanson Co. stock (see contra).........................	18,000	$ 2,400
30,000	Accounts payable..	$30,000	
	Less security: notes receivable and accrued interest (see contra).	14,300	15,700
	Unsecured creditors:		
35,000	Notes payable...	$35,000	
800	Add accrued interest	800	35,800
72,000	Accounts payable		72,000
	Estimated liability on notes receivable discounted..................		5,000
	Estimated liability on damage suits pending...........................		20,000
	Stockholders' equity:		
100,000	Capital stock..		
12,000	Additional paid-in capital..		
(44,500)	Deficit..		
$278,250	Total unsecured liabilities..		$150,900

immediately beneath the items to which they apply and would be recorded in the Book Value column in parentheses to indicate that they represent subtraction items.

Certain items that are not listed on the balance sheet may require recognition on the statement of affairs. These items would include assets that have been written off but that do have some realizable value upon liquidation, claims for expenses that are expected to emerge as a result of liquidation activities, and claims that have been regarded in the past as contingent but that are expected to make an ultimate claim upon assets in liquidation. When an item that does not appear on the balance sheet is presented on the statement of affairs, the Book Value column is left blank. Such items in this illustration are the free asset, Patents; the liability with priority, Estimated Liquidation Expenses; and the unsecured liabilities, Estimated Liability on Notes Receivable Discounted and Estimated Liability on Damage Suits Pending.

Creditors with priority. Balances of creditors who have legal priority are listed and summarized, but these balances are not extended to the Amount Unsecured column. This column is used for claims that are both unsecured and without priority. Provision is made for claims with priority by subtracting this total from the total estimated amount of assets available to satisfy claims of unsecured creditors.

Fully secured creditors. A creditor who is secured by property estimated to realize as much as or more than the amount of the claim is assured of full payment from the proceeds of such property. Consequently nothing is reported in the Amount Unsecured column. The property that is pledged as security on such a claim is shown on the asset side of the statement as an asset pledged with a fully secured creditor. If the property is expected to realize more than the claim that will be made against it, such excess is extended to the Estimated Amount Available column. This amount is a part of the total to become available for payment to unsecured creditors. In the statement of affairs for Superior Products, Inc., the mortgage bonds are reported as fully secured. Land and buildings pledged on the bonds are reported as assets pledged with fully secured creditors.

Partly secured creditors. A creditor who is secured by property estimated to realize less than the amount of the claim is only partly secured. The amount of the claim in excess of the estimated value of the pledged property is extended to the Amount Unsecured column. This amount is a part of the total of the unsecured or general claims against the debtor. The property that is pledged as security for such a claim is shown on the asset side of the statement as an asset pledged with a partly secured creditor. Since the total asset proceeds will be required to meet the claim on which the asset has been pledged, none of the asset value is reported as available to unsecured creditors. In the statement of affairs for Superior Products, Inc., certain notes payable and certain accounts payable are reported as partly secured. The notes receivable and the pledged portion of the Hanson Company's stock are reported as assets pledged with partly secured creditors.

Unsecured creditors. Balances for creditors who are unsecured and without priority are extended to the Amount Unsecured column. The amounts that are expected to be realized on all assets that are not pledged, i.e., the "free assets," are extended to the Estimated Amount Available column.

Capital. The capital balances for the enterprise are reported under the heading "Capital" or "Stockholders' Equity," but these balances are not extended to the Amount Unsecured column, which is used for amounts due to creditors. A deficit is reported in the Book Value column in parentheses to indicate that it is a subtraction item.

Calculation of deficiency to unsecured creditors. The amount that is estimated to become available for unsecured creditors is calculated on the asset side of the statement and the total for creditors with priority is subtracted from this amount. The remainder is the estimated amount available for unsecured creditors without priorities. The difference between the total unsecured liabilities and the amount that is available to meet such claims represents the estimated deficiency to be absorbed by the general creditors. The asset and the liability sides of the statement of affairs are brought into balance by adding the deficiency to the amount available to unsecured creditors.

Special column for loss or gain on realization of assets. A column headed "Loss (Gain) on Realization of Assets" is shown on the asset side of the statement of affairs. The differences between the book values of assets and the amounts estimated to be realized on their sales are reported in this column. Estimated gains on realization are shown in parentheses so that they may be subtracted from estimated losses in computing the estimated net loss on realization.

Accrued interest on assets and liabilities. Accrued interest items should be added to the principal to which they relate. When an asset has been pledged, both the asset and any related interest accumulations are considered as security on the debt. For example, in the illustration both notes receivable of $14,000 and accrued interest of $300 on these notes are shown as pledged on accounts payable of $30,000.

A pledged asset is security for both the principal of the debt and any interest accruals on this principal. For example, bonds payable of $50,000 and accrued interest of $750 on the bonds are shown as fully secured, and the sum of the principal and interest is subtracted from the pledged properties consisting of land and buildings.

Single balance sheet item shown in several places on the statement of affairs. In certain instances an asset or a liability that appears as a single item on the balance sheet appears in several places on the statement of affairs. For example, Superior Products, Inc., owns 500 shares of Hanson Co. stock. Three hundred shares are pledged; the remaining shares are unpledged. The Hanson Co. stock is therefore shown in two sections on the asset side of the statement of affairs: $3/5$ of the value of the asset is shown as pledged; $2/5$ of the value of the asset is shown as free. The balance sheet of Superior Products, Inc., also shows notes payable of $55,000. Notes of $20,000 are secured by assets that are estimated to realize less than the amount of the obligation; remaining notes are unsecured. These facts are indicated by presenting notes of $20,000 as partly secured and notes of $35,000 as unsecured.

Assets requiring additional expenditures before realization. It may be advisable or necessary to complete the work begun on certain assets before they are offered for sale. In these cases, the costs to be incurred in completing the assets and the values of the assets upon completion must be estimated. The net amount recoverable can then be estimated. For example, in the illustration it is estimated that the work in process can be sold for $25,000 after completion costs estimated at $4,500. The work in process is reported at $20,500, the estimated net recoverable amount.

Preparing estimates of amounts that may be paid to unsecured creditors. An estimate of the amount that may ultimately be paid to unsecured creditors is obtained by dividing the estimated amount available for unsecured creditors without priority by the total unsecured liabilities. In the illustration it is estimated that $96,700 will become available to meet unsecured liabilities of $150,900. Consequently it is estimated that the unsecured creditors without priority will receive 64% of their respective claims, or 64 cents on the dollar. This information may be indicated in the lower section of the statement as illustrated.

Special Problems in the Preparation of a Statement of Affairs

Several special matters that may arise were not illustrated in the preceding statement of affairs. These matters are discussed in the following paragraphs.

Amounts recoverable from partners. Individual partners who are personally solvent may and will be required to make contributions to the partnership towards payment of firm obligations. The amounts estimated to be recoverable from such partners should be reported as free assets on the partnership's statement of affairs.

Amounts recoverable from stockholders. When corporate assets include subscriptions on capital stock, contracts with subscribers will be enforced and amounts estimated to be recoverable should be reported as free assets. When a discount on capital stock is reported in the capital section of the balance sheet and the amount of such a discount is recoverable from stockholders by creditors in the event of insolvency, the recoverable discount should be included as a free asset on the statement of affairs.

Interests in affiliated units. When a company has affiliated branch units, assets and liabilities of the branches should be combined with those of the home office for purposes of the statement of affairs. When a company has controlling interests in stock of subsidiary companies, consolidation is not appropriate in view of the separate legal entities involved. Investments in stock of subsidiary companies, receivables from subsidiaries, and payables to subsidiaries are reported on the statement of affairs under appropriate asset and liability headings. When a subsidiary is insolvent, the statement of affairs for an insolvent parent would show an ownership interest in such a subsidiary with no value. Receivables from the subsidiary would be reported at the amounts recoverable as indicated by the statement of affairs prepared for the subsidiary.

Prepaid expenses. Although prepaid expenses may be included in the asset section at amounts estimated to be recoverable, exceptions are made when it is possible that certain prepaid expenses will expire or be consumed before liquidation is completed. For example, when the length of time required for liquidation is unknown, conservatism would suggest that no realizable value be reported for prepaid insurance items even though refunds on a short-rate basis could possibly result.

Deficiency Statement

A *deficiency statement* to indicate the source of the deficiency to unsecured creditors is usually prepared to accompany the statement of affairs. A deficiency statement for Superior Products, Inc., is shown on page 594.

Alternative Form of the Statement of Affairs

The statement of affairs has been described and illustrated in its conventional form. Alternative forms for this statement have been suggested, one of which is illustrated on page 595. The statement is prepared from the same data as used in the previous example. Preparation of the statement in the alternative form calls for the following steps:

(1) Account balances are listed at their book values as reported on the balance sheet.
(2) These balances are then restated, with assets listed at their estimated realization values, liabilities at the amounts payable upon liquidation, and the stockholders' equity at the difference between assets and liabilities as restated.
(3) Liabilities as restated are extended to columns headed "Creditors" — (1) "With Priority," (2) "Fully Secured," (3) "Partly Secured," and (4) "Unsecured." When a liability is only partly secured, the portion of the liability that will be satisfied by the pledge is reported in the Partly Secured column and the balance of the liability is reported in the Unsecured column.
(4) Assets as restated are extended to columns headed "Assets Available to Creditors" — (1) "With Priority," (2) "Fully Secured," (3) "Partly Secured," and (4) "Unsecured." When an asset is pledged with a fully secured creditor, the portion of the asset required to

Superior Products, Inc., Debtor
Deficiency Statement
May 15, 19X2

Estimated losses on realization of assets:		
Land and buildings	$ 25,000	
Hanson Co. stock	10,000	
Notes receivable	1,000	
Accounts receivable	12,000	
Finished goods	1,000	
Work in process	1,500	
Miscellaneous supplies	1,000	
Prepaid insurance	1,200	
Machinery and equipment	22,000	
Goodwill	20,000	$ 94,700
Additional liabilities:		
Estimated liquidation expenses	$ 12,500	
Estimated liability on notes receivable discounted	5,000	
Estimated liability on damage suits pending	20,000	37,500
Estimated gross loss		$132,200
Deduct:		
Estimated gains on realization of assets:		
Materials	$ 500	
Additional assets:		
Patents	10,000	10,500
Estimated net loss		$121,700
Loss to be borne by owners:		
Capital stock	$100,000	
Additional paid-in capital	12,000	
	$112,000	
Less deficit	44,500	67,500
Estimated deficiency to unsecured creditors		$ 54,200

satisfy the claim is reported as available to the fully secured creditor and the balance of the asset is reported as available to unsecured creditors.

(5) The amount required to satisfy creditors with priority is transferred from the column "Assets Available to Creditors — Unsecured" to the column "Assets Available to Creditors — With Priority."

The statement of affairs in the alternative form can be prepared quickly, and it provides a satisfactory presentation of the status of the different creditor groups. However, this form is not widely used, and it should be assumed in questions, exercises, and problems that, in the absence of any specific designation, reference is made to the statement of affairs in its conventional form.

Functions Served by the Statement of Affairs

To creditors of an insolvent concern, the statement of affairs is more significant than the balance sheet. The statement of affairs assists creditors in determining what policy should be adopted or what action should be taken with respect to the insolvent. Analysis of the statement helps them to decide whether an extension of time, a reorganization, a liquidation, or some other form of action is in their best interests.

Superior Products, Inc., Debtor
Statement of Affairs
May 15, 19X2

Alternative Form

Liabilities and Stockholders' Equity	Book Value	Adjusted	Creditors			
			With Priority	Fully Secured	Partly Secured	Un- secured
Taxes payable	$ 600	$ 600	$ 600			
Wages payable	1,200	1,200	1,200			
Notes payable	55,000	55,000			$18,000	$ 37,000
Accounts payable	102,000	102,000			14,300	87,700
Accrued interest on notes payable	1,200	1,200				1,200
Accrued interest on bonds	750	750		$ 750		
First mortgage bonds	50,000	50,000		50,000		
Estimated liquidation expenses		12,500	12,500			
Estimated liability on notes receivable discounted		5,000				5,000
Estimated liability on damage suits pending		20,000				20,000
Capital stock	100,000	100,000				
Additional paid-in capital	12,000	12,000				
Deficit	(44,500)	(166,200)				
Totals	$278,250	$194,050	$14,300	$50,750	$32,300	$150,900

Assets	Book Value	Adjusted	Assets Available to Creditors			
			With Priority	Fully Secured	Partly Secured	Un- secured
Cash	$ 1,750	$ 1,750				$ 1,750
Notes receivable	15,000	14,000			$14,000	
Accounts receivable (net)	31,500	19,500				19,500
Accrued interest on notes receivable	300	300			300	
Finished goods	15,000	14,000				14,000
Work in process	22,000	20,500				20,500
Materials	10,000	10,500				10,500
Miscellaneous supplies	1,500	500				500
Prepaid insurance	1,200					
Stock of Hanson Co. (500 shares)	40,000	30,000			18,000	12,000
Land	35,000 }	55,000		$50,750		4,250
Buildings (net)	45,000 }					
Machinery and equipment (net)	40,000	18,000				18,000
Goodwill	20,000					
Patents		10,000				10,000
	$278,250	$194,050				
Creditors with priority			$14,300			(14,300)
Totals			$14,300	$50,750	$32,300	$96,700

Total unsecured creditors	$150,900
Estimated amount available to unsecured creditors without priority	96,700
Estimated deficiency to unsecured creditors	$ 54,200
Estimated amount payable per dollar of unsecured liability: $96,700 ÷ $150,900	64¢

A solvent enterprise may prepare a statement of affairs to accompany an application for a loan or a credit line. In such instances the statement is utilized to impress prospective creditors with the satisfactory condition of the enterprise and the absence of risk if additional credit is granted. When the statement of affairs is presented as an exhibit for credit purposes, the usual balance sheet classifications can be used. Assets may be reported at "going concern" values rather than at amounts that would be recovered upon forced liquidation. A statement of affairs prepared by a solvent concern will show an amount available to unsecured creditors exceeding the total of unsecured claims. Such excess is reported on the liabilities and capital side of the statement in bringing the statement into balance.

QUESTIONS

1. What is meant by insolvency?

2. (a) What remedies are available to creditors without resort to the courts when claims are not paid when due? (b) What remedies are available under statutes or court jurisdiction?

3. Distinguish between a reorganization and a liquidation under the Bankruptcy Act.

4. What conditions must be met if a corporate reorganization under the Bankruptcy Act is to be effective?

5. Distinguish between voluntary and involuntary bankruptcy.

6. (a) Distinguish between secured creditors and creditors with priority. (b) What claims have preferential priority under the Bankruptcy Act?

7. Explain the order of payment of debts in bankruptcy liquidation proceedings.

8. Describe the nature of a dividend authorized by a bankruptcy judge.

9. Under what circumstances will a discharge in bankruptcy be denied?

10. (a) What is meant by bankruptcy "offenses"? (b) What is the effect of such offenses upon the bankruptcy action?

11. How does classification and presentation of assets and liabilities on the statement of affairs differ from classification and presentation of these items on the balance sheet?

12. Distinguish between the valuation procedures that are employed on the statement of affairs and those employed on the balance sheet.

13. In preparing a statement of affairs, indicate the sources from which a trustee may obtain reliable estimates or information concerning the probable realization of the following assets:

(a) Merchandise inventory.
(b) Land and buildings.
(c) Securities.
(d) Goodwill.

(e) Prepaid insurance.
(f) Notes receivable.
(g) Patents.
(h) Accounts receivable.

14. Explain how each of the following items will appear on a statement of affairs:

(a) *Estimated liquidation costs*, $2,500.

(b) *First mortgage bonds*, $25,000, upon which interest of $300 is accrued, secured by land and buildings with a book value of $40,000, estimated to realize $30,000.

(c) *Land and buildings* pledged to holders of bonds (see [b]).

(d) *Deficit*, $5,000.

(e) *Cash overdraft*, $1,500.

(f) *Probable judgments on damage suits pending*, $5,000.

(g) *Taxes payable*, $350.

(h) *Goodwill*, $20,000, upon which it is believed nothing will be realized.

(i) *Work in process*, book value of $15,000, estimated to realize $16,000 after additional costs of completion estimated at $1,500.

(j) *Notes receivable*, $15,000.

(k) *Notes receivable*, $20,000, upon which interest of $600 is accrued; notes are estimated to be 80% collectible; one half of the notes are pledged on notes payable of $10,000 on which interest of $400 is accrued.

(l) *Notes payable* secured by notes receivable (see [k]).

(m) *Patents*, fully amortized but estimated to realize $5,000.

(n) *Wages payable*, $800.

15. How would each of the following account balances be reported on the statement of affairs?

(a) Accumulated depreciation.

(b) Deferred income taxes.

(c) Appropriation for contingencies.

(d) Allowance for doubtful accounts.

(e) Allowance for container deposits made by customers.

(f) Appropriation for self-insurance.

16. How would each of the following balances be reported on the statement of affairs for the Burtchett Co.?

(a) Subscriptions receivable — preferred stock.

(b) Discount on common stock.

(c) Deficit.

(d) Paid-in capital from sale of treasury stock.

(e) Dividends payable on preferred stock.

17. (a) State how the estimated amount payable on unsecured claims is calculated. (b) In developing a statement of affairs for the Coburn Co., accountants summarize their conclusions with the following statement, "It appears that 68.31 cents on the dollar will become available to unsecured creditors if forced liquidation takes place." Do you have any criticism of the foregoing statement?

18. You are asked to prepare a statement of affairs for the Walsh Co. You find the following items under the investments heading on the balance sheet for the Walsh Co.:

(1) A balance with a domestic branch carried at a value of $120,000.

(2) Stock of a 100% owned subsidiary carried at a cost of $300,000.

(3) Advances of $60,000 to the 100% owned subsidiary.

State how each balance will be reported on a statement of affairs.

19. You are preparing a statement of affairs for the partnership of X, Y, and Z. In the course of your analysis of financial position, you determine that X and Y are personally solvent and will be able to meet the deficiency of the partnership to its creditors. How will you show this on the statement?

20. What is the nature and the purpose of the deficiency statement?

21. Describe the statement of affairs when it is prepared in its alternative form as illustrated in the chapter. Do you believe that this form has advantages over the conventional form?

22. What use may be made of the statement of affairs by a solvent enterprise?

EXERCISES

1. The Wallace Company is insolvent. The data listed below are developed in the course of preparing a statement of affairs. Indicate how these data should be reported on the statement.

    (a) Notes payable, $60,000, on which interest of $1,400 is accrued; included in the foregoing are notes of $15,000 on which interest of $300 is accrued and which are secured by U.S. bonds of $10,000 (see [b]).

    (b) U.S. bonds, $50,000 par and market value, on which there is accrued interest at 8% for three months.

2. Melody, Inc., has work in process costing $16,500. Completion of such goods is expected to require materials costing $5,000 and labor and other costs of $8,500. When completed, it is estimated that the goods can be sold for $35,000. Materials on hand cost $20,000; materials other than those required for the completion of goods in process are estimated to bring $13,500. Finished goods cost $22,000 and are estimated to have a sales value of $24,500. How would these facts be reported on the statement of affairs?

3. The following balances are found on the books of the Mason Company. State how each balance would appear on a statement of affairs prepared for this company.

Cash balance in savings account with Y bank.................................	$ 3,500
Cash overdraft in checking account with Y bank	(4,500)
Cash balance representing sinking fund accumulation with Z bank	16,500
Cash overdraft in checking account with Z bank	(1,500)
Total cash per books...	$14,000

4. P. M. Lee, trustee for Craig, Inc., prepares a statement of affairs for this company on January 31. Indicate how the following data would be reported on the statement of affairs prepared on this date:

    (a) 200 shares of Griffin stock costing $20,000, par $100, market value per share, $110; 100 shares are pledged to creditors whose claims total $10,500; remaining shares are unpledged.

    (b) Work in process costing $20,000, estimated to realize $18,000 after completion, which requires materials of $500 and additional labor of $2,000.

(c) Materials costing $12,000, estimated to realize $12,500 after the withdrawal of materials required to complete work in process in (b).

(d) Accounts receivable with a book value of $25,000, estimated to realize $20,000, pledged to holders of notes of $22,500.

5. The trustee for Harrison Mills, Inc., prepares a statement of affairs which shows that unsecured creditors whose claims total $60,000 may expect to receive approximately $36,000 if assets are sold for the benefit of creditors. How much may each of the following creditors hope to receive?

(a) A. G. Payne is an employee who is owed $150.

(b) C. A. Kambel holds a note for $1,000 on which interest of $50 is accrued; nothing has been pledged on the note.

(c) F. R. Steel holds a note of $6,000 on which interest of $300 is accrued; securities with a book value of $6,500 and a present market value of $5,000 are pledged on the note.

(d) R. T. Taylor holds a note for $2,500 on which interest of $150 is accrued; property with a book value of $2,000 and a present market value of $3,000 is pledged on the note.

6. The land and buildings owned by the Winn Corporation are sold to satisfy creditors and realize $40,000. Liabilities of the Winn Corporation are as follows:

Wages payable	$ 350
Taxes payable	150
Accrued interest on notes payable	400
Accrued interest on mortgage payable	500
Notes payable	22,000
Accounts payable	53,000
Mortgage payable (secured by land and buildings)	20,000

State the amount to be paid to each of the creditor groups upon distribution of the proceeds of $40,000 by the trustee in bankruptcy.

7. A statement of affairs for the Fox Company shows an estimated amount available for unsecured creditors of $60,000 and a deficiency of $15,000 to this group. What is the estimated amount payable on each dollar of unsecured claims?

8. From the following data, prepare a deficiency statement for the Belfour Company.

Stockholders' equity, per books:	
Capital stock	$100,000
Deficit	15,500
Balance	$ 84,500
Estimated gains on realization of assets:	
Land and buildings	$ 22,500
Estimated losses on realization of assets:	
Accounts receivable	$ 6,600
Inventories	24,000
Prepaid insurance and other prepaid expenses	600
Machinery and equipment	20,000
Goodwill and patents	45,000
	$ 96,200

Estimated claims requiring settlement, not recorded on books:

Liquidation costs..	$ 5,000
Contingent liabilities...	7,500
	$ 12,500

9. A review of the assets and liabilities of the Chambers Company, in bankruptcy on November 30, 19X6, discloses the following:

(a) A mortgage payable of $100,000 is secured by land and buildings valued at $160,000.

(b) Notes payable of $50,000 are secured by furniture and equipment valued at $40,000.

(c) Liabilities other than those referred to total $120,000, which includes claims with priority of $15,000.

(d) Assets other than those referred to have an estimated value of $45,000.

Prepare a statement of affairs in the alternative form illustrated in the chapter.

PROBLEMS

18-1. The following balances are found in the general ledger for the McKinney Company on November 1, 19X5:

Accounts Payable...	167,500
Accounts Receivable..	62,500
Additional Paid-In Capital — Premium on Sale of Stock..................	20,000
Allowance for Doubtful Accounts...	5,000
Accumulated Depreciation — Buildings...................................	40,000
Accumulated Depreciation — Machinery and Equipment..................	70,000
Buildings..	105,000
Capital Stock	200,000
Cash	15,750
Deficit..	71,750
Goodwill	50,000
Inventories	115,000
Investments...	45,000
Land	52,500
Machinery and Equipment...	125,000
Mortgage Payable, secured by land and buildings........................	100,000
Notes Payable...	40,000

The books do not show the following accruals: wages, $850; taxes, $2,000; interest on notes, $1,250; interest on mortgage, $2,500. Nothing will be realized on goodwill. The investments have a market value of $27,500 and have been pledged as security to holders of the notes. An offer of $125,000 has been received for land and buildings, and an offer of $15,000 has been received for machinery and equipment. It is estimated that inventories will realize $85,000 after their completion, which will require additional costs of $12,500. It is estimated that 15% of the accounts receivable will prove uncollectible. Expenses of liquidation are estimated at $15,000.

Instructions: (1) Prepare a statement of affairs.
(2) Prepare a deficiency statement.

18-2. The balance sheet for Barker Company shows the following items on January 31, 19X7:

Assets		
Cash..		$ 4,850
Accrued interest on notes receivable..		500
Notes receivable...		20,000
Accounts receivable	$45,000	
Less allowance for doubtful accounts....................	1,500	43,500
Merchandise inventory		40,000
Prepaid insurance..		500
Furniture and fixtures..	$12,000	
Less accumulated depreciation............................	8,000	4,000
Delivery equipment..	$20,000	
Less accumulated depreciation............................	2,000	18,000
Goodwill..		25,000
Total assets		$156,350

Liabilities and Stockholders' Equity	
Accrued salaries and wages...	$ 400
Accrued interest on notes payable	800
Notes payable..	50,000
Accounts payable..	68,000
Capital stock	50,000
Premium on stock	5,000
Deficit	(17,850)
Total liabilities and stockholders' equity	$156,350

A trustee appointed on January 31 obtains the following data:

(a) It is estimated that assets will realize the following amounts:
    Notes receivable and accrued interest......................... $13,400
    Accounts receivable 37,500
    Merchandise inventory ....70% of book value
    Prepaid insurance.. Nothing
    Furniture and fixtures.. 4,500
    Delivery equipment 14,000
    Goodwill.. Nothing

(b) Notes payable of $20,000 on which interest of $200 is accrued are secured by merchandise inventory with a book value of $30,000.

(c) Notes payable of $15,000 on which interest of $450 is accrued are secured by the delivery equipment.

(d) The company is contingently liable on notes receivable discounted of $15,000; however, it is believed that notes of only $2,000 may have to be paid without recovery.

(e) Liquidation expenses are estimated at $6,000.

Instructions: (1) Prepare a statement of affairs.
(2) Prepare a deficiency statement.

18-3. A trustee was appointed on July 1, 19X2, to take charge of the Crocker Company. At that time the following balance sheet was available:

Assets

Cash		$ 4,050
Accounts receivable	$40,000	
Less allowance for doubtful accounts	500	39,500
Finished goods		42,000
Work in process		35,000
Materials		20,000
Prepaid insurance		1,000
Patterns, jigs, and tools		20,000
Land		30,000
Buildings	$80,000	
Less accumulated depreciation	30,000	50,000
Machinery and equipment	$75,000	
Less accumulated depreciation	40,000	35,000
Intangibles		1
Total assets		$276,551

Liabilities and Stockholders' Equity

Accrued wages	$ 3,850
Accrued interest on notes	2,400
Accrued interest on bonds	1,500
Notes payable	63,500
Accounts payable	90,000
First mortgage bonds	60,000
Common stock	100,000
Additional paid-in capital	15,500
Deficit	(60,199)
Total liabilities and stockholders' equity	$276,551

It is estimated that assets will realize the following amounts: accounts receivable, $36,500; finished goods, $36,000; work in process after costs of $15,000 required for completion, $40,000; materials, $14,000; prepaid insurance, no value; patterns, jigs, and tools, $4,000; land and buildings, $70,000; machinery and equipment, $8,000; intangibles, $2,500.

One half of the finished goods on hand is pledged to holders of notes of $25,000; interest of $600 is applicable to these notes.

Additional accrued wages of $400 are not shown on the balance sheet. Liquidation expenses are estimated at $12,500.

Instructions: (1) Prepare a statement of affairs.

(2) Prepare a deficiency statement.

(3) Prepare a statement to show how much each creditor may expect to receive upon liquidation.

18-4. A trustee is appointed on March 30, 19X5, to take charge of Wentworth Company. The balance sheet on that date is shown on page 603.

Accounts receivable are classified as follows: good, $20,000; doubtful, $18,000 with an estimated value of $4,250; bad, $12,000. Good accounts of $10,000 are pledged to one of the trade creditors who is owed $8,000. It is believed that all common stock subscriptions will be collected.

The Weber Company has offered to purchase certain assets for amounts as follows: all of the finished goods, $20,000; work in process upon completion, $26,500; and patents, $5,000. It is estimated that completion of the work in

Assets

Cash..		$ 15,400
Accounts receivable...	$ 50,000	
Less allowance for doubtful accounts................	7,000	43,000
Common stock subscriptions receivable		10,000
Finished goods		40,000
Work in process		24,000
Materials...		20,000
Prepaid insurance...		1,000
Tools		20,000
Land..		20,000
Buildings	$105,000	
Less accumulated depreciation..........................	20,000	85,000
Machinery...	$ 70,000	
Less accumulated depreciation..........................	12,000	58,000
Goodwill..		35,000
Patents..		30,000
Total assets..		$401,400

Liabilities and Stockholders' Equity

Accrued interest on mortgage...	$ 1,400
Accrued interest on notes payable	2,500
Accrued wages and salaries..	4,500
Mortgage note payable	50,000
Notes payable...	91,500
Accounts payable...	95,000
Preferred stock...	50,000
Common stock..	125,000
Common stock subscribed	25,000
Deficit	(43,500)
Total liabilities and stockholders' equity	$401,400

process will require materials, $6,000, and wages and other expenditures, $10,000. Finished goods with a book value of $18,000 are pledged to holders of notes of $15,000. Interest of $300 applies on these notes.

Materials that will remain after completion of work in process are estimated to have a value of $15,000. Tools are estimated to have a value of $12,000. Machinery is estimated to have a value of $27,500 and the mortgaged land and buildings a value of $55,000. Nothing will be realized on goodwill and prepaid insurance. The company is contingently liable on notes receivable discounted amounting to $10,000; however, it is estimated that notes discounted of only $3,000 will have to be paid without recovery. The estimated expenses of liquidation are $12,000.

Instructions: (1) Prepare a statement of affairs.

(2) Prepare a deficiency statement.

(3) Prepare a statement to show how much each creditor may expect to receive upon liquidation.

18-5. The Cummings Company of San Diego has a branch in Santa Ana and a wholly owned subsidiary in Riverside, the Sun Company. The Sun Company was forced into bankruptcy on June 30, 19X1. A balance sheet for the Sun Company prepared on this date follows:

Assets		Liabilities and Stockholders' Equity	
Accounts receivable.................	$ 60,000	Cash overdraft — National	
Merchandise inventory	90,000	Bank	$ 10,000
Plant and equipment...............	105,000	Accounts payable	90,000
		Due to Cummings Co.	80,000
		Mortgage secured by plant and	
		equipment	30,000
		Capital stock	75,000
		Deficit	(30,000)
Total	$255,000	Total	$255,000

The Santa Ana branch balance sheet on this date shows:

Assets		Liabilities	
Cash......................................	$ 10,000	Accounts payable	$ 40,000
Accounts receivable.................	40,000	Home office	60,000
Merchandise inventory	50,000		
Total	$100,000	Total	$100,000

The balance sheet for the Cummings Company on June 30, 19X1, follows:

Assets		Liabilities and Stockholders' Equity	
Cash......................................	$ 20,000	Accounts payable	$140,000
Accounts receivable.................	80,000	Notes payable — State Bank....	60,000
Advances to Sun Co.	80,000	Wages payable.......................	2,500
Branch office current	60,000	Taxes payable........................	4,500
Investment in Sun Co.	75,000	Mortgage secured by plant and	
Plant and equipment...............	100,000	equipment	60,000
		Capital stock	100,000
		Retained earnings...................	48,000
Total	$415,000	Total	$415,000

It is assumed in the case of each business that accounts receivable and inventories will realize 60% of book value; plant and equipment items, 50% of book value.

Instructions: Prepare a statement of affairs for the Cummings Company, showing the probable amount available to creditors of this company upon liquidation. (Show all calculations that are required in support of your conclusions.)

18-6. The Peerless Corporation advises you that it is facing bankruptcy proceedings. As the company's CPA you are aware of its condition.

The balance sheet of the Peerless Corporation at June 30, 19X3, is shown on page 605.

Supplementary data:

   (1) Cash includes a $500 travel advance that has been expended.
   (2) Accounts receivable of $40,000 have been pledged in support of bank loans of $30,000. Credit balances of $5,000 are netted in the accounts receivable total.

Assets

Cash...	$ 2,000
Accounts receivable, less allowance for doubtful accounts	70,000
Inventory, finished goods..	60,000
Inventory, materials	40,000
Prepaid expenses..	5,000
Marketable securities..	20,000
Land...	13,000
Buildings, less accumulated depreciation.................................	90,000
Machinery, less accumulated depreciation................................	120,000
Goodwill..	20,000
Total assets...	$440,000

Liabilities and Stockholders' Equity

Accrued wages	$ 15,000
Accounts payable..	80,000
Notes payable...	135,000
Mortgages payable	130,000
Common stock...	100,000
Retained earnings (deficit)...	(20,000)
Total liabilities and stockholders' equity	$440,000

(3) Marketable securities consist of government bonds costing $10,000 and 500 shares of Bartlett Company stock. The market value of the bonds is $10,000, and the market value of the stock is $18 per share. The bonds have accrued interest due of $200. The securities are collateral for a $20,000 bank loan.

(4) Appraised value of materials is $30,000 and of finished goods is $50,000. For an additional cost of $10,000, the materials would realize $70,000 as finished goods.

(5) The appraised value of plant assets is: land, $25,000; buildings, $110,000; machinery, $75,000.

(6) Prepaid expenses will be exhausted during the liquidation period.

(7) Accounts payable include $15,000 of withheld payroll taxes and $6,000 owed to creditors who had been reassured by the president that they would be paid. There are unrecorded employer's payroll taxes in the amount of $500.

(8) Wages payable are not subject to any limitations under bankruptcy laws.

(9) Mortgages payable consist of $100,000 on land and buildings and a $30,000 chattel mortgage on machinery. Total unrecorded accrued interest for these mortgages amounted to $2,400.

(10) Estimated legal fees and expenses in connection with the liquidation are $10,000.

(11) Probable liability on judgment in a pending damage suit is $50,000.

(12) You have not rendered an invoice for $5,000 for last year's audit and you estimate a $1,000 fee for liquidation work.

Instructions: (1) Prepare a statement of affairs.
(2) Compute the estimated settlement per dollar of unsecured liabilities.

(AICPA adapted)

18-7. The Hardy Corporation is in financial difficulty because of low sales. Its stockholders and principal creditors want an estimate of the financial results of the liquidation of assets and liabilities and the dissolution of the corporation.

The corporation's post-closing trial balance on December 31, 19X8, is as follows:

Cash	1,000	
Accounts Receivable	20,500	
Allowance for Doubtful Accounts		350
Inventories	40,000	
Supplies	3,000	
Downhill Railroad 5% Bonds	5,000	
Accrued Bond Interest Receivable	750	
Advertising	6,000	
Land	4,000	
Building	30,000	
Accumulated Depreciation — Building		5,000
Machinery and Equipment	46,000	
Accumulated Depreciation — Machinery and Equipment		8,000
Accounts Payable		26,000
Notes Payable — Bank		25,000
Notes Payable — Officers		20,000
Payroll Taxes Payable		800
Wages Payable		1,500
Mortgage Payable		42,000
Mortgage Interest Payable		500
Capital Stock		50,000
Retained Earnings	29,100	
Appropriation for Product Guarantees		6,200
	185,350	185,350

The following information has been collected in anticipation of a meeting of the stockholders and the principal creditors to be held on January 2, 19X9:

(1) Cash includes a $300 protested check from a customer. The customer stated that the funds to honor the check would be available in about two weeks.

(2) Accounts receivable include accounts totaling $10,000 that are fully collectible and that have been assigned to the bank in connection with the notes payable. Included in the unassigned receivables is an uncollectible account of $150. The allowance for doubtful accounts of $350 now on the books will adequately provide for other uncollectible accounts.

(3) Purchase orders totaling $9,000 are on hand for the corporation's products. Inventory with a book value of $6,000 can be processed at an additional cost of $400 to fill these orders. The balance of the inventory, which includes obsolete materials with a book value of $1,200, can be sold for $10,500.

(4) In transit at December 31 but not recorded on the books was a shipment of defective merchandise being returned by a customer. The president of the corporation had authorized the return and the refund of the purchase price of $250 after the merchandise had been inspected. Other than this return, there is no other defective merchandise that

would bear upon the appropriation for product guarantees. The merchandise being returned has no salvage value.

(5) The supplies consist of advertising literature, brochures, and other sales aids. These could not be replaced for less than $3,700.

(6) The Downhill Railroad bonds are recorded at face value. The 50 bonds were purchased in 19X5 for $600, and the adjustment to face value was credited to Retained Earnings. At December 31, 19X8, the bonds were quoted at 18. (Accrued interest, if any, is included in quoted price.)

(7) The advertising account represents the future benefits of a 19X8 advertising campaign. Ten percent of certain advertising expenditures were placed in the account. The president stated that this amount was too conservative and that 20% would result in a more realistic measure of the market that was created.

(8) The land and the building are in a downtown area. A firm offer of $50,000 has been received for the land, which would be used as a parking lot; the building would be razed at a cost of $12,000 to the buyer. Another offer of $40,000 was received for the real estate, which the bidder stated would be used for manufacturing that would probably employ some Hardy employees.

(9) The highest of the offers received from used machinery dealers was $18,000 for all of the machinery and equipment.

(10) One creditor, whose account for $1,000 is included in the accounts payable, confirmed in writing that 90¢ on the dollar would be acceptable if the payment were made by January 10.

(11) Wages payable include year-end adjustments of $325 payable to certain factory employees for their overtime during the busy season.

(12) The mortgage payable is secured by the land and the building. The last two monthly principal payments of $200 each were not made.

(13) Estimated liquidation expenses amount to $3,200.

(14) For income tax purposes the corporation has the following net operating loss carryovers (tax rate, 50%):

19X6............	$10,000
19X7............	12,000
19X8............	8,000

Instructions: (1) Prepare a statement of affairs.

(2) Prepare a schedule that computes the estimated settlement per dollar of unsecured liabilities.

(AICPA adapted)

18-8. The Malone Company has been forced into bankruptcy as of April 30, 19X4. The balance sheet was prepared by the company bookkeeper as of April 30, 19X4, as shown on page 608.

Additional information:

(1) Of the total accounts receivable, $10,300 are believed to be good. The other accounts are doubtful, but it seems probable that 20% finally can be collected.

Assets

Cash..	$ 2,700
Accounts receivable...	39,350
Notes receivable...	18,500
Inventories:	
Finished machines..	12,000
Work in process...	35,100
Materials...	19,600
Supplies	6,450
Tools	14,700
Prepaid expenses...	950
Plant and equipment:	
Land...	20,000
Buildings	75,000
Machinery..	80,900
Total..	$325,250

Liabilities and Stockholders' Equity

Note payable to the First National Bank.....................................	$ 15,000
Notes payable to suppliers..	51,250
Accounts payable..	52,000
Accrued salaries and wages...	8,850
Accrued property taxes..	2,900
Employees' taxes withheld	1,150
Accrued payroll taxes	600
Accrued interest on bonds	1,800
First mortgage bonds payable..	90,000
Accumulated depreciation — buildings	33,750
Accumulated depreciation — machinery	32,100
Common stock ($100 par)...	75,000
Deficit	(39,150)
Total..	$325,250

(2) A total of $15,000 of the notes receivable has been pledged to secure the note payable to the First National Bank. All except $2,500 of these appear to be good. Interest of $800 is accrued on the $12,500 of good notes pledged and $300 is accrued on the $15,000 payable to the bank. The remaining notes are not considered collectible.

(3) The finished machines are expected to be sold for one third above their cost, but expenses in disposing of them will equal 20% of their sales price. Work in process can be completed at an additional cost of $15,400, of which $3,700 would be material used from the materials inventory. The work in process, when completed, will probably sell for $40,000 and selling expenses will be 20% of sales price. The materials not used will realize $8,000. Most of the value of tools consists of special items. After completion of work in process, the tools should sell for $3,000. The supplies inventory, which will not be needed to complete work, should sell for $1,000.

(4) Land and buildings are mortgaged as security for bonds. They have an appraised value of $95,000. The company recently purchased $20,000 of machinery on a conditional sales contract. It still owes $12,000 principal on this contract, which is included in the notes payable. These machines have a current used value of $10,000. Depreciation taken on these machines amounts to $1,800. The remaining machinery is believed to be salable at $10,000, but the cost of selling it may be $1,000.

Instructions: (1) **Prepare a statement of affairs, showing the estimated deficiency to unsecured creditors.**

(2) **Compute the percentage of probable payments to the $52,000 accounts payable.**

(AICPA adapted)

18-9. The Circle Furniture Co., Inc., has been finding it more and more difficult to meet its obligations. Although its sales volume appeared to be satisfactory and it was showing a profit, the requirements for capital for inventory and time contracts were greater than the company could provide. Finally, after pledging all of its installment accounts, it found itself unable to meet the bills falling due on October 10, 19X8. It is the opinion of the management that if it could obtain an extension of time in which to pay its obligations it could meet its liabilities in full. The corporation has arranged for a meeting of creditors to determine if the company should be granted an extension or be forced into bankruptcy.

The trial balance of the company on September 30, 19X8, is as follows:

Circle Furniture Co., Inc.
Trial Balance
September 30, 19X8

Cash on hand	500	
Cash in bank	1,620	
Installment contracts — pledged	215,000	
Allowance for doubtful contracts		13,440
Accounts receivable — 30-day	20,830	
Allowance for doubtful accounts		1,050
Inventories — January 1, 19X8	151,150	
Prepaid insurance	1,490	
Autos and trucks	22,380	
Accumulated depreciation — autos and trucks		14,960
Land	10,240	
Buildings	89,760	
Accumulated depreciation — buildings		7,530
Furniture and equipment	12,500	
Accumulated depreciation — furn. and equip.		2,140
Organization expense	880	
Trade accounts payable		132,100
Contract payable — furniture and equipment		5,800
Chattel mortgage on auto and trucks		10,000
Bank loan — secured by installment contracts		161,250
Taxes payable		14,220
Accrued salaries and wages		4,680
Accrued interest		10,990
Notes payable — stockholder		100,000
First mortgage payable		49,000
Capital stock		100,000
Retained earnings	65,290	
Sales		708,900
Purchases	527,630	
Expenses and miscellaneous income (net)	216,790	
	1,336,060	1,336,060

The following additional data are available:

(1) Depreciation, doubtful accounts, and prepaid and accrued items had all been adjusted as of September 30, 19X8.

(2) All installment contracts had been pledged with the bank on September 30, 19X8; the bank had deducted its interest to date and had increased the company loan to equal 75% of the face amount of the contracts in accordance with a loan agreement. It was estimated that a forced liquidation would result in a loss of $40,000 from the face amount of the contracts.

(3) Thirty-day accounts receivable were not pledged and it was estimated that they would provide $16,500 on a liquidation basis.

(4) It was estimated that since January 1, 19X8, the company had made a gross profit of 33⅓%, but that the inventories would provide only $100,000 on a forced liquidation.

(5) Cancellation of the insurance would provide $990.

(6) All the autos and trucks were covered by a chattel mortgage, and their total market value was $8,000.

(7) The store had been remodeled in 19X7 and the furniture and equipment had been acquired on contract. Because of its special nature, it was estimated that on a forced sale no more than $5,000 could be expected.

(8) The land and the buildings were subject to a 6% first mortgage on which interest had been paid to July 30, 19X8. It was estimated that the property could be sold for $75,000.

(9) The notes payable to stockholders had not been subordinated to general creditors. The notes carried a 6% rate of interest, but no interest had been paid since December 31, 19X6.

(10) Because prior income tax returns disclosed a large available net operating loss carryover, no current income tax need be considered.

(11) The cost of liquidation proceedings was estimated to be $5,000.

(12) There appeared to be no other values on liquidation and no unrecorded liabilities.

Instructions: (1) Prepare a statement of affairs.

(2) Prepare a statement of estimated deficiency to unsecured creditors.

(3) Compute the percentage of recovery by the unsecured creditors if the company were to be forced into liquidation.

(AICPA adapted)

18-10. The Allen-Barnes Partnership, of which Allen is manager, has had difficulty in meeting its obligations as the debts matured. The bookkeeper prepared the trial balance on April 15, 19X0, shown on page 611.

An analysis of the accounts revealed the following:

(1) Cash in First Bank, $8,000; in Second Bank, $12,000.

(2) Of the accounts receivable, 60% are good and fully collectible, 30% are doubtful and considered to be only 80% collectible, and the remaining 10% are worthless.

(3) All notes are good and are pledged as security on notes payable of $50,000 to the Factor House, with accrued interest of $500.

(4) Of the notes that were discounted at the Manning Bank, it is estimated that one amounting to $2,000 will not be paid at maturity or thereafter.

Cash...	20,000	
Accounts Receivable..	100,000	
Allowance for Doubtful Accounts...............................		4,000
Notes Receivable..	58,000	
Notes Receivable Discounted.....................................		12,000
Finished Goods..	15,000	
Work in Process..	20,000	
Materials	9,000	
Prepaid Insurance...	1,200	
Property Held in Trust...	18,000	
Land	12,000	
Building..	33,000	
Machinery and Equipment, cost	9,000	
Accumulated Depreciation...		6,000
Interest Receivable..	700	
Payroll Taxes Payable..		200
Real Estate Taxes		1,200
Wages Payable		3,450
Notes Payable		60,000
Accounts Payable		125,700
Mortgage Payable — 4%		40,000
Equipment Contract Payable (purchased on a conditional sales contract)...		6,400
Interest Payable		1,000
Allen, Capital..		15,975
Barnes, Capital..		1,975
Trust Principal..		18,000
	295,900	295,900

(5) All finished goods will be sold for 20% less than their cost. Work in process cannot be sold until finished and can be completed by incurring labor and material costs of $9,000, of which $3,000 will be from the materials inventory. The balance of the materials inventory will realize $5,000.

(6) The prepaid insurance, which expires October 15, has a short-term cancellation value of $900 on April 15.

(7) Property held in trust is in the form of stocks and bonds with realizable value of $24,000. The partnership is entitled to a fee of $600 per year, payable April 15, for their services. Cash was not available in the trust for the payment; therefore the fee was not recorded.

(8) The machinery and equipment with a book value of $8,000 will realize $5,000.

(9) The land and the building may be sold for $38,000; however the mortgage holder has indicated a willingness to cancel the debt and to assume all encumbrances for the surrender of title to the real estate. Interest on the mortgage was paid on January 15.

(10) Wages and commissions were last paid in full on December 31. Commission sales personnel were dismissed on February 15. Accrued wages in the trial balance are:

Bookkeeper (to April 15)	$1,400
Commission sales personnel (to February 15)	300
Allen, managing partner (to April 15)...............................	1,750
	$3,450

(11) The partnership owes the Second Bank a note of $10,000.

(12) The estimated administrative expenses are $3,000.

(13) Although Allen has personal liabilities that are approximately equal to personal assets, Barnes's personal assets exceed personal liabilities by $2,800.

Instructions: (1) Prepare a statement in good form, showing the estimated deficiency, if any, to unsecured creditors.

(2) Prepare a statement showing the estimated amounts available for each class of creditors.

(AICPA adapted)

18-11. Using the data in Problem 18-1 for the McKinney Company, prepare a statement of affairs in the alternative form.

18-12. Using the data in Problem 18-2 for Barker Company, prepare a statement of affairs in the alternative form.

19
Insolvency –
Administration

When an insolvent individual or organization cannot reach a mutually satisfactory settlement with creditors, legal remedies may be sought through the courts. Either the insolvent debtor or the creditors may apply to a federal bankruptcy court or to a state court of equity for the appointment of a trustee, an assignee, or a receiver to take charge of the insolvent's business.

Upon recognizing the need for protection of creditors, owners, or others having an interest in the business and after application by such parties, the courts will appoint a person to assume control of the assets of an insolvent individual or a company. Such authority is assumed by state and federal courts under powers granted by statute or under the common law. During the period of insolvency, the debtor is removed from control, and the usual rights of creditors to legal action are suspended. The appointee of the court, operating under the laws relating to insolvency and under instructions of the court, acts in a fiduciary capacity to protect the equities and the rights of the different parties.

The title given the court appointee may vary with the particular court having jurisdiction. In federal bankruptcy cases, an independent party designated to administer the affairs of an insolvent is referred to as a *trustee*. On the other hand, it is quite common for the debtor to be permitted to continue operating the business under the supervision of the court, who designates the insolvent as a *debtor in possession*. State courts often appoint a *receiver* or *assignee* to administer the affairs of an insolvent.

The qualifications, duties, and responsibilities of the assignee, trustee, debtor in possession, or receiver are quite similar. Each person must maintain records to show the course of operations, reorganization, or dissolution. The standards and the procedures that are considered in this chapter are applicable in the case of any person who may be placed in charge of the assets of a debtor. For simplicity and convenience, however, such appointees will be referred to as trustees.

Although a trustee is ordinarily appointed to direct liquidation and set-tlement with creditors, the trustee is frequently appointed with the expectation that financial solvency may be restored and properties returned to the control of former owners. The trustee assumes control of the assets, converts some or all of these assets into cash, and compromises and pays off claims. Significant decisions are made only with the advice and the approval of the court having jurisdiction. When rehabilitation of the business is effected, the trustee returns the property to its original management.

If solvency cannot be restored by continuing operations of the properties, the trustee may attempt a reorganization of the business, reducing in part or in whole the debtor's equity. If this process appears inexpedient or proves unsuccessful, assets are sold and creditors are paid off in accordance with their legal rights.

TRUSTEE'S REPORTS

During the trustee's administration, reports of operations are required at regular intervals by the court, creditors, owners, and perhaps governmental agencies and other interested groups. A specific system of accounting is not usually prescribed by law or by the courts. However, a system should be designed that will provide all of the data required in reporting to the different parties. The trustee's activities must be fully accounted for in order to prove that all responsibilities have been properly and faithfully fulfilled.

Upon assuming control, the trustee submits to the court a list of the assets taken over as authorized by court order. Creditors may request a statement of affairs at this time. Thereafter interim statements of position and operations, supported by schedules summarizing receipts, disbursements, and other significant data, are required. Reports that cover the entire period of stewardship are required upon termination of control.

Insolvency activities normally call for the adoption of a double-entry system of bookkeeping. Ordinarily, separate books are maintained by the trustee unless liquidation is to take place immediately, in which case the old books may be used to record the winding up process.

When separate books are maintained, these ordinarily report the transactions to which the trustee is a party. Eventually, these transactions are summarized and entered on the debtor's books. The trustee's records are used in preparing periodic summaries of operations. However, in the preparation of financial statements for the business unit as a whole, it will be necessary to combine the account balances on the trustee's books and on the debtor's books.

Whether the company books are continued or a new set of books is opened by the trustee, a careful distinction should be maintained in the records between original assets and liabilities and those emerging in the course of bankruptcy proceedings. A distinction between original assets taken over by the trustee and new assets acquired is necessary as a result of the difference in the trustee's responsibilities with respect to the two classes of assets. In the case of new assets, the trustee's responsibilities embrace both their acquisition and their realization; in the case of original assets, the trustee's responsibilities are limited only to their realization. In the case of new receivables, for example, the trustee must exercise satisfactory diligence both in granting credit and in realizing such claims. In the case of old receivables, however, losses arising from an unsound credit policy of the past cannot be attributed to the trustee. The responsibilities of the trustee with respect to old and new debt are also different. In the case of new debt, the trustee is responsible both for its incurrence and for its appropriate liquidation. In the case of original debt, the trustee is responsible only for its settlement in accordance with the instructions by appropriate authority. New debt may also have certain legal preferences over old debt, calling for a clear distinction between the two classes of debt in the accounts.

TRUSTEESHIP ACCOUNTS

When the trustee maintains a set of books summarizing bankruptcy activities, transactions are recorded on the separate trustee's books and on the books of the debtor in the manner described in the following paragraphs.

Assumption of Control by Trustee

Trustee's books. When a trustee is appointed by a court, title to part or all of the assets of the debtor is granted to the trustee. The trustee debits the appropriate asset accounts for those assets transferred by the court action and credits the debtor company. The account with the company summarizes the extent of the trustee's accountability to the debtor. Ordinarily the values of the assets on the company books are retained for purposes of the trustee's books. When both an asset account and a valuation account are shown for a property item, both the asset and the valuation account balances are established on the trustee's books. Assets taken over and to be realized may be designated "Old" to distinguish them from assets that are subsequently acquired by the trustee. Ordinarily, existing obligations of the debtor are not transferred but are left on the debtor's books; however, any liabilities emerging from the trustee's activities are recorded on the trustee's books. A distinction is thus maintained between original obligations and those incurred by the trustee.

Debtor's books. On the debtor's books, asset accounts are credited, and valuation accounts are debited for all assets taken over by the trustee. A reciprocal account with the trustee is debited. This reciprocal account summarizes the net assets of the debtor that are reported on the trustee's books.

Operations by the Trustee

Trustee's books. The trustee records transactions in the usual manner, with the following exceptions:

(1) When liabilities existing prior to the bankruptcy proceedings appear on the original books, payment of such liabilities by the trustee should be reported by a debit to the debtor account balance and a credit to Cash. However, instead of reducing the debtor balance directly, the charge is normally made to a temporary account with the debtor, such as "Debtor's Liability Paid — Accounts Payable, Old." The trustee's books then offer full data relating to the settlement of the debtor's obligations. Account balances reporting the payment of debts are closed into the debtor's account at the end of the period.

(2) Losses and gains that have accrued prior to the appointment of the trustee should be identified with the debtor. Such losses and gains can be recorded directly in the debtor's account, with the losses and gains recognized in nominal accounts on the debtor's books. However, instead of transferring such items to the debtor's books, the losses or gains are normally recorded on the trustee's books in nominal accounts identified with the debtor, such as "Debtor — Uncollectible Accounts Expense, Old," and "Debtor — Gain on Sale of Securities." These balances are closed into the trustee's income summary account at the end of the period.

(3) The trustee's appointment is a charge to administer and realize the assets of the debtor. The trustee thus takes credit for the proceeds from asset realization as well as any revenue emerging during the course of administration, including rental income, interest income, and dividend income. The trustee, however, is not charged with responsibility for the obligations that were assumed by the debtor. Payment of original indebtedness, as well as interest expense, penalties, and debt call premiums, are made by the trustee only upon orders by appropriate authority. Under the circumstances, any charges relating to the old indebtedness are identified with the debtor and are not recognized in the evaluation of the trustee's activities. As in the case of losses in (2), charges arising from an old debt can be transferred to the debtor's books. Oridinarily, however, such charges are recorded on the trustee's books in nominal accounts identified with the debtor, such as "Debtor — Interest Expense on Mortgage." These balances, too, are closed into the trustee's income summary account at the end of the period.

Debtor's books. The books of the debtor are not affected by the trustee's transactions that are reported in the usual manner in the trustee's books. For transactions in the three special classes mentioned, the following procedures are used:

(1) The discharge of obligations reflected on the debtor's books is normally recorded as soon as payment is made by the trustee. Data concerning the unpaid balances of original obligations are thus available at any time. Payment of an obligation by the trustee is recorded by a debit to the liability account and a credit to the trustee's account. When this practice is followed, the balance of the debtor's account on the trustee's books will not be the same as the balance of the trustee's account on the debtor's books until the

　　　trustee closes the balances in the debtor's liability paid accounts into the debtor's account at the end of the period.

(2)　When losses and gains are identified with the debtor rather than with bankruptcy activities and are recorded directly in the debtor's account by the trustee, such items are recorded on the debtor's books by entries to appropriate loss or gain accounts, with an offsetting entry to the trustee's account. The debtor's account on the trustee's books and the trustee's account on the debtor's books will be reciprocal, then, insofar as such items are concerned. However, when the trustee maintains a special class of nominal accounts for such special losses and gains, their recognition on the debtor's books is deferred until all activities are summarized at the end of the period.

(3)　When charges on old obligations are incurred by the trustee and are recorded directly in the debtor's account by the trustee, such items would be recorded on the debtor's books in a manner similar to that explained in (2). When such expenses are reported in special nominal accounts on the trustee's books, their recognition on the debtor's books is deferred until all activities are summarized at the end of the period.

Adjusting and Closing the Books

Trustee's books. The trustee's accounts are adjusted and closed at periodic intervals and also just before control is returned to the original owners. Adjustments are made in the usual manner. Revenue and expense accounts relating to trusteeship operations are closed into an income summary account in ascertaining the net income or loss identified with the trustee's administration. When special debtor loss, gain, and expense balances are reported on the trustee's books, they are closed into the income summary account, and the balance in the latter account reflects the net change in capital for the period. The balance in the income summary account is transferred to the debtor's account. Balances in debtor's liability paid accounts are also closed into the debtor's account at this time.

Debtor's books. An increase in capital as summarized on the trustee's books is recognized by a debit to the trustee's account and a credit to the appropriate capital account. A decrease would be recorded by a debit to the capital balance and a credit to the trustee's account. The debtor's account on the trustee's books and the trustee's account on the debtor's books are now reciprocal. When nominal accounts summarizing special income items are reported on the debtor's books, they too are transferred to capital.

Return of Control to Debtor

Trustee's books. Upon return of control to the debtor, the debtor's account, the asset valuation accounts, and the liability accounts are debited and the asset accounts are credited. The books of the trustee are then closed.

Debtor's books. When assets are returned to the debtor and liabilities incurred by the trustee are assumed by the debtor, the asset accounts are debited and the asset valuation accounts, the liability accounts, and the trustee's account are credited.

STATEMENTS PREPARED BY THE TRUSTEE

A balance sheet and an income statement for a business in bankruptcy are required periodically by the various interested parties. Such statements can be prepared only by combining account balances reported on the books of the trustee and on the books of the debtor. Trial balances for the trustee's books and the debtor's books before adjusting and closing are first prepared. Balances of the accounts in both sets of books are then combined by means of a work sheet.

A work sheet may include columns for adjustments and for eliminations. Accounts are brought up to date in the adjustment columns. The elimination columns are used in eliminating the reciprocal accounts by offsetting the balance of the trustee's account on the books of the debtor against the debtor's account on the books of the trustee. If the balances of the debtor's liability paid accounts in the trustee's books have not been closed into the account with the debtor, the balance of the trustee's account on the debtor's books must be offset against the combined balances of the debtor account and the debtor's liability paid accounts on the trustee's books. Account balances are now extended to the statement columns. Revenue, gain, expense, and loss balances are carried to the income statement columns. Asset, liability, and capital balances are carried to the balance sheet columns. The net change in capital as a result of trusteeship operations is calculated and the income statement and balance sheet columns on the work sheet are brought into balance. The work sheet is then used for the preparation of financial statements.

The balance sheet is prepared in its usual form. In preparing the income statement, a distinction is normally made between expense and revenue items identified with the trustee and similar items identified with the debtor. Presentation of the net income or loss from trusteeship operations may be followed by a summary of debtor revenue and expense items.

ACCOUNTING FOR TRUSTEESHIP ILLUSTRATED

To illustrate the entries on the books of the trustee and the debtor and the preparation of financial statements to summarize trusteeship operations, assume that the Miles Corporation is unable to meet current obligations as they mature, and I.B. Owens is appointed as trustee on March 31, 19X7. Creditors and stockholders agree that an attempt should be made to rehabilitate the business. If this proves unsuccessful, the trustee is to sell the business assets, pay off the creditors, and distribute remaining funds to the stockholders. The trustee is authorized to take over all of the business assets. A balance sheet prepared just prior to appointment of the trustee appears below.

Miles Corporation
Balance Sheet
March 31, 19X7

Assets

Current assets:

Cash...		$ 1,000
Notes receivable..		15,000
Accounts receivable..	$ 25,000	
Less allowance for doubtful accounts....................	1,000	24,000
Accrued interest on notes receivable......................		150
Merchandise inventory		50,000
Total current assets		$ 90,150

Investments:

Common stock of X Co..	$ 16,000	
Preferred stock of Y Co..	4,000	
Total investments		20,000

Plant and equipment:

Land		$15,000	
Buildings	$60,000		
Less accumulated depreciation	7,800	52,200	
Furniture and fixtures...............................	$ 6,000		
Less accumulated depreciation	1,950	4,050	
Total plant and equipment.......................................			71,250
Total assets...			$181,400

Liabilities and Stockholders' Equity

Liabilities

Current liabilities:

Notes payable		$ 35,000
Accounts payable		30,000
Accrued interest on notes payable............................		250
Accrued interest on mortgage		400
Total current liabilities		$ 65,650

Long-term debt:

6% First mortgage payable		40,000
Total liabilities...		$105,650

Stockholders' Equity

Capital stock	$100,000	
Less deficit	24,250	
Total stockholders' equity..		75,750
Total liabilities and stockholders' equity........................		$181,400

The transactions and the entries on the books of the trustee and the corporation during the period of trusteeship are shown on pages 620 to 627.

A work sheet is prepared at the end of the year in developing the financial statements. The work sheet is shown on pages 628 and 629. The income statement prepared from this work sheet is given on page 630. The balance sheet is given on page 631.

Transaction

Assumption of Control by the Trustee
March 31, 19X7

(1) Assets taken over by trustee:

Cash..		$ 1,000
Notes receivable..		15,000
Accounts receivable	$25,000	
Less allowance for doubtful accounts..........................	1,000	24,000
Accrued interest on notes receivable..............................		150
Merchandise inventory		50,000
Common stock of X Co...		16,000
Preferred stock of Y Co..		4,000
Land		15,000
Buildings	$60,000	
Less accumulated depreciation	7,800	52,200
Furniture and fixtures...	$ 6,000	
Less accumulated depreciation	1,950	4,050
		$181,400

Operations of the Trustee
March 31–December 31

(2) Sales on account... $210,000

---

(3) Purchases on account $112,000

---

(4) Accounts receivable (new) were reduced by the following:

Cash collections	$158,500
Notes received in payment..	30,000
Sales returns and allowances	1,500
Sales discounts allowed...	2,000
	$192,000

---

(5) Collection on accounts receivable, old, $22,000; remaining accounts were written off as uncollectible.

---

(6) Collection on notes receivable, old, $15,000, and interest, $450.

---

(7) Collection on notes receivable (new), $18,000, and interest, $200.

Trustee's Books		Corporation's Books	
Cash...............................	1,000	I. B. Owens, Trustee	181,400
Notes Receivable, Old...........	15,000	Allowance for Doubtful Ac-	
Accounts Receivable, Old......	25,000	counts.................................	1,000
Accrued Interest on Notes		Accumulated Depreciation of	
Receivable, Old....................	150	Buildings.............................	7,800
Merchandise Inventory..........	50,000	Accumulated Depreciation of	
Common Stock of X Co.	16,000	Furniture and Fixtures	1,950
Preferred Stock of Y Co.	4,000	Cash.................................	1,000
Land...................................	15,000	Notes Receivable...............	15,000
Buildings............................	60,000	Accounts Receivable..........	25,000
Furniture and Fixtures	6,000	Accrued Interest on Notes	
Allowance for Doubtful Ac-		Receivable.......................	150
counts.............................	1,000	Merchandise Inventory.......	50,000
Accumulated Depreciation		Common Stock of X Co.	16,000
of Buildings	7,800	Preferred Stock of Y Co......	4,000
Accumulated Depreciation		Land	15,000
of Furniture and Fixtures....	1,950	Buildings...........................	60,000
Miles Corp., Debtor............	181,400	Furniture and Fixtures	6,000
Accounts Receivable............. 210,000			
Sales................................	210,000		
Purchases 112,000			
Accounts Payable..............	112,000		
Cash................................... 158,500			
Notes Receivable.................	30,000		
Sales Returns and Allowances	1,500		
Sales Discount.....................	2,000		
Accounts Receivable..........	192,000		
Cash...................................	22,000		
Allowance for Doubtful Ac-			
counts, Old..........................	1,000		
Corporation — Uncollectible			
Accounts Expense, Old	2,000		
Accounts Receivable, Old...	25,000		
Cash...................................	15,450		
Notes Receivable, Old........	15,000		
Accrued Interest on Notes			
Receivable, Old	150		
Interest Income.................	300		
Cash...................................	18,200		
Notes Receivable..............	18,000		
Interest Income.................	200		

Transaction

(8) Accounts payable (new) were reduced by the following:

Cash payments...	$ 46,000
Notes issued in payment..	40,000
Purchases returns and allowances...............................	1,500
Purchases discounts received	2,500
	$ 90,000

(9) Payment of accounts payable, old... $ 30,000

(10) Payment of notes payable, old, $35,000, and interest, $950.

(11) Payment of notes payable (new), $15,000, and interest, $300.

(12) Sale of securities:

	Book Value	Amount Realized
Common stock of X Co..	$16,000	$ 8,500
Preferred stock of Y Co..	4,000	4,500
	$20,000	$13,000

(13) Payment of operating expenses:

Sales salaries	$ 22,000
Other selling expense..	18,600
Office expense..	8,000
Other general expense...	12,000
Trustee fees...	6,500
	$ 67,100

Adjusting Entries,
December 31

(14) To transfer beginning merchandise inventory to Income Summary, $50,000.

(15) To record ending inventory, $36,000.

(16) To provide for doubtful accounts (new accounts), $450.

Trustee's Books			Corporation's Books		
Accounts Payable	90,000				
Cash		46,000			
Notes Payable		40,000			
Purchases Returns and Allowances		1,500			
Purchases Discount		2,500			
Corporation Liability Paid — Accounts Payable, Old	30,000		Accounts Payable	30,000	
Cash		30,000	I. B. Owens, Trustee		30,000
Corporation Liability Paid — Notes Payable, Old	35,000		Notes Payable	35,000	
Corporation Liability Paid — Accrued Interest on Notes Payable, Old	250		Accrued Interest on Notes Payable	250	
Corporation — Interest Expense on Notes Payable, Old..	700		I. B. Owens, Trustee		35,250
Cash		35,950			
Notes Payable	15,000				
Interest Expense	300				
Cash		15,300			
Cash	13,000				
Corporation — Loss on Sale of X Co. Stock	7,500				
Common Stock, X Co.		16,000			
Preferred Stock, Y Co.		4,000			
Corporation — Gain on Sale of Y Co. Stock		500			
Sales Salaries Expense	22,000				
Other Selling Expense	18,600				
Office Expense	8,000				
Other General Expense	12,000				
Trustee Fees	6,500				
Cash		67,100			
Income Summary	50,000				
Merchandise Inventory		50,000			
Merchandise Inventory	36,000				
Income Summary		36,000			
Uncollectible Accounts Expense	450				
Allowance for Doubtful Accounts		450			

Transaction		
To record depreciation: (17) Furniture and fixtures...	$	450
To record depreciation: (18) Buildings..	$	1,800
(19) To record accrued interest on notes receivable..........................	$	200
(20) To record accrued interest on notes payable (new).....................	$	300
(21) To record accrued interest on mortgage...................................	$	1,800

Closing Entries,
December 31

(22) To close trustee's revenue and expense accounts into the income summary account.

(23) To close corporation expense, loss, and gain accounts into the income summary account.

Trustee's Books		Corporation's Books
Depreciation of Furniture and Fixtures..............................	450	
Accumulated Depreciation of Furniture and Fixtures....	450	
Depreciation of Buildings	1,800	
Accumulated Depreciation of Buildings	1,800	
Accrued Interest on Notes Receivable...........................	200	
Interest Income.................	200	
Interest Expense	300	
Accrued Interest on Notes Payable	300	
Corporation — Interest Expense on Mortgage, Old.........	1,800	
Accrued Interest on Mortgage................................	1,800	
Sales.....................................	210,000	
Purchases Returns and Allowances..................................	1,500	
Purchases Discount..............	2,500	
Interest Income....................	700	
Sales Returns and Allowances...............................	1,500	
Purchases	112,000	
Sales Salaries Expense.......	22,000	
Other Selling Expense........	18,600	
Office Expense..................	8,000	
Depreciation of Furniture and Fixtures.....................	450	
Depreciation of Buildings ...	1,800	
Uncollectible Accounts Expense...............................	450	
Other General Expense.......	12,000	
Trustee Fees.....................	6,500	
Sales Discount..................	2,000	
Interest Expense	600	
Income Summary	28,800	
Income Summary	11,500	
Corporation — Gain on Sale of Y Co. Stock	500	
Corporation — Interest Expense on Notes, Old...........	700	
Corporation — Interest Expense on Mortgage, Old......	1,800	
Corporation — Uncollectible Accounts Expense.......	2,000	
Corporation — Loss on Sale of X Co. Stock	7,500	

Transaction
(24) To record increase in retained earnings for the nine-month period.
(25) To close corporation liabilities paid accounts.

Return of Control to Debtor,
January 2, 19X8

(26) Assets and liabilities returned to corporation:

Cash..		$ 33,800
Notes receivable...		12,000
Accounts receivable...	$18,000	
Less allowance for doubtful accounts...........................	450	17,550
Accrued interest on notes receivable...............................		200
Merchandise inventory...		36,000
Land		15,000
Buildings	$60,000	
Less accumulated depreciation	9,600	50,400
Furniture and fixtures...	$ 6,000	
Less accumulated depreciation	2,400	3,600
Total assets..		$168,550
Notes payable		$ 25,000
Accounts payable		22,000
Accrued interest on notes payable..................................		300
Accrued interest on mortgage		1,800
Total liabilities...		$ 49,100

Trustee's Books		Corporation's Books	
Income Summary 3,300		I. B. Owens, Trustee 3,300	
Miles Corp., Debtor............	3,300	Retained Earnings.............	3,300

Trustee's Books		Corporation's Books	
Miles Corp., Debtor.............. 65,250			
Corporation Liability			
Paid — Accounts Payable,			
Old	30,000		
Corporation Liability			
Paid — Notes Payable, Old.	35,000		
Corporation Liability			
Paid — Accrued Interest on			
Notes Payable, Old	250		

Trustee's Books		Corporation's Books	
Miles Corp., Debtor.............. 119,450		Cash 33,800	
Notes Payable...................... 25,000		Notes Receivable.................. 12,000	
Accounts Payable................. 22,000		Accounts Receivable............. 18,000	
Accrued Interest on Notes		Accrued Interest on Notes	
Payable...............................	300	Receivable...........................	200
Accrued Interest on Mortgage	1,800	Merchandise Inventory.......... 36,000	
Allowance for Doubtful Ac-		Land.................................... 15,000	
counts................................	450	Buildings............................. 60,000	
Accumulated Depreciation of		Furniture and Fixtures 6,000	
Buildings.............................	9,600	Notes Payable..................	25,000
Accumulated Depreciation of		Accounts Payable..............	22,000
Furniture and Fixtures	2,400	Accrued Interest on Notes	
Cash	33,800	Payable............................	300
Notes Receivable..............	12,000	Accrued Interest on Mort-	
Accounts Receivable..........	18,000	gage................................	1,800
Accrued Interest on Notes		Allowance for Doubtful Ac-	
Receivable.........................	200	counts.............................	450
Merchandise Inventory.......	36,000	Accumulated Depreciation	
Land..................................	15,000	of Buildings	9,600
Buildings...........................	60,000	Accumulated Depreciation	
Furniture and Fixtures	6,000	of Furniture and Fixtures....	2,400
		I. B. Owens, Trustee	119,450

Miles Corporation,
Work Sheet,

	Trial Balances	
	Dr.	Cr.
Corporation's Books		
I. B. Owens, Trustee	116,150	....
Accrued Interest on Mortgage	....	400
6% First Mortgage Payable	....	40,000
Capital Stock	....	100,000
Retained Earnings	24,250	....
Trustee's Books		
Cash	33,800	....
Notes Receivable	12,000	....
Accounts Receivable	18,000	....
Merchandise Inventory	50,000	....
Land	15,000	....
Buildings	60,000	....
Accumulated Depreciation of Buildings	....	7,800
Furniture and Fixtures	6,000	....
Accumulated Depreciation of Furniture and Fixtures	....	1,950
Notes Payable	....	25,000
Accounts Payable	....	22,000
Miles Corporation, Debtor	....	181,400
Sales	....	210,000
Sales Returns and Allowances	1,500	....
Sales Discount	2,000	....
Purchases	112,000	....
Purchases Returns and Allowances	....	1,500
Purchases Discount	....	2,500
Sales Salaries Expense	22,000	....
Other Selling Expense	18,600	....
Office Expense	8,000	....
Other General Expense	12,000	....
Trustee Fees	6,500	....
Interest Income	....	500
Interest Expense	300	....
Corporation — Interest Expense on Notes, Old	700	....
Corporation — Uncollectible Accounts Expense, Old	2,000	....
Corporation — Loss on Sale of X Co. Stock	7,500	....
Corporation — Gain on Sale of Y Co. Stock	....	500
Corporation Liability Paid — Accounts Payable, Old	30,000	....
Corporation Liability Paid — Notes Payable, Old	35,000	....
Corporation Liability Paid — Accrued Interest on Notes Payable, Old	250	....
	593,550	593,550
Income Summary	....	....
Uncollectible Accounts Expense	....	....
Allowance for Doubtful Accounts	....	....
Depreciation of Furniture and Fixtures	....	....
Depreciation of Buildings	....	....
Accrued Interest on Notes Receivable	....	....
Accrued Interest on Notes Payable	....	....
Corporation — Interest Expense on Mortgage, Old	....	....
Increase in Retained Earnings	....	....

Debtor
December 31, 19X7

Adjustments		Eliminations		Income Statement		Balance Sheet	
Dr.	Cr.	Dr.	Cr.	Dr.	Cr.	Dr.	Cr.
....	....	....	116,150	....	....	....	....
....	(21) 1,800	....	....	....	....	....	2,200
....	....	....	....	....	....	....	40,000
....	....	....	....	....	....	....	100,000
....	....	....	....	....	....	24,250	....
....	....	....	....	....	....	33,800	....
....	....	....	....	....	....	12,000	....
....	....	....	....	....	....	18,000	....
(15)36,000	(14)50,000	....	....	....	....	36,000	....
....	....	....	....	....	....	15,000	....
....	....	....	....	....	....	60,000	....
....	(18) 1,800	....	....	....	....	....	9,600
....	....	....	....	....	....	6,000	....
....	(17) 450	....	....	....	....	....	2,400
....	....	....	....	....	....	....	25,000
....	....	....	....	....	....	....	22,000
....	....	181,400	....	....	....	....	....
....	....	....	....	....	210,000	....	....
....	....	....	....	1,500	....	....	....
....	....	....	....	2,000	....	....	....
....	....	....	....	112,000	....	....	....
....	....	....	....	....	1,500	....	....
....	....	....	....	....	2,500	....	....
....	....	....	....	22,000	....	....	....
....	....	....	....	18,600	....	....	....
....	....	....	....	8,000	....	....	....
....	....	....	....	12,000	....	....	....
....	....	....	....	6,500	....	....	....
....	(19) 200	....	....	....	700	....	....
(20) 300	....	....	....	600	....	....	....
....	....	....	....	700	....	....	....
....	....	....	....	2,000	....	....	....
....	....	....	....	7,500	....	....	....
....	....	....	....	....	500	....	....
....	....	....	30,000	....	....	....	....
....	....	....	35,000	....	....	....	....
....	....	....	250	....	....	....	....
(14)50,000	(15)36,000	....	....	50,000	36,000	....	....
(16) 450	....	....	....	450	....	....	....
....	(16) 450	....	....	....	....	....	450
(17) 450	....	....	....	450	....	....	....
(18) 1,800	....	....	....	1,800	....	....	....
(19) 200	....	....	....	....	....	200	....
....	(20) 300	....	....	....	....	....	300
(21) 1,800	....	....	....	1,800	....	....	....
91,000	91,000	181,400	181,400				
				247,900	251,200	205,250	201,950
....	....	....	....	3,300			3,300
				251,200	251,200	205,250	205,250

Miles Corporation, Debtor
I. B. Owens, Trustee
Income Statement
March 31–December 31, 19X7

Gross sales..			$210,000
Less: Sales returns and allowances..		$ 1,500	
Sales discount		2,000	3,500
Net sales			$206,500
Cost of goods sold:			
Merchandise inventory, March 31, 19X7....................................		$ 50,000	
Purchases..	$112,000		
Less: Purchases returns and allowances............. $1,500			
Purchases discount 2,500	4,000	108,000	
Merchandise available for sale..		$158,000	
Less merchandise inventory, December 31, 19X7......................		36,000	122,000
Gross profit..			$ 84,500
Operating expenses:			
Selling expenses:			
Sales salaries expense...		$ 22,000	
Other selling expense		18,600	$ 40,600
General expenses:			
Office expense...		$ 8,000	
Depreciation of furniture and fixtures..................................		450	
Depreciation of buildings..		1,800	
Uncollectible accounts expense		450	
Other general expense..		12,000	
Trustee fees..		6,500	29,200	69,800
Operating income			$ 14,700
Other revenue and expense items:			
Interest income		$ 700	
Interest expense..		600	100
Income from trustee's operations			$ 14,800
Corporation revenue and expense items:			
Corporation expenses:			
Interest expense on notes, old.......................... $ 700			
Interest expense on mortgage, old 1,800	$ 2,500		
Corporation losses:			
Uncollectible accounts expense, old $2,000			
Loss on sale of X Co. stock............................ 7,500	9,500		
Total corporation expenses and losses.......................................		$ 12,000	
Less corporation gains:			
Gain on sale of Y Co. stock..		500	
Net corporation loss..			11,500
Increase in retained earnings			$ 3,300

Miles Corporation, Debtor
I. B. Owens, Trustee
Balance Sheet
December 31, 19X7

Assets

Current assets:		
Cash...		$ 33,800
Notes receivable..		12,000
Accounts receivable...	$ 18,000	
Less allowance for doubtful accounts................................	450	17,550
Accrued interest on notes receivable.................................		200
Merchandise inventory		36,000
Total current assets		$ 99,550
Plant and equipment:		
Land	$15,000	
Buildings	$60,000	
Less accumulated depreciation	9,600	50,400
Furniture and fixtures..	$ 6,000	
Less accumulated depreciation	2,400	3,600
Total plant and equipment..		69,000
Total assets...		$168,550

Liabilities and Stockholders' Equity

Liabilities

Current liabilities:		
Notes payable		$ 25,000
Accounts payable		22,000
Accrued interest on notes payable....................................		300
Accrued interest on mortgage		2,200
Total current liabilities		$ 49,500
Long-term debt:		
6% First mortgage payable		40,000
Total liabilities...		$ 89,500

Stockholders' Equity

Capital stock...	$100,000	
Less deficit	20,950	
Total stockholders' equity		79,050
Total liabilities and stockholders' equity		$168,550

QUESTIONS

1. (a) Describe the nature of the debtor in possession. (b) What are the duties of a trustee?

2. Describe the accounting system that must be employed by an appointee of a court who is to take charge of a debtor's assets.

3. What reports and statements are required of the trustee by a court?

4. What circumstances should be considered in determining whether a trustee should continue with the use of original company books or should establish a new set of books to summarize trusteeship activities?

5. In accounting for a bankruptcy trustee, why are distinctions made between:

    (a) Assets originally acquired by the company and assets subsequently acquired by the trustee?

    (b) Liabilities originally incurred by the company and liabilities subsequently incurred by the trustee?

    (c) Revenue and expense items related to the company and revenue and expense items related to the trustee?

6. When separate books are to be maintained by the trustee, what entries would be made on the books of the trustee and on the books of the corporation for each of the following transactions?

    (a) The trustee takes over certain assets of the company.

    (b) The trustee converts assets taken over into cash.

    (c) The trustee pays off corporation debts.

    (d) The trustee distributes remaining cash to stockholders in the form of a dividend in final liquidation.

7. Give two alternative procedures that may be followed on both the company's books and the trustee's books for the payment of interest on indebtedness originally incurred by the company.

8. What entry would be made on the books of the Success Corporation and on the separate books of trustee M. A. Turner for each of the following transactions of the trustee?

    (a) Took over control of the corporate assets.

    (b) Sold merchandise on account.

    (c) Received payment on accounts receivable, old.

    (d) Received payment on accounts receivable, new.

    (e) Wrote off worthless accounts, old, against allowance established prior to trusteeship.

    (f) Received payment on notes receivable, old, and interest earned prior to trusteeship.

    (g) Received interest on securities held by the corporation as an investment.

    (h) Sold part of the securities held at a loss.

    (i) Purchased merchandise on account.

    (j) Paid accounts payable, new.

    (k) Paid mortgage note and accrued interest on the note, part of the interest having accrued prior to trusteeship.

    (l) Paid expenses of trusteeship.

    (m) Paid remaining operating expenses.

    (n) Adjusted the accounts for the following items prior to return of the corporate assets to the former management:

        (1) Ending inventory.

        (2) Accrued interest on securities held.

        (3) Depreciation on furniture and equipment.   *(continued)*

(4) Accrued operating expenses.

(5) Provision for doubtful accounts on accounts receivable, new.

(6) Prepaid operating expenses.

9. (a) What entries are made in closing revenue and expense items on the trustee's books at the end of the period? (b) What entries are made on the company books in recognizing the results of trusteeship activities and in closing revenue and expense items that are reflected on the company books?

10. Assuming that financial solvency is restored and a trustee returns a business to the control of its original owners, what entries would be made on the books of the trustee and on the books of the company upon such a transfer?

11. Assuming that financial solvency cannot be restored and a trustee makes payment to all of the creditors according to the terms of a composition, what entries would be made on the books of the trustee and on the books of the company in recording the settlement and corporate dissolution?

12. What special procedures are followed in combining debtor and trustee account balances in the preparation of financial statements at the end of the period?

EXERCISES

1. Prepare the entries that would appear on the separate books of Ruth Parks, bankruptcy trustee for the Madison Co., in recording the following transactions. Assets were transferred to the trustee's books, but original liabilities were left on the company records.

(a) Merchandise is purchased for $15,000, with trustee's certificates of indebtedness issued for such goods.

(b) Sales on account are $80,000.

(c) Company accounts payable of $12,000 are paid.

(d) Trustee's certificates of $8,500 are paid.

(e) Collections on company accounts receivable of $14,000 are made; accounts totaling $1,500 prove worthless and are written off.

(f) Collections on trustee's accounts of $46,000 are made; accounts totaling $650 prove worthless and are written off.

(g) Company notes payable of $15,000 and accrued interest of $450 are paid; the company books report a liability for accrued interest of $150 as of the date of the last closing.

(h) Furniture and fixtures with a cost of $10,000 and a book value of $6,000 are sold for $5,600.

2. The bankruptcy trustee for the Monarch Co. keeps separate books. The following transactions, among others, are completed in July:

(1) The trustee acquires company bonds of $10,000 at a market price of 86 plus accrued interest of $200; the bonds are retired. (The obligation was carried on the company's books.)

(2) The trustee sells 500 shares of Wallace Corp. stock, with a cost to the company of $15,750, at 22½ less brokerage commissions and costs of $140. (The asset was carried on the trustee's books.)

Prepare the entries that would appear on the books of the trustee and on the books of the company, assuming that:

(a) Gains, losses, and expense items identified with the debtor are reflected on the trustee's books and are closed into the trustee's account at the end of the period.

(b) Gains, losses, and expense items identified with the debtor are reflected on the company's books and are closed into a company income summary account at the end of the period.

3. The following account balances were taken from the books of A. L. Shaw, bankruptcy trustee for Bloom Motors, Inc., and from the books of the company:

Trustee's Books

Bloom Motors, Inc., Debtor	$66,000
Liabilities Paid — Bloom Motors, Inc.	15,000
Sales	80,000
Cost of Goods Sold	56,000
Operating Expenses	14,000
Bloom Motors, Inc. — Loss on Sale of Investments	16,000

Company's Books

A. L. Shaw, Trustee	$51,000
Interest on Mortgage	2,500

Prepare the closing entries that are required on (a) the trustee's books and (b) the company's books.

4. The bankruptcy trustee for the Wescott Co. shows on the separate trustee-ship books only the revenue and expense items relating to normal trading transactions. Company charges and gains and losses on the sale of assets or the liquidation of indebtedness are reported on the company books. The trustee's books carry both old and new assets and new liabilities. Old liabilities are reported on the company books. What entries would be made on the two sets of books for the following?

(a) The trustee pays off company notes of $20,000 and interest of $500; the company books show accrued interest of $150 at the date of the last closing; $350 represents interest of the current period.

(b) Company investments costing $22,500 are sold for $30,000.

(c) Company 6% bonds of $50,000 are acquired by the trustee at a price of 62 plus accrued interest for 3 months; bonds are canceled.

(d) Company plant and equipment items costing $6,000, with a book value of $4,400, are sold for $1,600.

(e) Normal operations, which are summarized in the trustee's income summary account, show a net income of $6,200. The income summary account is closed. The trustee's income is recognized on the company books, and this balance as well as company revenue and expense accounts are closed.

5. The balance sheet of the Michigan Company is summarized as follows:

Assets	$100,000	Liabilities......................	$50,000
Deficit	10,000	Capital stock..................	60,000

A trustee is appointed who conducts the business for 6 months. The trustee pays all of the old liabilities and returns to the company assets of $120,000 and new liabilities of $40,000. Prepare the entries to be made on the trustee's books and on the company's books:

    (a) At the time control is assumed by the trustee.

    (b) At the time the trustee pays off the old liabilities.

    (c) At the time the trustee determines the income and closes the income summary account and the liabilities paid accounts.

    (d) At the time the trustee turns the business back to the company.

6. The following account balances are found on the books of the Potter Co. and its assignee for the benefit of creditors, Jane Taylor. Taylor has converted all of the assets, with the exception of land and buildings, into cash.

	Assignee's Books		Company Books	
	Dr.	Cr.	Dr.	Cr.
Jane Taylor, Assignee..............			114,000	
Potter Co., Debtor...................		114,000		
Cash.......................................	20,500			
Land and Buildings.................	65,000			
Trade Accounts Payable				35,000
Mortgage Note........................				40,000
Capital Stock..........................				50,000
Retained Earnings			12,500	
Income Summary....................	28,500			1,500
	114,000	114,000	126,500	126,500

Land and buildings are transferred to holders of the mortgage note in final settlement of this claim. Available cash is distributed to trade creditors in final liquidation of their claims.

Prepare the entries that are required on each set of books in recording the settlements and the dissolution of the business.

PROBLEMS

19-1. The balance sheet for the McDonald Company on April 1, 19X3, is shown on page 636.

    On this date W. A. Krell was appointed as trustee to assume control of the business. The trustee conducted the business until December 31, 19X3, when it was returned to management. Transactions completed by the trustee were:

    Materials purchased on account, $36,000; $12,000 remains unpaid on December 31; discounts received were $650.

    Freight paid on materials purchased, $3,200.

    Direct labor paid, $41,000; $600 is accrued on December 31.

    Manufacturing expenses paid, $27,600; $750 is accrued on December 31.

    General expenses paid, $18,600; $960 is accrued on December 31.

Assets		Liabilities and Stockholders' Equity	
Cash..	$ 8,000	Notes payable	$ 41,000
Notes receivable......................	21,350	Accounts payable	61,300
Accounts receivable .. $57,500		Accrued interest on notes	
Less allow. for		payable..............................	200
doubtful accounts.. 1,200	56,300	Accrued interest on mortgage	
Accrued interest on notes		note	100
receivable...........................	150	6% Mortgage note payable.......	20,000
Finished goods	24,800	Capital stock, $10 par	100,000
Work in process......................	18,500	Retained earnings..................	5,500
Materials	19,000		
Land	15,000		
Buildings.................. $40,000			
Less accumulated			
depreciation 8,000	32,000		
Machinery $50,000			
Less accumulated			
depreciation 17,000	33,000		
Total	$228,100	Total	$228,100

Sales on account, $199,700; $21,500 remains uncollected on December 31; discounts allowed were $1,800.

Selling expenses paid, $26,500; $1,350 is accrued on December 31.

Collections on accounts of April 1, $51,050; remaining accounts were written off as uncollectible.

Payments on accounts of April 1, $61,300.

Collections on notes of April 1, $20,000, and interest, $600; notes of $1,350 and accrued interest of $30 as of April 1 were written off as uncollectible.

Payments on notes payable of April 1, $41,000, and interest on these notes, $1,360.

Payment of semiannual interest on mortgage notes, $600; $400 is accrued on December 31.

Additional adjustments required December 31, 19X3, were:

Allowance for doubtful accounts, 2% of accounts.
Depreciation of buildings, $1,500.
Depreciation of machinery, $3,750.
Materials inventory, $16,000.
Work in process inventory, $17,600.
Finished goods inventory, $21,850.
Amount owed to trustee (payable in January), $9,000.

Instructions: (1) Prepare the necessary journal entries for the separate books of the trustee and for the books of the corporation: (a) to record transfer of corporation assets to the trustee; (b) to record the transactions for the period; (c) to adjust and close the books; (d) to record the return of the business to the corporation.

(2) Prepare (a) a balance sheet as of December 31, 19X3, and (b) an income statement supported by a schedule to show the cost of goods manufactured for the period April 1–December 31, 19X3.

19-2. A. T. Call was appointed trustee on May 1, 19X8, when the Robbins Corporation was unable to meet its current obligations as they matured. A balance sheet for the corporation prepared on this date is as follows:

Assets		Liabilities and Stockholders' Equity	
Cash..	$ 5,750	Notes payable	$ 35,000
Notes receivable......................	25,000	Accounts payable	65,000
Accounts receivable .. $65,000		Accrued interest on notes	
Less allow. for		payable..............................	1,050
doubtful accounts.. 1,300	63,700	Capital stock	50,000
Accrued interest on notes		Retained earnings...................	10,050
receivable............................	400		
Merchandise inventory	40,000		
Furniture and fixtures $15,000			
Less accumulated			
depreciation 3,750	11,250		
Vick Corporation stock (750			
shares at $20)	15,000		
Total	$161,100	Total	$161,100

The business was conducted by Call until December 31, 19X8, when it was returned to the control of the corporation. Transactions completed by the trustee during the period of trusteeship were as follows:

Sales on account, $140,000.
Purchases on account, $80,000.
Reductions in accounts receivable (new):

Cash collections	$78,000
Sales returns and allowances	3,000
Sales discounts allowed...	4,000
	$85,000

Collections on notes receivable, old, $24,000, and interest, $650; notes receivable, old, $1,000, and accrued interest of $100 as of May 1 were written off as uncollectible.
Collections on accounts receivable, old, $55,000; remaining accounts were written off as worthless.
Sale of 500 shares of Vick Corporation stock, $12,000.
Reductions in accounts payable (new):

Cash payments	$12,500	
Notes issued in payment...	18,000	
Purchases returns and allowances.............................	2,000	
Purchases discounts received.................................	500	$33,000

Payment of notes payable, old, $25,000, and interest, $1,400 (includes all of accrued interest as of May 1).
Payment of accounts payable, old, $65,000.
Payment of operating expenses:

Selling expenses	$18,500	
General expenses (including expenses of trustee)	23,300	$41,800

Additional data for adjustments on December 31 were as follows:

Merchandise inventory, $33,250.
Provision for doubtful accounts, 2% of accounts receivable.
Depreciation of furniture and fixtures, 10% per year.

Accrued expenses:
Selling expenses	$250	
General expenses	300	
Interest on notes payable (old)	150	
Interest on notes payable (new)	200	$900

Instructions: (1) Prepare the necessary journal entries for the separate books of the trustee and for the books of the corporation: (a) to record transfer of corporation assets to the trustee; (b) to record the transactions for the period; (c) to adjust and close the books; (d) to record the return of the business to the corporation.

(2) Prepare (a) a balance sheet as of December 31, 19X8, and (b) an income statement for the period May 1–December 31, 19X8.

19-3. X and Y, partners, were unable to meet their maturing obligations and were required to turn over the business to Z, a bankruptcy trustee, on July 1, 19X1. The condition of the business as shown by a balance sheet prepared on June 30, 19X1, was as follows:

Assets			Liabilities and Capital	
Cash		$ 4,000	Notes payable	$ 7,500
Notes receivable		3,750	Accounts payable	34,700
Accounts receivable		28,450	Accrued interest on notes pay-	
Merchandise inventory		17,600	able	300
Furniture and fixtures ..	$1,800		X, capital	10,000
Less accumulated			Y, capital	7,500
depreciation	300	1,500		
Cash surrender value of life in-				
surance		4,700		
Total		$60,000	Total	$60,000

Transactions completed by the trustee during the period of July 1, 19X1, to June 30, 19X2, were as follows:

Accounts receivable of $20,000 were pledged on an advance from the AAA Finance Co.; the trustee collected cash of $14,400 after a 4% deduction for finance charges.

Settlement was made on notes payable by payment of $7,850, which included accrued interest to date of payment, $350.

Of the unpledged accounts receivable, accounts of $7,500 were subsequently collected and remaining accounts were written off as uncollectible.

Notes receivable of $2,500 were collected; remaining notes were written off as worthless.

Settlement was made on accounts payable by the payment of cash of $15,500 and the balance in the form of 12 equal monthly installment notes. The notes are all dated July 1, 19X1, and provide for interest at 5% payable upon their maturities; the first note is due on August 1, 19X1.

All of the accounts that were pledged were subsequently collected. The loan from the AAA Finance Co. was paid off with interest at 6% for 2 months.

Purchases on account during the period of trusteeship were $40,000; sales on account were $75,000.

Operating expenses of $12,500 were paid in cash.

The installment notes were paid as they came due.

Trustee's expenses and fees totaled $6,500; $3,500 had been paid and the balance is payable on August 1, 19X2.

On June 30, 19X2, the trustee adjusted and closed the books before returning the business to its owners. On this date, customers' balances not yet collected amounted to $13,600; trade creditors' balances of $12,000 had not yet been paid; operating expenses of $760 were accrued. An inventory disclosed merchandise costing $16,500 on hand. Depreciation was recognized on furniture and fixtures at 10%. An allowance on the balance of the customers' accounts was established at 5%.

Instructions: (1) Prepare journal entries for the separate books of the trustee and for the books of the partnership: (a) to record transfer of partnership assets to the trustee; (b) to record the trusteeship transactions for the period; (c) to adjust and close the books; (d) to record the return of the business to the partnership.

(2) Prepare (a) a balance sheet as of June 30, 19X2, and (b) an income statement for the period of trusteeship ending June 30, 19X2.

19-4. The Curtis Co. cannot meet its obligations and a general assignment of assets for the benefit of creditors is made at the beginning of 19X9. Roger Wilson, assignee, attempts to restore solvency; but on April 30, 19X9, it is decided that this is impossible and that interests of the creditor group will be best served by immediate liquidation. On this date balances on the books of the assignee and on the books of the company are:

	Assignee's Books		Company's Books	
	Dr.	Cr.	Dr.	Cr.
Cash	25,500			
Accounts Receivable	30,000			
Merchandise Inventory	40,000			
Roger Wilson, Assignee			135,000	
Land			15,000	
Buildings			60,000	
Accumulated Depreciation of Buildings				7,500
Machinery and Equipment	35,000			
Accumulated Depreciation of Machinery and Equipment		15,000		
Patents	25,000			
Accounts Payable		20,000		66,000
6% Mortgage Note Payable (interest payable 4/30 and 10/31)				50,000
Accrued Interest on Mortgage Note				500
Curtis Co. in Assignment		135,000		
Capital Stock				100,000
Retained Earnings			14,000	
Sales		30,000		
Cost of Goods Sold	28,000			
Selling Expenses	6,500			
General Expenses	10,000			
	200,000	200,000	224,000	224,000

Transactions for April 30–June 30 follow:

(a) On May 1, land and buildings are turned over to the holder of the mortgage note in full settlement of the note and unpaid interest to that date. No entries have been made for accrued interest and depreciation for 19X9. The building is being depreciated over a 16-year life.

(b) Collections on accounts receivable total $15,000; remaining accounts are sold to the Crawford Finance Company for $4,500.

(c) Grace Hall agrees to purchase the merchandise for $20,000 and the machinery and equipment for $9,800. Payment is made on June 30. No depreciation has been recognized on machinery and equipment for 19X9; the depreciation rate on this asset is 8% per year. Hall also pays $2,000 for the patents.

(d) Payments of miscellaneous assignment expenses total $1,800. The assignee's fee of $3,000 is paid.

(e) Accounts payable incurred by the assignee are paid in full.

(f) The balance of cash is distributed as a final payment on June 30 to old trade creditors.

Instructions: (1) Prepare the entries on the books of the assignee and the company to record the course of liquidation and to close the two sets of books.

(2) Prepare an income statement summarizing activities of the assignee and the Curtis Co. for the period January 1–June 30.

19-5. Joan Cole took over the business of Wesson Stores, Inc., on July 1, 19X7, as a trustee. Trial balances of the company books and the trustee's books on December 31, 19X7, follow. On this date the trustee has merchandise on hand amounting to $20,750.

	Wesson Stores, Inc. Dr.	Wesson Stores, Inc. Cr.	Joan Cole, Trustee Dr.	Joan Cole, Trustee Cr.
Cash			28,420	
Accounts Receivable — Old			37,800	
Accounts Receivable — New			39,680	
Merchandise Inventory, July 1, 19X7			25,300	
Fixtures			91,500	
Accumulated Depreciation				17,500
Trademark			12,500	
Accounts Payable — New				19,600
Wesson Stores, Inc., Debtor				214,400
Sales				200,500
Purchases			126,400	
Depreciation			5,490	
Selling Expenses			22,800	
General Expenses			14,110	
Trustee's Expenses			1,500	
Wesson Stores, Inc., Liabilities Paid — Accounts Payable, Old			35,000	
Wesson Stores, Inc., Liabilities Paid — Interest on Mortgage			4,000	
Wesson Stores, Inc. — Loss from Accounts Receivable, Old			7,500	
Joan Cole, Trustee	175,400			
Mortgage Payable (due December 31, 19X9)		50,000		
Capital Stock		150,000		
Deficit	20,600			
Interest Expense	4,000			
	200,000	200,000	452,000	452,000

Instructions: Prepare as of December 31, 19X7, an income statement and a balance sheet to be submitted to creditors as interim reports. Submit a work sheet in support of your statements.

19-6. Coast Sales Company, having insufficient cash to continue operations, turned over the business to L. E. King, a trustee, on December 31, 19X5. Account balances on the company's books as shown by a balance sheet prepared on this date were as follows:

Assets		Liabilities and Stockholders' Equity	
Cash...	$ 10,860	Accounts payable	$125,000
Accounts receivable................	54,700	Capital stock	150,000
Inventory (cost)	82,940	Retained earnings...................	23,500
Advance to Cranston Co...........	50,000		
Plant and equip-			
ment $125,000			
Less accumulated			
depreciation........ 25,000	100,000		
Total	$298,500	Total	$298,500

The trustee took over the assets at the balance sheet figures, except for inventory, which was taken over at the prevailing market price for the inventory, $70,000. The trustee operated the business for a year and then returned the business to the control of the stockholders on December 31, 19X6.

The following transactions were completed by the trustee during the year:

Sales on account totaled $184,350, of which $145,400 had been collected.

Purchases on account amounted to $95,400, of which $75,400 had been paid.

All of the old accounts receivable were collected, except for balances of $9,500 that were written off as uncollectible.

At the time the trustee took over the assets, the Cranston Co. was undergoing liquidation. The trustee subsequently recovered 45¢ on the dollar on the advance made to this company.

Company accounts payable were all paid in cash, except for a $25,000 balance on which a 90-day non-interest-bearing note due January 15, 19X7, was issued.

Payments representing general and selling expenses amounted to $27,440.

The trustee charged $6,000 for fees and expenses; $4,000 was paid in cash, and the balance is due February 15, 19X7.

The merchandise inventory on December 31, 19X6, amounted to $82,500.

Depreciation of $12,500 was recorded.

Instructions: (1) Prepare a work sheet to summarize the activities during the period of trusteeship.

(2) Prepare an income statement summarizing activities during the period of trusteeship.

(3) Prepare a balance sheet for the business on December 31, 19X6, after its return to the stockholders.

19-7. The Triangle Corporation contemplates dissolution primarily because one of the three stockholders may be regarded as unfriendly. Arthur and Brooks, two of the stockholders, agree to form a partnership. A balance sheet of the Triangle Corporation on December 16, 19X8, is shown on the following page.

The Triangle Corporation
Balance Sheet
December 16, 19X8

Assets

Current assets:
Cash	$ 95,000
Receivables — less allowance, $22,000	135,000
Inventories	225,000
Investments	20,000
Total current assets	$475,000

Property — stated at appraisal value determined as of December 16, 19X8 .... $125,000
Less accumulated depreciation .... 27,500 ... 97,500

Treasury preferred stock (par value, $40,000), at cost	47,250
Other assets	10,000
Prepaid expenses	4,500
Total assets	$634,250

Liabilities and Stockholders' Equity

Current liabilities:
Note payable — Crandall, stockholder	$ 30,000
Accounts payable — trade	110,000
Accrued liabilities	8,000
Accrued federal income tax	24,000
Total current liabilities	$172,000
Contingent liabilities	50,000

Stockholders' equity:
Capital stock:
Preferred stock — $100 par (entitled to $110 in liquidation); authorized, 1,000 shares; in treasury, 400 shares; outstanding, 600 shares $100,000
Common stock — no-par; authorized, 200,000 shares; issued and outstanding, 100,000 shares stated at nominal value of $1 per share 100,000
Additional paid-in capital 150,000
$350,000

Revaluation capital arising from property appraisal as at December 16, 19X8 50,000
Retained earnings ..... 12,250 ... 412,250

Total liabilities and stockholders' equity $634,250

The following data are available:

(1) The capital stock records of the corporation as at December 16, 19X8, indicate that there are three stockholders who have retained their respective interests since corporate organization more than 20 years ago, as shown by the following tabulation:

Stockholder	Total Paid In	Preferred Shares	Preferred Paid In	Common Shares	Common Paid In
Arthur	$115,000	300	$30,000	35,000	$ 85,000
Brooks	105,000	100	10,000	40,000	95,000
Crandall	90,000	200	20,000	25,000	70,000
	$310,000	600	$60,000	100,000	$250,000

(2) In accordance with a reorganization agreement, the corporation will acquire the stock interest of Crandall, and thereafter the corporation will be dissolved by an appropriate disposition of its net assets.

(3) To finance the acquisition of the stock interest of Crandall, the property was appraised as a basis for an $80,000 mortgage satisfactorily arranged by the corporation with a bank. The appraisal made as at December 16, 19X8, and reflected in the general books is summarized as follows:

	Appraisal	Books Before Appraisal	Revaluation Captial
Property......................................	$125,000	$70,000	$55,000
Accumulated depr.....................	27,500	22,500	5,000
	$ 97,500	$47,500	$50,000

(4) The stock interest of Crandall is to be acquired by the cash payment of $110 per share for the preferred stock and $3 per share for the common stock. Such reacquired stock is to be canceled.

(5) After acquisition of the stock interest of Crandall, disposition of the net assets of the corporation in complete liquidation and dissolution is to be made as follows:

(a) The note payable to Crandall is to be paid.

(b) The investments (having a quoted market value of $36,000 as at December 16, 19X8) reflected in the balance sheet of the corporation are to be distributed at the market value (incident to the complete liquidation) to Brooks.

(c) The contingent liabilities resulted from guarantees under contract, which are to be settled by the corporation at 25 cents on the dollar.

(d) The remaining assets are to be acquired and the liabilities (including the $80,000 mortgage) are to be assumed by a partnership organized by Arthur and Brooks. Brooks invests cash in the partnership as necessary to achieve an equal partnership interest with that of Arthur.

Instructions: Prepare a balance sheet for the partnership of Arthur and Brooks as of December 16, 19X8, after giving effect to the dissolution of the predecessor organization in accordance with the reorganization agreement.

(AICPA adapted)

19-8. The Bergstrom Company cannot meet its obligations and C. Phillips is appointed trustee on April 28, 19X3. The books are closed on that date and the following trial balance is prepared:

Debits

Cash	800
Receivables	1,400
Finished Goods	100,000
Materials and Supplies...................	15,000
Goods on Consignment (out)..........	220,000
Employees' Bonds	4,700
Prepaid Insurance	800
Machinery and Equipment..............	507,300
	850,000

Credits

Accounts Payable	110,000
Bank Overdraft	1,000
Bank Loans	105,000
Baker, Inc.	250,000
Acceptances	23,000
Collateral Notes Payable	4,700
Lease — Machinery	30,000
Accrued Interest on Lease	2,000
City Taxes Accrued	4,000
Mortgage on Machinery	100,000
Accrued Interest on Mortgage	3,000
Accumulated Depreciation	7,300
Capital Stock — Preferred	100,000
Capital Stock — Common	100,000
Retained Earnings	10,000
	850,000

On November 20, 19X3, the trustee, having disposed of all assets except $400 of accounts receivable that are considered doubtful, calls upon you to prepare an interim statement for the information of shareholders and creditors. An examination of the company's and the trustee's books and records discloses the following:

(a) Cash receipts:

Collections of accounts receivable	$ 1,000
Rebate upon cancellation of all insurance	100
Proceeds from surrender of insurance policy on life of manager	1,000
Sales of finished goods during trusteeship	75,000
Rent of sublet portion of the building	1,000
Unclaimed wages	500
Interest on bank account	200
Sale of all goods and supplies on hand after operations were discontinued	25,000
Sale of all machinery and equipment owned	200,000
	$303,800

(b) Cash disbursements:

City taxes	$ 4,000
Interest on city taxes	400
Mortgage	100,000
Interest on mortgage	5,000
Labor, materials, and other operating and general expenses during trusteeship	61,000
	$170,400

(c) Of the stocks on hand at April 28, finished goods costing $60,000 were sold during the trusteeship and $9,000 of materials and supplies were used.

(d) The accounts payable are understated by $10,000 and include an item of $5,000 in dispute.

(e) The merchandise on consignment was pledged as collateral to the advances by Baker, Inc., and was accepted by them in part payment of these advances at full book value.

(f) The collateral notes payable were for accommodation of employees and were secured by deposit of bonds. The notes were paid by the employees and the bonds returned to them.

(g) The lease covered machinery worth $30,000 used by the company under a lease agreement. It was returned by the trustee and was accepted in full satisfaction of this agreement and all interest accrued.

(h) Claims were filed for all liabilities except an item of $7,000 of accounts payable.

(i) Trustee's fees need not be considered.

Instructions: (1) Prepare a columnar work sheet summarizing the foregoing data.

(2) Prepare a balance sheet and an income statement summarizing activities of the trustee.

(AICPA adapted)

20
Insolvency — Statement of Realization and Liquidation

A summary of the course of operations of a business under the direction of a trustee and involving the realization of assets and the liquidation of indebtedness may be presented in the form of a special report called the *statement of realization and liquidation*.

Operations by a trustee are presented on the statement of realization and liquidation in a manner that permits a summary of the net business gain or loss for the period covered. The statement is usually accompanied by supplementary schedules summarizing changes in cash and in capital. It may also be accompanied by formal reports in the form of a balance sheet, an income statement, and a retained earnings statement.

The preparation of the statement of realization and liquidation in its conventional form is illustrated in the first part of the chapter. In the remainder of the chapter, alternative forms of this statement are presented.

STATEMENT OF REALIZATION AND LIQUIDATION IN CONVENTIONAL FORM

In its conventional form, the statement of realization and liquidation is composed of asset, liability, and revenue and expense sections, with subdivisions in each of these sections as follows:

Assets

Assets to be realized	Assets realized
Assets acquired	Assets not realized

Liabilities

Liabilities liquidated	Liabilities to be liquidated
Liabilities not liquidated	Liabilities assumed

Revenues and Expenses

Supplementary charges	Supplementary credits

The basic procedures that are employed in the preparation of the statement of realization and liquidation in its conventional form will be illustrated by means of a simple set of facts. Assume that Helen West is appointed trustee of the Apex Company on December 1, 19X2. The financial position of the Apex Company as shown by a balance sheet prepared on this date is as follows:

Apex Company
Balance Sheet
December 1, 19X2

Assets		Liabilities and Stockholders' Equity		
Cash	$ 5,000	Accounts payable		$ 65,000
Marketable securities	15,000	Capital stock	$50,000	
Accounts receivable	30,000	Less deficit	15,000	35,000
Merchandise (cost)	50,000			
Total	$100,000	Total		$100,000

Transactions in December that did not involve cash were as follows:

Sales of merchandise on account	$ 5,000
Purchases of merchandise on account	1,500

Cash receipts and disbursements for December are summarized as follows:

Cash receipts:

Sale of merchandise	$25,000
Collection of accounts receivable	11,500
Sale of the marketable securities	18,500
Interest on marketable securities	150
	$55,150

Cash disbursements:

Payment of accounts payable	$35,000
Payment of expenses of trustee	7,500
	$42,500

At the end of December, assets remaining to be realized and liabilities remaining to be liquidated are as follows:

Assets

Accounts receivable:

Balance, December 1		$30,000
Add sales on account in December		5,000
		$35,000
Deduct: Collections on account in December	$11,500	
Balances determined to be uncollectible	1,500	13,000
Balance, December 31		$22,000

Merchandise:

Balance, December 1	$50,000
Add merchandise acquired in December	1,500
	$51,500
Deduct cost of goods sold in December	31,500
Balance, December 31	$20,000

Liabilities

Accounts payable:

Balance, December 1	$65,000
Add purchases on account in December	1,500
	$66,500
Deduct payments on account in December	35,000
Balance, December 31	$31,500
Accrued expenses balance, December 31	$ 350

A statement of realization and liquidation for the Apex Company, together with cash and capital schedules, appears on pages 649 and 650. The statement and the supporting schedules were developed by analyzing data in terms of debit and credit and by "posting" the data.

For purposes of posting, the left-hand side of the statement of realization and liquidation is viewed as composed of debit sections; the right-hand side of the statement is viewed as composed of credit sections. The following steps are employed in the process of summarizing trustee activities on the statement and the accompanying schedules. The items in the statement and schedules are identified by the numbers corresponding to these steps.

(1) Beginning balance sheet data are reported on the statement and the supplementary schedules as follows:
(a) The cash balance is reported as a debit in the cash schedule.
(b) Remaining assets are listed as debits in the asset section of the statement under the heading "Assets to be realized."
(c) Liabilities are listed as credits in the liability section of the statement under the heading "Liabilities to be liquidated."
(d) Capital balances are reported as credits in appropriately titled capital schedules.

(2) Current transactions other than those involving cash are analyzed and their effects are reported on the statement as follows:
(a) Sales on account are reported as a debit to Accounts Receivable in the asset section of the statement under the heading "Assets acquired" and a credit to Sales in the revenue and expense section under the heading "Supplementary credits."
(b) Purchases on account are reported as a debit to Purchases in the revenue and expense section of the statement under the heading "Supplementary charges" and a credit to Accounts Payable in the liability section under the heading "Liabilities assumed."

(3) Cash receipts and disbursements are reported on the statement and the accompanying schedules as follows:
(a) Cash receipts are reported as debits in the cash schedule and as credits either in the asset section of the statement under the heading "Assets realized" or in the revenue and expense section under the heading "Supplementary credits," whichever is appropriate.
(b) Cash disbursements are reported as debits either in the liability section of the statement under the heading "Liabilities liquidated" or in the revenue and expense section under the heading "Supplementary charges," whichever is appropriate, and as credits in the cash schedule.

Apex Company, Debtor
Helen West, Trustee
Statement of Realization and Liquidation
For Month Ended December 31, 19X2

Assets

Assets to be realized:		Assets realized:	
(1) Marketable securities............	$ 15,000	(3) Marketable securities............	$18,500
(1) Accounts receivable..............	30,000	(3) Accounts receivable..............	11,500
(1) Merchandise	50,000	Assets not realized:	
Assets acquired:		(4) Accounts receivable..............	22,000
(2) Accounts receivable..............	5,000	(4) Merchandise	20,000

Liabilities

Liabilities liquidated:		Liabilities to be liquidated:	
(3) Accounts payable	35,000	(1) Accounts payable	65,000
Liabilities not liquidated:		Liabilities assumed:	
(4) Accounts payable	31,500	(2) Accounts payable	1,500
(4) Accrued expenses................	350		

Revenues and Expenses

Supplementary charges:		Supplementary credits:	
(2) Purchases.........................	1,500	(2) Sales on account	5,000
(3) Payment of expenses of		(3) Interest on marketable securi-	
trustee	7,500	ties......................................	150
		(3) Sales for cash......................	25,000
			$168,650
		(5) Net loss	7,200
Total	$175,850	Total	$175,850

Apex Company, Debtor
Helen West, Trustee
Supplementary Schedules To Accompany Statement of Realization and Liquidation
For Month Ended December 31, 19X2

Cash

19X2			19X2		
Dec. 1 (1)	Balance	$ 5,000	Dec. 1–31 (2)	Payment of accounts payable.....	$35,000
1–31 (3)	Cash sales of merchandise	25,000	(2)	Payment of expenses of trustee..	7,500
(3)	Collections on accounts receivable	11,500	Dec. 31	Balance........................	17,650
(3)	Proceeds from sale of marketable securities	18,500			
(3)	Collection of interest on marketable securities	150			
		$60,150			$60,150
19X3					
Jan. 1	Balance............................	$17,650			

Capital Stock

	19X2		
	Dec. 1	(1) Balance.................	$50,000

Retained Earnings

19X2			19X2		
Dec. 1	(1) Balance	$15,000	Dec. 31	Balance	$22,200
31	(5) Net loss for December ...	7,200			
		$22,200			$22,200
19X3					
Jan. 1	Balance	$22,200			

(4) Ending asset and liability balances are reported on the statement as follows:

(a) Assets still to be realized are listed under the asset section heading "Assets not realized."

(b) Liabilities still to be liquidated are listed under the liability section heading "Liabilities not liquidated."

(5) The loss or the gain on liquidation may now be summarized by adding the amounts on the left-hand side and the right-hand side of the statement. A left-hand side excess indicates a loss emerging from liquidation, and the loss is reported on the right-hand side of the statement to bring the totals on each side of the statement into balance. A right-hand side excess would indicate a gain from liquidation, and such a gain would be reported on the left-hand side of the statement in bringing the totals on each side of the statement into balance. The loss or the gain may now be reported in the supplementary capital schedule. Capital accounts then report the capital at the end of the period.

It should be observed that the final loss or gain on the statement of realization and liquidation represents a combination of three factors:

(1) The loss or the gain emerging from asset changes summarized in the asset section of the statement.

(2) The loss or the gain emerging from liability changes summarized in the liability section of the statement.

(3) Revenue and expense items summarized in the revenue and expense section of the statement.

In the case of the Apex Company, the loss of $7,200 emerges from these categories as follows:

					Loss or (Gain)
Assets:					
Assets to be realized		$ 95,000	Proceeds from asset realization	$30,000	
Assets acquired		5,000	Assets not realized	42,000	
		$100,000		$72,000	$28,000
Liabilities:					
Applied to liability liquidation		$ 35,000	Liabilities to be liquidated .	$65,000	
Liabilities not liquidated		31,850	Liabilities assumed	1,500	
		$ 66,850		$66,500	350
Revenues and expenses:					
Supplementary charges		$ 9,000	Supplementary credits	$30,150	(21,150)
Net loss					$ 7,200

Certain transactions can be treated in alternative manners on the statement of realization and liquidation. In the previous illustration, the following alternatives are available:

Transaction	Treatment	Alternative
Sale of merchandise on account.	Dr. Assets acquired Cr. Supplementary credits	Dr. Assets acquired Cr. Assets realized
Purchase of merchandise on account.	Dr. Supplementary charges Cr. Liabilities assumed	Dr. Assets acquired Cr. Liabilities assumed
Uncollectible accounts written off.	No entry. (Loss emerges from recognition of accounts receivable at a reduced value under the heading "Assets not realized.")	Dr. Supplementary charges Cr. Assets realized
Accrued expenses at end of period.	No entry. (Charge emerges from recognition of amount payable under the heading "Liabilities not liquidated.")	Dr. Supplementary charges Cr. Liabilities assumed

A check on the calculation of the loss or the gain on realization and liquidation may be provided by summarizing the balances reported on the statement and the accompanying schedules as follows: the balance of cash in the cash schedule plus other assets under the heading "Assets not realized" must be equal to the liabilities under the heading "Liabilities not liquidated" plus capital as reported in the capital schedules. Data for the Apex Company summarized in this manner follow:

Apex Company, Debtor
Balances per Statement of Realization and Liquidation
and Accompanying Schedules
December 31, 19X2

Assets		Liabilities and Stockholders' Equity		
Cash.................................	$17,650	Liabilities not liquidated....................		$31,850
Assets not realized..........................	42,000	Capital stock	$50,000	
		Less deficit	22,200	27,800
Total	$59,650	Total		$59,650

Financial statements may be prepared to accompany the realization and liquidation summaries. Financial statements prepared for the Apex Company are as follows:

Apex Company, Debtor
Helen West, Trustee
Income Statement
For Month Ended December 31, 19X2

	Book Value	Proceeds	Loss or (Gain)
Losses and gains on asset realization:			
Marketable securities	$15,000	$18,500	$(3,500)
Merchandise..	31,500	30,000	1,500
Accounts receivable	13,000	11,500	1,500
Excess of gains over losses...			$ (500)
Expenses during course of realization and liquidation..........			7,850
			$ 7,350
Other revenue — interest on marketable securities			(150)
Net loss...			$ 7,200

Apex Company, Debtor
Helen West, Trustee
Balance Sheet
December 31, 19X2

Assets		Liabilities and Stockholders' Equity		
Cash..	$17,650	Accounts payable		$31,500
Accounts receivable.........................	22,000	Accrued expenses.............................		350
Merchandise	20,000			
		Total liabilities.................................		$31,850
		Stockholders' equity:		
		Capital stock	$50,000	
		Deficit, Dec. 1 $15,000		
		Add loss for		
		December.. 7,200	22,200	27,800
Total	$59,650	Total		$59,650

STATEMENT OF REALIZATION AND LIQUIDATION
IN ALTERNATIVE FORM

The statement of realization and liquidation prepared in the conventional form just illustrated is subject to certain limitations:

(1) The statement fails to point out those individual factors responsible for the gain or the loss for the period. The final net gain or loss results from a combination of elements — revenue and expense items summarized in a revenue and expense section, gains and losses reflected in a summary of asset proceeds, gains and losses reflected in summaries of liability liquidation, and gains and losses reflected in changed values assigned to ending assets and liabilities.

(2) The statement fails to provide a full summary of the nature of asset and liability changes. Beginning and ending asset and liability account balances are presented, but there is no reconciliation of these balances in view of credits to assets for cash proceeds that may be more or less than asset book value and charges to liabilities for cash payments that similarly may involve amounts other than book value. Furthermore, the statement fails to offer support for asset and liability changes arising from adjusting data.

These limitations can be overcome by an alternative approach in the preparation of the statement. Transactions can be reported on the statement of realization and liquidation in a manner consistent with the procedure that is employed in recording the transactions. All transactions are analyzed just as they would be for recording purposes and are then "posted" to the statement and its supporting schedules.

Sale of an asset is analyzed in terms of the reduction in the book value of the asset and the resulting loss or gain from realization. The reduction in asset book value is reported under the heading "Assets realized," and the loss or the gain on realization is reported as a supplementary charge or credit. Liquidation of a liability is analyzed in terms of the reduction in the book value of the liability and any loss or gain from settlement. The reduction in the liability book value is reported under the heading "Liabilities liquidated" and the loss or the gain on liquidation is reported as a supplementary charge or credit. Adjusting data require analysis in terms of their effects upon assets, liabilities, and revenues and expenses, and they are reported on the statement in accordance with such an analysis.

Recording transactions and adjustments on the statement and the schedules in accordance with the procedure that is followed in the accounts will make available a complete summary of revenue and expense items in the revenue and expense section of the statement. Furthermore, ending asset balances become the direct product of beginning asset balances, increases in assets arising from acquisitions, and decreases in assets resulting from asset sales. Ending liability balances are the direct product of beginning liability balances, increases in liabilities arising from new obligations assumed, and decreases resulting from the liquidation of liabilities. An organized and clear reporting of revenues and expenses is made available through this procedure, and a full reconciliation of changes in asset and liability items is afforded.

The following examples illustrate the nature of the analysis and the posting process that is employed on the statement of realization and liquidation in recording current transactions.

Realization of assets: Cash received is reported as a debit in the cash schedule; the reduction in the book value of the asset is reported as a credit under the heading "Assets realized"; the loss or the gain on realization is reported as a debit or a credit under the heading "Supplementary charges" or "Supplementary credits."

Liquidation of liabilities:	The reduction in the book value of the liability is reported as a debit under the heading "Liabilities liquidated"; cash paid is reported as a credit in the cash schedule; a loss or a gain from settlement is reported as a debit or a credit under the heading "Supplementary charges" or "Supplementary credits."
Revenue:	Cash received is reported as a debit in the cash schedule; the revenue is reported as a credit under the heading "Supplementary credits." If the revenue is receivable, a debit to the receivable would be reported under the heading "Assets acquired."
Merchandise purchases or expense:	The cost or expense is reported as a debit under the heading "Supplementary charges." The payment of cash for purchases or expense is reported as a credit in the cash account. If the expense is payable, a credit to a payable would be reported under the heading "Liabilities assumed."

The following examples illustrate the procedures employed on the statement in recording the adjusting data at the end of the period:

Beginning inventory:	The beginning inventory, an element of cost of goods sold, is recorded as a debit under the heading "Supplementary charges"; the beginning inventory is canceled in the asset section by a credit under the heading "Assets realized."
Ending inventory:	The ending inventory as an asset item is recorded as a debit under the heading "Assets acquired"; the ending inventory as a subtraction from goods available for sale is recorded as a credit under the heading "Supplementary credits."
Depreciation:	The expense is recorded as a debit under the heading "Supplementary charges"; the reduction in the book value of the asset for cost amortization is recorded as a credit under the heading "Assets realized."
Accrued expense:	The expense is recorded as a debit under the heading "Supplementary charges"; the payable is recorded as a credit under the heading "Liabilities assumed."
Accrued revenue:	The receivable is recorded as a debit under the heading "Assets acquired"; the revenue is recorded as a credit under the heading "Supplementary credits."
Prepaid expense:	When an expense balance includes an amount that is to be deferred: the asset is recorded as a debit under the heading "Assets acquired"; the reduction in the expense balance is recorded as a credit under the heading "Supplementary credits."
Deferred revenue:	When a revenue balance includes an amount that is to be deferred: the reduction in the revenue balance is recorded as a debit under the heading "Supplementary charges"; the liability is recorded as a credit under the heading "Liabilities assumed."

After the current transactions and the adjustments are recorded, the ending asset and liability balances are determined as follows:

Assets not realized = Assets to be realized + Assets acquired − Assets realized
Liabilities not liquidated = Liabilities to be liquidated + Liabilities assumed − Liabilities liquidated

As a final step in the preparation of the statement of realization and liquidation, the debits and the credits in the revenue and expense section are summarized. The section is balanced and the net loss or gain is reported as a charge or a credit in the appropriate capital schedule.

Preparation of the statement of realization and liquidation in the alternative form is illustrated for the Miles Corporation, based on the facts given in the preceding chapter. Asset, liability, and capital balances for the Miles Corporation at the beginning of trusteeship were given on page 619. Transactions and adjusting data for the Miles Corporation during the period of trusteeship are listed and analyzed in terms of their effects upon the statement in the section that follows. The statement of realization and liquidation and the supporting schedules prepared from these data are shown on pages 658–660. Transactions and adjustments are numbered the same as in the illustration in the preceding chapter.

Data	Analysis and Entry		

(1) Beginning balances:
Cash.... $ 1,000 Liabilities..... $105,650
(List in detail.)
Other
Assets.. 180,400
(List in Capital
detail.) Stock........... 100,000
  Deficit .... (24,250)
_____   _____
$181,400 $181,400
	Dr. Cash — Cash Schedule ....
	Dr. Other Assets (as named) —
	"Assets to be realized"...............
	Dr. Retained Earnings — Retained
	Earnings Schedule......................
	  Cr. Liabilities (as named) —
	  "Liabilities to be liquidated".....
	  Cr. Capital Stock — Capital
	  Stock Schedule ....
		1,000
		
		180,400
		
		24,250
			
			105,650
			
			100,000

(2) Sales on account, $210,000.	Dr. Accounts Receivable —
	"Assets acquired" ....
	  Cr. Sales — "Supplementary
	  credits".................................
		210,000	
			
			210,000

(3) Purchases on account, $112,000.	Dr. Purchases — "Supplementary charges".................................... Cr. Accounts Payable — "Liabilities assumed"	112,000	 112,000

(4) Accounts receivable (new) were reduced by the following:
Cash collections............................ $158,500
Notes received in payment............. 30,000
Sales returns and allowances 1,500
Sales discounts allowed................ 2,000
  _____
  $192,000
	Dr. Cash — Cash Schedule ....
	Dr. Notes receivable — "Assets acquired" ....
	Dr. Sales Returns and Allowances — "Supplementary charges"........
	Dr. Sales Discount — "Supplementary charges" ....
	  Cr. Accounts Receivable — "Assets realized".....................
		158,500
		
		30,000
		
		1,500
		
		2,000
			
			192,000

(5) Collection on accounts receivable, old (carried at book value of $24,000), $22,000; remaining accounts were written off as worthless.	Dr. Cash — Cash Schedule .... Dr. Allowance for Doubtful Accounts, Old — "Assets realized"... Dr. Uncollectible Accounts Expense, Old — "Supplementary charges".................................... Cr. Accounts Receivable, Old — "Assets realized".....................	22,000 1,000 2,000	 25,000

Data	Analysis and Entry		
(6) Collection on notes receivable, old:	Dr. Cash — Cash Schedule	15,450	
Principal balances......................... $ 15,000	Cr. Notes Receivable, Old — "Assets realized".....................		15,000
Accrued interest 150	Cr. Accrued Interest on Notes Receivable, Old — "Assets realized"....................................		150
Interest....................................... 300	Cr. Interest Income — "Supplementary credits"		300
$ 15,450			
(7) Collection on notes receivable (new):	Dr. Cash — Cash Schedule	18,200	
Principal balances......................... $ 18,000	Cr. Notes Receivable — "Assets realized".................................		18,000
Interest....................................... 200	Cr. Interest Income — "Supplementary credits"		200
$ 18,200			
(8) Accounts payable (new) were reduced by the following:	Dr. Accounts Payable — "Liabilities liquidated"	90,000	
Cash payments .... $ 46,000	Cr. Cash — Cash Schedule........		46,000
Notes issued in payment................ 40,000	Cr. Notes Payable — "Liabilities assumed"..............................		40,000
Purchases returns and allowances .. 1,500	Cr. Purchases Returns and Allowances — "Supplementary credits"...........................		1,500
Purchases discounts received 2,500	Cr. Purchases Discount — "Supplementary credits"..........		2,500
$ 90,000			
(9) Payment of accounts payable, old, $30,000.	Dr. Accounts Payable, Old — "Liabilities liquidated"	30,000	
	Cr. Cash — Cash Schedule........		30,000
(10) Payment of notes payable, old:	Dr. Notes Payable, Old — "Liabilities liquidated"	35,000	
Principal balances......................... $ 35,000	Dr. Accrued Interest on Notes Payable, Old — "Liabilities liquidated"....................................	250	
Accrued interest 250	Dr. Interest Expense on Notes Payable, Old — "Supplementary charges"................................	700	
Interest....................................... 700	Cr. Cash — Cash Schedule........		35,950
$ 35,950			
(11) Payment of notes payable (new):	Dr. Notes Payable — "Liabilities liquidated"	15,000	
Principal balances......................... $ 15,000	Dr. Interest Expense — "Supplementary charges"	300	
Interest....................................... 300	Cr. Cash — Cash Schedule........		15,300
$ 15,300			
(12) Sale of securities:	Dr. Cash — Cash Schedule	13,000	
Common stock of X Co. (book value, $16,000)................................... $ 8,500	Dr. Loss on Sale of X Co. Stock — "Supplementary charges"	7,500	
Preferred stock of Y Co. (book value, $4,000) 4,500	Cr. Common Stock of X Co. — "Assets realized".....................		16,000
$ 13,000	Cr. Preferred Stock of Y Co. — "Assets realized".....................		4,000
	Cr. Gain on Sale of Y Co. Stock — "Supplementary credits"......		500

Data	Analysis and Entry		
(13) Payment of operating expenses: Sales salaries expense.................... $ 22,000 Other selling expense .... 18,600 Office expense.............................. 8,000 Other general expense.................. 12,000 Trustee fees................................. 6,500 $ 67,100	Dr. Sales Salaries Expense — "Supplementary charges" .... Dr. Other Selling Expense — "Supplementary charges" .... Dr. Office Expense — "Supplementary charges" .... Dr. Other General Expense — "Supplementary charges" .... Dr. Trustee Fees — "Supplementary charges" .... Cr. Cash — Cash Schedule........	22,000 18,600 8,000 12,000 6,500	 67,100
(14) To recognize beginning inventory as an element of cost of goods sold, $50,000.	Dr. Merchandise Inventory (March 31) — "Supplementary charges" .. Cr. Merchandise Inventory (March 31) — "Assets realized".	50,000	 50,000
(15) To recognize ending inventory as an asset and as a subtraction from goods available for sale in arriving at cost of goods sold, $36,000.	Dr. Merchandise Inventory (Dec. 31) — "Assets acquired"............. Cr. Merchandise Inventory (Dec. 31) — "Supplementary credits"	36,000	 36,000
(16) To provide for doubtful accounts (new accounts), $450.	Dr. Uncollectible Accounts Expense (allowance provision) — "Supplementary charges" .... Cr. Allowance for Doubtful Accounts — "Assets realized"	450	 450
(17) To record depreciation of furniture, and fixtures, $450.	Dr. Depreciation of Furniture and Fixtures (allowance provision) — "Supplementary charges" .... Cr. Accumulated Depreciation of Furniture and Fixtures — "Assets realized"......................	450	 450
(18) To record depreciation of buildings, $1,800.	Dr. Depreciation of Buildings (allowance provision) — "Supplementary charges" .... Cr. Accumulated Depreciation of Buildings — "Assets realized"..	1,800	 1,800
(19) To record accrued interest on notes receivable, $200.	Dr. Accrued Interest on Notes Receivable — "Assets acquired"...... Cr. Interest Income (accrued) — "Supplementary credits".........	200	 200
(20) To record accrued interest on notes payable (new), $300.	Dr. Interest Expense (accrued) — "Supplementary charges" .... Cr. Accrued Interest on Notes Payable — "Liabilities assumed"	300	 300
(21) To record accrued interest on mortgage, $1,800.	Dr. Interest Expense on Mortgage, Old (accrued) — "Supplementary charges"................................. Cr. Accrued Interest on Mortgage — "Liabilities assumed" ...	1,800	 1,800
(22) To transfer net gain to retained earnings, $3,300.	Dr. Increase in Retained Earnings — "Supplementary charges"........ Cr. Increase in Retained Earnings — Retained Earnings Schedule	3,300	 3,300

Miles Corporation, Debtor
I. B. Owens, Trustee
Statement of Realization and Liquidation
March 31–December 31, 19X7

Assets

Assets to be realized:		
Notes receivable, old......................		$15,000
Accounts rec., old $25,000		
Less allow. for doubtful		
accounts	1,000	24,000
Accrued interest on notes receivable, old		150
Merchandise inventory (March 31)..		50,000
Land		15,000
Buildings......................... $60,000		
Less accumulated depr.	7,800	52,200
Furniture and fixtures...... $ 6,000		
Less accumulated depr.	1,950	4,050
Common stock of X Co..................		16,000
Preferred stock of Y Co.................		4,000
		$180,400
Assets acquired:		
(2) Accounts receivable		$210,000
(4) Notes receivable		30,000
(15) Merchandise inventory (Dec. 31).....................................		36,000
(19) Accrued interest on notes receivable		200
		$276,200
		$456,600

Assets realized:		
(4) Accounts receivable		$192,000
(5) Accounts rec., old.... $25,000		
Less allow. for doubtful accounts....	1,000	24,000
(6) Notes receivable, old		15,000
(6) Accrued interest on notes rec., old		150
(7) Notes receivable		18,000
(12) Common stock of X Co.		16,000
(12) Preferred stock of Y Co.		4,000
(14) Merchandise inventory (March 31)		50,000
(16) Allowance for doubtful accounts		450
(17) Accumulated depr. of furniture and fixtures....................		450
(18) Accumulated depr. of bldgs....		1,800
		$321,850
Assets not realized:		
Notes receivable...........................		$ 12,000
Accounts receivable $18,000		
Less allow. for doubtful accounts	450	17,550
Accrued interest on notes rec.........		200
Merchandise inventory (Dec. 31)		36,000
Land		15,000
Buildings......................... $60,000		
Less accumulated depr.	9,600	50,400
Furniture and fixtures...... $ 6,000		
Less accumulated depr.	2,400	3,600
		$134,750
		$456,600

Liabilities

Liabilities liquidated:		
(8) Accounts payable...................		$ 90,000
(9) Accounts payable, old...........		30,000
(10) Notes payable, old................		35,000
(10) Accrued int. on notes pay., old		250
(11) Notes payable......................		15,000
		$170,250
Liabilities not liquidated:		
Notes payable		$ 25,000
Accounts payable		22,000
Accrued interest on notes payable..		300
Accrued interest on mortgage		2,200
6% first mortgage payable		40,000
		$ 89,500
		$259,750

Liabilities to be liquidated:		
Notes payable, old		$ 35,000
Accounts payable, old		30,000
Accrued int. on notes payable, old..		250
Accrued interest on mortgage		400
6% first mortgage payable		40,000
		$105,650
Liabilities assumed:		
(3) Accounts payable..................		$112,000
(8) Notes payable.......................		40,000
(20) Accrued interest on notes payable......................................		300
(21) Accrued interest on mortgage.		1,800
		$154,100
		$259,750

Income

Supplementary charges:		Supplementary credits:	
(3) Purchases	$112,000	(2) Sales	$210,000
(4) Sales returns and allowances..	1,500	(6) Interest income	300
(4) Sales discount	2,000	(7) Interest income	200
(5) Uncollectible accounts expense, old	2,000	(8) Purchases returns and allowances	1,500
(10) Interest expense on notes, old	700	(8) Purchases discount	2,500
(11) Interest expense	300	(12) Gain on sale of Y Co. stock	500
(12) Loss on sale of X Co. stock	7,500	(15) Merchandise inventory (Dec. 31)	36,000
(13) Sales salaries expense	22,000	(19) Interest income (accrued)	200
(13) Other selling expense	18,600		
(13) Office expense	8,000		
(13) Other general expense	12,000		
(13) Trustee expense	6,500		
(14) Merchandise inventory (March 31)	50,000		
(16) Uncollectible accounts expense (allowance provision)	450		
(17) Depr. of furniture and fixtures (allowance provision)	450		
(18) Depr. of buildings (allowance provision)	1,800		
(20) Interest expense (accrued)	300		
(21) Interest expense on mortgage, old (accrued)	1,800		
	$247,900		
(22) Increase in retained earnings..	3,300		
	$251,200		$251,200

Miles Corporation, Debtor
I. B. Owens, Trustee
Supplementary Schedules To Accompany Statement of Realization and Liquidation
March 31–December 31, 19X7

Cash

Mar. 31 Balance	$ 1,000	(8) Payment of accts. payable	$ 46,000
(4) Collection of accounts receivable	158,500	(9) Payment of accts. pay., old	30,000
(5) Collection of accounts receivable, old	22,000	(10) Payment of notes payable, old, $35,000; accrued interest on notes payable, old, $250; and current interest, $700	35,950
(6) Collection of notes receivable, old, $15,000; accrued interest on notes receivable, old, $150; and current interest, $300	15,450	(11) Payment of notes payable, $15,000, and current interest, $300	15,300
(7) Collection of notes receivable, $18,000, and current interest, $200	18,200	(13) Payment of operating expenses	67,100
(12) Proceeds from sale of common stock of X Co., $8,500, and preferred stock of Y Co., $4,500	13,000	Dec. 31 Balance	33,800
	$228,150		$228,150
Jan. 1 Balance	$ 33,800		

Capital Stock

	Mar. 31 Balance	$100,000

Retained Earnings

Mar. 31 Balance............................. $ 24,250	Dec. 31 (22) Increase in retained earnings...................... $ 3,300
	31 Balance.............................. 20,950
$ 24,250	$ 24,250
Jan. 1 Balance................................ $ 20,950	

A check on the accuracy of the statement of realization and liquidation and supporting schedules is afforded by the following summary:

Miles Corporation, Debtor
Balances per Statement of Realization and Liquidation and Accompanying Schedules
December 31, 19X7

Assets	Liabilities and Stockholders' Equity	
Cash... $ 33,800	Liabilities not liquidated.................... $ 89,500	
Assets not realized............................ 134,750	Capital stock..................... $100,000	
	Less deficit 20,950	79,050
Total $168,550	Total $168,550	

The financial statements that may be prepared to accompany the realization and liquidation statement for the Miles Corporation were illustrated in the previous chapter.

STATEMENT OF REALIZATION AND LIQUIDATION — WORK SHEET FORM

Previous illustrations utilized a statement and related schedules in summarizing the process of realization and liquidation. Realization and liquidation data can also be presented by means of a work sheet. Although such a presentation represents a departure from the conventional approach, nevertheless it offers a clearer and better organized presentation of data and is developed in a manner similar to that employed in preparing other financial statements. The work sheet approach may take a number of different forms. One form is illustrated on pages 662 and 663. The statement is based upon the facts in the previous example. The following steps are employed in the development of the statement:

(1) Beginning balances are listed in the first pair of columns in trial balance form but are divided into four groups: (a) cash, (b) other assets, (c) liabilities, and (d) stockholders' equity. In listing the accounts, adequate space is left within each group to provide for

transactions and new accounts to be added in summarizing activities for the period.

(2) Transactions are recorded in a second pair of columns. The four classes of items mentioned in (1) are headed in the second pair of columns as follows:

Cash		Other Assets	
Receipts	Disbursements	Acquired	Realized

Liabilities		Stockholders' Equity	
Liquidated	Assumed	Charges	Credits

Transactions are analyzed in terms of their effects on assets, liabilities, and stockholders' equity, and are then applied in debit and credit form to the accounts in the different sections within the Transactions columns. Transactions are thus analyzed and recorded on the work sheet in the same manner in which they would be analyzed and recorded on the books.

(3) Ending asset and liability balances are determined by combining ending balances and changes reported in the Transactions columns and are listed in the third pair of columns. The original balances for the stockholders' equity are carried to the third pair of columns. Income statement data in the last section of the Transactions columns are summarized and the net income or loss is determined. The income or loss is entered as a balancing figure in the revenue and expense section of the Transactions columns and as a balancing figure in the third pair of columns, where it represents an addition to or a subtraction from the beginning balances previously listed.

The work sheet form for realization and liquidation reporting offers in a single exhibit the following data:

(1) Beginning and ending asset, liability, and capital balances.
(2) A reconciliation of beginning and ending balances for each item.
(3) A full statement of cash receipts and disbursements.
(4) A full listing of revenue and expense items and the net change in capital therefrom.

With a complete summary of financial and operating data available in this form, any data requested by the court, creditors, or other parties can be conveniently located on the work sheet and transferred to the appropriate reports and schedules.

Miles Corporation, Debtor
I. B. Owens, Trustee
Statement of Realization and Liquidation
March 31–December 31, 19X7

Item	Balances March 31, 19X7	Transactions — Cash Receipts	Transactions — Cash Disbursements	Transactions — Other Assets Acquired	Transactions — Other Assets Realized	Balances December 31, 19X7
Cash balance, March 31	1,000					
Collection of accounts receivable		(4) 158,500				
Collection of accounts receivable, old		(5) 22,000				
Collection of notes receivable, old; accrued interest on notes receivable, old; and current interest		(6) 15,450				
Collection of notes receivable and current interest		(7) 18,200				
Payment of accounts payable			(8) 46,000			
Payment of accounts payable, old			(9) 30,000			
Payment of notes payable, old; accrued interest on notes payable, old; and current interest						
Payment of notes payable and current interest			(10) 35,950			
Proceeds from sale of common stock of X Co. and preferred stock of Y Co.		(12) 13,000	(11) 15,300			
Payment of operating expenses			(13) 67,100			
Cash balance, December 31						33,800
Notes receivable, old	15,000				(6) 15,000	
Accounts receivable, old	25,000				(5) 25,000	
Allowance for doubtful accounts, old	1,000			(5) 1,000		
Accrued interest on notes receivable	150			(19) 200	(6) 150	200
Merchandise inventory	50,000			(15) 36,000	(14) 50,000	36,000
Common stock of X Co.	16,000				(12) 16,000	
Preferred stock of Y Co.	4,000				(12) 4,000	
Land	15,000					15,000
Buildings	60,000					60,000
Accumulated depreciation of buildings	7,800				(18) 1,800	9,600
Furniture and fixtures	6,000					6,000
Accumulated depreciation of furniture and fixtures	1,950				(17) 450	2,400
Accounts receivable				(2) 210,000	(4) 192,000	18,000
Notes receivable				(4) 30,000	(7) 18,000	12,000
Allowance for doubtful accounts					(16) 450	450

			Liabilities: Liquidated	Liabilities: Assumed		
Notes payable, old		35,000	(10) 35,000			
Accounts payable, old		30,000	(9) 30,000			
Accrued interest on notes payable, old		250	(10) 250			
Accrued interest on mortgage		400		(21) 1,800		2,200
6% first mortgage bonds		40,000				40,000
Accounts payable			(8) 90,000	(3) 112,000		22,000
Notes payable			(11) 15,000	(8) 40,000		25,000
Accrued interest on notes payable				(20) 300		300
			Stockholders' Equity: Charges	**Stockholders' Equity: Credits**		
Capital stock		100,000				100,000
Retained earnings	24,250				24,250	
Sales				(2) 210,000		
Purchases			(3) 112,000			
Sales returns and allowances			(4) 1,500			
Sales discount			(4) 2,000			
Uncollectible accounts expense, old			(5) 2,000			
Interest income				(6) 300 (7) 200 (19) 200		
Purchases returns and allowances				(8) 1,500		
Purchases discount				(8) 2,500		
Interest expense on notes, old			(10) 700			
Interest expense			(11) 300 (20) 300			
Loss on sale of common stock of X Co.			(12) 7,500			
Gain on sale of preferred stock of Y Co.				(12) 500		
Sales salaries expense			(13) 22,000			
Other selling expense			(13) 18,600			
Office expense			(13) 8,000			
Other general expense			(13) 12,000			
Trustee fees			(13) 6,500			
Income summary (beginning and ending inventories)			(14) 50,000	(15) 36,000		
Uncollectible accounts expense			(16) 450			
Depreciation of buildings			(18) 1,800			
Depreciation of furniture and fixtures			(17) 450			
Interest expense on mortgage			(21) 1,800			
	216,400	216,400	247,900	251,200	205,250	201,950
Increase in retained earnings			3,300			3,300
			251,200	251,200	205,250	205,250

QUESTIONS

1. Distinguish between the functions served by the statement of affairs and the statement of realization and liquidation.

2. Describe the nature of the statement of realization and liquidation.

3. How are original assets, liabilities, and capital reported for purposes of realization and liquidation reports?

4. (a) What sections of the statement of realization and liquidation or its supplementary schedules are affected by cash receipts? (b) What sections of the statement or the schedules are affected by cash payments?

5. How are the following data reported on the statement of realization and liquidation and the supplementary schedules?

    (a) Assets taken over by a trustee.
    (b) Sale of assets taken over at a loss.
    (c) Payment to creditors of amounts owed.
    (d) Distribution of cash to owners in the form of a final liquidating dividend.

6. How are the following data reported on the statement of realization and liquidation prepared in its conventional form?

    (a) Additional assets discovered.
    (b) Additional liabilities discovered.
    (c) Assets determined to be worthless in the course of liquidation.
    (d) Composition of creditors, with payments to be made to creditors in four equal quarterly installments.

7. Explain the sources that contribute to the net income or loss when the statement of realization and liquidation is prepared in its conventional form, with the income or loss determined by adding the amounts on each side of the statement.

8. What alternative analyses of the following transactions may be made in reflecting these transactions on the statement of realization and liquidation prepared in the conventional form?

    (a) Sale of merchandise.
    (b) Accrued revenue.
    (c) Uncollectible accounts written off.
    (d) Settlement of an obligation at less than its book value.

9. (a) What are the limitations of the statement of realization and liquidation prepared in its conventional form? (b) What modifications can be introduced in the statement to overcome these limitations?

10. When transactions are analyzed in terms of debit and credit and are applied to the statement of realization and liquidation and the supplementary schedules, what are the offsetting debits and credits for each of the following transactions? (Give the statement section or schedule affected.)

    (a) Purchase of merchandise on account.
    (b) Liquidation of liabilities at less than the book value of such obligations.

    (c) Sale of securities at a profit.

    (d) Payment of expenses.

11. When adjustments are analyzed in terms of debit and credit and are applied to the statement of realization and liquidation and the supplementary schedules, how would the following adjusting data be recorded in the statement sections and the schedules?

    (a) Recognition of beginning inventory as an element in the calculation of cost of goods sold.

    (b) Recognition of ending inventory as an asset and an element in the calculation of cost of goods sold.

    (c) Accrued expenses.

    (d) Amortization of deferred costs.

    (e) Accrued revenue.

    (f) Prepaid expense balances that have expired.

    (g) Expense prepayments.

    (h) Deferred revenue balances that have been earned.

    (i) Deferred revenue.

12. The accountant for the Lea Co., which is in bankruptcy proceedings, feels that the preparation of a statement of realization and liquidation makes unnecessary the development of the usual financial statements. Do you agree?

13. What advantages can you suggest for the preparation of the realization and liquidation report in work sheet form?

EXERCISES

1. The following balance sheet is prepared for the Warden Co. on December 1, when Mary Gonzales is appointed trustee to take over control:

Assets		Liabilities and Stockholders' Equity	
Cash.................................	$ 12,000	Accounts payable	$ 55,000
Receivables......................	36,000	Capital stock..................	50,000
Merchandise	40,000	Retained earnings..........	(2,000)
Furniture and fixtures (net)............................	15,000		
Total..............................	$103,000	Total	$103,000

Transactions in December are summarized as follows:

Cash receipts:
    Sale of merchandise $24,000
    Collection of receivables:
      Company receivables $18,500
      Trusteeship claims...   450   18,950
                               $42,950

Cash disbursements:
    Purchase of merchandise............ $ 750
    Expenses....................................   1,400
                                 $ 2,150

Sales of merchandise on account in December totaled $1,800. Company receivables of $650 were written off as worthless. At the end of December the merchandise on hand is valued at $22,500. Depreciation of furniture and fixtures is $250.

(a) Prepare a statement of realization and liquidation in conventional form together with supporting schedules.
(b) Prepare a condensed balance sheet as of December 31 to prove the gain or the loss for December.

2. Indicate how the following transactions for the Leo Sales Co. in bankruptcy will be reported on the statement of realization and liquidation and the supplementary schedules prepared in the conventional form.

(a) Sale of merchandise on account, $25,000.
(b) Collections on accounts receivable, $13,500; uncollectible accounts of $500 are written off.
(c) Sale of securities costing $17,000 for $16,400.
(d) Purchase of merchandise on account, $17,500.
(e) Payment of selling expenses, $4,750, of which $800 had accrued prior to bankruptcy.
(f) Depreciation of furniture and fixtures, $275.
(g) Trade of delivery truck with a book value of $1,200 for a new truck costing $2,200; $1,000 is allowed on the trade-in, and the balance is paid in cash.
(h) Payments on accounts payable, $9,800, after a $200 discount.

3. From the following data and transactions, prepare a statement of realization and liquidation and supporting schedules for Jaspar and Kalman in the alternative form.

(a) The beginning balance sheet on October 1 is as follows:

Assets		Liabilities and Capital	
Cash..............................	$ 5,000	Notes payable..................	$ 25,000
Marketable securities.......	20,000	Accounts payable.............	34,500
Accounts receivable.........	25,000	Accrued interest on notes	
Merchandise	40,000	payable.........................	500
Furniture and fixtures		Jaspar, capital.................	30,000
(net).............................	10,000	Kalman, capital	10,000
Total..............................	$100,000	Total..............................	$100,000

During October:
(b) Marketable securities are sold for $11,500.
(c) Merchandise sales are as follows: cash sales, $8,500; sales on account, $6,500.
(d) Collections of $12,000 are made from customers; accounts of $400 are written off as worthless.
(e) Payment of $10,000 is made on notes payable and $300 for accrued interest.
(f) Payment of $21,500 is made on account.

(g) Payment of $2,200 is made for expenses.
(h) At the end of October, the following adjusting data are recognized:
    Merchandise on hand is valued at $22,500.
    Accrued interest on notes payable on this date is $330.
    Depreciation of furniture and fixtures for October is $250.

4. Assuming preparation of the statement of realization and liquidation and the supplementary schedules for the Wesley Co. in the alternative form, give the effects of the following data on the statement and the schedules in terms of offsetting debits and credits:

(a) Balances relating to a company bond issue as of December 1, when trusteeship became effective, were as follows: bonds payable, $100,000; discount on bonds, $2,500; accrued interest on bonds, $1,000. Outstanding bonds were acquired at a cost of $86,500, which included a payment of accrued interest of $1,500.
(b) Balances relating to a company investment as of December 1 were as follows: $20,000 bonds of Ward Co., book value (cost plus prior accumulation of discount), $17,750; accrued interest on bonds, $300. Bonds were sold at a price of $21,400, which includes receipt of accrued interest of $325.
(c) Balances relating to unsecured creditors were as follows: notes payable, $20,000; accrued interest on notes payable, $1,500; accounts payable, $38,500. Settlement was made with this group of creditors by means of a composition whereby they agreed to accept 60¢ on the dollar, with 15¢ paid in December and the balance paid in the first three months of the following year in equal monthly installments.

5. The partnership of L and M is unable to repay a maturing bank loan. Upon petition to the court by the bank, N is appointed as trustee and takes over the control of the firm on July 15. The following balance sheet is prepared from the books of the partnership on this date:

Assets		Liabilities and Capital	
Cash..............................	$ 3,250	Accounts payable.............	$ 6,500
Accounts receivable.........	12,000	Bank loan........................	20,000
Inventory (at cost)............	21,350	Accrued interest on bank	
Supplies	800	loan.............................	500
Furniture and fixtures		L, capital	10,000
(net).............................	7,600	M, capital........................	8,000
Total..............................	$45,000	Total..............................	$45,000

Transactions during the period of trusteeship from July 15–August 31 are as follows:

(a) The accounts receivable are sold for $8,000.
(b) A part of the inventory costing $5,000 is sold for $4,500; the balance of the inventory is accepted by the original supplier at a 30% discount.
(c) Supplies of $150 are used.
(d) The loan from the bank is paid, together with additional interest of $150.
(e) Accounts payable of $3,500 are paid.
(f) Trustee's expenses of $295 are paid.

Prepare a statement of realization and liquidation with supporting schedules in the alternative form.

6. Assuming preparation of the statement of realization and liquidation for the Process Co. in work sheet form, indicate in terms of offsetting debits and credits how the following adjustments would be reported on the work sheet:

(a) Depreciation of equipment	$ 4,500
(b) Leasehold amortization	1,500
(c) Accrued interest on investments	350
(d) Accrued salaries and wages	600
(e) Rent expense that is prepaid	60
(f) Rental income that is received in advance	200
(g) Beginning inventory that is to be recognized in cost of goods sold	35,000
(h) Ending inventory	21,500

PROBLEMS

20-1. The Young Steamship Co. is unable to meet its current obligations, partly because of losses suffered and partly because of inability to transfer its foreign deposits back to the United States. Upon petition of creditors, the Moore Steamship Co. is appointed trustee. On February 12, 19X4, the trustee takes over the control of the business. The following balance sheet is prepared from the books of the Young Steamship Co. on this date:

Assets			Liabilities and Stockholders' Equity			
Cash	$	51,200	Accounts payable		$	202,500
Freights receivable		81,800	Accrued expenses			39,500
Merchandise		42,000	6% mortgage payable			600,000
Prepaid expenses		35,000	Capital			
Foreign deposits		123,500	stock.... $1,400,000			
Vessels (net)		1,800,000	Less			
Furniture and fixtures			deficit...	83,500		1,316,500
(net)		25,000				
Total		$2,158,500	Total			$2,158,500

Transactions of the trustee up to December 31, 19X4, are as follows:

(a) Cash receipts:

Collections on freights receivable (after a discount of $6,800 is allowed to a shipper in settlement of a dispute that may have cost more to arbitrate)	$ 75,000
Freights received on new shipping contracts (after 5% of the total freight being withheld by agents pending settlement)	427,500
Proceeds from sale of merchandise	91,800
	$594,300

(b) Cash disbursements:

Fuel oil	$165,000
Operating expenses (including accrual of $39,500)	133,000
Cash purchases of merchandise	50,000
Accounts payable (after discounts of $4,500)	198,000
Prepaid expenses..	40,000
Trustee's expenses	17,500
Interest on mortgage..	36,000
	$639,500

(c) Foreign deposits of $108,000 are utilized to pay for merchandise pur-
chased abroad and shipped back by own vessels. The merchandise is
subsequently sold to wholesalers at a 15% discount. (Proceeds are listed
under cash receipts.)

(d) Adjustments for the following are required at the end of the year.

Accounts payable — fuel oil..	$ 35,000
Merchandise on hand..	25,000
Prepaid expenses...	18,500
Accrued expenses..	26,800
Depreciation of vessels...	100,000
Depreciation of furniture and fixtures.............................	5,000

Instructions: (1) Prepare a statement of realization and liquidation in conventional form together with supporting schedules.

(2) Prepare a balance sheet as of December 31, 19X4.

20-2. The Bailey Storage Co. is unable to meet its obligations. On March 1, 19X2,
C. C. Hill is appointed trustee. A balance sheet prepared from the books of the
Bailey Storage Co. on this date is as follows:

Assets			Liabilities and Stockholders' Equity	
Cash..................................		$ 8,200	Accounts payable	$ 28,400
Notes receivable......................		14,500	6% mortgage on warehouse	50,000
Accounts receivable................		31,050	Accrued interest on mortgage	
Supplies		2,050	(up to March 1, 19X2)...........	1,000
Trucks..................	$25,000		Capital stock	40,000
Less accumulated			Retained earnings..................	8,400
depreciation.....	10,500	14,500		
Warehouse.............	$75,000			
Less accumulated				
depreciation.....	17,500	57,500		
Total		$127,800	Total	$127,800

The trustee operates the business until the end of the year and returns control of the business to the stockholders at that time.

Transactions during the period of trusteeship are as follows:

(a) Cash receipts:

Notes receivable, old..	$ 13,800
Accounts receivable, old...	28,000
Accounts receivable, new	140,000
	$181,800

(b) Cash disbursements:

Accounts payable, old	$ 28,400
Accounts payable, new..	27,600
Mortgage payable (installment payment on November 1, 19X2)	15,000
Interest on mortgage (paid on May 1 and November 1)	3,000
Operating expenses...	84,400
Trustee's expenses and fees	8,000
New trucks (after trade-in allowance of $12,500).............	10,000
	$176,400

(c) Billings to customers for truckage and storage services, $153,450. Purchases on account for gas, oil, parts, and other supplies, $35,000.

(d) A 10-month, 6% note dated April 1, 19X2, for $3,000 is received from a customer in settlement of an old account receivable. Balances of old accounts and notes receivable after collections are written off as worthless at the end of the year.

(e) Five trucks having a total book value of $10,000, but with an original cost to the company of $20,000, are traded in for 5 new trucks on July 1, 19X2. The new trucks are estimated to have a total scrap value of $5,000 after a 5-year service life.

(f) Adjustments on December 31, 19X2, are as follows:

Supplies on hand...	$ 4,500
Accrued operating expenses	1,500
Depreciation of old trucks (including depreciation for the period March 1–July 1, 19X2, for the 5 trucks traded) ...	3,000
Depreciation of warehouse	5% per year

Instructions: (1) Prepare a statement of realization and liquidation in conventional form together with supporting schedules.

(2) Prepare a balance sheet as of December 31, 19X2.

20-3. Horace Sloan, a partner in the investment banking firm of Ross and Sloan, died on December 31, 19X6. The assets and the liabilities of the firm at that date were as follows:

Cash in Bank	11,526.90	
Life Insurance Funds Receivable.....................	44,700.02	
Marketable Securities	978,663.77	
Notes and Accounts Receivable	23,268.63	
Bonds of Brown Lumber Co., bankrupt, at 25% of par..	56,250.00	
75% Interest in Logs, Lumber, Machinery, and Logging Equipment	22,604.25	
Notes Payable...		500,000.00
Accrued Interest		1,500.00
Liability as Guarantors of Note of Brown Lumber Co., bankrupt....................................		38,170.31
Accounts Payable..		14,357.33
Agreement to Repurchase $10,000 of Brown Lumber Co. Bonds at 97½.............................		9,750.00
Capital — Phillip Ross, 40%		229,294.37
Capital — Horace Sloan, 60%.........................		343,941.56
Totals	1,137,013.57	1,137,013.57

Phillip Ross, surviving partner, was appointed trustee to continue the business for a limited period of time.

The transactions to September 30, 19X7, were as follows:

(1) The amount due for life insurance was collected.

(2) $712,554.07 was realized on securities that cost $619,483.

(3) $3,725 was expended in exercising stock rights related to the marketable securities, with the original and newly acquired shares among those unsold at September 30.

(4) Notes and accounts receivable realized $17,429.30, but of the balance outstanding at September 30 only $1,000 was considered collectible.

(5) Foreclosure proceedings were instituted on the bonds of the Brown Lumber Co. In the final settlement, $4,603.97 was realized in cash and the firm acquired a ¾ interest in 10,000 acres of timberland.

(6) The interest in logs, lumber, machinery, and logging equipment realized $2,725.09.

(7) A claim receivable for damages, which was pending on December 31, 19X5, but not entered on the books, was settled for $3,000.

(8) The notes payable, with interest amounting to $27,500, were paid.

(9) The liability as guarantors of the note of the Brown Lumber Co. was discharged by payment of $36,149.73.

(10) One $1,000 bond of the Brown Lumber Co. had been lost or stolen and therefore could not be produced. The remaining bonds were repurchased. (It is assumed that there will be no company liability on the bond that is not produced.)

(11) The accounts payable, together with an additional item of $1,275 owing at December 31 but not discovered until later, were duly paid.

(12) The sum of $200,000 was withdrawn in the proportion of the partners' investments.

(13) Expenses incurred, exclusive of interest, totaled $7,328.30, of which $432.15 was unpaid on September 30, 19X7.

(14) Income amounted to $14,732.03, of which $2,500 had not been received on September 30, 19X7.

Instructions: Prepare a statement of realization and liquidation in conventional form for the use of the trustee and of the executor of the estate of the deceased partner.

(AICPA adapted)

20-4. A balance sheet prepared for Rusk Sales as of March 1, 19X9, is shown on page 672.

A summary of transactions of the trustee for this company for the period March 1–July 1 follows:

Transactions, March 1–July 1:
  Sales on account, $36,000.
  Purchases on account, $12,000.
  Reductions in accounts receivable — new:
    Cash collections, $30,000.
    Sales returns, $1,000.

Assets			Liabilities and Capital	
Accounts			Cash overdraft	$ 1,500
receivable........	$20,000		Notes payable....................	15,000
Less allowance			Accrued interest on notes	
for doubtful			payable.........................	500
accounts......	1,000	$19,000	Accounts payable..............	25,000
Merchandise inventory.......		30,000	M. A. Rusk, capital	16,000
Furniture and				
fixtures	$ 5,000			
Less				
accumulated				
depreciation	1,000	4,000		
Securities..........................		5,000		
Total..................................		$58,000	Total	$58,000

Reductions in accounts receivable — old:
  Cash collections, $14,000.
  Accounts of $2,000 were written off as uncollectible; remaining accounts are believed
    to be collectible.
Sale of securities, $8,000.
Payment of accounts payable — new, $4,000.
Payment of notes payable — old, $15,000, and interest, $1,000.
Payment of accounts payable — old, $18,000.
Payment of operating expenses, $10,000.

Data for adjustments, July 1:
  Merchandise inventory, $18,500.
  Depreciation of furniture and fixtures, $100.
  Accrued operating expenses, $500.
  Prepaid operating expenses, $350.

Instructions: Prepare a statement of realization and liquidation in the alternative form together with supplementary schedules.

20-5. Using the data given in Problem 19-1 for the McDonald Company (page 635), prepare a statement of realization and liquidation in the alternative form together with supplementary schedules.

20-6. Using the data given in Problem 19-2 for the Robbins Corporation (page 636), prepare a statement of realization and liquidation in the alternative form together with supplementary schedules.

20-7. The Wain Sales Company was on the verge of insolvency. Accordingly, a trustee, B. C. Bell, was appointed by the court to take legal possession of the company's assets as at February 1, 19X2. A new set of books was opened by the trustee to reflect properly the transactions during the period of trusteeship. A proper segregation is to be made between transactions originating prior to and during the trusteeship. At January 31, 19X3, the business was turned back to the company.

A post-closing trial balance of the company on February 1, 19X2, is as follows:

Cash..	48,000	
Notes Receivable	90,000	
Notes Receivable Discounted		10,000
Accrued Interest on Notes Receivable	3,000	
Accounts Receivable	138,000	
Allowance for Doubtful Accounts		7,500
Inventory..	174,200	
Capital Stock Subscriptions Receivable	20,500	
U.S. Government Bonds...	25,000	
Buildings..	121,400	
Accumulated Depreciation — Buildings.....................		56,540
Prepaid Insurance	1,400	
Deficit...	47,040	
Notes Payable...		127,500
Accrued Interest on Notes Payable...........................		9,800
Accounts Payable..		296,000
Mortgage Payable on Buildings		60,000
Accrued Interest on Mortgage Payable.....................		1,200
Common Stock..		100,000
	668,540	668,540

The transactions during the year of trusteeship are summarized as follows:

Cash collections:

Notes receivable — old (gross $79,000, less notes written off $8,090)........	$ 70,910
Interest on notes receivable, including accrued interest of $3,000	4,400
Accounts receivable — old (gross $110,000, less discount of $2,000 and uncollectible accounts written off, $3,500)..	104,500
Capital stock subscriptions receivable ($1,000 uncollectible).....................	19,500
Securities considered worthless February 1, 19X2, and not included in post-closing trial balance	4,700
Trustee's certificates issued, interest at 4½%...	120,000
Accounts receivable — new (gross $225,000, less discount of $10,600)	214,400
Interest on U.S. Government bonds	500
Total cash collections..	$538,910

Cash payments:

Notes receivable discounted, not paid by makers (remaining $7,500 as at February 1, 19X2, paid by makers at maturity)	$ 2,500
Notes payable — old	65,200
Accounts payable — old (retired at a discount of 10%)	45,000
Accounts payable — old (retired at face amount).....................................	210,000
Accounts payable — new (gross $124,000, less discount of $2,000)...........	122,000
Interest on notes payable, including accrual of $9,800...............................	11,000
Interest on mortgage payable, including accrual of $1,200	2,600
Trustee's certificates...	40,000
Interest on trustee's certificates	5,810
Trustee's fees..	8,000
Total cash payments	$512,110

Other transactions:

Sales of merchandise (before discounts)...	$260,000
Purchases of merchandise (before discounts)	110,000
Selling expenses	33,000
General expenses...	13,000

Adjustments at January 31, 19X3:

Merchandise inventory	$120,000
Depreciation of buildings	3,600
Accrued taxes..	3,700
Accrued interest on notes receivable...	300
Provision for doubtful accounts — new accounts receivable	800
Insurance expired	300
Interest on old notes payable..	2,800
Interest on old mortgage payable	1,200

Instructions: (1) Prepare a statement of realization and liquidation summarizing the trustee's transactions by setting forth accountability at the beginning of trusteeship, the operations during trusteeship, and the condition at the consummation of trusteeship.

(2) Prepare summary statements of assets and liabilities conveyed to company management at the termination of the trusteeship period.

(AICPA adapted)

20-8. Using the data given in Problem 19-6 for the Coast Sales Company (page 641), prepare a statement of realization and liquidation in work sheet form.

20-9. Using the data given in Problem 19-3 for the X and Y partnership (page 638), prepare a statement of realization and liquidation in work sheet form.

20-10. The Sherbourne Company was unable to meet its obligations. As a result, Wilma Bond was appointed trustee on February 6, 19X6. The following trial balance was taken from the books as of that date:

Debits

Cash	764
Accounts Receivable......................	5,928
Merchandise...................................	16,536
Prepaid Expenses...........................	704
Fixtures..	12,342
Total debits	36,274

Credits

Accounts Payable...........................	15,987
Notes Payable...............................	3,500
Accrued Wages, Taxes, etc.	1,275
Accrued Rent.................................	600
Accumulated Depreciation	3,803
Capital Stock	10,000
Retained Earnings	1,109
Total credits	36,274

In the period from February 5 to April 30, 19X6, the trustee's actions resulted in the following:

(1) An audit of the accounts receivable disclosed that there were an additional $423 of accounts receivable that had not been recorded on the books.

(2) Merchandise costing $8,310 was sold for cash.

(3) A portion of the fixtures, which cost $5,376 and had accumulated depreciation of $942, was sold.
(4) Accounts receivable totaling $1,882 were collected. Other accounts amounting to $741 have been determined to be worthless.
(5) Claims have been approved and paid for $903 of the wages and taxes that were accrued at February 5. Wage claims for $125 that were unrecorded on February 5 have also been approved and paid. Other claims have not yet been paid.
(6) Expenses for wages and supplies used in liquidating the business to April 30 amounted to $1,245. Fees for the trustee need not be considered.
(7) Rent under leases has continued to accrue in the amount of $900. Interest of $70 has accrued on notes payable.
(8) Cash receipts and cash disbursements show the following:

Cash Receipts

Collection of accounts....................	$1,882
Sales of merchandise.....................	9,108
Sale of fixtures.............................	1,000

Cash Disbursements

Accrued wages and taxes	$1,028
Expenses of the trustee..................	1,245

Instructions: Prepare a statement of realization and liquidation in work sheet form for the period ended April 30, 19X6.

(AICPA adapted)

21
Estates and Trusts – General Estate Procedures

Parties who are entrusted with the care, management, and disposition of properties on behalf of others and who are accountable for such activities act in a *fiduciary* capacity and are referred to as *fiduciaries*. Receivers, assignees, or trustees who are appointed to take over control of the assets of insolvents act in the capacity of fiduciaries. Parties who are named by a court to assume control of an estate and parties who, by terms of a trust instrument, are appointed to manage properties for the benefit of others act in a similar capacity.

This chapter and the one that follows describe the accounting procedures used by those parties who are charged with the administration of properties of an estate and of a trust. For an understanding of the accounting, the nature of the activities and responsibilities of such parties as well as the legal framework within which they operate must be understood. The statutes and body of law governing the activities of those parties administering estates and trusts vary in the different states. Also the legal requirements as to accounting frequently differ. The rules and the procedures described are those that generally apply to estates and trusts. The accounting methods and reports illustrated are those that are normally adopted or required.

ADMINISTRATION OF AN ESTATE

Upon the death of a person, it becomes necessary for some party to assume control and administration of the property of the deceased and to make appropriate disposition of this property. If the decedent has left a will, the property will be disposed of in accordance with the terms of the will. In the absence of a will, state inheritance laws govern the disposition of the property.

A person who has left a will is said to have died *testate* and is referred to as the *testator*. In the absence of a will, the person is said to have died *intestate.* When there is a will, this document may name a person to carry out its provisions. If such a person is willing and able to administer the estate, the court will confirm the appointment, and the person will be referred to as an *executor.* When a will fails to name a person or when the party named is unqualified to act in settling the estate, the court will appoint a person to act in such a capacity, and this person will be referred to as an *administrator-with-the-will-annexed* or *administrator c.t.a. (cum testamento annexa).* In the absence of a will, the court appointee is simply referred to as an *administrator.* The executor or the administrator is referred to as the *personal representative* of the deceased.

The *law of decedents' estates,* also known as the *probate law,* governs the administration and the distribution of the property of a decedent. This law is administered by courts that are variously known as *probate, surrogate's,* or *orphans'* courts. A petition to the court of proper jurisdiction by any party having an interest in the estate begins estate proceedings. Such a petition is known as an *application for probate* or *application for grant of administration.* If there is a will, it must be ruled valid or *probated* by a court of probate jurisdiction before it becomes operative. If, after hearings, the court is satisfied that the will is genuine, that it was made by a party who was legally competent at the time, and that it represents the last expression of the decedent relative to the distribution of the property, the court will order that the terms of the will be carried out. The will is then said to be *admitted to probate.*

The court confirms the appointment of the executor named in a will by issuing *letters testamentary.* It confirms the appointment of an administrator by issuing *letters of administration.* These instruments evidence the authority of the individual to act as the personal representative of the deceased and to assume title to the properties of the estate. The executor or the administrator is considered a fiduciary operating under court control. In the case of any questions as to the appropriate distribution of properties of the estate, the court may be asked to interpret the terms of the will or to designate the legal rules that are applicable.

RESPONSIBILITIES OF THE EXECUTOR OR THE ADMINISTRATOR

Upon appointment by the court, the personal representative becomes responsible for the collection, conservation, and distribution of the property of the decedent. For court, tax, and accounting purposes, an inventory of the estate properties is prepared. Funeral and administrative expenses, legal debts of the decedent, estate and inheritance taxes, and other expenses are paid from the estate. Properties are converted into cash when necessary to meet such requirements. After providing for the payment of all estate expenses and debts, the personal representative distributes remaining properties to the legal beneficiaries. Finally, the personal representative is required to account to the court and to other parties of interest with respect to estate administration and distribution. These responsibilities are described in detail in the following pages.

Administration of Estate Properties

The personal representative takes title to the estate properties, and throughout the administration process, any properties belonging to the estate are sought and taken possession of when found. These estate properties must be prudently managed, protected, and conserved until they are distributed. In the absence of special instructions in the will, the personal representative is normally not required to invest estate funds or to operate a business left by the decedent. When the estate includes a partnership interest, liquidation of the partnership will be required in the absence of special provisions in the will or in the articles of partnership. The responsibility of the personal representative is ended only after all of the properties have been properly distributed and the court has formally approved the course of administration.

The personal representative is normally required to submit to the court an inventory of all the properties identified with the estate. A full description should be provided for each property item in the inventory, and values must be assigned to each item. The personal representative may be able to arrive at satisfactory valuations for many of the items in the inventory. For certain items it may be necessary or required by law to consult outside authority.

State laws specify those assets that pass directly to beneficiaries, in accordance with testamentary dispositions or rules of succession, and those that pass to the estate. Ordinarily, laws provide that title to real property shall pass directly to the legal beneficiaries upon the death of the decedent and that only personal property shall pass into the possession and control of the personal representative. In many states a portion of the decedent's personal properties in the form of household and personal effects and a limited amount of cash pass directly to the surviving spouse or to the decedent's children. Ordinarily, real and personal properties that pass directly to beneficiaries are not included in the decedent's inventory, which is limited to those properties for which the representative is held accountable by law. However, schedules listing real and personal properties excluded from the inventory should be submitted to the court so that the court may be informed of all of the properties left by the decedent.

When a valid contract has been made by the decedent for the sale of real estate, the receivable for the contract sales price is recognized as personal property and comes into the possession of the personal representative for distribution. Although title to the real estate passes to the legal beneficiary, the latter is required to relinquish such title upon the fulfillment of the contract. A contract by the decedent to purchase real estate is recognized as realty and thus is identified with the legal beneficiary. Any payment that is required on such a contract represents a claim against the personal property of the deceased. A mortgage receivable owned by the decedent represents personalty. A mortgage payable on real estate frequently follows the real estate and thus represents a claim to be met by the party acquiring title to the realty. In some states, however, the mortgage may have to be paid by the estate, with the beneficiary taking the property free of the mortgage.

Among the property items that are included in the personal representative's inventory are the following:

> Cash in checking and savings accounts, cash on hand, cash in decedent's safety deposit box, etc.
> Valuables in the decedent's possession, in safety deposit box, etc.
> Advancements to legatees or heirs.
> Notes and accounts receivable.
> Accrued interest on notes (up to and including the date of the decedent's death).
> Recoverable judgments and other claims.
> Accrued rents receivable.
> United States bonds.
> Corporate bonds.
> Accrued interest on bonds (up to and including the date of decedent's death.)
> Corporate stock.
> Dividends declared on corporate stock.
> Ownership interest in a business or partnership.
> Real estate that becomes a part of the estate by terms of the will.
> Life insurance when the estate is named the beneficiary.

The values that are assigned to the individual property items are normally those that are applicable or acceptable for inheritance and estate tax purposes. For many items, satisfactory valuations may be found by consulting brokers, appraisers, or other experts or by referring to current market quotations. For certain items, valuation will present serious difficulties calling for various approaches under the different circumstances encountered. Particularly difficult problems are encountered in determining the value to be assigned to such properties as a going business, an interest in a partnership, stock in a closely held corporation, royalty rights, and copyrights.

When properties are discovered after the original inventory has been filed, supplements to the original inventory are prepared and submitted to the court.

Payment of Debts of the Estate

Debts of the estate must be fully met before any property may properly be distributed to the beneficiaries. State laws generally set a limited period, frequently six months, within which creditors of the decedent must file their claims or forfeit any legal rights that they may have. Ordinarily, laws require that the executor or the administrator must advertise for claims by placing legal notices in specified newspapers or journals for a certain period. The executor rejects invalid claims and establishes appropriate defenses when claims can be avoided. Approved claims are paid.

When assets of the estate are insufficient to meet all debts, the personal representative recognizes certain priorities as set by state statutes. The law frequently provides that claims against the estate shall have priority in the following order:

(1) Estate administration expenses.
(2) Funeral expenses.
(3) Expenses of last illness.
(4) Allowances for the support and the maintenance of the deceased's dependents for a limited period when provided by law.
(5) All debts entitled to preference under the laws of the United States and of the state.
(6) Certain wage claims of employees of the decedent.
(7) Judgment creditors.
(8) All other debts.

Taxes Paid by the Estate

The executor or the administrator is responsible for the settlement of all taxes relating to the decedent or to the estate, including income tax and estate tax.

Income tax. Income tax on the decedent's income for the period from the date of the last income tax return to the date of death is considered to be a liability of the decedent, and thus must be paid by the estate. Furthermore, the payment of income tax on the income of the estate during the period of its administration may be required.

Federal tax laws require the preparation of fiduciary income tax returns for an estate with a gross income of $600 or more in its taxable year. Estates are taxed generally in the same manner as individuals, using the rate structure applicable to married persons filing separate returns, although they are not entitled to the zero bracket deduction.

To the extent that income is distributed to beneficiaries, the estate may be viewed as a conduit. The estate may be able to deduct such distributions in calculating its own taxable income, and the income distributed to beneficiaries is generally taxable to them, retaining the same character as it had in the hands of the estate.

Federal estate tax. The federal estate tax is a levy on an individual's *right to give* his or her estate to others upon death. This tax, as other expenses and debts of the decedent, is paid by the estate and reduces the amount ultimately available to beneficiaries.

The estate tax is based on the decedent's total or *gross estate* less certain allowable deductions and exemptions. A decedent's gross estate includes all property owned at the date of death, whether real or personal, tangible or intangible, regardless of location. Property considered to be owned at the date of death includes property transferred by gift within three years prior to death, property subject to a general power of appointment, and the full value of certain property held in joint tenancy with right of survivorship. Thus the classification of property includible in the gross estate is quite broad.

In arriving at the value of the gross estate, the executor or the administrator is offered the option of stating property values as of (1) the date of the decedent's death or (2) the date six months after the decedent's death, or in the case of property disposed of at an earlier date, the value at such date of disposition. Deductions are allowed from the gross estate for funeral and administrative expenses, commissions and fees, claims against the estate, unpaid mortgages, a marital deduction for certain properties that pass to a surviving spouse, and bequests for public, charitable, and religious organizations.

The gross estate, less allowable deductions, represents the *taxable estate*. Because the estate tax is integrated with the federal gift tax, a tentative tax is calculated on the sum of the taxable estate plus the amount of taxable gifts made after 1976 but before three years prior to the date of death. The tentative tax is reduced by the gift taxes paid on gifts made after 1976. Credits are allowed against the tax for state death taxes paid (within limits) and for a statutory amount which is normally $47,000. The tentative tax less the allowable credits is the net tax for which the estate is liable.

Distribution of Estate Properties After Payment of Debts and Taxes

When a beneficiary other than the estate is named in a life insurance policy, insurance payment is made directly to the named beneficiary. When the estate is named as the beneficiary, payment is made to the personal representative. Property held in joint tenancy with right of survivorship passes directly to the joint tenant, although it may be includible in the gross estate of the decedent for death tax purposes. Title to all other personal property passes to the personal representative, who distributes it to the beneficiaries. Title to real estate normally passes directly from the decedent to the beneficiary by will or by law unless (1) it becomes a part of the estate by the terms of the will or (2) it is made available to the personal representative by court order to provide cash for payment of debts of the estate.

After appropriate provisions have been made for the payment of all claims against the estate, the personal representative may take steps to distribute the remaining estate properties.

In the absence of a will naming the persons who are to receive the estate property available for distribution, property is distributed by the personal representative in accordance with the state laws relating to intestate succession. These laws specify the distributions that are required in view of the various marriage and blood relationships between the decedent and the surviving relatives. Certain states distinguish between the distribution of real and personal property of the intestate. In these states, the persons who are to inherit real property are determined by the *laws of descent* and the persons who are to share in the distribution of personal property are determined by the *laws of distribution*. The persons receiving properties under the laws of descent and distribution are referred to as the *heirs* or *next of kin*.

When there is a will, the disposition of personal property by the terms of the will is known as a *legacy* or *bequest*. The person named to receive such property is referred to as a *legatee*. The disposition of real property by the terms of a will is known as a *devise*. The person named to receive such property is called a *devisee*.

Testamentary dispositions of personal property are classifed as follows:

Specific legacies: Dispositions of particular items. For example: "My gold watch to my son," "My 100 shares of X Co. common stock to my wife," or "Forgiveness of the $1,000 owed me by my brother, Jack."

Demonstrative legacies: Dispositions of cash or other personal property payable out of a particular fund or asset accumulation. For example: "$1,500 from the balance of my account at the State Bank to my chauffeur."[1]

General legacies: Dispositions that are not specifically designated and are payable out of the general assets of the estate. For example: "$10,000 to the Children's Hospital."

Residuary legacies: Dispositions of the personal property remaining after distribution of the other legacies named. For example: "The rest, remainder, and residue of my personal property to be divided between my brothers, John and Henry."

Real property dispositions may be classified as *specific devises, general devises,* and *residuary devises*. A residuary disposition in the form of the "remainder of my property" would cover all remaining property, both real and personal.

If a will fails to dispose of all the property, such a failure is referred to as a condition of *partial intestacy*, and undisposed properties are distributed in accordance with the laws of descent and distribution. State laws frequently provide that a surviving spouse, in lieu of testamentary dispositions, may elect to take a share of the estate as specified by law. Such an elective share is frequently defined as that portion of the properties that the surviving spouse would have received if the decedent had died intestate.

It has already been suggested that the personal representative must make provision for the payment of all estate expenses and debts before distributing properties to the various beneficiaries. The personal representative who makes certain distributions and is then unable to satisfy estate claims in full may be held personally liable to creditors.

When payment of debts makes it impossible to pay the legacies in full as provided for in the will, the abatement or ademption of certain classes of legacies is necessary. *Abatement* refers to a proportionate reduction or scaling down of legacies of a certain class. *Ademption* refers to the complete revocation of legacies of a certain class. In the absence of provisions to the contrary in a will, laws of the state normally call for the abatement or the complete revocation of legacies by classes in the following order: (1) residuary legacies, (2) general legacies, and (3) demonstrative and specific legacies. When all the personal property is insufficient to satisfy the claims

---

[1]When a fund is insufficient to satisfy the amount of the demonstrative legacy, the amount of the deficiency would be regarded as a general legacy.

against the estate, the court may approve the lease, mortgage, or sale of the real property descended or devised.

In certain cases a legacy may not require payment. This *failure of legacies* may be authorized by law or the court as a result of such circumstances as the death of a legatee prior to the decedent's death, the loss or destruction of specific property bequeathed, or a disposition that is regarded as contrary to public policy.

Amounts that are earned on specific legacies after the date of the decedent's death accrue to the respective beneficiaries. When collection of such earnings is made by the estate, the earnings are paid to the legatee together with the specific legacy. Certain legacies may be subject to deductions or offsets for such items as (1) payments made by the executor on behalf of respective beneficiaries, e.g., inheritance and transfer taxes and fees, and (2) debts due to the decedent by respective beneficiaries. Parents during their lifetimes may transfer properties to their children as advancements on the shares of the estates to which they will be entitled. When there is no will, children who have received advancements from the decedent for amounts that exceed their distributable shares of the estate are entitled to no further distributions but are not required to return such excesses. If the advancements are less than their shares, they are entitled to the difference between their distributable shares of the estate and the advancements. Gratuitous transfers of property prior to death are construed as absolute gifts and not as advancements except when the latter can be proved.

State laws normally provide that, at the discretion of the executor or the administrator, the distribution of legacies may be deferred for a certain period, normally from six months to a year. Furthermore, laws frequently provide that interest shall accrue on legacies that are unpaid after a specified time after death or petition for probate. Payment of interest for such an overdue period is recognized as a charge against the earnings of the properties whose distribution was deferred. When a payment is made to a legatee in advance of a statutory waiting period, such a payment may be subject to a charge for interest for the period of advancement. In the latter instance, the distributable estate is increased by the amount of the interest earned. In making an advance payment, the personal representative should require bond to assure recovery of the advance if such action later becomes necessary.

Intermediate and Final Accountings

The executor or the administrator is required to report to the court and to other interested parties on the progress of estate administration and distribution. The nature of the report varies in character. In some cases certain reports may be required at regular intervals during the course of administration. When an estate is of short duration, reports may be required only when the personal representative has completed estate administration and requests a formal discharge. Reports summarizin tivities and progress that are submitted during the course of estate administration are referred to as *intermediate accountings*. A report submitted upon fulfillment of the responsibilities of administration is called a *final accounting*. Vouchers evidencing completed transactions may be submitted to the court, together with the reports. The report frequently found in accounting to the court takes the form of the *charge and discharge statement*. This report is illustrated later in the chapter.

The compensation or the commissions allowed to the executor or the administrator may be provided by terms of the will or may be fixed by the court or by statute. Commissions when computed in accordance with statute are based upon the value of the estate that is handled by the personal representative. A fund may be set aside for remuneration of the personal representative. The court must approve the payment of the commissions. In making the final accounting, the personal representative requests approval for the payment of commissions and for the distribution of remaining estate properties. If everything is in order, the court approves the accounting and issues a decree authorizing remaining distributions. Upon receiving further evidence from the personal representative that distributions have been completed, the court declares the estate to be closed and the settlements to be final and binding upon all parties.

ACCOUNTING FOR THE ESTATE

The nature and the form of the books and the records to be maintained by the executor or the administrator are not prescribed by law. Books and accounts should be kept in sufficient detail to make possible the convenient preparation of the reports required by the court and other parties of interest. Ordinarily, the reports are prepared in a form that shows the properties coming into the possession of the personal representative and the disposition of such properties. Accounts, then, must provide a record of the estate properties and their changes. It is normally desirable to record transactions of the estate in double-entry form.

General Principles of Estate Accounting

Data concerning properties and how the personal representative has handled the responsibilities relative to such properties are provided by records maintained in the following manner:

(1) Asset accounts are debited and Estate Principal (or Estate Corpus) is credited for property items originally coming into the possession of the personal representative. Estate Principal summarizes the personal representative's accountability for estate properties.

(2) Increases in estate properties from asset discoveries, the sale or conversion of estate properties at a gain, proceeds from the lease, mortgage, or sale of real properties as authorized by the court, and estate income are recorded by debits to appropriate asset accounts and

credits to nominal accounts that indicate the sources of the increased accountability on the part of the personal representative. Credit balances in the nominal accounts are ultimately closed into Estate Principal.

(3) Decreases in estate properties from the sale or the conversion of properties at a loss, the payment of expenses and debts of the decedent, the payment of estate expenses, and distributions to beneficiaries are recorded by credits to appropriate asset accounts and debits to nominal accounts that explain the reductions in the personal representative's accountability. Debit balances in the nominal accounts are ultimately closed into Estate Principal. The full distribution of estate assets will cancel the balance in Estate Principal.

Recording Transactions of an Estate

Entries to record the transactions of the estate are described in the following paragraphs.

Opening the estate books. The estate inventory is the basis for the opening entry on the books for the estate. Individual estate assets are debited and the account Estate Principal is credited. Asset accounts are debited at the appraised values as of the date of the decedent's death as reported on the asset inventory submitted to the court.

Discovery of assets after opening estate books. When assets of the decedent are discovered after the inventory has been filed with the court, appropriate asset accounts are debited and the account Assets Subsequently Discovered is credited. The assets are recorded at their value as of the date of the decedent's death.

Disposal of assets. As properties, including accrued income items as of the date of death, are converted into cash, Cash is debited and the appropriate asset accounts are credited. If assets realize less than their book values, Losses on Disposal of Assets is debited. If assets realize more than their book values, Gains on Disposal of Assets is credited.

Collection of income accruing to the estate. Collections of income earned after the date of the decedent's death on assets belonging to the estate are recorded by debits to Cash and credits to Collections of Income.

Collection of amounts accruing to a legatee. When the personal representative collects amounts that were earned after the date of the decedent's death on assets specifically bequeathed and thus accruing to a legatee, Cash is debited and an account with the legatee is credited. The subsequent payment of cash to the legatee is recorded by a debit to the account with the legatee and a credit to Cash.

Payment of funeral and administrative expenses. Payments of funeral expenses, expenses of the last illness, court fees, attorneys' fees, accountants' fees, appraisers' fees, fiduciaries' fees, bonding costs, estate tax, and other administrative expenses are recorded by debits to Funeral and Administrative Expenses and credits to Cash.

Payment of debts of decedent. Payments of debts of the decedent and income taxes on the income earned prior to death are recorded by debits to Debts of Decedent Paid and credits to Cash.

Payment or delivery of legacies. Payments or transfers of legacies are recorded by debits to the account Legacies Paid or Delivered and credits to the appropriate asset accounts. When it is required that legacies be recorded at their fair market values as of the date of distribution, Legacies Paid or Delivered is debited for such values, assets are credited at amounts reported on the books, and loss or gain balances are debited or credited for the differences.

Payment of amounts chargeable to a legatee. When the personal representative makes payment of a charge that is to be borne by the legatee (state inheritance taxes, for example), an account with the legatee is debited and Cash is credited. The subsequent receipt of cash from the legatee is recorded by a debit to Cash and a credit to the account with the legatee. The legatee may not be required to reimburse the estate but may be paid the legacy less the amount previously paid by the estate. The balance in the legatee's account is transferred to Legacies Paid or Delivered.

Payment of expenses chargeable to income. Payments of expenses incurred after the date of the decedent's death and applicable to the earnings of the estate are recorded by debits to Expenses Chargeable to Income and credits to Cash.

Distribution of net income. Distributions of cash representing estate net income — the difference between collections of income and payments of expenses chargeable against such income — are recorded by debits to Distribution of Income and credits to Cash.

Closing the executor's books. Accounts before closing and their balances are as follows:

Debits	Credits
Losses on Disposal of Assets	Estate Principal
Funeral and Administrative Expenses	Assets Subsequently Discovered
Debts of Decedent Paid	Gains on Disposal of Assets
Legacies Paid or Delivered	Collections of Income
Expenses Chargeable to Income	
Distributions of Income	

In closing the books, the nominal accounts with debit and credit balances are transferred to Estate Principal. After the nominal accounts are closed, Estate Principal will be equal to the assets still on hand. When all of the estate assets have been distributed, transfer of the nominal accounts to Estate Principal will cancel this balance.

Illustration of Accounting for an Estate

The following example is designed to illustrate the basic procedures that are required in accounting for the estate. The special problems that are encountered when estate assets are transferred to a trust and when principal-income distinctions must be made are considered and illustrated in an example in the next chapter. The example in the next chapter also illustrates the schedules that are prepared to support the charge and discharge statement.

Assume that Walter Bragg dies testate on May 31, 19X4. The will is admitted to probate on July 10, 19X4. The will does not name an executor and the court appoints a daughter, Linda Bragg, to act as administrator-with-the-will-annexed, and she is issued letters of administration.

The will provides for the following:

(1) Specific bequests of 500 shares of Gaylord Corp. preferred stock and all of the Gaylord Corp. bonds are made to the daughter, Linda.
(2) A general bequest of $1,000 is made to the Children's Hospital.
(3) After payment of debts, expenses, and legacies, the home, the remaining estate properties, and any estate income are to be distributed to the widow, Anna Mae.

On July 25, Linda Bragg files with the court of probate jurisdiction an inventory of estate assets as follows:

Cash in bank	$ 2,400
Personal effects	350
Automobile	1,500
United States savings bonds, Series E, (redemption value on May 31)	6,250
Gaylord Corp. 6% preferred stock, 1,000 shares, $10 par	10,550
Dividends declared on Gaylord Corp. 6% preferred stock	150
Gaylord Corp. 4% bonds, $6,000 face value	5,675
Accrued interest on Gaylord Corp. 4% bonds from Feb. 1	80
Total inventory of assets	$26,955

In this example it is assumed that laws of the state do not require the executor to include in the inventory those assets for which no responsibility or control is assumed; hence the home that passes directly to the widow is not reported. In certain states it is required that real estate be inventoried even though it passes directly to heirs or devisees. Further, it may be desirable to report such property on the executor's books even though it passes directly to the named beneficiaries, since it must be included as a part of the estate subject to federal estate taxes. In the instances mentioned, real estate can be recorded on the books of the executor as a part of the beginning inventory. Entries to report that such assets had passed to respective beneficiaries would then be made.

The entries to record the inventory and the subsequent transactions completed by the administrator in accounting for the Bragg estate follow:

Transaction	Entry

May 31
(1) Assets at appraised values per inventory filed with the court by Linda Bragg:
Cash.. $ 2,400
Personal effects 350
Automobile 1,500
U.S. savings bonds 6,250
Gaylord Corp. 6% preferred stock, 1,000 shares, $10 par 10,550
Dividends declared on Gaylord Corp. 6% preferred stock 150
Gaylord Corp. 4% bonds, $6,000 face value 5,675
Accrued interest on Gaylord Corp. 4% bonds.. 80
                              $26,955
	Cash 2,400
	Personal Effects................... 350
	Automobile.......................... 1,500
	U.S. Savings Bonds 6,250
	Gaylord Corp. 6% Preferred Stock 10,550
	Dividends Receivable on Gaylord Corp. 6% Preferred Stock 150
	Gaylord Corp. 4% Bonds 5,675
	Accrued Interest on Gaylord Corp. 4% Bonds.................. 80
	    Estate Principal................. 26,955

June 10 (2) Collected dividends on Gaylord Corp. 6% preferred stock, $150.	Cash .... 150 Dividends Receivable on Gaylord Corp. 6% Preferred Stock 150
July 1 (3) Interest was credited on cash in bank, $20.	Cash .... 20 Collections of Income......... 20
July 15 (4) Paid funeral expenses, $850.	Funeral and Administrative Expenses............................. 850 Cash 850
July 26 (5) Sold automobile for $1,325.	Cash .... 1,325 Losses on Disposal of Assets.. 175 Automobile 1,500

July 31
(6) Sold 500 shares of Gaylord Corp. 6% preferred stock at 10¾.
	Cash 5,375
	    Gaylord Corp. 6% Preferred Stock 5,275
	    Gains on Disposal of Assets 100

Aug. 1
(7) Received semiannual payment on Gaylord Corp. 4% bonds, $120.
	Cash 120
	    Accrued Interest on Gaylord Corp. 4% Bonds.......... 80
	    Linda Bragg 40

Aug. 15 (8) Discovered deposit of $225 with Security Savings and Loan Association.	Cash — Security Savings and Loan Association.................. 225 Assets Subsequently Discovered 225

Transaction	Entry		
Sept. 11 (9) Received dividends on Gaylord Corp. 6% preferred stock, $75.	Cash .... Linda Bragg	75	75
Sept. 15 (10) Paid debts of decedent, $1,800.	Debts of Decedent Paid......... Cash	1,800	1,800
Sept. 15 (11) Paid general legacy to Children's Hospital, $1,000.	Legacies Paid or Delivered..... Cash	1,000	1,000
Dec. 1 (12) Paid inheritance tax: On legacies distributable to Linda Bragg .... $ 180 On legacies distributable to Anna Mae Bragg .... 150 $ 330	Linda Bragg .... Anna Mae Bragg................... Cash	180 150	330
Dec. 6 (13) Paid court and administrative expenses, $240.	Funeral and Administrative Expenses............................. Cash	240	240
Dec. 8 (14) Received cash from Linda Bragg in settlement of balance due: Inheritance tax paid by estate, due from Linda............................... $ 180 Less interest and dividends collected by estate on specific legacies, accruing to Linda .... 115 Balance due..................................... $ 65	Cash .... Linda Bragg	65	65

Dec. 8
(15) Distributed specific legacies to Linda Bragg:
Gaylord Corp. 6% preferred stock, 500 shares; Gaylord Corp. 4% bonds, $6,000 face value.
	Legacies Paid or Delivered.....
	    Gaylord Corp. 6% Preferred Stock...............................
	    Gaylord Corp. 4% Bonds ....
		10,950	5,275
			5,675

A trial balance of the accounts maintained by Linda Bragg as of December 10, 19X4, and a charge and discharge statement prepared from the data on the trial balance are shown on page 690. The charge and discharge statement is submitted to the court with a request that the administrator be permitted to make final distribution of remaining estate properties.

The final accounting as submitted by Linda Bragg is approved by the court, and the administrator is permitted to distribute remaining assets to the residuary beneficiary. Entries to record this distribution and to close the estate books follow the charge and discharge statement.

Estate of Walter Bragg
Linda Bragg — Administrator-with-the-Will-Annexed
Trial Balance
December 10, 19X4

Cash	5,310	
Cash — Security Savings and Loan Association	225	
Personal Effects	350	
U.S. Savings Bonds	6,250	
Anna Mae Bragg	150	
Estate Principal		26,955
Assets Subsequently Discovered		225
Gains on Disposal of Assets		100
Collections of Income		20
Losses on Disposal of Assets	175	
Funeral and Administrative Expenses	1,090	
Debts of Decedent Paid	1,800	
Legacies Paid or Delivered	11,950	
	27,300	27,300

Estate of Walter Bragg
Linda Bragg — Administrator-with-the-Will-Annexed
Charge and Discharge Statement
May 31, 19X4–December 10, 19X4

I Charge Myself With:		
Original principal of estate	$26,955	
Assets subsequently discovered	225	
Gains on disposal of assets	100	
Collections of income	20	$27,300
I Credit Myself With:		
Losses on disposal of assets	$ 175	
Funeral and administrative expenses	1,090	
Debts of decedent paid	1,800	
Legacies paid or delivered	11,950	15,015
Balance		$12,285
Consisting of:		
Cash		$ 5,310
Cash — Security Savings and Loan Association		225
Personal effects		350
U.S. savings bonds		6,250
Claim against Anna Mae Bragg		150
Total		$12,285

Transaction	Entry

Dec. 28		Legacies Paid or Delivered..... 12,265	
(16)		Distributions of Income......... 20	
Distributed residuary assets to Anna		Cash	5,310
Mae Bragg:		Cash — Security Savings	
Cash	$ 5,310	and Loan Association........	225
Cash — Security Savings and Loan		Personal Effects...............	350
Association	225	U.S. Savings Bonds...........	6,250
Personal effects	350	Anna Mae Bragg...............	150
U.S. savings bonds	6,250		
Claim against Anna Mae Bragg (inher-			
itance tax paid)	150		
	$12,285		

Transaction	Entry		
(17) To close the nominal accounts into Estate Principal.	Estate Principal......................	26,955	
	Assets Subsequently Discovered......................................	225	
	Gains on Disposal of Assets ...	100	
	Collections of Income............	20	
	Losses on Disposal of Assets...............................		175
	Funeral and Administrative Expenses..........................		1,090
	Debts of Decedent Paid......		1,800
	Legacies Paid or Delivered ..		24,215
	Distributions of Income......		20

QUESTIONS

1. (a) Define the term *fiduciary*. (b) Give four different situations that require participation by a fiduciary.

2. Define each of the following terms: (a) testator, (b) intestate, (c) admission to probate, (d) letters of administration, (e) bequest.

3. Distinguish between:

(a) Administrator and executor.
(b) Legatee and devisee.
(c) Specific legacy and demonstrative legacy.
(d) General legacy and residuary legacy.

(e) Laws of descent and laws of distribution.
(f) Abatement and ademption.
(g) Intermediate accounting and final accounting.

4. Define each of the following terms: (a) partial intestacy, (b) advancement, (c) legacy failure.

5. List the duties of the executor or administrator.

6. (a) What properties normally appear on the inventory that is presented to the court by the personal representative of the decedent? (b) What values are reported for properties inventoried and how are such values ascertained? (c) Under what circumstances will real property be included in the inventory? (d) Under what circumstances will life insurance policies be included in the inventory?

7. State which of the following items are normally included in the inventory submitted to the court:

(a) Interest in a partnership.
(b) Down payment made by the decedent for purchase of land.
(c) Refundable advance to an heir.
(d) Mortgage note receivable on property sold by decedent.
(e) Deposit on real estate purchase contract entered into by decedent.
(f) Corporate first mortgage bonds.

8. What is the estate tax?

9. (a) What priorities are set by law in the payment of claims against the estate? (b) What is the order of abatement or ademption of legacies when required in the settlement of estate claims? (c) Will real property generally or specifically devised ever be used for the payment of estate claims? Explain.

10. (a) State the sources for an increase in the personal representative's accountability. (b) State the sources for a decrease in the personal representative's accountability.

11. In accounting for an estate, what entries are made when:

    (a) Estate books are opened and properties are recorded at appraised values.
    (b) Property is sold at more than its appraised value.
    (c) Property belonging to the decedent is discovered during the course of administration.
    (d) Income is collected, a part of which had accrued as of the date of the decedent's death and was included in the beginning inventory.
    (e) Expenses of last illness are paid.
    (f) Property is sold at less than its appraised value.
    (g) Income is collected on a legacy not yet distributed.
    (h) The legacy referred to in (g) is paid, together with the income collected thereon.
    (i) Debts of the decedent are paid.
    (j) Remaining assets are distributed to the residuary legatee.
    (k) Accounts of the estate are closed.

12. Give the entries that would be made on the books for the estate of Barbara Bailey as a result of the following:

    (a) An inventory for the estate shows the decedent to have left cash, certain valuables, a first mortgage note receivable on property that the decedent had sold 3 months ago, together with 3 months' accrued interest on the note, and corporate bonds, together with 2 months' accrued interest on the bonds. The mortgage note is specifically bequeathed to a son, while the balance of the estate after payment of expenses, etc., is to be transferred to the surviving spouse.
    (b) A dividend is received and investigation discloses that the decedent is an owner of certain shares of stock; the dividend had been declared prior to date of death.
    (c) The bonds are sold at an amount in excess of their appraised value plus accrued interest for 5 months.
    (d) Interest for 6 months is collected on the mortgage note.
    (e) Funeral and administrative expenses are paid.
    (f) Legacies are distributed and estate accounts are closed.

13. The estate of Henry Dakin pays the following taxes. State how each payment would be reflected in the accounts:

    (a) Federal income tax on earnings of the decedent prior to date of death.
    (b) Federal income tax on estate income for year after decedent's death.

(c) State death taxes requiring reimbursement from beneficiaries.

(d) Federal estate taxes.

(e) Local real estate taxes accrued prior to decedent's death.

(f) Local real estate taxes on property that is owned by the estate.

14. Describe the charge and discharge statement.

EXERCISES

1. A.C. Parker died on March 15. Prepare the entries that will appear on the estate books as a result of the following:

(a) An inventory was filed with the court as follows:

Cash..	$4,560
R Co. common stock, 100 shares..	6,000
S Co. 6% bonds, $5,000 face value....................................	5,150
Accrued interest on bonds, Jan. 15–Mar. 15......................	50
Personal effects and household effects..............................	2,600

(b) Funeral expenses and expenses of last illness were paid, $1,600.

(c) Interest was collected on S Co. bonds for 6 months.

(d) Dividends of $60 were received on R Co. common stock. The stock is bequeathed by will to Billy Parker, a son, and the stock, together with the cash dividend, is transferred to the son.

(e) S Co. 6% bonds are sold at 104 plus accrued interest on September 15.

(f) Debts of decedent are paid, $6,000.

(g) The court approves the payment of administrative expenses of $450 and the distribution of the balance of the estate to the surviving spouse.

2. What entries would be made on the books of the estate of Wilma Massey for the following transactions:

(a) 500 shares of 6% preferred stock of the W Company, with par value of $50 per share, are sold at 55. The shares are carried at a value of $53.50 as of the date of decedent's death.

(b) 5% bonds of the X Company, with a face value of $20,000, are sold at 103½ plus accrued interest for 3 months. The bonds are carried on the books at their appraised value, $20,250.

(c) 200 shares of stock of Y Company are discovered in a safety deposit box of the decedent. The stock had a value of $4,000 on the date of death and a dividend of 37½ cents per share had been declared on each share just prior to the date of the decedent's death.

(d) Interest for 6 months is collected on 6% bonds of the Z Company with a face value of $20,000. At the date of the decedent's death, interest for 2 months had accrued and had been recorded as a part of the estate inventory. The bonds are a specific legacy distributable to B.

(e) Certain personal effects of the decedent, reported on the inventory as without value, realized $350.

3. A trial balance for the estate of Joseph Kelly on March 31 follows:

Cash..	4,200	
Estate Principal		46,250
Assets Subsequently Discovered..		1,250
Gains on Disposal of Assets..		3,700
Collections of Income		400
Losses on Disposal of Assets	6,500	
Funeral and Administrative Expenses	2,200	
Debts of Decedent Paid	12,000	
Legacies Paid or Delivered..	11,550	
Devises Delivered...	15,000	
Expenses Chargeable to Income..	150	
	51,600	51,600

(a) Using the preceding data, prepare a charge and discharge statement.

(b) Assuming that the court authorizes the distribution of cash on hand to the residuary legatee, prepare the entry to record the distribution and to close the estate books.

4. Personal property left by Andrew Allen on the date of his death is valued at $40,000. Testamentary dispositions to his children include:

Specific legacy to Betty, property included in the inventory at.......		$ 3,500
Demonstrative legacy to Carl, cash in F & M Bank, included in the inventory at		1,650
General legacies:		
To Don..	$25,000	
To Nancy...	10,000	
To Frank..	5,000	40,000

Assets of the estate other than cash and the specific legacy are sold at $1,500 less than inventoried values. Funeral and administrative expenses and debts of the decedent totaling $12,500 are paid. The executor then distributes legacies to Don, Nancy, and Frank. Assuming that the laws provide for the pro rata abatement of general legacies in the event that all legacies cannot be met, state how the cash is to be distributed to the individual beneficiaries.

5. Residuary assets of the estate of Z are to be distributed among beneficiaries as follows: A, 25%; B, 25%; C, 12½%, D, 12½%; E, 8⅓%; F, 8⅓%; G, 8⅓%. Distribution of the residuary estate is authorized by the court on May 1, 19X7. On this date there is cash on hand of $66,000 and the books show that there was an advance of $15,000 to A on July 1, 19X5, on which interest at the rate of 6% per year has accrued.

(a) How should the cash on hand be distributed?

(b) Prepare the entries to close the estate books.

PROBLEMS

21-1. Sally Brent died on April 30, 19X2. Brent left a will providing for the following disposition of her properties:

Personal residence — to spouse, Warren Brent.
Household furniture — bequeathed to spouse.
Jewelry — bequeathed to spouse.

Cash of $10,000 — bequeathed to daughter, Edith B. Powers.

Balance of estate after payment of debts, expenses, taxes, and other distributions — to be divided equally between Edith B. Powers and son, James Brent.

James Brent was named executor of the estate. Assets of the decedent as of the date of death were valued as follows:

Residence	$60,000
Life insurance payable to spouse	50,000
Household furniture	4,200
Jewelry...	6,000
Dividends on Kern Steel common, payable May 5 to stockholders	
of record April 10	1,250
Kern Steel common..	52,375
Cash in checking account...	4,400

A summary of cash receipts and disbursements related to estate activities up to December 1, 19X2, follows:

Cash Receipts		Cash Disbursements	
Collection of dividends	$ 1,250	Expenses of last illness and funeral expenses......................	$ 3,600
Proceeds from sale of Kern Steel stock.....................................	50,650	Debts of the decedent..............	23,250
Collection of note receivable in name of decedent (note was found in July)	850	Federal and state death taxes.....	1,250
		Attorneys' and accountants' fees	1,600

James Brent submitted a statement to the court on December 1, 19X2, summarizing his activities as executor and requesting permission for the distribution of the remaining estate assets. Brent agreed to waive all commissions and fees.

Instructions: Prepare a charge and discharge statement for the period April 30–December 1, accompanied by a schedule showing the proposed distribution of estate assets on this date.

21-2. Clyde C. Cook died on January 20, 19X3. An inventory filed by Marilyn James, his executrix, listed the following:

Cash in commercial account...	$ 515
Cash in savings account..	4,400
Series E U.S. savings bonds (redemption value).............................	7,825
Stock, A Co., 500 shares	15,600
Stock, B Co., 100 shares...	3,600
Dividends receivable on B Co. stock...	100
Automobile...	2,400

Cook's will provides for the following legacies:

To Children's Hospital, cash of $5,000
To son, Carl: automobile
250 shares of A Co. stock
50 shares of B Co. stock
To widow: properties not otherwise disposed of by will, and estate income.

The following transactions took place during the course of administration:

(a) Funeral expenses and expenses of last illness were paid, $1,350.
(b) Dividends were collected on B Co. stock, $100.

(c) Dividends were received on A Co. stock, $250.

(d) The U.S. savings bonds were redeemed at $7,875.

(e) Debts of the decedent were paid, $4,410.

(f) The legacy to the Children's Hospital was paid.

(g) The legacy to the son was distributed.

(h) The executrix received permission from the court to pay administration expenses and fees totaling $1,450 and to distribute the estate income and remaining estate assets to the widow. This was done on July 31, 19X3.

Instructions: (1) Prepare the entries to record the transactions of the executrix.

(2) Prepare a charge and discharge statement summarizing the course of estate liquidation.

(3) Prepare the entries to close the books of the estate.

21-3. Alex Bender died on July 1, 19X1. Richard Wells, who was named administrator-with-will-annexed, filed the following inventory with the probate court:

Cash	$ 6,450
6% preferred stock, Y Co., 100 shares, $100 par	10,500
4% bonds, Z Co., $5,000 face value	5,200
Accrued interest on Z Co. bonds	50
Household furniture	1,600
Automobile	2,000

The following testamentary dispositions were made by Bender: (1) $2,500 each to two nephews, James and Billy Bender; (2) the automobile, 50 shares of Y Co. preferred stock and $2,500 in Z Co. bonds to a sister, Amelia Bender; (3) the remainder of the estate, including any estate income, to the Good Samaritan Foundation, a charitable organization.

During the course of administration, the following transactions were completed by Wells:

(a) Paid funeral and administrative expenses, $2,200.

(b) Received interest on Z Co. bonds for 6 months, $100.

(c) Received a semiannual dividend on Y Co. stock, $300.

(d) Sold bonds of Z Co., $2,500 face value, for $2,525 plus accrued interest for 3 months.

(e) Sold 50 shares of Y Co. stock for $5,000.

(f) Paid debts of the decedent, $3,600.

(g) Distributed the specific and general legacies.

(h) Made application to the court and received its approval for the distribution of the estate income and remaining estate assets. The distribution was made on January 10, 19X2.

Instructions: (1) Prepare the entries to record the estate transactions.

(2) Prepare a charge and discharge statement summarizing estate liquidation.

(3) Prepare the entries to close the books of the estate.

21-4. Robert Story died on May 1, 19X7, and his daughter Patricia was named executrix for the estate. The will provided that, after payment of funeral and administrative expenses, debts of the decedent, and bequests to charitable organizations, the remaining estate was to be distributed to the widow, Rita, and to the daughter, Patricia, in the ratio of 2-to-1 respectively.The will also provided that the widow's share of the estate was to be invested in an annuity for her support during her lifetime.

Patricia Story kept no records of the transactions of the estate, but had a list of cash receipts and disbursements up to November 30, 19X7, as follows:

Cash receipts:

Cash on hand in banks, May 1, 19X7	$27,500
Savings accounts discovered	6,500
Proceeds from sale of 1,000 shares of Fielding Corp. common stock (appraised at 21½ per share on May 1, 19X7)	23,000

Cash payments:

Funeral and administrative expenses...	$ 1,150
Debts of decedent paid...	3,500
Advance to Rita Story	3,500
Payment on exercise of 1,200 rights of Lane Co. common stock (received 600 shares of the Lane Co. common stock on exercise of rights).................	33,000
General legacies to charity:	
Community Hospital	5,000
Community Home for Orphans..	5,000
Inheritance tax paid on behalf of Rita Story...	2,200

After the payment of funeral and administrative expenses, the debts of the decedent, and the general legacies, Patricia Story distributed the shares of Fielding Corp. common stock in the ratio specified. Shares of Fielding Corp. common stock belonging to the widow were sold with the permission of the court. Patricia Story withheld the proceeds from the sale and later used it for payment of part of the 600 shares of the Lane Co. common stock received through the exercise of rights. After exercising the rights of Lane Co. common stock, she made a similar distribution of the shares of Lane Co. common stock. Lane Co. common stock was valued at $50 on May 1, 19X7.

On December 1, 19X7, the court ordered Patricia Story to submit a charge and discharge statement. She engaged an accountant to prepare the statement for her. In preparing the statement, the accountant found that Patricia Story had made an overdistribution, both to herself and to the widow.

Instructions: (1) Prepare entries to record the inventory of the estate on May 1, 19X7, and to record the transactions of the executrix up to November 30, 19X7, with proper charges to the accounts of the legatees for the excess distributions.

(2) Prepare a charge and discharge statement for the executrix as of December 1, 19X7.

21-5. On April 1, 19X8, just before making final distribution of the estate of Martha Duncan, the executor's books show the following asset balances:

Cash..	$42,800
Discount Sales Co. Stock	7,200
Claim against Norman Duncan......	16,000

The estate is distributable as follows: ½ to the spouse, John Duncan; ⅓ to a son, Norman; and the balance equally to two daughters, Betty and Lorraine. An advance had been made by the estate to Norman on July 1, 19X7, with the permission of the court. It was agreed that interest at 6% would be charged on the loan to the date when final distribution is made to estate beneficiaries.

On April 1 it is agreed that the spouse shall take over the stock of the Discount Sales Co. at its present value of $7,500. The executor's commission of $1,200 is paid and the remaining available cash is distributed to the appropriate parties.

Instructions: Prepare the entries in general journal form to record the final distribution of estate assets and to close the estate books on April 1. Indicate how the cash is distributed among the various beneficiaries, showing calculations.

21-6. Under the terms of the will of Jackson Holmes, who died in 19X4, the beneficiaries were:

> Mary Holmes, widow of testator, who was left a special bequest of $50,000 payable immediately, and in addition a life interest in ½ of the residuary estate, with the right of appointment.
> Kathryn Holmes, his daughter, who was left ¼ of the residuary estate. One half of this was left outright and the other half was to remain in trust, with the right of appointment.
> Jenny Holmes, his daughter, who was left a life interest in ⅛ of the residuary estate, with the right of appointment.
> John Holmes, his son, who was also left a ⅛ interest in the residuary estate, to be paid to him outright.

The testator specified that, because of unsatisfactory market conditions, the trustees have the power and the right to defer liquidation of any of the assets until, in their opinion, conditions are favorable and may, in their discretion, make intermediate distributions of principal from the funds so realized to the beneficiaries who are entitled thereto. The income from the estate was to be distributed annually in the proportion of the beneficiaries' interests.

On December 31, 19X6, the following advances were made on account of principal:

> Kathryn Holmes $150,000
> John Holmes................................. 100,000

The special bequest to Mary Holmes had not been paid on this date.

The trustees rendered their first accounting to the surrogate as at December 31, 19X6, on which date all income, after paying therefrom all expenses applicable to income, was paid to the beneficiaries.

The surrogate's decree on the accounting of December 31, 19X6, specified that (1) in considering the distribution of future income, all intermediary payments of principal should be treated as advances to the beneficiaries; (2) in order to make a fair and equitable division of income, interest at 6% per annum should be charged and credited.

The income for 19X7 amounted to $450,000 after all expenses applicable to income had been paid. No further distribution of principal had taken place.

Instructions: Prepare a statement showing the amounts payable to each beneficiary on December 31, 19X7. (AICPA adapted)

21-7. Janice Thompson died on July 7, 19X6. Her will appointed two executors to administer her estate and provided for the payment of funeral and other necessary expenses and of general bequests as follows: $10,000 to the Cemetery on the Mount; $15,000 to Mary, a sister; and $5,000 to each executor in lieu of fees.

The testator at the date of death possessed the following: cash, $52,000; accounts receivable, $18,000; non-interest-bearing notes receivable, $10,000; first-mortgage bonds, 6%, interest payable on January 1 and July 1, with a principal amount of $18,000 and an appraised value of $15,000; Western Development Corp. bonds, 3%, interest payable on January 15 and July 15, with a face value of $100,000, and an appraised value of $101,500; 5,000 shares of Shell Mining Company no-par stock costing $50,000, appraised as valueless; 1,000 shares of Atlas Amusement Corporation stock, $100 par, appraised at $102 per share; semiprecious stones, $5,280; clothing, $1,375; furniture, $7,500.

A summary of cash transactions from July 7, 19X6, to September 30, 19X7, is as follows:

Cash receipts:

Accounts receivable collected (remainder uncollectible)	$15,000
Proceeds from sale of $70,000 of Western Development Corp. bonds on January 15, 19X7, at 102 without interest	71,400
Dividends:	
$2.50 per share of Atlas Amusement Corporation stock, declared payable to stockholders of record on July 5, 19X6, and paid on July 25, 19X6	2,500
$2.50 per share of Atlas Amusement Corporation stock, declared payable to stockholders of record on January 5, 19X7, and paid on January 25, 19X7	2,500
Proceeds from sale of 5,000 shares of Shell Mining Company stock at $.10 per share	500
Refund of 19X6 overpayment of United States income tax (estimated tax paid, $5,725; actual tax payable, $5,350)	375
Proceeds from sale of furniture	5,150
Other transactions: short-term notes were collected at maturity; interest on all investments was collected.	

Cash disbursements:

Funeral expenses, etc.	$ 1,750
Administrative expenses (corpus, $5,250; income, $1,250)	6,500
Legal and accounting services incident to probating will	3,750
Debts of testator	14,450
United States Treasury Department — tax deficiency, 19X3, and interest thereon, $72	522
Playa Company, 4½% bonds — $20,000 acquired on September 16, 19X6, at 101 (interest dates, March 15 and September 15; bonds mature on September 15, 19X9)	20,580
Short-term notes, $5,000; 6% short-term notes purchased out of corpus on January 16, 19X7, at 100½; interest payable on January 15 and July 15, maturing in 6 months from date of purchase.	
Other transactions: general bequests were paid in full, with Mary taking semiprecious stones at appraised value to apply against bequest of $15,000; clothing was given to charity.	

Instructions: (1) Prepare the entries to be made on the books of the executors for the period July 7, 19X6, to September 30, 19X7, and on September 30, 19X7.

(2) Prepare a charge and discharge statement covering activities for the period indicated. (AICPA adapted)

21-8. The will of Peter Brown, who died on December 31, 19X2, provided cash bequests of $40,000 to Sandra Brown, his widow, and $15,000 each to two children, with the residuary estate to be divided equally among the three beneficiaries. Sandra Brown was appointed executrix and trustee without fees or other compensation.

By court order Sandra Brown was to receive a family allowance of $4,000 a month, commencing January 1, 19X3, payable from income or from any cash principal available if the income should be inadequate. The estate never had enough cash available to pay the full allowance nor could any part of the cash bequests be paid. Accordingly a considerable liability to Sandra Brown had accumulated toward the end of 19X8 for the unpaid portion of the family allowance, as shown by the following trial balance of the estate ledger at December 31 of that year:

Cash	200	
Securities	20,000	
Building A	200,000	
Accumulated Depreciation — Building A		36,000
Building B	160,000	
Accumulated Depreciation — Building B		38,400
Mortgage — Building B		32,000
Revolving Fund — Building A	1,800	
Revolving Fund — Building B	2,400	
Sandra Brown — Family Allowance		288,000
Sandra Brown — Paid on Account	178,000	
Estate Corpus		168,000
	562,400	562,400

The balance in the estate corpus account was made up as follows:

Appraisal of assets	$365,000
Deduct funeral expenses, etc.	15,000
	$350,000
Add income:	
Dividends received	6,000
Rentals, after deducting expenses and mortgage interest to date	100,000
	$456,000
Deduct family allowance	288,000
Balance	$168,000

For want of cash, the beneficiaries decided to settle all liabilities by transfer of property, and they requested their attorney to petition the court for approval of the following agreement to take effect as of December 31, 19X8:

> Building B and its revolving fund are to be conveyed to Sandra Brown subject to the mortgage. In turn she agrees to waive all of her claim against the estate for expenditures not refunded to her, including one of $5,000 for estate income taxes paid by her and not collected from the estate, and in addition to pay attorney's fees of $6,000 for the estate. Furthermore, all beneficiaries agree to have the family allowance discontinued after December 31, 19X8, and also to waive their claims to the cash bequests.

The court gave its approval to the agreement and ordered an intermediary accounting by the trustee as of December 31, 19X8.

Instructions: (1) Prepare the entries required to adjust the trial balance.

(2) Prepare a columnar work sheet showing the trial balance before and after adjustment.

(3) Prepare a statement of Sandra Brown's account.

(4) Prepare a statement of estate corpus.

(5) Prepare the trustee's intermediary accounting in the form of a charge and discharge statement. (AICPA adapted)

22
Estates and Trusts — Principal and Income

A *trust* relationship is formed when a person or persons are appointed to hold certain properties for the benefit of others. The person who creates the trust is variously known as the *donor, trustor, settlor, creator*, or *founder*. Those who are to receive the benefits of the trust are its *beneficiaries*. The person who assumes possession of the property and holds and manages it in the interests of the beneficiaries is known as the *trustee*. The trustee may be an individual or a corporate entity. The trustee acquires legal title to trust property, and the beneficiaries possess equitable or beneficial title to such property.

Trusts commonly provide for two classes of beneficiaries: (1) those who are entitled to the income from the properties in trust for a certain time; (2) those who are entitled to the properties composing the principal of the trust at the end of the period indicated. The person who is to receive the income from a trust is known as the *income beneficiary* or *cestui que trust*. The person entitled to the income during his or her life is referred to as a *life tenant* or *life beneficiary*. The person who is to receive the principal of the trust upon termination of the tenancy of the income beneficiary is called the *principal beneficiary* or *remainderman*. The income beneficiary may also be the principal beneficiary when the trust provides that trust income is to be distributed to a certain party until reaching a certain age, whereupon this same party is to receive the principal properties of the trust. Trust income as well as trust principal may be distributable to more than one person.

LIVING AND TESTAMENTARY TRUSTS

A living person may transfer title to properties to a trustee who is to hold them for the benefit of others. Such a trust is known as a *living trust* or *inter vivos trust*. Transfer of properties is generally effected by a written agreement known as a *declaration of trust*. The creator of the trust may make any desired provisions for the distribution of income and principal of the trust to the named beneficiaries. The trustor may reserve the right to revise the terms of the trust or actually to revoke the trust in the event that family circumstances or business conditions make such a change desirable. The trust is then known as a *revocable living trust*. A trust in which the trustor does not reserve the right to revoke or to alter constitutes an outright gift and is an *irrevocable living trust*. The declaration of trust should indicate the date on which the trust becomes effective.

A trust may be established by the terms of a will. A trust established by will is in effect a legacy or a devise of certain properties. A portion or all of the estate properties is made subject to the control and the management of a trustee for the benefit of the parties named as beneficiaries. Income and principal distributions are made in accordance with the terms of the trust. A trust established by terms of a will is known as a *testamentary trust*. The testamentary trust becomes effective upon the date of the decedent's death.

When real estate is left in trust by will, title passes directly from the deceased to the trustee. When personalty is left in trust, the trustee obtains title upon distribution of the property by the executor or the administrator. Amounts earned on such property and collected by the executor or the administrator from the date of the decedent's death but not distributed to the income beneficiary are also transferred to the trustee. When a trust is to be composed of the residuary assets of the estate, the trust properties are not finally determinable until the estate is declared terminated, and the trustee can assume no trust responsibilities until granted title to the properties.

RESPONSIBILITIES OF THE TRUSTEE

A trustee has those powers expressly granted by the trust as well as those powers that are required to carry out its purposes. The duties and the responsibilities of the trustee are normally similar to those of the executor or the administrator. A trustee acquires legal title to the trust property, which must be managed, conserved, and protected. Principal funds must be kept invested and income-producing. Investments are made in accordance with the requirements of state laws except when contrary provisions are found in the trust declaration. Whenever necessary, properties are sold or exchanged. The trustee is responsible for the collection of income and its appropriate distribution. Upon termination of the trust, the trustee is responsible for the distribution of principal. All income and principal distributions must be made in accordance with the instrument establishing the trust and also in accordance with statutory law. Finally, as in the case of the executor or the administrator, the trustee is required to render to the court of appropriate jurisdiction and to other interested parties a full accounting for the trust properties. Periodic reports may be prepared, and a final accounting may be required upon the final distribution of properties and request by the trustee for a formal discharge. The trustee is liable for any failure to meet the stated responsibilities under the trust in a reasonable and prudent manner.

A will may name the same individual as both executor of the estate and as trustee for a trust created by its terms. As executor, the individual acts to wind up the estate with powers and duties consistent with this responsibility. As trustee, the individual administers the trust in accordance with requirements of the trust declaration and with the statutory law pertaining to trusts. The fiduciary must maintain separate books for activities as executor and separate books for activities as trustee. When properties of the estate are formally turned over to the trust, the books of the estate will report the transfer of such properties out of the estate and the books of the trust will report their receipt. If several trusts are created by the will, a separate accountability for each trust is required.

PRINCIPAL AND INCOME OF THE TRUST DISTINGUISHED

In both living and testamentary trusts, careful distinction must be made between property composing the *principal* or *corpus* of the trust and property composing the *income* of the trust. The distinction between principal and income is made by law except when a contrary treatment is prescribed by the provisions of the trust instrument. This distinction is important because the principal of the trust belongs to the remainderman and is to be distributed to this party upon termination of the trust, while the income belongs to the income beneficiary and is distributable during the trust period. When the income beneficiary and the remainderman are different parties, failure to distinguish properly between principal and income will result in gain to one party and in loss to the other. Even when the income beneficiary is ultimately to receive the trust principal, improper distinctions between principal and income will result in trust distributions that do not meet the conditions set by the party who established the trust.

Properties acquired by the trust as a result of gift, legacy, or devise, and designated as ultimately to become available to the remainderman, form the trust principal. Proceeds from the sale of such properties, or any new properties acquired with the original assets or their proceeds, are likewise principal. Gains or losses on the disposal of principal assets increase or decrease the amount of the trust principal. In the case of a testamentary trust, properties of the decedent on the date of death, whether determined and inventoried as of the date of death or discovered at some later date, represent principal.

Debts relating to principal assets require payment from these assets. Thus a mortgage on real estate transferred to a trust requires settlement from principal assets. Proceeds from a mortgage placed after the asset transfer constitute principal, and settlement of such a mortgage is made from principal. When a trust is to be composed of the residuary assets of an estate, the debts of the decedent and the debts relating to estate liquidation, including taxes and surviving spouse's sustenance when allowed, are paid from principal assets and reduce the amount ultimately to be recognized as trust principal.

The earnings or yield from the use of principal assets, such as interest, dividends, rents, and royalties, represent trust income. Expenses that relate to the production of income, such as interest, taxes, costs of caring for income-producing properties, and legal expenses, are charges against trust income. The difference between the gross income and the expenses chargeable against such income becomes available for distribution to the income beneficiary. Distributions to the income beneficiary must leave trust principal unimpaired.

Accounting records of the trustee must maintain the distinction between principal and income items if the trustee's responsibilities to principal and income beneficiaries are to be met. The trustee is required periodically to submit statements summarizing accountabilities to both principal and income beneficiaries. Such reports normally take the form of the charge and discharge statement, prepared in two sections: the first section is devoted to principal assets and reports the principal assets held by the trustee at the beginning of the period, the changes in such principal assets during the period, and the balance of principal assets held at the end of the period; the second section is devoted to income assets and reports any income assets held by the trustee at the beginning of the period, income assets becoming available during the period, distributions and expenses paid out of income assets during the period, and any balance of income assets held at the end of the period. Statements submitted by the trustee must be accompanied by vouchers and other evidence offering full support for the summaries.

Analysis of Trust Receipts and Disbursements

Each receipt and disbursement by the trustee requires analysis to determine whether it is to be treated as principal or as income. In distinguishing between principal and income, the trustee is bound by any specific provisions in the trust instrument or by the creator's intent if determinable from the trust instrument. In the absence of express or implied rules in the instrument creating the trust, the trustee follows statutory requirements of the state or the specific rulings of the court of trust jurisdiction. Some progress has been made towards uniformity on rules governing classification of items as principal and income. Several states have adopted the Uniform Principal and Income Act or a part of the provisions embodied in this Act. The general rules governing the classification of cash receipts and payments are considered in the paragraphs that follow.

Interest income and expense. Statutory law generally provides that interest income is accruable for classification purposes. Accrued interest income at the beginning of an income beneficiary's tenancy (the date of death of the party creating a testamentary trust, for example) is considered principal. Accrued interest income at the date of termination of the income beneficiary's tenancy (the date of death of a life tenant, for example) is considered income. Only interest earned during the period of the income beneficiary's tenancy qualifies as income and is distributable to this party. Collections of interest, then, must be analyzed and identified as to that portion representing income and to be made available to an income beneficiary and that portion representing principal and to be retained for the principal beneficiary. Laws generally make an exception to the accrual rule for interest that is credited on savings accounts: interest credited by a bank during the period of tenancy is allowed in full to the income beneficiary; interest credited after termination of the tenancy is allowed to the principal beneficiary.

The "purchase" of accrued interest upon the acquisition of securities from principal funds calls for subsequent analysis of interest receipts and the replenishment of principal for such an outlay. A "sale" of accrued interest upon the disposal of securities calls for analysis of the sales proceeds with recognition of the accrued interest as income and the balance of the proceeds as a return of principal.

Ordinarily, interest expense is accruable. Thus an income beneficiary is chargeable only for interest accruing during his or her tenancy. Accrued interest expense at the beginning of an income beneficiary's tenancy is regarded as a principal debt. Accrued interest expense at the date of termination of an income beneficiary's tenancy is regarded as an income debt. Payments of interest expense require analysis to determine that portion chargeable against principal and reducing the amount ultimately available to the principal beneficiary and that portion chargeable against income and thus reducing the amount distributable to the income beneficiary.

Rental income and rental expense. State laws generally require the accrual of rental income and rental expense. Rentals identified with the period of tenancy are income items, and rentals accruing prior to or after the period of tenancy are principal items. Similar rules of accrual commonly apply to royalty income. Ordinarily, compensation does not have to be made to an income beneficiary for rents and royalties applicable in part to the tenancy period but collected by the testator prior to death.

Dividends. Dividends are not accruable. The general rule is that the declaration date determines the classification of dividends as principal or income. Dividends that are declared within the period of the income beneficiary's tenancy are income; dividends declared prior to such tenancy or after such tenancy are principal. In some states, however, the classification is determined in terms of the record date, the date when the company refers to its books for a list of the stockholders who are entitled to dividends. When the record date falls within the tenancy period, the dividends are recognized as income; when the record date precedes the tenancy period, the dividends are recognized as principal. Dividend declaration dates or dividend payment dates have no significance when the latter rule is in effect.

To illustrate the application of these rules, assume that a trust becomes effective upon the death of the testator on November 10. Cash dividends on stock of the estate are declared on November 1 payable on December 1 to stockholders of record November 15. If the declaration date is controlling, dividends when collected are recognized as principal; if the record date is controlling, the dividends when collected are recognized as income.

State laws may provide that certain dividends or portions of certain dividends must be regarded as principal even though they are related to the period of the income beneficiary's tenancy. Laws of most states provide that all cash dividends within the tenancy period represent income accruing to the income beneficiary. Many states have adopted the view that whether ordinary and regular or extraordinary and irregular, all cash dividends shall be regarded as income and all stock dividends as principal. It is the form of the dividend that determines its classification. This is known as the "Massachusetts Rule" and has been adopted in the Uniform Principal and Income Act.

Some states, however, follow the "Pennsylvania Rule," which provides that a distinction must be made between ordinary dividends and extraordinary dividends. Although ordinary and regular dividends are regarded as income, extraordinary dividends must be apportioned between principal and income so that there is no impairment of principal. This rule applies to all dividends, whether cash, stock, property, or scrip. Apportionment is based on the periods when the earnings used as a basis for dividends were accumulated. A dividend or that portion of a dividend declared from earnings accumulated prior to the commencement of the trust is regarded as principal; a dividend or that portion of a dividend declared from earnings accumulated during the period of the trust is regarded as income.

Liquidating dividends. The foregoing discussion was related to dividends representing distributions of corporate earnings. Liquidating dividends representing the proceeds from wasting assets or from corporate liquidation are generally regarded as distributions of capital and are classified as principal.

Stock rights. Stock rights and the proceeds from the sale of stock rights are generally regarded as principal. This rule has been adopted in the Uniform Principal and Income Act.

Profit realized on contract completed after death. When a contract remains to be completed after a person's death, the profit is not accrued but is calculated at the conclusion of the contract and the full amount is considered principal.

Income from crops and livestock. When farm lands are held in trust, any crops harvested during the income beneficiary's tenancy are regarded as income; costs of maintaining the farm lands and harvesting the land are chargeable to income. The income from a first crop of a testamentary trust requires no apportionment but accrues to the income beneficiary. Livestock born during an income beneficiary's tenancy is likewise income. The income beneficiary is normally charged for any shrinkage in the original livestock supply. If principal is to be unimpaired, the supply of livestock at the termination of the income beneficiary's tenancy should be equal to the supply at the beginning of the tenancy period.

Depreciation, depletion, and amortization. No charge is generally required against income for depreciation or obsolescence of trust properties unless specifically provided for in the trust instrument. There is no reimbursement to principal for the normal impairment in properties through such natural causes. The prevailing view holds that, if the party creating the trust had intended that the principal beneficiary recover a sum equal to depreciation or obsolescence during the tenancy period, specific requirements to that effect would have been included in the trust instrument.

When trust properties include certain wasting assets such as mines, oil wells, or timberlands, or intangibles such as leaseholds, patents, and copyrights, it is generally held that income must be reduced by amounts equal to the depletion or the amortization charges. When a charge against income for asset depletion or amortization is appropriate, a portion of the proceeds from sales equal to this charge is withheld during the period of tenancy and is regarded as principal. Proceeds from activities relating to wasting assets, then, are divided into two parts: (1) the amount required to keep the principal unimpaired and (2) the balance representing income. In the trust instrument, it is possible to provide that no charge shall be made against income for asset depletion or amortization.

Operating, maintenance, and repair charges. All ordinary expenses in the operation of income properties are chargeable to income. Such expenses as insurance, taxes, repairs, and rental fees are proper charges to income. Normal and recurring maintenance expenses and repairs on properties are chargeable against the income from properties, but extraordinary repairs, betterments, and additions are normally chargeable against principal on the theory that these result in principal benefits. When an expenditure benefits both principal and income, the court may authorize apportionment of the expenditure between principal and income. In the case of unimproved or non-income-producing properties, carrying charges are generally absorbed by principal.

Partnership profits. Profits of a partnership up to the date that the deceased partner's interest is calculated are generally regarded as principal. When the books are closed as of the date of death, the deceased's interest on this date represents principal, and any income related to this interest thereafter represents income. When the partnership agreement provides for closing the books at the end of the fiscal period in the regular manner, the interest of the decedent determined as of this date is generally regarded as principal.

Insurance premiums on real estate. Insurance premiums on properties are charged against income. Amounts collected on insurance policies as a result of a property loss are treated as a recovery of principal.

Property tax, estate tax, and income tax payments. In general, taxes on real estate are not considered to accrue. Taxes that were assessed and became a lien on the property prior to the period of tenancy are usually charges against principal; taxes becoming a lien during the tenancy period are usually charges against income. Special assessment taxes during the period of tenancy may be chargeable against either principal or income, or may be apportioned between both, depending upon the extent to which the levies are related to the permanent improvement of properties. The federal estate tax is chargeable against principal. Income taxes on the gains resulting from the sale of principal assets are chargeable against principal; income taxes on accumulations of income are chargeable against income.

Trust fees and expenses. Fees and expenses of administering a trust are identified with principal or income, depending upon the parties who benefit by the services performed. The expenses of creating the trust are generally charged against principal. When estate assets are to be transferred to a trust, all administrative expenses, including probate and legal expenses of preparing the estate for the trust, are chargeable to principal. After the trust has been set up, expenses pertaining to the production and collection of income are charged to income; expenses relating to the preservation of principal are charged to principal. Charges identified with changes in investments are generally considered principal and reported as a cost of the principal assets acquired. Fees based upon sums of income and principal paid out would be charged against income and principal respectively. Certain fees and expenses may be related to both principal and income, suggesting allocation between the two. Under such circumstances, directions from the court may be sought as a basis for the allocation.

Receipt of bond interest — amortization of bond premium and discount. When a testamentary trust holds bonds originally acquired by the deceased, courts have held that bond interest collected during the period of tenancy accrues in full to the income beneficiary. No adjustment in income is required even though the bonds are inventoried at a premium or at a discount. Upon the sale of the bonds or upon their maturity, the difference between the value of the bonds at the date of death and the amount received on their sale is treated as a principal gain or loss. In the absence of specific provisions for bond premium or bond discount amortization, it is assumed that the intent of the testator was to make the interest actually collected on the bonds available to the income beneficiary.

When bonds are purchased by a trustee at a premium, courts generally have supported the amortization of premium and the payment to the income beneficiary of the bond interest reduced by such amortization. Interest received, then, is considered to be composed of two parts: (1) an amount equal to the premium amortization that is principal and (2) the balance representing income. However, when bonds are purchased by a trustee at a discount, courts generally have not supported the amortization of discount on bonds and the payment to the income beneficiary of an amount in excess of the interest actually received. The ultimate recovery of an amount exceeding bond cost is treated as a principal gain.

The Uniform Principal and Income Act has adopted a consistent position for bonds taken over at the commencement of a trust as well as for bonds purchased at either a premium or a discount during a period of trust tenancy. The Act provides that no adjustment be made for premium or discount amortization, the income beneficiary being entitled to amounts actually received as interest. Upon the sale or the maturity of the bonds, any loss or gain represented by the difference between their inventoried value or cost and their sales proceeds or maturity value applies to principal. When bonds are acquired at a discount, the income beneficiary still receives no more than the interest actually collected; however, the amount of interest collected is not reduced when bonds are acquired at a premium.

Accounting for the Testamentary Trust

Since the testamentary trust is normally operative from the date of the testator's death even though the assets are not to be turned over to the trustee until the estate is terminated, a careful distinction between principal and income items must be made on the books of the executor or the administrator until separate books for the trust are set up. The entries described in the following paragraphs are made on the estate books in accounting for income items.

Collection of income. Receipts representing income accruing to the income beneficiary are recorded by debits to Income Cash and credits to Collections of Income. When an account is maintained for Income Cash, cash representing a part of the principal of the estate is designated as Principal Cash. With income from a number of different sources, a separate income account for each class of income may be maintained.

Payment of expenses identified with income. Expenses chargeable against income are paid out of income cash. The account Expenses Chargeable to Income is debited and Income Cash is credited. Here, too, separate accounts may be maintained to report the different expense items. The titles of such accounts should indicate the trust income relationship.

Distributions of income. Distributions of income cash to the income beneficiary are recorded by debits to the account Distributions of Income and by credits to Income Cash. When there are a number of income beneficiaries, separate distribution accounts with each beneficiary may be maintained.

Closing nominal income accounts. Nominal income account balances may be closed at regular intervals and also before trust assets on the estate books are transferred to the trustee. Income accounts before closing appear with debit and credit balances as follows:

Debits	Credits
Income Cash	Collections of Income
Distributions of Income	
Expenses Chargeable to Income	

To close the accounts, Collections of Income is debited, Distributions of Income and Expenses Chargeable to Income are credited, and Estate Income is credited. The balance in Estate Income is then equal to the balance of the income assets.

Transfer of trust assets to trustee. When the estate transfers principal assets to a trust, the asset accounts to form the principal of the trust are credited and an account Principal Assets Transferred to Trustee is debited. The balance of the latter account is ultimately closed into Estate Principal. Income assets that have not been distributed to the beneficiary are also transferred to the trust. The asset accounts are credited and an account Income Assets Transferred to Trustee is debited. The balance of the latter account is ultimately closed into Estate Income.

Maintaining Books for the Trust

When trust books are opened, accounts with the principal assets are debited and Trust Principal is credited. Trust Principal measures the accountability of the trustee to the principal beneficiary. Any assets identified with the income beneficiary are recorded by debits to the income asset accounts and a credit to Trust Income. Trust Income measures the accountability to the income beneficiary. Thereafter transactions are recorded with appropriate distinction between principal and income items. At the end of the trust fiscal period, nominal accounts reporting changes in the trust principal, such as Gains on Disposal of Principal Assets, Losses on Disposal of Principal Assets, and Expenses Chargeable to Principal, are closed into Trust Principal. Nominal accounts reporting changes in trust income, such as Collections of Income, Expenses Chargeable to Income, and Distributions of Income, are closed into Trust Income.

It should be observed that accounting for the trust is normally maintained on a cash basis. Distributions to an income beneficiary must be limited to the amount of income cash available. Under these circumstances, the cash basis provides for income measurement that is consistent with the limitations that are found in income distribution. However, accruable income and expense must be recognized both at the beginning of the income beneficiary's tenancy and upon termination of the tenancy. For example, any accrued interest receivable on the date of the commencement of a trust must be recognized as increasing principal and any accrued interest payable on this date must be recognized as decreasing principal. Receipts and disbursements relating to such accrued items during the trust period are recorded as changes in Principal Cash, since income accrues to the income beneficiary only from the commencement of the tenancy. Furthermore, any accrued interest receivable on the date of the termination of an income beneficiary's tenancy must be recognized as a part of trust income and any accrued interest payable on this date must be recognized as a charge against trust income. While past distributions to the income beneficiary were limited to the income available in the form of cash, settlement upon termination of the tenancy period calls for the payment of income adjusted for accruable items.

ACCOUNTING FOR THE ESTATE-TO-TRUST DEVELOPMENT ILLUSTRATED

Accounting for an estate whose assets are ultimately transferred to a trust is illustrated in the example that follows. Paul Davis, who died on May 1, 19X5, left a will naming William C. Ross as executor and trustee. The will was admitted to probate and letters testamentary were issued by the court to Ross on May 15. The will provided that:

Home, furniture, personal effects, and cash of $15,000 were to go to the widow, Joan Davis.

The personal library was bequeathed to Southeastern University.

Co. X Bonds were bequeathed to the son, Henry.

After payment of debts, expenses, legacies, and estate and inheritance taxes, remaining property was to be held by William C. Ross in trust, the income from the trust to be paid to the widow and, upon her death, the trust principal to be paid to the son.

The inventory filed by the executor as of May 1 and subsequent transactions are recorded as follows:

Transactions		Entries on Estate Books[1]		
May 1		*Principal Cash................	2,800	
(1) Assets at appraised values per inventory filed with the court by William C. Ross:		Estate Principal..........		2,800
Cash...............................	$ 2,800	Automobile....................	1,500	
Automobile	1,500	Furniture and Personal		
Furniture and personal effects	4,500	Effects.........................	4,500	
Library............................	2,000	Library	2,000	
Co. A stock (100 shares)..................	11,500	Co. A Stock....................	11,500	
Dividends on Co. A stock declared April 15, to stockholders of record April 25, payable May 25	150	Dividends Receivable on Co. A Stock....................	150	
		Co. X 6% Bonds	10,000	
Co. X 6% bonds............................	10,000	Accrued Interest on Co. X		
Accrued interest on Co. X bonds, December 1–May 1............................	250	Bonds	250	
		Co. Y 6% Bonds	25,000	
Co. Y 6% bonds............................	25,000	Accrued Interest on Co. Y		
Accrued interest on Co. Y bonds, December 1–May 1............................	625	Bonds	625	
		Life Insurance Policy	20,000	
Life insurance policy payable to estate..	20,000	Estate Principal..........		75,525

---

[1]Entries with asterisks on this and the following pages would appear in special cash journals as illustrated on pages 718 and 719.

Transactions	Entries on Estate Books		
May 20 (2) Collected life insurance policy.	*Principal Cash	20,000	
	Life Insurance Policy ...		20,000
May 25 (3) Collected dividends on Co. A stock.	*Principal Cash	150	
	Dividends Receivable on Co. A Stock		150
June 1 (4) Collected interest for 6 months on Co. X 6% bonds.	*Principal Cash	300	
	Accrued Interest on Co. X Bonds		250
	Henry Davis		50
June 1 (5) Collected interest for 6 months on Co. Y 6% bonds.	*Principal Cash	625	
	Income Cash	125	
	Accrued Interest on Co. Y Bonds		625
	Collections of Income		125
June 10 (6) Sold automobile.	*Principal Cash	1,350	
	Losses on Disposal of Assets	150	
	Automobile		1,500
June 12 (7) Paid funeral expenses.	*Funeral and Administrative Expenses	600	
	Principal Cash		600
June 15 (8) Transferred cash, furniture, and personal effects to Joan Davis.	*Legacies Paid or Delivered	15,000	
	Principal Cash		15,000
	Legacies Paid or Delivered	4,500	
	Furniture and Personal Effects		4,500
June 15 (9) Transferred library to Southeastern University.	Legacies Paid or Delivered	2,000	
	Library		2,000
June 18 (10) Transferred Co. X bonds and interest collected on bonds from April 30 to Henry Davis.	Legacies Paid or Delivered	10,000	
	Co. X 6% Bonds		10,000
	*Henry Davis	50	
	Principal Cash		50
September 1 (11) Received payment of $1,000 note dated March 1 and interest at 6% for six months from R. G. Stapp. (The executor had no knowledge of this asset until September 1.)	*Principal Cash	1,010	
	Income Cash	20	
	Assets Subsequently Discovered		1,010
	Collections of Income		20
September 1 (12) Distributed available income cash to Joan Davis.	*Distributions of Income	145	
	Income Cash		145

Transactions	Entries on Estate Books
September 5 (13) Collected dividends on Co. A stock.	*Income Cash.................. 150 Collections of Income... 150
September 15 (14) Paid debts filed against the decedent: A. C. Parker, $450; P. O. Thomas, $3,200; State Bank (on note), $2,000.	*Debts of Decedent Paid... 5,650 Principal Cash............. 5,650

September 15
(15) Sold Co. A stock.
	*Principal Cash............... 11,800
	   Company A Stock 11,500
	   Gains on Disposal of Assets....................... 300

October 1
(16) Paid estate taxes and miscellaneous administrative expenses.
	*Funeral and Administrative Expenses................... 6,385
	   Expenses Chargeable to Income......................... 15
	     Principal Cash............. 6,385
	     Income Cash.............. 15

Statements for the Estate-to-Trust Development

A trial balance of principal and income accounts on the estate books on October 1, 19X5, a charge and discharge statement prepared from the trial balance and ledger accounts, and schedules prepared in support of the charge and discharge statement appear as follows:

Estate of Paul Davis
William C. Ross, Executor
Trial Balance
October 1, 19X5

	Principal Accounts		Income Accounts	
	Dr.	Cr.	Dr.	Cr.
Principal Cash..	10,350			
Co. Y 6% Bonds.......................................	25,000			
Estate Principal.......................................		78,325		
Assets Subsequently Discovered		1,010		
Gains on Disposal of Assets......................		300		
Losses on Disposal of Assets.....................	150			
Funeral and Administrative Expenses..........	6,985			
Debts of Decedent Paid............................	5,650			
Legacies Paid or Delivered	31,500			
Income Cash...			135	
Collections of Income...............................				295
Expenses Chargeable to Income			15	
Distributions of Income			145	
	79,635	79,635	295	295

Estate of Paul Davis
William C. Ross, Executor
Charge and Discharge Statement
May 1–October 1, 19X5

First, as to Estate Principal
  I Charge Myself With:
    Original principal of estate (Schedule A) $78,325
    Assets subsequently discovered (Schedule B)..............   1,010
    Gains on disposal of assets (Schedule C).....................   300 $79,635

  I Credit Myself With:
    Losses on disposal of assets (Schedule D)................... $ 150
    Funeral and administrative expenses (Schedule E)........   6,985
    Debts of decedent paid (Schedule F)..........................   5,650
    Legacies paid or delivered (Schedule G)......................   31,500   44,285

  Balance as to Estate Principal (Schedule H).................... $35,350

Second, as to Estate Income
  I Charge Myself With:
    Collections of income (Schedule I).............................. $ 295

  I Credit Myself With:
    Expenses chargeable to income (Schedule J)............... $ 15
    Distributions of income (Schedule K)..........................   145   160

  Balance as to Estate Income — Consisting of Income Cash $ 135

  (Balances of estate principal and estate income are subject to deductions for executor's commissions.)

Schedule A — Original Principal of Estate, May 1, 19X5
  Cash... $ 2,800
  Automobile...   1,500
  Furniture and personal effects   4,500
  Library..   2,000
  Co. A stock..   11,500
  Dividends receivable on Co. A stock   150
  Co. X 6% bonds   10,000
  Accrued interest on Co. X bonds   250
  Co. Y 6% bonds   25,000
  Accrued interest on Co. Y bonds   625
  Life insurance policy   20,000
  Total.. $78,325

Schedule B — Assets Subsequently Discovered
  Note dated March 1 accruing interest at 6%, signed by R. G. Stapp .. $ 1,000
  Accrued interest on note on May 1   10
  Total... $ 1,010

Schedule C — Gains on Disposal of Assets
  Proceeds on sale of Co. A stock on September 15............ $11,800
  Co. A stock, per inventory, May 1....................................   11,500
  Gain .... $ 300

Schedule D — Losses on Disposal of Assets
  Automobile, per inventory, May 1..................................... $ 1,500
  Proceeds on sale of automobile on June 10.....................   1,350
  Loss .... $ 150

Schedule E — Funeral and Administrative Expenses
  Funeral expenses... $ 600
  Taxes..   4,000
  Administrative expenses   2,385
  Total.. $ 6,985

Schedule F — Debts of Decedent Paid
A. C. Parker	$ 450
P. O. Thomas	3,200
State Bank	2,000
Total	**$ 5,650**

Schedule G — Legacies Paid or Delivered
Joan Davis	$19,500
Henry Davis	10,000
Southeastern University	2,000
Total	**$31,500**

Schedule H — Balance as to Estate Principal
Principal cash	$10,350
Co. Y 6% bonds	25,000
Total	**$35,350**

Schedule I — Collections of Income
Interest on Co. Y bonds for period May 1–June 1	$ 125
Interest on R. G. Stapp note, May 1–August 1	20
Dividends on Co. A stock, September 5	150
Total	**$ 295**

Schedule J — Expenses Chargeable to Income
Administrative expenses	$ 15

Schedule K — Distributions of Income
Payment to Joan Davis, September 1	$ 145

Closing Entries for the Estate

The final accounting as submitted by William C. Ross is approved by the court, and the executor is allowed commissions of $2,025 allocable $2,000 to principal and $25 to income. The court authorizes William C. Ross to act as trustee for the testamentary trust that names Joan Davis, the life tenant, and Henry Davis, the remainderman. The entries that are required on October 1 in closing the temporary accounts on the estate books are as follows:

Transactions	Entries on Estate Books		
October 1 (17) Commissions paid for administration.	*Funeral and Administrative Expenses	2,000	
	Expenses Chargeable to Income	25	
	Principal Cash		2,000
	Income Cash		25
October 1 (18) To close principal accounts.	Estate Principal	44,975	
	Assets Subsequently Discovered	1,010	
	Gains on Disposal of Assets	300	
	Losses on Disposal of Assets		150
	Funeral and Administrative Expenses		8,985
	Debts of Decedent Paid		5,650
	Legacies Paid or Delivered		31,500

Transactions	Entries on Estate Books		
October 1 (19) To close income accounts.	Collections of Income......	295	
	Distributions of Income		145
	Expenses Chargeable to Income...................		40
	Estate Income............		110

Account balances on the executor's books after closing would be as follows:

	Principal Accounts		Income Accounts	
	Dr.	Cr.	Dr.	Cr.
Principal Cash..	8,350			
Co. Y 6% Bonds.....................................	25,000			
Estate Principal.......................................		33,350		
Income Cash			110	
Estate Income				110
	33,350	33,350	110	110

The entries on the executor's books to record the transfer of principal and income assets to the trustee and to close the remaining accounts are as follows:

Transactions	Entries on Estate Books		
October 1 (20) Transferred principal assets to William C. Ross, trustee.	*Principal Assets Transferred to William C. Ross, Trustee	8,350	
	Principal Cash.............		8,350
	Principal Assets Transferred to William C. Ross, Trustee	25,000	
	Co. Y 6% Bonds		25,000
October 1 (21) To close principal accounts.	Estate Principal.............	33,350	
	Principal Assets Transferred to William C. Ross, Trustee..............		33,350
October 1 (22) Transferred income assets to William C. Ross, trustee.	*Income Assets Transferred to William C. Ross, Trustee	110	
	Income Cash		110
October 1 (23) To close income accounts.	Estate Income................	110	
	Income Assets Transferred to William C. Ross, Trustee.............		110

Accounting for the Trust

The opening entries on the trustee's books and the entries that are made for the transactions that take place during the trust's fiscal period, which is to be the calendar year, follow. A charge and discharge statement would be prepared to summarize activities of the trust for the partial period ending December 31.

Transactions	Entries on Trust Books		

October 1
(24) Took over principal and income assets from William C. Ross, executor.
	*Principal Cash................
	   Trust Principal ....
	
	Co. Y 6% Bonds ....
	   Trust Principal ....
	
	*Income Cash..................
	   Trust Income ....
		8,350
		
		25,000
		
		110
			8,350
			
			25,000
			
			110

October 31
(25) Purchased $7,500 Co. Z 6% bonds, interest payable annually on December 31, at 104 plus accrued interest. Bonds mature 50 months from this date.
	*Co. Z 6% Bonds ....
	Accrued Interest on Co. Z
	  Bonds ....
	   Principal Cash.............
		7,800
		
		375
			
			8,175

December 1 (26) Collected interest for 6 months on Co. Y 6% bonds.	*Income Cash.................. Collections of Income...	750	750
December 15 (27) Distributed available income cash to Joan Davis.	*Distributions of Income... Income Cash...............	860	860

December 31
(28) Collected interest on Co. Z bonds, $450, interest being divided between principal and income as follows:
To principal —
  Accrued interest on date of purchase paid from principal cash.... $375
  Premium amortization for two months, 2/50 × $300 (it is assumed that state laws provide for the principal recovery of original bond outlay, with amortization on a straight-line basis).................. <u>12</u>
  $387
 	
To income —
  Interest collected, $75, less premium amortization, $12............. <u>63</u>
  $450
	*Principal Cash................
	Income Cash..................
	  Accrued Interest on Co.
	  Z Bonds.....................
	  Co. Z 6% Bonds ....
	  Collections of Income...
		387
		63
			
			375
			12
			63

December 31 (29) To close temporary accounts.	Collections of Income...... Trust Income .... Distributions of Income	813 47	 860

Special Cash Journals for Executor and Trustee

Special columnar cash receipts and cash payments journals are generally desirable in recording cash transactions of the executor and the trustee. Cash transactions for William C. Ross, Executor, could be recorded in a

CASH

Date		Account Credited	Explanation	Post. Ref.
May	1	Estate Principal...............................	Cash left by decedent.........................	
	20	Life Insurance Policy........................	Collected insurance............................	
	25	Dividends Receivable on Co. A Stock..	Collected dividend	
June	1	⎰Accrued Interest on Co. X Bonds	Collected accrued interest	
		⎱Henry Davis....................................	Collected legacy interest	
	1	⎰Accrued Interest on Co. Y Bonds	Collected accrued interest	
		⎱Collections of Income......................	Collected interest income	
	10	Automobile	Sold automobile at loss.....................	
Sept.	1	⎰Assets Subsequently Discovered	Collected note and accrued int.	
		⎱Collections of Income......................	Collected interest income	
	5	Collections of Income......................	Collected dividend income	
	15	Co. A Stock — Gains on Disposal of Assets	Sold stock at gain	

CASH

Date		Account Debited	Explanation	Post. Ref.
June	12	Funeral and Administrative Expenses	Paid funeral expense..........................	
	15	Legacies Paid or Delivered................	Paid cash legacy to widow..................	
	18	Henry Davis	Paid interest collected on legacy..........	
Sept.	1	Distributions of Income....................	Paid income to widow	
	15	Debts of Decedent Paid	Paid creditors	
Oct.	1	⎰Funeral and Administrative Expenses	Paid principal charges	
		⎱Expenses Chargeable to Income........	Paid income charges	
Oct.	1	⎰Funeral and Administrative Expenses	Paid principal commissions..................	
		⎱Expenses Chargeable to Income........	Paid income commissions	
	1	Principal Assets Transferred to William C. Ross, Trustee	Transferred principal cash to trustee....	
	1	Income Assets Transferred to William C. Ross, Trustee...........................	Transferred income cash to trustee......	

cash receipts journal and a cash payments journal as illustrated below. Similar special columnar cash journals could be provided to record the cash transactions completed by William C. Ross acting as trustee.

RECEIPTS

Principal Cash Dr.	Income Cash Dr.	Disposal of Assets			Collections of Income Cr.	Sundry Credits
		Loss Dr.	Asset Cr.	Gain Cr.		
2,800						2,800
20,000			20,000			
150			150			
300			250			
						50
625			625			
	125				125	
1,350		150	1,500			
1,010						1,010
	20				20	
	150				150	
11,800			11,500	300		
38,035	295	150	34,025	300	295	3,860

PAYMENTS

Principal Cash Cr.	Income Cash Cr.	Funeral and Administrative Expenses Dr.	Debts of Decedent Paid Dr.	Legacies Paid or Delivered Dr.	Expenses Chargeable to Income Dr.	Distributions of Income Dr.	Sundry Debits
600		600					
15,000				15,000			
50				50			
	145					145	
5,650			5,650				
6,385		6,385					
	15				15		
27,685	160	6,985	5,650	15,050	15	145	
2,000		2,000					
	25				25		
8,350							8,350
	110						110
10,350	135	2,000			25		8,460

1. (a) What is meant by a trust? (b) Name the parties to a trust.

2. Distinguish between:

(a) Trust principal and trust income.
(b) Testamentary trust and inter vivos trust.
(c) Income beneficiary and remainderman.
(d) Revocable trust and irrevocable trust.

3. (a) When does the testamentary trust acquire title to (1) real properties and (2) personal properties? (b) When does the tenancy of the income beneficiary begin?

4. What are the usual responsibilities of the trustee?

5. What books should be maintained by a party who is named in a will as both executor of an estate and trustee of a trust created by the will?

6. Which of the following items are generally considered principal and which are considered income?

(a) Assets discovered after death of the testator.
(b) Gain on the sale of a principal asset.
(c) Cash dividend of which 30% is declared by the corporation to be liquidating.
(d) Extra cash dividend.
(e) Proceeds from sale of stock rights.
(f) Accrued interest on bonds as of death of the testator.
(g) Gain on sale of securities acquired and sold after death of the testator.
(h) Profit on executory contract completed after death of the testator.
(i) Income from sale of crops after death of the testator.
(j) Accrued interest on bonds as of termination of a trust.
(k) Recovery of insurance as a result of property loss by fire.

7. Which of the following items are generally considered to decrease principal and which are considered to decrease income?

(a) Specific legacies distributed.
(b) Legal fees for defending estate against certain claims.
(c) Funeral and administrative expenses of the estate.
(d) Cost of supporting surviving spouse for short period after death of testator.
(e) Federal estate tax paid.
(f) Expenses of probating will.
(g) Commission to executor for distributing estate assets.
(h) Loss on failure to collect account receivable of testator.
(i) Legal fees for collection of rents on property.
(j) Depreciation of real estate.
(k) Depletion of wasting assets.
(l) Property taxes assessed after death of testator.
(m) Cost of harvesting crops after death of testator.

(n) Ordinary repairs on real estate.
(o) Commission to trustee on distribution of income cash.
(p) Special assessment tax on real estate for street improvements.
(q) Interest on mortgage on real estate.
(r) Federal income tax on gain from sale of real estate.
(s) Federal income tax on income accumulated for the benefit of the income beneficiary.
(t) Accounting and legal fees in winding up trust activities.
(u) Real estate taxes that were a lien on date of testator's death.
(v) Loss on sale of a principal asset.
(w) Principal asset written off as worthless.
(x) Inheritance taxes paid on a trust-estate.
(y) Federal income taxes on decedent's last tax return.
(z) Special amounts allowed by law to surviving spouse.

8. What two views are held with respect to the treatment of "extraordinary" cash dividends as principal and income? Which rule prevails?

9. What two views are held with respect to the treatment of stock dividends as principal and income? Which rule prevails?

10. (a) What general rules are followed in the measurement of income accruing to the income beneficiary when property is subject to (1) depreciation and (2) depletion? (b) What entries are made in recording depreciation and depletion on the trustee's books?

11. Assuming the following conditions for bonds held in trust, indicate in each case how the net income accruing to the income beneficiary is generally measured:

How Acquired	Value at which Carried
(1) Transfer from estate	Premium
(2) Purchase by trustee	Premium
(3) Transfer from estate	Discount
(4) Purchase by trustee	Discount

12. The executor for P. M. Bours listed 1,000 shares of Uranium, Inc., at no value in the estate inventory. As a result of valuable discoveries on the properties of this company four months after date of death, the stock became actively traded in over-the-counter dealings. A dividend was declared and paid. Shortly after receiving the dividend, the executor sold the stock. Income of the estate is payable to the surviving spouse, and the principal of the estate is ultimately to be distributed to a surviving daughter. How would the dividend and the sale of the stock be reported on the estate books?

13. In accounting for a trust, what entries would be made when:

(a) The trust is opened and principal assets are recorded at appraised values.
(b) Trust assets are sold at a gain.
(c) Bonds are purchased at a premium plus 2 months' accrued interest.
(d) Semiannual interest is collected on the bonds referred to in part (c). (The law requires that income be reduced by regular bond premium amortization.)

(continued)

   (e) The costs of setting up the trust are paid.

   (f) Income is distributed, and the trustee withdraws 2% of the income distribution as a commission.

   (g) All nominal accounts are closed at the end of the trust fiscal period.

EXERCISES

1. Peter Green, executor for the estate of Lee Andrews, collects the following items. What entries would be made for each of these receipts in distinguishing properly between principal and income?

   (a) Dividends of $300 on X Company stock, declared prior to date of death.

   (b) Interest of $450 on Y Company bonds, $150 having accrued prior to date of death.

   (c) Rentals from properties owned, $400, $250 having accrued prior to date of death.

   (d) Interest of $600 on Z Company bonds, $100 having accrued prior to date of death. One half of the Z Company bonds represents a specific legacy.

2. P. C. Thatcher died on June 30, 19X2, leaving a will in which B. D. Schire was named executor. Among other assets, the executor took over bonds of $10,000 appraised at $10,275, with interest at 6% payable annually on December 31. The bonds mature on December 31, 19X7. What entries would be made on December 31, 19X2, when interest is collected and the proper amount of cash is paid to the income beneficiary?

3. In Exercise 2, state how the entries would differ if Schire, as trustee, acquired the bonds at $10,275 on June 30 and made payment to the income beneficiary on December 31? (Assume that the law requires the amortization of bond premium in calculating income.)

4. Under the terms of the will of J. A. Bailey, $40,000 is to be transferred to a trust to be administered by Judy Barker. The transfer of cash is made on February 1, 19X3, and on March 1 Barker acquires $35,000 of 6% bonds of the Wescott Co. at 104½ plus accrued interest for 3 months. Interest is collected on the bonds on June 1 and December 1. Bonds mature in 8 years and 9 months after date of purchase, and bond premium is amortized over this period in arriving at the income distributable to the income beneficiary, Paul Bailey. Income distributions are made on June 15 and December 15. The trustee recognizes no accruals at the end of the calendar year.

   (a) Prepare the entries that would be made on the books of the trustee in 19X3.

   (b) Prepare a charge and discharge statement as to principal and income.

5. The following trial balance is taken from the books of the estate of Richard Harmon on May 1, 19X0:

	Principal Accounts		Income Accounts	
	Dr.	Cr.	Dr.	Cr.
Principal Cash..	25,000			
Stock of Ramsey Co.	67,500			
York Co. 3% Bonds	48,000			
Estate Principal..		179,500		
Assets Subsequently Discovered		3,500		
Gains on Disposal of Assets........................		2,000		
Losses on Disposal of Assets......................	4,800			
Funeral and Administrative Expenses..........	3,750			
Debts of Decedent Paid............................	7,950			
Legacies Paid or Delivered	28,000			
Income Cash			1,750	
Collections of Income...............................				4,500
Expenses Chargeable to Income			250	
Distributions of Income			2,500	
	185,000	185,000	4,500	4,500

Prepare entries (a) to close the temporary accounts and to record the transfer of estate assets to the trust and (b) to open the trust books.

6. Jack Lemmon, named trustee under a testamentary trust for the benefit of Ellen Hill, took control on April 1, 19X8, of 250 acres of farm land, including unharvested crops, appraised at a value of $45,000; a house appraised at $8,500; and a savings account of $4,950. Income from the trust is to be distributed to Ruth Hill for the support of the income beneficiary until the time when Ellen reaches 21, when the entire trust principal is to be turned over to her.

The trustee completed the following transactions for the period April 1, 19X8–December 31, 19X8:

(a) Paid $1,450 for harvesting crops planted by the deceased, and sold the entire crop for $8,800.
(b) Sold the house and the farm land for $52,000.
(c) Purchased $55,000 of California Power Co. bonds at 100½.
(d) Received bond interest of $1,100 and interest from savings deposit of $100.
(e) Distributed the trust income after deducting fees of $200.

Prepare entries to record the activities of the trustee.

PROBLEMS

22-1. Frank Culver died on November 12, 19X5. His will named Sandra Scott executrix of his estate and also trustee under a testamentary trust. The will provided that, upon settlement of the estate, remaining assets were to be placed in trust, with the income paid to the widow of the decedent for her lifetime and the principal of the trust passing to certain charities upon the widow's death. Scott winds up estate affairs and her estate books show the following account balances on September 15, 19X6, just before she established separate books for the trust:

Principal Cash	$ 43,500
Securities — Stocks and Bonds	24,000
Culver Building on Wilshire Blvd.	135,000
Mortgage Payable on Culver Building	60,000
Income Cash	350
Losses on Disposal of Assets	2,800
Funeral and Administrative Expenses	8,500
Debts of Decedent Paid	14,000
Legacies Paid or Delivered	82,000
Expenses Chargeable to Income	4,200
Estate Principal	238,950
Distributions of Income	17,450
Assets Subsequently Discovered	1,850
Gains on Disposal of Assets	9,000
Collections of Income	22,000

Instructions: (1) Prepare a charge and discharge statement summarizing estate activities.

(2) Prepare the entries to close the accounts on the estate books and to report the transfer of assets to the trustee.

(3) Prepare the entries to open the books of the trust.

22-2. Carolyn Stoneman died on June 1, 19X1, leaving a will in which she named John Burke as executor and trustee. Property is to be disposed of as follows:

Home, furniture, and automobile to husband.
Library to Edgewood State College.
10 shares of X Co. preferred stock and $5,000 of Y Co. bonds to the executor as a legacy.
Proceeds of insurance policy of $10,000 as well as all of the rest, residue, and remainder of the real and personal property to be placed in the hands of Burke as trustee. Income from this property is to accrue to a son who will receive the trust principal upon reaching the age of 21.

An inventory was filed by the executor as follows:

Balance in checking account	$ 1,500
Household furniture	8,500
Automobile	3,500
Library	4,000
Apartment house	60,000
X Co. 6% preferred stock, $100 par, 50 shares	5,350
Regular quarterly dividend on preferred stock, declared May 10 and payable to stockholders of record May 25	75
Y Co. 6% bonds, interest payable semiannually on February 1 and August 1 (valued at par)	15,000
Accrued interest on Y Co. bonds	300
Insurance policy (payable to estate)	10,000

The following transactions are completed by the executor:

(a) Quarterly dividend on preferred stock is collected on June 10.
(b) Insurance policy is collected.
(c) Household furniture and automobile are turned over to husband.
(d) The library is transferred to Edgewood State College.
(e) Interest on bonds, $450, is collected on August 1.
(f) The executor withdraws his legacy on August 15.
(g) Remaining bonds are sold at 102 plus accrued interest on September 1.

(h) The preferred stock is sold for 102½.
(i) Funeral, administrative expenses, and taxes are paid, $7,200.
(j) A bank deposit of $1,250 in the name of Carolyn Stoneman is discovered.
(k) Debts of the decedent are paid, $6,500.
(l) The apartment house is sold for $61,500 on August 20; $16,500 is received in cash, and a 6% mortgage note is received for the balance. Income collected on the real estate to the date of the sale totaled $1,850; expenses paid were $1,200.
(m) Income cash was distributed to the son on September 1.
(n) On September 1 Burke closed executor accounts and opened new books to record his activities as trustee.

Instructions: (1) Prepare general journal entries for Burke as executor.
(2) Prepare a trial balance and a charge and discharge statement, together with supporting schedules.
(3) Prepare the journal entries to close the estate books.
(4) Prepare the entry to open the trust books.

22-3. The estate of Wilbur Ward is appraised as of the date of his death, March 1, as follows:

Cash in bank	$ 3,600
Apartment house	40,000
6% mortgage note on 12th St. property, interest payable June 1 and December 1	30,000
Unimproved real estate	4,500
Personal and household effects	10,000
Billings Co. 6% bonds, interest payable January 1 and July 1 (valued at par)	15,000
Cross Co. common stock	3,000
Accrued interest on bonds	150
Accrued interest on mortgage note	450

Disposition of the property under the will is as follows:

Bert Parker is to act as executor and trustee and is to receive bonds of $5,000, plus expenses, as compensation for his services.
Personal and household effects are to be turned over to the widow. The son, John, is granted a legacy of $5,000, and two granddaughters are allowed $2,500 each.
The executor shall dispose of such securities as may be necessary in liquidating the liabilities of the estate. After payment of legacies, expenses, and debts, residual property shall be held in trust by the trustee, with income to be payable to the widow and trust assets to belong to the son upon her death.

During the period of executorship, March 1 to November 1, the following events took place:

Interest of $900 was collected on the mortgage note, and $450 was collected on the Billings Co. bonds.
Dividends of $60 were received on the Cross Co. common stock.
Cross Co. common stock was sold for $2,600, and Billings Co. bonds with a face value of $5,000 were disposed of for $5,100 plus accrued interest to the date of sale, $25.
Apartment house rental receipts totaled $3,600; however, $150 represented collection of rentals accrued prior to March 1. Repairs, maintenance, and taxes paid on this property totaled $1,650.
The executor paid debts of $2,200, funeral expenses and expenses of last illness of $950, and legal, probate, and administrative expenses of $800. In addition, $1,500

was paid to the State Bank on a note dishonored by George Connally. This note had been endorsed by the decedent. It is believed that collection will be made from the maker of the note.

All of the legacies were distributed in accordance with the provisions of the will, except that the son, with the consent of all parties, accepted the unimproved real estate in full settlement of his legacy. In addition, cash of $2,000 was paid to the widow.

On November 1 the executor filed his report with the court. The court approved final distribution of the estate according to the terms of the will, and the executor thereupon closed the estate books and opened books as trustee.

Instructions: (1) Prepare the entries in general journal form to record the transactions of the executor on the estate books.

(2) Prepare a pre-closing trial balance and a charge and discharge statement, together with accompanying schedules, to be submitted to the court.

(3) Prepare the entries to close the temporary principal accounts and income accounts.

(4) Prepare the entries to transfer principal and income assets to the trustee and to close the estate books.

(5) Prepare the opening entries on the books of the trustee.

22-4. Laura Briggs is appointed to act as trustee for a trust fund of $106,000. Income is to be paid to Andrew Scott, and the principal is to be paid to Scott when he reaches the age of 25.

On June 30, 19X2, Briggs receives the cash and on July 1 purchases $100,000 of Coast Utilities Co. 4½% bonds, paying 103 plus accrued interest. Interest on the bonds is payable semiannually on April 1 and October 1. The bonds mature on October 1, 19X8.

The trustee collects interest regularly in 19X2 and 19X3. In making income distributions out of the trust, the trustee is entitled to withdraw 5% of such amounts as her commission. Trust income is distributed at the end of 19X2 and 19X3. (State laws provide that bond premium shall be amortized in determining amounts available for income beneficiaries.)

Instructions: (1) Prepare in general journal form the entries to record the transactions on the books of the trustee, including the closing entries that would be prepared at the end of 19X2 and 19X3.

(2) Prepare charge and discharge statements as to principal and income for 19X2 and for 19X3.

22-5. Clarence Ross acts as trustee under terms of a testamentary trust made by Robert Searles, deceased. Income of the trust is payable to Alma Searles. At her death, the trust principal is to be divided equally among four children, Andrew, Barbara, Charles, and Delores. On December 31, 19X1, trust account balances are as follows:

Valley County 5% fifteen-year bonds, interest payable April 1 and October 1, bonds dated October 1, 19X1; face value, $30,000 ...	$34,500*
Principal Cash..	5,500
Trust Principal	40,000

*Valley County bonds were purchased on October 1, 19X1, after the trust was formed.

On March 1, 19X2, the trustee purchased $5,000 of Riverside 4½% bonds, paying $5,150 plus accrued interest of $75. Interest is payable semiannually at the beginning of May and November, and bonds mature on May 1, 19X6.

Interest on bonds was collected regularly and all available income cash was distributed to the life tenant on July 1 and December 31, 19X2 and 19X3. The trustee in making remittances deducts 2% as a commission. This rate is allowed Ross on all cash distributions made by him on behalf of the trust.

Alma Searles died on May 1, 19X4. At the direction of the court, the trustee sold the bonds at the following amounts:

Valley County 5% Bonds	$32,000 plus accrued interest to June 1
Riverside 4½% Bonds	$ 5,100 plus accrued interest to June 1

Alma Searles's will provided that any equity that she might have in the trust income upon her death should be paid to her daughter Delores. The trustee made final distribution of trust assets in accordance with the foregoing stipulations.

Instructions: (1) Prepare in general journal form the entries to record the transactions on the books of the trustee, including the closing entries that would be prepared at the end of each calendar year and also upon termination of the trust on June 1, 19X4. (Assume that state laws require premium amortization in determining amounts available to the income beneficiary. Amortization entries are made only when interest is collected.)

(2) Prepare charge and discharge statements as to the principal and income for 19X2, for 19X3, and for the period January 1–June 1, 19X4.

22-6. Charles Murray, executor for the estate of Nancy Warner, and trustee, takes charge of the following assets on January 4, 19X9:

Cash	$ 45,000
Product Development Co. stock, 10,000 shares, market value	82,500
Condominium in Sky High Mountains, appraised value	56,500
Land in Sunset City, appraised value	250,000

The will provides that, after payments of funeral and administrative expenses, debts of the decedent, federal and state taxes, and bequests to charities, the residue and remainder of the real and personal property is to be placed in the hands of Murray as trustee. Paul Warner is to be sole life tenant of the trust income. He is to receive a minimum of $15,000 per year. If net trust income after allowance for expenses and trustee's fees is not equal to this minimum, the deficiency is to be paid out of principal.

From January 4, 19X9 to March 31, 19X9, the executor made the following cash disbursements: funeral and administrative expenses, $4,200; debts of decedent, $8,500; advance to Paul Warner, $5,000; bequests to charity, $20,000; income tax of decedent for 19X8, $1,720; and fees of executor, $2,000.

On March 31, 19X9, the executor closed his accounts and opened new books to record his activities as trustee.

From April 1, 19X9 to December 31, 19X9, cash transactions of the trustee were as follows:

Cash receipts:

Dividends on Product Development Co. stock, declared after death of decedent	$ 5,000
Proceeds from sale of lots (the land was divided into 45 Class A lots, 80 Class B lots, and 40 Class C lots):	

Class A lots sold, 15 @ $3,600	$ 54,000
Class B lots sold, 50 @ $2,600	130,000
Class C lots sold, 20 @ $1,500	30,000
Gross proceeds from sale	$214,000
Less commissions to agents	10,700
Net proceeds	203,300
Interest received on $150,000 Sunset City bonds	2,250
Income from operations of the Sky High Condominium as a resort hotel	6,950

Cash disbursements:

Cost of grading and surveying in subdividing land into lots	$ 8,000
Cost of remodeling the Sky High Condominium	21,500
Investment in Sunset City bonds at par	150,000

Other disbursements:
 Trustee's fees allowed and paid as follows:
  5% of net trust income before allowance for fees.
  2% of net gain on sale of principal assets.
 Allowance to Paul Warner less advance.

Instructions: (1) Prepare general journal entries for the executor, including entries to close the estate books.

(2) Prepare entries for the trustee to record trust activities.

(3) Prepare a charge and discharge statement for the trustee, covering the period April 1, 19X9, to December 31, 19X9.

22-7. The will of Ann Benson, deceased, directed that her executor, Carl Dewing, liquidate the entire estate within two years of the date of her death and pay the net proceeds and income, if any, to Sunnydale Orphanage. Benson died on February 1, 19X7, after a brief illness.

An inventory of the decedent's property was prepared, and the fair market value of all items was determined. The preliminary inventory, before the computation of any appropriate income accruals on inventory items, follows:

	Fair Market Value
First National Bank checking account	$ 6,000
$60,000 City of Laguna school bonds, interest rate 2% payable January 1 and July 1, maturity date 7/1/X9	59,000
2,000 shares of Jones Corporation capital stock	220,000
Term life insurance; beneficiary — estate of Ann Benson	20,000
Personal residence ($45,000) and furnishings ($5,000)	50,000

During 19X7 the following transactions occurred:

(1) The interest on the City of Laguna school bonds was collected. The bonds were sold on July 1 for $59,000, and the proceeds and interest were paid to the orphanage.

(2) The Jones Corporation paid cash dividends of $1 per share on March 1 and December 1, as well as a 10% stock dividend on July 1. All dividends were declared 45 days before each payment date and were payable to holders of record as of 40 days before each payment date. On September 2, 1,000 shares were sold at $105 per share, and the proceeds were paid to Sunnydale Orphanage.

(3) Because of a depressed real estate market, the personal residence was rented furnished at $300 per month commencing April 1. The rent is paid monthly, in advance. Real estate taxes of $900 for the calendar year of 19X7 were paid. The house and furnishings have estimated lives of 45

years and 10 years respectively. The part-time gardener-repairer was released after being paid 4 months' wages totaling $500 on April 30 for
services performed.
(4) The First National Bank checking account was closed and the balance of
$6,000 was transferred to an estate bank account.
(5) The term life insurance was paid on March 1 and deposited in the estate
bank account.
(6) The following disbursements were made:
  (a) Funeral expenses, $2,000.
  (b) Final illness expenses, $1,500.
  (c) April 15 income tax remittance, $700.
  (d) Attorney's and accountant's fees, $12,000.
(7) On December 31, the balance of the undistributed income, except for
$1,000, was paid to the beneficiary. The balance of the cash on hand
derived from the corpus of the estate was also paid to the beneficiary on
December 31. As of December 31, 19X7, the executor resigned and
waived all commissions.

Instructions: Prepare a charge and discharge statement separately stated as
to principal and income, together with its supporting schedules, on behalf of the
executor of the estate of Ann Benson for the period from February 1, 19X7,
through December 31, 19X7.

(AICPA adapted)

22-8. Alfred Tucker died in an accident on May 31, 19X2. His will, dated February 28, 19X1, provided that all just debts and expenses be paid and that his
property be disposed of as follows:

Personal residence — devised to Betty Tucker, widow.
United States Treasury bonds and Puritan Co. stock — to be placed in trust. All in-
  come to go to Betty Tucker during her lifetime, with right of appointment upon her
  death.
Seneca Co. mortgage notes — bequeathed to Carol Tucker Watson, daughter.
Cash — a bequest of $10,000 to Donald Tucker, son.
Remainder of estate — to be divided equally between the two children, Carol Tucker
  Watson and Donald Tucker.

The will further provided that during the administration period Betty Tucker
was to be paid $300 a month out of estate income. Estate and inheritance taxes
are to be borne by the residue. Donald Tucker was named as executor and
trustee.
  An inventory of the decedent's property was prepared. The fair market value
of all items as of the date of death was determined. The preliminary inventory,
before the computation of any appropriate income accruals on inventory items,
follows:

Personal residence property	$ 45,000
Jewelry — diamond ring...	9,600
York Life Insurance Co. — term life insurance policy on life of	
Alfred Tucker; beneficiary — Betty Tucker, widow	120,000
Granite Trust Co. — 3% savings bank account, Alfred Tucker, in	
trust for Paul Watson (grandchild), interest credited January	
and July 1; balance May 31, 19X2...	400
Fidelity National Bank — checking account; balance May 31,	
19X2..	143,000

$100,000 United States Treasury bonds, 3%, 19X9, interest payable March 1 and September 1	$100,000
$9,700 Seneca Co. first mortgage notes, 6%, 19X6, interest payable May 31 and November 30...	9,900
800 shares Puritan Co. common stock.......................................	64,000
700 shares Meta Mfg. Co. common stock...................................	70,000

The executor opened an estate bank account to which he transferred the decedent's checking account balance. Other deposits, through July 1, 19X3, were as follows:

Interest collected on bonds:	
$100,000 United States Treasury:	
September 1, 19X2...	$ 1,500
March 1, 19X3	1,500
Dividends received on stock:	
800 shares Puritan Co.:	
June 15, 19X2, declared May 7, 19X2, payable to holders of record May 27, 19X2...	800
September 15, 19X2...	800
December 15, 19X2...	1,200
March 15, 19X3	800
June 15, 19X3..	800
Net proceeds of June 19, 19X2, sale of 700 shares Meta Mfg. Co...	68,810

Payments were made from the estate's checking account through July 1, 19X3, for the following:

Funeral expenses	$ 2,000
Assessments for additional 19X0 federal and state income taxes ($1,700) plus interest ($110) to May 31, 19X2.........................	1,810
19X2 income taxes of Alfred Tucker for the period January 1, 19X2, through May 31, 19X2, in excess of amounts paid by the decedent on Declarations of Estimated Tax.............................	9,100
Federal and state fiduciary income taxes, fiscal years ending June 30, 19X2 ($75) and June 30, 19X3 ($1,400)	1,475
Federal and state estate taxes	58,000
Monthly payments to Betty Tucker: 13 payments of $300	3,900
Attorney's and accountant's fees	25,000

The executor waived his commission. However, he desired to receive his father's diamond ring in lieu of the $10,000 specific legacy. All parties agreed to this in writing, and the court's approval was secured. All other specific legacies were delivered by July 15, 19X2.

Instructions: Prepare a charge and discharge statement as to principal and income, together with supporting schedules, to accompany the attorney's formal court accounting on behalf of the executor of the estate of Alfred Tucker for the period from May 31, 19X2, through July 1, 19X3. (Alfred Tucker was not a resident of a community property state.) The following supporting schedules should be included: (1) Original Principal of Estate; (2) Gains on Disposal of Estate Assets; (3) Losses on Disposal of Estate Assets; (4) Funeral, Administrative, and Other Expenses; (5) Debts of Decedent Paid; (6) Legacies Paid or Delivered; (7) Balance as to Estate Principal, July 1, 19X3; (8) Proposed Plan of Distribution of Estate Assets; (9) Collections of Income; (10) Distributions of Income.

(AICPA adapted)

22-9. Sam Williams, Jr. died on January 15, 19X7. His will named Helen Wilson as his executrix. His records disclosed the following estate:

Cash in bank..	$ 3,750
6% note receivable, including $50 accrued interest	5,050
Stocks	50,000
Dividends declared on stocks..	600
6% mortgage receivable, including $100 accrued interest	20,100
Real estate — apartment house	35,000
Household effects...	8,250
Dividend receivable from Sam Williams, Sr. trust fund..................	250,000
Total...	$372,750

On July 1, 19X0, the late Sam Williams, Sr. created a trust, with his son Sam Williams, Jr. as life tenant and his grandson as remainderman. The assets in the fund consist solely of the outstanding capital stock of Williams, Inc., namely, 2,000 shares of $100 each. At the creation of the trust, the book value, as well as the market value, of the Williams, Inc., shares was $400,000, and at December 31, 19X6, it was $500,000. On January 2, 19X7, Williams, Inc., declared a 125% cash dividend payable February 2, 19X7, to shareholders of record January 12, 19X7.

The executrix' transactions from January 15 to 31, 19X7, were as follows:

Cash receipts:

Jan. 20	Dividends	$ 1,500.00
25	6% note receivable..	5,000.00
	Interest accrued on note	58.33
	Stock sold, inventoried at $22,500	20,000.00
	6% mortgage sold...	20,100.00
	Interest accrued on mortgage	133.33
28	Sale of assets not inventoried	250.00
29	Real estate sold..	30,000.00
		$77,041.66

Cash disbursements:

Jan. 20	Funeral expenses..	$ 1,750.00
23	Decedent's debts..	8,000.00
25	Decedent's bequests..	10,000.00
31	Advance to widow...	1,500.00
		$21,250.00

Instructions: Prepare a charge and discharge statement as to principal and income for the executrix, covering the period from January 15 to January 31, 19X7.

(AICPA adapted)

22-10. Wallace Weber died January 1, 19X3, and left his property in trust for his daughter, Amy. The income was to be paid to her as long as she lived, and at her death the trust was to go to his nephew, Werner Weber. He appointed Joanne Brooks trustee at a fixed fee of $5,000 per annum. All expenses of settling the estate were paid and accounted for by the executor before the trustee took it over.

Amy died on September 30, 19X6, and left all her property in trust to her cousin, Phillip Marsh. Joanne Brooks was appointed executrix and trustee of her estate, and she agreed not to make any additional charges for these services. All income was to be paid to Phillip Marsh. The estate, which consisted solely of Amy's unexpended income from the Wallace Weber trust, was immediately invested in 9% certificates of deposit.

The property received under the will of Wallace Weber on January 1, 19X3, was:

10,000 shares of the K. O. Corporation, valued at $100 each.
$300,000 bonds of the K. O. Corporation, paying interest on June 30 and December 31 at 6% per annum.

In the 5 years ended December 31, 19X7, the trustee received the following dividends on the stock:

February 1, 19X3	$40,000
February 1, 19X4	40,000
February 1, 19X5	40,000
February 1, 19X6	60,000
February 1, 19X7	60,000

During this period the trustee made the following payments:

Expenses:		
$100 a month, totaling		$ 6,000
Trustee's fees:		
$5,000 per annum, totaling		$ 25,000
To beneficiaries:		
Amy Weber:		
19X3	$27,250	
19X4	35,000	
19X5	25,000	
19X6	37,000	$124,250
Werner Weber:		
19X6	$17,000	
19X7	46,000	$ 63,000
Phillip Marsh:		
19X7		$ 3,000

The undistributed income was left on deposit in the bank and drew no interest.

Instructions: Prepare trustee's statements covering the 5 years ended December 31, 19X7, showing the beneficiaries' interests.

(AICPA adapted)

22-11. Sam Hill died September 30, 19X8, leaving a will and appointing three executors to administer his estate. The will provided for the payment of funeral expenses, debts, and other necessary expenses, and for the specific bequests listed on page 733.

The balance of the estate was to be held in trust, and the income thereof was to be paid in equal shares to the three children of the testator during their natural lives. The first distribution from income was to be made December 31, 19X9.

Cemetery, for upkeep of burial plot...	$ 2,500
Hospital	2,000
Church...	5,000
Relative..	10,000
Executors ($5,000 each in lieu of fees)	15,000
	$34,500

On the death of each of the life beneficiaries, the proportionate part of the estate as of that date was to revert to that beneficiary's issue surviving, if any; otherwise, it was to remain in trust.

At the date of death the testator possessed the following: cash, $25,000; accounts receivable, $55,000; 5½% first mortgage bonds, interest June 30 and December 31, par and appraised value, $100,000; U.S. Treasury 2¾% bonds, interest May 15 and November 15, par and appraised value, $50,000; 1,000 shares Astor Mining Company stock, $5 par, appraised as valueless; 1,000 shares of Boston Industries, Inc., stock, $100 par, appraised at $110; clothing, $1,000; jewelry, $5,000; furniture, $10,000.

Receipts were as follows: $40,000 of U.S. Treasury bonds sold on November 15, 19X8, at 102; accounts receivable collected, $50,000 (balance worthless); dividends on Boston Industries, Inc., declared prior but paid subsequent to death of testator, $4,000; dividend of same company declared and paid subsequent to death of testator, $2,000; furniture sold for $9,000; Astor Mining Company stock sold at 25 cents per share; bank interest earned after death, $1,250; refund of federal taxes for 19X7, $500; all interest collected on investments.

Disbursements were as follows: funeral expenses, $2,500; administration expenses (chargeable to corpus), $8,000; legal services, $3,000; debts of testator, $15,000; 19X8 federal and state taxes to date of death, $3,100; specific bequests as indicated, with relative taking jewelry at appraised value against bequest of $10,000.

Other transactions: clothing given to charity.

Instructions: Prepare as of November 30, 19X9, (a) a summary statement of executors as to principal, showing assets remaining in the estate; and (b) a summary statement of executors as to income. (For purposes of this problem, ignore the factors of inheritance, transfer, and other taxes not specified in the problem.)

(AICPA adapted)

23
Governmental Units — The General Fund

All phases of the financial activities of a governmental unit, whether federal, state, or local, are determined and controlled by law. Laws determine how revenues of the governmental unit are to be raised. Laws determine how the revenues are to be allocated among the different governmental activities and the specific purposes for which they may be spent. Standards and procedures for handling receipts and disbursements and for accounting and reporting for the governmental unit must likewise conform with the law.

The plan developed by a governmental unit for the expenditures of a given period and for the means of financing these expenditures is known as a *budget*. The budget prepared in accordance with legal requirements and enacted into law becomes the basis for the management and control of the financial activities of the period. Changes in a budget may be made during the period by appropriate legislative action. Financial actions must adhere to the plans and requirements established by the budget and supplementary legislative provisions.

EFFECTS OF LEGAL CONTROLS UPON ACCOUNTING

In accounting for a business firm and for a governmental unit, transactions are analyzed and recorded in books of original entry and in ledger accounts, and are summarized periodically on statements reporting financial position and operating results. In accounting for the business firm, emphasis is placed on the satisfactory measurement of net income arising from the sale of goods or services. Financial operations of the governmental unit, however, are not directed toward achieving a net income but toward raising sufficient revenue to meet the cost of the services that the unit is called upon to render. Although revenues and expenditures of the governmental unit are recorded and summarized in accounting for its activities, no adjustments are normally made for depreciation and certain accrued and pre-paid items that would require recognition in measuring net income.

On the other hand, accounting for the governmental unit involves certain responsibilities that go beyond those found in accounting for a business. Accounts of the governmental unit must provide financial data that will enable officials of the government to administer affairs in accordance with the legislative intent as provided by the budget and other applicable laws and regulations. Further, the accounts must summarize governmental activities and show how these activities meet legal requirements.

The National Council on Governmental Accounting (NCGA), the authoritative standard-setting body in the governmental accounting area, has emphasized the dual requirements of accounting and financial reporting for governmental units by stating:

> A governmental accounting system must make it possible both: (a) to present fairly and with full disclosure the financial position and results of financial operations of the funds and account groups of the governmental unit in conformity with generally accepted accounting principles; and (b) to determine and demonstrate compliance with finance-related legal and contractual provisions.[1]

Accounting for a governmental unit requires the recognition of different *funds* that have been established for that unit. A fund is defined by the NCGA as:

> "a fiscal and accounting entity with a self-balancing set of accounts recording cash and other financial resources, together with all related liabilities and residual equities or balances, and changes therein, which are segregated for the purpose of carrying on specific activities or attaining certain objectives in accordance with special regulations, restrictions, or limitations."[2]

Funds are established by constitution, statute, charter, or ordinance, or by appropriate action by the legislative or administrative branch of the government. The purpose of fund accounting is to permit the identification of resources that cannot be commingled, due to special restrictions imposed on their use by legal or contractual requirements. The number of separate funds established by a governmental unit may vary from one to more than a hundred. Each fund requires a separate accounting. The accounting for a fund will measure assets, liabilities, fund equities, and revenues and expenditures.

Governmental accounting is frequently referred to as *fund accounting* in view of the recognition of the fund as the accounting entity. Governmental accounting is also referred to as *budgetary accounting* because budgetary accounts are incorporated in the system of accounts. Fund or budgetary accounting is applicable to all levels of government, including the federal gov-

---

[1]Statement 1, *Governmental Accounting and Financial Reporting Principles* (Chicago: Municipal Finance Officers Association of the United States and Canada, March 1979), p. 2.
[2]*Ibid.*

ernment, state government, counties, cities, school districts, and other special taxing units. Such accounting is also employed with certain modifications by nonprofit service organizations whose activities are related to funds and whose operations are frequently controlled by budgets. Such organizations include schools, hospitals, charities, religious organizations, and fraternal groups.

Many governmental units carry on major business enterprises furnishing utilities or other special services to the public. The operations of such enterprises follow closely the operations that would be found in private enterprises. Such enterprises call for accounting and reporting procedures that parallel those found in a comparable private business firm.

CLASSIFICATION OF ACCOUNTS OF A GOVERNMENTAL UNIT

Accounts within funds are classified into balance sheet and operating statement accounts. Further classifications are applied to the revenue and expenditure accounts. Extended classifications may be called for in governmental accounting to facilitate effective planning, control, and reporting. Classification serves in budget preparation and execution, in reporting, in cost analysis, in comparative analyses, and in the development of statistical summaries.

Classes of funds

The NCGA has classified funds used by governmental units according to the types of activities that are financed, as follows:

GOVERNMENTAL FUNDS

(1) *The General Fund* — to account for all financial resources except those required to be accounted for in another fund.
(2) *Special Revenue Funds* — to account for the proceeds of specific revenue sources (other than special assessments, expendable trusts, or for major capital projects) that are legally restricted to expenditure for specified purposes.
(3) *Capital Projects Funds* — to account for financial resources to be used for the acquisition or construction of major capital facilities (other than those financed by proprietary funds, Special Assessment Funds, and Trust Funds).
(4) *Debt Service Funds* — to account for the accumulation of resources for, and the payment of, general long-term debt principal and interest.
(5) *Special Assessment Funds* — to account for the financing of public improvements or services deemed to benefit the properties against which special assessments are levied.

PROPRIETARY FUNDS

(6) *Enterprise Funds* — to account for operations (a) that are financed and operated in a manner similar to private business enter-

prises — where the intent of the governing body is that the costs (expenses, including depreciation) of providing goods or services to the general public on a continuing basis be financed or recovered primarily through user charges; or (b) where the governing body has decided that periodic determination of revenues earned, expenses incurred, and/or net income is appropriate for capital maintenance, public policy, management control, accountability, or other purposes.

(7) *Internal Service Funds* — to account for the financing of goods or services provided by one department or agency to other departments or agencies of the governmental unit, or to other governmental units on a cost-reimbursement basis.

FIDUCIARY FUNDS

(8) *Trust and Agency Funds* — to account for assets held by a governmental unit in a trustee capacity or as an agent for individuals, private organizations, other governmental units, and/or other funds. These include (a) Expendable Trust Funds, (b) Nonexpendable Trust Funds, (c) Pension Trust Funds, and (d) Agency Funds.[3]

A general fund will be used in every governmental unit. The number of special funds in any governmental unit will vary, depending upon the nature and variety of the special activities carried on by the unit and the legal provisions that have been adopted for separately financing such activities. The NCGA recommended the following principle with regard to the number of funds:

Governmental units should establish and maintain those funds required by law and sound financial administration. Only the minimum number of funds consistent with legal and operating requirements should be established, however, since unnecessary funds result in inflexibility, undue complexity, and inefficient financial administration.[4]

In addition to the eight classes of funds listed, the NCGA recommends that special account groups be established to provide information concerning general fixed assets and general long-term debt. Although the general fixed assets and the general long-term debt account groups do not qualify as funds as previously defined, the terms "funds" and "fund accounting" are normally interpreted broadly to include these groups that are required for a full accounting.

Governmental Revenues Classified

A governmental unit normally obtains revenues from many sources. A primary classification of revenues for budgetary, recording, and statement purposes is normally made in terms of revenue *source*. Revenues of a municipality, for example, are normally classified under the following headings:

---

[3]*Ibid.*
[4]*Ibid.*

Taxes   Revenue from use of money and
Licenses and permits   property
Fines, forfeits, and penalties   Charges for current services
Revenue from other agencies

Subclassifications would be provided for significant revenue sources within the above categories. For example, tax sources may be subdivided to show taxes on real property, taxes on personal property, sales taxes, and interest and penalties on delinquent taxes. Licenses and permits may be subdivided in categories such as motor vehicle licenses, building permit fees, and inspection charges.

Instead of classifying revenues by source as described, revenues are frequently classified according to the *organization unit* making the collection. Revenues, then, would be classified in terms of the department, bureau, or division responsible for their collection.

Governmental Expenditures Classified

A primary classification of expenditures is usually made in terms of governmental *function*. Expenditures of a municipality, for example, may be classified by function under the following headings:

General government   Libraries
Public safety   Recreation
Transportation   Public service enterprises
Sanitation and waste removal   Interest on debt
Health and hospitals   Redemption of bonds
Public welfare   Miscellaneous
Schools

Expenditures according to function may be further subclassified in terms of *activities, character,* and *object*. To illustrate, general governmental expenditures may be subclassified in terms of *activities* as administrative, legislative, and judicial. Information concerning the *character* of expenditures is offered by subclassifying expenditures as (1) current operations, (2) capital outlay, and (3) debt retirement. Information concerning the *object* of expenditures is offered by further analysis of the current expenditure items just mentioned in terms of (1) personal services for salaries and wages, (2) contractual services, consisting of work done under special contract, (3) material and supply acquisitions, and (4) other charges.

A functional classification of expenditures may be accompanied by a further subclassification in terms of *organization units*. The basis for such classification is the department, bureau, or division responsible for certain activities, character, and object.

All of the classifications that have been suggested are shown in the headings of the following statement that summarizes expenditures for a department of health, one of the units involved in the health and hospitals function of a governmental unit:

Function: Health and Hospitals

	Current Operations				Capital Outlays			Debt Retirement
	Personal Services	Con-tractual Services	Materials and Supplies	Other Charges	Land	Buildings	Equipment	
Department of Health —								$10,000
Bureau of Regulation and Inspection:							$6,500	
Inspection of Milk and Dairy Products	$4,000	$1,500	$1,200	$300				
Inspection of Other Foods and Drugs	5,000	2,000	1,500	200				
Sanitary Inspection	1,200		300	150				

Revenues and expenditures are classified only in certain funds. Classifications are appropriate in accounting for general fund revenues and expenditures when receipts are collected from many sources and are applied to many functions. Classification would not apply in the case of a debt service fund that is restricted to the accumulation of moneys for the retirement of bonds. In the latter case, revenues are normally acquired from a single source and applied to a single purpose.

ACCOUNTING FOR THE GOVERNMENTAL UNIT

Accounting for the governmental unit begins with the adoption of a budget by the responsible legislative body. The budget lists the proposed expenditures and also the sources for financing those expenditures. Adoption of the budget provides legal authorization for expenditures in accordance with the plan. This authorization to commit governmental resources is called an *appropriation*. The budget that authorizes expenditures is at the same time a device that limits expenditures. Expenditures may not exceed the amounts specified for each function or organization unit as well as for each object within the categories named. The statements that are prepared at the end of each period compare actual expenditures with the amounts appropriated in terms of the classifications established within the budget.

Upon adoption of the budget, certain revenue-producing measures may have to be put into effect. Although legislation may already be effective with respect to sales tax rates, licenses, and fees, special action may be required in setting tax rates for real and personal property and charges for certain services. Once the revenue-raising rates are set, no further action or control is involved. Subsequent accounting reports provide comparisons of actual revenue with revenue requirements as established in the budget.

A general ledger is maintained for each fund. The ledger contains asset, liability, and fund balance accounts and revenue and expenditure accounts.

Revenue and expenditure detail provided in the accounts may be summarized in accordance with the classifications to be used in reporting activities. Separate subsidiary ledgers are maintained when necessary.

A balance sheet is prepared for each fund at the end of the period. The
balance sheet may be accompanied by a statement summarizing fund operations for the period. The nature of the latter statement varies with the
different funds. In some instances operating data consist of a summary of
revenues and expenditures; in other instances the details of revenues and
expenses are presented, focusing on the maintenance of capital; in certain
instances both types of data are given. Balance sheets and operating statements are often supported by schedules offering supplementary detail.
Governmental units may also prepare interim statements within the fiscal
period. Frequently, separate statements for each fund are accompanied by
combined statements showing the financial condition and the results of operations for all funds of each type and for all of the funds of the governmental unit.

The National Council on Governmental Accounting has recommended a
body of principles to be employed in accounting for state and local governments. These principles include the fund definitions previously referred to,
as well as those which follow:

ACCOUNTING FOR FIXED ASSETS AND LONG-TERM LIABILITIES

A clear distinction should be made between (a) fund fixed assets
and general fixed assets and (b) fund long-term liabilities and general
long-term debt.

a. Fixed assets related to specific proprietary funds or Trust
   Funds should be accounted for through those funds. All other
   fixed assets of a governmental unit should be accounted for
   through the General Fixed Assets Account Group.
b. Long-term liabilities of proprietary funds, Special Assessment
   Funds, and Trust Funds should be accounted for through
   those funds. All other unmatured general long-term liabilities
   of the governmental unit should be accounted for through the
   General Long-Term Debt Account Group.

VALUATION OF FIXED ASSETS

Fixed assets should be accounted for at cost or, if the cost is not
practicably determinable, at estimated cost. Donated fixed assets
should be recorded at their estimated fair value at the time received.

DEPRECIATION OF FIXED ASSETS

a. Depreciation of general fixed assets should not be recorded in
   the accounts of governmental funds. Depreciation of general
   fixed assets may be recorded in cost accounting systems or
   calculated for cost finding analyses; and accumulated depreciation may be recorded in the General Fixed Assets Account
   Group.

b. Depreciation of fixed assets accounted for in a proprietary fund should be recorded in the accounts of that fund. Depreciation is also recognized in those Trust Funds where expenses, net income, and/or capital maintenance are measured.

ACCRUAL BASIS IN GOVERNMENTAL ACCOUNTING

The modified accrual or accrual basis of accounting, as appropriate, should be utilized in measuring financial position and operating results.

a. *Governmental fund* revenues and expenditures should be recognized on the modified accrual basis. Revenues should be recognized in the accounting period in which they become available and measurable. Expenditures should be recognized in the accounting period in which the fund liability is incurred, if measurable, except for unmatured interest on general long-term debt and on special assessment indebtedness secured by interest-bearing special assessment levies, which should be recognized when due.

b. *Proprietary fund* revenues and expenses should be recognized on the accrual basis. Revenues should be recognized in the accounting period in which they are earned and become measurable; expenses should be recognized in the period incurred, if measurable.

c. *Fiduciary fund* revenues and expenses or expenditures (as appropriate) should be recognized on the basis consistent with the fund's accounting measurement objective. Nonexpendable Trust and Pension Trust Funds should be accounted for on the accrual basis; Expendable Trust Funds should be accounted for on the modified accrual basis. Agency Fund assets and liabilities should be accounted for on the modified accrual basis.

d. *Transfers* should be recognized in the accounting period in which the interfund receivable and payable arise.

BUDGETING, BUDGETARY CONTROL, AND BUDGETARY REPORTING

a. An annual budget(s) should be adopted by every governmental unit.

b. The accounting system should provide the basis for appropriate budgetary control.

c. Budgetary comparisons should be included in the appropriate financial statements and schedules for governmental funds for which an annual budget has been adopted.

TRANSFER, REVENUE, EXPENDITURE, AND EXPENSE ACCOUNT CLASSIFICATION

a. Interfund transfers and proceeds of general long-term debt issues should be classified separately from fund revenues and expenditures or expenses.

b. Governmental fund revenues should be classified by fund and source. Expenditures should be classified by fund, function (or program), organization unit, activity, character, and principal classes of objects.
c. Proprietary fund revenues and expenses should be classified in essentially the same manner as those of similar business organizations, functions, or activities.

COMMON TERMINOLOGY AND CLASSIFICATION

A common terminology and classification should be used consistently throughout the budget, the accounts, and the financial reports of each fund.

INTERIM AND ANNUAL FINANCIAL REPORTS

a. Appropriate interim financial statements and reports of financial position, operating results, and other pertinent information should be prepared to facilitate management control of financial operations, legislative oversight, and, where necessary or desired, for external reporting purposes.
b. A comprehensive annual financial report covering all funds and account groups of the governmental unit — including appropriate combined, combining, and individual fund statements; notes to the financial statements; schedules; narrative explanations; and statistical tables — should be prepared and published.
c. General purpose financial statements may be issued separately from the comprehensive annual financial report. Such statements should include the basic financial statements and notes to the financial statements that are essential to fair presentation of financial position and operating results (and changes in financial position of proprietary funds and similar Trust Funds).[5]

The remaining pages of this chapter and the chapter that follows describe the operations of governmental funds and illustrate the application of the principles that have been described. Accounting for the general fund is described in this chapter; accounting for other funds and the account groups that have been mentioned is described in the following chapter.

GENERAL FUND

Every governmental unit has a general fund. This most important fund finances all of the normal activities of the unit. Revenues that are not specifically allocated by law to some special fund accrue to the general fund. Activities or projects that are not to be financed by some special fund make their demands upon the resources of the general fund.

---

[5]*Ibid.*, pp. 3–4.

Entries for the General Fund

To illustrate the accounting for the general fund of a governmental unit, general fund transactions for the City of A and the entries to record these transactions are listed on pages 744–747. An explanation of these entries is given below and on pages 747–749.

Adoption of budget. [See transaction (1).] At the beginning of the fiscal period, the budgeted revenues and appropriations are recorded by a debit to Estimated Revenues and a credit to Appropriations. Estimated Revenues may be interpreted as the total estimated resources to be available for the period; Appropriations may be interpreted as the total planned expenditures. When the budget shows an excess of estimated revenues over appropriations, Fund Balance is credited in the opening entry. This excess is the fund increase that is estimated to result from activities of the current period. When the budget shows an excess of appropriations over estimated revenues, Fund Balance is debited in the opening entry. In such an instance, assets carried over from prior periods are to be used in financing current activities.

Accounts that report budgetary estimates of revenues or budgetary limitations on expenditures are referred to as *budgetary accounts*. Accounts that express the results of actual transactions of the governmental unit are termed *operating accounts*. During the course of activities of the fiscal period, budgetary accounts serve as comparison and control devices; but at the end of the period the financial position and the results of activities must be expressed in terms of what actually occurred.

Revenues. [See transactions 2, 3, 4, and 9.] When tax levies are made, when accrued revenue is recognized, or when collections of previously unrecognized revenue are made, an appropriate asset account is debited and the account Revenues is credited. Certain increases in the general fund may represent contributions from other funds. For example, cash may be received regularly from public utilities or other public enterprises to finance general fund activities. Cash balances in terminated funds may likewise be transferred to the general fund and thus become available to that fund. Although their impact on the general fund balance is the same as revenues from outside sources, such internal transfers are termed "other financing sources" to distinguish them from revenues.

The account Revenues may be viewed as an offset to the account Estimated Revenues. The collection of revenue that has already been recognized in the accounts by a receivable is recorded by a debit to Cash and a credit to the receivable. At the end of the period the balances in the accounts Estimated Revenues and Revenues are closed. If actual revenues are greater than estimated revenues, the closing entry consists of a debit to Revenues, a credit to Estimated Revenues, and a credit to Fund Balance. If actual revenues are less than estimated revenues, Fund Balance is debited. Fund Balance is thus corrected to reflect the actual revenue of the period.

A subsidiary *revenues ledger* is maintained to show revenue detail. As revenues are recognized, individual accounts are credited for revenue amounts. The sum of the credits must agree with the total reported in the account Revenues in the general ledger. The account Revenues controls the credits in the subsidiary revenues ledger.

The subsidiary account balances are closed when the controlling account balance is closed and the revenue excess or deficiency is carried to Fund Balance. In the example, subsidiary accounts were indicated for only major revenue sources. Ordinarily, dozens, and in some cases hundreds, of subsidiary accounts would be maintained in reporting the individual sources of revenue.

General Fund Books

Transaction	Entry		
(1) Adoption of budget for fiscal year ending June 30, 19X4, indicating estimated revenues of $1,000,000 and providing for appropriations of $960,000.	*General ledger:* Estimated Revenues	1,000,000	
	Appropriations		960,000
	Fund Balance		40,000
	Details of revenue estimates:		
	General Property Taxes .... $ 620,000		
	Business Taxes 45,000		
	Sales Taxes 105,000		
	Motor Vehicle Licenses 60,000		
	Municipal Court Fines 35,000		
	Interest on Bank Deposits 5,000		
	Rents 20,000		
	Return of Taxes Collected by State 100,000		
	Charges for Private Police Service 10,000		
	$1,000,000		
	Subsidiary appropriations ledger — *credits:*		
	General Government .... $ 48,000		
	Police Department 242,000		
	Fire Department 122,500		
	Highways 85,000		
	Sanitation and Waste Removal 90,000		
	Health and Hospitals............ 137,500		
	Public Welfare 130,000		
	Debt Service Fund 10,000		
	Government's Share of Special Assessments 20,000		
	Establishment of Internal Service Fund.................... 25,000		
	Establishment of Utility Fund 50,000		
	$ 960,000		
(2) Accrual of revenue resulting from property tax levy.	*General ledger:* Taxes Receivable	600,000	
	Revenues..		600,000

Transaction	Entry		
(2) *continued*	*Subsidiary taxpayers ledger — debits:* Individual taxpayers accounts............................ $600,000 *Subsidiary revenues ledger — credit:* General Property Taxes......... $600,000		
(3) Receipt of other revenues.	*General ledger:* Cash.. Revenues..	380,000	380,000
	Subsidiary revenues ledger — credits: Business Taxes.................... $ 43,500 Sales Taxes......................... 96,000 Motor Vehicle Licenses......... 65,000 Municipal Court Fines.......... 32,000 Interest on Bank Deposits..... 6,500 Rents................................. 20,000 Return of Taxes Collected by State............................. 106,250 Charges for Private Police Service.......................... 10,750 $380,000		
(4) Collection of taxes previously accrued.	*General ledger:* Cash.. Taxes Receivable.................................	560,000	560,000
	Subsidiary taxpayers ledger — credits: Individual taxpayers accounts............................ $560,000		
(5) Expenditures and transfers made in accordance with appropriations (expenditures include purchases of equipment and purchases of supplies from internal service fund. Transfers include required contributions to debt service fund and special assessment fund, and establishment of internal service and utility funds).	*General ledger:* Transfers.. Expenditures... Vouchers Payable............................... Due to Internal Service Fund................ Due to Debt Service Fund.................... Due to Special Assessment Fund.......... Due to Utility Fund.............................	105,000 595,000	555,000 65,000 10,000 20,000 50,000
	Subsidiary appropriations ledger — debits: General Government............ $ 31,500 Police Department............... 197,200 Fire Department.................. 35,000 Highways............................ 40,000 Sanitation and Waste Removal.................................... 88,000 Health and Hospitals............ 86,500 Public Welfare..................... 116,800 Debt Service Fund............... 10,000 Government's Share of Special Assessments.............. 20,000 Establishment of Internal Service Fund.................... 25,000 Establishment of Utility Fund 50,000 $700,000		

Transaction	Entry		
(6) Estimates of budgetary commitments that will result from orders placed for supplies and equipment.	*General ledger:* Encumbrances .... Fund Balance Reserved for Encumbrances	250,000	250,000
	Subsidiary appropriations ledger — debits: General Government .... $ 15,200 Police Department .... 44,250 Fire Department .... 85,250 Highways .... 42,500 Sanitation and Waste Removal .... 1,800 Health and Hospitals .... 48,500 Public Welfare 12,500 $250,000		
(7) Liquidation of encumbrances ($200,000) upon receipt of invoices and determination of actual expenditures relating to encumbrances ($195,000).	*General ledger:* Fund Balance Reserved for Encumbrances .. Encumbrances	200,000	200,000
	Subsidiary appropriations ledger — credits: General Government .... $ 12,000 Police Department .... 38,400 Fire Department .... 60,800 Highways .... 36,000 Sanitation and Waste Removal .... 1,750 Health and Hospitals .... 39,500 Public Welfare 11,550 $200,000		
	General ledger: Expenditures .... Vouchers Payable	195,000	195,000
	Subsidiary appropriations ledger — debits: General Government .... $ 11,200 Police Department .... 37,500 Fire Department .... 59,750 Highways .... 36,600 Sanitation and Waste Removal .... 1,750 Health and Hospitals .... 36,900 Public Welfare 11,300 $195,000		
(8) Payment of vouchers and billings.	*General ledger:* Vouchers Payable .... Due to Internal Service Fund .... Due to Debt Service Fund .... Due to Special Assessment Fund .... Due to Utility Fund .... Cash	665,000 55,000 10,000 20,000 50,000	 800,000
(9) To close revenues and estimated revenues accounts at the end of the fiscal year.	*General ledger:* Revenues .... Fund Balance .... Estimated Revenues	980,000 20,000	 1,000,000

Transaction	Entry

(9) *continued*.

To close revenues ledger balances:

	Debits
General Property Taxes.........	$600,000
Business Taxes....................	43,500
Sales Taxes........................	96,000
Motor Vehicle Licenses.........	65,000
Municipal Court Fines	32,000
Interest on Bank Deposits.....	6,500
Rents	20,000
Return of Taxes Collected by State...............................	106,250
Charges for Private Police Service...........................	10,750
	$980,000

---

(10) To close appropriations, expenditures, transfers, and encumbrances accounts at the end of the fiscal year.

General ledger:

Appropriations......................................	960,000	
Transfers		105,000
Expenditures.....................................		790,000
Encumbrances		50,000
Fund Balance....................................		15,000

To close appropriations ledger balances:

	Debits
General Government	$2,100
Police Department...............	1,450
Fire Department	3,300
Highways...........................	1,900
Sanitation and Waste Removal...................................	200
Health and Hospitals............	5,100
Public Welfare.....................	950
	$15,000

Expenditures and Transfers. [See transactions (5), (6), (7), (8), and (10).] As expenditures are incurred, the account Expenditures is debited and appropriate liability accounts are credited. Certain payments that are made by the general fund represent contributions to other funds to finance their special activities. For example, general fund appropriations may include sums for the establishment of a special internal service fund, the contribution to a debt service fund for the retirement of bonds, or the contribution to a special assessment fund for the construction of certain local improvements. Amounts payable by the general fund to other funds as contributions to capital should not be recorded as expenditures, but as "transfers." Payments to other funds for goods or services in accordance with budgetary appropriations are recorded by debits to Expenditures and credits to liability accounts with the particular funds. The expenditures account balance may be viewed as an offset to the account Appropriations. A debit to Expenditures, then, is a reduction in the balance of appropriations that are still available for spending during the year. The payment of a voucher or an interfund obligation is recorded by a debit to the appropriate liability account and a credit to Cash.

To insure that appropriations will not be overexpended, it is desirable to recognize in the accounts not only expenditures that have actually been incurred but also future expenditures that have been committed by the issuance of purchase orders. When purchase orders are issued, the account Encumbrances is debited and the account Fund Balance Reserved for Encumbrances is credited for the estimated commitment. When the orders are filled and the exact charges are received, the entries originally recording the commitments are reversed and the expenditures are recorded at their actual amounts. Although appropriations may be encumbered for such items as orders for supplies and contracts for services, encumbrances are not recognized for regularly recurring expenditures such as payrolls. Charges for regularly recurring expenditures are recognized only at the time expenditures are made. When encumbrances are recorded, the balances of the account Encumbrances and the account Expenditures are both properly viewed as offsets to the account Appropriations. They both use up budgetary authority, although encumbrances do not result in a decrease in Fund Balance until an actual obligation exists.

Frequently there is authority for subdividing total appropriations into monthly or quarterly *allotments*. Allotments limit expenditures within the month or the quarter to fractional parts of the entire appropriation. Unexpended allotment balances are carried forward within the fiscal year to the next allotment period. Allotment schedules contribute to a continuing control over expenditures and help avoid the need for special appropriations to meet shortages in the later stages of the budget period.

Appropriations usually expire upon the close of the budget period. At the end of the period, the accounts Encumbrances, Transfers, Expenditures, and Appropriations are closed. When the sum of the actual expenditures and commitments is less than the budgeted appropriations, the closing entry consists of a debit to Appropriations and credits to Encumbrances, Transfers, Expenditures, and Fund Balance. Fund Balance then reports the effects of the actual charges and encumbrances of the fiscal period rather than the original appropriation amount. Closing the accounts as described leaves Fund Balance Reserved for Encumbrances with a credit balance that is carried into the succeeding period. The reserve is viewed as a part of the fund balance rather than as a liability. The encumbrance procedure is no more than an earmarking of appropriations, since a fund cannot be charged for goods and services before they are actually received.

A subsidiary *appropriations ledger* is maintained to offer information and control over expenditures. Accounts in this ledger normally provide full detail concerning original appropriations, allotments, expenditures, and encumbrances. Individual appropriation accounts are credited for original appropriations. The sum of the credits to these accounts must agree with the total reported in the account Appropriations in the general ledger.

Upon incurring transfers or expenditures, individual appropriation accounts are debited, thus reducing the credit balances that report amounts available for expenditure. Encumbrances are also recognized by debits reducing individual appropriation account balances. When the orders are received and the exact charges are known, the encumbrances are canceled, the actual expenditures are recorded, and the credit balances in the appropriation accounts are corrected to show the actual unexpended and unencumbered balances at that point.

The sum of the debits to the individual appropriation accounts for transferred expenditures must agree with the total reported in the transfers and expenditures accounts in the general ledger, and the sum of the debits for encumbrances must agree with the total reported in the encumbrances account in the general ledger. The appropriations account thus controls the credits in the subsidiary ledger and the transfers, expenditures, and encumbrances accounts summarize and control the debits made to the subsidiary accounts.

A debit balance cannot appear in a subsidiary appropriation account at the end of the fiscal period if actual expenditures, transfers, and encumbrances for the budgeted item have been limited to the amount of the appropriation. A credit balance in a subsidiary appropriation account at the end of the period indicates that the appropriation exceeded actual expenditures, transfers, and encumbrances for the item. A credit excess of Appropriations over Expenditures, Transfers, and Encumbrances should be matched by a similar credit total in the subsidiary accounts. The subsidiary accounts are closed when the controlling account balances are closed and the net change in Fund Balance is recorded.

In the example, subsidiary accounts were indicated only for expenditures summarized in terms of function. In practice, a separate account would be required for each appropriation as set by the budget. Normally the budget would provide appropriations for the various governmental functions analyzed in terms of organization unit and object.

The nature of the control of the balances of the appropriations, encumbrances, and expenditures accounts over subsidiary appropriations accounts is illustrated below and on page 750.

Encumbrances	Expenditures	Appropriations	Fund Balance
(2) 36,000 | (3) 34,000	(3) 62,600 | (4) 62,600	(4) 66,000 | (1) 66,000	(4) 1,400
| (4) 2,000			

SUBSIDIARY APPROPRIATIONS LEDGER

Salaries — Police Dept.

Date	Explanation	Encumbrances			Expenditures		Unen-cumbered Balance
		Dr.	Cr.	Bal.	Dr.	Total	
7/1	Appropriation per budget..						(1) 40,000
7/31	Payment of salaries..........				(3) 2,600	2,600	37,400
6/30	Payment of salaries..........				(3) 3,000	40,000	—

Supplies — Police Dept.

Date	Explanation	Encumbrances Dr.	Encumbrances Cr.	Encumbrances Bal.	Expenditures Dr.	Expenditures Total	Unen-cumbered Balance
7/1	Appropriation per budget..						(1) 6,000
7/2	Order placed for supplies (Order #715)................	(2) 600		600			5,400
7/7	Receipt of supplies (Order #715)........................		(3) 600		(3) 585	585	5,415
7/8	Purchase of supplies........				(3) 50	635	5,365
6/30	Balances.........................			500		5,100	400
	To close......................			500	(4) 400	5,500	—

Equipment — Police Dept.

Date	Explanation	Encumbrances Dr.	Encumbrances Cr.	Encumbrances Bal.	Expenditures Dr.	Expenditures Total	Unen-cumbered Balance
7/1	Appropriation per budget..						(1) 20,000
6/30	Balances.........................			1,500		17,500	1,000
	To close......................			1,500	(4) 1,000	18,500	—

Explanation of Controlling Account — Subsidiary Relationships

(1) *Entries to record budgeted appropriations:* In reporting estimated revenues and appropriations per budget at the beginning of the period, Estimated Revenues is debited, and Appropriations and Fund Balance are credited. The credit of $66,000 to Appropriations in the general ledger is accompanied by individual credits to the subsidiary appropriations accounts for this total.

(2) *Entries to record encumbrances:* In recording encumbrances, Encumbrances is debited and Fund Balance Reserved for Encumbrances is credited. The debit of $36,000 to Encumbrances in the general ledger is accompanied by individual debits to the subsidiary appropriation accounts for this total.

(3) *Entries to record expenditures and the liquidation of encumbrances:* In recording expenditures, Expenditures is debited and Vouchers Payable is credited. When encumbrances are liquidated, an entry is made debiting Fund Balance Reserved for Encumbrances and crediting Encumbrances. The debit of $62,600 to Expenditures in the general ledger is accompanied by individual debits to the subsidiary accounts for this total. For encumbrances that are liquidated with the recognition of expenditures, a credit of $34,000 to Encumbrances in the general ledger is accompanied by individual credits to the subsidiary appropriation accounts for this total, and unencumbered balances in the subsidiary accounts are adjusted for the differences

between the credits for encumbrances that are canceled and the debits for expenditures that are now recognized.

(4) *Entries to close the expenditures accounts:* In closing an excess of appropriations over encumbrances and expenditures at the end of the period, Appropriations is debited, Encumbrances and Expenditures are credited, and Fund Balance is credited. The debit of $66,000 to Appropriations and credits of $2,000 to Encumbrances and $62,600 to Expenditures are accompanied by total debits of $1,400 to the subsidiary appropriation accounts, canceling the unencumbered balances (credits) in these accounts.

General Fund Statements

A general fund is established upon the organization of a governmental unit and continues for the life of that unit. Accounts are closed periodically, with assets, liabilities, and fund balances being carried into the subsequent period. Entries to record the budget and the transactions of the new period are then applied to the balances carried over. To simplify the illustration for the City of A, no opening balances were given. A general fund trial balance prepared on June 30, 19X4, after the accounts are closed, would appear as follows:

City of A
General Fund
Trial Balance
June 30, 19X4

Cash	140,000	
Taxes Receivable	40,000	
Vouchers Payable		85,000
Due to Internal Service Fund		10,000
Fund Balance Reserved for Encumbrances		50,000
Fund Balance		35,000
	180,000	180,000

Statements are developed from this trial balance together with data supplied by the general ledger and the subsidiary account detail. At least four statements should be prepared: (1) a balance sheet, (2) a statement analyzing the changes in fund balance, (3) a statement comparing actual revenues with estimated revenues, and (4) a statement comparing expenditures, transfers, and encumbrances with appropriations. Cash reports and various other analytical and comparative summaries may be developed to accompany the basic exhibits mentioned.

Balance sheet. The balance sheet that is prepared at the end of the fiscal period reports the assets, the liabilities, and the fund balance showing the portion reserved for encumbrances and the unreserved fund balance. A general fund balance sheet for the City of A as of June 30, 19X4, would reflect the closing entries for revenue and appropriation items previously given and would appear as shown below.

City of A
General Fund
Balance Sheet
June 30, 19X4

Assets		Liabilities and Fund Equity		
Cash	$140,000	Vouchers payable		$ 85,000
Taxes receivable	40,000	Due to internal service fund		10,000
		Fund balance:		
		Reserved for encumbrances	$50,000	
		Unreserved	35,000	85,000
Total assets	$180,000	Total liabilities and fund equity		$180,000

Other assets that might appear on the general fund balance sheet include petty cash funds, temporary investments, accrued interest on investments, delinquent taxes, interest and penalties receivable on taxes, tax liens receivable, amounts due from other funds, and supply inventories. Other liabilities that might appear are items such as contracts payable, amounts due to other funds, taxes collected in advance, and notes payable.

Although the balance sheet prepared at the end of a fiscal period reports the financial status of the city as it enters into a new fiscal period, balance sheets prepared at different intervals during the course of the period should reflect budgetary as well as operating balances. A balance sheet for the City of A, prepared as of December 31, 19X3, for example, should reflect those revenues estimated to be collectible for the remainder of the period as well as the appropriations that apply to the remainder of the period. Balance sheet data would be obtained from a trial balance prepared as of this date. To illustrate, assume that a trial balance for the City of A on December 31, 19X3, shows the following information:

City of A
General Fund
Trial Balance
December 31, 19X3

Cash	156,000	
Taxes Receivable	260,000	
Estimated Revenues	1,000,000	
Revenues		760,000
Vouchers Payable		110,000
Due to Internal Service Fund		12,000
Due to Special Assessment Fund		20,000
Fund Balance Reserved for Encumbrances		62,500
Appropriations		960,000
Transfers	20,000	
Expenditures	466,000	
Encumbrances	62,500	
Fund Balance		40,000
	1,964,500	1,964,500

A balance sheet prepared on this date would appear as follows:

City of A
General Fund
Balance Sheet
December 31, 19X3 (Interim Report)

Assets and Estimated Revenues			Liabilities, Appropriations, and Fund Equity			
Cash..		$156,000	Vouchers payable.......................................			$110,000
Taxes receivable.............................		260,000	Due to internal service fund........................			12,000
Estimated revenues...............	$1,000,000		Due to special assessment fund			20,000
Less revenues collected to			Fund balance reserved for encumbrances....			62,500
date.............................	760,000	240,000	Appropriations..........................	$960,000		411,500
			Less: Expenditures and transfers to date.........	$486,000		
			Encumbrances on Dec. 31, 19X3............	62,500	548,500	
			Unreserved fund balance...........................			40,000
			Total liabilities, appropriations, and fund			
Total assets and estimated revenues...........		$656,000	equity..			$656,000

Analysis of changes in fund balance. The unreserved fund balance of the general fund indicates the resources that can be employed in financing future general fund appropriations. Changes in the fund balance arise during the fiscal period as a result of the difference between governmental revenues and the charges against those revenues. A statement of changes in unreserved fund balance shows changes for the past period. Ordinarily, the statement is prepared in a manner that discloses both budgetary estimates as to changes in fund balance for the year and actual revenues, expenditures, transfers, and other debits and credits that affect the fund balance. The analysis of changes in the unreserved fund balance for the City of A for the year ended June 30, 19X4, may be prepared as shown on page 754.

It is possible to prepare the statement of changes in fund balance in a form that reports the net change arising from the difference between total revenues and total expenditures and transfers. In this form, where budgetary comparisons are not made, Fund Balance Reserved for Encumbrances is not shown separately, because encumbrances are commitments of budgetary authority rather than actual expenditures. Thus, Fund Balance Reserved for Encumbrances is treated as a part of Fund Balance. The following statement illustrates this format:

City of A
General Fund
Analysis of Changes in Fund Balance
For Year Ended June 30, 19X4

Fund balance, July 1, 19X3		—
Add excess of revenues over expenditures and transfers for year ended June 30, 19X4:		
Revenues...	$980,000	
Expenditures and transfers	895,000	$85,000
Fund balance, June 30, 19X4		$85,000

City of A
General Fund
Analysis of Changes in Unreserved Fund Balance
For Year Ended June 30, 19X4

	Estimated	Actual	Excess (Deficiency) of Actual Compared with Estimated
Unreserved fund balance, July 1, 19X3*......................	—	—	
Add: Fund balance reserved for encumbrances, July 1, 19X3*	—	—	
Revenues, 19X3–19X4.....................................	$1,000,000	$980,000	($20,000)
Total balance and additions...	$1,000,000	$980,000	($20,000)
Deduct: Expenditures chargeable to fund balance reserved for encumbrances, July 1, 19X3*	—	—	
Expenditures, 19X3–19X4...........................	$ 855,000	$790,000	($65,000)
Transfers to other funds..............................	105,000	105,000	
Fund balance reserved for encumbrances, June 30, 19X4...		50,000	50,000
Total deductions	$ 960,000	$945,000	($15,000)
Unreserved fund balance, June 30, 19X4....................	$ 40,000	$ 35,000	($5,000)

*When there are beginning balances for the unreserved fund balance and the fund balance reserved for encumbrances, these balances would be shown in both estimated and actual columns.

Statement of revenue — estimated and actual. Statements summarizing operations of the governmental unit are prepared at the end of the period to accompany statements reporting financial position. A revenue statement summarizes actual revenues for the period and compares them with original estimates in the budget. The statement thus shows the extent to which individual revenues met original expectations and offers a basis for developing revenue estimates for future budgets. The statement is prepared from the detail in the subsidiary revenue ledger and estimates included in the budget. In the revenue statement for the City of A, on page 755, it should be observed that totals on this statement support the revenues summary as listed on the analysis of changes in fund balance.

Statement of expenditures, transfers, and encumbrances — compared with appropriations. An expenditures, transfers, and encumbrances statement summarizes actual expenditures, transfers, and encumbrances for the period and compares them with the appropriations authorized for the period. The statement thus indicates the extent to which departments have remained within the limits set by the budget and offers a basis for future appropriation planning. The statement is prepared from the detail reported in the subsidiary appropriations ledger. Part of an expenditures and encumbrances statement for the City of A is illustrated on page 756. It should be noted that totals on this statement support the expenditures summary as listed on the analysis of changes in fund balance.

City of A
General Fund
Statement of Revenue — Estimated and Actual
For Year Ended June 30, 19X4

Revenue by Source	Estimated Revenue	Actual Revenue	Excess (Deficiency) of Actual Compared with Estimated
General property taxes...	$ 620,000	$600,000	($20,000)
Business taxes..	45,000	43,500	(1,500)
Sales taxes...	105,000	96,000	(9,000)
Motor vehicle licenses...	60,000	65,000	5,000
Municipal court fines...	35,000	32,000	(3,000)
Interest on bank deposits...	5,000	6,500	1,500
Rents...	20,000	20,000	—
Return of taxes collected by state	100,000	106,250	6,250
Charges for private police service.............................	10,000	10,750	750
Totals...	$1,000,000	$980,000	($20,000)

Combined Statement of Revenues, Expenditures, and Changes in Fund Balance. The separate statements of revenues, expenditures, and changes in fund balance may be combined into a single statement to disclose general fund operations. The advantage of such a statement is that it highlights the interrelationships among the factors that affect the fund balance. It should be kept in mind, however, that an excess of revenues over expenditures and transfers is not necessarily a sign of effective management, since achieving such an excess is not an objective of the governmental unit. The combined statement merely points out the factors that have affected the fund balance during the year.

A combined statement for the General Fund of the City of A would appear as follows:

City of A
General Fund
Statement of Revenues, Expenditures, and Changes in Fund Balance
For Year Ended June 30, 19X4

	Budgeted	Actual	Excess (Deficiency) of Actual over Budget
Revenues	$1,000,000	$980,000	($20,000)
Expenditures	855,000	790,000	65,000
Excess of revenues over expenditures..	$ 145,000	$190,000	$45,000
Other financing sources (uses) — transfers to other funds	(105,000)	(105,000)	–0–
Excess of revenues over expenditures and other uses	$ 40,000	$ 85,000	$45,000
Fund balance, July 1, 19X3.............	—	—	—
Fund balance, June 30, 19X4..........	$ 40,000	$ 85,000	$45,000

City of A
General Fund
Statement of Expenditures, Transfers, and Encumbrances
Compared with Appropriations
For Year Ended June 30, 19X4

Function, Activity, and Object	Authorizations			Expenditures and Transfers	Unexpended Balance	Encumbrances Outstanding at End of year	Unencumbered Balance
	Appropriations	Encumbrances Outstanding at Beginning of Year	Total				
General government:							
Legislative:							
Personal services.........	$ 15,000	—	$ 15,000	$ 15,000	$ —	$ —	$ —
Contractual services......	5,000	—	5,000	4,000	1,000	750	250
Equipment................	3,000	—	3,000	—	3,000	2,800	200
	$ 23,000	—	$ 23,000	$ 19,000	$ 4,000	$ 3,550	$ 450
Executive:							
Personal services........	$ 10,000	—	$ 10,000	$ 10,000	$ —	$ —	$ —
Contractual services.....	2,000	—	2,000	1,000	1,000	600	400
Totals................	$960,000	—	$960,000	$895,000	$65,000	$50,000	$15,000

SPECIAL CONSIDERATIONS RELATING TO
REVENUES AND EXPENDITURES

Certain matters related to accounting for revenues and expenditures were not illustrated in the example for general fund accounting. In the following paragraphs, these matters are discussed.

Tax Revenues

When losses are expected to emerge in the course of collection of a tax levy, it is appropriate to establish an allowance for uncollectible taxes upon recognizing the asset and the related revenue. For example, in the previous illustration for the City of A, the tax levy of $600,000 was recorded by a debit to Taxes Receivable and a credit to Revenues for this amount. Assuming that only $590,000 is estimated to be recoverable, the following entry would be made:

```
General ledger:
Taxes Receivable...........................................................    600,000
    Allowance for Uncollectible Taxes ...................................               10,000
    Revenues .................................................................              590,000

Subsidiary taxpayers ledger — debit:
    Individual taxpayers accounts ........................  $600,000

Subsidiary revenues ledger — credit:
    General Property Taxes ...............................  $590,000
```

On the balance sheet prepared at the end of the period, the allowance account is subtracted from the asset balance.

When the due date for payment has passed and taxes are delinquent, both receivable and allowance balances should be transferred to accounts that indicate the delinquent nature of the taxes. Collection of delinquent taxes together with interest and penalties is recorded as a recovery of the delinquent taxes balance and as additional revenue. When interest and penalties have accrued on delinquent taxes at the end of a period, an asset would be established for the accrual and an allowance would be recognized for the estimated loss related to such accrual. The following entries record (1) tax delinquencies, (2) recoveries on delinquent balances, and (3) the accrual of interest and penalties on delinquent balances at the end of a period:

```
(1) General ledger:
    Taxes Receivable — Delinquent ...................................    40,000
    Allowance for Uncollectible Taxes...............................    10,000
        Taxes Receivable.................................................              40,000
        Allowance for Uncollectible Taxes — Delinquent........              10,000

    Subsidiary taxpayers ledger:
    No entries.
```

(2) *General ledger:*

Cash	11,000	
Taxes Receivable — Delinquent		10,000
Revenues..		1,000
Subsidiary taxpayers ledger — credits:		
Individual taxpayers accounts	$10,000	
Subsidiary revenues ledger — credit:		
Interest and Penalties	$ 1,000	

(3) *General ledger:*

Interest and Penalties Receivable................................	1,200	
Allowance for Uncollectible Interest and Penalties Receivable...		350
Revenues..		850
Subsidiary taxpayers ledger — debits:		
Individual taxpayers accounts	$ 1,200	
Subsidiary revenues ledger — credit:		
Interest and Penalties	$ 850	

When delinquent taxes are converted into tax liens, receivable balances for taxes, interest, and penalties should be transferred to a tax lien receivable account, and allowance balances related to the original asset accounts should be transferred to a tax lien allowance account. Any costs involved in establishing the tax liens are added to the tax lien balance. Collection of tax liens is recorded by debits to Cash and credits to Tax Liens Receivable. In the event of failure to collect a tax lien and upon appropriate authorization, the tax lien is offset against the allowance. Entries to record (1) the conversion of delinquent taxes into tax liens, (2) collections of tax liens, and (3) the write-off of uncollectible tax liens follow:

(1) *General ledger:*

Tax Liens Receivable...	31,200	
Allowance for Uncollectible Taxes — Delinquent...........	10,000	
Allowance for Uncollectible Interest and Penalties Receivable...	350	
Taxes Receivable — Delinquent		30,000
Interest and Penalties Receivable............................		1,200
Allowance for Uncollectible Tax Liens		10,350
Subsidiary tax liens ledger — debits:		
Individual taxpayers accounts	$31,200	
Subsidiary taxpayers ledger — credits:		
Individual taxpayers accounts	$31,200	

(2) *General ledger:*

Cash	12,000	
Tax Liens Receivable...		12,000
Subsidiary tax liens ledger — credits:		
Individual taxpayers accounts	$12,000	

(3) *General ledger:*

Allowance for Uncollectible Tax Liens	5,000	
Tax Liens Receivable...		5,000
Subsidiary tax liens ledger — credits:		
Individual taxpayers accounts	$ 5,000	

Revenues Received in Advance

In certain instances taxes may be collected in advance of the period in which they accrue or are due. In such cases a liability balance is recognized in the accounts. When the tax assessment is made, Taxes Receivable is debited and Revenues is credited for the amount of the assessment. At this time the advance may be applied against the receivable balance. The entries that are made upon (1) tax collection and (2) application of such collections to the receivables are as follows:

(1) *General ledger:*
Cash 12,000
    Taxes Collected in Advance...................................... 12,000
Subsidiary taxpayers ledger (for succeeding period) — credits:
    Individual taxpayers accounts $12,000

(2) *General ledger:*
Taxes Collected in Advance.. 12,000
    Taxes Receivable.. 12,000
Subsidiary taxpayers ledger:
    No entries — credits to receivable balances for amounts paid were recognized by previous entry.

Proceeds from Issue of Bonds

When cash from the issue of bonds is made available to the general fund, it is recognized in the accounts of the general fund as "financing" rather than revenue. The bond liability balance is not reported in the general fund because bonds make no current claim on general fund resources. The liability balance, however, is reported in the general long-term debt account group, which is described later. The receipt by the general fund of proceeds from a bond issue is recorded by the following entry:

General ledger:
Cash.. 100,000
    Other Financing Sources.. 100,000
Subsidiary financing ledger — credit:
    Proceeds from Issue of Bonds...................... $100,000

Revenues from Sale or Salvage of Fixed Assets

When cash from the sale or salvage of fixed assets becomes available to the general fund, it is recognized in the general fund accounts as revenue. The decrease in the property item is not reported in the general fund but is reported in the separate general fixed assets account group in which the asset was originally recorded. This procedure is described later. The receipt of cash from property sales or salvage is recorded as follows:

General ledger:
Cash.. 2,500
    Revenues.. 2,500
Subsidiary revenues ledger — credit:
    Proceeds from Sale of Obsolete Equipment............ $2,500

Expenditures in Liquidation of Encumbrances of Prior Period

In the illustration for the City of A, the credit to Fund Balance Reserved for Encumbrances was accompanied by a debit to Encumbrances. The encumbrance balance, like the expenditures balance, was treated as a charge against current revenues. The reserve balance at the end of the period was regarded as a portion of a fund balance awaiting charges to emerge from the liquidation of encumbrances. In the new fiscal period, expenditures emerging from previous authority and commitments should be distinguished from those that are made under current appropriations. The liquidation of prior period encumbrances that are not related to current appropriations should be charged against the fund balance reserve. Expenditures and encumbrances of the current period should be separately reported as charges related to current appropriations. To accomplish this distinction in expenditures, the fund balance reserved for encumbrances carried over from a prior period should be identified with the prior period and distinguished from the reserve relating to encumbrances of the current period.[6] As expenditures relating to prior year commitments are made, an expenditures account indicating a relationship to the prior period should be debited. Ordinarily encumbrances can be fully liquidated within the succeeding period. At the end of this period, the balance of expenditures related to the prior period is closed against the fund balance reserve, and any reserve excess or deficiency is carried to fund balance.

For example, assume in the previous illustration for the City of A that in the fiscal year ended June 30, 19X5, expenditures of $48,500 are made in full liquidation of encumbrances of $50,000 existing at the end of the prior year. The entries to record the liquidation of the encumbrances during the period and the cancellation of related expenditures and reserve balances on June 30, 19X5, follow:

General ledger:
Expenditures Chargeable Against Fund Balance Reserved for Encumbrances — Prior Year.....................................	48,500	
Vouchers Payable..		48,500

General ledger:
Fund Balance Reserved for Encumbrances — Prior year......	50,000	
Expenditures Chargeable Against Fund Balance Reserved for Encumbrances — Prior Year...................................		48,500
Fund Balance		1,500

The analysis of changes in fund balance for the year ended June 30, 19X5, will show an increase of $1,500 arising from the liquidation of prior year encumbrances.

Some governmental units offset the encumbrances and fund balance reserved for encumbrances balances at the end of the period and recognize outstanding encumbrances in making appropriations for the new period.

---

[6]In practice, the fund balance reserved for encumbrances account would be dated to show the year to which it was related.

Under such circumstances, the balance sheet prepared at the end of the period shows no reserved fund balance. Following the entry recognizing appropriations for the new period, Encumbrances is debited and Fund Balance Reserved for Encumbrances is credited for unliquidated balances of the preceding period. Liquidation of the encumbrances is then charged against appropriations of the new period instead of against a fund balance reserve carried over from a preceding period. Laws of the governmental unit should indicate the encumbrance procedure that is to be followed.

Purchases of Fixed Assets

Purchases of properties such as equipment, buildings, and land from resources of the general fund require authorization in the form of appropriations just as any current expenditure item. Acquisitions of assets are made in accordance with budgetary provisions and are recorded as expenditures in the usual manner. The property item does not appear as an asset of the general fund, since it does not represent a resource that is to be employed in meeting claims against this fund. The property item, however, is reported in the general fixed assets account group, which is described later. The purchase of a property item by the general fund is recorded by the following entry:

```
General ledger:
Expenditures ...............................................   40,000
    Vouchers Payable.......................................            40,000

Subsidiary appropriations ledger — debit:
Acquisition of Land.....................................  $40,000
```

Prepayments and Inventories

In certain instances it may be the policy of the governmental unit to report on the balance sheet prepayments and supplies inventories. Because such assets are not in a form to become available in meeting subsequent appropriation demands, the balance sheet should show a reservation of the fund balance equal to the sum of these asset balances. When materials and supplies inventories are to be reported on the balance sheet, the following entry may be made in the ledger at the end of the period:

```
Materials and Supplies Inventories .........................   8,500
    Fund Balance Reserved for Materials and Supplies Invento-
    ries ...........................................................            8,500
```

No change needs to be made in these balances during the course of the fiscal period. New purchases may be treated as expenditures. Assuming that inventories at the end of the next period are valued at $8,200, an entry to recognize the reduction in the inventories balance is made as follows:

```
Fund Balance Reserved for Materials and Supplies Inventories.   300
    Materials and Supplies Inventories .......................            300
```

Retirement of Bonded Debt

Long-term general obligation bonds issued by a governmental unit may be retired directly by payment from the general fund, or from amounts accumulated for that purpose in a separate debt service fund. When payment of bonded debt is to be made by the general fund, this utilization of resources can be made only if there is budgetary authorization for such payment. Thus a debit would be made to a "financing uses" account, which may be viewed as an offset to appropriations in the same manner as Expenditures, which is used to record payments for current salaries, materials, or equipment. If payment is to be made from a debt service fund, any general fund contributions to that fund would be recorded as transfers by the general fund and treated in a similar fashion.

Recognition of the amount payable directly by the general fund would be made by an entry as follows:

```
General ledger:
Financing Uses .............................................     65,000
    Matured Bonds Payable ..............................                  65,000
Subsidiary appropriations ledger — debit:
    Retirement of Bonds.....................  $65,000
```

Payment of the matured obligations is recorded as follows:

```
Matured Bonds Payable ................................     65,000
    Cash........................................................                  65,000
```

If the bond retirement is to be handled through a debt service fund, the transfer from the general fund would be recorded as follows:

```
General ledger:
Transfers.......................................................     65,000
    Due to Debt Service Fund............................                  65,000
Subsidiary appropriations ledger — debit:
    Retirement of Bonds.....................  $65,000
```

The payment to the debt service fund would be recorded as follows:

```
Due to Debt Service Fund................................     65,000
    Cash........................................................                  65,000
```

Normally, general obligation bonds for which a sinking fund accumulation is required should be handled through the use of a debt service fund. Periodic transfers from the general fund may be made before the retirement date to meet accumulation requirements. From the general fund viewpoint, such transfers would be recorded in the same manner as described. The treatment of these transactions within the debt service fund is discussed in Chapter 24.

Interest payments that are to be made currently by the general fund on bonds outstanding as well as on maturing issues are recorded as expenditures in the accounts. Decreases in a governmental units' general obligation debt are not shown in the general fund but are summarized in the separate general long-term debt account group, which is described later.

QUESTIONS

1. What are the essential differences between accounting for a commercial enterprise and accounting for a governmental unit?

2. What information should be provided by accounts and statements of a governmental unit?

3. (a) Define the term *fund* as employed in governmental accounting. (b) How is a fund established?

4. How may the major governmental revenues be classified?

5. Give five bases for classification of governmental expenditures. Show by example the expenditures that would be listed under each classification given.

6. Describe the nature and the purpose of the governmental budget.

7. Describe the purpose of the general fund.

8. Distinguish between *budgetary* accounts and *operating* accounts.

9. What entries would be made in the general and subsidiary ledgers in recording the general fund budget?

10. Explain how each of the following differ: (a) appropriation, (b) allotment, (c) encumbrance, and (d) expenditure.

11. What accounts in the general ledger control the detail reported in the revenues ledger and the appropriations ledger?

12. (a) What is the significance of the entries in the subsidiary revenues ledger? (b) What is the significance of the debit and credit entries in the subsidiary appropriations ledger? (c) In the appropriations ledger, what is the significance of an account with a credit balance?

13. The City of Bell, after adoption of an appropriation ordinance, makes a number of supplementary appropriations during the course of the fiscal period. How should such supplementary appropriations be recorded in the general and subsidiary ledgers?

14. Give the entries that would be made in the general ledger and the subsidiary ledgers of the general fund for each of the following transactions:

    (a) A budget is adopted, providing for an excess of appropriations over estimated current revenues.
    (b) General property taxes accrue; the accrual is recognized together with a provision for estimated losses on such taxes.
    (c) Other revenues are collected.
    (d) Orders are placed for materials, and encumbrances are recognized in the accounts for such orders.
    (e) Certain items ordered in (d) are received and expenditures are recognized in the accounts.
    (f) Payrolls are approved for payment.
    (g) Checks are written in payment of vouchers.
    (h) Collections are made on general property taxes. *(continued)*

(i) General property taxes not collected are recognized in the accounts as delinquent.

(j) Charges are made by an internal service fund for services rendered to the general fund and are recognized in the accounts.

(k) At the end of the period:
   (1) Accrued interest and penalties on delinquent taxes are recognized, together with a provision for possible losses on this item.
   (2) Inventories and supplies on hand in the various departments are reported in the accounts.

(l) Estimated revenues exceed revenue balances for the period; revenue accounts are closed.

(m) Appropriations exceed expenditures, transfers, and encumbrances for the period; accounts are closed.

15. What statements are prepared to summarize general fund operations for the year? What information is offered by each of these?

16. How will the balance sheet for the general fund prepared during the fiscal year differ from that prepared at the end of the fiscal year?

17. Describe the form that may be employed for (a) the analysis of changes in unreserved fund balance, (b) the statement of revenues — estimated and actual, and (c) the statement of expenditures and encumbrances — compared with appropriations.

18. Explain how you would treat the following matters in the accounts of a general fund:

(a) Taxes are assessed and it is estimated that 2% of the assessments will prove uncollectible.

(b) Uncollected taxes at the end of the year are delinquent; accrued interest and penalties are recognized on such delinquencies.

(c) Certain receivables are uncollectible and the city council authorizes that they be written off against an allowance that was recognized on such uncollectibles.

(d) Sums are collected representing taxes not yet accrued or recorded on the books.

19. The town of Wescott wishes to show prepayments and materials and supplies on hand on the general fund balance sheet at the end of each period. What accounting procedures would you recommend be employed to achieve this purpose?

20. What arguments can you give for excluding fixed assets in the preparation of the general fund balance sheet?

21. What arguments can you give for excluding charges for depreciation in the preparation of the general fund operating reports?

EXERCISES

1. Prepare the entries to record the following general fund transactions for the City of Balfour:

(a) Revenues for 19X8–X9 are estimated at $150,000; appropriations are made in the amount of $145,000.

(b) A general tax levy is set at $120,000; the tax accrual is recognized in the accounts, together with an allowance for uncollectible taxes estimated at $2,500.

(c) Orders estimated to cost $70,000 are placed for materials and supplies, and encumbrances are recorded.

(d) Certain materials and supplies ordered in (c) are received; invoices total $56,000 for items originally estimated to cost $57,500.

(e) Tax anticipation warrants (bonds) of $25,000 are sold to obtain cash in advance of tax collections.

(f) Payrolls of $50,000 are approved for payment.

(g) Property taxes totaling $105,000 levied in (b) are collected; remaining taxes are recognized in the accounts as delinquent.

(h) Licenses, fines, fees, etc., totaling $40,000 are collected.

(i) Tax anticipation warrants are paid, together with interest of $500.

(j) Payments totaling $90,000 are made on vouchers for materials, supplies, and payrolls relating to (d) and (f).

(k) An obligation of $6,000 to a city public service enterprise for services rendered during the year is recognized in the accounts.

(l) Vacant land is purchased for future construction at a cost of $15,000; cash payment is made on the purchase.

(m) Accounts are closed at the end of the year.

2. A trial balance for the general fund of the city of Grandview, prepared on June 30, 19X3, the end of a fiscal year, follows:

Cash..	200,000	
Taxes Receivable — Delinquent	35,000	
Allowance for Uncollectible Taxes — Delinquent...		5,000
Estimated Revenues	1,200,000	
Vouchers Payable		45,000
Due to Other Funds...		15,000
Taxes Collected in Advance................................		3,500
Fund Balance Reserved for Encumbrances, 19X1–X2...		35,000
Fund Balance Reserved for Encumbrances, 19X2–X3...		40,000
Appropriations...		1,300,000
Fund Balance...		138,000
Revenues..		1,175,000
Encumbrances	40,000	
Expenditures..	1,250,000	
Expenditures Chargeable to Fund Balance Reserved for Encumbrances, 19X1–X2..................	31,500	
	2,756,500	2,756,500

All of the encumbrances relating to 19X1–X2 were liquidated during the year. Prepare the necessary adjusting and closing entries.

3. Prepare the entries required in the general fund to record the following transactions, assuming that required payments are made by the general fund and receipts become available to this fund:

(a) Desks were ordered for operating departments at an estimated cost of $15,000, the purchase to be financed out of the general fund.
(b) The desks were received. The actual cost of $15,400 was paid.
(c) Equipment costing $10,000 and carried in the general fixed asset account group was sold for $650.
(d) A fire truck costing $5,000 was traded in for another truck. The price of the new truck was $6,200, but $1,000 was allowed on the old truck.
(e) A library building that had been financed through the issuance of bonds was torn down. The original cost of the building was $75,000 and the cost of dismantling the building was $2,500. Cash of $1,500 was realized from the salvage.

4. Prepare the entries affecting the general ledger as well as subsidiary accounts of the general fund for the following transactions:

(a) The appropriation for salaries in the public welfare department is increased by $400, a general appropriation for contingencies having been provided by the budget for salary changes of this nature.
(b) The appropriation for contractual services in the public welfare department is reduced by $500 and the appropriation for personal services is increased by this amount when it is decided that a project is to be completed by departmental employees.
(c) A supplementary appropriation for a permanent advance of $30,000 to an internal service fund is made after the budget has already been recorded in the accounts.
(d) A supplementary appropriation of $1,500 is made for salary of a collection clerk as a result of a new policy adopted whereby charges are to be made for certain services rendered by the public welfare department; it is estimated that revenues from this source will total $4,000.

5. A trial balance prepared for the City of Knox appears as follows:

Cash	180,000	
Receivables (net)	215,000	
Payables		160,000
Fund Balance Reserved for Encumbrances — Prior Year		45,000
Fund Balance Reserved for Encumbrances — Current Year		60,000
Fund Balance		187,500
Estimated Revenues	1,000,000	
Revenues		860,000
Appropriations		980,000
Expenditures — Current Year	800,000	
Expenditures — Prior Year	37,500	
Encumbrances — Current Year	60,000	
	2,292,500	2,292,500

(a) Prepare a balance sheet from the foregoing summary, assuming that the balances reflect transactions as of May 31, one month prior to the end of the city's fiscal period, and that budgetary accounts are to be reflected on the statement.

(b) Prepare a balance sheet from the foregoing summary, assuming that the balances reflect transactions as of June 30, the end of the city's fiscal period, and that budgetary accounts are not to be reflected on the statement.

6. From the following account balances taken from the ledger of the general fund for the City of W at the end of the fiscal year ending June 30, 19X7, prepare a statement summarizing fully the changes in unreserved fund balance for the year:

Unreserved fund balance, June 30, 19X6, $315,000.

Revenues, July 1, 19X6–June 30, 19X7: estimated, $750,000; actual, $734,000.

Expenditures, July 1, 19X6–June 30, 19X7: appropriations, $820,000; expenditures, $755,000; fund balance reserved for encumbrances, June 30, 19X7, $35,000.

Fund balance reserved for encumbrances, July 1, 19X6, $36,000; expenditures, July 1, 19X6–June 30, 19X7, in full liquidation of encumbrances as of July 1, 19X6, $34,500.

Credit to fund balance, July 1, 19X6–June 30, 19X7: proceeds from sale of city properties no longer being used, $180,000.

PROBLEMS

23-1. A general fund trial balance for Welcome City on July 1, 19X0, was as follows:

Cash	117,500	
Taxes Receivable — Delinquent	15,000	
Allowance for Uncollectible Taxes — Delinquent		10,000
Vouchers Payable		70,000
Fund Balance Reserved for Encumbrances		15,000
Fund Balance		37,500
	132,500	132,500

During the fiscal year ended June 30, 19X1, the following transactions took place:

(a) A budget was adopted, reporting estimated revenues of $340,000 and authorizing expenditures of $350,000.

(b) Taxes were levied totaling $250,000, of which $15,000 was estimated uncollectible.

(c) Taxes were collected as follows:
Prior year, $12,500 (remaining balances were written off).
Current year, $225,000.

(d) Other revenues collected, $95,000.

(e) Orders were placed for equipment, materials, and supplies, $230,000.

(f) Vouchers were approved as follows:

In full liquidation of encumbrances outstanding on June 30, 19X0	$ 12,500
In liquidation of current encumbrances reported at $200,000	205,000
For current salaries	115,000

(g) Vouchers were paid, $370,000.

(h) Unpaid taxes were transferred to the delinquent account.

Instructions: (1) Prepare general journal entries for the year to record the transactions and to close the accounts.

(2) Prepare (a) a balance sheet and (b) an analysis of changes in unreserved fund balance in condensed form.

23-2. A balance sheet for the general fund for Ocean View City shows balances as follows on June 30, 19X5:

Cash..	$22,500	Vouchers payable.........................		$14,000
Taxes receivable — delinquent	16,000	Fund balance:		
		Reserved for		
		encumbrances.........	$20,000	
		Unreserved	4,500	$24,500
	$38,500			$38,500

The following transactions took place during the fiscal year ended June 30, 19X6:

(a) Budget estimate of revenue, $200,000.

(b) Budget appropriations, $195,000.

(c) Taxes levied for purposes of this fund, $100,000.

(d) Cash borrowed from a special revenue fund pending tax collections, $40,000.

(e) Delinquent taxes collected, $3,500, plus interest and penalties of $750.

(f) Current taxes collected, $90,000, plus interest and penalties, $1,500. Balance of current taxes was transferred to delinquent taxes account.

(g) Other revenues collected, $90,000.

(h) Repayments to the special revenue fund on balance borrowed, $30,000.

(i) Orders placed for equipment, materials, and supplies estimated to cost $60,000.

(j) Vouchers approved in full liquidation of encumbrances outstanding on June 30, 19X5, $19,500.

(k) Vouchers approved for purchases of materials and supplies, $45,000.

(l) Vouchers approved for salaries, $90,000.

(m) Vouchers approved for purchases of equipment, $26,000.

(n) Transfer to debt service fund for payment of matured bonds, $20,000, and interest, $1,000.

(o) Vouchers paid, $179,000; transfers, $21,000.

(p) Unliquidated encumbrances on June 30, 19X6, $12,000.

Instructions: (1) Prepare the entries in general journal form to record the transactions and to close the accounts at the end of the period.

(2) Prepare (a) a balance sheet and (b) an analysis of changes in fund balance in condensed form.

23-3. A balance sheet for the Lakeside City general fund on April 30, 19X8, showed the following balances:

Cash..	$172,500	Vouchers payable.....................		$155,000
Taxes receivable (19X7–X8)........	30,000	Fund balance:		
Taxes receivable (19X6–X7)........	10,000	Reserved for		
		encumbrances	$35,000	
		Unreserved	22,500	57,500
	$212,500			$212,500

The following transactions took place during the fiscal year, May 1, 19X8–April 30, 19X9.

(a) A budget was approved:
Estimated revenues:

From taxes, licenses, fees, and other regular revenue sources	$720,000
From issuance of general bonds	200,000

Appropriations:

For general government activities.....................................	$600,000
For the retirement of general bonds maturing on January 1, 19X9	300,000

(b) Taxes levied for general fund activities, $450,000.
(c) Collection of taxes:
   19X6–X7, $7,500 plus interest and penalties, $3,150.
   19X7–X8, $21,000 plus interest and penalties, $4,200.
   19X8–X9, $425,000.
(d) Receipt of proceeds from general bond issue, $200,000.
(e) Collection of other revenues, $250,000.
(f) Orders placed at estimated costs as follows:

Equipment..	$ 65,000
Materials and supplies	200,000

(g) Vouchers approved in full liquidation of encumbrances outstanding on April 30, 19X8, as follows:

	Encumbrances	Vouchers Payable
Equipment	$15,000	$15,000
Materials and supplies........................	20,000	19,200

(h) Vouchers approved in liquidation of encumbrances currently incurred as follows:

	Encumbrances	Vouchers Payable
Equipment	$ 50,000	$ 52,500
Materials and supplies........................	175,000	174,250

(i) Transfer to debt service fund for payment of general bonds maturing on January 1, 19X9, $300,000, plus interest, $7,500.
(j) Vouchers approved for payment of salaries, $260,000.
(k) Vouchers approved for payment of other current expenditures, $60,000.
(l) Vouchers paid, $592,500; transfers, $307,500.

Instructions: (1) Prepare the entries in general journal form to record the transactions of the general fund and to close the accounts at the end of the period.

(2) Prepare (a) a balance sheet and (b) an analysis of changes in fund balance in the form illustrated on page 754.

23-4. The following is a general fund balance sheet for Fairfield City on June 30, 19X2:

General Fund

Assets

Cash...		$ 140,000
Taxes receivable:		
19X0–X1..	$21,000	
19X1–X2..	44,000	65,000
Total assets...		$ 205,000

Liabilities and Fund Equity

Vouchers payable...		$ 80,000
Tax anticipation notes payable		65,000
Fund balance:		
Reserved for encumbrances.............................	$25,000	
Unreserved	35,000	60,000
Total liabilities and fund equity............................		$ 205,000

A budget for 19X2–X3 is adopted as follows:

Estimated Revenues

Taxes..	$ 765,000
Licenses and permits	125,000
Fines, forfeits, and penalties....................................	30,000
Revenue from use of money and properties.............	20,000
Revenue from other agencies	200,000
Charges for current services......................................	90,000
	$1,230,000

Appropriations

General government..	$ 130,000
Public safety	300,000
Highways	90,000
Sanitation and waste removal....................................	50,000
Health and hospitals	45,000
Public welfare..	40,000
Schools..	420,000
Libraries	35,000
Recreation	20,000
Contribution to pension fund......................................	5,000
Interest on debt...	30,000
Redemption of long-term debt (transfer to debt service fund)	40,000
	$1,205,000

Taxes levied for the year 19X2–X3 were $775,000.

A cash receipts and disbursements statement for the year ended June 30, 19X3, follows:

Receipts

Taxes: 19X0–X1...	$ 20,000	
19X1–X2...	32,000	
19X2–X3...	725,000	$ 777,000
Licenses and permits		130,000
Fines, forfeits, and penalties..		32,000
Revenue from use of money and properties.............................		16,500
Revenue from other agencies		190,000
Charges for current services..		80,000
Tax anticipation notes		300,000
Total receipts		$1,525,500

Disbursements

General government...		$ 110,000
Public safety		250,000
Highways		80,000
Sanitation and waste removal...		50,000
Health and hospitals		44,000
Public welfare..		32,000
Schools...		350,000
Libraries		32,000
Recreation		20,000
Contribution to pension fund...		5,000
Redemption of tax anticipation notes		238,000
Interest on debt..		30,000
Redemption of long-term debt..		40,000
Prior year's indebtedness:		
Vouchers payable...	$80,000	
Tax anticipation notes	65,000	145,000
Prior year's encumbrances (in full liquidation of reserve)		23,500
Total disbursements..		$1,449,500

Unpaid invoices and unliquidated encumbrances related to 19X2–X3 appropriations were outstanding on June 30, 19X3, as follows:

	Unpaid Invoices	Encumbrances	Total
General government..........................	$12,000	$ 4,500	$ 16,500
Public safety	35,000	10,000	45,000
Highways...	6,000		6,000
Schools	15,000	40,000	55,000
	$68,000	$54,500	$122,500

Uncollected taxes for the year 19X0–X1, $1,000, were written off against the fund balance.

Instructions: (1) Prepare journal entries to record transactions for the year ended June 30, 19X3, indicating postings to the general ledger accounts and also to the subsidiary ledger accounts.

(2) Prepare for the year ended June 30, 19X3, (a) a balance sheet, (b) an analysis of changes in fund balance, (c) a statement of revenue — estimated and actual, and (d) a statement of expenditures and encumbrances compared with appropriations.

23-5. The following is a general fund balance sheet for Beach City on January 1, 19X7:

General Fund

Assets

Cash..		$ 235,000
Taxes receivable:		
19X5...	$33,500	
19X6...	67,500	101,000
Total assets		$ 336,000

Liabilities and Fund Equity

Vouchers payable...		$ 140,000
Tax anticipation notes payable		90,000
Fund balance:		
Reserved for encumbrances	$50,000	
Unreserved..	56,000	106,000
Total liabilities and fund equity.................................		$ 336,000

A budget for 19X7 is adopted as follows:

Estimated Revenues

Taxes..	$1,250,000
Licenses and permits	150,000
Fines, forfeits, and penalties.......................................	55,000
Revenue from use of money and properties..................	40,000
Transfers from other agencies	275,000
Charge for current services	65,000
	$1,835,000

Appropriations

General government..	$ 180,000
Public safety	350,000
Highways..	250,000
Sanitation and waste removal.......................................	55,000
Health and hospitals	70,000
Public welfare...	60,000
Schools...	650,000
Libraries	50,000
Recreation	30,000
Contribution to pension fund..	15,000
Interest on debt..	35,000
Redemption of debt (transfer to debt service fund)...................	60,000
	$1,805,000

Taxes levied for the year 19X7 were $1,238,000.

Uncollected taxes for 19X5, $3,500, were written off against the fund balance.

A cash receipts and disbursements statement for the year ended December 31, 19X7, follows:

773

Receipts

Taxes: 19X5	$ 30,000	
19X6	55,000	
19X7	1,195,000	$1,280,000
Licenses and permits		152,000
Fines, forfeits, and penalties		58,000
Revenue from use of money and properties		45,000
Transfers from other agencies		280,000
Tax anticipation notes		500,000
Charge for current services		64,500
Total receipts		$2,379,500

Disbursements

General government		$ 145,000
Public safety		317,500
Highways		185,000
Sanitation and waste removal		48,000
Health and hospitals		65,000
Public welfare		59,500
Schools		612,000
Libraries		47,500
Recreation		28,000
Contribution to pension fund		15,000
Redemption of tax anticipation notes		460,000
Interest on debt		35,000
Redemption of debt		60,000
Prior year's indebtedness:		
Vouchers payable	$140,000	
Tax anticipation notes	90,000	230,000
Prior year's encumbrances (in full liquidation of reserve)		52,000
Total disbursements		$2,359,500

Unpaid invoices and unliquidated encumbrances related to 19X7 appropriations were outstanding on December 31, 19X7, as follows:

	Unpaid Invoices	Encumbrances	Total
General government	$20,500	$ 12,000	$ 32,500
Public safety	18,000	14,000	32,000
Highways		57,500	57,500
Sanitation and waste removal	6,500		6,500
Schools	15,000	21,500	36,500
	$60,000	$105,000	$165,000

Instructions: (1) Prepare journal entries to record transactions for the year ended December 31, 19X7, indicating postings to the general ledger accounts and also to the subsidiary ledger accounts.

(2) Prepare for the year ended December 31, 19X7, (a) a balance sheet, (b) an analysis of changes in fund balance, (c) a statement of revenue — estimated and actual, and (d) a statement of expenditures and encumbrances compared with authorizations.

23-6. The following information pertains to the operations of the general fund of Z County. Functions of this county government include operating the county jail and caring for the county courts.

Funds to finance the operations are provided from a levy of county tax against the various towns of the county, from the state distribution of unincorporated business taxes, from an assessment against the towns and against the state for the boarding of prisoners, and from interest on savings accounts.

The balances in the accounts of the fund on January 1, 19X9, were as follows:

Cash in Savings Accounts	60,650
Cash in Checking Accounts	41,380
Cash on Hand (undeposited prisoners' board receipts)	320
Inventory of Jail Supplies	3,070
Due from Towns and State for Boarding of Prisoners	3,550
General Fund Balance	108,970

The budget for 19X9 as adopted by the county commissioners provided for the following items of revenue and appropriations:

(1)	Town and county taxes	$20,000
(2)	Jail operating costs	55,500
(3)	Court operating costs	7,500
(4)	Unincorporated business tax	18,000
(5)	Board of prisoners (revenue)	5,000
(6)	Commissioners' salaries and expenses	8,000
(7)	Interest on savings	1,000
(8)	Miscellaneous costs	1,000

The fund balance was appropriated in sufficient amount to balance the budget. At December 31, 19X9, the jail supply inventory amounted to $5,120, cash of $380 was on hand, and $1,325 of prisoners' board bills were unpaid. The following items represent all of the transactions that occurred during the year, with all current bills vouchered and paid by December 31, 19X9:

Item (1) was transacted exactly as budgeted.	
Item (2) cash expenditures amounted to	$55,230
Item (3) amounted to	7,110
Item (4) amounted to	18,070
Item (5) billings amounted to	4,550
Item (6) amounted to	6,670
Item (7) amounted to	1,050
Item (8) amounted to	2,310

During the year, $25,000 was transferred from the savings accounts to the checking accounts.

Instructions: From the above information, prepare a work sheet with columns to show:

(a) The transactions for the year. (Journal entries are not required.)
(b) Variances between budgeted and actual revenues and expenditures for the year.
(c) Balance sheet of the general fund, December 31, 19X9.

(AICPA adapted)

23-7. The following data were taken from the accounts of the Town of Farmdale after the books had been closed for the fiscal year ended June 30, 19X5:

	Balances 6–30–X4	19X5 Changes Debits	19X5 Changes Credits	Balances 6–30–X5
Cash..	$180,000	$ 955,000	$ 880,000	$255,000
Taxes Receivable.....................	20,000	809,000	781,000	48,000
	$200,000			$303,000
Allowance for Uncollectible Taxes......	$ 4,000	6,000	9,000	$ 7,000
Vouchers Payable	44,000	880,000	889,000	53,000
Due to Internal Service Fund.............	2,000	7,000	10,000	5,000
Due to Debt Service Fund.................	10,000	60,000	100,000	50,000
Fund Balance Reserved for Encumbrances......................................	40,000	40,000	47,000	47,000
Fund Balance.................................	100,000	20,000	61,000	141,000
	$200,000	$2,777,000	$2,777,000	$303,000

The following additional data are available:

(1) The budget for the year provided for estimated revenues of $1,000,000 and appropriations of $965,000.
(2) Expenditures totaling $895,000, in addition to those chargeable against Fund Balance Reserved for Encumbrances, were made.
(3) The actual expenditure chargeable against Fund Balance Reserved for Encumbrances was $37,000.

Instructions: Prepare a work sheet to compare estimated revenues with actual revenues and encumbrances and expenditures with appropriations and other authorizations. The work sheet should have the following column headings: Columns 1–4, "Name of Account"; Column 5, "Balance Sheet, June 30, 19X4"; Columns 6 and 7, "19X5 Transactions" (Debit and Credit); Column 8, "Estimated Revenues"; Column 9, "Actual Revenues"; Column 10, "Encumbrances and Expenditures"; Column 11, "Appropriations and Other Authorizations"; Column 12, "Balance Sheet, June 30, 19X5." (Formal journal entries are not required.)

(AICPA adapted)

23-8. The account balances of the general fund of McArthur Township at the beginning of 19X3 include:

Cash	1,300
Taxes Receivable..	3,500
Accounts Payable..	800
Fund Balance Reserved for Encumbrances.................................	1,100

The cash receipts for the year were:

From taxes of prior years...	$ 3,200
From taxes of the current year	76,000
Other current revenues	16,000
Sales of old equipment..	600
Temporary loans...	20,000

The disbursements for the year were as follows:

Accounts payable of the preceding year.......................................	$	800
Invoices for current operations:		
(a) Covering all orders and contracts outstanding at beginning of		
year...		1,200
(b) Incurred during year..		80,000
Payment of bonds falling due during year (transfer to debt service		
fund)...		10,000
Purchase of fixed assets..		4,000
Permanent petty cash advance made to city finance office..............		500
Supplies purchased for central storeroom established during year ...		4,000
Payment of temporary loans		15,000

During the year $1,600 of supplies purchased were issued to departments whose operating costs are met from this fund. The balance of stock on hand at the end of the year represents a minimum inventory that the municipality proposes to maintain in the storeroom.

The only taxes considered collectible at the end of 19X3 are those of the current year amounting to $7,000. Unfilled orders and contracts outstanding at the end of 19X3 amounted to $900.

Instructions: (1) Prepare a work sheet to summarize activities of the general fund for 19X3.

(2) Prepare a general fund balance sheet as of December 31, 19X3.

(3) Prepare a statement summarizing in detail the changes in the general fund balance for 19X3.

(AICPA adapted)

23-9. Information relating to the general fund for the Town of Clayton for the year ended April 30, 19X8, follows:

(a) Fund balance at May 1, 19X7, consisting entirely of cash, $2,350.
(b) Budget estimate of revenue, $185,000.
(c) Budget appropriations, $178,600.
(d) Tax levy, $115,620, against which an allowance of $4,000 is set for estimated losses in collection.
(e) Tax receipts, $112,246, with penalties of $310 in addition.
(f) Receipts from temporary loans, $20,000, all of which were repaid during period with interest of $300.
(g) Balance of encumbrances unliquidated, April 30, 19X8, $3,250.
(h) Vouchers approved for operating expenditures, $146,421.
(i) Vouchers approved for capital expenditures, $21,000.
(j) Transfer to Debt Service Fund for payment of bonds falling due during the year, $5,000, and for interest on the bonds, $2,000.
(k) Miscellaneous revenue received, $74,319.
(l) Rebate of current year's taxes collected in error, $240.
(m) Warrants issued and payable on demand, $169,400.
(n) Refund on an expense voucher on which an excess payment was made, $116.

Instructions: (1) Prepare the entries to record the data listed.
(2) Prepare entries to close the books for the year ended April 30, 19X8.

777

(3) Prepare a balance sheet as of April 30, 19X8.
(4) Prepare a statement of revenue, expenditures, and fund balance for the year ended April 30, 19X8.

(AICPA adapted)

23-10. Account balances for the general fund of the City of Homewood, on January 1, 19X1, were as follows:

Cash	1,000
Taxes Receivable — Delinquent	8,000
Accounts Payable	7,000
Fund Balance Reserved for Encumbrances	1,500
Fund Balance	500

Transactions for 19X1 were as follows:

(a) The budget that was adopted for 19X1 provided for taxes of $275,000, special assessments of $100,000, fees of $15,000, and license revenues of $10,000. Appropriations were $290,000 for general fund operations, and $100,000 for the purpose of establishing an internal service fund.
(b) All taxes and special assessments became receivable.
(c) Cash receipts for the general fund included:

Taxes from 19X1	$260,000
Special assessments	100,000
Fees	16,000
Licenses	9,500
Taxes Receivable — Delinquent	5,000
Interest on Taxes Receivable — Delinquent	500

Tax liens were obtained on the remainder of the delinquent taxes.
(d) Contracts amounting to $75,000 were let by the general fund.
(e) Billings for services rendered by the internal service fund to the general fund totaled $40,000.
(f) General fund disbursements were as follows:

Internal service fund	$100,000
Accounts payable of the preceding year	7,000
Outstanding orders at beginning of the year were received and paid for	2,000
Operating expenditures incurred during year	145,000
Supplies purchased for central storeroom established during year	5,000
Contracts let during year	30,000
Permanent advance to newly created petty cash fund	1,000
Services performed by internal service fund	35,000
Salaries paid during year	30,000

(g) All unpaid taxes became delinquent.
(h) Supplies inventory in the general fund amounted to $2,000 on December 31, 19X1. This amount is to be shown on the general fund balance sheet.

Instructions: Prepare as of December 31, 19X1, a work sheet reflecting the transactions, closing entries, and balance sheet for the general fund.

(AICPA adapted)

23-11. The Good Haven Township's adjusted trial balance for the general fund at the close of its fiscal year ended June 30, 19X4, is as follows:

Cash..	1,100	
Taxes Receivable — Current (note 1)	8,200	
Allowance for Uncollectible Taxes — Current................		150
Taxes Receivable — Delinquent	2,500	
Allowance for Uncollectible Taxes — Delinquent...........		1,650
Miscellaneous Accounts Receivable.............................	4,000	
Allowance for Uncollectible Accounts..........................		400
Due from Internal Service Fund....................................	5,000	
Expenditures (note 2)..	75,500	
Encumbrances	3,700	
Revenues (note 3)..		6,000
Due to Utility Fund..		1,000
Vouchers Payable		2,000
Fund Balance Reserved for Encumbrances — Prior Year.		4,400
Fund Balance Reserved for Encumbrances....................		3,700
Surplus Receipts (note 4)		700
Appropriations..		72,000
Fund Balance...		8,000
	100,000	100,000

Note 1. The current taxes and miscellaneous accounts receivable, recorded on the accrual basis as sources of revenue, amounted to $50,000 and $20,000 respectively. These items have been recorded on the books subject to a 2% provision for uncollectible accounts.

Note 2. Includes $4,250 paid during the fiscal year in settlement of all purchase orders outstanding at the beginning of the fiscal year.

Note 3. Represents the difference between the budgeted (estimated) revenue of $70,000 and the actual revenue realized during the fiscal year.

Note 4. Represents the proceeds from sale of equipment damaged by fire.

Instructions: (1) Prepare in columnar form an analysis of changes in fund balance for the year ending June 30, 19X4, with column headings for "Estimated," "Actual," and "Excess or Deficiency of Actual Compared with Estimated."

(2) Prepare a balance sheet at June 30, 19X4.

(AICPA adapted)

23-12. A partial general ledger trial balance (before adjustments) of the general fund of the City of Brookville at December 31, 19X7, is shown on page 779.

The unencumbered balance of the fire department's appropriation at December 31, 19X7, was $10,025. As legally authorized, the city council voted to carry this balance over to 19X8 in the rounded amount of $10,000. The action of the city council has not been recorded in the accounts.

Unfilled purchase orders for the general fund at December 31, 19X7, totaled $20,000.

Instructions: (1) Prepare the adjusting journal entry or entries for general fund accounts at December 31, 19X7.

Supplies Inventory (Physical Inventory 12/31/X7)	10,000	
Estimated Revenue — Miscellaneous	20,000	
Estimated Revenue — Taxes	95,000	
Appropriations		112,000
Revenue — Miscellaneous		21,600
Revenue — Taxes		95,500
Encumbrances	20,000	
Expenditures	80,000	
Expenditures Chargeable Against Prior Years' Encumbrances	7,100	
Fund Balance Reserved for Encumbrances (Balance, 1/1/X7, $7,000)		27,000
Fund Balance Reserved for Supplies Inventory (Balance at 1/1/X7)		12,000
Fund Balance		3,300

(2) Prepare the closing journal entry or entries for general fund accounts at December 31, 19X7.

(3) Prepare in columnar form an analysis of changes in fund balance for the year with the following column headings: "Estimated," "Actual," and "Excess or Deficiency of Actual Compared with Estimated."

(AICPA adapted)

24
Governmental Units – Special Funds

To achieve the important objective of determining and demonstrating compliance with finance-related legal and contractual provisions, accounting for governmental units requires segregating resources into separate entities called funds. The number of funds found in any governmental unit will vary with the nature of the special activities carried on by the unit and the legal provisions that have been adopted for separate financing of such activities. Accounting for the general fund was described in the preceding chapter; accounting for special funds and for account groups is discussed in this chapter.

SPECIAL REVENUE FUNDS

A *special revenue fund* is established when charter, statute, or contract requires that specific taxes or special revenue sources are to be used to finance a particular activity. Special revenue funds, then, are established when certain revenue is to be used exclusively for particular purposes such as schools, parks, libraries, or special improvements. A special revenue fund may be created to serve certain broad purposes or to serve some narrow and limited purpose. In either case resources can be applied only to the particular fund objective. A fund may be a special revenue fund of the general governmental unit but may be viewed as comparable to a general fund of a lower-level unit. For example, the governmental unit views the "school fund" as a special revenue fund, whereas the school fund is the "general fund" in terms of operations of the school system as a whole.

The authority for administering a special revenue fund may rest with the general governing body, but frequently the authority is delegated to a special body. A special revenue fund to finance school activities may be administered by a school board. A special revenue fund to finance recreational activities may be administered by a recreational commission. In some instances, the body responsible for the administration of the fund has the power to levy taxes or to establish the revenue measures that are required to finance activities. When a special revenue fund is to finance a number of activities, planning and control of expenditures will be required. Expenditures are controlled by a budget in the same manner as in the general fund.

A special revenue fund calls for the establishment of a general ledger and appropriate subsidiary ledgers. Upon adoption of a budget, entries are made in estimated revenues, appropriations, and fund balance accounts. During the course of activities, revenues and expenditures and encumbrances are summarized in the general ledger and are reported in detail in the subsidiary records. The statements that report the activities of a special revenue fund are similar to the statements of the general fund. Accounting for a special revenue fund is the same as accounting for the general fund.

CAPITAL PROJECTS FUNDS

Whenever major capital projects such as buildings, bridges, or other structures are to be financed by sources other than special assessments, trust funds, or proprietary funds, a *capital projects fund* is established to account for the financial resources used. A separate capital projects fund with its own self-balancing set of accounts is established for each project, and the fund continues in existence until the project is completed and the money disposed of properly.

Financial resources for a capital project usually are provided by the sale of long-term bonds, although grants from other governments and contributions from the general fund are also common sources. If a project is financed through the issuance of bonds, the bond liability is not recorded in the capital projects fund, but in the general long-term debt account group. The cost of the project itself is not recorded in the capital projects fund, but in the general fixed assets account group. The role of the capital projects fund, then, is strictly to account for the source and disposition of financial resources used to pay for the project.

Entries for Capital Projects Fund

To continue the example for the City of A in the preceding chapter, assume that this city approves a general bond issue to finance the acquisition of land and the construction of government buildings. Capital projects fund transactions and the entries to record these transactions follow:

Capital Projects Fund Books

Transaction	Entry		
Authorization of bond issue.	Estimated Other Financing Sources................ Appropriations	100,000	100,000
Sale of bonds.	Cash.. Other Financing Sources............................	100,000	100,000
Expenditure for purchase of land made relative to purpose of bond issue.	Expenditures .... Vouchers Payable..	20,000	20,000
Placing of orders and estimate of expenditures that will arise from commitments.	Encumbrances.. Fund Balance Reserved for Encumbrances ...	25,000	25,000
Placing of contract with construction company for work on project.	Encumbrances.. Fund Balance Reserved for Encumbrances ...	50,000	50,000
Liquidation of certain encumbrances ($15,000) upon receipt of invoices, and determination of expenditures relating to encumbrances ($16,000).	Fund Balance Reserved for Encumbrances ...... Encumbrances.. Expenditures .... Vouchers Payable..	15,000 16,000	15,000 16,000
Completion of contract by construction company and authorization for payment of same, less 10% retention pending final approval of project.	Fund Balance Reserved for Encumbrances ...... Encumbrances.. Expenditures .... Vouchers Payable.. Contracts Payable — Retained Percentage ...	50,000 50,000	50,000 45,000 5,000
Payment of vouchers.	Vouchers Payable.. Cash..	70,000	70,000
To close the appropriations, encumbrances, and expenditures accounts at the end of the period.	Appropriations .... Expenditures .... Encumbrances.. Fund Balance	100,000	86,000 10,000 4,000
To close the other financing sources accounts at the end of the period.	Other Financing Sources.............................. Estimated Other Financing Sources..............	100,000	100,000

A trial balance for the capital projects fund after posting the entries is shown on page 783.

Authorization of bond issue. The authorization of a bond issue is recorded by a debit to the account Estimated Other Financing Sources and a credit to the account Appropriations for the amount of the bonds to be issued. These are budgetary accounts. Estimated Other Financing Sources

City of A
Capital Projects Fund
Trial Balance
June 30, 19X4

Cash	30,000	
Vouchers Payable		11,000
Contracts Payable — Retained Percentage		5,000
Fund Balance Reserved for Encumbrances		10,000
Fund Balance		4,000
	30,000	30,000

may be viewed as the total resources estimated to become available to the fund. Appropriations may be viewed as the total spending authorized to be made from resources of the fund.

Proceeds from issuance of bonds. When bonds are sold at par, Cash is debited and Other Financing Sources is credited. If the bonds are sold at a premium, a bond premium account is also credited. The disposition of the premium balance is made in accordance with applicable legal requirements. If the premium becomes available for capital projects fund purposes, the premium is transferred to the appropriations account. If the premium is to be made available to the general fund for general purposes or to a debt service fund for bond interest payments or for bond retirement, the premium may be transferred to a payable account with such a fund. The subsequent payment of cash cancels the payable. If the bonds are sold at a discount, a bond discount account is debited for the amount of the discount. As in the case of a premium, disposition of the discount depends upon legal requirements. If the discount reduces the amount available for capital projects fund purposes, the discount is closed into the appropriations account. If the discount is to be recovered from some other fund in meeting capital projects fund requirements, a receivable balance with such other fund is established and the discount balance is closed. The subsequent receipt of cash cancels the receivable. The liability arising from the issue of the bonds is not reported in the capital projects fund but is recognized in the general long-term debt account group.

Expenditures and encumbrances. When a capital projects fund is to finance construction activities, the orders or contracts that are placed in carrying out the purpose of the bond issue are recorded by debits to Encumbrances and credits to Fund Balance Reserved for Encumbrances. As orders are filled and contracts are completed, original encumbrance entries are reversed and the actual expenditures are recorded by debits to Expenditures and credits to the appropriate liability accounts.

The authorization for expenditures is not limited to a specified time but is effective until completion of the project. However, it is desirable to close the expenditures account at the end of each fiscal period so that the portion of the project that has been completed may be summarized. The encumbrances account is also closed at the end of the period. However, the balance in the corresponding fund balance reserve account is shown separately in preparing a capital projects fund balance sheet.

Properties constructed for general governmental purposes from capital projects fund proceeds are not reported in the capital projects fund but are recognized in the separate general fixed assets account group. When construction is only partly completed at the end of the period, expenditures to date are reported in the general fixed assets account group as Construction in Progress.

When the project is completed, the fund balance is matched by cash of an equivalent amount. Cash remaining in the capital projects fund is disposed of in accordance with legal requirements. Normally, the cash must be transferred to the fund that is responsible for ultimate retirement of the bonds. The transfer of cash to the general fund or to a debt service fund is recorded by a debit to Fund Balance and a credit to Cash. Capital projects fund accounts have now been closed and the fund is no longer operative. The fund receiving cash from the capital projects fund debits Cash and credits Other Financing Sources. If Construction in Progress was previously recognized in the separate general fixed assets account group, this balance is canceled and the property item is recorded at its full cost.

When capital projects fund proceeds are used for the purchase of certain properties, the purchase is recorded by a debit to Expenditures. Accounts are closed as previously indicated. Recognition of the properties that are acquired through capital projects fund expenditures is made in the general fixed assets account group.

Capital Projects Fund Statements

Statements for each capital projects fund are prepared periodically. These statements normally consist of a balance sheet, a statement comparing expenditures and encumbrances with appropriations, and a statement of cash receipts and disbursements. Statements may be accompanied by special schedules that offer detailed support of statement items. When there are a number of capital projects funds, combined statements may be prepared with separate columns reporting financial data relating to the individual funds and total columns summarizing the data for all of the capital projects funds. Although each fund should be reported separately in a comprehensive financial report, only the combined statement for all capital projects funds is normally included in the basic financial statements of the governmental unit. The statements for the capital projects fund for the City of A are illustrated on the following page. It should be observed that the building project is still uncompleted with certain encumbrances remaining to be liquidated, and certain invoices and contracts remaining to be paid.

City of A
Capital Projects Fund
Balance Sheet
June 30, 19X4

Assets		Liabilities, Appropriations, and Fund Equity		
Cash..	$30,000	Vouchers payable.............................		$11,000
		Contracts payable — retained percentage..		5,000
		Fund balance:		
		Reserved for encumbrances	$10,000	
		Unreserved	4,000	14,000
Total assets......................................	$30,000	Total liabilities, appropriations, and fund equity		$30,000

City of A
Capital Projects Fund
Statement of Expenditures and Encumbrances
Compared with Appropriations
For Year Ended June 30, 19X4

Amount appropriated, January 20, 19X4..	$100,000
Less expenditures, January 20–June 30, 19X4..................................	86,000
Unexpended balance..	$ 14,000
Less encumbrances, June 30, 19X4...	10,000
Unencumbered balance, June 30, 19X4	$ 4,000

City of A
Capital Projects Fund
Statement of Cash Receipts and Disbursements
For Year Ended June 30, 19X4

Receipts:		
Proceeds from sale of bonds, January 20, 19X4.............................		$100,000
Disbursements:		
Purchase of land..	$20,000	
Payments on construction contract.............................	45,000	
Payment of other miscellaneous costs and expenses......	5,000	70,000
Cash balance, June 30, 19X4..		$ 30,000

A balance sheet for a capital projects fund may show asset and liability balances other than those listed in the example. Other assets may include accounts receivable and amounts due from other funds. Liabilities may include accounts payable, contracts payable, judgments payable, and amounts due to other funds.

The statement comparing expenditures and encumbrances with appropriations may show changes in the amount appropriated other than those in the illustration. For example, there may be additions to or deductions from the appropriations balance for bond premiums and discounts, for contributions from other funds, and for transfers to other funds.

SPECIAL ASSESSMENT FUNDS

A *special assessment fund* is established whenever public improvements are to be financed in part or in whole by special levies on properties benefiting therefrom. The special assessment fund accounts for the collection of special assessment levies and also reports the application of such monies to the particular purpose for which they were raised.

Special assessment improvements are made only after appropriate authorization by the legislative body or favorable vote by the property owners affected. When a project has been approved, a special assessment fund is established for the project, and the authorization as well as subsequent transactions are recorded in the special assessment fund books. A separate special assessment fund is established for each special assessment project authorized.

When cash is collected from property owners at the time improvements are made, accounting for a special assessment fund is similar to that for the capital projects fund previously illustrated. Ordinarily, however, special assessments are collected over a number of years and it becomes necessary to finance construction from the proceeds of special assessment bonds or other long-term loans. Such obligations are claims against the benefited properties and are retired as the special assessments are collected from property owners. Thus, special assessment bonds payable are treated as a liability of the particular special assessment fund, and are not included in the general long-term debt account group. Special assessment taxpayers are normally charged interest on any deferred payments and this interest is used to pay the interest on the special assessment indebtedness. When construction is financed by bonds or other loans, the special assessment fund must show the original receipt of funds and their use for the authorized project, and also the subsequent collection of special assessments and the application of such proceeds to the retirement of special assessment fund indebtedness.

Entries for Special Assessment Funds

To illustrate the accounting for a special assessment fund, assume that street improvements are authorized within the City of A, the cost of such improvements to be shared by the city and by the property owners who benefit from the improvements. Special assessment fund transactions and the entries that are made to record such transactions follow:

Special Assessment Fund Books

Transaction	Entry		
Authorization of project.	Estimated Revenues — Current......................	10,000	
	Estimated Revenues — Deferred	90,000	
	Estimated Other Financing Sources................	20,000	
	Appropriations..		120,000
Charge to general fund for its share of cost, and assessments levied against property owners.	Special Assessments Receivable — Current.....	10,000	
	Special Assessments Receivable — Deferred ...	90,000	
	Due from General Fund.................................	20,000	
	Revenues		10,000
	Deferred Revenues..................................		90,000
	Other Financing Sources............................		20,000
Receipt of general fund's share of cost and first half of current assessments.	Cash...	25,000	
	Due from General Fund.............................		20,000
	Special Assessments Receivable — Current..		5,000
Issuance of bonds to finance construction activities.	Cash...	95,000	
	Bonds Payable		95,000
Cost incurred for construction.	Expenditures	20,000	
	Vouchers Payable....................................		20,000
Placing of orders for construction materials.	Encumbrances...	10,000	
	Fund Balance Reserved for Encumbrances ...		10,000
Placing of contract with construction company for work on project.	Encumbrances...	80,000	
	Fund Balance Reserved for Encumbrances ...		80,000
Completion of contract by construction company and authorization for payment, less 10% retention pending final approval of project.	Fund Balance Reserved for Encumbrances	80,000	
	Encumbrances...		80,000
	Expenditures	85,000	
	Vouchers Payable.....................................		76,500
	Contracts Payable — Retained Percentage ...		8,500
Payment of vouchers.	Vouchers Payable..	90,000	
	Cash...		90,000
Receipt of second half of current assessments together with interest on unpaid assessments.	Cash...	7,000	
	Special Assessments Receivable — Current..		5,000
	Revenues		2,000
Retirement of part of bond issue together with interest on bonds.	Bonds Payable...	4,000	
	Expenditures	1,900	
	Cash...		5,900
To record accrued interest on special assessments receivable — deferred at the end of the period.	Interest Receivable......................................	450	
	Revenues		450
To record accrued interest on bonds payable at the end of the period.	Expenditures	400	
	Interest Payable.......................................		400

Transaction	Entry		
To close appropriations, encumbrances, and expenditures accounts at the end of the period.	Appropriations... Expenditures .... Encumbrances... Fund Balance	120,000	107,300 10,000 2,700
To close revenues and other financing sources accounts at the end of the period.	Revenues .... Other Financing Sources............................... Estimated Other Financing Sources.............. Estimated Revenues — Current.................... Fund Balance	12,450 20,000	20,000 10,000 2,450
To close estimated revenues — deferred account at the end of the period.	Fund Balance .... Estimated Revenues — Deferred	90,000	90,000

A trial balance taken after posting the entries is as follows:

City of A
Special Assessment Fund
Trial Balance
June 30, 19X4

Cash..	31,100	
Special Assessments Receivable — Deferred.................	90,000	
Interest Receivable..	450	
Bonds Payable..		91,000
Vouchers Payable		6,500
Contracts Payable — Retained Percentage....................		8,500
Interest Payable		400
Fund Balance Reserved for Encumbrances....................		10,000
Fund Balance..	84,850	
Deferred Revenues		90,000
	206,400	206,400

Authorization of project. The authorization of a project to be financed by special assessments is recorded by debits to the accounts Estimated Revenues and Estimated Other Financing Sources and a credit to the account Appropriations. Estimated Revenues and Estimated Other Financing Sources may be viewed as the total resources estimated to become available in fulfilling the objectives of the fund. Appropriations may be viewed as the total amount authorized to be spent by the fund.

Proceeds from special assessments and from borrowing. The amount that the governmental unit is to contribute as its share of the project cost and the assessments against property owners are recorded by debits to appropriate receivable accounts and credits to Revenues or Other Financing Sources. Because the deferred portion of assessments receivable is not available for current operations, that amount is credited to a liability account, rather than being recognized as revenue. Subsidiary ledgers are established and individual debits are made to accounts with special assessment taxpayers. As cash is received from the governmental unit and from taxpayers during the construction period, Cash is debited and the receivable balances are credited. Accounting for taxes follows the same procedures described in the preceding chapter for the general fund.

When borrowing is necessary to meet construction requirements, Cash is debited and Bonds Payable (or other appropriate liability account) is credited. Subsequent collections of assessments are applied to the liquidation of the bonded indebtedness. Subsequent collections of interest on special assessments are applied to the payment of interest on the bonded indebtedness. Collections, then, are recorded by debiting Cash and crediting special assessment receivable accounts and Revenue. Accrued interest on special assessments receivable at the end of the period is recognized by a debit to Interest Receivable and a credit to Revenue.

The issue of bonds at a premium or at a discount creates special problems. When bonds are issued at a premium, Cash is debited for the amount of the obligation, and the amount of the premium, and Bonds Payable and Premium on Bonds are credited. The premium balance is amortized over the life of the bond issue, and periodic debits to the premium are accompanied by credits to Expenditures. When bonds are issued at a discount, Cash is debited for the bond issue proceeds, Discount on Bonds is debited for the amount of the discount, and Bonds Payable is credited. The discount balance is amortized over the life of the bond issue, and periodic credits to the discount are accompanied by debits to Expenditures. Special assessments collections, in either case, require analysis in terms of the amount to be applied to the liquidation of bonded indebtedness and the amount to be applied to the payment of interest on such indebtedness.

Encumbrances and expenditures. Encumbrances and expenditures are recorded just as in the capital projects fund. They are closed at the end of each period. A credit balance in the fund balance account upon the completion of the project would indicate a remaining fund balance. This balance would be used for the abatement of special assessments still owing, for rebates to be made to special assessment taxpayers, or for disposal in some other manner in accordance with the law. When special assessment expenditures are made for the acquisition or the development of properties properly recognized as fixed assets, the property items are recognized at their acquisition or during the course of their construction in the general fixed assets account group just as projects financed by a capital projects fund.

Payments of bonds and interest on bonds from special assessment proceeds are recorded by debits to Bonds Payable and to Expenditures and by credits to Cash. Accrued interest on bonds at the end of the period is recognized by a debit to Expenditures and a credit to Interest Payable.

A deficit upon ultimate settlement of special assessment indebtedness calls for a cash transfer in accordance with legal requirements. The law frequently provides that if there is a fund balance, cash is to be transferred to the general fund. A deficit is generally made up by a transfer of cash from the general fund. The general fund debits Transfers upon transferring cash to a special assessment fund to finance construction activities, to absorb a construction deficit, or to cover an interest shortage. The general fund credits Other Financing Sources upon receiving excess cash from a special assessment fund.

Negative fund balance. While bonds of the special assessment fund are outstanding, it is common for the fund balance to be negative. This is due to the concept of revenue recognition used in all governmental fund types as applied to the particular circumstances of the special assessment fund.

In governmental funds, revenue is recognized when it is both measurable and available. In the case of special assessment tax levies, the current portion which will be collected within the next twelve months is regarded as "available," but the deferred portion is not. Thus, the receivable for deferred special assessments is recorded with a corresponding liability — Deferred Revenues — rather than a revenue account. Over the years, as the installments become current they will be recognized as revenue with the corresponding reduction in the liability, but in the early years of the fund operation they would not.

On the other hand, the amounts recognized as expenditures for the project to be financed by special assessments will reflect the full amount of the assessments, both current and deferred. Because cash is needed to pay for the project costs, bonds are issued to make up for the uncollected assessments. But the bonds issued are recorded as a liability in the special assessment fund and thus do not affect the fund balance.

Other fund types do not have this problem. In the capital projects fund, for example, bond proceeds are treated as "other financing sources" which increase the fund balance. In proprietary fund types, expenditures for capital projects are recognized as assets and thus do not decrease the fund balance. This is because the measurement focus of proprietary fund types is on capital maintenance rather than flows of short-term financial resources.

The appearance of a deficit when the fund is operated in a prudent manner is likely to mislead readers of special assessment fund statements. This issue could be resolved in several alternative ways. One solution would be for the deferred assessments to be recognized as revenues. Assuming that they are measurable, they could be regarded as available in the sense that they will provide the means for paying off liabilities of the fund as they come due. Another alternative would be to treat bond proceeds as "other financing sources" which increase the fund balance, as is done with capital projects funds. This would require separate recognition of the bond obligation in an account group comparable to general long-term debt. These solutions are not in conformity with current generally accepted accounting principles, however.

Special Assessment Fund Statements

Statements are prepared periodically for each special assessment fund. These statements normally consist of a balance sheet, a statement comparing expenditures and encumbrances with appropriations, and a statement of cash receipts and disbursements. When there are several special assessment funds, combined statements may be prepared, with separate columns reporting financial data for the individual special assessment funds and total columns summarizing the data for all of the special assessment funds. The balance sheet for the special assessment fund of the City of A is illustrated as follows. The other statements are similar to those previously illustrated for the capital projects fund.

City of A
Special Assessment Fund
Balance Sheet
June 30, 19X4

Assets		Liabilities and Fund Equity	
Cash..	$ 31,100	Vouchers payable	$ 6,500
Special assessments receivable — deferred....................................	90,000	Contracts payable — retained percentage....................................	8,500
Interest receivable.........................	450	Bonds payable	91,000
		Interest payable	400
		Deferred Revenues	90,000
		Fund balance reserved for encumbrances.....................................	10,000
		Fund balance	(84,850)
Total assets	$121,550	Total liabilities and fund equity	$121,550

A balance sheet for a special assessment fund may show assets and liabilities other than those reported in the example. Assets may include assessments receivable — delinquent, current, and deferred; special assessment liens receivable; penalties receivable on special assessments; amounts due from the general fund for its share of cost; and amounts due from other funds. Liabilities may include contracts payable, judgments payable, and amounts due to other funds.

A special assessment fund is terminated only after its receivables have been fully realized and its obligations fully liquidated. Special assessments receivable to be collected in years to come and bonds to be paid from such proceeds are reported on successive balance sheets until receivables are fully realized and bonds are fully liquidated.

DEBT SERVICE FUNDS

A *debt service fund* is established whenever resources are accumulated for the specific purposes of retiring and making interest payments on bonds of the governmental unit. Books of the debt service fund report the accumulation of the fund and also the application of assets to the particular purpose for which they were accumulated.

Cash deposits are normally made to the debt service fund at regular intervals. The source of such deposits may be contributions from the general fund or a special revenue fund, or specific debt service fund levies included in the general tax assessments. Cash deposited in the fund is invested, and the earnings on these investments further increase the amount available for bond retirement. When serial bonds are issued, a fund accumulation is not required, for cash is applied periodically to the direct retirement of the serial maturities. Normally, serial bond maturities, as well as periodic interest on both serial bonds and term bonds, are met through direct payment by the general fund or special revenue funds.

Deposits that must be made to a debt service fund to accumulate for bond retirement are usually specified in the indenture contract at the time the bonds are issued. These amounts may be arbitrary sums or they may be equal periodic sums calculated actuarially so that such deposits at an assumed interest rate will accumulate to the required amount at some future date. When deposits are calculated actuarially and earnings differ from the assumed rate, deposits may be adjusted or cash transfers may be made to or from the general fund so that scheduled amounts are deposited.

Entries for Debt Service Funds

Assume that the City of A is required to establish a debt service fund for the ultimate retirement of the bonds that were issued for the construction of certain public properties, referred to in an earlier example. Debt service fund transactions and the entries to record such transactions on the fund books follow, and a trial balance after recording these transactions is on page 793.

Debt Service Fund Books

Transaction	Entry		
Charge to source providing installment contribution.	Due from General Fund................................. Other Financing Sources................................	10,000	10,000
Receipt of payment from general fund.	Cash... Due from General Fund....................................	10,000	10,000
Investment of cash.	Investments... Cash...	9,800	9,800
Receipt of interest.	Cash... Revenues	300	300
To record accrued interest at the end of the period.	Interest Receivable... Interest Revenue..	50	50

To close accounts at the end of the period.	Other Financing Sources.................................
	  Revenues ....
	  Fund Balance ....
		10,000
		350
			10,350

Proceeds from contributions and from earnings. The debt service fund is not usually subject to budgetary control. The provisions of the bond indenture normally determine the amounts to be accumulated. Therefore, no entry to recognize the adoption of the budget is made. If a portion of the

City of A
Debt Service Fund
Trial Balance
June 30, 19X4

Cash...	500	
Interest Receivable...	50	
Investments..	9,800	
Fund Balance		10,350
	10,350	10,350

taxes is to be made directly available to the debt service fund in satisfying deposit requirements, Taxes Receivable is debited and Contribution Revenues is credited. Accounting for the collection of taxes will follow the same procedures as for the general fund. If the contribution is to be made by the general fund or a special revenue fund, a receivable account with such a fund is debited to establish the claim and the transfers account is credited. When the contribution is received, Cash is debited and the receivable account is credited.

Accounting for debt service fund investments of a governmental unit is similar to accounting for sinking fund investments of a business firm. Amounts collected on investments are recorded by debits to Cash and credits to appropriate revenue accounts. At the end of the period, adjustments to recognize any revenue accruals are made. At this time, too, entries would be made for the amortization and accumulation of any premiums or discounts on fund investments. After adjustments, the individual revenue account balances are closed.

Retirement of bonds will require the sale of fund securities. Gains and losses on such sales are carried to Fund Balance. A deficit in a debt service fund and insufficient funds to meet maturing indebtedness is made up in accordance with legal requirements. Generally, the shortage is met by a general fund contribution. The receipt of such a contribution is recorded by a debit to Cash and a credit to Other Financing Sources. An excess balance in the debt service fund will result in a transfer of cash to some other fund in accordance with legal requirements. Such a transfer is recorded by a debit to Transfers and a credit to Cash. The general fund records a transfer of cash to meet normal interest requirements or a debt service fund shortage by a debit to Expenditures. The receipt of cash from a debt service fund is recorded by a credit to Other Financing Sources.

Expenditures. When bonds that are to be paid from the debt service fund mature, they should be recognized on the fund books by a debit to Fund Balance and a credit to Matured Bonds Payable. Upon payment of the bonds, the liability account is closed. Until the time the bonds mature, they are carried in the general long-term debt account group. When they mature and are recognized on the books of the debt service fund, the balances are closed in the general long-term debt account group.

Debt Service Fund Statements

Statements are prepared periodically for each debt service fund. Statements normally include a balance sheet, a statement comparing sinking fund accumulations with requirements, a statement analyzing the changes in the fund balance, and a statement of cash receipts and disbursements. When there are a number of debt service funds, combined debt service fund statements may report individual fund data and combined data. Investment balance detail can be provided in the form of supporting schedules. The balance sheet for the debt service fund of the City of A is illustrated as follows:

City of A
Debt Service Fund
Balance Sheet
June 30, 19X4

Assets		Liabilities and Fund Equity	
Cash..	$ 500	Fund balance	$10,350
Interest receivable	50		
Investments	9,800		
Total assets......................................	$10,350	Total liabilities and fund equity	$10,350

Assets other than those shown in the example may be included on a debt service fund balance sheet. Among these assets are cash with fiscal agents for payment of bonds; taxes receivable — current and delinquent, and related allowances for uncollectible taxes; tax liens receivable; interest and penalties receivable; and amounts due from other funds.

INTERNAL SERVICE FUNDS

Internal service funds or *revolving funds* are created upon establishing service units that are to offer certain goods or services to the different governmental departments. Service funds are established with the expectation that they will be able to provide goods and services at costs that are less than what the governmental departments would otherwise have to pay to outsiders. Representative of internal service funds are central stores, garages, printing establishments, cement and asphalt plants, and prison industries.

Operations of the internal service fund are similar to those of a private business organization, and accounting for the fund normally parallels that of a commercial organization. Costs are incurred in connection with operations, but the internal service fund recovers its costs through charges that it makes to governmental departments that benefit from its services. Ordinarily expenditures of the fund are not restricted by appropriation measures. Operations of the fund are based upon the demands made upon it by the various departments, and such demands are limited to the amounts appropriated to respective departments for its goods or services.

Entries for Internal Service Funds

Assume that the City of A establishes a central print shop offering printing services to the various city departments. Internal service fund transactions, the entries that are made to record such transactions, and a trial balance taken after recording the transactions follow:

Internal Service Fund Books

Transaction	Entry		
Establishment of internal service fund by contribution from general fund in accordance with budgetary appropriation.	Cash.. Capital Contribution by General Fund	25,000	25,000
Purchase of equipment, materials, and supplies.	Equipment .... Materials and Supplies.................................... Vouchers Payable...	10,000 26,000	36,000
Billings to gereral fund for services rendered.	Due from General Fund.................................... Revenue from Services	40,000	40,000
Expenses incurred.	Expenses.. Vouchers Payable...	25,000	25,000
Cash received from general fund on billings.	Cash.. Due from General Fund...............................	30,000	30,000
Payment of vouchers.	Vouchers Payable... Cash...	50,000	50,000
Materials and supplies used during the period.	Expenses.. Materials and Supplies..............................	14,000	14,000
To record depreciation of equipment.	Expenses.. Accumulated Depreciation of Equipment......	500	500

To close revenue and expense accounts at the end of the period.	Revenue from Services ....
	    Expenses..
	    Retained Earnings..
		40,000	39,500
			500

City of A
Central Print Shop Internal Service Fund
Trial Balance
June 30, 19X4

Cash..	5,000	
Due from General Fund......................................	10,000	
Materials and Supplies......................................	12,000	
Equipment	10,000	
Accumulated Depreciation of Equipment...........................		500
Vouchers Payable...		11,000
Capital Contribution by General Fund		25,000
Retained Earnings...		500
	37,000	37,000

The internal service fund is established by a contribution from the general fund or from some other fund, or possibly from money provided by the issuance of bonds. Cash is debited and a capital account reporting the source of the contribution is credited. Revenue and expense items of the internal service fund are recorded just as they would be for a similar business enterprise. Materials and supplies purchased by the fund may be carried on a perpetual inventory basis, with debits to expense recognized as these items are consumed or transferred. Property and equipment items acquired by the fund are carried on its own books, and depreciation is recognized as a part of the cost of goods and services for billing purposes. Billings thus recover the depreciation sustained and provide funds for the ultimate replacement of the depreciable properties. At the end of the period, adjustments are made for prepaid and accrued items, for depreciation and amortization, and for inventories, as for a business. Revenue and expense balances are closed, and the net income or loss from operations is carried to Retained Earnings.

Ordinarily an internal service fund bills the departments that it serves for no more than the cost of the services rendered. Cost accounting records may be maintained in arriving at charges that will cover material, labor, and overhead costs. When charges are made at approximate cost, the capital of the fund will remain steady. When charges are made that produce a net income, the transfer of cash to the general fund may be authorized at different intervals. Such transfers are recorded on the internal service fund books by debits to Retained Earnings and credits to Cash. When an internal service fund operates regularly at a net loss, replenishment of its capital by the general fund at intervals may be authorized. The transfer of cash in such an instance is recorded on the internal service fund books by a debit to Cash and a credit to Transfers. When the transfers account is closed to Retained Earnings, the deficit is eliminated. The general fund receiving cash from an internal service fund credits Other Financing Sources. The transfer of cash to an internal service fund in establishing the fund or in meeting a capital deficiency is recorded by a debit to Transfers.

Internal Service Fund Statements

Statements are prepared periodically for each internal service fund. Statements normally include a balance sheet, a statement of operations, and an analysis of changes in retained earnings. When there are several funds, combined statements may report individual fund data and combined data. The internal service fund balance sheet for the City of A is shown as follows. The statement of operations and the analysis of changes in retained earnings would be similar to those normally prepared for a private business unit.

City of A
Central Print Shop
Balance Sheet
June 30, 19X4

Assets			Liabilities, Capital, and Retained Earnings		
Cash..		$ 5,000	Vouchers payable...............................		$11,000
Due from general fund........................		10,000	Capital contribution by general fund		25,000
Materials and supplies........................		12,000	Retained earnings...............................		500
Equipment...........................	$10,000				
Less accumulated deprecia-tion.................................	500	9,500	Total liabilities, capital, and retained		
Total assets		$36,500	earnings..		$36,500

FIDUCIARY FUNDS

Governmental units frequently hold and operate assets in the capacity of trustee or agent. Separate *trust funds* and *agency funds* are established for properties so controlled. In its capacity as trustee or as agent, the governmental unit is faced with special responsibilities. It must carry out its duties in accordance with trust or agency requirements as well as the applicable general law. A full accounting for the discharge of its responsibilities in either capacity is required.

Trust and agency funds are so similar that they are generally treated as a single class for governmental accounting purposes. In certain cases the accounting for such funds is very simple and the fund books are maintained for only a short period. An example would be an expendable fund established when the governmental unit receives a grant that is immediately spent, or when the governmental unit makes certain cash collections that are immediately distributed to other units. In other instances the accounting may be rather complex and the fund may continue for a considerable time or indefinitely. Examples would be an expendable fund established when the governmental unit takes over tax-delinquent properties and makes cash distributions to other governmental units in satisfaction of their liens as cash is realized on such properties; or a nonexpendable fund established when the governmental unit receives a grant, with the principal to remain intact and only the income to be used for public purposes. Whether simple or complex problems are involved, accounting for the governmental trust or agency is similar to that employed for such a relationship in the private sector.

Entries for a Trust Fund

Assume that cash is received by the City of A for the establishment of a trust fund. Income of the fund is to become available for certain public purposes, but the principal of the fund is to remain unexpendable. Transactions for the trust fund, entries to record the transactions, and a post-closing trial balance for the fund appear as follows:

Trust Fund Books

Transaction	Entry		
Receipt of cash.	Principal Cash.. Trust Fund Principal Balance.......................	50,000	50,000
Investment of cash.	Investments.. Principal Cash...	45,000	45,000
Receipt of income, which is to be used for a specific purpose.	Income Cash.. Income...	1,500	1,500
Payments chargeable to income in accordance with trust requirements.	Expenditures Chargeable to Income .... Income Cash...	1,200	1,200
To close the accounts at the end of the period.	Income.. Expenditures Chargeable to Income .... Trust Fund Income Balance.........................	1,500	1,200 300

City of A
Trust Fund
Trial Balance
June 30, 19X4

Principal Cash...	5,000	
Investments..	45,000	
Trust Fund Principal Balance..		50,000
Income Cash...	300	
Trust Fund Income Balance..		300
	50,300	50,300

A clear distinction must be maintained between principal assets and income assets when only the latter are expendable. Income and income payment account balances are closed at the end of each period. An excess of income over income expenditures would indicate that income had not been wholly expended, and such a balance could be used to satisfy spending requirements in subsequent periods.

When a fund is nonexpendable both as to principal and as to income, as in the case of a fund established to make loans to public employees, no principal-income distinction for assets is necessary. Fund capital can be summarized in a single account or can be divided into original capital and the retained earnings or the deficit emerging from the fund activities. The same procedures would apply for a fund that is fully expendable as to principal and income, as in the case of a fund for pensions to employees.

Trust Fund Statements

Statements are prepared periodically for each trust fund and each agency fund. Statements normally include a balance sheet, a statement accounting for changes in fund principal and income balances, and a statement of cash receipts and disbursements. When there are several agency and trust funds, combined statements may report individual and combined data. The balance sheet for the trust fund of the City of A is shown as follows. The remaining statements would be the same as those prepared for the private trust.

City of A
Trust Fund
Balance Sheet
June 30, 19X4

Assets		Liabilities and Fund Balances	
Principal cash	$ 5,000	Trust fund principal balance	$50,000
Investments	45,000	Trust fund income balance	300
Income cash	300		
Total assets	$50,300	Total liabilities and fund balances	$50,300

ENTERPRISE FUNDS

Many governmental units own and operate certain utilities and other enterprises that offer services to the public. Examples of utilities include water plants, electric plants, gas plants, and transportation systems. Examples of other enterprises include airports, docks, and public housing. Operations of such utilities and other enterprises are normally self-supporting; the rates charged to the public cover the costs of providing services. *Enterprise funds* are established to account for the properties and the operations of the public enterprises.

Accounting for Enterprise Funds

Operations of publicly owned enterprises are similar to those of privately owned businesses, and accounting is normally the same as that for private units. Accounting for public units, as for private units, must provide at regular intervals full data concerning both the financial position and the results of operations.

Original acquisition of an enterprise may be financed from amounts contributed by the general fund or by a special revenue fund, from amounts raised by a general bond issue, or from amounts raised by the sale of enterprise bonds that are to be retired from earnings of this unit. When cash for the purchase of properties is received from a general or a special revenue fund, the enterprise fund debits Cash and credits a capital account that identifies the fund making the contribution. When cash is received from the issue of bonds of the general governmental authority, the enterprise fund debits Cash and credits Capital Contributed by General Bond Issue. When cash is raised by means of its own bonds secured by a lien on its revenues or a mortgage on its properties, the enterprise debits Cash and credits

Bonds Payable or Mortgage Bonds Payable. Following the receipt of cash, entries are recorded on the books of the enterprise for the purchase of land and buildings and other properties.

Revenues and expenses are recorded on the books of the enterprise just as they would be recorded on the books for a similar private enterprise. At the end of each period appropriate adjustments are made in arriving at financial position and the results of operations. The net income or loss from operations is summarized and transferred to Retained Earnings.

When cash representing a portion or all of the net income is transferred by the enterprise fund to the general fund or to some special revenue fund to finance governmental activities, the entry on the enterprise books is a debit to Retained Earnings and a credit to Cash. The general fund or special revenue fund in receiving cash from an enterprise credits Other Financing Sources. The general fund or special revenue fund in transferring cash to an enterprise fund to establish the fund or to meet a capital deficiency debits Transfers. When another fund transfers cash to an enterprise fund in payment for services, it debits the expenditures account.

Enterprise Fund Statements

Statements are prepared periodically for each enterprise fund. Statements normally include a balance sheet, a revenue and expense statement, and a statement analyzing changes in retained earnings. Supporting schedules normally accompany the statements. Statements and supporting schedules are similar to those for private enterprises. An enterprise fund balance sheet for the City of A is as follows:

City of A
Enterprise Fund
Balance Sheet
June 30, 19X4

Assets

Current assets:			
Cash...		$ 35,500	
Accounts and notes receivable...	$ 40,000		
Less allowance for doubtful accounts...............................	1,500	38,500	
Materials and supplies..		12,000	
Prepaid expenses...		6,500	$ 92,500
Restricted assets:			
Cash and investments for debt service			30,000
Utility plant in service:			
Land		$ 50,000	
Structures and improvements	$150,000		
Less accumulated depreciation...	20,000	130,000	
Equipment..	$ 60,000		
Less accumulated depreciation...	15,000	45,000	225,000
Deferred costs:			
Unamortized bond issue costs...			2,500
Total assets...			$350,000

Liabilities, Contributions, and Retained Earnings

Liabilities:
  Current liabilities:
    Vouchers payable.. $ 60,000
    Accrued expenses...   5,000 $ 65,000
  Bonds payable...   200,000
                                                                                                              $265,000

Contributions and retained earnings:
  Capital contribution by general fund .... $ 50,000
  Retained earnings appropriated for debt service....................... 30,000
  Unappropriated retained earnings   5,000   85,000
Total liabilities, contributions, and retained earnings.................................... $350,000

GENERAL FIXED ASSETS ACCOUNT GROUP

There is a need for a full accountability for the fixed assets of a governmental unit. As indicated in previous sections, internal service, trust and agency, and enterprise funds report fixed asset acquisitions on their respective books. However, the general fund, special revenue funds, capital projects funds, and special assessment funds do not report fixed assets on their respective books but simply debit an expenditures account. Fixed assets acquired by the latter funds are referred to as the *general fixed assets* and are summarized in a separate self-balancing *general fixed assets account group*.

General fixed assets when acquired by purchase are recorded at cost. When properties are acquired by gift, they are recorded at their appraised value. Normally no recognition is made in the accounts for depreciation on general fixed assets. Cost allocation procedures for general fixed assets would serve little purpose when there is no concern with a determination of net income. Physical checks of property items are made at various intervals and differences between items on hand and items reported on the books are investigated and reconciled.

Entries for the General Fixed Assets Group

Transactions and entries affecting the general fixed assets records for the City of A and a trial balance after transactions have been recorded are as follows:

General Fixed Assets Books

Transaction	Entry		
Acquisition of equipment through expenditures of general fund.	Equipment .... Investment in General Fixed Assets — From General Fund Revenues	65,000	65,000

Transaction	Entry		
Equipment retired during period (original cost, $6,000, financed by general fund).	Investment in General Fixed Assets — From General Fund Revenues .... Equipment	6,000	 6,000

To record land acquired and buildings in process of construction at the end of the year through expenditures of capital projects fund.	Land ....
	 Structures and Improvements in Progress ....
	    Investment in General Fixed Assets — From
	    Bonds ....
		20,000
		 66,000
			
			 86,000

To record improvements in process at the end of the year through expenditures of special assessment fund.	Structures and Improvements in Progress ....
	    Investment in General Fixed Assets — From
	    Property Owners' Share of Special Assess-
	    ments ....
	    Investment in General Fixed Assets — From
	    Government's Share of Special Assessments .
		105,000	
			
			 85,000
			
			 20,000

City of A
General Fixed Assets
Trial Balance
June 30, 19X4

Equipment	59,000	
Structures and Improvements in Progress	171,000	
Land	20,000	
Investment in General Fixed Assets — From General Fund Revenues		59,000
Investment in General Fixed Assets — From Bonds		86,000
Investment in General Fixed Assets — From Property Owners' Share of Special Assessments		85,000
Investment in General Fixed Assets — From Government's Share of Special Assessments		20,000
	250,000	250,000

The acquisition of a general fixed asset is recorded in the general fixed assets account group by a debit to the appropriate asset account and a credit to Investment in General Fixed Assets. Frequently, instead of a single investment credit balance indicating total general asset holdings, separate investment balances are established to indicate the different sources of general fixed assets financing, such as general fund revenues, bonds, special assessments, and grants. General fixed assets in the process of construction are reported as "in progress" until their completion, when the full cost is recorded. The entries for the expenditures for fixed assets are not made in the general fixed assets account group but are made in the books of the funds financing the acquisitions, as described in earlier sections.

Subsidiary accounts are provided to show general fixed assets detail. The subsidiary record describes each asset, reports its cost, and offers supplementary information including its location and other significant data.

When a general fixed asset is retired, the original entry recording the acquisition is reversed. The account Investment in General Fixed Assets is debited and the appropriate asset balance is credited.

Statements for the General Fixed Assets Group

Statements are prepared periodically from the general fixed assets group books. Statements normally include a statement of general fixed assets and a statement summarizing changes in the different classes of general fixed assets during the course of the period. A statement of general fixed assets prepared for the City of A is as follows:

City of A
Statement of General Fixed Assets
June 30, 19X4

Land..	20,000	Investment in general fixed assets financed from:	
Structures and improvements in progress....................................	171,000	General fund revenues	$ 59,000
Equipment.....................................	59,000	Bonds	86,000
		Property owners' share of special assessments	85,000
		Government's share of special assessments	20,000
Total..	$250,000	Total	$250,000

GENERAL LONG-TERM DEBT ACCOUNT GROUP

Long-term debt of the governmental unit, with the exception of that reported directly in special assessment funds or enterprise funds, is known as the *general long-term debt*. Total general long-term debt maturity amounts are summarized in a separate self-balancing *general long-term debt account group*.

Entries for the General Long-Term Debt Group

Transactions and entries affecting the general long-term debt records for the City of A and the resulting trial balance appear as follows:

General Long-Term Debt Books

Transaction	Entry		
To record bonds issued to finance improvements.	Amount To Be Provided for Retirement of Bonds...................................... Sinking Fund Bonds Payable	100,000	100,000
To record increase in debt service fund for retirement of bonds.	Amount Provided for Retirement of Bonds .... Amount To Be Provided for Retirement of Bonds..	10,350	10,350

City of A
General Long-Term Debt
Trial Balance
June 30, 19X4

Amount Provided for Retirement of Bonds......................	10,350	
Amount To Be Provided for Retirement of Bonds............	89,650	
Sinking Fund Bonds Payable..		100,000
	100,000	100,000

Total amounts owed as principal on long-term debt are reported as liabilities, with offsets in the form of balances reporting the amounts available and the amounts to be provided in the future to meet such obligations. Upon the issuance of bonds, Amount To Be Provided for Retirement of Bonds is debited, and Bonds Payable is credited. Cash received upon issuing such bonds is not reported in the general long-term debt books but is accounted for in the capital projects funds as described earlier.

When a debt service fund is established for the retirement of bonds, the addition of resources to the fund is recorded in the general long-term debt group of accounts by a debit to Amount Provided for Retirement of Bonds and a credit to Amount To Be Provided for Retirement of Bonds. When debt service fund bonds mature and the debt service fund establishes a liability for matured bonds payable, the issue is canceled on the general long-term debt books by a debit to Bonds Payable and a credit to Amount Provided for Retirement of Bonds.

When payment of bonds is to be made from current revenues, recognition of maturing serial bonds or term bonds on the books of the debt service fund calls for an entry in the general long-term debt books debiting Bonds Payable and crediting Amount To Be Provided for Retirement of Bonds.

Statements for the General Long-Term Debt Group

Statements are prepared periodically from the general long-term debt group books. Statements normally include a statement of general long-term debt and statements summarizing changes in the individual long-term debt balances during the course of the period. A statement of general long-term debt for the City of A is as follows:

City of A
Statement of General Long-Term Debt
June 30, 19X4

Amount provided for retirement of bonds..	$ 10,350	General bonds — sinking fund bonds payable.............................	$100,000
Amount to be provided for retirement of bonds.............................	89,650		
Total...	$100,000	Total..	$100,000

It may be observed that some governmental units combine the general fixed assets and the general long-term debt items in a single set of books. In such instances the following procedures are frequently followed: (1) acquisition of fixed assets is recorded by a debit to the asset accounts and a credit to Excess of Fixed Assets over Long-Term Debt; (2) the disposal of a fixed asset is recorded by an entry reversing the entry made at the time of the asset acquisition; (3) the issue of general bonds is recorded by a debit to Excess of Fixed Assets over Long-Term Debt and a credit to Bonds Payable;

(4) the retirement of general long-term debt is recorded by an entry reversing the entry made at the time of the bond issue. A statement for the general fixed assets and long-term debt group would show fixed assets balanced by bonds payable and an excess of fixed assets over long-term debt.

The foregoing practice can be criticized on the grounds that there is normally no relationship between a governmental unit's general fixed assets and general long-term debt that would suggest their presentation on a single statement with a netted balance. Many of the fixed assets are acquired from current revenues, special assessments, and grants rather than from bond issues. On the other hand, general long-term debt, although in some instances incurred to finance fixed asset acquisitions, may also be incurred to meet general and special revenue fund deficits, to establish internal service funds, and to acquire public utilities and other enterprises. Normally bondholders can look only to the governmental unit's taxing powers and not to the fixed assets for settlement of its general long-term debt. Under these circumstances, general fixed assets and general long-term debt represent two separate aspects of a governmental unit's financial status. A combined statement of general fixed assets and general long-term debt is not considered to be in conformity with current generally accepted accounting principles.

COMBINED STATEMENTS

In addition to the separate statements for the different funds described on the preceding pages, it is normally desirable to prepare statements that show combined financial and operating data. A balance sheet may be prepared that shows assets, liabilities, and balances for all of the funds of a governmental unit. Certain summaries of revenues and expenditures for different funds can be presented in combined form to show the results of related activities. A statement of cash receipts and expenditures may report the cash transactions for all of the funds.

A combined balance sheet for the City of A may be prepared as illustrated on pages 806 and 807. The Combined Balance Sheet — All Funds, while showing a total column which aggregates account balances for all funds, also presents in columnar form the combined balance sheet data for each separate fund type. Because of the need for accountability of each individual fund, a combined balance sheet for all funds cannot take the place of separate fund balance sheets. A combined balance sheet may give the reader a general overview of the entire range of activities of the governmental unit, but individual fund financial statements are necessary to provide full accountability.

Note that the total column in which all balance sheet data are aggregated is marked "Memorandum Only." Totals for different fund types are not meaningful, since their measurement focuses are different.

City of A
Combined Balance Sheet — All Funds
June 30, 19X4

Assets	General Fund	Capital Projects Fund	Special Assessment Fund	Debt Service Fund	Central Print Shop	Trust Fund	Enterprise Fund	General Fixed Asset Accounts	General Long-Term Debt Accounts	Total (Memorandum Only)
Cash	$140,000	$30,000	$31,100	$500	$5,000	$5,300	$35,500			$247,400
Accounts and notes receivable (net)							38,500			38,500
Taxes receivable	40,000									40,000
Interest receivable			450	50						500
Due from general fund					10,000					10,000
Materials and supplies					12,000		12,000			24,000
Prepaid expenses							6,500			6,500
Investments				9,800		45,000				54,800
Cash and investments for debt service							30,000			30,000
Special assessments receivable — deferred			90,000							90,000
Land							50,000	$20,000		70,000
Structures and improvements (net)							130,000			130,000
Structures and improvements in progress								171,000		171,000
Equipment (net)					9,500		45,000	59,000		113,500
Unamortized bond issuance costs							2,500			2,500
Amount available and to be provided for retirement of bonds									$100,000	100,000
Totals	$180,000	$30,000	$121,550	$10,350	$36,500	$50,300	$350,000	$250,000	$100,000	$1,128,700

Liabilities									
Vouchers payable	$ 85,000	$ 11,000	$ 6,500		$11,000		$ 60,000		$ 173,500
Due to internal service fund	10,000								10,000
Accrued expenses							5,000		5,000
Interest payable			400						400
Contracts payable — retained percentage		5,000	8,500						13,500
Bonds payable			91,000				200,000	$100,000	391,000
Deferred revenues			90,000						90,000
Total liabilities	$ 95,000	$16,000	$196,400		$11,000		$265,000	$100,000	$ 683,400
Fund Equities									
Fund balance reserved for encumbrances	$ 50,000	$10,000	$10,000						$ 70,000
Fund balance	35,000	4,000	(84,850)	$10,350					(35,500)
Unappropriated retained earnings					$ 500		$ 5,000		5,500
Retained earnings appropriated for debt service							30,000		30,000
Capital contribution by general fund					25,000		50,000		75,000
Trust fund principal balance						$50,000			75,000
Trust fund income balance						300			300
Investment in general fixed assets								$250,000	250,000
Total fund equities	$ 85,000	$14,000	$ (74,850)	$10,350	$25,500	$50,300	$ 85,000	$250,000	$ 445,300
Totals	$180,000	$30,000	$121,550	$10,350	$36,500	$50,300	$350,000	$250,000	$100,000	$1,128,700

QUESTIONS

1. (a) Name and describe eight types of funds that might be found in a municipality. (b) Which of the funds named carry fixed assets among their resources? (c) Which of the funds named carry long-term indebtedness among their liabilities?

2. (a) What purposes are served by a special revenue fund? (b) How does such a fund originate? (c) How do special revenue fund operations compare with those of the general fund?

3. (a) Indicate the different purposes for which a general long-term debt may be incurred. (b) Assuming that bond proceeds are employed for public improvements, name the funds or account groups affected through such use and give the entries that would appear on the books of each. (c) What statements are prepared for a capital projects fund during the course of its operations?

4. Would you recommend that a system of encumbrances be employed in a capital projects fund? Give reasons for your answer.

5. What purposes are served by a special assessment fund? How does such a fund originate?

6. (a) Describe the nature of a debt service fund. (b) Assuming that the fund is ultimately applied to the retirement of bonds, name the funds affected by such action and give the entries that are made on the books of each.

7. (a) Describe the nature of an internal service fund. (b) What is the purpose of recognizing depreciation in summarizing activities in this fund? (c) Would you recommend that billings for goods and services be made at cost, at more than cost, or at less than cost? Give reasons for your answer.

8. List the possible dispositions of a remaining fund balance in:

    (a) the general fund.
    (b) a capital projects fund.
    (c) a special assessment fund.
    (d) a debt service fund.
    (e) an internal service fund.

9. Describe and give an example for each of the following:

    (a) An agency fund.
    (b) A trust fund that is expendable as to both principal and income.
    (c) A trust fund that is expendable as to income but nonexpendable as to principal.
    (d) A trust fund that is nonexpendable as to both principal and income.

10. (a) Give three examples of utilities that may be owned and operated by a governmental unit. (b) Give three examples of other enterprises that may be owned and operated by a governmental unit.

11. Give the entries that would be made on the general fixed assets books for each of the following transactions:

    (a) Certain equipment is acquired for general government purposes in accordance with special revenue fund appropriations.

(b) Certain equipment acquired by a special revenue fund is scrapped.

(c) Bonds are issued for construction of public buildings and the buildings are partly completed in the current period.

(d) Certain special assessment improvements begun in a previous period are completed in the current period.

(e) Certain buildings originally financed from general fund revenues are destroyed by fire.

12. Give the entries that would be made in the general long-term debt account group for each of the following transactions:

(a) Term bonds are issued for the construction of a freeway.

(b) Cash is transferred from the general fund to a debt service fund to provide for the ultimate retirement of bonds issued in (a).

(c) Serial bonds are issued for the construction of public buildings.

(d) Payment is made by the general fund of current serial bond maturities as well as interest on serial bonds.

13. Indicate for each account that follows the different funds or other books of account in which it might appear:

(a) Amount To Be Provided for Retirement of Bonds.

(b) Appropriations.

(c) Fund Balance Reserved for Encumbrances.

(d) Matured Bonds Payable.

(e) Deferred Revenues.

(f) Equipment.

(g) Expenditures.

(h) Estimated Revenues.

(i) Taxes Receivable.

(j) Bonds Payable.

(k) Interest Receivable.

14. Describe the nature of the combined balance sheet for a governmental unit.

EXERCISES

1. What are the entries to record the following transactions of a special revenue fund for the City of X?

(a) The budget is adopted providing for estimated revenues of $100,000 and appropriations of $90,000.

(b) Revenues totaling $105,000 are collected.

(c) Orders are placed for materials and supplies estimated to cost $40,000.

(d) Materials and supplies billed at $34,000 are received. These were estimated to cost $35,000 and were included in (c).

(e) Payments of $30,000 on billings relating to (d) are made.

(f) Salaries totaling $45,000 are paid.

(g) Accounts are closed at the end of the period.

2. What are the entries to record the following transactions of a capital projects fund for the City of X?

   (a) Bonds of $100,000 are authorized for the construction of a sewer sys-
       tem.
   (b) Bonds are sold at par.
   (c) Construction is completed at a cost of $95,000.
   (d) Accounts are closed and the remaining cash is transferred to the general
       fund.

3. What are the entries to record the following transactions of a special assessment fund for the City of X?

   (a) Improvements are authorized at a cost of $100,000. Forty percent of the
       cost is to be borne by the city, the balance by taxpayers.
   (b) Payment is received for the city's share of cost, and $60,000 is borrowed
       from an internal service fund to finance construction, pending collection
       of assessments from taxpayers.
   (c) Construction is completed at a cost of $100,000.
   (d) Collection of special assessments of $60,000 is made.
   (e) Payment is made to the internal service fund.
   (f) Accounts are closed.

4. Prepare the entries to record the following transactions of a central materials
storeroom on the books of this fund and on the books of any of the other funds
that are affected:

   (a) The general fund transfers $10,000 to a central materials storeroom in
       establishing the fund.
   (b) Materials are purchased and paid for, $8,000.
   (c) Salaries of $1,000 are paid.
   (d) Materials that cost $5,000 are requisitioned by the general fund depart-
       ments. Overhead at the rate of 6% is added to the cost of materials in
       the charge to these departments.
   (e) The book inventory of materials at the end of the period exceeds the
       physical inventory by $150.

5. The following transactions, among others, were completed by the City of
Monica. Prepare the journal entries to record the transactions on the books of all
of the funds affected.

   (a) Bonds of $100,000, for which a debt service fund had been established,
       matured and were paid by the debt service fund.
   (b) Bonds of $100,000 were authorized and sold at par to finance a general
       fund deficit. Bonds pay 4% interest and are due in 10 years.
   (c) Twenty-year, 4½% bonds of $200,000 were sold at par to finance con-
       struction.
   (d) The project financed from the bonds referred to in (c) was completed.
       The construction expenditures balance in the amount of $197,000 was
       closed; the balance in the capital projects fund was transferred to the
       debt service fund.
   (e) Special assessment improvements in the amount of $500,000 were au-
       thorized. Special assessment notes of $350,000 were sold at par to fi-
       nance current construction. Assessments of $350,000 were levied on pri-
       vate property, the remainder of the cost to be paid by the municipality.
       The municipality authorized the issuance of 10-year, 5% bonds in financ-

ing its share of the cost, $150,000. The bonds were sold at a premium of $1,000. Bond proceeds were transferred to the special assessment fund.

6. The following transactions are completed by the City of Fairview during the course of a fiscal period. Prepare the entries that would be made on the general fixed assets and general long-term debt books.

(a) Equipment to be paid for by the general fund is ordered at an estimated cost of $20,000 and is subsequently received at a cost of $19,400.
(b) Buildings originally acquired by expenditures of $40,000 from the general fund are dismantled, and salvage of $1,500 is recovered; salvage proceeds were made available to the general fund.
(c) Equipment costing $2,500 is destroyed by fire.
(d) Equipment originally acquired by an expenditure of $5,000 from the general fund is no longer useful and is traded in for similar new equipment costing $6,500. A $500 trade-in allowance is received on the old equipment.
(e) Bonds of $100,000 due in 10 years and with interest at 8½%, payable semiannually, are issued for an addition to a library. The addition is completed at a cost of $95,000 and $5,000 is transferred from the capital projects fund to a debt service fund.

PROBLEMS

24-1. In 19X2 Garden City authorizes the widening of First Street at a cost of $500,000. The project is to be financed one fourth by general fund contributions and the balance by property owners in the special assessment district.

The city pays its share of the cost in 19X2, and $375,000 is borrowed from Garden City Bank to finance construction activities pending collection of special assessments.

Payments of $100,000 are made to property owners in 19X2 for the land required in the street widening project. In December, 19X2, a contract is awarded to the Peerless Construction Co. for the work to be done at an estimated cost of $400,000.

The project is completed in 19X3 and settlement is made with the contractors at $415,000. The general fund contributes $15,000 to complete payment on the contract.

Collections are made from the property owners of the full amount of the special assessments, plus interest and penalties totaling $39,000, during the period 19X3–19X7. During this period collection proceeds are used to pay off the obligation to the bank, together with interest charges over the 5-year period totaling $33,200. At the end of 19X7 the balance of special assessment fund cash is transferred to the general fund and the special assessment books are closed.

Instructions: (1) Prepare all of the entries that are required on the books of the special assessment fund for the period 19X2–19X7.

(2) Prepare a balance sheet for the special assessment fund showing its position as of December 31, 19X2.

24-2. The following are the transactions of a central storehouse during 19X5:

(a) The fund is established by a contribution of $100,000 by the general fund.

(b) Supplies of $125,000 are purchased on account.

(c) Salaries and miscellaneous expenses of $4,000 are paid.

(d) Supplies costing $56,000 are requisitioned by general fund departments. The general fund is billed for the cost of supplies plus 6% of such cost, which is estimated to cover departmental overhead.

(e) Cash of $45,000 is received on general fund billings.

(f) Payments of $112,500 are made on account.

(g) The following information is recorded at the end of the fiscal period. Accrued salaries and expenses are $400. A physical count of the supplies on hand shows an inventory that is $160 less than the book inventory.

Instructions: (1) Prepare the journal entries to record the transactions of the central storehouse, including adjusting and closing entries at the end of 19X5.

(2) Prepare (a) a balance sheet and (b) a statement of operations for the year ended December 31, 19X5.

24-3. The ledger balances of the Water Department of Valley City on December 31, 19X7, were as follows:

Cash — operating fund	$ 588,800	Accounts payable — trade	$ 47,000
Cash — consumers' deposits	17,000	Accounts payable — township	56,000
Postage on meter	1,000	Water consumers' deposits	67,000
Accounts receivable:		Revenue bonds payable	300,000
Consumer billing	65,000	Accumulated depreciation	1,200,000
Service	17,000	Retained earnings	4,500,000
Sundry	700	Revenue	1,500,000
Due from other funds	—	Expense:	
Supplies inventory	140,000	Production	340,000
Merchandise on order and in		Distribution	151,000
transit	145,000	Office	90,000
Investments — consumers'		Administrative and general	105,000
deposits	50,000	Cost of installations, repairs	
Property	6,000,000	and parts	140,000
Unfilled orders and contracts	145,000	Interest on consumers' de-	
Warrants payable	50,100	posits	600
Due to other funds	—	Interest on bonds	9,000
Advance service payments	—	Allowances and adjustments	5,000

NOTE: *Revenue bonds mature serially $30,000 each year.*

Examination of the records disclosed the following additional data:

(a) Included in error in accounts payable — trade:

(1) For reimbursement of metered postage .... $ 500

(2) Due to other city funds 18,500

(b) Items included in book inventory that were not received until 19X8 2,000

(c) Computation of inventory items chargeable to distribution expense understated 1,000

(d) Classified as accounts payable trade, should be accounts payable township 10,000

(e) Unfilled orders not of record 1,000

(f) 19X8 expense purchases recorded as 19X7 liabilities and charged to expense as follows:

    (1) Production expense... $500

    (2) Distribution expense.. 500

    (3) Office expense.. 500

    (4) Administrative and general expense 500

(g) Included in accounts receivable — service, but actually due from other funds.. 500

(h) Credit balances included in accounts receivable — service, advance service payments... 1,000

(i) Included in accounts receivable sundry but due from other city funds.. 50

(j) Required adjustment to reduce unfilled orders and contracts to proper estimates 2,600

(k) Purchase order included in unfilled orders and contracts. This order is a duplication of a previously recorded expenditure 40,000

(l) Unrecorded receivable from township for water 5,000

Instructions: (1) Prepare a work sheet showing the original trial balance, the adjustments, and the extended operating and balance sheet accounts for the Water Department of Valley City for the year ended December 31, 19X7.

(2) Prepare a balance sheet as of December 31, 19X7.

(3) Prepare an operating statement for the year ended December 31, 19X7.

(AICPA adapted)

24-4. The following information pertains to the operation of the water fund of the City of S. Included in the operations of this fund are those of a special replacement fund for the Water Department, the accounts of which are a part of the accounts of the water fund.

The balances in the accounts of this fund on January 1, 19X5, were:

Cash...	$ 6,126
Accounts receivable	7,645
Supplies.....................................	13,826
Investments of replacement fund..	21,700
Permanent property......................	212,604
Accounts payable.........................	4,324
Customers' deposits	1,500
Replacement fund reserve............	21,700
Retained earnings	21,773
Bonds payable	60,000
Municipal contribution.................	152,604

The following items represent the total transactions of the fund for the year ended December 31, 19X5.

(a) Services billed... $146,867

(b) Accounts collected 147,842

(c) Uncollectible accounts of prior years written off 1,097

(d) Invoices and payrolls approved for current expense.............. 69,826

(e) Invoices approved for purchase of water department supplies.. 31,424

(f) Supplies issued for use in operation 32,615

(g) Supplies secured from general fund and used in operation (cash transferred to general fund) 7,197

(h) Vouchers approved for payment of bonds and interest of $3,000 23,000

(i) Depreciation entered as charge against current income and credited to replacement reserve 10,600

(j) Deposits received 400

Deposits refunded 240

(k) Invoices approved for replacements of equipment that cost $6,200 7,800

(l) Invoices approved for additions to plant 12,460

(m) Vouchers approved for purchase of securities necessary to fully invest the replacement fund .... compute

(n) Income received on investments 1,102

(o) Warrants drawn for invoices, payrolls and vouchers approved 147,316

Instructions: Prepare from the above information (1) a balance sheet of the fund as of December 31, 19X5, (2) an operating statement of the water department for 19X5, and (3) an analysis of the retained earnings of the water fund for 19X5.

(AICPA adapted)

24-5. Trial balances for Bensonville City on July 1, 19X3, were as follows:

General Fund

Cash.	35,000	
Delinquent Taxes Receivable.	30,000	
Allowance for Uncollectible Delinquent Taxes		10,000
Inventories.	22,500	
Vouchers Payable		60,000
Fund Balance Reserved for Encumbrances		7,500
Fund Balance Reserved for Inventories		22,500
Fund Balance.	12,500	
	100,000	100,000

General Fixed Assets

Land	120,000	
Buildings and Improvements	400,000	
Equipment.	66,500	
Investment in General Fixed Assets.		586,500
	586,500	586,500

General Long-Term Debt

Amount To Be Provided for Retirement of Bonds	250,000	
Bonds Payable.		250,000
	250,000	250,000

The budget adopted for the fiscal year 19X3–19X4 was as follows:

Estimated revenues	$220,000
Appropriations	207,500
Available fund balance	$ 12,500

The city council levied taxes of $125,000 for the year. Uncollectible taxes were estimated at 5%. Collections on the current tax levy totaled $115,000. Collections on delinquent taxes were $12,500 which included penalties and interest of $1,000. Receipts from other sources during the year totaled $90,000.

Vouchers relating to current-year commitments totaling $200,000 were approved and included the following: salaries and services, $115,000; buildings and improvements, $50,000; equipment, $25,000; interest on bonds, $10,000. The cost of buildings and improvements exceeded the original estimate, and a supplementary appropriation of $15,000 was passed by the City Council to permit the completion of this project. Vouchers totaling $7,000 in liquidation of all of the prior-year commitments were approved. On June 30, 19X4, there were unliquidated commitments of $20,000 for equipment. Orders for the equipment had been placed pursuant to current appropriations, but equipment had not yet been received. Vouchers paid during the year totaled $215,000.

During the year, equipment of $11,500 that was no longer usable was retired. Inventories on hand at the end of the year totaled $18,000. Unpaid taxes were transferred to the delinquent taxes account.

Instructions: (1) Prepare the entries in general journal form to record the transactions of the general fund and to close the accounts at the end of the year.

(2) Prepare a balance sheet and an analysis of changes in fund balance in condensed form for the general fund.

(3) Prepare the required entries in general journal form for the general fixed assets account group.

(4) Prepare statements at the end of the year for the general fixed assets account group.

24-6. Mills City maintains only one fund, the general fund, and two account groups. Statements for Mills City at the end of 19X8 show the following balances:

General Fund

Cash..		$52,250	Vouchers payable.........................	$36,000
Delinquent taxes receivable...........................	$25,000		Fund balance reserved for encumbrances..................................	15,000
Less allowance for uncollectible taxes..............	10,000	15,000	Unreserved fund balance	16,250
		$67,250		$67,250

Statement of General Fixed Assets

Land, buildings, and improvements	$ 400,000		Investment in fixed assets financed from:	
Equipment............................	850,000		General fund revenues....	$ 800,000
			Bonds	450,000
	$1,250,000			$1,250,000

Statement of General Long-Term Debt

Amount to be provided for retirement of bonds	$600,000	Bonds payable..........................	$600,000

Transactions of the city during 19X9 were as follows:

(a) A budget for 19X9 was adopted as follows:

Estimated revenues:

Taxes — 19X9	$400,000	
Licenses and permits	60,000	
Fines and penalties	40,000	
Revenues from other agencies	35,000	$535,000

Appropriations:

General government	$100,000	
Public safety	180,000	
Highways	60,000	
Sanitation and health	45,000	
Charities	30,000	
Bond retirement and interest	120,000	$535,000

(b) Taxes of $420,000 were levied; an allowance of $20,000 was established for possible losses on tax collections, and revenue of $400,000 was recognized on the levy.

(c) Cash receipts during 19X9 were as follows:

Delinquent taxes	$ 6,000	
Current taxes	380,000	
Licenses and permits	64,000	
Fines and penalties	39,500	
Revenues accruing from state government	35,000	$524,500

(d) Vouchers were approved during 19X9 for the following:

General government	$ 96,750	
Public safety	166,000	
Highways	49,600	
Sanitation and health	44,000	
Charities	29,800	
Bond retirement	100,000	
Interest on bonds	20,000	
In full liquidation of encumbrances outstanding on January 1, 19X9	14,200	$520,350

These expenditures included a total of $50,000 for equipment and $35,000 for buildings and improvements.

(e) Checks drawn in payment of vouchers totaled $525,250.

(f) Current encumbrances unliquidated at the end of 19X9 were as follows:

General government	$ 1,800	
Public safety	11,600	
Highways	10,000	$23,400

Instructions: (1) Prepare the entries in general journal form to record the transactions of the general fund and to close the accounts at the end of the period.

(2) Prepare for the general fund: (a) a balance sheet, (b) a statement of revenue — estimated and actual, (c) a statement of expenditures and encum-

brances — compared with authorizations, and (d) an analysis of changes in fund balance.

(3) Prepare the entries in general journal form required on the general fixed assets books.

(4) Prepare statements at the end of the year for the general fixed assets.

24-7. Statements for the City of X on June 30, 19X7, showed balances as follows:

General Fund

Cash	$50,000	Vouchers payable	$30,000
Taxes receivable — delinquent	25,000	Fund balance reserved for encumbrances	20,000
		Unreserved fund balance	25,000
	$75,000		$75,000

General Fixed Assets

Land and improvements	$700,000	Investment in general fixed assets financed from bonds	$950,000
Equipment	250,000		
	$950,000		$950,000

General Long-Term Debt

Amount to be provided for payment of principal	$1,280,000	Bonds payable	$1,280,000

Transactions of the city for the year ended June 30, 19X8, follow:

(a) The budget for the year showed revenues estimated at $750,000 and appropriations of $745,000.

(b) A bond issue was authorized for the construction of a recreation center at a cost of $100,000, and bonds were sold at par. The interest rate on the bonds is 10%; bonds mature at the end of 10 years.

(c) A debt service fund was established for retirement of the recreation center bonds. Required contributions for the first year were $9,000, and required earnings were $400. Interest on the bonds will be paid by the general fund.

(d) Taxes of $500,000 were assessed to finance general fund activities.

(e) A street widening project of $125,000 was authorized.

(f) Property owners were assessed $75,000 for the street project, the city to contribute the balance. Contributions from each source were payable in 10 equal annual installments.

(g) Contracts were entered into with Fulton and Flagg, Inc., for construction of the recreation center at a cost of $80,000 and with Powers Construction Co. for the street widening at a cost of $85,000.

(h) Taxes were collected as follows:

General taxes — delinquent	$ 5,000
General taxes — current	480,000
Special assessment taxes	7,200

Unpaid current taxes were transferred to delinquent tax accounts.

(i) Additional revenues collected by the general fund totaled $235,000.

(j) General fund encumbrances outstanding on June 30, 19X7, were fully liquidated by the approval of vouchers for $18,250. Various equipment items costing $2,400 were included in this total.

(k) Vouchers were approved for current expenditures of the general fund totaling $690,000. This amount included $50,000 for the current maturities of general bonds which are not covered by a debt service fund, $20,000 for interest on bonds, and $65,000 representing the cost of various equipment items.

(l) General fund encumbrances outstanding on June 30, 19X8, total $35,000.

(m) Vouchers totaling $716,500 were paid by the general fund.

(n) The general fund transferred cash of $9,000 to the debt service fund and $5,000 to the special assessment fund. (These items are not included in the expenditures or payments mentioned previously.)

(o) Bonds of $112,500 were sold by the special assessment fund at par to finance completion of the project.

(p) The debt service fund acquired U.S. Government bonds at par as an investment, paying $8,500 plus accrued interest, $150.

(q) Interest of $450 was collected on investments by the debt service fund. Accrued interest on the bond investments on June 30, 19X8, is $60.

(r) Payment of $20,500 was made to property owners for land required in the street widening project.

(s) Billing was received for work done to date and payment was made as follows: to Fulton and Flagg, Inc., $50,000; to Powers Construction Co., $25,000.

Instructions: (1) Prepare the entries in general journal form that would be required on the books of each of the funds and account groups for the City of X, including any entries required on June 30, 19X8, the end of the fiscal year.

(2) Prepare a combined balance sheet for the City of X as of June 30, 19X8.

24-8. The following budget was proposed for 19X4 for the Blue Valley School District general fund:

General fund balance, January 1, 19X4.....................................	$128,000
Revenues:	
Taxes...	112,000
Investment income..	4,000
Total...	$244,000
Expenditures:	
Operating...	$120,000
County treasurer's fees...	1,120
Bond interest..	50,000
General fund balance, December 31, 19X4................................	72,880
Total...	$244,000

A general obligation bond issue of the school district was proposed in 19X3. The proceeds are to be used for a new school. There are no other outstanding bond issues. Information about the bond issue follows:

Face: $1,000,000
Interest rate: 10%
Bonds dated: January 1, 19X4
Coupons mature: January 1 and July 1 beginning July 1, 19X4
Bonds mature serially at $100,000 per year starting January 1, 19X6.

The school district uses a separate bank account for each fund. The general fund trial balance at December 31, 19X3, follows:

Cash..	28,000	
Temporary Investments — U.S. 8% Bonds, interest payable May 1 and November 1	100,000	
Fund Balance...		128,000
	128,000	128,000

The county treasurer will collect the taxes and charge a standard fee of 1% on all collections. The transactions for 19X4 were as follows:

January 1 — The proposed budget was adopted, the general obligation bond issue was authorized, and the taxes were levied.
February 28 — Tax receipts from the county treasurer, $49,500, were deposited.
April 1 — The bond issue was sold at 101 plus accrued interest. It was directed that the premium be used for payment of interest.
April 2 — The school district disbursed $47,000 for the new school site.
April 3 — A contract for $950,000 for the new school was approved.
May 1 — Interest was received on temporary investments.
July 1 — Interest was paid on bonds.
August 31 — Tax receipts from the county treasurer, $59,400, were deposited.
November 1 — Payment was made on new school construction contract, $200,000.
December 31 — Operating expenses of $115,000 were paid during the year.

Instructions: Prepare journal entries to record the 19X4 transactions in the following funds or account groups:

(1) General fund.
(2) Capital projects fund.
(3) General fixed assets.
(4) General long-term debt.

(AICPA adapted)

24-9. The city hall capital projects fund was established on July 1, 19X6, to account for the construction of a new city hall financed by the sale of bonds. The building was to be constructed on a site owned by the city.

The building construction was to be financed by the issuance of 10-year, $2,000,000 general obligation bonds bearing interest at 10%. Through prior arrangements, $1,000,000 of these bonds were sold on July 1, 19X6. The remaining bonds are to be sold on July 1, 19X7.

The only funds in which transactions pertaining to the new city hall were recorded were the city hall capital projects fund and the general fund. The capital projects fund's trial balance on June 30, 19X7, follows:

Cash..	893,000	
Expenditures..	140,500	
Encumbrances	715,500	
Accounts Payable		11,000
Fund Balance Reserved for Encumbrances...........		723,000
Appropriations...		1,015,000
	1,749,000	1,749,000

An analysis of the expenditures account follows:

	Debit
(a) A progress billing invoice from General Construction Company (with which the city contracted for the construction of the new city hall for $750,000 — other contracts will be let for heating, air conditioning, etc.) showing 10% of the work completed	$ 75,000
(b) A charge from the general fund for work done in clearing the building site..	11,000
(c) Payments to suppliers for building materials and supplies purchased	14,500
(d) Payment of interest on bonds outstanding............................	40,000
	$140,500

An analysis of the fund balance reserved for encumbrances account follows:

	Debit (Credit)
(a) To record contract with General Construction Company........	($750,000)
(b) Purchase orders placed for materials and supplies...............	(55,000)
(c) Receipt and payment of materials and supplies	14,500
(d) Payment of General Construction Company invoice less 10% retention	67,500
	($723,000)

An analysis of the appropriations account follows:

	Debit (Credit)
(a) Face value of bonds sold..	($1,000,000)
(b) Premium realized on sale of bonds....................................	(15,000)
	($1,015,000)

Instructions: (1) Prepare a work sheet for the city hall capital projects fund at June 30, 19X7, showing:

(a) Preliminary trial balance.
(b) Adjustments.
(c) Adjusted trial balance.

(2) Prepare the adjusting journal entries for the following funds and groups of accounts (closing entries are not required):

(a) General fixed assets.
(b) General fund.
(c) General long-term debt.   (AICPA adapted)

24-10. The Village of Hope, by referendum on November 30, 19X2, was authorized to sell bonds, the proceeds of which were to be used for constructing a municipal building to provide adequate facilities for the offices and departments of the village. The cost of the building was estimated to be $90,000, and the ordinance provided for the issuance of general obligation bonds in that amount, at an interest rate of 9% per annum. Bonds were to be dated January 1, 19X3, and were to become due and payable in equal annual installments on January 1 of each year for nine years beginning in 19X5. Interest was to be due semiannually on January 1 and July 1, except that the first coupon was to be due on July 1, 19X4. Bonds were to be payable out of the proceeds of a direct annual tax sufficient to pay the principal and interest when due.

The village advertised for bids on the bonds, and on January 15, 19X3, the bids were opened and the bonds were awarded to Municipal Bond Co.

The following transactions occurred:

(a) November 30, 19X2 — Bonds were authorized in accordance with the referendum.

(b) February 1, 19X3 — Bonds were sold to Municipal Bond Co. and a certified check was received in the amount of $94,086, including premium and accrued interest at an annual rate of 9% to date of sale.

(c) February 10, 19X3 — Initial architectural fees of $2,000 were paid to the firm that prepared the plans and specifications and was to have construction supervision. The fee for their services was to be 6% of the building cost.

(d) April 15, 19X3 — The general contractor had bid $81,400 to construct the building. The first contractor's estimate in the amount of $30,000 was received from the architect, properly approved. The estimate was paid, less 10% retained until the building was accepted by the village.

(e) July 30, 19X3 (entry as of September 1, 19X3) — The appropriation ordinance of the village for the fiscal year ending August 31, 19X4, was adopted. The ordinance contained provision for the retirement of the bonds due on January 1, 19X5, and interest due through that date. It has been the experience of the village that the tax levy should provide an additional 3% to provide for uncollectible taxes.

(f) September 20, 19X3 — The final contractor's invoice was received in the amount of $54,500, including approved extras totaling $3,100. The invoice was paid less a 10% retention. At the same time, an invoice in the amount of $2,000 was paid to the architects.

(g) December 21, 19X3 — Final approval of the building was given by the architect and the board of trustees and final payments were made to the general contractor and the architect.

Instructions: Journalize the preceding transactions. Prepare entries for each of the applicable funds, and key the entries to the transaction letter indicated. No entries need to be considered to close out the various revenue and expenditure accounts at August 31, 19X3.

(AICPA adapted)

24-11. Bonds of $5,000,000 are authorized by the voters of Oak City for the construction of a health center. The following transactions take place in 19X1:

(a) The bonds are sold at par, $5,000,000. Bonds pay interest at 10% and are due at the end of 10 years.
(b) Land is purchased for cash at a cost of $1,200,000.
(c) A contract is entered into for construction of the center at a cost of $3,200,000.
(d) Payments are authorized on the construction contract totaling $1,700,000.

The project is completed in 19X2 when the following transactions take place:

(a) The contractors are paid the balance owed on the contract, $1,500,000, plus extras of $160,000.
(b) Payments are made for miscellaneous expenditures totaling $406,200, incurred during the course of construction.
(c) A debt service fund is established through general fund appropriations of $300,000 per year. Transfer of $300,000 is made by the general fund and, in addition, bond interest amounting to $500,000 is transferred from general fund appropriations.
(d) The balance of cash in the capital projects fund is transferred to the debt service fund.

Instructions: (1) Prepare all of the entries required on the capital projects fund books for 19X1 and 19X2. Assume that closing entries are made at the end of 19X1 and also upon completion of the project.

(2) Prepare a balance sheet for the capital projects fund as of December 31, 19X1.

(3) Prepare any entries affecting (a) the general fund books, (b) the general fixed assets account group, (c) the general long-term debt account group, and (d) the debt service fund books.

24-12. Sunshine City entered into the following transactions during the year 19X6:

(a) A bond issue was authorized by vote to provide funds for the construction of a new municipal building, which it was estimated would cost $500,000. The bonds were to be paid in 10 equal installments from a debt service fund, payments being due March 1 of each year. Any balance of the capital projects fund is to be transferred directly to the debt service fund.
(b) An advance of $40,000 was received from the general fund to underwrite a deposit of $60,000 on the land contract. The deposit was made.
(c) Bonds of $450,000 were sold for cash at 102. It was decided not to sell all of the bonds because the cost of the land was less than was expected.
(d) Contracts amounting to $390,000 were let to Michela and Company, the lowest bidder, for the construction of the municipal building.
(e) The temporary advance from the general fund was repaid and the balance on the land contract was paid.
(f) Based on the architect's certificate, warrants were issued for $320,000 for the work completed to date.
(g) Warrants paid in cash by the treasurer amounted to $310,000.
(h) Due to changes in the plans, the contract with Michela and Company was revised to $440,000; the remainder of the bonds were sold at 101.

(i) Before the end of the year the building had been completed and additional warrants amounting to $115,000 were issued to the contractor in final payment for the work. All warrants were paid by the treasurer.

Instructions: (1) Record the transactions and the closing entries in capital projects fund T accounts. Designate the entries in the T accounts by the letters that identify the data.

(2) Prepare applicable fund balance sheets as of December 31, 19X6, considering only the proceeds and the expenditures from capital projects fund transactions.

(AICPA adapted)

24-13. In a special election held on May 1, 19X7, the voters of the city of Necknar approved a $10,000,000 issue of 20-year, 6% general obligation bonds. The proceeds of this sale will be used to help finance the construction of a new civic center. The total cost of the project was estimated at $15,000,000. The remaining $5,000,000 will be financed by an irrevocable state grant which has been awarded. A capital projects fund was established to account for this project and was designated the Civic Center Construction Fund. The formal project authorization was appropriately recorded in a memorandum entry.

The following transactions occurred during the fiscal year beginning July 1, 19X7, and ending June 30, 19X8:

(a) On July 1, the general fund loaned $500,000 to the Civic Center Construction Fund for defraying engineering and other expenses.
(b) Preliminary engineering and planning costs of $320,000 were paid to Akron Engineering Company. There had been no encumbrance for this cost.
(c) On December 1, the bonds were sold at 101. The premium on bonds was transferred to the Debt Service Fund.
(d) On March 15, a contract for $12,000,000 was entered into with Candu Construction Company for the major part of the project.
(e) Orders were placed for materials estimated to cost $55,000.
(f) On April 1, a partial payment of $2,500,000 was received from the state.
(g) The materials that were previously ordered were received at a cost of $51,000 and paid.
(h) On June 15, a progress billing of $2,000,000 was received from Candu Construction for work done on the project. As per the terms of the contract, the city will withhold 6% of any billing until the project is completed.
(i) The General Fund was repaid the $500,000 previously loaned.

Instructions: (1) Prepare journal entries to record the transactions in the Civic Center Construction Fund for the period July 1, 19X7, through June 30, 19X8, and the appropriate closing entries at June 30, 19X8.

(2) Prepare journal entries to record the transactions in any other funds and account groups that may be required.

(AICPA adapted)

24-14. The City of Fairview, organized twenty years ago, has never kept accounts on a double-entry system. During 19X8 the city council employed you to install a system of accounts. You made a study and determined the values of assets and liabilities in order to inaugurate the proper system as of January 1, 19X9, the beginning of the city's fiscal year, as follows:

(a) City taxes receivable — 19X8 and prior years (including 10% considered uncollectible) .... $ 21,900

(b) Investment in securities:
    (1) Earmarked to bond retirement..................................... 136,680
    (2) Donated by J. C. Belmont on July 1, 19X8, the net income from which is to supplement library operations. The cost of all the stock to Belmont was $50,000. Appraised value on July 1 65,400

(c) Cash:
    (1) For general operations, including $3,000 in petty cash.... 18,000
    (2) Earmarked to investments for bond retirement (represents interest earned over the actuarial estimate)........... 840
    (3) Balance of cash donated by J. C. Belmont, the net income from which is to supplement library operations...... 12,000
    (4) Undistributed balance of cash received from J. C. Belmont investments and apartment rents......................... 3,000

(d) Buildings:
    (1) For general operations.. 235,000
    (2) Apartment building donated by J. C. Belmont on July 1, 19X8. Net income to be used in the operation of the library. Cost of completion to Belmont ten years ago, $96,000 (exclusive of cost of land) with estimated life of 50 years, no salvage. Appraised value on July 1, 19X8..... 90,000

(e) Equipment:
    (1) For general use... 280,000
    (2) Apartment furniture purchased with donated cash, October 1, 19X8, estimated life 10 years, no salvage. Cost .. 36,000

(f) Streets and curbs built by special assessment funds in prior years. (All collected.) The city contributed ⅓ of the cost....... 300,000

(g) Land:
    (1) For general use... 60,000
    (2) For apartment building site...................................... 10,000

(h) Supplies:
    (1) For general operation 1,800
    (2) For apartment house operation, purchased by income cash.. 300
    (3) Originally purchased for general operation, transferred to and used in library operations; no settlement has been made.. 2,400

(i) Vouchers payable — for general operations......................... 16,000

(j) 10%, 30-year bonds payable. (Issued for purchase of land, buildings and equipment.)... 400,000

Instructions: List the funds or account group titles that would be required for the city on the basis of this information, leaving at least 15 lines between each title. Under each title make one summary journal entry that will record all of the required accounts and amounts in that fund or account group.

(AICPA adapted)

24-15. The balance sheet for the Town of Z was prepared on June 30, 19X4, as follows:

Town of Z
Balance Sheet
June 30, 19X4

Assets

Current:		
Cash..	$ 50,000	
Taxes receivable (including special assessments of $80,000)...	100,000	
Supply inventories	10,000	
Investments of trust funds.....................................	30,000	$ 190,000
Fixed:		
Land..	$100,000	
Buildings	800,000	
Equipment...	50,000	950,000
		$1,140,000

Liabilities and Fund Equity

Current:		
Accounts payable..		$ 10,000
Fixed:		
General obligation bonds payable..........................	$350,000	
Special assessment bonds payable	75,000	425,000
Fund equities:		
General fund	$ 35,000	
Trust funds	40,000	
Capital projects fund..	25,000	
Special assessment fund	5,000	
Capital fund	600,000	705,000
		$1,140,000

During the first month of its fiscal year starting July 1, 19X4, the following events took place relative to the general fund:

- (a) A budget was adopted that provided for property taxes of $210,000 for general municipal purposes and for estimated revenue of $23,000 from fees. Appropriations were $180,000 for current operations, $20,000 for debt service, and $35,000 for street and other capital improvements.
- (b) During July, purchase orders of $9,400 were placed, $3,150 of which were received and vouchered at an actual net cost of $3,078. Payroll amounting to $5,185 was vouchered, and $14,000 of accounts payable were paid.
- (c) $21,000 of 19X3–19X4 taxes were collected, $18,350 of which were special assessments. Also, $466 of delinquent taxes and penalties were collected. These taxes had been written off and no amount was in the cur-

rent budget for such collections. Miscellaneous fees collected amounted to $2,060.

(d) Inventory of supplies at the end of the month was $10,400.

Instructions: (1) Rearrange the balance sheet as of June 30, 19X4, in acceptable form.

(2) Prepare a balance sheet for the general fund at the end of the first month of the new fiscal year, July 31, 19X4.

(AICPA adapted)

Check Figures

Prob. No.	Check Figures
1-1	(2) Partners' capitals, Dec. 31, 19X0: Allen, $69,770; Bailey, $24,930.
1-2	(3) Partners' capitals, July 1, 19X6: Baker, $31,500; Carr, $47,250.
1-3	(3) Partners' shares of profits: Cross, $20,000; Deming, $10,000.
1-4	(4) Bonus to Clark, $4,760.
1-5	Capitals, Dec. 31, 19X7: Evans, $55,522; Gale, $56,583.
1-6	Bonus to Miller, $1,620.
1-7	Capitals, Sept. 1, 19X2: Bedford, $34,720; Brown, $55,280.
1-8	Distribution of cash, Nov. 1, 19X9: M, $16,350; N, $825; O, $2,825.
1-9	Marsh overcharge, $850.
1-10	Total required earnings, $64,666.67.
1-11	Capitals after cash distribution: X, $41,640; Y, $20,820; Z, $6,940.
1-12	Distribution of cash, June 30, 19X7: B, $11,016; C, $11,191; D, $7,791.
1-13	A, Capital, Dec. 31, 19X9, $30,040.
2-1	Capitals, April 1, 19X8: Collins, $78,125; Cox, $46,875; Curry, $31,250.
2-2	(5) Goodwill, $6,400.
2-3	(3) Goodwill, $12,000.
2-4	(6) Bonuses: to M, $7,500; to N, $2,500.
2-5	Capitals, Dec. 31, 19X3: X, $59,225; Y, $40,375; Z, $57,000.
2-6	Capitals, Dec. 31, 19X6: Caine, $53,000; Osman, $16,400; Roberts, $3,000.
2-7	Corrected balances, Dec. 31, 19X9: A, $32,125; B, $33,625; C, $51,900.
2-8	Distribution of cash, Jan., 19X5: Ross, $11,330; Sears, $4,850; Thomas, $1,320.
2-9	(2) Capitals: D, $54,450.51; E, $46,837.89.
2-10	Capitals in new partnership: A, $90,000; B, $135,000; C, $67,500; D, $157,500.
2-11	Corrected profits, 19X5, $4,000.
2-12	Income distribution: Alston, $5,650; Bailey, $5,650; Carter, $14,650.
2-13	Partners' equities, Nov. 1, 19X8: A, $26,750; B, $80,250; C, $121,000; D, $18,100; F, $10,700.
2-14	Goodwill on Catron's books, $14,600.
3-1	Cash distribution: Gordon, $9,125; Haller, $1,525.
3-2	(e) Payment to C, $38,000.
3-3	Payment by Carl to Decker and Eaton, $1,400 each.
3-4	Payments to partners: A, $35,000; D, $8,750.
3-5	(2) Amount available for P's personal creditors, $16,750.
3-6	(3) Payments to Z by W and Y, $500 each.

Prob. No.	Check Figures
3-7	Payment to partners: A, $5,000; B, $2,500.
3-8	(3) Amount owed by Ball to Allen, $4,940.
3-9	M receives 15 shares of Bay Corp., and 140 shares of Cory Stores.
3-10	(2) Amount that must be realized on sale of assets, $49,850.
4-1	Investment by Tucker in July, $4,200.
4-2	Investment by Hoffman in October, $2,200.
4-3	October installment to partners: A, $18,250; B, $10,950; C, $7,300.
4-4	April installment to partners: D, $8,750; E, $6,750; F, $4,500.
4-5	April installment to partners: on loans, K, $1,240; N, $100; on capitals, L, $720; M, $720; N, $620.
4-6	March distribution: Quade, $2,948; Rogers, $4,422; Stanford, $4,422; True, $1,858.
4-7	(2) Cash return to partners in August: F, $9,500; G, $3,125; H, $2,375.
4-8	(2) Cash to partners in March: R, $23,625; S, $14,175; T, $7,200.
4-9	(2) Cash to partners in February: W, $18,750; X, $3,750; Y, $8,750; Z, $8,750.
4-10	First $4,500 to A.
4-11	(2) Cash to partners: Burke, $2,450; Cox, $5,550; Drake, $1,700.
4-12	(2) Cash distribution for September: Arthur, $41,500; Brown, $26,400; Cook, $8,600.
4-13	Payment by Drew to Carter in final settlement, $177.
4-14	(1) Payment by Newman in final settlement: to Lane, $20,330; to Morris, $29,650.
4-15	(1) Payment by Olson in final settlement: to Moore, $69,600; to Morris, $54,550.
4-16	(c) A receives $1,280: $1,005 from B and $275 from C.
5-1	(1) Gross profit on sale, $57,200.
5-2	Net loss for 19X4, $7,604.58.
5-3	Total realized gross profit, $52,080.
5-4	(2) Net loss for 19X4, $13,585.
5-5	(3) Net loss for 19X8, $3,150.
5-6	Realized gross profit, $117,000.
5-7	Total realized gross profit, $57,625.
5-8	(1) Total realized gross profit, $172,852.50.
5-9	(3) Net loss on defaults, $854.40. (4) Total realized gross profit, $105,120.40.
5-10	(3) Total deferred gross profit, 12/31/X3, $37,384.
5-11	(2) Total realized gross profit, $11,403.13. (3) Gain on repossession, $6,653.33.
5-12	(2) Taxable income, $16,850.
5-13	(3) Balance of principal, Dec. 31, $1,420.77.
5-14	(3) Interest expense for Oct., $464.24.
5-15	(4) Loss on repossession, $64.36.
5-16	(1) Gross profit percentage, 37.75; (4) Total realized gross profit, 19X7, $99,024.86.
6-1	(2) Consignor's profit, $270.
6-2	(3a) Consignor's profit, $390.
6-3	(3a) Consignor's profit, $284.
6-4	(2) Consignor's profit: July, $252; August, $189.
6-5	(3a) Consignor's profit, $436.
6-6	Net income for 19X4, $30,685.
6-7	Net income for 19X0, $62,356.
6-8	(1) Inventory, Dec. 31, 19X8, $288,210.
6-9	Balances after corrections: A, $750 Cr.; B, $1,350 Dr.
6-10	(2e) Realized profit on cash sales, $3,000; on installment sales, $1,260.
6-11	Net income after income tax for year, $167,246.25.
7-1	Net income for month, $1,955.
7-2	Branch net loss for year, $1,650.
7-3	Combined net income for January, $3,665.

Prob. No.	**Check Figures**

7-4   Combined net income for 19X6, $12,050.
7-5   (1) Corrected balances, $61,360.
7-6   (1) Corrected balances, $57,460.
7-7   (2) Corrected balances in home office account, $132,165.

8-1   (2) Branch profit after adjustment, $1,750.
8-2   (2) Branch profit after adjustment, $1,860.
8-3   (2) Combined net income for 19X8, $112,150.
8-4   (2) Combined net income for 19X0, $4,500.
8-5   (2) Combined net income for 19X5, $2,374.
8-7   Branch net income, $14,170; home office net income, $30,000.
8-8   (1) Branch net income, $22,600; home office net income, $39,000.
8-9   (2) Adjusted Branch net income, $2,756.
8-10   Branch net income, $21,000; home office net income, $83,000.

9-1   (2) Columbia Corp. stockholders' equity, $796,000.
9-2   (4) DEF, Inc., stockholders' equity, $6,370,000.
9-3   Plan A: capital stock, $7,200,000; Plan B: preferred stock, $6,000,000; common stock, $2,000,000.
9-4   (3) Company T stock outstanding, $2,800,000.
9-5   (3) Retained earnings, $2,200,000.
9-6   (2) Retained earnings, $4,850,000.
9-7   (1b) Deficit, June 30, 19X6, $30,000; (2b) Retained earnings, June 30, 19X6, $2,270,000.
9-8   Purchase: goodwill, $100,000.
9-9   (1b) 4.8 shares of G Corp. for each share of D Corp.
9-10   (2) Net income of Z Corp. during period of control by Y Corp., $95,000.
9-11   (1) Total sales price, $11,214,000. (2) Net loss after federal tax benefit, $1,371,750.

10-1   Minority interest, $76,000.
10-2   Controlling interest, $30,513,000.
10-3   Minority interest, $30,000.
10-4   (1) Minority interest, $80,000. (2) Minority interest, $75,000.
10-5   (4) Minority interest, $11,000.
10-6   (3) Goodwill, $12,500.
10-7   Minority interest, $48,500.
10-8   Minority interest, $64,500.
10-9   (2) Minority interest, $122,500.
10-10   (2) Minority interest, $20,000.
10-11   (1) Controlling interest, $3,775,000. (2) Controlling interest, $2,650,000.

11-1   (2c) Retained earnings: Dec. 31, 19X0, $249,402; Dec. 31, 19X1, $231,342; Dec. 31, 19X2, $246,082.
11-2   (1) Minority interest, $111,536.
11-3   (2) Minority interest: Dec. 3, 19X3, $100,500; Dec. 31, 19X4, $113,000.
11-4   (2) Minority interest, $90,000.
11-5   (2) Minority interest, $67,633.
11-6   (3) Minority interest, $135,000.
11-7   (2) Minority interest, $49,515.
11-8   (2) Minority interest, $60,250.

12-1   (1b) Miller purchase: adjustment of machinery value, $7,500; North purchase: adjustment of machinery value, $3,000.
12-2   Controlling interest, Dec. 31, 19X1, $720,000; Dec. 31, 19X2, $588,800.
12-3   (3) Controlling interest, $428,225.
12-4   (3) Controlling interest, $619,065.
12-5   Controlling interest, $590,500.
12-6   (2) Controlling interest, $2,802,860.

Prob. No.	Check Figures
12-7	Controlling interest, $5,169,296.
12-8	Retained earnings, P, Inc., $2,464,571.
12-9	(1) Due from Marsh Sales, as corrected (on Dodge Mfg. Co. books), $104,975.97.
13-1	(2) Minority interest, $98,153; controlling interest, $1,190,530.
13-2	Retained earnings, $115,480.
13-3	Minority interest, $131,922; controlling interest, $1,411,050.
13-4	Minority interest, $127,550.
13-5	Minority interest, $75,667; controlling interest, $292,000.
13-6	Minority interest, $109,334; controlling interest, $1,128,336.
13-7	Appraisal adjustments: Snell, Inc., $26,000; Todd, Inc., $40,000.
14-1	Minority interest, $55,125; controlling interest, $696,706.
14-2	Minority interest, $58,415; controlling interest, $647,400.
14-3	Consolidated retained earnings, $487,217.
14-4	Goodwill, $24,687; consolidated retained earnings, $666,573.
14-5	Minority interest, $41,875; controlling interest, $833,069.
14-6	Controlling interest, $514,248.
14-7	Controlling interest, $475,917.
14-8	(3) Dec. 31, 19X2: goodwill, $10,832; retained earnings, $178,832.
14-9	Controlling interest, $616,463.
14-10	Controlling interest, $981,000.
14-11	Minority interest, $378,750; controlling interest, $5,525,000.
14-12	Controlling interest, $1,855,277.
15-1	Minority interest, $15,400; controlling interest, $366,900.
15-2	Minority interest, $101,020; controlling interest, $1,268,264.
15-3	Controlling interest, $565,610.
15-4	Minority interests: in Co. C, $190,500; in Co. B, $312,000.
15-5	(2) Minority interest, $105,560; controlling interest, $1,315,760.
15-6	Minority interest, $174,500; controlling interest, $1,033,387.
15-7	Minority interest, $272.12 deficit.
15-8	(1) Minority interest, $87,128.38. (2) Minority interest, $85,000.
15-9	Controlling interest, $1,166,869.
15-10	Minority interest, $13,684; controlling interest, $252,141.
15-11	(2) Profit of Co. F recognized by Co. P for year, $16,442.31.
15-12	Minority interest, $51,900; controlling interest, $907,367.
15-13	(2) Co. R stockholders receive $49,000.
15-14	Amount paid per share of Co. S stock: $29.48.
15-15	Shares in new company: to Co. R shareholders, 27.98 percent; to Co. S shareholders, 27.18 percent.
16-1	Net income: to minority interest, $8,750; to controlling interest, $123,000.
16-2	Net income: to minority interest, $1,900; to controlling interest, $32,100.
16-3	Net income to minority interest, $10,020; net loss to controlling interest, $4,920.
16-4	Net income to controlling interest, $186,500.
16-5	Consolidated net income, $16,550.
16-6	Net income: to minority interest, $5,295; to controlling interest, $85,005.
16-7	Consolidated net income, $66,630.
16-8	(2) Co. B retained earnings on date of acquisition, $100,000.
16-9	Consolidated net income, $715,000.
16-10	Net loss: to minority interest, $5,145; to controlling interest; $41,240.
16-11	Income to controlling interest, $148,619.
16-12	Consolidated income, $146,525.
16-13	Consolidated income, $764,382.
16-14	Net income: to minority interest, $2,125; to controlling interest, $82,125.
16-15	Consolidated income: $304,450.

**Prob.
No.**   **Check Figures**

17-1   Combined income for year, $54,670.
17-2   (3) Branch income for year, $139,565.
17-3   (2) Combined net income, $47,650; stockholders' equity, Dec. 31, $444,650.
17-4   (2) Combined net income, $39,880; stockholders' equity, Dec. 31, $217,320.
17-5   (2) Branch net income after bonus: in pounds, £4,691.19; in dollars, $10,089.39.
17-6   (3) Consolidated income, $354,120; stockholders' equity, Dec. 31, $1,286,620.
17-7   (2) Minority interest, $25,698; controlling interest, $419,742.
17-8   Exchange adjustment (loss) $28,460.

18-1   Deficiency, $20,225.
18-2   Deficiency, $24,950.
18-3   Deficiency, $34,100.
18-4   Deficiency, $59,250.
18-5   Deficiency of Cummings Co., $75,000.
18-6   Deficiency, $18,200.
18-7   Deficiency, $10,250.
18-8   Deficiency, $32,640.
18-9   Deficiency, $110,430.
18-10   Deficiency, $6,300.
18-11   Deficiency, $20,225.
18-12   Deficiency, $24,950.

19-1   Increase in retained earnings during trusteeship, $12,250.
19-2   Decrease in retained earnings during trusteeship, $3,850.
19-3   (2) June 30, 19X2: X, Capital, $14,880; Y, Capital, $12,380.
19-4   Decrease in retained earnings during assignment, $86,000.
19-5   Increase in retained earnings during trusteeship, $14,150.
19-6   Increase in retained earnings during trusteeship, $18,510.
19-7   Capitals, Dec. 16, 19X8: Arthur, $162,500; Brooks, $162,500.
19-8   Decrease in retained earnings during trusteeship, $337,800.

20-1   Decrease in retained earnings, $170,800.
20-2   Increase in retained earnings, $18,660.
20-3   Increase in partners' capitals, $54,476.89.
20-4   Increase in capital, $2,750.
20-5   Increase in retained earnings, $12,250.
20-6   Decrease in retained earnings, $3,850.
20-7   Increase in retained earnings, $13,200.
20-8   Increase in retained earnings, $18,510.
20-9   Increase in partners' capitals, $9,760.
20-10   Decrease in retained earnings, $5,294.

21-1   Legacy to daughter, $18,725.
21-2   Total legacies paid or delivered, $27,230.
21-3   Total legacies paid or delivered, $19,675.
21-4   Excess distribution to Patricia, $4,550.
21-5   Cash paid to John, $25,410.
21-6   Cash paid to John, $51,750.
21-7   Balance to estate, $255,680.
21-8   (5) Balance to estate, $186,000.

22-1   Balance as to estate principal, Sept. 15, $142,500.
22-2   Balance as to estate principal, Sept. 1, $75,225.
22-3   Balance as to estate principal, Nov. 1, $78,100.
22-4   Balance as to trust principal, Dec. 31, 19X2, $106,000; distributions of income, 19X3, $3,819.
22-5   Distributions of income: 19X2, $1,299.48; 19X3, $1,361.22; 19X4, $778.61.

Prob.
No.   **Check Figures**

22-6   Balance as to trust principal, Dec. 31, 19X9, $469,472.
22-7   Balance as to estate principal, Dec. 31, 19X7, $170,000.
22-8   Balance as to estate principal, July 1, 19X3, $281,450.
22-9   Balance as to estate principal, Jan. 31, 19X7, $345,850.
22-10   Net income to beneficiaries, Wallace Weber Trust, 19X3–19X7, $299,000.
22-11   Balance as to estate principal, Nov. 30, 19X9, $290,340.63.

23-1   Unreserved fund balance, $27,500.
23-2   Unreserved fund balance, $3,250.
23-3   Unreserved fund balance, $36,400.
23-4   Unreserved fund balance, $93,500.
23-5   Unreserved fund balance, $105,500.
23-6   Fund balance, Dec. 31, $83,370.
23-7   Unreserved fund balance, June 30, $141,000.
23-8   Unreserved fund balance, $2,700.
23-9   Unreserved fund balance, April 30, 19X8, $11,014.
23-10   Unreserved fund balance, $5,000.
23-11   Unreserved fund balance, $11,900.
23-12   Unreserved fund balance, Dec. 31, $9,300.

24-1   (2) Total assets, $775,000.
24-2   Net loss for year, $1,200.
24-3   Net income, $665,400.
24-4   Net income, $23,634.
24-5   Unreserved general fund balance, (deficit) $22,250.
24-6   Unreserved general fund balance, $26,000.
24-7   Combined total assets, $2,773,760.
24-8   (3) Total investment in fixed assets, $247,000.
24-9   Adjusted trial balance totals, $2,749,000.
24-10   Capital projects fund: total expenditures, $89,570.
24-11   Capital projects fund: unreserved fund balance, $600,000.
24-12   (2) Debt service fund: cash, $14,500.
24-13   General fixed assets: construction work in process, $2,371,000.
24-14   General fund: fund balance, $21,110.
24-15   (2) General fund: total assets and estimated revenues, $264,400.

Index

A

Abatement, *def.*, 682
Accounting,
 budgetary, 735
 effects of legal controls upon, 734
 fund, 735
Accounting Principles Board,
 see American Institute of Certified Public Accountants
Account sales, *def.*, 157
Accounts of a foreign affiliate,
 translation of, 542
Activities of governmental expenditures, *def.*, 738
Ademption, *def.*, 682
Administration,
 of an estate, 676
 of estate properties, 678
Administrator, *def.*, 677
 c.t.a. (*cum testamento annexa*), 677
 responsibilities of, 677
 see also Personal representative
Administrator-with-the-will-annexed, *def.*, 677
Admitted to probate, *def.*, 677
Affiliated companies, *def.*, 273
Affiliated group,
 as defined by Internal Revenue Code, 279
Affiliates,
 connecting, 458
Agency,
 accounting for an, 185
 and branch distinguished, 184
 operations of an, 184
Agency fund,
 see Fiduciary fund
Allotments, *def.*, 748
American Accounting Association,
 position on adoption of installment method of accounting, 133
 position on mutual holdings, 476
American Institute of Certified Public Accountants,

comparison of consolidation and the equity method, 313
definition of corporate joint ventures, 105
interpretation of Opinion 17 on goodwill amortization when control of a subsidiary is not achieved on first purchase, 419
position on accounting for investments for corporate joint ventures, 105
position on adoption of installment method of accounting, 134
position on allocation of intercompany profits to majority and minority interests, 378
position on an excess of net assets over cost in business combinations accounted for as a purchase, 247
position on applying the equity method when parent control is not achieved on first purchase, 417
position on capital from consolidation, 292
position on consolidation for pooling of interests subsequent to acquisition, 354
position on deciding upon consolidation policy, 279
position on degree of ownership in subsidiary to support consolidation, 278
position on difference between investment cost and asset values on purchase of subsidiary interest, 413
position on disclosure of assets and liabilities of unconsolidated subsidiaries, 332
position on dividends from pre-acquisition retained earnings, 348
position on elimination of intercompany profits, 371
position on intercompany profits on assets, 371
position on length of goodwill amortization period for investment in a subsidiary, 419
position on mutual holdings, 476
position on pooling of interests as business combinations, 245-246
position on preparation of consolidated statements under conditions of pooling interests, 295